Jimmy Swaggart Bible Commentary

Ezekiel

JIMMY SWAGGART BIBLE COMMENTARY

- Genesis (639 pages) (11-201)
- Exodus (639 pages) (11-202)
- Leviticus (435 pages) (11-203)
- Numbers
  Deuteronomy (493 pages) (11-204)
- Joshua
  Judges
  Ruth (329 pages) (11-205)
- I Samuel
  II Samuel (528 pages) (11-206)
- I Kings
  II Kings (560 pages) (11-207)
- I Chronicles
  II Chronicles (528 pages) (11-226)
- Ezra
  Nehemiah
  Esther (288 pages) (11-208)
- Job (320 pages) (11-225)
- Psalms (688 pages) (11-216)
- Proverbs (320 pages) (11-227)
- Ecclesiastes
  Song Of Solomon (245 pages) (11-228)
- Isaiah (688 pages) (11-220)
- Jeremiah
  Lamentations (688 pages) (11-070)
- Ezekiel (508 pages) (11-223)
- Daniel (403 pages) (11-224)
- Hosea
  Joel
  Amos (496 pages) (11-229)
- Obadiah
  Jonah
  Micah
  Naham
  Habakkuk
  Zephaniah *(will be ready Spring 2013)* (11-230)
- Matthew (625 pages) (11-073)
- Mark (606 pages) (11-074)
- Luke (626 pages) (11-075)
- John (532 pages) (11-076)
- Acts (697 pages) (11-077)
- Romans (536 pages) (11-078)
- I Corinthians (632 pages) (11-079)
- II Corinthians (589 pages) (11-080)
- Galatians (478 pages) (11-081)
- Ephesians (550 pages) (11-082)
- Philippians (476 pages) (11-083)
- Colossians (374 pages) (11-084)
- I Thessalonians
  II Thessalonians (498 pages) (11-085)
- I Timothy
  II Timothy
  Titus
  Philemon (687 pages) (11-086)
- Hebrews (831 pages) (11-087)
- James
  I Peter
  II Peter (730 pages) (11-088)
- I John
  II John
  III John
  Jude (377 pages) (11-089)
- Revelation (602 pages) (11-090)

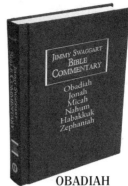

OBADIAH
JONAH
MICAH
NAHAM
HABAKKUK
ZEPHANIAH

For prices and information please call: 1-800-288-8350
Baton Rouge residents please call: (225) 768-7000
Website: www.jsm.org • Email: info@jsm.org

Jimmy Swaggart Bible Commentary

Ezekiel

World Evangelism Press

ISBN 978-1-934655-01-6
11-223 • COPYRIGHT © 2005 World Evangelism Press®
P.O. Box 262550 • Baton Rouge, Louisiana 70826-2550
Website: www.jsm.org • Email: info@jsm.org • (225) 768-8300
13 14 15 16 17 18 19 20 21 22 23 24 25 26 27 28 / RRD / 18 17 16 15 14 13 12 11 10 9 8 7 6 5 4 3
All rights reserved. Printed and bound in U.S.A.
No part of this publication may be reproduced in any form or by any means
without the publisher's prior written permission.

TABLE OF CONTENTS

1. Ezekiel 1   2. Index 500

THE BOOK OF EZEKIEL

(1) "NOW IT CAME TO PASS IN THE THIRTIETH YEAR, IN THE FOURTH MONTH, IN THE FIFTH DAY OF THE MONTH, AS I WAS AMONG THE CAPTIVES BY THE RIVER OF CHEBAR, THAT THE HEAVENS WERE OPENED, AND I SAW VISIONS OF GOD.

(2) "IN THE FIFTH DAY OF THE MONTH, WHICH WAS THE FIFTH YEAR OF KING JEHOIACHIN'S CAPTIVITY,

(3) "THE WORD OF THE LORD CAME EXPRESSLY UNTO EZEKIEL THE PRIEST, THE SON OF BUZI, IN THE LAND OF THE CHALDEANS BY THE RIVER CHEBAR; AND THE HAND OF THE LORD WAS THERE UPON HIM."

The construction is:

1. The heavens were opened to Ezekiel, and he saw visions of God.
2. Him being a captive by the Babylonians in no way hindered the flow of the Spirit in his heart and life.
3. His Prophetic Ministry begins here with the Word of the Lord coming to him.

VISIONS

The moving of the Holy Spirit signifies Spiritual Life.

As it regards the *"Visions,"* that which the Lord gives to His people, it pertains most of all to a Revelation of Himself. While instruction follows and information is given, it is ever the business of the Holy Spirit to draw us into a deeper relationship with the Lord. That's why Paul said, *"That I may know Him"* (Phil. 3:10).

CAPTIVITY

Many false Prophets in Jerusalem were

NOTES

predicting that the Babylonian Power was going to be overthrown, with Judah raised once again to her original splendor. Only Jeremiah and Ezekiel, and the few gathered around them were saying otherwise. To be sure, their Message of continued captivity didn't set well at all! I'm certain that Ezekiel, along with Jeremiah, would very much have enjoyed prophesying *"peace and safety,"* however, that would not have been the Word of the Lord.

PRESENT TIMES

Exactly as Judah of old, the modern Church abounds with false prophets. Many are denying the coming Rapture of the Church. Many are saying that there is no such thing as a coming Great Tribulation. They're claiming that the situation in the world is getting better and better, with the *"Church"* coming to terms with the major religions of the world, and with Christianity becoming more and more recognized, which will usher in the coming of the Lord. But the Bible doesn't say that!

In fact, the Scriptures tell us, *"Now the Spirit speaks expressly, that in the latter times* (the times in which we now live) *some shall depart from the Faith, giving heed to seducing spirits, and doctrines of devils"* (I Tim. 4:1). Paul also wrote, *"This know also, that in the last days perilous times shall come"* (II Tim. 3:1); and then, *"For when they shall say, Peace and safety; then sudden destruction comes upon them, as travail upon a woman with child; and they shall not escape"* (I Thess. 5:3).

Ezekiel was a captive to the Babylonian Power, but he was still a free man. He who is free in his spirit, is free indeed! Those in Jerusalem who were prophesying smooth things were claiming they were free, but in reality, they were prisoners to their own ungodly direction, for there is no freedom outside of Jesus Christ!

THE WORD OF THE LORD

The Scripture emphatically states *"The Word of the LORD came to Ezekiel."* In this Passage, it is clear that the indwelling Holy Spirit speaks to the human spirit, and does so constantly, at least to those who have proper relationship with the Lord. But let it be known: Whatever the Spirit says will always be 100 percent according to the Word of God.

THE CROSS

Due to the Cross, the Heavens are now open to a far greater extent than they were in the time of Ezekiel. The great barrier between God and man, and we speak of the barrier of sin, has been forever removed by the Cross of Christ, inasmuch that *"whosoever will, let him take of the Water of Life freely"* (Rev. 22:17).

(4) "AND I LOOKED, AND BEHOLD, A WHIRLWIND CAME OUT OF THE NORTH, A GREAT CLOUD, AND A FIRE INFOLDING ITSELF, AND A BRIGHTNESS WAS ABOUT IT, AND OUT OF THE MIDST THEREOF AS THE COLOR OF AMBER, OUT OF THE MIDST OF THE FIRE.

(5) "ALSO OUT OF THE MIDST THEREOF CAME THE LIKENESS OF FOUR LIVING CREATURES. AND THIS WAS THEIR APPEARANCE; THEY HAD THE LIKENESS OF A MAN.

(6) "AND EVERY ONE HAD FOUR FACES, AND EVERY ONE HAD FOUR WINGS.

(7) "AND THEIR FEET WERE STRAIGHT FEET; AND THE SOLE OF THEIR FEET WAS LIKE THE SOLE OF A CALF'S FOOT: AND THEY SPARKLED LIKE THE COLOUR OF BURNISHED BRASS.

(8) "AND THEY HAD THE HANDS OF A MAN UNDER THEIR WINGS ON THEIR FOUR SIDES; AND THEY FOUR HAD THEIR FACES AND THEIR WINGS.

(9) "THEIR WINGS WERE JOINED ONE TO ANOTHER; THEY TURNED NOT WHEN THEY WENT; THEY WENT EVERY ONE STRAIGHT FORWARD.

(10) "AS FOR THE LIKENESS OF THEIR FACES, THEY FOUR HAD THE FACE OF A MAN, AND THE FACE OF A LION, ON THE RIGHT SIDE: AND THEY FOUR HAD THE FACE OF AN OX ON THE LEFT SIDE; THEY FOUR ALSO HAD THE FACE OF AN EAGLE."

The exegesis is:

1. In this Vision given to the Prophet, he saw things, which the eyes of man had never before beheld.

2. These Living Creatures are *"Cherubims"* (Chpt. 10).

3. They have to do with the Throne of God. What Ezekiel saw is very similar to that which was seen by John in his Vision (Rev. 4:6-9).

THE HOLY SPIRIT

More than likely, the *"whirlwind, which came out of the north,"* refers to the Holy Spirit. This we do know, everything done on this Earth by the Godhead comes through the Person, Ministry, Work, and Office of the Holy Spirit.

Ezekiel related his Vision exactly as he saw it, and it all pertains to the Glory of God, which to be frank, is beyond our comprehension. The abode of God is so far above this mortal coil that there is no way that we can properly grasp or understand the Glory of Jehovah. And if we could understand it, that would mean that it would be no greater than we are, which means that it wouldn't be worth knowing.

A DREAM

A dear lady in California was saved through our Television Ministry. She had a wonderful experience in the Lord, which drastically changed her lifestyle. If I remember correctly, she was in her late sixties at the time of her Salvation.

Not long after she was saved, she contracted the dreaded disease of cancer. We prayed earnestly for her healing, but the Lord did not see fit to extend this particular blessing, and soon it became apparent that she would die.

Since she had only been saved for a very short time, she was somewhat fearful of death. She asked me any number of times, *"What will it be like? What is Heaven like?"*

All I could tell her was that which is given to us in the Bible. But then, a few weeks before she died, I had a dream about the situation. I dreamed that she died and was ushered into the place that we refer to as *"Heaven."* In my dream, Frances, Frances' Mother, and I accompanied this dear lady to her eternal abode.

And that's the part I wish to relate to you.

I did not see the Glory that Ezekiel saw, but the following is that which stood out so vividly in my memory.

That which I saw was a pastoral scene, with the great Throne of God at a distance. I could see it, but I could not see any of its features. I remember telling the dear lady that the area where we were belonged to her. She answered by asking, *"I've only been saved a short time, so how could I have all of this?"*

I do not know how I knew it was hers, but I did know, and I encouraged her again that this belonged to her. But the thing that was so remarkable was the Presence of God that seemed to permeate the air. I have never in my life had such a feeling of serenity, of peace, of love! The atmosphere was so serene, that I remember that I did not want to leave. I had to literally pull myself away from this ideal setting.

I said to the dear sister, *"We're going to have to leave now, but we will be back before too very long."*

Almost immediately after experiencing the dream, I called the dear sister in question, and related to her what I had seen in the dream, and what I had experienced. It seemed to console her, and to fill her with assurance. She passed away a few days later, and she is there now, in that place called *"Heaven."* Since that time, Frances' Mother has also gone on to be with the Lord, residing there in that place that I saw in my dream that night so long ago.

THE CHERUBIM

The Cherubims are mentioned many times in the Old Testament, but only once in the New, and that referring back to the Old (Heb. 9:5). However, as stated, that which John saw in the Fourth Chapter of Revelation was the same that Ezekiel saw, with one exception — John's Cherubim had *"six wings,"* while Ezekiel's had four. Actually, both John and Ezekiel called them *"Living Creatures,"* but the New Testament translators, unfortunately, called them *"beasts"* in the Fourth Chapter of Revelation.

In the Book of Genesis, the Cherubim were assigned to the Tree of Life in Eden (Gen. 3:24). A similar symbolic function was credited to the golden Cherubim, which were placed at either end of the Cover (Mercy Seat) of the Ark of the Covenant (Ex. 25:18-22).

Figures of Cherubim formed part of the lavish decorations of Solomon's Temple (I Ki. 6:26). Two of these, carved in olive wood and overlaid with gold, dominated the inner Sanctuary. Using eighteen inches for the cubit, they were fifteen feet high. They were facing each other, with two wings meeting in the middle and two wings touching the walls at either end, thereby covering the entire Holy of Holies. Cherubim were also carved in the form of a frieze around the wall of Solomon's Temple, and they appeared together with animal representations on decorative panels forming part of the base of the huge brass basin (Molten Sea), which contained the water for ritual oblations (the Brazen Laver).

These Creatures, which are totally unlike anything seen by man, seem to serve one purpose, a constant symbolism of the Holiness of God. Actually, those John saw are Cherubim, which they certainly seem to be, and *"they rest not day and night, saying, Holy, Holy, Holy, LORD God Almighty, which was, and is, and is to come"* (Rev. 4:8).

Some have said that they appear at the gate of Eden, guarding the Way of Life, upon the Veil of the Tabernacle and the Temple, predicting the coming Incarnation, upon the Mercy Seat witnessing to the Atonement, and in the Fourth Chapter of Revelation, leading the song in celebration of Redemption.

(11) "THUS WERE THEIR FACES: AND THEIR WINGS WERE STRETCHED UPWARD; TWO WINGS OF EVERY ONE WERE JOINED ONE TO ANOTHER, AND TWO COVERED THEIR BODIES.

(12) "AND THEY WENT EVERY ONE STRAIGHT FORWARD: WHITHER THE SPIRIT WAS TO GO, THEY WENT; AND

THEY TURNED NOT WHEN THEY WENT.

(13) "AS FOR THE LIKENESS OF THE LIVING CREATURES, THEIR APPEARANCE WAS LIKE BURNING COALS OF FIRE, AND LIKE THE APPEARANCE OF LAMPS: IT WENT UP AND DOWN AMONG THE LIVING CREATURES; AND THE FIRE WAS BRIGHT, AND OUT OF THE FIRE WENT FORTH LIGHTNING.

(14) "AND THE LIVING CREATURES RAN AND RETURNED AS THE APPEARANCE OF A FLASH OF LIGHTNING.

(15) "NOW AS I BEHELD THE LIVING CREATURES, BEHOLD ONE WHEEL UPON THE EARTH BY THE LIVING CREATURES, WITH HIS FOUR FACES."

The diagram is:

1. Verse 12 proclaims the fact that the Holy Spirit gives the direction.

2. Quite possibly, the great Lamp symbolizes the Holy Spirit, and reveals the energy which moves the Cherubims and the wheels.

3. The wheels, it seems, represent direction, hence the *"eyes"* of Verse 18.

THE GLORY OF GOD

To try to explain these things is beyond the comprehension of mere mortals. Ezekiel had this Vision and saw what he was writing about, but did not even make an attempt to explain what he saw. What Ezekiel saw is far beyond what we presently know and would, therefore, have to be beyond our comprehension. Admittedly, many commentators have attempted to explain this phenomenon, but even the best Hebrew Scholars can only come up with guesswork. So, I'm going to treat this Vision, as glorious as it was, in the following manner.

THE CROSS

When we think of God, Who left this magnificent glory, a glory, as stated, beyond our comprehension, and came down to this mortal coil, in order to die upon a Cross that we might be saved, then and only then, can we get a feeling of the love that was shown to the human race by this redemptive act. In fact, all of this shown to Ezekiel had but one destination, and that was the Cross. Actually, the entirety of the Bible can be summed up as the story of the Cross. While

NOTES

the Lord Jesus Christ was, and is, the Source of all things, at least which pertain to Righteousness, the Cross is the means by which it is all done. Now, that is a statement that you need to carefully inspect.

JESUS CHRIST IS THE SOURCE AND THE CROSS IS THE MEANS

The following is an extremely abbreviated view of God's Prescribed Order of Victory. He only has one order — not ten, not five, not even two — just one!

As simple as it is, the world rejects it out of hand, and the Church basically does the same. But yet, it is God's Way, and it is the story of the Bible. It is as follows:

THE CROSS

The Believer must grasp the fact that every single thing that we receive from the Lord, irrespective as to what it might be, all and without exception, is made possible by what Jesus did at the Cross (Gal. 6:14).

FAITH

Without exception, the object of our faith must always be the Cross of Christ. This is very, very important! While there has been more teaching and preaching on Faith in the last several decades than possibly any other time in history, there is probably less true Faith being evidenced today than ever before. The trouble is not a lack of faith, but rather things other than the Cross being made the object of one's Faith. The only faith that God will recognize is Faith that ever makes the Cross its object. We must never forget that (Rom. 6:3-14).

THE HOLY SPIRIT

Jesus is the Source, but it is the Holy Spirit Who does the actual work within our lives, making available to us that for which Jesus has paid such a price at the Cross. Before the Cross, the Holy Spirit, due to the sin problem being incompletely addressed by the blood of bulls and goats (which was woefully, insufficient), the Spirit of God was very limited as to what He could do, even on behalf of the great Faith worthies. However, when Jesus died on the Cross, pouring out His Life's Blood, which satisfied the demands of a thrice-Holy God, the sin debt was forever removed, at least for all who will believe. Now, the Holy Spirit has the latitude to do within our hearts and lives all things which are necessary. While He doesn't demand much of us, He does demand one thing:

He demands that we ever make the Cross the object of our Faith. Listen to Paul:

"For the Law (a law devised by the Godhead in eternity past) *of the Spirit* (Holy Spirit) *of Life* (the Holy Spirit is the Superintendent of Life, so to speak, and Christ is the Source of Life) *in Christ Jesus* (refers to what Christ did at the Cross, all on our behalf), *has made me free from the Law of sin and death"* (Rom. 8:2).

This tells us that the *"means"* by which the Holy Spirit works, which is the Cross, is so ironclad that it is referred to as a *"Law."*

What I've just given you is the means by which the Believer can walk in total and perpetual victory, in that sin will no longer have dominion over him (Rom. 6:14). It is the Cross which has made it possible for all Believers to live eternally in the splendor and glory which Ezekiel describes.

(16) "THE APPEARANCE OF THE WHEELS AND THEIR WORK WAS LIKE UNTO THE COLOUR OF A BERYL: AND THEY FOUR HAD ONE LIKENESS: AND THEIR APPEARANCE AND THEIR WORK WAS AS IT WERE A WHEEL IN THE MIDDLE OF A WHEEL.

(17) "WHEN THEY WENT, THEY WENT UPON THEIR FOUR SIDES: AND THEY TURNED NOT WHEN THEY WENT.

(18) "AS FOR THEIR RINGS, THEY WERE SO HIGH THAT THEY WERE DREADFUL; AND THEIR RINGS WERE FULL OF EYES ROUND ABOUT THEM FOUR.

(19) "AND WHEN THE LIVING CREATURES WENT, THE WHEELS WENT BY THEM: AND WHEN THE LIVING CREATURES WERE LIFTED UP FROM THE EARTH, THE WHEELS WERE LIFTED UP.

(20) "WHITHERSOEVER THE SPIRIT WAS TO GO, THEY WENT, THITHER WAS THEIR SPIRIT TO GO; AND THE WHEELS WERE LIFTED UP OVER AGAINST THEM: FOR THE SPIRIT OF THE LIVING CREATURE WAS IN THE WHEELS.

NOTES

(21) "WHEN THOSE WENT, THESE WENT; AND WHEN THOSE STOOD, THESE STOOD; AND WHEN THOSE WERE LIFTED UP FROM THE EARTH, THE WHEELS WERE LIFTED UP OVER AGAINST THEM: FOR THE SPIRIT OF THE LIVING CREATURE WAS IN THE WHEELS.

(22) "AND THE LIKENESS OF THE FIRMAMENT UPON THE HEADS OF THE LIVING CREATURE WAS AS THE COLOUR OF THE TERRIBLE CRYSTAL, STRETCHED FORTH OVER THEIR HEADS ABOVE."

The composition is:

1. The appearance of these Living Creatures was totally unlike anything that Ezekiel (or anyone else, for that matter) had ever seen.

2. There is a beauty about all of this that is absolutely indescribable.

3. Along with this beauty, *"means,"* and *"power,"* are also portrayed, presenting to us that which is incomparable.

THE SPIRIT WORLD

For clarification purposes, I am going to restate something I've already stated: It is virtually impossible to fully understand these things which Ezekiel saw. And the reason for the impossibility is that the great Prophet was given a glimpse into the Spirit world of Righteousness. As a result, he could only describe what he saw. There is precious little instruction given regarding the meaning of all this, but yet, it is all so very, very important.

I have searched Commentary after Commentary and read after many Scholars, even some who were proficient in Hebrew, but none had any understanding of what Ezekiel actually saw. So, I feel it would be far more profitable to address this all-important subject, as it regards this Chapter, in the following manner:

This which unfolds before us in this Chapter — so grand, so glorious, so wonderful, so powerful, and so beautiful — is that which the Lord desires to bring us into. In other words, every Saint of God can expect to enjoy the glory of the Spirit world of Righteousness, and do so forever, and forever, but only because of what Jesus did at the Cross. It was the Cross, and the Cross alone, which opened up the way, which took down the barrier between God and man (Eph. 2:13-18).

So, all of this of which we here read is pointing toward the coming of the Son of God, Who would pay the price for lost humanity by giving Himself in Sacrifice, upon the Cross of Calvary. If we understand this, then our lack of understanding about all the particulars of this Vision, are not really that important. If the Lord had wanted us to understand every facet of this which He showed the great Prophet, then He would have given Ezekiel the explanation of all things. But the reason He didn't is that such is not the emphasis. The emphasis is what the Lord would ultimately do in order to bring mankind to Himself. Again, we point to the Cross.

(23) "AND UNDER THE FIRMAMENT WERE THEIR WINGS STRAIGHT, THE ONE TOWARD THE OTHER: EVERY ONE HAD TWO, WHICH COVERED ON THIS SIDE, AND EVERY ONE HAD TWO, WHICH COVERED ON THAT SIDE, THEIR BODIES.

(24) "AND WHEN THEY WENT, I HEARD THE NOISE OF THEIR WINGS, LIKE THE NOISE OF GREAT WATERS, AS THE VOICE OF THE ALMIGHTY, THE VOICE OF SPEECH, AS THE NOISE OF AN HOST: WHEN THEY STOOD, THEY LET DOWN THEIR WINGS.

(25) "AND THERE WAS A VOICE FROM THE FIRMAMENT THAT WAS OVER THEIR HEADS, WHEN THEY STOOD, AND HAD LET DOWN THEIR WINGS.

(26) "AND ABOVE THE FIRMAMENT THAT WAS OVER THEIR HEADS WAS THE LIKENESS OF A THRONE, AS THE APPEARANCE OF A SAPPHIRE STONE: AND UPON THE LIKENESS OF THE THRONE WAS THE LIKENESS AS THE APPEARANCE OF A MAN ABOVE UPON IT.

(27) "AND I SAW AS THE COLOUR OF AMBER, AS THE APPEARANCE OF FIRE ROUND ABOUT WITHIN IT, FROM THE APPEARANCE OF HIS LOINS EVEN UPWARD, AND FROM THE APPEARANCE OF HIS LOINS EVEN DOWNWARD, I SAW AS IT WERE THE APPEARANCE OF FIRE, AND IT HAD BRIGHTNESS ROUND ABOUT.

(28) "AS THE APPEARANCE OF THE BOW THAT IS IN THE CLOUD IN THE DAY OF RAIN, SO WAS THE APPEARANCE OF THE BRIGHTNESS ROUND ABOUT.

NOTES

THIS WAS THE APPEARANCE OF THE LIKENESS OF THE GLORY OF THE LORD. AND WHEN I SAW IT, I FELL UPON MY FACE, AND I HEARD A VOICE OF ONE WHO SPOKE."

The structure is:

1. This Vision experienced by Ezekiel has similarities to the Vision of John the Beloved on the Isle of Patmos, portrayed in Revelation, Chapters 4 and 5.

2. One can probably best describe this which was portrayed to Ezekiel as *"the Glory of the Lord."*

3. The response of the Prophet to this wondrous display was that he *"fell upon his face."*

THE GLORY OF GOD

The Bible Student must understand that the privilege for the Child of God to one day become a part of this display of Glory, which will last forever and forever, is granted only by the Cross of Christ. As we have stated, and will no doubt state other times in this Volume, while Christ is the Source of all that we receive, the Cross is the means by which it is granted unto us, and the Cross alone is the means.

Unfortunately, the modern Church has been so moved away from the Cross that, for all practical purposes, it hardly knows where it has been, where it is, or where it is going.

The Cross of Christ is not a mere doctrine. It is the foundation on which all Doctrine is built. If Bible Doctrine is not built on the foundation of the Cross it will, in some way, be wrong. It's just that simple!

Listen to what Peter said:

"Forasmuch as you know that you were not redeemed with corruptible things, as silver and gold, from your vain conversation (lifestyle) *received by tradition from your fathers;*

"But with the Precious Blood of Christ, as of a lamb without blemish and without spot:

"Who verily was foreordained before the foundation of the world, but was manifested in these last times for you" (I Pet. 1:18-20)

This Passage plainly tells us that the first Doctrine formulated by the Godhead, as it refers to Redemption, was the Cross. God through foreknowledge knew that He would make man; through foreknowledge, He also knew that man would fall. To save man, who was God's highest creation, the Cross would be the means by which this was done, which necessitated God becoming Man, which we refer to as the *"Incarnation."*

So, one can trace all false doctrine, all false directions, and all error to a misinterpretation or a misunderstanding of the Cross of Christ.

It is the Cross alone which makes it possible for Believers to have the Glory of God, which Ezekiel was privileged to see. When it was revealed to him, he fell on his face, even as many do (Rev. 1:17).

"Amazing Grace! How sweet the Sound,
"That saved a wretch like me!
"I once was lost, but now I'm found,
"Was blind, but now I see."

" 'Twas grace that taught my heart to fear,
"And Grace my fears relieved;
"How precious did that Grace appear
"The Hour I first believed!"

"Thro' many dangers, toils, and snares,
"I have already come;
"Tis Grace hath bro't me safe thus far,
"And Grace will lead me home."

CHAPTER 2

(1) "AND HE SAID UNTO ME, SON OF MAN, STAND UPON YOUR FEET, AND I WILL SPEAK UNTO YOU.

(2) "AND THE SPIRIT ENTERED INTO ME WHEN HE SPOKE UNTO ME, AND SET ME UPON MY FEET, THAT I HEARD HIM WHO SPOKE UNTO ME."

The overview is:

1. The entire Glory of God is outlined here and elsewhere; man falling on his face before it proclaims man's fallen state as a result of the fall in the Garden of Eden.

2. The phrase, *"Son of Man, stand upon your feet,"* reflects the *"Born-Again"* experience, and the lifting of man up from his fallen state. This is life and power.

3. One of the greatest descriptions of the fallen state is man fallen to the earth and unable, at least within his own power, to arise. He keeps trying, and keeps falling back! Only Christ can stand man upright on his feet, spiritually speaking, of which the Resurrection was a type.

THE HOLY SPIRIT

The Power of God, which emanated from the Glory of God, knocked Ezekiel off his feet, or so it seems; as well, he could not arise without that same power, and we refer to the Holy Spirit, lifting him up.

Everything done on the Earth by the Godhead, with one exception, was done, and is done, through the Person, Power, Office, Agency, and Ministry of the Holy Spirit. In fact, the Bible opens its pages with the words, *"And the Spirit of God moved upon the face of the waters"* (Gen. 1:2).

In fact, the only work in which the Holy Spirit hasn't been the sole Agent is the first Advent of Christ. Even then, the Holy Spirit superintended all that was done, including Christ's conception, His birth, His Life and Ministry, and above all, His Death on the Cross of Calvary, as well as His Resurrection (Rom. 8:11). In fact, there is evidence that Jesus didn't die until the Holy Spirit told Him that He could die (Heb. 9:14).

However, in Old Testament Times, the Holy Spirit, despite the fact that He is God, actually the third Person of the Triune Godhead, was limited as to what He could do on Earth. The reason was the sin debt owed by man to God, which the blood of bulls and goats could not remove (Heb. 10:4).

But when Jesus died on the Cross, thereby forever settling the sin debt owed by man, in other words, wiping the slate clean, at least for those who will believe, which satisfied the demands of a thrice-Holy God, this opened the door for the Holy Spirit to abide in the hearts and lives of Believers forever. Jesus said, *"I will pray the Father, and He shall give you another Comforter, that He may abide with you forever* (and that He did).

"Even the Spirit of Truth; Whom the world cannot receive, because it sees Him not, neither knows Him: but you know Him; for He

dwells with you, and shall be in you" (Jn. 14:16-17).

The Master plainly said here that the Holy Spirit only dwelt *"with"* Believers before the Cross, but now, due to the Cross, and the sin debt being paid, the Holy Spirit dwells *"in"* Believers.

So, the Cross opened up an entirely new vista as it regards the Holy Spirit, and all that He does on this Earth in the hearts and lives of Believers.

(3) "AND HE SAID UNTO ME, SON OF MAN, I SEND YOU TO THE CHILDREN OF ISRAEL, TO A REBELLIOUS NATION THAT HAS REBELLED AGAINST ME: THEY AND THEIR FATHERS HAVE TRANSGRESSED AGAINST ME, EVEN UNTO THIS VERY DAY.

(4) "FOR THEY ARE IMPUDENT CHILDREN AND STIFFHEARTED. I DO SEND YOU UNTO THEM; AND YOU SHALL SAY UNTO THEM, THUS SAITH THE LORD GOD.

(5) "AND THEY, WHETHER THEY WILL HEAR, OR WHETHER THEY WILL FORBEAR, (FOR THEY ARE A REBELLIOUS HOUSE,) YET SHALL KNOW THAT THERE HAS BEEN A PROPHET AMONG THEM."

The synopsis is:

1. Ezekiel receives his commission.
2. The phrase, *"Whether they will hear, or whether they will forbear,"* lends more weight to the probable failure of his mission, wholly or in part.
3. For the first time, the Lord designates the calling of *"a Prophet"* to Ezekiel.

THE PROPHET

The words in the Fifth Verse, *"And they,"* concerned Judah, Jerusalem, and the Exiles, and are used in a strong denouncing sense. It is as if the Holy Spirit is saying that the effort is futile, but love will make the effort, even unto the bitter end. The Exiles consisted of the first deportations, which included Daniel in the first (605 B.C.), and Ezekiel in the second (597 B.C.), with both deportations probably totaling approximately 20,000 people, along with the people of the Northern Kingdom who had been taken captive nearly one hundred and thirty years before. Due to this length of time, this number, counting the Northern Kingdom, could have risen to as much as 100,000, or even far more! These were scattered all over Babylonia, as the Book of Esther proclaims (Esther 9:30).

In Old Testament Times, the Office of the Prophet was used by the Lord to lead and guide Israel. In fact, Samuel was the first one to stand in that Office. While there were Prophets before him, their influence was necessarily limited, simply because the nation of Israel had not yet been formed.

The Old Testament Prophet acted as a mouthpiece for God, receiving a Message from Him and proclaiming it in accordance with His Commands.

A PREACHER OF RIGHTEOUSNESS

While the Office of the Prophet definitely involved itself in *"foretelling,"* still, the greater thrust of the Prophetic Ministry was in *"forthtelling,"* or in other words, they served as *"Preachers of Righteousness."* This means that many Prophetic Messages were addressed not merely to the head but also to the heart of the listeners. They abound in pictures calculated to arouse strong feelings of sorrow for sin, of gratitude to God, or of determination to follow the Commands of God. In view of this, it is quite natural that there should be evidence of strong emotion on the part of the Prophets and also of their hearers. This, however, is very different from saying that the Prophet was compelled only by his feelings, or that his Message was produced exclusively by his emotions.

The Message of the true Prophet, at least if it was in the realm of *"forthtelling,"* was almost always negative. It was designed to address false directions, and the spiritual apathy of the people, and in fact, it still functions in this manner presently.

Almost all of the time, Prophets are treated harshly by their listeners. People do not enjoy being called to account. They do not enjoy having to deal with wrong direction or wrong doing; so, for the most part, they turn on the Prophet, and seek to silence his voice. That's what Jesus was speaking of when He said: *"Oh Jerusalem, Jerusalem, you who kill the Prophets, and stone them who are sent unto you, how often would I have gathered your children together, even as a hen gathers her chickens under her wings, and you would not"* (Mat. 23:37). This means that garlands of appreciation are seldom laid upon the necks of Prophets. But the man who stands in the Office of the Prophet (and that Office still exists presently [Eph. 4:11]) must expect the abuse. It comes with the territory.

Incidentally, even though the Office of the Prophet still exists today, it is now the Apostle whom the Lord uses to lead and guide the Church, which is normally done by the type of Message given to the Apostle. So, regarding leadership, it was the Prophet in Old Testament Times, and it is the Apostle in New Testament Times.

(6) "AND YOU, SON OF MAN, BE NOT AFRAID OF THEM, NEITHER BE AFRAID OF THEIR WORDS, THOUGH BRIERS AND THORNS BE WITH YOU, AND YOU DO DWELL AMONG SCORPIONS: BE NOT AFRAID OF THEIR WORDS, NOR BE DISMAYED AT THEIR LOOKS, THOUGH THEY BE A REBELLIOUS HOUSE.

(7) "AND YOU SHALL SPEAK MY WORDS UNTO THEM, WHETHER THEY WILL HEAR, OR WHETHER THEY WILL FORBEAR; FOR THEY ARE MOST REBELLIOUS.

(8) "BUT YOU, SON OF MAN, HEAR WHAT I SAY UNTO YOU; BE NOT THOU REBELLIOUS LIKE THAT REBELLIOUS HOUSE: OPEN YOUR MOUTH, AND EAT THAT I GIVE YOU.

(9) "AND WHEN I LOOKED, BEHOLD, AN HAND WAS SENT UNTO ME; AND, LO, A ROLL OF A BOOK WAS THEREIN;

(10) "AND HE SPREAD IT BEFORE ME; AND IT WAS WRITTEN WITHIN AND WITHOUT: AND THERE WAS WRITTEN THEREIN LAMENTATIONS, AND MOURNING, AND WOE."

The diagram is:

1. The presentation of the Gospel to rebellious hearts arouses tremendous opposition.

2. God's Word is to be proclaimed, whether the people accept it or not!

3. The Prophet is warned against the natural weakness of the human heart, which, in the face of rebellion, is prone to compromise.

4. The Message that Ezekiel was to deliver was not one of glad tidings, but instead of *"lamentations, mourning, and woe."*

NOTES

THE NEGATIVE MESSAGE

The true moral character of those to whom the Prophet was to minister, is declared as hard-faced, stubborn-hearted, and rebellious as briars, thorns, and scorpions. Unfortunately this description is also true of modern congregations; and, when, through faithful Preachers, the Spirit of God declares the fact, only a few accept His testimony, humbly and contritely seeking the Saviour; but the majority are filled with rage.

The Message of the Cross addresses false doctrine as nothing else. While there presently is much false doctrine, perhaps that which is doing the most damage to the modern Church is the *"Word of Faith"* Message, so-called. In reality, it's no faith at all, at least that which God will honor.

This doctrine ridicules the Crucifixion, referring to it as *"past miseries"* and the *"worst defeat in human history."* It is said by their champions that those who preach the Cross are preaching death; instead, they claim, the Preacher must preach the Throne, etc. That seems strange when one hears the words of the Apostle Paul: *"For the preaching of the Cross is to them who perish foolishness, but unto us who are saved it is the power of God"* (I Cor. 1:18).

Paul didn't say, *"For the preaching of the throne,"* or *"the preaching of the Resurrection,"* but rather, *"the preaching of the Cross."* Now one can accept what these modern teachers say, or one can accept that said by Paul. One cannot accept both.

When the Cross is demeaned or ignored, as it definitely is in these circles, such proclaims the fact that such a Doctrine is blatantly dishonest, at least as it regards the Word of God. One cannot have it both ways; it is either right, or it is wrong! And the Word of Faith Doctrine is Scripturally wrong!

BE NOT AFRAID OF THEM

Some time during the year 2000, the Lord began to move upon me and upon other Preachers in this Ministry, especially upon my son Donnie, to cry out against this Message. It is one thing to cry out against false doctrine which is opposed by most Christians, but something else to cry out against false doctrine that is accepted by most Christians, as is the Word of Faith Message. Even though most all the Preachers associated with our Ministry have cried out, and are crying out, against this wayward direction, it is Donnie on whom the Lord has specifically laid His Hand, who has cried out against this doctrine, and has done so in no uncertain terms. He has pointed out the falseness of the Message, using the very words of the Preachers and Teachers themselves, and then identified the false Messengers. In other words, no one had any trouble knowing exactly what he was talking about or of whom he was speaking.

Upon hearing the Message, a few humbled themselves and repented; however, rage has filled the hearts and lives of most. And that rage has been directed against Donnie, which of course, causes much pain and hurt — more than most will ever know. In fact, I firmly believe that my son stands in the Office of the Prophet. To be sure, he hasn't given himself that designation, but it is my personal feeling that this is the Office in which the Lord has placed him.

We have lost friends and supporters, even at the very times we needed them the most; however, the obligation and responsibility of the true Prophet of God presents itself as very simple. He must hear from the Lord, and then deliver what he feels the Lord has given him to deliver. The Message must not be trimmed; it must not be compromised; irrespective as to whether it is accepted or rejected, the man of God is to deliver his soul. He has no alternative or choice! To be sure, he must expect the rage! But above all, he must obey God.

To be frank, the modern Church, at least in the last few decades, has very little heard the voice of the true Prophet. Oh, yes! There have been many who claim to be Prophets, but for the most part, the Biblical signs were missing.

Let us say it again:

At times, the Prophet of God will foretell, but the greater thrust of his Ministry will always be as a *"Preacher of Righteousness"* (II Pet. 2:5).

"I know the Lord will make a way for me.
"I know the Lord will make a way for me.
"If I live a holy life, shun the wrong, and do the right,
"I know the Lord will make a way for me."

CHAPTER 3

(1) "MOREOVER HE SAID UNTO ME, SON OF MAN, EAT THAT YOU FIND; EAT THIS ROLL, AND GO SPEAK UNTO THE HOUSE OF ISRAEL.

(2) "SO I OPENED MY MOUTH, AND HE CAUSED ME TO EAT THAT ROLL.

(3) "AND HE SAID UNTO ME, SON OF MAN, CAUSE YOUR BELLY TO EAT, AND FILL YOUR BOWELS WITH THIS ROLL THAT I GIVE YOU. THEN DID I EAT IT; AND IT WAS IN MY MOUTH AS HONEY FOR SWEETNESS.

(4) "AND HE SAID UNTO ME, SON OF MAN, GO, GET THEE UNTO THE HOUSE OF ISRAEL, AND SPEAK WITH MY WORDS UNTO THEM.

(5) "FOR YOU ARE NOT SENT TO A PEOPLE OF A STRANGE SPEECH AND OF AN HARD LANGUAGE, BUT TO THE HOUSE OF ISRAEL;

(6) "NOT TO MANY OF A STRANGE SPEECH AND OF AN HARD LANGUAGE, WHOSE WORDS YOU CANNOT UNDERSTAND. SURELY, HAD I SENT YOU TO THEM, THEY WOULD HAVE HEARKENED UNTO YOU.

(7) "BUT THE HOUSE OF ISRAEL WILL NOT HEARKEN UNTO YOU; FOR THEY WILL NOT HEARKEN UNTO ME: FOR ALL THE HOUSE OF ISRAEL ARE IMPUDENT AND HARDHEARTED.

(8) "BEHOLD, I HAVE MADE YOUR FACE STRONG AGAINST THEIR FACES, AND YOUR FOREHEAD STRONG AGAINST THEIR FOREHEADS.

(9) "AS AN ADAMANT HARDER THAN FLINT HAVE I MADE YOUR FOREHEAD: FEAR THEM NOT, NEITHER BE DISMAYED AT THEIR LOOKS, THOUGH THEY BE A REBELLIOUS HOUSE.

(10) "MOREOVER HE SAID UNTO ME, SON OF MAN, ALL MY WORDS THAT I SHALL SPEAK UNTO YOU RECEIVE IN YOUR HEART, AND HEAR WITH YOUR EARS.

(11) "AND GO, GET YOU TO THEM OF THE CAPTIVITY, UNTO THE CHILDREN OF YOUR PEOPLE, AND SPEAK UNTO THEM, AND TELL THEM, THUS SAITH THE LORD GOD; WHETHER THEY WILL HEAR, OR WHETHER THEY WILL FORBEAR."

The composition is:

1. The phrase, *"Eat that you find,"* is a reminder that the true Prophet does not choose his Message (Acts 4:20), but delivers what is given unto him by the Lord.

2. The Word of God is ever sweet to a spiritual palate. But it is bitter to the flesh, for it judges its nature and activities, and announces the wrath of God, which is coming upon it.

3. Before the Preacher can speak with effect to his fellowmen, he must personally experience the sweetness and bitterness of the Word of God, as given forth by the Holy Spirit.

THE WORD OF GOD

In the Vision given to Ezekiel, the Prophet was told to eat a particular roll, which was evidently a scroll of the Word of God, which was the manner in which the Word of God was written in those days. As well, Ezekiel did not literally eat anything; all of this was done in the Vision, but it was just as real to the Prophet as though he had literally eaten it.

The Word of God was sweet as honey in his mouth, but it is always bitter to the *"flesh."* The Word of God ever judges the flesh, which speaks of man's efforts, personal abilities, and personal strength, which God can never honor.

Paul said: *"There is therefore now no condemnation to them which are in Christ Jesus, who walk not after the flesh, but after the Spirit"* (Rom. 8:1).

"Walking after the flesh" refers to the Believer attempting to live for God by means other than Faith in Christ and the Cross. *"Walking after the Spirit"* refers to the Believer abiding strictly by the Word of God, which always leads the Believer to Christ and the Cross.

Ezekiel's Prophecies began about five or six years before the destruction of Jerusalem, after the nation had gone so far that even Repentance (although saving the individual) would not have saved the nation or the city.

In Verse 7, the Lord told the Prophet that the House of Israel would not hear the Message, even though it came directly from the Lord. The two words, *"impudent"* and *"hardhearted,"* tell us why Israel would not hear the Word of the Lord.

The word *"impudent"* means to be contemptuous, in the sense of holding the Word of God in contempt and exhibiting a cocky boldness. The word *"hardhearted"* means *"unfeeling and pitiless."*

If the Gospel is offered and then rejected, the heart grows progressively harder. Spiritually speaking, the individual is not left in a neutral position.

THE ANOINTING

It is not easy to preach to people when it is obvious that they are rejecting the Message. As they reject the Message, invariably, they also reject the Messenger!

The intimation in these statements is that the hearts of these individuals had grown hard, because they had determined in their mind that they would not serve God. The idea is one of free will, which determines the position of the heart.

These individuals have purposely, stubbornly, and willfully, in the face of Light, determined to reject God's Way in favor of their own. Their position was a willful, clear, thought-out choice, hence, their hardness! As a result, God would give Ezekiel the spiritual and mental strength to bring about a purposeful heart in order to stand against their obstinacy in delivering his Message.

Ezekiel's Message was primarily to those in captivity in the Babylonian Empire. As previously stated, there were many thousands held there by their captors.

Concerning Israel, Verse 11 uses the phrase, *"thy people,"* instead of *"My people."* In fact, Jehovah no longer recognized them as His.

Ezekiel's responsibility was to deliver the Message, rather than their response to it. He is to *"speak unto them, and tell them, Thus saith the Lord GOD."*

(12) "THEN THE SPIRIT TOOK ME UP, AND I HEARD BEHIND ME A VOICE OF A GREAT RUSHING, SAYING, BLESSED BE THE GLORY OF THE LORD FROM HIS PLACE.

(13) "I HEARD ALSO THE NOISE OF THE WINGS OF THE LIVING CREATURES THAT TOUCHED ONE ANOTHER, AND THE NOISE OF THE WHEELS OVER AGAINST THEM, AND A NOISE OF A GREAT RUSHING.

(14) "SO THE SPIRIT LIFTED ME UP, AND TOOK ME AWAY, AND I WENT IN BITTERNESS, IN THE HEAT OF MY SPIRIT; BUT THE HAND OF THE LORD WAS STRONG UPON ME.

(15) "THEN I CAME TO THEM OF THE CAPTIVITY AT TEL-ABIB, THAT DWELT BY THE RIVER OF CHEBAR, AND I SAT WHERE THEY SAT, AND REMAINED THERE ASTONISHED AMONG THEM SEVEN DAYS.

(16) "AND IT CAME TO PASS AT THE END OF SEVEN DAYS, THAT THE WORD OF THE LORD CAME UNTO ME, SAYING,"

The structure is:

1. It is the Holy Spirit Who energized the Cherubim and the wheels, and then took hold of Ezekiel to energize him.

2. The *"bitterness"* of Verse 14 probably refers to the unwillingness of the Prophet to be the bearer to the people of a Message of lamentation, mourning, and woe.

3. The *"Hand of the LORD"* strong upon him gave him the courage and strength to overcome his reluctance, and sanctified his anger.

THE HOLY SPIRIT

In Verses 12 and 14, the word "Spirit" should have been capitalized, because it is speaking of the Holy Spirit, and His involvement in all of this. As we've already stated, everything done on this Earth by the Godhead, with the exception of what Christ did at the Cross, has been done through the Person and Ministry of the Holy Spirit. In fact, nothing is going to be done for God on this Earth, unless it is birthed, carried out, and finished by the Holy Spirit. While the Spirit of God uses men and women to accomplish His tasks, He does so only as they are pliable in His hands. As is obvious, the Holy Spirit is God!

All of these things happening to the Prophet are taking place in Vision only. But of course, it is just as real as literal events.

THE MODERN CHURCH AND THE HOLY SPIRIT

At the time of this writing (May, 2003), there are probably less people presently being baptized with the Holy Spirit than at any time since the great Latter Rain outpouring began at the turn of the Twentieth Century (Joel 2:23). The Denominations which are supposed to be Pentecostal, according to their own admission, now have less, much less, than fifty percent of their people who are Spirit-baptized. The modern Church presently operates, at least for the most part, without the Holy Spirit. This means that precious little is actually being done for the Lord. The Denominational world, and I speak of the Baptist, Methodist, etc., have totally rejected the Baptism with the Holy Spirit, with the evidence of speaking with other tongues; consequently, what little light they once had is now being lost; for light rejected, is light withdrawn.

The Pentecostal Denominations, which claim to believe in the Baptism with the Holy Spirit, as stated, are seeing, at this present time, precious few baptized with the Spirit. In fact, almost no emphasis is placed on the Holy Spirit, other things being dominant. As a result, in these circles, very little is being done for the Lord.

The Charismatic world, which boasts of tens of thousands of Churches over this land and around the world, falls into the same category. Far too many of them are into the *"greed gospel,"* with many saying, even as the Ephesian Disciples, *"We have not so much as heard whether there be any Holy Spirit"* (Acts 19:2).

If the Reader thinks I sound negative, the situation is actually far worse than I have reported.

A PERSONAL WORD

If I remember correctly, it was either in late winter of 1992, or early spring. At any rate, the Morning Prayer meeting was in progress. There must have been approximately eight or ten people present, if that.

After praying for a few minutes, the Spirit of the Lord began to come upon me in a strong way. I was imploring the Lord to help me, for I knew that it was impossible for us to survive without His help. I was crying to Him for strength, which I so desperately needed, and for victory to be paramount, which could only be carried out by the Holy Spirit. In other words, as the Spirit of God dealt with me, and did so strongly, I was made to see my many shortcomings, my many weaknesses, and my many flaws, and I knew that He Alone could give me what was needed for these problems to be addressed.

And then at a given time, the Lord spoke to my heart as it regards the Church world as a whole. He took me to the First Chapter of the great Prophet Isaiah, and He said to me, *"You are seeking Me for help regarding yourself, which you desperately need, but the entirety of the Church world also needs this help."* And then He said, *"The whole head is sick, and the whole heart faint. From the sole of the foot even unto the head there is no soundness in it; but wounds, and bruises, and putrifying sores: they have not been closed, neither bound up, neither mollified with ointment"* (Isa. 1:5-6).

And then the Lord related something else to me, which, at the present time, I do not feel the liberty to relate. But this much I will say:

A MIGHTY MOVE OF GOD

I personally feel in my spirit that the Lord is about to do something great and mighty. I do not necessarily think that the institutionalized Church will be very much changed, but I do feel that hearts which are hungry and thirsty for God are going to see that hunger and that thirst satisfied. I believe the Lord is going to move in a greater way than possibly He has ever moved before.

In October of 1991, the Lord told me to begin two prayer meetings a day: one in the morning, and one in the evening. That has been twelve years ago, and I still hold to that which the Lord instructed me to do. During these twelve years, I have sensed many mighty movings of the Holy Spirit upon my person, and the Lord has spoken many things to my heart. Among those things which He has spoken, I believe, is the Promise of a definite Move of God, which possibly will eclipse anything that has ever been done in the past. God's revelations of Himself never diminish, but always increase. In other words, what He does now incorporates what He did previously, but adds to that which was previously done. That is His method. He never diminishes, but always increases. And whatever is done, it is always the Holy Spirit Who does the doing.

Jesus said: *"If any man thirst, let him come unto Me, and drink.*

"He who believes on Me, as the Scripture has said, out of his innermost being shall flow rivers of Living Water.

"But this spoke He of the Spirit, which they who believe on Him should receive" (Jn. 7:37-39).

(17) "SON OF MAN, I HAVE MADE YOU A WATCHMAN UNTO THE HOUSE OF ISRAEL: THEREFORE HEAR THE WORD AT MY MOUTH, AND GIVE THEM WARNING FROM ME.

(18) "WHEN I SAY UNTO THE WICKED, YOU SHALL SURELY DIE; AND YOU GIVE HIM NOT WARNING, NOR SPEAK TO WARN THE WICKED FROM HIS WICKED WAY, TO SAVE HIS LIFE; THE SAME WICKED MAN SHALL DIE IN HIS INIQUITY; BUT HIS BLOOD WILL I REQUIRE AT YOUR HAND.

(19) "YET IF YOU WARN THE WICKED, AND HE TURN NOT FROM HIS WICKEDNESS, NOR FROM HIS WICKED WAY, HE SHALL DIE IN HIS INIQUITY; BUT YOU HAVE DELIVERED YOUR SOUL.

(20) "AGAIN, WHEN A RIGHTEOUS MAN DOES TURN FROM HIS RIGHTEOUSNESS, AND COMMIT INIQUITY, AND I LAY A STUMBLINGBLOCK BEFORE HIM, HE SHALL DIE: BECAUSE YOU HAVE NOT GIVEN HIM WARNING, HE SHALL DIE IN HIS SIN, AND HIS RIGHTEOUSNESS WHICH HE HAS DONE SHALL NOT BE REMEMBERED; BUT HIS BLOOD WILL I REQUIRE AT YOUR HAND.

(21) "NEVERTHELESS IF YOU WARN THE RIGHTEOUS MAN, THAT THE RIGHTEOUS SIN NOT, AND HE DOES NOT SIN,

HE SHALL SURELY LIVE, BECAUSE HE IS WARNED; ALSO YOU HAVE DELIVERED YOUR SOUL."

The diagram is:

1. The substance of Ezekiel's Message is given in Verses 17 through 21, and the dual character of the Christian Ministry is found in the instructions: *"Hear the Word at My Mouth"* and *"Give them warning from Me."*

2. As Ezekiel was a *"Watchman unto the House of Israel,"* likewise, every true Preacher of the Gospel falls into the same category, i.e., as a *"Watchman unto the Church."*

3. In Verses 18 through 21, the unscriptural doctrine of Unconditional Eternal Security is hereby refuted.

A WATCHMAN

In the ancient world, watchmen walked the walls in order to spot any hostile action against the city. They were also there to give word to the King of any person approaching the city wall (II Sam. 18:24-27; II Ki. 9:17-20). In times of hostility, the dangers of the night were especially feared, and the watchmen eagerly looked forward to the break of day (Isa. 21:11).

As a Watchman, Ezekiel was to *"hear the Word at My Mouth, and give them warning from Me."*

ETERNAL SECURITY

As a Preacher of the Gospel and a student of the Word, I definitely believe in eternal security, but that which one could say is *"conditional."* Verses 18 through 21 graphically proclaim the conditions. In other words, there is no such thing as an unconditional eternal security. The idea that one can be saved, and then, no matter what they do thereafter, can remained saved, and make Heaven their eternal home, in truth, presents a *"fool's hope."* The entirety of the Book of Hebrews militates against the false doctrine of Unconditional Eternal Security.

Some Christian Jews, during the time of the Early Church, were turning their back on Christ, and going back into Judaism. The Believer's connection with Christ is based solely upon Faith in Christ. When Faith in Christ ceases to be, and reverts to something else, as it evidently was with some of those Christian Jews, Paul severely warned them that it is *"impossible for those who were once enlightened, and have tasted of the Heavenly Gift, and were made partakers of the Holy Spirit,*

"And have tasted the good Word of God, and the powers of the world to come,

"If they shall fall away, to renew them again unto Repentance; seeing they crucify to themselves the Son of God afresh, and put Him to an open shame" (Heb. 6:4-6).

This doesn't mean that a backslider cannot come back to Christ, but it does mean if a Believer ceases to believe in Christ, which means he ceases to trust in what Christ has done at the Cross, then that person becomes an unbeliever, and if he remains in that situation, he will lose his soul.

The Apostle also said: *"For if we sin willfully, after that we have received the knowledge of the Truth, there remains no more Sacrifice for sins,*

"But a certain fearful looking for of judgment and fiery indignation, which shall devour the adversaries.

"He who despised Moses' Law died without Mercy under two or three witnesses:

"Of how much sorer punishment, suppose ye, shall he be Thought worthy, who has trodden under foot the Son of God, and has counted the Blood of the Covenant, wherewith he was Sanctified, an unholy thing, and has done despite unto the Spirit of Grace?" (Heb. 10:26-29).

Once again, the *"willful sin"* of which the Apostle wrote was that of forsaking Christ — more particularly, forsaking what He had done for us at the Cross. They *"counted the Blood of the Covenant,"* which refers to the Cross, as *"an unholy thing."*

Now remember, these are individuals who had truly been saved, but they lost their way through unbelief, even as millions have done since then.

It is Faith in Christ which brings one to Salvation, and Faith in Christ which keeps one in Salvation; if that Faith is lost, or, more particularly, shifted to something else, the person reverts to the status of unbeliever, and is in a lost condition; unless he comes back to Christ, which is a renewal of Faith, he cannot be saved.

WHAT IS THE STATUS OF THEM WHO HAVE NEVER HAD THE PRIVILEGE TO HEAR THE GOSPEL?

Verse 18 tells us what their status is. Regrettably and sadly, they are lost. But there is a chilling statement at the end of that Verse. It says:

"When I say unto the wicked, you shall surely die: and you give him not warning, . . . his blood will I require at your hand."

God has sent His Son to this world, Who paid a terrible price at Calvary's Cross, in order for man to be saved. In other words, Heaven has already done all that Heaven can do about the Salvation of man. It is the business of the Church to take the Gospel to the world. And to a degree, the Church has done that.

However, ignorance of the Gospel never presents a ticket to Salvation. The rudiments of Salvation can only come to the individual when that person expresses Faith in Christ and what Christ did at the Cross. The believing sinner may not understand very much about Christ, but He must express Faith. He must realize that he is lost, and that the only Saviour is the Lord Jesus Christ. Then, and then only, can he be saved (Rom. 10:9-10, 13; Eph. 2:8-9).

If ignorance of the Gospel is equal to Salvation, then the best way to get all people saved is to close all Churches, stop all Preaching, stop printing any more Bibles, in order that the entirety of the population of the world may remain ignorant, and thereby saved; however, I think it is obvious as to the fallacy of such thinking. So, sadly and regrettably, those who have never heard the Gospel, and who die in that condition, will be eternally lost.

As well, it is the business of the Child of God, and I speak of every single Believer, to do everything within his personal power, in the realm of prayer and in the realm of giving of our finances, to take this Gospel to the furthest reaches of this globe. But tragically, untold millions of dollars are spent on projects which claim to be the Gospel, but aren't the Gospel. So, such money is wasted, as would be obvious!

THE MINISTRY OF THE WATCHMAN

The problem of the Church is Preachers preaching what people want to hear, instead of what they need to hear. This is the age of the Church population having *"itching ears."* Paul said:

"For the time will come when they will not endure sound Doctrine; but after their own lusts shall they heap to themselves teachers, having itching ears;

"And they shall turn away their ears from the Truth, and shall be turned unto fables" (II Tim. 4:3-4).

The problem of *"itching ears"* has always persisted, but it is worse now than ever. But the greater problem is that it is no trouble whatsoever for these people to find Preachers who will accommodate those *"itching ears."* The land and the world are full of them.

This is the age of *"feel-good"* Churches. It's the age when no Gospel at all is preached, or else things are preached about the Gospel, but with the Gospel not actually being preached. And what do I mean by that statement?

Unless the Preacher is preaching the Cross, he's not actually preaching the Gospel (I Cor. 1:17-18, 21, 23; 2:2). That doesn't mean that he preaches about the Cross every time he preaches, but it does mean that the Cross must be at the foundation of all that he does preach.

The true Watchman must hear from Heaven, and then deliver to the people what the Lord has given him to preach.

PERSONAL EXPERIENCE

If I remember correctly, the year was 1982. Our Telecast was aired in quite a number of countries in the world, translated into various languages. We were having some of the largest crowds in the history of Evangelism, with tens of thousands being brought to a saving knowledge of Jesus Christ, and I exaggerate not!

While in prayer one Saturday morning, the Spirit of the Lord came upon me and began to reveal some things to me. The Lord informed me that I was to deliver a Message to the people. The Message to the Denominational world was that they were to embrace the Holy Spirit. The Message to the Pentecostal and Charismatic world was that they must come back to the Holy Spirit. And then I was to deliver a Message to the Catholic Church, which was simple and to the point: *"The just shall live by Faith."*

The Lord then told me that if I obeyed Him, many people would be saved, and many lives would be changed, but I would have to pay a terrible price. He went on to say, *"Your own will turn against you."*

I did not answer immediately, trying to understand the import of what I was being told.

Concerning the last of His instructions, I had little or no knowledge about the Catholic Church. Raised in North Louisiana, where there were almost no Catholics, I had little or no occasion whatsoever to deal with these people. And beside that, Catholic Charismatics were sending us hundreds of thousands of dollars, which we desperately needed for the Work of God.

Naturally, upon hearing something that I knew was going to create a firestorm, to be sure, I, of course, *"tried the spirits,"* to make certain that what I was hearing was from the Lord.

When the Holy Spirit reveals something to someone, He very seldom lets the matter rest; generally, he keeps dealing with the person, even as He did with me. I got to the place where I couldn't sleep at night, and then I knew that what I had been given was from the Lord, and that I must do my very best to do what He had told me to do.

To be sure, a firestorm of unprecedented proportions did burst upon this Ministry.

For one thing, I began to preach, and over worldwide Television, that Catholic Charismatics must come out of that system. I did not doubt that the Lord had saved them, and had even baptized some with the Holy Spirit. Still, they could not remain in that false doctrine. They had to come out!

I think those statements caused more anger than anything else. It flew in the face of what they were being told by most Pentecostals and Charismatics. They were being told to remain in the Catholic Church, but I was telling them they must leave.

One particular Charismatic leader wrote me and said, *"With one Message, you have destroyed more than I have taken a lifetime to build."* Of course, he was telling the Catholic Charismatics to remain in the Catholic Church. I read his letter with great interest. Either the Message I was preaching was far stronger than I realized, or else he had not built very much.

The vituperation and the anger burst upon us like a thunderstorm. The Lord was exactly right; my own turned against me. However, I would rather have the Lord on my side, and everybody against me, than to have everybody on my side, and the Lord be against me.

As a *"Watchman,"* it was my business to hear from the Lord, and to deliver what He told me to deliver. I was not to add to the Message, or to take from the Message.

Exactly as the Lord said, we saw tens of thousands brought to a saving knowledge of Jesus Christ, for which we give the Lord all the praise and all the glory.

When the Lord told the Prophet Ezekiel that he was to be a Watchman unto the House of Israel, He was saying the same thing to all God-called Preachers.

One day, every single Preacher of the Gospel, and once again, I speak of those who are truly God-called, will stand before the Lord to give account for everything we've preached, and our motives for preaching it. We must ever keep that in mind.

(22) "AND THE HAND OF THE LORD WAS THERE UPON ME; AND HE SAID UNTO ME, ARISE, GO FORTH INTO THE PLAIN, AND I WILL THERE TALK WITH YOU.

(23) "THEN I AROSE, AND WENT FORTH INTO THE PLAIN: AND, BEHOLD, THE GLORY OF THE LORD STOOD THERE, AS THE GLORY WHICH I SAW BY THE RIVER OF CHEBAR: AND I FELL ON MY FACE.

(24) "THEN THE SPIRIT ENTERED INTO ME, AND SET ME UPON MY FEET, AND SPOKE WITH ME, AND SAID UNTO ME, GO, SHUT YOURSELF WITHIN YOUR HOUSE.

(25) "BUT YOU, O SON OF MAN, BEHOLD, THEY SHALL PUT BANDS UPON YOU, AND SHALL BIND YOU WITH THEM, AND YOU SHALL NOT GO OUT AMONG THEM:

(26) "AND I WILL MAKE YOUR TONGUE CLEAVE TO THE ROOF OF YOUR

MOUTH, THAT YOU SHALL BE DUMB, AND SHALL NOT BE TO THEM A REPROVER: FOR THEY ARE A REBELLIOUS HOUSE.

(27) "BUT WHEN I SPEAK WITH YOU, I WILL OPEN YOUR MOUTH, AND YOU SHALL SAY UNTO THEM, THUS SAITH THE LORD GOD; HE WHO HEARS, LET HIM HEAR; AND HE WHO FORBEARS, LET HIM FORBEAR: FOR THEY ARE A REBELLIOUS HOUSE."

The overview is:

1. In these Verses, we find that, under the control of the Holy Spirit, the lips are taught when to be dumb, and when to speak.

2. To hear the Word from the Mouth of the Lord, the servant of the Lord must be willing to withdraw into the *"plain,"* or *"low place,"* for it is there that the Master speaks with the servant, and afresh reveals Himself in His glory to him.

3. The *"Glory of the LORD"* can be falsely imitated, but never duplicated. It is done so with noise, show, pomp, ceremony, activity, and action, but all of the flesh, and which cannot please God (Rom. 8:8).

THE GLORY OF THE LORD

The *"Glory of the LORD,"* is, among other things, a revelation of the Power and Presence of God as manifested by the Holy Spirit. It is the highest honor God can pay an individual — the Revelation of His Glory! It is that which makes the Church a living organism; and yet, most Churches, Preachers, and Christians have never experienced such even one time! Actually, most in Christendom do not even believe in it, do not want it, or desire it, and thereby strongly oppose it! These are Churches where the Holy Spirit is not present, and in fact, is not wanted.

THE CONTROL OF
THE HOLY SPIRIT

When under the control of the Holy Spirit, a control, incidentally, which must be freely given, the lips are taught when to be dumb and when to speak.

The *"bands"* referred to in Verse 25 speak of the rebellion of the exiles against the Word of God. They would not hear what Ezekiel had to say; they would seek to stop his Message, as those in Jerusalem sought to stop the Message of Jeremiah.

"The Holy Spirit is here, where Saints in prayer agree,
"As Jesus' parting Gift is near, each pleading company."

"Not far away is He, to be by prayer bro't nigh,
"But here in present majesty, as in His Courts on high."

"He dwells within our soul, an ever welcome guest;
"He reigns with absolute control, as Monarch in the breast."

"Obedient to Your Will, we wait to feel Your Power;
"Oh Lord of Life, our hopes fulfill, and bless this hallowed hour."

CHAPTER 4

(1) "THOU ALSO, SON OF MAN, TAKE THEE A TILE, AND LAY IT BEFORE YOU, AND PORTRAY UPON IT THE CITY, EVEN JERUSALEM:

(2) "AND LAY SIEGE AGAINST IT, AND BUILD A FORT AGAINST IT, AND CAST A MOUNT AGAINST IT; SET THE CAMP ALSO AGAINST IT, AND SET BATTERING RAMS AGAINST IT ROUND ABOUT.

(3) "MOREOVER TAKE THOU UNTO YOU AN IRON PAN, AND SET IT FOR A WALL OF IRON BETWEEN YOU AND THE CITY: AND SET YOUR FACE AGAINST IT, AND IT SHALL BE BESIEGED, AND YOU SHALL LAY SIEGE AGAINST IT. THIS SHALL BE A SIGN TO THE HOUSE OF ISRAEL.

(4) "LIE THOU ALSO UPON YOUR LEFT SIDE, AND LAY THE INIQUITY OF THE HOUSE OF ISRAEL UPON IT: ACCORDING TO THE NUMBER OF THE DAYS THAT YOU SHALL LIE UPON IT YOU SHALL BEAR THEIR INIQUITY.

(5) "FOR I HAVE LAID UPON YOU THE YEARS OF THEIR INIQUITY, ACCORDING TO THE NUMBER OF THE DAYS, THREE HUNDRED AND NINETY DAYS: SO SHALL YOU BEAR THE INIQUITY OF THE HOUSE

OF ISRAEL.

(6) "AND WHEN YOU HAVE ACCOMPLISHED THEM, LIE AGAIN ON YOUR RIGHT SIDE, AND YOU SHALL BEAR THE INIQUITY OF THE HOUSE OF JUDAH FORTY DAYS: I HAVE APPOINTED YOU EACH DAY FOR A YEAR.

(7) "THEREFORE YOU SHALL SET YOUR FACE TOWARD THE SIEGE OF JERUSALEM, AND YOUR ARM SHALL BE UNCOVERED, AND YOU SHALL PROPHESY AGAINST IT.

(8) "AND, BEHOLD, I WILL LAY BANDS UPON YOU, AND YOU SHALL NOT TURN THEE FROM ONE SIDE TO ANOTHER, TILL YOU HAVE ENDED THE DAYS OF YOUR SIEGE."

The diagram is:

1. It has been argued that these symbolisms instructed by the Lord of Ezekiel were only envisioned and not carried out in fact; however, all the evidence is otherwise.

2. This was taking place in Babylonia, approximately four years before Jerusalem would be destroyed by Nebuchadnezzar; therefore, the time of destruction is drawing near, which the Lord desires to portray to the exiles.

3. The *"iron pan,"* as portrayed by the Holy Spirit, is that Nebuchadnezzar's siege, at least when it comes, will be so expertly drafted, that its victorious outcome is certain.

SIGNS

At this particular time, there is no doubt that false prophets were proclaiming that shortly the Exiles would be restored to Jerusalem, with Judah regaining its supremacy. Inasmuch as the Exiles desired to hear this Message, and it was no doubt popular, Ezekiel's Message, which was the opposite, proclaiming Jerusalem's destruction, was not happily received. Therefore, the Holy Spirit will use every method of approach, including symbolisms, that the true Message be understood.

The *"three hundred and ninety days,"* were to represent the *"three hundred and ninety years of their iniquity."* It pertained to the time when the Northern Kingdom of Israel split away from Judah and Benjamin under Jeroboam. It would be about four years before the three hundred and ninety years were fulfilled, which is when Jerusalem fell.

The three hundred and ninety years represented the Lord's extreme displeasure with the Northern Kingdom, as a result of their splitting the nation and going into idol worship (I Ki. 12:16-20, 28-30). As would be obvious, they were out of the Will of God.

The forty years pertained to the entire Prophetic Ministry of Jeremiah, ending with the fall of Jerusalem, and having begun in the thirteenth year of the reign of Josiah.

In all of this, we see the Lord dealing with the people, in order that they not believe that which was false, but would rather believe His Prophets. Regrettably, as far as is known, the Lord at that time only had two Prophets, who were Jeremiah and Ezekiel, while no doubt the false Prophets abounded. As stated, the false prophets were claiming that the Babylonian siege would be lifted, and Judah would be restored to her place of prominence. This is what the people wanted to hear. Jeremiah and Ezekiel were prophesying the very opposite, that which the people did not want to hear.

SIGNS OF THE TIMES

Judah and Jerusalem were coming down to the very end before Judgment would fall. The reasons were gross sin and repeated spurnings of the Call of God. Likewise, the modern Church follows suit.

We are at the very end of the Church Age; Judgment is about to be poured out on this world, in the form of the great Tribulation (Mat. 24:21). All of this means that the Rapture could take place at any time; however, precious few modern Believers are actually looking for the Rapture, and in fact, most don't know anything about the Rapture. Incidentally, the Rapture and the Resurrection are one and the same (I Thess. 4:13-18; I Cor., Chpt. 15). The great sign at present is Israel, which has always been God's Prophetic time clock. Another sign is the terrible spiritual declension of the Church. Concerning these times, Paul said: *"Now the Spirit* (Holy Spirit) *speaks expressly* (pointedly), *that in the latter times* (the times in which we now live) *some shall depart from the Faith* (Jesus Christ and Him Crucified), *giving heed to seducing spirits and doctrines of Devils"* (I Tim. 4:1).

While there are no signs in the Bible referring to the Rapture, there are multitudinous signs as it regards the Second Coming. And if we see many signs already in progress regarding the Second Coming, of which we have named a few, then this should make us realize just how near the Rapture must be.

(9) "TAKE THOU ALSO UNTO YOU WHEAT, AND BARLEY, AND BEANS, AND LENTILES, AND MILLET, AND FITCHES, AND PUT THEM IN ONE VESSEL, AND MAKE THEE BREAD THEREOF, ACCORDING TO THE NUMBER OF THE DAYS THAT YOU SHALL LIE UPON YOUR SIDE, THREE HUNDRED AND NINETY DAYS SHALL YOU EAT THEREOF.

(10) "AND YOUR MEAT WHICH YOU SHALL EAT SHALL BE BY WEIGHT, TWENTY SHEKELS A DAY: FROM TIME TO TIME SHALL YOU EAT IT.

(11) "YOU SHALL DRINK ALSO WATER BY MEASURE, THE SIXTH PART OF AN HIN: FROM TIME TO TIME SHALL YOU DRINK.

(12) "AND YOU SHALL EAT IT AS BARLEY CAKES, AND YOU SHALL BAKE IT WITH DUNG THAT COMES OUT OF MAN, IN THEIR SIGHT.

(13) "AND THE LORD SAID, EVEN THUS SHALL THE CHILDREN OF ISRAEL EAT THEIR DEFILED BREAD AMONG THE GENTILES, WHITHER I WILL DRIVE THEM."

The composition is:

1. As it regards the coming siege of Jerusalem, the diet, such as it was, would be measured because of the scarcity of food.

2. As Ezekiel went through the regimen each day, the sameness of the procedure could not help but have a lasting effect on the Exiles, as it portrayed by Prophetic symbolism that which was coming shortly to Jerusalem.

3. To *"drink also water by measure"* showed that water, as well, would be at a premium, even as food, in the coming siege, which of course, the false prophets said would never occur.

THE WORD OF THE LORD

In a besieged city, the supply of wood soon fails, with cow chips or *"cow dung"* being used instead to make a fire for cooking.

The implication by the Lord, even as given in Verse 12, was that this supply also would soon fail because of the animals being eaten, and that the population would be forced to use the dried contents of the cesspools of Jerusalem, hence the command by Jehovah to *"bake it with dung that comes out of man, in their sight."*

Surely, the implication of the symbolic Prophecy on the viewers was not lost as Ezekiel carried it out day-by-day, and in its exactness and sameness.

The questions must be asked, *"Why wouldn't the people heed the Prophecies of Jeremiah in Jerusalem, or those of Ezekiel in Babylonia?"* and *"Could not the people tell the difference between the Prophecies of Jeremiah and Ezekiel and those of the false prophets?"*

The truth is, they couldn't! Once again, they didn't want to believe what the two Prophets were saying, because it was not what they liked or desired!

But the upshot of all of this was, Judah would not admit her sinful, hard hearted, rebellious spirit against the Lord. At this time, all evidence shows that Judah was very religious. All the activities in the Temple were being carried out on a daily basis. In fact, prosperity filled the land.

They reasoned that God would never allow the heathen to come into the Temple; according to this reasoning, Jerusalem would never fall. So, the Prophecies of Jeremiah and Ezekiel were not only rejected, but were greatly resented.

It all has to do with the evil hearts of men.

All sin in some way is a departure of one's Faith from the Cross of Christ to something else. While Israel, at that time, was continuing to offer up Sacrifices, their Faith was in the ritual, instead of what the Sacrifices represented — namely the coming Redeemer, and the price He would pay on the Cross. It is the same presently!

Satan has been very successful at shifting the Faith of the Church away from the Cross to other things. To be sure, he really doesn't care too very much about what the other things are, knowing that such a direction, whatever it might be, will bring severe spiritual trouble. Men do not mind being religious; in fact, they enjoy being religious. Someone has well said, *"The doing of religion is the worst narcotic there is."*

Because of Judah's rebellious spirit, she had gone into idol worship, and service to the Lord had become mere ritual. The sin and the evil were becoming worse by the day, but yet, unrecognized by Judah.

When the Church loses sight of sin, when it has a wrong opinion of sin, this is one of the surest signs of spiritual declension. If one doesn't properly understand the price that had to be paid to address the terrible problem of sin, which was the Cross, then one cannot understand how bad that sin actually is. The heart becomes hardened, because of the deceitfulness of sin (Heb. 3:13).

(14) "THEN SAID I, AH LORD GOD! BEHOLD, MY SOUL HAS NOT BEEN POLLUTED; FOR FROM MY YOUTH UP EVEN TILL NOW HAVE I NOT EATEN OF THAT WHICH DIETH OF ITSELF, OR IS TORN IN PIECES; NEITHER CAME THERE ABOMINABLE FLESH INTO MY MOUTH.

(15) "THEN HE SAID UNTO ME, LO, I HAVE GIVEN YOU COW'S DUNG FOR MAN'S DUNG, AND YOU SHALL PREPARE YOUR BREAD THEREWITH.

(16) "MOREOVER HE SAID UNTO ME, SON OF MAN, BEHOLD, I WILL BREAK THE STAFF OF BREAD IN JERUSALEM: AND THEY SHALL EAT BREAD BY WEIGHT, AND WITH CARE; AND THEY SHALL DRINK WATER BY MEASURE, AND WITH ASTONISHMENT:

(17) "THAT THEY MAY WANT BREAD AND WATER, AND BE ASTONIED ONE WITH ANOTHER, AND CONSUME AWAY FOR THEIR INIQUITY."

The structure is:

1. Ezekiel, as a Priest, had faithfully followed the Law of Moses, and had done his best to keep himself from any kind of defilement. That of which he speaks is noted in Exodus 22:31; Leviticus 7:24; 11:39-40; 17:15.

2. The Sixteenth Verse pertains to the terrible famine, which would ensue as a result of the siege of Jerusalem, which was described by Jeremiah upon its fulfillment (Lam. 4:8-10).

3. To the horror of the famine and its physical privation, there was to be added the consciousness that it was caused by their own sins, which could have been avoided, had they only repented.

INIQUITY

Clearly and plainly, the Lord proclaims the fact that all of the suffering which was to come upon Judah, which would be unimaginable in its scope, and which would effect every single individual, with untold thousands dying of starvation, or killed by the Babylonians, all were caused *"by their iniquity."*

Untold numbers of times, they could have heeded the admonition to repent, but they would not repent; because judgment had been again and again threatened, and had not yet come to pass, they rested in their false security that judgment would never come.

But let the Reader understand this:

God is longsuffering, not willing that any should perish, but that all should come to Repentance. Therefore, let it be known: His delay is not the result of approval or inattention, but is rather that of Mercy. But despite the delays, and the extended Mercy, Judah would not repent, but rather grew worse, inasmuch as sin always has a downward slide.

"Are you weary, are you troubled? Are you sore distressed?

"Come to Me, saith One, and, coming, be at rest.

"Has He marks to lead me to Him, if He be my guide?

"In His feet and hands are wound prints, and His side.

"Is there diadem, as Monarch, that His brow adorns?

"Yes, a crown, in very surety, but of thorns."

"If I find Him, if I follow, what His greatness here?

"Many a sorrow, many a labor, many a tear.

"If I still hold closely to Him, what has He at last?

"Sorrow vanquished, labor ended, Jordan passed."

CHAPTER 5

(1) "AND YOU, SON OF MAN, TAKE YOU

A SHARP KNIFE, TAKE YOU A BARBER'S RAZOR, AND CAUSE IT TO PASS UPON YOUR HEAD AND UPON YOUR BEARD: THEN TAKE YOU BALANCES TO WEIGH, AND DIVIDE THE HAIR.

(2) "YOU SHALL BURN WITH FIRE A THIRD PART IN THE MIDST OF THE CITY, WHEN THE DAYS OF THE SIEGE ARE FULFILLED: AND YOU SHALL TAKE A THIRD PART, AND SMITE ABOUT IT WITH A KNIFE: AND A THIRD PART YOU SHALL SCATTER IN THE WIND; AND I WILL DRAW OUT A SWORD AFTER THEM.

(3) "YOU SHALL ALSO TAKE THEREOF A FEW IN NUMBER, AND BIND THEM IN YOUR SKIRTS.

(4) "THEN TAKE OF THEM AGAIN, AND CAST THEM INTO THE MIDST OF THE FIRE, AND BURN THEM IN THE FIRE; FOR THEREOF SHALL A FIRE COME FORTH INTO ALL THE HOUSE OF ISRAEL.

(5) "THUS SAITH THE LORD GOD; THIS IS JERUSALEM: I HAVE SET IT IN THE MIDST OF THE NATIONS AND COUNTRIES THAT ARE ROUND ABOUT HER."

The overview is:

1. Again, the Lord uses symbolism to portray the desired Message. It is the symbol of the *"barber's razor."*

2. The symbolic action predicted that the fire, i.e., the Wrath of God, and pestilence, and famine should destroy approximately one third of the nation, with war destroying a second third, and the Exiles representing the third part, which would be *"scattered in the wind."* Many of these also were to perish by sword and famine.

3. According to these Prophecies, the carnage was terrible, with hundreds of thousands ruthlessly slaughtered when Jerusalem finally fell, along with many thousands who died of plague and starvation. The shaved head and beard would truly be a fitting symbol!

4. The judgment was to be so complete that even those who thought they had escaped, by whatever means, would find the *"fire"* of judgment chasing them, of which they could not escape. None, no matter how clever could outwit Jehovah.

5. The phrase, *"This is Jerusalem,"* is strong indeed! She, representing the nation, was placed in the center of the nations in order to shed upon them the light of the Gospel. But she rebelled against Truth more than the heathen, multiplied idols, and sank morally lower than her neighbors.

THIS IS JERUSALEM

The term of Verse 5, *"This is Jerusalem,"* is said by the Lord in the spirit of scorn, because of sin. Jerusalem was to be the light of the nations, the light to point not only those of Israel toward the Lord, but also the Gentiles. This was where the Lord had His Temple constructed. It was where the Sacrifices were offered morning and evening. It was where God dwelt in the Holy of Holies in the Temple, dwelt between the Mercy Seat and the Cherubim. It was the only city on the face of the Earth that had a knowledge of God, which meant that it was privileged as no other city of that day was privileged.

As a result, it knew the ways of the Lord; it had His Word, which made it light years ahead of any of the other nations of the world. But all to no avail! It turned the Light into darkness, Salvation into sin, strength into weakness, Heaven into Hell.

And even though this was God's City, the place where He had chosen to portray His Name, still, let it ever be understood that God cannot abide sin, and the sin of Jerusalem had become worse and worse. When the Lord of Glory now speaks of His City, and we speak of His City on Earth, He speaks with scorn. So, the questions must also be asked, *"What is He saying presently about the Church? What is He saying presently about me? About you?"*

Let the reader understand that God can only speak well of us, as our Faith is anchored firmly in Christ. It is to Christ, and to Christ Alone, that He said, *"This is My Beloved Son, in Whom I am well pleased"* (Mat. 3:17). So, He is pleased with us, only as we are in Christ. And one can be in Christ only by a portrayal of Faith in the Sacrifice of Christ, which is the price paid on Calvary's Hill. Faith placed in anything else is spurious, unacceptable to God, and is rejected out of hand. And if that is true, and it definitely is, then where does that put the present Church, which little exercises Faith in Christ and Him Crucified?

Is the Lord presently looking down and saying, with scorn and contempt, as He said of Jerusalem of old, *"This is the Church?"*

(6) "AND SHE HAS CHANGED MY JUDGMENTS INTO WICKEDNESS MORE THAN THE NATIONS, AND MY STATUTES MORE THAN THE COUNTRIES THAT ARE ROUND ABOUT HER: FOR THEY HAVE REFUSED MY JUDGMENTS AND MY STATUTES, THEY HAVE NOT WALKED IN THEM.

(7) "THEREFORE THUS SAITH THE LORD GOD; BECAUSE YOU MULTIPLIED MORE THAN THE NATIONS THAT ARE ROUND ABOUT YOU, AND HAVE NOT WALKED IN MY STATUTES, NEITHER HAVE KEPT MY JUDGMENTS, NEITHER HAVE DONE ACCORDING TO THE JUDGMENTS OF THE NATIONS THAT ARE ROUND ABOUT YOU;

(8) "THEREFORE THUS SAITH THE LORD GOD; BEHOLD, I, EVEN I, AM AGAINST YOU, AND WILL EXECUTE JUDGMENTS IN THE MIDST OF YOU IN THE SIGHT OF THE NATIONS.

(9) "AND I WILL DO IN YOU THAT WHICH I HAVE NOT DONE, AND WHEREUNTO I WILL NOT DO ANYMORE THE LIKE, BECAUSE OF ALL YOUR ABOMINATIONS.

(10) "THEREFORE THE FATHERS SHALL EAT THE SONS IN THE MIDST OF YOU, AND THE SONS SHALL EAT THEIR FATHERS; AND I WILL EXECUTE JUDGMENTS IN YOU, AND THE WHOLE REMNANT OF YOU WILL I SCATTER INTO ALL THE WINDS.

(11) "WHEREFORE, AS I LIVE, SAITH THE LORD GOD; SURELY, BECAUSE YOU HAVE DEFILED MY SANCTUARY WITH ALL YOUR DETESTABLE THINGS, AND WITH ALL YOUR ABOMINATIONS, THEREFORE WILL I ALSO DIMINISH YOU; NEITHER SHALL MINE EYE SPARE, NEITHER WILL I HAVE ANY PITY.

(12) "A THIRD PART OF YOU SHALL DIE WITH THE PESTILENCE, AND WITH FAMINE SHALL THEY BE CONSUMED IN THE MIDST OF YOU: AND A THIRD PART SHALL FALL BY THE SWORD ROUND ABOUT YOU; AND I WILL SCATTER A THIRD PART INTO ALL THE WINDS, AND I WILL DRAW OUT A SWORD AFTER THEM.

(13) "THUS SHALL MINE ANGER BE ACCOMPLISHED, AND I WILL CAUSE MY FURY TO REST UPON THEM, AND I WILL BE COMFORTED: AND THEY SHALL KNOW THAT I THE LORD HAVE SPOKEN IT IN MY ZEAL, WHEN I HAVE ACCOMPLISHED MY FURY IN THEM."

The exegesis is:

1. Judah rebelled against truth more than the heathen, multiplied idols, and sank morally lower than her neighbors.

2. After Judah had changed the Laws of God, the Laws of the surrounding nations were more Righteous than those of God's chosen.

3. *"I, even I,"* presents a solemn formula, which emphasizes the certainty of the Wrath of God.

4. Righteousness must, from its nature, be restless till evil is judged. Then it is comforted. Such was the effect of the judgment of sin at Calvary; and those who recognize this Gospel fact, and take refuge in the great God and Saviour, the Lord Jesus Christ, Who is the Redeemer, taste the sweetness of the Divine comfort.

THE CHANGING OF THE WORD OF GOD

Twisting and perverting the Word was the great sin of Judah; it is the great sin of the modern Church as well!

The Bible teaches Salvation by Grace through Faith, and that refers to Faith in Christ and what He did at the Cross (Eph. 2:8-9). It teaches the Baptism with the Holy Spirit, which is received subsequent to Salvation, and is always accompanied by speaking with other tongues, as the Spirit of God gives the utterance (Acts 2:4; 10:45-46; 19:1-7). It teaches Divine Healing according to believing prayer and the Will of God (James 5:14).

It teaches the Rapture of the Church, which could take place at any time (I Thess. 4:13-18). It teaches a Great Tribulation which is to come upon this world, during which time the man of sin, the Antichrist, will make his debut, and seek to destroy Israel (Rev., Chpts. 6-19). The Bible teaches the Second Coming, which will take place at the conclusion of the Great Tribulation, when the Lord Jesus Christ will come back to this Earth with a host of Angels, and with every Saint of God who has ever lived, who will be with Him (Rev., Chpt. 19).

The Word of God also teaches a coming thousand-year reign of Christ, Who will rule this Earth in Righteousness and Glory (Rev., Chpt. 20). The Bible also teaches the Perfect Age, which will follow the Great White Throne Judgment (Rev. 20:11-15), and will come about after the renovation of this Earth and the Heavens by Fire (II Pet. 3:12-13). This Perfect Age, when the Lord transfers His Headquarters from Heaven to Earth, will last forever and forever (Rev., Chpts. 21-22).

THE CROSS OF CHRIST

The central theme of the Word of God is, *"Jesus Christ and Him Crucified"* (Gen. 3:15; Isa., Chpt. 53; I Cor. 1:17-18, 21, 23; 2:2; Gal. 6:14; Eph. 2:13-18; Col. 2:14-15).

The entirety of the Word of God strains toward the Cross of Christ. This means that everything before the Cross looked forward to that coming event, and everything after the Cross, looks backward to that accomplished event, which makes possible all the things of the future.

The Sacrificial System was instigated by the Lord from the time of the Fall. In fact, even before that system was introduced, the Lord told Satan through the serpent: *"And I will put enmity* (animosity) *between you and the woman, and between your seed* (unredeemed humanity) *and her Seed* (the Lord Jesus Christ); *it* (He) *shall bruise your head* (the victory of the Cross), *and you shall bruise his Heel* (the sufferings of the Cross)" (Gen. 3:15).

In the Fourth Chapter of Genesis, we find the stage set, and a portrayal of what will come, as it regards this animosity between *"your seed and her Seed."* The Lord gave to the fallen First Family the means by which they could have communion with Him and have forgiveness of sins. That *"means"* was the Sacrifice of a clean animal, which was a symbol of the One Who was to come, the Lord Jesus Christ, and Who would be the ultimate Sacrifice, and the Altar, which was a Type of the Cross. The Sacrificial System was not to change until Christ would come, a time period of approximately 4,000 years.

There was no difference between the two brothers, Cain and Abel, but there was an eternal difference between their Sacrifices. They are both corrupt branches of a decayed tree, both born outside Eden, both guilty sinners, with no moral difference, and both sentenced to death.

The words *"by Faith"* in Hebrews 11:4 teach us that God had revealed, as stated, a way of approach to Him (Rom. 10:17). Abel accepts this Way, Cain rejects it. Abel's Altar speaks of Repentance, of Faith, and of the Precious Blood of Christ, the Lamb of God without blemish. Cain's Altar tells of pride, unbelief, and self-righteousness.

Abel's Altar is beautiful to God's eye, and repulsive to man's. Cain's Altar is beautiful to man's eye and repulsive to God's. These *"Altars"* exist today: around the one, that is Christ and His atoning Work, few are gathered; around the other, many. God accepts the slain Lamb and rejects the offered fruit; and the offering being rejected, so of necessity is the offerer. According to Hebrews 11:4, God *"testified over"* Abel's gifts, i.e., He sent fire from Heaven.

God loves Cain; wishing to bless him also, He tells him that if he will make an Offering similar to his brother's, it will be accepted; that the Lamb for the Sin-Offering was close at hand, lying at the door entrance of the Tabernacle before which the brothers were standing; that He would give him, if obedient, dominion over the whole Earth, and dispose his brother to willingly accept that Government, as He had disposed Eve to willingly accept subjection to Adam.

Cain rejects this love, invites his brother into the field, and murders him. Adam sins against God, and Cain sins against man. In their united conduct, we have sin and all its forms, and that on the first page of human history.

Cain's religion was too refined to slay a Lamb, but not too cultured to murder his brother. God's way of Salvation fills the heart with love; man's way of salvation inflames it with hatred. *"Religion has ever been the greatest cause of bloodshed"* (Williams).

THE CROSS, THE ONLY WAY

Also on the first page of human history, we have the Salvation pattern laid out, simple, gracious, benevolent, loving, and totally effective. Man is to offer up a clean animal, in this case, a lamb, as a Sacrifice on the Altar, with its hot blood poured out at the base of the Altar, which typified the price that God demanded as it regards payment for sin — a price that man could not hope to pay. To be saved, in the offering up of the Sacrifices, all man had to do was believe in the One represented by the Sacrifices, trusting God that He would eventually come in order to redeem this fallen race.

But as beautiful and wonderful as that *"Gift of God"* actually is, man finds it almost impossible to accept. He must change the Sacrifice, even as did Cain. He is perfectly content to build an Altar, even as did Cain, but he is loathe to accept the Sacrifice given by God on that Altar, the Lord Jesus Christ. So, he substitutes his own. Or possibly, he does it the other way. He rejects the Altar, while accepting Christ. Paul said that such constitutes *"another Jesus, which produces another spirit, and presents another Gospel"* (II Cor. 11:4).

So, in one way or the other, the rejection of the Sacrifice, or the rejection of the Altar, man seeks to substitute his own inventions; and perhaps one can say that the situation, possibly, has never been worse than at the present.

DEPARTING FROM THE FAITH

Paul said: *"Now the Spirit speaks expressly, that in the latter times some shall depart from the Faith, giving heed to seducing spirits, and doctrines of Devils"* (I Tim. 4:1).

"The Faith" refers to Christ and what Christ did at the Cross. Satan has been very successful in the last several decades at pushing the Church away from the Cross. Consequently, at the present time, there is less preaching of the Cross than at any time since the Reformation. And let me quickly say the following:

To properly understand the Bible, one has to properly understand the Cross. Realizing that there is very little understanding of the Cross presently, and I speak of both Salvation and Sanctification, this means that there is very little true understanding of the Word of God. In fact, without a proper understanding of the Cross, an awful perversion of the Word is the result, which is very similar to what happened to Judah of old. So, the question must be asked, *"Why is the Cross rejected, or else perverted as to its true meaning?"*

There may be many reasons, but I personally think that two particular reasons address the great body of thought as it regards false direction. They are:

UNBELIEF

We teach and believe that Jesus addressed every single thing which man lost in the Fall at the Cross (Col. 2:14-15; Eph. 1:10). This means that Jesus addressed every vice, every iniquity, and every transgression, atoning for all sin. The glorious Scripture says: *"For by one Offering He has perfected forever them who are Sanctified"* (Heb. 10:14).

In fact, the Cross not only addressed the Fall of man, but it also addressed the great revolution of Satan carried out against God sometime in eternity past (Eph. 1:10). Admittedly, we do not presently have all the benefits of what Jesus did at the Cross, in fact, only the *"Firstfruits"* (Rom. 8:23), the balance awaiting the coming Resurrection (I Cor. 15:51-58). But, to be sure, there are presently enough benefits available to us, all because of the Cross, that we can live a victorious life, in that the sin nature not have dominion over us in any capacity, with total victory over the world, the flesh, and the Devil (Rom. 8:14).

DOESN'T THE MODERN CHURCH BELIEVE THIS GREAT TRUTH OF TOTAL VICTORY IN THE CROSS?

With some few exceptions, *"No!"*

There are two reasons this is so: A. When the explanation of the Cross is given, actually as it was taught by Paul so long ago, and given to him by the Lord Jesus Christ (Gal. 1:12), it is mostly rejected. And let it be understood: Light rejected is Light withdrawn, and the end result is never good.

B. The advent of humanistic psychology. In the first place, psychology doesn't work anyway. And in the second place, to accept humanistic psychology in place of the Cross of Christ, especially by Preachers who claim to be Spirit-filled, is tantamount to blasphemy. And that's exactly what the major Pentecostal Denominations have done, at least in the United States and Canada, and I'm afraid in most of the balance of the world as well. There is, I would pray, an exception here and there, but not many!

If one truly believes the Cross, it obviously cancels out humanistic psychology. And if one accepts humanistic psychology, that cancels out the Cross. It is impossible to wed the two. The former comes from the wisdom of this world, which is *"sensual and devilish"* (James 3:15). The latter, i.e., *"the Cross,"* comes entirely from God, as is obvious. The two cannot mix!

So, the only reason I can see that religious men accept humanistic psychology as the answer to the perversions of man, is simply because of unbelief as it regards the Cross of Christ. You either believe that the answers for sin, perversion, immorality, and transgression of any type, which refer to the moral depravity of mankind, are found totally in the Cross, or else you don't believe it. There is no gray area, no middle ground.

There is an additional culprit, which has made great inroads into the modern Church, and is, in my personal opinion, possibly the most insidious of all. I speak of the *"Jesus Died Spiritually Doctrine,"* promoted by most Word of Faith Churches.

THE JESUS DIED SPIRITUALLY DOCTRINE

Many Christians who subscribe totally to the Word of Faith Doctrine have probably never even heard the term, *"Jesus Died Spiritually";* however, that is the foundation doctrine of most Word of Faith Churches. The truth is, that which they refer to as *"Faith"* is no Faith at all, at least that which God will recognize!

First of all, there is no room for the Cross in the theology in of the Word of Faith Doctrine. Actually, the Cross is repudiated as it regards this teaching. It is referred to as *"past miseries"* or *"the greatest defeat in human history."*

To deal with the Word of Faith Doctrine, I will copy verbatim a Message I wrote for the August 2002 Issue of The Evangelist Magazine.

THE WORD OF FAITH DOCTRINE

I'm going to address myself in this article to something that is very touchy, but yet which I definitely feel must be addressed.

I want to deal with statements made by Brother Kenneth K. Hagin in the April Issue of his magazine, 2002.

Even though I will have to take a strong stand against statements made by Brother Hagin, I do so not at all with any rancor in my heart against this dear man. He is older than I am, and I defer to his age; however, I definitely do not defer to his doctrine. I will be as gentle as possible, but at the same time, I will also be as straightforward as possible.

WHAT RIGHT DO I HAVE?

Some may argue that inasmuch as Brother Hagin is older than this Evangelist, I have no right to say anything. I remind the reader that Paul was younger than Simon Peter. In fact, Peter was looked at in the Early Church as the Prince of the Apostles. He had been personally selected by Christ, and had walked with Christ for some three and one half years. In fact, he was the spokesman for the original Twelve. But yet, Paul rebuked him, and did so publicly, even though he (Paul) was the junior.

I refer to Galatians, Chapter 2, where Paul rebuked Peter, and did so publicly, because of the Law/Grace issue. To Peter's credit, the great Apostle took this stinging rebuke, although it must have been hard on the flesh. May all of us have the Grace that Peter definitely possessed.

THE WORD OF FAITH DOCTRINE

That which I will say concerns the foundation of the Word of Faith Doctrine, which I believe is unscriptural and, therefore, totally in error. If we are wrong about the Atonement, then, in some way, we will be wrong about everything else as it regards what we teach concerning the Bible. I realize that's a strong statement, but I believe it to be true. Whereas the Atonement is the foundation of the Gospel, the Cross is the foundation of the Atonement. If one divorces the Cross from the Atonement, one has destroyed the Atonement, which is the most serious offense that can be committed.

I'm going to address some of Brother Hagin's statements, and do so according to the Word of God.

These statements were made in his advertisement of a booklet he was offering, as stated, in the April Issue 2002, of his monthly magazine.

THE CROSS, A PLACE OF
DEFEAT OR VICTORY?

Brother Hagin said in the advertisement, *"The Cross is a place of defeat."* How in the world could any Preacher read the Bible and come up with a conclusion that the Cross is a place of defeat? In fact, it was the greatest place of victory in the entirety of the history of mankind. The life of Christ wasn't taken from Him at the Cross. He laid it down voluntarily and willingly. He said:

"I lay down My life, that I might take it again.

"No man takes it from Me, but I lay it down of Myself. I have power to lay it down, and I have power to take it again" (Jn. 10:17-18).

If the Romans or the Jews had taken His Life from Him, then one could refer to the Cross as a place of defeat. However, considering that He purposely went to the Cross, and purposely laid down His Life, one could hardly refer to such as a defeat.

As stated, the Cross was the place of the greatest victory that man has ever known. Paul said: *"Blotting out the handwriting of Ordinances that was against us, which was contrary to us, and took it out of the way, nailing it to His Cross;*

"And having spoiled principalities and powers, He made a show of them openly, triumphing over them in it" (Col. 2:14-15).

Plainly and unmistakably, Paul tells us that Jesus Christ satisfied the demands of the broken Law, demands which were incumbent upon every human being, and He did so by and through His Death on the Cross. In other words, He nailed the charges against us to *"His Cross,"* in effect, stating, *"Paid in Full."*

When He did this, He atoned for all sin.

NOTES

And sin being the legal means by which Satan held men in captivity, Satan was totally defeated, along with all of his cohorts. In other words, he lost his legal right, due to the Atonement, to hold man in captivity, at least for those who will believe (Jn. 3:16).

In fact, Brother Hagin, in one sense of the word, is right when he said: *"The Cross is actually a place of defeat";* but his understanding is backwards. It was the place of defeat for Satan, and not Christ or Believers.

IS THE RESURRECTION THE
PRINCIPAL PLACE OF VICTORY?

Considering the Cross is a place of defeat, our Brother maintains that the Resurrection is the place of victory. Is that correct? Listen again to Paul. He said: *"For the preaching of the Cross is to them who perish foolishness; but unto us which are saved it is the Power of God"* (I Cor. 1:18).

Paul <u>didn't</u> say: *"For the preaching of the Resurrection. . . ."*

If the Resurrection was the place of victory, then why did he say, *"the preaching of the Cross . . . is the Power of God"*?

Notice again what Paul said: *"But God forbid that I should glory* (boast), *save in the Cross of our Lord Jesus Christ, by Whom the world is crucified unto me, and I unto the world"* (Gal. 6:14).

Once again, he <u>didn't</u> say: *"But God forbid that I should glory, save in the Resurrection of our Lord Jesus Christ. . . ."* In fact, the teachers of the Word of Faith do exactly that. They boast of the Resurrection, while demeaning the Cross.

Why do they do this?

THE JESUS DIED
SPIRITUALLY DOCTRINE

Even as I've already stated previously, most of the followers of the Word of Faith Doctrine have never heard of the terminology, *"the Jesus Died Spiritually Doctrine."* But yet, this Doctrine is the foundation of the belief system of the Word of Faith. Let's address it briefly:

They teach that Christ became a sinner on the Cross, hence them calling it a place of defeat. As a sinner, He died and went to Hell, they say, and we speak of the burning side of Hell. There He suffered the horrible agonies of the dammed for three days and nights, with Satan and his demons celebrating the defeat of Christ. At the end of those three days and nights, the Lord said, *"It is enough,"* and Jesus was then *"born-again,"* and then Resurrected from the dead.

There is no shred of that found in the Word of God. In fact, one of their principal Teachers made the statement as it regards the teaching of this subject, *"You won't find it in the Bible; it has to be revealed to your spirit."* Let me say this:

That which I cannot find in the Bible, I will not accept. The dear lady who said that is right about one thing: This particular Jesus Died Spiritually Doctrine cannot be found in the Bible. What, actually, does the Bible say?

JESUS DIED PHYSICALLY, NOT SPIRITUALLY

Peter said: *"For Christ also has once suffered for sins* (the Cross), *the just for the unjust, that He might bring us to God, being put to death in the flesh, but quickened by the Spirit* (Holy Spirit)*"* (I Pet. 3:18).

This Passage, as is plainly obvious, says that Jesus was *"put to death in the flesh,"* which means that He did not die spiritually.

For one to die spiritually, one has to register unbelief toward God, which separates that person from God, and unless they repent, they will be separated eternally (Jn. 16:8-11).

They would argue that they do not teach that Jesus became a sinner on the Cross; however, I remind the Reader that a person doesn't need to be born-again, unless that person is a sinner. God does not send Righteous people to Hell. Furthermore, a person can become a sinner only by sinning. While One Who is perfectly Righteous can bear the penalty of sin, one cannot become a sinner without sinning. And what does the Bible say about Christ?

"Wherefore He is able also to save them to the uttermost who come unto God by Him, seeing He ever lives to make intercession for them.

"For such an High Priest became us, Who is Holy, harmless, undefiled, separate from sinners, and made higher than the Heavens" (Heb. 7:25-26).

The Old Testament Sacrifices were Types of Christ. The animal had to be *"without blemish"* (Ex. 12:5). In fact, if Christ had sinned even once, or had become a sinner in any respect, He would not have been qualified to serve as a Sacrifice. God could not accept a polluted Sacrifice, only one that was *"Holy, harmless, undefiled, and separate from sinners."*

Christ was made to bear the sin penalty, which was physical death, and did so by offering up Himself as a Sacrifice. He did not in any way become a sinner. Paul said:

"For He (God the Father) *has made Him* (Christ) *to be sin for us,* (a Sin-Offering), *Who knew no sin; that we might be made the Righteousness of God in Him"* (II Cor. 5:21).

In connection with this, Isaiah prophesied: *"Yet it pleased the LORD to bruise Him; He has put Him to grief: when you shall make His soul an Offering for sin"* (Isa. 53:10).

HELL?

There is no record in the Bible that Jesus went into the burning side of Hell. He definitely did go into the Paradise side of that place, and there liberated all the Righteous souls who awaited the Cross (Eph. 4:8-9). And I remind the Reader that He liberated these people, which included all the Old Testament Saints, before His Resurrection. If, in fact, our Redemption is to be placed in the Resurrection, then Christ did wrong by liberating these people before the Resurrection.

After the Cross, and before the Resurrection, Christ also preached to the fallen Angels who were held in prison, then located in the heart of the Earth (I Pet. 3:19-20; Jude, Vss. 6-7).

The Scripture also says: *"For You* (God the Father) *will not leave My soul in Hell* (speaking of Jesus)*; neither will You suffer Your Holy One to see corruption"* (Ps. 16:10).

It is speaking here of the grave and Paradise, and not the burning side of Hell. As stated, the Scripture plainly says that God the Father would not suffer Christ, Who is referred to here as *"Your Holy One,"* to see *"corruption."*

If Christ had sinned in any manner, He could not have been referred to as a *"Holy One."* And the Scripture plainly says that

He would not see *"corruption,"* which means that even though He became a Sin-Offering, fulfilling the Old Testament Types, He was in no way corrupted by becoming a sinner.

FIRSTBORN?

Our Word of Faith friends claim that Christ was *"born-again,"* and of all places, in Hell. They derive this from Romans, Chapter 8. Paul said: *"For whom He did foreknow, He also did predestinate to be conformed to the Image of His Son, that He might be the Firstborn among many Brethren"* (Rom. 8:29).

The word *"Firstborn,"* as used here by Paul, in the Greek, is *"prototokos."* The Greek Scholars tell us that the translation *"Firstborn,"* although the best that can be done in English, is not a proper translation. In fact, they say there is no word in English that would properly translate *"prototokos."*

Its actual meaning is that the one so called is the instigator or father of the subject at hand. In other words, Christ is the One Who made it possible, through the Cross, for all men to be *"born-again."*

For instance, Paul also said: *"Who (Christ) is the Image of the Invisible God, the Firstborn of every creature"* (Col. 1:15).

This doesn't mean that Christ is a creature, because, as God, He has always existed (Jn. 1:1). It simply means that Christ is the Creator of all things (Jn. 1:3). Paul said again: *"And He (Christ) is the Head of the body, the Church: Who is the beginning, the Firstborn from the dead; that in all things He might have the preeminence"* (Col. 1:18).

The *"Firstborn from the dead"* means that His Resurrection has made it possible for all Believers to be Resurrected. In other words, He, the Creator of all things, the Originator of Salvation, is also *"the Resurrection and the Life."* That's the reason that He addressed Martha as He did. He said to her: *"I am the Resurrection, and the Life: he who believes in Me, though he were dead, yet shall he live"* (Jn. 11:20-25). Jesus is the Creator; Jesus is Salvation; Jesus is the Resurrection.

No, the word *"Firstborn"* doesn't mean that Jesus died as a sinner and was Born-Again, as sinners are Born-Again when they accept Christ, but rather that He is the Originator of Salvation and its manner.

THE VEIL IN THE TEMPLE

When Jesus died on the Cross, the Scripture says, *"The Veil of the Temple was rent in twain from the top to the bottom"* (Mat. 27:51).

It is believed that the last Words uttered by Christ before He died were: *"It is finished: Father into Your hands I commend My Spirit"* (Jn. 19:30; Lk. 23:46). Incidentally, if He died as a sinner and went to the burning side of Hell, as the Word of Faith Doctrine teaches, how could He refer to God at that last moment as His *"Father,"* and how could He commend His Spirit to the Father? Sinners don't do such!

As well, the moment He died, before His Resurrection, the Scripture says the Veil in the Temple, which separated the Holy Place from the Holy of Holies, was torn from top to bottom. This signified that Redemption was now complete, because the debt was paid, and God had accepted that payment. This means that all can come directly to God through Jesus Christ. If Salvation awaited the Resurrection, as our dear Brother Hagin states, then we must conclude that God ripped the Veil prematurely, which we know He didn't!

MY GOD, MY GOD, WHY HAVE YOU FORSAKEN ME?

Jesus uttered those words on the Cross sometime between 12 noon and 3 p.m. in the afternoon. (He was placed on the Cross at 9 a.m., the time of the morning Sacrifice. He died at 3 p.m., the time of the evening Sacrifice, totally fulfilling Old Testament Types. Under Mosaic Law, a Sacrifice was offered every morning at 9 a.m., and every afternoon at 3 p.m.

At 12 noon, which the Bible refers to as the *"sixth hour,"* it says, *"There was a darkness over all the Earth until the ninth hour"* (Lk. 23:44). The *"ninth hour,"* was 3 p.m., when Jesus died. So, for some three hours, *"darkness (was) over all the Earth."* During that time, Christ cried, *"My God, My God, Why have You forsaken Me?"*

Our Word of Faith friends teach that this is when Jesus became a lost sinner, etc.

During this three-hour period, Christ was bearing the sin of the world, in effect, bearing its penalty, which would result in physical death. God could not look upon this scene, and for the obvious reasons. He is thrice-Holy, which means that even though Christ was His only Son, He could not look upon Him as He was bearing the sin penalty.

However, when Jesus would die, the debt would then be paid, and God could once again look upon Him, thereby helping Him, hence Him saying when He died, *"Father, into Your hands I commend My Spirit"* (Lk. 23:46). Had God forsaken Him altogether, as our Word of Faith friends teach, then Jesus, as we have stated, could not have referred to Him at the time of His death as *"Father,"* and neither could He commend His Spirit to God. But He could do this, because the moment He died, the price was looked at by God as totally and completely paid. It did not await the Resurrection for this to happen, having been completed at His death.

THE RESURRECTION

In no way do we mean to demean the Resurrection of Christ. In fact, the Resurrection was totally necessary; however, let the Reader understand that the Resurrection was never in doubt. The idea of Jesus suffering in the burning pit of Hell, with demons dancing in hellish glee, never happened. As stated, Satan was defeated at the Cross, not in Hell.

Jesus Atoned for all sin. Had there been one sin left unatoned, Jesus could not have risen from the dead. The Scripture plainly says: *"For the wages of sin is death; but the Gift of God is Eternal Life through Jesus Christ our Lord"* (Rom. 6:23).

So, if one sin had been left unatoned, Jesus would have remained dead! There would have been no Resurrection! But due to the fact that Jesus atoned for all sin, and that He did so through His Death, and His Death Alone, there was no way that Satan could hold Him in death, nor any of the Old Testament Saints, for that matter. As stated, Satan was defeated at the Cross, which means that his defeat did not await the Resurrection (Col. 2:14-15).

IS IT THE CROSS OR THE THRONE?

Brother Hagin said, *"We preach a 'Cross' religion, and we need to preach a 'throne' religion."*

In the first place, we shouldn't preach *"religion"* at all, religion being that which is totally devised by man, and not God. Christianity is not a *"religion,"* but rather a *"relationship,"* and with a man, the Man, the Lord Jesus Christ.

But be that as it may, should we, in fact, as Preachers of the Gospel, preach a *"throne religion,"* as our dear brother said?

Again, we go to Paul. He said: *"For the preaching of the Cross is to them who perish foolishness; but unto us who are saved it is the Power of God"* (I Cor. 1:18).

Paul didn't say anything here about *"preaching the throne,"* but rather about *"preaching the Cross."* In fact, our Word of Faith friends fulfilled the first part of this Verse as given by Paul. The preaching of the Cross is to them *"foolishness."* But Paul called it *"the Power of God."*

He also said: *"For after that in the Wisdom of God the world by wisdom knew not God, it pleased God by the foolishness of preaching* (the foolishness of preaching the Cross) *to save them who believe"* (I Cor. 1:21).

He didn't say anything here about *"preaching the Throne,"* but rather *"preaching the Cross."*

And then he said: *"But we preach Christ Crucified"* (I Cor. 1:23). He didn't say, *"We preach Christ on the Throne."*

While it is true that Christ is no longer on a Cross, that He is, in fact, seated by the Right Hand of the Father, and that actually every Saint is seated with Him (Eph. 2:6), He is there and we are there because of what He did at the Cross. Listen again to Paul:

"For if we have been planted together in the likeness of His Death, we shall be also in the likeness of His Resurrection" (Rom. 6:5).

This plainly tells us that we can be *"Resurrection people"* only as we understand that *"We have been planted together in the likeness of His Death."* In other words, if we do not have a correct view of the Cross, we will not have a correct view of the Resurrection.

IS PREACHING THE CROSS PREACHING DEATH?

Brother Hagin said in his advertisement,

"When you preach the Cross, you are preaching death." I don't mean to be unkind, but that statement, which I have quoted verbatim, comes perilously close to blasphemy.

Our Brother is saying that if you preach the Cross, and people believe what you preach, it will lead to their spiritual declension, possibly even the loss of their souls. Let's see what the Word says:

Paul said: *"But now in Christ Jesus you who sometimes were far off are made nigh by the Blood of Christ. . . .*

"And that He might reconcile both (Jews and Gentiles) *unto God in one body by the Cross, having slain the enmity thereby"* (Eph. 2:13, 16).

Paul is preaching the Cross here, so is he preaching death?

Paul also said: *"Know ye not, that so many of us as were baptized into Jesus Christ were baptized into His Death?*

"Therefore we are buried with Him by baptism into death: that like as Christ was raised up from the dead by the Glory of the Father, even so we also should walk in newness of life.

"For if we have been planted together in the likeness of His Death, we shall be also in the likeness of His Resurrection" (Rom. 6:3-5).

Paul is not speaking of Water Baptism, as some claim, but rather the Crucifixion of Christ, and our part in Christ as our Substitute.

He then said: *"Likewise reckon ye also yourselves to be dead indeed unto sin* (the sin nature), *but alive unto God through Jesus Christ our Lord"* (Rom. 6:11).

The Apostle is saying here that we as Believers are dead unto the sin nature, even though the sin nature itself is not dead, and we are this by what Christ did at the Cross and our Faith in that Finished Work. The word *"reckoned"* refers to that which we believe, or that in which we have our Faith, i.e., *"the correct object of Faith, which must be the Cross."*

While it is certainly true that I have the likeness of His Resurrection, I have that likeness only because of what He did at the Cross and my Faith in that Finished Work.

Listen again to the Apostle: *"But we preach Christ Crucified"* (I Cor. 1:23). As previously stated, the Apostle didn't say, *"But we preach Christ Resurrected."* Why not?

He preached Christ Crucified, simply because that's where the victory is found. That's where the *"Power of God, and the Wisdom of God"* (I Cor. 1:24) are found.

When Paul told the Galatians how to live a Godly life, listen to what he said:

"I am Crucified with Christ: nevertheless I live; yet not I, but Christ lives in me: and the life which I now live in the flesh I live by the Faith of the Son of God, Who loved me, and gave Himself for me" (Gal. 2:20).

Again, I call your attention to the fact that the Apostle didn't say, *"I am Resurrected with Christ,"* but rather, *"I am Crucified with Christ."*

Notice again what the Apostle said:

"For Christ sent me not to baptize, but to preach the Gospel: not with wisdom of words, lest the Cross of Christ should be made of none effect" (I Cor. 1:17).

Again, you should notice what he didn't say. He didn't say, *"Lest the Resurrection of Christ should be made of none effect."*

And let us quote again: *"For the preaching of the Cross* (not the preaching of the Resurrection) *is to them who perish foolishness; but unto us which are saved it is the Power of God"* (I Cor. 1:18).

Now either Brother Hagin is right, or else the Apostle is right. You can't have it both ways. Brother Hagin said that the preaching of the Cross is death, while the Apostle said, *"The Preaching of the Cross . . . is the Power of God."*

The Cross of Christ is a Finished Work, which took place many centuries ago, which has continuing results, results which will never be discontinued, and which will never have to be repeated. It is the benefits of which we speak. As we've already stated, Christ is not still on the Cross, but rather seated by the Right of Hand of God (Heb. 1:3), and we Believers are seated with Him (Eph. 2:6). But we must ever understand that we occupy this place and position all because of what Christ did at the Cross. That's why Paul said that he must not major in Water Baptism, or any other Ordinance of the Church, etc., *"lest the Cross of Christ be made of none effect."* And that's what our dear Brother has done. He has made the Cross of Christ of none effect, and there could be no greater sin for a Preacher to commit.

THE MAKING OF THE CROSS OF CHRIST OF NONE EFFECT

Let me say it again: For the Preacher of the Gospel to deliberately make the Cross of Christ of none effect, as the Word of Faith Doctrine does, is the greatest sin of all. It consigns Believers, at least those who follow that teaching, to spiritual oblivion. Ultimately, they will say, as Paul said, *"O wretched man that I am! Who shall deliver me from the body of this death?"* (Rom. 7:24).

In fact, the entirety of the Seventh Chapter of Romans portrays the experience of the Apostle Paul immediately after he was saved and Baptized with the Holy Spirit, but not yet knowing the victory of the Cross. Trying to live for God outside of the victory of the Cross and our Faith in that Finished Work leaves us without the help of the Holy Spirit. But thank God, the Great Apostle earnestly sought the Lord, and the Lord gave him the meaning of the New Covenant, which in reality is the meaning of the Cross, in other words, what Jesus accomplished for us as our Substitute on the Cross. There is no victory outside the Cross! There is no Spiritual Growth or Fruit of the Spirit outside of the Cross. In fact, the Holy Spirit works exclusively within the parameters of the Finished Work of Christ. And if we step outside of those parameters, we are, in effect, committing *"spiritual adultery"* (Rom. 7:1-4).

We are married to Christ, but if we try to live this Christian life outside of Faith in His Finished Work, the Holy Spirit constitutes such action as *"spiritual adultery."* In other words, we are being unfaithful to Christ. And that's exactly what our dear Brother is doing, plus all those who follow the Word of Faith teaching. Listen again to Paul:

"For the Law of the Spirit of Life in Christ Jesus has made me free from the Law of sin and death" (Rom. 8:2).

This one Passage tells how the Holy Spirit works. It is found in the phrase, *"In Christ Jesus."* In fact, Paul uses that term, or one of its derivatives, over a hundred times in his fourteen Epistles. Every single time, it refers to what Jesus did at the Cross, all on our behalf. This is the way the Holy Spirit works, at least as it regards victory within our lives. He only requires of us that we evidence Faith in the Cross of Christ, and continue to do so, for that's where our victory was won (Rom. 6:11).

SATAN'S LAST FLING AT THE CHURCH

I believe the Rapture of the Church is very near. World events are shaping up as it regards the fulfillment of Bible Prophecy concerning the Endtime. It is my personal belief that the Word of Faith Doctrine is Satan's masterstroke. It is propagated by those who claim to be Spirit-filled, and thereby, Spirit-led. They claim that their Doctrine is based squarely on the Bible; however, as I trust I have amply proven, their Doctrine is definitely <u>not</u> based on the Word of God, but rather on a twisted perversion of the Word.

The Word of Faith Doctrine has gradually deteriorated, because it is leaven, until its major emphasis now is money. To Brother Hagin's credit, he has opposed this emphasis, but the money emphasis is prevalent simply because of the falseness of the Doctrine. And until you change the Doctrine, which means to come back to the Cross, the problem will not solve itself, but will rather increase. As Paul said, *"A little leaven leaventh the whole lump"* (Gal. 5:9).

THE CROSS OF CHRIST

No person who honestly surveys the Word of God can come to any conclusion but that Paul *"preached the Cross."* He preached the Cross as it regards *"Salvation"* for the sinner, and he preached the Cross as it regards *"Sanctification"* for the Saint. Paul's Epistles plainly bear that out.

Consequently, the Apostle said: *"But though we, or an Angel from Heaven, preach any other gospel unto you than that which we have preached unto you, let him be accursed."* And then he said it again: *"As we said before, so say I now again, If any man preach any other gospel unto you than that you have received, let him be accursed"* (Gal. 1:8-9).

Paul is saying that if anybody preaches anything except the Cross, he's preaching *"another Gospel,"* which cannot be accepted, and which will bring the curse of God upon him, which could result in the loss of the soul (Gal. 1:6-9).

Again, I emphasize that we're dealing here with the Atonement, which is the Foundation of the Gospel, and actually is the Gospel. If we miss it on this, and the Word of Faith Doctrine misses badly, then we've missed it everywhere else as well.

Satan, I believe, has saved this particular false gospel for these last days, and he has been amazingly successful!

GOD'S PRESCRIBED ORDER OF VICTORY

To take all that Paul said, and reduce it down to a very abbreviated statement, God's Prescribed Order of Victory is the following:

1. THE CROSS: The Believer must understand that every single thing that comes to him from God comes exclusively through what Jesus did for us at the Cross. Christ is the Source, while the Cross is the means.

2. OUR FAITH: The object of our Faith must ever be the Cross of Christ. If we place it in something else, we are, in effect, committing spiritual adultery (Rom. 7:1-4).

3. THE HOLY SPIRIT: Understanding that everything comes to us through the Finished Work of Christ, and that this must ever be the Object of our Faith, then the Holy Spirit will work mightily on our behalf. To be sure, it is impossible for the Believer to live a Christian life, at least as he should live, without the help of the Holy Spirit. In fact, everything that the Godhead does on this Earth, except what Jesus did at the Cross, is done by and through the Person, Agency, Work, and Ministry of the Holy Spirit. And, as previously stated, He works exclusively within the Finished Work of Christ, which means that our Faith must ever be anchored in that great Sacrifice. This being the case, we can live the Resurrection life, but outside of this, such a life is impossible (Rom. 6:3-14; 7:1-4; 8:1-2, 11; I Cor. 1:17-18, 21, 23; 2:2, 5; Gal. 6:14; Eph. 2:13-18; Col. 2:14-15).

JUDGMENT

God must judge sin. As a result, the sinner can throw himself on the Cross of Calvary, where God judged the sins of the world in the death of His Son, our Saviour, the Lord Jesus Christ, Who in effect, took the Judgment for us, or else, one can ignore that remedy; however, one does so at one's peril.

Judah would not trust in the Sacrifice of Christ; because they refused to trust in that Sacrifice, God had no alternative but to pronounce Judgment, and a Judgment so severe that it beggars description. In fact, one can tell by the Judgment of God on sin just how bad that sin actually is. How foolish we are to forsake the Cross! But I'm afraid that's exactly what the modern Church has done.

Because Judgment didn't come immediately, Judah thought it wouldn't come, and that despite the fact that both Jeremiah and Ezekiel were prophesying almost daily that Judgment was coming. Then, as now, they didn't believe it!

But ultimately the Judgment came, as ultimately the Judgment always comes. Let us state it again: God must judge sin. He has no alternative but to do so. Jesus suffered our Judgment on the Cross when He became the Sin-Bearer of the world. He, and He Alone, paid the price that we could not pay. If we accept what He has done for us, the terrible storm cloud of God's wrath against sin is appeased; however, if we reject that price, that Sacrifice, that Finished Work, and that Judgment, then God has no alternative but to pour that Judgment out on us, which will ultimately conclude in the Lake of Fire (Rev. 20).

DOES GOD JUDGE BELIEVERS?

No! At least not in the type of Judgment that's visited upon unbelievers. He chastises Believers, which refers to the fact of correcting Believers.

The Judgment of God upon sin is punitive, i.e., is meant to punish, because there is no other alternative. Believers, however, have placed their Faith and trust in Christ, Who has taken the Judgment in our place (Jn. 3:16).

When it comes to chastisement, such is

visited upon Believers in order to correct us. The Scripture plainly says:

"And you have forgotten the exhortation which speaks unto you as unto children, My son, despise not thou the chastening of the Lord, nor faint when you are rebuked of Him:

"For whom the Lord loves He chastens, and scourges every son whom He receives.

"If you endure chastening, God deals with you as with sons; for what son is he whom the Father chastens not?

"But if you be without chastisement, whereof all are partakers, then are you bastards, and not sons.

"Furthermore we have had fathers of our flesh which corrected us, and we gave them reverence: shall we not much rather be in subjection unto the Father of spirits, and live?

"For they verily for a few days chastened us after their own pleasure; but He for our profit, that we might be partakers of His Holiness.

"Now no chastening for the present seems to be joyous, but grievous: nevertheless afterward it yields the peaceable fruit of Righteousness unto them which are exercised thereby" (Heb. 12:5-11).

(14) "MOREOVER I WILL MAKE YOU WASTE, AND A REPROACH AMONG THE NATIONS THAT ARE ROUND ABOUT YOU, IN THE SIGHT OF ALL WHO PASS BY.

(15) "SO IT SHALL BE A REPROACH AND A TAUNT, AN INSTRUCTION AND AN ASTONISHMENT UNTO THE NATIONS THAT ARE ROUND ABOUT YOU, WHEN I SHALL EXECUTE JUDGMENTS IN YOU IN ANGER AND IN FURY AND IN FURIOUS REBUKES. I THE LORD HAVE SPOKEN IT.

(16) "WHEN I SHALL SEND UPON THEM THE EVIL ARROWS OF FAMINE, WHICH SHALL BE FOR THEIR DESTRUCTION, AND WHICH I WILL SEND TO DESTROY YOU: AND I WILL INCREASE THE FAMINE UPON YOU, AND WILL BREAK YOUR STAFF OF BREAD:

(17) "SO WILL I SEND UPON YOU FAMINE AND EVIL BEASTS, AND THEY SHALL BEREAVE YOU: AND PESTILENCE AND BLOOD SHALL PASS THROUGH YOU; AND I WILL BRING THE SWORD UPON YOU. I THE LORD HAVE SPOKEN IT."

The diagram is:

1. Of all the suffering experienced by Judah, perhaps the worst of all was the *"reproach among the nations . . . in the sight of all who pass by."*

2. The phrase, *"So it shall be a reproach and a taunt,"* refers to Jerusalem, which was to be the great object lesson in God's education of mankind.

3. The Chapter ends with the words, *"I the LORD have spoken it,"* which is the final stroke of all, guaranteeing that even though the words came from Ezekiel, they, of necessity, belong to the Lord. As such, they were guaranteed of fulfillment.

I THE LORD HAVE SPOKEN IT

We see from all of this that the Lord has the final say in everything, as it regards those who belong to Him. And in fact, this goes for the entirety of the world.

Satan has latitude only as the Lord allows him such. He cannot do more than the Lord allows, and even must seek permission to do that (Job, Chpts. 1-2). In fact, the Lord uses Satan constantly, even as the Book of Job brings out, to carry forth Judgment. While Satan's purposes may be something else altogether, still, God is still in charge of all things.

Understanding this, Believers should seek the Will of the Lord in all things, which of course, the Holy Spirit desires fully to bring about (Rom. 8:27).

We must ever understand, and do so fully, that the words, *"I the LORD have spoken it,"* refer to the present time, exactly as then. God's Word cannot be treated with contempt. It cannot be perverted, twisted, ignored, or set aside. If so, Judgment will be the ultimate result!

On the other hand, to obey the Word is the ingredient of life. It is the blessing of all things (Ps. 119).

"My soul, in sad exile, was out on life's sea,
"So burdened with sin, and distressed,
"Till I heard a sweet voice saying, Make me your choice,

"And I entered the haven of rest."

"I yielded myself to His tender embrace,
"And faith taking hold of the Word,
"My fetters fell off, and I anchored my soul
"The haven of rest is my Lord."

"The song of my soul, since the Lord made me whole,
"Has been the old story so blest
"Of Jesus, Who'll save whosoever
"Will have a home in the haven of rest."

CHAPTER 6

(1) "AND THE WORD OF THE LORD CAME UNTO ME, SAYING,

(2) "SON OF MAN, SET YOUR FACE TOWARD THE MOUNTAINS OF ISRAEL, AND PROPHESY AGAINST THEM,

(3) "AND SAY, YOU MOUNTAINS OF ISRAEL, HEAR THE WORD OF THE LORD GOD; THUS SAITH THE LORD GOD TO THE MOUNTAINS, AND TO THE HILLS, TO THE RIVERS, AND TO THE VALLEYS; BEHOLD, I, EVEN I, WILL BRING A SWORD UPON YOU, AND I WILL DESTROY YOUR HIGH PLACES.

(4) "AND YOUR ALTARS SHALL BE DESOLATE, AND YOUR IMAGES SHALL BE BROKEN: AND I WILL CAST DOWN YOUR SLAIN MEN BEFORE YOUR IDOLS.

(5) "AND I WILL LAY THE DEAD CARCASES OF THE CHILDREN OF ISRAEL BEFORE THEIR IDOLS; AND I WILL SCATTER YOUR BONES ROUND ABOUT YOUR ALTARS.

(6) "IN ALL YOUR DWELLING PLACES THE CITIES SHALL BE LAID WASTE, AND THE HIGH PLACES SHALL BE DESOLATE; THAT YOUR ALTARS MAY BE LAID WASTE AND MADE DESOLATE, AND YOUR IDOLS MAY BE BROKEN AND CEASE, AND YOUR IMAGES MAY BE CUT DOWN, AND YOUR WORKS MAY BE ABOLISHED.

(7) "AND THE SLAIN SHALL FALL IN THE MIDST OF YOU, AND YOU SHALL KNOW THAT I AM THE LORD."

NOTES

The overview is:

1. As the prior Message attacked idolatry in the city of Jerusalem, so this Message (Chpts. 6-7) attacked it in the Land of Israel.

2. Ezekiel did not speak his own words, but the Word that came to him from Jehovah, and he delivered it in the very words given to him.

3. *"Abomination of desolation"* expresses the moral and material result of idolatry.

IDOLATRY

As is overly obvious in these Passages, Judah, which had been given the true way of worship, had forsaken the true worship of God, and had set up idols all over the land, and of every description, and offered up worship unto these demon spirits, for all idolatry is the result of demon powers (I Tim. 4:1).

As Jeremiah, in the city of Jerusalem, was prophesying against these terrible evils, and doing so on a daily basis, Ezekiel was instructed by the Lord to direct his Prophecies as well toward the land of Judah, even though he was in Babylonia.

There was no doubt information of certain kinds passing between Judah and the Exiles in Babylonia, and the Lord would have Judah to know that His Word was in the mouths of two or more witnesses. As we've already stated, the false Prophets were claiming that the Babylonians would be repulsed and Jerusalem and Judah would be spared, but God says otherwise!

JUDGMENT

As is recorded in these Chapters, and especially this Chapter, that which the Lord said through His Prophet was seemingly enough to make anyone repent. In no uncertain terms, and plain language, the Lord said, *"I will lay the dead carcases of the Children of Israel before their idols; and I will scatter your bones round about your Altars."* He then said, *"In all your dwelling places the city shall be laid waste, and the high places shall be desolate."* And then He said, *"And you shall know that I am the LORD."*

But yet the people would not turn, would not repent, would not forsake their evil ways.

Sin hardens the heart, and those who are thus afflicted do not think correctly. In fact, they cannot think correctly. They do not rightly *"hear,"* and they do not rightly *"see."* That's the reason that Jesus kept saying in His Messages to Israel, *"He who has ears to hear, let him hear* (Mat. 11:15; 12:1; 13:9, 15-16, 43; 28:14; Mk. 2:23; 4:9, 23; Lk. 1:44; 4:21, etc.).

IDOLATRY AND THE MODERN CHURCH

When most Christians think of idolatry, they think of heathenistic idols, which existed in Bible Times; they seldom equate idolatry with the present times. Listen to the Word of God:

Paul listed *"idolatry"* as one of the works of the flesh (Gal. 5:19-21). John the Beloved closed out his first Epistle by saying, *"Little children keep yourselves from idols"* (I Jn. 5:21). Paul warned Christians, *"Now these things were our examples, to the intent we should not lust after evil things, as they also lusted.*

"Neither be ye idolaters, as were some of them" (I Cor. 10:6-7).

Idolatry presents itself as anything in the heart which seeks to take the place of Christ. Someone has said that our devotion must be to God first, family second, and business third, etc. No! That is wrong as well.

It must be the Lord first, the Lord second, the Lord third, the Lord fourth, etc. If the Lord is given proper place within our hearts and lives, everything else will fall into place in the sphere of our devotion to Him. So, when we think of idols, we should forget about the idols of Biblical heathenism, and understand that idolatry is anything which seeks to take the place of Christ.

To be frank, religion is the worst idolatry. While anything can be an idol, such as family, business, money, pleasure, sports, power, place, or position, etc., I think one can say without fear of exaggeration that the idol of religion, with untold millions worshiping at its altars, has doomed more human beings than possibly every other idol combined.

THE CROSS

In 1997, the Lord in answer to several years of soul searching prayer, and I speak of prayer on a daily basis, even morning and night, began to open up to me the Message of the Cross, in fact, that for which I had so long sought. The Revelation that He began to give on that memorable day has not stopped even unto this hour. In fact, it is open ended, and for the simple reason that the New Covenant is the *"Everlasting Covenant,"* and as such, it cannot be exhausted (Heb. 13:20). To totally plumb its depths, and to totally scale its heights, I think would be impossible.

Among the many things the Lord has shown me is this very thing to which we are addressing ourselves, i.e., idolatry in the modern Church.

The Gospel is *"Jesus Christ and Him Crucified"* (I Cor. 1:23). Paul said:

"For Christ sent me not to baptize, but to preach the Gospel: Not with wisdom of words, lest the Cross of Christ should be made of none effect" (I Cor. 1:17). In this Passage, the Apostle tells us that the *"Gospel"* can be summed up in the short phrase, *"the Cross."* In fact, Paul uses the word *"Cross"* as a figurative name for the entire Work of Redemption (I Cor. 1:18; Gal. 5:11; 6:12, 14; Eph. 2:16; Phil. 2:8; 3:18; Col. 1:20). So, as stated, the Gospel is, *"Jesus Christ and Him Crucified,"* summed up by the word *"Cross."*

If we allow anything to be added to that simple Gospel, or taken from that simple Gospel, then we have created an idol. Paul also said: *"But I fear, lest, by any means, as the serpent beguiled Eve through his subtilty, so your minds should be corrupted from the simplicity that is in Christ.*

"For if he who comes preaches another Jesus, whom we have not preached, or if you receive another spirit, which you have not received, or another gospel, which you have not accepted, you might well bear with him" (II Cor. 11:3-4).

ANOTHER JESUS, ANOTHER SPIRIT, AND ANOTHER GOSPEL

What did Paul mean by the terms, *"another Jesus, another spirit, and another Gospel"*?

If Christ is placed in any role except as the Sacrifice for sin, pure and simple, you have manufactured *"another Jesus."* If this is done, and to be sure, it is done constantly, it is produced by *"another spirit,"* which means that the Holy Spirit is not the author of such. It all plays out to *"another gospel,"* which will save no one, deliver no one, and set no captives free.

The Jesus then produced becomes an idol, because it's not the Jesus of the Word of God, but rather, a *"Jesus"* of man's own making.

There are millions presently, who claim to believe in Christ, but who equate their particular Denomination with some type of supposed spirituality. In other words, they believe that by belonging to their particular Denomination, such association carries with it some type of spirituality. This is idolatry, pure and simple!

Such could be said for a local Church, or a particular Doctrine, or even Preachers. We Protestants are quick to point out the idolatry of Catholicism, but I wonder if we aren't guilty of the same sin!

So, as the Lord began to open up the Cross to me, showing me that Jesus Christ and Him Crucified must ever be the Object of our Faith, and that alone as the Object of our Faith, I began to see more clearly the insidiousness of institutionalized religion. No, it's not wrong to belong to a Denomination, or to belong to a particular Church; but at the same time, we must always understand what these things truly are, and that they carry no spiritual connotation, at least within themselves.

Whenever the Cross is fully embraced, which speaks of the Sacrifice of Christ as meeting our every need, many will find that they are no longer welcome in the particular Church with which they have been associated, possibly for many years. Men love their idols, and religious men love their idols most of all! And to be sure, the Cross tears down every idol of the mind, the heart, the soul, and the spirit. If properly embraced, it lays waste all of man's claims to spirituality, holding up the Sacrifice of Christ as the Gospel, the only Gospel!

PAUL AND THE CROSS

It was to Paul that the meaning of the New Covenant was given (Gal. 1:11-12), which, in effect, is the meaning of the Cross. As well, one could turn it around and say, *"The meaning of the Cross is the meaning of the New Covenant."* In fact, its greatest symbolism, or Ordinance, is the *"Lord's Supper,"* which totally and completely portrays the Death of Christ (I Cor. 11:23-30).

Satan, during the time of Paul, powerfully came against this great Message of Grace, which is the Message of the Cross, because the Cross is the means by which Grace is given to the needy soul. Satan's great effort then was to add the Law of Moses, which actually had originally been given by God, to the Message of Grace, which, of course, is impossible. Either one cancels out the other; nevertheless, Satan tried, and tried desperately, using Believers, so-called, to carry out his insidious efforts. In fact, he almost always uses those inside the Church to carry forth his schemes. Unfortunately, he seems to always have plenty of takers for his evil suggestions. In fact, Satan's traps are sprung so readily, and presented so carefully, that many times, even the most dedicated can be deceived. Simon Peter is a perfect example.

I feel that one could say, and do so without exaggeration, that Simon Peter was one of the Godliest men who ever lived. He was the prince of the Apostles in his day, personally chosen by Christ, and served as the spokesman for all of the chosen Twelve, and I speak of his post-Resurrection Ministry. However, witness the occasion, as it says:

"But when Peter was come to Antioch, I (Paul) *withstood him to the face, because he was to be blamed.*

"For before that certain came from James, he did eat with the Gentiles: but when they were come, he withdrew and separated himself, fearing them which were of the circumcision.

"And the other Jews dissembled likewise with him; insomuch that Barnabas also was carried away with their dissimulation (hypocrisy).

"But when I saw that they walked not uprightly according to the Truth of the Gospel, I said unto Peter before them all, If you, being a Jew, live after the manner of Gentiles (which he evidently was doing), *and not as do the Jews* (looking to the Law), *why do you compel the Gentiles* (now) *to live as do the Jews?"* (Gal. 2:11-14).

Some may read this, and pass it off as

relatively insignificant; however, what Peter did was a grievous sin, and could have destroyed the entirety of the Work of God on Earth, had Paul not taken the proper stand.

Peter's sin was twofold:

First of all, it was man-fear (Gal. 2:12), and second, it was a repudiation of the Grace of God, which meant that Peter was reverting back to Law. Considering who he was, as stated, if left unchecked, it could have destroyed the Church; this was Satan's intention, and he nearly succeeded.

To Peter's credit, even though he was older than Paul, it seems that he took the rebuke graciously, and repented of his actions; but, to be sure, it was no small matter. In fact, all sin has its origination with improper faith, which means that faith is transferred from Christ and Him Crucified to something else.

Had Peter continued in that direction, this thing, *"the Law,"* would have become an idol, even as it had already become for many Christian Jews of that time.

How many modern Preachers are preaching something other than the Cross as it regards our Sanctification?

THE ONLY WAY TO LIVE FOR GOD

The Believer is to ever understand that the *"Source"* of all things from God is Christ. But as well, we are to ever understand that the *"means"* by which these things are given to us is the Cross. And when I say *"everything,"* I mean *"everything"*!

Consequently, as the Believing sinner must look to Christ and the Cross for Salvation, even though he understands little of what it all means, likewise, the Believer is to continue to look to Christ and the Cross for strength to live this Christian life. To continue to look to the Cross, even on a daily basis, is so very, very important, so important in fact that we simply cannot live for God as we ought to, unless we have a proper interpretation of the Cross as it refers to our daily Sanctification. But regrettably, most Christians have no knowledge whatsoever of this of which I speak, irrespective that there is nothing more important for the Child of God. Read carefully the Words of our Lord.

TAKE UP THE CROSS DAILY

Jesus said: *"If any man will come after Me, let him deny himself, and take up his cross daily, and follow me"* (Lk. 9:23).

Every true Christian knows that Jesus said this, so they know that it is true, but most have a wrong interpretation of what He meant.

When He said, *"Let him deny himself,"* many think that He is speaking of asceticism, which is the denial of all things which are comfortable or pleasurable, etc. As well, when He spoke of *"taking up the Cross,"* they equate that with suffering. So, a false interpretation has successfully neutralized this Passage, which, in Truth, is one of the most glorious Commands given in the entirety of the Word of God.

First of all, when Jesus spoke of *"denying one's self,"* he wasn't speaking of asceticism, or any such thing. He was meaning that we must deny our own strength, ability, acumen, intelligence, knowledge, and efforts, as it regards the living of this Christian life. All such things, as noble as they might seem to be, are but *"walking after the flesh"* (Rom. 8:1). To do such means that one does not trust Christ, but rather himself, which, sadly, is the state of most modern Christians.

When He spoke of taking up the Cross, he wasn't speaking of suffering, but rather trusting in the benefits of the Cross, which constitutes the most glorious, the most wonderful, thing that anyone could ever enjoy. This is the secret of all life. This is what Jesus was talking about when He said, *"The thief cometh not, but for to steal, and to kill, and to destroy: I am come that they might have life, and that they might have it more abundantly"* (Jn. 10:10). In other words, taking up the Cross is *"more abundant life."* Every single true Believer has *"more abundant life,"* but, unfortunately, only a precious few are enjoying *"more abundant life."* And the reason they aren't enjoying this wonderful privilege is because they don't understand the Cross.

DAILY

And then to add the final thought to this great Passage given by Christ, the Lord told us that we must *"take up the Cross daily."* What did He mean by that?

He meant that one must consciously face each new day with the realization that Jesus has paid it all, and that we are going to trust that which He has done, and trust that exclusively. This means that we will not trust ourselves, but Christ, and Christ Alone, and, more specifically, what He did for us at the Cross.

The Cross is something which took place nearly two thousand years ago. It was a perfect Sacrifice and, therefore, will never need to be repeated; however, it has continuing results, results which will never be discontinued. And it is those *"results,"* or, better said, *"benefits,"* of which we speak.

Of course, Christ is not on the Cross, but rather at the Right Hand of the Majesty on High (Heb. 1:3). In fact, spiritually speaking, we are also now seated with Him in Heavenly Places (Eph. 2:6); however, we must always remember that He is there, and we are with Him, solely because of what He has done at the Cross.

One must realize just how important the Cross is, when Jesus tells us that we must *"take it up daily."* But unfortunately, most Christians park the Cross at their initial Salvation experience, and somehow have come to think that they have gone beyond the Cross. They think of the Cross as elementary, not realizing that it's impossible to go beyond the Cross. To do so, is to lose one's way completely.

In fact, the Cross is not a goal, but rather a gateway to all the great things of God. The Cross opens to us the mighty Baptism with the Holy Spirit, the Fruit of the Spirit, Gifts of the Spirit, Hope, Peace, Faith, Grace, Love, Power, the Anointing, Financial prosperity, Divine Healing, Justification, Sanctification, and Glorification, the last one yet to come, in fact, everything!

If the Reader thinks that I stress the Cross too much, I would counter by saying that it's impossible to stress the Cross too much. The problem has been that it's not been stressed nearly enough. In fact, it has been all but ignored, actually repudiated in many places. Please allow me to come back to the original thought.

Considering the spiritual condition of the modern Church, I'm not so certain, as it regards idols, if the modern Church is any better off, if at all, than Judah and her idols of old!

(8) "YET WILL I LEAVE A REMNANT, THAT YOU MAY HAVE SOME WHO SHALL ESCAPE THE SWORD AMONG THE NATIONS, WHEN YOU SHALL BE SCATTERED THROUGH THE COUNTRIES.

(9) "AND THEY WHO ESCAPE OF YOU SHALL REMEMBER ME AMONG THE NATIONS WHITHER THEY SHALL BE CARRIED CAPTIVES, BECAUSE I AM BROKEN WITH THEIR WHORISH HEART, WHICH HAS DEPARTED FROM ME, AND WITH THEIR EYES, WHICH GO A WHORING AFTER THEIR IDOLS: AND THEY SHALL LOATHE THEMSELVES FOR THE EVILS WHICH THEY HAVE COMMITTED IN ALL THEIR ABOMINATIONS.

(10) "AND THEY SHALL KNOW THAT I AM THE LORD, AND THAT I HAVE NOT SAID IN VAIN THAT I WOULD DO THIS EVIL UNTO THEM.

(11) "THUS SAITH THE LORD GOD; SMITE WITH YOUR HAND, AND STAMP WITH YOUR FOOT, AND SAY, ALAS FOR ALL THE EVIL ABOMINATIONS OF THE HOUSE OF ISRAEL! FOR THEY SHALL FALL BY THE SWORD, BY THE FAMINE, AND BY THE PESTILENCE.

(12) "HE WHO IS FAR OFF SHALL DIE OF THE PESTILENCE; AND HE WHO IS NEAR SHALL FALL BY THE SWORD; AND HE WHO REMAINS AND IS BESIEGED SHALL DIE BY THE FAMINE: THUS WILL I ACCOMPLISH MY FURY UPON THEM.

(13) "THEN SHALL YOU KNOW THAT I AM THE LORD, WHEN THEIR SLAIN MEN SHALL BE AMONG THEIR IDOLS ROUND ABOUT THEIR ALTARS, UPON EVERY HIGH HILL, IN ALL THE TOPS OF THE MOUNTAINS, AND UNDER EVERY GREEN TREE, AND UNDER EVERY THICK OAK, THE PLACE WHERE THEY DID OFFER SWEET SAVOUR TO ALL THEIR IDOLS.

(14) "SO WILL I STRETCH OUT MY HAND UPON THEM, AND MAKE THE LAND DESOLATE, YES, MORE DESOLATE THAN THE WILDERNESS TOWARD DIBLATH, IN ALL THEIR HABITATIONS: AND THEY SHALL KNOW THAT I AM THE LORD."

The composition is:

1. *"You shall know that I am Jehovah."* This formula occurs in this actual form twenty-one times in Ezekiel, but only twice elsewhere (Ex. 10:2; I Ki. 20:28).

2. The force of this formula is: *"You shall make the experience that I am the Living God* (in contrast to dead idols) *Whose Promises and Judgments are realities, and not empty words."*

3. *"I am broken."* This may be translated; *"I have broken."* The one translation means that God's heart was broken with Israel's determined idolatry; the other, because of that idolatry, He broke His Covenant with them. Both are true.

THE REMNANT

In a sense, there have always been two Israels. No, I'm not speaking of Judah and Israel proper, but the nation as a whole.

There was always the small *"remnant,"* which served God, and the far, far greater majority, which didn't, even though they were all referred to as Israelites.

The *"Remnant"* spoken of in Verse 8 doesn't necessarily mean that these were obedient to the Lord, although it is certain that some of them were. But the fact remains, by comparison with the entirety of the population of Israel, the number who truly loved the Lord, who truly followed Him, and who truly obeyed Him, at least to the best of their ability, was small indeed! It is the same with modern Church.

In the United States alone, approximately one hundred million people claim to be Born-Again. What that number truly is, only God knows; however, we are given some indication. The Scripture says:

"Enter ye in at the straight gate: for wide is the gate, and broad is the way, that leads to destruction, and many there be which go in thereat:

"Because straight is the gate, and narrow is the way, which leads unto life, and few there be who find it" (Mat. 7:13-14).

So, we know from this that despite the claims of many, only a *"few,"* by comparison to the many, will find it.

Why do that many profess, when only a few possess?

NOTES

Jesus tells us in the very next Verse. He said: *"Beware of false prophets, which come to you in sheep's clothing, but inwardly they are ravening wolves"* (Mat. 7:15).

The Judah of Ezekiel's day had her share of false prophets, while the Prophets of the Lord were few.

Exactly as Ezekiel said, *"Thus saith the LORD,"* or words to that effect, the false prophets were saying the same thing. In other words, they were claiming that the Lord was the Author of their statements, the same as the true Prophets.

WHY WILL PEOPLE FOLLOW FALSE PROPHETS?

That's a good question!

Whenever people abandon the Cross, whether Judah of old, or modern Christians, they become a target for false doctrine; they are unable to tell the true from the false. In fact, the very reason for them rejecting the Cross, which speaks of self-will, is that which attracts them to the false prophets.

Far too many professing Christians desire Preachers who will tell them what they want to hear, instead of what they need to hear. And, to be blunt, there are plenty of Preachers who are ready and willing to accommodate them.

For instance, the modern "greed Gospel," which is a product of the Word of Faith Doctrine, finds a ready clientele, simply because there seems to be a modicum of greed in all of us. Especially when Preachers cover this greed with Scriptures, which seems to legitimize it, it becomes the Apple ready to be bitten.

As well, millions embrace the unscriptural Doctrine of Unconditional Eternal Security, simply because they desire to keep sinning. Always remember: Any doctrine that excuses sin, or ignores sin, is not of God. As stated, the Lord Jesus Christ went to the Cross in order to deliver us from sin. Paul said: *"Who gave Himself for our sins, that He might deliver us from this present evil world, according to the Will of God and our Father"* (Gal. 1:4). So, the Lord does not save us *"in"* sin, but rather *"from"* sin. He has given us the means through the Cross, and through the Cross alone that we might have victory over all sin.

No, the Bible doesn't teach sinless perfection, which, in fact, we will not have until the trump sounds; however, the Bible does teach, *"sin shall not have dominion over you"* (Rom. 6:14). At the Cross of Calvary, both the power of sin was broken, and the guilt of sin was removed.

Again, Paul said:

"Knowing this, that our old man is Crucified with Him, that the body of sin might be destroyed (the power of sin was broken), *that henceforth we should not serve sin* (the guilt of sin is removed)*"* (Rom. 6:6). So, if we allow sin to dominate us as Believers, this means that we aren't taking advantage of what Christ has done for us at the Cross, and that error occurs because we are unaware of what He has done for us at the Cross as it regards Sanctification, or else we simply do not believe what He has done, in effect, making something else the object of our Faith.

Some three times in this Sixth Chapter of Ezekiel, the Holy Spirit through the Prophet said, *"And they shall know that I am the LORD"* (Vss. 7, 13, 14). We can know that in the realm of Judgment, or in the realm of victory. The choice is ours!

"Face-to-face with Christ my Saviour,
"Face-to-face, what will it be?
"When with Rapture I behold Him,
"Jesus Christ Who died for me."

"Only faintly now I see Him,
"With the darkling Veil between,
"But a blessed day is coming,
"When His Glory shall be seen."

"What rejoicing in His Presence,
"When all are banished grief and pain;
"When the crooked ways are straightened,
"And the dark things shall be plain."

"Face-to-face! Oh blissful moment!
"Face-to-face to see and know,
"Face-to-face with my Redeemer,
"Jesus Christ Who loves me so."

CHAPTER 7

(1) "MOREOVER THE WORD OF THE LORD CAME UNTO ME, SAYING,

(2) "ALSO, THOU SON OF MAN, THUS SAITH THE LORD GOD UNTO THE LAND OF ISRAEL; AN END, THE END IS COME UPON THE FOUR CORNERS OF THE LAND.

(3) "NOW IS THE END COME UPON YOU, AND I WILL SEND MY ANGER UPON YOU, AND WILL JUDGE YOU ACCORDING TO YOUR WAYS, AND WILL RECOMPENSE UPON YOU ALL YOUR ABOMINATIONS.

(4) "AND MY EYE SHALL NOT SPARE YOU, NEITHER WILL I HAVE PITY: BUT I WILL RECOMPENSE YOUR WAYS UPON YOU, AND YOUR ABOMINATIONS SHALL BE IN THE MIDST OF YOU: AND YOU SHALL KNOW THAT I AM THE LORD.

(5) "THUS SAITH THE LORD GOD; AN EVIL, AN ONLY EVIL, BEHOLD, IS COME.

(6) "AN END IS COME, THE END IS COME: IT WATCHES FOR YOU; BEHOLD, IT IS COME.

(7) "THE MORNING IS COME UNTO YOU, O YOU WHO DWELL IN THE LAND: THE TIME IS COME, THE DAY OF TROUBLE IS NEAR, AND NOT THE SOUNDING AGAIN OF THE MOUNTAINS.

(8) "NOW WILL I SHORTLY POUR OUT MY FURY UPON YOU, AND ACCOMPLISH MY ANGER UPON YOU; AND I WILL JUDGE YOU ACCORDING TO YOUR WAYS, AND WILL RECOMPENSE YOU FOR ALL YOUR ABOMINATIONS.

(9) "AND MY EYE SHALL NOT SPARE, NEITHER WILL I HAVE PITY: I WILL RECOMPENSE YOU ACCORDING TO YOUR WAYS AND YOUR ABOMINATIONS THAT ARE IN THE MIDST OF YOU; AND YOU SHALL KNOW THAT I AM THE LORD WHO SMITES."

The diagram is:

1. This Prophecy preceded by only a short time the third and final siege of Jerusalem.

2. This siege resulted in the destruction of the City and the Temple, and the banishment into slavery of the few Hebrews who survived the slaughter of the inhabitants.

3. The Prophecy asserts the justice of the Divine anger, and points to the aggravated idolatry which provoked that Wrath (Williams).

THE TIME IS COME

Due to the fact that Judah would not repent, and that despite the untold warnings from Jeremiah and Ezekiel, the Holy Spirit through Ezekiel cries, *"the time is come,"* i.e., *"the end is come upon the four corners of the land."* This was the Word of the Lord, which came through both Jeremiah and Ezekiel, but false Prophets were proclaiming the very opposite! As Ezekiel was saying, *"It is come,"* they were saying, *"It will not come."* Actually, the false Prophets were predicting that the Exiles would be restored to Jerusalem presently and that the time of danger was over. What actually happened proclaims to one and all the falseness of their Message.

KINGDOM NOW PHILOSOPHY

A quite large segment of the Church is presently teaching that the world is getting better and better, with Christianity gradually taking the ascendancy over the world, with ultimately the Church then telling the Lord that He can now come back, which will usher in the Millennial Reign; actually, some are even teaching that we're already in the Millennial Reign.

At the same time, they are teaching that there will be no Rapture of the Church, no coming Great Tribulation, claiming that this was fulfilled in A.D. 70, when Jerusalem was defeated by the Roman Tenth Legion, with over one million Jews dying.

While that was certainly bad, it in no way compares with the Words of Christ, when He said: *"For then shall be Great Tribulation, such as was not since the beginning of the world to this time, no, nor ever shall be"* (Mat. 24:21).

While A.D. 70 was very bad for Israel, which actually destroyed it as a nation, still, it didn't compare with Hitler's Holocaust, which saw some six million Jews slaughtered during that carnage. To be frank, Satan engineered that horror, because he knew that it was time for Prophecy to be fulfilled as it regards Israel once again becoming a nation, which they did in 1948. Even a cursory investigation of Revelation, Chapters 6 through 19, portrays the glaring and obvious fact that these Chapters have not yet been fulfilled. This is the Great Tribulation of which Jesus spoke, and which is soon to come upon this world.

No, things are not getting better and better, but rather worse and worse.

In the last Epistle written by the Apostle Paul, he said: *"This know also, that in the last days perilous times shall come."*

He then went on to list what men would become, and, to make it even more shocking, we must realize that he was speaking here of Believers, so-called. He then said, *"Having a form of Godliness, but denying the power thereof: from such turn away"* (II Tim. 3:1, 5).

The phrase, *"denying the power thereof,"* refers to denying the Holy Spirit, and thereby denying the Cross. The Cross is what made it possible for the Holy Spirit to use His Power on our behalf. Paul also said:

"For the preaching of the Cross is to them who perish foolishness; but unto us which are saved it is the Power of God" (I Cor. 1:18).

How is the *"Cross"* the Power of God?

It is used in this manner by the Holy Spirit as He gave such to Paul, simply because it was the Cross which made it possible for the Holy Spirit to come into hearts and lives, and to use His Power on our behalf. The terrible sin debt was totally and completely paid at the Cross, and this is what made it possible for the Holy Spirit to abide within our hearts and lives, and do so forever (Jn. 14:16-17).

THE END

In Verse 2, the Prophet said, *"An end, the end has come upon the four corners of the land."* This refers to the Spirit of the Lord being lifted from the Temple in Jerusalem, which will spell the doom of the City, and which is outlined in Chapter 11. The scepter of power, as the leader of the nations, then passed from the faltering hands of Judah to a heathen Monarch, and has resided there ever since, which is called *"the times of the Gentiles"* (Lk. 21:24). If the Holy Spirit is removed, then the Church is of no more consequence.

A PERSONAL ILLUSTRATION

If I remember correctly, the year was 1960, or else very close to that particular time. Frances and I, along with Donnie, who was then very small, were in a Church in Mobile, Alabama, in Revival. I hesitate to use the word *"Revival,"* simply because it did not begin that way at all.

The people of this Church had just completed a new Sanctuary, which was then one of the most beautiful in that particular Denomination. If I remember correctly, it seated approximately a thousand people, which was large for that particular time.

It seemed that we were getting no place at all with the meetings. The Lord wasn't moving and I was having difficulty trying to preach. It was so disconcerting that I called home and told my Sister not to send any more mail, because we were going to close out that coming Sunday night.

Every day I would go out in back of the little Motel where we were staying, and would seek the Face of the Lord regarding the Service that particular evening. After about the third or fourth night with nothing happening, the Lord began to deal with my heart, urging me to preach on the Baptism with the Holy Spirit. Now, don't misunderstand! I was not at all reluctant to do what the Lord wanted done. I just wasn't sure if I was hearing from the Lord. The Services were bad enough without me trying to preach something that the people were going to totally reject. So, it continued on for two or three more days, with the Lord increasingly encouraging me to preach on the Baptism with the Holy Spirit.

I remember that particular morning, some days later, as I was walking beneath the trees, praying behind the Motel. I said to the Lord, *"I can't shake this thing, so it must be You, telling me to preach accordingly."* So, I prepared the Message for that particular night.

If I remember correctly, it was Friday night, but then again, my memory may be faulty. At any rate, the Service that night began as usual. The Crowd was fair, and after the Service was turned to me, I went to the piano and sang two or three songs, as I usually did.

I then came back to the pulpit, opened my Bible, announced my Text, read the Scripture, bowed my head and prayed, and then began to preach. As stated, my subject was the Baptism with the Holy Spirit.

THE MOVING OF THE SPIRIT

I don't suppose I had been preaching but just a few minutes, when I felt the anointing begin to come, which was the first time I had sensed such in the entirety of this meeting. And when it came that night, it came with a mighty Move.

When it hit me, it hit the entirety of the congregation. People began to raise their hands and praise the Lord. And then to my surprise, the Pastor, who was sitting behind me on the platform, whizzed past me, jumped the railing, and started down the aisle. A good many people followed him, and it was not just a case of emotionalism. It was a Move of God.

I really did not personally give an Altar Call that night, for the Holy Spirit gave the Altar Call Himself. Without me bidding the people, they began to stream down the aisles to come to the Altars. In fact, some fell halfway, unable to get to the front, as a roar of praise began to come up from the Sanctuary.

HE'S BACK

A little later in the Altar Service, two young ladies kneeling at the Altar went through to the mighty Baptism with the Holy Spirit and began to speak with other tongues.

A man ran upon the platform where I was singing and worshiping — a big man. He must have stood six feet, six inches tall, and must have weighed at least 250 to 260 pounds. I found out later that he was a contractor in that Church, and had actually been the one who had built this beautiful edifice.

I remember that he picked me up. I'm six feet tall, and at the time of this writing (2003), I weigh 200 pounds. But then I weighed about 140 pounds. Like a rag doll, he picked me up and began to whirl me around. But it was what he said that I have never forgotten.

He was weeping and praising the Lord all at the same time, and he kept saying it over and over, *"Brother Swaggart, He's back, He's back."* To be frank, I didn't know exactly what he was talking about at the beginning. When he finally put me down, he said this to me:

"Brother Swaggart, we haven't had a single person Baptized with Holy Spirit in

this Church in the last two years. We were fearful that He had departed, and wouldn't come back." But then with tears rolling down his face, he said it again and again, *"He's back! He's Back!"* He was referring to those two girls who had just prayed through to the Baptism, and others which would follow in a few minutes.

THE HOLY SPIRIT

Ladies and gentleman, without the Holy Spirit, the Church is nothing. And the most dangerous thing that can happen to a Church is when it can successfully operate without the Spirit. And regrettably, that seems to be the case with untold thousands of Churches at this particular time.

Even as I dictate the words of this illustration I have just given to you concerning the Meeting in Alabama, I sense strongly the Presence of God.

I can think of nothing worse than the absence of the Holy Spirit. And I can think of nothing greater than the Presence of the Holy Spirit. However, the Lord was about to leave Israel, and that being done, which would happen shortly, there would be nothing left.

We as Believers are functional for the Lord, and serve a purpose for the Lord, only as we provide a suitable Temple for the habitation of the Spirit. Listen again to Paul: *"In Whom* (Christ) *you also are built together for an habitation of God through the Spirit"* (Eph. 2:22).

(10) "BEHOLD THE DAY, BEHOLD, IT IS COME: THE MORNING IS GONE FORTH; THE ROD HAS BLOSSOMED, PRIDE HAS BUDDED.

(11) "VIOLENCE IS RISEN UP INTO A ROD OF WICKEDNESS: NONE OF THEM SHALL REMAIN, NOR OF THEIR MULTITUDE, NOR OF ANY OF THEIRS: NEITHER SHALL THERE BE WAILING FOR THEM.

(12) "THE TIME IS COME, THE DAY DRAWS NEAR: LET NOT THE BUYER REJOICE, NOR THE SELLER MOURN: FOR WRATH IS UPON ALL THE MULTITUDE THEREOF.

(13) "FOR THE SELLER SHALL NOT RETURN TO THAT WHICH IS SOLD, ALTHOUGH THEY WERE YET ALIVE: FOR THE VISION IS TOUCHING THE WHOLE MULTITUDE THEREOF, WHICH SHALL NOT RETURN; NEITHER SHALL ANY STRENGTHEN HIMSELF IN THE INIQUITY OF HIS LIFE.

(14) "THEY HAVE BLOWN THE TRUMPET, EVEN TO MAKE ALL READY; BUT NONE GOES TO THE BATTLE: FOR MY WRATH IS UPON ALL THE MULTITUDE THEREOF.

(15) "THE SWORD IS WITHOUT, AND THE PESTILENCE AND THE FAMINE WITHIN: HE WHO IS IN THE FIELD SHALL DIE WITH THE SWORD; AND HE WHO IS IN THE CITY, FAMINE AND PESTILENCE SHALL DEVOUR HIM.

(16) "BUT THEY WHO ESCAPE OF THEM SHALL ESCAPE, AND SHALL BE ON THE MOUNTAINS LIKE DOVES OF THE VALLEYS, ALL OF THEM MOURNING, EVERY ONE FOR HIS INIQUITY.

(17) "ALL HANDS SHALL BE FEEBLE, AND ALL KNEES SHALL BE WEAK AS WATER.

(18) "THEY SHALL ALSO GIRD THEMSELVES WITH SACKCLOTH, AND HORROR SHALL COVER THEM; AND SHAME SHALL BE UPON ALL FACES, AND BALDNESS UPON ALL THEIR HEADS."

The composition is:

1. Israel had turned the Blessing of God into license. Instead of these Blessings humbling them, which they would have if Judah had constantly been aware of their Source, in their self-Righteousness, they credited themselves as the source.

2. Such is caused by *"pride,"* and, unless taken out by Repentance, will only grow worse until it *"buds,"* i.e., abscesses and runs over as a cup of iniquity.

3. Repentance motivated by personal suffering because of misconduct is false repentance. True Repentance is born of a sense of sin against God.

THE JUDGMENT OF GOD

Unfortunately, most of the Book of Ezekiel is made up of God's pronouncements of Judgment, and we speak of Judgment on Judah, and even His glorious City Jerusalem — a Judgment such as Judah and Jerusalem had never seen. But yet, the people would not listen at all!

Even as we've already stated, and will no doubt address it again, the people were hearing two sets of Prophets. In all Truth, there were only Jeremiah and Ezekiel who were prophesying for the Lord, Jeremiah in Jerusalem, and Ezekiel in Babylonia. How many false prophets there were, we aren't told; however, I am certain that the number was quite large. In fact, the false Prophets grew rich, because they were saying what the people wanted to hear.

Jeremiah and Ezekiel were saying that Judah was so far gone that it was now too late to repent. While Repentance would definitely help any particular individual, as far as the nation was concerned, it had crossed the line of no return. In Truth, Judah had become so hardened toward the Word of the Lord that there was no thought of them turning, despite the great Prophecies of both Jeremiah and Ezekiel.

In a sense, it has never been any different than that, although, at that particular time, on the very eve of Judgment, there have probably been few times in history that the situation was more critical than then. But yet, I must ask, *"How much different is it between then and now, as it regards the modern Church?"*

To be frank, false prophets now abound; but, as then, it's not so easy to ascertain the difference between the false and the true.

Both presently are saying, *"Thus saith the Lord!"* Both are claiming to have heard from God, but now, as then, the false Prophets are telling the people what they want to hear. In other words, they are prophesying smooth things to them. What the people need to hear, they are not relating to people whatsoever, and for many and varied reasons, with money being the greatest reason of all.

The true Prophet of God has to be willing, first of all, to say what the Lord tells him to say, which is never easy to say. And as well, they have to be willing to take the abuse that is most definitely going to come, and that isn't easy either! As I've said elsewhere in this Volume, this Ministry (Jimmy Swaggart Ministries) has been called of God to take a certain stand relative to certain false Doctrine. As well, we have been called of

NOTES

God to proclaim the Cross, perhaps as it has not been proclaimed in recent times. Those two, the Prophetic Message and the Cross, are not designed to win friends. And to be frank, the abuse has been exceptional.

But only one thing matters, and that is making certain that we've heard from the Lord, and then delivering what He has told us to deliver, neither adding to, nor taking from.

PRIDE HAS BUDDED

Verse 10 begins with the words, *"Behold the day."* It refers to the *"Day of Wrath"* that's soon to come. The phrase, *"The rod has blossomed,"* refers to Nebuchadnezzar who was ready to strike.

The phrase, *"Pride has budded,"* refers to Israel's determined sin, which demanded the rod, and is here unique. It means *"proud luxuriance."*

One can look at Judah of old as a microcosm of the present concerning the entire world. *"Pride has budded,"* and as Judah and Jerusalem were on the eve of destruction, likewise the world is staring full face into the coming Great Tribulation. *"The great day of His Wrath is come, and who shall be able to stand?"* (Rev. 6:17).

In Verse 12, the Lord makes the statement, *"Let not the buyer rejoice, nor the seller mourn."* The idea of the Verse is this:

In the first two deportations, some of the wealthy class and the nobles were spirited off to Babylon. As a result, they were forced to sell their estates at give-away prices, which caused *"the seller to mourn, and the buyer to rejoice."* Ezekiel is saying that in either case the joy or the sorrow would be transient. In Verse 13, the Lord said, *"For the seller shall not return to that which is sold, although they were yet alive,"* refers to the year of Jubilee. The idea is, the false Prophets were claiming the immediate restoration of the Exiles, and when the year of Jubilee rolled around, which came every fifty years, the land would then revert to its original owner; however, the Lord is saying through the Prophet that none of these sellers and buyers would live to see the Jubilee.

(19) "THEY SHALL CAST THEIR SILVER IN THE STREETS, AND THEIR GOLD

SHALL BE REMOVED: THEIR SILVER AND THEIR GOLD SHALL NOT BE ABLE TO DELIVER THEM IN THE DAY OF THE WRATH OF THE LORD: THEY SHALL NOT SATISFY THEIR SOULS, NEITHER FILL THEIR BOWELS: BECAUSE IT IS THE STUMBLINGBLOCK OF THEIR INIQUITY.

(20) "AS FOR THE BEAUTY OF HIS ORNAMENT, HE SET IT IN MAJESTY: BUT THEY MADE THE IMAGES OF THEIR ABOMINATIONS AND OF THEIR DETESTABLE THINGS THEREIN: THEREFORE HAVE I SET IF FAR FROM THEM.

(21) "AND I WILL GIVE IT INTO THE HANDS OF THE STRANGERS FOR A PREY, AND TO THE WICKED OF THE EARTH FOR A SPOIL: AND THEY SHALL POLLUTE IT.

(22) "MY FACE WILL I TURN ALSO FROM THEM, AND THEY SHALL POLLUTE MY SECRET PLACE: FOR THE ROBBERS SHALL ENTER INTO IT, AND DEFILE IT.

(23) "MAKE A CHAIN: FOR THE LAND IS FULL OF BLOODY CRIMES, AND THE CITY IS FULL OF VIOLENCE.

(24) "WHEREFORE I WILL BRING THE WORST OF THE HEATHEN, AND THEY SHALL POSSESS THEIR HOUSES: I WILL ALSO MAKE THE POMP OF THE STRONG TO CEASE; AND THEIR HOLY PLACES SHALL BE DEFILED.

(25) "DESTRUCTION COMES; AND THEY SHALL SEEK PEACE, AND THERE SHALL BE NONE.

(26) "MISCHIEF SHALL COME UPON MISCHIEF, AND RUMOR SHALL BE UPON RUMOR; THEN SHALL THEY SEEK A VISION OF THE PROPHET; BUT THE LAW SHALL PERISH FROM THE PRIEST, AND COUNSEL FROM THE ANCIENTS.

(27) "THE KING SHALL MOURN, AND THE PRINCE SHALL BE CLOTHED WITH DESOLATION, AND THE HANDS OF THE PEOPLE OF THE LAND SHALL BE TROUBLED: I WILL DO UNTO THEM AFTER THEIR WAY, AND ACCORDING TO THEIR DESERTS WILL I JUDGE THEM; AND THEY SHALL KNOW THAT I AM THE LORD."

The structure is:
1. The *"strangers"* and *"wicked"* of Verse 21, and the *"robbers"* of Verse 22, were the Babylonians. They robbed and profaned the Temple. Verse 22 also says, *"My face will I turn from them."* It means that God would not strike dead the Chaldean soldiers who would intrude into the Holy of Holies. He would avert His Face so as not to witness the intrusion. This fact affirmed the rupture between God and Israel.

2. The Seventh Chapter closes the first section of the Book of Ezekiel. It belongs to the River Chebar and the captives, and predicts the Judgment that should come on the whole nation. It will be a complete Judgment, for it would fall on the four corners of the land. The nation having failed in its Testimony for God, the execution of the Judgment was now the only Testimony to the existence and nature of God. How sad that under the circumstances then present, Judgment should be the only possible testimony (Williams).

THE STUMBLINGBLOCK OF THEIR INIQUITY

The phrase of Verse 19, which says, *"They shall cast their silver in the streets, and their gold shall be removed,"* actually says, *"They shall cast their silver idols . . . and their gold idols. . . . "* This was the stumblingblock of their iniquity.

Judah had traded Jehovah for a stupid looking idol made of metal or wood. Consequently, they became like the idol they worshiped, dumb, stupid, senseless, and without spiritual intelligence. Such characterizes almost all the present world.

When the Judgment does fall, Judah will throw away these gold and silver idols, for their absolute uselessness will be obvious to all. Only Jehovah could help, and they had long since turned their backs on Him.

These Verses portray the moral level to which Judah and Jerusalem had fallen in their rebellion against God, and proclaimed the justice of Judgment.

Verse 20 says, *"As for the beauty of His ornament, He set it in Majesty."* This refers to the Temple in Jerusalem.

The phrase, *"Their detestable things therein,"* refers to the Hebrew idolaters who set up the idols in the Temple. It is unthinkable that these abominable things were set up in the very Temple of God; and yet they were, and worse yet, by God's chosen people.

As well, we must take stock of our own lives, realizing, just as Judah set these detestable things in the Temple in the very Presence of God, we also, who are Temples of the Holy Spirit, may have things in our lives which are just as abominable now as then (I Cor. 3:16-17).

Verse 21 says, *"And I will give it into the hands of the strangers for a prey."* This refers to the Temple, as well as all of its ornaments, being given to the Chaldeans, who were *"strangers"* to God.

Inasmuch as these beautiful ornaments, which had been given by God, were not being used for Righteous purposes, therefore, the Lord would give these beautiful furnishings to the wicked for a *"spoil."* His people had turned it into wickedness, so why not give it to the *"wicked"!*

"My secret place" of Verse 22 refers to the *"Holy of Holies,"* where resided the Ark of the Covenant, the Mercy Seat, and the Cherubim, and where God resided.

No one was to go into this place except the High Priest, and then only once a year, on the great Day of Atonement, and then with blood, which was sprinkled on the Mercy Seat. But the Lord says that when the Chaldean soldiers broke into the Holy of Holies, even as they did do, He would not strike them dead, as He would have done to Hebrews, had they entered this place unlawfully.

In fact, the Babylonian soldiers did break into the entirety of the Temple, including the Holy of Holies. In fact, the Temple was totally destroyed.

However, even though the Babylonians took many sacred vessels from the Temple, which had been built by Solomon, and was no doubt the most expensive structure ever built, when they broke into the Holy of Holies, the Ark of the Covenant wasn't there. Tradition says that Jeremiah had had it removed before this time, and that he had hidden it in a cave; however, whether that is true or not is anyone's guess. But two things are certain: there was no Ark of the Covenant in the Holy of Holies when the Babylonians entered; and, if it was hidden in a cave, it's never been found.

THE HOLY PLACES

Verse 24 says, *"And their Holy Places shall be defiled."* The Holy Spirit is speaking of all the idols set up in Judah, as well as those set up in the Temple, even now referring to the actual Holy of Holies in the Temple as being no different than the idol Temples of the heathen, because Judah had long since ceased to look to it in the right spirit. So, the Lord put the Temple into the same position as the heathen altars.

Does the Holy Spirit liken some Churches to the same position as Islam, Buddhism, or Hinduism? In this Passage, He likens His very dwelling place to heathen altars; therefore, He does no less today to those Churches which do not *"rightly divide the Word."*

The thinking was that the Babylonians, in the last few years, had already made two excursions into the land and had effected two deportations of the rich and skillful, and a third intrusion would, therefore, be similar to the previous two. However, the Holy Spirit through the Prophet informs the inhabitants of Judah and Jerusalem that the third excursion will have no similarity to the prior ones. The other two would be a mere pin-prick in comparison to the damage done by a meat-cleaver; therefore, any false hopes of a serene occupation are dashed by the Prophet. However, they didn't listen to the Prophet of God, rather choosing to listen to the false Messengers.

AN EXAMPLE

Unfortunately, the twin Books of Jeremiah and Ezekiel, are read and studied very little by the modern Church. We would do well to study these two Books just as much as we study the Psalms, or the Epistles, or the Gospels. The warnings given, while applied to Judah of old, still, are examples for us presently. Paul said: *"Now all these things happened unto them for examples: and they are written for our admonition, upon whom the ends of the world are come.*

"Wherefore let him who thinks he stands take heed lest he fall" (I Cor. 10:11-12).

As we have already stated, and will keep stating, God cannot abide sin in any form. Sin must be dealt with, and there's only one way it can be dealt with, and that's through heart-broken Repentance, and looking to the Cross where sin was addressed once and for all. There is no other remedy but the Cross! And the trouble with the world, and even the Church, is that they all think there is a remedy other than the Cross. There isn't, and there never will be!

The Lord loved His chosen people, the Israelites, just as He presently loves the Church. But God's love cannot wink at sin. God expects more presently, even in this dispensation of Grace, than He did in Old Testament Times. Most of the Church world doesn't know that, but it happens to be true. Let me say it in a little different way:

Paul said: *"And the times of this ignorance* (Old Testament Times) *God winked at; but now* (this Dispensation of Grace) *commands all men everywhere to repent"* (Acts 17:30).

The above Passage doesn't mean that God, during Old Testament Times, condoned sin, for God can never condone sin. It merely means that God didn't bring Judgment on sin quite as swiftly during those times, because of ignorance.

The only people on the face of the Earth at that time who knew anything about God were the Israelites. Even then, their knowledge was limited, due to the fact that the Holy Spirit could not work then as He works now, because of the terrible sin debt over mankind, which the blood of bulls and goats could not take away (Heb. 10:4).

But since the Cross, the Holy Spirit can now abide permanently in the hearts and lives of all Believers, which He definitely does. As well, every Believer can also be Baptized with the Holy Spirit, which gives the Holy Spirit greater latitude within our lives.

While the unredeemed are still just as spiritually dead now as they were before the Cross, still, the influence of Christianity has definitely been felt over the entirety of the world. As a result, God holds this world more accountable now than then, and the same holds for the Church.

We should read these words as it regards the Prophecies given by Ezekiel, and we should tremble when we read them.

"My hope, blessed Jesus, is anchored in Thee,

"Thy Righteousness only now covereth me,
"Thy Blood, shed on Calvary, now is my plea;
"My hope, my hope, my hope is in Thee."

"I stand on the Rock that no temp'st can shake,
"And life from Thy hands every moment I take,
"Thy love will endure when all others forsake;
"My hope, my hope, my hope is in Thee."

"My hope for eternity rests in Thy hand,
"My heart deeply longs for that fair better land,
"Where one day complete in Thyself I shall stand;
"My hope, my hope is in Thee."

CHAPTER 8

(1) "AND IT CAME TO PASS IN THE SIXTH YEAR, IN THE SIXTH MONTH, IN THE FIFTH DAY OF THE MONTH, AS I SAT IN MY HOUSE, AND THE ELDERS OF JUDAH SAT BEFORE ME, THAT THE HAND OF THE LORD GOD FELL THERE UPON ME.

(2) "THEN I BEHELD, AND LO A LIKENESS AS THE APPEARANCE OF FIRE: FROM THE APPEARANCE OF HIS LOINS EVEN DOWNWARD, FIRE; AND FROM HIS LOINS EVEN UPWARD, AS THE APPEARANCE OF BRIGHTNESS, AS THE COLOUR OF AMBER.

(3) "AND HE PUT FORTH THE FORM OF AN HAND, AND TOOK ME BY A LOCK OF MY HEAD; AND THE SPIRIT LIFTED ME UP BETWEEN THE EARTH AND THE HEAVEN, AND BROUGHT ME IN THE VISIONS OF GOD TO JERUSALEM, TO THE DOOR OF THE INNER GATE THAT LOOKS TOWARD THE NORTH; WHERE WAS THE SEAT OF THE IMAGE OF JEALOUSY, WHICH PROVOKES TO JEALOUSY.

(4) "AND, BEHOLD, THE GLORY OF THE GOD OF ISRAEL WAS THERE,

ACCORDING TO THE VISION THAT I SAW IN THE PLAIN."

The overview is:

1. Ezekiel's second Prophecy begins here and closes at Chapter 11. It concerns Jerusalem, and exposes the hypocrisy, abominations, and violence existing there.

2. Five years later, the City and the Temple were completely destroyed by the Chaldeans.

3. The Wrath of God fell on the guilty City; and this Chapter and the following expose the abominations which justified that Wrath.

ABOMINATIONS

The Vision which Ezekiel mentions in Verse 1 took place *"in the sixth year,"* referring to his sixth year of captivity, which was approximately five years before the destruction of Judah and Jerusalem.

The occasion of this particular Prophecy, which will be startling to say the least, even as we shall see, took place in his house, with the elders of Judah, who were of the Exiles, and who evidently had come to hear the Prophet speak. As he was ministering, he said, *"The hand of the Lord GOD fell there upon me."*

That which will be portrayed to him is striking indeed! Even though he is in Babylonia, hundreds of miles away from Jerusalem, the Lord will give him visions of the evil activity carried on in the very confines of the Temple itself! It seems somewhat strange that the Lord would give this to Ezekiel who was in captivity, when it was not given to Jeremiah who was Prophesying in the very Temple itself, or, at least, very near. Perhaps it was because of the type of Ministry given to both Prophets.

JEREMIAH

Jeremiah's Ministry consisted of Prophetic announcements emboldened by symbolism, with only a small amount of visionary activity. However, Ezekiel's Ministry, although also consisting of Prophetic announcement, consisted of Visions into the Spirit world, as perhaps no other man ever experienced, with the exception of Daniel and John the Beloved, the latter while on the Isle of Patmos. Ezekiel would be shown the reason for Jeremiah's Prophetic announcements. Consequently, the Holy Spirit gives the Bible student a look into the Spirit world, which is the reason for actions carried out by the Lord. It is one thing to hear *"Thus saith the Lord,"* and quite another thing to know the reason for such pronouncements. Ezekiel, in panoramic view, so to speak, as if coming through on a Television screen, is shown in glaring detail the reasons for the actions of Jehovah. The Reader must not allow these all-important lessons to be lost upon him!

At any rate, both the Ministries of Jeremiah and Ezekiel complemented each other, and placed together presented the entirety of the Message that the Lord had given to Judah and Jerusalem.

A VISION OF GOD

Verse 2 proclaims a Vision of Jehovah, as given to Ezekiel, on this particular day. Evidently, the Elders who were gathered did not see what Ezekiel saw; this appearance was strictly reserved for the Prophet.

The fiery appearance that Ezekiel saw had the likeness of man. In reality, it was the God of Israel, and was accompanied by the Glory; and He it was Who spoke in Vision to the Prophet. This is the same as Ezekiel saw in the previous Vision outlined in Chapter 1. The Prophet, in effect, is actually seeing the Spirit Body of Jehovah.

Some have stated, as we have previously said, that this is merely an anthropomorphism, which means that this is not really what God looks like, but merely a form He takes on in order that man may understand Him. However, there is no basis for such in Scripture, and if true, would mean that Ezekiel's Vision in some way, was a lie.

Some refer to the words of John, *"No man has seen God at any time,"* to prove their point (Jn. 1:18). However, the Greek word for *"seen"* is *"horao,"* which means to either see with the eye or fully comprehend with the mind. In this case, it means to *"fully comprehend with the mind,"* and the Verse should read, *"No man has ever fully comprehended God at any time in all His fullness, save the Only Begotten Son."*

Therefore, what Ezekiel saw was an actual Vision of God in His Spirit Body, which is actually what He looks like, but which Glory can change constantly if so desired, and which Ezekiel little understood or comprehended, as would be obvious!

THE VISION

The Third Verse proclaims the Lord taking Ezekiel by the hair of his head and transporting him to Jerusalem, where he will see the cause of the coming Judgment. This means that Ezekiel did not literally go to Jerusalem, but rather saw all of these things in a Vision.

The *"door of the inner gate that looks toward the North"* was actually the *"Gate of the Altar,"* the most conspicuous part of the Temple where the people gathered in large numbers.

THE IMAGE OF JEALOUSY

This was probably the Asherah, which was set up close to the *"Brazen Altar."* This idol was upon a pedestal, wounding with jealousy the love that shone forth in the Glory of God. The scene that meets the eye is unthinkable, to say the least!

It is believed that the *"Asherah,"* which, incidentally, was made in all sizes, some of wood, some of stone, and some of precious metals, was actually a replica of the male reproductive organ. The people worshiped it, in a sense, as the god of fertility, trying to ascertain the origin of life. All type of perversions and sexual abominations were carried on as it regards the worship of this *"god."*

When one realizes that this thing was erected by the side of the Brazen Altar, which was a Type of Christ and the price that He would pay in order to redeem fallen humanity, one then begins to see the depths to which the people of God had fallen.

How could these people who were the recipients of the Word of God, the people of the Book, those who had given the world the Prophets, who were to serve as the womb of the Messiah, come to this place?

I believe I know the answer to that. It is the same with all spiritual declension.

THE CROSS

If this heathenistic, obscene idol was actually set up by the side of the Brazen Altar, it was placed there for a purpose other than worship. In some way, the Children of Israel had long since lost the true meaning of what the Sacrificial System was all about, which, in fact, was meant to portray the coming Redeemer, and the price that He would pay in order to set men free. The Sacrificial System had merely become a ceremony to them.

So, they may have reasoned that inasmuch as the Brazen Altar typified death, this obscene idol, the man's reproductive member, in their thinking, typified life. This means that they had completely lost the idea of life coming out of death, typified by the Cross, of which the Brazen Altar was a symbol. In other words, death was required, and the death of a perfect, innocent victim, of which Christ Alone fit the description, and of which the innocent Lambs were a Type. This death would pay the price for fallen humanity, which would alleviate the sin debt, at least for all who believed. Upon Faith, life could then be given, of which Christ was the Source, with the Cross as the means by which this would be done, and of which, as stated, the Sacrificial System was a type.

So, the Cross was denigrated by the thinking of Judah of that particular time, with the life source being reckoned as something else, in this case, a heathenistic, vulgar idol. Now this question begs to be asked:

MODERN ABOMINATIONS

If there was no excuse for Judah of old, and there wasn't, then where does that put the modern Church? The Cross is now a fact; the Holy Spirit has come; the Word of God is complete. All this means that the New Covenant affords much more knowledge about the great Plan of God. In other words, if there was no excuse for Judah, then surely there is no excuse for the modern Church and its rejection or denial of the Cross. The sin in the eyes of God must be the same, and even worse.

While the modern Church has not replaced the Cross with a vulgar idol, at least not in the natural, other things have replaced it. Therefore, we must say, *"An idol is an idol, is an idol"!*

This is the reason I encourage all over whom we might have at least a modicum of influence to read the Book of Ezekiel. We need to understand that if God rejected Judah,

His chosen people, then how do we think we can fare any better, when our situation is possibly just as bad, and maybe even worse. Listen again to Paul:

"Boast not against the branches. But if you boast, you bear not the root, but the root you.

"You will say then, the branches (Israel) *were broken off, that I* (the Church) *might be grafted in.*

"Well; because of unbelief they (Israel) *were broken off, and you* (the Church) *stand by Faith. Be not highminded, but fear:*

"For if God spared not the natural branches (Israel), *take heed lest He also spare not you"* (Rom. 11:18-21).

The Lord dealt with Israel in two ways: as a nation, and as individuals. While the situation finally became so bad that He had to destroy the nation, individuals within the nation, at least the few who believed the Lord, were saved.

There are similarities to God's dealings with the Church presently. He deals with the Church as a whole, and He deals with individuals. But the Church, unlike the nation of Israel, is splintered in many and varied segments. Basically, His Spirit has left the institutionalized Church, at least those who have rejected His Word, and deals mostly with individuals. While emphasis has always been tendered greatly toward individuals in the great Plan of God, it is even more so under the New Covenant.

THE LORD'S SUPPER

There are two great Ordinances in the Church. They are Water Baptism, which is entered into at one time, which is at conversion, and the Lord's Supper, which is repeatedly engaged. As such, the latter would be a greater example, even as it is meant to be.

Paul said some things regarding Judgment, in respect to the Lord's Supper, that I'm afraid most Believers little understand. The account is found in I Corinthians 11:24-32.

This account, as given by the Holy Spirit to Paul, tells us that the broken bread typifies His physical body, which was given on the Cross as a Sacrifice. The cup proclaims His shed Blood, which typifies the price that was paid, which, in essence, was the pouring out of His Life.

So, the Lord's Supper portrays the New Covenant as nothing else, because it portrays the Cross as nothing else.

The Apostle said: *"Wherefore whosoever shall eat this bread, and drink this cup of the Lord, unworthily, shall be guilty of the Body and Blood of the Lord"* (I Cor. 11:27).

What did Paul mean by eating and drinking *"unworthily"*?

Sinless perfection is not demanded for the Believer to partake of the Lord's Supper; however, one thing is demanded, and that is that we know and understand that everything we have from the Lord comes to us totally through the Sacrifice of Christ. This means that if the Cross is not the Object of our Faith, then we are partaking of this Supper *"unworthily,"* and consequently, *"shall be guilty of the Body and Blood of the Lord."* Now let's see what the Apostle meant by that?

UNWORTHILY

He then said, *"For he who eats and drinks unworthily, eats and drinks damnation to himself, not discerning the Lord's Body"* (I Cor. 11:29). This means that the Believer does not properly understand that everything he receives from the Lord comes to him totally and completely through Christ and what Christ did at the Cross. If he thinks he receives such from any other means, he is *"not discerning the Lord's Body."* Now what is the result of that?

The Apostle then said: *"For this cause many are weak and sickly among you, and many sleep"* (I Cor. 11:30). This Thirtieth Verse should give us cause for deep contemplation. It means, if we do not properly understand the Cross, which this Ordinance typifies, such thinking and such wrong direction can bring on sickness; it also means (and this is chilling indeed!), by the words, *"and many sleep,"* that Christians can die prematurely, because they do not properly discern the Lord's Body.

Now that doesn't mean that every Christian who dies at a young age falls into this category; however, it definitely does mean that many do! That's how important that a proper understanding of the Cross is.

To sum up, this means that much sickness

(not all), and much premature death (not all), among Christians are caused by Christians taking the Lord's Supper without the Cross being the complete Object of their Faith. That's how important that the Cross is. While the Lord doesn't deal with the Church in the same manner that he dealt with Judah of old, simply because the Church is not a nation, still, in individual ways, His Judgment is just as severe now as then, or even more so.

The Cross of Christ is the only source of protection for the Child of God. And by that, we're not speaking of the wooden Cross itself, for that has no validity at all, but, rather, that which the Cross produced, which speaks of benefits that come to us even unto this hour, and, in fact, ever shall be (Heb. 13:20).

So, the point I'm attempting to make is, we must not read these Chapters in Ezekiel and allow its lessons to be lost upon us.

(5) "THEN SAID HE UNTO ME, SON OF MAN, LIFT UP YOUR EYES NOW THE WAY TOWARD THE NORTH. SO I LIFTED UP MY EYES THE WAY TOWARD THE NORTH, AND BEHOLD NORTHWARD AT THE GATE OF THE ALTAR THIS IMAGE OF JEALOUSY IN THE ENTRY.

(6) "HE SAID FURTHERMORE UNTO ME, SON OF MAN, SEE YOU WHAT THEY DO? EVEN THE GREAT ABOMINATIONS THAT THE HOUSE OF ISRAEL COMMITTED HERE, THAT I SHOULD GO FAR OFF FROM MY SANCTUARY? BUT TURN YOU YET AGAIN, AND YOU SHALL SEE GREATER ABOMINATIONS.

(7) "AND HE BROUGHT ME TO THE DOOR OF THE COURT; AND WHEN I LOOKED, BEHOLD A HOLE IN THE WALL.

(8) "THEN SAID HE UNTO ME, SON OF MAN, DIG NOW IN THE WALL: AND WHEN I HAD DUG IN THE WALL, BEHOLD A DOOR.

(9) "AND HE SAID UNTO ME, GO IN, AND BEHOLD THE WICKED ABOMINATIONS THAT THEY DO HERE.

(10) "SO I WENT IN AND SAW; AND BEHOLD EVERY FORM OF CREEPING THINGS, AND ABOMINABLE BEASTS, AND ALL THE IDOLS OF THE HOUSE OF ISRAEL, PORTRAYED UPON THE WALL ROUND ABOUT.

NOTES

(11) "AND THERE STOOD BEFORE THEM SEVENTY MEN OF THE ANCIENTS OF THE HOUSE OF ISRAEL, AND IN THE MIDST OF THEM STOOD JAAZANIAH THE SON OF SHAPHAN, WITH EVERY MAN HIS CENSER IN HIS HAND; AND A THICK CLOUD OF INCENSE WENT UP.

(12) "THEN SAID HE UNTO ME, SON OF MAN, HAVE YOU SEEN WHAT THE ANCIENTS OF THE HOUSE OF ISRAEL DO IN THE DARK, EVERY MAN IN THE CHAMBERS OF HIS IMAGERY? FOR THEY SAY, THE LORD SEES US NOT; THE LORD HAS FORSAKEN THE EARTH.

(13) "HE SAID ALSO UNTO ME, TURN THEE YET AGAIN, AND YOU SHALL SEE GREATER ABOMINATIONS THAT THEY DO.

(14) "THEN HE BROUGHT ME TO THE DOOR OF THE GATE OF THE LORD'S HOUSE WHICH WAS TOWARD THE NORTH; AND, BEHOLD, THERE SAT WOMEN WEEPING FOR TAMMUZ.

(15) "THEN SAID HE UNTO ME, HAVE YOU SEEN THIS, O SON OF MAN? TURN YOU YET AGAIN, AND YOU SHALL SEE GREATER ABOMINATIONS THAN THESE.

(16) "AND HE BROUGHT ME INTO THE INNER COURT OF THE LORD'S HOUSE, AND, BEHOLD, AT THE DOOR OF THE TEMPLE OF THE LORD, BETWEEN THE PORCH AND THE ALTAR, WERE ABOUT FIVE AND TWENTY MEN, WITH THEIR BACKS TOWARD THE TEMPLE OF THE LORD, AND THEIR FACES TOWARD THE EAST; AND THEY WORSHIPPED THE SUN TOWARD THE EAST.

(17) "THEN HE SAID UNTO ME, HAVE YOU SEEN THIS, O SON OF MAN? IS IT A LIGHT THING TO THE HOUSE OF JUDAH THAT THEY COMMIT THE ABOMINATIONS WHICH THEY COMMIT HERE? FOR THEY HAVE FILLED THE LAND WITH VIOLENCE, AND HAVE RETURNED TO PROVOKE ME TO ANGER: AND, LO, THEY PUT THE BRANCH TO THEIR NOSE.

(18) "THEREFORE WILL I ALSO DEAL IN FURY: MY EYE SHALL NOT SPARE, NEITHER WILL I HAVE PITY: AND THOUGH THEY CRY IN MY EARS WITH A LOUD VOICE, YET WILL I NOT HEAR THEM."

The synopsis is:

1. Four pictures of abominations (Vss. 5-17), each succeeding picture revealing a deeper depth of idolatrous iniquity, are set out in these Verses.

2. The four abominations are:

A. The Asherah;

B. Egyptian idolatry;

C. The worship of Tammuz, the son of the Queen of Heaven; and,

D. Sun-worship.

3. Four times in the Hebrew Scriptures, the Holy Spirit addresses the Messiah as *"the Branch,"* that is, as the *"Author of Life."* Satan's parody of this was the Asherah.

THE IMAGE OF JEALOUSY

Both Verses 3 and 5 speak of the *"image of jealousy."* Once again, it is speaking of the *"Asherah,"* which represented the male reproductive member. It is most probable that the great golden image of Nebuchadnezzar was a phallus.

We see this idol mentioned first in the Bible in Exodus 34:13-14. It was at this time that God portrayed His Name as *"Jealous,"* consequently, the Holy Spirit using the phrase in Verse 3, *"the image of jealousy, which provokes to jealousy,"* and in Verse 5, *"this image of jealousy."* Of this, we will have more to say in a moment.

EGYPTIAN IDOLATRY

Verses 10 through 12 proclaim the greater abomination of the chamber of Egyptian idolatry; and here stood all the seventy members of the Hebrew Synod, so to speak, worshiping the loathsome reptiles portrayed on the walls.

These were probably forerunners of the Sanhedrin. Traditionally, they originated with the seventy Elders who assisted Moses (Numbers 11:16-24). They were actually the rulers of Israel, exercising not only civil jurisdiction according to Jewish Law, but also criminal jurisdiction.

In Christ's day, the Sanhedrin were just as wicked, or more so, as in the days of Ezekiel, with only two of its members taking the part of Christ, Joseph of Arimathaea and Nicodemus.

The deep pain of this scene is sharpened by the presence of Jaazaniah. His father Shaphan had taken part in Josiah's reformation (II Ki., Chpt. 22) and two of his brothers were friendly to Jeremiah (Jer. 26:24; 36:10, 25). We must remember that all of this heathenistic worship was going on in the confines of the Temple, where God dwelt between the Mercy Seat and the Cherubim, in the Holy Holies. That's the reason He said in Verse 6, *"Do you see what they do? even the great abominations that the house of Israel commits here, that I should go far off from My Sanctuary"*?

Even as we will find in Chapter 11, the Temple had now become a *"God-deserted"* place. His visitation now would be one of Judgment and, therefore, as a Destroyer. In Truth, and sadly, the Lord has left most Churches. Why does He leave?

FALSE DOCTRINE

All false Doctrine is caused in one way or the other by demon spirits. Paul said:

"Now the Spirit (Holy Spirit) *speaks expressly* (pointedly), *that in the* latter *times* (the times in which we now live) *some shall depart from the Faith* (Jesus Christ and Him Crucified), *giving heed to seducing spirits, and doctrines of devils"* (I Tim. 4:1).

While false Doctrine has always abounded in the Work of God, we are told here in the words of Paul, as given to him by the Holy Spirit, that this problem would compound itself in the last of the last days, actually, the times in which we now live. In fact, there is more false doctrine today, I personally think, then at any time since the Reformation.

There are myriads of false doctrines, but the two which possibly affect the Church more adversely, at this present time, than all others are: A. Unconditional Eternal Security; and, B. The Word of Faith Doctrine, which espouses the Jesus Died Spiritually idea. This latter doctrine completely denies the Cross, referring to it as *"past miseries"* or as the *"greatest defeat in human history."*

In brief, it claims that Jesus became a sinner on the Cross, thereby dying and going to Hell as a sinner, and suffered there for three days and nights, and we speak of the burning side of Hell. They teach that Demons tortured Him during this particular time, when, at the end of that three days and nights, God said, *"It is enough,"* and Jesus was then *"Born-Again,"* even as any sinner is Born-Again, and Born-Again we might quickly add, in Hell itself. He was then Resurrected, they teach. So, according to this teaching, the great Redemption Plan was carried out in the pit of Hell, with the Cross playing no part whatsoever.

Now there is one great thing about this: there's not a single word of it found anywhere in the Bible. It is a fictitious fabrication from beginning to end. In fact, one of its leading proponents said, *"You won't find this in the Bible, it has to be given to you by Revelation from the Lord."*

I beg to disagree! If it's not in the Bible, you can rest assured that whatever is being given to whomever is not from the Lord, but rather from deceiving spirits.

Let me bluntly state, and in no uncertain terms, that Salvation was afforded, bought, and paid for, at the Cross of Christ (Jn. 3:16; Rom. 6:3-5; I Cor. 1:17-18, 23; 2:2; Gal., Chpt. 5; 6:14; Eph. 2:13-18; Col. 2:14-15).

THE HOLY SPIRIT

Regrettably and sadly, the Holy Spirit is little present in most Churches. In fact, where there are genuine movings of the Spirit, such places are not easily found.

At the turn of the Twentieth Century, the great Latter Rain outpouring of the Holy Spirit began, as Prophesied by Joel (Joel 2:23). Regarding this outpouring, tens of thousands of Baptists, Methodists, and Lutherans, etc., were Baptized with the Holy Spirit, with the evidence of speaking with other tongues; however, these Denominations, as an institutionalized Church, completely rejected the Holy Spirit, for to reject His manner of Baptism is to reject the Spirit Himself (Acts 2:4).

In times past, many of these Denominations produced great Preachers who preached a great Salvation Message, resulting in many people being saved; however, since their rejection of the Holy Spirit, there is actually very little presently going on in these particular Churches, at least as far as the Lord is concerned. While there is much religious machinery, actually more than ever, very little is being truly done for the Lord, simply because the Holy Spirit is little there, if at all, at least as it regards these particular Churches. And without Him, there can be nothing done for the Lord.

Regrettably, most of the Pentecostal Denominations, which owe their very existence to the outpouring of the Holy Spirit, little stress any more the Baptism with the Spirit. In fact, I'm told that only about 38 percent of the people who attend Assemblies of God Churches even claim to be Baptized with the Holy Spirit. I suppose that the Church of God, the second largest Pentecostal Denomination, would probably fall into the same category.

In truth, there are probably less people being baptized with the Holy Spirit presently than at any time since the great Latter Rain outpouring began at the turn of the Twentieth Century.

On a personal note, my son Donnie is being used by the Lord, along with a few other Preachers, to see a goodly number Baptized with the Spirit in his meetings, and that all over the world. For that we are extremely thankful to the Lord; however, as wonderful as that is, it is just a drop in the proverbial bucket, compared to what ought to be taking place at this time.

SIN

Every true Christian, due to the Divine Nature, hates sin. But the truth is, at least at this particular time, most modern Christians have an erroneous viewpoint of sin.

Many think, because this is the Dispensation of Grace, that the Lord overlooks sin. Others are just simply taught to confess the fact that they are the *"Righteousness of God,"* and as such, ignore sin. They also teach that if the Preacher preaches against sin, he is merely creating a sin consciousness in the hearts of his listeners, which will cause them to sin. So, in their interpretation, the Preacher should never preach about sin, etc.

That's strange, when Paul mentioned sin some seventeen times in the Sixth Chapter of Romans alone. And, we must remember, Paul was writing to Believers. This foolish teaching of not mentioning sin comes from the Word of Faith Doctrine.

Most of the Church leaders presently have

turned to humanistic psychology in their efforts to address the sin problem, whatever that sin problem might be.

So, an improper view of sin has wrought havoc in the lives of most Christians.

THE CROSS

There's only one answer for sin, and that's the Cross of Christ. There is no other cure, no other remedy, and no other solution, only the Cross!

The truth is, the problem with humanity is the problem of sin, and that includes the Church as well.

Paul said: *"For in that He died, He died unto sin once"* (Rom. 6:10). He also said: *"But this Man* (the Lord Jesus Christ), *after He had offered One Sacrifice for sins forever, sat down on the Right Hand of God"* (Heb. 10:12). He then said, *"For by one Offering* (the offering of Himself on the Cross) *He has perfected forever them who are Sanctified"* (Heb. 10:14).

So, we learn from this, plus many other Passages in the Word of God which could be given, that the only answer for sin is the Cross.

To be brief, the Believer can live a victorious, overcoming Christian life, only by understanding that the Cross of Christ is the means by which the Lord gives us everything. Consequently, the Cross must ever be the Object of our Faith, which then gives the Holy Spirit great latitude to work within our lives (Rom. 8:1-2, 11).

THE BENEFITS OF THE CROSS

When we speak of the Cross, we're not putting Jesus back on the Cross. In fact, Jesus is at the Right Hand of the Father in Heaven, and we, spiritually speaking, are seated with Him in Heavenly Places (Heb. 1:3; Eph. 2:6). However, what we all must realize is that Jesus holds that position, and we are with Him, solely because of what He did for us at the Cross.

The Cross is an act which was carried out nearly 2,000 years ago, which will never have to be repeated; however, it has continuing benefits, benefits which continue to this hour, which will actually ever continue (Heb. 13:20). It's the *"benefits"* of which we speak,

NOTES

all provided by the Cross.

So, if the Believer thinks that he can leave the Cross at Salvation, or at any time, this shows that he little understands the Cross. In fact, the entirety of the meaning of the New Covenant can be summed up in the meaning of the Cross, which speaks to what Jesus did there, all on our behalf.

Believers have an erroneous viewpoint of sin, simply because they have an erroneous viewpoint of the Cross. And unless we make the Cross the foundation of all that we are in Christ, we will conclude by preaching false doctrine, and the Holy Spirit will simply vacate the Temple (I Cor. 3:16-17).

TAMMUZ

Tammuz was the son of the Queen of Heaven, at least that which someone had fabricated out of nothing, because it did not exist.

As today, so at that time, the favorite Divinity of women was the Virgin and her child. She was supposed to lose her son, and later on to find him. A festival of weeping celebrated the loss, and the recovery, by a festival of rejoicing. These were two of the greatest festivals of the ancient sacred year. These women were weeping in the Temple of Jehovah, not for their sins, but for Tammuz!

THE SUN WORSHIPERS

The final and most appalling form of idolatrous abomination was that of the High Priest and the Chiefs of the twenty-four Courses of Aaron standing in the Holy Place with their backs to the Most Holy Place, worshiping the sun!

Sun-worship is believed by some to be purest form of idolatry. Here it is declared to be the most impure, for it was at that time associated with the Branch, i.e., Asherah (Vs. 17).

Four times in the Hebrew Scriptures, the Holy Spirit addresses the Messiah as *"the Branch,"* that is, as the Author of Life. Satan's parody of this was the Asherah — the Greek Phallus. The ancients, in their effort to reach back to the origin of life and worship it as a god, arrived at the lowest depth of moral and intellectual degradation by the institution of Phallic worship (the worship of the man's reproductive member).

This was the deepest depth of abomination, and is affirmed by the words of burning indignation: *"Lo, they put the branch to My nose!"* (Vs. 17).

Someone misinterpreted the Text, and said, *"Lo, they put the branch to their nose,"* when, in reality, the actual Text reads, *"My nose."*

Some worshipers put a certain kind of plant to their faces when adoring the sun, and it is thought that the reference in Verse 17 is to this fact. But such an action would not call forth the indignation which burns in the language of the Verse, or explain why this fourth picture revealed the greatest abomination.

They were thrusting this vulgar idol into the very Face of God!

Idolatry blinds. The God of Glory was actually present, at least at this time, in His Temple, but the Priests and Elders declared He was not there (Vs. 12). This blindness is affirmed in the following Chapter.

The heart that is governed by any form of idolatry, whether material, scientific, or philosophic, is insensible to fellowship with God, and cannot see His Glory as revealed in the Face of Jesus Christ (II Cor. 4:6) (Williams).

"I can see far down the mountain,
where I've wandered many years.
"Often hindered on my journey by the
ghosts of doubts and fears.
"Broken vows and disappointments,
thickly strewn along the way.
"But the Spirit has led unerring, to the
land I hold today."

CHAPTER 9

(1) "HE CRIED ALSO IN MY EARS WITH A LOUD VOICE, SAYING, CAUSE THEM WHO HAVE CHARGE OVER THE CITY TO DRAW NEAR, EVEN EVERY MAN WITH HIS DESTROYING WEAPON IN HIS HAND.

(2) "AND, BEHOLD, SIX MEN CAME FROM THE WAY OF THE HIGHER GATE, WHICH LIES TOWARD THE NORTH, AND EVERY MAN A SLAUGHTER WEAPON IN HIS HAND; AND ONE MAN AMONG THEM WAS CLOTHED WITH LINEN, WITH A WRITER'S INKHORN BY HIS SIDE: AND THEY WENT IN, AND STOOD BESIDE THE BRASEN ALTAR.

(3) "AND THE GLORY OF THE GOD OF ISRAEL WAS GONE UP FROM THE CHERUB, WHEREUPON HE WAS, TO THE THRESHOLD OF THE HOUSE. AND HE CALLED TO THE MAN CLOTHED WITH LINEN, WHICH HAD THE WRITER'S INKHORN BY HIS SIDE;"

The exegesis is:

1. The last Verse of the previous Chapter and the first Verse of this Chapter should be read together, and the contrast between the *"loud voice"* of the idolaters and the *"loud voice"* of the God of Judgment noticed (Williams).

2. These seven beings were evidently supernatural. Six were Ministers of Wrath, and one of Grace.

3. The one man of Grace, clothed in linen, stands for Righteousness. He alone had the *"writer's inkhorn by his side,"* signifying that he would mark the ones who were Righteous.

THE SPIRIT WORLD

This Chapter gives us a view into the spirit world of the action of God concerning the destruction of Jerusalem. The glutted population of the city had no idea that such was happening, as indeed it was! Those marked for death actually happened some four to five years before the deed of destruction was brought about, and could have changed even up to the last moment upon true, heartfelt Repentance by any individual.

This Chapter will reveal the minute detail in which Judgment is poured out, even down to the exact individual. Such is no less true today! One has to wonder if the Lord is *"marking"* America for Judgment?

Verse 2 proclaims seven men, in reality, seven Angels, for they were all supernatural beings, with *"six"* delegated for slaughter, and *"one"* delegated for Salvation.

Concerning the reason that six men were chosen, some have suggested that there were six idolaters for every true worshiper; however, it is very doubtful that there were that many true worshipers in Jerusalem at that time. So, the number *"six"* must suggest something else!

MAN

Six is the number of man. Man was created on the sixth day. As an example, Goliath had six pieces of armor. And Nebuchadnezzar's image was marked by three sixes, *"666"*: Sixty cubits high (90 feet), six cubits broad (9 feet), and proclaimed by six instruments of music (Dan. 3:1, 7). The great superman of the future will be recognized by the number *"666."*

The *"one"* added to the *"six,"* totaling seven, speak of God's perfection, and perfection in all He does. Therefore, His Judgment is perfect!

THE BRAZEN ALTAR

We find that all seven of these supernatural beings stood beside the Brazen Altar, which signified Calvary.

At the Brazen Altar, sin was atoned for and forgiven. However, the introduction of man's idol religion thrust this Altar aside. Nevertheless, even though thrust aside by man, it definitely was not thrust aside by God, in fact, could not be! As stated, this Altar foreshadowed Calvary. From that Altar, the Ministers of Wrath and Mercy went forth. The Minister of Grace went first, with those of Wrath after him.

So, it is today, and so it shall be. The Grace of God acts from Calvary, and the Wrath of God will act from Calvary. Calvary is the center of the Divine activities in Grace and Judgment. God's controversy with man concerns His dearly-beloved Son, and the Atonement that Christ made for sin.

Man's religious efforts, energized by Satan, are continually directed to the substitution of another way of life than that provided by God at Golgotha. Thus, they dishonor Christ.

If man accepts Christ and what He did at the Cross, Judgment is abated, because Jesus took the Judgment at Calvary. If man refuses Christ, then the Judgment comes upon the Christ rejecter, because sin must be judged. It's either judged in Christ, or it's judged in the life of the individual. The latter is not a very pleasant prospect.

(4) "AND THE LORD SAID UNTO HIM, GO THROUGH THE MIDST OF THE CITY, THROUGH THE MIDST OF JERUSALEM, AND SET A MARK UPON THE FOREHEADS OF THE MEN WHO SIGH AND WHO CRY FOR ALL THE ABOMINATIONS THAT BE DONE IN THE MIDST THEREOF.

(5) "AND TO THE OTHERS HE SAID IN MY HEARING, GO YE AFTER HIM THROUGH THE CITY, AND SMITE: LET NOT YOUR EYE SPARE, NEITHER HAVE YE PITY:

(6) "SLAY UTTERLY OLD AND YOUNG, BOTH MAIDS, AND LITTLE CHILDREN, AND WOMEN: BUT COME NOT NEAR ANY MAN UPON WHOM IS THE MARK; AND BEGIN AT MY SANCTUARY. THEN THEY BEGAN AT THE ANCIENT MEN WHICH WERE BEFORE THE HOUSE.

(7) "AND HE SAID UNTO THEM, DEFILE THE HOUSE, AND FILL THE COURTS WITH THE SLAIN: GO YE FORTH. AND THEY WENT FORTH, AND SLEW IN THE CITY."

The diagram is:

1. Some think the white-robed Minister pictured Israel's True and Great High Priest, the Lord Jesus Christ (Rev., Chpts. 7, 14).

2. We find here that the Grace of God acts from Calvary, and the Wrath of God will act from Calvary, as well!

3. Verse Six says the Judgment begins at the House of God (I Pet. 4:17). There is a throb of anguished love in the words, *"My Sanctuary."*

THE HOUSE OF GOD

The Fourth Verse proclaims the fact that all who were Righteous in Jerusalem, as small as that number was, were to have a mark set upon them. Of course, those upon whom the mark was set had no knowledge of what was taking place. This happened in the spirit world, but was as real as anything could ever be. Actually, the reality of this particular time would not take place for another four to five years.

So, we learn from all of this how minutely the Lord works in the spirit world, actions which bring about things on Earth.

Verses 5 and 6 proclaim the *"six"* going about, and consigning the balance of the population, those who were not Righteous, to the slaughter. In other words, they were marked for death at the coming invasion.

Of course, the question begs to be asked: *"Could these individuals have changed their situation, in other words, the righteous becoming unrighteous, and the unrighteous becoming righteous?"*

Yes, they could have! Chapter 3 of this Book proclaims that fact. Whether any of this actually happened, we aren't told!

As we see from Verse 6, the Judgment began at the Sanctuary of the Lord, and spoke of those in the previous Chapter who were worshiping idols in the Sanctuary.

SEPTEMBER 11, 2001 (9-11-01)

As it regards the terrible events of September 11, 2001, when Muslims purposely crashed two airplanes into the twin towers of New York City, plus one airplane into the Pentagon, in Washington D.C., several Preachers over Television claimed that the reason that the Lord allowed this to happen to America was because of the homosexuals and the abortions, etc.

While these sins are certainly grievous, as would be obvious, and while the Lord certainly takes a dim view of such activity, that was not what caused the deaths of nearly four thousand people, with their loss affecting tens of thousands, as well as hurting the economy of our nation. It was the Church, which caused the problem, and what do we mean by that?

Peter said, *"For the time is come that judgment must begin at the House of God: and if it first began at us, what shall the end be of them who obey not the Gospel of God?"* (I Pet. 4:17).

The cause of this problem, even as the Word of God proclaims, is not the fault of the unredeemed, but rather the fault of the professing redeemed.

Whenever the Church of the Living God is on fire for God, and is striving to obey the Word of God, this brings blessing upon that particular Church, as well as the city in question, or even an entire nation. And, of course, when we speak of *"the Church,"* we're speaking of the Church as a whole, not just a local Church in a particular city, even though the latter is very, very important. The condition of the Church as a whole in any nation has a lot to do with the blessing or the lack of such, as it regards any particular nation.

In fact, it doesn't take many Righteous people in any area to sway the situation toward the positive. The Judgment of Sodom and Gomorrah proclaims that fact (Gen., Chpt. 18). This tells us that the number of Righteous people in Judah, and Jerusalem, was abysmally small.

The September 11, 2001 horrors should have been a wake-up call, not only to this country, but also to the Church as a whole. But it seems like it has been little heeded, if at all!

DESTRUCTION

The destruction that would be brought about by God did not take place at that moment, but, in the mind of God, it was already a foregone conclusion.

The question should be asked, *"How many at this very moment around the world has the Lord already marked for destruction, even though they personally have no knowledge of such?"*

"Marked for destruction" is a foreboding thought. But this is exactly what Ezekiel saw in the spirit world, several years before it would actually come to pass in brutal horror.

As it should be obvious from these Passages, the Lord delights not at all in Judgment. In fact, He does everything within Heaven's power to turn people away from that which demands Judgment. But the problem is, men do not turn very quickly, or very easily. And in truth, most won't turn at all.

The world has become so psychologized that any more, it doesn't think of God in the realm of Judgment at all. The psychological way claims that man is inherently good, and if something happens to cause him to be bad, it's always external forces that do such. The Bible says the very opposite! The Bible teaches that man is born in sin and is inherently evil, and for there to be a change, man must be *"Born-Again"* (Jn. 3:3).

Of course, as the world of psychology measures the situation, man is not due any Judgment at all, but God says the very opposite.

Men can accept Jesus Christ as the Saviour today, or they will face Him as the Judge tomorrow.

(8) "AND IT CAME TO PASS, WHILE THEY WERE SLAYING THEM, AND I WAS LEFT, THAT I FELL UPON MY FACE, AND CRIED, AND SAID, AH LORD GOD! WILT YOU DESTROY ALL THE RESIDUE OF ISRAEL IN YOUR POURING OUT OF YOUR FURY UPON JERUSALEM?

(9) "THEN SAID HE UNTO ME, THE INIQUITY OF THE HOUSE OF ISRAEL AND JUDAH IS EXCEEDING GREAT, AND THE LAND IS FULL OF BLOOD, AND THE CITY FULL OF PERVERSENESS: FOR THEY SAY, THE LORD HAS FORSAKEN THE EARTH, AND THE LORD SEES NOT.

(10) "AND AS FOR ME ALSO, MY EYE SHALL NOT SPARE, NEITHER WILL I HAVE PITY, BUT I WILL RECOMPENSE THEIR WAY UPON THEIR HEAD.

(11) "AND, BEHOLD, THE MAN CLOTHED WITH LINEN, WHICH HAD THE INKHORN BY HIS SIDE, REPORTED THE MATTER, SAYING, I HAVE DONE AS YOU HAVE COMMANDED ME."

The composition is:

1. In the Vision, Ezekiel saw the slaughter that would take place some four or five years later.

2. We learn from this that all-important events, especially as it concerns *God's people*, are first decided in Heaven before these things take place on Earth.

3. All of this shows that God cannot spare even His Own, no matter how much He loves them, if they persist in disobedience, resulting in gross sin and iniquity. God can never be taken for granted. We must always remember that. The phrase, *"And I was left,"* of the Eighth Verse, refers to all the Priests marked for death except Ezekiel. His question to the Lord, *"Will You destroy all?"* portrays the fact that precious few were actually marked for Salvation by *"the Man clothed with linen."*

FEW

As it was then, so it is now. The Churches are filled with people who, for the most part, do not know God. Religion abounds, but very little personal relationship with Christ! Millions claim to be *"Born-Again,"* when the far greater majority have never come to a saving knowledge of Jesus Christ. From the dawn of time, it has been as Christ said, *"Few*

NOTES

there be who find it" (Mat. 7:13-14). Actually, from the time of Adam to Noah, a period of some 1,600 years, the Bible only records two individuals being saved, who were Abel and Enoch (Heb. 11:4-5).

If one is to carefully observe the history of Israel, God's chosen people, one will find that throughout their approximate 2,000-year history, only a few, at least in comparison to the whole, truly knew God. It is the same today!

HER SIN IS EXCEEDING GREAT

The Lord had said of Sodom and Gomorrah, *"Their sin is very grievous,"* portraying the similarity between Israel and Judah and Sodom and Gomorrah. The Lord had said of His people, *"The iniquity of the House of Israel and Judah is exceeding great."*

In a sense, Judah's sin was far greater because they were sinning against light, whereas Sodom and Gomorrah had no light. Actually, Jesus would later say concerning Capernaum and the whole of Judah: *"That it shall be more tolerable for the land of Sodom in the Day of Judgment, than for you"* (Mat. 11:24).

Judah had taken the position, due to their spiritual declension, that God took no active part in the affairs on Earth, and even with His people. They thought of Him as only an Observer, if that! Why would they say that?

They had the same spirit that much of the modern Church has presently, claiming that the days of miracles are over, etc. The modern Church, being almost entirely a man-made institution, has forsaken the Bible, and if attention is given to it, it is denied. Even if the exact terminology is not used, the modern Church conducts itself as if *"the LORD has forsaken the Earth."*

As well, they claimed that the Lord did not see their sins. The proponents of Unconditional Eternal Security claim the same thing! They claim if a person is saved, Grace covers any and all sins they may commit and, therefore, the Lord does not even see the sins of a Believer.

While it is true that the Lord does not see the sins which are washed and cleansed upon proper Repentance, still, He most definitely sees the sins of Believers which are unconfessed and unrepented (I Jn. 1:6-10).

NO MORE PITY

In Verse 10, the Lord said, *"And as for Me also, My eye shall not spare, neither will I have pity."* Actually, three times it is declared that pity will not be shown (8:18; 9:5, 10); but this is not the triple language of pleasure but of agony. It is love compelled to keep reminding itself of the sad necessity of Judgment.

Let it ever be understood that God takes no delight in sending Judgment. Actually, He will bear long before such is brought about; however, if pleas for Repentance, offered time and time again, continue to be ignored, the Righteousness of God demands that sin ultimately be Judged. The Lord stands ready to forgive, to cleanse, to wash, and to make whole any person, who will come to Him ardently seeking His Mercy and Grace, which He freely gives; however, He also demands a turning away from sin. But let the Reader understand: The turning away from sin can only be brought about in one capacity.

GOD'S PRESCRIBED ORDER OF VICTORY

What I'm going to relate in the next few paragraphs could be some of the most important material that you, the Reader, have ever come across. It is the simple Truth of God's Word, but yet, that of which the modern Church is little aware.

God has a way of victory. If we as Believers are to walk in victory, and I'm speaking of victory over all sin, then we must go God's Way, the Way laid down in His Word. No, the Bible doesn't teach sinless perfection, but it does teach that *"sin shall not have dominion over you"* (Rom. 6:14).

Not knowing God's Prescribed Order of Victory, which we will give to you momentarily, the Church casts about, seeking to find a way of victory, all of their own making, all to no avail!

Sometime back, I spent at least two hours on the phone with one of the most noted Preachers in the United States. His prescription for victory over sin was that such is caused by demon spirits; therefore, the evil spirit causing sin in the life of any particular Believer must be rebuked, but it must be done by a Preacher who understands these things, so the man said, etc.

It is certainly true that demon spirits become involved any time sin to any degree is manifested; however, there is nothing in the Bible that corroborates what our dear Brother said. In other words, it is not possible for any Preacher to lay hands on you, and to rid you of your sin. While the laying on of hands is definitely Scriptural, and will definitely help, still, unless the Believer knows and understands God's Prescribed Order of Victory, that Believer cannot walk in the victory for which Jesus paid such a price.

When we speak of sin we're speaking of habitual sin, in other words, something that's in the life of a Believer over which he has repeatedly tried to find victory, all to no avail. Let me hurriedly say this:

WORKS OF THE FLESH

When most Christians think of this of which we speak, their mind automatically goes to alcohol, drugs, immorality, nicotine, gambling, etc. Now, the vices definitely are terrible sins! But, believe it or not, there are many more types of sins which also are referred to as *"works of the flesh."*

Paul said: *"Now the works of the flesh are manifest, which are these; Adultery, fornication, uncleanness, lasciviousness,*

"Idolatry, witchcraft, hatred, variance, emulations, wrath, strife, seditions, heresies,

"Envyings, murders, drunkenness, revellings, and such like" (Gal. 5:19-21).

As we can see here, the many sins listed, and even some not listed, cover the waterfront. In other words, there are many things here of which modern Christians are guilty, of which they do not really think of as sin, but which in reality is sin.

For instance, very few people would think of false doctrine as sin; however, it comes under the heading of *"heresies."* So, the point I'm trying to make is this:

While most Christians would not be engaged in the vices that we mentioned above, to be sure, if the Christian doesn't understand the Cross, without the shadow of a doubt, one or more of the sins listed by Paul in the Fifth Chapter of Galatians are going to manifest themselves in the lives of Believers in some way.

Actually, these things mentioned are really the result of the major sin that's causing the problems.

REBELLION AGAINST GOD'S WAY

The Christian needs to look beyond the particular act of sin that he constantly commits to the cause of this problem. That's where the real trouble is. When we look at particular sins, which Paul named, etc., we are really looking at the symptoms of the real problem, and if all we address is the symptom, we'll never really find victory. Do you understand that of which I speak?

To really solve a problem, we have to go to the cause of the problem. So, what is the cause of bondage in the lives of Christians, or sin of any nature?

The real cause is, they are trying to live for God in the wrong way. All sin is a failure of Faith in some way. And what do we mean by that?

Whether we realize it or not, we Believers get off on a wrong track, or fail God in some way, or even become snared in bondages, simply because of a failure of Faith. In other words, our Faith is deficient in some manner.

And what we mean by that is this:

FAITH

Faith is really a very simple thing. It is merely the act of believing God, i.e., *"believing His Word."* I would certainly trust that most, if not all, Christians certainly fall into that category. They believe the Word of God. So, that means that Faith itself is really not the problem. The real problem is the correct object of Faith. That's where Christians go wrong.

The Object of our Faith, without exception, must be in Christ and what Christ did for us at the Cross. Now let's deal with that for a moment.

Christ must never be separated from the Cross, which refers to what He did there. No, Christ is not still on the Cross; He is rather seated by the Right Hand of the Father in Heaven (Heb. 1:3). As well, we are seated with Him in Heavenly Places, spiritually speaking (Eph. 2:6). The idea is, everything I receive from the Lord comes by the means of the Cross. God does not change. He was the same 5,000 years ago as He is now. It's the Cross, however, that has made it possible for Him to give you and me great things. Always the Cross!

So, the Believer must have his Faith anchored in the Cross, not allow it to be moved from the Cross, ever understanding that all that we receive from the Lord comes by the means of the Cross.

THE HOLY SPIRIT

Every Believer must understand that the life we need to live, the Christlikeness we must have, and the Righteousness and the Holiness which must be paramount in our lives cannot be brought about by our own machinations, ability, strength, power, or anything that we might have. All of it is a work of the Holy Spirit. To be sure, we have to be willing that these things be made paramount in our lives, but that's about all that we can supply — an obedient heart and a willing mind. The Holy Spirit has to do everything else (Rev. 22:17).

But we must remember that the Holy Spirit works exclusively within the parameters of the Finished Work of Christ. Jesus said: *"I will pray the Father, and He shall give you another Comforter, that He may abide with you forever;*

"Even the Spirit of Truth; Whom the world cannot receive, because it sees Him not, neither knows Him: but you know Him; for He (the Holy Spirit) *dwells with you, and shall be in you"* (Jn. 14:16-17).

Now why is it that the Holy Spirit did not dwell in Believers before the Cross, but only with them?

It was because the blood of bulls and goats could not take away sins, only cover them; therefore, the sin debt remained (Heb. 10:4). It was not until the Cross that all sin could be taken away, which it was (Jn. 1:29). That's how important the Cross is. It is where the Covenant was cut, which is an everlasting Covenant (Heb. 13:20), of which we will say more later in this Volume.

Now the Holy Spirit doesn't require very much of us, only that our Faith ever rest in the Finished Work of Christ, i.e., *"the Cross."* That seems a simple enough thing; however, it proves to be a tremendous hurdle for many

Believers. For some reason, it's difficult for many Christians, even so-called religious leaders, to place their Faith exclusively in the Cross of Christ. There are many reasons for that, but I suspect one of the main reasons is, when we do that, place our Faith in the Cross, and do so exclusively, this eliminates everything else. To be sure, religious man loves his works, which God cannot accept.

When the Believer's Faith is anchored in the Cross, and the Cross exclusively, the Holy Spirit can then work in one's life, which means that the Believer can then have victory over all type of sin, with sin no longer having dominion over him (Rom. 6:14).

This is God's Prescribed Order of Victory. He only has one prescribed order, because no other is needed. If the Believer goes God's Way, the Believer will receive all the benefits; otherwise, the Believer will continue to struggle, will not have victory within his or her life, and, no matter what he does, still will not have victory; the problem, whatever it might be, will actually continually get worse. Leaven has to be removed, which is a Biblical symbol of sin, or else it will ultimately corrupt the whole (Gal. 5:9).

I've given you, in abbreviated form, God's Prescribed Order of Victory. The Believer cannot live for God by any other method. This is the way laid out, which is the way of the Cross, and the way of the Cross alone!

CONTINUED VICTORY?

Some Christians erroneously think that if they place their Faith exclusively in the Cross of Christ, then there will never be another temptation, and there will never be another failure.

The truth is, Satan is not going to discontinue his efforts against the Child of God, irrespective that you are believing and acting correctly. He will seek to discourage you. He will test your Faith, and do so stringently, and be allowed by the Lord to do so. But if you will keep believing, and I'm referring to believing in Christ and what Christ did at the Cross, you will ultimately see victory. It may take longer for some than for others; but, to be sure, the Word of God cannot fail. If we function according to God's Prescribed Order, the Scripture plainly says, *"Sin shall not have dominion over you"* (Rom. 6:14).

If modern Christians could go back to the time of Ezekiel, and could survey the Jews in Judah and Jerusalem, as it regards their spiritual condition, I think it would quickly become obvious that where they began to fail is when they had a failure of Faith as it regards the Sacrifices. They began to look at them as mere rituals or ceremonies, forgetting the very purpose of the Sacrifices, which was to point to the coming Redeemer, Who would be the Lord Jesus Christ. A failure of Faith always begins with an incorrect interpretation of the Cross, of which the Jewish Sacrifices were a Type. An improper understanding of the Cross, a rebellion against the Cross, an ignoring of the Cross, an outright denial of the Cross, and even ignorance of what the Cross really is, always lead to a failure of Faith, which, in effect, is sin itself, which leads to acts of sin. To rebel against God's Way, which is *"Jesus Christ and Him Crucified,"* is sin. In fact, it is the worst sin of all, because it leads to spiritual wreckage.

That's the reason that the Church world is in its present condition of spiritual lethargy and apathy; through whatever reason, it has rebelled against the Cross, which is God's only way of Salvation and Victory.

"Keep thyself pure! Christ's soldier true,
"Through life's loud strife, He calls to you.
"Thy Captain speaks: His Word obey;
"So shall thy strength be as thy day."

"Keep thyself pure! When lusts assail,
"When flesh is strong, and spirit frail,
"Fight on a fadeless crown, to win
"Christ will give victory over sin."

"Oh Holy Spirit, keep us pure,
"Grant us Your strength when sins allure;
"Our bodies are Thy Temple, Lord;
"Be Thou in thought and act adored."

CHAPTER 10

(1) "THEN I LOOKED, AND, BEHOLD,

IN THE FIRMAMENT THAT WAS ABOVE THE HEAD OF THE CHERUBIMS THERE APPEARED OVER THEM AS IT WERE A SAPPHIRE STONE, AS THE APPEARANCE OF THE LIKENESS OF A THRONE.

(2) "AND HE SPOKE UNTO THE MAN CLOTHED WITH LINEN, AND SAID, GO IN BETWEEN THE WHEELS, EVEN UNDER THE CHERUB, AND FILL YOUR HAND WITH COALS OF FIRE FROM BETWEEN THE CHERUBIMS, AND SCATTER THEM OVER THE CITY. AND HE WENT IN IN MY SIGHT.

(3) "NOW THE CHERUBIMS STOOD ON THE RIGHT SIDE OF THE HOUSE, WHEN THE MAN WENT IN; AND THE CLOUD FILLED THE INNER COURT.

(4) "THEN THE GLORY OF THE LORD WENT UP FROM THE CHERUB, AND STOOD OVER THE THRESHOLD OF THE HOUSE; AND THE HOUSE WAS FILLED WITH THE CLOUD, AND THE COURT WAS FULL OF THE BRIGHTNESS OF THE LORD'S GLORY.

(5) "AND THE SOUND OF THE CHERUBIMS' WINGS WAS HEARD EVEN TO THE OUTER COURT, AS THE VOICE OF THE ALMIGHTY GOD WHEN HE SPEAKS."

The structure is:

1. We learn in this Chapter that the *"Living Creatures"* of Chapter 1 are named here *"Cherubims."*

2. The departure of the Glory, i.e., *"the Holy Spirit,"* from the Temple is the Vision of this Chapter.

3. He retires unwillingly. His throne was the most Holy Place (8:4); He then withdrew to the threshold (9:3); then, above the threshold (10:1, 4); then He retired to the Eastern Gate; finally, to the Mount of Olivet on the East side of the City (11:23). Thus, did the God of Israel in lingering love forsake His City and Temple, not to return till the future day, which has not yet come, but which is proclaimed in Ezekiel 43:2-7.

THE CHERUBIMS

These Visions which Ezekiel had of the Glory of God, outlined in Chapters 1 and 10, portray nothing that is mechanical, but all that is spiritual, therefore, alive. While these Visions in the Spirit world are so glorious as to defy description, at the same time, they are beyond our comprehension. There's absolutely nothing on earth that even remotely resembles these Living Creatures, these Cherubims, as described by the Prophet. But yet, this is something that every Saint of God will enjoy forever and forever. I think this is one of the reasons that Paul made the following statement:

"It is not expedient for me doubtless to glory. I will come to Visions and Revelations of the Lord.

"I knew a man in Christ above fourteen years ago, (whether in the body, I cannot tell; or whether out of the body, I cannot tell: God knows;) such an one caught up to the third Heaven (he was speaking of himself).

"And I knew such a man, (whether in the body, or out of the body, I cannot tell: God knows;)

"How that he was caught up into Paradise, and heard unspeakable words, which it is not lawful for a man to utter" (II Cor. 12:1-4).

As we said in Commentary regarding Chapter 1, to try to explain this that Ezekiel saw is, for all practical purposes, an impossible task. The better thing that we can say is that this which is so wonderful has been made possible to the Child of God through what Christ did at the Cross, and that alone! In other words, we will live in the very midst of that forever and forever. What a delightful thought!

GOD'S JUDGMENT AGAINST SIN

The phrase, *"Coals of fire from between the Cherubims,"* as given to us in Verse 2, is the same as 1:13. It signifies God's Judgment against sin.

The *"coals of fire"* were not literal in the sense that we understand it, but were very literal in the spiritual sense.

In Isaiah's Vision (Isa. 6:6), the work of the fire was to purify, but here to destroy. The Glory of God, as here portrayed, of which the most consecrated receives only a tiny touch, is so far beyond human comprehension in its majesty, glory, power, and wonder that the few, as Ezekiel, who have been privileged to see it can little understand what they have actually seen! However, the Holy Spirit did not see fit to explain it further, but only to portray it, thereby, leaving it up to man to believe or not believe. Such demands Faith, which is the manner of God's dealings with the human family.

THE GLORY OF THE LORD

Verse 4 says, *"Then the Glory of the LORD went up from the Cherub, and stood over the threshold of the house,"* which is its entrance. It is as if He does not want to go, but has no choice but to leave, because He is not wanted. One can literally feel the pathos of the heart of God in this description.

How many times has the Lord left an individual, not because He desired to do so, but, rather, because He was no longer wanted or desired?

This house that was meant to be *"filled with the cloud of glory,"* as portrayed here, is rather filled with idols and *"every form of creeping things, and abominable beasts"* (8:10). As such, He, and we speak of the Holy Spirit, could no longer remain. Let us also state that the Holy Spirit cannot remain in the heart and life of anyone who fills their Temple with such abominations (I Cor. 3:16).

ALMIGHTY GOD

It is beautiful and yet amazing that the Holy Spirit uses the Name, *"Almighty God,"* in Verse 5. In the Hebrew, it means *"El Shaddai,"* which means *"The Breasted One,"* or *"The All-Sufficient One."*

The title, *"Almighty God,"* was first used in reference to Abraham (Gen. 17:1). So, that was, in effect, the beginning of the nation of Israel. The Lord then told them that He was the All Sufficient One, Who could supply their every need, and now He mentions it again, to let them know that they could have had anything they desired, but instead they went toward the Evil One. It is too late now, at least for the nation of Israel, but it still wasn't too late for individuals. At any time the individual would turn to God, they could then, and they can now, experience all that God is, which He desires to expend on our behalf.

Why is it that the far greater majority of mankind doesn't want the blessings of God, which meet our every need, but rather opt for other things?

DECEPTION

The greatest culprit as it regards individuals refusing the Lord, or else refusing His Way, while all the time they think they have His Way, is the problem of deception. Probably one could say without fear of exaggeration or contradiction that *"deception"* is Satan's greatest tool. The reason it is so great is because Satan is deceived himself. In other words, he can read the Bible just like anyone else can; however, he doesn't believe the Bible. He believes that he will ultimately come out victorious in this struggle between good and evil.

As someone has well said, the individual who is dead wrong, but believes he is dead right, and argues his point, does so with conviction. Satan does the same thing!

Due to the Fall, the heart of man is corrupt. Even after the person is saved, they have to be very careful that their hearts remain pure before God. It is so easily corrupted, because of self-will.

Most every person who is rebelling against God, whether they are doing so intentionally or unintentionally, believes in their heart that they are right. And self-will helps them to believe that, even though they are totally wrong!

For instance, the people in Jerusalem and Judah claim that the Lord is with them, and was not with the Exiles in Babylonia; however, the very reverse was true. The ones in Jerusalem reasoned that they had the Temple, the Sacrifices, and all the accoutrements of the Law; therefore, they listened to the false Prophets who told them that everything was going to work out all right, and refused the true Prophets, because the latter were not saying what they desired to hear. That problem has always persisted, and probably it persists worse now than ever before.

Churches are being filled with people who want to appease their conscience, but who really do not want to hear the True Gospel. In other words, they do not want the Spirit of God. Consequently, the far greater majority of modern Churches have become *"social centers with religious overtones."*

(6) "AND IT CAME TO PASS, THAT WHEN HE HAD COMMANDED THE MAN

CLOTHED WITH LINEN, SAYING, TAKE FIRE FROM BETWEEN THE WHEELS, FROM BETWEEN THE CHERUBIMS; THEN HE WENT IN, AND STOOD BESIDE THE WHEELS.

(7) "AND ONE CHERUB STRETCHED FORTH HIS HAND FROM BETWEEN THE CHERUBIMS UNTO THE FIRE THAT WAS BETWEEN THE CHERUBIMS, AND TOOK THEREOF, AND PUT IT INTO THE HANDS OF HIM WHO WAS CLOTHED WITH LINEN: WHO TOOK IT, AND WENT OUT.

(8) "AND THERE APPEARED IN THE CHERUBIMS THE FORM OF A MAN'S HAND UNDER THEIR WINGS.

(9) "AND WHEN I LOOKED, BEHOLD THE FOUR WHEELS BY THE CHERUBIMS, ONE WHEEL BY ONE CHERUB, AND ANOTHER WHEEL BY ANOTHER CHERUB: AND THE APPEARANCE OF THE WHEELS WAS AS THE COLOUR OF A BERYL STONE.

(10) "AND AS FOR THEIR APPEARANCES, THEY FOUR HAD ONE LIKENESS, AS IF A WHEEL HAD BEEN IN THE MIDST OF A WHEEL.

(11) "WHEN THEY WENT, THEY WENT UPON THEIR FOUR SIDES; THEY TURNED NOT AS THEY WENT, BUT TO THE PLACE WHERE THE HEAD LOOKED THEY FOLLOWED IT; THEY TURNED NOT AS THEY WENT.

(12) "AND THEIR WHOLE BODY, AND THEIR BACKS, AND THEIR HANDS, AND THEIR WINGS, AND THE WHEELS, WERE FULL OF EYES ROUND ABOUT, EVEN THE WHEELS THAT THEY FOUR HAD.

(13) "AS FOR THE WHEELS, IT WAS CRIED UNTO THEM IN MY HEARING, O WHEEL."

The overview is:

1. The Vision of the Throne superintending the Judgment assured Israel that their national calamities were not accidental, but providential. This great truth nourishes God's people in all ages.

2. Righteousness is the foundation of Divine action, whether in Redemption or Judgment.

3. The Righteousness of God in His Judgment of sin at Calvary, and in His faithfulness in fulfilling His Promises to the Believer, is the foundation of the Christian's assurance of Salvation; and it is the Righteousness of God which assures eternal condemnation to the rejecter of Christ.

THE WHEELS

In some way, it seems that these *"wheels,"* as strange as they seem to be, are alive, which means they aren't mechanical. In fact, Verse 12 says that the wheels *"were full of eyes round about, even the wheels that they four had."*

How does one explain such? Had the Holy Spirit wanted us to know more about these things, He would have given us more information.

Expositors believe that this which Ezekiel saw was no less than the Chariot-Throne of the King of the Universe. But beyond that, we have very little knowledge, because as previously stated, there's nothing on Earth that even remotely resembles such a thing. We're speaking here of degrees of power, which is beyond our comprehension. And beside the Power and the Glory, which are of indescribable beauty, are, as well, beyond our ability to grasp. Please allow me to say the following:

THE CROSS

In the beginning, the human race was created by God to live in His domain. In other words, this Earth could have been a Paradise, and was intended to be a Paradise, but sin spoiled it all.

But the Lord has made a way, through the Cross, that man can come back to Him and ultimately enjoy the indescribable glory and beauty of all that God is. We as Believers, at present, have no idea as to the full meaning of these things of which Ezekiel saw in his Vision. Still, there will be a day that we will know exactly what it all means, and will actually be a part of all that God is. Due to the significance of all of this, please allow me to break it down to a more understandable level.

JESUS IS THE SOURCE, WHILE THE CROSS IS THE MEANS

I have already made the statement any number of times, *"Jesus Christ is the Source, while the Cross is the Means,"* and will continue to use the phrase throughout this Volume, because it so very, very important.

Anyone who is a Believer knows that Jesus Christ is the Source of all things that we receive from God. In fact, the entirety of the story of the Bible is the story of Jesus Christ. In Prophecy, He appears immediately after the Fall, with the Lord telling Satan through the Serpent that the Seed of the woman, Who is Christ, would bruise his head, which speaks of the head of Satan, which would be done at the Cross (Gen. 3:15).

Every Sacrifice presented in the Old Testament, which, in fact, is the central theme of the Old Testament, is a portrayal of Christ, and what He would do in order to redeem fallen humanity. As someone has well said, the *"the Old Testament is the New Testament concealed, while the New Testament is the Old Testament revealed."* In fact, the New Testament, which in reality is the New Covenant, cannot be understood, unless one first of all understands the Old Testament, i.e., *"Old Covenant."*

It is sad, but much of the Charismatic world, and I speak of Charismatic Churches, etc., has little knowledge of the Old Testament. While of course, there are exceptions to this, as a whole, what I'm saying is correct. As such, they have little knowledge of the New Testament, despite the great claims.

THE CROSS IS THE MEANS

While the part of the Christian world which is truly Born-Again knows and understands that the Lord Jesus Christ is the Source of all Blessings, it little knows and understands that the Cross is the Means by which all of this is done. Let the Reader understand that the Cross was not just an incident. Neither was it an execution or an assassination. In other words, the Cross was the intended destination.

Through foreknowledge, the Lord knew that man would fall, and it was decided in the High Courts of Heaven that man would be redeemed by God becoming Man, and going to the Cross. This was determined even before the foundation of the world (I Pet. 1:18-20). So, when Christ was conceived in the womb of the Virgin Mary, and was done so by decree of the Holy Spirit (Mat. 1:18), it was all for but one purpose, and that was for Christ to go to the Cross. While everything the Lord did was of supreme significance, and I speak of His Perfect Life, His Healings and Miracles, and His Resurrection and Ascension, still, it was the Cross alone which purchased our Redemption.

If Christ had not gone to the Cross, His Perfect Life, Healings, and Miracles would have been to no avail; for those things, as wonderful as they are, could not have saved anyone. As well, if we place the emphasis of Redemption on the Resurrection, or the Ascension, or Christ seated at the Right Hand of Majesty on High (Heb. 1:3), then we miss the point altogether.

While all of these things are of immense significance, all depended on the Cross.

Considering that Jesus atoned for all sin at the Cross, the Resurrection then was never in doubt. The idea of Satan and demon spirits trying to stop Christ from being raised from the dead has no basis in the Scriptures. But at the same time, had there been one sin left unatoned, Jesus could not have risen from the dead. The Scripture plainly says: *"The wages of sin is death; but the Gift of God is Eternal Life through Jesus Christ our Lord"* (Rom. 6:23). But with all sin atoned, which it was at the Cross, then death held no more sway, and could not keep Christ in the nether world.

So, once the Cross was a fact, the Resurrection of Christ was guaranteed. As we've already stated, we dare not minimize anything that Christ did, for everything that He did was of utmost significance; however, we also must understand that the Cross is the Central theme of the Redemption Plan, which means that it is the central theme of the entirety of the Bible.

For instance, the Lord has always had an abundance of Grace. But before the Cross, He could not dispense Grace as He now does. The same could go for every attribute of God. But the Cross opened up the way for God to give us all manner of His Gifts. Listen to Paul:

"But unto every one of us is given Grace according to the measure of the Gift of Christ (which was made possible by the Cross).

"Wherefore He said, When He ascended

up on high, He led captivity captive, and gave Gifts unto men" (Eph. 4:7-8).

The *"Gifts"* of which Paul spoke concerned not only *"Apostles, Prophets, Evangelists, Pastors, and Teachers,"* but everything else we might need, which includes Grace, Love, Power, Peace, etc. In fact, the Cross addressed every single thing that man lost at the Fall.

WHAT DID THE CROSS ACCOMPLISH?

In brief, the Cross made it possible for the Holy Spirit to work in our hearts and lives in a completely new dimension.

If it is to be noticed, Christ said very little about the Holy Spirit during His Earthly Ministry, with the exception of the last week before His Death. In fact, He said more about the Holy Spirit during that time than the balance of His Life and Ministry combined (Jn., Chpts. 14-16).

With all sin atoned, which it was at the Cross, this means that the terrible sin debt which man owed to God, which the blood of bulls and goats could not take away (Heb. 10:4), the Holy Spirit could then come into the hearts and lives of all Believers, and there abide forever, which could not be done before the Cross (Jn. 14:16-17). The Cross made it all possible, and the Cross alone!

It is the Holy Spirit Who brings us all of that for which Christ paid such a price, but He is able to do these things only by the means of the Cross.

HOW THE HOLY SPIRIT WORKS

If the Believer knows how the Holy Spirit works, or rather what gives Him latitude to work, then the Believer can see great things accomplished in his life. But the tragedy is that the great majority of the modern Church have little idea as to how the Holy Spirit works.

As we previously said in this Volume, the Denominational world, by and large, has rejected the Holy Spirit, which means that almost nothing is done for God in those circles.

Worse still, the Pentecostal world, for all practical purposes, is on the very edge of denying the Holy Spirit, exactly as their Denominational Brothers.

I remember some years ago, seeing a letter written by the General Superintendent of the Assemblies of God, and sent to all the District Superintendents. I'm quoting from memory, so I'll have to paraphrase:

He said, *"It has been called to our attention that very few people are presently being Baptized with the Holy Spirit in our Churches."* He then went on to encourage the District Superintendents to encourage Pastors to *"Preach on the Holy Spirit."*

While I applaud the dear Brother's concern, I'm afraid it's going to take more than a request to alleviate the situation. In fact, as I dictate these notes on June 1, 2003, there are probably fewer Believers presently being Baptized with the Holy Spirit than at any time in the last one hundred years, in fact, the span of time concerning the Latter Rain (Joel 2:23).

Approximately three years ago, the Lord gave Donnie (our son) a special Faith to pray for Believers to be Baptized with the Holy Spirit. Since that time, he has seen thousands Baptized with the Spirit, which continues unto this hour, and I pray shall even increase in the future. But the truth is, precious few Pentecostal and Charismatic Preachers are any more preaching the Holy Spirit. For all practical purposes, the Holy Spirit is presently, at least for the most part, ignored. This is a tragedy of unprecedented proportions.

THAT WHICH THE LORD GAVE TO ME CONCERNING THE HOLY SPIRIT

I personally believe that the Revelation of the Cross, which the Lord has given unto this Evangelist, which is predicated totally on that given to the Apostle Paul, but yet, takes the Believer, I believe, to a higher height and a deeper depth regarding Paul's writings than heretofore known. All Revelation is progressive, and by that, I mean the following:

The Word of God is complete. This means that nothing must be subtracted from it, and nothing must be added to it. So, what I'm giving you is not something new. It's that which the Lord gave to Paul, but which I believe has been little understood, if at all, until this particular time. It is that which Paul taught, but which has by and large been lost during the past Centuries.

I have been an avid Bible student all of my life. I've read the Bible completely through over fifty times. To say I love the Word of God would be an understatement. I'm certain that many of you holding this Book in your hands fall into the same category. In fact, your taking the time to study these contents portrays a love for God and His Word.

In all of my years of study, I have read some few Messages which emphasize the Cross. But I have read none which portrays the Holy Spirit relative to the Cross. I'm certainly not saying that such material doesn't exist, but I am saying that I have never seen such. Let me lay a little groundwork:

A PERSONAL EXPERIENCE

If I remember correctly, it was March of 1988. My whole world had come to pieces. The fault most definitely was mine, even as failure is always the fault of the individual involved. But the truth is I didn't exactly know how it was my fault. Let me be more specific:

In those days, I was one of the strongest proponents of the Cross as it regards Salvation, and saw literally hundreds of thousands brought to a saving knowledge of Jesus Christ; however, I had no knowledge whatsoever of the Cross as it regards our Sanctification. And looking back, there wasn't a single person with whom I was acquainted who understood the part the Cross plays in our everyday living before God. Now let me say this:

If the Believer, even a Preacher, doesn't understand the Cross as it regards Sanctification, it is not possible for such a Believer to live for the Lord in the way he ought to live. It simply cannot be done!

Now, I didn't say that a person couldn't be saved. Anyone who trusts Christ is saved (Jn. 3:16; Rom. 10:9-10, 13). But the truth is, and it's so important that I must say it again, unless the Believer understands the Cross as it regards our everyday walk before God, in other words, our Sanctification, such a Believer cannot live a victorious, overcoming Christian life. While such a person is saved, the Truth is, many are *"miserably saved."* There are no exceptions!

This means that, in some way, works of the flesh are going to manifest themselves in the hearts and lives of such Believers. It becomes more tragic still, when we realize that virtually the entirety of the Church falls into this category. And I say that simply because the modern Church doesn't understand at all the part the Cross plays in our every day living for God. Listen to Paul:

LAW

"For Christ sent me not to Baptize, but to preach the Gospel: not with wisdom of words, lest the Cross of Christ should be made of none effect" (I Cor. 1:17).

He also said: *"Christ is become of no effect unto you, whosoever of you are justified by the Law; you are fallen from Grace"* (Gal. 5:4).

If the Believer does not trust Christ and the Cross, in some way, the Believer is depending on Law, which refers to any type of Law. I speak of Laws made up by Denominations, by individual Preachers, in the mind of an individual, etc. In other words, if our Faith is not in Christ and the Cross, then it's in Law, whether we understand such or not.

Back to this particular day in March of 1988, as stated, my entire world had fallen to pieces, and I did not know what to do. In fact, all I could do was to take it to the Lord in prayer. I had stayed home from the office that day, intending to spend the day in prayer, trying to seek direction.

In fact, I had done such at least once a week, for some years. I would read about 30 minutes in the Bible, and then seek the Lord for approximately the same amount of time, repeating the process all day. I don't exactly remember as to what time it was that morning, but I will never forget what took place.

When I begin to pray, I don't think in all of my life that I've ever sensed such oppression by the powers of darkness. The oppression was so severe that I didn't think I could stand it.

The Evil One began to speak to me, telling me to take what little money I had in the bank (if I remember, it was about $800), and just get in my car and drive away and disappear.

"You have disgraced your family," he said. *"You have also disgraced the Work of God, so you might as well quit."*

There was a fence nearby where I was praying, and I stood beside the fence, and said to the Lord, *"Please help me, no human being can stand this type of pressure!"*

THE HOLY SPIRIT

I don't exactly remember how long that terrible oppression continued; however, I do know that a few minutes of such seems like hours. At any rate, all of a sudden, even without any warning, there was a change.

It was like the Lord said to Satan, *"that's enough"!* Then the Holy Spirit came upon me in such a mighty way. It all happened instantly. One moment, the oppression was so horrible that I could hardly stand it, and the next moment, all of that was gone! Instead, the Spirit lifted me up, and then the Lord began to speak to my heart.

He said to me, *"I am going to show you some things about the Holy Spirit which you do not now know."*

I knew it was the Lord speaking to my heart, but my immediate thoughts were, the Holy Spirit is God, and there is so much about Him that I don't know, or anyone for that matter! And yet, I knew the Lord was speaking to me relative to the terrible oppression I was encountering. The Lord did not reveal to me then that of which He spoke. He gave me great strength, lifted me up, and encouraged me to go forward, but said nothing else as it regards what He said He would show me. In fact, it was about nine years before He would reveal to me that of which He spoke to my heart that morning in 1988.

During those intervening years, I sought His face constantly, asking Him to show me how the Believer could live victorious over the world, the flesh, and the Devil. There were mighty movings of the Holy Spirit during these times, but still the answer didn't come. In 1991, the Lord spoke to my heart, and told me to begin two prayer meetings a day, which we instituted immediately. In fact, I continue that regimen even unto this moment.

Time and time again, during these prayer meetings, the Lord in those intervening years would move upon me mightily, but still, I knew these *"movings,"* as wonderful as they were, were not that which the Lord had spoken to my heart, which He would give me. And then in 1997, some nine years after the fact, the Lord opened up to me that which He had promised those years before. In some of the previous Commentaries, I gave the year as 1996; however, on further investigation, I believe it was 1997. I'm embarrassed that I don't remember the exact year, but to tell the truth, when the Lord began to open up to me the Revelation of the Cross, it has been so exciting, so glorious, and so wonderful, that my thoughts were not exactly on the specific date, but rather on what the Lord was doing, and what I knew He was going to do.

The following is what the Lord gave to me, at least the progressive Revelation, as it regards the Holy Spirit, and what He had promised me in 1988. Elsewhere in this Volume, I will deal with the Revelation of the Cross in its entirety.

THE LAW OF THE SPIRIT OF LIFE IN CHRIST JESUS

When the Lord began to reveal to me the meaning of the Cross, and how it was the solution to every problem, I was so overjoyed with happiness, because I knew I had found the way of Victory. But at the same time, I knew that as wonderful as was this great Revelation, there was much more to come. I importuned the Lord to help me to keep my heart open for even greater Revelation. I know the Holy Spirit was prompting me to pray this type of prayer, and I was to later find out just exactly how correct this was.

Paul told us that this New Covenant, which, in effect, is the story of the Cross, is *"The Everlasting Covenant"* (Heb. 13:20).

This means that it's absolutely impossible for this great Revelation given to the Apostle so long ago to be exhausted.

During the intervening time, and I speak of the beginning of the Revelation unto the time that He gave me knowledge of the Holy Spirit, which He had long ago promised, I wondered in my mind as to exactly how the Holy Spirit played His part in all of this. As stated, I have read innumerable Books, with some few of them addressing the Cross, but none addressing the Holy Spirit relative to the Cross.

And then one particular morning, while doing our morning program over Radio, *"A*

Study In The Word," it happened!

The Lord began to open up to my heart the great Truth that the Holy Spirit works entirely within the confines of the Finished Work of Christ. In other words, it's the Cross that gives the Holy Spirit the legal means for Him to do the things which He does. To give the Scriptural proof for this, the Lord took me once again to the words of Paul:

"For the Law of the Spirit of Life in Christ Jesus has made me free from the Law of sin and death" (Rom. 8:2).

And then He gave me: *"But if the Spirit* (Holy Spirit) *of Him* (God the Father) *Who raised up Jesus from the dead dwell in you, He* (God the Father) *Who raised up Christ from the dead shall also quicken your mortal bodies by His Spirit Who dwells in you"* (Rom. 8:11).

He is not speaking here of the coming Resurrection, which most Believers think, but instead, our everyday living for God. He said here that He would *"quicken our mortal bodies,"* which speaks of our present bodies, in other words, giving us power to live the life we ought to give. But Romans 8:2 holds the secret to all of this.

HOW THE SPIRIT WORKS

Paul used the term, *"For the Law of the Spirit of Life."* What did he mean by that?

First of all, he is speaking of a *"Law"* devised by the Godhead in eternity past, which means that the Lord will ever function within this Law. While men may violate it constantly, God never will.

Paul also used the term *"the Spirit of Life."* This refers to the fact that the Holy Spirit superintends all Life, which flows from Christ, Who is ever its Source; that's what Jesus was speaking of when He said:

"If any man thirst, let him come unto Me and drink.

"He who believes on Me, as the Scripture has said, out of His innermost being shall flow rivers of Living Water.

"But this spoke He of the Spirit, which they who believe on Him should receive" (Jn. 7:37-39).

The key to this *"Law"* by which the Holy Spirit works is found in the phrase, *"in Christ Jesus."* Whenever Paul uses this term, or

NOTES

one of its derivatives, such as *"in Him,"* or *"in Whom,"* without exception, He is speaking of the Finished Work of Christ on the Cross. This means that all the Holy Spirit does for us, whatever that might be, is predicated strictly on the Sacrifice of Christ (Eph. 2:13-18). So, how do we enter into this?

THE CROSS OUR OBJECT OF FAITH

The Holy Spirit, in His Work within our lives, doesn't demand much of us, but He definitely does demand the following:

He demands that our Faith ever be in the Cross of Christ. In other words, the Cross must ever be the Object of our Faith. Listen to our Lord as He refers to the Holy Spirit:

"Howbeit when He, the Spirit of Truth, is come, He will guide you into all Truth: For He shall not speak of Himself; but whatsoever He shall hear, that shall He speak: and He will show you things to come.

"He shall glorify Me: for He shall receive of Mine, and shall show it unto you" (Jn. 16:13-14).

The short phrase, *"For He shall receive of Mine,"* refers to what Jesus did at the Cross, all on our behalf. Let us state it again:

Every single thing the Holy Spirit does for us is all, and without exception, predicated on the Sacrifice of Christ. What Jesus did at the Cross gives the Holy Spirit the legal right to do what He must do within our lives. Before the Cross, even as we have previously stated (Jn. 14:16-17), the Holy Spirit was very limited in what He could do in the lives of Believers, simply because animal blood was insufficient to take away sins. That awaited the coming Redeemer, Who would set the record straight, and do so by paying the debt in full, owed by man to God.

WHY JESUS WENT TO THE CROSS

Some people have the idea that it was Satan who forced Christ to go to the Cross. No! Satan had absolutely nothing to do with the Cross. While he did put it in the hearts of the Pharisees and Sadducees to demand of Pilate that Christ be placed on a Cross, this was done because the evil hearts of these people, knowing that the Word of God stated that anyone who was placed upon the tree was cursed by God (Deut. 21:22-23), which would, they thought, turn the people against Christ, thereby, erasing all ideas that He was the Messiah. Christ went to the Cross to satisfy the demands of a thrice-Holy God. It was God Who had been offended! The sins that man had committed were crimes against God, which means that man owed a debt to God that He could not pay. And yet, the debt had to be paid!

So, the only way this debt could be paid was by God becoming man, which He did, and paying the price Himself on the Cross. The Sacrifice, which was demanded, had to be perfect, so man could not fit that bill. There must not be any taint of sin about this Sacrifice, and due to the fact that man is born in sin, he is, therefore, shot down, so to speak, before he even begins. So, a perfect Sacrifice had to be offered; it had to be offered on a Cross; and God becoming Man was the only way this could be carried out (Isa. 7:14).

WHY A CROSS?

It had to be a Cross! But of course the question begs to be asked, *"Why a Cross?"* Would not stoning have sufficed? Or death in any form?

No! It had to be a Cross. And now, lets look at the reason why.

As we've already stated, the Sacrificial, Atoning Death of the Lord Jesus Christ was decided in the High Courts of Heaven, even before the foundation of the world (I Pet. 1:18-20). This means that the Cross is the Foundation Doctrine, on which all other Doctrine must be built. It was to Abraham that the Lord portrayed the manner in which Redemption would be brought about. It would be through death. Thus, the Lord, in portraying this great Plan to Abraham, did so by using an object lesson that was so graphic that Abraham would have absolutely no difficulty understanding what was being said or done. God demanded that Abraham offer up his son, Isaac as a human Sacrifice. Of course, we know that God stopped the hand of the Patriarch at the last moment; but, as far as Abraham was concerned, he was fully committed to the deed, as hurtful as it was.

Some people claim that God demanded this of Abraham because the Patriarch loved his son Isaac too much, etc. No, that's not the case at all! He was portraying to the Patriarch the manner in which Redemption would be provided.

In fact, when He stopped Abraham at the last moment, He then revealed Himself to the Patriarch by the name of *"Jehovah-Jireh,"* which means *"the LORD will provide"* (Gen. 22:9-14). Provide what?

God would provide a Saviour, a Redeemer. Man's problem is sin, and he needs a Saviour. And that Saviour would be Jesus Christ, Who would redeem man by giving His Perfect Life as a Sacrifice.

However, even though the Lord portrayed to Abraham that the death of an innocent victim was necessary in order to redeem humanity, He did not tell the Patriarch by what means this death would be brought about. That Revelation was given to Moses about four hundred years later.

THE CROSS, THE MEANS OF HIS DEATH

In the wilderness experience, the Word of God states that the Children of Israel *"spoke against God, and against Moses"* (Num. 21:5). They express doubt as it regards God, and they blamed Moses. They said:

"Wherefore have you brought us up out of Egypt to die in the wilderness? For there is no bread, neither is there any water; and our soul hates this light bread (Manna [Num. 21:5]).

The Scripture then says, *"And the LORD sent fiery serpents among the people, and they bit the people; and much people of Israel died"* (Num. 21:6).

The people then enjoined Moses to pray for them that the Serpents be taken away. The Scripture then said:

"And the LORD said unto Moses, Make thee a fiery serpent, and set it upon a pole: and it shall come to pass, that everyone who is bitten, when he looks upon it, shall live" (Num. 21:8).

The pole was a Type of the Cross. Therefore, the Lord showed Moses the means by which this death of the Redeemer would be brought forth. It would be on a Cross!

WHY A SERPENT?

In observing this scenario, one may well

ask one's self the question, as to why God demanded that a serpent be made of copper and placed on the pole? Why not a Dove? Or a Lamb?

The serpent was demanded, because sin, which originated with Satan, whom the Scripture refers to as *"that old serpent, called the Devil"* (Rev. 12:9), was that which the Lord had to address. In other words, Jesus went to the Cross in order to break the power of sin, and remove its guilt (Rom. 6:3-6).

As well, the death of Christ must address every sin, irrespective as to how bad it might be. In other words, Jesus had to atone for all sin, past, present, and future, even the most vile of transgressions. That's why the Cross, i.e., *"the Tree,"* was demanded.

Whenever an Israelite committed a dastardly crime, which demanded death, he was stoned to death, with his body then placed upon a tree as a spectacle to all, stating that he was cursed by God (Deut. 21:22-23). That's why Jesus couldn't die by any means or method other than the Cross.

WAS JESUS CURSED BY GOD ON THE CROSS?

No!

The Scripture says concerning this: *"Christ has redeemed us from the Curse of the Law, being made a curse for us: for it is written, Cursed is every one who hangs on a tree"* (Gal. 3:13).

Christ was not cursed by God, but was rather *"made a Curse."* There is a vast difference in the two.

Christ could not be cursed by God, simply because there was no sin in His Life of any degree. So, instead, He was *"made a curse,"* which means, that He suffered the blow of death, in the giving of Himself as a Sacrifice. In that manner, He atoned for all sin; consequently, the power of sin was broken, and the guilt of sin was removed (Rom. 6:6).

(14) "AND EVERY ONE HAD FOUR FACES: THE FIRST FACE WAS THE FACE OF A CHERUB, AND THE SECOND FACE WAS THE FACE OF A MAN, AND THE THIRD THE FACE OF A LION, AND THE FOURTH THE FACE OF AN EAGLE,

(15) "AND THE CHERUBIMS WERE LIFTED UP. THIS IS THE LIVING CREATURE THAT I SAW BY THE RIVER OF CHEBAR.

(16) "AND WHEN THE CHERUBIMS WENT, THE WHEELS WENT BY THEM: AND WHEN THE CHERUBIMS LIFTED UP THEIR WINGS TO MOUNT UP FROM THE EARTH, THE SAME WHEELS ALSO TURNED NOT FROM BESIDE THEM.

(17) "WHEN THEY STOOD, THESE STOOD; AND WHEN THEY WERE LIFTED UP, THESE LIFTED UP THEMSELVES ALSO: FOR THE SPIRIT OF THE LIVING CREATURE WAS IN THEM.

(18) "THEN THE GLORY OF THE LORD DEPARTED FROM OFF THE THRESHOLD OF THE HOUSE, AND STOOD OVER THE CHERUBIMS.

(19) "AND THE CHERUBIMS LIFTED UP THEIR WINGS, AND MOUNTED UP FROM THE EARTH IN MY SIGHT: WHEN THEY WENT OUT, THE WHEELS ALSO WERE BESIDE THEM, AND EVERY ONE STOOD AT THE DOOR OF THE EAST GATE OF THE LORD'S HOUSE; AND THE GLORY OF THE GOD OF ISRAEL WAS OVER THEM ABOVE.

(20) "THIS IS THE LIVING CREATURE THAT I SAW UNDER THE GOD OF ISRAEL BY THE RIVER OF CHEBAR; AND I KNEW THAT THEY WERE THE CHERUBIMS.

(21) "EVERY ONE HAD FOUR FACES APIECE, AND EVERY ONE FOUR WINGS; AND THE LIKENESS OF THE HANDS OF A MAN WAS UNDER THEIR WINGS.

(22) "AND THE LIKENESS OF THEIR FACES WAS THE SAME FACES WHICH I SAW BY THE RIVER OF CHEBAR, THEIR APPEARANCES AND THEMSELVES: THEY WENT EVERY ONE STRAIGHT FORWARD."

The structure is:

1. All of this represents the Chariot Throne of God.

2. The Cherubims, in some way, represent the Creation of God.

3. We also know that, in some way, they also represent the Holiness of God.

THE CHERUBIMS

Verse 14 gives a description that is slightly different from the first description given by

Ezekiel in 1:10. Here, the *"Cherub"* is substituted for the *"ox."* As well, it is first in order here, instead of being, as there, the third.

How do we explain the difference?

In this second Vision, the Prophet seems to recognize that these were Cherubims, in other words, the same Creatures that John would later see on the Isle of Patmos. And the Glory of the Lord made the face of the *"ox"* look Cherubic.

The Glory of the Lord makes all things beautiful, and it alone can do such! Men do their best to beautify the ugly or to delay the ravages of age, but ultimately and eventually fail. However, the Glory of the Lord, shining on the face of an ox, can make it look like the face of a Cherub.

In order to do this, in other words to make all of this possible for sinful man, the Son of God laid aside His *"beauty"* (Phil. 2:7), i.e., the Glory of God, in order that our ugliness may be the recipient of His Beauty.

Verse 18 proclaims the fact that the *"Glory of the LORD"* now begins to depart from the Temple. In effect, this was the Holy Spirit. He had resided in the Temple since its dedication by Solomon over four hundred years before. Now, it says, *"It (He) departed from off the threshold of the house."* That which made the house great is now gone! Jesus would later say, *"For whether is greater, the gold, or the Temple that sanctifies the gold?"* (Mat. 23:17). Now that which sanctified the Temple is gone.

Verse 22 declares the fact that these Cherubims *"went everyone straight forward."* This tells us that with *"the Father of Lights, there is no variableness, neither shadow of turning"* (James 1:17).

*"In loving-kindness Jesus came My soul
and Mercy to reclaim,
"And from the depths of sin and shame,
through Grace He lifted me."*

*"He called me long before I heard, before my sinful heart was stirred,
"But when I took Him at His word,
Forgiven He lifted me."*

*"His brow was pierced with many a
thorn, His hands by cruel nails
were torn,*

*"When from my guilt and grief, forlorn,
in love He lifted me."*

*"Now on a higher plain I dwell, and
with my soul I know 'tis well,
"Yet how or why, I cannot tell, He
should have lifted me."*

CHAPTER 11

(1) "MOREOVER THE SPIRIT LIFTED ME UP, AND BROUGHT ME UNTO THE EAST GATE OF THE LORD'S HOUSE, WHICH LOOKED EASTWARD: AND BEHOLD AT THE DOOR OF THE GATE FIVE AND TWENTY MEN; AMONG WHOM I SAW JAAZANIAH THE SON OF AZUR, AND PELATIAH THE SON OF BENAIAH, PRINCES OF THE PEOPLE.

(2) "THEN SAID HE UNTO ME, SON OF MAN, THESE ARE THE MEN WHO DEVISE MISCHIEF, AND GIVE WICKED COUNSEL IN THIS CITY:

(3) "WHICH SAY, IT IS NOT NEAR; LET US BUILD HOUSES: THIS CITY IS THE CALDRON, AND WE BE THE FLESH.

(4) "THEREFORE PROPHESY AGAINST THEM, PROPHESY, O SON OF MAN.

(5) "AND THE SPIRIT OF THE LORD FELL UPON ME, AND SAID UNTO ME, SPEAK; THUS SAITH THE LORD; THUS HAVE YOU SAID, O HOUSE OF ISRAEL: FOR I KNOW THE THINGS THAT COME INTO YOUR MIND, EVERY ONE OF THEM.

(6) "YOU HAVE MULTIPLIED YOUR SLAIN IN THIS CITY, AND YOU HAVE FILLED THE STREETS THEREOF WITH THE SLAIN.

(7) "THEREFORE THUS SAITH THE LORD GOD; YOUR SLAIN WHOM YOU HAVE LAID IN THE MIDST OF IT, THEY ARE THE FLESH, AND THIS CITY IS THE CALDRON: BUT I WILL BRING YOU FORTH OUT OF THE MIDST OF IT.

(8) "YOU HAVE FEARED THE SWORD; AND I WILL BRING A SWORD UPON YOU, SAITH THE LORD GOD.

(9) "AND I WILL BRING YOU OUT OF THE MIDST THEREOF, AND DELIVER

YOU INTO THE HANDS OF STRANGERS, AND WILL EXECUTE JUDGMENTS AMONG YOU.

(10) "YOU SHALL FALL BY THE SWORD; I WILL JUDGE YOU IN THE BORDER OF ISRAEL; AND YOU SHALL KNOW THAT I AM THE LORD.

(11) "THIS CITY SHALL NOT BY YOUR CALDRON, NEITHER SHALL YOU BE THE FLESH IN THE MIDST THEREOF; BUT I WILL JUDGE YOU IN THE BORDER OF ISRAEL:

(12) "AND YOU SHALL KNOW THAT I AM THE LORD: FOR YOU HAVE NOT WALKED IN MY STATUTES, NEITHER EXECUTED MY JUDGMENTS, BUT HAVE DONE AFTER THE MANNERS OF THE HEATHEN WHO ARE ROUND ABOUT YOU."

The diagram is:

1. The *"Spirit"* referred to in Verse 1 is the Holy Spirit.

2. Ezekiel is given a Vision of certain men in Jerusalem, who were opposing the Lord. He is told to *"Prophesy against them."*

3. The Word of the Lord, which came through Ezekiel, was very negative, to say the least. We would do well presently to heed its admonition.

THE HOLY SPIRIT

Verse 1 says, *"Moreover the Spirit lifted me up,"* which refers to the Holy Spirit. Three times, it says the Spirit lifted the Prophet up (3:14; 8:3; 11:1). It also says that the Spirit carried him (37:1); and four times it says the Spirit took him up (3:12; 8:3; 11:24; 43:5). The *"twenty-five men"* mentioned in this Verse could have been those mentioned in 8:16, however, those were probably Priests, and at least two of these are named as *"Princes of the people."* These are seen in a different locality. Irrespective of who they were, they represented rebellion against God.

Jeremiah was Prophesying in Jerusalem that the Chaldean invasion was near at hand; he likened it to a boiling cauldron (Jer. 1:11-16); and he sent a Message to the captives to build houses, because their exile would last seventy years (Jer. 29:5).

The princes in Jerusalem, which certainly included these *"twenty-five men,"* greatly opposed him, ridiculed his preaching, and put him in prison. Pelatiah appears to have been the leader, and was judged by God in that he died (Vs. 13).

WICKED COUNSEL

Verse 2 refers to the Holy Spirit giving Ezekiel information and direction. This was God's method then of dealing with His Prophets, and His method now! He would say two things about these men:

1. *"These are the men who devise mischief"*: This probably refers to the opposition against Jeremiah and the putting of him in prison.

2. *"And give wicked counsel in this city"*: This referred to any counsel which contradicted the Prophecies of Jeremiah and Ezekiel, but mostly referred to Jeremiah, because he was the one Prophesying in Jerusalem.

These men denied any coming invasion by the Babylonians, and that their city would be destroyed along with the Temple, which Jeremiah and Ezekiel were saying would definitely happen. They were as well claiming that the captives in Babylonia would soon be released and allowed to come back to Judah. In other words, they were proclaiming the opposite of what the Lord was saying through His Prophets, Jeremiah, and Ezekiel.

The false Message of false Prophets always strikes a chord with those whose motives are not to do the Will of God, but rather their own will. To be sure, it's not as simple as it seems. Most all people who believe false Doctrine believe they are doing the right thing, when, in reality, they aren't. They do that because they are deceived. Sometimes the Message of the Lord is not pleasant. In fact, it can be very negative, which strikes at the wrong doing of individuals, which most do not enjoy hearing. So, the vituperation is saved for those who are preaching the Truth, which is never a very pleasant experience for those who must deliver the negative Message.

As I've mentioned elsewhere in this Volume, we at this particular Ministry have felt led of the Lord to address certain, particular false Doctrines. I speak primarily of the *"Word* of Faith Doctrine." Most have not been too very happy about that. Even though the ones who know what we're preaching is the Truth, and desperately needs to be addressed, still will say very little in our favor, simply because they don't want to take the heat.

A group of Preachers viewed one of Donnie's Videos, which contained one of our Campmeeting Services where he had addressed this false Doctrine head-on. When the Video was finished, these Preachers were asked, *"Is he preaching the Truth"?* To a man, they said, *"Yes, what he's saying is the Truth, and desperately needs to be preached."* However, they added, *"But we aren't going to preach it,"* and neither will they stand behind us; however, there's only one thing that really matters, and that is hearing from the Lord, and delivering what He has said to deliver. The great question is, *"Is what we are preaching the Truth?"* That's all that really matters!

Unfortunately, as these men in Verse 2, many Preachers *"give wicked counsel,"* and no one, or rather precious few, oppose them.

THE FALSE MESSAGE

Verse 3 says, *"Which say, it is not near."* This referred to these Princes and others in Jerusalem who were claiming that no invasion by the Babylonians was near. It was the opposite of what the Lord was saying!

The true Prophets, and we speak of Jeremiah and Ezekiel, were saying that the captives should build houses in Babylonia, because the captivity was going to be long, while the false Prophets were saying the opposite, *"Let us build houses"* in Jerusalem, because our future is secure.

The phrase, *"This City is the cauldron, and we be the flesh,"* claims that the inhabitants of Jerusalem were as secure as if surrounded by iron (a cauldron is an iron pot of sorts).

PROPHESY

The Holy Spirit tells the Prophet to strongly oppose the false Message of these false Prophets. In Verse 4, the phrase, *"Therefore Prophesy against them,"* meant that the Message was to be pointed and direct, leaving absolutely no doubt as to what was being said, who was saying it, or to whom it was directed.

NOTES

It must be understood that all of these Prophets, both false and true, were claiming Divine inspiration and, therefore, that their Message was the correct one. Therefore, it was left up to the people to choose that which was right. Then, as now, they chose the Message that was the most pleasing to the ear because of their spiritual declension.

THE MONEY GOSPEL

By and large, the modern *"Faith Message"* has deteriorated to the point that money, almost exclusively, is the emphasis. Years ago it started out with the emphasis being on Divine Healing. While healing is certainly Scriptural, the manner in which it was being proposed was not Scriptural. False Doctrine, if not corrected, never gets better of its own, but rather worse. It's the case of a little leaven ultimately leavening the whole lump. So now, almost the entirety of the Faith Message is centered up on money, which appeals to greed, of which all of us seem to have at least a modicum of this vice.

So, it gathers a large crowd, because flesh appeals to flesh. Tragically, the only ones getting rich are the Preachers, with the people getting nothing, simply because what they are being told is unscriptural. Why don't they see that?

The spirit that permeates that false Message is the same spirit that prompts the gambler to keep putting his money in the slot machine, because the jackpot is right around the corner. Above all, they repudiate the Cross.

As stated, we have felt led of the Lord to cry out against this ungodly direction. As a result, we have been cursed, maligned, ridiculed, and caricatured, with the future seemingly to be more of the same. But once again, as Ezekiel had no choice but to *"Prophesy against them,"* we have no choice either!

SPEAK

Verse 5 says, *"And the Spirit of the LORD fell upon me, and said unto me, speak."*

If the Preacher of the Gospel is to bless the hearts and lives of his listeners, he must have the same *"Spirit of the LORD"* upon him as Ezekiel. As well, and despite the unbelief from modern Preachers, it is promised in the Word of God: *"And you shall receive the Gift of the Holy Spirit.*

"For the Promise is unto you, and to your children, and to all who are afar off, even as many as the Lord our God shall call" (Acts 2:38-39).

Without this, the Preacher only utters words out of his own mind, or, if from the Word of God, without unction.

The Word, *"Speak,"* refers to the Message given to Ezekiel by the Holy Spirit, and the demand by the Holy Spirit that it be strongly spoken to the people. The responsibility of the true Prophet is not the response of the people, but that the Message is delivered as given by God.

THE MIND OF MAN

The phrase, *"For I know the things that come into your mind, everyone of them,"* proclaims the Omniscience of the Lord, in that He knows all things, past, present, and future.

The things which were in the minds of the people in Jerusalem, as it concerned the events at hand, had to do with their response to the Messages of Jeremiah and Ezekiel. While the Word of the Lord was being delivered to these people, they were refusing that Word, and rather thinking other things, in other words, accepting the false Messages of the false Prophets. This angered the Lord, because He knew to where it would lead.

Concerning our minds, Paul said, *"Let this mind be in you, which was also in Christ Jesus"* (Phil. 2:5).

DEATH

The *"Mind of Christ"* was His obedience to the Father, even *"unto death, even the death of the Cross,"* because that was the Will of God (Phil. 2:7-8).

If we are to please God, this must be our mind as well! Does this mean that God wants us to die, as He did Christ?

Yes it does, but in a totally different way.

When Christ died, He died for us, and, as it is known, He died on a Cross. In effect, His Death was our death (Rom. 6:3-5). But that which died of us was the *"old man,"* which refers to what we were before coming

NOTES

to Christ. Due to that death, we have been raised with the Lord in *"newness of life"* (Rom. 6:4). But we must ever understand, that this *"new life"* which we now have, came to us as a result of what Christ did at the Cross, and is maintained by what Christ did at the Cross. So, our *"minds"* must always be after Christ, and what He did in order to give us Salvation and Victory.

But I'm afraid the *"Cross"* is not in the minds of most Believers. They have instead believed error, which will always fall out to great hurt, and could even result in the loss of the soul, and nothing could be worse than that!

JUDGMENT MULTIPLIED

The idea of Verse 6 is that the terrible destruction coming upon Jerusalem is not the fault of God, but the fault of the spiritual leaders and their rebellion against God. Therefore, the Lord lays the blame at their feet.

He says, *"You have multiplied your slain in this city,"* meaning that the Judgment is far worse than it would have been, because of the false Prophecies, which instigated even deeper rebellion. The word, *"multiplied,"* refers to Judgment multiplied because the rebellion multiplied.

Therefore, about four or five years later, when the Babylonians would destroy Jerusalem, with the horror of this destruction exploding upon them, these *"religious leaders,"* in observing this horrible blood-letting, were to understand that the fault was theirs alone.

STRANGERS

The gist of Verses 7 through 9 is that Judah and Jerusalem had walked in the ways of the heathen; therefore, they would suffer punishment at the hands of the heathen as a Righteous retribution.

The phrase from Verse 9, *"And deliver you into the hands of strangers,"* refers, of course, to the Chaldeans. However, Israel would never know true freedom after this, and would actually rebel against the true freedom Christ offered.

After being ruled by the Chaldeans, they were ruled by the Medes, and the Persians, then the Greeks, and finally the Romans. In

A.D. 70, they were destroyed as a nation, and further delivered into the *"hands of strangers"* all over the world, where they wandered as outcasts for nearly 2,000 years.

Even though a nation since 1948, still, their struggle has been obvious. It will continue to deepen until, in desperation, they accept the Antichrist as the Messiah, and will then face the worst tribulation of all, coming close to extinction (Mat. 24:21), and will be saved only by the Coming of the Lord (Rev., Chpt. 19).

I WILL JUDGE YOU

Verse 10 says, *"I will judge you in the border of Israel,"* which refers to the Princes as being carried to Riblah and there put to death. This is where Zedekiah's sons were slain before his eyes, and then they put out his eyes, and *"bound him with fetters of brass, and carried him to Babylon"* (II Ki. 25:6-7). As well, the Chaldeans no doubt killed many other Princes and Nobles at this time.

Therefore, some five or six years before the actual fulfillment of these Prophecies, the Lord warned, in exact detail, exactly what would happen. Yet, Zedekiah and these Princes would not repent, but continued in their path of rebellion.

Why?

The major reasons are unbelief and the fear of man. This characterizes not only Zedekiah and these Princes, but almost all of the human family, as well. As the Word of God was little heeded then, it is little heeded now, even though the dire predictions brought on by rebellion are carefully spelled out. Men simply do not believe the Bible; or, if they do, they fear the scorn of other men and refuse to stand up for Christ.

However, irrespective of the reason, Judah, as well as all humanity, even down to the single individual, *"shall know that I am the LORD."*

Unbelief, even though ensconced in the major religions of the world, does not preclude the surety of Judgment.

THE BIBLE

Verses 10 through 12 proclaim the major reasons for the coming Judgment.

The Lord not only tells Judah what He will do, but the reason for it being done! The reason is twofold:

1. They ignored the Law of God, refusing to *"walk in His statutes"* or to *"execute His Judgments."*

As the Bible then was the criteria, the Bible now is the criteria. Regrettably, much of the modern Church, instead of Believing God, is doing the same as Judah of old.

2. Verse 12 says, *"Have done after the manners of the heathen who are round about you."* If the Bible is not followed, the *"heathen are"*! The Church can either follow the word of man or the Word of God. It cannot follow both. And if the word of man does not coincide with the Word of God, God calls it *"heathenistic."*

As an example, the modern Church little believes any more that the Lord delivers, but instead, seeks the ways of the heathen, i.e., *"psychology."*

Judah of old thought she could accept some of the ways of the heathen, incorporating them in the Ways of the Lord, and could, therefore, draw the line where so desired. However, such cannot be! A little leaven will soon leaven the entire lump (Gal. 5:9). Consequently, almost all the modern Church has been psychologized to the point that the entire lump is leavened.

When the Church forsakes Christ as Deliverer, they also forsake Him as Truth, and then deny His Glory. As a result, most Churches, whatever their affiliation, are totally man-led, man-guided, and, therefore, bereft of any Moving of the Holy Spirit. God actually looks at them as *"heathen,"* just as He looks at the Muslim, the Hindu, etc.

(13) "AND IT CAME TO PASS, WHEN I PROPHESIED, THAT PELATIAH THE SON OF BENAIAH DIED. THEN FELL I DOWN UPON MY FACE, AND CRIED WITH A LOUD VOICE, AND SAID, AH LORD GOD! WILL YOU MAKE A FULL END OF THE REMNANT OF ISRAEL?

(14) "AGAIN THE WORD OF THE LORD CAME UNTO ME, SAYING,

(15) "SON OF MAN, YOUR BRETHREN, EVEN YOUR BRETHREN, THE MEN OF YOUR KINDRED, AND ALL THE HOUSE OF ISRAEL WHOLLY, ARE THEY UNTO WHOM THE INHABITANTS OF JERUSALEM

HAVE SAID, GET YOU FAR FROM THE LORD: UNTO US IS THIS LAND GIVEN IN POSSESSION.

(16) "THEREFORE SAY, THUS SAITH THE LORD GOD; ALTHOUGH I HAVE CAST THEM FAR OFF AMONG THE HEATHEN, AND ALTHOUGH I HAVE SCATTERED THEM AMONG THE COUNTRIES, YET WILL I BE TO THEM AS A LITTLE SANCTUARY IN THE COUNTRIES WHERE THEY SHALL COME.

(17) "THEREFORE SAY, THUS SAITH THE LORD GOD; I WILL EVEN GATHER YOU FROM THE PEOPLE, AND ASSEMBLE YOU OUT OF THE COUNTRIES WHERE YOU HAVE BEEN SCATTERED, AND I WILL GIVE YOU THE LAND OF ISRAEL.

(18) "AND THEY SHALL COME THITHER, AND THEY SHALL TAKE AWAY ALL THE DETESTABLE THINGS THEREOF AND ALL THE ABOMINATIONS THEREOF FROM THENCE.

(19) "AND I WILL GIVE THEM ONE HEART, AND I WILL PUT A NEW SPIRIT WITHIN YOU; AND I WILL TAKE THE STONY HEART OUT OF THEIR FLESH, AND WILL GIVE THEM AN HEART OF FLESH:

(20) "THAT THEY MAY WALK IN MY STATUTES, AND KEEP MY ORDINANCES, AND DO THEM: AND THEY SHALL BE MY PEOPLE, AND I WILL BE THEIR GOD.

(21) "BUT AS FOR THEM WHOSE HEART WALKS AFTER THE HEART OF THEIR DETESTABLE THINGS AND THEIR ABOMINATIONS, I WILL RECOMPENSE THEIR WAY UPON THEIR OWN HEADS, SAITH THE LORD GOD."

The structure is:

1. The captives in Babylonia had no material Temple, yet God Himself would be to them a Sanctuary for the *"little while"* their exile was to last, i.e., the predicted seventy years.

2. They would then return and purge Zion from every detestable thing. This had a fulfillment in the return under Ezra and Nehemiah, and by the consequent reformation which those leaders so vigorously carried out.

3. The Prophecy of the *"new spirit"* and the *"new heart"* belonged to the future. It will take place at the Second Coming.

DEATH

The Princes in Jerusalem opposed Jeremiah, even as they opposed Ezekiel, and ridiculed his preaching, and put him in prison. Judging by his solemn death, Pelatiah of Verse 13 appears to have been the leader of those who *"gave wicked counsel in Jerusalem."* The emphasis is that his death was a Judgment from God.

Sickness and premature death certainly don't always fall into the realm of a Judgment from God; however, if the truth were known, such Judgment continues to be extended presently, even as it was in Old Testament Times. More than likely, the death of Pelatiah was looked at by the inhabitants of Jerusalem as something unfortunate, and they probably would not have linked his death with the Judgment of God. When the words of Ezekiel ultimately came to them, their spiritual blindness would have hidden this fact from their eyes. When people rebel against God, their powers of discernment are greatly affected. They actually come to the place that they little know what is of God, and what isn't of God. And to be sure, Satan is a master at making that which definitely is of God, seem as if it isn't, and that which is definitely not of God, seem as if though it is.

A LITTLE SANCTUARY

Verse 16 proclaims the fact, due to the rebellion of Judah, and their refusal to repent, it was now the Will of God for His chosen people to be taken as captives into these heathen countries. Yet, He promised to be with them, even saying, *"Yet, will I be to them as a little Sanctuary in the countries where they shall come."*

The idea is that it is *"The Presence of Jehovah"* that makes the Sanctuary, not the Sanctuary that secures the Presence.

The Temple had become a shrine to Jerusalem; they thereby worshiped the Temple instead of the God of the Temple. Such is much of the modern Church!

THUS SAITH THE LORD

Verse 17 gives us the Promise of God that the Lord ultimately would bring Israel back to her Promised Land, by saying, *"I will give you the Land of Israel."*

This was partially fulfilled upon the return of the Exiles some seventy years after the first deportation. However, its total fulfillment speaks of a future time, which was not fulfilled in 1948 when Israel once again, after nearly 2,000 years of wandering, became a nation. The actual fulfillment concerns the Coming of the Lord, when He will then defeat the Antichrist, as well as all the enemies of Israel, with them accepting Him as Saviour and Messiah, and will then be given all the *"Land of Israel."*

A NEW SPIRIT

Verses 19 through 21 proclaim that which is going to take place in Israel at a future time. In fact, these Prophecies have not been fulfilled even yet. It is as if the Lord, knowing the disconcertment of those in Judah who truly still loved the Lord, that the nation would be destroyed, never to rise again, gives them a Prophecy of the future, which truly proclaims a coming glad day.

The Lord promises to give Israel a *"a new spirit"* and, in essence, a *"new heart."* Then He says that they will *"walk in My statutes, and keep My Ordinances."* He then further adds, as Verse 20 proclaims, *"And they shall be My people, and I will be their God."*

This will take place in the coming Millennial Reign when Christ has been accepted by Israel as Saviour and Messiah. But in the meantime, as Verse 21 says, Judah will answer for her rebellion against God; as we shall see, it will not be a pretty sight to behold.

(22) "THEN DID THE CHERUBIMS LIFT UP THEIR WINGS, AND THE WHEELS BESIDE THEM; AND THE GLORY OF THE GOD OF ISRAEL WAS OVER THEM ABOVE.

(23) "AND THE GLORY OF THE LORD WENT UP FROM THE MIDST OF THE CITY, AND STOOD UPON THE MOUNTAIN WHICH IS ON THE EAST SIDE OF THE CITY.

(24) "AFTERWARDS THE SPIRIT TOOK ME UP, AND BROUGHT ME IN A VISION BY THE SPIRIT OF GOD INTO CHALDEA, TO THEM OF THE CAPTIVITY. SO THE VISION THAT I HAD SEEN WENT UP FROM ME.

(25) "THEN I SPOKE UNTO THEM OF THE CAPTIVITY ALL THE THINGS THAT THE LORD HAD SHOWED ME."

The overview is:

1. Having reluctantly left the Temple, the Holy Spirit then forsook the city, lingering for awhile, with sorrowing love, upon the Mount of Olives.

2. Some five hundred years later, the Glory returned to that Mount, veiled in the sinless flesh of the Messiah, and once more Love looked upon the beloved but rebellious city and wept over it (Lk. 19:41). A few weeks later He ascended up from that Mount; and in a yet future day and the glory of His Second Advent, His feet shall stand upon it (Zech. 14:4). Then shall Israel have one heart and a new spirit (Williams).

3. The Prophet, awakening from his trance, communicated to his hearers the things shown to him in the Vision, and the hearts of the little flock were comforted with the wonderful Revelation that Israel's God of Glory was in their midst as a Sanctuary — a true and pure Temple; that He would continue so to be for the whole period of the captivity; that He shared their exile with them; and that He would certainly restore them to their homeland.

THE GLORY OF GOD

"The Glory of the God of Israel," as portrayed in Verse 22, was the strength of this Land, City, and People, and yet, they little knew or understood it.

The *"Glory of God"* made Israel unique among the nations of the world. Without a powerful army or defenses, they were still the strongest and most powerful nation in the world of that day, and actually served under God as the leader of all nations and kingdoms. They were a people of miracles because of the *"Glory of God."* But yet, they did not realize it, and forsook the *"Glory of God"* for heathen idols and practices.

As Judah and Jerusalem little understood the Source of their strength, likewise, the modern Church follows suit. It thinks that education, philosophy, money, political power, and position are its strength, when in reality, they are its weakness. Its strength, if any at all, is the *"Glory of God."* It is that which the world does not and cannot understand; sadly, the majority of the Church does not understand, either!

It is sad that in more than three hundred thousand Churches in America, most have never known one moment of the Glory of God. As well, sadly, thousands of others, even tens of thousands, that once knew His Glory, no longer do!

The strength of the Church is the *"Glory of God."* If it has the *"Glory,"* it has everything, and if it does not have the *"Glory,"* it has nothing, despite all the other things it might have.

DEPARTURE

Verse 23 is without a doubt one of the saddest Verses in the entirety of the Bible. The Holy Spirit, Who is Israel's power and strength, is leaving, although reluctantly. He is no longer wanted or desired; therefore, He has no choice but to leave.

Thankfully, Ezekiel also saw His return, as proclaimed in 43:2-5; however, this will be in the coming Millennial Reign, after Israel has accepted Christ as her Lord, Saviour, and Messiah.

The major factor which must be observed here is the fact that the Holy Spirit will not stay where He isn't wanted. To be sure, He loved these people with an undying love, but the abominations became so overriding, that He had no choice but to leave.

Before the Cross, the Holy Spirit dwelt in the Temple, in the Holy of Holies, between the Mercy Seat and the Cherubims. This was Israel's distinction above the other nations of the world, but what a distinction it was! They had access to leading, guidance, power, blessings, and prosperity, as no other nation on the face of the Earth; in fact, God meant for them to be a light to the other nations of the world. But regrettably, instead of leading the other nations, they became like the other nations, and even went into deeper idolatry and transgression. So, despite repeated warnings, there came a time that the Holy Spirit left. Although the Lord, even as He stated, would be a *"little Sanctuary"* in far off Babylonia, still, they would now become a defeated, whipped, beleaguered people.

THE HOLY SPIRIT AT THE PRESENT TIME

All of this should be a lesson to us in the modern Church, and, in fact, is meant to be a lesson.

It is my personal contention that with the advent of the Latter Rain outpouring of the Holy Spirit upon this world, and the rejection of this moving of the Spirit by most of the Denominational world, these particular Churches, are, by and large, left without the Spirit. And without the Holy Spirit, there may be much religious machinery, but nothing is done for God.

And then, regrettably, most of the Pentecostal Denominations seemingly are following suit. The Holy Spirit is less and less looked to, less and less depended on, with the ways of the world gradually taking His place, until I fear that most Pentecostal Denominations are on the verge of the departure of the Spirit.

Of course, since the Cross, the Holy Spirit deals with mankind in a totally different manner. While the Holy Spirit definitely dealt with individuals in Old Testament Times, His greater revelation was in the realm of a corporate structure. He doesn't deal that way at the present time, working exclusively through individuals. The Cross changed everything, making it possible for much more intimate contact and help.

But still, even in the heart and life of an individual, if unbelief characterizes such a person, and if such an avenue continues, the Holy Spirit, exactly as He did Israel of old, will simply leave (Heb. 6:4-6; 10:26-29).

THE VISION

The phrase, *"And brought me in a Vision,"* of Verse 24, proclaims the fact that Ezekiel did not go to Jerusalem literally, but only in a *"Vision."*

Now the Vision ends, and the Prophet is once again with his people in *"Chaldea"* in spirit, exactly as he had always been in body.

Verse 25 records the Prophet relating to his compatriots what the Lord had shown him. They were no doubt very much comforted with the wonderful revelation that Israel's

God of Glory was in their midst as a Sanctuary, a True and Pure Temple; that He would continue to be so for the entire period of the captivity that He shared their exile with them; and that He would certainly restore them ultimately to the homeland.

"I think when I read that sweet story of old,
"When Jesus was here among men,
"How He called little children as lambs to His fold,
"I should like to have been with Him then."

"I wish that His Hands had been placed on my head,
"That His arms had been thrown around me,
"And that I might have seen His kind look when He said,
"Let the little ones come unto Me."

"Yet still to His footstool in prayer I may go,
"And ask for a share in His Love;
"And if I thus earnestly seek Him below,
"I shall see Him and hear Him above."

CHAPTER 12

(1) "THE WORD OF THE LORD ALSO CAME UNTO ME, SAYING,

(2) "SON OF MAN, YOU DWELL IN THE MIDST OF A REBELLIOUS HOUSE, WHICH HAVE EYES TO SEE, AND SEE NOT; THEY HAVE EARS TO HEAR, AND HEAR NOT: FOR THEY ARE A REBELLIOUS HOUSE.

(3) "THEREFORE, THOU SON OF MAN, PREPARE THEE STUFF FOR REMOVING, AND REMOVE BY DAY IN THEIR SIGHT; AND YOU SHALL REMOVE FROM YOUR PLACE TO ANOTHER PLACE IN THEIR SIGHT: IT MAY BE THEY WILL CONSIDER, THOUGH THEY BE A REBELLIOUS HOUSE.

(4) "THEN SHALL YOU BRING FORTH YOUR STUFF BY DAY IN THEIR SIGHT, AS STUFF FOR REMOVING: AND YOU SHALL GO FORTH AT EVENING IN THEIR SIGHT, AS THEY WHO GO FORTH INTO CAPTIVITY.

(5) "DIG THOU THROUGH THE WALL IN THEIR SIGHT, AND CARRY OUT THEREBY.

(6) "IN THEIR SIGHT SHALL YOU BEAR IT UPON YOUR SHOULDERS, AND CARRY IT FORTH IN THE TWILIGHT: YOU SHALL COVER YOUR FACE, THAT YOU SEE NOT THE GROUND: FOR I HAVE SET YOU FOR A SIGN UNTO THE HOUSE OF ISRAEL.

(7) "AND I DID SO AS I WAS COMMANDED: I BROUGHT FORTH MY STUFF BY DAY, AS STUFF FOR CAPTIVITY, AND IN THE EVENING I DIGGED THROUGH THE WALL WITH MY HAND; I BROUGHT IT FORTH IN THE TWILIGHT, AND I BORE IT UPON MY SHOULDER IN THEIR SIGHT."

The Synopsis is:

1. In this object lesson, the Prophet predicted the attempted escape of King Zedekiah. The Prophecy preceded the event by about five years.

2. This object lesson was necessary because of the unbelief of the captives.

3. False Prophets were promising restoration to them and victory to Zedekiah.

A REBELLIOUS HOUSE

Jerusalem, despite the false Prophecies of the false Prophets, would not, and, in fact, at this late stage, could not be saved. Verse 2 tells us why! They had *"eyes to see"* and *"ears to hear,"* but they would not see or hear, because of their rebellion. Living for God is the greatest, most wonderful, glorious life there could ever be. The world has nothing that even remotely approaches that which is given by the Lord. The world, with its unredeemed, is spiritually dead, and cannot grasp or understand anything about the Lord. So, to them, living for God is about the same as a prison sentence. However, there are serious consequences for the Believer, as represented here by Judah and Jerusalem, if one seeks to function contrary to God's Will. Probably the core problem for this is exactly that which the Lord speaks of Judah; it is rebellion. A long time before, Samuel the Prophet said: *"Rebellion is as the sin of witchcraft, and stubbornness is as iniquity, and idolatry"* (I Sam. 15:23).

"Rebellion and stubbornness" are a manifestation of failure to conform to Truth. It is the tap-root of all evil. It characterized Judah of old, and characterizes almost all of humanity, even from the beginning!

The Bible is the Word of God, and, as such, is the only Message from God to man. To rebel against it shows unbelief, and is rebellion against God. So, the Holy Spirit would say of almost all the world, and for all time, *"They are a rebellious house."*

HOW IS REBELLION AS THE SIN OF WITCHCRAFT?

At first glance, the statement seems to be a misnomer; however, the Holy Spirit doesn't make mistakes.

"Witchcraft" is the effort to manipulate the spirit world of darkness in some way. It seeks to divine the future, to ward off evil spirits, or to place a curse on others. This is referred to in some circles as *"black magic."* However, there is another side to witchcraft, which is referred to as *"white magic."* This is the effort by individuals, who erroneously use the Word of God in an attempt to manipulate the spirit world of light, in other words, to get God to do certain things, etc. Both means are evil!

"Rebellion" fits into this mold of *"Witchcraft,"* simply because it seeks to serve God in a way and manner that is unscriptural. In other words, such individuals rebel against the plain, clear, written Word of God.

To help us understand that better, one could say that it is an attempt to live for God outside of His Biblical Plan, which is *"Jesus Christ, and Him Crucified"* (I Cor. 1:17-18, 21, 23; 2:2).

It should be readily understood that God doesn't respond favorably to manipulation in any manner. If we live this life according to God's Way, which is the Way of the Cross, then we will reap the benefits, which are multitudinous. If we seek to live for God by other means, no matter how good it may seem on the surface, the end result will not be positive. Anything other than a yielding to Christ and His Finished Work can only be construed as *"rebellion."*

ZEDEKIAH

Verses 3 through 7 portray an object lesson of the attempted escape and capture of Zedekiah, King of Judah, at this particular time.

This concerned the siege of Jerusalem by Nebuchadnezzar, which lasted about two years when it finally came, which was about four years from the time of Ezekiel's prophecy.

During that time, Zedekiah, according to the false Prophets, thought that Egypt was certainly going to come to the rescue of Jerusalem. However, Egypt did not come, and finally Nebuchadnezzar breached the walls of the city, with his soldiers coming in with great anger and fury. At the last moment, Zedekiah thought surely he could escape, and possibly even set up a Kingdom in exile.

The Prophet in his object lesson was not to take the *"stuff"* through the door of the house, but instead, *"dig through the wall,"* thus illustrating Zedekiah's escape attempt by going through a broken part of the wall of Jerusalem.

Once again, Ezekiel was to do this in the sight of the people, illustrating the fact that God would carefully observe all that Zedekiah was doing, thereby foiling his attempt to escape the Judgment of God.

What must of have been Zedekiah's response when he read these predictions from Ezekiel, as he, at the same time, heard the similar Prophecies of Jeremiah?

This object lesson was necessary, even in Babylonia, because of the unbelief of the captives. False Prophets were promising restoration to them and victory to Zedekiah.

The phrase, *"For I have set you for a sign unto the House of Israel,"* portrays the symbolic acts as being given by God, describing accurately as to exactly what would happen in the not too distant future. Sadly and regrettably, they were ignored by almost all.

SIGNS

As well, the *"signs"* are abundant today regarding the near Rapture of the Church, but sadly ignored! Also, the Rapture of the Church, within itself, will be the greatest sign of all concerning the Endtime, but even this, it seems from the Word of God, will be ignored by the world as it continues on its path of rebellion.

Concerning all of these things, and we speak of Endtime events, the nation of Israel is, and has always been, God's Prophetic time clock. And yet, despite the fact that Israel is now a nation, and has been since 1948, which is within itself a tremendous fulfillment of Bible Prophecy, still, there's almost no warning from the modern Church concerning the lateness of the hour.

Too much and too often, the modern Church has degenerated into a mere social club, or else is referring myriads to psychologists, while it denies the delivering power of Christ, which is accomplished through the Cross, or else is teaching people how to get rich by confessing their greatness before God.

A storm is rapidly and surely approaching this world, which Jesus called *"Great Tribulation,"* and said it would be worse than any that had preceded it, and nothing afterward would be like it (Mat. 24:21).

He went on to say that it would be so bad that unless the Lord shortens the days, *"no flesh would be saved,"* i.e., the entirety of humanity. However, He said those days of destruction would be shortened (Mat. 24:22).

And yet, despite this time being upon us, there are very few Messages from behind modern pulpits telling the people to *"prepare to meet God,"* but instead, *"another Gospel, presenting another Jesus, and by another spirit,"* is too often presented (II Cor. 11:4)!

Verse 7 says that Ezekiel obeyed the Lord respecting the object lesson. How many of the people took this lesson seriously, and how many ridiculed the *"sensationalism"* of the Prophet?

(8) "AND IN THE MORNING CAME THE WORD OF THE LORD UNTO ME, SAYING,

(9) "SON OF MAN, HAS NOT THE HOUSE OF ISRAEL, THE REBELLIOUS HOUSE, SAID UNTO YOU, WHAT DOEST THOU?

(10) "SAY THOU UNTO THEM, THUS SAITH THE LORD GOD; THIS BURDEN CONCERNS THE PRINCE IN JERUSALEM, AND ALL THE HOUSE OF ISRAEL WHO ARE AMONG THEM.

(11) "SAY, I AM YOUR SIGN: LIKE AS I HAVE DONE, SO SHALL IT BE DONE UNTO THEM: THEY SHALL REMOVE AND GO INTO CAPTIVITY.

(12) "AND THE PRINCE THAT IS AMONG THEM SHALL BEAR UPON HIS SHOULDER IN THE TWILIGHT, AND SHALL GO FORTH: THEY SHALL DIG THROUGH THE WALL TO CARRY OUT THEREBY: HE SHALL COVER HIS FACE, THAT HE SEE NOT THE GROUND WITH HIS EYES.

(13) "MY NET ALSO WILL I SPREAD UPON HIM, AND HE SHALL BE TAKEN IN MY SNARE: AND I WILL BRING HIM TO BABYLON TO THE LAND OF THE CHALDEANS; YET SHALL HE NOT SEE IT, THOUGH HE SHALL DIE THERE.

(14) "AND I WILL SCATTER TOWARD EVERY WIND ALL WHO ARE ABOUT HIM TO HELP HIM, AND ALL HIS BANDS; AND I WILL DRAW OUT THE SWORD AFTER THEM.

(15) "AND THEY SHALL KNOW THAT I AM THE LORD, WHEN I SHALL SCATTER THEM AMONG THE NATIONS, AND DISPERSE THEM IN THE COUNTRIES.

(16) "BUT I WILL LEAVE A FEW MEN OF THEM FROM THE SWORD, FROM THE FAMINE, AND FROM THE PESTILENCE; THAT THEY MAY DECLARE ALL THEIR ABOMINATIONS AMONG THE HEATHEN WHITHER THEY COME; AND THEY SHALL KNOW THAT I AM THE LORD."

The synopsis is:

1. All, as fore-pictured, came to pass (II Ki., Chpt. 25; Jer., Chpt. 39). Zedekiah, disguised so as not to be recognized, and with a few articles for the journey, forsook Jerusalem by night through a hole made in the city wall, and fled to Jericho. But God using the Chaldean army as a net, he was captured and brought to Riblah; and, His eyes having been put out, transported to Babylon where he died.

2. Josephus says that this Prophecy was sent to Zedekiah; but he, declaring that Jeremiah (Jer. 21:7) contradicted Verse 13 of this Chapter, it stating he should not see Babylon, and Jeremiah predicting he would be carried there, concluded to believe neither. Regrettably, he has many imitators at the present time.

3. The few reserved from destruction (Vs. 16) were spared that they might vindicate God's action by informing the nations of the

abominations which justified it. Daniel 9:5-14 illustrates this prediction (Williams).

CAPTIVITY

It seems at first that Ezekiel did not understand the meaning of what the Lord wanted him to do as it regards the object lesson, but he carried it out without fail. However, the next morning, as Verse 8 proclaims, through the Prophecies given him, it became clear as to the meaning of this symbolic action.

He told the people who had gathered to hear him that *"this burden concerns the Prince in Jerusalem,"* which referred to Zedekiah, who referred to himself as the King of Judah.

Actually, the phrase, *"Prince,"* instead of *"King,"* was used by the Holy Spirit because, at least in the mind of God, Zedekiah was not the true King of Judah, only one who served as a stopgap-measure. In the mind of God, Jehoiachin was the last King, at least in the line of David, to sit on the Throne. (He was also called Coniah.)

The Lord called Jehoiachin a *"despised broken idol,"* and said, *"For no man of his seed shall prosper, sitting upon the throne of David, and ruling any more in Judah"* (Jer. 22:28-30).

(Actually, Zedekiah was Jehoiachin's uncle, with the word, *"Brother,"* at least in this account, meaning *"next of kin"* — II Chronicles 36:10.)

Exactly as Verse 13 predicted, all came to pass (II Ki., Chpt. 25; Jer., Chpt. 39).

Let it be ever known that the Word of the Lord cannot fail!

While only Ezekiel prophesied in Captivity and Jeremiah in Jerusalem, at least as far as is known, who actually represented the Lord, most probably, false Prophets abounded. As then, so now!

At any time, Zedekiah could have repented before God and heeded the Word of the Lord. Even though he would have been carried as a captive into Babylon, he would have been spared the blindness and being treated as a slave.

Let it be known that before he became a captive of the Babylonians, He was a captive to his own self-will and man-fear. As such,

NOTES

he listened to the wrong voices, and, as such, it brought upon him disaster! And so it is with the entirety of the world.

How many presently are heeding the Word of the Lord? If the truth were known, for every one Church that truly preaches the Gospel, a hundred others don't!

THE SWORD

The idea of Verse 14 pertains to all who would attempt to help Zedekiah escape the Babylonians. Irrespective of their plans and their efforts to escape the sword, the Lord says the very opposite, *"I will draw out the sword after them."*

Thus, the false expectations of the captives that they would immediately be restored to their native land, and the equally false expectations of the people of Jerusalem that the Babylonians would never conquer them, were all destroyed by the symbolic Prophecy of these Verses.

Zedekiah, and Ahab before him, tried, but in vain, to outwit God. Their action was the more wicked because God in His love and pity told them beforehand of their fate if they persisted in their folly. He did not want them to perish.

Let it ever be known that all who refuse to flee from the wrath to come must get to know God in Judgment. Those who obey the command shall get to know Him in Grace, even as Verse 16 implies.

THE POWER OF GOD

The phrase from Verse 16, *"But I will leave a few men of them,"* refers to the total control held by the Lord regarding this people.

This is unsettling to the carnal heart, but a source of deep spiritual comfort to those who truly love the Lord.

The Child of God, truly loving the Lord, desires the Holy Spirit to have minute control. However, it is control that must be freely given by the Believer, for the Lord will not forcibly take such control as far as Blessing is concerned. However, if Judgment is necessary, as here, He will take as much control as is needed. This we must never forget!

(17) "MOREOVER THE WORD OF THE LORD CAME TO ME, SAYING,

(18) "SON OF MAN, EAT YOUR BREAD WITH QUAKING, AND DRINK YOUR WATER WITH TREMBLING AND WITH CAREFULNESS;

(19) "AND SAY UNTO THE PEOPLE OF THE LAND, THUS SAITH THE LORD GOD OF THE INHABITANTS OF JERUSALEM, AND OF THE LAND OF ISRAEL; THEY SHALL EAT THEIR BREAD WITH CAREFULNESS, AND DRINK THEIR WATER WITH ASTONISHMENT, THAT HER LAND MAY BE DESOLATE FROM ALL THAT IS THEREIN, BECAUSE OF THE VIOLENCE OF ALL THEM WHO DWELL THEREIN.

(20) "AND THE CITIES THAT ARE INHABITED SHALL BE LAID WASTE, AND THE LAND SHALL BE DESOLATE; AND YOU SHALL KNOW THAT I AM THE LORD."

The exegesis is:

1. There is every reason to believe that Ezekiel felt every emotion concerning the extent of the Prophecy given, as, in this case, famine and fear.

2. The weak being lorded over by the strong characterizes spiritual declension.

3. The only thing standing between the nations of the world and total anarchy is the Spirit of God and the Word of God.

THE WORD OF THE LORD

As Verse 18 proclaims, the bystanders, upon observing the Prophet, would have witnessed one obviously trembling in terror. Ezekiel must feel the same panic, fear, and catastrophe, even though hundreds of miles away, that the inhabitants of the doomed city of Jerusalem would soon experience. The emotion of it, at least on Ezekiel's part, must have been awful indeed!

As well, the modern Preacher of the Gospel, upon receiving the Message from the Lord, should be animated exactly as the Message he proclaims. If it is one of Judgment, he should feel the Judgment exactly as the lost will soon feel it.

As well, if his Message is one of joy, Faith, and rejoicing, it, as well, should be experienced; if the Preacher does not weep over the lost and shout with the Redeemed, he, by and large, is preaching a sermon instead of a Message given directly by Lord.

Too much modern preaching is void of feeling and of passion. It is this way primarily because the Messenger has not heard from God.

DESOLATION

Judah had known comparative prosperity for the last several decades, which prompted her to believe that all was well spiritually, when the opposite was the case.

The evidence is the Lord had long since ceased to deal with the people by chastisement, because all hope of their Repentance had long since faded, except for possibly lone individuals. While continuing to warn Judah through Ezekiel and Jeremiah of the impending doom, otherwise, it seemed as if He left them to their own devices; consequently, they mistook their prosperity for the Blessings of God, when it was anything but that.

The modern Church, I'm afraid, functions in the same capacity. As far as the United States is concerned, the Church has never been richer, and has never had larger crowds. The claim is made that this is the great Blessing of God, which, if the case, signifies God's approval.

Nothing could be further from the truth!

The modern Church characterizes the Laodicean Church of Revelation, Chapter 3. The Lord said of that Church: *"Because you say, I am rich, and increased with goods, and have need of nothing; and knowest not that you are wretched, and miserable, and poor, and blind, and naked"* (Rev. 3:17).

In fact, one, I think, could regrettably say that there are fewer people being saved presently than at any time since the Reformation. As well, there are fewer people being Baptized with the Holy Spirit than at any time since the great Latter Rain outpouring, which commenced at approximately the turn of the Twentieth Century.

While a 500-pound man may be big, no one would even remotely say that he is healthy. That is the same for the modern Church; it is big and fat, but definitely not spiritually healthy.

I AM THE LORD

The phrase from Verse 20, *"And you shall know that I am the LORD,"* has reference to the fact that Judah and Jerusalem little recognized Jehovah as Lord of the past or of the present. It is inconceivable to think such, and yet, is any different today?

Despite their present prosperity, Judah is about to know *"waste and desolation."*

Belonging to the Lord, as did the Children of Israel, brings about tremendous Blessings and advantages; however, there is a responsibility that goes along with belonging to Christ. If that responsibility is abrogated, and men begin to live as if the Word of God was not to be taken seriously, the God of Grace and Glory can quickly turn into the God of Judgment.

Some have the erroneous idea that this particular time being the dispensation of Grace, then God no longer calls men to account. But that's not what the Bible says.

Paul said: *"And the times of this ignorance God winked at; but now Commands all men everywhere to Repent"* (Acts 17:30).

The idea, as presented here and sanctioned by the Holy Spirit, is that God functions in the realm of Judgment presently to a greater extent than He did under the Old Covenant. A moment's thought will tell us the reason why.

Due to the Cross and the vast spread of the Gospel, much spiritual light has been given to the world. By and large, it has rejected that Light. Therefore, when the situation goes from bad to worse, weather patterns wreak havoc, but in truth, it is Judgment from God.

A reporter asked me once, if *"AIDS"* was a Judgment from God?

I only remember the question, and I have little recollection of what my answer then was; however, I would have to answer presently in the affirmative, *"Yes, AIDS is a Judgment from God."* What men sow is what men reap! Men have sowed to the wind, and they reap the whirlwind!

(21) "AND THE WORD OF THE LORD CAME UNTO ME, SAYING,

(22) "SON OF MAN, WHAT IS THAT PROVERB THAT YOU HAVE IN THE LAND OF ISRAEL SAYING, THE DAYS ARE PROLONGED, AND EVERY VISION FAILS?

(23) "TELL THEM THEREFORE, THUS SAITH THE LORD GOD; I WILL MAKE THIS PROVERB TO CEASE, AND THEY SHALL NO MORE USE IT AS A PROVERB IN ISRAEL; BUT SAY UNTO THEM, THE DAYS ARE AT HAND, AND THE EFFECT OF EVERY VISION.

(24) "FOR THERE SHALL BE NO MORE ANY VAIN VISION NOR FLATTERING DIVINATION WITHIN THE HOUSE OF ISRAEL.

(25) "FOR I AM THE LORD: I WILL SPEAK, AND THE WORD THAT I SHALL SPEAK SHALL COME TO PASS; IT SHALL BE NO MORE PROLONGED: FOR IN YOUR DAYS, O REBELLIOUS HOUSE, WILL I SAY THE WORD, AND WILL PERFORM IT, SAYS THE LORD GOD."

The composition is:

1. So corrupt and unbelieving is man that he turns the patience and longsuffering of God into a mocking Proverb, as evidenced in Verse 22.

2. But the day will surely come when the vain visions of popular Preachers will be proved false, and the sure Words of God's Book demonstrated true.

3. To be sure, whatever God has said, He will perform it, even as Verse 25 proclaims.

THE PROVERB

Verse 22 proclaims the fact that the people, hearing Message after Message and seeing nothing happen, simply did not believe that Judgment was near, or that any of this would come to task. The idea is proclaimed in the words, *"The days are prolonged."*

Likewise, the words, *"And every vision fails,"* simply means that the people did not believe Jeremiah or Ezekiel had heard from God. In other words, their Messages of coming Judgment were a standing joke, and were not taken seriously. It was passed off with a wave of the hand, accompanied by a smirk, or with the favorite derogatory quip of the hour.

The same thought is addressed by Simon Peter, where he said, *"Knowing this first, that there shall come in the last days scoffers, walking after their own lusts,*

"And saying, Where is the Promise of His Coming? For since the Fathers fell asleep, all things continue as they were from the beginning of the Creation" (II Pet. 3:3-4).

As the inhabitants of Judah and Jerusalem of old, modern scoffers discount the Bible and its predictions. As well, the modern Church little preaches a coming Rapture or

Judgment. It little preaches it, because it little believes it!

Men, even Christians, little understand the Lord. Most of the time He speaks far in advance. Because the delay of the prediction, the Faith of many fail.

Verse 23 proclaims the fact that it had become customary in Israel to say that God's Day of Judgment was a long way off, and that the Visions of the Prophets fail to materialize. To the careless and cynical, God declares that the people will no more use this Proverb, because Judgment will soon be levied.

The popular Preachers of that day were claiming the very opposite of what Jeremiah and Ezekiel were proclaiming. They were proclaiming peace and prosperity, while the true Prophets were proclaiming coming doom. To be sure, it was much easier to believe the false Message than the true, as it is today!

Actually, the fulfillment of these Prophecies was only about four or five years away. Jeremiah had now been Prophesying about thirty-five years, and Ezekiel only about a year. Upon rejecting Jeremiah's Message, the people had steadedly grown harder. As such, they were even less inclined to believe Ezekiel than they had Jeremiah. Nevertheless, the time of fulfillment was steadily drawing nearer.

THE FALSE MESSAGE

The *"Vain vision and flattering divination"* of Verse 24 pertained to the Messages of the false Prophets. The Holy Spirit is saying that soon their Messages will be shown as to what they really are, i.e., lies.

Regrettably, most of that which comes from modern pulpits must be labeled by the Holy Spirit as *"vain visions and flattering divination."*

The modern Charismatic Faith Message, which is no Faith at all, proclaims any Message that convicts of sin as condemnation, and condemns any such Preaching.

Another large segment of the Church, proclaiming Unconditional Eternal Security, soothes the wicked consciences of men by telling them that even though they may lose fellowship with God, they cannot lose sonship!

The Pentecostal world is far too often *"denying the power thereof,"* by mouthing psychological platitudes (II Tim. 3:5).

I WILL SPEAK

And God did speak! However, precious few listen to anything He had to say. And Judah went to her doom!

Is it any different presently? Paul addressed by saying: *"For the time will come when they will not endure sound Doctrine; but after their own lusts shall they heap to themselves teachers, having itching ears;*

"And they shall turn away their ears from the Truth, and shall be turned unto fables" (II Tim. 4:3-4).

In 1997 the Lord began to open up to me the Message of the Cross, telling me that the Cross held the solution for every problem, as it regarded sin or the effects of sin. The Cross alone deals with this matter.

Many Christians understand the Cross, at least to a small degree as it regards Salvation, but virtually none, at this particular time, understand the Cross as it regards Sanctification. But the tragedy is, once this Message is delivered to them, and done so with striking clarity, the far greater majority, have no interest. They, in effect, are writing their own Bible by their actions. This means they have rebelled against God's Prescribed Order, and have developed their own order. God is speaking loudly at this time, a time, incidentally, in which humanity desperately needs to hear His Voice, but how many are truly listening?

(26) "AGAIN THE WORD OF THE LORD CAME UNTO ME, SAYING,

(27) "SON OF MAN, BEHOLD, THEY OF THE HOUSE OF ISRAEL SAY, THE VISION THAT HE SEES IS FOR MANY DAYS TO COME, AND HE PROPHESIES OF THE TIMES THAT ARE FAR OFF.

(28) "THEREFORE SAY UNTO THEM, THUS SAITH THE LORD GOD; THERE SHALL NONE OF MY WORDS BE PROLONGED ANY MORE, BUT THE WORD WHICH I HAVE SPOKEN SHALL BE DONE, SAYS THE LORD."

The structure is:

1. The unbelief of Verse 27 develops into the skepticism of Verse 22.

2. The false expectations of the Captives that they would be immediately restored

to their native land, and the equally false expectations of the people of Jerusalem that the Babylonians would never conquer them, were all destroyed by the symbolic Prophecy of Verses 3 through 7.

3. This new Message to Ezekiel is to counteract the claims of those who desired to believe the false Prophets, claiming that Ezekiel's Prophecies, although real and true, nevertheless pertained to a distant time. The Lord instead claims through the Prophet that the fulfillment of these Prophecies is near at hand. He says, *"They shall not be prolonged anymore."*

JUDGMENT

The words, *"There shall none of My words be prolonged anymore,"* tells us that Judgment had been prolonged in order that Judah and Jerusalem may repent, but all to no avail! Now the Holy Spirit says, *"The prolonging has ended."*

It is a dire prediction, and is guaranteed a fulfillment because it concludes with, *"saith the Lord GOD."*

"I know who holds the future, and I
   know who holds my hand,
"With God things don't just happen,
   everything by Him is planned;
"So, as I face tomorrow, with its prob-
   lems large and small,
"I'll trust the God of Miracles, give to
   Him my all."

CHAPTER 13

(1) "AND THE WORD OF THE LORD CAME UNTO ME, SAYING,

(2) "SON OF MAN, PROPHESY AGAINST THE PROPHETS OF ISRAEL WHO PROPHESY, AND SAY THOU UNTO THEM WHO PROPHESY OUT OF THEIR OWN HEARTS, HEAR YE THE WORD OF THE LORD;

(3) "THUS SAITH THE LORD GOD; WOE UNTO THE FOOLISH PROPHETS, WHO FOLLOW THEIR OWN SPIRIT, AND HAVE SEEN NOTHING!

(4) "O ISRAEL, YOUR PROPHETS ARE LIKE THE FOXES IN THE DESERTS.

(5) "YOU HAVE NOT GONE UP INTO THE GAPS, NEITHER MADE UP THE HEDGE FOR THE HOUSE OF ISRAEL TO STAND IN THE BATTLE IN THE DAY OF THE LORD.

(6) "THEY HAVE SEEN VANITY AND LYING DIVINATION, SAYING, THE LORD SAYS: AND THE LORD HAS NOT SENT THEM: AND THEY HAVE MADE OTHERS TO HOPE THAT THEY WOULD CONFIRM THE WORD.

(7) "HAVE YOU NOT SEEN A VAIN VISION, AND HAVE YOU NOT SPOKEN A LYING DIVINATION, WHEREAS YOU SAY, THE LORD SAYS IT; ALBEIT I HAVE NOT SPOKEN?

(8) "THEREFORE THUS SAITH THE LORD GOD; BECAUSE YOU HAVE SPOKEN VANITY, AND SEEN LIES, THEREFORE, BEHOLD, I AM AGAINST YOU, SAITH THE LORD GOD.

(9) "AND MY HAND SHALL BE UPON THE PROPHETS WHO SEE VANITY, AND WHO DIVINE LIES: THEY SHALL NOT BE IN THE ASSEMBLY OF MY PEOPLE, NEITHER SHALL THEY BE WRITTEN IN THE WRITING OF THE HOUSE OF ISRAEL, NEITHER SHALL THEY ENTER INTO THE LAND OF ISRAEL; AND YOU SHALL KNOW THAT I AM THE LORD GOD."

The diagram is:

1. As the prophecy of the prior Chapter denounced false expectations, so that of this Chapter denounced the authors of them.

2. The false prophets were following their own spirit, and not the Holy Spirit, as Verse 3 proclaims.

3. They preached what the people wished to hear, and not what the Lord said to preach.

FALSE PROPHETS

The Message now to be given will no doubt arouse great enmity against the Prophet. It will now be directed toward the false prophets and prophetesses, and will pull no punches.

Verse 2 proclaims the fact that, as there were false prophets and prophetesses in Jerusalem, there were such among the Exiles as well! The Holy Spirit will now direct His attention to them in no uncertain terms!

While it was true that these people prophesied, still, it was not from the Lord but *"out of their own hearts."* As such, they said what the people wanted to hear, not what the Lord wanted said.

The real test of Truth is not a sign, wonder or prediction coming to pass; it is the Truth itself — the Word of God as plainly written (Deut. 4:2; 12:32; 29:29; Isa. 8:20; 55:11; Jn. 8:32-36; II Tim. 3:15-17; Rev. 22:18-19).

Anything contrary to what is plainly stated in Scripture is false regardless of its seeming inspiration. God allows some signs and wonders to prove men, temptations to test one's love for Him, and heresies to make manifest Truth (I Cor. 11:18-19; II Jn. 7-11). There would be no way of manifesting light if there were no darkness.

The sadness is that most Christians do not know the Word of God well enough to know what is true or what is false; therefore, they are easy prey for Satan!

The Holy Spirit admonishes the Believer to *"hear ye the Word of the LORD,"* and not the word of man!

FOOLISH PROPHETS

Verse 3 says that these *"foolish prophets"* spoke *"out of their own spirit,"* which means that they did not follow the Holy Spirit. They preached what the people wished to hear, in this case, a speedy restoration to the land of Judah.

The preaching of the false prophets was subjective (lacking in reality or substance, and relating to personal mental characteristics). The preaching of the true Prophet was objective (existing independent of mind and expressing the use of Truth without distortion by personal feelings or prejudices). In other words, the true Prophet preached from the Word of God. As today, so at all times, man sets inward religious emotional desires above outward Divine Revelation and desires a Christ without a Bible.

God calls these, as then, *"foolish prophets,"* and further says, *"they have seen nothing."* Such characterizes almost all modern pulpits. They do not preach the Word of God, but preach that which is from their own minds, or the minds of other men and have no revelation whatsoever from the Lord.

THE GAPS AND THE HEDGE

If there are *"gaps"* in the *"hedge,"* it is the business of true Prophets to fill in those gaps. They were to do so by preaching the true Gospel, which would shore up Israel's spiritual defenses.

But Verse 5 states that instead of doing this, the *"foolish prophets"* made merchandise of the time by telling the people a lie instead of the Truth. They made them feel comfortable in their sins, and further told them that peace and prosperity were just around the corner, which slandered the prophecies of Jeremiah and Ezekiel and, in effect, slandered God.

Made to feel comfortable and told what they wanted to hear, the people gladly contributed to the coffers of these false prophets. To be sure, there were precious few who contributed toward the support of Jeremiah and Ezekiel.

Tragically, much of the modern Church, because of lack of knowledge of the Bible, supports *"foolish prophets,"* which, in actuality, supports Satan.

The truth is, most money given to that which purports to be the Work of God, is in fact, not the Work of God, but the work of Satan. Admittedly, it is disguised, being transformed into an angel of light, but nevertheless Satan (II Cor. 11:13-15).

The phrase *"To stand in the battle in the day of the LORD"* means that these false prophets did not come to the defense of the Gospel. They were instead doing the opposite.

To carry on the Work of God is always a *"battle."* Satan opposes it at every turn, and most effectively opposes it by *"angels of light."* They claim to be of the Lord, but are not of the Lord. They prophesy in the Name of the Lord, but their message does not come from the Lord, but actually from their own minds.

VANITY AND LYING DIVINATION

The phrase in Verse 6, *"They have seen vanity and lying divination,"* means that they have believed their own lies and have tried to confirm their own predictions. They did so by claiming, *"The LORD says,"* when in fact, *"The LORD has not sent them,"* and had not said anything, at least not to them.

The phrase, *"And they have made others to hope,"* means that their word was so convincing that it was easy to believe.

Basically, their prophecies were in this vein: They claimed that inasmuch as Judah was God's Land and Jerusalem His City, with the people His People, and above all, the Temple being His, where in fact, He resided between the Mercy Seat and the Cherubims, such guaranteed His Divine Protection and, therefore, the Babylonians would be stopped.

It was an easy message to believe, because much of it was true. The Land was His Land, along with the City and the People. As well, the Temple was His Dwelling Place, etc. So, a lie went to the hearts of the people on the back of Truth. The false prophets made the message very convincing, and, thereby, gave a false hope to the people, which it seems they actually believed themselves.

The Truth was that even though part of their message was true, still, because of the great sins of the people and their refusal to repent, the Lord was forsaking the Land, City, People (most of the people) and the Temple. This they would not believe, as most today will not believe.

Presently, there are religious Denominations which the Lord greatly used in years past, and because of the past work done, many, as in Judah of old, refuse to believe the Lord has forsaken these respective Denominations, because of their departure from His Word and refusal to repent. Consequently, their false prophets proclaim the same message, basically, as the false prophets of Judah. Spiritually speaking, the results will be the same!

A VAIN VISION

All prophets, both false and true, claim to speak for God. The True Prophets, as few as they are, do speak for the Lord, while the false, of course, do not, and in fact, cannot! Only the Believers who are genuinely anchored in the Word will be able to discern the difference. Were it easy to discern the difference, these emphatic prophecies of warning would not have been given here and elsewhere.

At the present time, there are many who claim to be prophesying in the name of the Lord, but for the most part, the far, far greater number are not from the Lord. Predictions are made, with names and even dates being given at times, but which do not come to pass. The tragedy is, the Church seems to question this not at all. It looks like someone would take notice that these prophecies are false. But yet, they keep holding these individuals up, these false prophets, as men of God, supporting them with their money, irrespective of the falseness of their message. Why do they do that?

As we have been stating, most modern Christians have such little knowledge of the Word of God, which above all, must be the true criteria of all things. Not knowing the Word, they fall for anything. And to be sure, Satan knows how to dress up his wares, to where it looks right, at least after a fashion, and so it is easily believed by gullible, scriptural illiterates.

To believe that which the Lord has not said, and after a period of time becomes obvious that He has not said it, is to believe a lie. But the following must be noted:

SPIRITUAL HARM

When people believe a lie, they are not left as they were found. In other words, they go deeper into the spiritual quagmire of wrong direction, which makes it even harder for them to be extricated from their unbelief.

Verse 8 says, *"Because you have spoken vanity, and seen lies,"* refers to the gilded messages they have put together out of their own minds which deceived the people.

Nevertheless, it must be astutely remembered that they claimed to be of God just as much as Jeremiah and Ezekiel. In fact, almost every single Preacher in the world and for all time claims to be of God and speaking the Truth of God. The Truth is that only a few actually are of God and speak in Truth the Word of God.

The word *"vanity"* means *"empty nothings,"* which constituted the messages of these individuals. As well, they *"saw lies"* because they did not see the Word of God.

It is very easy for men to believe lies because it was by *"the lie"* that Adam and Eve fell in the Garden of Eden. Therefore, the manner of their Fall constitutes a continued weakness. Man lies easily and easily believes a lie.

DOOM OF THE FALSE PROPHETS

The phrase in Verse 9, *"And My Hand shall be upon the prophets who see vanity, and who divine lies,"* means for evil and not for good! Also, it is not for correction, but for destruction. It does not speak of a series of difficulties designed to lead the individual to God, but instead designed for the loss of their souls.

Therefore, the acclamation is terrible indeed! All those who claim to preach the Gospel, but, in fact, do not, and even though they sincerely think they do, but in Truth do not, could be eternally lost.

This does not speak of those who preach all the Light they have, even though not having all the Light. Perhaps that would be true, at least in some measure, concerning all Preachers, even the most Godly! However, it does speak of those who preach a lie and call it the Word of God, even those who sincerely think they are right, but in fact are deceived.

THE PREACHING OF THE CROSS

I think anyone who honestly studies the Word of God would have to come to the conclusion that Paul preached the Cross. To that Apostle the meaning of the New Covenant was given, which, in effect, was the meaning of the Cross. Consequently, and according to the guidelines of the Holy Spirit, the Apostle made the Cross the very centerpiece of the Gospel. While everything that Christ did was of utmost significance, still, it was the Cross which brought about man's Redemption, and the Cross alone! (Rom. 6:3-14; 8:1-2, 11; I Cor. 1:17-18, 21, 23; 2:2; Gal., Chpt. 5; 6:14; Eph. 2:13-18; Col. 2:14-15).

And when we talk about Paul preaching the Cross, we are speaking of the Cross as the means of Salvation and Sanctification.

ROMANS

The Epistle of Paul to the Romans, in effect, is the Theology of the Church. To fail to understand this Epistle is to fail to understand Christianity, and the tragedy is, most do not understand Romans. The following will give you an abbreviated outline as to what this great Book is all about.

NOTES

The first three Chapters proclaim the fact that man is lost, and as the Holy Spirit positioned the terminology, man is totally lost, meaning that there is no way that he can redeem himself. Both Gentiles and Jews are treated alike! They (we) are all in need of a Saviour, Who is Jesus Christ.

Chapters Four and Five proclaim the theology of Redemption, which is *"Justification by Faith."* It tells us that man cannot be saved by merit, by works, but only by Faith, and we speak of Faith in Christ and what Christ did at the Cross. Paul labors to bring forth the point that man cannot earn his Salvation, irrespective as to what he might do. He is justified only by evidencing faith in Christ and the Finished Work on the Cross.

Immediately after he broaches *"Justification by Faith,"* Chapter Six proclaims *"Sanctification by Faith."* In other words, in this Chapter we are told how to live for God. And if we do not understand this Chapter, then we simply do not know how to live for the Lord. As the Lord has only one way of Salvation, likewise He has only one way of victory, i.e., *"Sanctification."*

GOD'S PRESCRIBED ORDER OF VICTORY

Paul takes the Believer to the Cross in Romans 6:3-5. In those three Verses, he tells us that we were *"baptized into His Death,"* and *"buried with Him by Baptism into Death,"* and *"raised with Him in newness of life."* Now please understand. Paul is not speaking here of Water Baptism, but rather the Crucifixion of Christ, and our Faith in that Work. The moment the believing sinner evidences Faith in Christ to be saved, in effect, in the Mind of God, that person is literally placed *"in Christ,"* Who is our Substitute and our Representative Man. In effect, *"in Christ"* the believing sinner has died, which means what he was, no longer is. He is raised, as stated, *"in newness of life."* The Apostle said:

"Knowing this, (referring to Rom. 6:6) *that our old man is Crucified with Him, that the body of sin might be destroyed* (the power of sin broken), *that henceforth we should not serve sin"* (the sin nature is no longer to have sway in our hearts and lives).

Knowing and understanding this, in other words, that everything is in the Cross, meaning that everything comes to us by means of the Cross, we are to *"likewise reckon ourselves to be dead indeed unto sin* (the sin nature), *but alive unto God through Jesus Christ our Lord"* (Rom. 6:11).

This is where Faith comes in. The Believer is to ever make the Cross of Christ the Object of his Faith and never allow it to be moved to something else. This is God's Way and it is a way that will never change. The Eleventh Verse did not say that the sin nature is dead, rather that we are dead indeed unto the sin nature.

HOW DO WE STAY DEAD?

We stay dead to the sin nature by making certain that our Faith is ever placed in the Cross of Christ, understanding that the Cross is the means by which all things are given unto us.

When this is done, the Holy Spirit, Who works exclusively within the parameters of the Finished Work of Christ, will help us to live the life that we ought to live (Rom. 8:1-2, 11). That being the case, *"sin shall not have dominion over you."* (Rom. 6:14).

In brief, that which I have just given to you is God's Prescribed Order of Victory. As stated, He has no other order, only this one, and simply because it is enough.

ROMANS, CHAPTER 7

The Holy Spirit intends for the Believer, immediately after being saved, to go on into Romans 6. But the problem is, Romans 6 is so little understood presently, that most Believers fail to take advantage of this which the Lord has done for them through the Cross, which alone can help them to live a victorious life; consequently, trying to live for the Lord in all the wrong ways, instead, they plunge into Romans 7, which hinders Spiritual Growth, which spells defeat, and leaves the individual saying with Paul, *"O wretched man that I am! Who shall deliver me from the body of this death?"* (Rom. 7:24). All of this is because the Believer doesn't understand Romans 6, which has caused many to simply quit. Let me say it again:

If the Believer doesn't understand Romans,

NOTES

Chapter 6, which alone tells us how to successfully live for the Lord, the Believer is going to automatically plunge into Romans Chapter 7, which means he is trying to live for the Lord in the wrong way, and the end result will always be defeat.

The serious Bible student has probably wondered why the material in Romans 7 is placed between Chapters 6 and 8. Logically, the material in Chapter 7 seems that it ought to be where Chapter 6 is placed; however, the Holy Spirit had Paul to place the teaching of Chapter 7 in the chronological order which He wanted and desired. The reason is this:

It is not the Will of God for any Believer to have to undergo the experience of Romans 7. While it is true that Paul had to undergo this bitter experience; however, this was before the meaning of the New Covenant was given, so Paul did not really know God's Prescribed Order of Victory, and neither did anyone else in the world at that particular time. In fact, it was to Paul that this Revelation was given, which he gave to us in his Epistles (Gal. 1:12).

Once the Lord gave to Paul the meaning of the New Covenant, which, in effect, is the meaning of the Cross, Paul then gave it to us, which we have here in this great Epistle to the Romans, and elsewhere for that matter. So, it is not God's Will that any Believer has to live a life of spiritual failure, which characterizes Romans 7. It is His Will that the new convert go immediately into Chapter 6, enjoying the victory which the Cross brings. But as stated, unfortunately, there has been so little teaching on the Cross in the last few decades that the modern Church, for all practical purposes, is Cross illiterate!

VICTORY!

As someone has said, Romans, Chapter 6 presents the mechanics of the Holy Spirit, which tells *"how"* this life is lived. Romans, Chapter 8 tells us *"what"* the Holy Spirit will do within our lives, once we know *"how"* He works.

Unfortunately, most Believers, not understanding Romans 6, jump immediately from Romans, Chapters 4 and 5, to Chapter 8, completely bypassing Chapter 6. The trouble is they really aren't in Chapter 8, but rather in Chapter 7, while all the time loudly confessing how they are in Chapter 8.

The modern Church has been taught that we are to confess our way to victory, etc. While confession is definitely important, there is nothing in the Bible that tells us we can confess our way to victory. Jesus said, *"You shall know the Truth, and the Truth shall make you free"* (Jn. 8:32).

So we presently have the Church loudly confessing Romans 8, when in reality they are not in Romans 8, and for the following reason:

It is impossible for one to go to the *"victory"* of Romans 8 while skipping Romans 6, so they bog down in Romans 7, trying to live for God in all the wrong ways, while all the time loudly confessing how victorious they are; however, noise has never equaled reality.

The great *"victory"* of Romans 8 can only be obtained by the Child of God once they are properly anchored in the Cross of Romans 6. The Holy Spirit works exclusively within the parameters of the Finished Work of Christ, and in no other manner. Listen again to Paul:

"The Law of the Spirit of Life in Christ Jesus has made me free from the Law of sin and death" (Rom. 8:2).

This tells us emphatically as to how the Holy Spirit works. He works within the confines of a *"Law,"* which was established by the Godhead, even before the foundation of the world (I Pet. 1:18-20). This *"Law"* in which He works is found *"in Christ Jesus,"* which unequivocally proclaims what Jesus did at the Cross. So, the Holy Spirit works exclusively within the parameters of the Sacrifice of Christ. If we as Believers attempt to function in any other manner, in other words try to live for God by other means, whatever those means might be, and ever how good they may look on the surface, the end result will always be failure. The reason is simple: when the Believer allows his Faith to be placed in something other that the Cross, this means that he is being unfaithful to Christ, and, in effect, is committing spiritual adultery (Rom. 7:1-4). To be certain, the Holy Spirit will not have any truck whatsoever with such activity. So the Believer is left on his own, which means the Holy Spirit is not helping him, which spells defeat.

UNBELIEF

Immediately after Chapter 8, Paul deals with Israel regarding Chapters 9, 10, and 11. The serious Bible student may misunderstand as to why the teaching is given in these three Chapters as it regards Israel. At first glance, it seems out of place; however, once the Bible student knows what the Holy Spirit is doing through Paul, then it becomes very clear as to why Israel is used as an object lesson.

Israel lost her way with God because of unbelief. She simply would not accept God's Redemption Plan in Christ Jesus and the Cross, so she was cut down, and because there was no alternative. The idea is this:

The Holy Spirit through Paul is telling the Church that if we register unbelief toward Christ and the Cross, then what happened to Israel will happen to the Church. Unbelief destroyed Israel and unbelief will destroy the Church!

WHAT IS THE CONDITION OF THE MODERN CHURCH?

I firmly believe that the Lord has given to this Ministry the Revelation of the Cross, which is not new, but that which was taught by Paul, but which the Church has by and large lost, all in order that the Church be given another opportunity.

The Church is presently in pitiful condition. As previously stated elsewhere in this Volume, there are less people truly being saved presently than probably at any time since the Reformation. As well, there are fewer Believers being Baptized with the Holy Spirit presently than at any time, I think, since the Latter Rain outpouring which began at about the beginning of the Twentieth Century. So this means that the modern Church is in perilous condition. In fact, even as again we have already stated, the modern Church is symbolized by the Laodicean Church (Rev. 3:14).

That Church said and this Church says, *"I am rich, and increased with goods, and have need of nothing."* But the Master answered by saying, *"And knowest not that you *are wretched, and miserable, and poor, and blind, and naked"* (Rev. 3:17).

The only thing that can turn the modern Church to the right direction is the Message of the Cross. I believe that the Lord has raised up this Ministry to proclaim that very Message, which we are doing through Television, Radio, and these Commentaries.

When the Cross is abandoned, ignored, or ridiculed, the Church cannot honestly anymore call itself *"Christian,"* but is rather, at least in some ways, *"Pagan."* I realize that is a strong statement, but I believe it to be true. Let me say it again:

The Cross is the Foundation of Christianity, in effect, the Foundation of the entirety of the Plan of God as it regards Redemption (I Pet. 1:18-20). So the Church must be brought back to the Cross.

I do not know how many Ministries around the world have been touched by the Holy Spirit as it regards the Message of the Cross. But I do know that the Lord has touched Jimmy Swaggart Ministries, and that we are doing all that we can to propagate the greatest story ever told.

Once again, we go back to Paul's warning to the Church as it regards what happened to Israel. The Apostle said:

"Boast not against the branches. But if you boast, you bear not the root, but the root you.

"You will say then, the branches were broken off, that I might be grafted in.

"Well; because of unbelief they were broken off, and you stand by Faith. Be not highminded, but fear:

"For if God spared not the natural branches, take heed lest He also spare not you" (Rom. 11:18-21).

(10) "BECAUSE, EVEN BECAUSE THEY HAVE SEDUCED MY PEOPLE, SAYING, PEACE; AND THERE WAS NO PEACE; AND ONE BUILT UP A WALL, AND, LO, OTHERS DAUBED IT WITH UNTEMPERED MORTER:

(11) "SAY UNTO THEM WHICH DAUB IT WITH UNTEMPERED MORTER, THAT IT SHALL FALL: THERE SHALL BE AN OVERFLOWING SHOWER; AND YOU, O GREAT HAILSTONES, SHALL FALL; AND A STORMY WIND SHALL REND IT.

(12) "LO, WHEN THE WALL IS FALLEN, SHALL IT NOT BE SAID UNTO YOU, WHERE IS THE DAUBING WHEREWITH YOU HAVE DAUBED IT?

(13) "THEREFORE THUS SAITH THE LORD GOD; I WILL EVEN REND IT WITH A STORMY WIND IN MY FURY; AND THERE SHALL BE AN OVERFLOWING SHOWER IN MY ANGER, AND GREAT HAILSTONES IN MY FURY TO CONSUME IT.

(14) "SO WILL I BREAK DOWN THE WALL THAT YOU HAVE DAUBED WITH UNTEMPERED MORTER, AND BRING IT DOWN TO THE GROUND, SO THAT THE FOUNDATION THEREOF SHALL BE DISCOVERED, AND IT SHALL FALL, AND YOU SHALL BE CONSUMED IN THE MIDST THEREOF: AND YOU SHALL KNOW THAT I AM THE LORD.

(15) "THUS WILL I ACCOMPLISH MY WRATH UPON THE WALL, AND UPON THEM WHO HAVE DAUBED IT WITH UNTEMPERED MORTER, AND WILL SAY UNTO YOU, THE WALL IS NO MORE, NEITHER THEY WHO DAUBED IT;

(16) "TO WIT, THE PROPHETS OF ISRAEL WHICH PROPHESY CONCERNING JERUSALEM, AND WHICH SEE VISIONS OF PEACE FOR HER, AND THERE IS NO PEACE, SAYS THE LORD GOD."

The overview is:

1. The false prophets preached a message of *"peace"* when in reality there was no peace, but war! The modern false prophets are preaching prosperity, when the truth is there is no spiritual prosperity.

2. Every house built, no matter how seemingly strong it might be, if it is not built on the *"rock,"* it will not stand.

3. As Verse 12 proclaims, the modern Church, as Israel of old, is being deceived.

4. Verse 13 records the fact, with the Lord using two words regarding His response to these false prophets, *"anger"* and *"fury"*.

A FALSE PEACE

Verse 10 proclaims the false prophets proclaiming *"peace,"* which *"seduced the people"* by lulling them into a false security, and in doing so, so to speak, it narcotized their consciences. The false message has a tendency to do that.

As a symbol of this falseness, the Holy Spirit used the phrase *"a wall daubed with untempered mortar."* The *"untempered mortar"* was a *"stucco"* or *"plaster,"* which is hardly better than whitewash. While it hid the defects and gave it a semblance of solidity, the truth was the *"untempered mortar"* contained nothing that would hold the wall together. So, when bad weather came, it would crumble.

Most of that which is heard in modern Churches falls into the same category. It sounds good to the unspiritual ear, but in fact, is not the Word of God.

THE MESSAGE OF THE CROSS

The Message which the Holy Spirit strongly desires at present is the Message of the Cross. The Church must be brought back to the Cross, which is its firm foundation. All other supposed foundations are false, and when the storms come, the house built on those foundations, even as our Lord said, will not stand (Mat. 7:24-27).

As we have already said several times in this Volume, there are fewer people being saved today than at any time since the Reformation, and there are fewer people being Baptized with the Holy Spirit than at any time since the beginning of the Latter Rain outpouring, which began at about the turn of the Twentieth Century.

Why?

The Church has so badly strayed from its True Foundation, which is the Cross, that it has come to the place where the Holy Spirit cannot truly work. Oh yes, many things are presently claimed. We hear about miracles galore, but these so-called miracles are *"untempered mortar."* In other words, there is no substance to them. Precious few are saved, baptized with the Spirit, and delivered, and, despite all the claims, precious few are healed.

The Cross of Christ is the Foundation of the Christian Faith (I Pet. 1:18-20). Listen to Paul:

"According to the Grace of God which is given unto me, as a wise masterbuilder, I have laid the foundation, and another builds thereon. But let every man take heed how he builds thereupon.

NOTES

"For other foundation can no man lay than that is laid, which is Jesus Christ" (I Cor. 3:10-11).

Anytime that Paul mentions our Lord, he is speaking of what Christ has done at the Cross, and that exclusively. Concerning this, the Apostle said:

"Wherefore henceforth know we no man after the flesh: yes, though we have known Christ after the flesh, yet now henceforth know we Him no more" (II Cor. 5:16).

What did he mean by that statement?

He meant that most Believers look to Christ, or try to follow Him *"after the flesh,"* which refers to any means or way other than the Cross. Unfortunately, at this present time (2003), almost the entirety of the Church attempts to follow Christ *"after the flesh,"* which means they aren't following Him *"after the Spirit"* (Rom. 8:1).

Before people can begin to be saved, and Believers baptized with the Holy Spirit, and the Lord truly begin once again to work in the midst of His people, the Church must be brought back to the Cross. That, and that alone, is the True Foundation, and on that Foundation only will the Holy Spirit work!

IT SHALL FALL!

Verse 11 proclaims the Lord saying to the Prophet, as it concerned the wall built with *"untempered mortar,"* and in no uncertain terms, *"it shall fall."*

The false gospel may look good at the present time. Everyone may be acclaiming its promises. The Churches may be full, as people with itching ears rush to *"see the show."* But no matter what it may seem to be at present; no matter what people may think; no matter how big the crowds are presently; no matter how much money it may seem to have; the Holy Spirit has said, *"it will fall!"*

During the time of Jeremiah and Ezekiel, their crowds were sparse and their messages were met with ridicule, while the messages of the false prophets were acclaimed far and wide. Nevertheless, the true Message was in the hearts of Jeremiah and Ezekiel, and definitely not in the hearts of the false prophets. And no matter what it seemed to be at the present, the Holy Spirit had said *"it will fall."* And fall it did!

THE WRATH OF GOD

Verses 12 through 16 proclaim God's anger against the wall built with *"untempered mortar,"* which refers to a house of cards, so to speak.

The false prophets were attempting to proclaim *"peace"* on the foundation of a false message. There is no peace in that type of message, as there can be no peace in that type of message.

The Message of Jeremiah and Ezekiel was the very opposite of that which the people desired to hear, and as such, they rebelled against it. However, had they heeded, and consequently repented, they would have saved themselves untold sorrow and heartache. While it is true, at least at this late date, that they still would have gone into captivity, if Repentance had been forthcoming, the Lord would have seen to it that the City was spared and possibly the Temple, with them being treated favorably by their captors. But such was not to be, primarily because of these false prophets.

FALSE PROPHETS

The essence of the false prophet is that he calls the people *"after other gods, which you have not known"* (Deut. 13:2), thus teaching *"rebellion against the LORD your God, Who brought you out of the Land of Egypt"* (Deut. 13:5, 10).

As well, the false prophet is a man who does not confront sin or call the people to holiness (Jer. 23:21-22). The message of the false prophet is one of peace, without regard to the moral and spiritual conditions which are basic to peace, whereas the True Prophet has a Message of Judgment upon sin.

THE TRUE PROPHET

That does not mean that True Prophets cannot have a Message of peace, when in Truth, there can be a time when peace is the Message of God; but it will always be in Exodus' terms, that peace can come only when Holiness is satisfied concerning sin. The voice of the True Prophet is always the voice of the Law of God. Thus, false prophets are men of borrowed testimony, feigned authority, and self-appointed ministry, whereas the True Prophet stands in the counsel of Jehovah and hears His Voice, and has been sent by Him.

The *"Exodus"* term refers, of course, to the Children of Israel being delivered from Egyptian bondage, which is a symbol of God's people separating themselves from the world, unto God.

THE OFFICE OF THE PROPHET

Many claim that after the time of the Old Testament, the Ministry or Office of the Prophet is no more. However, Prophecy and the Prophets form the greatest line of continuity between the Old Testament and the New Testament. This is evident from the attitude of Christ and the Apostles to Old Testament Prophets, from the continuance of the phenomenon of Prophecy, both up to and after the Ministry of Christ, from the prophetic character of His Own Ministry, from the placing of the inspiration of New Testament Apostles alongside that of Old Testament Prophets, and from the general outpouring of the Holy Spirit — the Spirit of Prophecy — upon the Church, leading to a continuing acceptance of Prophets and prophesying in New Testament Churches.

The Old Testament Prophetic line did not end with Malachi, but with John the Baptist, as our Lord expressly declares (Mat. 11:13).

The customary division into two Testaments unfortunately obscures this marvelous unity of God's program of Revelation, but the line is continuous from Moses to John — and indeed beyond him, unto the present day.

THE WORDS OF CHRIST

Christ promised His Disciples that after His Ascension, He would send them His Holy Spirit, Who would empower them to bear witness to Him in the world, and would bear witness with them (Lk. 24:48-49; Jn. 14:26; 15:26-27; Acts 1:8). That this includes prophetic inspiration is clear from Matthew 10:19-20; John 16:12-15; etc.

One of the major results of the effusion of the Holy Spirit on all flesh is that *"they shall prophesy,"* including not only prophetic words, but also visions and dreams (Acts 2:18). Every Christian is potentially a *"Prophecy,"* for the Spirit given generally to the Church for its testimony to Christ is *"the Spirit of Prophecy"* (I Cor. 14:31; Rev. 19:10).

THE OFFICE OF THE PROPHET

The Office of the Prophet is somewhat different than the mere potential available to all Believers (Eph. 4:11; I Cor. 12:10; 14:5). While there are many Spirit-filled Christians who have the *"gift of prophecy"* (I Cor. 12:10), these do not necessarily stand in the *"Office of the Prophet."* The simple Gift of Prophecy, as one might say, speaks unto men to edification, and exhortation, and comfort (I Cor. 14:3). But the Office of the Prophet is totally different.

The man or woman who stands in the *"Office of the Prophet"* at times is used of God to *"foretell"* events, which are to come to pass in the near or distance future. As well, and more specifically, even as the Ministries of Jeremiah and Ezekiel bear out, the God-called Prophet is a *"Preacher of Righteousness"* (II Pet. 2:5). While all Preachers should be Preachers of Righteousness, still, the one who truly stands in the Office of the Prophet will have a greater authority about his Message than other Preachers. As well, the Lord will lead him to address subjects and false doctrine in a way and manner in which others will not be used.

THE SPIRITS OF THE PROPHETS

The spirits of Prophets are subject to Prophets (II Cor. 14:32), so that Prophecy is neither to be abused by people succumbing to any supposedly uncontrollable ecstatic frenzy, nor to be exercised without the check of other members of the Body, notably the Elders and other Prophets weighing or discerning the accuracy and reliability of utterances purporting to issue from the Holy Spirit (I Cor. 14:29-33).

It was doubtless such abuses which led the Apostle Paul to write: *"Do not quench the Spirit. Do not despise prophesying, but test everything; hold fast what is good"* (I Thess. 5:19-21) — with a similar balance to that shown by him towards *"tongues"* (I Cor. 14:39-40).

Testing or weighing prophetic utterances is all the more necessary in view of the warnings of both the New Testament and the Old Testament against false prophets and false prophecy, by which Satan seeks to lead the unwary astray (Mat. 7:15; 24:11, 24; II Pet. 2:1; I Jn. 4:1).

It is deplorable that presently, prophecies are uttered by so-called prophets with the dates and specifics outlined, but which do not come to pass. And yet the Church, seemingly oblivious to the falseness of these messages and these messengers, pass it off as if it did not happen. False prophets give out false messages; therefore, both the false message and the false prophet should be set aside, and identified as to what they truly are.

As well, false prophets will, on occasion, work miracles (Mk. 13:22), but as in the Old Testament (Deut. 13:1-5), are not to be given credence merely on that account. The testing of any prophetic utterance will be in accordance with our Lord's warning, *"You will know them by their fruits"* (Mat. 7:20), and will include their conformity to the teachings of Scripture, of Christ, and of His Apostles in both content and character.

Also, Paul stresses the fact that even with True Prophets, this gift is unprofitable and jarring in its exercise, unless it proceeds from a loving heart and is ministered in a loving way in the Church (I Cor. 12:31; 13:3).

PREACHING AND TEACHING

Some have argued that preaching and teaching are what is spoken of regarding New Testament Prophecy; however, while evangelistic proclamation, or even a teaching ministry, may on occasion approximate to Prophecy, they are not the same. While the Office of the Prophet certainly includes Preaching and Teaching, it by no means is limited to that. The Office of the Prophet presently differs not at all with those in the Old Testament or the New Testament, with but one exception.

THE WORD OF GOD

Whereas all Prophets (both past and present) are used of God to give a fresh Revelation of Divine Truth, as guidance to the Church, nation or individual, or to warn or to encourage by way of prediction as well as by reminders, such will also be in full accord with the written Word of Scripture, by which all such utterances must be tested. As such, this Word, will never serve as a doctrinal innovator (new doctrine), but to deliver the Word the Spirit gives in line with the Truth *"once for all delivered to the Saints"* (Jude, Vs. 3), which will challenge and encourage our Faith. In other words, if Prophecy is not according to the Word of God, it must be rejected out of hand.

Some of the Prophets of old, whether in the Old Testament or the New Testament, uttered that which not only was the Word of God, but as well, in Truth, became the Written Word of God as a Standard of Truth for all ages. However, such Revelation ended with the Apostle John giving us the Book of Revelation, which closed the Canon of Scripture (Rev. 22:21).

While that which is presently given by True Prophets of God is definitely the Word of God, it will always coincide perfectly with that which is already given (the Bible), and will never add to it, inasmuch as the Canon of Scripture, as stated, is finished and, thereby, completed.

PERSECUTION

Always in the New Testament, the Prophets of both Testaments are regarded as the pioneers of Faith, who stand on the front line in every age and reap the full blast of the wind of persecution stirred up in the world by the Devil against the people of God (Mat. 23:37; Lk. 11:47-50; Acts 7:52; I Thess. 2:15; Rev. 11:3-8; 16:6; 18:20, 24).

While the world will seldom accept the words of the True Prophet of God, regrettably and sadly, far too often the Church will not accept them either. And for the most part, persecution against the True Prophet of God comes from the Church. As Israel of old, the Church does not enjoy having its sins pointed out, and its wayward direction corrected.

The great yardstick of the True Prophet is, and ever must be, is he proclaiming *"Truth?"* If he is, then his word must be accepted.

But if the word proclaimed is known to be Truth, and yet the Church does not desire to accept that Truth, invariably, not being able to attack the Message, it will attack the Messenger. Fault will be found with the manner in which he delivers the Message or with his person, always which is a sure sign that the Message is being rejected.

APOSTLES AND PROPHETS

Regarding leadership, the Old Testament Church was led by the Ministry of the Prophets. They were the bearer of Truth, the dispenser of the Word, the signpost of direction, and as stated, above all, Preachers of Righteousness. Those who stand in the Office of the Prophet in this Dispensation of Grace, in a sense, fill the same role, but with one exception. It is the *"Apostle"* now who serves as the de facto leader of the Church. This is borne out in the Book of Acts and the Epistles.

Apostles are those who are given a special Message by the Lord, emphasizing the Word of God in a certain aspect. In other words, the Message the Lord has given the Apostle, which will always coincide perfectly with the Word of God, is meant to lead the entirety of the Church, in effect, serving as direction. To be sure, all true Apostles will not have the same emphasis, but will definitely have the same foundation, which is the Word of God.

As well, Apostles, as evidenced by the New Testament Apostles, can serve, and, in fact, do serve at times, in all aspects of the five-fold Callings of *"Apostles, Prophets, Evangelists, Pastors and Teachers"* (Eph. 4:11). We find this in the Ministry of Paul, and in fact, all other Apostles, which information is given in the Book of Acts and the Epistles.

It is ironical, the Apostleship of Paul, perhaps the greatest Apostle of all, was not accepted by some in the Early Church, with him continually having to proclaim his calling into the Office of the Apostle (Rom. 1:1; I Cor. 1:1; II Cor. 1:1; Gal. 1:1; etc.).

(17) "LIKEWISE, THOU SON OF MAN, SET YOUR FACE AGAINST THE DAUGHTERS OF YOUR PEOPLE, WHICH PROPHESY OUT OF THEIR OWN HEART; AND PROPHESY THOU AGAINST THEM.

(18) "AND SAY, THUS SAITH THE LORD GOD; WOE TO THE WOMEN WHO SEW PILLOWS TO ALL ARMHOLES, AND MAKE KERCHIEFS UPON THE HEAD OF EVERY STATURE TO HUNT SOULS! WILL YOU HUNT THE SOULS OF MY PEOPLE,

AND WILL YOU SAVE THE SOULS ALIVE WHO COME UNTO YOU?

(19) "AND WILL YOU POLLUTE ME AMONG MY PEOPLE FOR HANDFULS OF BARLEY AND FOR PIECES OF BREAD, TO SLAY THE SOULS WHO SHOULD NOT DIE, AND TO SAVE THE SOULS ALIVE WHO SHOULD NOT LIVE, BY YOUR LYING TO MY PEOPLE WHO HEAR YOUR LIES?

(20) "WHEREFORE THUS SAITH THE LORD GOD; BEHOLD, I AM AGAINST YOUR PILLOWS, WHEREWITH YOU THERE HUNT THE SOULS TO MAKE THEM FLY, AND I WILL TEAR THEM FROM YOUR ARMS, AND WILL LET THE SOULS GO, EVEN THE SOULS THAT YOU HUNT TO MAKE THEM FLY.

(21) "YOUR KERCHIEFS ALSO WILL I TEAR, AND DELIVER MY PEOPLE OUT OF YOUR HAND, AND THEY SHALL BE NO MORE IN YOUR HAND TO BE HUNTED; AND YOU SHALL KNOW THAT I AM THE LORD.

(22) "BECAUSE WITH LIES YOU HAVE MADE THE HEART OF THE RIGHTEOUS SAD, WHOM I HAVE NOT MADE SAD; AND STRENGTHENED THE HANDS OF THE WICKED, THAT HE SHOULD NOT RETURN FROM HIS WICKED WAY, BY PROMISING HIM LIFE:

(23) "THEREFORE YOU SHALL SEE NO MORE VANITY, NOR DIVINE DIVINATIONS: FOR I WILL DELIVER MY PEOPLE OUT OF YOUR HAND: AND YOU SHALL KNOW THAT I AM THE LORD."

The synopsis is:

1. The "*pillows*" symbolized the teaching which gave a false rest, and regrettably, which the people wished to hear.

2. The ornamental coverings for the head picture attractive and pleasing doctrines which obscure the facts of death and the judgment to come.

3. These false prophets and false prophetesses promised "*life*" to their listeners, but in effect, killed them, i.e., "*destroyed them spiritually.*"

PILLOW PROPHETS

As verses 17 through 23 proclaim, there were prophetesses, which of course speak of women who claim to function in that Office.

NOTES

No doubt, there were some, if not many of these, along with the men who were false prophets, in both Judah and Babylonia, with the latter referring to the Exiles. While women certainly can function in this Office, these particular ones were false.

The Holy Spirit, through Ezekiel, used the symbolism of "*pillows,*" to portray the easy message of these prophetesses and the "*rest*" which they promised. A false message will bring about a temporal "*rest,*" or as the Holy Spirit has already said in Verse 10, a temporary peace.

But we must remember, even as Verses 18 through 20 proclaim, it is souls which are at stake, which means that what is being addressed is the single most important thing in the world. Jesus said: *"For what is a man profited, if he shall gain the whole world, and lose his own soul? Or, what shall a man give in exchange for his soul?"* (Mat. 16:26).

The idea is, those who listened to these false prophets, whether men or women, died eternally lost. And to be sure, it was much easier to believe the false prophets than it was the Lord's True Prophets, Jeremiah and Ezekiel. In fact, it has always been that way.

THE MESSAGE OF THE CROSS

Bringing this scenario up to this present time, it is basically the same now as then. The message hasn't changed, whether false or true, and God's Way certainly hasn't changed, and, in fact, never will change.

Having sought the Lord for years, even doing so day and night, and with tears, and I exaggerate not, in 1997 the Lord began to open up to me the Message of the Cross. It was the answer to my tears, my pleas, my petitions, my quest. To be sure, during those intervening years, the Lord moved mightily upon my heart many times, but I knew that this for which I sought had not yet been given. And when it did come, I knew beyond the shadow of a doubt, and instantly, that this was the Lord. That which He told me, "*The solution which you seek is found in the Cross,*" was totally and completely Scriptural. In fact, He took me first of all to Romans Chapter 6 and began to open it up to me. As I dictate these notes in June 2003, nearly six years have passed, and that Revelation is still unfolding, still revealing itself. I have an idea, as previously stated in this Volume, that this Revelation will never end.

The truth is, it is impossible to exhaust what Christ has done for us at the Cross. The magnitude of that victory, I think, will never be totally plumbed, as it regards its height and its depth, as well as its length and its breadth. That's why Paul referred to it as the *"Everlasting Covenant"* (Heb. 13:20). When I think of the magnitude of what the Lord has given me, and when I consider, even as Paul said, *"Unto me, who am less than the least of all Saints, is this Grace given"* (Eph. 3:8), I can only stand amazed!

THE ACCEPTANCE OF THE CROSS

And then, when I immediately began to preach and teach this Message, this Message of Victory, this Message of Deliverance, I just knew that once this great Revelation of the Cross was made known, that all Believers would instantly accept its provision. To my dismay, I found the very opposite. While a few believed, most didn't!

Why?

While we have already addressed this in this Volume as it regards *"unbelief,"* the reasons must be looked at as to why the unbelief is present in the heart of a Believer, which within itself is an oxymoron.

For one to accept the Cross, one must reject everything else. All of man's glosses, additions, in fact, all the ways of man must be given up, and in totality. There is nothing that strikes at the very heart of the person like the Cross. It exposes all false doctrine, it exposes all self-will, and in fact, everything that is wrong. And when one doesn't understand the Cross, to be sure, much is wrong. And the truth is, most people do not want to give up their pet sins, their self-will, their place and position, etc.

The Cross demands total and complete allegiance to Christ, which means that such total allegiance to man, which religion demands, is totally eliminated. This puts one on a collision course with most religious Denominations, most Preachers, all erroneous doctrine, in effect, exposing it all.

Those who preach a false message, which brings about a false rest, are always popular. The Church, by and large, receives them with open arms. I found to my dismay, that most of the Church rejects the Cross, and for all of the reasons I've given, plus many we haven't addressed.

The Cross tears down all religious pretense, and to be sure, religious men love their pretense. As someone has said, *"The doing of religion is the most powerful narcotic there is."*

So, the Holy Spirit ends this Thirteenth Chapter of Ezekiel by saying, *"with lies you have made the heart of the righteous sad, whom I have not made sad; and strengthened the hands of the wicked, that he should not return from his wicked way, by promising him life."*

The Lord refers to this as *"vanity,"* which means *"empty nothings,"* and *"divinations,"* which is a form of witchcraft, which these prophetesses referred to as being *"Divine,"* meaning that they claimed that their message was of the Lord.

God give us true Preachers who will preach the Word without fear, without favor, without compromise. That alone is the Salvation of a people.

> *"Naught have I gotten but what I received,*
> *"Grace has bestowed it since I have believed,*
> *"Boasting excluded, pride I abase,*
> *"I'm only a Believer saved by Grace!"*
>
> *"Once I was foolish, and sin ruled my heart,*
> *"Causing my footsteps from God to depart;*
> *"Jesus has found me, happy my case;*
> *"I now am a Believer saved by Grace!"*
>
> *"Tears unavailing, no merit had I;*
> *"Mercy had saved me, or else I must die;*
> *"Sin had alarmed me, fearing God's face;*
> *"But now I'm a Believer saved by Grace!"*
>
> *"Suffer a sinner whose heart overflows,*
> *"Loving his Saviour to tell what he knows;*

"Once more to tell it would I embrace,
"I'm only a Believer saved by Grace!"

CHAPTER 14

(1) "THEN CAME CERTAIN OF THE ELDERS OF ISRAEL UNTO ME, AND SAT BEFORE ME.

(2) "AND THE WORD OF THE LORD CAME UNTO ME, SAYING,

(3) "SON OF MAN, THESE MEN HAVE SET UP THEIR IDOLS IN THEIR HEART, AND PUT THE STUMBLINGBLOCK OF THEIR INIQUITY BEFORE THEIR FACE: SHOULD I BE INQUIRED OF AT ALL BY THEM?

(4) "THEREFORE SPEAK UNTO THEM, AND SAY UNTO THEM, THUS SAITH THE LORD GOD; EVERY MAN OF THE HOUSE OF ISRAEL WHO SETS UP HIS IDOLS IN HIS HEART, AND PUTS THE STUMBLINGBLOCK OF HIS INIQUITY BEFORE HIS FACE, AND COMES TO THE PROPHET; I THE LORD WILL ANSWER HIM WHO COMES ACCORDING TO THE MULTITUDE OF HIS IDOLS;

(5) "THAT I MAY TAKE THE HOUSE OF ISRAEL IN THEIR OWN HEART, BECAUSE THEY ARE ALL ESTRANGED FROM ME THROUGH THEIR IDOLS."

The diagram is:

1. However fair the outward profession of Faith in God may be, the Holy Spirit can unmask the evil lodged within the heart.

2. Some of the Elders of Israel sought for Divine guidance, but the Holy Spirit through the Prophet tells them that the idols are in their hearts.

3. God cannot have fellowship with evil; and He, therefore, not only refuses to answer such prayers, but He replies to them with just Judgment.

4. Servants of the Lord should, like Ezekiel, courageously tell such applicants that God does not hear the prayer of the lip if iniquity is cherished in the heart (Ps. 66:18).

IDOLS

The *"Elders of Israel,"* of Verse 1, concerned those among the captives. They had evidently come to Ezekiel asking for prayer and guidance, but like so many; they wanted God's help but not God's Way. They wanted Salvation without giving up their sin. As they represented Israel of old, they represent the modern Church as well.

When the Lord spoke to Ezekiel concerning the petitions of these people, it was a word that they did not desire to hear. In fact, what they would hear would not at all be to their liking. Therefore, as most, they would seek another Church to attend! In fact, most people attend a Church where they can hear what they desire to hear, instead of a Church where they can hear what they need to hear. They need to hear the Word of God and all of the Word of God. They must, as well, obey it!

Verse 3 says, *"These men have set up their idols in their heart."* It goes to the very seat of the problem.

What type of idols?

These men were not falling down before heathenistic idols, as did the population of Babylonia. Idols were in their heart, and what does that mean?

Even though this word was given to these individuals some 2,500 years ago, it is still just as appropriate presently, as it was then. An idol of the heart is anything, which comes between the person and the Lord, whatever it might be! It is easy to make an idol out of anything, even legitimate things. One's family is certainly legitimate; however, if our family is put before God, then it becomes an idol. As well, religion is probably the greatest idol of all!

THE HOLY SPIRIT

Only the Holy Spirit can unmask the idols lodged within the heart. That is His business and He does it well, at least when given the opportunity.

Idols in the Old Testament consisted of graven and molten images, pillars, the Asherah and Teraphim.

The Old Testament polemic against idolatry, carried on chiefly by Prophets and Psalmists, recognizes the same two Truths, which Paul was later to affirm: that the idol was nothing, but, nevertheless there was demonic spiritual force to be reckoned with, and the idol, therefore, consisted of a definite spiritual negative, to say the least (Isa. 44:6-20; I Cor. 8:4; 10:19-20). Thus, the idol is nothing at all: man made it (Isa. 2:8); its very composition and construction proclaim its futility (Isa. 40:18-20; 41:6-7; 44:9-20). The Prophets derisively named them *"Gillulim,"* which meant *"dung pellets."*

However, even though the idol was nothing, no one could touch an idol and come away unscathed. Man's contact with the false god infects him with a deadly spiritual blindness of heart and mind (Isa. 44:18). Though what he worships is mere *"ashes,"* yet, it is full of the poison of spiritual delusion (Isa. 44:20). Those who worship idols become like them (Ps. 115:8; Jer. 2:5; Hos. 9:10), because of the reality of evil power (demon spirits) behind the idol.

THE NEW TESTAMENT AND IDOLS

The New Testament recognizes, as did the Holy Spirit through Ezekiel, that the peril of idolatry exists even where material idols are not fashioned. In other words, as here stated, they are set up in the heart.

The association of idolatry with sexual sins in Galatians 5:19-20 is outlined. As well, covetousness is linked with idolatry (I Cor. 5:11; Eph. 5:5; Col. 3:5).

John, having urged the finality and fullness of Revelation in Christ, warns that any deviation from the Bible is idolatry (I Jn. 5:19-21). The idol is whatever claims that loyalty which belongs to God Alone (Isa. 42:8).

(6) "THEREFORE SAY UNTO THE HOUSE OF ISRAEL, THUS SAITH THE LORD GOD; REPENT, AND TURN YOURSELVES FROM YOUR IDOLS; AND TURN AWAY YOUR FACES FROM ALL YOUR ABOMINATIONS.

(7) "FOR EVERY ONE OF THE HOUSE OF ISRAEL, OR OF THE STRANGER WHO SOJOURNS IN ISRAEL, WHICH SEPARATES HIMSELF FROM ME, AND SETS UP HIS IDOLS IN HIS HEART, AND PUTS THE STUMBLINGBLOCK OF HIS INIQUITY BEFORE HIS FACE, AND COMES TO A PROPHET TO ENQUIRE OF HIM CONCERNING ME; I THE LORD WILL ANSWER HIM BY MYSELF:

(8) "AND I WILL SET MY FACE AGAINST THAT MAN, AND WILL MAKE HIM A SIGN AND A PROVERB, AND I WILL CUT HIM OFF FROM THE MIDST OF MY PEOPLE; AND YOU SHALL KNOW THAT I AM THE LORD.

(9) "AND IF THE PROPHET BE DECEIVED WHEN HE HAS SPOKEN A THING, I THE LORD HAVE DECEIVED THAT PROPHET, AND I WILL STRETCH OUT MY HAND UPON HIM, AND WILL DESTROY HIM FROM THE MIDST OF MY PEOPLE ISRAEL.

(10) "AND THEY SHALL BEAR THE PUNISHMENT OF THEIR INIQUITY: THE PUNISHMENT OF THE PROPHET SHALL BE EVEN AS THE PUNISHMENT OF HIM WHO SEEKS UNTO HIM;

(11) "THAT THE HOUSE OF ISRAEL MAY GO NO MORE ASTRAY FROM ME, NEITHER BE POLLUTED ANY MORE WITH ALL THEIR TRANSGRESSIONS; BUT THAT THEY MAY BE MY PEOPLE, AND I MAY BE THEIR GOD, SAITH THE LORD GOD."

The composition is:

1. To set idolatrous objects before the eyes causes moral stumbling to the feet, while to set the Words of God's Book before the eyes, guards the feet from stumbling (Prov. 3:21-23).

2. A verbal reply was refused to these Elders, and a terrible response, in action, directly from the Hand of God Himself, promised.

3. But God loved and pitied these hypocrites, and the fact of this love added to the certitude and horror of the just doom that was impending over them. He cried to them to repent, no longer to keep far from Him, and He would receive and acknowledge them as His loved people — *"My People."*

4. It is the Cross alone, and Faith in that Finished Work, which can remove all idols from the heart.

REPENTANCE

The answer of the Lord to these Elders who had come to Ezekiel was, *"Repent, and turn yourselves from your idols; and turn away your faces from all your abominations"* (Vs. 6). The verbiage used by the Lord, *"turn"* and *"turn away,"* is an apt description of Repentance, which means *"to do an about face,"* in other words, to start going in the opposite direction.

WHAT IS TRUE REPENTANCE?

To merely repent of the act, which is what almost all Christians do, that is if they repent at all, does not at all address the problem, but actually, only the symptom. While the Lord will definitely hear such a petition (I Jn. 1:9), the truth is, what is causing particular sins, that is if symptoms only are addressed, remains in place, and will cause the same sins again, and again!

Now what do we mean by addressing the real problem?

The real problem is that Faith and trust have been placed in something other than the Cross, which denies the help of the Holy Spirit to the individual Christian; consequently, this is the real sin — rebellion against God's Prescribed Order, which is the Cross of Christ. In fact, the only answer for sin is the Cross. So, for the problem to be correctly addressed, whatever it might be, we must go to the real cause, thereby repenting to the Lord for our dependence on things, whatever they might be, other than Christ and Him Crucified.

Now because all of this is so very, very important, let me say it again.

REPENTANCE AND THE CROSS

Most Christians have never stopped to think as to the cause of their sinful failure, whatever that sinful failure might be. And the tragedy is, almost all sinful failure in the hearts and lives of Believers is habitual, meaning that it's happened over and over again, and for years. In fact, it steadily gets worse, because *"a little leaven* (corruption) *leaventh* (corrupts) *the whole lump"* (Gal. 5:9).

But the Truth is, precious few Christians have been taught anything about the cause of sin, so the cause has been left unaddressed, which means that the sin cycle continues, and for all the obvious reasons. Let's look a little closer at the real cause.

THE SIN NATURE

In the Sixth Chapter of Romans, the Apostle Paul addresses *"sin"* seventeen times. In the original Text, which refers to the Greek language, some fourteen times,

NOTES

he uses what is referred to as *"the definite article,"* which is the word *"the"* in front of the word *"sin."* So, in the original Text, it reads *"the sin,"* which means that he is not speaking of acts of sin, but rather the principle of sin, or rather, the sin nature. Two of the other times, the word *"sin"* is used as a noun, so, this means he is still referring to the sin nature. Only one time is he referring to acts of sin (Rom. 6:15).

WHAT IS THE SIN NATURE?

It is a result of the Fall in the Garden of Eden. One might say that one is bent in a certain direction, which is a direction of evil, instigated by Satan, and that it is his *"nature"* to do evil.

For instance, if it is to be noticed, a parent doesn't have to teach the child to lie, to steal, etc., the child will just do it automatically, portraying the sin nature. The child has to be taught not to lie, not to steal, etc.

Again, this is what Jesus was referring to when He said, *"For from within, out of the heart of men, proceed evil thoughts, adulteries, fornications, murders"* (Mk. 7:21).

To further illustrate that of which I speak, one can take a metal pipe, which is tall and straight, and is so in every direction. But if that pipe is bent, even though it is straightened back out, if pressure is applied, it will bend, and in the same spot where it was originally bent. It is the same with the sin nature. Man has a *"bent,"* which propels him toward evil due to the Fall. In fact, the sin nature totally rules and controls every unsaved person. In other words, everything they do militate towards sin.

When the believing sinner accepts Christ, due to the Cross, the sin nature is made ineffective, even though it still remains with the Christian. If the Christian functions according to the Word of God, he will have no trouble out of the sin nature whatsoever; however, if he doesn't function according to the Word of God, he will find himself being controlled by the sin nature, exactly as he was, at least in some manner, before he was saved.

THE FIRST THING

The first thing the Lord portrayed to me in the Revelation of the Cross was the *"sin nature."* He showed me what it was, how it worked, and did so from the Sixth Chapter of Romans. I found out later, that this was the very first thing that was shown to the Apostle Paul, as is evidenced, in the Seventh Chapter of Romans, which portrays the Apostle's personal experience immediately after he was saved and Baptized with the Holy Spirit. Not understanding at that time the Message of the Cross, the Apostle tried to live for God by means of the *"law,"* which made for a miserable existence. To Paul's credit, there was no one else in the world at that time who knew the Message of the Cross, that glorious Message being first of all delivered to Paul (Gal. 1:12). Paul then gave the Message of the Cross to us in his fourteen Epistles, but above all, in the Book of Romans. The modern Church addresses the sin nature in a variety of ways. Let's look at those ways, all of them being wrong, with the exception of one, and that is Grace.

IGNORANCE

Irrespective of the fact that a proper knowledge is required, that is, if the Believer is going to live Christlike. But the truth is, the modern Church is basically ignorant as it regards the *"sin nature,"* because it is seldom mentioned behind most pulpits.

Most Believers may have heard the term, but have absolutely no knowledge as to exactly what it is. In other words, due to the paucity of preaching and teaching on the subject, ignorance reigns in this arena.

However, this is an ignorance that can lead to spiritual wreckage. Please understand that this ignorance is not bliss. The effects of the sin nature will be just as real in such a person's life, causing all types of problems.

At least one of the reasons that there is such an appalling ignorance concerning this all-important subject is because of ignorance regarding the Cross, as it regards our Sanctification. In fact, I think it is impossible for one to properly understand the Cross, unless one properly understands the sin nature. The bitter truth is, the modern Church understands the Cross almost not at all.

DENIAL

There is a great segment of the Church, more specifically, the Word of Faith Doctrine, which denies the presence of the sin nature in the heart and life of the Believer. While they possibly believe that such existed before conversion, they claim that the sin nature no longer exists after one comes to Christ.

My answer to that is this: if there is no sin nature in the heart and life of the Believer, then why did Paul address it so graphically in the Sixth Chapter of Romans, and elsewhere? In fact, the Apostle tells us that through Christ and what He did at the Cross, and our Faith in that Finished Work, that we are *"dead unto the sin nature"*; however, he doesn't say that the sin nature is dead, only that we are dead to that nature (Rom. 6:11).

No! I hardly think that the Holy Spirit would have gone to all the trouble He did in giving Paul this information, and being as graphic about it as He was, regarding something that doesn't exist. And please remember, the Sixth Chapter of Romans is not written to the unsaved, but rather to Believers.

Yes! As the Text abundantly brings out, as it regards the Sixth Chapter of Romans, with the definite article *"the"* placed some fourteen times before the word *"sin,"* we know that Paul is speaking there of the *"evil nature"* or *"the sin nature."*

To be sure, once the trump sounds, and this physical body is redeemed (Rom. 8:23), the sin nature will then be forever gone. But until then, it remains.

However, and as previously stated, if it is addressed according to the Word of God, it will be dormant in the life of the Believer, causing no problem whatsoever. It is only when the Believer tries to live for God by means of *"law"* instead of *"Grace,"* that the sin nature becomes a real problem, actually ruling and reigning in the life of the Believer (Rom. 6:12).

LICENSE

Unfortunately, there are many Christians who know somewhat about the sin nature, and use it as a *"license"* to sin. For instance, they misinterpret Romans 7:15. Paul said there:

"For that which I do I allow (understand) *not: for what I would, that do I not; but what I hate, that do I."*

Paul addressed this by asking the question,

"What shall we say then? Shall we continue in sin (the sin nature), *that Grace may abound?*

"God forbid. How shall we, who are dead to the sin nature, live any longer therein?" (Rom. 6:1-2).

Every Believer must understand, even as this Sixth Chapter of Romans graphically bears out, the Lord doesn't save us in sin, but rather from sin. The Cross addressed every aspect of sin, and if we properly understand the Cross, Victory will be ours instead of defeat.

STRUGGLE

Unfortunately, many good Christians address the sin nature, whether they understand much about the sin nature or not, by a continuous *"struggle"* with sin, thinking that this is what Christianity is supposed to be like. But once again, this is not Biblical as well!

While at times, I will admit, there is a struggle, that of which I speak is a far cry from the *"struggle"* of the person who is trying to defeat the sin nature by means other than the Cross. In fact, such a struggle, which is unscriptural, makes the Christian experience miserable. If the truth were known, many, if not most, Christians are miserably saved. And it's all because of this constant *"struggle."*

Listen to our Lord: *"Come unto Me, all you who labor and are heavy laden, and I will give you rest.*

"Take My yoke upon you, and learn of Me; for I am meek and lowly in heart: and you shall find rest unto your souls.

"For My yoke is easy, and My burden is light" (Mat. 11:28-30).

Please notice that Jesus keeps talking about *"rest."* Does this of which our Lord is speaking match up with the constant *"struggle"* of many good Christians? I think not!

What do I mean by the statement, *"good Christian"*?

The very fact of the *"struggle,"* and please believe me, this can be a struggle of unprecedented proportions, proclaims the truth that these people, whoever they might be, are *"good Christians."* The person who isn't a good Christian won't struggle too very much against sin, as should be obvious. The struggle

NOTES

of which I speak pertains to those who truly love the Lord, and who truly want to please the Lord, and desire to be what God wants them to be. They see the problems in their lives, which are wrong, and they struggle against those problems, and do so with great zeal and effort, all to no avail. Why?

Paul said, as it regards this: *"I do not frustrate the Grace of God: for if Righteousness come by the Law, then Christ is dead in vain"* (Gal. 2:21).

Now let's look at the only way that the sin nature can be successfully approached, with victory guaranteed.

GRACE

The Christian is to understand that while he has a sin nature, that he, as stated, is *"dead to the sin nature,"* which means that it has no control over him whatsoever. This is all because of the Cross (Rom. 6:3-5, 11). For the Believer to be what he ought to be in the Lord, there must be an uninterrupted flow of Grace to the Believer's heart and life. How does this come about?

First of all, the Grace of God is simply the Goodness of God; it is administered by the Holy Spirit. In fact, Christ is the Source, while the Cross is the means. In this, as Paul taught us in Romans, Chapter 6, the Believer is to ever understand, exactly as just stated, that the Cross of Christ is the *"means"* by which all of these wonderful things are administered to us, and done so by the Holy Spirit (Rom. 8:2).

Understanding this, the Believer is to ever make the Cross the Object of his Faith, even as Paul proclaims to us in the Sixth Chapter of Romans (Vss. 3-5). The Cross ever being the Object of our Faith, the Holy Spirit can then work unfettered within our hearts and lives, bringing about the fruit of the Spirit, as well as Gifts of the Spirit, in other words, developing Righteousness and Holiness within our lives, which He Alone can do. But it's all, and without exception, based on the Cross.

It is not possible for Grace to come to the Believer as it should, unless the Believer properly understands the Cross, as it regards the Believer's Sanctification, which refers to how one lives for God, even on a daily basis (Lk. 9:23).

If the Believer doesn't understand the

Cross, at least as it regards our Sanctification, without fail, the Believer is going to revert to Law of one type or the other. What do we mean by that?

THE LAW

When Paul refers to the "Law" in any one of his fourteen Epistles, he is either speaking of the Law of Moses, and especially the moral part of that Law, which is the Ten Commandments (Ex., Chpt. 20), or else he is speaking of any type of Law that we make up ourselves, or our Church makes up, or our Denomination, or Preachers, etc.

Most of the time, the laws that we make up are good within themselves, just as the Law of Moses was good (Rom. 7:12). Because the laws which we fabricate are good, and I'm referring to laws that we try to live by in order to be Righteous or Holy, etc., this deceives us. Because they are good, it seems to us that this is the way to go; however, all it tends to do is to frustrate the Grace of God, which means to stop the Grace of God, which then leaves the Believer in a perilous situation (Gal. 2:21).

GRACE OR LAW

There are only two places for humanity to be, and that is either *"Law"* or *"Grace."* As is obvious, every single unsaved person on the face of the Earth is under Law, which immediately condemns him or her, etc. But the sad fact is, while most Christians think they are under Grace, in fact, they are under Law. Let's examine why?

Many Christians think that because this is the dispensation of Grace, that Grace just automatically comes to them. Were that the case, why did Paul talk about *"frustrating the Grace of God"* (Gal. 2:21), or even *"falling from Grace"?* (Gal. 5:4).

No, Grace doesn't automatically come to Believers, just because this is the Dispensation of Grace. When it comes to Grace, God had just as much Grace three thousand years ago as He does now. The difference is, because the blood of bulls and goats could not take away sins (Heb. 10:4), the sin debt remained on each and every human being, even Believers, which greatly limited the Lord as to what He could do, which means that Grace was limited as well.

The truth is, every single thing that God has ever done with man, and that from the beginning, has always been by Grace (Eph. 2:8-9). Otherwise, man could have experienced nothing good from God whatsoever. Because if man tries to function by Law, he is automatically condemned, which demands the Wrath of God. Faith in Christ and what Christ did at the Cross, all typified by the offering up of clean animals in Old Testament Times, enabled God to show Believers at that time at least a modicum of Grace.

But it awaited the Cross of Calvary before the sin debt could be lifted, because the Blood of Jesus Christ, God's Son, then atoned for all sin. Grace can now flow in an uninterrupted stream to the Child of God, all because of the Cross.

So, the reason that Believers do not experience the Grace of God as they should is because their Faith is in something other than the Cross, and that something, whatever name they may apply to it, is none other than *"Law."* And again, I quote Paul: *"If Righteousness come by the Law, then Christ is dead in vain"* (Gal. 2:21).

The idea is that there is no way that a person can attain to Righteousness, which refers to victory over all sin, by trying to live for God through a system of Laws. It is impossible! If he could do so, Jesus didn't need to come down here and die on a Cross, which is exactly what the Apostle is saying (Gal. 2:21).

Once again, let us reiterate, if the Believer doesn't understand the Cross as it regards Sanctification, the Believer is going to revert to Law. No matter what he calls it, no matter what he thinks, whether he understands it or not, he is living by *"Law,"* which guarantees that the *"sin nature"* is going to come alive within his heart and life, and begin to rule and reign, causing untold problems and difficulties.

WHAT DO WE MEAN, UNDERSTAND THE CROSS AS IT REFERS TO SANCTIFICATION?

Almost every Christian understands the Cross, at least after a fashion, as it regards Salvation. Probably one of the greatest statements, and one of the most beautiful statements, is *"Jesus died for me."* But the tragedy is, most have been taught, whether by example, or whether by erroneous teaching, to park the Cross at their Salvation experience. They are then told to go on to deeper and greater things.

Let it ever be understood, if any Believer goes beyond the Cross, he loses his way, which means instead of *"going on,"* he is rather *"going backwards."* There is nothing beyond the Cross, the Cross actually being the Foundation of all Doctrine, which means that every single thing that we receive from the Lord is based upon His great Sacrifice (Heb. 13:20; Eph. 2:13-18).

But when one mentions *"Sanctification,"* which refers to how we live for God, most people have never linked the Cross whatsoever to this all-important aspect of the Believer's life, which, in effect, is his life — and despite the fact that Paul graphically explains all of this to us in Romans, Chapter 6.

The trouble is, Believers, because of ignorance, downright unbelief, or trying to live for God by means of *"Law,"* which we've already discussed, can never be acceptable to the Lord, and for all the obvious reasons.

First of all, man cannot keep the Law anyway; as well, Jesus has already kept it for us, as it regards His Perfect Life; and He also satisfied its just demands by the Sacrificial Offering of Himself on the Cross, which paid the penalty for all sin, thereby satisfying the demands of the broken Law (Col. 2:14-15).

The Cross is just as important to my Sanctification as it is to my Salvation. In fact, there is no difference in our response to the Cross as it regards either one. The problem with Believers is, we think we can live for God by our own imaginations and means, which mean that we are actually writing our own Bible, and devising a way of Salvation other than that which the Lord has given us. We certainly don't think of it in that vein, but that's exactly what it is! In fact, for anyone to try to live for God by means other than Christ and the Cross is grossly insulting Christ. To be brief, as it regards our Sanctification, the Believer is to ever understand, even as we've already explained time and time again, that the Cross has made everything possible that

NOTES

we receive from the Lord; consequently, our Faith is to ever be anchored in the Finished Work of Christ (Rom. 6:3-14). That being the case, the Holy Spirit, Who works exclusively within the framework of the Sacrifice Christ, will work grandly within our lives, bringing about that which needs to be brought about, which He Alone can do (Rom. 8:1-2, 11).

DECEPTION

Verses 7 through 11 proclaim a powerful truth.

If a Prophet is deceived, and desires to stay in that deception, Verse 9 plainly says, *"I the LORD have deceived that Prophet."* In other words, if that's the road that such an individual desires to travel, the road of deception, the Lord plainly states here that He will aid the process. That is a chilling thought!

The Judgment of such a Preacher is pronounced, because they lead many people astray. In fact, every single Believer in this world is either walking in victory, or the lack thereof, because they have listened to a certain Preacher. If the Preacher leads them correctly, which means that he leads them according to Scripture, they are blessed indeed! Otherwise, to be blunt and simple, they are cursed (Gal. 1:8-9).

DECEPTION AND THE CROSS

Unbelief is a part and parcel of deception.

As the Lord helps us to proclaim this grand Message of the Cross, which is, and which has always been, the primary Message in the sight of God, I marvel as I watch the response of Preachers to this Message. Some express no interest, while others outright reject the Foundation of the Christian Faith.

When this is done, this says that the person, whoever they might be, has willfully set and charted a course for himself or herself which is the opposite of the Word of God. That being the case, the Lord allows things to happen which will speed them on their course even at a faster rate. In other words, He will help them, even as Ezekiel proclaims, to become more and more deceived. As stated, it is chilling, because it guarantees the loss of the soul of such a person.

Paul said: *"Now the Spirit speaks expressly, that in the latter times some shall depart from the Faith, giving heed to seducing spirits, and doctrines of devils"* (I Tim. 4:1).

(12) "THE WORD OF THE LORD CAME AGAIN TO ME, SAYING,

(13) "SON OF MAN, WHEN THE LAND SINS AGAINST ME BY TRESPASSING GRIEVOUSLY, THEN WILL I STRETCH OUT MY HAND UPON IT, AND WILL BREAK THE STAFF OF THE BREAD THEREOF, AND WILL SEND FAMINE UPON IT, AND WILL CUT OFF MAN AND BEAST FROM IT:

(14) "THOUGH THESE THREE MEN, NOAH, DANIEL, AND JOB, WERE IN IT, THEY SHOULD DELIVER BUT THEIR OWN SOULS BY THEIR RIGHTEOUSNESS, SAITH THE LORD GOD.

(15) "IF I CAUSE NOISOME BEASTS TO PASS THROUGH THE LAND, AND THEY SPOIL IT, SO THAT IT BE DESOLATE, THAT NO MAN MAY PASS THROUGH BECAUSE OF THE BEASTS.

(16) "THOUGH THESE THREE MEN WERE IN IT, AS I LIVE, SAYS THE LORD GOD, THEY SHALL DELIVER NEITHER SONS NOR DAUGHTERS; THEY ONLY SHALL BE DELIVERED, BUT THE LAND SHALL BE DESOLATE.

(17) "OR IF I BRING A SWORD UPON THAT LAND, AND SAY, SWORD, GO THROUGH THE LAND; SO THAT I CUT OFF MAN AND BEAST FROM IT:

(18) "THOUGH THESE THREE MEN WERE IN IT, AS I LIVE, SAYS THE LORD GOD, THEY SHALL DELIVER NEITHER SONS NOR DAUGHTERS, BUT THEY ONLY SHALL BE DELIVERED THEMSELVES.

(19) "OR IF I SEND A PESTILENCE INTO THAT LAND, AND POUR OUT MY FURY UPON IT IN BLOOD, TO CUT OFF FROM IT MAN AND BEAST:

(20) "THOUGH NOAH, DANIEL, AND JOB, WERE IN IT, AS I LIVE, SAYS THE LORD GOD, THEY SHALL DELIVER NEITHER SON NOR DAUGHTER; THEY SHALL BUT DELIVER THEIR OWN SOULS BY THEIR RIGHTEOUSNESS.

(21) "FOR THUS SAITH THE LORD GOD; HOW MUCH MORE WHEN I SEND MY FOUR SORE JUDGMENTS UPON JERUSALEM, THE SWORD, AND THE FAMINE, AND THE NOISOME BEAST, AND THE PESTILENCE, TO CUT OFF FROM IT MAN AND BEAST?

(22) "YET, BEHOLD, THEREIN SHALL BE LEFT A REMNANT THAT SHALL BE BROUGHT FORTH, BOTH SONS AND DAUGHTERS: BEHOLD, THEY SHALL COME FORTH UNTO YOU, AND YOU SHALL SEE THEIR WAY AND THEIR DOINGS: AND YOU SHALL BE COMFORTED CONCERNING THE EVIL THAT I HAVE BROUGHT UPON JERUSALEM, EVEN CONCERNING ALL THAT I HAVE BROUGHT UPON IT.

(23) "AND THEY SHALL COMFORT YOU, WHEN YOU SEE THEIR WAYS AND THEIR DOINGS: AND YOU SHALL KNOW THAT I HAVE NOT DONE WITHOUT CAUSE ALL THAT I HAVE DONE IN IT, SAYS THE LORD GOD."

The overview is:

1. In Jeremiah 15:1, guilty Jerusalem was told that the intercession of Moses and Samuel (Ex. 32:11-14; Num. 14:13-20; I Sam. 7:8-12) would fail to avert her coming doom; in this Chapter, it is added that the presence in Jerusalem of Noah, Daniel, and Job would also fail to preserve it from destruction.

2. Noah's family owed their Salvation to him (Gen. 6:9, 18; 7:1), Daniel's companions were similarly saved (Dan. 2:12, 17, 49), and Job's three friends were pardoned because of Job's intercession (Job 42:7-9).

3. Neither this Chapter nor Jeremiah 15 can be quoted in support of the supposed value of intercession of dead Saints. The argument is the reverse; for Jeremiah 15:1 declares that Moses and Samuel being dead, their value as intercessors cease; and even if they were alive, their intercession would be unavailing.

PROSPERITY

Verse 13 proclaims the fact that the prosperity of a nation is directly linked to the spiritual prosperity of the people. The process may not be instant, but it is sure.

The greatest asset of the United States, and of any other nation for that matter, is the Born-Again Saints residing in that particular country. Of course, the nations in question do not know that. Even the United States, which one could say is probably more Christian than any other nation in the world, doesn't understand at all that of which I speak. It dismisses true Christians as being of no consequence, never once even remotely realizing that the Blessing of God upon any place, even an entire nation, is brought about primarily because of the Righteous souls in that particular place.

NOAH, DANIEL, AND JOB

The Fourteenth Verse, even though negative, proclaims the power of intercession by the Godly on behalf of the ungodly. The Lord has allowed Righteous men and women to enter into the carrying out of His Will and Plan by their Intercession. Actually, it is far greater than Him just allowing participation. Instead, at least in many cases, the carrying out of His Will is predicated on the Intercession of the Saints. Regrettably, Intercession, at least as listed here, is, for all practical purposes, a lost art in modern Christendom. Christians have been taught to confess the deed done, which will guarantee it being quickly carried out; however, such is not taught in Scripture. While a proper confession is certainly desired, still, interceding before God is that which brings about the desired result, even though at times it may require many years to do so.

But Judah and Jerusalem were so far gone, spiritually speaking, that even if Noah and Job were alive at that time in Judah (Daniel was then alive, and in Babylon), their Intercession would have no affect on the coming Judgment. While individual Repentance would always be accepted by the Lord, as far as the nation of Judah was concerned, as well as the city of Jerusalem, the Lord is emphatically stating that there is no point in praying for their Deliverance. While it would be three or four years before the Judgment would come, come surely it would!

From this, we learn that God has pronounced Judgment on certain nations, even though it may be a length of time before the Judgment is carried out.

Four times the Holy Spirit repeats the phraseology of Noah, Daniel, and Job not being able to deliver Judah, even if Noah,

Daniel and Job were then alive (Vss. 14, 16, 18, 20). Such repetition is meant to impress upon all the severity of the situation. One can feel the urgency of the Holy Spirit, with the terminology becoming stronger as the nearness of the Judgment approaches. At least one of the reasons for the repetition, and even the naming of Patriarchs alive and dead, is the idea held by Israel that inasmuch as the great Patriarchs were their blood, this would guarantee their protection. Tragically, there were not enough of these Patriarchs; as well, Salvation is a personal thing. As someone has well said, *"God has no grandchildren."*

"Oh for a closer walk with God,
"A calm and Heavenly frame,
"A light to shine upon the road
"That leads me to the Lamb!"

"Where is the blessedness I knew
"When first I saw the Lord?
"Where is the soul refreshing view
"Of Jesus and His Word?"

"The dearest idol I have known,
"Whatever that idol be,
"Help me to tear it from Thy Throne,
"And worship only Thee."

"So shall my walk be close with God,
"Calm and serene my frame;
"So purer light shall mark the road
"That leads me to the Lamb."

CHAPTER 15

(1) "AND THE WORD OF THE LORD CAME UNTO ME, SAYING,

(2) "SON OF MAN, WHAT IS THE VINE TREE MORE THAN ANY TREE, OR THAN A BRANCH WHICH IS AMONG THE TREES OF THE FOREST?

(3) "SHALL WOOD BE TAKEN THEREOF TO DO ANY WORK? OR WILL MEN TAKE A PIN OF IT TO HANG ANY VESSEL THEREON?

(4) "BEHOLD, IT IS CAST INTO THE FIRE FOR FUEL; THE FIRE DEVOURS BOTH THE ENDS OF IT, AND THE MIDST OF IT IS BURNED. IS IT MEET FOR ANY WORK?

(5) "BEHOLD, WHEN IT WAS WHOLE, IT WAS MEET FOR NO WORK: HOW MUCH LESS SHALL IT BE MEET YET FOR ANY WORK, WHEN THE FIRE HAS DEVOURED IT, AND IT IS BURNED?

(6) "THEREFORE THUS SAITH THE LORD GOD; AS THE VINE TREE AMONG THE TREES OF THE FOREST, WHICH I HAVE GIVEN TO THE FIRE FOR FUEL, SO WILL I GIVE THE INHABITANTS OF JERUSALEM.

(7) "AND I WILL SET MY FACE AGAINST THEM; THEY SHALL GO OUT FROM ONE FIRE, AND ANOTHER FIRE SHALL DEVOUR THEM; AND YOU SHALL KNOW THAT I AM THE LORD, WHEN I SET MY FACE AGAINST THEM.

(8) "AND I WILL MAKE THE LAND DESOLATE, BECAUSE THEY HAVE COMMITTED A TRESPASS, SAITH THE LORD GOD."

The construction is:
1. Israel, in the Scriptures, is symbolized as a vine, as an olive, and as a fig-tree.
2. The vine symbolized spiritual privilege.
3. The one business of the vine is to bear grapes. Otherwise it is worthless, except as firewood (Jn. 15:6). Israel was the vine brought out of Egypt whose one duty and privilege was to bear moral fruit unto God (Mat. 21:33-46).

THE VINE

This short Chapter pertains to Judah and what she should have been under God. The Lord is very graphic in His description, and what He said concerning Judah and Jerusalem of old can, as well, be said of each and every individual who follows the Lord.

The question of Verse 2, *"What is the Vine Tree more than any tree?"* refers to the Truth that if the Vine does not bring forth fruit, it is no more valuable than any other tree in the forest. Its sole function is to bear fruit.

Actually, Israel, at least within herself, was weaker than all the other nations round about her. And yet, it was the supreme nation, but only because of the Power of God, which was resident only as it bore fruit.

Likewise, the Church is of no earthly or heavenly consequence if it does not bear fruit. However, if it bears fruit, it serves as a light to a darkened world, as well as life, which Source is Christ.

Israel's problem was that it became lifted up in its own pride, which brought about self-righteousness. It forgot that its Blessings were solely from the Lord and not from its own intellect, wisdom, or righteousness. In doing this, it began to hold on to the world with one hand and God with the other. However, the Lord will not share place with anything or anyone! He is all or not at all! As Israel of old, so the Church of today!

WORTHLESS

The analogy drawn by the Holy Spirit in Verse 3 is that the Vine can be used for nothing except to bear fruit. It is useless and valueless even as timber, and actually not fit to even make simple pegs *"on which to hang a vessel."*

Israel was raised up for one purpose, to show forth the Grace and Glory of God. That was her only purpose in the world. And yet, she forgot that purpose and had to be destroyed.

Likewise, the only purpose of the Church is to call men out of an evil, worldly system, and do so by declaring the Grace and Glory of the Lord, very similar to Israel of old. As we have stated many times, it is not the purpose of the Church to save society, but instead, to save men out of society; consequently, society is doomed, which means the moment the Church becomes political, it is no longer spiritual.

REBELLION

The whole of this Chapter, and especially Verse 8, proclaims the fact that the cause of the doom of Judah is that it perversely fell into determined rebellion. In other words, Judah sinned against Light. Consequently, they were not merely sinners as the surrounding nations; they were worse for they were apostates, transgressors, and rebels. As stated, they sinned against Light, for to them alone had been given the Law, i.e., the Bible.

The sole mission of the Church is to proclaim the Gospel, which is, *"Jesus Christ and Him Crucified"* (I Cor. 1:17, 23). This means that the Church is not to be an entertainment center, a social center, or a political center. Neither is it to be an economic bellwether, nor a counseling center for psychology.

If that is correct, and it definitely is, where does this leave the modern Church, which is steeped in these things?

Man's problem is sin. It is the business of the Church to point this out. Man's solution is the Lord Jesus Christ. It is the business of the Church to point this out. Everything else is incidental, and of no consequence. So, for the Church to be what the Church ought to be, its sole interest must be Christ, and its sole Message must be the Cross (I Cor. 2:2).

> *"Almighty Lord, Whose Sov'reign light extends o'er every nation,*
> *"We bless You for the Gospel light that brought to us Salvation.*
> *"And unto Thee we raise our prayerful all in darkness dwellings;*
> *"That they with us Thy light may share, with us Thy praise be telling."*

> *"O, hear us when we call on Thee for all the truth possessing*
> *"That they may ever ready be to share the heav'nly blessing*
> *"To send to Earth's remotest shore the glad Gospel Story*
> *"That all who hear may then adore Jesus, the King of Glory."*

> *"As with Thine eyes Lord, may we see the world in darkness lying;*
> *"And may Thy love the motive be to save the lost, the dying.*
> *"The precious harvest waiting lies, but few the workers number*
> *"O Church of Christ! Arise! Arise! Arouse thee from thy slumber!"*

> *"O Lord; the impulse must be Thine, forgive our sloth, our dullness;*
> *"O quicken us with Life Divine, with all Thy Spirit's fullness.*
> *"So may our love and faith increase, our fervor and devotion*
> *"To speed the messengers of peace O'er every land and ocean."*

> *"There evermore be with them, Lord, and evermore befriend them;*

NOTES

> *"Be Thou their Shield and Great Reward to succour and defend them.*
> *"Prosper their faithful ministry, 'til, in the day appointed,*
> *"The kingdoms of the world shall be the realm of Thine Anointed."*

CHAPTER 16

(1) "AGAIN THE WORD OF THE LORD CAME UNTO ME, SAYING,

(2) "SON OF MAN, CAUSE JERUSALEM TO KNOW HER ABOMINATIONS,

(3) "AND SAY, THUS SAITH THE LORD GOD UNTO JERUSALEM; YOUR BIRTH AND YOUR NATIVITY IS OF THE LAND OF CANAAN; YOUR FATHER WAS AN AMORITE, AND YOUR MOTHER AN HITTITE.

(4) "AND AS FOR YOUR NATIVITY, IN THE DAY YOU WERE BORN YOUR NAVEL WAS NOT CUT, NEITHER WERE YOU WASHED IN WATER TO SUPPLE YOU; YOU WERE NOT SALTED AT ALL, NOR SWADDLED AT ALL.

(5) "NO EYE PITIED YOU, TO DO ANY OF THESE UNTO YOU, TO HAVE COMPASSION UPON YOU; BUT YOU WERE CAST OUT IN THE OPEN FIELD, TO THE LOATHING OF YOUR PERSON, IN THE DAY THAT YOU WERE BORN.

(6) "AND WHEN I PASSED BY YOU, AND SAW YOU POLLUTED IN YOUR OWN BLOOD, I SAID UNTO YOU WHEN YOU WERE IN YOUR BLOOD, LIVE; YES, I SAID UNTO YOU WHEN YOU WERE IN YOUR BLOOD, LIVE.

(7) "I HAVE CAUSED YOU TO MULTIPLY AS THE BUD OF THE FIELD, AND YOU HAVE INCREASED AND WAXED GREAT, AND YOU ARE COME TO EXCELLENT ORNAMENTS: YOUR BREASTS ARE FASHIONED, AND YOUR HAIR IS GROWN, WHEREAS YOU WERE NAKED AND BARE.

(8) "NOW WHEN I PASSED BY YOU, AND LOOKED UPON YOU, BEHOLD, YOUR TIME WAS THE TIME OF LOVE; AND I SPREAD MY SKIRT OVER YOU, AND COVERED YOUR NAKEDNESS: YES, I SWORE UNTO YOU AND ENTERED INTO A

COVENANT WITH YOU, SAYS THE LORD GOD, AND YOU BECAME MINE.

(9) "THEN WASHED I YOU WITH WATER; YES, I THOROUGHLY WASHED AWAY YOUR BLOOD FROM YOU, AND I ANOINTED YOU WITH OIL.

(10) "I CLOTHED YOU ALSO WITH BROIDERED WORK, AND SHOD YOU WITH BADGERS' SKIN, AND I GIRDED YOU ABOUT WITH FINE LINEN, AND I COVERED YOU WITH SILK.

(11) "I DECKED YOU ALSO WITH ORNAMENTS, AND I PUT BRACELETS UPON YOUR HANDS, AND A CHAIN ON YOUR NECK.

(12) "AND I PUT A JEWEL ON YOUR FOREHEAD, AND EARRINGS IN YOUR EARS, AND A BEAUTIFUL CROWN UPON YOUR HEAD.

(13) "THUS WERE YOU DECKED WITH GOLD AND SILVER; AND YOUR RAIMENT WAS OF FINE LINEN, AND SILK, AND BROIDERED WORK: YOU DID EAT FINE FLOUR, AND HONEY, AND OIL: AND YOU WERE EXCEEDING BEAUTIFUL, AND YOU DID PROSPER INTO A KINGDOM.

(14) "AND YOUR RENOWN WENT FORTH AMONG THE HEATHEN FOR YOUR BEAUTY: FOR IT WAS PERFECT THROUGH MY COMELINESS, WHICH I HAD PUT UPON YOU, SAYS THE LORD GOD."

The structure is:

1. In this prophecy the apostasy of Jerusalem and Judah is presented under the figure of an unfaithful wife.

2. *"A Syrian ready to perish"* was Abraham their founder. Religiously he was a Canaanite, having an Amorite for a father and a Hittite for a mother, and possessing neither moral beauty, worthfulness, nor social position. Such was the squalid and foul birth of Jerusalem.

3. The interpretation of this Prophecy belongs to that city and nation, but an application truly describes the moral condition of all men by natural birth; for these Verses give a true picture of man's essential corruption.

JERUSALEM

Verse 2 proclaims *"Jerusalem"* as the subject, because she, as the Capital where the Temple was located, answers for the entirety of Judah. As Jeremiah prophesied in Jerusalem, Ezekiel prophesied in captivity. But yet, his Message, even though doubtlessly read by those in Jerusalem, would explain to the Exiles the reason for their captivity.

Most people, at least when speaking of God, have a tendency to think their punishment greater than their sin deserves. This Chapter will show the exact opposite to be the truth. Jeremiah would say after Jerusalem was destroyed, *"It is of the LORD's mercies that we are not consumed"* (Lam. 3:22).

David said: *"He has not dealt with us after our sins; nor rewarded us according to our iniquities"* (Ps. 103:10).

Whenever the chastised begin to understand the justness of God's chastisement and that the Lord has surrounded His chastisement with Mercy, and consequently, he is not receiving not nearly what he deserves, then, he is coming to the place desired by the Holy Spirit where Restoration can begin.

This Prophecy was given about four to five years before the fall of Jerusalem. Therefore, her *"abominations"* were laid out before her, and as such, she had no excuse.

CANAAN

The phrase of Verse 3, *"Your birth and your nativity,"* refers to the origin of Jerusalem, which was not heavenly, but earthly. Such is said because religious pride had so filled Jerusalem, as she held herself far above other cities and nations spiritually, that she no longer saw herself for what she really was. With a striking blow, the Holy Spirit, through the Prophet, strikes at her pride by saying, *"Your birth is of the Land of Canaan."*

Such would have been extremely distasteful to the prideful ear of the inhabitants of Jerusalem. The very name *"Canaan"* conjured up people who did not know God and had been little dealt with by God. They were heathen, idol worshipers, and consequently, knew nothing of the Word of the Lord as it had been given to the Patriarchs and Prophets.

Furthermore, the Holy Spirit strikes the blow even harder when He says, *"Your father was an Amorite, and your mother an Hittite."* Consequently, the Holy Spirit prods the people of Jerusalem by speaking to them as if they were descendants, not from Abraham, Isaac, and Jacob, but from the earlier heathen inhabitants of what was afterwards the Land of Israel.

In other words, the Holy Spirit is telling the inhabitants of Jerusalem that for all their lifted up religious pride, they were, in reality, no better, or even as righteous, as the surrounding heathen.

The modern Believer, as well, must ever understand, that he was brought out of the vilest of the vile, in other words, from total depravity; as such, it is only by the Grace of God that we are what we are. Paul said: *"But by the Grace of God I am what I am"* (I Cor. 15:10).

HER BEGINNINGS

Verses 4 and 5 do not portray God's lack of care, but that of surrounding nations.

The nations which surrounded Jerusalem and Israel never really accepted them in the family of nations and cities. They did not then and they do not now, even as the world does not accept the Child of God!

As I write (2003), these words continue to hold true, inasmuch as the majority of the world little considers Israel as a nation, but rather an interloper. Even though Jerusalem is the Capital of present Israel, the nations, including America, have never recognized it as such, but instead call Tel Aviv her Capital.

Israel has always suffered this ignominy because of her strange posture. As the other nations of the world are ruled by men, this nation was intended to be ruled by God. As such, it was to be a Light unto the nations, leading them out of darkness. Sadly, in that it failed; still, according to Prophecy, it will one day succeed.

Irrespective of its success or its failure, the Prophecy of nearly a thousand years before Ezekiel had said: *"Lo, the people shall dwell alone, and shall not be reckoned among the nations"* (Num. 23:9). And yet, in the coming Kingdom Age, Israel will be the greatest nation of all, and because of the very reason she has been spurned through the ages, the Lord Jesus Christ.

It is ironical, the One she hates is the cause of the hatred against her, and will yet be the cause of her blessing and honor given her.

GRACE

Verses 6 through 14 proclaim the fact of the Grace of the Redeemer in loving such a foul being, making her His Bride, and giving her such a priceless trousseau. Such surpass all human experience.

The word *"live"* is given in Verse 6, pertains to Spiritual Life being imparted to this people as a city and nation. Such is possible only by God, and cannot be instigated by man in any shape, form, or fashion.

As Verse 7 proclaims, Israel really became a nation under the advent of David as King. Under Saul, who was man's choice, as David was God's choice, Israel little came together as a unified people. Only under David, of which these Passages speak, did Israel become a cohesive unity. All was because of God, and is emphasized by the phrase, *"I have caused you. . . ."* Such proclaims the Lord as the Author of their Blessing and *"increase"* and the fact that they *"waxed great."*

LOVE

Verses 8 through 14 proclaim the fact that a mighty Prince, Who of course is the Lord, would take an abandoned infant and make her His Queen. Such is none other than amazing; but what adds to the wonder of it all is that this Divine Prince knew beforehand that His Bride would forsake Him, and ultimately betray and crucify Him.

Such affection is impossible among men, for when a man adopts a child, he hopes for a recompense in the love of the child; but who would adopt a child knowing beforehand that the child would hate and murder its benefactor?

The love that provided such a marriage, as described in Verses 10 through 14 is a love that passes knowledge.

(15) "BUT YOU DID TRUST IN YOUR OWN BEAUTY, AND PLAYED THE HARLOT BECAUSE OF YOUR RENOWN, AND POURED OUT YOUR FORNICATIONS ON EVERY ONE WHO PASSED BY; HIS IT WAS.

(16) "AND OF YOUR GARMENTS YOU

DID TAKE, AND DECKED YOUR HIGH PLACES WITH DIVERS COLORS, AND PLAYED THE HARLOT THEREUPON: THE LIKE THINGS SHALL NOT COME, NEITHER SHALL IT BE SO.

(17) "YOU HAVE ALSO TAKEN YOUR FAIR JEWELS OF MY GOLD AND OF MY SILVER, WHICH I HAD GIVEN YOU, AND MADE TO YOURSELF IMAGES OF MEN, AND DID COMMIT WHOREDOM WITH THEM,

(18) "AND TOOK YOUR BROIDERED GARMENTS, AND COVERED THEM: AND YOU HAVE SET MY OIL AND MY INCENSE BEFORE THEM.

(19) "MY MEAT ALSO WHICH I GAVE YOU, FINE FLOUR, AND OIL, AND HONEY, WHEREWITH I FED YOU, YOU HAVE EVEN SET IT BEFORE THEM FOR A SWEET SAVOR: AND THUS IT WAS, SAYS THE LORD GOD.

(20) "MOREOVER YOU HAVE TAKEN YOUR SONS AND YOUR DAUGHTERS, WHOM YOU HAVE BORNE UNTO ME, AND THESE HAVE YOU SACRIFICED UNTO THEM TO BE DEVOURED. IS THIS OF YOUR WHOREDOMS A SMALL MATTER,

(21) "THAT YOU HAVE SLAIN MY CHILDREN, AND DELIVERED THEM TO CAUSE THEM TO PASS THROUGH THE FIRE FOR THEM?

(22) "AND IN ALL YOUR ABOMINATIONS AND YOUR WHOREDOMS YOU HAVE NOT REMEMBERED THE DAYS OF YOUR YOUTH, WHEN YOU WERE POLLUTED AND BARE, AND WERE POLLUTED IN YOUR BLOOD.

(23) "AND IT CAME TO PASS AFTER ALL YOUR WICKEDNESS, (WOE, WOE UNTO YOU! SAYS THE LORD GOD;)"

The synopsis is:

1. While the sin of idolatry, and not of immorality, is intended by the expressions used in these Verses, yet it is true that the forms of idol-worship here struck at were marked by the grossest immorality, elevated into actions of religious devotion.

2. The phrase in Verse 16, *"the like things shall not come,"* present such a frenzied fever of debauchery that has never been previously, and shall never again be witnessed.

3. The phrase, *"images of men"* in Verse 17, indicates phallus-worship.

SPIRITUAL ADULTERY

As the previous Verses were glorious to behold, conversely, almost the entirety of the remainder of this Chapter is painful to behold.

The reason for Israel's apostasy can be traced to the opening statement in Verse 15, *"But you did trust in your own beauty,"* meaning that she looked on her glory as her own and did not recognize that everything in it was the Gift of God (Hos. 2:8).

This is what caused the downfall of Lucifer, *"Your heart was lifted up because of your beauty,"* as will later be described by the Prophet (Ezek. 28:17). Consequently, pride was the culprit and was so bad when Christ came that they murdered the Lord of Glory in the Name of the Lord.

The phrase, *"And played the harlot because of your renown,"* refers to spiritual harlotry.

Jehovah was Israel's husband; she proved unfaithful to Him by worshipping other gods (Isa. 53:5).

The phrase, *"his it was,"* is a statement of extreme scorn, referring to Israel conducting herself spiritually as a harlot, giving her body to any and all.

SPIRITUAL ADULTERY AND THE MODERN CHURCH

The Holy Spirit through Paul addresses this subject again in the New Testament. It is described in the first four verses of Chapter 7 in Romans. In these four Verses, Paul describes the Believer as being married to Christ; consequently, Christ is to supply our every need, which He definitely has, and definitely does, through the Cross (Gal. 6:14; Eph. 2:13-18).

In these verses, the Apostle also likens a woman who is married to her husband, but goes and marries another, while her first husband is still alive. He said of such a one, *"she shall be called an adulteress"* (Rom. 7:3).

So, the Apostle likens to *"spiritual adultery"* any Believer who trusts in anything, no matter how good it may seem to be on the surface, and no matter how good it may actually be, other than the Cross.

When we realize that such Believers are placed in the same category as Israel of old, even as it regards her spiritual harlotry, then the matter becomes serious indeed!

Regrettably, the term *"spiritual adultery"* has little been heard by most modern Christians. And please understand, we are speaking of spiritual adultery, and not the literal act itself, as should be obvious. We are speaking of unfaithfulness to Christ.

As Believers, we are intended to look to Christ exclusively for everything. As I have repeatedly stated, Christ is the *"Source"* and the Cross is the *"Means."* So if we look elsewhere than the Cross, which the far greater majority of the modern Church is doing, God looks at such an individual as a *"spiritual adulterer."* It's a serious charge! In fact, it causes as much rupture in the relationship between the Lord and Believers as such in the physical sense would cause in a marriage. And one can well imagine what such activity would do to a marriage.

Satan, in the last few decades, has been so successful in pushing the Church away from the Cross, that anymore the modern Church has no true foundation. It doesn't know where it's been, where it is, or where it's going. All of this is because it has drifted and strayed from the Cross.

As such, Believers are trying to live for God in all the wrong ways, making everything in the world the object of their faith instead of that which is the True Object, the Cross. As such, they are living in a state of *"spiritual adultery."* It is gross unfaithfulness to Christ!

The blame for all of this can be laid at the doorstep of many things; however, the biggest culprit of all is, I think, the Word of Faith doctrine. Satan has structured this doctrine with great care and finesse; consequently, it is accepted by the far greater majority of the modern Church. Even those who know of its wrongness are fearful of addressing this monster. They simply don't want the abuse! So they say nothing!

But while men applaud this particular doctrine, God refers to it as *"spiritual adultery."* Plus any method made by anyone to attempt to bring about Righteousness by Law. Such simply cannot be done (Gal. 2:21).

THE INCREASE OF WICKEDNESS

Verse 17 says, *"And made to yourself images of men and did commit whoredom with them."* This is thought by many scholars to intimate phallus-worship, i.e., the Asherah — the male reproductive organ.

Verse 18 refers to this filthy idol, the Asherah, being placed in the very Holy of Holies beside the Ark of the Covenant, or at least in the Holy Place beside the Altar of Worship. It is thought by some that Manasseh did this (II Chron. 33:3-7).

It is with horror that we read these words, and yet, is the modern Church any different?

Many have brought contemporary Christian music into their Churches, which is purposely styled after the acid rock music of the world, which is demon inspired, hence called *"contemporary,"* which means to be similar to its worldly counterpart.

As well, psychology has become the salvation of the Church, with the psychologist becoming its savior. As such, the Church has departed from the Wisdom of God, which is His Word, and opted for the Wisdom of the world, which is sensual and devilish (James 3:15).

The latter phrase of Verse 19, *"And thus it was, says the Lord GOD,"* means *"I saw it; it is really true, says Adonai-Jehovah."* The sense here is, how could such a shameful object of worship, made of wood, stone, or metal, give *"rest"* to either heart or conscience?

The term, *"sweet savour,"* refers here to *"a savour of rest."* In other words, they attributed their blessing to the idol instead of Jehovah.

As well, the modern Church is attributing its *"sweet savour"* to psychology instead of the Word of God. To be sure, as the *"sweet savour"* was taken away from Israel, it is being taken from the modern Church as well!

As Israel forsook Christ by forsaking the Brazen Altar, which typified His coming death at Calvary, and substituted other forms of worship, they then took the punishment for their sins away from Him and placed it upon themselves. The modern Church follows suit!

(24) "THAT YOU HAVE ALSO BUILT UNTO YOU AN EMINENT PLACE, AND

HAVE MADE YOU AN HIGH PLACE IN EVERY STREET.

(25) "YOU HAVE BUILT YOUR HIGH PLACE AT EVERY HEAD OF THE WAY, AND HAVE MADE YOUR BEAUTY TO BE ABHORRED, AND HAVE OPENED YOUR FEET TO EVERYONE WHO PASSED BY, AND MULTIPLIED YOUR WHOREDOMS.

(26) "YOU HAVE ALSO COMMITTED FORNICATION WITH THE EGYPTIANS YOUR NEIGHBOURS, GREAT OF FLESH; AND HAVE INCREASED YOUR WHOREDOMS, TO PROVOKE ME TO ANGER.

(27) "BEHOLD, THEREFORE I HAVE STRETCHED OUT MY HAND OVER YOU, AND HAVE DIMINISHED YOUR ORDINARY FOOD, AND DELIVERED YOU UNTO THE WILL OF THEM WHO HATE YOU, THE DAUGHTERS OF THE PHILISTINES, WHICH ARE ASHAMED OF YOUR LEWD WAY.

(28) "YOU HAVE PLAYED THE WHORE ALSO WITH THE ASSYRIANS, BECAUSE YOU WERE UNSATIABLE; YES, YOU HAVE PLAYED THE HARLOT WITH THEM, AND YET COULD NOT BE SATISFIED.

(29) "YOU HAVE MOREOVER MULTIPLIED YOUR FORNICATION IN THE LAND OF CANAAN UNTO CHALDEA; AND YET YOU WERE NOT SATISFIED HEREWITH.

(30) "HOW WEAK IS YOUR HEART, SAYS THE LORD GOD, SEEING YOU DO ALL THESE THINGS, THE WORK OF AN IMPERIOUS WHORISH WOMAN;

(31) "IN THAT YOU BUILD YOUR EMINENT PLACE IN THE HEAD OF EVERY WAY, AND MAKE YOUR HIGH PLACE IN EVERY STREET; AND HAVE NOT BEEN AS AN HARLOT, IN THAT YOU SCORN HIRE;

(32) "BUT AS A WIFE THAT COMMITS ADULTERY, WHICH TAKES STRANGERS INSTEAD OF HER HUSBAND!

(33) "THEY GIVE GIFTS TO ALL WHORES: BUT YOU GIVE YOUR GIFTS TO ALL YOUR LOVERS, AND HIRE THEM, THAT THEY MAY COME UNTO YOU ON EVERY SIDE FOR YOUR WHOREDOM.

(34) "AND THE CONTRARY IS IN YOU FROM OTHER WOMEN IN YOUR WHOREDOMS, WHEREAS NONE FOLLOWS YOU TO COMMIT WHOREDOMS: AND IN THAT YOU GIVE A REWARD, AND NO REWARD IS GIVEN UNTO YOU, THEREFORE YOU ARE CONTRARY."

The exegesis is:

1. The Philistines never did forsake their gods for those of Egypt and Chaldea; hence, they were religiously superior to the Hebrews.

2. The *"Holy Land"* became morally *"the Land of Canaan"* because of its adoption of the foul and ancient religion of Canaan.

3. Idolatry weakens the heart, i.e., the moral perception; but *"the Way of the LORD is strength to the upright"* (Prov. 10:29).

PLAYED THE WHORE

These verses proclaim the fact that since sin is against God, He cannot be complacent towards it or indifferent with respect to it, hence the detailed account given in these Passages, as well as the entire Bible. He reacts inevitably against it. This reaction is specifically His wrath. The frequency with which Scripture mentions the Wrath of God compels us to take account of its reality and meaning. God judges sin, as God must judge sin!

God considered Israel as His Covenant wife. She was unfaithful to Him in that she gave worship and adoration to *"strangers instead of her husband,"* i.e., Jehovah (Vs. 32).

The degree of sin, even as these Passages proclaim, becomes painfully obvious in that God's chosen had fallen to a level beneath their heathen counterparts. These people sinned against Light, inasmuch as they were the only people on the face of the Earth who were privileged to have knowledge of Jehovah. In sinning against Light, their sin was far worse than that of their surrounding neighbors.

THE INDICTMENT

The phrase of Verse 34, *"And the contrary is in you from other women in your whoredoms,"* refers to other nations which remain true to their gods, and did not take upon themselves the worship of the gods of other countries, whereas Judah forsook the worship of Jehovah, engaging in the worship of foreign gods. In this, they were contrary to other nations.

The phrase, *"Whereas none follows you to commit whoredoms,"* meant that Judah, at least among these nations, was alone in committing this foul sin.

The phrase, *"And in that you give a reward,"* is meant to refer to the practice of harlots. Such were paid for their services, but Judah was so eager to sin that she actually paid others (spiritually speaking) to accept her services, i.e., worship of their gods, which was spiritual adultery. Consequently, the Holy Spirit said, *"You are contrary."*

It would have been bad enough for Judah to have forsaken Jehovah even if she had been paid for it; however, she not only forsook Jehovah and was not paid for it, but instead, paid others to allow her to worship their gods.

What an indictment!

(35) "WHEREFORE, O HARLOT, HEAR THE WORD OF THE LORD:

(36) "THUS SAITH THE LORD GOD; BECAUSE YOUR FILTHINESS WAS POURED OUT, AND YOUR NAKEDNESS DISCOVERED THROUGH YOUR WHOREDOMS WITH YOUR LOVERS, AND WITH ALL THE IDOLS OF YOUR ABOMINATIONS, AND BY THE BLOOD OF YOUR CHILDREN, WHICH YOU DID GIVE UNTO THEM;

(37) "BEHOLD, THEREFORE I WILL GATHER ALL YOUR LOVERS, WITH WHOM YOU HAVE TAKEN PLEASURE, AND ALL THEM THAT YOU HAVE LOVED, WITH ALL THEM THAT YOU HAVE HATED; I WILL EVEN GATHER THEN ROUND ABOUT AGAINST YOU, AND WILL DISCOVER YOUR NAKEDNESS UNTO THEM, THAT THEY MAY SEE ALL YOUR NAKEDNESS.

(38) "AND I WILL JUDGE YOU, AS WOMEN WHO BREAK WEDLOCK AND SHED BLOOD ARE JUDGED; AND I WILL GIVE YOU BLOOD IN FURY AND JEALOUSY.

(39) "AND I WILL ALSO GIVE YOU INTO THEIR HAND, AND THEY SHALL THROW DOWN YOUR EMINENT PLACE, AND SHALL BREAK DOWN YOUR HIGH PLACES: THEY SHALL STRIP YOU ALSO OF YOUR CLOTHES, AND SHALL TAKE YOUR FAIR JEWELS, AND LEAVE YOU NAKED AND BARE.

(40) "THEY SHALL ALSO BRING UP A COMPANY AGAINST YOU, AND THEY SHALL STONE YOU WITH STONES, AND THRUST YOU THROUGH WITH THEIR SWORDS.

NOTES

(41) "AND THEY SHALL BURN YOUR HOUSES WITH FIRE, AND EXECUTE JUDGMENTS UPON YOU IN THE SIGHT OF MANY WOMEN: AND I WILL CAUSE YOU TO CEASE FROM PLAYING THE HARLOT, AND YOU ALSO SHALL GIVE NO HIRE ANY MORE.

(42) "SO WILL I MAKE MY FURY TOWARD YOU TO REST, AND MY JEALOUSY SHALL DEPART FROM YOU, AND I WILL BE QUIET, AND WILL BE NO MORE ANGRY.

(43) "BECAUSE YOU HAVE NOT REMEMBERED THE DAYS OF YOUR YOUTH, BUT HAVE FRETTED ME IN ALL THESE THINGS; BEHOLD, THEREFORE I ALSO WILL RECOMPENSE YOUR WAY UPON YOUR HEAD, SAYS THE LORD GOD: AND YOU SHALL NOT COMMIT THIS LEWDNESS ABOVE ALL YOUR ABOMINATIONS.

(44) "BEHOLD, EVERYONE WHO USES PROVERBS SHALL USE THIS PROVERB AGAINST YOU, SAYING, AS IS THE MOTHER, SO IS HER DAUGHTER.

(45) "YOU ARE YOUR MOTHER'S DAUGHTER; WHO LOATHES HER HUSBAND AND HER CHILDREN; AND YOU ARE THE SISTER OF YOUR SISTERS, WHICH LOATHED THEIR HUSBANDS AND THEIR CHILDREN: YOUR MOTHER WAS AN HITTITE, AND YOUR FATHER AN AMORITE.

(46) "AND YOUR OLDER SISTER IS SAMARIA, SHE AND HER DAUGHTERS WHO DWELL AT YOUR LEFT HAND: AND YOUR YOUNGER SISTER, WHO DWELLS AT YOUR RIGHT HAND, IS SODOM AND HER DAUGHTERS.

(47) "YET HAVE YOU NOT WALKED AFTER THEIR WAYS, NOR DONE AFTER THEIR ABOMINATIONS: BUT, AS IF THAT WERE A VERY LITTLE THING, YOU WERE CORRUPTED MORE THAN THEY IN ALL YOUR WAYS."

The diagram is:

1. The Holy Spirit through the Prophet addresses Judah as, *"O harlot!"*

2. Such terminology as given by the Holy Spirit shows how far Judah had fallen in her forsaking God, and actually is now being led by demon spirits.

3. Judah had attempted to become like the other nations, which she thought would

make her stronger, but in reality made her weaker. Likewise, the Church thinks that being accepted by the world signifies great strength, when, in reality, it signifies great spiritual weakness.

THE WORD OF THE LORD

In the previous verses we are told of the depth of Judah's sin, while in the following Verses we are told of her punishment.

The very thing that Judah was seeking to avoid, which was dominion by the surrounding countries, she avoided not at all. Her strength was Jehovah, but she denied Him and accepted Satan. By comparison, she did the same as Adam and Eve, in that she traded Lords. Whereas Jehovah had been her Lord, now Satan becomes her Lord and proves to be a hard taskmaster.

Verse 38 proclaims the fact that Judah and Jerusalem are now murderesses. This was because of the offering of little children in sacrifice to Moloch, and innocent people being put to death by evil magistrates in order to steal their land, etc. As they had shed blood, their blood would be shed.

THE FAIR JEWELS

Verse 39 proclaims Judah being taken by the Chaldeans, and Jerusalem being destroyed! This was about four years yet into the future.

One would think that the severity of these Prophecies, as given by both Jeremiah and Ezekiel, would at least make Jerusalem stop and listen, but tragically, there was no favorable response. In Jerusalem, Jeremiah would no doubt have been killed had he not been especially protected by the Lord. Ezekiel, although not in as imminent a danger as Jeremiah, due to being among the Exiles, still, was opposed. The false prophets in Jerusalem and among the Exiles were busily proclaiming peace and prosperity, which, of course, was the very opposite of the Word of the Lord, and, as well, much easier to believe.

The phrase, *"And shall take your fair jewels"* refers to the holy utensils in the Temple, with all representing Christ. As well, and as Ezekiel had portrayed in his Eleventh Chapter, the Holy Spirit would shortly vacate the premises, if not already having done so, which

NOTES

would leave Jerusalem *"naked and bare."*

JUDGMENT

Verse 42 contains the word *"fury,"* which is an apt response of the Lord against sin.

Various terms are used in the Old Testament respecting the sense of God's anger against sin. It is apparent that the Old Testament is permeated with references to the Wrath of God. Often more than one of the terms, such as *"fury," "wrath," "indignation,"* appear together in order to strengthen and confirm the thought expressed. There is intensity in the terms themselves and in the constructions in which they occur to convey the notions of displeasure, fiery indignation, and holy vengeance.

The wrath of God is, therefore, a reality, and the language and teaching of Scripture are calculated to impress upon us the severity by which it is characterized. There are three observations which particularly require mention.

THE WRATH OF GOD

First, the wrath of God must not be interpreted in terms of the fitful passions so commonly associated with anger in man. It is the deliberate, resolute displeasure which the contradiction of His holiness demands.

Second, it is not to be construed as vindictiveness, but as holy indignation; nothing of the nature of malice attaches to it. It is not malignant hatred, but righteous detestation.

Third, we may not reduce the wrath of God to His Will to punish. Wrath is a positive outgoing of dissatisfaction as sure as that which is pleasing to God involves satisfaction. We must not eliminate from God what we term *"emotion."* The wrath of God finds its parallel in the human heart exemplified in a perfect manner in Christ (Mk. 3:5; 10:14).

The epitome of sin's liability is, therefore, the holy wrath of God. Since sin is never impersonal, but exists in, and is committed by, persons, the wrath of God consists in the displeasure to which we are subjected; we are the objects.

The penal inflictions which we suffer are the expressions of God's wrath. The sense of guilt and torment of conscience or reflections is our consciousness of the displeasure of God. The essence of final perdition (eternal Hell) if His Mercy is rejected will consist in the infliction of God's indignation (Isa. 30:33; 66:24; Dan. 12:2; Mk. 9:43, 45, 48).

MERCY

Set over against the wrath of God against sin is the Mercy of God in His undeniable effort to deliver the sinner from sin. The entire story of the Bible is an account of God's supreme effort in the realm of Salvation for the sinner. That Redemption is centered in Jesus Christ, the Last Adam, His Eternal Son, the Saviour of sinners.

In Christ, God conquered sin, which was carried out at the Cross (Col. 2:14-15). Such are the great glad tidings of the Bible. Therefore, the invitation to all is given to come and drink of the Water of Life freely, that sin may be washed and cleansed and the sinner may find peace and eternal rest in the Lord Jesus Christ. No message can even remotely compare with this Message; consequently, it has been called *"The Greatest Story Ever Told."* It is the story of the lostness of man and his Redemption by the Lord Jesus Christ through the Cross, at least for all who will believe (Jn. 3:16).

Sadly, Judah of old would not believe and went to her doom, as multiple millions today will not believe and go to their doom!

CALVARY

The phrase of Verse 42, *"And I will be quiet, and will be no more angry,"* refers to the cause of the sin being removed.

This statement, as well, exemplifies the anger of God against sin being appeased by the death of Christ at Calvary. Even though Christ had not sinned, He took upon Himself our sins, and as well the penalty thereof, which was the Judgment of God (II Cor. 5:21). Therefore, the death of Christ at Calvary was as much to appease the anger of God against sin as it was to redeem man from the terrible effect of sin, which was death.

At Calvary, Christ carried out this task, thereby reconciling man to God (II Cor. 5:17-19). Hence, Paul would say: *"And, having made peace through the Blood of His Cross, by Him to reconcile all things unto Himself; by Him, I say, whether there be things in Earth, or in things in Heaven.*

"And you, who in times past were alienated and enemies in your mind by wicked works, yet now has He reconciled

"In the Body of His Flesh through death, to present you Holy and unblamable and unreprovable in His sight" (Col. 1:20-22).

One can only shout, *"Hallelujah!"*

ABOMINATIONS

The phrases of Verse 47, *"Walking after their ways,"* and the *"Doing after their abominations,"* portray the fact that these nations influenced Judah instead of Judah influencing these nations.

One of the greatest enemies of the modern Church is the world. Satan ever seeks to force the Church into the ways and abominations of the world. He too often succeeds!

As Judah of old was to be separate from the surrounding nations, likewise, the modern Believer is to do likewise. Paul said: *"Wherefore come out from among them, and be ye separate, saith the Lord, and touch not the unclean thing, and I will receive you"* (II Cor. 6:14-18).

If the relationship with Christ is what it ought to be, the world holds no attraction. However, if that relationship dims, then the world begins to look far more attractive!

The phrase, *"You were corrupted more than they in all your ways,"* refers to Judah sinning against Light, whereas the other nations of the world at that time had no light.

But yet, while the Bible definitely teaches *"separation,"* in no way does it teach *"isolation."* In fact, the only *"Light"* in the world is that provided by the Child of God. That's the reason that Jesus said of Believers: *"You are the Light of the world."* He then said, *"A city that is set on a hill cannot be hid,*

"Neither do men light a candle, and put it under a bushel, but on a candlestick; and it gives light unto all who are in the house.

"Let your light so shine before men that they may see your good works, and glorify your Father which is in Heaven" (Mat. 5:14-16).

However, Christians are like ships on the ocean. As long as the ship remains on the ocean, it can be of extremely valuable service to mankind; however, if the ocean gets in the ship, problems begin to multiply fast. It is the same with the Believer!

We are in the world, and in the world we are to let our light shine; however, if the world gets in us, this stops the light from shining!

(48) "AS I LIVE, SAITH THE LORD GOD, SODOM YOUR SISTER HAS NOT DONE, SHE NOR HER DAUGHTERS, AS YOU HAVE DONE, YOU AND YOUR DAUGHTERS.

(49) "BEHOLD, THIS WAS THE INIQUITY OF YOUR SISTER SODOM, PRIDE, FULLNESS OF BREAD, AND ABUNDANCE OF IDLENESS WAS IN HER AND IN HER DAUGHTERS, NEITHER DID SHE STRENGTHEN THE HAND OF THE POOR AND NEEDY.

(50) "AND THEY WERE HAUGHTY, AND COMMITTED ABOMINATION BEFORE ME: THEREFORE I TOOK THEM AWAY AS I SAW GOOD.

(51) "NEITHER HAS SAMARIA COMMITTED HALF OF YOUR SINS; BUT YOU HAVE MULTIPLIED YOUR ABOMINATIONS MORE THAN THEY, AND HAVE JUSTIFIED YOUR SISTERS IN ALL YOUR ABOMINATIONS WHICH YOU HAVE DONE.

(52) "YOU ALSO, WHICH HAVE JUDGED YOUR SISTERS, BEAR YOUR OWN SHAME FOR YOUR SINS THAT YOU HAVE COMMITTED MORE ABOMINABLE THAN THEY: THEY ARE MORE RIGHTEOUS THAN YOU: YES, YOU SHOULD BE MORE CONFOUNDED ALSO, AND BEAR YOUR SHAME, IN THAT YOU HAVE JUSTIFIED YOUR SISTERS.

(53) "WHEN I SHALL BRING AGAIN THEIR CAPTIVITY, THE CAPTIVITY OF SODOM AND HER DAUGHTERS, AND THE CAPTIVITY OF SAMARIA AND HER DAUGHTERS, THEN WILL I BRING AGAIN THE CAPTIVITY OF YOUR CAPTIVES IN THE MIDST OF THEM:

(54) "THAT YOU MAY BEAR YOUR OWN SHAME, AND MAY BE CONFOUNDED IN ALL THAT YOU HAVE DONE, IN THAT YOU ARE A COMFORT UNTO THEM.

(55) "WHEN YOUR SISTERS, SODOM AND HER DAUGHTERS, SHALL RETURN TO THEIR FORMER ESTATE, AND SAMARIA AND HER DAUGHTERS SHALL RETURN TO THEIR FORMER ESTATE, THEN YOU AND YOUR DAUGHTERS SHALL RETURN TO YOUR FORMER ESTATE.

(56) "FOR YOUR SISTER SODOM WAS NOT MENTIONED BY YOUR MOUTH IN THE DAY OF YOUR PRIDE,

(57) "BEFORE YOUR WICKEDNESS WAS DISCOVERED, AS AT THE TIME OF YOUR REPROACH OF THE DAUGHTERS OF SYRIA, AND ALL WHO ARE ROUND ABOUT HER, THE DAUGHTERS OF THE PHILISTINES, WHICH DESPISE YOU ROUND ABOUT.

(58) "YOU HAVE BORNE YOUR LEWDNESS AND YOUR ABOMINATIONS, SAITH THE LORD."

The exegesis is:

1. Financial prosperity was the cause of Sodom's moral fall, which caused them to commit an abomination, and did so in the face of God, which was the sin of homosexuality; consequently, He took them away (Gen. 18:21). The pattern is identical in the modern United States.

2. The Lord here proclaims Jerusalem as more guilty than Sodom — not positively but relatively (II Ki. 21:9).

3. The future restoration of Jerusalem, together with Samaria and Sodom, is predicted in Verses 53 through 63.

4. The amazing nature of the Grace that will perform this regeneration is preceded by the argument of Verses 53 through 59, which appears to be that Jerusalem had no more claim to forgiveness and restoration than either Sodom or Samaria, and that, therefore, her recovery was as eternally hopeless as theirs. This principle of Grace reappears in Romans 11:32.

But a Grace rich enough to forgive Jerusalem must, in its nature, be rich enough to forgive her less guilty companions for there is no difference; all have sinned.

5. But it is humbling to religious pride to be compelled to seek mercy in the company of the degraded and fallen, and of those formerly despised.

SODOM, SAMARIA, AND JERUSALEM

When Judah was placed beside Sodom, she was found wanting! Such is almost beyond imagination. And yet Christ would say concerning the Israel of His day: *"That it shall be more tolerable for the land of Sodom in the day of Judgment, than for you"* (Mat. 11:24).

Someone has said that if God does not judge America, He will have to apologize to Sodom and Gomorrah.

THE FOUR SINS OF SODOM

Verses 49 and 50 proclaim the four sins which characterized Sodom, and thereby the cause of her destruction:

1. *"Pride"*: This sin headed the list as it is the foundation sin of all sin. It is the sin that caused the fall of Lucifer; it is, therefore, the sin that characterizes the whole of humanity (Isa., Chpt. 14; Ezek., Chpt. 28)

2. *"Fullness of Bread"*: Financial prosperity was at least one of the causes of Sodom's moral fall. *"They became haughty"* (i.e., against God) and committed *"a certain abomination before Me"* (or against *"My Face,"* which was the sin of homosexuality); *"Therefore I took them away when I had seen it"* (Gen. 18:21).

The entire political spectrum of America is based on financial prosperity or the lack of it. In other words, the *"dollar"* has become the *"god"* of this country. As a result, even among many other terrible sins, *"homosexuality"* stands out as becoming more and more rampant over the nation. It must be remembered that this is the sin which God says is *"in His Face,"* meaning that it will not be tolerated.

Homosexuality is a sin against nature, and against God, and more than all against God. It is an evil tampering with His Creation, instigated by Satan. Irrespective of the claim, no homosexual is born a homosexual, even though all babies are born with proclivities toward certain perversions, which again is the result of the Fall. The answer to all of this is Jesus Christ and the Cross, and it is the only answer.

CAN A HOMOSEXUAL BE SAVED?

Well of course a homosexual can be saved, the same as an alcoholic, or a gambler, or a murderer, etc.; however, once the homosexual comes to Christ, as any other individual, that particular sin stops. God doesn't save people in sin, but rather from sin. In fact, that's the very premise of Redemption. Paul said:

"Who gave Himself for our sins, that He might deliver us from this present evil world,

NOTES

according to the Will of God and our Father" (Gal. 1:4).

Again I state, Jesus came to this world, died on a Cross, that *"He might deliver us from"* not *"deliver us in"*!

Again, Paul said: *"Do you not know that the unrighteous shall not inherit the Kingdom of God? Be not deceived: neither fornicators, nor idolaters, nor adulterers, nor effeminate, nor abusers of themselves with mankind* (homosexuals),

"Nor thieves, nor covetous, nor drunkards, nor revilers, nor extortioners, shall inherit the Kingdom of God.

"And such were some of you: but you are washed, but you are Sanctified, but you are Justified in the Name of the Lord Jesus, and by the Spirit of our God" (I Cor. 6:9-11).

3. *"Abundance of idleness"*: entertainment was Sodom's most remarkable product, as entertainment is America's most marketable product!

America once filled the world with the products of our factories and manufacturing concerns. Presently (2003), Hollywood and Disney are fast becoming our greatest exports. This is because of the *"abundance of idleness"* in the industrialized nations.

4. *"Neither did she strengthen the hand of the poor and needy"*: A false religion is selfish, it neglects the poor, hence, the condition of this segment of society and most nations of the world.

ABOMINATION

Verse 50 labels homosexuality as an *"abomination."*

It is not spelled out here, even as the principal sin of calf worship of Samaria was not spelled out, evidently because the Holy Spirit thought it wiser to dwell on the sins which were common to the two cities rather than on the vice, which, though it existed in Jerusalem (II Ki. 23:7), was probably not prevalent there.

From the phrase of the Fiftieth Verse, *"Therefore I took them away as I saw good,"* we learn that everything that happens in this world, whether good or bad, is either caused or allowed by the Lord.

For instance, we note that the storm which came up on the Sea of Galilee when Christ and His Disciples were crossing this body of water, was not sent by the Lord, but instead by Satan; however, Satan could not have done so unless first receiving permission from the Lord (Mk. 4:35-41; Job, Chpt. 1). Even though caused by Satan and allowed by the Lord, still, Christ would portray His Power in calming the storm, and the Lord would be glorified.

Therefore, disruptions of the elements, such as storms, tornados, hurricanes, etc., are called *"acts of God,"* and rightly so! Many take exception to this, claiming the Lord is not responsible for such; however, if He was not responsible, this would mean, at least in some areas, that Satan had greater power than Jehovah. Even the most elementary Bible Student will have to admit that such is not true; however, we learn from the first two Chapters of Job that Satan had to seek permission from the Lord before committing specific acts on Earth. The Bible also teaches that when the Judgment is allowed, the Righteous suffer with the unrighteous (Mat. 5:45).

The Bible is replete with the Truth that because of sin, Judgment is visited upon a nation, or even certain parts of a nation in the form of famine, storms, and war, etc. (I Ki. 8:46; 11:14, 23; 17:1; Gen. 41:29-30; Ex., Chpts. 7-12; Acts 2:19-20; 12:21-23; Rev., Chpts. 6-19).

Also the number of Righteous people in any area (those who have the Righteousness of Christ and not self-righteousness) very well determine the degree of Judgment, if any at all (Gen. 18:23-32).

Many may look at certain areas of the world which seem to prosper greatly and which contain few Righteous, if any at all, and think to discount the fact of Righteous influence; nevertheless, God's Patience and Mercy will tarry long, even for years or even decades and sometimes even centuries, but such is not to be looked at as approval, but rather the goodness of God designed to lead men to Repentance (Rom. 2:4-6). Barring Repentance, sooner or later Judgment will come (Gen. 15:16).

HUMBLED

Verses 51 through 57 proclaim the fact that the Lord judged Judah and Jerusalem to be more vile even than Sodom and the northern Kingdom of Samaria, with the latter having been defeated by the Assyrians, many years before. The reason was simple:

Sodom had very little witness of the Lord, while Samaria definitely had much more witness; however, Judah had the greatest witness on the face of the Earth. The Temple resided in Jerusalem, where God dwelt in the Holy of Holies, between the Mercy Seat and Cherubims. Sin against Light is the worst sin of all.

Therefore, it is humbling to religious pride to be compelled to seek mercy in the company of the degraded and fallen, and of those formerly despised. So the pride of Judah and Jerusalem had to be broken, even as the pride of Sodom and Samaria had to be broken. This is the sin, the sin of pride, which destroyed the Israel of Jesus' day.

He said of the Scribes and the Pharisees, the most devoted religious group in Israel at that time: *"Verily I say unto you, That the publicans and the harlots go into the Kingdom of God before you"* (Mat. 21:31).

Publicans were tax-collectors, and, therefore, looked at by Israel as traitors to God and to His people. It is obvious as to what harlots were! So how could Jesus say that these two particular forlorn classes could be saved, but that the religious crowd couldn't?

The reason is simple: The *"harlots"* and the *"publicans"* knew what they were; therefore, it was not too difficult to get them to repent; however, the religious self-righteous, full of pride, would never admit what they actually were. As well, to be told that they had to come the same way as these *"harlots"* and *"publicans"* was that which they could not abide. As stated, it is very humbling to religious pride to be compelled to seek mercy in the company of the degraded and fallen. In fact, that's what keeps untold millions out of the Kingdom of God.

PRIDE

Because of *"pride,"* millions think, and because of certain things, that they are better than others. The very idea that they would have to humble themselves and fall at the feet of the world's Redeemer, exactly as the harlots, etc., presents itself as repulsive unto them. But that's the way that all must come. And let me say one final thing about this:

The world is fond of supplying its own ethics, which it thinks justifies itself. In fact, it doesn't mind Jesus too very much, if we are speaking of His ethics. Actually, the ethics of all good men (good, supposedly) should be followed, with Jesus as merely one among many.

But when it comes to accepting Jesus as Saviour, which means that man is a poor, lost, helpless sinner, with all in the same boat, so to speak, and despite their so-called ethics, and that the only solution is the Cross of Christ, which again states how bad that man actually is, virtually all of the world balks at that.

But it's worse yet, when the Church follows suit. In fact, religious ethics are the worst of all! Such are put in the place of Calvary, which means that the Believer, while admitting his need of the Cross as a sinner coming to Christ, after being saved, dispenses with the Cross. As a result, pride and self-righteousness are the result. As such, they love to categorize sin. And to be told that they have to repent the same as the one who commits vile sins, they reject it out of hand, which means they are rejecting the Cross.

ETHICS

Christian ethics are no better than the ethics of the world. That may come as a surprise to most, but it happens to be true. The reason is simple: Such Christians put ethics in the place of the Cross. In other words, their Salvation is now ensconced in their ethics, whatever those ethics might be, which means that they periodically change, and, in fact, change even with the individual. The Cross is then forgotten, and, in many circles, even denied.

Let the Reader understand that there is no time in the existence of the human being, even after being saved, even after being baptized with the Holy Spirit, that one can dispense with the Cross. That's why Jesus told us that we must *"deny ourselves, and take up the Cross daily"* (Lk. 9:23). My Salvation and my Victory are not at all in my ethics, whatever those ethics might be, but solely in Christ and the Cross. So the sin of the Church is basically the sin of the world. It refuses to humble itself at the Cross. It cites its Denomination as being sufficient or its particular local Church, or its good works, etc. Once again, we go back to what Christ said:

"The publicans and the harlots go into the Kingdom of God before you" (Mat. 21:31).

(59) "FOR THUS SAITH THE LORD GOD; I WILL EVEN DEAL WITH YOU AS YOU HAVE DONE, WHICH HAVE DESPISED THE OATH IN BREAKING THE COVENANT.

(60) "NEVERTHELESS I WILL REMEMBER MY COVENANT WITH YOU IN THE DAYS OF YOUR YOUTH, AND I WILL ESTABLISH UNTO YOU AN EVERLASTING COVENANT.

(61) "THEN YOU SHALL REMEMBER YOUR WAYS, AND BE ASHAMED, WHEN YOU SHALL RECEIVE YOUR SISTERS, YOUR ELDER AND YOUR YOUNGER: AND I WILL GIVE THEM UNTO YOU FOR DAUGHTERS, BUT NOT BY YOUR COVENANT.

(62) "AND I WILL ESTABLISH MY COVENANT WITH YOU; AND YOU SHALL KNOW THAT I AM THE LORD:

(63) "THAT YOU MAY REMEMBER, AND BE CONFOUNDED, AND NEVER OPEN YOUR MOUTH ANY MORE BECAUSE OF YOUR SHAME, WHEN I AM PACIFIED TOWARD YOU FOR ALL THAT YOU HAVE DONE, SAYS THE LORD GOD."

The diagram is:

1. The *"oath"* and *"Covenant"* formed the marriage bond of Sinai. Jerusalem was unfaithful to that bond; but not so her Heavenly Lord. On the contrary, under the New Covenant, He will make an everlasting marriage-bond with her, giving her, at the same time, as bridesmaids, so to speak, her sisters Sodom and Samaria; and then will she learn by experience (know) what a wonderful husband is Immanuel; and her personal boasting will be silenced, for His praise only will fill her mouth.

2. *"Thy Covenant"* and *"My Covenant"* presents Sinai contrasted with Golgotha.

3. *"Pacified"* of Verse 63 means *"forgiven."* It is the propitiation. This propitiation was consummated at Calvary. It provides the righteous ground upon which God may meet and forgive the vilest sinners without injury

to the Righteousness which is the establishment of His Throne; for if God were to forgive sins unrighteously, He would wreck His Throne and cease to be God.

THE EVERLASTING COVENANT

It is ironical and yet beautiful; even in the midst of the predictions concerning the destruction of Jerusalem and Judah, the Lord looks ahead to a coming glad day when He will establish the *"Everlasting Covenant."* Then Israel will be restored. While that has not yet been done, and will not be done until the Second Coming, still, that which makes it possible has been done, and I speak of the Cross, which Paul referred to as *"The Everlasting Covenant"* (Heb. 13:20).

Verse 59 proclaims Israel as having broken the Law of Moses, described here as the *"Oath"* and the *"Covenant."*

The serious Bible student knows that man, even the Children of Israel, God's Chosen, could not keep the Law. In fact, the *"Law"* was like a mirror which showed man what he was, but gave him no power to change what he was.

Due to the Fall, man within himself, is totally lacking in capability as it regards the keeping of the Law. And that goes even for modern Believers, even those baptized with the Holy Spirit. And yet, the moral Law must be kept, which speaks of the Ten Commandments (Ex., Chpt. 20).

Going back to Israel before the Cross, even though they could not keep the Law, which became quickly obvious, they were still to adhere to its principles and precepts, and do so faithfully, leaning heavily on the Sacrificial System, with their faith anchored in that which the Sacrifices represented, namely the coming Redeemer, Who would be the Lord Jesus Christ. Every time they killed a lamb as it regarded Sacrifice, they were to understand, even as the hot blood poured out into the basin, that an innocent victim was dying in their stead, which symbolized the coming Redeemer, to Whom the Prophets constantly pointed (Isa., Chpt. 53).

But the truth is, Israel of old, even as we are here studying, forgot the Law, repudiated it, ignored it, or changed it to their own fancy.

THE MODERN BELIEVER AND THE LAW

The Apostle Paul told us exactly what position the Law must take, and we speak of the moral part of the Law of Moses, in the life of the Believer. In truth, it is to have no part at all, *"For you are not under the Law, but under Grace"* (Rom. 6:14).

But yet the moral Law is definitely to be kept in the heart and life of the Christian, and this being so, how is it to be done if we are not to address ourselves to Law in any fashion?

First of all, let's see what happens to the Believer who tries to live in some fashion under Law, which, regrettably, most of the modern Church does, and because it doesn't understand the Cross as it regards Sanctification.

THE CHRISTIAN WHO TRIES TO LIVE UNDER LAW

Now most Believers would automatically claim that they are not living under law, and in fact, have nothing to do with law. Most loudly trumpet the Grace of God, etc. But the facts are otherwise, whether the Believer understands it or not. Let us say it again:

If the Believer doesn't understand the Cross at it regards Sanctification, and virtually none do, and because it has not been preached behind the pulpit, there is no other place to be but law.

Most Christians, at least in their minds, draw up a list of *"dos and don'ts"* and try to live by that particular ethic. Or else they try to live by an ethic that someone else has drawn up, which, pure and simple, is *"law."* Now what does Paul say about that:

He said: *"For I was alive without the Law once* (when he gave his heart to Christ): *but when the Commandment* (Law) *came, sin revived* (the sin nature revived), *and I died* (I failed the Lord in that I sinned)" (Rom. 7:9).

Not knowing or understanding anything about the Grace of God at this particular time, and we refer to the time that Paul had got saved, he set about to live for God, regrettably, as most Christians do presently, and that is by *"keeping the Commandments, etc."* And when he sought to do this, he found the sin nature reviving in his life, and instead of keeping the Commandments, he found himself breaking the Commandments.

And then he said: *"Was then that which is good* (the Law) *made death unto me? God forbid."* Paul is saying here that the Law is not to be blamed for his failure. He then went on to say: *"But sin* (the sin nature), *that it might appear sin, working death in me by that which is good,"* proclaims the fact that the Law was good, and, as such, was not the cause of his failure; nevertheless, when he set about to try to keep the Law, and we continue to speak of the moral law, he found he couldn't do such and, therefore, it became the occasion of his failure (Rom. 7:13).

But in this Passage, and as stated, Paul makes it abundantly clear that the Law is not at fault as it regards his failing to do right; it was rather his wrong approach to the Law. Now the upshot of all of this is:

As stated, God demands of every Christian that we definitely keep the moral law of God. To be sure, if it was wrong to steal 3,500 years ago, it's wrong presently, etc. Moral law cannot change. So this shoots down the idea that the Christian need not bother or worry about sin, because Grace covers it. Again we state, God does not save us in sin, but rather, from sin (Rom. 6:1-2).

So the Christian must understand, if he tries to live for the Lord in the wrong way, which is by Law, which sadly and regrettably, most of the modern Church is attempting to do, such a direction will never come out to victory, only failure. The reason is, the Holy Spirit will not help a Believer in such an endeavor, and to be sure, any Righteousness and Holiness in our lives can be developed only by the Holy Spirit. Let's look at the right way to do this thing.

THE CHRISTIAN AND GRACE

Paul also said: *"I am crucified with Christ* (he takes us back to the Cross, actually Rom. 6:3-5): *nevertheless I live, yet not I, but Christ lives in me: and the life I now live in the flesh I live by the Faith of the Son of God, Who loved me, and gave Himself for me"* (Gal. 2:20).

In this one statement, which tells the Believer how to live for the Lord, which is by Grace, he begins with the Cross and ends with the Cross. Why did he do this?

He takes us back to Romans 6:3-5, which proclaims the fact that when you, the Believer, were saved, you were *"baptized into the death of Christ."* He was your Substitute, and your identification with Him placed you, at least in the mind of God, into His death.

You were then *"buried with Him by baptism into death."* This refers to what you were in your unsaved state. You died with Him, and now you are buried with Him, which means that all that you were in your unsaved state is now dead and buried.

You were then raised with Him *"in newness of life,"* which refers to His Resurrection. You are now able to live the Resurrection Life, but only as you understand that *"you have been planted together* (with Him) *in the likeness of His Death"* (Rom. 6:3-5).

Please understand: When you came to Christ, the Lord did not merely rehabilitate you, or refurbish you, but rather made of you a *"new creation"* (II Cor. 5:17). The old you died, and there is a new man that has taken his place (Col. 3:10).

HOW TO LIVE YOUR LIFE!

You are now to live your life by looking exclusively to Christ and what He has done for you at the Cross. As stated, when Paul told us how to do this, and we again speak of Galatians 2:20, he began this Verse by addressing himself to the Cross, and he closed the Verse by addressing himself to the Cross, which means, and unequivocally so, that the Believer is to look exclusively to the Cross of Christ. As we have repeatedly stated, and will continue to state, Christ is the *"Source,"* while the Cross is the *"Means."*

That's why Paul said: *"For Christ sent me not to baptize* (water baptism), *but to preach the Gospel: not with wisdom of words, lest the Cross of Christ should be made of none effect"* (I Cor. 1:17).

Paul is not knocking Water Baptism here, but merely stating that it must not be the emphasis, nor anything else for that matter, only the Cross. The Cross must be the center, the foundation, of all that the Believer is and believes. But the trouble with the modern Church is that it has made other things the emphasis. It has emphasized

Water Baptism, or the Lord's Supper, or joining the Church, or giving money to the Work of Lord, or witnessing to souls, or belonging to a particular Denomination, etc. While those things may or may not be good, if the emphasis is placed on those things, we are then turning them into law, which the Holy Spirit will never sanction.

Paul then said: *"For the preaching of the Cross is to them who perish foolishness; but unto us which are saved it is the Power of God"* (I Cor. 1:18).

The Greek word *"logos,"* which is translated *"preaching"* in this Verse, should have been translated *"Word"* or *"Message,"* for that's what it means. It should read, *"For the Word of the Cross. . . ."*

At any rate, we are told here that the *"preaching of the Cross,"* or the *"Word of the Cross,"* is that which contains the *"Power."*

How does the Cross contain Power? Let's explain that!

THE CROSS AND THE HOLY SPIRIT

In fact, there is no Power in the Cross as a wooden beam, which should be obvious. As well, there was no Power per se in the death of Christ, for, in fact, Jesus died in weakness (II Cor. 13:4); however, it must be understood, that it was a contrived weakness, meaning that He allowed Himself to be crucified (Jn. 10:17-18).

The *"Power"* comes in, according to what the Cross accomplished. At the Cross, Jesus atoned for all sin, which makes it possible for the Holy Spirit to now abide in the hearts and lives of Believers on a permanent basis (Jn. 14:16-17). And to be sure, the Power is in the Holy Spirit (Acts 1:8).

THE REVELATION

When the Lord first began to open up to me the Revelation of the Cross, even as I am attempting to give it to you here, such was the most glorious day in the Lord that I've ever experienced, other than when I was saved and baptized with the Holy Spirit.

As I rejoiced in this great Revelation, which I knew was the answer to my petition, and, in fact, that for which I had sought the Lord for so long, knowing that our victory is in the Cross, I wondered at that time, how the Holy Spirit fit into this. Of course, I knew that He did; but at that time, I did not understand exactly how. In fact, as I've already related in this Volume, the Lord had spoken to me in the spring of 1988 at a most crucial time in my life and Ministry that He would show me things about the Holy Spirit that I did not then know. While I knew much about the Holy Spirit at that time, at the same time, I knew I was missing something. And at the same time, I knew there was so much about the Holy Spirit I didn't know, as would be obvious, for the simple reason that the Holy Spirit is God.

It was some nine years before the Lord revealed to me that which He had stated on that March morning in 1988.

He revealed to me that the Cross of Christ is a legal work, and that the Holy Spirit works entirely within the confines of the legal work of the Cross of Christ. To show me this, He took me again to Romans:

"For the Law of the Spirit of Life in Christ Jesus has made me free from the Law of sin and death" (Rom. 8:2).

So in this Passage and others, we are told that the Believer must understand that everything he receives from the Lord comes to him exclusively by and through the Cross of Christ. That's what the words, *"in Christ Jesus,"* actually mean. The Holy Spirit works exclusively within the parameters of the Cross, and so much so that it is called *"The Law of the Spirit of Life."* That and that alone can give you victory over the *"Law of sin and death."*

Now of course, even as the Reader understands, the *"Law"* mentioned here has nothing to do with the Law of Moses, or any law which we might devise ourselves, but rather that which was ordained by the Godhead in eternity past, as it regarded how the Holy Spirit would work.

When the Believer places his faith exclusively in the Cross of Christ, and leaves his faith there, to be sure, the Holy Spirit will grandly help that Believer, and then the moral law will always be kept.

In fact, this is the *"Everlasting Covenant,"* mentioned in Verse 60, and which Paul again quoted in Hebrews 13:20.

When Jesus died on the Cross, the Lord

was *"pacified,"* even as Ezekiel 16:63 proclaims, which means that the Justice and Righteousness of God were forever satisfied at the Cross. The emphasis must always be the Cross, and the Cross alone! The Holy Spirit will honor nothing else.

"Are you able, said the Master, to be crucified with Me?
"Yes, the sturdy dreamers answered, to the death we followed Thee."

"Are you able to relinquish, purple dreams of power and fame,
"To go down into the garden, or to die a death of shame?"

"Are you able to remember, when a thief lifts up his eyes,
"That his pardoned soul is worthy, of a place in Paradise?"

"Are you able, when the shadows close around you with the sod,
"To believe that spirit triumphs, to commend your soul to God?"

"Are you able? Still the Master whispers down eternity
"And heroic spirits answer, now, as then, in Galilee."

CHAPTER 17

(1) "AND THE WORD OF THE LORD CAME UNTO ME, SAYING,
(2) "SON OF MAN, PUT FORTH A RIDDLE, AND SPEAK A PARABLE UNTO THE HOUSE OF ISRAEL;
(3) "AND SAY, THUS SAITH THE LORD GOD; A GREAT EAGLE WITH GREAT WINGS, LONGWINGED, FULL OF FEATHERS, WHICH HAD DIVERS COLOURS, CAME UNTO LEBANON, AND TOOK THE HIGHEST BRANCH OF THE CEDAR:
(4) "HE CROPPED OFF THE TOP OF HIS YOUNG TWIGS, AND CARRIED IT INTO A LAND OF TRAFFIK; HE SET IT IN A CITY OF MERCHANTS.
(5) "HE TOOK ALSO OF THE SEED OF THE LAND, AND PLANTED IT IN A FRUITFUL FIELD; HE PLACED IT BY GREAT WATERS, AND SET IT AS A WILLOW TREE.
(6) "AND IT GREW, AND BECAME A SPREADING VINE OF LOW STATURE, WHOSE BRANCHES TURNED TOWARD HIM, AND THE ROOTS THEREOF WERE UNDER HIM: SO IT BECAME A VINE, AND BROUGHT FORTH BRANCHES, AND SHOT FORTH SPRIGS.
(7) "THERE WAS ALSO ANOTHER GREAT EAGLE WITH GREAT WINGS AND MANY FEATHERS: AND, BEHOLD, THIS VINE DID BEND HER ROOTS TOWARD HIM, AND SHOT FORTH HER BRANCHES TOWARD HIM, THAT HE MIGHT WATER IT BY THE FURROWS OF HER PLANTATION.
(8) "IT WAS PLANTED IN A GOOD SOIL BY GREAT WATERS, THAT IT MIGHT BRING FORTH BRANCHES, AND THAT IT MIGHT BEAR FRUIT, THAT IT MIGHT BE A GOODLY VINE."

The composition is:

1. The punishment of King Zedekiah illustrates the heat of God's anger against falsehood, deceit, and breach of covenants.
2. The predictions of this Prophecy up to Verse 21 were fulfilled about five years later.
3. The historic facts reviewed by the Prophecy and recorded in the Scripture concerned Nebuchadnezzar's second siege of Jerusalem; the dismissal of Jehoiakim to Babylon; the selection and elevation to the throne of Judah of his uncle Zedekiah, who took in the Name of Jehovah an oath of fidelity to the Babylonian Monarch; the breach of that oath by the alliance with the Egyptians; the consequent third and final siege and capture of the city; its destruction and that of the Temple by fire; and the severe punishment pronounced upon Zedekiah and his sons and his princes. These were put to death in the presence of the unhappy king; he himself was then blinded, loaded with chains, and lodged in the prison at Babylon where he died.
4. Zedekiah's rebellion robbed the nation of its limited prosperity, caused its total dispersion, and put an end to the only Kingdom on Earth that God had recognized as His.

A PARABLE

Verses 1 through 8 present another warning

given to Zedekiah by the Lord through the Prophets Jeremiah and Ezekiel. All of this is astounding, especially in view of the fact that he did not heed them.

At this time, the false Prophets were busily telling him what he and the people wanted to hear, and it was much easier to believe their Prophecies than that given by the Lord. As peace and prosperity was the false cry of that day, it is the false cry of this day as well! Sadly, the major part of the modern Church specializes in that false doctrine.

The *"great eagle with great wings"* of Verse 3 speaks of Nebuchadnezzar. The phrase, *"Came unto Lebanon,"* actually speaks of Jerusalem, where the houses were built of cedar from Lebanon.

The phrase, *"And took the highest branch of the cedar,"* speaks of Jehoiahcin being taken captive after serving only three months as King of Judah (II Kings 24:8, 15-16).

Verse 4 says, *"He cropped off the top of his young twigs,"* and speaks of the more imminent citizens of Jerusalem being taken captive along with Jehoiachin. This was the second deportation by Nebuchadnezzar, and took place about eleven years before the third and final deportation, which completely destroyed Jerusalem and the Temple.

The phrase of Verse 5, *"He took also of the seed of the Land,"* refers to Nebuchadnezzar making Zedekiah King of Judah in place of Jehoiachin.

The phrase, *"And planted it in a fruitful field,"* refers to the possibility of Zedekiah's reign. But being fruitful, with the Land of Judah enjoying prosperity, if he had only submitted himself to Nebuchadnezzar, as directed by the Lord; however, this he did not do, which resulted in Judah and Jerusalem becoming very unfruitful, i.e., *"destroyed."*

The phrase, *"He placed it by great waters, and set it as a willow tree,"* referred to the Lord having Nebuchadnezzar to choose Zedekiah with every opportunity given for prosperity, as a *"willow tree"* can grow abundantly if near *"great waters."* So, repeatedly, the Lord attempted to save Judah and Jerusalem from destruction.

The phrase of Verse 6, *"And it grew,"* refers to prosperity under Zedekiah at least for a short time.

NOTES

The phrase, *"And became a spreading vine of low stature,"* means a base, or weak, kingdom enjoying a measure of prosperity.

The phrase, *"Whose branches turn toward him, and the roots thereof were under him,"* refers to the prosperity of Judah being sustained by Nebuchadnezzar, with the pronoun *"him"* referring to that Monarch.

The phrase, *"So it became a vine, and brought forth branches, and shot forth sprigs,"* means that the Kingdom of Judah ceased to be a lofty cedar enjoying independence, and instead became a lowly vine subject to the Gentile Monarch.

This was by Divine appointment; but Zedekiah's rebellion robbed the nation of this limited prosperity, and actually plunged it into total destruction.

As it regards Blessings from the Lord, we must ever understand that there must be *"obedience to the Lord." "Obedience"* and *"Blessings"* go hand in hand! We cannot expect Blessing if disobedience is rendered. We must not allow the lesson of Zedekiah, Judah, Jerusalem, the false Prophets, and the true Prophets, Jeremiah and Ezekiel, to be lost upon us.

Verse 7 speaks of *"another great eagle with great wings and many feathers."* This was Pharaoh-Hopra, King of Egypt.

If it is to be noticed, the description of this Kingdom by the Holy Spirit is not nearly so graphic as that of the Kingdom of Babylon. The Babylonian Kingdom described in Verse 3 is said to be *"longwinged"* and with *"divers colors,"* which are omitted respecting Egypt, noting that Egypt was not so strong, nor did her sway extend over so great a variety of nations as Babylon.

The phrase of Verse 7, *"And behold, this vine did bend her roots toward him,"* refers to Zedekiah courting the alliance of Pharaoh and trusting in his chariots.

The first two words, *"And behold,"* denote the foolishness of such action as pointed out by the Holy Spirit, and the absurdity in doing such a thing!

The phrase, *"That he might water it by the furrows of her plantation,"* refers to Pharaoh assuring Zedekiah that he could protect him against the Babylonian Monarch; however, as the future proved, and as the Lord through the Prophets repeatedly said, the boast of Pharaoh carried no weight.

Verse 8 proclaims the fact that if Zedekiah had obeyed the Prophets of the Lord, placing himself and Judah under the domain of Nebuchadnezzar, which the Lord demanded, then Judah would have had a fair measure of prosperity. The vine might have borne fruit. As well, the terrible blood bath that followed, along with the destruction of Jerusalem and the Temple, might have been avoided.

But Zedekiah would not heed the Word of the Lord as it came from Jeremiah and Ezekiel, but rather the Word of the false Prophets, who were predicting that the Babylonian yoke was going to be overthrown, and that Egypt would help get this done. It was not to be, even as it could not be!

When we disobey the Word of the Lord, it always brings a negative result. When we obey the Word of the Lord, there is always a positive result. We must never forget that.

(9) "SAY THOU, THUS SAITH THE LORD GOD; SHALL IT PROSPER? SHALL HE NOT PULL UP THE ROOTS THEREOF, AND CUT OFF THE FRUIT THEREOF, THAT IT WITHER? IT SHALL WITHER IN ALL THE LEAVES OF HER SPRING, EVEN WITHOUT GREAT POWER OR MANY PEOPLE TO PLUCK IT UP BY THE ROOTS THEREOF.

(10) "YES, BEHOLD, BEING PLANTED, SHALL IT PROSPER? SHALL IT NOT UTTERLY WITHER, WHEN THE EAST WIND TOUCHES IT? IT SHALL WITHER IN THE FURROWS WHERE IT GREW.

(11) "MOREOVER THE WORD OF THE LORD CAME UNTO ME, SAYING,

(12) "SAY NOW TO THE REBELLIOUS HOUSE, KNOW YE NOT WHAT THESE THINGS MEAN? TELL THEM, BEHOLD, THE KING OF BABYLON IS COME TO JERUSALEM, AND HAS TAKEN THE KING THEREOF, AND THE PRINCES THEREOF, AND LED THEM WITH HIM TO BABYLON;

(13) "AND HAS TAKEN OF THE KING'S SEED, AND MADE A COVENANT WITH HIM, AND HAS TAKEN AN OATH OF HIM: HE HAS ALSO TAKEN THE MIGHTY OF THE LAND:

(14) "THAT THE KINGDOM MIGHT BE BASE, THAT IT MIGHT NOT LIFT ITSELF UP, BUT THAT BY KEEPING OF HIS COVENANT IT MIGHT STAND.

(15) "BUT HE REBELLED AGAINST HIM IN SENDING HIS AMBASSADORS INTO EGYPT, THAT THEY MIGHT GIVE HIM HORSES AND MUCH PEOPLE. SHALL HE PROSPER? SHALL HE ESCAPE WHO DOES SUCH THINGS? OR SHALL HE BREAK THE COVENANT, AND BE DELIVERED?

(16) "AS I LIVE, SAITH THE LORD GOD, SURELY IN THE PLACE WHERE THE KING DWELLS THAT MADE HIM KING, WHOSE OATH HE DESPISED, AND WHOSE COVENANT HE BROKE, EVEN WITH HIM IN THE MIDST OF BABYLON HE SHALL DIE.

(17) "NEITHER SHALL PHARAOH WITH HIS MIGHTY ARMY AND GREAT COMPANY MAKE FOR HIM IN THE WAR, BY CASTING UP MOUNTS, AND BUILDING FORTS, TO CUT OFF MANY PERSONS:

(18) "SEEING HE DESPISED THE OATH BY BREAKING THE COVENANT, WHEN, LO, HE HAD GIVEN HIS HAND, AND HAS DONE ALL THESE THINGS, HE SHALL NOT ESCAPE."

The structure is:

1. The treaty with Egypt, which prosperity did not succeed, even as it could not succeed, because it was against the Word of the Lord.

2. We also find here the evil of Zedekiah's conduct in breaking an oath made in the name of Jehovah, and we speak of the oath he made to Nebuchadnezzar.

3. God's loving purpose was the peace and prosperity of His people, which He had deemed necessary, to be in subjection to the Gentiles, in this case, Nebuchadnezzar; and that they should be a witness for Him. In doing so, they would have been His recognized people, and a light to lighten the Gentiles. But their rebellion lost this prosperity and that glory.

THE BROKEN COVENANT

The question of Verse 9, *"Thus saith the Lord GOD; shall it prosper?"* refers to the alliance between Zedekiah and Pharaoh. The answer is *"no, it will not prosper"*; for he Nebuchadnezzar would uproot Zedekiah and destroy his Kingdom with an effort that needed neither great power nor many soldiers.

Verse 10 once again asks the question, *"Shall it prosper"?*

Not only will it not prosper, but it will instead *"utterly wither."*

The phrase, *"When the east wind touches it,"* refers to Nebuchadnezzar who came from the east.

The phrase, *"It shall wither in the furrows where it grew,"* means that this alliance with Egypt will die aborning.

Usually the Holy Spirit does not explain so fully the meaning of Parables, but here He does so in order that there be no mistake whatsoever concerning what is being said. In other words, this action portrays the Truth that the Lord was doing all within His Power to save Judah and Jerusalem from the coming blood bath; however, He would not violate the free moral agency of Zedekiah, as he will not violate the free moral agency of anyone and, therefore, Zedekiah, along with Judah and Jerusalem, went to their doom!

Verse 12 is the same as Verses 3 and 4, which speak of Nebuchadnezzar taking Jehoiachin and the Princes to Babylon, which was the second deportation. There were three in all.

The phrase of Verse 13, *"And has taken of the king's seed, and made a covenant with him,"* refers to Zedekiah being made king of Judah. When Zedekiah was made king, He made a Covenant with Nebuchadnezzar, and did so in the name of the Lord, which, in effect, was the Will of the Lord that he would submit himself to the heathen Monarch. But after a period of time, he rebelled against Nebuchadnezzar, and sought the help of Pharaoh of Egypt, attempting to throw off the Babylonian yoke, despite the fact that Jeremiah and Ezekiel were telling him to do otherwise.

The idea of the latter part of Verse 13, along with Verse 14, is that it was Nebuchadnezzar's policy to deprive Judah of all its elements of strength — to leave it *"base."* Even masons, smiths, and carpenters were carried off, lest they should be used for warlike preparations (II Ki. 24:16).

The phrase, *"That it might not lift itself up,"* means that Judah had no ability within itself to sustain military action, but yet, it would remain a viable Kingdom, sustained by Nebuchadnezzar *"by keeping the Covenant."*

The phrase, *"It might stand,"* refers to God's loving purpose, which was the peace and prosperity of His people in subjection, at least at this time, to the Gentiles. Had they obeyed Him fully, submitting themselves to Nebuchadnezzar, as the Lord demanded, they would have still enjoyed a modicum of blessing. But this they did not do, and this they would not do.

The phrase of Verse 15, *"But he rebelled against him in sending his ambassadors into Egypt,"* refers to Zedekiah actively seeking an alliance with the Egyptians, which was totally opposed to the Will of God, and which would bring ruin to Judah.

EGYPT

At no time in Bible history did the Lord sanction any type of alliance with Egypt, which He used as a type of the world, but with one exception; this was the time that Joseph was made Viceroy in Egypt, and his Father Jacob was instructed by the Lord to take the entirety of the family of God into this land (Gen. 46:1-4). Even then, the Prophecy was given that, *"I will also bring you up again,"* meaning that they would be brought out of Egypt, which they were. Their sojourn in Egypt at that time was two hundred and fifteen years.

As well, and due to Judah's failure, the Lord had other plans regarding the Gentile Kingdoms, which did not include Egypt.

The phrase, *"That they might give him horses and much people,"* refers to the chariots and horses of Egypt, which, throughout its entire history, seemed to have been its chief element of strength. Zedekiah, in listening to his false Prophets, was made to believe that the power of Egypt was greater than the power of the Chaldeans. The Holy Spirit repeatedly said otherwise (Vss. 3, 7).

The phrase of Verse 16, *"Surely in the place where the king dwells who made him king,"* refers to Nebuchadnezzar, who lived in Babylon, who made Zedekiah King of Judah.

The phrase, *"Even with him in the midst of Babylon he shall die,"* refers to the prison in Babylon, where Zedekiah was taken after being blinded. This was to be the outcome of the alliance with Egypt.

The Prophecy was probably written and given when the hopes of Zedekiah and his counselors were at their highest point, when the Chaldeans had, in fact, raised the siege of Jerusalem in anticipation of the arrival of the Egyptian Army (Jer. 37:5-11). Ezekiel, like Jeremiah, declared that the relief would be but temporary.

Verse 17 proclaims the fact that Zedekiah expected Egypt to come with a mighty army, and drive away the Babylonians.

While it is true that Egypt came against Nebuchadnezzar during the siege of Jerusalem, and the Babylonians raised the siege (Jer. 37:11) just long enough to repulse Hophra, still, it is not known whether much of a battle occurred or not, or whether Egypt on facing the Babylonians retreated. At any rate, the siege was quickly resumed by Nebuchadnezaar, with Jerusalem falling some months later.

The phrase of Verse 18, *"Seeing he despised the oath by breaking the Covenant,"* refers to the Covenant made by Zedekiah with the Babylonian King, but now breaking, which infuriated Nebuchadnezzar.

The phrase, *"He shall not escape,"* refers to Zedekiah in attempting to escape the Babylonians when the city failed!

(19) "THEREFORE THUS SAITH THE LORD GOD; AS I LIVE, SURELY MY OATH THAT HE HAS DESPISED, AND MY COVENANT THAT HE HAS BROKEN, EVEN IT WILL I RECOMPENSE UPON HIS OWN HEAD.

(20) "AND I WILL SPREAD MY NET UPON HIM, AND HE SHALL BE TAKEN IN MY SNARE, AND I WILL BRING HIM TO BABYLON, AND WILL PLEAD WITH HIM THERE FOR HIS TRESPASS THAT HE HAS TRESPASSED AGAINST ME.

(21) "AND ALL HIS FUGITIVES WITH ALL HIS BANDS SHALL FALL BY THE SWORD, AND THEY WHO REMAIN SHALL BE SCATTERED TOWARD ALL WINDS: AND YOU SHALL KNOW THAT I THE LORD HAVE SPOKEN IT."

The overview is:

1. Zedekiah freely agreed by Covenant to rule Judah under Nebuchadnezzar.

2. He took an oath to obey him, but rebelled after serving for several years.

3. He turned to Egypt for help, and for this God cursed him.

COVENANT

Zedekiah had made a Covenant with Nebuchadnezzar. It was God's Will that this Covenant be made, so the breaking of this Covenant, which Zedekiah did, was a sin against Jehovah Himself as the God of faithfulness and truth. If it is to be noticed, the Lord referred to this Covenant as *"My Covenant,"* so the breaking of it was a serious matter indeed!

Inasmuch as this Covenant was of the Lord, and that Zedekiah had treated it lightly, even despised it, the consequences for this Monarch would be frightful!

Zedekiah, as many modern Christians, was looking in the wrong direction. It was not necessarily Pharaoh, the King of Egypt, or Nebuchadnezzar, the King of Babylon that he had to fear, but rather God Almighty. In other words, it was the Lord who was guiding events, as it is the Lord Who always guides events. While Zedekiah may have thought he was breaking a Covenant with Nebuchadnezzar, in effect, he was breaking the Covenant of the Lord.

As modern Believers, we must not allow this lesson to be lost on us. It is not my will or even the will of someone else that really matters, but rather the Will of God. Everything the Believer does has significance. And everything the Believer does should be done in the Light of the Lord. In other words, what does the Lord want, which necessitates us praying about everything.

Zedekiah ignored the Lord, which means that he ignored what the Lord was saying through the Prophets Jeremiah and Ezekiel. Regrettably, he believed the false Prophets. As a result, not only would it be a sad day for him, but a sad day for all of Israel.

Verse 21 says, *"All his bands shall fall by the sword,"* refers to the terrible carnage, which developed when Jerusalem fell to the Babylonians. The Babylonians ruthlessly slaughtered multiple tens of thousands, or even hundreds of thousands. Nebuchadnezzar, angry because of Zedekiah's breaking of the Covenant and resistance against him, when finally taking Jerusalem, literally laid it waste.

As well, the words, *"And you shall know that I the LORD have spoken it,"* refer to the fact that what the Lord speaks will come to pass.

That's at least one of the reasons that the Word of God must be interpreted correctly. But the sad truth is, during this sad day of Judah's history, and as well at the present time, the Word of God is little consulted, but is rather ignored, or else perverted.

THE CONVERSION OF ZEDEKIAH?

The phrase of Verse 20, *"I will bring him to Babylon, and will plead with him there for his trespass that he has trespassed against Me,"* suggests that in his earthly prison and physical blindness, Grace gave him inward eyesight and spiritual freedom. In other words, it seems that he finally made his peace with God, even after long years of rebellion. Jeremiah 32:5 and 34:4-5 intimates this. It is tragic that it takes such chastisement to bring one to one's senses, but I'm afraid that often times this is the case.

(22) "THUS SAITH THE LORD GOD; I WILL ALSO TAKE OF THE HIGHEST BRANCH OF THE HIGH CEDAR, AND WILL SET IT; I WILL CROP OFF FROM THE TOP OF HIS YOUNG TWIGS A TENDER ONE, AND WILL PLANT IT UPON AN HIGH MOUNTAIN AND EMINENT:

(23) "IN THE MOUNTAIN OF THE HEIGHT OF ISRAEL WILL I PLANT IT: AND IT SHALL BRING FORTH BOUGHS, AND BEAR FRUIT, AND BE A GOODLY CEDAR: AND UNDER IT SHALL DWELL ALL FOWL OF EVERY WING; IN THE SHADOW OF THE BRANCHES THEREOF SHALL THEY DWELL.

(24) "AND ALL THE TREES OF THE FIELD SHALL KNOW THAT I THE LORD HAVE BROUGHT DOWN THE HIGH TREE, HAVE EXALTED THE LOW TREE, HAVE DRIED UP THE GREEN TREE, AND HAVE MADE THE DRY TREE TO FLOURISH: I THE LORD HAVE SPOKEN AND HAVE DONE IT."

The composition is:

1. The Kingdom predicted in Verses 22 through 24 is that of the Messiah.
2. The lofty top of the cedar is the Royal Family of David. Its top most and tender twig, the Messiah (Isa. 53:2); the high mountain, Zion.
3. All the nations of the Earth during the coming Kingdom Age, which is the interpretation of Verse 24, will submit themselves to the great King of Israel and enjoy the prosperity of His Kingdom. The high and green tree of man's proud dominion will be brought down and dried up, and the low and dry tree of despised Israel will then be made to flourish.

RESTORATION

The Kingdom predicted in Verses 22 through 24 is that of the Messiah during the coming Kingdom Age. It refers to the Restoration of Israel, which means that Israel will then accept Christ as her Lord, her Saviour, and her Messiah. This will be at the Second Coming.

The phrase from Verse 23, *"In the mountain of the height of Israel will I plant it,"* refers to Jerusalem and the mountain on which it is built. This very Verse, among others, is the very reason that this area has been contested for so long. Satan will go to any length to keep this Prophecy from being fulfilled; however, he will not succeed.

Even at the present, the Muslims claim a part, or all, of Jerusalem. Nevertheless, their claim is false, and even though Israel is presently a long way from God, still, these Passages plus many others promise a coming Restoration when Christ will finally be accepted as Israel's True King.

The Lord did not say that the possibility existed that such would come to pass, but the phrase, *"Will I plant it,"* guarantees its fulfillment.

The phrase, *"And bear fruit,"* means that it has seldom borne fruit in the past, but will definitely do so at that glorious future time. The reason Israel has not borne fruit in the past is because she would not abide in Christ. And it is only in Christ that one can bear fruit (Jn. 15:1-6).

The phrase, *"And under it shall dwell all fowl of every wing,"* refers to the Gentile nations of the world, which will, at that time, look to Christ for all prosperity. They will not be disappointed!

The phrase, *"In the shadow of the branches*

thereof shall they dwell," refers to Israel at that time being the dominant nation of the world, and all blessings flowing from Christ through it to all the nations.

The *"high tree"* of Verse 24, refers to the nations of the world, which have exalted themselves against God and His Will. He will bring them down, which will be done at the Second Coming (Dan. 2:35).

The *"low tree"* and the *"dry tree"* represent Israel, and what it has been in the past, because of its rejection of the Lord. But the Lord has promised that Israel will be restored. He said that he would *"exalt the low tree,"* and would *"make the dry tree to flourish."*

The phrase of Verse 24, *"I the LORD have spoken and have done it,"* refers to the fact that in the Mind of God, it has already been done, because He has spoken it. In fact, the happenings of this present time (2003), as it regards Israel, pertain to events which will lead to this coming glad day. Admittedly, Israel will face some hard days just ahead, in fact, the hardest they have ever faced. It is called, *"The time of Jacob's trouble."* But then the Lord said, *"But he shall be saved out of it"* (Jer. 30:7). It is the coming Great Tribulation, which is just ahead on the world scene (Mat. 24:21). But even though the dark night is definitely coming, it also will definitely be followed by a bright morning (Zech. 13:1).

"Like a river glorious is God's Perfect Peace,
"Over all victorious in its bright increase;
"Perfect, yet it flows fuller every day;
"Perfect, yet it grows deeper all the way."

"Hidden in the hollow of His Blessed Hand,
"Never foe can follow, never traitor stand.
"Not a surge of worry, not a shade of care,
"Not a blast of hurry touch the Spirit there."

"Every joy or trial falls from above,
"Traced upon our dial by the Son of Love.

NOTES

"We may trust Him fully, all for us to do;
"They who trust Him wholly find Him wholly True."

CHAPTER 18

(1) "THE WORD OF THE LORD CAME UNTO ME AGAIN, SAYING,

(2) "WHAT DO YOU MEAN, THAT YOU USE THIS PROVERB CONCERNING THE LAND OF ISRAEL, SAYING, THE FATHERS HAVE EATEN SOUR GRAPES, AND THE CHILDREN'S TEETH ARE SET ON EDGE?

(3) "AS I LIVE, SAITH THE LORD GOD, YOU SHALL NOT HAVE OCCASION ANY MORE TO USE THIS PROVERB IN ISRAEL.

(4) "BEHOLD, ALL SOULS ARE MINE; AS THE SOUL OF THE FATHER, SO ALSO THE SOUL OF THE SON IS MINE: THE SOUL THAT SINNETH, IT SHALL DIE.

(5) "BUT IF A MAN BE JUST, AND DO THAT WHICH IS LAWFUL AND RIGHT,

(6) "AND HAS NOT EATEN UPON THE MOUNTAINS, NEITHER HAS LIFTED UP HIS EYES TO THE IDOLS OF THE HOUSE OF ISRAEL, NEITHER HAS DEFILED THIS NEIGHBOUR'S WIFE, NEITHER HAS COME NEAR TO A MENSTRUOUS WOMAN.

(7) "AND HAS NOT OPPRESSED ANY, BUT HAS RESTORED TO THE DEBTOR HIS PLEDGE, HAS SPOILED NONE BY VIOLENCE, HAS GIVEN HIS BREAD TO THE HUNGRY, AND HAS COVERED THE NAKED WITH A GARMENT;

(8) "HE WHO HAS NOT GIVEN FORTH UPON USURY, NEITHER HAS TAKEN ANY INCREASE, THAT HAS WITHDRAWN HIS HAND FROM INIQUITY, HAS EXECUTED TRUE JUDGMENT BETWEEN MAN AND MAN,

(9) "HAS WALKED IN MY STATUTES, AND HAS KEPT MY JUDGMENTS, TO DEAL TRULY; HE IS JUST, HE SHALL SURELY LIVE, SAITH THE LORD GOD."

The structure is:

1. The miseries suffered by the people in Jerusalem, because of the Babylonian war, were declared by them to be due to their father's sins, for they concluded themselves to be Righteous. Hence, their proverb of Verse 2,

repeated in Verse 19, and its principle insisted on in Verses 25 and 29.

2. That is: they charge God with injustice, for man always throws the blame upon God, as Adam did (Gen. 3:12).

3. Ezekiel's Message vindicated God's Justice, and showed the equity of His moral government. It based itself upon the Divine plan, afterwards revealed, by which God can righteously declare a sinner to be a justified person (Williams).

4. Descendants are personally not punished for the sins of their ancestors, unless they persevere in them. It is otherwise with national judgments; but God always did, and always does, promise individual forgiveness to sinners who repent. His ways are therefore equal.

A FALSE DIRECTION

This Chapter deals with erroneous conclusions of the people regarding the Law of Moses. The Lord through the Prophet will direct His attention to the error, which characterizes Judah at that time.

In fact, millions have died eternally lost because they misinterpreted the Bible and did not *"rightly divide the Word of Truth."* The twisting of Scriptures to one's own destruction has persisted from the very beginning, and is even more predominant presently (II Pet. 3:16).

The Proverb of Verse 2, *"The fathers have eaten sour grapes, and the children's teeth are set on edge,"* proclaims Judah blaming their fathers' past years for their present miseries. So, in actuality, they were charging God with injustice, for man, as stated, always throws the blame on God, as did Adam (Gen. 3:12). This Proverb was probably derived from Exodus 20:5, where it says, *"I the LORD your God am a jealous God, visiting the iniquity of the fathers upon the children unto the third and fourth generation of them who hate Me."* However, they had taken this statement much farther than the Lord intended, failing to refer to the words *"of them who hate Me"*; further, Deuteronomy 24:16 says, *"Every man shall be put to death for his own sin."* In other words, the Word of God tells us that we are not responsible for the sins of others.

NOTES

It is certainly true that if the fathers sin, the children will certainly be affected in an adverse way; however, there is no inference whatsoever that a future generation, if they, in fact, live for God, will have to pay for the sins of the fathers.

As in Ezekiel's day, so in that of his Lord's (Mat. 23:32, 34, 36), that Hebrews believed themselves to be Righteous and attributed their misfortunes to the misconduct of their ancestors. However, this Chapter, along with Matthew 23:32, as well as others, prove that descendants are personally not punished for the sins of their ancestors, unless they persevere in those sins. God always promises individual forgiveness to sinners who repent (II Chron. 7:14; Rom. 10:13; I Jn. 1:9; Rev. 22: 17).

SOULS

Verse 4 emphatically declares that Judah was suffering for their own sins, not the sins of their Fathers. The phrase, *"The soul that sins, it shall die,"* proclaims the Truth that God judges each person upon his own actions, not for the actions of others. Men are loathe to take responsibility for their own actions, which true Repentance demands.

Modern psychology is probably one of the greatest culprits of all in that it claims that all men are basically good, and if they are bad, it is the fault of their parents, or other things. Consequently, psychology claims that if a person can only be placed in the right environment, given the correct education and is correct politically, their problems can be solved.

The Bible completely refutes this lie in that it says that all men are sinners, and their sin is the cause of their problems; and the only answer for it is Christ Jesus (Rom. 3:23; 6:23; 5:8).

LAWFUL AND RIGHT

Verses 5 through 9 are not the promotion of Salvation by works, but instead that if a person has truly repented and is attempting to do *"that which is lawful and right,"* such action will portray itself in a positive way in his life.

The Righteous principle upon which God acts in pardoning original sin and personal sins is revealed in Romans 3:21-26.

The phrase of Verse 5, *"But if a man be*

just," pertains to the sinner turning to God, and then attempting to do that *"which is lawful and right."* This completely refutes the unscriptural Doctrine of Unconditional Eternal Security, which states that a person can be saved and continue to live in sin. While Salvation saves from sin, it does not mean, however, that a person will never sin again; it does mean that an individual will attempt with all of his strength to do *"that which is lawful and right."* Anything else makes a mockery out of the Word of God and places Salvation as only a theory, which, in effect, does not change men's lives. Actually, the very foundation of Bible Salvation is that men's lives are gloriously and wondrously changed (II Cor. 5:17).

The idea of these statements, as given by the Lord through the Prophet, is that if a man repents, whatever sins his Father committed will have no bearing on him. The sin begins and stops with the individual who commits it, even though its effects may definitely carry over to the children, and others.

In other words, if a Father (or Mother) is an alcoholic, thereby squandering the family income, the children definitely will suffer in a physical, material, and even spiritual sense; however, the accountability for that sin (or whatever sin) will stop with the one who committed it. The idea of all that is said in these Verses is that when a person truly comes to the Lord, his life will definitely be affected, and changed, even in a drastic way. The idea that the only difference between the Redeemed and the unredeemed is the Blood of Christ is fallacious indeed! There is a vast difference in the Redeemed and the unredeemed, that is, if one is truly redeemed.

As stated, this doesn't mean that the Redeemed will never again sin, but it definitely does mean that the change in one's life is obvious to all. And if not, in other words, the person is continuing unabated in the old lifestyle, this is a sure sign that the Salvation of such a person is a profession only. In other words, they haven't really been Born-Again.

In fact, multiple millions throng Churches, claiming Salvation, but who, in reality, have never been Born-Again. Concerning such, Jesus plainly said, *"Wherefore by their fruits you shall know them."* He then went on to say: *"Not every one who says unto Me, Lord, Lord, shall enter into the Kingdom of Heaven; but he who does the Will of My Father which is in Heaven"* (Mat. 7:20-21).

VICTORY OVER SIN

Before the Cross, the Holy Spirit was greatly limited in that which He could do for the Believer. To be sure, He helped immeasurably, as would be obvious, but due to the fact that the blood of bulls and goats could not take away sins (Heb. 10:4), this meant that the sin debt remained, which presented the limitations. Therefore, all Believers before the Cross, even the Godliest, did not have near the capacity to live a Holy life as Believers since the Cross have that capacity. As stated, the Holy Spirit definitely was with them (Jn. 14:17), but at that time, He was not in them. So, Believers before the Cross had to present to the Lord a willing mind and an obedient heart, which meant that they wanted to do the Will of God, and would strive to do the Will of God, to the best of their ability. Even as now, their Salvation was anchored in the Faith which they exhibited toward the One Who was to come, namely the Lord Jesus Christ, Who was represented by the Sacrifices. But as far as living a Holy life was concerned, while all before the Cross were to do their best, they were limited in victorious living, because of the reason stated.

VICTORY SINCE THE CROSS

Due to the fact of the sin debt being paid by the Cross of Calvary, the Holy Spirit can now come into the heart and life of the Believer to abide permanently (Jn. 14:16-17), which He couldn't do before the Cross. As a result, the Believer now has the Personal help of the Spirit as it regards victorious living. And if we as Believers follow the admonition of the Spirit, which is given to us in the Word of God, irrespective as to whom we might be, whether weak or strong, victory can be ours in every capacity. No, the Bible doesn't teach sinless perfection, but it does teach that *"sin shall not have dominion over you"* (Rom. 6:14). The problem is that not one Christian out of a thousand, and I don't think I'm exaggerating, has any idea as to how the Holy Spirit works. As we've stated elsewhere in this Volume, most take Him for granted, if He is given any consideration at all.

In fact, I remember asking a Preacher once, who had finished four years of post-graduate study in one of the most prestigious Seminaries in the land, what he had learned about the Holy Spirit during that period of time?

I'll never forget his answer. He sat there for a moment, thinking, and then finally answered. *"Brother Swaggart, I can't remember that I heard the Holy Spirit mentioned once in the entirety of the four years I was in that graduate school."* While he went to state that he was certain that he had heard the name called during that period of time, but nothing stuck in his mind as it regarded what was said about the Holy Spirit, which means, that very little information was given. That's about the same as a lawyer going to four years of Law School, and graduating without having studied anything about Law, or any other such like endeavor.

All of this shows us just how far that the Church has drifted from the leadership of the Holy Spirit. When it comes to Pentecostals, most think that speaking with other Tongues, or the Operation of one or two Gifts of the Spirit, are the end result of the Holy Spirit. While those things are definitely important, they have little or nothing to do with victorious living. In fact, most Christians have no knowledge as to how the Holy Spirit affects victorious living, except that the Holy Spirit has Power. While He definitely does, the idea is that He use that Power on our behalf. Now once again, let me state the same thing I've just stated, but in a little different way.

Most Pentecostals and Charismatics think that this Power is automatically used on behalf of the Child of God. In other words, they think that being Baptized with the Spirit with the evidence of speaking with other Tongues automatically grants one this power. It doesn't! Because it's so important, let me say it again: It doesn't!

THE POWER OF THE SPIRIT

With the Holy Spirit using His Power on our behalf, which He certainly desires to do, there is absolutely nothing that cannot be done; the sole reason is that the Holy Spirit is God. As a result, He is Almighty. This means that things which we cannot do, and no matter how hard we try, are no problem for Him whatsoever, and for all the obvious reasons. But the great question is: How can I get the Holy Spirit to consistently use His Power on my behalf?

A LAW

Whether we realize it or not, everything the Holy Spirit does within our hearts and lives is done through particular legal means. In other words, it's a *"Law."* Something has given Him the legal means to work within our lives, and that something is the Cross of Christ.

Man owed a just debt to God, which He, incidentally, couldn't pay; but Christ paid it all at the Cross, at least for all who will believe (Jn. 3:16). This was a legal debt, which was satisfied by a legal Sacrifice, which, of course, was Christ. This is what gives the Holy Spirit the right to live permanently within our hearts and lives. The reason he couldn't do that before the Cross is because He didn't have the legal right to do so, in that the sin debt couldn't be paid by animal blood. Now listen to what Paul said:

"For the Law (the Law of which we speak, which was devised by the Godhead in eternity past) *of the Spirit* (Holy Spirit) *of Life* (all life comes from Christ, through the Spirit) *in Christ Jesus* (the Law of which we speak is that which Jesus did at the Cross) *has made me free from the Law of sin and death"* (Rom. 8:2).

As is obvious here, the Holy Spirit works in the confines of this particular *"Law,"* which refers to Christ and what Christ did at the Cross, all on our behalf. For the Holy Spirit to use His great Power on our behalf, He only requires one thing, and that is for us to exhibit our Faith exclusively in Christ and the Cross (Rom. 6:3-14; I Cor. 1:17-18, 23; 2:2; Gal. 6:14).

FAITH IN THE CROSS

Why is what I've just said so very hard for most people? And I continue to speak of the Believer exhibiting his Faith exclusively in Christ and the Cross.

It is hard because the Believer must give

up all hope of victory otherwise, which means that he places no confidence in the flesh at all. Paul said: *"For I know that in me* (that is, in my flesh), *dwelleth no good thing"* (Rom. 7:18). It's hard for the Believer to come to that place that he admits such.

Once the Cross is looked at objectively, in other words, from a total Scriptural position, we find that our dependence on all things other than the Cross must go, which speaks of our own good works, our Church, our Denomination, etc. No, it doesn't mean we are to quit our Church, but it does mean that we are to understand that the true Church is the end result of the Cross, and not the other way around. There's something in man, even the most consecrated Believers, which likes to believe that we can do whatever needs to be done. But the truth is, we can't!

There is only one way that the Believer can walk in victory, and I'm speaking of the fact that sin no longer has dominion over us, and that is by understanding that the Cross was an absolute necessity, and that it must ever be the Object of our Faith. Then and only then, will the Holy Spirit exert His Almighty Power on our behalf, which alone can give us what we need to live this life. That's what Paul was talking about when he said: *"There is therefore now no condemnation to them which are in Christ Jesus, who walk not after the flesh, but after the Spirit"* (Rom. 8:1).

(10) "IF HE BEGET A SON WHO IS A ROBBER, A SHEDDER OF BLOOD, AND WHO DOES THE LIKE TO ANY ONE OF THESE THINGS,

(11) "AND WHO DOES NOT ANY OF THOSE DUTIES, BUT EVEN HAS EATEN UPON THE MOUNTAINS, AND DEFILED HIS NEIGHBOUR'S WIFE.

(12) "HAS OPPRESSED THE POOR AND NEEDY, HAS SPOILED BY VIOLENCE, HAS NOT RESTORED THE PLEDGE, AND HAS LIFTED UP HIS EYES TO THE IDOLS, HAS COMMITTED ABOMINATION,

(13) "HAS GIVEN FORTH UPON USURY, AND HAS TAKEN INCREASE: SHALL HE THEN LIVE? HE SHALL NOT LIVE; HE HAS DONE ALL THESE ABOMINATIONS; HE SHALL SURELY DIE; HIS BLOOD SHALL BE UPON HIM."

The structure is:

1. The second case cited here is that of the bad son of a good father; the argument is that this fact aggravates his guilt, and that the merits of his Father shall not, and cannot, shield him from punishment.

2. These examples in this Chapter are given by the Holy Spirit because of the erroneous conclusions of the people of Judah.

3. Some felt that inasmuch as they were the children of Abraham, Isaac, and Jacob, this surely would insure their Salvation. In fact, they continued to think this, even during the time of Christ (Mat. 3:9).

INDIVIDUAL RESPONSIBILITY

The Holy Spirit makes it clear in this Chapter that individual responsibility is always required. In other words, the buck cannot be passed to others. Irrespective as to what one's family might be, whether good or bad, God will judge each person on the acts of that particular person, and not the acts of someone else.

The reason for this teaching is that man is forever loathe to admit culpability, rather desiring to blame someone else for the situation, which began, as stated, with Adam.

As well, some like to think, even millions, that if their parents, or else a husband or wife, are righteous, that somehow their Righteousness will cover the wayward direction of the sinner. It won't! While the Righteousness of a family or mate is definitely a blessing, and will be a tremendous blessing to all who are connected with such Righteousness, it will not protect the one who is wayward. While sin cannot be transmitted to someone else by proxy, neither can Righteousness!

(14) "NOW, LO, IF HE BEGET A SON, WHO SEES ALL HIS FATHER'S SINS WHICH HE HAS DONE, AND CONSIDERS, AND DOES NOT SUCH LIKE,

(15) "WHO HAS NOT EATEN UPON THE MOUNTAINS, NEITHER HAS LIFTED UP HIS EYES TO THE IDOLS OF THE HOUSE OF ISRAEL, HAS NOT DEFILED HIS NEIGHBOUR'S WIFE.

(16) "NEITHER HAS OPPRESSED ANY, HAS NOT WITHHOLDEN THE PLEDGE, NEITHER HAS SPOILED BY VIOLENCE,

BUT HAS GIVEN HIS BREAD TO THE HUNGRY, AND HAS COVERED THE NAKED WITH A GARMENT,

(17) "WHO HAS TAKEN OFF HIS HAND FROM THE POOR, WHO HAS NOT RECEIVED USURY NOR INCREASE, HAS EXECUTED MY JUDGMENTS, HAS WALKED IN MY STATUTES; HE SHALL NOT DIE FOR THE INIQUITY OF HIS FATHER, HE SHALL SURELY LIVE."

The overview is:

1. This third case presented here further illustrates the impartiality of God's justice.

2. It is that of a good son of a bad father, such as Josiah and Hezekiah, and it is stated that just as the Righteous conduct of a father is not credited to an unrighteous son, so the wickedness of a father is not charged to the account of a Godly son.

3. The repetition in detail of actions injurious to others is an evidence of God's love to mankind, and how His Nature revolts against all injustice and selfishness.

4. So far from God punishing a man for the sins of others, He will not even punish him for his own sins, if he repents and avails himself of God's Salvation, which is Christ.

RIGHTEOUSNESS

The Holy Spirit goes to all lengths to place responsibility upon the individual involved, whether of unrighteousness or of Righteousness.

If one is to notice in these Passages and repeat it over and over, if a person claims to love God, they will also love their fellowman and will treat them accordingly.

The criteria followed by the Holy Spirit throughout the entire Bible is *"Loving God with all one's heart, and one's neighbor as one's self"* (Lk. 10:27).

Christianity that shows no love for one's fellowman, despite the loud profession, also has no love for God. The two cannot be divorced!

All of this tells us that the Father is not responsible for the sins of his son, as the son is not responsible for the sins of the Father. Each person in the eyes of God is responsible for his own sins.

However, the Father, at least in some measure, is always responsible for the sins of the son, in the sense that if he raises him in the way he should go, when he is old, he will not depart from it (Prov. 22:6). Therefore, if the son does depart from the ways of God, in some measure the Father has not raised him correctly, and is, at least to some degree, responsible, and will pay for it in the actions of his wayward son. However, the boy's sins will be borne by himself alone!

(18) "AS FOR HIS FATHER, BECAUSE HE CRUELLY OPPRESSED, SPOILED HIS BROTHER BY VIOLENCE, AND DID THAT WHICH IS NOT GOOD AMONG HIS PEOPLE, LO, EVEN HE SHALL DIE IN HIS INIQUITY.

(19) "YET SAY YE, WHY? DOES NOT THE SON BEAR THE INIQUITY OF THE FATHER? WHEN THE SON HAS DONE THAT WHICH IS LAWFUL AND RIGHT, AND HAS KEPT ALL MY STATUTES, AND HAS DONE THEM, HE SHALL SURELY LIVE.

(20) "THE SOUL THAT SINNETH, IT SHALL DIE. THE SON SHALL NOT BEAR THE INIQUITY OF THE FATHER, NEITHER SHALL THE FATHER BEAR THE INIQUITY OF THE SON: THE RIGHTEOUSNESS OF THE RIGHTEOUS SHALL BE UPON HIM, AND THE WICKEDNESS OF THE WICKED SHALL BE UPON HIM."

The synopsis is:

1. So, as there will be absolutely no room for speculation, the Holy Spirit proclaims the Truth that the ungodly Father is not saved as a result of the Godly son, as the ungodly son is not saved as a result of a Godly Father.

2. Over, and over the Holy Spirit emphasizes the responsibility of the individual for his own sins.

3. The phrase, *"The soul that sins, it shall die,"* is an emphatic statement, which means that God will hold each person responsible for his own actions, not for the actions of others.

PERSONAL RESPONSIBILITY

The phrase in the Twentieth Verse, *"The soul that sins, it shall die,"* completely shoots down the erroneous Doctrine of the *"Family curse,"* or *"Generational curse,"* as it is sometimes called.

This erroneous doctrine teaches that judgment for grievous sin can pass down to several generations. Consequently, Christians are taught that if they are having problems, whether physical, financial, emotional, domestic, or spiritual, that it is because of a *"Family curse."* As a result, they need to find a Preacher who understands these things, and who will lay hands on them, rebuking the Family curse, and thereby setting them free.

While it may sound good to the carnal ear, it is definitely not Scriptural.

To be sure, there are all types of curses on the human race, all because of sin. That includes family curses, generational curses, and probably any other type of curse of which one could think. However, all of those curses are totally broken and obliterated at conversion. Listen to the Scripture:

"Therefore if any man be in Christ, he is a new creature: old things are passed away; behold, all things are become new" (II Cor. 5:17).

As well, Paul said: *"Christ has redeemed us from the curse of the Law, being made a curse for us: for it is written, cursed is everyone who hangs on a tree:*

"That the Blessing of Abraham might come on the Gentiles through Jesus Christ; that we might receive the Promise of the Spirit through Faith" (Gal. 3:13-14).

As should be plainly obvious, even as the Word of God plainly tells us, once the person comes to Christ, the entire cycle of curses, and of whatever nature, is broken.

ERRONEOUS INTERPRETATION

This erroneous teaching is derived from the misinterpretation of several Passages. One will suffice:

"Thou shall not bow down yourself to them, nor serve them: for I the LORD your God am a jealous God, visiting the iniquity of the fathers upon the children unto the third and fourth generation of them who hate Me" (Ex. 20:5).

Those who teach this erroneous Doctrine failed to include the phrase, *"them who hate Me."*

To be sure, the *"iniquity of the fathers,"* whatever that might be, will definitely go down several generations, if the offspring continue to hate the Lord, i.e., *"disobeying His Word."* As we have stated, there are all types of curses, which continue to wreak their havoc on the human race, even destroying entire families until someone in that family gives their heart to Christ. The curse is then broken.

THE KEY TO VICTORY

Christians have problems, simply because they do not understand the Cross as it regards their Sanctification, etc. And until they understand the Cross in this capacity, which will help them to *"walk after the Spirit,"* their problems are going to continue, irrespective as to what type of Godly manifestations they may experience, or whoever might pray for them. Jesus said: *"You shall know the Truth, and the Truth shall make you free"* (Jn. 8:32).

So, that means that the Preacher, by the laying on of hands, or even by Gifts of the Spirit being put into operation, cannot deliver a person from bondage to victory. While those things mentioned are definitely Scriptural in their own right, we err when we attempt to use them out of context.

Any manifestation from the Lord is desirable and helpful. As well, Godly Preachers laying hands on people will definitely be a Blessing. But those things, within themselves, will not deliver anyone. It takes the *"Truth"* to do that, and we're speaking of Christ and what Christ has done at the Cross. Faith in the Finished Work of Christ is the *"Truth"* of which our Lord spoke, and which alone will set the captive free. Understanding that, then the *"laying on of hands,"* will then be the Blessing it is intended to be. But when we try to replace the Cross with manifestations or other things, as right as these other might be in their own way, the victory which is sought will not be found.

(21) "BUT IF THE WICKED WILL TURN FROM ALL HIS SINS THAT HE HAS COMMITTED, AND KEEP ALL MY STATUTES, AND DO THAT WHICH IS LAWFUL AND RIGHT, HE SHALL SURELY LIVE, HE SHALL NOT DIE.

(22) "ALL HIS TRANSGRESSIONS THAT HE HAS COMMITTED, THEY SHALL NOT BE MENTIONED UNTO HIM: IN HIS RIGHTEOUSNESS THAT HE HAS DONE HE SHALL LIVE.

(23) "HAVE I ANY PLEASURE AT ALL THAT THE WICKED SHOULD DIE? SAITH THE LORD GOD: AND NOT THAT

HE SHOULD RETURN FROM HIS WAYS, AND LIVE?

(24) "BUT WHEN THE RIGHTEOUS TURNS AWAY FROM HIS RIGHTEOUSNESS, AND COMMITS INIQUITY, AND DOES ACCORDING TO ALL THE ABOMINATIONS THAT THE WICKED MAN DOES, SHALL HE LIVE? ALL HIS RIGHTEOUSNESS THAT HE HAS DONE SHALL NOT BE MENTIONED: IN HIS TRESPASS THAT HE HAS TRESPASSED, AND IN HIS SIN THAT HE HAS SINNED, IN THEM SHALL HE DIE."

The exegesis is:

1. We are plainly told in Verse 21 that if the wicked will turn from his sins, then he will be forgiven and cleansed.

2. The Lord also states that if the Righteous man turns back to wickedness, and stays in that wicked condition, then he will lose his soul.

3. All of this completely shoots down the erroneous Doctrine of Unconditional Eternal Security.

PREDESTINATION

These Passages plainly condemn the erroneous manner in which the subject of Predestination is mostly addressed. First of all, the Passages tell us, and in no uncertain terms, that the matter of Salvation is left up to the individual. While the sinner cannot institute a desire for God on his own, and the desire must be introduced by the Holy Spirit, still, the free moral agency of the sinner is never abrogated by the Spirit. While the unsaved is totally depraved, which means they are spiritually dead, which means they can have no correct thoughts toward God, at least of their own capacity, which means that the Holy Spirit must do the doing as it regards the conviction of the soul, and, in fact, everything that pertains to the Salvation of the individual, still, even though all of these things are brought to bear on the heart of the unsaved, even as the Word of God is presented to them, the Holy Spirit will never force the issue. While He will definitely move and convict, in order for the individual to be saved, he still has to say *"yes"* to that which the Holy Spirit has done. The Scriptural exhortation always is, *"whosoever will"* (Jn. 3:16; Rev. 22:17).

NOTES

While Predestination as rightly taught in the Word of God is definitely a viable Doctrine, as stated, it must be correctly taught. The Lord has predestined many things, but never individuals.

For instance, Paul said: *"For whom He did foreknow, He also did predestinate to be conformed to the Image of His Son, that He* (Jesus) *might be the firstborn* (the Originator of Redemption) *among many Brethren"* (Rom. 8:29).

This Passage, as do all others which teach the Doctrine of Predestination, proclaims that certain things are predestinated to be done after the person comes to Christ. And even then, the act to be carried out, in this case, *"conformation to the Image of His Son,"* is predicated on obedience as it regards the Believer. If the Believer properly obeys, it is predestinated that this particular work of *"conformation"* will be carried out.

The idea that God has already predestinated every single person as it regards Heaven or Hell, and there is nothing they can do about the situation, is not taught in the Word of God. As stated, the theme of the Scripture is, *"whosoever will"* (Rom. 10:13; Rev. 22:17).

As the Twenty-first Verse proclaims, *"If the wicked will turn from all his sins that he has committed, and will keep all of the Lord's Statutes and do that which is lawful and right, he shall surely live, he shall not die."*

This pertains to a person who has heard the Gospel, and is thereby given the opportunity to be saved. But he must favorably take that opportunity, or he will be eternally lost.

UNCONDITIONAL ETERNAL SECURITY

The Twenty-fourth Verse of this Chapter plainly refutes the Unscriptural Doctrine of Unconditional Security, which teaches that once a person is truly saved, they cannot be lost, no matter what they do. As stated, this is plainly and clearly refuted in this Twenty-fourth Verse.

Now, you the Reader can believe what the Scripture plainly says in this Twenty-fourth Verse, or else you can believe Preachers who proclaim the opposite of what the Word of God tells us.

Unconditional Eternal Security is a popular Doctrine, because it condones an ungodly lifestyle. In fact, there are untold millions in Hell right now, who possibly wouldn't be there, if they had not believed this false doctrine preached to them by some so-called Preacher.

It is Faith in Christ and the Cross which brings us into Salvation. It is Faith in Christ and the Cross which keeps us in Salvation. If such Faith is abrogated, which means that Christ and the Cross are no longer the object of one's Faith, the soul of that person will be lost. We get in by Faith and we stay in by Faith; if Faith is lost, which it has been with millions, which always results in the type of lifestyle mentioned in the Twenty-fourth Verse, such a person reverts from a saved condition to a lost condition. The Scripture plainly says, *"In them shall he die,"* meaning that if such a person stays in that condition, they will be eternally lost.

(25) "YET YOU SAY, THE WAY OF THE LORD IS NOT EQUAL. HEAR NOW, O HOUSE OF ISRAEL; IS NOT MY WAY EQUAL? ARE NOT YOUR WAYS UNEQUAL?

(26) "WHEN A RIGHTEOUS MAN TURNS AWAY FROM HIS RIGHTEOUSNESS, AND COMMITS INIQUITY, AND DIES IN THEM; FOR HIS INIQUITY THAT HE HAS DONE SHALL HE DIE.

(27) "AGAIN, WHEN THE WICKED MAN TURNS AWAY FROM HIS WICKEDNESS THAT HE HAS COMMITTED, AND DOES THAT WHICH IS LAWFUL AND RIGHT, HE SHALL SAVE HIS SOUL ALIVE.

(28) "BECAUSE HE CONSIDERS, AND TURNS AWAY FROM ALL HIS TRANSGRESSIONS THAT HE HAS COMMITTED, HE SHALL SURELY LIVE, HE SHALL NOT DIE.

(29) "YET SAITH THE HOUSE OF ISRAEL, THE WAY OF THE LORD IS NOT EQUAL. O HOUSE OF ISRAEL, ARE NOT MY WAYS EQUAL? ARE NOT YOUR WAYS UNEQUAL?

(30) "THEREFORE I WILL JUDGE YOU, O HOUSE OF ISRAEL, EVERY ONE ACCORDING TO HIS WAYS, SAITH THE LORD GOD. REPENT, AND TURN YOURSELVES FROM ALL YOUR TRANSGRESSIONS; SO INIQUITY SHALL NOT BE YOUR RUIN.

(31) "CAST AWAY FROM YOU ALL YOUR TRANSGRESSIONS, WHEREBY YOU HAVE TRANSGRESSED; AND MAKE YOU A NEW HEART AND A NEW SPIRIT: FOR WHY WILL YOU DIE, O HOUSE OF ISRAEL?

(32) "FOR I HAVE NO PLEASURE IN THE DEATH OF HIM WHO DIES, SAITH THE LORD GOD: WHEREFORE TURN YOURSELVES, AND LIVE YE."

The diagram is:

1. The question of Verse 23 is answered in Verse 32.

2. Conversion and regeneration can only be affected by the Holy Spirit. But the sinner is responsible to repent and to seek this new moral nature.

3. Directly the sinner tries to provide himself with this new moral nature, He discovers His helplessness; broken in spirit and casting himself on God for Salvation, the Holy Spirit reveals Christ to him, and thus works the mighty Miracle of the New Birth.

EQUAL

God's Ways are always equal, because He demands the same of all, irrespective of their status, position, gender, or the period of time in which they live.

Man's ways are grossly unequal because unrighteous judges can be bought off. Legislators make laws, which favor some and abuse others, with prejudice, racial, and religious bias playing their insidious parts relative to mankind. To be frank, the ways of man are so unequal as to be preposterous! And as unequal as man's ways are, as equal are God's Ways!

JUDGMENT

In Verse 30, the Holy Spirit through the Prophet now gives an Altar Call. It is one of the clearest most impassioned pleas found in the entire Bible.

The phrase, *"Therefore I will judge you,"* is a chilling thought to the human family, and is disbelieved by almost all! Modern psychology denies a coming Judgment, because it denies man's personal responsibility for his moral actions, claiming that others are to blame, whereas the Bible declares the very opposite, as this very Chapter stipulates.

The Old Testament makes it clear that the ultimate Ruler of the Universe is God. All human governing authority is derived from Him, whether known or not. Often, where the Old Testament speaks of God as Judge, it is His ultimate Sovereignty as Governor of the Universe, and not simply His role as Moral Arbiter, that is in view.

God's judicial acts are but one aspect of His Rule. To affirm God as Judge is to assert that he is Governor of all, not only with every right to command, but also with responsibility to vindicate and to condemn.

The New Testament, like the Old, strongly affirms God as ultimately the only qualified Judge. James emphasizes the Old Testament concept of a Judge as a Ruler when he writes, *"There is only one Lawgiver and Judge, the One Who is able to save and destroy. But you — who are you to judge your neighbor?"* (James 4:12).

In this dominant legal or judicial sense, only God has the right or knowledge to judge (Jn. 8:15-16). All will have to *"give an account to Him Who is ready to judge the living and the dead"* (I Pet. 4:5; II Tim. 4:1, 8; Heb. 10:30; 12:23; 13:4). The fact that God Alone is confident to pronounce Judgment on human beings is basic to our grasp of what the Bible says about Judging.

CONDEMNATION

Yet, God is not eager to judge. John writes that Jesus was sent into the world, not to condemn, but so that all who believe might be saved (Jn. 3:17). The verdict of condemnation is passed on to the lost by their own condition and actions as stated in these Passages in Ezekiel. Jesus, the Light, has come into the world; those who love darkness will reject Him and turn away (Jn. 3:19-21). The Father *"has entrusted all Judgment to the Son"* (Jn. 5:22); therefore, a person's response to Christ has become the dividing line between life and death (Jn. 5:19-30).

REPENTANCE

Romans picks up the theme and portrays God, moved by kindness, waiting patiently in order that people will respond and repent (Rom. 2:4). But *"For those who are self-seeking and who reject the Truth and follow evil, there will be wrath and anger"* (Rom. 2:8).

Those who reject the Divine pardon must in the end stand before God as Judge. In that Judgment, based on evaluation of each person's works (Rev. 20:12), God will *"give to each person according to what he has done"* (Rom. 2:6). Those who know the revealed Law of God will be judged by its standard. But even those who do not know the Will of God as unveiled in the written Word have *"the requirements of the Law written on their hearts"* (Rom. 2:15). God has created human beings with a moral sense, which gives inner testimony to right and wrong. Tragically, human beings are so warped by sin that the inner witness accuses but does not lead to Righteous living.

So, the day is coming when God will act as the moral Governor of our Universe. He will put aside His patience in order to carry out the verdict that people pronounced against themselves by their actions and by their refusal to accept God's pardon in Jesus.

The phrase, *"Repent, and turn yourselves from all your transgressions,"* addresses itself to one's sins and how those sins can be pardoned. If not, the Scripture emphatically states, *"iniquity shall be your ruin."*

Consequently, the sins of the unbeliever can be addressed in one of two ways:

1. Repentance: This means that one is sorry for his sins and accepts Christ's Atoning Work at Calvary where He was judged for our sins. If true Repentance is engaged, no Judgment comes to the Believing sinner, but, in Truth, was poured out in its entire wrath on Christ at Calvary.

2. The Great White Throne Judgment: If one does not allow his sins to be put away by Christ, then he will have to suffer the Judgment of those sins at the Great White Throne Judgment (Rev. 20:11-15).

So, one has a choice of accepting the Judgment upon Christ or upon Himself.

REGENERATION

Conversion and Regeneration can only be effected by the Holy Spirit. But the sinner is responsible to repent and to seek this new moral nature. Directly he tries to provide himself with these, he discovers his helplessness; broken in spirit and casting himself on God for Salvation, as stated, the Holy Spirit reveals Christ to him, and thus works the mighty Miracle of the New Birth.

In Verse 31, the phrase, *"The making of a*

new heart and a new spirit," refers to Regeneration. It means *"to begat again"* or *"to birth."* It means a making anew or renewing.

SIN

This Doctrine must be considered in the context of man in sin (Jn. 3:6; Eph. 2:1-3, 5). The effects of sin on human nature are considered to be so serious that, without the New Birth, the sinner cannot see, let alone enter into the Kingdom of God (Jn. 3:3, 5; I Cor. 2:6-16).

The initiative in regeneration is ascribed to God (Jn. 1:13); it is from above (Jn. 3:3, 7) and of the Spirit (Jn. 3:5, 8). The same idea occurs in Ephesians 2:4-5; I John 2:29; 4:7. This Divine act is decisive and once for all. It carries with it far-reaching effects.

RIGHTEOUSNESS

The abiding results are doing Righteousness, not committing sin, loving one another, believing that Jesus is the Christ, and overcoming the world, which can only come about as the Believer evidences Faith exclusively in Christ and the Cross (Gal. 6:14). These results indicate that in spiritual matters man is not altogether passive. He is passive in the New Birth; God acts on him. But the result of such an act is far-reaching activity; he actively repents, believes in Christ, and henceforth walks in newness of life (Rom. 6:3-5).

THE NEW BIRTH

John 3:8 serves to warn us that there is much in this subject that is inscrutable. Yet, we must inquire as to what actually happens to the individual in the New Birth.

It would be safe to say that there is no immediate change in the personality itself; the person is the same. But now he is differently controlled. Before the New Birth the sin nature controlled the man and made him a rebel against God; now, since conversion to Christ, the Spirit controls him and directs him toward God, or at least that's the way it should be.

The regenerate man walks after the Spirit, lives in the Spirit, is led by the Spirit, and is commanded to be filled with the Spirit (Rom. 8:4, 9, 14; Eph. 5:18); however, such a Believer is not perfect; he has to grow and progress (I Pet. 2:2), but in every department of his personality he is so directed.

We may define Regeneration as a drastic act on fallen human nature by the Holy Spirit, leading to a change in the person's whole outlook. He can now be described as a new man who seeks, finds, and follows God in Christ, all made possible by what Christ did at the Cross and our Faith in that Finished Work.

Without the *"new heart and new spirit,"* spiritual death, which is separation from God, will lead to eternal death. That's the reason Jesus said to Nicodemus, *"Verily, verily, I say unto you, Except a man be Born-Again, he cannot see the Kingdom of God"* (Jn. 3:3). The Born-Again experience is received by Repentance and Faith in Christ (Jn. 3:14-18; Acts 20:21).

As well, the awareness of the need of conversion can only be brought about by revelation of the Holy Spirit on the human heart, which comes about as the Word of God is preached, proclaimed, or witnessed in some manner. Jesus said:

"Verily, verily, I say unto you, Except a man be born of water and of the Spirit, he cannot enter into the Kingdom of God" (Jn. 3:5).

(Water is used here in a figurative sense of Salvation (Jn. 4:14; Isa. 12:3); of the Spirit Baptism (Jn. 7:37-39); and of cleansing by the Word of God (Jn. 15:3; Eph. 5:26).

Since men are cleansed and Born-Again by the Word (James 1:18; I Pet. 1:23), it is clear that being Born-Again of water means being Born-Again by the Word of God.)

TURN, AND LIVE

Twice the Holy Spirit emphasizes the Truth that the Lord has no pleasure in the death of the wicked. The repetition is not by accident. As this Word was spoken in Verse 23, likewise it is repeated in Verse 32, in order that the Reader or Hearer may fully understand the great lengths God has gone to in order to save mankind. Therefore, this Altar Call is concluded with the words, *"Wherefore turn, and live."*

One would have to conclude that, of all the utterances of Ezekiel, this is one of the most noble. With this, he takes his place by the side of the greatest of the Prophets as a Preacher of Repentance and Forgiveness.

As well, one feels the heart of God in these Passages as in few Passages in the Word of God. As this was the Message of Ezekiel of old, as well as all the True Prophets and Apostles, likewise, it should be the Message of every Preacher of the Gospel presently — *"Turn, and Live."*

"Consider Him, let Christ your pattern be,
"And know that He has apprehended thee
"To share His very Life, His Power Divine,
"And in the likeness of your Lord to shine."

"Consider Him, and thus your life shall be
"Filled with self-sacrifice and purity;
"God will work out in you the pattern true,
"And Christ's example ever keep in view."

"Consider Him, your Great High Priest above
"Is interceding in untiring love,
"And He will have you thus within the veil
"By Spirit-breathed petitions to prevail."

"Consider Him, and as you run the race,
"Keep ever upward looking in His Face;
"And thus transformed, illumined you shall be,
"And Christ's Own Image shall be seen in thee."

CHAPTER 19

(1) "MOREOVER TAKE THOU UP A LAMENTATION FOR THE PRINCES OF ISRAEL,

(2) "AND SAY, WHAT IS YOUR MOTHER? A LIONESS: SHE LAY DOWN AMONG LIONS, SHE NOURISHED HER WHELPS AMONG YOUNG LIONS.

(3) "AND SHE BROUGHT UP ONE OF HER WHELPS: IT BECAME A YOUNG LION, AND IT LEARNED TO CATCH THE PREY; IT DEVOURED MEN.

(4) "THE NATIONS ALSO HEARD OF HIM; HE WAS TAKEN IN THEIR PIT, AND THEY BROUGHT HIM WITH CHAINS UNTO THE LAND OF EGYPT.

(5) "NOW WHEN SHE SAW THAT SHE HAD WAITED, AND HER HOPE WAS LOST, THEN SHE TOOK ANOTHER OF HER WHELPS, AND MADE HIM A YOUNG LION.

(6) "AND HE WENT UP AND DOWN AMONG THE LIONS, HE BECAME A YOUNG LION, AND LEARNED TO CATCH THE PREY, AND DEVOURED MEN.

(7) "AND HE KNEW THEIR DESOLATE PALACES, AND HE LAID WASTE THEIR CITIES; AND THE LAND WAS DESOLATE, AND THE FULNESS THEREOF, BY THE NOISE OF HIS ROARING.

(8) "THEN THE NATIONS SET AGAINST HIM ON EVERY SIDE FROM THE PROVINCES, AND SPREAD THEIR NET OVER HIM: HE WAS TAKEN IN THEIR PIT.

(9) "AND THEY PUT HIM IN WARD IN CHAINS, AND BROUGHT HIM TO THE KING OF BABYLON: THEY BROUGHT HIM INTO HOLDS, THAT HIS VOICE SHOULD NO MORE BE HEARD UPON THE MOUNTAINS OF ISRAEL."

The composition is:

1. The first nine Verses of this Lamentation picture the nation of Israel as a lioness, and bewail the fate of her two whelps, Jehoahaz (Vss. 3-4) and Jehoiakim (Vss. 5-9).

2. The Mourner is Immanuel.

3. The terrible iniquity, which characterizes these two *"Princes of Israel,"* helped push the nation towards spiritual oblivion, hence, this admonition given by the Holy Spirit.

THE LAMENTATION

Verse 1 portrays the woe brought upon the nation of Judah by the ungodly actions of two of its Kings, Jehoahaz, and Jehoaiakim.

Israel was to be the spiritual leader of the world, pointing other nations toward God. Tragically, she did the very opposite! The Church is to do the same, but, also tragically, at least at this present hour, it is little better, if at all, than Judah of old!

The phrase of Verse 2, *"What is your mother?"* refers to Jerusalem as the great lion, and in a good sense (Isa. 29:1).

The phrase, *"She lay down among lions,"* refers to the surrounding heathen nations, which she was supposed to lead to God, but instead was led astray herself! She adopted their cruelty and ferocity, thereby losing the Glory of God.

God calls His people to separation from the world so that they may have power in testifying against it, may thus help it, and so be a true witness for God. But the bent of the natural will is to imitate the world and be as much like it as possible.

The phrase, *"She nourished her whelps among young lions,"* refers to Jehoahaz and Jehoiakim taking their cue from the *"young lions,"* i.e., Kings of the surrounding nations, rather than from the Lord.

THE SPIRIT OF THE WORLD

The greatest danger of the modern Church is being led by the world, as these Kings of Judah, instead of by the Lord. It is so easy to adopt the ways of the world and ignore the Ways of God. The Ways of God are not come by easily. The consecration and dedication must be complete, with a constant seeking of the Face of the Lord in order to find the leading of the Holy Spirit. Regrettably, most will not humble themselves to that degree of consecration.

This is not meant to imply that one can earn such by these actions, but that there must be dedication.

As well, the world constantly beckons, and even among one's own, being led by the Holy Spirit, most of the time, is met with scorn and derision instead of approval and commendation. Consequently, there are very few presently who do not receive their *"nourishment,"* from the *"young lions,"* i.e., ways of the world.

JOSIAH

Is noticeable that the Holy Spirit gives the account of the ungodliness of these Kings, with the intimation of the Godliness of their Father Josiah. Such is intended to fit the admonition of the previous Chapter, which spoke of the son who was a *"robber, a shedder of blood, and idol worshiper"* (Ezek. 18:10-13).

The Holy Spirit in that chapter proclaimed the Truth that the Righteousness of the father (Josiah) could not be handed down to the sons, Jehoahaz and Jehoiakim, and that his Righteousness would not forestall the Judgment that would come upon them because of their many sins.

JEHOAHAZ

The phrase in Verse 3, *"One of her whelps,"* referred to Jehoahaz who reigned only three months and was taken captive to Egypt (II Ki. 23:31-33).

He was the eighteenth king of Judah and took the Throne upon his father's death (Josiah) at Megiddo. Jeremiah called him "Shallum" (Jer. 22:11-12), an indication that Jehozhaz was his Throne name.

CHAINS

The phrase in Verse 4, *"The nations also heard of him,"* refers to Egypt and its allies beginning to be alarmed as they watched the aggressive policy of Jehoahaz, as he sought to assert his independence. Consequently, they laid a snare for him, and *"He was taken in their pit."* As stated, he was taken prisoner by Pharaoh-Necho and brought in chains to Egypt.

The *"chains"* spoken of always ensnare those who look to the world instead of God.

Jehoahaz, with the example of his Godly father Josiah before him, could have known true prosperity had he only looked to the Lord instead of the *"young lions"*; however, he chose the world and was rewarded with *"chains."* His example is identical to all who follow in his footsteps.

JEHOIAKIM

There has been a dispute, as it regards Verse 5, as to whether this Passage relates to Jehoiakim or Jehoiachin; however, the description more aptly fits Jehoiakim who reigned eleven years, rather than Jehoiachin who only reigned three months.

The phrase in Verse 5, *"Now when she saw that she had waited,"* refers to Jerusalem waiting in vain for Jehoahaz to be released from his captivity in Egypt. The *"young lion,"* as stated, is Jehoiakim, who was made King in his brother's place.

IDOLATRY

The phrase of Verse 6, *"And he went up and down among the lions,"* refers to him associating with the heathen nations exactly as did his brother, Jehoahaz.

The phrase, *"He became a young lion,"* refers to him ardently seeking to make Judah as the idol worshipers around him.

The phrase, *"And learned to catch the prey, and devoured men,"* refers to his cruelty, of which his Kingdom was noted.

To pay the Egyptian dues imposed upon him by Pharaoh, he levied heavy land taxes (II Ki. 23:35). He also built costly royal buildings, using forced labor (Jer. 22:13-17), and is described as an oppressive covetous ruler. The reforms of his father, Josiah, were forgotten in the reversion to idolatry and introduction of Egyptian rites (Ezek. 8:5-17). He shed much innocent blood (II Ki. 24:4) and had the Prophet Urijah murdered for opposing him (Jer. 26:20-21).

He opposed the Prophet Jeremiah greatly (Jer. 36:26) and personally burned the scroll from which Jehudi read the words of the Prophet to him.

Josephus the Jewish Historian said, *"He was unjust and wicked by nature, and was neither reverent toward God, nor kind to man."*

DESOLATION

The phrase of Verse 7, *"And he knew their desolate palaces,"* means that he plundered the nation in order to pay Egypt, and to build his costly edifices.

The phrase, *"And the land was desolate,"* refers not only to spiritual desolation, but also to the economic hardship imposed upon the people.

The phrase, *"And the fullness thereof, by the noise of his roaring,"* refers to his violent nature in imposing his will upon Judah.

BABYLON AND EGYPT

The phrase of Verse 8, *"Then the nation set against him on every side,"* refers to the anger of Babylon because of his dallying with Egypt.

In 605 B.C., which was Jehoiakim's fourth year as King of Judah, Nebuchadnezzar defeated the Egyptians at Carchemish and won control of Israel as far as the Egyptian border (Jer. 25:1; 46:2). About a year later, Jehoiakim, with other rulers, went before Nebuchadnezzar to submit to him as a vassal state (Jer. 36:9-29).

However, in 601 B.C., another battle between the Egyptians and the Babylonians came about, and the Babylonians were defeated. At that time, Jehoiakim transferred his loyalty, despite the warnings of the Prophet Jeremiah, to the Egyptians. This angered Nebuchadnezzar, who immediately set out to regain the lost territory, and who began to make excursions into Judah. On March 16, 597 B.C., he captured Jerusalem. He then seized Jehoiakim and appointed a King of his own choice (II Chron. 36:6-8).

HOW SHOULD THIS HISTORY AFFECT MODERN CHRISTIANS?

In the first place, every single thing which we read in the Bible is the Word of God, which means that it is of an inestimable value, and is given to us for a great purpose.

Second, every single thing in the Word of God, beginning with Genesis 1:1, is a portrayal of the march of Redemption, and all that pertain to that march, which ultimately played out to your Salvation. Nothing could be more important than that!

Third, we are meant to learn from all of these examples. In other words, we are plainly told that we must not make the same mistakes that these particular individuals made. Concerning all of this, Paul said:

"Now all these things happened unto them for examples: and they are written for our admonition, upon whom the ends of the world are come" (I Cor. 10:11).

WITHOUT GOD

The phrase of Verse 9, *"And they put him in ward and chains,"* refers to the anger against him by Nebuchadnezzar, because of siding with Egypt. Consequently, he would treat him brutally!

The phrase, *"And brought him to the King of Babylon,"* does not mean that he was taken to Babylon, but that he was taken before Nebuchadnezzar. Even though the Scripture does not say how he died, it is believed that he died on the way to Babylon, drawn and cast forth and unburied.

From now on, he would *"roar"* in chains, but not on the *"mountains of Israel."* He was 36 when he died, without God, and unlamented!

(10) "YOUR MOTHER IS LIKE A VINE IN YOUR BLOOD, PLANTED BY THE WATERS: SHE WAS FRUITFUL AND FULL OF BRANCHES BY REASON OF MANY WATERS.

(11) "AND SHE HAD STRONG RODS FOR THE SCEPTRES OF THEM WHO BORE RULE, AND HER STATURE WAS EXALTED AMONG THE THICK BRANCHES, AND SHE APPEARED IN HER HEIGHT WITH THE MULTITUDE OF HER BRANCHES.

(12) "BUT SHE WAS PLUCKED UP IN FURY, SHE WAS CAST DOWN TO THE GROUND, AND THE EAST WIND DRIED UP HER FRUIT: HER STRONG RODS WERE BROKEN AND WITHERED; THE FIRE CONSUMED THEM.

(13) "AND NOW SHE IS PLANTED IN THE WILDERNESS, IN A DRY AND THIRSTY GROUND.

(14) "AND FIRE IS GONE OUT OF A ROD OF HER BRANCHES, WHICH HAS DEVOURED HER FRUIT, SO THAT SHE HAS NO STRONG ROD TO BE A SCEPTRE TO RULE. THIS IS A LAMENTATION, AND SHALL BE FOR A LAMENTATION.

The structure is:

1. The vine of Verse 10, *"and its strong rod"* and *"a rod of her branches,"* (Vss. 11, 14) was Zedekiah.

2. Israel, as a vine, enjoyed, under the overlordship of Babylon, a limited prosperity.

3. Verse 12 predicted Judah's violent end; and Verse 14 foretold that Zedekiah's treachery would be the cause of the destruction of the City and Temple by fire. It also foretold that no King should henceforth reign on the Throne of Israel.

4. Verse 13 describes Israel's miserable state during the Seventy Years of the Captivity.

5. *"This shall be for a Lamentation"* pertains to Zedekiah, whose doom was still future, at the time that this lament was given by the Spirit to the Prophet.

FRUITFUL

The phrase of Verse 10, *"Thy mother is like a vine,"* is referred to in Ezekiel 17:6, and refers to Judah as a Vine.

The phrase, *"In your blood,"* refers to David's sons who occupied the Throne of Judah, according to the Commandment of the Lord.

The phrase, *"Planted by the waters,"* refers to the Grace of God which nourished Judah and gave her opportunity for great prosperity, which for a time she enjoyed, which pertained to the Judah of the past.

The phrase, *"She was fruitful and full of branches by reason of many waters,"* refers to the Blessings of God given unto her, which made her the envy of the nations, until she rebelled against God, and lost those blessings.

The phrase of Verse 11, *"And she had strong rods for the scepters of them who bear rule,"* refers to the kingly line of David, which was God-appointed and thereby blessed.

The phrase, *"And her stature was exalted among the thick branches,"* refers to the glory of her Kings among the nations, because they were appointed by God. In fact, Israel at that time was above all the nations of the world, because of the blessings of God upon His people.

BECAUSE OF SIN

Verse 12 says, *"But she was plucked up in fury."* This refers to the Judgment of God, which came upon her because of her rebellion against God. In fact, the Judgment came in stages, even over many years, with pressure being applied to a greater extent each time, hoping to bring Israel to Repentance. But it was all to no avail!

Babylon invaded Judah in 605 B.C., because the Lord allowed it, because of the sin of the people. At that time, quite a few of the prominent Israelites were carried captive into Babylon. During this first deportation, Daniel and the three Hebrew children were taken into captivity, with an indefinite number of others. Jehoiakim was King at that time. Many of the vessels of the Temple were also taken at that time (II Ki. 24:14).

The second deportation took place under Jehoiachin, in which Mordecai and Esther, along with Ezekiel, were taken into Babylon. About 10,000 others were also taken in this particular deportation. This happened in 597 B.C.

The last deportation would take place under Zedekiah, which was about four years from the time of this Prophecy, and would result in the total destruction of Jerusalem, along with hundreds of thousands being slaughtered. As said, *"she was to be cast down to the ground."*

The phrase, *"And the east wind dried up her fruit,"* refers to the Babylonians who came from the East.

The phrase, *"Her strong rods were broken and withered; the fire consumed them,"* refers to her King Zedekiah who would be taken and *"broken,"* i.e., blinded, with the city destroyed by fire. As stated, this pertains to about four years in the future, from the time it was prophesied by Ezekiel.

ZEDEKIAH

The phrase from Verse 13, *"And now she is planted in the wilderness,"* presents a double meaning:

First of all, it referred to Judah's spiritual state at the time of Ezekiel's Prophecy, which was likened to a *"wilderness."*

Whereas Israel had once been *"planted by the waters,"* i.e., the Blessings of God, now she is *"in a dry and thirsty ground,"* i.e., with no spiritual sustenance whatsoever, because of her rebellion against the Lord.

As well, it speaks of the captivity that is coming which describes Israel's miserable state during the Seventy Years of captivity.

The phrase in Verse Fourteen, *"And fire is gone out of a rod of her branches,"* refers to the evil capacity of her Kings after Josiah, and the Judgment of God which will swiftly come in upon them. As such, all the glory described in Verses 10 and 11 is now gone, and sin *"has devoured her fruit."*

The phrase, *"So that she has no strong rod to be a Scepter to rule,"* refers to Zedekiah at present, who was a weak King, to say the least!

The phrase, *"This is a lamentation,"* refers to Jehoahaz and Jehoaichin, whose punishment was already then a matter of accomplished history.

The phrase, *"And shall be for a Lamentation,"* refers to Zedekiah, whose doom was still future at the time this lament was given by the Spirit to the Prophet. But Zedekiah would not heed, even as untold millions presently will not heed!

"Oh happy day that fixed my choice
"On Thee my Saviour and my God!
"Well, may this glowing heart rejoice
"And tell its raptures all abroad."

"Oh happy bond that seeks my vows
"To Him Who merits all my love!
"Let cheerful anthems fill His house,
"While to that sacred shrine I move."

"Tis done, the great transactions done,
"I am my Lord's and He is mine;
"He drew me, and I followed on,
"Charmed to confess the voice Divine."

"Now rest, my long divided heart,
"Fixed on this blissful center, rest;
"Nor ever from my Lord depart,
"With Him of every good possessed."

CHAPTER 20

(1) "AND IT CAME TO PASS IN THE SEVENTH YEAR, IN THE FIFTH MONTH, THE TENTH DAY OF THE MONTH, THAT CERTAIN OF THE ELDERS OF ISRAEL CAME TO ENQUIRE OF THE LORD, AND SAT BEFORE ME.

(2) "THEN CAME THE WORD OF THE LORD UNTO ME, SAYING,

(3) "SON OF MAN, SPEAK UNTO THE ELDERS OF ISRAEL, AND SAY UNTO THEM, THUS SAITH THE LORD GOD; ARE YOU COME TO ENQUIRE OF ME? AS I LIVE, SAITH THE LORD GOD, I WILL NOT BE ENQUIRED OF BY YOU.

(4) "WILL YOU JUDGE THEM, SON OF MAN, WILL YOU JUDGE THEM? CAUSE THEM TO KNOW THE ABOMINATIONS OF THEIR FATHERS:

(5) "AND SAY UNTO THEM, THUS SAITH THE LORD GOD; IN THE DAY WHEN I CHOSE ISRAEL, AND LIFTED UP MY HAND UNTO THE SEED OF THE HOUSE OF JACOB, AND MADE MYSELF KNOWN UNTO THEM IN THE LAND OF EGYPT, WHEN I LIFTED UP MY HAND UNTO THEM, SAYING, I AM THE LORD YOUR GOD;

(6) "IN THE DAY THAT I LIFTED UP

MY HAND UNTO THEM, TO BRING THEM FORTH OF THE LAND OF EGYPT INTO A LAND THAT I HAD ESPIED FOR THEM, FLOWING WITH MILK AND HONEY, WHICH IS THE GLORY OF ALL LANDS:

(7) "THEN SAID I UNTO THEM, CAST YE AWAY EVERY MAN THE ABOMINATIONS OF HIS EYES, AND DEFILE NOT YOURSELVES WITH THE IDOLS OF EGYPT: I AM THE LORD YOUR GOD.

(8) "BUT THEY REBELLED AGAINST ME, AND WOULD NOT HEARKEN UNTO ME: THEY DID NOT EVERY MAN CAST AWAY THE ABOMINATIONS OF THEIR EYES, NEITHER DID THEY FORSAKE THE IDOLS OF EGYPT: THEN I SAID, I WILL POUR OUT MY FURY UPON THEM, TO ACCOMPLISH MY ANGER AGAINST THEM IN THE MIDST OF THE LAND OF EGYPT.

(9) "BUT I WROUGHT FOR MY NAME'S SAKE, THAT IT SHOULD NOT BE POLLUTED BEFORE THE HEATHEN, AMONG WHOM THEY WERE, IN WHOSE SIGHT I MADE MYSELF KNOWN UNTO THEM, IN BRINGING THEM FORTH OUT OF THE LAND OF EGYPT."

The structure is:

1. The fact of man's moral estrangement from God, and of his incurable attachment to any god rather than Jehovah, is demonstrated in this Chapter.

2. Israel's history demonstrates the hopeless moral corruption, mental and spiritual degradation, and blindness of man at large.

3. This fundamental doctrine is exceedingly offensive to human pride; but it shows the necessity of a new creation, without which no man can either recognize or experience Spiritual Revelation (I Cor. 2:14; II Cor. 5:17).

THE WORD OF THE LORD

The last Prophecy, concluding with the last Verse of the previous Chapter, began in Ezekiel Chapter 8:1. A little over eleven months passed during which the Prophecies of the intervening Chapters had been spoken, and written.

This Prophecy begins with the First Verse of this Chapter, and follows through to the conclusion of Chapter 23.

Ezekiel had now been prophesying a little over two years, and it will be about two and a half years before the Chaldeans will besiege Jerusalem.

The phrase of Verse 1, *"Certain of the Elders of Israel came to enquire of the LORD, and sat before me,"* denotes a desire to know what will happen in the future. The same thing was done some months before, as is recorded in Chapter 14, and could well have included many of the same Elders. Incidentally, the *"seventh year,"* as spoken in this Verse, pertains to the length of the Prophet's captivity up to this time.

There was a reason for these Elders coming. False prophets among the Exiles were at this time predicting a speedy Restoration to Judah (Jer. 28:11). The evidence is that these Elders desired Ezekiel to preach the same comfortable Message, but he refused to do so, and on the contrary, exposed the deep-seated idolatry of their hearts and announced an accession of the Wrath of God upon them.

Even though outwardly these Elders professed the worship of God, according to Verse 31, they inwardly loved idolatry. Such is gross hypocrisy! Such hypocrisy also characterizes modern Christendom, as it did ancient Israel.

In 8:1, Ezekiel uses the phrase, *"Elders of Judah,"* where here, he uses the phrase, *"Elders of Israel."* There is no contradiction, inasmuch as he uses the two words interchangeably. They both mean the same, as Judah now serves as the entirety of Israel.

THE PRESENT CHURCH

The scene with the Elders of Israel coming before Ezekiel, and which transpired about 2,500 years ago, is repeating itself presently; however, the situation now is even worse than then. At least these Elders came to Ezekiel, whereas at present, the modern Church has no desire to even hear what the Lord is actually saying.

Churches are presently filled with people, even running over at the seams, so to speak, who desire to hear a message to their liking. There is little interest or desire to hear the Message preached by Paul to Felix, the Message of *"Righteousness, temperance, and judgment to come"* (Acts 24:25). At least during Ezekiel's day, some were interested in hearing what the Prophet had to say, even though it was little believed. As stated, the situation has now deteriorated spiritually until there is no desire to even hear what *"The Spirit is saying to the Churches"* (Rev. 3:22).

In fact, concerning the Messages to the seven Churches of Asia, Churches which typify the entire Church Age, the last Word given by Christ is the warning *"He who has an ear, let him hear what the Spirit says unto the Churches."* Considering that that was the last word of Christ to the Church, it had best be heeded, as should be graphically understood!

THE HISTORY OF ISRAEL

In this Chapter, the Lord outlines five periods to which Ezekiel points in this Prophecy, during which the nation chose idols instead of God. They are:

1. In Egypt (Vss. 5-9).
2. In the wilderness (the fathers), (Vss. 10–17).
3. In the wilderness (the children), (Vss. 18-26).
4. In the Land (the Promised Land), (Vss. 27-29).
5. In Exile (Vss. 30-38).

The *"Elders"* had asked for the *"Word"* of the Lord, and now they will receive the *"Word of the Lord."* As stated, it will not be a pleasant Message. However, much better to receive the Truth, as negative as it may be, than to hear a sugar-coated lie, which characterizes so many pulpits.

In all of this, the nation of Israel demonstrates the hopeless moral corruption, mental and spiritual degradation, and blindness of man at large.

All of this is exceedingly offensive to human pride; but it shows, as stated, the necessity of a new creation, without which it is impossible for man to understand anything about God, as well as His Word (Jn. 3:3, 5; II Cor. 5:17).

THE INQUIRY

The inquiry which these Elders tendered was not that which would be entertained by the Lord, and, in fact, is never that which will be entertained by the Lord.

These Elders have not come before God in order for their sins to be forgiven and their lives changed, but instead that they may hear a pleasant Message regarding their soon to be deliverance from Babylonian captivity, or so they think!

Sadly and regrettably, millions presently come before God each week with the same attitude and spirit. They desire no change within their lives, consequently, they seek Churches without a Moving of the Holy Spirit in order that they may feel comfortable in their sin.

To these, the Lord also responds with incredulity, *"Are you come to enquire of Me?"*

There is sarcasm in the tone and the threat of judgment as we shall see, but yet, which seem to stir no positive response from these Elders. The entire response of the Lord is according to the long settled ways of these Elders, who claim God, and even claim to be the spiritual leaders of Israel in Exile, but who, in actuality, denied God's Word. Let me say it again, when one reads these words, one is, as well, reading the modern pulpit.

These individuals did not want God, nor anything of God. They readily believed the message of the false prophets, but still, there was a nagging fear in their hearts as Ezekiel was prophesying the very opposite. Since their last visit, they think possibly his Message may have changed! However, they will be quickly disappointed.

Someone made the remark the other day that I was no longer relevant to the modern Ministry, inasmuch as I was still preaching the same thing now, that I preached in the 1970's and 1980's, etc.

That's a strange statement, as if the Word of God changes.

Irrespective of the time frame, or the culture, or the people, the problem is sin. That doesn't change. Once again, the solution, irrespective of the culture, the people, or the time frame, is *"Jesus Christ and Him Crucified."* Preachers who change their message, do so for one of two reasons:

1. They are trying to accommodate their message to the passing wind of fancy, whatever that is.
2. They've been preaching something wrong, and they now desire to preach that which is right.

What I was preaching in the 1970's and 1980's saw hundreds of thousands brought to a saving knowledge of Jesus Christ. Inasmuch as the problem presently is the same, and the solution presently is the same, there is nothing to change about the Message that I preach.

The phrase of Verse 3, *"As I live, saith the Lord GOD, I will not be enquired of by you,"* presents a startling statement indeed! The Lord will not accede to their request, as He will not hear the prayers of anyone, who, as these, harbors iniquity in his heart (Ps. 66:18). Unforgiveness brings the same results (Mat. 6:14-15).

Even though this Passage is not specifically speaking of prayer, the end results are the same! These individuals wanted an answer from God, as millions of Christians today want answers from God. However, most modern Christians know little or nothing about prayer.

PRAYER

Most do not enquire of the Lord at all except during times of emergency. Even then, it is mostly a hit or miss affair, with a *"I'll try this"* attitude. In most cases, such is little better than putting money in a slot machine hoping for the desired results. Let not that person think they shall receive anything from the Lord.

God does not demand a perfect heart or even for one to be free from sin for prayer to be answered; however, He does demand that we desire holiness and be willing to confess and forsake all sin. In that context, He will always hear and answer (I Jn. 1:9).

In fact, the Bible emphasizes the simplicity of prayer. Believers are to pray about everything, confident that God hears our prayers, and that He cares and is able to act. God's people are implored to speak to Him, call on Him, and cry out to Him. He told Moses concerning Israel, *"I have surely seen the affliction of My people which are in Egypt, and have heard their cry by reason of their taskmasters; and I know their sorrows."*

He then said, *"I am come down to deliver them out of the hand of the Egyptians, and to bring them up out of that land unto a good land and a large, unto a land flowing with milk and honey"* (Ex. 3:7-8).

In the Hebrew, which concerns itself with the Old Testament, several words are used regarding prayer. The following include those most commonly used.

THE MEANING OF PRAYER

1. *"Palal"*: It is usually translated, *"to pray."* It is a call to God to assess a need presented and thus to act upon it. It also speaks of the dependence and humility of the one praying. As well, it is an appeal for a Divine decision.

2. *"Tepillah"*: This speaks of personal and corporate prayer with a sense of requesting intervention. It also speaks of confession and thanksgiving (Num. 21:7; I Sam. 2:1; II Chron. 33:18-19; Neh. 11:17).

3. *"Na"*: This is a Hebrew word expressing entreaty (Gen. 12:13).

4. *"Atar"*: This stresses the earnestness of the one praying and the intensity with which the request is made. Sometimes the word is associated with Sacrifice (II Sam. 24:25). As well, simple entreaty is included (Ex. 8:30-31).

5. *"Saal"*: This refers to asking or enquiring, which means to ask someone for something. The word is often used in the Old Testament of *"enquiring of the Lord."* It is clear from this Passage that the attitude of dependence suggested by this word is very important to God (Josh. 9:14; I Sam. 10:22; I Sam. 30:1-4).

6. *"Anah"*: This refers to a cry to God (Ps. 4:1; 69:16-17). It or its derivative, *"Sama,"* is also used to indicate humbling oneself before, and submission to, God (Ezra 8:21).

7. *"Paga"*: Means *"to meet"* or *"to encounter."* Its meaning is one of intercession as well (Isa. 53:12; Jer. 27:18).

8. *"Hanan"*: This means to cry to one who is able to act to meet the need of the supplicant.

Thus these different words used in the Hebrew, plus some we have not named, show how significant prayer was in the life of believing Israel. The use of these words, as well as their intrinsic meaning, reveal a beautiful dependence on God, as a Person, Who cares for His people, and Who acts to help them.

Prayer is an expression of personal relationship. This relationship is initiated by God, Who is recognized as Creator and Redeemer. The Holy Spirit is emphatic in this recognition.

Prayer, then, is the appeal of a child who recognizes his dependence. It is made to an all-powerful Person Who cares. Sometimes the appeal is motivated by need, and sometimes it pertains to praise, but nevertheless it is to God. He can be approached at any time, in any place.

It is very significant that the Old or New Testaments present no prayer liturgy. Prayer is not a matter of ritual religion. It is a living, vital expression of relationship. Thus, true prayer is always a matter of the heart (Jer. 29:12 –14), while false or meaningless prayer is only a matter of the lips (Isa. 29:13).

In the New Testament, it being originally in Greek, the words are of course, different, but yet their meaning is basically the same as the Old Testament. The New Testament emphasizes the fact that God hears and responds to the requests of His people (Mat. 6:8; 7:7-11; 18:19; 21:22; Jn. 14:13-14; 15:7, 16; 16:23; James 1:5; I Jn. 3:22; 5:13).

JESUS

Jesus soundly condemns a ritualistic and hypocritical approach to prayer. He presents true prayer as an intimate expression of relationship with a God Who is one's Father (Mat. 6:5-8). Jesus' model prayer known to us as the Lord's Prayer sums up this beautiful relationship.

We approach Him as we would a Father. We acknowledge and praise Him as the hallowed One in Heaven. We express our joyful submission to His Will. We acknowledge our dependence on the Lord for material and spiritual sustenance, and we ask for forgiveness. We acknowledge His right to direct our lives (Mat. 6:9-13).

THE CROSS

Jesus and what He did at the Cross, all on our behalf, are seen in the New Testament as the key to personal relationship with God that is central to prayer. Looking back on His Death and Resurrection, we understand what Jesus was saying when He taught His Disciples, *"I am the Way, the Truth, and the Life: no man comes unto the Father except by Me."* (Jn. 14:6). Through Jesus, and because of His Cross and Resurrection, we can *"approach the Throne of Grace with confidence,"* sure that we will *"receive Mercy and find Grace to help us in our time of need."* (Heb. 4:16).

However, a continuing intimate walk with Christ is vital to prayer. Jesus using the image of the Vine and Branches (Jn., Chpt. 15) told the Apostles, *"If you abide in Me, and My Words abide in You, you shall ask what you will, and it shall be done unto you."* (Jn. 15:7). That intimate relationship with Christ, enhanced as His Words reshape our personalities to fit with His Values and Character, brings us into so rich a harmony with the Lord that what we wish is what God desires us to ask (Jn. 16:23-24).

THE HOLY SPIRIT

As well, the Holy Spirit plays a unique role in the intimate exchange known as prayer. Actually, *"The Spirit Himself intercedes for us with groans that words cannot express"* (Rom. 8:26), and *"The Spirit intercedes* (helps us) *for the Saints in accordance with God's Will"* (Rom. 8:27). While the Spirit may, at times, assist us in prayer without our conscious awareness, our understanding clearly must be involved (I Cor. 14:13). Jesus told the Apostles that the Spirit would take from what belonged to Christ and make it known (Jn. 16:15).

As stated, prayer is a continuous expression of relationship. The New Testament speaks of prayer as a continuous, constant experience for Believers (Acts 1:14; I Thess. 5:17; II Thess. 1:11; I Tim. 5:5; I Cor. 7:5). Just as we talk with members of our family naturally and spontaneously, so we converse with God Who also shares our lives.

INTERCESSION

One of the most striking features of prayer, as it is portrayed in the Epistles, is its intercessory nature. We read again and again of prayer being offered by Believers for one another. In this, we learn that prayer is an expression of relationship within the Body of Christ, as well as an expression of a relationship with God. Out of the intimacy of shared lives grows a deep concern for others and their needs and this provides the primary content for the prayers in the Epistles.

The New Testament gives promise after promise of encouragement that our requests will surely be answered, that is, if we pray in the Will of God. This encouragement comes as a listing of indicators that reassure us that our relationship with God is vital and real. Those who seek, knock, and ask, receive what they request (Mat. 7:7-11).

Jesus told the Apostles that when two agreed regarding a matter, it would be done by God (Mat. 18:19). To pray *"in Jesus' Name"* means to identify with His Character and purposes (Jn. 14:13-14; 15:16; 16:23). The trust that we have in God calms our doubts and uncertainties and also testifies to us that God's answer will come. Only those who show contempt for God by questioning His ability or willingness to act in human affairs, and thus violate the relationship, will not be answered when they call (James 1:5).

As we obey the Lord, for obedience is a necessary requirement in relationship to God, we are assured that we live in a relationship with Him in which our prayers are heard and answered (I Jn. 3:22). As Scripture and the Holy Spirit testify to us that what we ask is in the frame work of God's Will, we can have confidence that what we ask for will be granted (I Jn. 5:14-15).

RELATIONSHIP

The Book of Psalms, actually the Prayer and Songbook of the Old Testament, best captures the warmth and intimacy of prayer that grows out of the Believer's relationship with the Lord.

In the New Testament, we are shown that each Person of the Trinity is deeply involved in prayer. We come to the Father through the Son, accompanied by the guidance of the Holy Spirit.

While there are actually no *"conditions"* that a person must meet before God will hear prayer, the Bible provides indicators that force our attention back to the quality of our personal relationship with God. Those whose lives demonstrate that they have no significant relationship with God (the unjust, the unconcerned, and the disobedient) have no basis on which to expect their prayers to be heard, much less answered. But those who experience a growing relationship with the Lord, marked by trust, obedience, love, harmony with other Believers, and a growing commitment to the Revealed Will of God, can rest assured. God does hear the prayers of those who live close to Him. Our prayers are heard, and they will be answered in His time.

ON A PERSONAL NOTE

Beginning in October of 1991, and continuing for about eleven years, we had two prayer meetings a day, morning and evening. To be frank, I still continue this prayer relationship with the Lord, twice a day, on a personal basis.

I've learned to take everything to the Lord in prayer. And to be sure, I personally cannot see how any Christian can maintain any type of relationship, at least without some type of prayer life. Most every assurance that I have received from the Lord has come while in prayer. By the help of the Lord, I will continue this regimen until the Rapture, or until the Lord calls me home.

During each prayer session, I generally pray about thirty minutes, always being very careful to *"enter into His gates with thanksgiving, and His courts with praise"* (Ps. 100:4). At some point, when I feel the moving of the Holy Spirit, I will begin to relate to the Lord our needs, ever seeking His Leading and Guidance in all things. As stated, I've learned to pray about everything, even those things which seem to be small and insignificant. It is the Lord Alone Who knows the way through the wilderness, so to speak!

When I was a child, prayer meetings were a constant part of my Christian experience. As well, when Frances and I first married, and I was just beginning to preach, evening prayer meetings on a daily basis with my Grandmother was a normal affair. In fact, at least after a fashion, she taught me how to pray.

She used to tell me, and in no uncertain terms, *"Jimmy, God is a big God, so ask big."* I've never forgotten that, and it has helped me to touch this world with the Gospel of Jesus Christ.

When she would speak to me in this manner, she would get a far away look in her eyes, seeming to see beyond the pale of the present into the future. I knew she was speaking by the Spirit, and to be sure, it left an indelible mark upon my heart. She taught me that God answers prayer and, as stated, she taught me to *"believe big."*

ABOMINATIONS

The question of Verse 4, *"Will you judge them, Son of man?"* is asked twice, and is meant to assume the position of relating the historical narrative of Judah, even up to the time they sat before Ezekiel. These Elders had come expecting a pleasant answer regarding their soon to be deliverance, or so they think! The Holy Spirit by *"causing them to know the abominations of their fathers,"* will, in no uncertain terms, proclaim the justness of God's actions, and furthermore, relate to these individuals their own culpability.

Men very readily enjoy hearing a Message of peace and prosperity, but not so much a Message of Judgment! Consequently, and much too often, people seek Churches which will either condone their sins, give them license to sin, or promise them health and wealth. Only those who truly seek the heart of God will attend Churches where the Holy Spirit has full latitude in the services, where He can not only bless, but convict as well; regrettably Ezekiel's Church, so to speak, was not very large.

EGYPT

Verses 5 through 8 reveal that in Egypt the Israelites were idolaters; that God raised up Prophets to plead with them there, but in vain. But despite that, the Lord delivered them.

The phrase, *"And made Myself known unto them in the land of Egypt,"* refers to the great power expended regarding their deliverance from Egyptian bondage.

The phrase, *"When I lifted up My Hand unto them, saying, I am the LORD your God,"* refers to all the idols of Egypt, and that Jehovah was to be the *"Lord your God,"* exclusive of all else. The phrase, *"I am,"* guarantees His ability to provide all that was needed, not only in their deliverance, but as well in their daily lives. The phrase also implies that they had been formerly worshipping idols, and we continue to speak of the time they were in Egypt, before their deliverance.

MILK AND HONEY

The phrase of Verse 6, *"Flowing with milk and honey,"* appears first in Exodus 3:8, and became proverbial.

NOTES

The entire Verse is also a portrayal of the great Plan of Redemption affording God's Salvation. The Lord not only delivers the believing sinner from bondage, but also delivers them to Blessing.

The phrase, *"Which is the glory of all lands,"* portrayed the Promised Land as the Land of Lands, or the *"Glory of all Lands."* As well, Salvation is the *"Glory of all Life"* (Jn. 10:10).

The description of Israel given here by the Holy Spirit, and done so in the physical and the material, is meant to portray the Spiritual Life in Christ. If it's lived the way it ought to be lived, and if the Believer takes full advantage of what Jesus did at the Cross, all on our behalf, then truly this life in Christ will *"flow with milk and honey,"* and will be the *"glory of all life."*

But the sad fact is, as it regards most true Believers, even as Israel little experienced in the physical what the land of Israel was meant to be, many times defeated by their enemies, and even made to be slaves in their own inheritance, and all because of not properly following the Lord, such is the same with many, if not most, in the present sense as it regards Christ.

MORE ABUNDANT LIFE

When the believing sinner comes to Christ, more abundant life instantly becomes the possession of the new Saint; however, the truth is, while all Believers definitely have more abundant life, only a precious few are actually enjoying this *"more abundant life"* (Jn. 10:10).

Why?

The truth is, most Believers simply do not know how to live for God. As a result, they suffer many adverse things which they should not have to suffer, and miss out on so many things which we are intended to have. While all Believers can live in the beauty and the bounty of Romans, Chapter 8, the truth is, virtually all of the modern Church is living in Romans, Chapter 7. And to be sure, *"O wretched man that I am, who shall deliver me from the body of this death?"* is hardly an example of *"more abundant life"* (Rom. 7:24).

In fact, the experience of Israel, which Paul said was given to us as an example, is in fact a perfect example of that of which I speak.

Even though God had personally selected this geographical area, which would be the home, so to speak, of His chosen people, and even though He described it as the land *"flowing with milk and honey,"* and the *"glory of all lands,"* the truth is, Israel little lived up to that which the Lord had prepared for them. In fact, and especially during the time of the Judges, they stayed in submission to enemy tribes, such as the Hivites, the Canaanites, the Amalekites, etc. about as much, or even more so, than they enjoyed a modicum of freedom. Actually, the situation at times became so bad, that the Children of Israel were even afraid to walk on the highways, for fear that their enemies would subjugate them to harassment, or even bodily harm (Judg. 5:6).

Under David and Solomon, Israel enjoyed tremendous prosperity and freedom, as well as under Josiah, Hezekiah, and Jehoshaphat. But ultimately, they so missed the Ways of the Lord, that eventually and ultimately, even as we are studying here concerning Ezekiel, they were driven from their land altogether, and made vassals of a foreign power.

Let me say it again: this is a perfect example of many modern Christians. Israel could have had all that God had prepared for them, but because of failure to walk in His Ways, they forfeited that which the Lord had planned for them. Most Christians are doing the same thing presently. What God has prepared for them, and has done so through Christ and what Christ has done at the Cross, is little realized in the hearts and lives of most Believers. That is tragic, but true!

THE REAL REASON IS AN IMPROPER UNDERSTANDING OF THE CROSS

The Message of the Cross, which in reality is the Message of the New Covenant, has been little preached in the last several decades. It has been so little preached, that for the most part, the Church is Cross illiterate. In fact, even the basic foundations of Salvation by Faith are being lost, with virtually no knowledge whatsoever as it regards Sanctification, in which the Cross is the foundation; however, as stated, most either have an improper understanding of the Cross, or no understanding at all.

NOTES

Most Christians, because of false teaching, pay lip service to the Cross as it regards their Salvation; however, as it regards their Sanctification, they know virtually nothing about it. In fact, the word *"Sanctification"* is a word almost altogether lost to the modern Church, despite the fact that the Doctrine of *"Sanctification"* is one of the cardinal Doctrines of the Bible. It simply means for one to be *"set apart unto Christ."* To say it a better way, *"one is set apart from the world, unto Christ,"* which means unto Christ totally and completely. Sanctification is true holiness! In fact, both words come from the same basic Greek root.

One of the reasons for this dilemma is that the basic goal of most modern Christians is not Christlikeness, but rather, material things. In other words, Christ and the Gospel are being used to acquire material things, which means that the Gospel, in actuality, is being grossly perverted.

The result has been, and is, a total bondage in one way or the other, for most Christians. We go back again to Israel of old! Even though their inheritance was a land *"flowing with milk and honey,"* and the *"glory of all lands,"* still, in many cases, it became a prison. However, the defeated condition of the Israel of those days of long ago was not the fault of the Lord, but rather the fault of Israel in leaving the Ways of the Lord, thereby manufacturing their own ways. It is the same presently!

LET MY PEOPLE GO

Irrespective as to how it has arrived at this sorry spectacle, and a spectacle I might quickly add which is far more dangerous than Israel of old, and because there is much financial prosperity presently, which many mistakenly conclude to be the Blessings of the Lord. While such certainly can be, in the present case, it seldom is. In other words, True Christianity has been abandoned for so long that virtually the entirely of the modern Church knows little or nothing about the true Blessings of the Lord. The modern Church is by and large a social gathering with religious overtones. Jesus is looked at as a great ethic or example, but not at all for the real purpose for which He came, which was to deliver men from sin. In fact, while most of the Church speaks of Christ as the Saviour, it is not known or understood as to what that really means. In other words, the Cross is not connected with Christ in modern thinking, as it must be, for true Christianity to be understood.

Sitting on the platform at Family Worship Center sometime back, Donnie was preaching. He casually mentioned what the Lord spoke to Moses, and that Moses was to tell Pharaoh. The words were, *"Let my people go!"*

Even though Donnie only said this in passing, the moment he said it, the Spirit of God came upon me in a great way. I sat there for some time weeping as the Lord dealt with my heart about His people. Most are in bondage, and the only thing that is going to set them free is the Message of the Cross (Rom. 6:3-14; 8:1-2, 11; I Cor. 1:17-18, 21, 23; 2:2; Eph. 2:13–18).

Sin was addressed at the Cross, and the Cross only! And it is sin that puts people in bondage, and the only delivering factor from sin is what Jesus did at the Cross. That is the reason and the purpose of the Cross, which makes everything else possible.

I personally believe that the Lord is going to take this Message of the Cross to the entirety of the world, possibly in a way that it has never been done before. In fact, I cannot see the Lord doing otherwise. As well, I believe this Ministry (Jimmy Swaggart Ministries) is going to play a great part in that. I am certain that the Lord has called many others in the same capacity, but whatever it is that the Lord wants us to do, and in whatever capacity, that is what we desire to do.

In 1997 when this great Revelation of the Cross was given to me, it definitely was for me, but it definitely was not for me only. It is meant for the entirety of the Body of Christ, as should be overly obvious! That's the reason we are exerting every effort regarding Television and Radio, plus the printed material, as well as every other means, to get out this Message. It is imperative that we do so.

IDOLS

The phrase of Verse 7, *"Idols of Egypt,"* proclaims the fact that some of the Children of Israel, while in Egypt, were idol worshippers. The Lord demanded their disengagement from such abominations.

No special mention of the idols of Egypt occurs in the Pentateuch; however, it is clear that this is the form of idolatry implied in the Second Commandment (Ex. 20:4-5). As well, the episode of the *"Golden Calf"* (Ex. 32:4) shows that the Children of Israel had been greatly influenced by Egypt.

Concerning this, *"Egypt"* is used, in a sense, as a type of the world, and of course, we speak of the Egypt of the time of the deliverance of the Children of Israel. The *"idols"* speak of all that pertain to that system.

Tragically, in modern Christendom, too often times idols (things of the world) are not shed by the Child of God upon coming to Christ. The fault, all too often, lies with the pulpit, in that the people much of the time, are not sufficiently warned!

Please allow me to again make the statement as given by John the Beloved, *"Little children, keep yourselves from idols"* (I Jn. 5:21).

The Apostle wasn't speaking of little figurines that some people use for good luck charms, or even of the type of *"idols"* worshipped by the heathen of Old Testament times. He was rather speaking of *"idols of the heart,"* which refer to anything of the world which comes before Christ. In fact, and again as we've already stated, religion is the greatest and most powerful idol of all.

MODERN TEACHING THAT EQUATES TO IDOLS

Millions equate their Church with Christ: in other words, being faithful to their Church is the same as being faithful to Christ. Millions equate particular doctrines with Christ. Millions equate their particular Denomination with Christ. And what do I mean by that?

Millions in almost every Denomination, if not all Denominations, equate their belonging to that Denomination as something spiritual. In fact, such an idea is given credence from behind many pulpits. As well, they are taught if they leave that particular Denomination, that they will lose their spirituality or even their souls. Consequently, *"fear"* becomes a part of their experience, and I speak of the fear of doing something that would be opposed to that particular Denomination.

The Truth is, such a spirit is of Satan, and such a Denomination, or Church, have become an idol. While the individuals associating themselves with such may equate it with Christ, the truth is, religious Denominations or particular Churches have nothing to do with Christ at all. While it's certainly not wrong to belong to a Denomination or Church, these things must always be kept in proper prospective.

These things I've stated, at least in spirit, are identical to what took place in Israel of old. Oftentimes they worshipped the heathenistic idols of the surrounding countries, and they equated those idols with Jehovah. It was something they could see, touch, and feel. And so, in their minds, when they worshipped this *"idol,"* whatever it may have been, they were worshipping Jehovah; however, they were not worshipping Jehovah, just as their modern counterparts are not worshipping the Lord by equating their Denomination or Church with Christ.

I'm afraid that presently this problem is more acute than it's ever been before in the history of the Church.

Some years ago, many, if not most Christians, not understanding the Cross at all as it refers to our Sanctification, made laws out of good things such as *"prayer,"* or *"Bible study,"* or *"witnessing."* While these things are very good in their own right, and while every good Christian is definitely going to have a strong prayer life, etc., if we think by the doing of those things that such brings about Holiness and Righteousness, we will find ourselves deceived. In other words, the victory for which we seek cannot be found in that direction. Jesus said, *"You shall know the Truth, and the Truth shall make you free"* (Jn. 8:32).

But at this present time (2003), prayer is almost a lost art, and so is Bible study, etc. The great throughway now to success and prosperity, at least as it is presently taught, is involvement and faithfulness to a particular Church. Pure and simple, such people have turned the Church, whatever the name on the door, into an idol. They have *"changed the Truth of God into a lie, and worshipped and served the creature more than the Creator, Who is blessed forever. Amen"* (Rom. 1:25).

NOTES

To say it another way, their faith is not in Christ and the Cross, but rather in their particular Church. So where does that leave these particular people?

SPIRITUAL CONDITION

To be frank, most who occupy themselves accordingly, are not even Born-Again. They are religious but not Righteous, at least with the type of Righteousness given by the Lord. In fact, they are woefully self-righteous. They are faithful to the Church, but they aren't faithful to Christ. They *"have a form of godliness, but deny the power thereof."* Concerning such, the Scripture plainly says, *"from such turn away"* (II Tim. 3:5).

Holy Spirit Power can only be registered in proper faith and proper faith is always that which has the Cross as its Object (Rom. 6:3-14; I Cor. 1:18; Gal. 6:14). Such Churches become social centers with religious overtones. Such Preachers merely proclaim an ethic, which sounds good to the carnal ear, but which in reality will serve no spiritual purpose whatsoever.

No! Regrettably and sadly, *"idols"* are still with us and, in fact, in a bigger and greater way than ever. While they might presently be more subtle, they are at the same time more lethal.

REBELLION

Verse 8 says, *"But they rebelled against Me, and would not harken unto Me."* All too often, this is the story of the modern Church. Refusing to heed the Word of God, and, thereby, rebelling against God, is the seed-bed of all spiritual declension. This one word, *"rebellion,"* proclaims the entire cause of the deterioration of relationship with Christ. It answers most questions regarding *"why?"*

In stark clarity and revealing detail, the Holy Spirit is presently beginning to bring the Message of the Cross to the Church world, possibly as He has never done so before. While there will definitely be some who will heed and herald this Message, which is not new, but rather that given to the Apostle Paul, but long since abandoned by the Church, the truth is, the far greater majority are rebelling, and will rebel against this *"Word of the Lord."*

I want to make it clear that some will definitely accept, and thank God for those. But most will not!

Why?

A long, long time ago, the Prophet Samuel answered that question. He said, *"Behold, to obey is better than sacrifice, and to hearken than the fat of rams.*

"For rebellion is as the sin of witchcraft, and stubbornness is as iniquity and idolatry" (I Sam. 15:22-23).

First of all, all *"rebellion,"* at least in the spiritual sense, is against the *"Word of the Lord."* This is evidenced by the phrase of Verse 8, *"But they rebelled against Me, and would not hearken unto Me."* That's at least one of the reasons why some seven times Jesus said to the seven Churches of Asia, which were types of the entire Church age, *"He who has an ear, let him hear what the Spirit says unto the Churches"* (Rev. 3:22). In fact, that was His last Word to the Church. Last words are always very important! And especially considering that they come from our Lord, we had best heed exactly what He has said.

Let's break down I Samuel 15: 22-23, and see what it says:

"Rebellion" and *"stubbornness"* are basically the same. *"Stubbornness"* is a refusal to accept the Word of the Lord. *"Rebellion"* is a position which opposes Truth, and the word *"stubbornness"* proclaims the fact that the individual knows what is right, but refuses to obey. All of it translates into *"witchcraft, iniquity, and idolatry."*

"Witchcraft," as it is used here, translates into a perversion of the Word of God, which means that the Word of God is not ignored, but is rather perverted, in other words, twisted to make it mean something that God never intended. Scores of Bible Doctrines have been done accordingly. The modern Word of Faith movement is a perfect example! By perverting the Word of God, in effect, the individual, to be plain and simple, is setting up another system, which is other than *"Jesus Christ and Him Crucified."* The word *"iniquity"* refers to the fact that all of this is gross sin. Consequently, what is done in this capacity becomes an *"idol,"* i.e., *"idolatry."*

Saul was given instructions, by the Lord through the Prophet Samuel, to destroy the entirety of the Amalekites, and all that was theirs, including the animals, etc. (I Sam. 15:3). Instead, Saul spared Agag, the Amalekite king, and *"the best of the sheep, and of the oxen, and of the fatlings, and of the lambs, and all that was good, and would not utterly destroy them"* (I Sam. 15:9). He claimed that he was going to offer these animals up in sacrifice, hence, Samuel telling him that *"to obey is better than sacrifice."*

These animals would not suffice, even though they definitely were the type of animals that were to be used in Sacrifice. Because they belonged to an ungodly, heathenistic king, they could not serve as types of Christ, which all sacrificial animals were supposed to serve. So, in effect, Saul was planning to offer up that to God which God could not accept.

It is the same presently as the modern Church worshipping *"another Jesus"* (II Cor. 11:4). Christ Alone can be accepted, and we speak of what he did at the Cross. If any other proposal is presented, which doesn't recognize Christ for Who He rightly is, and what He has rightly done, which speaks of the Cross, it must be rightly rejected.

So, Saul was rejected by God, because he attempted to offer a polluted Christ on the Cross, while the modern Church is even worse, in that it rejects the Cross altogether.

THE NAME OF THE LORD

Verse 9 says, *"But I wrought for My Name's sake,"* which refers to the deliverance of the Children of Israel out of Egypt. This tells us that the only reason they were spared was not because of their holiness, because they had none, but rather His Holiness and Name's sake.

The idea of Verse 9 is that Moses, when asked by the Children of Israel as to who sent him, he was to say unto them, *"I AM has sent me unto you"* (Ex. 3:14).

As well, Pharaoh would be told the same thing, when he asked the question, *"Who is the LORD?"* (Ex. 5:1-2). His question would be ruefully answered in the destruction of Egypt. In order that God's Name *"not be polluted before the heathen,"* the Lord, and despite Israel's idol worship in Egypt, would *"bring them forth out of the Land of Egypt."*

His honor was at stake, and not theirs!

(10) "WHEREFORE I CAUSE THEM TO GO FORTH OUT OF THE LAND OF EGYPT, AND BROUGHT THEM INTO THE WILDERNESS.

(11) "AND I GAVE THEM MY STATUTES, AND SHEWED THEM MY JUDGMENTS, WHICH IF A MAN DO, HE SHALL EVEN LIVE IN THEM.

(12) "MOREOVER ALSO I GAVE THEM MY SABBATHS, TO BE A SIGN BETWEEN ME AND THEM, THAT THEY MIGHT KNOW THAT I AM THE LORD WHO SANCTIFIES THEM.

(13) "BUT THE HOUSE OF ISRAEL REBELLED AGAINST ME IN THE WILDERNESS: THEY WALKED NOT IN MY STATUTES, AND THEY DESPISED MY JUDGMENTS, WHICH IF A MAN DO, HE SHALL EVEN LIVE IN THEM; AND MY SABBATHS THEY GREATLY POLLUTED: THEN I SAID, I WOULD POUR OUT MY FURY UPON THEM IN THE WILDERNESS, TO CONSUME THEM.

(14) "BUT I WROUGHT FOR MY NAME'S SAKE, THAT IT SHOULD NOT BE POLLUTED BEFORE THE HEATHEN, IN WHOSE SIGHT I BROUGHT THEM OUT.

(15) "YET ALSO I LIFTED UP MY HAND UNTO THEM IN THE WILDERNESS, THAT I WOULD NOT BRING THEM INTO THE LAND WHICH I HAD GIVEN THEM, FLOWING WITH MILK AND HONEY, WHICH IS THE GLORY OF ALL LANDS;

(16) "BECAUSE THEY DESPISED MY JUDGMENTS, AND WALKED NOT IN MY STATUTES, BUT POLLUTED MY SABBATHS: FOR THEIR HEART WENT AFTER THEIR IDOLS.

(17) "NEVERTHELESS MY EYE SPARED THEM FROM DESTROYING THEM, NEITHER DID I MAKE AN END OF THEM IN THE WILDERNESS."

The diagram is:

1. The Lord brought the Children of Israel out of Egyptian bondage because of His Holiness, and not because of theirs.

2. As it regards the "*Law,*" He gave them His Statutes, and said that they should "*live in them,*" and not "*by them,*" for life cannot be thus merited.

3. The Divine Title Jehovah-Mekaddishkem is given in Verse 12. It means, "*The Lord, The Sanctifier.*"

THE LAW

Verses 10 and 11 portray the "*Law,*" which was given to Israel in the wilderness. The phrase, "*He shall even live in them,*" referred to the Statutes of the Law, which would provide a quality of life heretofore unknown in the world. But Israel little took advantage of this which the Lord gave them, just as the Church little takes advantage of the Word of God, which is given to us.

The Law was given for many and varied reasons. Some of those reasons are as follows:

1. The "*Law*" was the Standard which God demanded of men, and we particularly speak of the Ten Commandments (Ex., Chpt. 20).

2. The Law was given that man might see how lacking in capability he was, as it regards the keeping of the Law. In other words, due to the Fall, man, even the Children of Israel couldn't keep the Law; consequently, the Sacrificial System was provided in the Law, which pointed to Christ, and what He would do at the Cross, in order that their infractions of the Law could be covered, which was done by the shed blood of these innocent animals.

3. While the Law was a mirror showing man what he actually was, it had no power to change man.

4. In the face of all of this, the Law of God, as given to the Children of Israel, was by far the most equitable Law on the face of the Earth. While there were many other laws in existence at that time, they were all devised by man and, therefore, were grossly unfair and unequal. In other words, the laws devised by men favored some while penalizing others.

The Law of God addressed every single facet of life and living.

All of the Law, in one way or the other, pointed to Christ, Who Alone would perfectly keep the Law and satisfy its just demands by dying on the Cross of Calvary. That's why the Scripture plainly says: "*For Christ is the end of the Law for Righteousness to everyone who believes*" (Rom. 10:4).

As stated Christ satisfied every demand of the Law.

HOW DOES THE LAW AFFECT THE MODERN CHRISTIAN?

It's not supposed to affect the Christian at all. The Scripture plainly says, *"You also are become dead to the Law by the Body of Christ"* (Rom. 7:4). What did Paul mean by that?

The term *"Body of Christ"* refers to Christ offering up His Perfect Body on the Cross in Sacrifice, which satisfied the demands of the broken Law (Gal. 3:13-14).

But if it is to be noticed, the Apostle didn't say that the Law was dead, but rather, that we are *"dead to the Law."* Now what did he mean by that?

While the Law is not dead, and we speak of the moral aspect of the Law, and because the moral aspect cannot die, still, we are dead to all of its aspects and precepts.

Does that mean that the moral law of the Ten Commandments is not incumbent upon modern Believers?

Not at all! They are, in fact, very much incumbent upon every Believer. If it was wrong to steal 3,000 years ago, it's wrong to steal now. If it was wrong to commit adultery then, it's wrong now, etc.

The idea is, we are to keep the Moral Law of God, but we are to do it strictly and totally through Christ. We are to look to Him exclusively as it regards what He did for us at the Cross, and then, the Holy Spirit will work mightily within our lives (Rom. 8:1-2, 11), guaranteeing the keeping of the moral law; however, this is not done by us subscribing to the Commandments, but rather, by us looking to Christ exclusively, Who was the perfect keeper of the Law, and as well, Who satisfied its just demands on the Cross. The Law will then be kept; however, it is all in Christ, and what Christ has done at the Cross.

THE OBJECT OF OUR FAITH

If we make the Law in any capacity, whether the Law of God, or laws we have made up ourselves, the object of our faith, we will fail every single time. Addressing this, Paul plainly said: *"For if Righteousness come by the Law, then Christ is dead in vain"* (Gal. 2:21).

The idea is, no Believer can bring about Righteousness within his life by subscribing to a system of law or laws. He can only do so by looking exclusively to Christ and what Christ has done at the Cross, which then gives the Holy Spirit latitude to work in our lives, bringing about that which we must have, and I refer to the fruit of the Spirit (Gal. 2:20).

The answer is not Law-keeping and in any capacity, but rather, *"Christ and Him Crucified."*

THE SABBATH

Verses 12 and 20, with Deuteronomy 5:15, suggest that prior to the Exodus, the Sabbath of Genesis 2:3 was not observed by men, but was given by God to Israel as He also gave circumcision as a sign of special relationship with these people.

The purpose of the Sabbath, which incidentally came every Saturday, was for *"rest."* It was meant to typify the *"rest"* which would be afforded by Christ, according to the work that He carried out at the Cross. As everything else about the Jewish Law pointed to Christ, so did the Sabbath. Jesus said: *"Come unto Me, all ye who labor and are heavy laden, and I will give you rest.*

"Take My yoke upon you, and learn of Me; for I am meek and lowly in heart: you shall find rest unto your souls.

"For My yoke is easy, and My burden is light" (Mat. 11:28-30). Consequently, when Jesus came, He fulfilled all the Law, including the Sabbath, meaning that it is no more in vogue.

Consequently, Churches which attempt to keep the Jewish Sabbath as a part of their ritual worship, are out of dispensation relationship and, therefore, are unscriptural.

If it is to be noticed, in the Book of Acts and the Epistles, the primary day of worship became the first day of the week, Sunday, which was the day that Jesus rose from the dead (Jn. 20:1, 19; Acts 20:7; I Cor. 16:2).

Any part of the old Jewish Law that modern Believers endeavor to keep, including the Jewish Sabbath, presents itself, whether intended or not, as a statement that Jesus did not satisfy the Law and, therefore, we must continue its precepts, which is an insult of the highest order toward Christ. As we've already stated in this Volume, the Scripture plainly says, and in no uncertain terms: *"For Christ is the end of the Law for Righteousness to everyone who believes"* (Rom. 10:4).

There is something in man, even ardent Believers, which desires to earn or merit one's Salvation or Sanctification. The only way that such a direction can be entered into is by law, whether the ancient Law of Moses, or religious laws which we devise ourselves. Probably one could say, without fear of contradiction, that the hardest thing for the Believer to do, is to trust not at all in religious works, whatever they might be, and do the contrary, trust solely in Christ and what He has done for us at the Cross. It would seem to be the easiest thing to do, especially considering, that there is no way that success can be gained by the Law route; however, despite the 100 percent failure rate, we seem determined to go that route. With many, even most, especially at this particular time, they do so out of ignorance, because they do not understand the Cross as it regards our Sanctification, which refers to the way and manner in which we live for the Lord. So they revert to Law, because there is no place else to go.

But even after we understand the Cross regarding *"walking after the Spirit,"* we have to portray a constant diligence that we not revert back into law, which is so easy to do.

SANCTIFICATION

The phrase of Verse 12, *"That they might know that I am the LORD Who sanctifies them,"* in the Hebrew contains the Divine Title *"Jehovah-Mekaddishkem."* It means, *"The Lord, The Sanctifier."* It portrays the Truth that man cannot sanctify Himself.

Sanctification is the cleansing process, which is carried out by the Holy Spirit. In other words, it *"makes one clean,"* whereas Justification *"declares one clean."*

There is no way the believing sinner can cleanse himself from the effects of original sin. Such is impossible! Therefore, it must be done by an outside power, which is *"the Lord, our Sanctifier"* (I Cor. 6:11).

Every Believer is instantly and wholly sanctified at the moment of conversion, which is an absolute necessity, before Justification can be carried out, which of course, is all done instantly, at least as far as we are concerned.

Concerning this, Paul said, after listing many types of sins and wickedness: *"And such were some of you: but you are washed, but you are sanctified, but you are justified in the Name of the Lord Jesus, and by the Spirit of our God"* (I Cor. 6:11).

One should notice the progression. First of all, the believing sinner is *"washed."* This in essence pertains to the Blood of Jesus Christ being applied to our hearts, lives, and sins, which is, in effect, the action part of the Sanctification process. This being done, the believing sinner is now clean, and is declared so, which is *"Justification by Faith"* (Rom. 5:1). As we have stated, it's impossible for the believing sinner to be *"justified,"* before he is *"sanctified."*

Now that is our *"position"* in Christ, which never changes. This means we are perfectly clean, and perfectly declared so, and all because of one's Faith in Christ, Who Alone is our Substitute; believing in Him, and what He has done for us at the Cross, grants the believing sinner all that Christ is, which is perfection before God. In other words, being *"in Christ,"* which refers to believing what He did for us at the Cross, grants to us the entirety of the victory purchased by Christ, and done so for us exclusively, and given to us upon Faith.

POSITION AND CONDITION

However, as we all know, even though the actual *"position"* of the Believer is perfect in Christ, and because it is in Christ, which position will never change, as long as the Believer continues to evidence Faith in Christ, the truth is, our *"condition"* is not exactly up to our *"position."* By *"condition,"* I am referring to our everyday life and living before God, in other words, our *"daily walk."*

Consequently, the Holy Spirit immediately sets out to bring our *"condition"* up to our *"position."* As the *"position"* never changes, conversely, our *"condition"* is up and down, even as the Believer soon realizes.

The only way that the *"condition"* can be brought up to the *"position"* is by the Believer continuing to evidence Faith in Christ and what Christ has done at the Cross on our behalf. Then and then only can the Holy Spirit carry out in our lives that which needs to be done. He doesn't require much of us, but He definitely requires that the Cross ever be the Object of our Faith, and that such never change.

As we've already stated in this Volume, Romans, Chapters 4 and 5 give us the means by which Justification is carried out, which is always by Faith, and never by works. And when we say *"by Faith,"* without exception, we are speaking of Faith in Christ, and what Christ did at the Cross. In other words, the Cross must ever be the Object of our Faith (Jn. 3:16; Rom. 10:9-10, 13; Rev. 22:17; Eph. 2:13-18; Col. 2:14-15).

Leaving Romans, Chapters 4 and 5, we then come to Chapter 6, which now tells the Believer how to live a victorious, overcoming Christian life. At the beginning of that Chapter, Paul anchors the Believer into the Cross (Rom. 6:3-5).

In Verses 6 through 10, the Apostle tells us how that, due to the Cross, we are now dead to what we once were, which means we are dead to the sin nature. The power of sin has been broken, and the guilt removed, all because of the Cross. Then in Verse 11, he brings our constant faith into view. He said: *"Likewise reckon* (account) *ye also yourselves to be dead indeed unto sin* (dead unto the sin nature), *but alive unto God through Jesus Christ our Lord."* Due to what Christ did for us at the Cross, and our continued Faith in that Finished Work, we are dead to the sin nature. He doesn't say here that the sin nature is dead, which in actuality it isn't, but rather that we are dead to its power; consequently, it is rendered ineffective; if we continue to evidence our Faith in Christ and the Cross, we will remain dead to the sin nature, and perpetual victory will be ours. The Holy Spirit through Paul said so.

"For sin (the sin nature) *shall not have dominion over you: for you are not under the Law, but under Grace"* (Rom. 6:14).

This in brief, which I have given unto you, is the manner and way in which the *"condition"* of the Believer is to be brought up to our *"position."* All of it is a work of the Spirit, which predicates what He does exclusively on and within the Finished Work of Christ (Rom. 8:1-2, 11).

This is the only means by which the Believer can walk in victory. That's why Paul also said: *"But God forbid that I should glory, save in the Cross of our Lord Jesus Christ, by Whom the world is crucified unto me, and I unto the world."* (Gal. 6:14).

THE WILDERNESS

When Fathers are hardened in sin, as Verses 13 through 17 will portray, hope has recourse in their children; but then, as now, these are found to possess the same corrupt nature as their parents, and consequently to love the same sins, as Verses 18 through 21 will also proclaim!

The terrible account of all these rebellions in the wilderness hardly needs to be portrayed here. Enough to say that Ezekiel's testimony to these Elders could not be denied regarding these accusations. They full well knew the history of their own people, and of the Mercy of God.

Once again, as in Egypt, Ezekiel proclaims the fact, in Verse 13, that the Lord strongly desired to *"pour out My fury upon them in the wilderness, to consume them."*

The idea is, as is plainly shown here, that Judah deserved destruction long before now! Their history was one of disobedience rather than of obedience, therefore, they had no argument, and it was only by the Grace of God, that they were allowed to continue up to this point.

As well, all of mankind stands to be judged accordingly. We are guilty! We do not merit Salvation, there is nothing we have ever done, even in the slightest way that could merit Salvation; therefore, Salvation is all of God and none of us. It is only by His Grace and Mercy that we have not been destroyed.

JUDGMENT

The expression as used in Verse 15, *"I lifted up My hand unto them,"* is used seven times in this Chapter (Vss. 5-6, 15, 23, 28, 42).

From this Passage, we learn how absolutely close that Israel came to being totally exterminated in the wilderness. It was only the intercession of Moses which caused them, after a fashion, to be spared (Num. 14:11-35). In fact, despite that intercession, that particular generation was destroyed, but their children were allowed to continue and go into the Promised Land.

DESPISING THE WORD OF GOD

Verse 16 says, *"Because they despised My Judgments,"* which meant, that they despised the Word of God. As a result, they did not *"walk in His Statutes."* As well, they *"polluted His Sabbaths,"* which means they did not keep them, and had no desire to keep them.

The phrase, *"For their heart went after their idols,"* proclaims the reason that they did these things.

Their *"heart"* was not after God, but rather after their own selfish pursuits, in actuality, idols. In other words, they brought Egyptian worship with them into the wilderness.

Unfortunately, all too often, Believers bring the worship of the world into their Christian experience, and what do we mean by that?

In effect, everything comes under the heading of *"worship."* We either worship things of the world, or we worship that which is of God. One may not think of attachments to the world as that of worship, but that's actually what it is.

Men bow down to the idols of entertainment, of social activity, of place and position, of money, etc. We have to be very careful, that we do not carry these things with us into our worship of the Lord. The Scripture plainly says: *"You shall have no other gods before Me. You shall not bow yourself down to them, nor serve them: For I the LORD your God am a jealous God"* (Ex. 20:3, 5).

THE MOSAIC LAW

The Mosaic Law was far more than merely a moral code delivered by Moses, but was rather meant to serve as the entirety of a lifestyle for God's people. Actually, it addressed itself to every facet of life and being. In essence, everything in the experience of the people of Israel was guided by the Law. It was the constitution of the nation, the basis for determining civil and criminal cases, as well as a guide to worship. It was also a personal guide to good family and social relationships, and a personal guide to relationship with the Lord.

Law comprised not only those regulations that define sin and established guilt, but also the sacrificial system through which the Believer might find atonement for sins. In essence, everything in the experience of the people of Israel was guided by the Law. To those who truly loved God, the Law was highly esteemed. Two of David's Psalms show us how highly esteemed the Law was among believing Israelites. They are Psalms 19 and 119. (It is not certain if David actually wrote Psalm 119, but there is a great deal of evidence that he did.)

THE CURSE OF THE LAW

And yet, the Law of God carried with it a terrible curse if not obeyed (Deut., Chpt. 28), but yet God gave no power for man to keep it. Some may think it cruel for the Lord to demand such and to attach a terrible penalty to failure, when He knew they would be unable to properly obey.

However, the Law was never intended to save men, but only to serve as a *"guardian to bring us unto Christ that we might be justified by Faith"* (Gal. 3:24). Paul would ask the question, *"Wherefore then serves the Law?"* or rather, *"What good is the Law?"* His answer was, *"it was added because of transgressions,"* meaning, to point out what was right and what was wrong (Gal. 3:19).

Among other reasons, the Law was given by God in order that man may see what sin was, and to see also his inability to obey the Law. He was then to throw himself on the Mercy and Grace of God, hence the giving of the Sacrifices, which were a type of the coming Christ.

As stated, the Law contained no salvation, only a curse! In fact, there was Righteousness in the Law, but for such Righteousness to be attained, the Law had to be perfectly kept, which man was unable to do, but which Jesus did on our behalf.

The curse of the Law was death, which pertained to all, because all were disobedient, even Moses.

Yet, with His Death at Calvary, *"Christ has redeemed us from the curse of the Law, being made a curse for us"* (Gal. 3:13).

In other words, Christ took the penalty of the curse, that, in fact, should have come upon us.

Him being made curse for us means that the curse was lifted from us, which means that the sin debt was forever paid. He did all of this that *"the Blessing of Abraham might come on the Gentiles through Jesus Christ;*

that we might receive the Promise of the Spirit through Faith" (Gal. 3:14).

Many do not understand that God would demand so much regarding the Law, and yet give man no power to do that which, within himself, was impossible.

However, if the Lord had given power to keep the Law, such would have only made man worse than he already was. Man's problem already was pride, and if power had been given to keep the Law, pride would have only increased. Actually, man is so incurably prideful and, therefore, evil (incurable within himself), that even the giving of the Law caused Israel to be even lifted up further in pride. Therefore, by the time that Christ came, they were so prideful in their self-righteousness that they actually thought they were keeping the Law. And yet Jesus told them, *"None of you keepeth the Law"* (Jn. 7:19).

However, and as stated, Christ kept the Law perfectly and, in effect, has transferred that perfection to the Believer (Gal. 2:19-21).

(18) "BUT I SAID UNTO THEIR CHILDREN IN THE WILDERNESS, WALK YE NOT IN THE STATUTES OF YOUR FATHERS, NEITHER OBSERVE THEIR JUDGMENTS, NOR DEFILE YOURSELVES WITH THEIR IDOLS:

(19) "I AM THE LORD YOUR GOD; WALK IN MY STATUTES, AND KEEP MY JUDGMENTS, AND DO THEM;

(20) "AND HALLOW MY SABBATHS; AND THEY SHALL BE A SIGN BETWEEN ME AND YOU, THAT YE MAY KNOW THAT I AM THE LORD YOUR GOD.

(21) "NOTWITHSTANDING THE CHILDREN REBELLED AGAINST ME: THEY WALK NOT IN MY STATUTES, NEITHER KEPT MY JUDGMENTS TO DO THEM, WHICH IF A MAN DO, HE SHALL EVEN LIVE IN THEM; THEY POLLUTED MY SABBATHS: THEN I SAID, I WOULD POUR OUT MY FURY UPON THEM, TO ACCOMPLISH MY ANGER AGAINST THEM IN THE WILDERNESS.

(22) "NEVERTHELESS I WITHDREW MY HAND, AND WROUGHT FOR MY NAME'S SAKE, THAT IT SHOULD NOT BE POLLUTED IN THE SIGHT OF THE HEATHEN, IN WHOSE SIGHT I BROUGHT THEM FORTH.

(23) "I LIFTED UP MY HAND UNTO THEM ALSO IN THE WILDERNESS, THAT I WOULD SCATTER THEM AMONG THE HEATHEN, AND DISPERSE THEM THROUGH THE COUNTRIES;

(24) "BECAUSE THEY HAD NOT EXECUTED MY JUDGMENTS, BUT HAD DESPISED MY STATUTES, AND HAD POLLUTED MY SABBATHS, AND THEIR EYES WERE AFTER THEIR FATHERS' IDOLS.

(25) "WHEREFORE I GAVE THEM ALSO STATUTES THAT WERE NOT GOOD, AND JUDGMENTS WHEREBY THEY SHOULD NOT LIVE;

(26) "AND I POLLUTED THEM IN THEIR OWN GIFTS, IN THAT THEY CAUSED TO PASS THROUGH THE FIRE ALL WHO OPEN THE WOMB, THAT I MIGHT MAKE THEM DESOLATE, TO THE END THAT THEY MIGHT KNOW THAT I AM THE LORD."

The composition is:

1. God commanded that the children should be passed over to Him and live. Idolatry commanded that they should be passed through to Moloch and die. It is the same presently with the world and with Christ.

2. God may be known experientially as a Saviour or as a Destroyer. He must be *"known"* as the latter by everyone who refuses to know Him as the former.

3. To Israel He showed both goodness and severity (Rom. 11:22); but neither action moved them from their idols, for man is by nature evil (Rom., Chpts. 3-8).

OBEDIENCE

Verses 18 through 21 proclaim the fact of the Lord pleading with *"their children in the wilderness,"* that they would not conduct themselves as had their fathers before them. The Lord is simply asking them to obey His Word. He asks the same of us today.

But sadly, the pleadings of the Lord were to no avail. The *"children"* rebelled exactly as did their fathers. They had the same corrupt nature as their parents, and consequently, loved the same sins.

MERCY

Verses 22 through 26 proclaim the anger

of the Lord registered against the Children of Israel in the wilderness. The situation, in fact, was so bad that He condemned the first generation to death, with them dying in the wilderness, and allowed the second generation to go into the Promised Land.

He did it so the heathen would not be able to mock His Name, claiming that He had brought them into the wilderness, and could not deliver them.

So when they finally went into the Promised Land, even after forty years of wandering in the wilderness, they were not to think that the Lord had allowed them to go into the Land because He approved of them. Actually, their being allowed to go into the Land of Israel had little to do with them, but with His *"Name."*

Verse 26 proclaims the fact that the Children of Israel, while in the wilderness, and despite the miracles of God, actually engaged in human sacrifice, in offering up their children unto Moloch. The sacrifice of children on that altar was the most abominable of all, as would be overly obvious!

THE MODERN CHURCH

I am positive that every Believer presently, and even those who really do not know the Lord despite what they might claim, would look with abhorrence of the offering up of children in sacrifice to heathenistic idols. The very thoughts of such create a revulsion in our hearts, even as it should.

However, let the modern Church understand the following:

If parents do not portray a Godly example in front of their children, and if they do not attend a Church where the Spirit of God is paramount, they will, in effect, conclude such a direction by sacrificing their children to the idols of the world. While it might be more subtle now than then, the end result is the same. The young man or young lady is destroyed!

The only thing that can keep our sons and daughters, in fact the only thing that can keep any of us, is the Power of God. But what did Paul say:

He said: *"This know also, that in the last days perilous times shall come."*

He then gave a long list of ungodly directions, and then concluded by saying: *"Having a form of godliness, but denying the power thereof: from such turn away"* (II Tim. 3:1-5).

And that's the state of the far greater majority of most Churches. They have a *"form of godliness,"* but that is the extent of their consecration. The truth is, they have *"denied the power."* What does that mean?

THE POWER

The power, of course, is in the Holy Spirit; however, He registers that power in our hearts and lives, thereby helping us to live the life we ought to live, by virtue of Christ and what Christ did at the Cross, and that exclusively (Rom. 8:2). So, for the Believer to have the Power of God manifested in his life, the Cross of Christ must ever be the Object of his Faith. But the truth is, the modern Church has denied the Cross, which means that they have *"denied the power thereof,"* which means that it is impossible for such individuals to live a Godly life. As previously stated, most Churches are mere social centers with religious overtones. Most Preachers, regrettably, are little more than social workers, or the proclaimers of a particular ethic, in other words, amateur psychologists. In fact, in the second largest Pentecostal Denomination in the world, the Church of God located in Cleveland, Tennessee, all of their preachers are strongly encouraged to get a degree in psychology. In fact, at the time of this writing (2003), their General Overseer is a practicing Psychologist. Consequently, all who attend such type Churches are colored by this particular direction.

In truth, this Denomination, plus the Assemblies of God, the largest Pentecostal Denomination in the world, have *"denied the power thereof,"* and because they are denying the Cross. They would not agree to such, but the truth is, one cannot accept the Cross and humanistic psychology at the same time. Either one cancels out the other.

Jesus plainly said: *"No man can serve two masters: for either he will hate the one, and love the other; or else he will hold to the one, and despise the other. You cannot serve God and mammon"* (Mat. 6:24).

The word *"mammon"* means *"confidence,"* meaning, that one cannot place confidence in God and the things of the world at the same time.

So the end result of all of this is, that the children will be lost.

If I remember correctly, the year was 1992. It was a service at Family Worship Center. I was preaching.

The Spirit of the Lord moved mightily upon me during the course of the Message, and spoke through me, saying, *"Unless we have Revival, our children are going to be lost."*

I've thought about that many times, but only of late do I fully understand, I think, what the Lord was then saying.

In fact, 1992 was some five years before the Lord would give me the Revelation of the Cross. But since that Revelation has been given, I now understand, at least after a measure, the spiritual condition of the modern Church, and its rejection of the Cross. That rejection will fall out to the loss of the sons and daughters of the present generation. In fact, it cannot be otherwise. It is the same as Israel of old, offering their sons and daughters as sacrifice to Moloch. If our faith and confidence are not exclusively in Christ and the Cross, there will be no power to live for God; consequently, the soul will be lost!

(27) "THEREFORE, SON OF MAN, SPEAK UNTO THE HOUSE OF ISRAEL, AND SAY UNTO THEM, THUS SAITH THE LORD GOD: YET IN THIS YOUR FATHERS HAVE BLASPHEMED ME, IN THAT THEY HAVE COMMITTED A TRESPASS AGAINST ME.

(28) "FOR WHEN I HAD BROUGHT THEM INTO THE LAND, FOR THE WHICH I LIFTED UP MY HAND TO GIVE IT TO THEM, THEN THEY SAW EVERY HIGH HILL, AND ALL THE THICK TREES, AND THEY OFFERED THERE THEIR SACRIFICES, AND THERE THEY PRESENTED THE PROVOCATION OF THEIR OFFERING: THERE ALSO THEY MADE THEIR SWEET SAVOUR, AND POURED OUT THERE THEIR DRINK OFFERINGS.

(29) "THEN I SAID UNTO THEM, WHAT IS THE HIGH PLACE WHEREUNTO YOU GO? AND THE NAME THEREOF IS CALLED BAMAH UNTO THIS DAY.

(30) "WHEREFORE SAY UNTO THE HOUSE OF ISRAEL, THUS SAITH THE LORD GOD; ARE YOU POLLUTED AFTER THE MANNER OF YOUR FATHERS? AND COMMIT YOU WHOREDOM AFTER THEIR ABOMINATIONS?

(31) "FOR WHEN YOU OFFER YOUR GIFTS, WHEN YOU MAKE YOUR SONS TO PASS THROUGH THE FIRE, YOU POLLUTE YOURSELVES WITH ALL YOUR IDOLS, EVEN UNTO THIS DAY: AND SHALL I BE ENQUIRED OF BY YOU, O HOUSE OF ISRAEL? AS I LIVE, SAITH THE LORD GOD, I WILL NOT BE ENQUIRED OF BY YOU.

(32) "AND THAT WHICH COMES INTO YOUR MIND SHALL NOT BE AT ALL, THAT YOU SAY, WE WILL BE AS THE HEATHEN, AS THE FAMILIES OF THE COUNTRIES, TO SERVE WOOD AND STONE."

THE STRUCTURE IS:

1. Israel committed a grave trespass against the Lord, i.e., they associated idols with God. This is also the great sin of many Churches, especially the Catholic Church.

2. The four *"theres"* of Verse 28 are employed to emphasize the contrast with the one divinely appointed place of acceptance, which is Calvary, as foreshadowed by Mt. Moriah.

3. Access to God, Forgiveness, and Righteousness, as Abel proved, can only be enjoyed through Christ's Atonement; for He is, as He Himself said, the one and only Way to God.

4. Ezekiel, by inspiration, refused to pray for his visitors. They must have been very angry with him, for instead of preaching to them the comfortable doctrines which the other prophets announced, he exposed their idolatries and hypocrisies, and predicted their eternal ruin.

5. The determined bent of the Hebrew mind to worship any god rather than Jehovah, and their efforts during some 3,500 years to become like other nations, and to be one of them, proved the existence of God and the inspiration of the Bible.

For their failure to be as other nations, despite all their efforts — and these efforts are still in operation — demonstrates the existence of a Will that plans the contrary, and has planned it for thousands of years; and their repeated rebellions against Jehovah, culminating in the Crucifixion of the Messiah, and continuing to the present day, reveal inspiration, for no nation refuses devotion to a god of its own invention. Had the Hebrews invented the God of Israel, they would have been loyal to Him.

THE HEATHEN

The phrase of Verse 27, *"Yet in this your fathers have blasphemed Me, in that they have committed a trespass against Me,"* actually says, *"they trespassed a trespass."* That is, they were guilty of a supreme trespass, i.e., they associated idols with God. This is the great sin of the Catholic Church in its Mary worship. It is, as well, the great sin of the Protestant Church in its worship of Denominations, i.e., denominationalism.

THERE

The word *"there"* in Verse 28, used four times, is meant to emphasize the fact, that Israel ignored the chosen place of Sacrifice as appointed by the Lord, and rather developed their own places of Sacrifice, called *"high places."* In fact, the very name *"high place"* convicted these worshippers of rebellion, and not of ignorance (Deut. 12:1-5).

In fact, the modern Church is not totally unlike the Israel of long ago. God's appointed place of worship was the Tabernacle, and wherever it was, He appointed its position, and then the Temple, which was built by Solomon. Anything else, and anyplace else, where sacrifices were offered, represented gross Rebellion against God. As stated, *"they trespassed a trespass."*

God's appointed place of sacrifice and worship represented Christ, and what He would do to redeem fallen humanity by way of the Cross. Consequently, there could be only one place, and that appointed by the Lord, and because there was only One Redeemer, the Lord Jesus Christ, and one place where He would affect Redemption, which was the Cross of Calvary.

However, the modern Church, in many ways, is very similar to Israel of old. Most preachers aren't preaching the Cross, but rather are preaching something else, which constitutes, in its own way, a modern *"high place."* That's why Paul said:

"But though we, or an Angel from Heaven, preach any other gospel unto you than that which we have preached unto you, let him be accursed.

"As we said before, so say I now again, if any man preach any other gospel unto you than that you have received, let him be accursed." (Gal. 1:8-9).

THE EXILES

The fifth period of Israel's idolatrous history is the subject of Verses 30 through 32. Every evidence points to the fact that the Exiles polluted themselves with idolatry after the manner of their fathers, for the word *"you"* of these Verses is emphatic.

The Lord certainly would have entertained a plea for Mercy and Forgiveness, if they had only repented, but barring that, His answer as expressed in Verse 31 was, *"As I live says the Lord GOD, I will not be enquired of by you."*

The expression, *"As I live,"* and as used by the Lord was to emphasize the absolute Truth of what was being spoken.

A WORD FROM THE LORD

These Passages plainly tell us that individuals harboring sin in their lives, in other words, who have no desire to truly follow the Lord, need not expect a *"Word from the Lord."* And yet, there are untold numbers of Christians who are actively seeking this Word from the Lord, which, in fact, has become a major business in the modern Church.

Self-called prophets are ready and willing to give this *"Word,"* all the time claiming that it is from the Lord.

If it is to be noticed, these self-called Prophets, when prophesying over the laity, always speak words of comfort and coming blessings. They do so, because they hope to get money from these people, and they usually do! If they attempt to prophesy over Preachers, it's almost always negative, because they almost never get money from that source.

The wisdom of the street, in secular terms, says, *"Follow the money."* And that's exactly what the self-called prophets do!

VAIN REASONING

The phrase of Verse 32, *"And that which comes into your mind,"* actually had to do with the Temple.

If the Temple were to be destroyed, as Jeremiah and Ezekiel were prophesying, this would mean, at least in the minds of these rebels against God, that they could no longer worship Jehovah, and would be free to "*be as the heathen,*" to "*serve wood and stone!*"

In their thinking, if Jehovah did not intend for them to do this, then there would be no destruction of the Temple, and no dispersion among the nations.

They had reasoned these things in their minds, because they did not desire to live for God. As well, they surely thought their knotty questions which they actually were not able to ask, but which the Holy Spirit revealed to the Prophet, would refute his prophecies.

I wonder what their thoughts were, when Ezekiel began to answer them, even though they had not even asked the question?

This should have been enough to have told them that what Ezekiel was prophesying was from the Lord. It should also have told them that those things which the false prophets were proclaiming were none other than lies. But regrettably, men see what they want to see, and think what they want to think.

(33) "AS I LIVE, SAYS THE LORD GOD, SURELY WITH A MIGHTY HAND, AND WITH A STRETCHED OUT ARM, AND WITH FURY POURED OUT WILL I RULE OVER YOU:

(34) "AND I WILL BRING YOU OUT FROM THE PEOPLE, AND WILL GATHER YOU OUT OF THE COUNTRIES WHEREIN YOU ARE SCATTERED, WITH A MIGHTY HAND, AND WITH A STRETCHED OUT ARM, AND WITH FURY POURED OUT.

(35) "AND I WILL BRING YOU INTO THE WILDERNESS OF THE PEOPLE, AND THERE WILL I PLEAD WITH YOU FACE TO FACE.

(36) "LIKE AS I PLEADED WITH YOUR FATHERS IN THE WILDERNESS OF THE LAND OF EGYPT, SO WILL I PLEAD WITH YOU, SAYS THE LORD GOD.

(37) "AND I WILL CAUSE YOU TO PASS UNDER THE ROD, AND I WILL BRING YOU INTO THE BOND OF THE COVENANT:

(38) "AND I WILL PURGE OUT FROM AMONG YOU THE REBELS, AND THEM WHO TRANSGRESS AGAINST ME: I WILL BRING THEM FORTH OUT OF THE COUNTRY

NOTES

WHERE THEY SOJOURN, AND THEY SHALL NOT ENTER INTO THE LAND OF ISRAEL: AND YOU SHALL KNOW THAT I AM THE LORD."

The structure is:

1. The predictions of Verses 33 through 44 belong to the future.

2. "*The uplifted hand*" promised Blessing; the "*stretched out arm*" assured Judgment.

3. The statements in this Prophecy appear to be that, as God at the first brought Israel out of Egypt into the wilderness (the wilderness of the land of Egypt), and judged them there, so will He, in the future, bring them out of the Egypt of the nations, and into the "*wilderness of the people,*" where He will plead with them, which is even yet future. In fact, this of which Ezekiel predicts, has already begun to come to pass, which one might say, actually began in 1948, and will be fulfilled in totality at the Second Coming.

RULE

Verses 33 through 38 pertain to the coming Great Tribulation, while Verses 39 through 44 proclaim the result of that Great Tribulation, which will be Israel coming back to God.

Verses 33 proclaims the fact of the words, "*Will I rule over you?*" that Israel could not abdicate their high position, and would, therefore, remain under the burden of its responsibilities.

The idea is, irrespective of Israel's rejection of the Lord, and even their Crucifixion of Him, which resulted in the destruction of their nation, they still must answer to the Lord, and are responsible to Him.

Actually, their formation into a nation in 1948 is possibly the greatest miracle of the past nearly 2,000 years. Never before have a people, as scattered as had been Israel, been brought together in a cohesive unit to form a nation. Such has never happened, with the exception of Israel.

Presently, they sit in the midst of a sea of Arabs, who threaten their destruction, and who have already attempted several times to destroy them, but to no avail. In the natural, there is no way that Israel could have become a nation, much less survive, especially considering the powerful forces arrayed against her. But she has survived, and because she belongs to God, and has a destiny yet to fulfill, which will ultimately bring her to Christ.

While the Lord is definitely leading and guiding them, even presently, it is from a distance. This leading will of necessity take them through great sorrows which are yet future, but will ultimately lead them home (Jer. 30:6).

The phrase of Verse 34, *"And will gather you out of the countries wherein you are scattered,"* concerns the beginning of its fulfillment, as stated, with the formation of Israel as a nation in 1948. Actually, they are still being brought out, with several hundreds of thousands in 1991 and 1992 coming out of the former Soviet Union.

The phrase, *"With a mighty hand,"* refers to blessing, which insured this gathering and their formation as a nation.

The phrase of Verse 35, *"And I will bring you into the wilderness,"* concerns the coming Great Tribulation, predicted by Christ, as well as many others (Mat. 24:21), refers to Revelation, Chapter 12. This flight of the sun-clothed woman, which is actually Israel, will take place at the mid-point of the Great Tribulation. At that time, the Antichrist will break his seven year pact with her, actually attacking her, and would destroy her, were it not for the intervention of the Lord. The area spoken of is ancient Petra (Isa. 16:1-5; 42:11-13; Hos. 2:14-23; Rev. 12:6, 13-16).

TRIBULATION

Verse 37 says, *"And I will cause you to pass under the rod,"* is primarily that of chastisement. This primarily will concern itself with the latter half of the Great Tribulation of three and one-half years, when Israel will come close to extinction. The Antichrist will seek to annihilate her and will come close to succeeding. Actually, the Prophet Zechariah predicts that two-thirds of Israel will be destroyed, leaving only one-third to accept Christ at His Second Advent (Zech. 13:8-9; 12:10; 13:1; Rom. 11:25-29).

The *"purging"* of Verse 38 has to do, and as we have stated, with the two-thirds of Israel which will be destroyed during the last three and one-half years of the Great Tribulation, and the Battle of Armageddon.

(39) "AS FOR YOU, O HOUSE OF ISRAEL,

NOTES

THUS SAITH THE LORD GOD; GO YE, SERVE YE EVERY ONE HIS IDOLS, AND HEREAFTER ALSO IF YOU WILL NOT HEARKEN UNTO ME: BUT POLLUTE YOU MY HOLY NAME NO MORE WITH YOUR GIFTS, AND WITH YOUR IDOLS.

(40) "FOR IN MY HOLY MOUNTAIN, IN THE MOUNTAIN OF THE HEIGHT OF ISRAEL, SAYS THE LORD GOD, THERE SHALL ALL THE HOUSE OF ISRAEL, ALL OF THEM IN THE LAND, SERVE ME: THERE WILL I ACCEPT THEM, AND THERE WILL I REQUIRE YOUR OFFERINGS, AND THE FIRSTFRUITS OF YOUR OBLATIONS, WITH ALL YOUR HOLY THINGS.

(41) "I WILL ACCEPT YOU WITH YOUR SWEET SAVOUR, WHEN I BRING YOU OUT FROM THE PEOPLE, AND GATHER YOU OUT OF THE COUNTRIES WHEREIN YOU HAVE BEEN SCATTERED; AND I WILL BE SANCTIFIED IN YOU BEFORE THE HEATHEN.

(42) "AND YOU SHALL KNOW THAT I AM THE LORD, WHEN I SHALL BRING YOU INTO THE LAND OF ISRAEL, INTO THE COUNTRY FOR THE WHICH I LIFTED UP MY HAND TO GIVE IT TO YOUR FATHERS.

(43) "AND THERE SHALL YOU REMEMBER YOUR WAYS, AND ALL YOUR DOINGS, WHEREIN YOU HAVE BEEN DEFILED; AND YOU SHALL LOATHE YOURSELVES IN YOUR OWN SIGHT FOR ALL YOUR EVILS THAT YOU HAVE COMMITTED.

(44) "AND YOU SHALL KNOW THAT I AM THE LORD WHEN I HAVE WROUGHT WITH YOU FOR MY NAME'S SAKE, NOT ACCORDING TO YOUR WICKED WAYS, NOR ACCORDING TO YOUR CORRUPT DOINGS, O YE HOUSE OF ISRAEL, SAITH THE LORD GOD."

The overview is:

1. *"Go ye, serve you every one his idols,"* is language that is meant to be ironical.

2. The acceptance of the worshipper is the result of the value of the victim offered in sacrifice for sin. Hence Believers are engraced in the Beloved One (Eph. 1:6), Christ; for we have no grace in ourselves.

3. The vindication of God's judicial action is the keynote to the Book of Ezekiel.

THE ELDERS

The Holy Spirit in Verse 39, through the Prophet, now brings the prophecy away from the future to the present. The Elders are here addressed.

The Lord tells them, "Go *ye, serve ye everyone his idols,*" but do not make the sin worse by the hypocrisy of unreal worship, by mixing up the name of Jehovah with the ritual of Moloch. By their double worship of Jehovah and idols, they were "*polluting*" His Holy Name.

The phrase, "*With your gifts,*" means that they were giving gifts to the Lord and to the idols.

Is the modern Church any different?

The only way that the Lord can be truly worshipped is for the Preacher and the people to properly understand the Cross. Otherwise, it will be a mixture of the world and the Holy Spirit, which, as exclaimed here, God will not accept.

Since the Reformation, the Church has never been more off course.

To attempt to fabricate worship outside of the parameters of the Cross presents the meanderings of the minds of men, or worse yet, the wisdom of the world, which is "*sensual and devilish*" (James 3:15).

AN EXAMPLE OF METHODS OTHER THAN THE CROSS

Some time back, I received a letter from an Assemblies of God Pastor. I was not acquainted with the Brother, but his letter was very interesting.

He went on to exclaim as to how he had found the answer to successful, victorious Christian living. The following is his description.

He had been asked to attend a meeting reserved for Preachers only, and headed up by the Pastor of one of the large Full Gospel Churches in the nation. The Preacher in charge was giving his "*new revelation*" to the assembled Preachers, which would tell them how to walk in victory.

According to his directions, they were to take a piece of paper, and write on that paper all of their sins, weaknesses, etc. With that finished, they were then to pair off, men with men, and women with women, all in the same auditorium, and read aloud to each other that which they had written on the paper.

The Pastor went on to declare that his list was not nearly as bad as others!

After reading aloud this long list of sins and weaknesses, they were then to tear the paper into little pieces, throw the pieces on the floor, and then jump up and down on the pieces, while shouting loudly, etc.

Now, as stated, our dear Brother claimed that this was the answer to the sin problem.

I answered his letter by merely stating, *"My Brother, there is no answer for sin except the Cross."* I did not elaborate further.

If this proposed solution was not so sad, it would be hilariously funny. But when one realizes that such stupidity is proposed by those who claim to be Spirit-filled, one is left wondering if these Preachers have ever read the Bible!

One can multiply that ridiculous foolishness a thousand times over, and one will have the beginning of the foolish ideas projected by men in this day and age, as it regards victorious living. Anything and everything except the Cross!

RESTORATION

Verses 40 through 44 now revert to prophecies concerning the future. Redeemed Israel, in the happy day of her future glory, will recognize, and confess, all her happiness to be due to the worthfulness of the Name of Jesus, not to any moral value in herself, for her "*ways*" were evil, and her "*doings*" corrupt.

These Passages pertain to the coming Millennial Reign, when Christ will personally reign supreme from Jerusalem, and the contesting of the Land will then end. For Verse 40 says, "*There shall all the House of Israel, all of them in the Land, serve Me.*" Even though the battle has raged regarding this Land (the Promised Land) for thousands of years, and rages presently greater than ever before, it will now end, and forever.

ACCEPTANCE

Verse 41 proclaims the fact of the Lord "*accepting*" Israel. There is no greater honor than for the Lord to say "*I accept you.*" He will do so only on the merit of the shed and applied Blood of the Lord Jesus Christ, His only Son, and our only Saviour.

The phrase of Verse 43, "*And you shall loathe yourselves in your own sight for all your evils that you have committed,*" concerns Israel's acceptance of Christ when they realize Who He is, and especially how they crucified Him, and brought upon themselves such judgment and sorrow (Zech. 12:10; 13:1).

(45) "MOREOVER THE WORD OF THE LORD CAME UNTO ME, SAYING,

(46) "SON OF MAN, SET YOUR FACE TOWARD THE SOUTH, AND DROP YOUR WORD TOWARD THE SOUTH, AND PROPHESY AGAINST THE FOREST OF THE SOUTH FIELD;

(47) "AND SAY TO THE FOREST OF THE SOUTH, HEAR THE WORD OF THE LORD, THUS SAITH THE LORD GOD; BEHOLD, I WILL KINDLE A FIRE IN YOU, AND IT SHALL DEVOUR EVERY GREEN TREE IN YOU, AND EVERY DRY TREE: THE FLAMING FLAME SHALL NOT BE QUENCHED, AND ALL FACES FROM THE SOUTH TO THE NORTH SHALL BE BURNED THEREIN.

(48) "AND ALL FLESH SHALL SEE THAT I THE LORD HAVE KINDLED IT: IT SHALL NOT BE QUENCHED.

(49) "THEN SAID I, AH LORD GOD! THEY SAY OF ME, DOES HE NOT SPEAK PARABLES?"

The synopsis is:

1. "*Set thy face*" of Verse 46 determines direction and certainty of accomplishment.

2. The fourfold repetition of the word "*south*" of Verses 46 through 47 made absolute Judah as the scene of approaching judgment.

3. The Wrath of God is symbolized here as fire (Verse 47), the green trees figure the righteous, the dry trees, the wicked.

THE WORD OF THE LORD

The balance of this Chapter speaks of the coming judgment upon Judah and Jerusalem, which was to take place shortly, about four years from the time that Ezekiel made these predictions. As is by now obvious, rebellion against God, ensconced in their idol worship, was basically the cause.

This exposure of the persistent attachment of Israel to idolatry justified God in His employment of the Babylonians to destroy Jerusalem and burn the Temple. If the Temple was no longer to be used in the worship of Jehovah, then it was of no earthly use.

Though the sufferings of the Exiles proved the falsehood of idolatry and of its prophets and the Truth of God's predicted wrath, yet they clung to their idols. Sadly, only a few of them repented and were restored with Ezra and Nehemiah to Israel. Such is the folly and incurable rebellion of the human heart.

For the most part, the Elders in Exile claimed that Ezekiel was proclaiming a fanciful story, a tale, or rather something that was unreal; likewise, the world presently says the same of the Bible. It ridicules the coming judgment day, as it ridicules Hell-fire. However, the unbelief and sarcasm negate not at all the veracity of the Word of God. Irrespective of the response, all will be fulfilled!

"I sing the love of God my Father,
　Whose Spirit abides within;
"Who changes all my grief to gladness,
　and pardons my every sin.
"Tho' clouds may lower dark and dreary,
　yet He has promised to be near;
"He gives me sunshine for my shadow,
　and beauty for ashes, here."

"I will sing the love of Christ, my Saviour, Who suffered upon the tree;
"That in the secret of His Presence, my bondage might freedom be.
"He comes to bind the brokenhearted;
　He comes the fainting soul to cheer;
"He gives me all of joy for mourning,
　and beauty for ashes, here."

"I sing the beauty of the Gospel that scatters, not thorns but flow'rs;
"That bids me scatter smiles and sunbeams wherever are lonely hours.
"The garment of His praise it offers, for heaviness of Spirit drear;
"It gives me sunshine for my shadow, and beauty for ashes, here."

CHAPTER 21

(1) "AND THE WORD OF THE LORD

CAME UNTO ME, SAYING,

(2) "SON OF MAN, SET YOUR FACE TOWARD JERUSALEM; AND DROP YOUR WORD TOWARD THE HOLY PLACES, AND PROPHESY AGAINST THE LAND OF ISRAEL,

(3) "AND SAY TO THE LAND OF ISRAEL, THUS SAITH THE LORD; BEHOLD, I AM AGAINST YOU, AND WILL DRAW FORTH MY SWORD OUT OF HIS SHEATH, AND WILL CUT OFF FROM YOU THE RIGHTEOUS AND THE WICKED.

(4) "SEEING THEN THAT I WILL CUT OFF FROM YOU THE RIGHTEOUS AND THE WICKED, THEREFORE SHALL MY SWORD GO FORTH OUT OF HIS SHEATH AGAINST ALL FLESH FROM THE SOUTH TO THE NORTH:

(5) "THAT ALL FLESH MAY KNOW THAT I THE LORD HAVE DRAWN FORTH MY SWORD OUT OF HIS SHEATH: IT SHALL NOT RETURN ANY MORE.

(6) "SIGH THEREFORE, THOU SON OF MAN, WITH THE BREAKING OF YOUR LOINS; AND WITH BITTERNESS SIGH BEFORE THEIR EYES.

(7) "AND IT SHALL BE, WHEN THEY SAY UNTO YOU, WHEREFORE SIGHEST THOU? THAT YOU SHALL ANSWER, FOR THE TIDINGS; BECAUSE IT COMES: AND EVERY HEART SHALL MELT, AND ALL HANDS SHALL BE FEEBLE, AND EVERY SPIRIT SHALL FAINT, AND ALL KNEES SHALL BE WEAK AS WATER: BEHOLD, IT COMES, AND SHALL BE BROUGHT TO PASS, SAITH THE LORD GOD."

The exegesis is :

1. The inclusion of the righteous with the wicked in national and universal judgments is one of the principles of God's moral government. It is important to recognize this principle.

He does not promise exemption to His people from the suffering which justly follows national sins; but He makes this great distinction — that the wicked perish under such suffering, while the righteous are sustained in it; and finally, in Resurrection, are delivered from it (Heb. 11:35).

2. The phrase of Verse 5, "*It shall not return anymore*," refers to the sword that shall not be returned to its sheath until it has accomplished its purpose.

3. The phrase, "*Because it comes,*" pertains to the sword of the Chaldeans, the instrument of God's wrath, and its certitude.

PROPHESY

This is a part of the Prophecy of the previous Chapter and continues without interruption. It pertains to the coming judgment upon Judah and Jerusalem, which will take place shortly from the time that Ezekiel gave these predictions, and goes into detail.

It would seem, and due to the minute detail, that the Exiles in Babylonia, as well as the people of Judah and Jerusalem, would surely have paid special heed to these predictions, especially considering the magnitude of the proposed destruction; however, the human heart is so incurably evil, and coupled with unbelief, at least pertaining to the things of God, man then, as now, is lulled into a spiritual stupor.

The phrase, "*Holy Places,*" of Verse 2 refers to the Temple in Jerusalem.

To which we alluded in the last Chapter, some of the Elders had reasoned that Prophecies concerning the destruction of the Temple were false, due to fact that the Temple must remain in order for the worship of the Lord to continue. And if the Lord destroyed the Temple, that would mean a refutation, at least in their minds, of the Law and the Promises that Lord had given to the Patriarchs and Prophets of old!

Therefore, they thought it was not possible that the Temple could be destroyed! However, their thinking was flawed, because they did not know the Word of God. The words of Moses, in Deuteronomy 28:15 through the conclusion of that Chapter, as well as many other places in the Bible, had foretold exactly what would happen to them if they forsook the Lord. They did not know the Word of God, because they had little interest in the Word of God.

These Elders hardly realized, as they sat before Ezekiel and he delivered the Word of the Lord to them, that what they were hearing would actually become just as much as part of the Bible as the Pentateuch, which they so ardently professed to believe! This is overly sad, when one realizes that we are speaking of the Church of that day. And yet, the modern Church, at least as a whole, is little different, if at all!

The phrase, "*And prophesy against the land of Israel*," is especially ominous. What follows is enough to bring anyone to Repentance, but not the heart festooned with unbelief!

UNBELIEF

These words, as given by the Holy Spirit, seem to have a resignation of doom, especially considering that these Prophecies have been coming forth, whether from Jeremiah or from Ezekiel, for over thirty-five years. Actually, the people were harder now than they had been at the beginning of the Prophecies given by Jeremiah. (He was quite a bit older than Ezekiel.)

As the Word of God is delivered and heard, with each negative response, the individual becomes harder! Therefore, at this stage, the hearts of the religious leaders and the people had become increasingly negative and skeptical toward the Word of the Lord.

Regrettably, the same thing is happening in modern America. There is presently a type of unbelief toward the Bible that is chilling. There is very little reverence or respect for the Name of the Lord. The blasphemy over television, as well as all other walks of life, has been increasingly vituperative and open. And yet this too, typically, mirrors the modern Church.

The phrase of Verse 3, "*Thus saith the LORD; Behold, I am against you*," records Judah's doom as nothing else!

Down through the centuries, Israel's strength exclusively was the Lord. They had gained their status and acquired their riches and prosperity all because of His Blessings. Now that He is against them, they have no support, strength, prosperity, or source of help. The surrounding nations, which they had sought to emulate in worship and lifestyle, had no love for them, and actually, would gloat over their defeat. Because of their rebellion against God, they were left absolutely defenseless.

The phrase, "*And will draw forth My sword out of his sheath*," refers to the coming carnage by Nebuchadnezzar, which was then about four years away. Hundreds of thousands would die! And yet, all of this could have been stopped by sincere Repentance before God.

THE RIGHTEOUS AND THE WICKED

The phrase, "*And will cut off from you the righteous and the wicked*," has two meanings:

1. The "*righteous*" would be cut off in the sense of the Lord not hearing their cries that Judah and Jerusalem be spared. Actually, the Lord had told Jeremiah to not even pray for the deliverance of these people, because such prayers would not be heard and would not be answered.

The phrase has no reference to the righteous being spiritually lost.

2. The "*wicked*" were to be cut off in death, destruction, and judgment. Their mocking would then cease! As well, they would see, before their very eyes, the fulfillment of every word that had been prophesied.

THE SWORD

Verses 4 through 7 proclaim the coming judgment on Judah and Jerusalem, which would be awful to behold.

The phrase of Verse 5, "*I the LORD have drawn forth My sword out his sheath*," refers to the Lord having total say over the disposition of these people, as well as every other nation in the world! The sword is referred to as "*My sword*," denoting God's independent action.

This refers not only to Judah of old, but as well to all nations and peoples, and for all time! This means that God either causes or allows all that takes place in the world.

THE CAUSE

Many modern Bible students would disagree with this, claiming that war, and such like, is caused by Satan; however, to believe such is to place the Lord in a subordinate position to Satan. Such is not the case, and even a rudimentary knowledge of the Scripture will quickly prove the error of such thinking.

The Lord is in total control of the planet, and all therein, as well as all else of His creation. Even though it is Satan who "*steals, kills, and destroys*," still, he must have permission from the Lord to act (Job, Chpts. 1-2).

At times, the Lord allows Satan certain latitude regarding war, the elements, judgment, etc. He allows such because of the wickedness of the people, or their purposes. Therefore, the phrase, "*Acts of God,*" as used concerning storms, etc., is correct.

Even though engineered and carried out by Satan, the parameters are designed by the Lord. These things are allowed because of required judgment on sin and sinners, and will, as stated in Verse 3, include both the righteous and the wicked.

THE BURDEN

The phrase of Verse 6, "*Sigh, therefore, thou son of man,*" refers to Ezekiel so burdened with the portent of this coming disaster, that it "*breaks his loins,*" i.e., breaks his heart.

The phrase, "*And with bitterness sigh before their eyes,*" refers to the Prophet being greatly moved, possibly even with heavy weeping before the eyes of these Elders. It was not an act, but an admonition from the Lord, that he was not to be ashamed of his emotion, but was rather to allow it full vent.

Even though they heard what the Prophet said, and they also saw how greatly he was affected by great emotion, they, it seems, were not at all affected. Thus, the picture here is of the hardened heart!

The phrase, "*Behold, it comes, and shall be brought to pass, saith the Lord GOD,*" of Verse 7 presents the proclamation, but was little believed by his listeners!

That which Ezekiel now experiences will be exactly what will happen to the entirety of the Exiles some four years later, when word was received of the fall and destruction of Jerusalem. This is emphasized in the words, "*for the tidings.*" These tidings would be awful indeed!

(8) "AGAIN THE WORD OF THE LORD CAME UNTO ME, SAYING,

(9) "SON OF MAN, PROPHESY, AND SAY, THUS SAITH THE LORD; SAY, A SWORD, A SWORD IS SHARPENED, AND ALSO FURBISHED:

(10) "IT IS SHARPENED TO MAKE A SORE SLAUGHTER; IT IS FURBISHED THAT IT MAY GLITTER; SHOULD WE THEN MAKE MIRTH? IT CONTEMNETH THE ROD OF MY SON, AS EVERY TREE.

(11) "AND HE HAS GIVEN IT TO BE FURBISHED, THAT IT MAY BE HANDLED: THIS SWORD IS SHARPENED, AND IT IS FURBISHED, TO GIVE IT INTO THE HAND OF THE SLAYER.

(12) "CRY AND HOWL, SON OF MAN: FOR IT SHALL BE UPON MY PEOPLE, IT SHALL BE UPON ALL THE PRINCES OF ISRAEL: TERRORS BY REASON OF THE SWORD SHALL BE UPON MY PEOPLE: SMITE THEREFORE UPON YOUR THIGH.

(13) "BECAUSE IT IS A TRIAL, AND WHAT IF THE SWORD CONTEMN EVEN THE ROD? IT SHALL BE NO MORE, SAITH THE LORD GOD.

(14) "THOU THEREFORE, SON OF MAN, PROPHESY, AND SMITE YOUR HANDS TOGETHER, AND LET THE SWORD BE DOUBLED THE THIRD TIME, THE SWORD OF THE SLAIN: IT IS THE SWORD OF THE GREAT MEN WHO ARE SLAIN, WHICH ENTER INTO THEIR PRIVY CHAMBERS.

(15) "I HAVE SET THE POINT OF THE SWORD AGAINST ALL THEIR GATES, THAT THEIR HEART MAY FAINT, AND THEIR RUINS BE MULTIPLIED: AH! IT IS MADE BRIGHT, IT IS WRAPPED UP FOR THE SLAUGHTER.

(16) "GO THEE ONE WAY OR OTHER, EITHER ON THE RIGHT HAND, OR ON THE LEFT, WHITHERSOEVER YOUR FACE IS SET.

(17) "I WILL ALSO SMITE MY HANDS TOGETHER, AND I WILL CAUSE MY FURY TO REST: I THE LORD HAVE SAID IT."

The diagram is:

1. The minuteness of detail in these predictions, years before they became history, is one of the striking facts of inspiration.

2. Is it a time for mirth, when God has just announced His coming wrath?

3. The Grace and love that here recognize idolatrous Judah as "*My people*" awaken wonder and worship in the heart (Verse 12).

THE SHARPENED SWORD

The Holy Spirit will now go into great detail regarding the coming carnage, which is meant to portray to the people the severity of the judgment, and hopefully, to instigate Repentance. However, the Repentance never materialized!

The phrase, "*A sword is sharpened, and also furbished,*" of Verse 9 speaks of the Divine mission of the Chaldean sword, i.e., the Babylonian army, and its success against Judah and against Ammon. This Prophecy preceded the destruction of Judah by some four years, and of Ammon, by ten years.

As stated, the minuteness of detail in these predictions, years before they became history, is one of the striking facts of inspiration.

The phrase of Verse 10, "*It is sharpened to make a sore slaughter,*" refers to the Lord handing the sharpened sword to the Chaldean slayer in order that it might be used against the Judean wrong-doer.

THE SLAYER

The phrase of Verse 11, "*To give it into the hand of the slayer,*" referring to the "*sword,*" speaks of Nebuchadnezzar. The Babylonian Monarch, no doubt, thought himself to be a free agent; but long before his campaign against Judah, his victory over Zedekiah, his recourse to divination at the parting of the high roads in northern Israel, and his victory over the Ammonites, all were here foretold.

The phrase, "*Because it is a trial,*" of Verse 13, refers to the judgment that is coming upon Judah.

The question, "*And what if the sword contemns even the rod?*" refers to Jehovah's sword despising the rod, and "*it shall be no more*" until the Messiah comes Whose right it is to rule.

Sadly, when Jesus actually did come, Israel rejected Him, which brought upon themselves total and complete ruin. But still, the day is coming, when the Lord Jesus Christ will definitely rule over Israel, and in fact, the entirety of the world.

The phrase of Verse 14, "*And let the sword be doubled the third time,*" predicts the third, and final, campaign against Jerusalem.

The first invasion took place in 605 B.C., with the second taking place in 597 B.C., and the last to occur in 586 B.C., which was some four years into the future.

The word "*doubled,*" as it refers to the sword, has reference to a well-tempered sword, which strikes an object and doubles, or bends, but does not break. Such a sword is justly described as the sword of a great one who inflicts deadly wounds, i.e., "*sword of the great,*" which kills all before it. In the sack of Jerusalem, that sword pursued its victims even into their innermost chambers.

The phrase of Verse 17, "*I will also smite My hands together,*" refers to the Lord signifying a task completed. Even though it was yet some four years into the future, in the mind of God it was already accomplished.

The phrase, "*And I will cause My fury to rest,*" refers to the Truth that His fury will not rest until every single prediction is fulfilled concerning the destruction of Judah and Jerusalem. To emphasize the certitude of this action, the Holy Spirit says, "*I the LORD have said it.*"

(18) "THE WORD OF THE LORD CAME UNTO ME AGAIN, SAYING,

(19) "ALSO, THOU SON OF MAN, APPOINT THEE TWO WAYS, THAT THE SWORD OF THE KING OF BABYLON MAY COME: BOTH TWAIN SHALL COME FORTH OUT OF ONE LAND: AND CHOOSE THOU A PLACE, CHOOSE IT AT THE HEAD OF THE WAY TO THE CITY.

(20) "APPOINT A WAY, THAT THE SWORD MAY COME TO RABBATH OF THE AMMONITES, AND TO JUDAH IN JERUSALEM THE DEFENCED.

(21) "FOR THE KING OF BABYLON STOOD AT THE PARTING OF THE WAY, AT THE HEAD OF THE TWO WAYS, TO USE DIVINATION: HE MADE HIS ARROWS BRIGHT, HE CONSULTED WITH IMAGES, HE LOOKED IN THE LIVER.

(22) "AT HIS RIGHT HAND WAS THE DIVINATION FOR JERUSALEM, TO APPOINT CAPTAINS, TO OPEN THE MOUTH IN THE SLAUGHTER, TO LIFT UP THE VOICE WITH SHOUTING, TO APPOINT BATTERING RAMS AGAINST THE GATES, TO CAST A MOUNT, AND TO BUILD A FORT.

(23) "AND IT SHALL BE UNTO THEM AS A FALSE DIVINATION IN THEIR SIGHT, TO THEM WHO HAVE SWORN OATHS: BUT HE WILL CALL TO REMEMBRANCE THE INIQUITY, THAT THEY MAY BE TAKEN.

(24) "THEREFORE THUS SAITH THE LORD GOD; BECAUSE YOU HAVE MADE YOUR INIQUITY TO BE REMEMBERED, IN THAT YOUR TRANSGRESSIONS ARE DISCOVERED, SO THAT IN ALL YOUR

DOINGS YOUR SINS DO APPEAR; BECAUSE, I SAY, THAT YOU ARE COME TO REMEMBRANCE, YOU SHALL BE TAKEN WITH THE HAND.

(25) "AND YOU, PROFANE WICKED PRINCE OF ISRAEL, WHOSE DAY IS COME, WHEN INIQUITY SHALL HAVE AN END,

(26) "THUS SAITH THE LORD GOD; REMOVE THE DIADEM, AND TAKE OFF THE CROWN: THIS SHALL NOT BE THE SAME: EXALT HIM WHO IS LOW, AND ABASE HIM WHO IS HIGH.

(27) "I WILL OVERTURN, OVERTURN, OVERTURN, IT: AND IT SHALL BE NO MORE, UNTIL HE COME WHOSE RIGHT IT IS; AND I WILL GIVE IT HIM.

The composition is:

1. Two arrows, one marked Ammon and the other Jerusalem, were placed in a quiver by Nebuchadnezzar, and whichever one the king drew was accepted as an omen. The liver of a beast or a fowl, offered in sacrifice, was also examined and its healthy, or unhealthy, condition accepted as favorable, or the reverse.

2. Zedekiah is the *"profane prince"* of Verse 25, and his *"crown"*, the *"diadem"* of Verse 26, was proclaimed that *"it shall not endure."* He was, in effect, the last king: he was *"high,"* but was *"abased;"* and there will be no other king until He Who is *"low,"* i.e., the despised Jesus of Nazareth, returns; unto Him shall the diadem be given; for it is His right.

3. Meanwhile, God overturns all efforts to give that crown to another.

THE KING OF BABYLON

From the time this prophecy was given, due to the slowness of travel in those days, there is a possibility that Nebuchadnezzar's army would shortly leave for the excursion into Judah.

The phrase of Verse 19, *"Appoint thee,"* refers to two different roads. When he reached Damascus or somewhere nearby, there was an intersection with one road leading to Rabbath, the capital of the Ammonites (Deut. 3:11; II Sam. 11:1), with the other leading to Jerusalem. Apparently, the Exiles and the people of Judah flattered themselves that Rabbath was the destination and, therefore, Judah would be spared.

It is probable that some period of time, maybe several weeks, was spent there while Nebuchadnezzar made his decision as to which way to go.

In listening to the false prophets, almost all the people of Judah, as well as those among the Exiles, believed that Judah would be spared. The Holy Spirit, if they only had listened, would here tell them otherwise!

The phrase, *"Choose it at the head of the way to the city,"* refers to the two directions and the manner in which Nebuchadnezzar made his decision.

The phrase of Verse 21, *"For the king of Babylon stood at the parting of the way,"* proclaims that which is very striking.

Two arrows, one marked Ammon and the other Jerusalem, were placed in a quiver, and whichever one the king drew out was accepted as an omen.

As well, and as previously stated, the liver of a beast or a fowl, offered in sacrifice, was also examined, and its healthy, or unhealthy, condition accepted as favorable, or the opposite.

However, and unknown to Nebuchadnezzar, the Lord would make the choice.

As one reads this Twenty-first Verse, one is reading the luck of the draw, i.e., chance prediction. This is the way of the world, and as such, provides no leading, except in a wrong direction, and most of the time is guided by demon spirits.

This time would be different, only because the Lord took a hand in the event; however, let no Christian think that the Lord takes a hand in fortune telling, crystal balls, tarot cards, psychics, horoscopes, or any other devious methods. All such methods are of Satan, and are guided by demon spirits.

For every decision to be made, the Will of the Lord is to be sought by the Believer. He has promised to hear, and to answer, as well as giving guidance and direction (Jn. 16:13-15; 16:23-26).

LEADING AND GUIDANCE

The question of leading and guidance by the Holy Spirit is surely important to all true Believers. Jesus' first words to His Disciples, at least as far as discipleship was concerned, were: *"Follow Me"* (Mat. 4:19). They were to do the following, He would provide the leading. That method is still in force.

Going to the Old Testament, there are a number of Hebrew words which express the idea of leading or guidance of the Lord. The following constitute some of the major examples:

NAHAH

This means to lead in the sense of conducting along the right path. A beautiful picture of this is found in Ex. 13:21: *"By day the LORD went ahead of them in a pillar of cloud to guide them on their way."* The image of guidance stresses the Presence of the Lord; God goes with Believers to show the way.

NAHAG

This conveys the idea of shepherding. God conducts us to His intended destination, going before us when we are responsive to His voice, and herding us when we stray.

NAHAL

This Hebrew word means *"to lead with care."* We sense the implications in Isa. 40:11. He tends His flock like a shepherd. He gathers the lambs in His arms and carries them close to His heart; He gently leads those who are young.

DARAK

This speaks of God leading His people in righteous paths. He guides the humble in what is right and teaches them His way (Ps. 25:4-5, 9).

In inquiring of the Lord, two Old Testament words express this concept.

DARAS

This means to *"seek with care."* Often, what is sought from the Lord is knowledge or advice in order to gain insight into a particular problem.

SAAL

This is used, as well, in statements about going to God for guidance.

It is important to God that His people show reliance on Him by requesting His specific guidance when difficult decisions must be made. God pronounces woe on those who rush to solve their own problems without looking to Him:

"Woe to the obstinate children, declares the LORD, to those who carry out plans that are not Mine, forming an alliance, but not by My Spirit, heaping sin upon sin; who go down to Egypt without consulting Me" (Isa. 30:1-2; Josh. 9:14).

The act of inquiring of the Lord reveals that the Believer has Faith that God is, that God is aware, and that God is involved in the life of the individual. Looking to God and seeking His Leading is an act of Faith.

As well, all of this shows us the willingness of God to show us His best way. Some, like Saul, who rejected and turned from God, might not be given guidance (I Sam. 28:6). But Believers need have no doubt that when they approach God for guidance, He hears and is pleased.

GOD'S WAYS

Throughout the Bible, the Lord at times used dreams in giving guidance, which He continues to do at this present time. Also, Prophets in both Old and New Testaments were used by the Holy Spirit. The following records a number of places where guidance is said to have come from the Holy Spirit (Lk. 4:1; Acts 13:2-3; 20:22; Rom. 8:14).

If one is to notice, the Bible does not provide a formula for Believers to follow in seeking God's guidance, nor does He provide a list of ways in which God leads. It does, however, provide a clear perspective that helps to approach this vital and practical issue. The Holy Spirit may use any number of means, including circumstances, Scripture, or even the advice of friends to guide our lives, providing it is Scriptural and applicable.

To which we have alluded, the Lord warned Israel, and all, that none of the practices used by the pagan peoples of Canaan to seek guidance were to be adopted by His people. These pagan ways are found in Deuteronomy, Chapter 18.

JERUSALEM

The phrase of Verse 22, *"At his right hand was the divination of Jerusalem,"* pertains to Nebuchadnezzar with his back to the north facing both Judah and Ammon, which lay due south. The road on the right led to

Jerusalem, while the one on the left led to Rabbath of the Ammonites. As he placed his hand into the quiver to pull out one of the arrows, and then looking at it, he found that it signified Jerusalem.

The phrase, "*To appoint captains,*" refers to orders and instructions being given for the siege of Jerusalem.

The phrase of Verse 23, "*And it shall be unto them as a false divination in their sight,*" refers to the false prophets in Jerusalem still continuing to preach peace and prosperity, and causing the king and the people to believe that Nebuchadnezzar was not going to come to Jerusalem. Up until the Babylonians were on top of them, they did not believe God's Word.

The phrase, "*To them who have sworn oaths,*" refers to Zedekiah who had sworn an oath to Nebuchadnezzar, but had dallied with the Egypt faction, conspiring to throw off the subjugation of the Babylonians. Zedekiah went to Babylon in 593 B.C., possibly to allay suspicion concerning his involvement in the plot (Jer. 51:59).

However, after Nebuchadnezzar laid siege to Jerusalem, the Egyptian army purposed to come to the rescue of Judah, whose aid might have already been sought. At this time, Zedekiah finally did revolt against Babylon (II Ki. 24:20), breaking his covenant (Ezek. 17:12-13).

Jeremiah the Prophet constantly warned Zedekiah of this treachery, seeing Babylonian overlordship as Divinely ordained (Jer. 27:12-14). Actually, the Lord looked at this oath made by Zedekiah to Nebuchadnezzar as an oath made to Jehovah.

THE DIADEM

The phrase in Verse 26, "*Remove the diadem,*" refers to the Mitre of the High Priest, who would no longer have a Temple nor an avenue for his services.

The phrase, "*And take off the crown,*" refers to the Throne of Judah being abolished by Nebuchadnezzar. The Mitre and the Crown shall alike pass away — taken from their unworthy wearers.

The phrase, "*This shall not be the same,*" refers to these two positions, King and High Priest, which would be no more, at least in this capacity.

Israel, after the dispersion and the rebuilding of the Temple, did once again reinstate the Office of the High Priest, but it never was the same as it had been.

The phrase, "*Exalt Him Who is low and abase him who is high,*" has a beautiful meaning, referring to Christ, Who will be exalted and Who was low, and Zedekiah, who was high, being abased.

Verse 27 with the phrase, "*I will overturn, overturn, overturn, it,*" refers to Judah being destroyed as a nation, and especially its supreme authority, and its Throne never again being established, at least "*until He come Whose right it is.*" This is the despised Jesus of Nazareth Who will return; unto Him shall the diadem be given, "*Whose right it is.*" Meanwhile, God overturns all efforts to give that crown to another.

The word "*overturn*" is repeated three times, proclaiming the absolute certitude of what is predicted. The nation of Israel will once again gain its place and position which God originally intended; however, it will not be until it accepts Jesus as its Lord, Master, Saviour, and Messiah. This will be done at the Second Coming (Zech. 13:1).

(28) "AND THOU, SON OF MAN, PROPHESY AND SAY, THUS SAITH THE LORD GOD CONCERNING THE AMMONITES, AND CONCERNING THEIR REPROACH; EVEN SAY THOU, THE SWORD, THE SWORD IS DRAWN: FOR THE SLAUGHTER IT IS FURBISHED, TO CONSUME BECAUSE OF THE GLITTERING:

(29) "WHILE THEY SEE VANITY UNTO YOU, WHILE THEY DIVINE A LIE UNTO YOU, TO BRING THEE UPON THE NECKS OF THEM WHO ARE SLAIN, OF THE WICKED, WHOSE DAY IS COME, WHEN THEIR INIQUITY SHALL HAVE AN END.

(30) "SHALL I CAUSE IT TO RETURN INTO HIS SHEATH? I WILL JUDGE YOU IN THE PLACE WHERE YOU WERE CREATED, IN THE LAND OF YOUR NATIVITY.

(31) "AND I WILL POUR OUT MY INDIGNATION UPON YOU, I WILL BLOW AGAINST YOU IN THE FIRE OF MY WRATH, AND DELIVER YOU INTO THE HAND OF BRUTISH MEN, AND SKILLFUL TO DESTROY.

(32) "YOU SHALL BE FOR FUEL TO THE FIRE; YOUR BLOOD SHALL BE IN THE MIDST OF THE LAND; YOU SHALL BE NO MORE REMEMBERED: FOR I THE LORD HAVE SPOKEN IT."

The overview is:

1. The Ammonites rejoiced at the destruction of Jerusalem. That was their "*reproach.*" But five years later they rebelled against the Chaldeans, who consequently invaded their country and destroyed them so effectually that they ceased to exist as a nation.

2. The Ammonites perished in their own land, whereas the captives of Israel, whom they reproached, still exist and will ultimately be restored.

3. After the judgment was rendered, the sword, having accomplished its purpose, was to be caused to return into its sheath.

AMMON

The phrase of Verse 28, "*Thus saith the Lord GOD concerning the Ammonites,*" refers to these ancient enemies of Israel. When Nebuchadnezzar took the road to Jerusalem instead of coming to Rabbath, the Ammonites thought surely they had escaped the judgment. This Prophecy proclaims differently!

The phrase, "*And concerning their reproach,*" concerns their rejoicing at the destruction of Jerusalem. As should be obvious, the Lord did not take kindly to that, even though Judah and Jerusalem were destined for judgment.

The phrase of Verse 29, "*While they see vanity unto you, while they divine a lie unto you,*" refers to the soothsayers among them who divined that Nebuchadnezzar would not attack them as he would Jerusalem, but they would be spared. The Holy Spirit calls their divination "*a lie.*"

As well, the divination of the prognosticators of this present age, whether in the Church or out of it, who divine coming peace and prosperity, is called by the Holy Spirit "*a lie!*" He says the very opposite:

"*This know also, that in the last days perilous times shall come*" (II Tim. 3:1).

The phrase, "*When their iniquities shall have an end,*" refers to their idea that they had escaped the judgment that had fallen on Judah and Jerusalem. The Holy Spirit is saying that the gloating shall have "*an end.*"

JUDGMENT

The phrase of Verse 30, "*I will judge you in the place where you were created,*" refers to Nebuchadnezzar bringing his army directly into the land of Ammon, and so destroying Ammon that she would no more exist.

Instead of gloating over the fall of Judah and Jerusalem, the Ammonites would have done well to have repented; however, as a worshipper of idols, they did not believe in Jehovah.

Actually, they were a relative of Israel, having descended from Benammi, Lot's younger son by his daughter, born in a cave near Zoar (Gen. 19:38). As Lot was a nephew of Abraham, they were regarded as relatives of the Israelites, who were commanded to treat them kindly (Deut. 2:19).

At the time of the Exodus from Egypt, Israel did not conquer Ammon (Deut. 2:19, 37; Judg. 11:15). However, the Ammonites were condemned for joining the Moabites in hiring Balaam, and were forbidden to enter the congregation of Israel to the tenth generation (Deut. 23:3-6).

The Ammonites worshipped Moloch as their god, which was one of the most repulsive of heathen deities (I Kings 11:1, 5, 7, 33); nevertheless, it was Jehovah Who signed their death warrant. The phrase of Verse 32, "*You shall be no more remembered,*" refers to any hope of restoration, as it regards Ammon, being dashed. It seems that God judged them even more severely than He did Sodom (Ezek. 16:53). The phrase, "*No more remembered,*" spells its eternal doom.

However, their destruction was not instantaneous, as they survived into the Second Century B.C., which was about 300 years after this Prophecy. Today there are no more Ammonites and there will never be again.

THE REASON FOR SUCH JUDGMENT

Some may question as to why the Lord would restore Sodom, which will take place in the coming Kingdom Age, especially considering its great wickedness, and not restore Ammon?

Sodom, as wicked as it was, so wicked in

fact, that it had to be destroyed, still, did not seek to hurt or hinder Abraham, but rather seemed to seek his favor. To the contrary, the Ammonites greatly opposed Israel, who despite their unrighteousness, were the people of God.

I think the evidence is clear that the Lord can tolerate gross wickedness, much more that He can the much greater wickedness of the opposition to His Word and His people. When He said, *"Touch not My Anointed and do My Prophets no harm,"* he meant exactly what He said (Ps. 105:15).

Consequently, Christians, or anyone for that matter, should be very careful as to how they treat a fellow Christian. As well, the attitude of some religious leaders in attempting to silence certain Ministries, especially those which are greatly anointed by the Lord, will bring upon themselves, ultimately so, a swift and sure destruction. Even though such destruction may not be obvious at the beginning, still, the Holy Spirit will immediately cease His Operation, as least in Blessing, the effect of which will immediately be felt, leading to spiritual rot, and thereby destruction.

Judah and Jerusalem had sinned terribly, so terrible, in fact, that God would bring about tremendous judgment upon them, and would use the Babylonians to do so; however, as it is here obvious, He took great umbrage at anyone else, other than the nation that He had appointed, doing them any harm, even to the point of gloating over their Fall. In that *"gloating,"* they destroyed themselves! We must never forget, even as the Word of God rings out, *"Vengeance is Mine; I will repay, saith the Lord"* (Rom. 12:19).

"I'm abiding today in Canaan land,
"In the sunlight of God's Love;
"And the Saviour's Face ever shines before me,
"As I journey to my home above."

"'Tis a foretaste of coming glory yonder,
"In that Land beyond the sky.
"Where in bliss untold I shall ever wander,
"In the blessed homeland by and by."

"Won't you enter the Land of peace and blessing,
"And its rapture with me share?
"All your sin and guilt to the Lord confessing,
"You will have a blessed welcome there."

CHAPTER 22

(1) "MOREOVER THE WORD OF THE LORD CAME UNTO ME, SAYING,

(2) "NOW, THOU SON OF MAN, WILL YOU JUDGE, WILL YOU JUDGE THE BLOODY CITY? YES, YOU SHALL SHOW HER ALL HER ABOMINATIONS.

(3) "THEN YOU SAY, THUS SAITH THE LORD GOD, THE CITY SHEDS BLOOD IN THE MIDST OF IT, THAT HER TIME MAY COME, AND MAKES IDOLS AGAINST HERSELF TO DEFILE HERSELF.

(4) "YOU ARE BECOME GUILTY IN YOUR BLOOD THAT YOU HAVE SHED; AND HAVE DEFILED YOURSELF IN YOUR IDOLS WHICH YOU HAVE MADE: AND YOU HAVE CAUSED YOUR DAYS TO DRAW NEAR, AND ARE COME EVEN UNTO YOUR YEARS: THEREFORE HAVE I MADE YOU A REPROACH UNTO THE HEATHEN, AND A MOCKING TO ALL COUNTRIES.

(5) "THOSE WHO BE NEAR, AND THOSE WHO BE FAR FROM YOU, SHALL MOCK YOU, WHICH ARE INFAMOUS AND MUCH VEXED.

(6) "BEHOLD, THE PRINCES OF ISRAEL, EVERY ONE WERE IN YOU TO THEIR POWER TO SHED BLOOD.

(7) "IN YOU HAVE THEY SET LIGHT BY FATHER AND MOTHER: IN THE MIDST OF YOU HAVE THEY DEALT BY OPPRESSION WITH THE STRANGER: IN YOU HAVE THEY VEXED THE FATHERLESS AND THE WIDOW.

(8) "YOU HAVE DESPISED MY HOLY THINGS, AND HAVE PROFANED MY SABBATHS.

(9) "IN YOU ARE MEN WHO CARRY TALES TO SHED BLOOD: AND IN YOU THEY EAT UPON THE MOUNTAINS: IN THE MIDST OF YOU THEY COMMIT LEWDNESS.

(10) "IN YOU HAVE THEY DISCOVERED

THEIR FATHERS' NAKEDNESS: IN YOU HAVE THEY HUMBLED HER WHO WAS SET APART FOR POLLUTION.

(11) "AND ONE HAS COMMITTED ABOMINATION WITH HIS NEIGHBOR'S WIFE; AND ANOTHER HAS LEWDLY DEFILED HIS DAUGHTER IN LAW; AND ANOTHER IN YOU HAS HUMBLED HIS SISTER, HIS FATHER'S DAUGHTER.

(12) "IN YOU HAVE THEY TAKEN GIFTS TO SHED BLOOD; YOU HAVE TAKEN USURY AND INCREASE, AND YOU HAVE GREEDILY GAINED OF YOUR NEIGHBOURS BY EXTORTION, AND HAVE FORGOTTEN ME, SAITH THE LORD GOD.

(13) "BEHOLD, THEREFORE, I HAVE SMITTEN MY HAND AT YOUR DISHONEST GAIN WHICH YOU HAVE MADE, AND AT YOUR BLOOD WHICH HAS BEEN IN THE MIDST OF YOU.

(14) "CAN YOUR HEART ENDURE, OR CAN YOUR HANDS BE STRONG, IN THE DAYS THAT I SHALL DEAL WITH YOU? I THE LORD HAVE SPOKEN IT, AND WILL DO IT.

(15) "AND I WILL SCATTER YOU AMONG THE HEATHEN, AND DISPERSE YOU IN THE COUNTRIES, AND WILL CONSUME YOUR FILTHINESS OUT OF YOU.

(16) "AND YOU SHALL TAKE YOUR INHERITANCE IN YOURSELF IN THE SIGHT OF THE HEATHEN, AND YOU SHALL KNOW THAT I AM THE LORD."

The synopsis is:

1. The series of Prophecies concerning Jerusalem, which begin here, coupled with the review of Israel's moral history in Chapter 20 and with the entire book of Jeremiah, have extraordinary interest because they mark the transference of the government of the world from Israel to the Gentiles.

2. And yet, in all of this, we see the unfailing faithfulness of God to His Covenant with Abraham.

3. Also, we see the justice of His action in the destruction of Jerusalem.

4. And yet, in all of this, all of these prophetic messages, on God's part, we see patience, tender care, love, oft-repeated forgiveness, countless interventions of Grace, and heaped-promises of Mercy, voiced by Spirit-filled messengers.

NOTES

5. On man's part, we see a demonstration of the entire vanity of his nature, the rebellion and folly of his will, his determined attachment to evil, and the radical corruption of his heart, which neither goodness nor severity could change. Thus did this lengthened test of fallen human nature effectually prove that the carnal mind is enmity against God, that it is not subject to the Law of God, neither indeed can be.

6. But these Prophecies reveal a future of blessing for man, based not upon his goodness, for it has been demonstrated that he has none, but founded upon, and secured by, a goodness reposing in the bosom of God — that is Christ (Williams).

7. The dominating keynote of Chapters 22 through 24 is the exposure of the moral condition of Jerusalem as a vindication of the justice of God in its destruction.

8. The blood-stained city was Jerusalem; "*her abominations*" are shown to have been the practice of idolatry, with its impure ceremonies, and the violation of the moral legislation of the Book of Leviticus.

9. The Divine purpose was that Israel should be apart from, and throned as Queen above, the nations of the Earth; but her own conduct caused her to lose that supremacy, and thus she profaned herself by making herself a common nation.

THE INIQUITY OF JERUSALEM

The phrase of Verse 2, "*Bloody city,*" as it is applied to Jerusalem by the Holy Spirit through the Prophet, is the same phraseology used by the Holy Spirit through the Prophet Nahum, which was applied to Nineveh (Nah. 3:1). That is more interesting indeed when one realizes that the Assyrians, with Nineveh their capital, were the cruelest of the cruel!

Therefore, the title "*bloody city,*" as applied by the Holy Spirit, denotes far more than a mild epithet. The Holy Spirit said this for a reason. Murder had become common place in Jerusalem, and the instigators of much of this shed blood were the civil rulers.

But a great part of the blood shed in the city, even as Verse 3 proclaims, was that of children sacrificed to Moloch, and of people murdered for the sake of gain.

The phrase of Verse 3, "*And makes idols*

against herself to defile herself," refers to her attempting to attract the favorable attention of surrounding nations, but, in fact, attracting no favorable attention, and incurring upon herself the Wrath of God.

The phrase is striking in that it portrays Jerusalem working against herself instead of for herself. In other words, the very thing she was doing, thinking to benefit, was, in fact, sewing the seed of her own destruction. Every modern Christian should take heed.

MODERN PREACHERS

All too often, modern preachers seek to gain the applause of other Preachers, and do so by compromising the Word of God. They think to better themselves, when in reality they are destroying themselves. The answer is found in the word *"defilement."* Anything is *"defilement"* which does not strictly abide by the Word of God.

Likewise, people seek to attend popular Churches. The criteria of the Holy Spirit is that if it is truly popular with God, it will not be popular with man. Popularity with man and popularity with God are two different things altogether! It should ever be noted, if one is popular with man, he cannot be popular with God. As well, if one is popular with God, he cannot be popular with man!

There was a prophecy given at Family Worship Center in Baton Rouge on the Sunday Night of July 31, 1994. Basically, it said that God was going to use this Ministry around the world; however, the hatred of the world and Church would be no less then than now! It said, *"As you are despised now, you will be despised then!"*

REPROACH

The phrase of Verse 4, *"Therefore have I made you a reproach unto the heathen, and a mocking to all countries,"* refers to the very opposite which Judah and Jerusalem thought they would attain. In adopting the idols of the surrounding nations, she thought surely she would gain their approval, but she found to her dismay that she gained only their *"reproach,"* and consequently, they mocked her!

How sad that Jerusalem, once famous and full of peace, should become infamous and full of confusion!

The phrase of Verse 6, *"Everyone were in you to their power to shed blood,"* refers to the fact that there was no restraint on the doer of evil other than the limitation of his capacity.

The phrase, *"To shed blood,"* is startling, especially considering that it was given by the Holy Spirit. This shows the degree of sin and the level to which the morals of the nation had fallen. It was caused by the Leadership of Judah, i.e., *"the Princes of Israel."*

It is an ironic thing! The United States was built on the foundation of the Word of God, as evidenced by our Founding Fathers. However, the Bible is today banned, basically, from most government buildings. In our courtrooms, the spectators can read pornography, but they cannot read the Bible. And now the Supreme Court of the United States has stricken down laws as it regards sodomy. As well, the shift is moving strongly toward allowing *"same sex marriages,"* which can be construed as none other than an abomination in the eyes of God. Such is a gross insult to the creation model of man and wife.

If one looks to history as it regards the destruction of Empires, one will see that three sins were always paramount:

1. Pedophilia.
2. Homosexuality.
3. Murder.

HOLY THINGS

The phrase of Verse 8, *"My holy things,"* refers to the entirety of the Law and the Divine Ordinances. They not only forsook them, but they *"despised them,"* proving that sin never remains static, but always involves itself in deterioration.

This Passage teaches us that it is not possible to disobey the Word of God without ultimately degenerating into a hatred of the Word of God. As the Word of God has the effect upon the human heart of either softening or hardening it, according to response, likewise, the response will not remain static, but always, if in the negative, degenerate into outright hatred and opposition. Hence, *"you have despised My holy things."*

Presently, the *"holy things of God"* are being profaned when religious men forsake the

Wisdom of the Word for the wisdom of men.

Presently, if there is a problem in a particular life, all too often the Church offers the services of the Psychologist as the answer and solution to the problem, and little seeks the Face of God, if at all.

COUNSELING

I heard a great Preacher say once, *"If the Preacher preaches as he ought to preach, which means that he faithfully preaches the Word of God, just about every question that a person has will ultimately be answered."* This means that most counseling, at least as we presently know such, is not Scriptural.

There certainly may be times that an individual would need to talk to a particular Preacher about particular decisions that need to be made; however, the greater thrust of counseling in modern Churches is almost altogether in the psychological realm, which in effect, is a denial of the Gospel, and more particularly, a denial of the Cross.

When it comes to spiritual weaknesses, sin, transgressions, iniquity, perversions, or anything that is morally wrong, the answer is not counseling, but the Cross. And quite possibly, one of the reasons that the Church has turned to humanistic Psychology is because it little understands the Cross. If looked at at all, the Cross is relegated to the initial Salvation experience, which pretty well concludes what is known by most as it regards the Cross. They have little understanding as to the part the Cross plays in our everyday, ongoing Christian walk. In fact, it plays more than a part, it is everything!

What Jesus did on the Cross not only made it possible for us to be Born-Again, but, as well, to live the life we ought to live after we come to Christ. In fact, nothing but a proper Faith in the Cross can bring about that for which Jesus has paid such a price (Jn. 10:10).

Even though the following is given more than this particular time in this Commentary, because of the great significance of that of which we speak, please allow me the liberty to briefly address it again.

The following is not necessarily a formula or a diagram, but mostly a direction which the Believer must go, as it regards proper living for the Lord.

FOCUS

The Believer must focus entirely and completely on Christ. Jesus is the answer for all things, because He Alone could be the answer for all things. He came as our Substitute; He, in effect, is our Representative Man. Identification with Him brings us this for which He came.

In fact, the entirety of the Bible, in one way or the other, points to Christ. He must be the Center of our world, meaning that everything must revolve around Him.

OBJECT OF FAITH

We must also understand that it's not only *"Who"* He is, but also *"What"* He has done. We speak of the Cross.

The very purpose of Christ coming to this world was to go to the Cross. This means that the Cross was not an incident, an accident, or an execution. It was the planned objective, actually planned by the Godhead from before the foundation of the world (I Pet. 1:18-20).

Had the Ministry of Christ stopped with His Virgin Birth, or His perfect Life, or His miracles and healings, as important and absolutely necessary as all of these things were, still, no one would have been saved. Salvation is effected totally and completely by what Christ did at the Cross; hence, the Cross must ever be the Object of our Faith. That's the reason that Paul said:

"Christ sent me not to baptize, but to preach the Gospel, not with wisdom of words, lest the Cross be made of none effect" (I Cor. 1:17).

Satan will do everything within his power to shift the object of our faith to other things, because he knows that the other things, as wonderful and Scriptural as they may be in their own right, will effect no positive results. He doesn't care if the Christian fasts until he can be pulled through a keyhole, because Satan knows, at least as it regards victory over sin, that while fasting will definitely help, it is not the answer.

The same can be said for anything else that one might mention in this capacity. I believe in manifestations, at least if they are truly of the Lord; however, manifestations, as wonderful as they may be, and as much as they may affect us, will not grant the individual victory in this life we are endeavoring to live. Jesus said: *"You shall know the Truth, and the Truth shall make you free"* (Jn. 8:32).

What we are giving you here is Truth. You are ever to make the Cross of Christ the Object of your Faith (Rom. 6:3-5, 11, 14).

POWER SOURCE

Once you understand that Jesus is your answer, and solely your answer, and that He is your answer as it regards what He did at the Cross, which incidentally, was done totally and completely on our behalf, and then we make the Cross the Object of our Faith, the Holy Spirit will then work mightily on our behalf. And to be sure, there is nothing the Holy Spirit cannot do, simply because He is God.

Paul said: *"For the Law of the Spirit of life in Christ Jesus has made me free from the law of sin and death"* (Rom. 8:2).

The Holy Spirit works so completely within the parameters of the Finished Work of Christ, that it is referred to in the Passage just quoted as a *"Law."* In fact, it is the very first Law that was established by the Godhead, and we speak of the Cross, which the Holy Spirit through Peter, said was *"devised from before the foundation of the world"* (I Pet. 1:18-20).

In fact, the Holy Spirit and the Crucified Christ work so closely together, that in the vision which John the Beloved had on the Isle of Patmos, they are seen as basically being indivisible. John said:

"And I beheld, and lo, in the midst of the Throne and of the four beasts, and in the midst of the Elders, stood a Lamb as it had been slain, having seven horns and seven eyes, which are the seven Spirits of God sent forth into all the Earth" (Rev. 5:6).

Incidentally, the *"slain Lamb,"* typifying what Christ did at the Cross, is the only way that the Throne of God can be reached. In fact, if anyone tries to come any other way, we are told in the Word of God, that the Holy Spirit will bar access (Eph. 2:13-18).

The *"seven horns"* speak of total dominion, which speaks of total victory over the world, the flesh, and the Devil. In other words, the Saint of God, if we take advantage of what Jesus did at the Cross, can have total victory over all sin. No, this doesn't mean sinless perfection, for the Bible doesn't teach such. But it does mean that *"sin shall not have dominion over you"* (Rom. 6:14).

The *"seven eyes"* stand for total and perfect illumination of the Word of God, as well as the Operation of the Holy Spirit. The idea is this:

The Believer cannot properly understand the Word unless the Believer ever makes the Cross the Object of his Faith. The *"seven eyes"* pertain to the Holy Spirit and His Perfect illumination, but is predicated, at least as far as the Believer is concerned, on the *"slain Lamb."* To know the Word and be led by the Spirit are the hallmarks of Victory for the Child of God, in fact, absolutely necessary, but are all based entirely on the Cross of Christ.

So, the power source is the Holy Spirit, but it's all predicated on the Cross (Rom. 8:1-2, 11).

RESULTS

If Christ is the central figure, and the Cross is ever the Object of our Faith, with the Holy Spirit then helping us, and doing so grandly, and because He works exclusively within the parameters of the Finished Work of Christ, to be sure, the results will be victory, victory, victory!

Now let's look at the same diagram, that is if we should refer to it as such, but look at it in the way that it's being done by most Christians.

WRONG WAY

Focus: Works.
Object of Faith: Performance.
Power source: Self.
Results: Defeat!

VILE SINS

Verses 9 through 12 proclaim, in no uncertain terms, the spiritual condition of Judah at the time of the Judgment.

Verse 10 proclaims the fact that *"incest"* had become common.

The phrase, *"In thee have they humbled her who was set apart for pollution,"* refers to women being forced to commit the sex act even during the time of their monthly period.

This was forbidden of the Lord, because the monthly period of the woman, which discharged impurities, was meant to portray as such, the Fall of man and the subsequent spiritual condition of all babies born thereafter, i.e., *"born in original sin."*

As a result of this serving as such a symbol, the Lord forbade intercourse during this particular time each month. By ignoring this command of the Lord regarding abstinence, at least at this time, in effect, the guilty party was refuting the lostness of man and the need for a Saviour.

The phrase of Verse 12, *"In thee have they taken gifts to shed blood,"* proclaims the fact that the taking of human life in Jerusalem had become common place. Presently, it is little different. Life is cheap, because the children are taught in public schools that man is a product of evolution; consequently, he has no soul; therefore, he faces no eternal judgment. Consequently, abortion is rampant because human life is cheap!

ABORTION

As stated, abortion is rampant, with the effected results being that human life becomes cheaper and cheaper. Why not? — especially considering that it is just a blob that is being removed from the mother's womb, or so is thought by these Christ-rejecters! No one likes to be told or reminded that they have committed murder when a baby is aborted for any purpose, but that is exactly what it is.

For long centuries, no decent person, and certainly no respected Christian, has advocated killing an unborn baby. Like any other act of killing, it is murder. This is the law of civilized nations, or at least should be, and more important, it is the Law of God. Yet now, godless people are saying, *"Kill the baby. It will be good for the mother's mental health."*

She doesn't want the child, it is reasoned, and has become pregnant because of force, fornication, or by accident. However, even though it may be by force (rape), still, the child is no less human, and must be treated accordingly. Whether it is wanted or not does not enter into the picture. Whether someone can afford to care for it, as well, does not enter into the picture. If that is a criteria, then all undesirables can be exterminated.

ALL MURDER IS WRONG

In the Old Testament, even before the Law, God said, *"whoso sheds man's blood, by man shall his blood be shed: for in the image of God made He man"* (Gen. 9:6). Under the Mosaic Law, God plainly commanded, *"He who smites a man, so that he die, shall surely be put to death"* (Ex. 21:12).

The death penalty for murder (cold-blooded murder) is also clearly implied in the New Testament: the ruler of a nation is *"the minister of God . . . for he bears not the sword in vain"* (Rom. 13:1-7). As well, murderers are kept outside the Heavenly Jerusalem (Rev. 21:8; 22:15).

To God, the killing of an unborn child is murder. The person guilty of that murder is subject to the same conviction and deserving of the same punishment, who maliciously pulls the trigger of a gun to kill another person.

The unborn child, even at the moment of conception, is a human being — a person. Some persons have foolishly said that the unborn child, up to the sixth or seventh month, is little more, as stated, than a *"blob"* of flesh; but that is simply not true. The little unborn baby is not just a part of the mother's body; he (or she) is a separate life altogether. All of the child's particular traits have already been charted in his genes. The sex of the child, the color of its eyes and hair, its physical features, its special talents and gifts, are all determined at the time of conception. Both the mother and the father of the child have already, at this point, passed down to their baby, every genetic characteristic they will contribute.

A PERSON

The Bible teaches that the child, from conception, is a person, and consequently, a living soul. David was inspired to say, *"Behold, I was shaped in iniquity, and in sin did my mother conceive me"* (Ps. 51:5). When David said, *"I was shaped,"* it was the Words of the Holy Spirit through David proclaiming the Truth that, from the moment of conception, he was the person who would later be known as David, the great King of Israel.

Again, the Psalmist David was inspired to write, *"You have covered me in my mother's womb. I will praise You; for I am fearfully and wonderfully made"* (Ps. 139:13-14). From the moment of conception and as the Holy Spirit gave the intent, David was, indeed, a person. It was David's body, his very substance, in the womb of his mother.

JEREMIAH

We have the same kind of teaching concerning Jeremiah, who said, *"Then the Word of the Lord came unto me, saying, before I formed you in the belly, I knew you; and before you came forth out of the womb I sanctified you, and I ordained you a Prophet unto the nations"* (Jer. 1:4-5).

God knew the Prophet Jeremiah before he was born. If, by abortion, this unborn child had been murdered, it would have been Jeremiah who died. The mother would not have known his name, but God would have. The mother might not have known that this was to be a mighty Prophet of God, but God would have known that too.

JOHN THE BAPTIST

John the Baptist was, *"filled with the Holy Spirit, even from his mother's womb"* (Lk. 1:15). Mary, the mother of Jesus, came to greet Elizabeth, *"and it came to pass, that when Elizabeth heard the salutation of Mary, the baby leaped in her womb"* (Lk. 1:41).

This unborn child, who would be known as *"John the Baptist,"* in the womb of his mother, may not have understood clearly why he leaped at the sound of the voice of Mary, *"the Mother of the Saviour,"* but God knew!

LITTLE CHILDREN

It is interesting to note the words of Jesus, *"Suffer the little children to come unto Me, and forbid them not: for of such is the Kingdom of God"* (Mk. 10:14). He was speaking in reference to the infants brought to be blessed by Him. The term used for *"infants"* in the Greek is *"brephos,"* which Young's analytical Concordance defines as *"a child born or unborn."* This means, then, that all the little ones who died before birth had an immortal soul (*"of such is the Kingdom of God"*), and they, to be sure, will meet us there.

ILLEGITIMATE?

Some have claimed that if the baby is illegitimate, then it should be aborted. Of course, the answer to that is you do not erase, correct, or even justify one's sin by committing another. To be frank, it is not the baby that is illegitimate, it is the parents. (In fact, there is no such thing as an illegitimate baby.)

The real answer to sin is Repentance and trusting the Saviour for forgiveness and for rearranging the soiled life. To compound sin upon sin is not the way to peace or mental health. Some persons say the end justifies the means, but it never does!

SAVING THE LIFE OF THE MOTHER?

There is always the question of aborting the baby to save the life, or preserve the health, of the mother. In some rare cases, this may be necessary, but rarely.

Murdering an unborn child is the same as murdering the incompetent, the retarded, the handicapped, the aged, or senile. If we are going to kill the unwanted, possibly there are many one-year olds, two-year olds, five-year olds, ten-year olds, even fifty-year olds who are unwanted. Why not just kill them, too?

It is easy to see how horrendous this terrible crime becomes when carried to its ultimate conclusion. To slay the innocent because he cannot protest or swear out a warrant is a sin. And the Scripture says, *"Be sure your sin will find you out"* (Num. 32:23). There is a God Who cares for the weak, the unloved, and the unprotected. He will bring to Judgment.

I have dealt with abortion, although it is not the only kind of murder committed, as is obvious. However, it is the most common kind of murder committed.

GREED

As sexual immorality and abortion have become commonplace, likewise, *"greed"* characterizes almost the entirety of humanity. Perhaps, this is the reason that Paul said, *"The love of money is the root of all evil"* (I Tim. 6:10).

The dollar sign has become the basis on which almost everything is done, even in the Church. To be frank, the *"health and wealth"* message, which is so presently popular in the Church, is a result of greed. The Holy Spirit uses the term *"you have greedily gained of your neighbors by extortion."* What an indictment!

As stated, the Holy Spirit, through Ezekiel, did not confine Himself to the mere enumeration of specific sins. These are traced to their source in that *"forgetting God"* is the starting-point and the consummation of all forms of evil. Paul said as much in Romans 1:28. When men forget God, the results are not pleasant to behold!

As well, it is not possible to forget God and not be engulfed by these hideous sins, which, without fail, will destroy civilization.

DISHONEST GAIN

The phrase from Verse 13, *"Behold, therefore I have smitten My hand at your dishonest gain which you have made,"* refers to the Lord using this gesture as one of indignant, and at it were, impatient command. He will no longer tolerate such actions in Judah and Jerusalem, and the gesture signifies a soon conclusion with a coming of great Judgment. The idea is, that God will stop the evil and use whatever means necessary to do so!

The phrase, *"Which has been in the midst of you,"* concerns great evil, and is to be removed by judgment, if it is not allowed to be removed by repentance.

One must remember that the demand for Repentance had been forthcoming, at least concerning this coming judgment, for at least thirty-five years. As a result, many think that because judgment does not come immediately, that it will not come at all! However, its coming, barring Repentance, is certain, with the time only as uncertain.

God is merciful, loving, kind, and longsuffering. He has no desire to bring such judgment, and if done, is only brought after long pleading with the recalcitrant one.

While dishonest gain has been the hallmark of the world, and from the very beginning, and because of man's unredeemed state, the worst dishonest gain of all is Preachers taking advantage of people, enticing them to give money, some even their very living, with the idea that such type of giving is going to make them millionaires, etc.

NOTES

While this problem, no doubt, has always plagued the Church, at least to a certain degree, it is more prevalent today than ever, and especially in the teaching of the *"Word of Faith Doctrine."* In fact, in that very popular doctrine, *"money"* is the emphasis. In fact, this emphasis is not shared with anything else in this perverse doctrine, but in fact, is total. In other words, *"money"* is the entire warp and woof of the *"Word of Faith"* philosophy.

THE WORD OF FAITH DOCTRINE

This doctrine began in the 1960s, and in fact, gained great headway in the 1970s, with the emphasis then being primarily on healing. However, the doctrine is grossly unscriptural, and in fact, there were no healings, at least as a result of this teaching.

To be brief, the foundational error of this false teaching is the *"Jesus Died Spiritually Doctrine."* Strangely enough, most of the followers of this particular philosophy have little knowledge as to that of which I've just stated. The primary reason is, the emphasis, as stated, is on money, and not correct Biblical teaching.

Also, most of the terminology used by the propagators of this false message is identical, or at least similar, to the terminology used as it regards correct Doctrine. In others words, they claim to believe in the Blood of Christ and the Cross, and at times will loudly trumpet such; however, the truth is, they don't believe in these factors at all, and will quickly add, that is if they are pushed, that it required something to be added to the Blood and to the Cross, in order for man to be saved.

That which they claim that must be added, pertains to Jesus dying spiritually on the Cross. By that, they mean that He died not only physically, but He died spiritually, which means, that He died as a lost sinner, having actually become one with Satan, and that when He died, He then went to the burning side of Hell, where all sinners go upon death.

They teach that He was tormented in Hell for some three days and nights, until God said, *"It is enough."* He was then, they continue to teach, born again, like any sinner is born again, and raised from the dead.

In other words, they teach that the price

for our Redemption was paid, not on the Cross, that being only a way-station in this odyssey, but rather in the pit of Hell, suffering as a sinner. Now the preposterous thing about all of this is, there's not a shred of any of this found in the Bible. In fact, it is the greatest attack on the Atonement, perhaps, that Satan has ever engineered. I believe it is his last great thrust before the Rapture of the Church. In other words, he saved his major thrust for the last period.

At least one of the reasons that this doctrine is so insidious, this attack on the Cross, this gross attack on the Atonement, is because those who are propagating this message, claim to be Spirit-filled. Therefore, they automatically gain a legitimacy in the minds of many.

As well, what they teach appeals solely to the flesh, catering to all the base motives in hearts and lives. It is legitimized, at least in the minds of many, by Scriptures being perverted and pulled out of context. And to be sure, the factor of greed, at least at it regards money, is present more or less, probably one could say, in all of us. Therefore, to be rich, and to have it seemingly legitimized by Scripture, is the pot of gold at the end of the rainbow.

In fact, as it regards this Word of Faith Doctrine, there is very little, if any, appeal for Righteousness, Holiness, and Christlikeness. Actually, the total emphasis is on self.

And let me venture this final thought on this particular subject:

THE GAMBLING SPIRIT

The spirit that captivates the hearts and lives of the millions who follow this doctrine, is, in effect, the same spirit which captivates the unredeemed who go into the Casinos, hoping they're going to hit it rich. In fact, regarding the dupes who support this perfidious doctrine, they are constantly being told that their great *"payday"* is right around the corner. They've got to keep giving, and in effect, increase their giving, even to the extent of mortgaging their homes.

The truth is, as it regard gambling in the world, the only ones getting rich are the owners of the Casinos, and in the realm of the Word of Faith doctrine, the only ones getting rich are the Preachers.

I maintain that the spirit that captivates

NOTES

both, the gambler on the street, and the gambler in the Church, i.e., *"functioning from a motive of greed,"* is one and the same spirit.

If it is to be noticed, very soon after the Word of Faith doctrine began to make inroads into the modern Church, the gambling fever took over this country, which has resulted in untold numbers of broken hearts and broken lives.

THE BLESSING OF THE LORD

All error, as someone has rightly said, rides into the Church on the back of Truth. In other words, there is always a modicum of truth mixed in with the error, which makes it palatable. God does bless His people, and does so abundantly, and does so in every way, which includes finances, etc. It is sad, even though the very emphasis of the Word of Faith Doctrine is money, the very thing which the followers of this philosophy seek to get, it constantly eludes them. In other words, it's all a façade, and simply because it is error, and the Holy Spirit cannot condone, sanction, or bless error.

But for those who truly love the Lord, and who truly give *"to prove the sincerity of their love"* (II Cor. 8:8), the Lord will definitely bless such efforts, and will do so abundantly. His Word plainly says: *"But this I say, he which sows sparingly shall reap also sparingly; and he which sows bountifully shall reap also bountifully"* (II Cor. 9:6).

Pure and simple, the money gained by false preachers, preaching a false doctrine, can only be concluded as *"dishonest gain,"* and will ultimately bring upon itself the Judgment of God.

THE INHERITANCE

Verses 13 through 16 proclaim, in no uncertain terms, that which the Lord said that He would do. Regrettably, the people of Judah and Jerusalem little believed the Word that was given. And all of that despite the fact, as Ezekiel delivered the Message, and is given in Verse 14, *"I the LORD have spoken it, and will do it."*

The phrase of Verse 16, *"And you shall take your inheritance in yourself in the sight of the heathen,"* refers to her inheritance being squandered by trying to become as the *"heathen."*

What was Judah's inheritance?

The Hebrew term is *"Yara,"* which means *"to become an heir,"* or *"to take possession."*

Another Hebrew word is *"Nahal,"* which indicates giving or receiving property as a permanent possession. Of special note is the stress laid on the idea of permanent possession. A central Old Testament concept is that God gave to the Hebrews the Land of Israel or as it is sometimes called, *"Palestine,"* as a permanent possession. That gift established that claim to the land *"forever."* Consequently, Israel's effort to completely occupy this ancient land presently, is considered by many in the State of Israel to be simply exercising an ancient right.

THE COVENANT

The Covenant of the Lord giving this particular territorial area known as *"Israel"* to Jacob's children, was made with Abraham (Gen. 13:14-18; 15:7, 18; 17:1-8).

A little over four hundred years later, Joshua took the land, and according to the directions given by the Holy Spirit, divided it among the Twelve Tribes, with plots given to each family as a permanent possession.

Although disobedient generations of Israelites might be driven from the land, God committed Himself, by Covenant, to give to the descendants of Abraham, Isaac, and Jacob *"all this land"* to be *"their inheritance forever"* (Ex. 32:13).

The Psalms praise God for His commitment and remind Israel that it is those who are in right relationship with God — the meek and the righteous (Ps. 37:11) — who will ultimately take full possession of the promised inheritance.

SIN

Israel, and because of sin, was now about to lose this possession, but still, they would be restored some seventy years later, albeit with a Gentile overlord.

When they crucified Christ, they were driven from the Land, and scattered all over the world. This expulsion took place in A.D. 70. Even though an element continued to try to maintain the possession, the Romans, in A.D. 135, once again totally dispersed them, where they wandered for about nineteen hundred years all over the world. In 1948, and according to Bible Prophecy, they once again became a State, albeit with great parts of the Land continuing to be contested.

The contesting will continue, when in the near future, in the time of the coming Antichrist, he, this man of sin, will make the greatest effort of all to dispossess these ancient people, which will trigger the Coming of the Lord (Rev., Chpt. 19). Then Israel, under Christ, will once again totally possess the Land, serving as the premier nation of the world, and all because of Christ.

A SPIRITUAL SYMBOL

As well, the Land of Israel, as a physical possession, is a symbol or shadow of the Believer's inheritance under the New Covenant. Paul wrote in Romans 8:17, *"If we are children, then we are heirs."* Even though having no connection with earthly law, still, Paul's statement, as given by the Holy Spirit, is a reflection of Roman inheritance Law.

In the Old Testament system, as in ours presently, a person must die before others became his heirs. In Roman law, it was birth, not death, that established heirship; therefore, in using the same principle, the Holy Spirit tells us that because we have been Born-Again through Faith in Christ, and have become God's Children, we have full rights as heirs to all that is our Father's (Rom. 9:6-8; Gal. 3:6-7, 28, 29).

As God's heirs, we are, in a real sense, currently *"owners"* of all the good things, tangible and intangible, to be found in God, and all made possible by the Cross. The Blessings we receive now are from the rich storehouse of His wealth, distributed at His will, but truly our own. One day we will possess fully what we currently own.

THE MAIN EMPHASIS OF THE BELIEVER'S INHERITANCE

It is exciting to see in the New Testament those things that are our inheritance. The main emphasis is on the Kingdom of God (Mat. 25:24; I Cor. 6:9-10; 15:50; Gal. 5:21; Eph. 5:5; James 2:5).

Because of the unique character of Roman Law, which was used by Paul as a model, the

New Testament can affirm both that we already do own in this wonderful inheritance, and that we will come into a full experience of it in the future. Because inheritance law was based on birth and not on the determination of one's heirs at the time of his death, we can be sure now that in Christ, and through the new birth, we have already come *"into an inheritance that can never perish, spoil, or fade — kept in Heaven for us"* (I Pet. 1:4).

Hallelujah!

Nevertheless, as Satan tried repeatedly to disengage Israel from its earthly inheritance, likewise, he attempts to do the same with the Heavenly Inheritance of the New Testament Child of God.

THE NEW COVENANT

As we have stated, under Roman Law, the child did not have to wait until the death of the parents before receiving his inheritance, but actually received it at birth; however, if he died, the inheritance was forfeited, as would be obvious. Likewise, if the Believer ceases to believe and spiritually dies through trespasses and sins, even as Israel of old, he will lose the inheritance.

The phrase, *"And you shall know that I am the Lord,"* refers to the Lord being the owner of the inheritance and, therefore, having the legal right to possess or dispossess as He wills.

One of the great reasons that the New Covenant is so much greater than the Old Covenant, is because the New Covenant is based on Christ, where the Old Covenant was based on individual performance. Paul said, *"and joint-heirs with Christ"* (Rom. 8:17). That's the reason that Faith only is required to gain and to maintain this inheritance (Jn. 3:16; Rom. 5:1; 10:9-10, 13), whereas obedience to a myriad of Laws was required under the Old Covenant, as Peter said, *"which neither our fathers nor we were able to bear"* (Acts 15:10).

Paul said: *"For if the inheritance be of the Law, it is no more of Promise, but God gave it to Abraham by Promise"* (Gal. 3:18). The Promise given to Abraham was *"Justification by Faith"* (Gen. 15:6).

THE CROSS

It is the Cross, and the Cross alone, which has made all of this possible. The Cross opened up the Way to God, which means that the Sacrifice of Christ was perfect, and perfectly accepted by God, and in every capacity. What man lost in the Fall, he regained at the Cross, for, in effect, Christ was the *"Last Adam,"* and the *"Second Man"* (I Cor. 15:45-47).

In fact, the theme of the entirety of the Bible is *"Jesus Christ and Him Crucified,"* typified in the Sacrifices of the Old Testament, and proclaimed as the meaning of the New Covenant, as given by Paul; hence, he said: *"We preach Christ crucified"* (I Cor. 1:23).

THE INFALLIBILITY OF THE NEW COVENANT

The New Covenant is so infallible, so perfect, that the Holy Spirit through Paul referred to it as, *"The Everlasting Covenant"* (Heb. 13:20). This means it will never have to be amended, added to, subtracted from, or replaced. It is perfect because it is in Christ.

All Covenants are entered into by two or more parties. The New Covenant is the same, but yet, totally different.

All the Covenants of old made by God with man were broken by man, and broken constantly. So, in a sense, the breaking of the Covenants by man rendered them ineffective. But the New Covenant cannot be broken, and let me explain why!

While the New Covenant is definitely a Covenant made between God and man, the great secret of the New Covenant is that Jesus Christ is both God and Man. In Himself, He satisfied all the demands of the Covenant, hence the necessity of the Incarnation and, therefore, it can never be broken. While man might fail, and in fact, does so repeatedly, Christ does not fail and, in fact, cannot fail.

THE CROSS, THE RATIFICATION OF THE COVENANT

All Covenants, at least the kind of which we speak, were ratified by the shedding of blood. In Old Testament times, an animal was sacrificed as a symbol of the covenant. Oftentimes, the fingers of the covenant parties were cut, with blood being shed, and mingled together, to ratify the covenant. To be sure, the New Covenant is no less ratified, and, in fact, has the greatest ratification of all.

The Cross, which was the scene of the shedding of Blood, the Blood of God's only Son became, therefore, the ratification of the Covenant. Blood had to be shed, and blood was shed. The difference was, however, whereas the blood that was shed in the past was either animal blood, or the impure blood of covenant partners, now, the Blood shed on the Cross of Calvary by the Son of the Living God was perfect and pure, never tainted by sin, and could, therefore, serve as an eternal ratification. Paul said:

"*But now in Christ Jesus* (through what He did at the Cross) *you who in times past were far off* (Gentiles) *are made nigh by the Blood of Christ.*

"*For He is our peace* (Justifying Peace) *Who has made both one* (Jews and Gentiles), *and has broken down the middle wall of partition between us* (the wall on the Temple compound, which was about four feet high, which separated the court of the Gentiles from the Court of Israel);

"*Having abolished in His Flesh* (His physical Body was the Perfect Sacrifice) *the enmity* (the estrangement caused by sin), *even the Law of Commandments contained in Ordinances,* (He satisfied on the Cross the demands of the Broken Law, which condemned all men); *for to make in Himself of twain one new man* (the Body of Christ), *so making peace* (justifying and sanctifying peace);

"*And that He might reconcile both* (Jews and Gentiles, for all must come the same way) *unto God in one Body* (the Church) *by the Cross* (where the Covenant was ratified), *having slain the enmity thereby* (removed the cause, which was sin):

"*And came and preached peace to you which were afar off* (preached Salvation to the Gentiles), *and to them who were nigh* (and as well to the Jews).

"*For through Him* (through Christ and what He did at the Cross) *we both* (Jews and Gentiles) *have access* (to the very Throne of God) *by one Spirit* (the Holy Spirit) *unto the Father*" (Eph. 2:13–18).

As is glaringly obvious in these Passages, it was the *"Cross"* which ratified the Covenant, because it was there where the Blood of the Son of God was shed, forever paying the price, hence, it is *"The Everlasting Covenant."*

NOTES

Once again, we must shout, *"Hallelujah!*

(17) "AND THE WORD OF THE LORD CAME UNTO ME, SAYING,

(18) "SON OF MAN, THE HOUSE OF ISRAEL IS TO ME BECOME DROSS: ALL THEY ARE BRASS, AND TIN, AND IRON, AND LEAD, IN THE MIDST OF THE FURNACE; THEY ARE EVEN THE DROSS OF SILVER.

(19) "THEREFORE THUS SAITH THE LORD GOD; BECAUSE YOU ARE ALL BECOME DROSS, BEHOLD, THEREFORE I WILL GATHER YOU INTO THE MIDST OF JERUSALEM.

(20) "AS THEY GATHER SILVER, AND BRASS, AND IRON, AND LEAD, AND TIN, INTO THE MIDST OF THE FURNACE, TO BLOW THE FIRE UPON IT, TO MELT IT; SO WILL I GATHER YOU IN MY ANGER AND IN MY FURY, AND I WILL LEAVE YOU THERE, AND MELT YOU.

(21) "YES, I WILL GATHER YOU, AND BLOW UPON YOU IN THE FIRE OF MY WRATH, AND YOU SHALL BE MELTED IN THE MIDST THEREOF.

(22) "AS SILVER IS MELTED IN THE MIDST OF THE FURNACE, SO SHALL YOU BE MELTED IN THE MIDST THEREOF; AND YOU SHALL KNOW THAT I THE LORD HAVE POURED OUT MY FURY UPON YOU."

The exegesis is:

1. The second of these Messages to Jerusalem (Vss. 17-22) had, in principle, a fulfillment about four or five years later; but its plenary fulfillment belongs to the future day of God's Judgment of the city during the reign of the false Messiah, i.e., *"the Antichrist."*

2. The point in these Verses, which the Holy Spirit uses as a symbol, appears to be that, in a crucible, silver may be extracted from baser metals, but that in the case of Jerusalem, the process only produced dross, i.e., *"the scum that forms on the surface of molten metal."*

3. As *"scum"* is skimmed from the top of molten metal and thrown away, so must Israel be treated accordingly!

DROSS

The entirety of this message, as stated, pertains to the Lord using the symbolism of metal being melted, which in the case of

Israel, was supposed to be *"silver."* But there was no silver there, only the *"dross,"* i.e., *"scum."* In other words, there was nothing salvageable about the people, at least at this time.

The New Testament counterpart to this, is found in the words of Simon Peter, *"that the trial of your faith, being much more precious than of gold that perishes, though it be tried with fire, might be found unto praise and honor and glory at the appearing of Jesus Christ"* (I Pet. 1:7).

Paul also addressed the subject by saying: *"Now if any man build upon the foundation gold, silver, precious stones, wood, hay, stubble;*

"Every man's work shall be made manifest, for the day shall declare it, because it shall be revealed by fire, and the fire shall try every man's work of what sort it is" (I Cor. 3:12-13).

As it regards the precious metals, which Paul uses as symbolism, standing for purity, and then the words hay and stubble, which stand for that which is unacceptable, in other words, they will not stand the test of fire, the end result is this:

How much in our lives pertains to that which is pure and how much that which is impure?

However, it must be understood that Paul is not speaking of one's Salvation, but rather *"every man's work,"* which stands for what we are doing with that which God has given us. With some, I fear, the loss will be total, meaning that the motives of such a one were unsatisfactory, as well as the efforts. But yet, such a person, although losing all reward, will not lose his soul, that depending solely on Faith in Christ (I Cor. 3:15).

The truth is, most people who claim Salvation, really aren't saved. Jesus said as much (Mat. 7:14). And then regarding those who are truly saved, our faith is tried constantly, in order to get out the impurities (I Pet. 1:7).

A PERSONAL EXPERIENCE

When Frances and I first married, for a few months, I had a job with a plumber, which in many ways, proved to be most interesting.

He taught me how to melt lead, which was used to caulk the joints of pipe. He had a small jet burner, of sorts, with a thick pot on top of the burner. The bars of lead would be put into the pot, with fire ultimately melting the lead.

When it melted, all the impurities in the lead would rise to the top, and was to be skimmed off, leaving only pure lead. That way the caulk, when applied to the pipe joints, would be sure.

Basically, this is what the Holy Spirit is doing in our lives by allowing us to be placed in the furnace of affliction, in order that our faith may be tested. As someone has said, *"all faith must be tested, and great faith must be tested greatly."* How much of it is pure, and how much of it is dross? Only applied pressure will reveal the answer to that question.

(23) "AND THE WORD OF THE LORD CAME UNTO ME, SAYING,

(24) "SON OF MAN, SAY UNTO HER, YOU ARE THE LAND THAT IS NOT CLEANSED, NOR RAINED UPON IN THE DAY OF INDIGNATION.

(25) "THERE IS A CONSPIRACY OF HER PROPHETS IN THE MIDST THEREOF, LIKE A ROARING LION RAVENING THE PREY; THEY HAVE DEVOURED SOULS; THEY HAVE TAKEN THE TREASURE AND PRECIOUS THINGS; THEY HAVE MADE HER MANY WIDOWS IN THE MIDST THEREOF.

(26) "HER PRIESTS HAVE VIOLATED MY LAW, AND HAVE PROFANED MY HOLY THINGS: THEY HAVE PUT NO DIFFERENCE BETWEEN THE HOLY AND PROFANE, NEITHER HAVE THEY SHOWN DIFFERENCE BETWEEN THE UNCLEAN AND THE CLEAN, AND HAVE HID THEIR EYES FROM MY SABBATHS, AND I AM PROFANED AMONG THEM.

(27) "HER PRINCES IN THE MIDST THEREOF ARE LIKE WOLVES RAVENING THE PREY, TO SHED BLOOD, AND TO DESTROY SOULS, TO GET DISHONEST GAIN.

(28) "AND HER PROPHETS HAVE DAUBED THEM WITH UNTEMPERED MORTER, SEEING VANITY, AND DIVINING LIES UNTO THEM, SAYING, THUS SAITH THE LORD GOD, WHEN THE LORD HAS NOT SPOKEN.

(29) "THE PEOPLE OF THE LAND HAVE

USED OPPRESSION, AND EXERCISED ROBBERY, AND HAVE VEXED THE POOR AND NEEDY: YES, THEY HAVE OPPRESSED THE STRANGER WRONGFULLY.

(30) "AND I SOUGHT FOR A MAN AMONG THEM, THAT SHOULD MAKE UP THE HEDGE, AND STAND IN THE GAP BEFORE ME FOR THE LAND, THAT I SHOULD NOT DESTROY IT: BUT I FOUND NONE.

(31) "THEREFORE HAVE I POURED OUT MY INDIGNATION UPON THEM; I HAVE CONSUMED THEM WITH THE FIRE OF MY WRATH: THEIR OWN WAY HAVE I RECOMPENSED UPON THEIR HEADS, SAITH THE LORD GOD."

The diagram is:

1. The third Prophecy reviews the moral condition of the city, and groups its inhabitants into four sections: Preachers, Priests, Princes, and People. All are declared to be corrupt, neither *"cleansed"* nor *"rained upon."*

2. The conscience that is not cleansed by the Precious Blood of Christ, and the heart that is not fertilized by the rain of the Holy Spirit, are necessarily unclean; however, the outward life may be adorned with religious ceremonies.

3. Pure and simple, the preachers of that day destroyed souls. They enjoyed large salaries, and they made many widows by urging their husbands to fight, and by promising them victory. They thus furnish a striking picture of present-day Preachers accepted by the world (I Jn. 4:5-6). The Preachers are mentioned first because their influence was greatest, and because the moral character of a people is determined by its creed.

4. The Priests did not suppress the Bible, of which they were the custodians; they violated it. In other words, they denied its inspiration and authority; they profaned its teachings, that is, they lowered the Book to the common level of other books.

5. The Princes, like the other three sections of society, had one main object in view — the amassing of wealth by fair means or foul.

THE CONSPIRACY

Verses 24 and 25 proclaim the *"conspiracy of her prophets."*

NOTES

The phrase of Verse 25, *"They have devoured souls,"* tells us, in no unmistakable terms, that it is *"souls,"* always souls, which are stake, and of which nothing is more important.

The *"conspiracy"* that plagues the land presently (2003) comes under the following headings, as it regards false doctrine:

1. Agreement: Tens of thousands of Preachers agree, for instance, with the false doctrine of the Word of Faith philosophy.

2. Fear: Many Preachers know that this doctrine is wrong, grossly wrong, but they will say nothing out of fear of losing their Churches, or the approval of other Preachers. Regrettably, many, if not most, Preachers seek to please other Preachers, rather than pleasing God.

3. Silence: Tens of thousands of Preachers know, beyond the shadow of a doubt, that the false doctrine of which we speak is making great inroads into the modern Church. They know it is wrong, grossly wrong! But for any number of reasons, they will not speak out. Mostly, they don't want to take the heat, which always comes to the few who seek to please the Lord.

So, in effect, whether intended or not, Satan has developed a *"conspiracy"* to keep false doctrine from being exposed. Regrettably and sadly, he is being very successful!

FALSE DOCTRINE

To be sure, there is certainly more false doctrines that the one primarily we have singled out, and I speak of the Word of the Faith philosophy; however, this particular doctrine is far more insidious, simply because it has made tremendous inroads into the Pentecostal and Charismatic worlds, in effect, decimating those ranks. But above all of that, it is the most powerful attack against the Atonement that Satan has ever engineered, especially as it regards the Full Gospel Message.

The phrase of Verse 25, *"They have taken the treasure and precious things,"* refers to the Glory of the True Gospel that was withheld from the people. The *"Cross"* is the answer and the only answer; however, this *"treasure"* and *"precious thing"* have been openly ridiculed by the Word of Faith Message, claiming that the Cross is little more than *"past miseries,"* and as some have said, *"the greatest defeat in human history."*

With the Message of the Cross for all practical purposes decimated in modern ranks, the Church is left in a position to where it doesn't know where it has been, where it is, or where it's going. It's like a rudderless ship. It is at the mercy of every passing wind of doctrine, hence, the gross stupidity of some manifestations, claimed to be of the Holy Spirit. Let me say it again:

The Denominational world has tried to preach the Cross without the Holy Spirit, with the end result being that, by and large, they presently preach much of nothing. The Pentecostal and Charismatic worlds have tried to preach the Holy Spirit without the Cross, and the consequence is that they are left without the Holy Spirit, and rather with *"spirits."*

HUMANISTIC PSYCHOLOGY

The phrase of Verse 26, *"They have put no difference between the holy and profane,"* can, of course, refer to many things; however, bringing all of this up to the present time (2003), psychological counseling fits the bill.

Even though the following have been given elsewhere in these Volumes, due to the fact that Commentaries are studied differently that other books, it is necessary, we think, to repeat them:

• The Bible is the Word of God (Jn. 1:1). The *"bible"* for psychology is man's opinion, which changes almost on a daily basis.

• The Bible holds all answers relative to human behavior (II Pet. 1:3). Psychology claims to hold all answers relative to human behavior, but denies the Bible.

• The Bible says man is an eternal soul (Jn. 3:16). Psychology has its roots in evolution.

• The Bible says man is a sinner (Rom. 3:23). Psychology says man is a victim.

• The Bible says the problem is man's evil heart (Jer. 17:9). Psychology says man's problem is his environment.

• The Bible says man is inherently evil (Rom. 3:10-18). Psychology says man is inherently good.

• The Bible treats the core of man's problem, which is an evil heart (Jn. 3:3). Psychology treats man's symptoms only.

• The Bible says that Jesus Christ and the Cross are the answer (Mat. 11:28-30). Psychology says psychotherapy is the answer.

• The Bible says that we should deny self (Mat. 16:24). Psychology says we should love self.

• The Bible directs us to the Spirit of God (Zech. 4:6). Psychology directs us to the flesh.

• The Bible directs us to Faith in God (Mk. 11:22). Psychology directs us to self-effort.

• The Bible directs us to Repentance (Acts 26:20). Psychology directs us to remorse.

• The Bible directs us to Restoration (Gal. 6:1). Psychology directs us to referral.

• The Bible directs us Truth (Jn. 17:17). Psychology directs us to man's opinions.

• The Bible directs us to personal responsibility (Rev. 22:17). Psychology directs us to irresponsibility.

• The Bible directs us to free will (Rev. 22:17). Psychology directs us to determinism (causes other than one's self).

• The Bible deals with a *"cure of souls"* (Mat. 11:28-30). Psychology deals with a *"cure of minds,"* but, in reality, cures nothing.

• The Bible says God's Truth is unchangeable (Ps. 119:89). Psychology says truth is determined by majority and culture.

• The Bible says it is sufficient (II Pet. 1:3). Psychology says the Bible is insufficient.

• The Bible leads us to love for God and man (Mat. 22:37-39). Psychology leads to love for self.

TO MAKE UP THE HEDGE AND STAND IN THE GAP

Verses 27 through 29 proclaim the acute spiritual condition of the leaders of the nation, which led Judah and Jerusalem astray. Verse 30 says, and concerning this, *"I sought for a man among them, who should make up the hedge, and stand in the gap before Me for the Land, that I should not destroy it: but I found none."*

This Passage is chilling indeed, for it portrays the Holy Spirit seeking to save the people and the Land from destruction, even up until the very last, but to no avail!

It is startling indeed, when one considers that there wasn't one single individual in the position of Leadership whom God could use for this all-important task. What an indictment!

For reasons we have already stated, the situation presently is little better, if any at all, than during those times of so long ago. Spiritually, the Church has never been in worse condition than it is now, at least since the Reformation.

Concerning Judah of old, neither a reformer (*"the hedge"*) nor an intercessor (*"the gap"*) were found in the guilty city to save it from destruction. So Verse 31 says, *"Therefore have I poured out My indignation upon them."*

I think the Bible student cannot help but see that God demands Repentance with forthcoming Revival, or else there will be judgment.

However, before there can be Revival, there must be a Reformation. In other words, the Church must turn back to the Bible, back to the Cross! And this the Holy Spirit is grandly seeking to do, even at this very moment.

Revival cannot be brought about on the foundation of false doctrine; it can only be brought about on the true foundation of the Word of God. And to be sure, the Cross is the foundation Doctrine of all doctrine, meaning that all doctrine must be based squarely on the Cross, or else it's not Scriptural (I Pet. 1:18-20).

As Judah and Jerusalem of old faced this intersection, so does the modern Church. It must have a Move of God, turning it back to the Cross, or else it will be judged. As well, the Church must be brought back to the Cross, or else the nation will be judged. And the Judgment, according to all Scripture, will be even more severe than it was upon Sodom and Gomorrah. They ultimately will be restored (Ezek. 16:53), but that which is lost to the modern Church will not be restored.

"Take the Name of Jesus with you,
"Child of sorrow and of woe.
"It will joy and comfort give you,
"Take it then wherever you go."

"Take the Name of Jesus ever
"As a shield from every snare;
"If temptations round you gather,
"Breathe that holy Name in prayer."

"O, the precious Name of Jesus;
"How it thrills our souls with joy,
"When His loving arms receive us
"And His songs our tongues employ!"

"At the Name of Jesus bowing,
"Falling prostrate at His feet,
"King of kings in Heaven, we'll crown Him
"When our journey is complete."

CHAPTER 23

(1) "THE WORD OF THE LORD CAME AGAIN UNTO ME, SAYING,

(2) "SON OF MAN, THERE WERE TWO WOMEN, THE DAUGHTERS OF ONE MOTHER:

(3) "AND THEY COMMITTED WHOREDOMS IN EGYPT; THEY COMMITTED WHOREDOMS IN THEIR YOUTH: THERE WERE THEIR BREASTS PRESSED, AND THERE THEY BRUISED THE TEATS OF THEIR VIRGINITY.

(4) "AND THE NAMES OF THEM WERE AHOLAH THE ELDER, AND AHOLIBAH HER SISTER: AND THEY WERE MINE, AND THEY BORE SONS AND DAUGHTERS. THUS WERE THEIR NAMES; SAMARIA IS AHOLAH, AND JERUSALEM AHOLIBAH.

(5) "AND AHOLAH PLAYED THE HARLOT WHEN SHE WAS MINE; AND SHE DOTED ON HER LOVERS, ON THE ASSYRIANS HER NEIGHBOURS,

(6) "WHICH WERE CLOTHED WITH BLUE, CAPTAINS AND RULERS, ALL OF THEM DESIRABLE YOUNG MEN, HORSEMEN RIDING UPON HORSES.

(7) "THUS SHE COMMITTED HER WHOREDOMS WITH THEM, WITH ALL THEM WHO WERE THE CHOSEN MEN OF ASSYRIA, AND WITH ALL ON WHOM SHE DOTED: WITH ALL THEIR IDOLS SHE DEFILED HERSELF.

(8) "NEITHER LEFT SHE HER WHOREDOMS BROUGHT FROM EGYPT: FOR IN HER YOUTH THEY LAY WITH HER, AND THEY BRUISED THE BREASTS OF HER VIRGINITY, AND POURED THEIR WHOREDOM UPON HER.

(9) "WHEREFORE I HAVE DELIVERED HER INTO THE HAND OF HER LOVERS, INTO THE HAND OF THE ASSYRIANS, UPON WHOM SHE DOTED.

(10) "THESE DISCOVERED HER NAKEDNESS: THEY TOOK HER SONS AND HER DAUGHTERS, AND SLEW HER WITH THE SWORD: AND SHE BECAME FAMOUS AMONG WOMEN; FOR THEY HAD EXECUTED JUDGMENT UPON HER."

The construction is:

1. The idolatry of the ancients was not the senseless worship of savages, but a highly developed, philosophical and cultured religion, beautified with impressive ceremonies, made awesome and mysterious by human sacrifice, and accepted by the deepest religious feelings of kings, princes, philosophers, scientists, and all classes of society, both cultured and uncultured.

2. But God, in order to make men sensible of the vileness and horror of a religion so approved by man, was obliged to use the imagery of this Chapter; for none other could express its bestiality and loathsomeness.

3. To charge the Bible with indelicacy in its condemnation of sin is as just as to condemn a mirror for reflecting the loathsome marks of a repugnant disease upon a man's face. The Bible and the mirror, being truth, can, neither of them, act contrary to their nature.

4. Aholah and Aholibah figure Samaria and Jerusalem. They were the daughters of one mother — Sarah.

5. This Chapter points out that the sin of Jerusalem was greater than that of Samaria; for Priests and people associated idolatry, in its most blood-stained form, with the worship of Jehovah.

6. Judgment had already destroyed Samaria and swept its people into captivity, and a similar doom was now impending over Jerusalem.

7. There was no moral difference between these sisters. The same conduct showed the same nature. The heart at the close was the same as at the beginning. They were the children of an idolater (Josh. 24:2); they were idolaters while still in Egypt (Josh. 24:14), and in the Wilderness (Acts 7:42-43); and now, after long years of Divine pleading and goodness and discipline, they were attached more than ever to their idols, including those brought from Egypt.

8. Thus, under this lengthened test of approximately one thousand years, was demonstrated the incurable idolatry of man's fallen nature.

WHOREDOMS

This Chapter clearly and yet graphically illustrates the sin and wickedness of both the Northern and the Southern Kingdoms of Samaria and Judah. The idea for exhaustive explanation, as given by the Holy Spirit, is that the reader not misunderstand the cause of the terrible judgment which had already come upon Samaria, and was shortly to come upon Judah. Even though the Judgments were terrible, still, the pleadings for repentance on the part of both Samaria and Judah were constant and longsuffering. Therefore, these two nations had no one to blame but themselves, as the individual has no one to blame but himself.

Over and over again, one can easily see in these narratives the terrible cause of judgment, the pleadings for repentance, and the refusal of the people to heed or hear. Therefore, one not only sees the terrible sin of the people, but also the great Grace of God.

The *"two women, the daughters of one mother"* figured, as stated, the Northern Kingdom of Samaria and the Southern Kingdom of Jerusalem, which prefigured Judah as well. They were *"the daughters of one mother,"* which refers to Sarah, who gave birth to Isaac, who sired Jacob, from whom sprang the twelve sons representing the Twelve Tribes of Israel.

From the birth of the sons of Jacob to the time of the split forming two nations was approximately seven hundred years. Even though during this time there were hints of dissatisfaction between the two factions, with Ephraim claiming supremacy, still, they remained one visible people through the reign of King Solomon. Under his son, Rehoboam, the rift widened, finally resulting in a split, with Nine Tribes forming the Northern Kingdom called Israel, Samaria, or Ephraim. Jeroboam became their king. Three Tribes, Judah and Benjamin, with Simeon being in the borders of Judah, made up the Southern Kingdom, with Jerusalem as its capital, and the nation called Judah.

This Chapter reviews their conduct from

Egypt to the final destruction of their city and the nation. Thus, under this lengthened test of about eleven hundred years was demonstrated the incurable idolatry of man's fallen nature.

Regrettably, idolatry continues today in a materialistic form in heathendom, and in varying mental and material forms in Christendom, and will reach its climax under the Antichrist.

The Lord looked at Israel as His wife, and He as their husband; consequently, the phrase of Verse 3, *"They committed whoredoms,"* speaks of her unfaithfulness to Him. The word, *"whoredoms,"* does not speak of sexual impurity, even though this, no doubt, was rampant, but rather idolatry.

SAMARIA

"Aholah" represents Samaria, and is primarily addressed in Verses 4 through 10. Samaria was destroyed about one hundred and thirty years before Judah was brought under the dominion of the Babylonians.

Israel's protection, whether the Northern or the Southern kingdoms, was Jehovah. With such protection, Israel was the most powerful nation in the world. Without it, they were *"naked!"* The only thing that could lift God's hand of protection was sin. To be *"naked"* meant to be open to the Judgment of God, which would allow heathen nations to have their way, as with Assyria.

Hoshea was the King of Israel when the Scripture says, *"The King of Assyria found conspiracy in Hoshea"* (II Ki. 17:4). Now Assyria will make inroads into the Northern Kingdom of Israel, and actually destroyed it as a nation. The reason given by the Holy Spirit was, *"that the children of Israel had sinned against the Lord their God"* (II Ki. 17:7-12).

The neighboring nations, which both Samaria and Judah attempted to imitate, secretly hated them, and openly rejoiced at their Fall. Actually, the Northern Kingdom of Israel went into oblivion and ceased forever to be a nation. From henceforth, all the Promises would reside in the Southern Kingdom of Judah, which herself would sin greatly, but yet would be restored, and ultimately will fulfill the Promises made to the Patriarchs and Prophets.

SPIRITUAL ADULTERY

This which I will presently address is a little different than that which the Lord addressed as it regarded Judah of those long years ago; still, the character or direction is the same.

If it is to be noticed, the Lord used extremely strong statements as it regards Judah and her sins, such as *"whoredoms"* and *"harlot,"* etc. While immorality, as we think of such, was, no doubt, rampant at that particular time in Judah, the crowning sin of which the Lord addressed, however, was Judah's unfaithfulness to Him. He was their husband, and by their worshipping idols, which pertained to other countries, they were being grossly unfaithful to Jehovah.

In the first four verses of Romans, Chapter 7, Paul says that we as Believers, as the Body of Christ, are in essence married to Christ (Rom. 7:4). As such, Christ is to meet our every need, which He does through the Cross, even as Paul characterized in Romans, Chapter 6. This means that the Believer is to understand, and ever do so, that Christ is always the *"Source"* for all things, and the Cross is the *"Means"* by which everything is done. In other words, the Cross made it possible for the Grace of God to flow to us in an uninterrupted manner, and to whatever degree is needed. But if the Believer ceases to look to Cross as the Means, but rather begins to trust something else, even though Christ continues to be named, in essence, such a Believer is committing *"spiritual adultery."*

Now the utmost tragedy of all of this is that virtually the entirety of the modern Church is living in a perpetual state of spiritual adultery, because, due to lack of proper teaching, they have almost no knowledge of the Cross, as it regards the Sanctification experience. Ignorant of the Cross, and what it means to our daily living, this means that the Believer will look to other things, and even though the other things may be good in their own right, those things, whatever they might be, will not bring victory to the Saint of God. The reason is simple:

THE HOLY SPIRIT

Whatever we as Believers do for the Lord, and whatever He does in us, and I mean in totality, must be done exclusively by the Holy

Spirit. We cannot save ourselves, sanctify ourselves, strengthen ourselves, or overcome within the capacity of ourselves. In fact, Jesus bluntly said: *"For without Me, you can do nothing"* (Jn. 15:5).

As Paul will tell us in Romans, Chapter 8, the Holy Spirit works entirely within the parameters of the Finished Work of Christ. In other words, it is the Cross which gave and which gives the Holy Spirit the legal right to do all that He does (Rom. 8:2). To be sure, His help is always available; however, it is available on only His terms. And what are those terms?

He doesn't ask much of us, only that we ever make the Cross the Object of our Faith (Rom. 6:3-11). If we do this, ever making the Cross the Object of our Faith, then the Holy Spirit will work mightily in our lives, and then we can walk in a state of perpetual victory — victorious over the world, the flesh, and the Devil (Rom. 8:11).

DOES A PROPER UNDERSTANDING OF THE CROSS GUARANTEE VICTORY?

Yes and No!

Let's say it this way.

When the Believer begins to properly understand the Cross as it regards his everyday walk before God, he then has the potential for total and complete victory within his life. And for that victory to be gained and maintained, faith must be maintained, and by that, we mean perpetual Faith in Christ and the Cross. In fact, Paul referred to this as the *"good fight of Faith"* (I Tim. 6:12). Actually, this is the only *"fight"* in which we are called upon to engage.

Satan will do everything within his power to move our Faith from Christ and the Cross to other things. And to be sure, he doesn't too very much care what those other things are, just as long as it's not the Cross. But if the Believer's faith begins to wane, which means that Satan is being successful, then victory will be lost.

The only way that the Believer can live an overcoming, victorious Christian life, and do so on a perpetual basis, victorious, as stated, over the world, the flesh, and the Devil, is by a continuous looking to Christ and the Cross. There is no other way, even as no other way is needed. But just because one knows that, doesn't necessarily guarantee victory. As stated, and we repeat, the Believer must ever understand, that his faith cannot waver, but must ever be anchored in Christ and the Cross. One must practice such on a daily basis. Jesus said so (Lk. 9:23).

The Cross is something which happened now nearly two thousand years ago. But it has benefits which continue, and in fact which will never be discontinued, and it's those benefits of which we speak. Let us say it again:

Christ is ever the *"Source,"* while the Cross is ever the *"Means."*

The *"fighting of this good fight of Faith"* is so critical, and so necessary of engagement, that Jesus said: *"If any man will come after Me, let him deny himself* (deny his own strength and abilities) *and take up his cross* (that which the Cross provides) *daily* (on a daily basis), *and follow Me"* (Lk. 9:23).

As we've already stated elsewhere in this Volume, as our Lord made the statement, the faith of which we speak, and I continue to speak of Faith in the Cross, must be renewed, so to speak, on a daily basis. That's how critical the situation actually is.

THE POWERS OF DARKNESS

One thing the Believer seemingly little understands is the magnitude of the Powers of Darkness which he faces. They are of far greater magnitude than we can even begin to realize. The idea is, within ourselves, we cannot even hope to overcome these powerful forces.

When one looks at the Book of Revelation, and the strange creatures which John describes, which come under the heading of demon spirits, etc., we then begin to see the magnitude of that which we face (Rev. 9:1-11, 17-19). That's the reason that Paul said: *"For we wrestle not against flesh and blood, but against principalities, against powers, against the rulers of the darkness of this world, against spiritual wickedness in high places"* (Eph. 6:12).

Understanding this, we should automatically realize that if we don't do this thing God's Way, spiritual wreckage will be the result. And to be sure, that *"Way"* is *"Jesus Christ and Him Crucified"* (I Cor. 1:23).

REPETITION

If it is to be noticed, as I'm certain it is, due to Satan hindering, it is not easy for the Believer to understand the Message of the Cross, as simple as it is; therefore, it is necessary that I repeat this great Truth over and over, even as Paul did.

I constantly have people coming up to me and saying, *"Brother Swaggart, I see it now!"* And some of these people have been hearing me preach and teach this for several years. So why does it take so long for some?

I cannot answer that, and I suppose the correct answers are as diverse as the number of people. The human being is a complex creation. No two of us are exactly alike. What is clear to one is not so clear to the other, even though it is explained in the same manner.

When the Lord first began to give me this great Revelation, which was in 1997, we immediately began to teach and preach this great Truth. After several months, I thought surely that the Lord would want me go to another subject. To be sure, I tried! It wasn't that I didn't want to do the Will of God, I just assumed, and wrongly as it turned out, that I should address other subjects.

It took a little while for the Lord to get through to me, that I wasn't to discontinue this teaching on the Cross until He told me otherwise. I'm now able to see why He has led me accordingly.

In the first place, there aren't many Preachers preaching and teaching the Cross. And second, Satan will oppose this Message as he opposes nothing else. The reason is simple!

The Cross was the place of Satan's defeat, and a total defeat (Col. 2:14-15; Eph. 2:13-18). So Satan will settle for Preachers preaching good things, while they do not preach the best thing. In fact, unless the Preacher preaches the Cross, which means that it is understood that all things come to us by virtue of the Cross, he's not really preaching the Gospel. He might be preaching about the Gospel, but he's not actually preaching The Gospel. Again, we state:

"But we preach Christ crucified, unto the Jews a stumblingblock, and unto the Greeks foolishness;

"But unto them which are called, both Jews and Greeks, Christ the power of God, and the Wisdom of God" (I Cor. 1:23-24).

This means that the *"power of God"* (I Cor. 1:18) and the *"Wisdom of God"* cannot be known and understood outside of a proper understanding of the Cross.

Not understanding that, the Believer will live in a state of *"spiritual adultery,"* which is the road to ultimate spiritual ruin.

(11) "AND WHEN HER SISTER AHOLIBAH SAW THIS, SHE WAS MORE CORRUPT IN HER INORDINATE LOVE THAN SHE, AND IN HER WHOREDOMS MORE THAN HER SISTER IN HER WHOREDOMS.

(12) "SHE DOTED UPON THE ASSYRIANS HER NEIGHBOURS, CAPTAINS AND RULERS CLOTHED MOST GORGEOUSLY, HORSEMEN RIDING UPON HORSES, ALL OF THEM DESIRABLE YOUNG MEN.

(13) "THEN I SAW THAT SHE WAS DEFILED, THAT THEY TOOK BOTH ONE WAY,

(14) "AND THAT SHE INCREASED HER WHOREDOMS: FOR WHEN SHE SAW MEN PORTRAYED UPON THE WALL, THE IMAGES OF THE CHALDEANS PORTRAYED WITH VERMILLION,

(15) "GIRDED WITH GIRDLES UPON THEIR LOINS, EXCEEDING IN DYED ATTIRE UPON THEIR HEADS, ALL OF THEM PRINCES TO LOOK TO, AFTER THE MANNER OF THE BABYLONIANS OF CHALDEA, THE LAND OF THEIR NATIVITY:

(16) "AND AS SOON AS SHE SAW THEM WITH HER EYES, SHE DOTED UPON THEM, AND SENT MESSENGERS UNTO THEM INTO CHALDEA.

(17) "AND THE BABYLONIANS CAME TO HER INTO THE BED OF LOVE, AND THEY DEFILED HER WITH THEIR WHOREDOM, AND SHE WAS POLLUTED WITH THEM, AND HER MIND WAS ALIENATED FROM THEM.

(18) "SO SHE DISCOVERED HER WHOREDOMS, AND DISCOVERED HER NAKEDNESS: THEN MY MIND WAS ALIENATED FROM HER, LIKE AS MY MIND WAS ALIENATED FROM HER SISTER.

(19) "YET SHE MULTIPLIED HER

WHOREDOMS, IN CALLING TO REMEMBRANCE THE DAYS OF HER YOUTH, WHEREIN SHE HAD PLAYED THE HARLOT IN THE LAND OF EGYPT.

(20) "FOR SHE DOTED UPON THEIR PARAMOURS, WHOSE FLESH IS AS THE FLESH OF ASSES, AND WHOSE ISSUE IS LIKE THE ISSUE OF HORSES.

(21) "THUS YOU CALL TO REMEMBRANCE THE LEWDNESS OF YOUR YOUTH, IN BRUISING YOUR TEATS BY THE EGYPTIANS FOR THE PAPS OF YOUR YOUTH.

(22) "THEREFORE, O AHOLIBAH, THUS SAITH THE LORD GOD; BEHOLD, I WILL RAISE UP YOUR LOVERS AGAINST YOU, FROM WHOM YOUR MIND IS ALIENATED, AND I WILL BRING THEM AGAINST YOU ON EVERY SIDE;

(23) "THE BABYLONIANS, AND ALL THE CHALDEANS, PEKOD, AND SHOA, AND KOA, AND ALL THE ASSYRIANS WITH THEM: ALL OF THEM DESIRABLE YOUNG MEN, CAPTAINS AND RULERS, GREAT LORDS AND RENOWNED, ALL OF THEM RIDING UPON HORSES.

(24) "AND THEY SHALL COME AGAINST YOU WITH CHARIOTS, WAGONS, AND WHEELS, AND WITH AN ASSEMBLY OF PEOPLE, WHICH SHALL SET AGAINST YOU BUCKLER AND SHIELD AND HELMET ROUND ABOUT: AND I WILL SET JUDGMENT BEFORE THEM, AND THEY SHALL JUDGE YOU ACCORDING TO THEIR JUDGMENTS.

(25) "AND I WILL SET MY JEALOUSY AGAINST YOU, AND THEY SHALL DEAL FURIOUSLY WITH YOU: THEY SHALL TAKE AWAY YOUR NOSE AND YOUR EARS; AND YOUR REMNANT SHALL FALL BY THE SWORD: THEY SHALL TAKE YOUR SONS AND YOUR DAUGHTERS; AND YOUR RESIDUE SHALL BE DEVOURED BY THE FIRE.

(26) "THEY SHALL ALSO STRIP YOU OUT OF YOUR CLOTHES, AND TAKE AWAY YOUR FAIR JEWELS.

(27) "THUS WILL I MAKE YOUR LEWDNESS TO CEASE FROM YOU, AND YOUR WHOREDOM BROUGHT FROM THE LAND OF EGYPT: SO THAT YOU SHALL NOT LIFT UP YOUR EYES UNTO THEM, NOR REMEMBER EGYPT ANY MORE."

The diagram is:

1. Judah, far from taking warning by the fate of her sister, Samaria, plunged deeper into the abominations of idolatry.

2. Impure love usually ends in open hatred. So Israel, in the end, hated the Egyptians, the Assyrians, and the Babylonians, and they hated her; likewise, the Christian who falls to a certain type of sin, concludes by hating that sin. But then it has done its damage!

3. Recalling old sins frequently leads to a resumption of them.

JUDAH

Judgment coming having already destroyed Samaria and sweeping its people into captivity, which was done approximately one hundred and thirty years before, now, a similar doom is impending over Jerusalem. She, far from taking warning from the fate of her sister, plunged deeper into the abominations of idolatry.

These facts, reaching a climax in this Chapter, vindicate God's action in the outpouring of His wrath upon them.

Why did the Holy Spirit judge Jerusalem and the Southern Kingdom of Judah as *"more corrupt"* (Vs. 11) than her Northern Sister? They were both engaged in idol worship, and yet, the Holy Spirit uses the words *"more than her Sister in her whoredoms."*

The Northern Kingdom of Israel did not have one single Godly King of the nineteen who reigned during the approximately two hundred and sixty years of their existence.

To the contrary, the Southern Kingdom of Judah had a number of Godly Kings who attempted to lead the nation toward God. As we have repeatedly stated, if Grace is shown and rejected, the condition of the person or nation always worsens! Of these Godly Kings, Jehoshaphat, Hezekiah, and Josiah, were quite possibly the Godliest. It seems they did all within their power to lead Judah toward God, but still, the people clung to idolatry.

Therefore, in view of the fact that more light was given to Judah than to her Northern counterpart, and considering her great rebellion, the Holy Spirit would say, *"She *was more corrupt."*

DEPENDENCE!

The phrase of Verse 12, *"She doted upon the Assyrians,"* was said of her Northern Sister as well! The splendor which had fascinated Samaria fascinated Judah also.

Jerusalem, as her Northern Sister, courted the alliance of the Kings of Assyria, as in the case of Ahaz (II Ki. 16:7-10) and Tiglath-Pileser. Even Hezekiah followed in the same line, trusting in Egypt — and afterwards rebelled. Manasseh, too, paid tribute and made Jerusalem the scene of a confluent idolatry, which included that of Assyria.

Perhaps the greatest temptation, even to the Godliest, is to lean on the arm of flesh. Consequently, these mighty empires were ever tempting shoulders to lean on; however, they always prove in the end to be destructive.

The Lord does not desire the Believer to depend even on good men. The Work of the Holy Spirit is that the person depend on the Lord exclusively. Jesus said, and concerning the Holy Spirit, *"He will guide you into all Truth"* (Jn. 16:13). Of course, the Holy Spirit uses, and constantly, the fivefold Ministry Gifts outlined in Ephesians 4:11. Nevertheless, such are always to point toward Christ and never to themselves.

It was God's intention that His people always look exclusively to Him for leading, guidance, protection, and help. It is the same presently, but yet, most Preachers look toward Denominations or at least another Preacher for their help, leading, or guidance. The Truth is, Denominations can provide no help at all, at least that which God will recognize, and other Preachers can only be of service as they point the individual to Christ and His Word.

The cause of all the failure then, and the cause of all the failure now, is a lack of dependence on the Word of God. They either did not know the Word, or else, they did not believe the Word. Consequently, it was said of Christ: *"He marveled because of their unbelief"* (Mk. 6:6).

COVERING

The idea of *"covering"* is big presently in modern Christian circles, and, in fact, I suppose, has always been, at least to a certain degree; however, due to the departure from the Holy Spirit, I think this problem is more acute now than ever.

By the word *"covering,"* we are speaking of Preachers who allow other preachers to be their *"covering"* for them, or even particular Denominations.

Even though this might be all the rage, the question is, *"Is it Scriptural?"*

No, it's not Scriptural, not even in the slightest. In fact, it is grossly unscriptural!

While I love all of my Brothers and Sisters in the Lord, and actively appreciate their advice and counsel, at least if it's according to the Word of God, the idea that some other poor, frail human being can serve as a covering for me, or anyone else for that matter, is ludicrous to say the least. They cannot even serve as a covering for themselves, much less others.

All of this is a work of the Evil One, endeavoring to shift dependence of the Believer to that other that Christ.

What does the Word of God say?

The Holy Spirit, through the Prophet Isaiah, said, *"Woe to the rebellious children, saith the LORD, who take counsel, but not of Me; and who cover with a covering, but not of My Spirit, that they may add sin to sin"* (Isa. 30:1).

And then our Lord said, to which we have already alluded: *"Howbeit when He, the Spirit of Truth, is come, He will guide you into all Truth: for He shall not speak of Himself; but whatsoever He shall hear, that shall He speak: and He will show you things to come.*

"He shall glorify Me: for He shall receive of Mine, and shall show it unto you" (Jn. 16:13-14).

Perhaps one can say, that this is the greatest sin of religious Denominations. More and more, the Preachers in these particular Denominations, and whatever they might be, are encouraged to look to the Denominational leadership for direction. In fact, in most of the modern Pentecostal Denominations, at least in the United States and Canada, the idea that Preachers are to seek the Lord for leading and guidance is frowned upon. These Preachers are greatly encouraged, and in some cases, demanded that they look strictly to Denominational leaders.

In fact, in one particular Pentecostal Denomination, when individuals come before the Missions Board for service on the foreign field and voice that they feel the Lord is leading them to a certain country, for the most part, this is ridiculed. In fact, much of the time, these individuals would be sent to another place, just to show them who is running the show. I think it would be very obvious as to how unscriptural such a situation is.

As a result, this particular Denomination, and I'm referring to the Assemblies of God, while having many Missionaries on the foreign field, is presently doing precious little for the Lord Jesus Christ. Many of these individuals are little more than amateur psychologists, with the Holy Spirit having precious little say in anything that is done. As a result, while there may be much activity, in fact, there is almost nothing being done for the Lord. And the truth is, there's not even much activity at the present time.

I realize that my statements are blunt, and they will arouse anger in some circles; however, what I'm saying is the Truth!

The moment the individual seeks to live this life, seeks to serve God, and to do so according to the direction of fellowmen, the results will not be pleasant. The only true *"Covering"* that a Believer is to have is the Lord Jesus Christ. Anything else is contrary to the Word and the Will of God.

THE BABYLONIANS

The phrase of Verse 15, *"After the manner of the Babylonians of Chaldea,"* refers to Judah wanting to be like her heathenistic counterparts.

Judah's beauty was the Presence of God which hovered over the Temple and, thereby, made the city of Jerusalem the greatest city in the world; however, there was no superficial ostentation as in other cities and nations, but instead a quiet simplicity. As long as they were close to God, they understood this as God's Way, the greatest Way on Earth. Not only were their natural wants provided, but the spiritual man, the most important of all, was abundantly fed. This, the surrounding nations could not have because they did not know Jehovah.

However, when Judah began to lose her way because of pulling further and further away from Jehovah, they lost the Presence and then the glitter of other nations became very enticing.

WORLDLINESS

Paul said: *"Be not unequally yoked together with unbelievers: for what fellowship has Righteousness with unrighteousness? And what communion has light with darkness?*

"And what concord has Christ with Belial? Or what part has he who believes with an infidel?

"And what agreement has the Temple of God with idols? For you are the temple of the Living God; as God has said, I will dwell in them, and walk in them; and I will be their God, and they shall be My people.

"Wherefore come out from among them, and be ye separate, saith the Lord, and touch not the unclean thing; and I will receive you,

"And will be a Father unto you, and you shall be My sons and daughters, saith the Lord Almighty" (II Cor. 6:14-18).

While the Bible definitely teaches, as is overly obvious here, separation from the world, it does not teach isolation. We are *"in the world,"* but, as Believers, we are not to be *"of the world."*

It's like a ship which sails on the water. As such, it can carry valuable cargo, and be of great service to mankind; however, if the water gets in the ship, catastrophe will be the result! It's the same with Believers. We are in the world, but we are not to be of the world.

What is worldliness?

Worldliness is simply *"following the ways of the world,"* instead of the *"ways of the Lord!"*

When we start looking to the world for solutions, we will find the solutions the world provides, and while it may be momentarily successful, the end result will not be pleasant or pretty.

Holiness is being led by the Holy Spirit, while worldliness is being led by man.

It would be amusing, were it not so sad, at the modern Church using *"Contemporary Music,"* claiming that such *"draws young people."*

Draws them to what?

They're sure not being drawn to the Lord!

To use the *"ways of the world"* to draw the young people is like using alcohol to draw the drunk, etc.

Pure and simple, it is the Holy Spirit Who draws people to Christ, young people included. And if the Holy Spirit doesn't do such, it simply cannot be done. Jesus said:

"No man can come to Me, except the Father which has sent Me draw him" (Jn. 6:44).

The Master then said:

"And I, if I be lifted up from the Earth, will draw all men unto Me.

"This He said, signifying what death He should die" (Jn. 12:32-33).

The truth is, we're filling up Churches presently with people who have never been Born-Again. They have been drawn to the Church by various means, but not by the Holy Spirit! Consequently, they are religious, but lost! To be like the world, is to be of the world, and to be of the world, is to not be of God.

John said: *"Love not the world, neither the things that are in the world. If any man love the world, the love of the Father is not in him"* (I Jn. 2:15).

ALIENATION

The phrase of Verse 18, *"Then My Mind was alienated from her, like as My Mind was alienated from her sister,"* has the sense of the following:

If a wife is unfaithful to her husband, oftentimes, after the unfaithful act, she grows disillusioned with her lover. Then her husband, because of her unfaithfulness and lack of Repentance, becomes disillusioned with her. She then finds herself rejected by all.

Judah found herself in this same position. Her alliances with the heathen were to prove to be empty promises; therefore, the friendship quickly deteriorated, and because of lack of Repentance, she alienated herself as well from the Lord. Ultimately, she was left with nothing, as all such excursions do.

The word *"alienation"* means, *"a withdrawing or separation of a person or his affections from an object or position of former attachment."*

Due to the idolatry of Judah, her sins alienated her from God, exactly as sin will alienate a person from God presently.

God's answer to sin is the Cross, and alone the Cross! So if a Believer rejects the Cross, or ignores the Cross, such a Believer is, at the same time, repudiating that which the Lord has done in order to salvage the lost sons of Adam's fallen race. When the Church does this, and I continue to speak of repudiating or ignoring the Cross, this alienates the Church from God, which causes Him to alienate Himself from the Church. Anything that alienates the Lord from us, as should be overly obvious, is serious indeed! And I personally believe that a repudiation or ignoring of the Cross is the greatest cause of such alienation. Listen to Paul:

"Examine yourselves, whether you be in the Faith; prove your own selves. Know you not your own selves, how that Jesus Christ is in you, except you be reprobates?" (II Cor. 13:5).

The phrase, *"In the Faith,"* refers to Faith in Christ and what Christ has done for us at the Cross. Failure to be *"in the Faith,"* is to place one's self in the position of being a *"reprobate,"* which is catastrophic, spiritually speaking.

PSYCHOLOGY

Recalling old sins frequently leads to a resumption of them.

Now in the clutches of Satan, and because of leaving the Ways of the Lord, the old idolatry of Egypt is now awakened within Judah. Verse 19 says, *"in calling to remembrance the days of her youth."* To be sure, she did not, at this time, recall to remembrance the movings of the Holy Spirit, but instead, *"wherein she had played the harlot in the land of Egypt."*

The abiding tactic of humanistic psychology is identical to the sin of Judah, *"in calling to remembrance the days of her youth."* Dragging out old sins, hurts, failures, or abuses are anathema to the Word of God. It not only does not, as psychology claims, disgorge the recessed affliction, but instead, opens the old wound. And yet, the Church has fallen for this lie hook, line, and sinker!

The Holy Spirit through Paul said: *"Forgetting those things which are behind, and reaching forth unto those things which are* before, I press toward the mark for the prize of the High Calling of God in Christ Jesus"* (Phil. 3:13-14).

Paul went on to say that those who did not follow those admonitions, *"are enemies of the Cross of Christ."*

He further said, *"whose end is destruction"* (Phil. 3:18-19).

When the individual properly repents before the Lord, the sin is washed away by the Precious Blood of Christ (I Jn. 1:7, 9).

If the sin is gone, in effect, washed away by the Precious Blood of Christ, then the Believer should remember them no more. They should not be spoken of, alluded to, or addressed in any fashion. The reason is, that sin or sins simply don't exist anymore.

One of the major avenues of humanistic psychology is to dredge up old hurts and sins. Not only does this not help, but it actually harms the person, and greatly so! Psychology takes the approach that talking about something helps it, whatever it is.

If one will use a little common sense, one would realize that talking about a physical illness in no way heals that illness. While the illnesses of which we speak aren't physical, nevertheless they are real hurts, and to be sure, they cannot be healed by merely discussing them. In fact, there is no healing outside of Christ, but in Christ, there is healing for every problem, irrespective as to how bad that problem might be.

Through our Ministry alone, we have seen untold numbers of people who were molested, sexually, domestically, and spiritually, in their younger years, completely set free by the Power of God. It is done simply by the individual being pointed toward Christ and the Cross, and them evidencing Faith in Christ and what Christ has done for us at the Cross. Let me give you a perfect Biblical illustration.

THE BITTER WATERS

Immediately after the Children of Israel were delivered from Egyptian bondage, the Scripture says that they *"went three days in the wilderness, and found no water,"* at least water they could drink. The Scripture further said, *"They could not drink of the waters of Marah, for they were bitter"* (Ex. 15:22-23).

NOTES

When Moses *"cried unto the Lord,"* the Scripture says, *"the Lord showed him a tree, which when he had cast into the waters, the waters were made sweet"* (Ex. 15:25).

The *"bitter waters"* served here as a symbol of all the bitterness which the Children of Israel had experienced in Egypt, and not for them only, but for all other Believers, as well, and for all time.

Life, at times, can be very cruel. Terrible things happen to people, even to little children. As well, bad things can definitely happen to good people.

But irrespective, these encounters, with many being serious indeed, can cause scars, which, in effect, imprison the individual. That's one of the reasons that our Lord said: *"The Spirit of the Lord is upon Me, for He has anointed Me . . . to heal the brokenhearted . . . to set at liberty them who are bruised"* (Lk. 4:18).

The only answer to this problem is the *"Tree,"* which symbolizes the Cross. The *"Tree"* was to be placed into these bitter waters, with them then turning sweet, in other words, drinkable.

This tells us that the *"bitterness"* of the past, whatever it may have been, can be healed only by the application of the Cross. If we put the Cross into those problems, a miraculous healing takes place; in fact, this is the only manner in which victory can be won over those terrible hurts of the past.

BY FAITH

The way this is done, is for the Believer to understand that Jesus addressed every single problem at the Cross (Col. 2:14-15). In other words, as it regards the Atonement, not one single thing was left undone or unaddressed. That's the reason that Paul referred to it as the *"Everlasting Covenant,"* meaning that it will never have to be amended (Heb. 13:20).

Once the Believer understands that the Cross is the *"Means"* by which all things are given to us by Christ, he then is to simply place his faith in that Finished Work, and the Holy Spirit will then perform the necessary work of healing within our hearts, erasing those problems, completely healing them, in effect, *"turning the bitter waters* sweet." (Rom. 8:11).

THE SERIOUSNESS OF SPIRITUAL ADULTERY

The phrase of Verse 20, *"For she doted upon their paramours,"* refers to the Egyptian Princes whose favor Judah courted. She threw herself into the idolatrous ritual of Egypt with an almost orgiastic passion. Ezekiel is probably speaking of the efforts of Zedekiah in his courtship of Egypt against the Babylonians.

The phrase of Verse 20, *"Whose flesh is the flesh of asses, and whose issue is like the issue of horses,"* is startling indeed! The Holy Spirit is actually using bestiality as an example of the sin which Judah committed.

To help us understand it even more, he is referring to a wife, who in her unfaithfulness, not only committed adultery with a man, but had sexual relations with an animal. He uses such as an example to portray Judah leaving His Presence for the presence of the idol-worshipping heathen.

In this statement, as well as others, the Bible student gets a general idea as to how the Lord views sin. It is to Him very personal, because it is directed at Him by Satan. In fact, Satan's greatest trump is when he can get one of God's children to disobey, which the Lord compares to unfaithfulness, i.e., spiritual adultery. Along with the repugnance of sin is the hurt felt by God at the unfaithfulness. It is the same, and even far greater, than a husband would feel upon the unfaithfulness of his wife, or vice versa.

The sin of rejecting the Cross, or ignoring the Cross, which is the state presently of almost all of the modern Church, is far worse, than any of us realize.

In the natural sense, it's bad enough for a wife to be unfaithful to her husband, or vice versa, and of course, we speak of doing such with another man; however, for the woman to submit herself to an animal, presents a perversion which is beyond compare.

The following explains this in the modern Christian realm:

SPIRITUAL PERVERSION

For the Believer to ignore the Cross as it regards his Sanctification, and to do so because of ignorance, is one thing; however, for the Believer to repudiate the Cross, after the light of the Cross has been given to him, as many in the modern Church are now doing, presents a perversion of the worst kind. In the physical sense, even as the Holy Spirit brings it out here, it is the same as *"bestiality."* If in fact that is correct, such a person has lost his soul. Let's say it again:

To not understand the Cross, and because it's not been properly taught, is one thing; however, for the Cross to be properly explained, and then for it to be repudiated or purposely ignored, which I again state the far greater majority of the modern Church is now doing, is a rejection of light, which will lead to total, complete, spiritual ruin.

The Cross of Christ is the dividing line between the True Church and the apostate Church. In fact, it has always been that way, but more so now than ever! Why?

We are living in the last of the last days. In other words, the Church has about run its course, with the Lord getting ready to bring Israel back to her rightful place, which will be done at the Second Coming (Rev., Chpt. 19). False doctrine presently abounds! Religious Denominations, at least for the most part, are so mixed up, that they hardly know what they believe anymore. So the Believer must look to the Cross, and the Cross alone!

Those who reject the Cross or attempt to join the Cross to works, even as the Judaizers attempted to join the Cross to the Law, will not succeed. The ultimate end will be destruction, because God, as I would hope is obvious, looks at such as a very grave sin. Some sins are worse than others; to be sure, the rejection of the Cross, other than blaspheming the Holy Spirit, is the greatest sin of all. It is the sin of rejecting God's Way, thereby instituting our own way instead!

GOD'S WAY

The phrase of Verse 22, *"Behold I will raise up your lovers against you,"* refers to the Babylonians, along with others, which would turn against Judah. In other words, the very safety and protection she thought she was securing would turn to be the very opposite!

The phrase, *"And I will bring them against you on every side,"* has reference to a hive of bees, when disturbed, suddenly attacking from all sides.

All of these words are given by Jeremiah and Ezekiel, and with startling detail as to what is soon to happen, but yet, Judah not at all believes it. At this time, Jerusalem is prosperous, at least for some, while others were greatly oppressed. Her alliances, at least she thinks, will bring her even greater prosperity. In her cleverness, she proposes to juggle the two juggernauts of Egypt and Babylon against each other and, thereby, escape. For a while it looks like her plans are succeeding; and, therefore, the Prophecies of both Jeremiah and Ezekiel seem unreal. Actually, her religious leaders call Jeremiah a *"bag of wind."*

While Judah was looking to Egypt, she seemingly fails to realize that it is the Lord, and not Egypt or Babylon, Who is pulling the strings. And because of her rebellion, the Lord will begin to work against Judah, which is appalling indeed!

When we as Believers look to anyone or anything except the Lord, which is the sin of the modern Church, exactly as it was the sin of Judah, we are purposely, whether we realize it or not, placing ourselves in a very perilous situation. While men may rule, God constantly overrules. To have man opposed to you is one thing, but to have God opposed to you is something else altogether. Man is very limited as to what he can do, in fact, not being able to do anything but what the Lord allows him to do. But God is all-powerful, all-knowing; therefore, He can do anything.

WHY WILL THE BELIEVER NOT LOOK TO GOD?

There are many reasons!

Most Christians don't know the Word of God well enough to know what the Lord wants. And then again, most Christians have such a weak relationship with the Lord, that again, it's almost like strangers.

When the Christian has a proper relationship, which means he has a proper prayer life and he hungers and thirsts after Righteousness, he will then desire to look exclusively to the Lord.

But let the Reader understand that all of this hinges on proper faith. And there can

NOTES

be no proper faith without the Cross ever being the Object of our Faith. In fact, to look to things other than the Cross simply means that we are looking to that other than the Lord. While such Christians may talk about the Lord incessantly, and claim that they are looking exclusively to Him, if they do not make the Cross the Object of their Faith, what they are saying is false. In fact, they are serving *"another Jesus, presented by another spirit, which presents another gospel"* (II Cor. 11:4).

SELF

The greatest hindrance to the Child of God, I think, is the problem of *"self."* While of course we are a *"self,"* and even though redeemed, we are still a *"self,"* and always will be. The idea is, we must place *"self"* entirely into Christ. Jesus said:

"If any man will come after Me, let him deny himself" (Lk. 9:23).

What did he mean by one *"denying oneself"*?

He is not speaking here of asceticism, but rather the denial of one's own ability and strength, in order to live this Christian experience, i.e., *"to follow Christ."* How does one deny oneself?

It can only be done, even as we've already stated, by one *"taking up one's Cross,"* and even doing so on a daily basis. Everything the Child of God needs, and needs to do, is found exclusively in the Cross of Christ. No intricate process is required or involved, only Faith. Once again, this refers to Faith in Christ and what Christ has done at the Cross. The Holy Spirit will take care of the balance.

DYING TO SELF!

Ever since I was a little kid in Church, I would hear Believers talk about, and Preachers preaching about, *"dying to self."*

In fact, the statement is correct. It simply means, that we are to die to our own personal efforts and abilities, when it comes to living for the Lord. As stated, it doesn't mean that we cease to be *"a self,"* for that we will ever be; however, *"dying to self"* is not really the question. The question is, how is it done?

To *"die to self,"* Christians try all sorts of things. They try giving up something they love. I heard of someone the other day, who gave up sugar in his tea, thinking that was *"dying to self."* It would be funny, if it weren't so sad, because the very ones laughing, probably, are trying something else just as ridiculous.

The truth is, there is no way that the Believer, irrespective as to what we might do, can *"die to self."* All of the efforts that we make are in the flesh and, thereby, unacceptable to the Lord.

We die to self simply by looking to Christ and the Cross, and as I have repeatedly stated, even over and over, and will continue to do so, ever making the Cross of Christ the Object of our Faith (Rom. 6:3-14; 8:1-2, 11; I Cor. 1:17-18, 21, 23; 2:2; Gal., Chpt. 5; 6:14; Eph. 2:13-18; Col. 2:14-15).

EGYPT

Verses 23 through 27 proclaim the idolatry of Judah.

The fact that Israel was an idolater in Egypt is again recalled, because she has never fully overcome the propensity toward this evil. It was at least in part the reason for her present spiritual declension and consequent judgment.

When the Lord delivered the Children of Israel from Egyptian bondage, they were delivered fully and completely, and no trace of this evil lifestyle was to remain; however, some of them clung to this evil, as many Christians today cling to things of the world.

At this very time, Zedekiah is working toward a political alliance between Judah and Egypt against the Babylonians; therefore, they are continuing to do what the Lord had commanded they not do, for any alliance also included the Egyptian cultus, which was the worship of their gods.

This lesson is seemingly lost on most of the modern Church. Any involvement with the world, such as taking up its lifestyle, etc., also means the involvement of oneself with the ways of the world, i.e., demon spirits. In other words, as an example, Christians who turn their radio dials to a country or rock station, are, as well, involving themselves in far more than just music. They are involving themselves in the fuel that powers this genre, i.e., demon spirits.

Many Religious Denominations have attempted to solve this problem by legislation, in other words, the making of rules forbidding particular things; however, such are always unsuccessful, simply because it is a throwback to law. The only answer is a proper relationship with Christ, which destroys any such desire.

The phrase, *"Nor remember Egypt any more,"* refers to the Lord extinguishing this hope forever, which He did! There would never be another foray in that direction.

(28) "FOR THUS SAITH THE LORD GOD; BEHOLD, I WILL DELIVER YOU INTO THE HAND OF THEM WHOM YOU HATE, INTO THE HAND OF THEM FROM WHOM YOUR MIND IS ALIENATED:

(29) "AND THEY SHALL DEAL WITH YOU HATEFULLY, AND SHALL TAKE AWAY ALL YOUR LABOUR, AND SHALL LEAVE YOU NAKED AND BARE: AND THE NAKEDNESS OF YOUR WHOREDOMS SHALL BE DISCOVERED, BOTH YOUR LEWDNESS AND YOUR WHOREDOMS.

(30) "I WILL DO THESE THINGS UNTO YOU, BECAUSE YOU HAVE GONE A WHORING AFTER THE HEATHEN, AND BECAUSE YOU ARE POLLUTED WITH THEIR IDOLS.

(31) "YOU HAVE WALKED IN THE WAY OF YOUR SISTER; THEREFORE WILL I GIVE HER CUP INTO YOUR HAND."

The composition is:

1. Again let us state, Israel was looking to man, when they should have been looking to God. He Alone, could do the doing.

2. In fact, the Lord would dictate as to exactly what these nations would do. While they thought it was their idea, all the time He was bringing about events, which would cause them to carry out His Will.

3. Rebellion against God brings about action from God, but action, to be sure, which is very negative.

THE DISPENSATION OF GRACE

Verses 28 through 31 proclaim the sure Judgment of God that is coming upon Judah and Jerusalem, *"because you have gone a whoring after the heathen and because you are polluted with their idols."*

Now many will look at these statements, as given through the Prophet Ezekiel, and conclude, that because we are presently living in the Dispensation of Grace, that God doesn't function in this manner any more. Nothing could be further from the truth!

Paul said in his Message to the Athenians: *"And the times of this ignorance* (ignorant of the Ways of the Lord) *God winked at; but now commands all men everywhere to repent"* (Acts 17:30).

This doesn't mean that God did not hold mankind at that particular time, accountable for their sins, which He most definitely did. It just means, that He didn't step in with Judgment, until there was no alternative.

But since the Cross, which has made Grace available to all, at least all who will believe, ignorance is not taken into account. So the Truth is, there is more judgment being poured out on the world on the whole, during this Dispensation of Grace, than it was during the time before the Cross.

In fact, the Holy Spirit, through Paul, plainly stated that if Believers took the Lord's Supper *"unworthily,"* they would be *"guilty of the Body and Blood of the Lord."* Consequently, the Apostle said, *"Let a man examine himself, and so let him eat of that bread, and drink of that cup."*

He then said, *"For he who eats and drink unworthily, eats and drinks damnation to himself* (brings a curse upon himself), *not discerning the Lord's Body.*

"For this cause many are weak and sickly among you, and many sleep" (even though they don't lose their souls, their lives are cut short) (I Cor. 11:24-31).

We should ever understand that the Lord says what He means, and means what He says. He rewards Righteousness, and He brings judgment upon unrighteousness. While He might tarry long before the Judgment comes, ultimately, it will come, in one way or the other.

(32) "THUS SAITH THE LORD GOD; YOU SHALL DRINK OF YOUR SISTER'S CUP DEEP AND LARGE: YOU SHALL BE LAUGHED TO SCORN AND HAD IN DERISION; IT CONTAINS MUCH.

(33) "YOU SHALL BE FILLED WITH DRUNKENNESS AND SORROW, WITH THE CUP OF ASTONISHMENT AND DESOLATION, WITH THE CUP OF YOUR SISTER SAMARIA.

(34) "YOU SHALL EVEN DRINK IT AND SUCK IT OUT, AND YOU SHALL BREAK THE SHERDS THEREOF, AND PLUCK OFF YOUR OWN BREASTS: FOR I HAVE SPOKEN IT, SAITH THE LORD GOD."

The structure is:

1. The drunkenness of anguish is recorded here, and anguish so great as to cause the captives to tear their bosoms.

2. And yet, for all of these warnings, Judah still would not repent. It is the same presently. The Word of God is replete with warnings concerning these last of the last days, but the Church takes little notice.

3. The problem then was unbelief, as the problem now is unbelief.

JUDGMENT

Verses 32 through 34 contain language so graphic, so all-encompassing, so total, so complete, as it refers to Judgment, that it will either have to be accepted, or totally rejected, meaning that Ezekiel was labeled as a false Prophet.

As we've already stated, at this particular time, those who were really false prophets were predicting peace and prosperity, just as the false prophets presently are predicting peace and prosperity. And, to be sure, it is much easier for the modern Church to believe the peace and prosperity message, rather than the message of judgment. The Churches that preach the *"everything is rosy"* doctrine, and *"how to be rich"* gospel, are full and overflowing. In other words, such a message caters to a large audience. Sadly and regrettably, the true need of the people is little met, if at all.

The need is victory over sin, which can only come about through the Cross of Christ. But as the Cross has never been attractive, likewise it's not attractive at present.

A short time ago, I was speaking with an Evangelist, whom, incidentally, I hold in high regard. He was making mention of the failure rate among Preachers, which, in fact, is far worse than even I had realized. And what is the answer of the modern Church as it regards this terrible dilemma? The answer is humanistic psychology, which of course, is no answer at all. Listen to Simon Peter:

"According as His Divine Power has given

unto us all things that pertain unto life and Godliness, through the knowledge of Him Who has called us to glory and virtue;

"Whereby are given unto us exceeding great and precious Promises: that by these you might be partakers of the Divine Nature, having escaped the corruption that is in the world through lust" (II Pet. 1:3-4).

Now either Peter told the Truth, as the Holy Spirit inspired him to say these things concerning *"all things being given to us in the Word of God, that pertain unto life and Godliness,"* or else Peter lied, and we need to look to other sources. I happen to believe that Peter told the truth; consequently, if the Church looks to other things, such as humanistic psychology, we are, in effect, saying, that the Apostle was lying; or in other words, that the Holy Spirit didn't know what He was talking about. And that's exactly the state in which the modern Church finds itself!

(35) "THEREFORE THUS SAITH THE LORD GOD; BECAUSE YOU HAVE FORGOTTEN ME, AND CAST ME BEHIND YOUR BACK, THEREFORE BEAR YOU ALSO YOUR LEWDNESS AND YOUR WHOREDOMS.

(36) "THE LORD SAID MOREOVER UNTO ME; SON OF MAN, WILL YOU JUDGE AHOLAH AND AHOLIBAH? YES, DECLARE UNTO THEM THEIR ABOMINATIONS;

(37) "THAT THEY HAVE COMMITTED ADULTERY, AND BLOOD IS IN THEIR HANDS, AND WITH THEIR IDOLS HAVE THEY COMMITTED ADULTERY, AND HAVE ALSO CAUSED THEIR SONS, WHOM THEY BORE UNTO ME, TO PASS FOR THEM THROUGH THE FIRE, TO DEVOUR THEM.

(38) "MOREOVER THIS THEY HAVE DONE UNTO ME: THEY HAVE DEFILED MY SANCTUARY IN THE SAME DAY, AND HAVE PROFANED MY SABBATHS.

(39) "FOR WHEN THEY HAD SLAIN THEIR CHILDREN TO THEIR IDOLS, THEN THEY CAME THE SAME DAY INTO MY SANCTUARY TO PROFANE IT; AND, LO, THUS HAVE THEY DONE IN THE MIDST OF MY HOUSE.

(40) "AND FURTHERMORE, THAT YOU HAVE SENT FOR MEN TO COME FROM FAR, UNTO WHOM A MESSENGER WAS SENT; AND, LO, THEY CAME: FOR WHOM YOU DID WASH YOURSELF, PAINTED YOUR EYES, AND DECKED YOURSELF WITH ORNAMENTS.

(41) "AND SAT UPON A STATELY BED, AND A TABLE PREPARED BEFORE IT, WHEREUPON YOU HAVE SET MY INCENSE AND MY OIL.

(42) "AND A VOICE OF A MULTITUDE BEING AT EASE WAS WITH HER: AND WITH THE MEN OF THE COMMON SORT WERE BROUGHT SABEANS FROM THE WILDERNESS, WHICH PUT BRACELETS UPON THEIR HANDS, AND BEAUTIFUL CROWNS UPON THEIR HEADS.

(43) "THEN SAID I UNTO HER WHO WAS OLD IN ADULTERIES, WILL THEY NOW COMMIT WHOREDOMS WITH HER, AND SHE WITH THEM?

(44) "YET THEY WENT IN UNTO HER, AS THEY GO IN UNTO A WOMAN WHO PLAYS THE HARLOT: SO WENT THEY IN UNTO AHOLAH AND UNTO AHOLIBAH, THE LEWD WOMEN.

(45) "AND THE RIGHTEOUS MEN, THEY SHALL JUDGE THEM AFTER THE MANNER OF ADULTERESSES, AND AFTER THE MANNER OF WOMEN WHO SHED BLOOD; BECAUSE THEY ARE ADULTERESSES, AND BLOOD IS IN THEIR HANDS."

The overview is:

1. The deepest depth of evil is the association of idolatry with God.

2. Idolatry was an old sin with Israel. An old sin is an easy sin.

3. Idolatry is spiritual adultery.

FORSAKING GOD

The phrase of Verse 35, *"Because you have forgotten Me, and cast Me behind your back,"* refers to Judah forsaking the Word of God, and thereby forsaking God. Forsaking Him always occurs if His Word is forsaken.

The phrase, *"Therefore bore you also your lewdness and your whoredoms,"* refers to idol worship with all its attendant demon spirits.

Judah had forgotten, as many modern Christians forget, that the two ways here represented, i.e., the ways of the world and the Ways of God, represent far more than meets the eye. The Ways of God, which are outlined in His Word, constitutes the Holy Spirit, with all that is right, good, noble, holy, righteous, true, and upright. Conversely, the ways of the world refer to the spirit world of darkness, populated and controlled by demon spirits, whose overall mission is to *"steal, kill, and destroy"* (Jn. 10:10).

One cannot have both!

THE SUBTLE WAYS OF SATAN

To give an example, just sometime back I picked up a letter off my desk to which was attached some advertisements and information pamphlets concerning an organization formed to help homosexuals in their efforts to leave that lifestyle, and to thereby walk with Christ. The list of its Board of Directors and Board of Reference contains the names of some of the most prominent Religious Leaders in America and Canada.

While I in no way question the motives of these individuals, I do strongly question their methods. They are attempting, through the field of psychology, with its psychological counseling and all that pertains to such efforts to bring about the desired results. To be blunt, such is impossible!

In the first place, man cannot deliver man, and irrespective of his educational background or secular training, the end results are always the same — failure.

If such will work, then Christ came all the way from Heaven and died on a cruel Cross for nothing (Gal. 2:21). Psychology strikes at the very heart of Bible Christianity. Its way is the wisdom of this world which James described as *"earthly, sensual, devilish"* (James 3:15).

He also described the *"wisdom that is from above* (the Bible), *is first pure* (undiluted by man), *then peaceable, gentle, and easy to be entreated, full of mercy and good fruits, without partiality, and without hypocrisy* (James 3:17).

Psychology claims that man can be rehabilitated with psychological methods. If such is true, which it is not, then, as we have stated, what Christ did at Calvary was unnecessary. No, these people may be well-intentioned, but they will reap no positive results, for all such efforts are doomed to failure.

Even though the Lord in some of these efforts is spoken of, still, the methods used are purely humanistic, and doomed to failure.

There is deliverance for homosexuals, or anyone else for that matter, but it is found only in Christ and what Christ has done for us at the Cross.

The tragedy is, the modern Church little believes in the delivering Power of God, simply because it little believes in the Cross. Concerning this, the Prophet Jeremiah said:

"For My people have committed two evils; they have forsaken Me the fountain of living waters, and hewed them out cisterns, broken cisterns, that can hold no water" (Jer. 2:13).

It is sad, when one realizes that almost all of the modern Church has bought into the psychological way. And in doing such, they have had to forsake the *"Way of the Lord."* As stated, it is impossible to have both.

Jesus said: *"No servant can serve two masters: for either he will hate the one and love the other, or else he will hold to the one and despise the other. You cannot serve God and mammon"* (Lk. 16:13).

(The word, *"mammon,"* as explained by Christ, is an egocentric covetousness, which claims man's heart and, therefore, estranges him from God.)

THE CROSS

It is the business of the Church to present to the world Christ as the Source, and the Cross as the Means. The Cross alone is to be held up as the answer to hurting humanity, and with the understanding, that it deals with all things. Paul said:

"But God forbid that I should glory (boast), *save in the Cross of our Lord Jesus Christ, by Whom the world is crucified unto Me, and I unto the world"* (Gal. 6:14).

The Apostle also said: *"For the preaching* (Word) *of the Cross is to them who perish foolishness; but unto us which are saved, it is the Power of God"* (I Cor. 1:18).

For the homosexual to be delivered, or anyone else, the *"Truth"* must be presented unto them (Jn. 8:32).

The Cross is the answer for their problem and, in fact, the only answer. There is Salvation in no other!

HOW IS THE CROSS THE POWER OF GOD?

Within itself, at least as far as the wooden beam is concerned, the Cross contained no power. To be frank, even the death of Christ, at least within itself, contained no power, as ought to be obvious. The *"Power"* has to do with the Holy Spirit, and the following is the way it works.

When Jesus died on the Cross, He died as a Sacrifice which atoned for all sin, thereby, satisfying the righteous demands of a thrice-Holy God. Jesus didn't go to the Cross to satisfy Satan, or to pay any debt to Satan. God doesn't owe Satan anything. Jesus went to the Cross because a just debt was owed to God, which man could not satisfy (Rom. 6:3-5).

To be sure, God has Power to regenerate man without the Cross; however, His righteous Nature will not allow a legal debt to go unpaid. While God, being all-powerful, can do anything, it must be ever remembered that He will do nothing opposite of His Nature, which is pure holiness, pure righteousness! So the debt had to be paid, and Jesus paid it by offering up Himself.

In fact, all of this was planned from before the foundation of the world (I Pet. 1:18-20).

Through foreknowledge, God knew that He would make the world, would create man, and that man would Fall; therefore, the Godhead determined, from before the foundation of the world, as to how man would be redeemed, which was by the Cross.

Now either you believe what the Bible says about the Cross, as it regards the deliverance of humanity, or else you don't believe it! There is no middle ground with the Cross. It is either, *"Jesus Christ and Him Crucified,"* as the answer to hurting humanity (I Cor. 1:23), or else you have put your faith in some other thing. As stated, there is no middle ground.

SPIRITUAL ADULTERY

The phrase from Verse 37, *"They who have committed adultery,"* refers to idol worship, as the Lord looks at Judah as His wife, and He her Husband (Isa. 54:5).

As the husband and wife relationship, ideally, is the closest relationship possible, at least between humans, from this symbolic expression, we are made to see the type of relationship with all Believers desired by the Lord. Actually, the highest relationship of all, at least in the spiritual sense, is the Believer's relationship with Christ (Rom. 5:1; 6:3-14; 8:1-2, 11). This determines all victory, overcoming power, leading, and guidance for the Believer. Therefore, Judah's idol worship was looked at by the Lord as unfaithfulness and, therefore, *"spiritual adultery."*

Actually, the application holds true respecting anything placed ahead of the Lord, or even on an equal basis! The idea is further strengthened by the phrase, *"And with their idols have they committed adultery."*

BLOOD ON THE HANDS

The phrase, *"And blood is in their hands,"* refers to the heathen nations to which Judah was responsible for taking the Word of the Lord, but yet failed to do so. In fact, they became worse in their abominations, even than the heathen.

The Lord had plainly told Ezekiel that if Judah, or any Believer for that matter, did not faithfully warn the wicked of their spiritual plight, that *"his blood will I require at your hand"* (Ezek. 3:18).

HUMAN SACRIFICE

The phrase, *"To pass for them through the fire, to devour them,"* had to do with Judah offering up her sons in human sacrifice to the hideous god Molech. It is difficult to imagine a person so depraved, especially one who has once known God, who would offer up his own flesh and blood in human sacrifice!

These children were not raised in the fear of God, but instead were raised to be offered to Molech.

While the modern Church may draw back from such with horror, the truth is, the modern Church is basically doing the same thing.

The other night, I happened to be looking at a *"Christian"* channel over television, and was grieved at what I saw. An entertainer (yes, we have Christian entertainers now!) was spot-lighting his new video. It was an imitation of rap music, with all the dancing, bucking, and grunting that went with such a production. He was talking about J. C. being in the house, etc. Incidentally, J. C. stood for Jesus Christ.

When the thing concluded, which sadly is not the exception but rather the norm, the host of the program, who is affiliated with the Assemblies of God, exclaimed as to how much he liked the video, and then asked where the performer had learned his dance technique!

The performer, Carman, replied that he had been taught by a dance instructor, whom both of them seemed to have known, etc.

The excuse is that such is needed to *"reach the youth."*

"Reach them for what?" I might quickly ask, because it certainly is not going to reach them for the Lord.

So what am I saying? I am saying, that through this abomination, which passes off for the gospel, young people are being led to *"Molech,"* just as the children of ancient Judah.

Sadder yet, most Christians so-called, think this which I have addressed is perfectly satisfactory. This only goes to show the state of the modern Church!

The idol worshippers in Judah claimed to be following Jehovah, as the idol worshippers today are claiming the same thing.

THE SANCTUARY

The phrase of Verse 38, *"Moreover, and this they have done unto Me,"* proclaims the Truth that the deepest depth of evil is the association of idolatry with God, which these Judaites did, and which, in essence, the modern Church is doing as well.

Verse 39 says that the Judaites would offer up their children as sacrifice in the morning, and then take a lamb to the Temple that afternoon and offer it as Sacrifice.

How could people become so spiritually blind?

How is the Church so spiritually blind today?

To be sure, the false prophets ignored all of this, constantly proclaiming peace and prosperity. The sins of Judah and Jerusalem were not touched by these false prophets, as the sins of this modern age are not touched by the present false prophets.

Look at the *"big names"* over what passes for Christian television! Are they warning people about sin? Are they preaching the Cross? The answer is *"no"* on both counts. They are preaching peace and prosperity, in other words, how to get rich.

Probably one can say without any fear of Scriptural contradiction, that presently, T.B.N. is the de facto leader of this apostasy. And yet, the modern Church pours hundreds of millions of dollars into these coffers, thinking all the time that they're supporting the Gospel of Jesus Christ, when in reality, they're supporting the work of the Devil.

CLEAR AND PLAIN PREACHING

I realize that many, in fact, most all, get very angry when we call names; however, I preach and I write what I believe the Lord has told me to say. I do not answer to man, but rather to God. My business is not trying to win a popularity contest, but rather to hear from Heaven, and then to faithfully deliver what *"Thus saith the Lord."*

I will not go so far as to say that everyone who is on the T.B.N. Channel falls into the same category, but I would definitely say that most all do! Religious evil is the worst evil of all. It must ever be remembered, that it was religious evil that crucified Christ, and, to be sure, were the time frames reversed, religious evil would crucify Him today, just as it did then.

A FALSE HELP

The phrase of Verse 40, *"And furthermore, that you have sent for men to come from far,"* refers to ambassadors which had been sent from time to time by both Samaria and Jerusalem to Egypt, Assyria, and Babylon, seeking alliances. In order to secure these alliances, they *"painted their eyes, and decked themselves with ornaments"* which means, they embraced the idol worship of that respective country.

Israel was intended by God to look to Him exclusively for all their needs, not to the heathen nations. Actually, this was not a suggestion, but a command. The reasons are obvious.

Not only could these nations not help Israel, but actually would cause great harm, as is portrayed in these Passages.

INTERCESSION AND THE HOLY SPIRIT

The phrase of Verse 41, *"And sat upon a stately bed,"* has reference to the Altar of Incense, which sat before the Veil immediately in front of the Holy of Holies in the Temple.

The phrase, *"Whereupon you have set My Incense and Oil,"* had to do with the Holy Incense, made of various spices, which was to be poured over the coals of fire brought from the Brazen Altar and placed on the Altar of Incense. It typified Christ in His High Priestly, intercessory role.

This Holy Incense, made of *"stacte, onycha, and galbanum, with pure frankincense,"* was to be used only in this capacity, and never to be used as a perfume applied to the physical bodies of the people (Ex. 30:34-38). If such were misused, it would mean the loss of the soul, *"cut off from the people."*

The intent of Verse 41 is to portray Judah giving praise and worship to idols, which praise and worship belonged only to God.

THE FLESH

The modern Christian should as well take all of this to heart, in that it is wrong to applaud the flesh, irrespective of the ability or talent, for praise and worship belong only to the Lord.

And yet, so much of Hollywood and the world have rubbed off on the Church that too often all of us has drifted from the true worship of the Lord to mere entertainment, which, in turn, receives our applause. How far we have strayed, and how so much this must grieve the Heart of God.

If the Lord would provide them, we should have excellent musicians and singers in our Churches; however, what is carried forth must never be placed in the realm of entertainment. It must always be to the Lord. Listen to the Psalmist:

"Rejoice in the Lord, O ye righteous, for praise is comely for the upright.

"Praise the Lord with harp: sing unto Him with the Psaltery and an instrument of ten strings.

"Sing unto Him a new song; play skillfully with a loud noise" (Ps. 33:1-3).

However, in all of this, the Lord must be glorified, and never the flesh. While our ability and talent certainly are to be used for the Lord, such ability and talent must not be applauded, but rather the Lord must be praised. In fact, man has nothing to offer, no matter how skillful he might be. It is the Lord Alone Who can meet our every need; consequently, the Lord Alone deserves our praise.

THE HEATHEN

Verses 42 through 45 proclaim the terrible state in which Judah and Jerusalem now find themselves. The phrase of Verse 42, *"And a voice of a multitude being at ease was with her,"* refers to the fact that Jerusalem had strayed so far from God, that now the heathen were *"at ease with her."* The reason being, Judah's religion was now no different that theirs!

What an indictment!

In Verse 44, the Lord calls Samaria and Jerusalem the *"lewd women."*

The phrase, as it speaks of Judah, that she *"played the harlot,"* has two references:

1. As a harlot, Judah was not only consenting to the idol worship of the heathen, but was actually pursuing and soliciting the activity.

2. The foreign powers, therefore, treated her as one, not holding back whatsoever in portraying even the most abominable (child sacrifice), which she eagerly accepted and practiced!

If it is to be noticed, the Holy Spirit, through the Prophet Ezekiel, in essence, said the same thing, while in different ways, over and over again. This was not without design. The Holy Spirit was trying to get through to these people the seriousness of their situation.

Likewise, as I am certain the Reader notices, I, too, am saying the same thing over and over, hopefully in different ways, to try somehow to awaken the Church. If the Holy Spirit followed this pattern, and He definitely did, then I have no alternative but to do the same.

(46) "FOR THUS SAITH THE LORD GOD; I WILL BRING UP A COMPANY UPON THEM, AND WILL GIVE THEM TO BE REMOVED AND SPOILED.

(47) "AND THE COMPANY SHALL STONE THEM WITH STONES, AND DISPATCH

THEM WITH THEIR SWORDS; THEY SHALL SLAY THEIR SONS AND THEIR DAUGHTERS, AND BURN UP THEIR HOUSES WITH FIRE.

(48) "THUS WILL I CAUSE LEWDNESS TO CEASE OUT OF THE LAND, THAT ALL WOMEN MAY BE TAUGHT NOT TO DO AFTER YOUR LEWDNESS.

(49) "AND THEY SHALL RECOMPENSE YOUR LEWDNESS UPON YOU, AND YOU SHALL BEAR THE SINS OF YOUR IDOLS: AND YOU SHALL KNOW THAT I AM THE LORD GOD."

The synopsis is:

1. Jerusalem suffered a just doom; her walls were beaten down with stones, her houses burned with fire, and her children slain with the sword.

2. This fearful doom was occasioned by their own conduct, and could not be ascribed to Divine injustice.

3. What we sow, we reap!

IDOLATRY

The *"lewdness"* of Verse 48 refers to idolatry. The Lord said, *"Thus will I cause lewdness to cease out of the land,"* which means that He would rid Israel of idolatry. If the people would not forsake it through Repentance, then they would forsake it through judgment.

The phrase of Verse 49, *"And they shall recompense your lewdness upon you,"* refers to Judah and Jerusalem receiving the very opposite of what they thought they would receive by their alliances. They thought that these heathen nations would help them, but, in fact, they instead turned on both Judah and Jerusalem.

The last phrase of Chapter 23, *"And you shall know that I am the Lord God,"* refers to the fact that if they would not know Him in Repentance, they would most definitely know Him in judgment.

We must not allow these lessons to be lost on us.

"Throw out the Lifeline across the dark wave,
"There is a brother whom someone should save;
"Somebody's brother! O, who then, will dare
"To throw out the Lifeline, his peril to share?"

"Throw out the Lifeline with hand quick and strong:
"Why do you tarry, why linger so long?
"See! He is sinking; O Hasten today
"And out with the Lifeboat! Away, then away!"

"Throw out the Lifeline to danger-fraught men
"Sinking in anguish where you've never been:
"Winds of temptation and billows of Woe
"Will soon hurl them out where the dark waters flow."

"Soon will the season of rescue be o'er,
"Soon will they drift to eternity's shore;
"Haste then, my brother, no time for delay,
"But throw out the Lifeline and save them today."

CHAPTER 24

(1) "AGAIN IN THE NINTH YEAR, IN THE TENTH MONTH, IN THE TENTH DAY OF THE MONTH, THE WORD OF THE LORD CAME UNTO ME, SAYING,

(2) "SON OF MAN, WRITE THEE THE NAME OF THE DAY, EVEN OF THIS SAME DAY: THE KING OF BABYLON SET HIMSELF AGAINST JERUSALEM THIS SAME DAY.

(3) "AND UTTER A PARABLE UNTO THE REBELLIOUS HOUSE, AND SAY UNTO THEM, THUS SAITH THE LORD GOD; SET ON A POT, SET IT ON, AND ALSO POUR WATER INTO IT:

(4) "GATHER THE PIECES THEREOF INTO IT, EVEN EVERY GOOD PIECE, THE THIGH, AND THE SHOULDER: FILL IT WITH THE CHOICE BONES.

(5) "TAKE THE CHOICE OF THE FLOCK, AND BURN ALSO THE BONES UNDER IT, AND MAKE IT BOIL WELL, AND LET THEM SEETHE THE BONES OF IT THEREIN.

(6) "WHEREFORE THUS SAITH THE

LORD GOD; WOE TO THE BLOODY CITY, TO THE POT WHOSE SCUM IS THEREIN, AND WHOSE SCUM IS NOT GONE OUT OF IT! BRING IT OUT PIECE BY PIECE, LET NO LOT FALL UPON IT.

(7) "FOR HER BLOOD IS IN THE MIDST OF HER; SHE SET IT UPON THE TOP OF A ROCK; SHE POURED IT NOT UPON THE GROUND, TO COVER IT WITH DUST;

(8) "THAT IT MIGHT CAUSE FURY TO COME UP TO TAKE VENGEANCE, I HAVE SET HER BLOOD UPON THE TOP OF A ROCK, THAT IT SHOULD NOT BE COVERED.

(9) "THEREFORE THUS SAITH THE LORD GOD; WOE TO THE BLOODY CITY! I WILL EVEN MAKE THE PILE FOR FIRE GREAT.

(10) "HEAP ON WOOD, KINDLE THE FIRE, CONSUME THE FLESH, AND SPICE IT WELL, AND LET THE BONES BE BURNED.

(11) "THEN SET IT EMPTY UPON THE COALS THEREOF, THAT THE BRASS OF IT MAY BE HOT, AND MAY BURN, AND THAT THE FILTHINESS OF IT MAY BE MOLTEN IN IT, THAT THE SCUM OF IT MAY BE CONSUMED.

(12) "SHE HAS WEARIED HERSELF WITH LIES, AND HER GREAT SCUM WENT NOT FORTH OUT OF HER: HER SCUM SHALL BE IN THE FIRE.

(13) "IN YOUR FILTHINESS IS LEWDNESS: BECAUSE I HAVE PURGED YOU, AND YOU WERE NOT PURGED, YOU SHALL NOT BE PURGED FROM YOUR FILTHINESS ANY MORE, TILL I HAVE CAUSED MY FURY TO REST UPON YOU.

(14) "I THE LORD HAVE SPOKEN IT: IT SHALL COME TO PASS, AND I WILL DO IT: I WILL NOT GO BACK, NEITHER WILL I SPARE, NEITHER WILL I REPENT; ACCORDING TO YOUR WAYS, AND ACCORDING TO YOUR DOINGS, SHALL THEY JUDGE YOU, SAITH THE LORD GOD."

The exegesis is:

1. The people boasted that Jerusalem was a cauldron (an iron pot) and they the food in it, and consequently, they were quite safe. This Prophecy (Vss. 1-14) informed them that the cauldron was corrupt and poisonous, and that its contents would be consumed.

2. The second Prophecy of this Chapter (Vss. 15-27) predicted that the destruction of the city and its inhabitants would be a calamity, so overwhelming as to extinguish public expression of private sorrow.

3. By Prophecy, the Exiles knew what the public could only have learned three months later by courier, owing to the distance of Jerusalem from the river Chebar.

PROPHECY FULFILLED

The phrase of Verse 1, *"Again in the ninth year, in the tenth month, in the tenth day of the month,"* coupled with the phrase of Verse 2, *"Even of this same day,"* signifies that, by Prophecy, the Exiles learned that on that very day, 590 B.C., Nebuchadnezzar laid siege to Jerusalem. For some thirty-eight years, Jeremiah had been prophesying of this time, and Ezekiel about four years. Tragically enough, even with Nebuchadnezzar at their door, and no one allowed to go in or come out of the city, the people still would not repent. Their hopes were on Egypt to come to their rescue, and not the Lord. Such shows the incurable disposition of their wicked hearts, in that they would rebel against the Lord until the very last.

The Apostle Paul grieved accordingly, sensing that terrible judgment in his day was coming upon Jerusalem, which it did. Jerusalem was invaded by the powerful tenth Roman Legion, under Titus, where over a million Jews were slaughtered in the carnage, with other hundreds of thousands sold as slaves at trifling prices (Rom. 9:1-3).

REBELLION

The phrase of Verse 3, *"And utter a parable unto the rebellious house,"* signifies the reason for the present dilemma of Judah. They were rebellious, and their rebellion was against God.

"Rebellion" is a critical concept in the Biblical doctrine of sin. As with other Biblical concepts, an understanding of rebellion hinges on core beliefs about the nature of relationships among human beings and between God and man. Rebellion means to be stubborn, hard, and determined not to respond to God. It means *"to rebel"* or *"to revolt"* indicating a violation of an established

relationship by a subordinate, and in this case, Judah against the Lord. This sin of rebellion involves a violation of God's Laws and Covenant requirements, and by it, Israel's relationship with God was repeatedly shattered.

Rebellion is one of the most serious concepts associated with sin. It portrays God as ultimate Sovereign, Who stooped to establish a well-defined relationship with mere human beings. Israel enjoyed many benefits through her unique Covenant relationship with Him. Yet, though God as the Superior in the relationship had been absolutely faithful to His Covenant obligations, Israel again and again proved unfaithful. She worshipped other gods, violated the Laws and Statutes that the Lord established, and stubbornly refused to acknowledge any fault.

HOW DOES GOD REACT TO REBELLION?

In respect to rebellion, the Lord offers His people two alternatives:

1. Turn to Him for Forgiveness and Salvation.

2. Persist in rebellion and be punished.

But however terrible the rebellion, there is no possibility that the purposes expressed in God's Covenant will be set aside (Isa. 46:8-11).

The Old Testament concept of rebellion is carried over into the New Testament as well! Spiritually, rebellion is a violation of the obligations established by the existence of a relationship with God.

That which protects the Believer today from rebellious attitudes and actions, is to *"fix our eyes on Jesus"* (Heb. 12:2), and keep our hearts open to God, obeying His Will as revealed in Scripture.

The primary key to responsiveness to ensure against rebellion in our heart is a simple but joyful trust in the Person of the Lord, and what He has done for us in the Sacrifice of Himself on the Cross. As we remain confident of His Love and Care, we remain open and responsive to Him (Heb. 3:7-19).

REBELLION AGAINST THE CROSS

As I've already noted several times in this Volume, in 1997 the Lord, in answer to soul-searching prayer, even day and night for nearly six years, began to open up to me the Message of the Cross, grandly and gloriously answering my petition.

How can the Believer live a victorious, overcoming Christian life, victorious, in effect, over the world, the flesh, and the Devil? And when I speak of *"victory,"* I'm speaking of perpetual victory, not just victory some of the time. No, I'm not speaking of sinless perfection, because the Bible doesn't teach such; however, I am definitely teaching that *"sin shall not have dominion over you"* (Rom. 6:14).

I cannot even begin to express to you, the Reader, how I felt as the Lord began to open up this great Truth to me concerning the Cross, which, in fact, continues unto this hour. To be sure, I had preached the Cross all of my life, literally seeing hundreds of thousands brought to a saving knowledge of Jesus Christ, and I exaggerate not. In fact, I preached the Cross so strong, claiming that it was the answer, and not humanistic psychology, that the leadership of the Assemblies of God, with whom I was then associated, grew incensed with me, in fact, to the point of hatred, which it seems, exists even unto this very hour.

But the truth of all of this is, I understood the Cross as it regards Salvation, and at the same time, I knew that Calvary was the answer to all of the problems of man, but I didn't know how. In other words, I had no idea as to how the Cross affects our Sanctification, our daily walk with God. As stated, I knew that it had a connection, but I simply did not understand what Paul taught as it regards this great subject, and as is found in Romans, Chapter 6.

Looking back, I did not know a single Preacher who understood this great Truth, actually the very foundation of the Gospel. Satan had been very successful in alienating the Church from the Cross. I think I can say without fear of Scriptural contradiction, that the Evil One used the Word of Faith Doctrine, as he used nothing else, to foster and nurture this false direction.

At any rate, the Holy Spirit soon made it real to me, that this Revelation of the Cross was not for me only, but for the entirety of the Church world. In fact, and as already stated elsewhere in this Volume, the Cross of Christ is the dividing line between the True Church and the apostate church.

THE RESPONSE OF THE CHURCH TO THE CROSS

While it is imperative that the Message of the Cross be delivered to the modern Church, and which we are attempting to do with all that is within our power, and as God helps us, still, I do not labor under an illusion that the Church as a whole is going to accept this of which we speak. To be sure, there will be many Believers who definitely will accept this Message, and will see their lives gloriously revolutionized; in other words, they will learn what true Christianity actually is. They will learn what Jesus was speaking about when He spoke of *"more abundant life"* (Jn. 10:10). But as far as the leadership of most Religious Denominations, I doubt very seriously if there will be much change. Why?

In the first place, the Cross addresses every single aspect of one's life, living, and walk with God. It leaves absolutely nothing out of the picture. It points out idols, of which religion is the biggest of all, and it points out relationships. The Cross lets us know exactly Who the Lord Jesus actually is, and what He has done. As well, the Cross shows us for what we are, and it's not a very pretty picture. Once the Message of the Cross is fully understood, such a Believer will then begin to fully understand just how much he needs Christ, and what He did for us at the Cross. Let me give you an example:

The Assemblies of God and the Church of God, the two largest Pentecostal Denominations in the world, have both embraced humanistic psychology as the answer to the ills of the human race. They have done so in an open, concentrated action, leaving absolutely no doubt as to where they stand regarding this all-important issue.

Now the truth is, it is impossible to embrace this worldly system, and at the same time embrace the Cross. So I ask you the question:

Do you think the leadership of the Assemblies of God and the Church of God, as well as all of the other Denominations, are going to publicly denounce this nefarious system of humanistic psychology, thereby, telling the world they had been wrong about this thing all of these years? I don't think so! Do you think they are going to publicly stand up before the world and say, *"The Cross of Jesus Christ and the Cross alone is the answer"*? I don't think so!

It would be my prayer that they would, but instead, I see them going even deeper in the other direction.

ANGER

Now you must understand, to make these statements as boldly as I am making them, and to preach this which I am giving to you in this Commentary, does not at all endear me to those particular Religious Leaders. In fact, and I do not think I exaggerate, they hate Jimmy Swaggart. I regret that; however, were we dealing with makes and models of automobiles, or preferences regarding ordinary things, that would be different; however, we are dealing with the eternal souls of men. And to be sure, there are millions in Hell right now, even hundreds of millions, who wish that someone had been bold enough, willing to take the heat, in order to tell them the truth. But few will!

BLOOD

The phrase in Verse 6, *"Woe to the bloody city,"* refers to the Law as commanded in Leviticus, Chapter 17, Verse 13.

It states there that blood should be hidden in the Earth. But Jerusalem's guilt was visible and open, and cried as loud for judgment as blood exposed upon the top of a rock; and God, therefore, dealt with her as a bloodstained city.

The phrase, *"And whose scum is not gone out of it,"* refers to the entirety being scum. In other words, when all the scum was to flow to the top, and ladled out, there would be nothing left!

The phrase of Verse 7, *"For her blood is in the midst of her; she set it upon the top of a rock; she poured it not upon the ground, to cover it with dust,"* refers to the fact that Judah and Jerusalem had become so corrupt and depraved, that they no longer tried to hide their sin, but instead, did it openly as in the Face of God, not even trying to *"cover it with dust."*

This spoke of human sacrifice, as well as violence carried out against helpless victims who could not defend themselves. We must remember that this description is given thusly by the Holy Spirit, that all may know the depths of her evil, and the cause of her judgment.

The phrase of Verse 8, *"I have set her blood upon the top of a rock, that it should not be covered,"* in its simplest form, means, that if they would not allow Christ to cover their sins, then their resulted judgment would be open to all.

The seriousness of these statements could not be overemphasized! The seed-bed of every adverse calamity is here portrayed.

LIES

The phrase of Verse 12, *"She has wearied herself with lies,"* refers to all that which was not the Word of God. Judah chose to believe the lie instead of believing the Truth. As well, they little realized that they were actually becoming a part of the Word of God, for the Prophecies given by both Jeremiah and Ezekiel were more than mere examples, but actually, were the very Word of God itself.

In their heeding the false prophets, and verbally and physically attacking God's True Prophets, they, in actuality, were attacking God Himself. To attack His Messenger is to attack Him! Consequently, in a sense, every single individual in the world, and for all time, is either in obedience or disobedience, becoming a part of the Word of God, for it governs all!

Jerusalem and Judah were in this terrible condition of impending judgment, because they believed a *"lie."* In one way or the other, the entirety of the human race falls into the same category.

THE WORD OF GOD

That is the reason that every Christian must avail himself of the knowledge of the Word of God. It alone holds the answers to the problems of life. It alone provides the solution! Therefore, the Bible should be as much a part of our daily lives as the food we eat.

Actually, Jesus said that man's very existence depended on food and the Bible (Mat. 4:4). It is tragic when one realizes that many, if not most, Christians have never even read the Bible completely through one time. Actually, it ought to be read completely through every six months, or at least once every year.

Being the Word of God, its treasures are inexhaustible. It is the only mirror that one can look into and truly see one's self. It, within its very content, will demand a close relationship with its Author, the Lord Jesus Christ (Jn. 1:1-4).

Many foolishly contend that they do not read the Bible, because they cannot understand it! This is at least one of the reasons that I believe the Lord has had us to write these Commentaries. Hopefully, they will make the Word of God a little easier to understand. If so, their value, or any true Bible help, for that matter, cannot be overestimated.

THE PURGE

The idea of Verse 13 is that the Lord will *"cause My fury to rest upon you,"* until all the filthiness is purged. As we have repeatedly stated, the filthiness can be purged by Calvary, or it can be purged by judgment, but purged it shall be!

The Old Testament views punishment, as described here, in a personal context. Punishment is the action of someone in a superior and responsible position when that action dramatically affects the situation of a subordinate adversely. God, as the moral Judge of the universe, has the right and the responsibility to evaluate and punish humankind.

In the view of the Old Testament, acts that are sinful make the sinner guilty and bring inevitable punishment. No one can sin without a subsequent and necessary change for the worse in his or her situation. Actually, the view of the New Testament is identical!

THE CROSS

Even though there are always adverse effects to sin, still, punishment can be escaped, as these Passages constantly proclaim, if one will hold fast to Christ and His Word. In fact, Jesus took the punishment for sin on the Cross that rightly should have come upon mankind. Upon Faith in Him, and the Cross, the Lord not only affords the Believer the

Salvation purchased at Calvary, but, as well, the penalty for sin is transferred from the sinner to Christ. This is the reason that judgment is sure, severe, and terribly destructive, if one will not accept what Christ did at the Cross.

Even though Calvary was yet in the future concerning the Old Testament, still, humanity was judged by God exactly as they are in the New Testament and, therefore, after Calvary. In the Mind of God, Calvary has always been, and whether looking forward to it, or backward to it, Faith in its astonishing work was ever honored.

In fact, every single Sacrifice offered up in the Old Testament was meant to be a picture and a portrayal, actually a symbolism of the coming Redeemer, the Lord Jesus Christ, Who would redeem mankind by the vicarious offering of Himself on the Cross. The slaughter of the lambs, the heifers, the oxen, the goats, all proclaim this coming event, which stands at the very intersection of time. So, all who were saved before the Cross were saved by looking forward to that coming event, which refers to faith expressed in that which God would do, symbolized by the Sacrifices. Men are now saved by looking backward to an accomplished fact, in other words, a victory already purchased by what Christ did at the Cross. In Old Testament times, it was a prophetic Jesus to Whom one looked; now, we look to an historical Jesus, for the Work is completed, and Christ now sits at the Right Hand of the Father in Heaven, meaning that His great Sacrifice has been fully accepted, and there by His very Presence, He makes intercession for all who believe Him (Heb. 1:3; 7:25; 10:12-14).

JUDAH

The gist of Verse 14 is that Judah has gone so far down the road of wickedness, that even Repentance would not spare the nation, although it would save the souls of those who truly repented. The phrase, *"I will not go back, neither will I spare, neither will I repent,"* is solemn indeed! It should be a statement that every person takes to heart.

Even though the Lord will never turn away a soul who comes to Him in humility and brokenness, still, with each deepening sin, certain barriers are crossed, with some things being lost, unable anymore to be retrieved.

Judah, as we have stated, is a prime example. For a little bit over thirty-eight years, the Prophecies from the lips of Jeremiah had been going forth, with Ezekiel joining him, at least to the Exiles, at the last. During this time, the offer was given for them to repent, which would have not only saved their souls, but their nation as well! But now, that is too late! The nation cannot be saved, it must go into captivity.

REPENTANCE

However, I dare not, even for a moment, leave the idea that a person can go so far that Repentance is of little value. Such is never the case! No condition is too sordid, terrible, or far gone, that Repentance cannot, at least to a degree, turn around. Always, the soul will be saved, which is by far the most important! As well, much suffering can be spared.

The Bible teaches us that no one has ever gone too far, but that if they will turn to the Lord, He will save, cleanse, wash, and miraculously bring about in them a change. Jesus said, *"All that the Father gives Me shall come to Me; and him who comes to Me I will in no wise cast out"* (Jn. 6:37; Rev. 22:17).

(15) "ALSO THE WORD OF THE LORD CAME UNTO ME, SAYING,

(16) "SON OF MAN, BEHOLD, I TAKE AWAY FROM YOU THE DESIRE OF YOUR EYES WITH A STROKE: YET NEITHER SHALL YOU MOURN NOR WEEP, NEITHER SHALL YOUR TEARS RUN DOWN.

(17) "FORBEAR TO CRY, MAKE NO MOURNING FOR THE DEAD, BIND THE TIRE OF YOUR HEAD UPON YOU, AND PUT ON YOUR SHOES UPON YOUR FEET, AND COVER NOT YOUR LIPS, AND EAT NOT THE BREAD OF MEN.

(18) "SO I SPOKE UNTO THE PEOPLE IN THE MORNING: AND AT EVENING MY WIFE DIED; AND I DID IN THE MORNING AS I WAS COMMANDED.

(19) "AND THE PEOPLE SAID UNTO ME, WILL YOU NOT TELL US WHAT THESE THINGS ARE TO US, THAT YOU DO SO?

(20) "THEN I ANSWERED THEM,

THE WORD OF THE LORD CAME UNTO ME, SAYING,

(21) "SPEAK UNTO THE HOUSE OF ISRAEL, THUS SAITH THE LORD GOD; BEHOLD, I WILL PROFANE MY SANCTUARY, THE EXCELLENCY OF YOUR STRENGTH, THE DESIRE OF YOUR EYES, AND THAT WHICH YOUR SOUL PITIES; AND YOUR SONS AND YOUR DAUGHTERS WHOM YOU HAVE LEFT SHALL FALL BY THE SWORD.

(22) "AND YOU SHALL DO AS I HAVE DONE: YOU SHALL NOT COVER YOUR LIPS, NOR EAT THE BREAD OF MEN.

(23) "AND YOUR TIRES SHALL BE UPON YOUR HEADS, AND YOUR SHOES UPON YOUR FEET: YOU SHALL NOT MOURN NOR WEEP; BUT YOU SHALL PINE AWAY FOR YOUR INIQUITIES, AND MOURN ONE TOWARD ANOTHER.

(24) "THUS EZEKIEL IS UNTO YOU A SIGN: ACCORDING TO ALL THAT HE HAS DONE SHALL YOU DO: AND WHEN THIS COMES, YOU SHALL KNOW THAT I AM THE LORD GOD.

(25) "ALSO, THOU SON OF MAN, SHALL IT NOT BE IN THE DAY WHEN I TAKE FROM THEM THEIR STRENGTH, THE JOY OF THEIR GLORY, THE DESIRE OF THEIR EYES, AND THAT WHEREUPON THEY SET THEIR MINDS, THEIR SONS AND THEIR DAUGHTERS,

(26) "THAT HE WHO ESCAPES IN THAT DAY SHALL COME UNTO YOU, TO CAUSE YOU TO HEAR IT WITH YOUR EARS?

(27) "IN THAT DAY SHALL YOUR MOUTH BE OPENED TO HIM WHICH IS ESCAPED, AND YOU SHALL SPEAK, AND BE NO MORE DUMB: AND YOU SHALL BE A SIGN UNTO THEM; AND THEY SHALL KNOW THAT I AM THE LORD."

The diagram is:

1. The Temple was the desire of the Hebrews' eyes, even as Ezekiel's wife was to him.

2. The Prophet was to be dumb to his people until the arrival, some three years later, of the messenger announcing the capture of Jerusalem by the Babylonians.

3. God took from Ezekiel his happiness, and with Paul he left the thorn, thus fitting them as Preachers the more fully to sympathize with suffering humanity, and, at the same time, fortifying them against falling. Both men accepted the discipline.

THE DESIRE OF THE EYES

The Word that is given here, and we speak of the balance of the Chapter, presents one of the most sacred object lessons that could be given. It speaks of the death of Ezekiel's wife, with the Holy Spirit using this as a symbol, even as we shall see. Ezekiel, at this time, was about thirty-four years old, with his wife possibly being a little younger.

That the Holy Spirit would allow us into the sacredness and privacy of this moment in the Prophet's life is done only that the desired lesson may be learned. And yet, the pathos is so great, that whatever we write could never begin to touch the poignancy of the experience.

Verse 16 says, *"Son of man, behold, I take away from you the desire of your eyes with a stroke."*

From the text, we have absolutely no idea if his wife had been ill before, or, as the words *"with a stroke"* suggest, did it fall on him out of the proverbial blue? Questions thick and fast arise, but with few answers, and yet, we will attempt to address ourselves to at least the most obvious, and that which the Holy Spirit desires to teach us.

WHY DID NOT THE LORD HEAL HER?

The reason will become more obvious the deeper we go; however, we do learn from this Passage, plus others, that the Lord can, and does, bring sickness, if He so desires! While a proper interpretation of the Bible, I believe, will portray all sickness as originating with the Fall and, thereby, Satan, still, the Lord, in that He controls all, can use such if He so desires.

We also learn from this that anything and everything that happens to a Believer is either caused, or at least allowed, by the Lord. Of course, that could be said for the whole of creation, inasmuch as the Lord controls all, with Satan working within the parameters drawn out for him (Job, Chpts. 1-2).

While the Lord definitely does heal, He, as should be obvious, doesn't do so all the time. While it's always God's Will to heal the sick, sometimes, even as here, it's not His Wisdom.

Anytime we are sick, we should ask the Lord for healing; however, if healing doesn't come, we shouldn't berate ourselves as lacking in faith, and neither should we blame the Lord. We should leave it in His Hands, knowing that His Grace is sufficient for all things.

WHY WOULD THE LORD DESIRE THAT HIS FAITHFUL PROPHET SUFFER SO?

One of the great ingredients of the Christian Faith is Trust. One who demands all the answers now would probably not understand were they given. The Lord, to be frank, is not obligated to explain all things to us, but we definitely are obligated to trust Him for all things. The record is complete. Trust placed in Him has never been disappointed.

When Paul asked that the thorn of contention and difficulties be removed, the Lord refused to do so. But He did say to Paul: *"My grace is sufficient for you: for My strength is made perfect in weakness"* (II Cor. 12:7-9). Unfortunately, much of the faith teaching so-called, in the last several decades, has led Believers to think that any type of trouble or problem, and especially sickness, are all because of a lack of faith on one's part. While that certainly might be true with some, it's definitely not true with all, and I greatly suspect that it's not true with many.

The Lord is not a glorified bellhop, Who goes about doing our bidding. And yet, I'm afraid that this is the posture in which the Lord has been placed in much of the modern faith teaching. Some have even been so foolish to claim that if Paul had their faith, he could have escaped all of his difficulties and problems, which he enumerates to us in his Epistles. I beg to differ! Anyone who would claim that they have more faith than Paul, to use a street term, is smoking something! But yet, many Christians are regrettably following such stupidity — and stupidity it is!

A SIGN

The death of the Prophet's wife was to be a sign to the Exiles. All personal feelings were to be lost, or else to seem a small thing in comparison with the desolation of Judah.

What the Lord asked of the Prophet was dire indeed! Not only would he lose his wife, *"the desire of his eyes,"* but he was not even allowed to weep over her loss. Such made the hurt far worse.

His loss was great, but the loss that the entirety of the nation (and the world for that matter) was about to experience made his loss seem insignificant. Judah, as the light of the world, was being extinguished. The portend of that was so great that it defied description!

THE CONSECRATION OF THE PROPHET

Verse 18 proclaims the fact that Ezekiel, knowing that his wife had but hours left to live, yet obeyed the Lord in conducting a service *"in the morning."* What must have been on his mind as he attempted to speak to the people that morning hour? But yet, the Lord *"commanded"* him to do this, and he faithfully obeyed.

The degree of consecration here evidenced is far beyond the pale of most! And yet, it is the type of consecration demanded of all.

Certainly he would have far rather spent these last hours of her life at her bedside, yet the day was spent, not in ministering at her deathbed, but in one last effort to impress the teachings of the time upon the seared consciences and hardened hearts of his countrymen and neighbors.

The text simply says, *"And at evening my wife died."* When she expired, he no doubt was by her side. His hand must have held hers and caressed her so tenderly and gently, but then the deadly *"stroke"* came, and she was gone. She would, as Paul said, *"be with Christ, which is far better"* (Phil. 1:23).

There is no way that one can know the sorrow that filled the Prophet's heart that eventful night. From the direction of the text, it seems the news spread fast concerning her death. To say the least, the people are lacking in understanding regarding his demeanor, especially in view of his great loss.

He did not conduct himself as all others when they lose a loved one. There were no tears, or no outward sign of mourning; consequently, they would ask the question, as Verse 19 proclaims, *"Will you not tell us what these things are to us, that you do so?"*

Therefore, his strange demeanor had the

effect it was meant to have — to arouse them to ask questions. And the questions they asked implied that they had some knowledge that his conduct was, in some way, connected with his Office of the Prophet, and the message he was to deliver.

THE SANCTUARY

It seems that the Lord had given Ezekiel little reason as to why his wife was to be taken, but now, and almost immediately after her death, the explanation will be given.

Of course, the explanation answered very few of his questions. No doubt, he must have wondered why the Lord could not have used something else as a symbol, rather than the death of his beloved? If those questions came, which they no doubt did, Ezekiel would have placed them in the Hands of the Lord, to be answered at a coming glad day when there will be no more sorrow, and He will wipe all tears away from our eyes (Rev. 21:4).

Ezekiel's wife was a symbol of the Temple, the *"desire of the eyes of Israel,"* as proclaimed in Verse 21. As his wife died, so the Temple must die.

There is something exquisitely heart-rending concerning the phrase, *"The desire of your eyes,"* speaking of the Temple, but yet was used of his wife in Verse 16.

There is no way that one could properly explain what the loss of the Temple meant to Israel, and for the entirety of the world for that matter! This was where God dwelt, between the Mercy Seat and the Cherubim. It was His building, and, in fact, the only building on Earth that had ever been designed by Him. From there, He governed His People with His Presence, constantly hovering over them. As such, and being the only place in the world where God resided, therefore, its loss would be awful indeed, not only for Israel, but for all of mankind.

Regarding Israel, the Temple was not only called *"the desire of your eyes,"* but as well *"the excellency of your strength,"* for God was their strength.

In just a few months, when it would be destroyed by Nebuchadnezzar, they would learn that there is a sorrow which is too deep for tears, something that is beyond observation. The state which the Prophet describes is not one of callousness, or impenitence, or despair. It is meant to portray to them the seriousness of the situation, which hopefully will be the beginning of Repentance.

It must be remembered that all of these things, the destruction of the Temple, and the city, as well as the loss of so many people, are to happen about one year to eighteen months into the future.

EZEKIEL

Verses 22 through 24 continue to exclaim the coming judgment upon Judah and Jerusalem, which will be so severe, that it will be beyond comprehension.

The phrase from Verse 24, *"Thus Ezekiel is unto you a sign,"* denotes there had been other signs, such as the *"tile,"* the *"barber's razor,"* and the *"vine tree,"* etc., so now the man himself is to be a sign in this hour of bereavement.

The phrase, *"And when this comes,"* refers to the destruction of Jerusalem being yet future, but only months away.

As well, the phrase, *"You shall know that I am the Lord GOD,"* is used repeatedly in the Book of Ezekiel. The statement is designed thusly by the Holy Spirit for a specific purpose.

The people had long since ceased reverencing and respecting the Lord. They did not believe His Word, nor did they consider Him to be the Master of their fate. This is the reason the Holy Spirit constantly refers to their actions as *"adultery,"* i.e., *"spiritual adultery."* They no longer respected Who He was, nor what He said! They had long since begun looking to heathen countries for leadership, guidance, and support, therefore, making alliances with them, and, as well, serving their gods.

Therefore, this affirmative statement as to the Lordship of Jehovah is repeated over and over, that the people may understand, that it was the Lord Who did the doing and said the saying. If they would not respect His plea for Repentance, they would respect His display of judgment.

THE CHURCH

The phrase of Verse 25, *"When I take from them their strength,"* refers to the Temple, which will be destroyed, and which is their strength, but not in the way in which they now see such. They had ceased to understand that the Temple, which was the dwelling place of Jehovah, at least on Earth, was, and due to Him residing there, the cause of all their blessing, prosperity, strength, and glory. This was the *"joy of their glory,"* and *"the desire of their eyes."* It is the same with the modern Church.

The strength of the Church is not buildings, education, conferred educational degrees, money, entertainment, place or position, but, instead, the Glory of God. Without the *"Glory,"* the Church is no more than any other earthly organization. Actually, concerning the far greater majority of that which refers to itself as *"Church,"* it has long ceased to be of God, that is, if it ever was; consequently, it is no more than any organization such as the Masons, or the Knights of Columbus, etc. Only where the Lord actually dwells, which is the Born-Again Believer, whose body is a temple of the Holy Spirit, is the True Church (I Cor. 3:16).

THE SPIRIT OF THE LORD

The Holy Spirit, resident within the Body, is the strength of the Church, and that alone! Buildings, organization, money, education, etc., count not at all, only the Spirit of God.

In the 1700's and the 1800's, the Baptist and Methodist organizations were mightily used of God to help steer America and Canada in the right direction. One could say, without fear of exaggeration, I think, that the Methodist Church, in those years, fanned the flame of revival to such an extent that these twin countries were set on a road of freedom that would lead to greatness. The greatness of this nation was born during those years. It is owed to the spiritual fervor of the Move of God at that time.

In the late 1800's, the spiritual fires of the Baptists and Methodists began to ebb, which occasioned the rise of those who called themselves *"Holiness,"* and because of becoming tired of religious formalism, and hungering for a Move of God, which would bring Righteousness. These as well greatly influenced America and the world. Sadly, after a period of time, this flame ebbed, and for the most part, succumbed to legalism.

Along about the turn of the Twentieth Century, hearts hungering for the Holy Spirit, and tired of formalism and legalism, began to importune the Lord for an outpouring of His Spirit. He did not disappoint them, and as a result of these hungry hearts, the Latter Rain, prophesied by Joel, began to be poured out on the entire world, which would, without doubt, usher in the greatest Move of God the world had ever known (Joel 2:23; Acts 2:1-4).

These people called themselves Pentecostals, because they taught the Acts 2:4 experience as a definite Work of Grace, subsequent to Salvation, given for Power, which brought the Church into a new dimension. In those days, it was not called a Denomination, and actually, it preferred to be referred to as a *"Movement"*; consequently, this *"Movement"* girdled the globe, with one of, if not, the most powerful missions effort ever known to man. Its priority was the taking of the Gospel of Jesus Christ to the entire world. This was done with very little organization, and even less money, but instead with the Power of the Holy Spirit, which made the Book of Acts alive again.

APOSTASY

Sadly, even as those who preceded us (for I am Pentecostal), we, at least for the most part, seem to have lost our way. When we were on the wrong side of the tracks, we looked to God; but now that material prosperity has come, there is little dependence anymore on the Moving and Operation of the Holy Spirit. We have forgotten that the *"strength, the joy of our glory, the desire of our eyes,"* is the Holy Spirit, Who always lifts up Christ. He Who made us great has been traded for psychology. The Wisdom of God has been traded for the wisdom of man.

To be sure, there is much religious machinery which generates much religious activity and, therefore, the appearance remains; however, the most dangerous thing that can happen to a Church is for it to be able to function without the Holy Spirit. It is striking evidence that He, at least for the most part, is gone, and we don't even know it!

THE REFORMATION

The Church, at least at times, talks about the need for Revival. While that is certainly true, the extended truth is, we cannot have Revival until we first have a Reformation. In other words, the Church must come back to the Cross, which means that the Biblical fundamentals of Christianity are once again embraced. The Lord cannot bless false doctrine; cannot function in the midst of false doctrine; will not work in that capacity.

In some ways, the Reformation now needed, is at least as dire as the Reformation brought about during the time of Martin Luther, or, even in some ways, more so. In many ways, the Reformation needed is identical to that particular time.

The Catholic Church, which gradually came into being, slowly took the Church into a Salvation by works, which, of course, the Lord could not accept. So, the Reformation begun by Martin Luther was designed by the Holy Spirit to take the Church back to the Cross, which is the foundation for *"Justification by Faith"* (Rom., Chpts. 4-5).

Again I state: This is at least one of the reasons that Jimmy Swaggart Ministries has survived. While we are certainly not the only one, still, I believe the Lord has brought us to this place in order that the great Word of the Cross might be given to a hurting world, and especially the Church, which we are doing everything within our power to carry out.

THE MESSAGE OF THE CROSS IS NOT OPTIONAL

The Word of the Cross is not something that one can take or leave. As previously stated, the Cross of Christ is the Foundation Doctrine of the entirety of Christianity (I Pet. 1:18-20). Without the Cross, there is no Biblical Christianity! So there must be a Reformation before there can be a Revival. As stated, this is not optional; it is the Cross or die! This is epitomized at the very dawn of the Word of God.

CAIN AND ABEL

Genesis, Chapter 4 gives us the account.

There was no difference between the brothers, Cain and Abel, but an eternal difference between their sacrifices. They were both corrupt branches of a decayed tree, both born outside Eden, both guilty, both sinners, no moral difference, and both sentenced to death. The words, *"by faith,"* as given to us in Hebrews 11:4, teach that God had revealed a way of approach to Him (Rom. 10:17). Abel accepts this way, Cain rejects it. Abel's Altar speaks of Repentance, of Faith, and of the Precious Blood of Christ, the Lamb of God, without blemish. Cain's altar tells of pride, unbelief, and self-righteousness.

THE ALTARS

Abel's Altar is beautiful to God's eye and repulsive to man's. Cain's altar, beautiful to man's eye, is repulsive to God's. These *"altars"* exist today: around the one, that is Christ and His Atoning Work, few are gathered; around the other, many are gathered. God accepts the slain lamb and rejects the offered fruit; and the offering being rejected, so of necessity is the offerer.

Cain's religion was too refined to slay a lamb, but not too cultured to murder his brother. God's Way of Salvation fills the heart with love; man's way of salvation enflames it with hatred. *"Religion"* has ever been the greatest cause of bloodshed.

The saga of Cain and Abel is pretty much the story of the entirety of humanity, and written on the first pages of human history. It is either the Cross, which is God's Way, or it's any one of ten thousands of ways devised by men, which God cannot accept, and which will ultimately be the occasion of His wrath. Paul said:

"For therein is the Righteousness of God revealed from faith to faith: as it is written, the just shall live by faith.

"For the Wrath of God is revealed from Heaven against all ungodliness and unrighteousness of men, who hold the Truth in unrighteousness" (Rom. 1:17-18).

REVEALED TRUTH

The phrase of Verse 26, *"In that day,"* refers to the time, and just a few months hence, when Jerusalem would be totally destroyed, and the few who would *"escape"* that carnage and, therefore, taken captive into Babylonia, would then tell the sad news to the Exiles. The news would be so horrible that it would defy description! All that Jeremiah and Ezekiel had prophesied, and the people had refused to believe, now, they would *"hear it with their ears."*

In all the forty years before, when the Lord, through Jeremiah, and then in the last few years through Ezekiel, had warned the people, much, if not all of this, could have been avoided! Their Messages were not heeded, but instead vilified. And now, word for word, they will hear all of the horrible details with an effect so drastic that they can hardly believe what they hear.

THE SIGN

After this Message, it seems that the Prophet was to speak no more to his people, but was instead, as Verse 27 says, to be *"dumb,"* and would remain so, until the arrival some months later of the messengers announcing the fall of Jerusalem to the Babylonians. This would include the total destruction of the Temple.

These months, or possibly even a little more than a year, of the silence imposed upon Ezekiel, would serve as another sign as well!

The silence spoke loudly for the Lord by saying, *"I have said all there is to say, and the deed is now done."*

No more offers for Repentance were given, at least by Ezekiel. No more pleas, warnings, or detailed explanation as to what was going to happen. All of that was now past. Only when the messenger came, bearing the terrible news of the fulfillment of all the Prophecies, would the Lord once again open the Prophet's mouth, with him then speaking the Word of the Lord regarding other countries, and, beautifully so, Israel's future restoration.

"Saviour, more than life to me,
"I am clinging, clinging close to Thee;
"Let Your precious Blood applied,
"Keep me ever, ever near Your side."

"Thro' this changing world below,
"Lead me gently, gently as I go;
"Trusting Thee, I cannot stray,
"I can never, never lose my way."

"Let me love Thee more and more,
"'Til this fleeting, fleeting life is o'er;
"'Til my soul is lost in love,
"In a brighter, brighter world above."

CHAPTER 25

(1) "THE WORD OF THE LORD CAME AGAIN UNTO ME, SAYING,

(2) "SON OF MAN, SET YOUR FACE AGAINST THE AMMONITES, AND PROPHESY AGAINST THEM;

(3) "AND SAY UNTO THE AMMONITES, HEAR THE WORD OF THE LORD GOD; THUS SAITH THE LORD GOD; BECAUSE YOU SAID, AHA, AGAINST MY SANCTUARY, WHEN IT WAS PROFANED; AND AGAINST THE LAND OF ISRAEL, WHEN IT WAS DESOLATE; AND AGAINST THE HOUSE OF JUDAH, WHEN THEY WENT INTO CAPTIVITY;

(4) "BEHOLD, THEREFORE I WILL DELIVER YOU TO THE MEN OF THE EAST FOR A POSSESSION, AND THEY SHALL SET THEIR PALACES IN YOU, AND MAKE THEIR DWELLINGS IN YOU: THEY SHALL EAT YOUR FRUIT, AND THEY SHALL DRINK YOUR MILK.

(5) "AND I WILL MAKE RABBAH A STABLE FOR CAMELS, AND THE AMMONITES A COUCHING PLACE FOR FLOCKS: AND YOU SHALL KNOW THAT I AM THE LORD.

(6) "FOR THUS SAITH THE LORD GOD; BECAUSE YOU HAVE CLAPPED YOUR HANDS, AND STAMPED WITH THE FEET, AND REJOICED IN HEART WITH ALL YOUR DESPITE AGAINST THE LAND OF ISRAEL;

(7) "BEHOLD, THEREFORE I WILL STRETCH OUT MY HAND UPON YOU, AND WILL DELIVER YOU FOR A SPOIL TO THE HEATHEN; AND I WILL CUT YOU OFF FROM THE PEOPLE, AND I WILL CAUSE YOU TO PERISH OUT OF THE COUNTRIES: I WILL DESTROY YOU; AND YOU SHALL KNOW THAT I AM THE LORD."

The composition is:

1. The Prophet, dumb to Israel, now speaks to seven neighboring nations; that is, to the world at large, under the dominion of Babylon.

2. One great lesson learned from this Chapter is: not to rejoice when God punishes guilty men, for that will bring His anger upon such as do so.

3. The Ammonites, the Moabites, the Edomites, and the Philistines have perished as nations, but the Israelites exist in millions. This fact is one of the many proving the inspiration of the Bible.

THE AMMONITES

"The Word of the LORD," coming to Ezekiel, will now address seven neighboring nations. These were under the dominion of Babylon, or soon would be. They are as follows:

1. Ammon (25:1-7).
2. Moab (25:8-11).
3. Edom (25:12-14).
4. Philistia (25:15-17).
5. Tyre (26:1-28:19).
6. Zidon (28:20-26).
7. Egypt (29:1-32:32).

Such proclaims the Lord's dominion over all Gentile powers, as well as Israel, and very specifically, as to how they related to Israel.

What is remarkable in these Prophecies by Ezekiel is that He has no message for Babylon, which, for Isaiah and Jeremiah, was the leading representative of the world powers considered in their antagonism to the Divine Kingdom.

As to why no word was given by Ezekiel concerning Babylon is known only to the Lord, as the Prophet only proclaimed what the Lord gave him. In fact, the omitting of Babylon does not show lack of inspiration on the part of Ezekiel, but instead, great inspiration. If he had been speaking out of his own mind, Babylon would, no doubt, have been the chief topic; however, that which he said was *"the Word of the LORD."*

The country of Ammon, with Rabbah as its chief city, bordered Israel on the east. The Jordan River separated the two countries (this is a part of present-day Jordan).

At the time of the Exodus, Israel did not conquer Ammon (Deut. 2:19, 37; Judg. 11:15); however, the Ammonites were condemned for joining the Moabites in hiring Balaam, and were forbidden to enter the congregation of Israel to the tenth generation (Deut. 23:3-6). The god of the Ammonites was Molech, and addressed as *"Milcom."*

After the return from exile, Tobiah, the governor of Ammon, hindered the building of the walls by Nehemiah (Neh. 2:10, 19; 4:3, 7). Inter-marriage between the Jews and the Ammonites was censured by both Ezra and Nehemiah (Ezra 9:1-2; Neh. 13:1, 23-31). They were, at least for the most part, bitter enemies of Israel. The Holy Spirit tells Ezekiel, as recorded in Verse 2, *"Prophesy against them."*

A JEALOUS GOD

The phrase of Verse 3, *"Thus saith the Lord GOD; because you said, Aha, against My Sanctuary, when it was profaned; and against the Land of Israel, when it was desolate; and against the house of Judah, when it went into captivity,"* proclaims the anger of the Lord registered against the Ammonites, because they gloated over the fall of Judah and Jerusalem. We learn from Jeremiah 40:14 that the name of the Ammonite King, at this time, was Baalis.

Psalm 83 and the Prophecy of Obadiah, along with Psalm 137, with Lamentations, Chapter 4 and Amos 1:11 should be read in connection with this Prophecy.

The Ammonites, the Moabites, the Edomites, and the Philistines have all perished as nations, but the Israelites exist in millions.

The Lord is a jealous God concerning His people, and that jealousy explodes into anger when a hand is lifted against them, and irrespective of their guilt. He Alone reserves the right to order and carry out chastisement. To be sure, His Judgment is swift in the sense that it is commanded, even though there may be a period of time before it is carried out.

These Passages, however, tell us that carried out it will be! His Word still is, *"Touch not My anointed, and do My Prophets no harm"* (Ps. 105:15).

While it is true that the Lord ordained the Babylonians to serve as His instrument of chastisement against Judah, still, they were unwitting participants; however, He did not ordain the *"Ammonites,"* or anyone else for that matter, to gloat over the Fall of His people.

ISRAEL

The phrase of Verse 4, the *"Men of the east,"* refers to Babylon. About five years after the destruction of Jerusalem, these nations, including Ammon, were conquered by the Chaldeans. They took over the *"palaces"* of the Nobles, and *"made their dwellings in them."*

The phrase, *"They shall eat your fruit, they shall drink your milk,"* refers to all the riches and possessions of the Ammonites, which were plundered by the Babylonians. Their *"Aha"* against the *"Temple, when it was profaned,"* was an expensive laugh!

We learn from these Passages, that the world of that day was judged in relationship to Israel. Nations and Empires rose and fell according to how they related to these people. Likewise, but perhaps in a more limited way, the world is judged by God as to how they relate to the Church, His Body (The True Church, not the apostate church); however, the nations then did not understand that, and neither do they now!

The might, power, and prestige of the United States are wrapped up in the number of people in this country who are truly Born-Again. The powers that be do not know that, neither would they believe it, were it related to them; however, it is the truth! The fortunes of this country ride exclusively upon the spiritual condition of those who are Born-Again.

Looking at the New Testament, we find that the mighty Roman Empire was addressed only as it impacted the Church, i.e., the Work of God on Earth. Otherwise, it was of no consequence!

THE LAND OF ISRAEL

The phrase of Verse 6, *"Stamped with the feet,"* means that the Ammonites danced with joy when the Temple was burned, and Jerusalem was destroyed. The Lord saw all of this, and would now call it to account.

"The Land of Israel," as stated in this Verse, even though sinful and wicked, was still very special to the Lord. Even though it had been soiled, defiled, and polluted, still, it was His Land, and His people; therefore, the rejoicing at their Fall was, in effect, an insult directly to Jehovah.

In these Passages, one can readily see the parental feelings of the Lord. Irrespective of how truant a child may be, and the degree of punishment the parent felt should be administered, still, for another person, and especially a stranger, to exult in the punishment administered by the parent will not solicit approval, but only anger. Thus it is with God as well!

DESTRUCTION

The phrase of Verse 7, *"And I will cause you to perish out of the countries: I will destroy you,"* was carried out about three hundred years later. It is known that the Ammonites survived into the Second Century B.C., but that they died out after that, and ceased to be a nation, exactly as the Lord had spoken through His Prophet.

We learn several things from all of these Verses. First of all, that God controls all nations, as should be obvious, even though most of the people in these nations know Him little or not at all.

As well, we learn that His dealings with these nations, which we refer to as *"heathen,"* are predicated to a great extent on their treatment of Believers, whether those Believers are in another country, or whether they are in the particular country proper. As would be obvious, the Church is different than Israel of old, it being a nation. The Church, to the contrary, is Worldwide, but, of course, is concentrated in some countries far more than in others.

Also, as we look at Israel presently, it is obvious that the Jews are a long, long way from God. They are out of Covenant, out of favor, and in a state of rebellion; however, the Lord has promised, through the Prophets, that they will ultimately be restored, with them becoming a nation in 1948, the beginning of the fulfillment of these many Prophecies. The final result will be that they will accept Christ as their Lord, Saviour, and Messiah, which will take place at the Second Coming (Rev., Chpt. 19; Zech., Chpt. 12).

But despite their present spiritual declension, they still belong to the Lord; consequently, the great Promise, given by God to Abraham so long, long ago, where He said: *"I will bless them who bless you, and curse him who curses you"* (Gen. 12:3) holds true unto this hour. This means that the Arab world is ultimately going to pay severely for their opposition to Israel. It also means that the other nations of the world, such as France and Germany, while not openly opposing Israel, at the same time, giving her little help as well, will ultimately be taken into account by God.

Also, if the Truth be known, the Blessings of God upon the United States are, at least in part, because of our help given to Israel. We must not forget that! As stated, what God told Abraham, so long ago, holds true even unto the present time and, in fact, will always hold true.

(8) "THUS SAITH THE LORD GOD; BECAUSE THAT MOAB AND SEIR DO SAY, BEHOLD, THE HOUSE OF JUDAH IS LIKE UNTO ALL THE HEATHEN;

(9) "THEREFORE, BEHOLD, I WILL OPEN THE SIDE OF MOAB FROM THE CITIES, FROM HIS CITIES WHICH ARE ON HIS FRONTIERS, THE GLORY OF THE COUNTRY, BETH-JESHIMOTH, BAAL-MEON, AND KIRIATHAIM,

(10) "UNTO THE MEN OF THE EAST WITH THE AMMONITES, AND WILL GIVE THEM IN POSSESSION, THAT THE AMMONITES MAY NOT BE REMEMBERED AMONG THE NATIONS.

(11) "AND I WILL EXECUTE JUDGMENTS UPON MOAB; AND THEY SHALL KNOW THAT I AM THE LORD."

The structure is:

1. All of these nations mentioned in this Chapter were conquered by the Babylonians about five years after the burning of the Temple in Jerusalem.

2. These nations, although disavowing Jehovah altogether in favor of their gods, got to know, to their sorrow, that the God of Israel exists, and that He judges sin.

3. When the time came, these nations were quick to realize, that their gods, fabricated out of their own evil minds, were no match at all for Jehovah. The Muslims had better realize that Allah falls into the same category. This figment of evil men's imagination has made war on the Lamb, but the Scripture say, *"And the Lamb shall overcome them: for He is Lord of lords and King of kings"* (Rev. 17:14).

THE HEATHEN

The Holy Spirit directs these words toward Moab and Seir. Their sin was the same as that of Ammon, in that they exulted in the Fall of Jerusalem.

Whereas it was satisfactory for Jehovah to say this about His people, He would not tolerate anyone else likening them *"unto all the heathen."*

It also seems that these, as well as the Ammonites, served in Nebuchadnezzar's army against Judah (II Ki. 24:2).

MOAB AND SEIR

Moab and Seir bordered Israel on the east, and lay immediately south of Ammon. Seir normally stands for Edom, but here appears as distinguished from it, the latter nation having a distinct message in Verse 12. It may be that Moabites occupied Mt. Seir, and retained possession of it and, therefore, Ezekiel coupled the two names together.

At any rate, in the Ninth Verse, Ezekiel seems to address himself mainly to Moab. The phrase from Verse 9, *"From his cities which are on his frontiers, the glory of the country,"* has in it a touch of irony. This area had once been assigned to the Tribe of Reuben, and it was afterwards claimed as belonging to the Israelites by right of conquest (Judg. 11:23).

Collectively, this area was the glory of the country of Moab, having the best pasturage, but now denied to them because it had never really been theirs to start with, belong originally to Israel.

If one is to notice, sometimes hundreds of years will pass before God calls to account, but call to account He ultimately will! Repentance will always forego His Judgment, but these heathen nations, although at times appealed to by the Lord, seldom engaged in such.

AMMONITES

Verse 10 proclaims the Holy Spirit making the statement the second time, that the *"Ammonites"* will be blotted out, having said basically the same thing in Verse 7. This is not idle repetition, but to denote the certitude of the promised action.

Every single Word in the Bible, as it was originally given by the Lord, has meaning and weight, all out of proportion to our ability to comprehend. Inasmuch as it is the Word of God, Jesus said, *"Heaven and Earth shall pass away, but My Words shall not pass away"* (Mat. 24:35).

JUDGMENT

The phrase of Verse 11, *"And they shall know that I am the LORD,"* pertains to heathen nations who did not recognize Jehovah at all; however, irrespective of their ideas concerning Jehovah, it was Jehovah at this time with Whom they must deal.

Presently, the nations of the world give little respect to the Lord of Glory, little understanding that He controls all. The idea that they worship idols, such as Buddha, or one called Allah, etc., in their minds absolves them of any responsibility toward the Lord; however, and irrespective of their belief, their responsibility to the Lord is the same. In Truth, the so-called gods of this present world do not exist, but function in the same capacity as the idols of the heathen nations surrounding Israel of old.

ISLAM

Since September 11, 2001, the United States has become very aware of the religion of Islam. Regrettably, many Christians have the mistaken idea that *"Allah"* is just another name for God. It isn't!

The name of *"Allah"* was chosen by Mohammed from the three-hundred-plus gods worshipped by the Arabs about fourteen centuries ago. Actually, the name, *"Allah,"* harks back to the moon-god of the ancient Babylonian Empire. It is a derivative of Baal, as are most of those heathen gods of so long ago.

While the Muslims, after a fashion, pay lip-service to the Lord Jesus Christ, they do not at all believe that He is the Son of God, or that He rose from the dead. They claim that He only swooned on the Cross, and did not actually die; consequently, after being placed in the tomb, He revived a short time later. They refer to Jesus as a Prophet, but claim that Mohammed is far greater.

The religion of Islam is controlled more by demon spirits, at least as far as its opposition to Christ is concerned, than any other religion in the world today. While all religions are inspired by Satan, which means they originated with Satan, Islam is the worst!

The nations of the world which embrace this travesty enjoy less freedom than any other people on the face of the Earth, at least if Islam has its way. Its women are afforded no freedom at all, in effect, treated as second-class citizens, or even as slaves.

Economically, every Muslim country is a basket case. Poverty and ignorance rule.

The richest of the Muslim nations is Saudi Arabia. Its per capita income is about $13,000 per year, while the per capita income in the United States is approximately $50,000 per year. And of that $13,000 for Saudi Arabia, the far greater majority of that goes to the ruling body, with the per capita income of the majority of the country hovering at about $6,000 per year.

Gross ignorance and superstition prevail in all Muslim countries, because this demon-inspired religion of Islam controls everything. There is no such thing as freedom of religion in any Muslim country, and there is no such thing as separation of Church and State. As well, Islam is, by far, the most violent religion on Earth, with 99 percent of all terrorist activity on Earth being carried out by Muslims.

Our President is dead wrong when he states to the American people that Islam is a great religion of love and peace. Nothing could be further from the truth! Let the Reader understand the following:

If the Muslims had their way, they would kill every single American in this nation, and anywhere else in the world, plus every Jew. They do not lack the will, only the way. We need to always keep that in mind.

While, of course, all Muslims aren't murderers, still, its leading factions definitely fall into that category.

WHAT SHOULD THE POLICY OF AMERICA BE TOWARD MUSLIM COUNTRIES?

First of all, we should deal with them on the basis of properly understanding who they are and what they are. We should also understand that they hate us, which I think they have amply proven, and graphically so. Consequently, agreements cannot be made with these people, simply because they do not respect any agreement. If, in fact, they do respect agreements, it will only be as long as it suits their purpose, and when that is done, the agreement is thrown aside, and they then proceed to do whatever it is they desire to do.

As well, we must realize that their religion is not one of love and peace, but rather the most violent on the face of the Earth; also, we must never forget that they have sworn, and do presently swear, our total destruction. As stated, they do not lack the will, only the way.

It would be in America's best interests if we secured our oil from other sources, and, in fact, traded not at all with any Muslim country.

We should let them know, and in no uncertain terms, that any terrorist activity against us is going to be met with like force, and in no uncertain terms.

And in conjunction with all of that, we must understand that the religion of Islam is the driving force behind all of the terrorism, ignorance, and slavery, which rules all Muslim countries, and which desires strongly to rule the United States.

Concerning Israel, we should understand that the true purpose of the Muslims is that every Jew die, and that the entirety of the Land of Israel belong to the Arabs. That is their intention and their goal. As we've already stated, no agreement made with these people will be kept by these people. So whatever we do regarding appeasement, we do at our own peril!

THE NATIONS OF THE WORLD

It seems that the Lord's dealings with modern nations fall into one of three patterns:

1. If they fit into His Plan, as Babylon of old did, He will then bring certain things to pass in order that the Plan be carried out. As He is God and, therefore, Omniscient, Omnipotent, and Omnipresent, He can do these things without infringing upon the free moral agency of the leaders of these respective countries.

2. If they impact His Church, the True Body, in an adverse way, the Lord will *"execute judgment,"* exactly as He did on Moab and others.

3. If they do not fit into His Plan, and do not adversely affect His Body, they are dealt with only according to their sins.

However, His Judgments, unless it affects His Plan, because He is kind, loving, and longsuffering, may be many years in coming.

(12) "THUS SAITH THE LORD GOD; BECAUSE THAT EDOM HAS DEALT AGAINST THE HOUSE OF JUDAH BY TAKING VENGEANCE, AND HAS GREATLY OFFENDED, AND REVENGED HIMSELF UPON THEM;

(13) "THEREFORE THUS SAITH THE LORD GOD; I WILL ALSO STRETCH OUT MY HAND UPON EDOM, AND WILL CUT OFF MAN AND BEAST FROM IT; AND I WILL MAKE IT DESOLATE FROM TEMAN; AND THEY OF DEDAN SHALL FALL BY THE SWORD.

(14) "AND I WILL LAY MY VENGEANCE UPON EDOM BY THE HAND OF MY PEOPLE ISRAEL: AND THEY SHALL DO IN EDOM ACCORDING TO MY ANGER AND ACCORDING TO MY FURY; AND THEY SHALL KNOW MY VENGEANCE, SAITH THE LORD GOD."

The overview is:

1. While nations may not have anything to do with Jehovah, all definitely, sooner or later, will answer to Jehovah.

2. There is only one God, manifested in three Persons, *"God the Father, God the Son, and God the Holy Spirit."*

3. It is Jesus Christ with Whom the present world must deal. It gave Him its answer some two thousand years ago, but His appearance the second time will be totally different than the first time.

EDOM

The idea of Verse 12 is that *"Edom"* had held a longstanding grudge against Judah, which went back to Esau (their founder) and Jacob (Gen. 27:36). Ezekiel also called it the *"perpetual hatred"* (35:5).

What had been malicious exultation passed into overt acts of hostility. The moment of Judah's weakness was seized as an opportunity for gratifying Edom's wicked desires. Therefore, the Lord would pronounce judgment against it!

Edom was stretched out along the south

of Judah from the border of Moab on the Dead Sea to the Mediterranean and the Arabian Desert; and it held the same relation to Judah as Moab and Ammon did to the Northern Kingdom. Being long bitter enemies of Israel, they rejoiced over the destruction of Jerusalem by the Chaldeans, and showed great cruelty to Jews who fled to them for refuge.

VENGEANCE

As the word, *"vengeance,"* is used in Verse 12 concerning Edom's anger against Judah, likewise, the Lord uses the same word against them. He says, *"And they shall know My Vengeance, saith the Lord GOD."*

There is an obvious emphasis in the repetition of this word. The Law of Divine Retribution will work out its appointed purpose — vengeance on those who sought vengeance. The Edomites shall reap as they have sown, and shall know that the vengeance of Jehovah is more terrible than their own.

In reference to the phrase of Verse 14, *"And I will lay My vengeance upon Edom by the hand of My people Israel,"* the Holy Spirit, through Amos the Prophet, states that its subjugation is connected with the Messianic Prophesy that the fallen Tabernacle of David should be raised up (Amos 9:12). This will be at the Coming of the Lord.

(15) "THUS SAITH THE LORD GOD; BECAUSE THE PHILISTINES HAVE DEALT BY REVENGE, AND HAVE TAKEN VENGEANCE, WITH A DESPITEFUL HEART, TO DESTROY IT FOR THE OLD HATRED;

(16) "THEREFORE THUS SAITH THE LORD GOD: BEHOLD, I WILL STRETCH OUT MY HAND UPON THE PHILISTINES, AND I WILL CUT OFF THE CHERETHIMS, AND DESTROY THE REMNANT OF THE SEA COAST.

(17) "AND I WILL EXECUTE GREAT VENGEANCE UPON THEM WITH FURIOUS REBUKES; AND THEY SHALL KNOW THAT I AM THE LORD, WHEN I SHALL LAY MY VENGEANCE UPON THEM."

The synopsis is:

1. The Philistines are now addressed.
2. The sin of the Philistines is pretty much the same as the Edomites.
3. The three gods of the Philistines were, *"Dagon, Ashtoreth, and Beelzebub."* To these gods, they offered sacrifices and wore charms in battle (Judg. 16:23; II Sam. 5:21).

THE PHILISTINES

The phrase of Verse 15, *"The old hatred,"* and as it concerned the Philistines, proclaims the fact that, for many years, even centuries, they had been the enemies of Israel. It is from their name that the modern name *"Palestine"* is derived.

The Philistines are descendants of Ham, through Mizraim and Casluhim (Gen. 10:13-14; I Chron. 1:11-12). As far back as Abraham and Isaac they are mentioned, with these Patriarchs having dealings with them.

Their area of settlement was along the coastal strip of the Mediterranean, between Egypt and Gaza. Their major cities were, *"Gaza, Ashkeklon, Ashdod, Ekron, and Gath"* (Josh. 13:2-3). There was more conflict between these people by the Israelites than possibly any other group. From time to time, they were used by God to chastise the Israelites (Judg. 3:2-3).

Just before Saul became King, the Ark of God was captured by the Philistines in a disastrous battle at Apek, and the shrine of Shiloh was destroyed (II Sam., Chpt. 4). At this time, the Philistines probably controlled Esdraelon, the coastal plain, Negeb, and much of the hill-country. They also controlled the distribution of iron and, thus, prevented the Israelites from having useful weapons (I Sam. 13:19-22).

After Saul became King, they continued to assert themselves, as when they challenged Israel at Ephes-Dammin, and David killed Goliath (I Sam., Chpts. 17-18).

After David became King, he drove the Philistines out of the hill-country, and struck a heavy blow in Philistia itself (II Sam. 5:25), putting an end to the power of the Philistines as a serious menace.

However, after the death of David, the Philistines continued to cause trouble throughout the Monarchy. They were still aggressive in the time of Ahaz (Isa. 9:8-12), and the last time they are mentioned in the Bible is the Prophecy of Zechariah, after the return from the Exile.

DAVID

Verses 16 and 17 emphatically state that God will *"execute great vengeance upon the Philistines."* The *"Cherethims"* are probably the same as the *"Cherithites."* These are mentioned several times as chiefs of the warriors of David (II Sam. 8:18; 15:18; 20:7, 23; I Ki. 1:38, 44).

As stated, David subjugated these people, and they were made to serve Israel, at least in his day.

As a symbol of the flesh, which they were, David, as a Type of Christ, conquered them and made them serve Israel. When he defeated Goliath, even though there were other wars, he, personally, never was defeated by them, but always was victorious, forcing them to serve him. Conversely, Saul was finally defeated by them at Gilboa; therefore, the picture of them as representative of the flesh, and Saul never overcoming the flesh, the Philistines ultimately killed him.

Thus, the modern Christian should learn from both David and Saul. Through the Spirit, David was ever victorious, while through the flesh, Saul ever failed! Satan cannot be defeated in the flesh, as typified by Saul, only by the Spirit, as typified by David.

THE FLESH AND THE SPIRIT

Continuing to address this subject according to New Testament teaching, of which the Old Testament personalities were types, listen to Paul:

"There is therefore now no condemnation to them which are in Christ Jesus, who walk not after the flesh, but after the Spirit" (Rom. 8:1).

Most Christians have absolutely no idea as to what *"walking after flesh"* actually means, or *"walking after the Spirit."*

Paul uses the term *"flesh"* to portray human ability, strength, and power. In other words, it's that which we attempt to do as Believers, without the help of the Holy Spirit.

"Walking after the Spirit," of course, refers to the Holy Spirit, and points to the Cross. In other words, the Believer, when *"walking after the Spirit,"* places his Faith exclusively in Christ, and what Christ has done at the Cross, all on our behalf. Most people think that *"walking after the Spirit"* is doing spiritual things, whatever that might be; in other words, being faithful to Church, reading one's Bible, witnessing to souls about the Lord, etc. While all of these things just mentioned are very good, and which every good Christian will most definitely do, they do not constitute *"walking after the Spirit."*

Every single thing the Holy Spirit does is done within the confines and the parameters of the Finished Work of Christ, even as we've already explained in this Volume, it is all *"in Christ Jesus,"* which refers to what Christ did at the Cross. In fact, even as Romans 8:2 proclaims, the manner in which the Spirit works within our lives is governed by a *"Law."* It is *"The Law of the Spirit of Life in Christ Jesus."*

So, *"walking after the Spirit"* concerns our daily walk before God, in other words, the manner and way that we conduct ourselves, our lifestyle, and speaks of our total dependence on Christ, with Christ and the Cross ever being the Object of our Faith (Rom. 6:3-14; I Cor. 1:17-18, 23; 2:2; Gal. 6:14).

Many people think that *"walking after the flesh"* is watching too much television, or being too interested in sports, or whatever, etc. While those things may or may not be a hindrance, such have nothing to do with *"walking after the flesh."*

"Walking after the flesh" portrays the Christian attempting to live this life, to follow Christ, by rules, regulations, laws, etc. In other words, *"walking after the flesh,"* whether one realizes it or not, is rebellion against God's Way, which is *"Jesus Christ and Him Crucified"* (Eph. 2:13-18; Col. 2:14-15). And let the Reader understand, if the Believer doesn't understand the Cross, as it refers to Sanctification, which Paul explains to us in Romans, Chapter 6, then without fail, such a Believer is going to *"walk after the flesh."* In fact, every Believer on the face of the Earth is either functioning in *"Grace"* or *"Law."* This means that every single Believer is attempting to live his life either by *"the Holy Spirit"* or *"the flesh."*

There are no other alternatives! Paul said: *"For you are not under the Law, but under Grace"* (Rom. 6:14).

While it's definitely true that Believers under the New Covenant are no longer under

Law in any capacity, the facts are, if the Christian doesn't understand the Cross, and I refer to his Sanctification, which means that he doesn't understand Grace, then by default, he will automatically be under Law. While it may not be the Law of Moses, but rather a law that he has devised himself, or his Church, or his Denomination, still, it is law, and will bring about its negative results.

"Law," whether the Law of God as given to Moses, or laws devised by men, and we're speaking of religious laws, such have no power to help men obey these laws, and considering that the Holy Spirit will not function in such an atmosphere, that leaves the Believer with only his personal strength, i.e., *"the flesh."* As repeatedly stated, such a course is guaranteed of failure.

THE GRACE OF GOD

Even though this is the Dispensation of Grace, many Believers, although constantly speaking of Grace, have little understanding as to what Grace actually is.

First of all, the Grace of God is simply the Goodness of God, freely given to undeserving Believers. And yes, we definitely are living in the Dispensation of Grace, all made possible by the Cross (Eph. 2:8-9).

However, the fact that we are living in the Dispensation of Grace doesn't mean that Grace is an automatic factor, even as some think. The truth is, the Grace of God can be *"frustrated"* (Gal. 2:21), and as well, a Believer can *"fall from Grace"* (Gal. 5:4). Now what does all of this mean?

The Believer who frustrates the Grace of God refers to functioning in both Law and Grace. Christians who do this, mostly do this out of ignorance. In other words, they do not understand the Cross, so that means they don't understand Grace, so that means that part of the time, they're functioning in *"law"* and part of the time, they're functioning in *"Grace."* To be sure, even as the Holy Spirit through Paul exclaims, it is a *"frustrating experience."*

With such a Believer, which characterizes untold millions, not only are they frustrating the Grace of God by their constant leanings on the flesh, but they are also frustrating themselves.

Many of these Christians are very consecrated, and the frustration only deepens, when the harder they try, the worse the situation becomes. It leaves them in the exact state that Paul proclaimed, when he said: *"For that which I do I understand not"* (Rom. 7:15). (The Greek word translated *"allow"* should have been translated *"understand,"* because that's what it means.)

Until such a Believer has the Cross properly explained to him (or her), they will continue to function in the realm of frustration.

FALLING FROM GRACE

This phrase, as Paul mentions in Galatians 5:4, is misunderstood by most Christians. I remember some years back hearing quite a few Preachers discuss this subject, with virtually all of them exclaiming that when one sinned, that one had *"fallen from Grace."* They better pray they are wrong, simply because, if that is correct, then every Believer on the face of the Earth has fallen from Grace. No, that's not what the statement means.

In Galatians, Chapter 5, Paul is dealing with Believers who are forsaking the way of the Cross and resorting to law, and in that case, the Law of Moses. And remember, these were Gentiles. He said to them, *"Behold, I Paul say unto you, that if you be circumcised, Christ shall profit you nothing"* (Gal. 5:2).

In other words, if these Galatians were going to place their Faith in the Law of Moses, even as the Judaizers were trying to get them to do, what Christ did at the Cross would be of no profit for them. That's when the Apostle then said:

"Christ is become of no effect unto you, whosoever of you are justified by the law (seek to be justified by the Law); *you are fallen from Grace"* (Gal. 5:4).

"Falling from Grace" refers to Believers who know and understand the Message of the Cross and turn away from that Message, or else they have properly heard the Message of the Cross, and refuse to accept it. When this is done, this means that such a Believer has rejected God's Way, which is the Cross, rather opting for another way, with the Holy Spirit bluntly saying through the Apostle *"You are fallen from Grace."*

Such a direction stops the Grace of God

from coming to such an individual; regrettably, this characterizes millions as well. And if individuals continue along this path, with *"Christ profiting them nothing,"* which refers to their rejection of what He has done for them at the Cross, even though they have once been saved, they will now lose their souls, at least if they stay on this erroneous path.

Let us say it again: it is either *"Grace"* or *"law."* It is either *"the Holy Spirit"* or *"the flesh."*

According to all of this, the Believer should ask himself, *"Am I 'walking after the flesh,' or 'walking after the Spirit'?"*

"Never be sad or desponding,
"If you have faith to believe;
"Grace for the duties before you,
"Ask of your God and receive."

"What if your burdens oppress you;
"What though your life may be drear;
"Look on the side that is brightest,
"Pray and your path will be clear."

"Never be sad or desponding,
"There is a morrow for thee;
"Soon you shall dwell in its brightness,
"There with the Lord you shall be."

"Never be sad or desponding,
"Lean on the arm of your Lord;
"Dwell in the depths of His mercy,
"You shall receive your reward."

CHAPTER 26

(1) "AND IT CAME TO PASS IN THE ELEVENTH YEAR, IN THE FIRST DAY OF THE MONTH, THAT THE WORD OF THE LORD CAME UNTO ME, SAYING,

(2) "SON OF MAN, BECAUSE THAT TYRUS HAS SAID AGAINST JERUSALEM, AHA, SHE IS BROKEN THAT WAS THE GATES OF THE PEOPLE: SHE IS TURNED UNTO ME: I SHALL BE REPLENISHED, NOW SHE IS LAID WASTE:

(3) "THEREFORE THUS SAITH THE LORD GOD; BEHOLD, I AM AGAINST YOU, O TYRUS, AND WILL CAUSE MANY NATIONS TO COME UP AGAINST YOU, AS THE SEA CAUSES HIS WAVES TO COME UP.

(4) "AND THEY SHALL DESTROY THE WALLS OF TYRUS, AND BREAK DOWN HER TOWERS: I WILL ALSO SCRAPE HER DUST FROM HER, AND MAKE HER LIKE THE TOP OF A ROCK.

(5) "IT SHALL BE A PLACE FOR THE SPREADING OF NETS IN THE MIDST OF THE SEA: FOR I HAVE SPOKEN IT, SAITH THE LORD GOD: AND IT SHALL BECOME A SPOIL TO THE NATIONS.

(6) "AND HER DAUGHTERS WHICH ARE IN THE FIELD SHALL BE SLAIN BY THE SWORD; AND THEY SHALL KNOW THAT I AM THE LORD.

(7) "FOR THUS SAITH THE LORD GOD; BEHOLD, I WILL BRING UPON TYRUS NEBUCHADNEZZAR KING OF BABYLON, A KING OF KINGS, FROM THE NORTH, WITH HORSES, AND WITH CHARIOTS, AND WITH HORSEMEN, AND COMPANIES, AND MUCH PEOPLE.

(8) "HE SHALL SLAY WITH THE SWORD YOUR DAUGHTERS IN THE FIELD: AND HE SHALL MAKE A FORT AGAINST YOU, AND CAST A MOUNT AGAINST YOU, AND LIFT UP THE BUCKLER AGAINST YOU.

(9) "AND HE SHALL SET ENGINES OF WAR AGAINST YOUR WALLS, AND WITH HIS AXES HE SHALL BREAK DOWN YOUR TOWERS.

(10) "BY REASON OF THE ABUNDANCE OF HIS HORSES THEIR DUST SHALL COVER YOU: YOUR WALLS SHALL SHAKE AT THE NOISE OF THE HORSEMEN, AND OF THE WHEELS, AND OF THE CHARIOTS, WHEN HE SHALL ENTER INTO YOUR GATES, AS MEN ENTER INTO A CITY WHEREIN IS MADE A BREACH.

(11) "WITH THE HOOFS OF HIS HORSES SHALL HE TREAD DOWN ALL YOUR STREETS: HE SHALL SLAY YOUR PEOPLE BY THE SWORD, AND YOUR STRONG GARRISONS SHALL GO DOWN TO THE GROUND.

(12) "AND THEY SHALL MAKE A SPOIL OF YOUR RICHES, AND MAKE A PREY OF YOUR MERCHANDISE: AND THEY SHALL BREAK DOWN YOUR WALLS, AND DESTROY YOUR PLEASANT HOUSES: AND THEY SHALL LAY YOUR STONES AND YOUR TIMBER AND YOUR DUST IN THE MIDST OF THE WATER.

(13) "AND I WILL CAUSE THE NOISE OF YOUR SONGS TO CEASE: AND THE SOUND OF YOUR HARPS SHALL BE NO MORE HEARD.

(14) "AND I WILL MAKE YOU LIKE THE TOP OF A ROCK: YOU SHALL BE A PLACE TO SPREAD NETS UPON: YOU SHALL BE BUILT NO MORE: FOR I THE LORD HAVE SPOKEN IT, SAITH THE LORD GOD."

The exegesis is:

1. The Prophecy concerning Tyre occupies this and the two following Chapters.

2. This Chapter sets out its sin (Vs. 2); its punishment (Vss. 3-6); the executors of its doom—Nebuchadnezzar (Vs. 7) and Alexander (Vs. 12); and the effect produced on other nations by her judgment (Vss. 15-16, 18, 21).

3. The *"eleventh year"* of Verse 1 pertains to the years that Ezekiel had been in Babylonia, and the time of the fall of Jerusalem. The tidings of the capture may have reached both Tyre and Telabib, with the Prophet having already heard of the response of Tyre.

4. There were two Tyres. The older city was built upon a promontory jutting out into the sea. It was captured by Nebuchadnezzar, and its ruins thrown into the sea by Alexander the Great. New Tyre was built upon an island at a little distance from the shore, and was captured by Alexander the Great.

5. The siege of Tyre by Nebuchadnezzar lasted thirteen years.

6. *"Many nations as waves"* of Verse 3 pertain to the first wave, which was the Babylonians, and the last wave of invasion being the Greeks. The Prophecy of the Chapter embraces both destructions. Nebuchadnezzar destroyed her walls; Alexander the Great scraped her dust, for, in order to attack New Tyre, he built a causeway to the island through the sea with the materials of the Old Tyre, and history records that his soldiers, in order to complete the causeway, gathered the dust of Old Tyre in baskets and emptied them into the waters. Today, as for centuries past, the site of the ancient city is a bare rock upon which fishermen dry their nets.

7. These Prophecies are a striking demonstration of the inspiration of Scripture.

TYRE

The Holy Spirit devotes this Chapter, plus Chapters 27 and 28, to Tyre. Some of the reasons are as follows:

A. The gloating of Tyre over the fall of Jerusalem.

B. Tyre is an example of the world attempting to rebuild the Garden of Eden without the Tree of Life, i.e., the Lord Jesus Christ.

C. Man was created by God as a tripartite being, composed of *"spirit, soul, and body."* (I Thess. 5:23). As such, he must be dealt with spiritually, materially, and physically.

Tyre is an example of the world attempting to ignore the spiritual, which is actually the most important part, and placing total emphasis on the material and the physical; consequently, she served as an example for the whole world, as sowing to the flesh, and for all time (Gal. 6:8).

D. As such, her King, Ithobalis II, was a type of Satan, as will be outlined in Chapter 28.

The phrase in Verse 1, *"And came to pass in the eleventh year, in the first day of the month,"* some think refers to the fifth month. If that is the case, Jerusalem had just fallen, and the Temple would be burned and destroyed six days from this moment (II Ki. 25:3, 8-9). The tidings of the Fall of Jerusalem may have reached both Tyre and Telabib, and Ezekiel may have already heard of the response of Tyre. The Lord would use this occasion to give some astounding Prophecies, not only of Tyre, but of the spirit world as well!

THE GLOAT OF SATAN OVER THE FALL OF JUDAH AND JERUSALEM

The phrase, *"Aha, she is broken that was the gates of the people,"* refers to Jerusalem that had become, at least in some measure, an international mart. Quite possibly, a goodly number of Gentiles from surrounding countries had become proselytes to the God of Israel and especially under the administrations of Hezekiah and Josiah. The number could have been quite large, causing considerable traffic as they came to the Temple to worship.

At any rate, her trade with other nations would have been considerable, enough at least to cause Tyre to exult over her Fall, thinking now that such commerce would come her way. The phrase, *"She is turned unto me: I shall be replenished,"* reinforces that idea.

In the mind of Tyre, which was one of the great trade centers of the world of that day, the destruction of Jerusalem would, therefore, enrich her by the transference of this traffic to her.

The gloating over the Fall of Jerusalem, as evidenced by almost all of the surrounding nations, shows that they had absolutely no understanding whatsoever of her worth and value even to them. Jerusalem was the only city in the world where God resided, and as such, if Jerusalem had walked in the Light of the Lord, and these nations had taken advantage of that Light, which was intended by the Lord, their enrichment would have known no bounds. It would have been an enrichment far greater than material things, for it would have satisfied the true hunger of the soul, as only Christ can do; therefore, her Fall was, in effect, their Fall, but they did not have enough spiritual sense to realize it.

THE FOUNDING OF TYRE

According to Herodotus, Tyre was founded in 2700 B.C. The city became prosperous and became the principal Phoenician port controlling the Phoenician coast. It was actually on the border of Israel on the north and next to the land allocated to the Tribe of Asher (Josh. 19:29).

By the time of David, Hiram I, King of Tyre, being David's friend, supplied materials for building the royal palace at Jerusalem (II Sam. 5:11; I Ki 5:1; I Chron. 15:1), a policy that was continued by Tyre during the reign of Solomon, when Hiram sent wood and stone for the construction of the Temple (I Ki. 5:1-12; II Chron. 2:3-16).

During this time, Hiram I, even though exposed to the God of Israel, continued to worship the deities Melqart and Astarte. However, because of his help to David and Solomon, the Lord blessed Tyre, in that this period was called *"The golden age of Tyre."* It became the merchant Prince of the Eastern Mediterranean.

After this time, Tyre suffered invasions, but by the time of Jeremiah and Ezekiel, had regained her autonomy and much of her former sea-trade; therefore, at the time of the Prophecies of both Jeremiah and Ezekiel concerning this city, she was strong, prosperous, and due to the Fall of Jerusalem, expecting to grow even more prosperous.

THE OPPOSITION OF GOD

The phrase of Verse 3, *"Therefore thus saith the Lord God; behold, I am against you, O Tyrus,"* presents a chilling scenario indeed!

In the last some five hundred years, Tyre, bordering Israel, had had the opportunity to know Jehovah. In fact, as stated, Hiram I aided David and Solomon greatly, especially as it regards the latter in the construction of the Temple.

As Solomon began construction on the Temple, he sent to Hiram, requesting help concerning *"cedar trees out of Lebanon"* (I Ki. 5:1-6). In this request, he greatly praised the *"Lord my God,"* and was, therefore, a great testimony to Hiram. Hiram answered in the affirmative and said *"Bless the LORD this day, which has given unto David a wise son over this great people"* (I Ki. 5:7); therefore, the knowledge of the Lord possessed by Hiram seemed to be greater than any of the other kings of the surrounding countries. Regrettably, it seems that he did not forsake his gods and serve Jehovah exclusively.

It must always be remembered, Light given, and then Light rejected, does not leave one in a static position, but worse!

DESTRUCTION

Verse 4 portrays two destructions:

The phrase, *"And they shall destroy the walls of Tyrus,"* refers to Nebuchadnezzar destroying her walls, while the phrase, *"I will also scrape her dust from her,"* refers to Alexander the Great building a causeway to attack the New Tyre. History records that his solders, in order to complete the causeway, gathered the dust of the Old Tyre in baskets and emptied them into the waters.

It took Nebuchadnezzar thirteen years to overthrow the city, according to Josephus.

While besieging Jerusalem, Nebuchadnezzar had driven Pharaoh back to Egypt. Tyre rejoiced over this and the Fall of Judah; and then, as in these Prophecies, her own downfall was predicted. The date of Nebuchadnezzar's siege was 587-574 B.C.

In 332 B.C., Alexander the Great laid siege to the island port for seven months and captured it only by building a moll to the island fortress, as stated!

Incidentally, Jesus took His Ministry to the district bordering Tyre and Sidon (Mat. 15:21-28; Mk. 7:24-31). The people of Tyre actually heard Him speak (Mk. 3:8; Lk. 6:17), and He cited Tyre as a heathen city which would bear less responsibility than those Galilean towns which constantly witnessed His Ministry (Mat. 11:21-22; Lk. 10:13-14). Christians were active in Tyre in the First Century (Acts 21:3-6), and there the Scholar Origen was buried (A.D. 254).

AND THEY SHALL KNOW THAT I AM THE LORD

If it is to be noticed, the phrase, *"And they shall know that I am the Lord,"* is used over and over again in the Book of Ezekiel, and has far greater meaning than meets the eye.

God, as the Maker and Creator of this world, including mankind, as well as the Heavens, demands allegiance, as He should! With the Fall in the Garden of Eden, Satan, by deception, was able to get mankind to change his allegiance from the Lord to himself. There the battle has raged from that day until this. Most of the world, whether they realize it or not, serves Satan. He, in one form or the other, is recognized as Lord. The Holy Spirit even calls him *"the god of this world,"* and says *"He has blinded the minds of them which believe not, lest the Light of the Glorious Gospel of Christ, Who is the Image of God, should shine unto them"* (II Cor. 4:4).

As a result of most of the world following Satan, they do not recognize God or His Word. Pharaoh said, *"Who is the Lord that I should obey His Voice to let Israel go?"* (Ex. 5:2).

So, the arrogance expressed against the God of the Bible continues even up to this present hour. Nevertheless, whether recognized or not, the Lord, countless times, has stepped in and brought Judgment.

The greatest challenge to His Supremacy will be during the coming Great Tribulation Period, with the rise of the Antichrist. It will be all the rebellions of the past, at least in spirit, rolled into one, with every effort made to rid the world, once and for all, of the Lord Jesus Christ. Instead, the opposite will happen, with the Second Coming of Christ (Rev., Chpt. 19).

As well, during that seven-year period of Great Tribulation, the Scripture says, *"For the great day of His wrath has come, and who shall be able to stand?"* (Rev. 6:17). Then, as in the Ezekiel account, *"They shall know that I am the Lord."*

SOVEREIGN

The phrase from Verse 7, *"Behold, I will bring upon Tyrus Nebuchadnezzar, King of Babylon,"* refers to the Lordship of Christ as Sovereign Ruler overall. While the Potentate, *"Nebuchadrezzar,"* at least at this time, would have little understood Who Jehovah was, still, his actions were channeled by the Lord of Glory.

The Lord, being Omnipotent (all-powerful), Omniscient (all-knowing), and Omnipresent (is present everywhere), could do this without infringing upon the King's free moral agency.

If one is to notice, as it regards Nebuchadnezzar, the title, *"a king of kings,"* is given to him by the Holy Spirit. This was so, for many other kings submitted to him. However, Christ Alone, as it regards the entirety of the World, is *"The King of Kings,"* and is the only One Who will ever serve in this capacity.

Therefore, one can see Nebuchadnezzar's charted course long before he had made his plans. Such is the Power of God!

NEBUCHADNEZZAR

Verses 9 through 11 proclaim the siege of Nebuchadnezzar against Tyre.

When the walls of Tyre were finally breached by Nebuchadnezzar, the might and power of his army and cavalry quickly overran the city. As the Scripture said in Verse 10, the dust from the horses filled the air as the horsemen quickly fanned out across the city, wreaking havoc. In other words, they had laughed when this happened to Jerusalem, now, and according the Word of Lord, it would happen to them.

Nebuchadnezzar laid siege to the walls of Jerusalem for about two years before it fell. The siege against Tyre took thirteen years.

During that time, no doubt, as the people in Jerusalem, they thought surely they would wear out the Babylonians. Thirteen years is a long time! Quite possibly, the people of Tyre knew of the Prophecies of Jeremiah and Ezekiel concerning this great city of Tyre, and how it would be overthrown, but refused to believe them.

Now, as then, most think if the Lord does not do something immediately, it will not be done; however, what He has stated will definitely come to pass, even though at times it may take many years to do so. Many think, that because of the delay, they are getting by, and, in other words, beating the game. Let no one think such! The Lord says what He means, and means what He says.

TWO INVASIONS

The *"he"* and *"his"* of Verses 9 through 11 is Nebuchadnezzar; the *"they"* of Verse 12, the soldiers of Alexander the Great. The two invasions were separated by about one hundred and fifty years.

The phrase of Verse 11, *"And your strong garrisons shall go down to the ground,"* may have been referring to the two famous columns standing in the temple of the Tyrian Hercules, one of gold, and the other of emerald, as symbols of strength, or as pedestals surmounted by a statue of Baal.

The phrase *"Thy dust in the midst of the water,"* as stated, refers to Alexander's invasion.

OLD TYRE

The phrase of Verse 13, *"And I will cause the noise of your songs to cease,"* refers to Tyre as being famous for its music, eminent no less for its culture than its commerce. Also, the phrase implies that the merriment continued during the seven months of siege by Alexander the Great, and that such action suggested that they believed he would not succeed. But succeed he did, and according to the Scripture. Then the music stopped.

The phrase of Verse 14, *"Thou shall be built no more,"* speaks of this *"rock"* where Old Tyre was located. Today, as for centuries past, the site of the ancient city, as here described, is a bare rock, upon which fishermen dry their nets, exactly as was prophesied.

NOTES

However, beginning somewhat before World War II, a New Tyre has been built somewhat inland, but stretching to the sea. It has between 10,000 and 20,000 population.

I was there right after the invasion by Israel in the *"Peace for Galilee"* campaign. This was in 1983. This city had been all but destroyed by Israeli artillery. Because of strong resistance by the Arabs, heavy fighting had taken place there with great destruction. The Israelis stated that they had requested that the Arabs surrender, but to no avail!

As I stood there that day, surveying the carnage, and thinking back over the many, many centuries of history regarding this place, my mind went back to the time of David, when it spoke of Hiram, king of Tyre, who was ever a lover of David, and how if they had followed David's God, their future would have been so different. However, such can be said for the entirety of the world.

(15) "THUS SAITH THE LORD GOD TO TYRUS; SHALL NOT THE ISLES SHAKE AT THE SOUND OF YOUR FALL, WHEN THE WOUNDED CRY, WHEN THE SLAUGHTER IS MADE IN THE MIDST OF YOU?

(16) "THEN ALL THE PRINCES OF THE SEA SHALL COME DOWN FROM THEIR THRONES, AND LAY AWAY THEIR ROBES, AND PUT OFF THEIR BROIDERED GARMENTS: THEY SHALL CLOTHE THEMSELVES WITH TREMBLING, THEY SHALL SIT UPON THE GROUND, AND SHALL TREMBLE AT EVERY MOMENT, AND BE ASTONISHED AT YOU.

(17) "AND THEY SHALL TAKE UP A LAMENTATION FOR YOU, AND SAY TO YOU, HOW ARE YOU DESTROYED, THAT WAS INHABITED OF SEAFARING MEN, THE RENOWNED CITY, WHICH WAS STRONG IN THE SEA, SHE AND HER INHABITANTS, WHICH CAUSE THEIR TERROR TO BE ON ALL WHO HAUNT IT!

(18) "NOW SHALL THE ISLES TREMBLE IN THE DAY OF YOUR FALL; YES, THE ISLES THAT ARE IN THE SEA SHALL BE TROUBLED AT YOUR DEPARTURE.

(19) "FOR THUS SAITH THE LORD GOD; WHEN I SHALL MAKE YOU A DESOLATE CITY, LIKE THE CITIES THAT ARE NOT INHABITED; WHEN I SHALL BRING UP THE DEEP UPON YOU, AND GREAT

WATERS SHALL COVER YOU;

(20) "WHEN I SHALL BRING YOU DOWN WITH THEM WHO DESCEND INTO THE PIT, WITH THE PEOPLE OF OLD TIME, AND SHALL SET YOU IN THE LOW PARTS OF THE EARTH, IN PLACES DESOLATE OF OLD, WITH THEM THAT GO DOWN TO THE PIT, THAT YOU BE NOT INHABITED; AND I SHALL SET GLORY IN THE LAND OF THE LIVING;

(21) "I WILL MAKE YOU A TERROR, AND YOU SHALL BE NO MORE: THOUGH YOU BE SOUGHT FOR, YET SHALL YOU NEVER BE FOUND AGAIN, SAITH THE LORD GOD."

The diagram is:

1. The *"and"* in the last line of Verse 20 would be better translated *"but."* The argument is that instead of the nations enriching Tyre because of the destruction of Jerusalem, they would impoverish her; and while her inhabitants would be shut up in Hell, the Messiah will be reigning in glory in the Land of the Living, which speaks of Jerusalem in the midst of the redeemed sons of Israel.

2. The close of the Chapter corresponds and contrasts with its beginning. Jerusalem destroyed and its citizens in captivity, Tyre enriched and her citizens clothed with glory; Tyre destroyed and its citizens in eternal captivity, and Jerusalem and her citizens rejoicing in the glory of Messiah's endless Life and Kingdom.

3. If men would only take the time to read these Prophecies, and see beyond question how they came to pass, the veracity of the Word of God would be easily recognized. The Bible is about one-third Prophecy, the only Book in the world of its kind. When predictions are made concerning the future, everything is laid on the line, so to speak! That's the reason there are no prophecies in the Koran, or any other so-called holy book.

THUS SAITH THE LORD

The phrase of Verse 15, *"Shall not the isles shake at the sound of your fall,"* more than likely included all cities and towns on the Indian Ocean and the Persian Gulf, inasmuch as the report of the Fall of Tyre was spread far and wide.

NOTES

The phrase, *"When the slaughter is made in the midst of you,"* refers to that which happened to Jerusalem happening likewise to Tyre. They had laughed, now they will laugh no more!

The phrase, *"Princes of the sea,"* taken from Verse 16, refers to the merchant princes who had made Tyre one of the greatest centers of commerce in the world. These are the ones who had gloated over the Fall of Jerusalem, thinking that the commerce of Jerusalem would now be theirs.

During the sieges by Nebuchadnezzar, and then later by Alexander the Great, they would *"clothe themselves with trembling."* As well, *"they sat upon the ground, and trembled at every moment."*

These lessons should be a grand example to the world, but sadly, they are little heeded by modern society, as all of the Bible is little heeded!

Due to the riches and power of Tyre, the surrounding countries did not think she would fall, and especially considering that it took Nebuchadnezzar thirteen years to subdue the city.

No contemporary account of this siege is available, at least that I am aware of; however, from the length of time it took the Babylonian Monarch, it must be gathered that he faced formidable odds. But it fell, and because the Lord said it would!

THE PLACE CALLED HELL

The phrase of Verse 20, *"When I shall bring you down with them who descend into the pit,"* is actually a portrayal of Hell itself and the people of Tyre shut up with the antediluvians, i.e. *"with the people of old time."*

The word, *"Hell,"* as it's used in the Bible, is a synonym for the underworld of departed spirits. Jesus said that this place is located *"in the heart of the Earth"* (Mat. 12:40). There are some five areas in this place referred to as *"Hell."* They are as follows:

TARTARUS

Fallen angels alone occupy this place. It seems that these are the angels which cohabited with women, producing a race of giants, which is mentioned in Genesis 6:4.

Jude mentioned these by saying: *"And

the angels which kept not their first estate, but left their own habitation, He has reserved in everlasting chains under darkness unto the judgment of the great day.

"Even as Sodom and Gomorrah and the cities about them in like manner, giving themselves over to fornication, and going after strange flesh, are set forth for an example, suffering the vengeance of eternal fire.

"Likewise also these filthy dreamers defile the flesh, despise dominion, and speak evil of dignities" (Jude Vss. 6-8).

The evidence is, our Lord immediately after His death on the Cross, went down into Paradise, and also preached to these fallen angels. The Scripture says:

"For Christ also has once suffered for sins, the just for the unjust, that He might bring us to God, being put to death in the flesh, but quickened by the Spirit:

"By which also He went and preached unto the spirits in prison;

"Which sometime past were disobedient" (I Pet. 3:18-20).

The word *"preached"* used here concerning Christ, is a different Greek word than normal. Preaching normally refers to the *"good news"* of the Gospel; however, the Greek word here translated *"preached"* actually refers to Christ making an announcement. What announcement He made, we aren't told.

As well, the word *"spirits"* speaks of angels and not men or demon spirits.

HELL

This is the place where all unsaved souls immediately go at death. Jesus graphically described this place regarding the illustration He gave concerning Lazarus and the rich man (Lk. 16:19-31).

He spoke of the rich man dying, and the Scripture says, *"And in Hell he lift up his eyes, being in torments"* (Lk. 16:23).

Jesus also plainly and clearly stated that Hell was a place of fire. He said of the rich man, who cried out to Abraham, *"Send Lazarus, that he may dip the tip of his finger in water, and cool my tongue, for I am tormented in this flame"* (Lk. 16:24).

So we know from this, that the fires of Hell are real.

Of course, the soul and the spirit of either the redeemed or the unredeemed are indestructible. Also, we know that Hell was not originally prepared for man, but rather *"prepared for the devil and his angels"* (Mat. 25:41).

Jesus plainly warned all of humanity, as He spoke of the Holy Spirit, He said: *"If I depart, I will send Him unto you.*

"And when He is come, He will reprove the world of sin, and of Righteousness, and of Judgment:

"Of sin, because they believe not on Me;

"Of Righteousness, because I go to My Father, and ye see Me no more;

"Of Judgment, because the prince of this world is judged" (Jn. 16:7-11).

In essence, He is saying that all of mankind which follows Satan will experience Satan's judgment, which is *"Hell."* Every person who has ever lived and died unsaved is now in Hell. They will be there until they stand at the Great White Throne Judgment, and are then transferred to the lake of fire.

PARADISE

Before the Cross, due to the insufficiency of animal blood to take away sin (Heb. 10:4), the sin debt still remained on all, even the great faith worthies of the Old Testament; consequently, when all Believers died before the Cross, they were taken by the angels (Lk. 16:22) into Paradise, which Jesus also referred to as *"Abraham's bosom"* (Lk. 16:22).

In effect, despite dying in the faith, all of these individuals were held as captives by Satan, even though the Evil One was not allowed to put them in the burning side of Hell. Concerning this, Jesus also said, concerning Paradise and Hell, *"And beside all this, between us and you there is a great gulf fixed: so that they which would pass from hence to you cannot; neither can they pass to us, who would come from thence"* (Lk. 16:26).

When Jesus died on the Cross, thereby forever settling the sin debt, at least for all who will believe, He went down into Paradise, sometimes referred to as Hell (Ps. 16:10). Concerning this, Paul said: *"Wherefore He said, When He ascended up on high, He led captivity captive, and gave gifts unto men.*

"Now that He ascended, what is it but that He also descended first into the lower parts of the Earth?" (Eph. 4:8-9).

The statement, *"He led captivity captive,"* means that all of the Old Testament Believers were being held captive by Satan, and because, as we have stated, *"the blood of bulls and goats could not take away sins"* (Heb. 10:4). In fact, all of these people, all of the Old Testament Greats, were awaiting the Cross. The moment the Cross was a fact, Satan had no more hold over these people.

Jesus, as it regards His trip down into Paradise, made all of these people who had been captives of Satan, His captives, and took them with Him; consequently, the place we now refer to as *"Paradise"* is empty.

Presently, whenever a Believer dies, due to what Christ did on the Cross, instantly, the soul and the spirit go to be with Christ in Heaven (Phil. 1:23).

THE BOTTOMLESS PIT

Some nine times in the Book of Revelation, the *"bottomless pit"* is mentioned. In this *"bottomless pit,"* even at this very moment, the Scripture tells us that demon locusts are locked up in this Abyss, and will be released in the coming Great Tribulation (Rev. 9:1-3).

The Scripture also tells us that there is an *"angel of the bottomless pit, whose name in the Hebrew tongue is Abaddon, but in the Greek tongue has his name Apollyon"* (Rev. 9:11).

We are also told of another powerful fallen angel who is now locked up in the *"bottomless pit,"* but who will be released in the coming Great Tribulation (Rev. 11:7; 17:8).

And then we are told that at the beginning of the Kingdom Age, which will commence with the Second Coming of the Lord, that Satan will be, as well, locked up in the bottomless pit, where he will remain throughout the Kingdom Age, of one thousand years (Rev. 20:1-3).

So, in this place are demon spirits and some fallen angels.

THE LAKE OF FIRE

Tartarus, Hell, and the bottomless pit are now occupied; however, Paradise is empty. At the Great White Throne Judgment, the Scripture tells us that all demons, fallen angels, and people who are in Tartarus, Hell, and the Bottomless Pit will then be transferred to the *"Lake of Fire."* The Scripture says, *"This is second death"* (Rev. 20:14). The Scripture also says that they will remain there *"forever and ever"* (Rev. 20:10).

THE CROSS

The only thing standing between mankind and eternal Hell is the Cross of Christ. If men reject Christ and the Cross, Hell, i.e., the Lake of Fire, will be their eternal abode; and to be sure, eternity is a long, long, time! In fact, it is *"forever and forever"* (Rev. 20:10). As well, if men accept Christ and reject the Cross, this is an acceptance that God cannot tolerate. Paul referred to such as *"another Jesus, fostered by another spirit, presenting another gospel"* (II Cor. 11:4).

It took the Cross to redeem man, and when men truly accept Christ, they are accepting what He has done to redeem us, which alone could redeem us, and I continue to speak of the Cross (Eph. 2:13-18; Jn. 3:3-16; Rev. 22:17).

PURGATORY

Is there such a place as purgatory?

No! It is, pure and simple, a fabrication of the Catholic Church.

The Roman Catholic Church has defined the existence of purgatory in the Decree of Union drawn at the Council of Florence in A.D. 1439 and again at the Council of Trent, which says:

"The Catholic Church, instructed by the Holy Spirit, has from sacred Scriptures and the ancient traditions of the fathers taught in sacred councils and very recently in the ecumenical synod, that there is a purgatory, and that the souls therein detained are helped by the suffrages of the faithful, but principally, by the acceptable sacrifice of the altar."

The Catholic Church also teaches that Christians can indulge themselves in two kinds of sin: *"mortal sins,"* which will damn the soul, and *"venial sins,"* which will not damn the soul but will consign it to purgatory. All souls, therefore, who die in venial sins, or with a temporal punishment of their sins still unpaid, must atone for them in purgatory, or so says the Catholic Church.

THE APOCRYPHA

The Roman Church gets some of her beliefs from some of the Apocryphal writings (II Maccabees 12:43-46). These writings were considered by the Jewish Rabbis as unworthy of being included in the Word of God.

The Roman Catholic Church goes on to say that because she is the infallible teacher of Divine Revelation, in the name of the Bible and tradition, she has the authority to declare the Apocrypha an article of faith. (At the conclusion of this article, we will deal with the Apocrypha.)

The Catholic Church further believes that the faithful on Earth, the Saints in Heaven, and the souls in purgatory are united together in love and prayer. According to her doctrine, the faithful on Earth still struggling to win the victory of Salvation, form the *"Church Militant,"* while the Saints in Heaven are the *"Church Triumphant,"* and the souls in purgatory, still suffering in order to be perfectly purified from the effects of sin, constitute the *"Church Suffering."*

ROMAN CATHOLIC EXPLANATION

To sum it all up, the Roman Catholic Church states that purgatory is the state or condition in which those who have died in a state of Grace, but with some attachment to sin, suffer for a time before they are admitted to the glory and happiness of Heaven. In this state and period of passive suffering, they are purified of venial sins, satisfy the demands of Divine justice for temporal punishment due for these sins, and are thus converted to a state of worthiness.

WHAT THE WORD OF GOD ACTUALLY TEACHES

What does the Word of God say concerning purgatory?

Nothing.

All of these teachings are contradicted by the New Testament. We are told that we *"have therefore . . . boldness to enter into the holiest by the Blood of Jesus, by a new and living way"* (Heb. 10:19-20).

The Apostle Paul taught that when sins are remitted, which is made possible by the Cross, and our Faith in that Finished Work, there is no more need of any other offering for sins. Thus Paul concluded his argument on the Priesthood of Christ. Christ's Offering is efficacious (effective) for all past, present, and future sins (but on the condition of proper confession of sin and meeting the terms of continued Grace, which is continued faith in Christ and the Cross). Hebrews 10:19-20 give the Child of God full access to Heaven. It is a grand conclusion to the doctrinal argument of the worthiness of every Child of God to enter the portals of glory. In other words, all Christians, by accepting the Blood Sacrifice paid for by our Saviour, have instant citizenship in Heaven. When a person comes to Christ, at that very moment, they are totally and completely saved. While we should grow in grace and knowledge of the Lord, there is no such thing as a person being more saved. At the moment of conversion, the Scripture says: *"You are washed, you are sanctified, you are justified in the name of the Lord Jesus, and by the Spirit of our God"* (I Cor. 6:11). Concerning sins committed by the Believer, the Scripture also says: *"and the Blood of Jesus Christ His Son cleanses us from all sin"* (I Jn. 1:7).

The Apostle also said: *"If we confess our sins, He is faithful and just to forgive us our sins, and to cleanse us from all unrighteousness"* (I Jn. 1:9).

The Catholic Church teaches a salvation by works. So the great question always is, *"How many works are enough?"* Of course, no one knows the answer to that question, so all must go to purgatory in order to be made worthy to enter Heaven.

Such a doctrine insults Christ, belittles the Cross, perverts the great price that Jesus paid in the offering up of Himself in Sacrifice in order to save lost humanity.

While a Roman Catholic can definitely come to Christ and be saved, the truth is, once they are saved, there is no way they can stay in that unscriptural system and remain saved. The Scripture plainly tells us, concerning the Holy Spirit: *"He will guide you into all Truth"* (Jn. 16:13). So there will be no mistake as to what is being said, the moment that a Catholic accepts Christ, if they are to maintain their Salvation, they must leave the Catholic Church.

It's easy to understand how mere pagans can teach the doctrine of purgatory (as was taught in Egypt, for example); however, no such excuse can be made for the Cardinals, Bishops, Monsignors, and Priests of the Roman Catholic Church. They are supposed to know better, but the truth is, most of them really don't know any better, because they are unredeemed.

DEEPENING ERROR

Prayers for the dead go hand in hand with purgatory. In Catholic doctrine, prayer cannot be completely effective without the Priests as intermediaries, and no priestly function can be rendered unless there is a special payment. Therefore, in every land, we find the Priesthood of the Catholic Church devouring widows' houses (Mat. 23:14, 29), and making merchandise of the tender emotions of sorrowing relatives sensitive to the immortal destiny of their beloved dead (II Pet. 2:3).

One of the oppressions under which people in Roman Catholic countries groan is the obligation to pay for special devotions whenever death takes a member of their family. Not only must they pay for funeral services and funeral dues for repose of the departed at the time of the burial, but the Priest pays repeated visits afterward to the family for the same purpose, and this entails a seemingly endless number of expenses.

The following was an advertisement that appeared in the August 11, 1946, *"Our Sunday Visitor,"* a popular Catholic weekly newspaper.

ARE YOU INSURED?

Write and ask about our plan to offer the Gregorian Masses after your death.
This is real insurance for your soul.

The Gregorian Masses for a soul in purgatory are thirty in number and must be offered consecutively. At that time (1946), the minimum price was $30 (in 2003 dollars, that would be approximately $600). It was believed and taught by those in the Roman Church that Christ appeared to Saint Gregory and promised He would release souls from purgatory on payment of the money.

PERSONAL KNOWLEDGE

I remember, years ago in Southern Louisiana, turning on the radio and hearing a particular program hosted by a Catholic Priest. He was telling the people to send in a certain amount of people on behalf of individuals who had died.

He went on to state that many of these loved ones were almost completely out of purgatory. All that remained was an arm or a leg.

This is at least one of the reasons the Roman Catholic Church is so rich: the tremendous amount of money pouring into its coffers each day by poor individual Catholics thinking they can retrieve the souls of departed loved ones from a place called purgatory — a place which, in fact, doesn't even exist.

THE BLOOD OF JESUS CHRIST

The Roman Catholic doctrine of purgatory is purely pagan and cannot, for a moment, stand in the light of Scripture. The Bible plainly tells us: *"He who has the Son has life; and he who has not the Son of God has not life"* (I Jn. 5:12).

Thus, the whole doctrine of purgatory is a system of purely pagan origins. It is dishonoring to God and deluding to men who continue to live in sin with a hope of atoning for it after death, thus cheating them out of their property, and above all, their salvation.

WHAT IS MEANT BY THE TERM "APOCRYPHA"?

At the end of the first Christian century, the Jewish Rabbis, at the Council of Gamnia, closed the Canon of Hebrew Books, which make up the Old Testament (those books considered authoritative). Their decision resulted from:

• The multiplication and popularity of sectarian apocryphal writings.
• The Fall of Jerusalem (A.D. 70), which created a threat to the religious tradition of the Jews.
• The disputes with Christians over their interpretation of the Jewish Scriptures in preaching and writing.

There was never any doubt about the five Books of the Law (Pentateuch), but, beyond that, various sects of Judaism disagreed. The prophetic collection was generally agreed upon by 200 B.C., but the major problem concerned the *"other writings."* Three criteria operated in deciding what books should occupy a place in the authoritative Old Testament Scriptures:

1. The content of each Book had to harmonize with the Law.

2. Since prophetic inspiration was believed to have begun with Moses (about 1450 B.C.) and ended with Ezra (about 450 B.C.), to qualify for the Canon and to be considered inspired, a Book had to have been written within that timeframe.

3. The language of the original manuscript had to be Hebrew.

On this basis, the thirty-nine Books of the Old Testament were selected for the Jewish Canon of Scriptures. Failing these criteria, the rest of the ancient Jewish writings came to be classified as *"Apocrypha"* or *"pseudepigrapha"* (literally, *"false writings"*).

THE NEW TESTAMENT

A number of Christian writings, other than those that came to be accepted for the New Testament, appeared early and were considered by some authorities to be worthy of Canonical status. *"The Didache," "the Epistle of Barnabas," "I and II Clement," "the Shepherd of Hermes," "the Apocalypse of Peter,"* and *"the Acts of Paul"* were some of the more popular ones. By the beginning of the Third Century, twenty-two of the writings of our present New Testament had been widely accepted. Four principles or considerations operated in determining what books should occupy a place in the authoritative New Testament Scriptures:

1. Was the Book written by an Apostle or by someone associated with an Apostle?

2. Was the Book's content of a spiritual nature?

3. Was the Book widely received by the Churches?

4. Was there evidence in the Book of Divine Inspiration?

As far as is known, it was the Easter letter of Archbishop Athanasius of Alexandria (A.D. 367) who first listed the twenty-seven Books of our New Testament as authoritative.

NOTES

Jerome, by his Latin translation of these same twenty-seven Books (A.D. 382), further established this list as Canonical for the Churches.

This is a brief explanation of how our Bible (thirty-nine Books in the Old Testament and twenty-seven in the New Testament) came to be established as the Word of God.

THE APOCRYPHA

This group of books, numbering about fourteen, is believed to be spurious; literally, *"false writings."* This in no way implies that the books do not contain some good things, nor does it mean they were written by evil men. It simply means they were believed not to be inspired; consequently, they were not placed in the Canon of Scripture.

Eleven of these Apocryphal books have been accepted by the Catholic Church, included in Roman Catholic Canon, and placed in the Douay Version of the Bible (Catholic).

Why were these books not considered inspired or Canonical (included in the Canon or Books of the Bible)? Some of the reasons will relate to the Old Testament; some, to the New Testament.

1. As far as the Old Testament was concerned, these particular books were not included in the Hebrew Canon of Scripture.

2. Our Lord, the Apostle Paul, nor any other writer in the New Testament, ever quoted from these spurious writings (Apocrypha). Yet, they quoted frequently in the New Testament from the Books that were included in the Hebrew Canon of Scripture, i.e., *"the Old Testament."*

3. Josephus, the Hebrew historian, expressly excluded these *"false writings"* or Apocrypha.

4. None of the Apocryphal books claim Divine inspiration.

5. The Apocryphal books have historical, geographical, and chronological errors.

6. For the most part, they teach and uphold doctrines that are contrary to the Scriptures (for instance, lying is sanctioned in some cases, magic is advocated and practiced in other cases, etc.).

7. As literature, they are considered to be myth and legend.

8. Their spiritual (and even moral) stance

is generally far below both the Old and New Testaments.

9. Respecting the Old Testament, most of these spurious books were written much later than the Books that were considered to be authoritative and inspired.

10. As we discussed in the explanation earlier respecting the New Testament writings, to be Canonized a Book had to have been written by an Apostle, or someone associated with an Apostle. The Book had to be spiritual, had to have been widely received by the Churches, and had to show evidence of Divine inspiration.

THE GOSPEL

Satan has done everything within his power to hinder, destroy, dilute, and outright do away with the Word of Almighty God. But through the Power of God, the Bible as we have it today (its sixty-six Books, both Old and New Testaments, from Genesis to Revelation) is the Word of God. Nothing else can be added to it.

When any person or any Church claim that other writings, other books, other so-called inspiration should be included in the Canon of Scripture, this is a work of the Evil One himself. Paul put it aptly when he said:

"Though we, or an angel from Heaven, preach any other gospel unto you than that which we have preached unto you, let him be accursed. As we said before, so say I now again, if any man preach any other gospel unto you than that you have received, let him be accursed" (Gal. 1:8-9).

THUS SAITH THE LORD

Verse 21 brings to a close this Twenty-sixth Chapter. At the beginning of the Chapter, Jerusalem is destroyed and its citizens are in captivity. Tyre is enriched, and her citizens are clothed with glory.

But at the close of this Chapter, according to the Word of the Lord, Tyre is pictured as destroyed, and its citizens in eternal captivity, while Jerusalem and her citizens rejoice in the Glory of the Messiah's endless Life and Kingdom.

The Word of the Lord will always come to pass; those who serve God will ultimately take best, and without fail!

NOTES

"Where cross the crowded ways of life,
"Where sound the cries of race and clan,
"Above the noise of selfish strife,
"We hear Your voice, O Son of Man!"

"In haunts of wretchedness and need,
"On shadowed thresholds dark with fears,
"From paths where hide the lures of greed,
"We catch the vision of Your tears."

"The cup of water given for Thee
"Still holds the freshness of Your Grace;
"Yet long these multitudes to see
"The sweet compassion of Your face."

"O Master, from the mountainside,
"Make haste to heal these hearts of pain,
"Among these restless throngs abide,
"O tread the city's streets again."

"'Til the sons of men shall learn Your love,
"And follow where Your feet have trod:
"'Til glorious from Your Heaven above
"Shall come the city of our God."

CHAPTER 27

(1) "THE WORD OF THE LORD CAME AGAIN UNTO ME, SAYING,

(2) "NOW, THOU SON OF MAN, TAKE UP A LAMENTATION FOR TYRUS;

(3) "AND SAY UNTO TYRUS, O THOU THAT ART SITUATE AT THE ENTRY OF THE SEA, WHICH ARE A MERCHANT OF THE PEOPLE FOR MANY ISLES, THUS SAITH THE LORD GOD; O TYRUS, THOU HAS SAID, I AM OF PERFECT BEAUTY.

(4) "YOUR BORDERS ARE IN THE MIDST OF THE SEAS, YOUR BUILDERS HAVE PERFECTED YOUR BEAUTY.

(5) "THEY HAVE MADE ALL YOUR SHIP BOARDS OF FIR TREES OF SENIR: THEY HAVE TAKEN CEDARS FROM LEBANON TO MAKE MASTS FOR YOU.

(6) "OF THE OAKS OF BASHAN HAVE THEY MADE YOUR OARS; THE COMPANY OF THE ASHURITES HAVE MADE YOUR

BENCHES OF IVORY, BROUGHT OUT OF THE ISLES OF CHITTIM.

(7) "FINE LINEN WITH BROIDERED WORK FROM EGYPT WAS THAT WHICH YOU SPREAD FORTH TO BE YOUR SAIL; BLUE AND PURPLE FROM THE ISLES OF ELISHAH WAS THAT WHICH COVERED YOU.

(8) "THE INHABITANTS OF ZIDON AND ARVAD WERE YOUR MARINERS: YOUR WISE MEN, O TYRUS, WHO WERE IN YOU, WERE YOUR PILOTS.

(9) "THE ANCIENTS OF GEBAL AND THE WISE MEN THEREOF WERE IN YOU YOUR CALKERS: ALL THE SHIPS OF THE SEA WITH THEIR MARINERS WERE IN YOU TO OCCUPY YOUR MERCHANDISE.

(10) "THEY OF PERSIA AND OF LUD AND OF PHUT WERE IN YOUR ARMY, YOUR MEN OF WAR: THEY HANGED THE SHIELD AND HELMET IN YOU; THEY SET FORTH YOUR COMELINESS.

(11) "THE MEN OF ARVAD WITH YOUR ARMY WERE UPON YOUR WALLS ROUND ABOUT, AND THE GAMMADIMS WERE IN YOUR TOWERS: THEY HANGED THEIR SHIELDS UPON YOUR WALLS ROUND ABOUT; THEY HAVE MADE YOUR BEAUTY PERFECT.

(12) "TARSHISH WAS YOUR MERCHANT BY REASON OF THE MULTITUDE OF ALL KIND OF RICHES: WITH SILVER, IRON, TIN, AND LEAD, THEY TRADED IN YOUR FAIRS.

(13) "JAVAN, TUBAL, AND MESHECH, THEY WERE YOUR MERCHANTS: THEY TRADED THE PERSONS OF MEN AND VESSELS OF BRASS IN YOUR MARKET.

(14) "THEY OF THE HOUSE OF TOGARMAH TRADED IN YOUR FAIRS WITH HORSES AND HORSEMEN AND MULES.

(15) "THE MEN OF DEDAN WERE YOUR MERCHANTS; MANY ISLES WERE THE MERCHANDISE OF YOUR HAND: THEY BROUGHT YOU FOR A PRESENT HORNS OF IVORY AND EBONY.

(16) "SYRIA WAS YOUR MERCHANT BY REASON OF THE MULTITUDE OR THE WARES OF YOUR MAKING: THEY OCCUPIED IN YOUR FAIRS WITH EMERALDS, PURPLE, AND BROIDERED WORK, AND FINE LINEN, AND CORAL, AND AGATE.

(17) "JUDAH, AND THE LAND OF ISRAEL, THEY WERE YOUR MERCHANTS: THEY TRADED IN YOUR MARKET WHEAT OF MINNITH, AND PANNAG, AND HONEY, AND OIL, AND BALM.

(18) "DAMASCUS WAS YOUR MERCHANT IN THE MULTITUDE OF THE WARES OF YOUR MAKING, FOR THE MULTITUDE OF ALL RICHES; IN THE WINE OF HELBON, AND WHITE WOOL.

(19) "DAN ALSO AND JAVAN GOING TO AND FRO OCCUPIED IN YOUR FAIRS: BRIGHT IRON, CASSIA, AND CALAMUS, WERE IN YOUR MARKET.

(20) "DEDAN WAS YOUR MERCHANT IN PRECIOUS CLOTHES FOR CHARIOTS.

(21) "ARABIA, AND ALL THE PRINCES OF KEDAR, THEY OCCUPIED WITH YOU IN LAMBS, AND RAMS, AND GOATS: IN THESE WERE THEY YOUR MERCHANTS.

(22) "THE MERCHANTS OF SHEBA AND RAAMAH, THEY WERE YOUR MERCHANTS: THEY OCCUPIED IN YOUR FAIRS WITH CHIEF OF ALL SPICES, AND WITH ALL PRECIOUS STONES, AND GOLD.

(23) "HARAN, AND CANNEH, AND EDEN, THE MERCHANTS OF SHEBA, ASSHUR, AND CHILMAD, WERE YOUR MERCHANTS.

(24) "THESE WERE YOUR MERCHANTS IN ALL SORTS OF THINGS, IN BLUE CLOTHES, AND BROIDERED WORK, AND IN CHESTS OF RICH APPAREL, BOUND WITH CORDS, AND MADE OF CEDAR, AMONG YOUR MERCHANDISE."

The composition is:

1. The Holy Spirit through Ezekiel continues to direct attention to Tyre. The reason for this prolonged account is that Tyre is a symbol of Satan's efforts to build an earthly kingdom, and thereby meeting the needs of man, but without God.

2. The spirit of the world is the greatest enemy of the Church, which Tyre represents.

3. We learn from all of this given by the Holy Spirit through the Prophet that irrespective as to what the world may have to offer, other than the Lord, all is a losing operation.

THE WORD OF THE LORD

As stated previously, The Holy Spirit

allotting so much time to the city of Tyre is of far greater import than merely a pronounced judgment due to her gloating over the Fall of Jerusalem. The reason for such detail, and given by the Holy Spirit at that, concerns itself with Tyre as a symbol of Satan's efforts to build an earthly kingdom, and thereby meeting the needs of man, but without God. As such, this city serves as a symbol of the world's corrupt system in the Old Testament, as rebuilt Babylon will serve in the New Testament. As the Lord destroyed the former, He, likewise, will destroy the latter (Rev., Chpt. 18).

FALSE DOCTRINE

Surely by now the Reader has noticed that we have dealt quite extensively with the Word of Faith doctrine in this Volume. There is a reason that we have devoted so much space to this particular philosophy.

The serious Bible student knows that Paul, during his day, dealt very extensively with the Law/Grace issue. Much of his writings are taken up with correction that was desperately needed, and because of the efforts of Satan to dilute, and thereby destroy, the great Message of Grace.

As the Law/Grace issue was Satan's great thrust in the time of the Early Church, it is my belief that the Word of Faith doctrine is his major thrust at this particular time. In a sense, I personally feel that this particular effort of the Evil One is far more dangerous than even that in Paul's day. At any rate, both, as should be obvious, fall into the same category.

In that last thirty or more years, the Word of Faith doctrine, which in reality is no faith at all, at least that which God will recognize, has made tremendous inroads into the Church. It has influenced virtually all of the Pentecostal and Charismatic church world. As it regards this particular doctrine, the salvation of souls is completely ignored. In fact, there is no one saved under this doctrine, simply because the Holy Spirit cannot use false doctrine in order to propagate the Gospel. While there may be a few people who truly do get saved in these particular Churches and meetings, it is definitely because of outside factors, and not because of the Word of Faith doctrine. Actually, they make almost no effort to get anyone saved, claiming that their ministry is that of *"enlightenment,"* in other words, to tell the Church *"how to get rich."*

It's amazing that something which is so blatantly unscriptural, so blatantly false, is yet accepted so widely. The great reason is that the greed factor plays a tremendous part in this acceptance, inasmuch as the emphasis of this doctrine is *"money."*

But that which makes this Doctrine so false, so ungodly, so unscriptural, is its repudiation of the Cross. As we've already said any number of times in this Volume, its primary preachers refer to the Cross as *"past miseries"* and *"the greatest defeat in human history."* Actually, Kenneth Hagin teaches that anyone who preaches the Cross is preaching death. He claims that we should rather preach the Resurrection and the Throne.

Paul said: *"For the preaching of the Cross is to them who perish foolishness; but unto us which are saved it is the Power of God"* (I Cor. 1:18).

Now one can accept the teaching of our dear brother, or one can accept the teaching of Paul. The choice is yours!

Again, Paul said: *"But we preach Christ Crucified"* (I Cor. 1:23). If it is to be noticed, the Apostle didn't say, *"But we preach Christ Resurrected."*

Well, of course, the Resurrection and the Exaltation of Christ are of extreme significance; however, the reason the Apostle proclaimed the Cross, and not the Resurrection, is because it was at the Cross where the price was paid for our Redemption, by Christ giving Himself as an Offering for sin, in fact, serving as a Sacrifice (Heb. 10:12-14). As important as the Resurrection is, it was not the Resurrection which redeemed us, but rather the Cross. And when we ignore the Cross, we have attacked the Atonement, which is the very heart of Christianity. In other words, if we take away the Cross, there is nothing left!

THE CHOICE

So the Church must make a choice! It can accept Paul, or it can accept these Word of Faith teachers. It cannot accept both. However, I want to make it crystal clear about my own personal choice. As the great Warrior Joshua said: *"As for me and my house, we will serve the Lord"* (Josh. 24:15).

Why would the majority of the Pentecostal and Charismatic Church world opt for this false doctrine, especially considering that it is so blatantly obvious as to its wrong direction?

As someone has well said, *"A lie can go around the world, while the truth is trying to get on its shoes."* The Fall of man in the Garden of Eden came about because of deception. As a result, man is very easily deceived, even those who claim to follow Christ.

All false doctrine appeals in some way to our baser motives. In this case, greed. So, to offset this, Scriptures are pulled out of context and perverted, with the idea then presented that all of this is very Scriptural.

As we've stated, the lure of this doctrine is *"money."* The people are made to believe that they are going to get rich by giving to this particular philosophy. Never mind that no one ever gets rich except the Preachers! The pot of gold for the dupes who fall for this line is always just around the corner.

ANGELS OF LIGHT

In one of Donnie's Messages, in our Fourth of July Campmeeting of 2003, he read some statements from two or three of the primary Faith teachers so-called. The statements were obviously unscriptural.

After reading the statements, he alluded to the fact that if most Believers would themselves read these statements in some publication, they would probably throw the book or the article aside, because it would be instantly obvious that what was being promoted was false doctrine; however, he then went on to say, that if a name is put to these statements, and especially one of the big names of the Faith philosophy, the thoughts of those reading this error would suddenly change.

Why?

Most would think, erroneously so, that these individuals are great men and women of God, and they must know more about the situation than I do, so I will accept what they've said, even though I don't quite understand it.

The truth is, these people are *"angels of light,"* which mean that what they say in some cases, and they do teach some truth, may sound right, but when one puts the entire body of teaching together, it becomes gross error.

Paul said: *"For such are false apostles, deceitful workers, transforming themselves into the apostles of Christ.*

"And no marvel; for Satan himself is transformed into an angel of light.

"Therefore it is no great thing if his ministers also be transformed as the ministers of righteousness; whose end shall be according to their works" (II Cor. 11:13-15).

Paul also said: *"For many walk, of whom I have told you often, and now tell you even weeping, that they are the enemies of the Cross of Christ:*

"Whose end is destruction, whose god is their belly, and whose glory is in their shame, who mind earthly things" (Phil. 3:18-19).

When one reads the entirety of the body of teaching of these people, which a great percentage of the Church has accepted, one must come to the conclusion that these people are *"enemies of the Cross."* No other conclusion can be reached!

SUCCESS

Verses 1 through 8 proclaim the great commercial efforts of Tyre and its great success. Many were made rich by its efforts, with this city held up as the model. In fact, the world holds up many models.

Just this morning, someone made mention of one of the most famous Actors in Hollywood, known worldwide, and worth many millions of dollars. But when asked what he desired, his answer was most revealing. He said, *"I want peace"*!

While most would not pay much attention to this simple statement, still, it speaks volumes. For all of his world-wide acclaim, for all of his money, for all of his popularity, none of it brought peace, as those things cannot bring peace.

A short time ago, one of the Rock stars, with all the adulation that such a position brings, put a pistol in his mouth and pulled the trigger, blowing his brains out. Why?

While Satan promises many things, even as he did with Tyre, and continues to do unto this hour, the truth is, the things which really satisfy, which really give peace of mind, which really give security, Satan cannot provide. As someone has well said, *"The soul of man is so big, that only God can fill it up."*

It may come as a shock to most that a little lady, living on Social Security, struggling to make ends meet, but still who has Jesus, has a degree of happiness, well-being, and security, that the richest man in the world, who doesn't know Christ, doesn't have, and in fact, cannot have.

If money brings happiness, how much does one need for that happiness to be found?

As we've already stated, the Holy Spirit devoted all of this time and attention to the city of Tyre and its activities and commerce, which appeals to man and the world and general, in order to portray Satan attempting to build Paradise without Christ.

DISCRIMINATION

The phrase of Verse 8, *"Your wise men, O Tyrus, who were in you, were your pilots,"* proclaims the special position of this city. The intent of this Verse is to proclaim the fact that the common sailors came from Zidon and Arvad, while Tyre furnished the officers. Thus Tyre is held as a cut above the others, as Satan intended! (Zidon, sometimes spelled *"Sidon,"* was about thirty miles north of Tyre.)

Class consciousness is rampant in the world and is a product of the status symbol of Satan. Even though democracy has attempted to level the playing field, nevertheless, it has only partially succeeded, with *"class"* and *"status"* still very much alive!

Bible Christianity, if truly followed, eliminates all class distinction. In the Early Church, as recorded in the Book of Acts and the Epistles, slaves were just a much a part of the local congregation as the wealthiest of the wealthy (Eph. 6:5-9).

Even though the terrible practice of slavery was not abolished due to Roman Law, nevertheless, regarding place and position in the Body of Christ, all were to be treated equally. Thankfully, and because of the Word of God, slavery was ultimately abolished, at least in most nations of the world.

America spilled the blood of over one-half million of its sons (both North and South) in order that this sordid stain be erased. Even though this was definitely the Will of God, still, racial prejudice and bias can never be eliminated by laws, as well-intentioned as they may be, but only by Jesus Christ and a proper knowledge of the Word of God.

A PERSONAL EXPERIENCE

Some time back, I received a letter from a Judge in the City of Baton Rouge, who asked if he could use our Church, Family Worship Center, as a model for the community. He went on to state in his letter that everyone was represented in our Church, brown, black, white, red, and yellow.

I was somewhat taken aback at his request, which we gladly consented to, but thinking that all Churches were the same. I found out this was not correct. Most of the major religious Denominations in America have a distinct color line. They are either all black, all brown, or all white. While this may be desirable in certain situations, as a whole, such is unbiblical!

If Bible Christianity is preached and practiced, it will appeal to all alike, erasing the color barrier, and every other culture barrier that may exist.

CULTURE

Actually, Bible Christianity has its own culture, which is God-given and God-designed, and therefore placing no one in a subservient role. The poor are just as welcome as the rich, the uneducated as the educated, with all color lines blotted out. If it's not that way, it is not true Bible Christianity.

Jesus did not say, *"Come unto Me, some of you who are weary and heavy laden,"* but, *"all you who are weary and heavy laden"* (Mat. 11:28-30).

I have preached all over the world: North America, Central America, South America, Europe, Asia, Africa and the Islands of the Sea. I've had some to tell me that our ministry would not go over in certain places because of the culture, etc. I found all of that to be completely untrue. And I'll tell you why!

First of all, the problem is sin, and it is the same the world over. As well, the solution is Christ, and He is the same the world over. If it is to be noticed, Paul didn't change his Message, irrespective as to where he preached.

The truth is, the culture of all people,

anywhere in the world, is ungodly, unscriptural, un-Christlike, and desperately needs to be changed.

Second, it can only be changed by the power of the Gospel of Christ. When the person gives their heart and life to the Lord Jesus, they then take unto themselves Bible culture, which is the same the world over, that is, if adhered to as it should be. As someone has well said, *"The ground is level at the foot of the Cross."*

BUSINESS

Verses 9 through 12 proclaim the *"business"* of Tyre.

The phrase of Verse 12, *"They traded in your fairs,"* refers to huge trade marts such as are conducted at the present in order to exhibit the merchandise of a particular country.

America says that her business is business! Likewise Tyre.

At this particular time, the business of Jerusalem was supposed to have been the taking of the Word of the Lord to the world. This they did not do, but corrupted themselves, which necessitated their destruction by the Lord. Jesus would say: *"Man shall not live by bread alone, but by every Word that proceeds out of the Mouth of God"* (Mat. 4:4). Tragically and sadly, inasmuch as Jerusalem has just been destroyed, the *"Word of the Lord"* is woefully curtailed.

Even though the Lord will mightily use Daniel as a witness to the most powerful leaders in the world, nevertheless, that which the Lord intended for Jerusalem, in that it would be light to all the world, has now been brought to a halt. (Jerusalem had ceased to shine the light long before she was destroyed, which, in effect, occasioned her destruction.)

Even though after the 70-year dispersion ended, and the Jews were restored to their Land, still, the Light, even though burning brightly at the first unto Ezra and Nehemiah, soon after their demise, began to flicker. There is some scriptural indication that at this time, Zechariah, the Prophet, was murdered between the Sanctuary and the Altar (Mat. 23:35; Lk. 11:51).

Actually, the spiritual Light grew so dim, that from the time of Malachi, an approximate four hundred year period, no Prophet was heard in Judah, until John the Baptist. Tragically, when Christ came, He was murdered by His own, with Israel being destroyed in A.D. 70, and scattered all over the world.

The flame burned brightly during the days of the Early Church, as recorded in the Book of Acts, with a great part of the world of that day being evangelized; however, in the Third Century, that flame once again began to flicker as the Church began to apostatize, finally degenerating into what is now known as the Catholic Church.

During the Dark Ages, which constituted several hundred years preceding the Reformation, the flame of the Church almost went out; however, with the Reformation, it once again began to burn brightly.

THE HOLY SPIRIT

At the turn of the Twentieth Century, with the advent of the Latter Rain, which instigated the outpouring of the Holy Spirit, the flame began to burn on a par with the Early Church. Up to the present, because of the outpouring of the Holy Spirit, the world has been evangelized to a greater degree than ever before; however, in the 1990's, the Church began to lose its way, with the ensuing of a spiritual drought, which has seriously affected World Evangelism. Nevertheless, there is a hunger in the hearts of some for an outpouring the Holy Spirit such as the world has never seen before, and, as well, the Promise of the Word of God that such is forthcoming (Acts 2:17-21).

THE UNITED STATES

As Judah of old, America has been chosen by God, among others, to be the bearer of that Light, but as Judah of old, is losing her way.

As we have stated, the motto of the nation is *"The business of America is business."*

There is certainly nothing wrong with business, that is, if it is conducted honestly and forthrightly; in fact, God will bless business endeavors, as He is certainly is not an enemy of commerce. In fact, the blessings of God in an economic sense on this nation, making it the envy of the world, is because of the Gospel of Jesus Christ. The powers-that-be may think that the secret of this success is the great educational institutions of this land, or our form of government, etc. While all of these things may play a part, the real cause of the blessing upon this great land is because of the hundreds of thousands of born again Believers in this country who love and serve Jesus Christ. In fact, there is no nation in the world that has experienced the outpouring of the Holy Spirit as the United States. Even as I dictate these words, I strongly sense the Presence of God. It is the Moving, the Operation, the Power of the Holy Spirit, Who, without fail, glorifies Christ, that is the secret of all we have that is good.

But tragically, the nation is losing its way, because the Church is losing its way, and the Church is losing its way, because the Church has left the Cross. The Holy Spirit will not work apart from the Sacrifice of Christ, which gives Him the latitude to do all the things which He alone can do.

THE TAKING OF THE GOSPEL TO THE WORLD

Beginning in the 1930's, and stretching through the 1980's, the greatest export of the United States was Preachers of the Gospel, whether men or women, taking the Message of Redemption to the entirety of the world. In the 1980's, our own particular Ministry was involved by Television and by Crusades all over the world. We saw literally hundreds of thousands brought to a saving knowledge of Jesus Christ. We are still endeavoring to do all within our power to take the message of Redemption to hurting humanity. There is no other hope. Christ Alone holds the answer!

But tragically, at the present time, most of the Missionaries going out to the foreign field, and that number is now less than ever, are little more than amateur psychologists. While there definitely are a few Godly men and women taking the Gospel to the far-flung reaches of the world, the majority do not fit into that category.

In the last couple of years that I was with a major Pentecostal Denomination, I started to see the trend turn. Humanistic psychology was held up as the answer to the ills and perversions of man; consequently, Missionaries were encouraged to fortify themselves with training in this field. As a result, almost nothing is presently going on regarding the foreign fields, as it concerns the Gospel of Jesus Christ. While there definitely are some wonderful things happening, it is not because of the present crop of Missionaries, at least for the most part, but rather because of seed that was planted many years ago.

The Righteousness of the man of God is Jesus Christ. The power of the man of God is the Holy Spirit. With those two factors, Christ and the Holy Spirit, literally anything can be done. Without Christ and the Spirit, nothing can be done, at least for the Lord.

JUDAH

Verses 13 through 17 proclaim the many countries of the world of that day which traded with Tyre. In all the listing of these various places, Verse 17 says, *"Judah, and the Land of Israel, they were your merchants: they traded in your market. . . ."*

If one carefully reads this Chapter, digesting the list of lands and countries, but when coming to the phrase, *"Judah, and the land of Israel,"* there is a quickening of the Spirit and a sense of the Presence of God. Even though the Holy Spirit does nothing to highlight its mention, nevertheless, the serious Bible student understands the significance of this tiny land. As we have said repeatedly in all of our Volumes of the Commentaries, their purpose was threefold:

THE WORD OF GOD

They were to be recipients of the Word of God, which they were, as every writer of the Bible was Jewish, except possibly Luke. Some Scholars believe that even Luke was Jewish, and even though I'm not a Scholar, I believe the same.

Due to having the Word of God, and being the only people in the world who did have the Word of God, they were to be a Light in the midst of darkness.

The worth of all of this could not be overestimated, as should be obvious. There are many books in the world which claim to be holy and sacred, such as the book of Mormon and the Koran, to name just two; however, the truth is, all of those books were figments of men's imaginations, and worse yet, instigated by Satan himself.

THE MESSIAH

The Jews were, so to speak, to be the womb of the Messiah, which they were. This would be in fulfillment of the Promise given to Abraham, where the Lord said to him, *"And in you shall all families of the Earth be blessed"* (Gen. 12:3). As the Word of the Lord was to provide Light to the world, the Messiah was to provide Redemption; actually, the written Word and the Living Word are synonymous (Jn. 1:1).

EVANGELISM

Israel, in being the Light to the world, which they were intended to be, were to evangelize the lost, bringing them to the God of *"Abraham, Isaac, and Jacob."* In this they failed, as both Jeremiah and Ezekiel so glaringly portrayed.

But one day, in the coming Kingdom Age, after they have accepted Christ as their Lord, Saviour, and Messiah, they will then fulfill that which God originally intended, taking the Gospel of Jesus Christ over the entirety of the world. It will take place after the Second Coming (Isa. 66:19).

MERCHANDISE

Verses 18 through 24 proclaim the different types of merchandise traded between these nations, with Tyrus as the chief commercial center.

The indication of these passages is that *"merchants"* brought their wares from great distances to Tyre, where they were exhibited and purchased, both wholesale and retail.

Once again, we emphasize that business and trade are not wrong within themselves, provided they're carried on honestly. In fact, when God really blesses a nation, business activity will be increased greatly, as would be obvious; however, the idea of all of this, as given by the Holy Spirit, is that all understand that these things, as important as they may be to the material and physical welfare of humanity, cannot satisfy the true cry of the soul. Man is not only a physical and a mental being, but, as well, he is a spiritual being. As such, only the Lord can satisfy the longing of the human heart. Only the Lord can touch the soul. Only the Lord can satisfy the cry of the human heart, which alone can make life worth living. That's why Jesus said:

"The thief comes not, but for to steal, and to kill, and to destroy, but I am come that they might have life, and that they might have it more abundantly" (Jn. 10:10).

(25) "THE SHIPS OF TARSHISH DID SING OF YOU IN YOUR MARKET: AND YOU WERE REPLENISHED, AND MADE VERY GLORIOUS IN THE MIDST OF THE SEAS.

(26) "YOUR ROWERS HAVE BROUGHT YOU INTO GREAT WATERS: THE EAST WIND HAS BROKEN YOU IN THE MIDST OF THE SEAS.

(27) "YOUR RICHES, AND YOUR FAIRS, YOUR MERCHANDISE, YOUR MARINERS, AND YOUR PILOTS, YOUR CALKERS, AND THE OCCUPIERS OF YOUR MERCHANDISE, AND ALL YOUR MEN OF WAR, WHO ARE IN YOU, AND IN ALL YOUR COMPANY WHICH IS IN THE MIDST OF YOU, SHALL FALL INTO THE MIDST OF THE SEAS IN THE DAY OF YOUR RUIN.

(28) "THE SUBURBS SHALL SHAKE AT THE SOUND OF THE CRY OF YOUR PILOTS.

(29) "AND ALL WHO HANDLE THE OAR, THE MARINERS, AND ALL THE PILOTS OF THE SEA, SHALL COME DOWN FROM THEIR SHIPS, AND THEY SHALL STAND UPON THE LAND;

(30) "AND SHALL CAUSE THEIR VOICE TO BE HEARD AGAINST YOU, AND SHALL CRY BITTERLY, AND SHALL CAST UP DUST UPON THEIR HEADS, THEY SHALL WALLOW THEMSELVES IN THE ASHES:

(31) "AND THEY SHALL MAKE THEMSELVES UTTERLY BALD FOR YOU, AND GIRD THEM WITH SACKCLOTH, AND THEY SHALL WEEP FOR YOU WITH BITTERNESS OF HEART AND BITTER WAILING.

(32) "AND IN THEIR WAILING THEY SHALL TAKE UP A LAMENTATION FOR YOU, AND LAMENT OVER YOU, SAYING, WHAT CITY IS LIKE TYRUS, LIKE THE DESTROYED IN THE MIDST OF THE SEA?

(33) "WHEN YOUR WARES WENT FORTH OUT OF THE SEAS, YOU FILLED MANY PEOPLE; YOU DID ENRICH THE

KINGS OF THE EARTH WITH THE MULTITUDE OF YOUR RICHES AND OF YOUR MERCHANDISE.

(34) "IN THE TIME WHEN YOU SHALL BE BROKEN BY THE SEAS IN THE DEPTHS OF THE WATERS YOUR MERCHANDISE AND ALL YOUR COMPANY IN THE MIDST OF YOU SHALL FALL.

(35) "ALL THE INHABITANTS OF THE ISLES SHALL BE ASTONISHED AT YOU, AND THEIR KINGS SHALL BE SORE AFRAID, THEY SHALL BE TROUBLED IN THEIR COUNTENANCE.

(36) "THE MERCHANTS AMONG THE PEOPLE SHALL HISS AT YOU; YOU SHALL BE A TERROR, AND NEVER SHALL BE ANY MORE."

The diagram is:

1. The *"hiss"* of Verse 36 is expressive of mental shock, corresponding to the low whistle which men give today on suddenly hearing of some great calamity.

2. The last phrase of Verse 36, *"and never shall be any more,"* has been fulfilled. Old Tyre was utterly destroyed in 600 B.C., and New Tyre in A.D. 400.

3. The mills of God grind slowly, but they grind exceedingly fine. In other words, they miss nothing.

RUIN

The phrase of Verse 25, *"The ships of Tarshish,"* proclaims the distance to which the trade extended. These *"ships"* referred to ocean-going vessels.

All of this, as stated, was Satan's effort to rebuild the Garden of Eden without the *"Tree of Life,"* i.e., the *"Lord Jesus Christ."* The Evil One claims to his hapless victims that he can do such by addressing only the material and the physical. Inasmuch as it is impossible for him to address the spiritual, which can only be done by the Lord, his dupes are deceived.

Beginning with Verse 26, and through the remainder of the Chapter, all the glory and the glamour of Tyre are predicted to be brought to ruin.

The phrase of Verse 26, *"Your rowers have brought you into great waters,"* has reference to a ship on the open sea which has been steered into a storm. As such, she will be destroyed, and that destruction will include the hurt of all who contributed to her prosperity.

Despite the riches, glamour, glory, power, influence, and recognition, still, all that Satan has and does will ultimately be brought to destruction. As it is without God, consequently, it has the stamp of death written upon it, even at the height of its strength. This includes kingdoms, nations, and even individuals! Satan promises much, but his way is the way of death, while God's Way is the way of life.

The idea of this Verse is that *"greater waters,"* i.e., turbulent times are faced by all, the righteous and the unrighteous; however, the unrighteous cannot sustain the storm, because they do not have God's help, and will therefore *"be broken in the midst of the seas."*

Verse 27 continues with the portrayal of the *"ruin"* of Tyre. As Tyre was ultimately destroyed, so were every other kingdom, empire, nation, and person in the world who have forgotten God.

Mighty Egypt, which was looked at as the ruler of the world for so long, is now but a shabby sexton of ancient tombs.

The mighty Assyrian Empire, which likewise ruled the world of its day, is now only an inscription in archeological digs.

Mighty Babylon, described by Daniel as the *"Head of Gold,"* is now nothing but a footnote in history's accounts.

Mighty Greece once ruled the world under Alexander the Great, and gave the world its great thinkers, but now has only the ruins of the Acropolis to remind her of former glory.

Mighty Rome once ruled the world, and did so for nearly one thousand years, but today, where are her Generals and Caesars? They are peanut vendors and organ grinders.

Spain's piratical ships once sailed the oceans, filling her coffers with gold from the New World. Today, she sits like a drowsy beggar, watching the hands of a broken clock.

In the 1930's, much of the world was ruled by Great Britain, an Empire which, incidentally, did more to contribute to modern civilization than any other, and because she gave the Bible to the world (the King James translation); however, Great Britain is no longer great because she is no longer Godly. Sadly, the United States follows in the same footsteps, because she too is forgetting God.

These twin Empires of Great Britain and the United States, which have contributed so much because of Christianity, seemingly little know or understand that the source of their prosperity is God. Without God, it ultimately comes crashing down.

I realize that since the United States presently is the only super-power in the world, she possibly thinks that there is no nation or group of nations that can stand up to her. In the natural, that is correct; however, the Lord is able to bring down the mightiest, whoever they might be, if they forget Him. This must not be forgotten, but tragically, I'm afraid it is, even by the Church.

Even though presently the Jews are a long way from God, still, because of Promises made by the Lord to them, they are coming back to the Lord; even though there will be some hard days ahead, still, their greatest days are yet to come.

Conversely, the mighty Empires of the past, which were so much stronger, richer, and more powerful than Israel, are nothing but a footnote in history, because they did not have God. That which belongs to the Lord survives and grows; ultimately, in Christ, they will rule the world.

MASADA

On a trip to Israel, not so long ago, we were standing on the top of Masada, looking down at the ruins of what had been the Roman encampment of nearly two thousand years ago, when they finally took Masada, with over one thousand Jews committing suicide.

After the Jewish guide had finished explaining the historical narrative of those times, for a few moments all were silent, looking down from this promontorial point.

I looked at him and softly said, *"Where is mighty Rome today? She is gone, while Israel is once again thriving."*

This Jewish guide turned and looked at me for a long time, and then finally spoke. *"I've never thought of that,"* he said, *"but it is true,"* he added!

It is true because of God.

Masada was one of the last holdouts of the Jews of nearly 2,000 years ago. Jerusalem had already fallen, with over one million Jews being slaughtered, and hundreds of thousands sold as slaves. As far as the world was concerned, this little tiny nation would be no more. But they reckoned without God.

In 1948, as all the world knows, Israel, once again, after nearly two thousand years of wandering among the nations of the world, finally was back in their land, and once again, a sovereign State. Oh yes, it took the miracle-working power of God to bring it to pass. But it was brought to pass.

PRESIDENT TRUMAN

President Truman occupied the White House at a most momentous time in history, the close of World War II, and the start of the cold war with the Soviet Union.

As he usually did every morning after his retirement, he would take a walk, oftentimes accompanied by reporters trying to get his take on certain world events.

Not long before he died, a reporter asked him the following question:

"Mr. President, what do you consider to be your greatest achievement while in office?"

As the reporter wrote the story some time later, he went on to mention that many thoughts entered his mind, as he thought about what the answer of the President would be! This was the man who had given the orders for the atomic bombs to be dropped on Nagasaki and Hiroshima, Japan. This is the man who instituted the Marshall Plan, which saved Western Europe from Soviet Communism.

The Reporter was expecting one of these momentous events to be named; however, the President said something that, in a sense, was something of a shock to the reporter.

"That I had the privilege of putting the weight, the might and the power, of the United States behind the formation of Israel as a nation," was the answer of President Truman.

The President was right! The little man from Independence, Missouri, had been used mightily by God in bringing this to pass.

I had the opportunity to hear an interview, which lasted well over an hour, with Clark Clifford, who had been an advisor to every President in the Democratic Party, from the time of Truman through the time of Jimmy Carter. This was shortly before he died.

While there were many, many experiences of which this statesman was a part, almost the entirety of the program had to do with his contribution as it regarded President Truman, and the formation of Israel as a State.

He mentioned the fact that he was the junior advisor to the President, which meant that he carried very little weight at all. He knew that powerful forces in the President's Cabinet, such as General Marshall, were totally opposed to the formation of Israel as a State. In fact, some in the President's Cabinet were advocating the purchase of some small country in Central America, allowing the Jews to go there.

You must remember, at this time, the world had a guilt conscience, including the United States, because of the horror of the holocaust. So they felt they had to do something.

Clark Clifford, being the junior member of the Cabinet, didn't have enough clout to ask for an audience with the President. So he wrote him a letter, as it regarded Israel. He encouraged the President to help these beleaguered people, who had suffered so much, to once again find a place; as he put it in his letter, that place must be their ancient homeland, and it must be called *"Israel."*

To his surprise, President Truman sent for him. It had been some weeks since the letter had been sent, so he had no idea that the President wanted to discuss his letter.

He walked into the Oval Office and stood before the desk, awaiting the President to speak to him. He then looked and saw his letter open on the President's desk. Evidently, President Truman had been reading that which Clark Clifford had written.

The President looked up at him, and in his short, curt manner, without any preliminary remarks, asked Clark Clifford, *"Why do you feel so strongly about the Jews, that they must have a homeland of their own, that it must be the same land portrayed in the Bible, and that it must be called 'Israel'?"*

The question, Mr. Clifford said, was straight to the point. He said he stood there for a few moments, saying nothing, actually not knowing really what to say. He wasn't a Jew, so he really didn't know why he felt so strongly about this.

He then said to the President, *"Mr. President, I feel the way that I do, because it's the right thing to do"*! He said the President looked at him for a few moments and said nothing. Without comment, he dismissed him, thanking him for his answer.

A few days later, President Truman announced to the world that he would throw the weight of his office, and the might and majesty of the United States, behind the formation of a State for the Jews, which should be in the land presently called *"Palestine,"* and that it should be named *"Israel."*

Yes, Mr. President, you were right when you stated that your greatest achievement while serving as the leader of this nation, and of the free world, was your influence as it regards the formation of Israel as a State. You were used of God, and mightily so!

DESTRUCTION

Verses 28 through 36 proclaim the destruction of one of the greatest cities in the world of that day, Tyre.

Verse 31 says, *"They shall weep for you with bitterness of heart and bitter wailing."* Riches were their god, and now that the riches are lost, they have nothing! Such are all who place their confidence in anything other than the Lord. Not only do they lose their souls, but as well, they lose the very thing for which they sold their souls.

The intention of the Holy Spirit is to proclaim the Truth that even if riches are obtained, plus station and position, still, it does not bring satisfaction of soul, or true happiness of heart. These things, at least in some ways, are important; nevertheless, the most important thing is the spirit of man, which can only be satisfied by the Lord.

Satan treats man as if he is a material and physical being only, when in reality, as stated, man is a spiritual, material, and physical being. Of the three, the spiritual is by far the most important, and, sadly, the most neglected.

However, even if riches, fame, wealth, and greatness are obtained, they will ultimately be lost, as history abundantly proclaims.

For those who seek the Lord and trust His Ways, they have found the True Riches, which can never be lost, but will only grow and multiply.

Verse 33 says, concerning Tyre, *"You did enrich the kings of the Earth with the multitude of your riches and of your merchandise."*

Because of Tyre's marketing abilities, most of the nations of the world, obviously, would never have wanted her destruction. So, why did Nebuchadnezzar desire to destroy her?

More than likely, Nebuchadnezzar's reasons would not have been plausible to anyone else, probably not even to himself; however, the Lord had chosen him as an instrument for the destruction of this city, and that's what would happen.

Likewise, many nations of the world could not understand why the leaders of the former Soviet Union, which looked so monolithic, allowed it to destruct before the eyes of the world! Decisions were made, however, which, in effect, made little sense. But yet, it was done because God commanded that it be done.

The birth of Christ was about five hundred years after the destruction of Tyre, whereas the Coming of the Lord will be almost immediately after the destruction of future Babylon. Then, as Christ was denied at His First Advent, He will be accepted at His Second Advent, and will set up a Kingdom, a Kingdom of Righteousness, which will rule the entire world, and will ultimately result in the coming down out of Heaven, the New Jerusalem, as the Lord transfers His Headquarters from Heaven to Earth.

Hallelujah!

"A friend have I who stands near,
"To comfort me and still each fear;
"It is my Lord and Saviour dear,
"Whom, having not seen, I love."

"In vain may fancy try to trace
"My Saviour's beauty and His grace;
"More fair than I can dream
"His face, Whom having not seen, I love."

"This precious hope I have each day
"Illumines all my earthly way;
"That He will take me home to stay,
"Whom, having not seen, I love."

"With that fair mansion in my view,
"My pilgrim journey I pursue;
"And strive my Saviour's will to do
"Whom, having not seen, I love."

CHAPTER 28

(1) "THE WORD OF THE LORD CAME AGAIN UNTO ME, SAYING,

(2) "SON OF MAN, SAY UNTO THE PRINCE OF TYRUS, THUS SAITH THE LORD GOD; BECAUSE YOUR HEART IS LIFTED UP, AND YOU HAVE SAID, I AM A GOD, I SIT IN THE SEAT OF GOD, IN THE MIDST OF THE SEAS; YET YOU ARE A MAN, AND NOT GOD, THOUGH YOU SET YOUR HEART AS THE HEART OF GOD:

(3) "BEHOLD, YOU ARE WISER THAN DANIEL; THERE IS NO SECRET THAT THEY CAN HIDE FROM YOU:

(4) "WITH YOUR WISDOM AND WITH YOUR UNDERSTANDING YOU HAVE GOTTEN YOURSELF RICHES, AND HAVE GOTTEN GOLD AND SILVER INTO YOUR TREASURES:

(5) "BY YOUR GREAT WISDOM AND BY YOUR TRAFFIC HAVE YOU INCREASED YOUR RICHES, AND YOUR HEART IS LIFTED UP BECAUSE OF YOUR RICHES:

(6) "THEREFORE THUS SAITH THE LORD GOD; BECAUSE YOU HAVE SET YOUR HEART AS THE HEART OF GOD;

(7) "BEHOLD, THEREFORE I WILL BRING STRANGERS UPON YOU, THE TERRIBLE OF THE NATIONS: AND THEY SHALL DRAW THEIR SWORDS AGAINST THE BEAUTY OF YOUR WISDOM, AND THEY SHALL DEFILE YOUR BRIGHTNESS.

(8) "THEY SHALL BRING YOU DOWN TO THE PIT, AND YOU SHALL DIE THE DEATHS OF THEM WHO ARE SLAIN IN THE MIDST OF THE SEAS.

(9) "WILL YOU YET SAY BEFORE HIM WHO SLAYS YOU, I AM GOD? BUT YOU SHALL BE A MAN, AND NO GOD, IN THE HAND OF HIM WHO SLAYS YOU.

(10) "YOU SHALL DIE THE DEATHS OF THE UNCIRCUMCISED BY THE HAND OF STRANGERS: FOR I HAVE SPOKEN IT, SAITH THE LORD GOD."

The structure is:

1. The dual personality of the Demoniac (Mk., Chpt. 5) corresponds to the dual personality of the Prince of Tyre, except that, in this case, Satan himself, not a subordinate, energized his victim.

2. As thus indwelt and energized, the Prince of Tyre is here a fore-picture of the Antichrist, and the city itself pictures the polished point of the spear wounding the people of God. Tyre, as a fortress of the Evil One, was planted in Immanuel's Land, and, as a source of moral corruption and falsehood, visualized the Kingdom of Darkness in its perpetual antagonism to the Kingdom of Light (Williams).

3. The King of Tyre, at this time, was Ethbaal II. Ethbaal means *"God Himself."* He claimed to be the great God. Antichrist will declare himself to be the Supreme God, as well (II Thess. 2:4).

THE WORD OF THE LORD

Regarding the Spirit world, this Chapter is one of the most remarkable in the Bible. The Holy Spirit, through Ezekiel, as He had concerned Himself with the city of Tyrus, now concerns Himself with its ruler, who is symbolic of Satan.

This Chapter plus Isaiah, Chapter 14 give us great insight into Lucifer, the ruler of darkness.

The phrase of Verse 1, *"The Word of the Lord,"* proclaims the fact, that everything here given, were not the mere thoughts of Ezekiel, with him in fact, only being the transmitting agent. It is the *"Word of the Lord,"* which means, as does the entirety of the Bible, that it is infallible, irrevocable, unchangeable, unalterable, and without error.

As we've already stated, the earthly Prince of Tyre at the time of Ezekiel was Ethbaal II. He claimed to be God.

Ethbaal took part with Pharaoh Hopra and Zedekiah in the league against Nebuchadnezzar. This is one of, if not the major reason, that he was attacked and ultimately defeated by the Babylonian Monarch.

As we have stated, the Holy Spirit gave such time and attention to this city of Tyre, and because it represents Satan endeavoring to rebuild the Garden of Eden, so to speak,

NOTES

without the Tree of Life, Who is the Lord Jesus Christ. In fact, he pictures himself as God, and makes all types of promises to those who follow him, even making some of them very rich, etc.

Satan is not only the *"prince of the power of the air"* (Eph. 2:2), but as well, he is the *"god of this world"* (II Cor. 4:4). It refers to the system of the world, which at the Second Coming, will be taken over by the Lord Jesus Christ, with all of its kingdoms destroyed (Dan. 2:34-35, 44, 45). So in Chapters 26 through 28, the Holy Spirit, through the Prophet, outlines the system of this world, its sponsor, and his ultimate defeat. To which we have already alluded, *"the prince of this world is judged"* (Jn. 16:11), which means that his eternal due will be the *"lake of fire"* (Rev. 20:10), along with all down through history who have followed him (Rev. 20:11-15).

THE PRINCE OF TYRUS

The phrase of Verse 2, *"I am a god, I sit in the seat of God,"* is very near Paul's description of the *"man of sin"* (II Thess. 2:3-4). Even though this passage speaks of the earthly *"Prince of Tyrus,"* nevertheless, it is Satan himself who energizes his victim.

As we look at all of this, we see Israel planted in the midst of the nations of the world, in fact, the only Light in the midst of the darkness, for they were the only people on Earth who had any knowledge of Jehovah. The balance of the world worshipped idols, even as the name of the *"Prince of Tyre"* represents — Ethbaal. He was named after *"Baal."* And now Israel's Light has gone out, and I hope that in all of this, we can see the utter tragedy of this terrible happening. With Israel gone, there will be nothing left to show the way.

While they were ultimately restored, there is a good possibility that their falling away delayed the coming of the Messiah by several hundreds of years. Before He could come, the nation would have to be restored, would have to regain at least a measure of its strength, with at least a remnant of its people evidencing Faith in the Lord.

ISRAEL AND THE CHURCH

The situation is presently very similar, but

yet in opposite directions.

Whereas Israel had to be brought back to the Promised Land, after their dispersion, which dispersion was seventy years, they came back only in small numbers. It took approximately four hundred years for the nation to come back to some semblance of its former glory, even then ruled by other nations, and because they were no longer worthy to hold the scepter of power, that having been given to the Gentiles upon the spiritual declension of Judah.

So when Jesus came, the nation was ruled by Rome, but despite its terrible self-righteousness, still, there was an element among its people, who were truly looking for the Messiah, truly expecting His coming, and thereby evidencing faith in that great Promise (Lk. 2:25-38).

With the Church, it is the very opposite. Whereas Israel had to regain faith, at least as it regarded those who truly believed, the Church is losing Faith. The Scripture plainly says of these last days, and by no less than our Lord Himself: *"Nevertheless when the Son of Man comes, shall He find faith on the Earth?"* (Lk. 18:8). The idea is, if the Rapture doesn't take place soon, there will be precious few on the Earth who truly have faith.

FAITH

As we've said elsewhere in this Volume, the subject of *"Faith"* has been addressed more in the last fifty years, than possibly the entirety of the previous centuries of the Church put together. Tens of thousands of books have been written on the subject, with almost all of them of little use, or even blatantly unscriptural. The reason?

All of this teaching that has been given, while grandly proclaiming the principle of faith, has addressed almost none at all what the true object of faith must be!

As it regards faith, every human being who has ever lived has had, and does have, faith; however, it's not the type of Faith that God will recognize. While the Scientist boasts that he will not accept anything on faith, at the same time, labors in the laboratory, evidencing faith in his efforts, that a solution will be found for whatever it is that he is seeking. So, whether he realizes it or not, he is functioning strictly on faith, as does everyone else.

The free market system is an excellent example. It has provided the greatest prosperity in the world, at least for the nations which embrace this concept. Communism attempted to function in the spirit of a controlled economy, but fell by the wayside after a little more than seventy years. The reason? It destroyed the faith of the people, which means that the free market economy is God's way, and because it is the way of faith.

But yet, and as stated, while all of this may be *"Faith,"* it is not the type of Faith that God will recognize, and which His Word teaches as it regards Saving Grace. In fact, the type of Faith which has been expounded in the Church for the last fifty years is little more than the type of faith which the world evidences. The only difference is, the modern promoters of their brand of faith claim to base everything they do on the Bible, while the world ignores the Bible. But the truth is, the object of faith as it regards the world is *"self,"* as the object of faith as it has been taught for the last fifty years in the Church, likewise, is *"self,"* even though it heavily laces its teaching with Scriptures — pulled out of context, I might quickly add.

THE CROSS OF CHRIST MUST EVER BE THE OBJECT OF FAITH

The Word of God is the story of the Cross, in essence, *"Jesus Christ and Him Crucified"* (I Cor. 1:23). In fact, in the very first Chapter of the Gospel according to John, we are given, in brief, a portrayal of this of which I speak.

John writes: *"In the beginning was the Word, and the Word was with God, and the Word was God.*

"The same was in the beginning with God.

"All things were made by Him; and without Him was not anything made that was made.

"In Him was life; and the Life was the Light of men" (Jn. 1:1-4).

This tells us, in no uncertain terms, that Jesus Christ is the *"Word of God."*

And then John said: *"And the Word was made flesh, and dwelt among us, and we beheld His glory, the glory of the only Begotten of the Father, full of Grace and Truth"* (Jn. 1:14).

So this tells us, that God became flesh, and as we shall see, He became *"flesh"* for a particular purpose and reason.

The Apostle then said: *"The next day John saw Jesus coming unto him, and said, Behold the Lamb of God, which takes away the sin of the world"* (Jn. 1:29).

So, we are told in these Passages that Jesus, Who is God, and the Word are the same. We are told that this *"Word"* became *"flesh"* for a particular reason. That reason was to go to the *"Cross,"* which was necessary if man was to be redeemed. The Son of God would give Himself as a vicarious (substitutionary), efficacious (effective) Sacrifice for sin, which in effect, would break its power and take away its guilt. This and this alone would satisfy the righteous demands of a thrice-Holy God (Rom. 6:6).

So we learn here that Jesus and the Word are the same, and that it all leads to the Cross.

Therefore, to properly claim the veracity of the *"Word,"* we must always understand the Word as it relates to the *"Cross."* In fact, the entirety of the story of the Bible is the story of Christ and Him Crucified, and also, as one might say, the entire story of Christ and Him Crucified is the story of the Bible. The very first Promise given after the Fall was the promise of Redemption and how it would be carried out, which pointed to the Cross (Gen. 3:15). Consequently, on the very first pages of history, we find Christ and the Cross.

THE BOOK OF REVELATION

In the Book of Revelation, the last book in the Bible, the term, *"Lamb,"* is used some twenty-eight times. In the last two Chapters alone, it is used seven times. This has great meaning.

The Book of Revelation is a compendium of the entirety of the span of time from the beginning to the end, with the emphasis, as is obvious, placed on the end time. So, the Holy Spirit using the title or the metaphor, *"Lamb,"* to describe the Lord Jesus Christ proclaims this as the theme of the entirety of the Bible. But it becomes even more obvious, when we realize that the Holy Spirit used the metaphor, *"Lamb,"* some seven times in the last two Chapters, especially considering, that those two Chapters present a world and a Kingdom of God which are totally without sin. Satan and all of his cohorts are locked away in the Lake of Fire, where they will remain forever and forever. God has transferred His Headquarters from planet Heaven, one might say, to planet Earth, where it will remain forever. In fact, the entirety of the Earth and the heavens have been cleansed and renovated and restored to a perpetual freshness and newness. There is no more trace of sin, iniquity, transgression, disobedience, ungodliness, all which characterize wreckage and ruin. So, why would the Holy Spirit, in this atmosphere, use the metaphor, *"Lamb,"* seven times in these final two Chapters?

Two reasons:

1. First of all, by using the title or the metaphor, *"Lamb,"* He is telling us that we have all of this, and will enjoy it forever and forever, and I speak of everything described in Revelation, Chapters 21 and 22, all because of what Jesus did at the Cross.

2. Inasmuch as the title or metaphor, *"Lamb,"* is used seven times, this, being God's number of perfection, tells us that what Jesus did was absolutely perfect. That's the reason that Paul could refer to this Covenant as *"The Everlasting Covenant"* (Heb. 13:20), which means that it will never have to be amended in any form.

As is obvious, the word, *"Lamb,"* even as John used the word (Jn. 1:29), is a metaphor for the Sacrifice of Christ, pointing back toward all the millions of lambs which were offered up under the Old Testament economy, as a symbolism for the Redeemer Who was ultimately to come.

FAITH AND ITS CORRECT OBJECT

So, the only type of Faith that God will recognize is the Faith which has the Cross as its object (Jn. 3:16; Rom. 6:3-14; 8:1-2, 11; I Cor. 1:17-18, 21, 23; 2:2, 5; Gal., Chpt. 5; 6:14; Eph. 2:13-18; Col. 2:14-15; Rev. 22:17).

Regrettably, most all the teaching on the subject of faith given in the last fifty years, when traced to its ultimate conclusion, has *"self"* as its object; consequently, and as repeatedly stated, it is a faith that God cannot recognize, hence, Jesus asking the question if faith would be found on the Earth when He comes back?

The Master also said, and plainly: *"If any man will come after Me, let him deny himself* (deny self as it regards our personal strength and ability), *and take up his cross daily* (the benefits of the Cross) *and follow Me."*

He then said: *"For whosoever will save his life shall lose it* (who tries to function in his own strength): *but whosoever will lose his life for My sake, the same shall save it"* (lose one's life in Christ, which brings Salvation) (Lk. 9:23-24).

I believe at least one of the reasons that this Ministry (I speak of Jimmy Swaggart Ministries) has gone through the suffering and sorrow which we have experienced, not at all excusing ourselves from our own culpability, is that we might be given the great Revelation of the Cross, which in effect, was the same thing which Paul taught. Without a Romans 7:24 experience, I'm not certain if I could ever have been brought to the place to where the Lord could open up to my heart this great Truth. To be sure, it has been given not only for me, but for the entirety of the Church, and for the world for that matter. The Church must be brought back to the Cross! And to be sure, all who will be saved will come back to the Cross. Now read those words very carefully, because I definitely believe they are from the Lord.

If the Message of the Cross is rejected, the Lord will likewise reject the rejecter. Listen again to Paul: *"Wherefore come out from among them, and be ye separate, saith the Lord, and touch not the unclean thing; and I will receive you,*

"And will be a Father unto you, and you shall be My sons and daughters, saith the Lord Almighty.

"Having therefore these Promises, dearly beloved, let us cleanse ourselves from all filthiness of the flesh and spirit, perfecting holiness in the fear of God" (II Cor. 6:17-18; 7:1).

PRIDE

The phrase of Verse 2, *"Thus saith the Lord God; because your heart is lifted up,"* denotes the foundation sin of all sin, *"pride."*

Pride, in the scriptural and spiritual sense, speaks of self-importance, and leads to acts of rebellion and willful disobedience. It implies arrogant insensitivity to others, matched with overwhelming self-confidence. This attitude leads to conduct that in turn brings destruction, for only God can rightly be the Source and Object of our pride. It is a lofty sense of self-importance.

The dangers of arrogance and pride are well documented. For even the Godly can be drawn away from God, when success stimulates pride (II Chron. 26:16-17). According to Proverbs, pride is an evil to be hated (8:13), leads to disgrace (11:2; 29:23), breeds quarrels (13:10), and goes before destruction (16:18).

In other words, pride is sin. Pride and arrogance involve a denial of our place as creatures, living in a world shaped and governed by the Creator, Who has given a Word that is to govern our lives. Thus the Old Testament makes it clear: God is committed to punish pride and arrogance. In almost identical phraseology, Isaiah twice declared: *"The eyes of the arrogant man will be humbled and the pride of men brought low: the LORD alone will be exalted in that day"* (Isa. 2:11, 17).

PRIDE AND JUDGMENT

The theme of judgment is often associated with this sin, which involves not only a basic denial of the significance of God, but also the foolish exaltation of the individual or the human race (Dan. 5:20; Lev. 26:19).

In the New Testament, the Greek word often used for pride, *"Hypselophroneo,"* is used in Romans 11:20 and I Timothy 6:17, and means one who presumptuously rests their confidence in something other than God Himself.

Another Greek word, *"Physioo,"* for pride is found in I Corinthians 4: 6, 18, 19; 5:2; 8:1; 13:4; and Colossians 2:18. These direct our attention to the inner impact of pride. Pride puffs us up and makes us arrogant and conceited. Believers are warned against becoming puffed up about following one leader over another or for belonging to one particular group rather than another. The Corinthian Church was warned against being puffed up while sin was permitted in the fellowship.

THE RIGHT KIND OF PRIDE

Not all pride is wrong. Paul desired the Believer to take pride, not in externals, but in what God is doing in men's hearts (II Cor. 5:12). Paul himself takes pride in the progress of the Corinthians in the Faith (II Cor. 7:4; 8:24).

We Believers can take pride in ourselves, without comparing ourselves with others, when we lovingly support one another (Gal. 6:4). Both poor and rich Believers — for very different reasons — can take pride in their new position in the Faith (James 1:9-10).

Pride, as a self-exalting attitude, is wrong. But God wants us to take a healthy pride, and to find joy in what He is doing in our lives. As arrogance, the wrong kind of pride is a source of sin, for only the humility that keeps us responsive to the Lord and His Word is appropriate in our relationship with One Who is truly the Living God.

PRIDE AND SATAN

This Chapter will show us that it was pride that caused Satan's Fall, when he took his eyes off God, his Creator, and placed them on himself. As this is the sin which dragged him down, it is the sin that he used to drag down Adam and Eve in the Garden of Eden.

Satan told Eve that if she would partake of the fruit of the Tree of the Knowledge of Good and Evil, which the Lord had warned against, that *"You shall be as gods, knowing good and evil"* (Gen. 3:5). Regrettably, Adam and Eve believed Satan's lie, disobeyed God, and fell, dragging the entire human race with them, for all of humanity, theoretically, were in Adam's loins. As the representative of the human race, so to speak, when he sinned, he sinned for all, and all would suffer its results.

Adam and Eve lost God-consciousness, falling to the far lower level of self-consciousness. Hence, man's preoccupation with self. And yet, he ever tries to improve self, knowing that something is wrong, but ever fails, as fail he must. Self can only be improved as it is hidden in Christ.

Adam and Eve lost the power to do good, and in its place, they now possess the power to do only evil.

(Man thinks that he does much good by his philanthropic acts; however, the good that he does comes from the same tree that spawns the evil, *"the Tree of the Knowledge of Good and Evil,"* and consequently, is diseased, and thereby, corrupt. Therefore, without God, man cannot truly do good.)

Thus, instead of becoming like God, Adam and Eve became unlike Him in that He has the power to do only good. It is morally impossible for Him to sin, whereas, it is morally impossible for Adam and his offspring to live above sin. When Adam fell, he lost that glorious sinlessness and innocent countenance, which was comparable to that of Elohim, and took upon his countenance, instead, the guilt of sin, which marks the entirety of the human family.

PRIDE AND HUMANITY

"Pride" was the sin used by Satan for the downfall of the human family, and *"The Lie"* was its means; and therefore, the human family is lifted up in pride and finds it much easier to believe a lie and be damned, than to believe the Truth and be saved, thus deceived.

Other than God's Word, and that which is built on the Word of God, all else is a lie. The Laws of Mathematics, Chemistry, and Physics, as well as all the Natural Sciences, are unfailing because they stem from God's Laws of Creation; however, the Social Sciences, such as Sociology, Anthropology, and Psychology, etc., are based on lies, because they have, by and large, ignored the Truth concerning these subjects, which is the Word of God, and instead, have substituted the word of man.

Thankfully, the Natural Sciences such as Mathematics, etc., cannot be changed by man, or else nothing would function. In other words, the bridges would fall down, and the airplanes wouldn't fly, etc.; therefore, these Laws cannot be tampered with, or perverted, whereas, the social laws can, and, in fact, have been!

The very reason the social sciences are tampered with, with the Word of God being denied, is because of pride. Man erroneously thinks he can solve his own social and spiritual problems, when, in reality, he only makes them worse. Regrettably, the Church has bought into this lie, actually repudiating the very cause of its existence, which is to point men to Christ. Instead, it points them to Freud, Maslow, Rogers, and Skinner, etc.

PRIDE AND ITS EFFECT

The phrase of Verse 2, *"And you have said, I am a god,"* mouths the same words, basically, as the coming Antichrist, when he *"sits in the Temple of God, showing himself that he is god"* (II Thess. 2:4).

The phrase, *"I sit in the seat of God,"* which the Antichrist will attempt to do, is the crowning sin of all mankind. Men love to play God. Hence the world spawning an Adolf Hitler, a Genghis Khan, or a strutting gangster, dictator, or an inner city kid with a .38 caliber revolver. Whether it's a Joseph Stalin subjugating 150,000,000 people, or one person terrorizing a neighbor, it all stems from Satan and the desire to be God; however, all such action is totally bereft of the Heavenly Father Who can only do good, and, is instead filled with evil in that it can only do bad.

MAN AND GOD

The phrase of Verse 2, *"Yet you are a man, and not God,"* marks the great difference between the created and the Creator. In this one sentence is the error of the human family. Man does not desire to place himself in the position of the created, hence, the lie of evolution. Neither does he want to recognize God as the Creator, therefore, he makes himself god.

The phrase, *"Though you set your heart as the heart of God,"* refers to pride. God has the right to think of Himself as God, because He is God. Man has no right to think such; however, his heart, which is desperately wicked, keeps trying to make him believe that he is the Creator instead of the created.

Man is easily deceived into believing this, because, in fact, he does have the power to create many things, a power given to him by his Creator; however, man is never the originator of the first cause, that alone being the domain of God. In other words, while man can create things, he can do so only by using that which God has already created. But because of his fallen, demented nature, he is easily deceived into believing that he is the Creator; however, the one he deceives the most is himself.

This is the reason the Lord says, *"But to this man will I look, even to him who is poor* (poor in spirit) *and of a contrite spirit, and trembles at my Word"* (Isa. 66:2).

NOTES

WISDOM

The phrase of Verse 3, *"Behold, you are wiser than Daniel,"* doesn't actually mean that he was, in fact, wiser than the great Prophet-Statesman. He only thought so in his own mind.

By now, the fame of Daniel had, no doubt, spread far and wide through the Chaldean Empire. He had long since performed the impossible (by the direction of the Holy Spirit) in proclaiming to Nebuchadnezzar, not only his forgotten dream, but, as well, its all-important meaning (Dan., Chpt. 2). Due to the Lord elevating him, he had been made *"ruler over the whole province of Babylon, and chief of the governors over all the wise men of Babylon"* (Dan. 2:48). As Daniel was given up to be the wisest man in the Babylonian Empire, and, therefore, the world of that day, this egotistical king of Tyre, Ithobalis II, boasts that he is wiser that the Prophet.

The phrase of Verse 3, *"There is no secret that they can hide from you,"* refers to him comparing himself to Daniel.

As he was very rich, and Tyre was one of the great trading centers of the world, and had been made so by his ability, at least in part, he had become very lifted up in himself. He, no doubt, had a small army of agents working for him, and scattered all over the world of that day, keeping him informed regarding business activities, political happenings, or anything that might be useful to this prideful king. As a result of many of the *"secrets"* of his contemporaries and competitors being found out and revealed to him, he becomes bigger and bigger in his own eyes. Of course, the difference in this man and Daniel is staggering.

This king's wisdom comes about by subterfuge, cleverness, wiliness, lying, and chicanery, whereas Daniel's wisdom, instead, comes from God. And Daniel was the man with whom the king of Tyre compared himself with a self-satisfied sense of superiority, and he, as the next Verse will show, found the proof of his higher wisdom in his wealth.

WEALTH

The phrase of Verse 4, *"With your wisdom and with your understanding,"* refers to its use to gain riches for the king of Tyre, as most of such wisdom in the world is used for the same purpose. Conversely, Daniel's wisdom was used to carry out the Will of God, which, among other things, made government better, the lot of the people better, as well as all-around prosperity. The difference in the two is staggering, and portrays the present world as well!

The former was of greed, while the latter was of purpose — God's purpose. To be frank, statesmen of this character have probably never been seen before or since, and because the Lord has never elevated anyone quite like He did Daniel.

In this Twenty-eighth Chapter of Ezekiel, and the example given of this earthly king, Ithobalis II, one easily observes the spirit of this world's system, which is the same now as then. This system cannot be changed, at least not by man, even Christian man, but is rather slated for destruction. It is sad when one realizes that a great part of the resources of the modern Church is setting about to change the world by political means, which is totally unscriptural. As we have stated, while it is certainly true that the Body of Christ can make the world's system better by its involvement, and is encouraged to do so, at least up to a point (Rom., Chpt. 13), still, the world's system will not truly be changed until the Coming of the Lord (Rev., Chpt. 19).

The mission of the Church is to preach the Gospel of Jesus Christ, for it alone can set the captive free, and is actually meant to save men out of society, instead of saving society.

The phrase of Verse 4, *"You have gotten yourself riches,"* refers to the basic intent of the world that has not changed from then until now. Paul, in writing to Timothy, said: *"The love of money is the root of all evil"* (I Tim. 6:10).

Money, within itself, is not sinful or wrong, only the love of it constitutes greed. Hence, the Church is warned that *"Godliness with contentment is great gain,"* and that, if God does see fit to bless with money, it should be used to take the Gospel to the world (Rom. 10:14-15).

THE GOSPEL OF GREED

The Word of Faith philosophy, which began in an unscriptural way, and because it began with a philosophy other than the Cross, has now degenerated, until basically, it is no more than a *"gospel of greed."* To be frank, *"money"* is the theme of this message, and money alone!

Little or no effort is made to get people saved, or Believers baptized with the Holy Spirit, or lives changed by the Power of God; these false teachers claim that their ministry has nothing to do with souls being saved, etc. but rather to teach the Church how to be rich; consequently, Christlikeness, Righteousness, Holiness, and the Fruit of the Spirit are not at all the theme, but rather *"money."* Even though this doctrine is so blatantly wrong, so obviously wrong, yet, it wants not at all for followers, as hundreds of millions of dollars pour into its coffers, and because, it seems, there is a modicum of greed in all of us. And when it is claimed, that all of this is according to the Word of God, the Church, which is basically illiterate as it regards the Bible, easily falls for this *"lie,"* and a lie it is, and because the greed overwhelms all else. In other words, a Scripture quoted here and there, and pulled out of context and perverted, justifies, at least in the minds of the greedy, that which is being promoted.

Pure and simple, it is a pyramid scheme, with only the ones at the top getting rich, and I speak of the Preachers. And to be sure, the money that goes into their pockets pertains not at all to the spread of the Gospel, the winning of souls to Christ, or lives changed by the Power of God, but only that more trappings of riches can be purchased, in order to continue to deceive the gullible. In other words, the Preachers flaunt their wealth, telling the millions of dupes who follow them, that if they will exercise the faith which is being proclaimed, that they, as well, can have such riches. As stated, it is a heady doctrine, in that it seems to be legitimized by the Word of God, which justifies the greed.

If the Church would only open its eyes and look, it would see that during the decade of the 90's, the decade of gospel greed, I might add, precious few people were saved, precious few baptized with the Holy Spirit, precious few truly healed, despite the staggering claims, and precious few lives truly changed.

And yet, there is a small amount of truth in this fallacious doctrine, even as there is a small amount of truth in all lies.

God does bless His people, and does so abundantly!

THE TRUE BLESSINGS OF GOD

But if it's truly God Who is doing the blessing, the money will be used in the right way, at least by those who want to do right.

If God gives individuals the wisdom to get wealth, they should take care of their families, and then use the remainder to help take the Gospel to the world. If we function in this manner, which is the way that God intends, we will find the Blessings not only continuing, but multiplying. In fact, the Holy Spirit, through Paul, said: *"But this I say, he who sows sparingly shall reap also sparingly; and he who sows bountifully shall reap also bountifully"* (II Cor. 9:6).

So, in this Passage, we are told that if we *"sow bountifully,"* which means to help finance the Gospel, that we will *"reap also bountifully,"* and in every capacity, whether it be physical, material, economical, domestic, and above all, spiritual.

It must be remembered that Chapters 8 and 9 of II Corinthians deal with money, as possibly no other Passages in the Word of God; however, it is money that is to be used for the Work of God, and not personal enrichment. The idea is this:

The Lord plainly tells us, that if we take care of His work, that He will take care of our work. In fact, whenever the believing sinner comes to Christ, he literally comes into the economy of God, which is the greatest economy of on Earth. Jesus said concerning this:

"Therefore I say unto you, Take no thought for your life, what you shall eat, what you shall drink; nor yet your body, what you shall put on. Is not the life more than meat, and the body than raiment?

"Behold the fowls of the air: for they sow not, neither do they reap, nor gather into barns; yet your Heavenly Father feeds them. Are you not much better than they?

"Which of you by taking thought can add one cubit unto his stature?

"And why take ye thought for raiment? Consider the lilies of the field, how they grow, they toil not, neither do they spin (trying to change the situation and do little more than go in circles):

"And yet I say unto you, that even Solomon in all his glory was not arrayed like one of these.

"Wherefore, if God so clothe the grass of the field, which today is and tomorrow is cast into the oven, shall He not much more clothe you, O you of little faith?

"Therefore take no thought, saying, What shall we eat? Or what shall we drink? Or, wherewithal shall be we clothed?

"(For after all these things do the Gentiles seek:) for your Heavenly Father knows that you have need of all of these things.

"But seek ye first the Kingdom of God and His Righteousness; and all these things shall be added unto you.

"Take therefore no thought for the morrow: for the morrow shall take thought for the things of itself. Sufficient unto the day is the evil thereof" (Mat. 6:25-34).

That which you have just read is *"the economy of God,"* which stops all worry and fretting, knowing that God will take care of us, and because we have sought first His Kingdom and His Righteousness.

THE OPPOSITE OF THE ECONOMY OF GOD

The Holy Spirit through Paul addressed this as well, warning Christians about the dangers of the love of money. He said:

"Perverse disputings of men of corrupt minds, and destitute of the truth, supposing that gain is Godliness: from such withdraw yourself.

"But Godliness with contentment is great gain.

"For we brought nothing into this world, and it is certain we can carry nothing out.

"And having food and raiment let us be therewith content.

"But they who will be rich fall into great temptation and a snare, and into many foolish and hurtful lusts, which drown men in destruction and perdition.

"For the love of money is the root of all evil: which while some coveted after, they have erred from the faith and pierced themselves through with many sorrows.

"But you, O man of God, flee these things; and follow after Righteousness, Godliness, Faith, Love, Patience, Meekness" (I Tim. 6:5-11).

I think if we look at the modern Word of Faith doctrine, and compare it to what Jesus said in Matthew, Chapter 6, and to what Paul said in I Timothy, Chapter 6, we would have to come to the conclusion that this gospel of greed being promoted by this erroneous philosophy is not after Christ, but falls into the category of coveting after money, with Paul then plainly saying, *"They have erred from the faith"* (I Tim. 6:10).

The true riches are in obeying what Christ said, as should be overly obvious.

It is ironical, the greed gospel, which promises riches for all of its followers, gives no riches at all, because God cannot bless a *"lie."* But those who truly follow Christ, which is the way of the Cross, with Paul using the term, *"the Faith,"* will be blessed immeasurably, with the true riches, which the world cannot take away.

DESTRUCTION

Verses 5 through 10 proclaim the fact, that, sooner or later, God will bring to heel the system of pride. He has no choice or else it would destroy all of mankind.

The phrase of Verse 6, *"Because you have set your heart as the heart of God,"* is the great sin of mankind, fueled by pride. It was not that the king of Tyrus had a heart that was after God, as did David, but rather that he ignored the Creator of the Universe, and declared himself to be God. This is the great sin of mankind, fueled by pride. Satan wants to be God, and actually declares himself God, which will come to a head in the man of sin in the coming Great Tribulation (II Thess. 2:4). Consequently, all his followers share this same quest, in one way or the other. It stems, as we have previously said, from the Fall in the Garden of Eden. Satan lied to Adam and Eve, telling them that if they would do certain things, i.e., disobey God, they would be *"as gods, knowing good and evil"* (Gen. 3:5). Therefore, this, ungodly man has tried to do from that day until now. It, in effect, says, as this king of old, *"I can be God, better than God can be God."*

NOTES

Therefore, in these Passages, which the Holy Spirit intends, one can easily see the root cause of man's intractable position. He will not admit, at least easily so, that he is not the master of his own destiny and the captain of his own fate.

To be saved, man has to admit that he is a loathsome sinner and unable to save himself, and must therefore throw himself on the Mercy and Grace of God, pleading for help. This, for prideful man, is very hard to do!

GOD'S ANSWER TO PRIDE

Verses 7 through 8, wrapped up in the phrase, *"They shall bring you down to the pit,"* and referring to enemies which God would bring upon the king of Tyre, in effect, consigns this man to Hell, and, in fact, all who follow in his train.

In the phrase of Verse 9, the Lord answers the prideful boasts of this tyrant by saying, *"Will you yet say before him who slays you, I am God?"* And then, in effect, he says, *"But you shall be a man* (find out that you are only a man), *and no God, in the hand of him who slays you."*

This has reference to the coming Babylonians, and the inferiority of the Tyrian Monarch. His self-exaltation, which characterizes so many dictators, will then be put to the test. He has been extremely prosperous, and therefore rich, and made that way by Satan, until he thinks he is invincible; nevertheless, he will face a superior force engineered by the True God of Glory, and will then know that he is only a mere man, *"and no God."* He will not be able to deliver himself from the *"hand of him who slays you."*

The tenor of these words proclaims the Truth that a reckoning day is coming for all, and irrespective of their power and station in life, who has set themselves against God. Jehovah controls all, sees all, and is all, and, therefore, Omnipotent (all-powerful), Omniscient (all-knowing), Omnipresent (everywhere).

It should be noted, that it takes very little power or riches to turn the head of even the strongest. That's the reason, *"that not many wise men after the flesh, not many mighty, not many noble, are called"* (I Cor. 1:26).

As well, let it be known and understood,

that God will ultimately judge all pride. And all erroneous doctrine, and irrespective as to what direction it might take, is fueled by pride; as such, those who believe such erroneous doctrine, whatever it might be, will ultimately be judged by God.

THE CROSS, THE ONLY SOLUTION FOR PRIDE

If the Believer doesn't have the Cross as the foundation doctrine for all that he believes, understanding that everything we receive from the Lord comes to us exclusively by Christ and what He did at the Cross, then a prideful attitude will definitely be the result. It cannot be otherwise! That's why Paul said:

"For the preaching of the Cross is to them who perish foolishness; but unto us which are saved it is the Power of God" (I Cor. 1:18).

He then said: *"For it is written, I will destroy the wisdom of the wise, and will bring to nothing the understanding of the prudent"* (I Cor. 1:19). The type of wisdom and understanding of which he here speaks is that which is fueled by pride. It is that which has rejected the Cross, in effect, referring to it as *"foolishness."*

In fact, the Holy Spirit, through Paul, also said: *"For after that in the wisdom of God the world by wisdom knew not God* (cannot know God by prideful intellect), *it pleased God by the foolishness of preaching* (the preaching of the Cross) *to save them who believe"* (I Cor. 1:21).

To sum up, the world, and regrettably even much of the Church, looks at the *"Cross,"* as *"foolishness."* It is all because of pride. If it is to be noticed, and how can it not be noticed, the Word of Faith doctrine, which has made the greatest inroad into the modern Church, repudiates the Cross, referring to it as *"past miseries"* and *"the greatest defeat in human history."* Let us say it again:

The only solution for the problem of *"pride,"* which is a problem for every single Believer, and because it fueled the Fall, is the Cross of Christ. The Cross is God's answer to pride and His only answer. That rejected, there is nothing left but destruction. Listen again to Paul:

"For many walk, of whom I have told you often, and now tell you even weeping, that they are the enemies of the Cross of Christ: "Whose end is destruction, whose God is their belly, and whose glory is in their shame, who mind earthly things" (Phil. 3:18-19).

THE GOSPEL OF SELF-ESTEEM

In the last few years, the world and the Church have promoted the nefarious scheme of the gospel of self-esteem. They claim that man's true problem is a low self-esteem, and that the solution is to increase such. Consequently, one of its Preacher-promoters claims that Christ died on Calvary to glorify His self-esteem. When he said this over a *"Christian"* television program, several Assemblies of God Preachers, who were conducting the interview, gave him a hardy *"Amen."*

How the mighty have fallen!

The word, *"esteem,"* as in *"self-esteem,"* means *"to set a high value on,"* or *"to regard highly and prize accordingly."*

In answer to this false doctrine, Jesus said, *"But if your eye be evil, your whole body shall be full of darkness. If therefore the light that is in you be darkness, how great is that darkness"* (Mat. 6:23).

The gospel of self-esteem is, pure and simple, *"another gospel, proclaiming another Jesus, by another Spirit"* (II Cor. 11:4). As such, it is man-made and man-oriented. It is totally unscriptural and contradictory to the True Gospel of the Lord Jesus Christ. The Bible says, and concerning man, *"For all have sinned, and come short of the Glory of God"* (Rom. 3:23).

It also says: *"There is none righteous, no, not one: there is none who understands, none who seek after God. They are all gone out of the way, they are together become unprofitable; there is none who does good, no, not one"* (Rom. 3:10-11).

In these and other Passages, we are reminded that the whole world is guilty, which refers to being sinful, before God — and that the purpose of the Old Mosaic Law was to emphasize that all men are guilty before God. Then we are told:

"But now the Righteousness of God without the Law is manifested (in Christ) *. . . being justified freely by His Grace through the Redemption that is in Christ Jesus"* (Rom. 3:21, 24).

Man's only hope does not lie in works, but in justification extended through God's Grace — which is all based on Redemption through the Cross.

All of this tells us that man's problem is *"sin,"* and not merely a low *"self-esteem."* Satan is ever projecting something other than the real problem, which, regrettably, many in the Church readily accept. But let all know and understand, man's problem is sin, and sin alone; as well, the only solution for that problem is the Cross of Christ. The Church must understand this, must preach this, must proclaim this, and this alone!

A NEW REFORMATION?

Robert Schuller, the foremost proponent of the self-esteem gospel, has called for a *"new reformation,"* stating that the Sixteenth Century Movement (under Luther and Calvin) was, in his words, a *"reactionary movement,"* because it emphasized that men are sinners. Schuller goes on to say:

"Once a person believes he is an 'unworthy sinner,' it is doubtful if he can honestly accept the saving Grace that God offers in Jesus Christ."

Schuller offers the following as a blueprint for bringing sinners to Salvation:

"If you want to know why Schuller smiles on television, if you want to know why I make people laugh once in a while, I'm giving them sounds and strokes, sounds and strokes (like you would a baby).

"It's a strategy. People who don't trust need to be stroked. People are born with a negative self-image. Because they do not trust, they cannot trust God."

If Schuller is right, Bible evangelistic practices are obviously wrong. We should, then, stop telling people they are sinners who need Jesus Christ as a Saviour. We must no longer convince them of their sin and rebellion against a Holy God. We must never speak of Hell, nor warn of the terrible, eternal consequences of rejecting the wonderful offer of Salvation that is all in Jesus Christ, as an unmerited gift from God.

Instead, we should begin to stroke men and women into Faith, smile them into the Kingdom of God, and elevate, thereby, their self-esteem.

But Schuller has an even broader concept in mind. He goes on to say:

"A theology of self-esteem also produces a theology of social ethics and a theology of economics — and these produce a theology of government. It all arises from one foundation: the dignity of a person who was created in the Image of God."

Basically, this self-esteem theology states that we need a new reformation and a new theology. What it also suggests — but does not openly state — is that we need a new Bible.

THE DOCTRINE OF SELF-ESTEEM IS A DOCTRINE OF DEVILS

Paul said: *"Now the Spirit speaks expressly, that in the latter times some shall depart from the faith, giving heed to seducing spirits, and doctrines of devils"* (I Tim. 4:1).

The doctrine of self-esteem strikes at the very heart of the Gospel of Jesus Christ. This, of course, states that man is a lost sinner who cannot save himself, and who thus desperately needs a Redeemer.

In order to place this new teaching into proper perspective, we should realize that so-called *"Christian psychologists"* and *"Psychiatrists"* transplanted it from outside the Church.

Bruce Narramore, a leading Evangelical Psychologist, who vigorously promotes self-worth teaching, explains in You're Someone Special:

"Under the influence of humanistic Psychologists, like Carl Rogers and Abraham Maslow, many of us Christians have begun to see our need for self-love and self-esteem."

Satan's threefold humanistic plan for taking over the world is basically simple, and you might be surprised at how well it correlates with this new theology of Narramore and others like him.

• Darwinism (Darwin) — the concept of evolution as it affects the social man.

• Marxism (Communism) — Satan's failed economic foundation.

• Freudianism (Psychology) — A profound influence on the morals of man.

Those three are Satan's three-pronged assault — social, economic, and moral. The self-esteem philosophy comes directly from Freudian principles and it does demand an entirely different theology, a theology apart from the Bible.

ALL TRUTH IS GOD'S TRUTH?

The proponents of this lie, and a lie it is, accept the cliché, *"all truth is God's truth,"* which is offered up by *"Christian"* psychologists to justify the *"self-help"* philosophies and *"new-speak"* theologies. It is an *"answer"* and sloganized format.

It doesn't matter, we are told, *"if Adler and Maslow* (psychologists) *were humanists. If they stumbled upon truth, so be it. We must accept truth — no matter its source."*

Most, if not all, *"Christian"* Psychologists hold that Jesus used Psychology in His Ministry. In other words, *"Jesus,"* they say, was *"a great Psychologist."* If that is the truth, then what kind of Psychology did Jesus use?

Was it Freudian? Or some other poor deceived individual?

Freud himself stated: *"I would trash the whole business, but I don't know what else to turn to."* How tragic that he never read St. John 14:6, which states:

"I am the Way, the Truth, and the Life."

Jesus didn't merely propose truth or merely proclaim truth. *"Jesus is Truth."* Without Him, there is no Truth. So that means that Truth is not the end result of philosophy, but is rather a man, The Man Christ Jesus.

All that purports to be Truth without Him is a lie. Psychotherapy — the wellspring of self-esteem philosophy — is a lie, and because it is not according to the Word of God, and basically, what is being touted as Truth today (all Truth is God's Truth) is little more than disconnected facts taken out of context.

Pavlov's dogs were trained to respond by salivating at the ringing of a bell, because they thought that food would be the result, and huge segments of the *"science"* of psychology are built on this minor point.

In keeping with this same policy of building great precepts on flimsy evidence, we are asked to accept this principle: *"Even though it's not in the Bible, it can still be Truth. And anything that is Truth is God's Truth, because all Truth originally comes from God. We must, therefore, avail ourselves of any and all 'helps' that fall into our hands, whatever their source is."*

This foolish rationalization has been purchased by the modern Church at a very high price — the expense of the Bible. As well, it should be quickly stated that all error is Satan's, and it always comes disguised as Truth.

Truth related by a liar becomes a lie.

Is man's problem one of low self-esteem?

No, it isn't! To be completely objective, this much-touted philosophy is the precise opposite of reality.

While some few definitely do have a problem of low self-esteem, as a whole, man's problem is not a low self-esteem, but, actually, one of inflated self-esteem, and this problem was evident at the Fall of man in the Garden of Eden, and even before that, when Lucifer fell.

As we have stated several times, even in this one Chapter, Satan told Adam and Eve, *"You shall be as gods, knowing good and evil"* (Gen. 3:4-5).

That's the problem! It is the ancient temptation Satan used to beguile Eve, and he is still using the same tired ruse today; therefore, the real problem with the human family, as with the Tyrian Monarch, is that they all see themselves as gods. It is the foundation for humanism. Man is the focal point, replacing God. The whole world, in fact, is fascinated and beguiled by the false god of man's self-importance.

MAN'S ATTEMPT TO PLAY GOD

Tragically, this is the basic source of all man-made philosophies that are permeating Church circles, even Pentecostal and Charismatic. These philosophies, such as Christian psychology, sociology, possibility thinking, positive thinking, the fourth dimension, dream your own dream, inner healing, self-esteem, etc., are man's attempt to play God.

In some Pentecostal and Charismatic circles, such as the Word of Faith doctrine, the following statements are made:

"We are little gods."

"As Adam was formerly god of the world and lost it, we have now regained it."

"We are now little gods under the Lord Jesus Christ."

This is a dangerous, man-centered philosophy that will undermine and grossly cheapen the magnificent Gospel of the Lord Jesus Christ.

Man's basic problem is that he does not want to admit that he is a sinner desperately needing a Saviour, the Saviour Jesus Christ.

As well, dominion teaching, which has changed somewhat in the last few years, falls into the same category. It is the teaching which claims that society can be Christianized by the political process, i.e., getting Christians in high office and changing laws. This teaching is also unscriptural, because it is man-centered, as well. Whenever any *"gospel"* ceases to be God-focused and Christ-centered, it becomes unscriptural and heretical.

SELF

A. W. Tozer writes:

"If self occupies any part of the Throne, we cannot say that Jesus Christ is on the Throne of our heart. Self is man's greatest enemy. It embodies selfishness, greed, and all that opposes God. If Jesus Christ is centered on the Throne, self is eradicated, actually being lost in Christ. And until self is totally lost in Christ, there can be no Christ-centered Throne in our lives."

Self-esteem caters to man's basest nature. As stated, this first became apparent at the Fall in the Garden. It will lead no one to Christ, it will lead, instead, to the enshrinement of self.

Jay E. Adams, in his book, The Biblical View of Self-Esteem, says:

"Any system that proposes to solve human problems, apart from the Bible and the Power of the Holy Spirit (as all of these pagan systems, including the self-worth systems do), is automatically condemned by Scripture itself. Nor does this system in any way depend upon the Message of Salvation. Love, joy, and peace are discussed as if they were not the Fruits of the Spirit, but merely the fruits of right views of one's self, which anyone can attain without the Bible or the Work of the Spirit in his heart.

"For these reasons, the self-worth system, with its claims of Biblical correspondencies, must be rejected. It does not come from the Bible. Any resemblance between Biblical teaching and the teaching of the self-worth originators is either contrived or coincidental."

Paul says this about self-esteem:

"Let nothing be done through strife or vainglory; but in lowliness of mind let each esteem other better than themselves" (Phil. 2:3).

This teaches the precise opposite of puffed-up self-opinions. It clearly tells us to have a humble view of ourselves, being ever aware of our own secret faults and shortcomings. This Scripture does not state that man's crying need is enhanced self-esteem. It says that man needs less emphasis on ego and self-gratification.

J. I. Packer said:

"Modern Christians spread a thin layer of Bible teaching over their mixture of popular psychology and common sense. But their over-all approach clearly reflects the narcissism — the 'selfism' or 'meism' as it is sometimes called — that is the way of the world in the modern west."

WHAT IS MAN?

In Psalms, Chapter 8, the Psalmist expresses amazement that God visits man by asking the question, *"What is man?"* Then in Psalms 62, we have the answer to this question: *"Nothing."* Man is nothing!

Obviously, God does not love man because of his moral traits, He loves him despite them. This is why the Psalmist expressed amazement. It is a testimonial to God's greatness, not man's. The Lord said this:

"If any man will come after Me, let him deny himself, and take up his cross, and follow Me, for whosoever will save his life will lose it: and whosoever will lose his life for My sake shall find it" (Mat. 16:24-25). The Lord is here telling us that we must put self in its rightful place, which is *"in Christ,"* and we can only do this by forsaking ego and *"taking up the Cross."* (Interestingly, Luke adds the word *"daily,"* which certainly seems to indicate that this is a problem that must be constantly analyzed and subdued afresh.)

TAKING UP THE CROSS

Taking up the Cross, in the Master's day, referred to the putting to death. It was then the method of execution. So the Lord is saying, *"You must treat yourself — with your sinful ways, priorities, and desires — like a criminal. Your sins must be condemned and utterly done away with, which can only be done by taking up the Cross."*

Let us say it again. The Cross is the only means by which the sinner can come to Christ and the Believer can live a consecrated life. Please note the following:

1. No man can come to God except through Christ.

2. No man can come to Christ unless he comes through the Cross.

3. No man can come to the Cross without a denial of self.

This certainly says something about the self-image that Christ expects us to have — and it is a far cry from the elevated self-esteem being promoted today. In St. John 16:8, Jesus tells us that the Work of the Holy Spirit is to *"reprove the world of sin,* (self) *righteousness, and of judgment."* This means, under the teaching of the Gospel (I Cor. 1:21), that the Holy Spirit convicts men of sin — not of low self-esteem. It clearly states, furthermore, that man is a sinner.

When, according to the Gospel, an individual is convicted (reproved) of sin, he is brought to a place of repentance. He suddenly sees himself as he is — which is *"lost, undone, and without God."*

In Peter's sermon on the Day of Pentecost (Acts, Chpt. 2) some 3,000 were saved. If you read Peter's Message, you will search in vain for any reference to elevating the listener's self-esteem. Instead, he said:

"Therefore let all the house of Israel know assuredly, that God has made that same Jesus, Whom you have crucified, both Lord and Christ" (Acts 2:36).

Peter didn't by any means appeal here to their vanities in an effort to raise their self-esteem.

This is what happened!

"Now, when they heard this, they were pricked in their heart, and said unto Peter and to the rest of the Apostles, men and brethren, what shall we do?" (Acts 2:37).

That is quite different from what Schuller said: *"Once a person believes he is an 'unworthy sinner,' it is doubtful if he can honestly accept the Saving Grace God offers in Jesus Christ."*

Actually, that is the only way a person can accept the Lord Jesus Christ!

In Peter's second great sermon, as quoted in Acts, Chapter 3, he once more ignored the matter of the listener's self-esteem. Instead, he refocused on the darker sides of their natures. *"But you denied the Holy One and the Just, and desired a murderer to be granted unto you; and killed the Prince of Life, Whom God has raised from the dead; whereof we are witnesses"* (Acts 3:14-15).

This time, five thousand people were saved!

Clearly, this is the God-approved principle of confronting men with the fact that they are sinners, and that they are lost without God. It then becomes the responsibility of the Holy Spirit to convict them and bring them to Jesus Christ, which He does as the true Word of God is preached to them.

And where does all of this leave the gospel of self-esteem?

ANOTHER GOSPEL

It leaves it in the realm of *"another gospel,"* because it brings people to a man-centered philosophy instead of Christ.

As a result, those who respond to this siren song of deceit, and deceit it is, are not truly born again. They do not turn to the Lord Jesus Christ as their Saviour, to be frank, it is impossible for them to do so, because the Gospel has not been preached to them; a vain philosophy has been tendered in its place. They are then confronted with the impossible task of saving themselves.

"And if the blind lead the blind, both shall fall into the ditch" (Mat. 15:14).

The self-esteem spirit was the hardest spirit to purge out of the Disciples. It was a battle that raged in their lives and ministries right up to the end.

"And there was also a strife among them, which of them should be accounted the greatest" (Lk. 22:24) — (which is the account of the Last Supper).

As well, we see the mother of James and John, who sought to have her sons seated at either side of Christ. You see, the self-esteem spirit is capable of invading any situation, no matter how holy in concept, and once there, can threaten the very future of that situation.

What it really amounts to is that man's standard of greatness lies in attaining the position where he will be served, while God's standard involves serving.

Man's standard is to humble others, while God's is to humble oneself. Failure to observe these Godly principles led to the downfall of both Lucifer and Adam. It was the *"You shall be as gods"* principle in action, and this is again being promoted by way of the self-esteem gospel.

If this spirit of high self-esteem had not been purged from the Disciples, the entirety of the Work of God would have fallen to the ground. And the only way it could be rooted out was for the Master to demonstrate the foot-washing spirit, which He did at the Last Supper.

"After that He poured water into a basin, and began to wash the Disciples' feet, and to wipe them with a towel wherewith He was girded" (Jn. 13:5).

HUMILITY

The Lord, in this act, was not instituting some new form of Church ritual; He was, instead, demonstrating the principle of humility that He wanted His Disciples, and all followers for that matter, to adopt in our lives and Ministry.

Paul said this, concerning Christ: *"Let this mind be in you, which was also in Christ Jesus:*

"Who, being in the form of God, thought it not robbery to be equal with God:

"But made Himself of no reputation, and took upon Him the form of a servant, and was made in the likeness of men:

"And being found in fashion as a man, He humbled Himself, and became obedient unto death, even the death of the Cross" (Phil. 2:5-8).

CIRCUMCISION

The phrase of Verse 10, *"You shall die the deaths of the uncircumcised by the hand of strangers,"* refers to dying lost.

The phrase, *"uncircumcised,"* referred to the rite of circumcision, which was a Covenant between God and Abraham, and which would incorporate all the Jewish people who would later be born. It meant this:

On the eighth day of life, a Hebrew boy was to have the fold of skin covering the end of his penis cut off. This rite was called *"Circumcision."*

After God reconfirmed His Covenant Promise to Abraham for the third and last time, the Lord said of his descendants: *"And the uncircumcised man child whose flesh of his foreskin is not circumcised, that soul shall be cut off from his people; he has broken My Covenant"* (Gen. 17:14). This meant that the uncircumcised Israelite was not covered by the Covenant Promise given to Abraham.

The rite symbolized submission to God, separation from the world, and belief in God's Covenant Promise.

It symbolized *"submission to God,"* because it portrayed faith in His Word and what it represented.

It symbolized *"separation from the world,"* because of the skin that was separated or cut away.

It symbolized *"belief in God's Covenant Promise,"* which referred to the coming Cross, because blood was shed.

As well, the Lord required a *"circumcision of the heart"* (Deut. 10:16; 30:6; Jer. 4:4), which is explained as a Faith-rooted, heart-and-soul love for God, that issues in obedience.

The New Testament argues that Abraham was *"justified by Faith"* even while he was uncircumcised, in fact, years before the rite was given. Therefore, circumcision was only a sign, a *"seal of the Righteousness that he had by Faith even when he was uncircumcised"* (Rom. 4:11; Gen. 15:6; 17:10-27).

THE NEW COVENANT

The sign, or rite, of Circumcision was not carried over into the New Covenant, and because this rite pointed to Christ, and with Christ coming, there was no longer any need for the symbol. Nevertheless, many Hebrew Christians struggled to impose Circumcision and the Mosaic Law on Gentile Christians (Acts 15:1). This was rejected at the Jerusalem Council (Acts 15:1-29).

Paul proclaimed constantly that God has never been concerned for the symbol, as was Circumcision, as a thing in itself. God cares for the reality. It is our heart response to

Him that counts. Thus, looking into hearts and examining those who have responded to Christ's Gospel, the Bible says: *"It is we who are the true circumcision, who worship by the Spirit of God who glory in Jesus Christ, and who put no confidence in the flesh"* (Phil. 3:3).

In Ezekiel's day, when one used the word, *"uncircumcised,"* he was speaking of those who were not followers of the Lord or His Word, and were therefore not in His Covenant, and thereby lost. Such was the king of Tyre.

It would mean the same presently as one who has not accepted Jesus Christ as his Saviour — one who is therefore lost!

(11) "MOREOVER THE WORD OF THE LORD CAME UNTO ME, SAYING,

(12) "SON OF MAN, TAKE UP A LAMENTATION UPON THE KING OF TYRUS, AND SAY UNTO HIM, THUS SAITH THE LORD GOD; YOU SEAL UP THE SUM, FULL OF WISDOM, AND PERFECT IN BEAUTY.

(13) "YOU HAVE BEEN IN EDEN THE GARDEN OF GOD: EVERY PRECIOUS STONE WAS YOUR COVERING, THE SARDIUS, TOPAZ, AND THE DIAMOND, THE BERYL, THE ONYX, AND THE JASPER, THE SAPPHIRE, THE EMERALD, AND THE CARBUNCLE, AND GOLD: THE WORKMANSHIP OF YOUR TABRETS AND OF YOUR PIPES WAS PREPARED IN YOU IN THE DAY THAT YOU WERE CREATED.

(14) "YOU ARE THE ANOINTED CHERUB THAT COVERS: AND I HAVE SET YOU SO: YOU WERE UPON THE HOLY MOUNTAIN OF GOD: YOU HAVE WALKED UP AND DOWN IN THE MIDST OF THE STONES OF FIRE.

(15) "YOU WERE PERFECT IN YOUR WAYS FROM THE DAY THAT YOU WERE CREATED, TILL INIQUITY WAS FOUND IN YOU.

(16) "BY THE MULTITUDE OF YOUR MERCHANDISE THEY HAVE FILLED THE MIDST OF YOU WITH VIOLENCE, AND YOU HAVE SINNED: THEREFORE I WILL CAST YOU AS PROFANE OUT OF THE MOUNTAIN OF GOD: AND I WILL DESTROY YOU, O COVERING CHERUB, FROM THE MIDST OF THE STONES OF FIRE.

(17) "YOUR HEART WAS LIFTED UP BECAUSE OF YOUR BEAUTY, YOU HAVE CORRUPTED YOUR WISDOM BY REASON OF YOUR BRIGHTNESS: I WILL CAST YOU TO THE GROUND, I WILL LAY YOU BEFORE KINGS, THAT THEY MAY BEHOLD YOU.

(18) "YOU HAVE DEFILED YOUR SANCTUARIES BY THE MULTITUDE OF YOUR INIQUITIES, BY THE INIQUITY OF YOUR TRAFFIC; THEREFORE WILL I BRING FORTH A FIRE FROM THE MIDST OF YOU, IT SHALL DEVOUR YOU, AND I WILL BRING YOU TO ASHES UPON THE EARTH IN THE SIGHT OF ALL THEM WHO BEHOLD YOU.

(19) "ALL THEY WHO KNOW YOU AMONG THE PEOPLE SHALL BE ASTONISHED AT YOU: YOU SHALL BE A TERROR, AND NEVER SHALL YOU BE ANY MORE."

The overview is:

1. The statements given concerning Satan, such as *"You seal up the sum,"* and *"You are the perfection of wisdom and beauty,"* refer to him prior to his Fall.

2. Verse 13 mentions *"Eden,"* the first mention since Genesis 4:16. To emphasize its reality, the words, *"Garden of God,"* are added. Eden, therefore, is pointed to and not a mere summer-garden of the prince of Tyre.

3. The precious stones detailed in Verse 13 are those of Genesis 2:11-12. Nine of these were found on the Breastplate of the High Priest.

4. The phrase of Verse 15, *"Iniquity was found in you,"* present pride as the form of this iniquity. This rebellion probably caused the catastrophe which occurred between the first and second Verses of Genesis, Chapter 1.

LUCIFER

The tenor of this Chapter will now change from the earthly Monarch, the *"Prince of Tyre,"* to his sponsor, Satan, of which the earthly king was a symbol. Consequently, in Verses 11 through 19, we are given much information concerning Satan, regarding his creation, Fall, and coming destruction. This is evidenced by the salutation given in Verse 12.

While the Holy Spirit, through the Prophet Ezekiel, refers to the *"king of Tyrus,"* he is actually referring to Satan. It is the law of double reference. It pertains to a particular individual being addressed, while someone else is meant.

An excellent example is given to us in an exchange between Peter and Christ.

The Scripture tells us how that Christ began to explain *"how that He must go unto Jerusalem, and suffer many things of the Elders and Chief Priests and Scribes, and be killed, and be raised again the third day."*

The Scripture then says that *"Peter took Him, and began to rebuke Him, saying, Be it far from You, Lord: this shall not be unto You."*

We now have the response of Christ, by Him saying to Peter: *"Get thee behind Me, Satan: you are an offense unto Me: for you savour not the things that be of God, but those that be of men"* (Mat. 16:21-23).

While Jesus was speaking to Peter, He was, in effect, addressing Satan. As stated, it is the law of double reference.

This doesn't mean that Peter was of the Devil, but it does mean, that as he rebuked Christ and the Cross, he, most definitely, at the time, was being used by Satan. In fact, anything that we say which is not strictly of the Word of God, when it pertains to the Lord, is of Satan. That's the reason the Believer must know the Word, and be very careful to abide by the Word.

WISDOM

The phrase of Verse 12, *"You seal up the sum,"* means that Lucifer, when created by God, was originally the perfection of wisdom and beauty. The word, *"sum,"* actually refers in the Hebrew to *"pattern."* The phrase intimates that Lucifer was the wisest and most beautiful Angel created by God, and served the Lord in Holiness and Righteousness for a given period of time, although we aren't told how long.

The word, *"seal,"* intimates that there was nothing more that God could have given to Lucifer regarding *"wisdom and beauty."* In fact, the Holy Spirit uses the phrase, *"Full of wisdom,"* seemingly meaning that no Angel or creature of God was this wise. It should be quickly added that he still retains this *"wisdom,"* although perverted, and, as such, mortals cannot hope to compete with him in this category, and are, therefore, so easily duped.

With this amazing wisdom, he has corrupted the world, caused billions to be eternally lost, and reeked havoc, disaster, and tragedy upon the whole of the human family. That is the reason sin is so subtle, deceptive, and crafty! It has as its instigator the wisest of all the Angels. As such, it crafts myriad philosophies which ensnare man in their deceptive intellectualism. Hence, the world is plagued with the religions of Buddhism, Islam, Mormonism, Hinduism, and Catholicism, etc. All of this, plus man's rebellion against God in a million other ways, is spawned by the wisdom of Satan. That is the reason Solomon said: *"There is a way that seems right unto a man, but the end thereof are the ways of death"* (Prov. 14:12).

GOD'S WISDOM

The only wisdom above Satan's wisdom is God's Wisdom, which is unlimited. Satan's wisdom, as should be obvious, is limited, and because he is a mere creature. Therefore, the Christian, if he hopes to succeed, is to avail himself of the Wisdom of God, i.e., the Bible. Only such wisdom will overcome the Evil One! But tragically, the Church, as a whole, is trading the Wisdom of God for the wisdom of man, i.e., Satan. These vain philosophies sound so good, especially to the unspiritual ear, because they are *"full of wisdom,"* but yet wisdom that has been darkened, and, therefore, perverted. Paul called it: *"philosophy and vain deceit, after the tradition of men, after the rudiments of the world, and not after Christ"* (Col. 2:8).

BEAUTY

The phrase of Verse 12, *"Perfect in beauty,"* means that he was the most beautiful of God's angelic creation, with the Holy Spirit labeling his beauty as *"perfect."*

Before Lucifer's Fall, his beauty, and eclipsed only by the beauty of Christ, must have been a wonder to behold! Undoubtedly, there is no way that mere mortals could have described that which was the handiwork of God. Consequently, he not only uses his *"fallen wisdom"* to seduce man, but, as well, his *"perfect beauty."* It is a tantalizing prospect!

Even though the result of his handiwork

is obvious for all to see, and is horribly ugly, still, fallen man cannot really see it for what it actually is, because of being tantalized by the *"beauty."*

For example, Hollywood portrays beauty as its calling card, even referring to its *"beautiful people."* Madison Avenue, the world's advertising center in New York City, sells beauty as its greatest commodity; likewise, the ability of talented sports figures is said to be *"beautiful to behold."*

However, this beauty is also corrupted, only being on the exterior, as Satan's is only exterior. He has long since corrupted his true beauty, with nothing left but the traces of what once was. Likewise, man's beauty, and irrespective of its degree or nature, soon decays, and, therefore, fades into ugliness. The actress is no longer beautiful! The actor is no longer handsome! The athlete can no longer perform!

From the opposite and, therefore, true, the True Beauty given by Christ is that which changes the heart and, therefore, the life, and because it is from God, never fades unless the person turns his back on God.

THE GARDEN OF GOD

The phrase of Verse 13, *"You have been in Eden the Garden of God,"* more than likely refers to the world before Adam.

Genesis 1:1 declares: *"In the beginning God created the Heaven and the Earth."* Exactly when this was, we aren't told!

Genesis 1:2 says: *"And the Earth was without form, and void: and darkness was upon the face of the deep."*

We know that God did not originally create the world in this condition, but that it came to this place of being *"without form, and void,"* because of some particular type of catastrophe which took place. It was, no doubt, the catastrophe of the Fall of Lucifer.

At a given point in time in eternity past, Lucifer led a revolution against God, with approximately one-third of the Angels throwing in their lot with him, a revolution which has lasted unto this particular time (Rev. 12:4). So the *"Eden"* that God is speaking of here existed before the *"Eden"* of Adam.

All of this presents some scriptural proof that a Kingdom existed upon planet Earth before the chaos of Genesis 1:2.

Except for the very sparse information given to us in the Word of God as it regards the world that then was, we have little knowledge. As well, it is not known as to how long it existed; however, I think, as stated, there is ample proof in Ezekiel, Chapter 28, with Isaiah, Chapter 14, and Genesis, Chapter 1, that Lucifer ruled that Kingdom, under God, and was righteous and holy until he fell.

AN ANGEL OF THE HIGHEST RANK

The phrase of Verse 13, *"Every precious stone was your covering,"* and with the list of stones given, pertains to a period of time other than his tempting Eve in the Garden of Eden. The entirety of this Verse pertains to Lucifer before his Fall, and elucidates his wisdom and beauty, and especially his beauty.

Of the precious stones detailed in this Verse, nine of these were found on the Breastplate of the High Priest. Three are missing, those in the third row of the Breastplate, the *"ligure, and agate, and amethyst"* (Ex. 28:19).

As the Scripture is silent as to exactly what this meant — the similarity between the High Priest and Lucifer — we can only draw from the obvious.

Aaron, the first High Priest, was a type of Christ. His robes pictured the needs of the people; his sacrifices, the claims of God. The Ephod, with its shoulder pieces and Breastplate, was the principal vestment. Thus arrayed, Aaron symbolized Christ in the mystery of His Divine Manhood, bearing His people on His Shoulders, the place of strength, and bound upon His heart, the place of love.

On the shoulders of the High Priest, the names of the Tribes were according to their birth, but on the heart, according as God chose them: but all the names were engraved on precious stones; that is, stones which shine the more brightly when more intensely shone upon.

In the pocket of the Breastplate were placed the mysterious stones, known as Urim and Thummin, by means of which the Divine judgment of a matter was made known to Israel. Thus robed, Aaron bore the Judgment of the congregation before the Lord and communicated the Judgment of the Lord to the congregation.

Therefore, if the Holy Spirit intended any similarity regarding these precious stones as the covering of Lucifer, and their sameness on the Breastplate of the High Priest (minus three), and especially that the Breastplate of the High Priest contained the Urim and the Thummin, which spoke of the Wisdom of God, Lucifer, as the High Priest, must have served as the closest liaison to the Most High. There is every evidence that his rank was the highest of all the Angelic Host. As it said, he was *"full of wisdom, and perfect in beauty."*

Inasmuch as he was so close to God the Son before his Fall, this explains, at least somewhat, the reason for his great hatred of Christ after his Fall.

MUSIC

The phrase of Verse 13, *"The workmanship of your tabrets and of your pipes,"* leads to another interesting conclusion.

The word, *"tabrets,"* has to do with music, with *"pipes"* having to do, once again, with a precious stone or gem. It is interesting to note, that good singers, at least in the music world, are referred to as having a *"good set of pipes."*

There is every indication from this Passage that Lucifer, along with his other high duties, had something to do with the Worship of God, which contained music. He is called *"O Lucifer, son of the morning"* (Isa. 14:12). As well, when the Earth was originally created, the Scripture says, *"The morning stars sang together, and all the sons of God shouted for joy"* (Job 38:4-7). So, if the idiom, *"son of the morning,"* can be linked to the *"morning stars,"* and relative to their singing, these Passages tell us that Lucifer, at least before his Fall, was greatly instrumental in leading the Worship of God.

This would explain Satan's tremendous power in using music to enslave a great part of the world. I speak of modern rock music, but yet all forms which are controlled by the Evil One.

It is ironic, that one of my first cousins, Jerry Lee Lewis, was one of the founders, so to speak, of modern rock 'n' roll music. He and Elvis Presley began at approximately the same time. Actually, Jerry Lee and I were raised together, learning to play piano together in Church. His talent in both singing and music was extraordinary even then!

Even though the nation was somewhat alarmed regarding this new form of music known as rock 'n' roll, still, those early days of the late 1950's proclaimed only its mildness in comparison to its ultimate degenerative form.

Known as hard rock, or acid rock, or rap, it would enslave millions, as it promotes drugs, alcohol, immorality, witchcraft, and death. The power of this music was understood only by its devotees. Movie stars and starlets flocked to the side of grungy performers, who, for the most part, could barely carry a tune. These individuals were looked at as gods, by a nation of teenagers and children, and, consequently, led them down a path of bondage and spiritual oblivion.

It was so strong, it produced a counter-culture shaping not only the music of the world but its language and its education. Anyone with even the briefest exposure of the modern commercial music industry cannot escape the realization that this is an area which has been completely subverted by Satan. The results would indicate that his efforts have produced awesome results.

THE BONDAGE OF DARKNESS

Some time ago, I happened to turn on late-night television. One of the talk shows was featuring a particular rock group from England. Their answers to the host's questions were actually little more than a succession of grunts. They could barely string together four or five words — much less offer intelligent answers to the questions presented.

Their mental condition finally became so evident (and so disturbing) that the host just shook his head and told them it was pointless to continue — allowing them to leave the stage. I watched them shuffle off, dirty, unshaven, with matted and filthy hair sticking out from their heads — and I couldn't help but notice their eyes glazed with drugs. *"These,"* I thought, as they ambled off the stage, *"are the gods of this present world."*

At another time, I chanced to flick on the morning news of one of the major networks. A rock concert had taken place the previous night, and there had been a riot with several people killed. I watched the female anchor of this early morning news program, as she spoke of the performing group with utter awe. Their name was delivered as though she was pronouncing the name of deity.

It was as if she was speaking of something sacred every time she mentioned their activities. I sat there in total astonishment as I listened to this supposedly intelligent woman (incidentally, a name recognized all over America), realizing that she was simultaneously deceiving and being deceived.

I wondered if she really comprehended the enormity of the influence she so glibly described. Here she was, treating this group as though they were an asset to society, rather than the enormous liability they are.

Seemingly, she did not realize that multiple thousands of young people would be directed down the road to hard drugs because of the energy of this group. Some would even die and suffer the agony of the damned. Untold heartache would be the price imposed upon thousands of parents, and all because of this group, much less scores of others in similar circumstances.

Presently, thousands of radio and television stations in the United States and elsewhere incessantly beat out the pounding rhythm of top-forty rock or videos. This music has become so pervasive and the lyrics so filthy that they defy description. It is actually a form of pornography being distributed over the airwaves.

Worse still, the average age of those turned to this type of music is *"thirteen."*

Illicit sex and sexual perversion are the main themes of rock music. It has ceased to be merely *"suggestive,"* as it was in the days of my cousin, Jerry Lee Lewis, and Elvis Presley, and has now become openly pornographic, especially considering the *"rap artists."*

Illicit sex, the drug culture, witchcraft, and rock music go hand in hand. How many hundreds of thousands — even millions — of young people have started out on the road to drugs because their *"gods"* of rock 'n' roll set the example? As a result of all this, teenage suicides have risen dramatically in recent years.

It started, as stated, with Elvis, Jerry Lee, and the Beatles. This was followed by hard rock and acid rock, and then punk rock. Then

NOTES

it was rap. And what will it be next? Whatever it will, of this one can be sure; it will be diabolical and Satanic in origin. The desire of Satan is always to *"steal, kill and destroy"* (Jn. 10:10).

It is not a pretty picture to understand that hundreds of thousands, or even millions, of young boys and girls are listening to this putrid rock — often through headphones and looking at videos — for many hours a day. It is more tragic still, when one realizes that the producers of this music, the major record companies in America, located in New York, Los Angeles, and Nashville, along with radio station owners and T.V. Cable companies, that play this malignant rot, are as blatantly amoral as mad scientists deliberately loosing a plague on a nation.

MONEY

What they're doing, they do for money!

No wonder the Bible tells us that *"the love of money is the root of all evil"* (I Tim. 6:10). In other words, such is comparable to a pestilent sore, draining out a Satanic poison, that will corrupt the hearts and lives of untold millions of young people, and cause the worst type of life (and death) imaginable. The tragic aspect of this whole sordid mess is that it's all done basically for profit.

As well, country-western music basically falls into the same category. Its sponsor is Satan, as well.

One country-western entertainer recently admitted that country music is one of the greatest destroyers of morals in the nation today. Still, he keeps right on making the music that is perverting the country.

Even though country music could not be put in the class of perverted pop music, still, its source is the same, the fomenter of evil, Satan himself. As such, it is little understandable how Christians could have an affinity for that whose sponsor is Satan.

CHRISTIAN CONTEMPORARY MUSIC

Sadder still, much of music that passes for *"Christian"* has been so compromised that it beggars description. The best that can be said of this offering is that it is a work of the flesh and definitely not of the Holy Spirit.

Contemporary Christian music is incompatible with true Biblical Christianity. Music should refresh the spirit and glorify God. Instead, this is exactly as its name implies — contemporary — which means, at least in this case, *"similar to the music offerings of the world."*

So-called Christian entertainers and song writers have done their best, in many cases, to write songs that have little reference to the Glory of God, and which actually can be interpreted as either earthly or spiritual. This music is designed to mimic, as closely as possible, the fetid music of the world. Some Churches have even degenerated to the point where they employ strobe lights to give the gathering the atmosphere of a rock 'n' roll concert — an effort to appease the moral decline of young people.

Hard-core contemporary Christian music — so-called — strives to make Christ acceptable to men, rather than men acceptable to Christ! It attempts to lower the Lord Jesus to mankind's basest level instead of elevating man to the level of Christ. It is not of God!

That which projects the spirit of the world cannot project the Spirit of God. It is of the world and it is not of God! This is why God's Word tells us from across the centuries: *"Wherefore come out from among them, and be ye separate, saith the Lord, and touch not the unclean thing"* (II Cor. 6:17).

When one sums up the music business of the world, the word of Simon Peter comes echoing back to us from across the corridors of time. Despite all the modern technology, despite a national heritage that has produced more advantages than any other country in the history of the world, we are today rewarded (for the love of money) with the exact words the Apostle delivered under the unction of the Holy Spirit: *"cursed children"* (II Pet. 2:14).

As Satan is the author of the other, he is the author, as well, of much of the music that is rendered in Churches.

MUSIC WAS ORIGINALLY CREATED BY GOD

It was originally designed by God to be used in worship, and, in fact, is one of, if not the highest form of worship designed by the Holy Spirit.

For instance, the Book of Psalms is the longest Book in the Bible. It contains one hundred and fifty Psalms, which actually are songs — songs, incidentally, given by the Holy Spirit to David and to others. For the Holy Spirit to give this much emphasis to these Songs, and to make this Book the longest in the Bible, tells us how important that singing along with musical instrumentation are to God, and especially as it relates to Worship. Listen to the Psalmist:

"Rejoice in the LORD, O ye righteous: for praise is comely for the upright.

"Praise the LORD with harp: sing unto Him with the Psaltery and an instrument of ten strings.

"Sing unto Him a new song; play skillfully with a loud noise" (Ps. 33:1-3).

And again: *"Praise ye the LORD. Praise God in His Sanctuary: Praise Him in the firmament of His power.*

"Praise Him for His mighty acts: praise Him according to His excellent greatness.

"Praise Him with the sound of the trumpet: praise Him with the psaltery and harp.

"Praise Him with the timbrel and dance: praise Him with stringed instruments and organs.

"Praise Him upon the loud cymbals: praise Him upon the high sounding cymbals.

"Let everything that hath breath praise the LORD. Praise ye the LORD" (Ps. 150).

All of this proclaims to us, plus many Psalms we haven't enumerated, that it is the desire of the Holy Spirit, and a strong desire at that, that Believers worship and praise the Lord with singing, accompanied by musical instruments.

In the New Testament, it is the same. Paul dealt with this. He said: *"Speaking to yourselves in Psalms and Hymns and Spiritual Songs, singing and making melody in your heart to the Lord"* (Eph. 5:19).

And then: *"Let the Word of Christ dwell in you richly in all wisdom; teaching and admonishing one another in Psalms and Hymns and Spiritual Songs, singing with grace in your hearts to the Lord"* (Col. 3:16).

As Paul used the word, *"Psalms,"* the Greek word is *"Psalmos,"* which means *"a set piece of music; a sacred song to be accompanied with harp or other instruments."*

THE STRUCTURE OF MUSIC

The manner in which music is structured, the way that God originally brought it into being, has within it the incorporation of the Divine Trinity. The sound of music is combined under three headings, all given by God:

1. Melody: this speaks of an ordered structure of sound that is referred to as the *"tune"* or *"melody."*

2. Harmony: this has to do with the accompanying voices or instruments regarding the different parts of music, such as lead, alto, bass, or tenor. It is interesting to note that before the Death and Resurrection of Christ, most music was written in the minor keys; consequently, all the Psalms were basically written in minor keys, because they were written before Christ.

After His Death and Resurrection, the writing of music gradually shifted from the minors to the majors. It was as if the Holy Spirit was making a statement through this all-important aspect of worship called music. Since the Cross, man has the far greater opportunity to be in Harmony with Christ.

3. Rhythm: this has to do with the measured beats of which all of the Psalms, in one way or the other, were written, and, as well, all music is written presently. As an example: if a song is written in four-fourths time, it means that there are four beats to the measure, etc. If used properly, all of this — Melody, Harmony, and Rhythm — are of God and are accepted by Him as a part of our Worship of God.

THE PERVERSION OF SACRED MUSIC

Referring to contemporary Christian music, so-called, the ordered structure of Melody, Harmony, and Rhythm has been tampered with until it is no more applicable to that which was originally ordained by God. In this type of music, the Melody little follows a prescribed pattern. As well, the Harmony has been interrupted; consequently, the ordered, structured spirit of man, recreated by the Holy Spirit, cannot favorably respond to such disorder. Therefore, to such music, true Biblical Worship is not possible.

In the mid-1980's, Frances and I, along with others, were in Russia and Eastern Europe for a series of Meetings. The city in question was Budapest, Hungary.

The building was packed to capacity that night, with some standing outside, unable to get it. After the worship, which was good, an individual was called on to sing. As he was Hungarian, he spoke through an English interpreter, that we may understand, and mentioned that his song that would sing was learned while on a recent trip to America.

It was a contemporary type of song, by which, as stated, is impossible to worship. Also, as stated, the Melody had no prescribed pattern, and the Harmony was as disordered as all music of that type. Not only did the Spirit of God not move as the young man sang, but a bad spirit seemed to come over the service. The people could not worship, sitting there staring, as the *"performer"* rendered his special.

Actually, he was a good singer, and, thankfully, when that song was concluded, he began to sing a song that was definitely ordered by the Holy Spirit. Instantly, the people began to worship, as their spirits witnessed with that which the song projected, namely, the Lord.

I sat there that night chagrined that he had brought back from American Churches that which could be labeled as none other than an insult to the Holy Spirit. However, I was also amazed at the total contrast.

THE BAROMETER OF THE CHURCH

Music, as it engages in worship of the Lord, is the barometer of the Church. If it is stilted, cold, and formal, the Church is the same. If it follows the *"contemporary"* path, one can be certain that the particular Church in question is little more than entertainment.

However, if it is truly Spirit-led, the music and singing will bring Heaven down to Earth, glorifying, not man, but the Lord Jesus Christ, with the people giving vent to their expression by playing music and singing, rendering Worship to the Lord.

THE ANOINTED CHERUB

The phrase of Verse 14, *"You are the anointed Cherub who covers,"* means that Lucifer was chosen and *"anointed"* by God for a particular task and service. As stated, this had something to do with the Worship of God, which pertained to God's creation (Job 38:4-7). His great beauty would have been associated with this, and would, as well, have to do with the *"precious stones,"* which were his *"covering."*

If in truth, *"Eden,"* which was the *"Garden of God,"* was on planet Earth before the chaos, Lucifer, along with his other duties, would have ruled this Kingdom with great ability, because he was *"full of wisdom,"* as given to him by the Lord.

The phrase, *"And I have set you so,"* refers to the Lord placing Lucifer in this great position, possibly the highest of any Angelic Being.

The phrase, *"You were upon the holy mountain of God,"* could mean one of two things:

1. It refers to the place where Lucifer had his kingdom and throne on Earth before Adam's time (Isa. 14:12-14).

2. This speaks of God's Throne in Heaven, with Lucifer given place and position relative to the Throne (Rev. 4:2-11). More than likely, this latter is correct, and due to the next phrase.

The phrase, *"You have walked up and down in the midst of the stones of fire,"* could very will have reference to a part of the Throne of God. Actually, in Ezekiel's vision of the Throne, he said that it had *"as the appearance of fire round about within it,"* which also pertained to the Person of God (Ezek. 1:26-27).

As well, the phrase, *"Walked up and down,"* as structured, seems to imply that not just any Angel would have been given such latitude.

PERFECTION

The phrase of Verse 15, *"You were perfect in your ways,"* presents a statement made by the Holy Spirit. This pertained to his service for God, before the Fall. In other words, for a period of time, he conducted himself exactly as he should have done, creating harmony in the domain of the Lord. There is no way to know how long this time was, as the Bible does not say. And yet, it is as if the Holy Spirit says these words, *"You were* (past tense) *perfect,"* with a sob!

The phrase, *"Till iniquity was found in you,"* refers, as is obvious, to his Fall. This took place before Adam, exactly how long, we aren't told.

Pride was the form of this iniquity (Lk. 10:17-18). As well, this rebellion, as stated, probably caused the catastrophe which occurred between the First and Second Verses of Genesis, Chapter 1.

The phrase, *"Till iniquity was found in you,"* proclaims to all the cause of all the pain, suffering, sickness, and sin that mankind has ever known. It is the cause of all death, sorrow, and heartache! It is the cause of all war, resulting in privation and want. The sorrow caused by this one statement is enough to fill a thousand worlds, for it has broken billions of hearts.

INIQUITY

As far as we know, this statement in Verse 15 proclaims the origin of evil in the universe; however, the Bible says little about this, in that it is concerned with sin and its origin in human life (I Tim. 2:14; James 1:13). Even though Satan's sin was pride, to which we have already alluded, still, sin in its highest form is an attempt to assert independence from God, and hence, to call in question the very nature and ordering of existence, whereby Lucifer lived as a creature in utter dependence upon the Grace and Provision of His Creator. This much we do know:

This rebellion against God, led by Lucifer, included a great part, if not all, of God's Creation. That stage of the rebellion must have lasted for quite some time, because the Scripture says that one-third of God's Angels rebelled with Lucifer in his attempt to usurp authority over his Creator (Rev. 12:4).

Incidentally, the very name, *"Lucifer,"* means *"light-bearer."* After his Fall, he became known as Satan, the Prince of Evil (Job 1:6-12; 2:1-7). He is also referred to as *"the ruler of this world"* (Jn. 14:30) and *"the prince of the power of the air"* (Eph. 2:2).

MERCHANDISE

The phrase of Verse 16, *"By the multitude of your merchandise they have filled the midst of you with violence, and you have sinned,"* has to do with unjust gain, damage, false accusations, injustice, and wrong dealing. In other words, as righteous and holy as Lucifer had been, he is now unrighteous and unholy; consequently, all of his followers, which include almost the entirety of the world, and for all time, follow in his footsteps, hence, the world is filled with *"violence."* He has constantly attempted to usurp authority over Jehovah, and uses any method to do so, mostly, humanity!

The Holy Spirit bluntly says: *"And you have sinned."* The standard for right and wrong is set by the Holy Spirit in the Word of God; however, man is loathe to accept the standard, desiring, instead, to substitute his own! Consequently, standards fluctuate accordingly. Incidentally, the word, *"merchandise,"* in the Hebrew, is *"rekullah,"* and means *"traffic."* Satan traffics in nothing but sin.

The phrase, *"Therefore I will cast you as profane out of the Mountain of God,"* has the same meaning as the *"Holy Mountain of God,"* given in Verse 14, and probably refers to the Throne of God. Whatever capacity he had once enjoyed in this noble, high, and holy position, he has now forfeited.

SIN

Sin always takes a person farther than he wants to go, and faster than he desires to go. But all of this, is far more complicated that a simple *"yes"* or *"no"*!

Sin carries with it all forms of deception, all the powers of darkness which fuel the deception, and is quite more extensive than anyone realizes.

In the first place, the idea that all people have to do to escape sin is to simply say *"no,"* is facetious indeed! While it is certainly possible to say *"no"* to certain types of sin, and as it regards each individual, it is not at all possible to say *"no"* to all types of sin, at least within one's own ability, strength, and power. This is where we miss it!

The unredeemed individual thinks that he can beat the game, and can stop whenever he so desires. Untold millions have found out, to their utter dismay, that they couldn't.

The Christian thinks that, inasmuch as he is now redeemed, and, thereby, a *"new creation"* in Christ Jesus (II Cor. 5:17), whereas he couldn't say *"no"* before he was saved, now, he thinks, such lies within his power. It doesn't!

As the unredeemed cannot stop the sin business, unless he accepts Christ and the Cross, the truth is, the Christian, likewise, cannot stop the sin business, at least in all of its forms, unless he maintains his faith in Christ and the Cross.

The thing about all of this is, no matter how far gone the unredeemed might be, they still have the free moral agency that they can say *"yes"* or *"no"* to Christ. That's about as far as their willpower can take them. God guards their free moral agency in this respect, but only in this respect.

As a Preacher of the Gospel, I have seen untold numbers of people, who were already in total bondage to the powers of darkness, with death the next step, instead, say *"yes"* to Christ, and they were gloriously redeemed and set free by the Power of God.

But, of course, it's not easy for many of the unredeemed to say *"yes"* to Christ, inasmuch as Satan continues to make them believe that they can beat the game themselves, even though they are on the trembling edge of disaster. That's the reason that many have to come to that trembling edge, before they will finally say *"yes."* They keep trying the methods of the world, or their own power and strength, which always miserably fail. But, irrespective that the Lord might be the last choice, still, He, with Mercy and Grace, will meet that soul which comes to Him, never turning one away (Jn. 6:37).

GOD'S PRESCRIBED ORDER OF VICTORY

Sin, however, continues to maintain all of its various forms, with Satan continuing to use his wiles to trip up the Child of God. To be sure, Satan knows God's prescribed order of victory, but most definitely, he doesn't want the Believer to know that prescribed order. In fact, Satan will do everything within his power to push the Believer in the wrong direction, desiring that the *"sin nature"* once again rule the Child of God, exactly as it did before the person came to Christ. That's why Paul gave so much instruction in the Sixth Chapter of Romans concerning the *"sin nature."* He plainly tells us: *"Let not the sin nature therefore reign in your mortal body, that you should obey it in the lusts thereof"* (Rom. 6:12).

Now, if there was no danger of this, the Holy Spirit, through the Apostle, would not have warned us. But the fact is, the *"sin nature"* can definitely rule and reign in one's mortal body, with the Christian, despite trying to do otherwise, *"obeying it in the lusts thereof."* Let me say it again:

If this danger was not acute, the Holy Spirit would not have devoted a great part of the Sixth Chapter of Romans to this problem. The awful truth is, the sin nature is ruling and reigning in the hearts and lives of most Christians, simply because they don't know *"God's prescribed order of victory."*

What is that prescribed order?

It is that which we've already addressed any number of times in this Volume, and because of the seriousness of the situation, will, no doubt, address it several times more. In brief, it is as follows, and then we will elaborate somewhat:

1. Christ and the Cross (Rom. 6:3-5).
2. Christ and the Cross must ever be the object of our faith (Rom. 6:11).
3. That being the case, the Holy Spirit will grandly work on our behalf (Rom. 6:14; 8:1-2, 11).

The idea is this:

The Believer must ever understand that while Christ is always the *"Source,"* the Cross is always the *"Means."* In other words, every single thing we receive from the Lord: Salvation, the Baptism with the Holy Spirit, Grace, Peace, Faith, Justification, Sanctification, the Fruit of the Spirit, the Gifts of the Spirit, etc., all, without exception, plus many we haven't named, are made possible by the Cross. That's the reason that the Cross must ever be the object of our Faith.

When it comes to *"sin,"* there's really nothing in the Word of God that tells us to say *"no"* to sin. Something to which we are dead should not be the source of conversation whatsoever. And Paul plainly states:

"Likewise reckon ye also yourselves to be dead indeed unto sin, but alive unto God through Jesus Christ our Lord" (Rom. 6:11).

DEAD TO THE SIN NATURE

When Paul said: *"Therefore if any man be in Christ, he is a new creature,"* the Holy Spirit, through the Apostle, meant exactly what was said (II Cor. 5:17). Whenever Jesus died on the Cross, and when we evidence faith in Him and His Finished Work, in the Mind of God, we died with Him (Rom. 6:3-5). In other words, the Lord didn't try to patch us up, but, rather, brought the *"old man"* to a place of death, which was done by the means of the Cross and our Faith in that Sacrifice, which then made it possible for us to be *"born again,"* i.e., a *"new creation"* (Jn. 3:3). Paul then said:

"For he who is dead (having died with Christ) *is freed from sin* (freed from the power of the sin nature [Rom. 6:7]).

But the Lord did not kill the *"old man"* (Rom. 6:6) with nothing to take its place. *"As Christ was raised up from the dead by the glory of the Father, even so we also should walk in newness of life"* (Rom. 6:4).

In other words, we were raised *"in the likeness of His Resurrection"* and done so in *"newness of life"* (Rom. 6:4-5).

We now have a *"new life"* and it's all in Christ and what He did at the Cross. Inasmuch as I am now dead to the sin nature, I should not converse with it at all. I am simply to say *"yes"* to Christ, and as it concerns all things. Then and only then can the Believer walk in perpetual victory, which means, that the Cross is ever the object of your faith, which also means that the Holy Spirit now has the legal right to work within our lives, thereby, helping us to defeat all sin. Listen again to Paul:

"But if the Spirit (Holy Spirit) *of Him* (God the Father) *Who raised up Jesus from the dead dwell in you* (and He does by virtue of our faith in Christ), *He Who raised up Christ from the dead shall also quicken* (make alive) *your mortal bodies* (our present physical bodies) *by His Spirit Who dwells in you"* (Rom. 8:11).

In other words, the Holy Spirit will guarantee my victory, exerting on my behalf the same power that raised Jesus from the dead, which, to be sure, can throw over any attack by Satan. But for the Holy Spirit to do this, and to continue to do such, our Faith must be ever anchored in the Cross, and must not stray from that great Sacrifice (Rom. 8:2).

That, and that alone, is *"God's prescribed order of Victory."*

THE DESTRUCTION OF SATAN

The phrase of Verse 16, *"And I will destroy you,"* has not even yet been fulfilled, but most certainly will be! Satan's destruction is recorded in Revelation 20:10; however, the truth is, Satan was totally and completely made ineffective at the Cross. There his power was completely broken, inasmuch as Jesus addressed everything that was lost in the Fall, excluding nothing!

Paul said: *"Blotting out the handwriting of ordinances that was against us, which was contrary to us, and took it out of the way, nailing it to His Cross:*

"And having spoiled principalities and powers, He made a show of them openly, triumphing over them in it" (Col. 2:14-15).

However, as is obvious, even though Satan is completely defeated, as of yet, we do not have all the benefits for which Jesus paid such a price. In fact, we presently only have the *"firstfruits"* (Rom. 8:23). The remainder will be received at the Rapture of the Church, when we will then experience the putting on of Glorified Bodies, in which there is no more sin nature, and it will then be impossible for the Glorified Saint to sin. As stated, that awaits the coming Resurrection (I Cor., Chpt. 15).

THE CONSENT OF THE GOVERNED

If Satan has been totally and completely defeated at Calvary, which he definitely was, then how is it, many Christians might ask, that he continues to cause so much trouble?

The reason, whether it pertains to the unredeemed or the redeemed, is because we do not take advantage of what Jesus has done for us at the Cross. In effect, and by default, we give Satan consent to govern us, when in fact, as every Believer certainly knows, we are to be governed by the Lord Jesus Christ.

Believers may deny that they give Satan consent; however, when we ignore *"God's prescribed order of victory,"* thereby seeking to devise a new way, which closes the door to the Holy Spirit, whether we realize it or not, we have given Satan consent to govern us, hence, Paul saying that we should not allow the sin nature to *"reign"* over us (Rom. 6:12).

The reason is either *"ignorance"* or *"unbelief."* And after several years of the Lord dealing with me as it regards this subject, I have come to the conclusion, while there is much ignorance, there is as much, if not more, unbelief.

I have watched Believers, even Preachers, who were facing ruin because of the sin nature ruling them, be given the Message of the Cross, but stubbornly deny its veracity. Many say, and rather stupidly I might add, *"While that's all right for some, it's not needed by all."* While such a ridiculous statement might be overlooked coming from the mouth of a new convert, to hear a Preacher say such a ridiculous thing is almost beyond comprehension. But *"unbelief"* is far more sinister than most realize.

The sad fact is, the Church has strayed so far from the Cross, that anymore, Churches have become glorified social centers with religious overtones, and the Pastors have become social workers. In other words, it's the business of the Church to point out the problem which affects man and which causes him his difficulties, which is sin, and the solution, Who is Christ and what He had done for us at the Cross. But are the Churches doing that?

I think the answer is overly obvious! As stated, and let us say it again, most Churches are no more than social centers with religious overtones, while the Pastor is little more than a social worker, if that!

Our business is to *"preach Christ and Him Crucified"* (I Cor. 1:23). If we fail to do that, then we have nothing to offer a hurting world. Our efforts are a waste of time, and our proposed solutions are no more than ridiculous prattle. Sadly and regrettably, that characterizes most Churches and most Preachers.

PRIDE

Verse 17 is freighted with information regarding the reason and cause for Lucifer's Fall, and, as well, lends some credence to his being the ruler of the Earth before Adam and Eve.

The phrase from Verse 17, *"Your heart was lifted up because of your beauty,"* tells us the reason for his Fall, which was pride. He took his eyes off Christ, noticing his own beauty, as it grew more and more glorious in his eyes, until at some point in time, his *"heart"* was changed from Christ to himself. As far as we know, this was the origin of evil in all of God's creation.

As a result of the manner in which Lucifer fell, he would use the same method on Adam and Eve, resulting in their fall, and which has plagued the entirety of the Earth ever since. As a result, this sin of *"pride"* has filled Hell with billions of souls, and cause untold heartache in this world. It usurps authority over God and is the giant wall that the Holy Spirit must break down in order to penetrate the human heart, and, thereby, to bring Salvation.

That's at least one of the reasons that the Preacher of the Gospel must have the Holy Spirit in his presentation of the Word. Only the Holy Spirit, acting upon the Word of God, can break down that barrier, which means that intellectualism, nor any other method of man, can be successful, regarding the reaching of the soul for Christ. Consequently, of all the sins listed, it seems that the Lord hates pride the most, because it is the first sin listed, *"a proud look"* (Prov. 6:16-19).

WISDOM CORRUPTED

The phrase, *"You have corrupted your wisdom by reason of your brightness,"* refers not to the loss of wisdom, but, instead, wisdom corrupted, hence, the insidious design practiced upon the human family. Jesus said that Satan: *"comes not but for to steal, and to kill, and to destroy"* (Jn. 10:10). He does these things wonderfully well, and by corrupted wisdom.

When one looks at the world's deception, and with the terrible pain that accompanies this condition, it would seem that all would flock to the Lord; however, that is not so!

People continue to go to destruction by the multiple hundreds of millions, simply because the way looks right to them, having been made so by this corrupted wisdom. The *"brightness"* and *"wisdom"* go hand in hand. The false way looks bright, and, therefore, is crowded!

NOTES

The phrase, *"I will cast you to the ground,"* actually has to do with the future, meaning it has not yet happened. John the Beloved tells us: *"And the great dragon was cast out, that old serpent, called the Devil, and Satan, which deceives the whole world: he was cast out into the Earth, and his angels were cast out with him"* (Rev. 12:9). This will take place at approximately the midpoint of the coming Great Tribulation.

Of course, Satan has lost his prestigious position which he once had with the Lord, even though, after a fashion, he still has access to the Throne of God (Job, Chpts. 1-2). But even that access, as stated, is soon to end.

The phrase of Verse 17, *"I will cast you to the ground, I will lay you before kings, that they may behold you,"* refers to the coming time during the Battle of Armageddon, when Satan will be totally defeated by the Lord at the Second Coming. At that time, John said: *"And I saw an Angel come down from Heaven, having the key of the bottomless pit and a great chain in his hand.*

"And he laid hold on the dragon, that old serpent, which is the Devil, and Satan, and bound him a thousand years,

"And cast him into the bottomless pit, and shut him up, and set a seal upon him, that he should deceive the nations no more, till the thousand years should be fulfilled: and after that he must be loosed a little season" (Rev. 20:1-3).

At the end of that time, exactly as stated, Satan will be loosed for *"a little season,"* and then the Scripture says: *"And the Devil who deceived them was cast into the lake of fire and brimstone, where the beast and the false prophet are, and shall be tormented day and night forever and ever"* (Rev. 20:10).

Satan will remain in the Lake of Fire forever and forever, and will be there with all the billions of dupes which he deceived, and as can be imagined, suffering untold humiliation, which will last forever.

THE TRAFFIC OF SIN

The phrase of Verse 18, *"You have defiled your sanctuaries by the multitude of your iniquities, by the iniquity of your traffic,"* refers to the domain which he had before the Fall, but which he spoiled by sin. As stated, we know very little about this particular revolution against God, but, which to be sure, has spilled over into our domain as well. In other words, this problem didn't really begin in the Garden of Eden, but, rather, when Satan, as here proclaimed, led his revolution against God. That battle between good and evil continues unto this hour, but it is almost over.

The Cross sealed Satan's doom, and the Second Coming will *"finish"* him as it regards his ambition to make himself God.

Many would ask the question, *"Cannot Satan read the Bible, and, thereby, learn of his coming fate?"*

Most definitely, Satan can read the Bible; however, the truth is, he simply doesn't believe the Bible, even as none of his followers believe the Bible.

As I dictate these notes on July 14, 2003, Satan still thinks he will overthrow God, thereby taking dominion over the Throne of God, to which he aspires (Isa. 14:14). But irrespective of what he thinks, he will not succeed!

The phrase, *"Therefore will I bring forth a fire from the midst of you, it shall devour you,"* refers to the wages of sin being death, and, ultimately, all who participate in such, including the once mighty Lucifer, being cast into the Lake of Fire (Mat. 25:41; Rev. 20:10). Pure and simple, the Lord here pronounces the ultimate doom of Satan, and all who follow him. We must never forget that! All who follow Christ will be saved, while all who follow Satan will be eternally lost.

The phrase, *"And I will bring you to ashes upon the Earth in the sight of all them who behold you,"* pertains, as stated, to the Lake of Fire, where Satan will be incarcerated forever, along with all of the billions who have followed him.

One can well imagine the passion of anger that will be evidenced against the Evil One, and will be evidenced forever. They believed his lies and were damned! Their pride and pomp are now ashes! They now realize what it is, not only to suffer the eternal damnation of being eternally lost, but, as well, will be separated from God forever, which, within itself, is even worse than all the other suffering, and all because of this one called *"Lucifer."* What he will suffer at their hands, and forever, is beyond the pale of imagination!

FOREVER

The phrase of Verse 19, *"And never shall you be anymore,"* is that for which Godly men have cried from the very beginning.

Many have wondered as to why the Lord has allowed Satan to continue. In fact, John said: *"But in the days of the voice of the seventh Angel, when he shall begin to sound, the Mystery of God should be finished, as He has declared to His Servants the Prophets"* (Rev. 10:7).

This *"mystery of God"* addresses itself as to why the Lord has allowed Satan to continue for this period of time. We aren't given the reason, hence, the word, *"mystery,"* being used; however, we do know, that God does all things well.

We must remember that this question looms far larger than the human race. It also incorporates all of God's creation, plus the myriad of Angels of His Kingdom.

We know that God has not allowed the Evil One to continue because of weakness on God's part. We also know that God has had a good reason for that which He has done. He does all things well! But this we do know, Satan's *"finish"* has already been recorded. This includes all fallen angels, as well as demon spirits.

Then the prayer of Christ that God's Will *"would be done on Earth, as it is in Heaven"* will finally be answered and brought to pass (Mat. 6:9-10).

(20) "AGAIN THE WORD OF THE LORD CAME UNTO ME, SAYING,

(21) "SON OF MAN, SET YOUR FACE AGAINST ZIDON, AND PROPHESY AGAINST IT,

(22) "AND SAY, THUS SAITH THE LORD GOD; BEHOLD, I AM AGAINST YOU, O ZIDON; AND I WILL BE GLORIFIED IN THE MIDST OF YOU: AND THEY SHALL KNOW THAT I AM THE LORD, WHEN I SHALL HAVE EXECUTED JUDGMENTS IN HER, AND SHALL BE SANCTIFIED IN HER.

(23) "FOR I WILL SEND INTO HER PESTILENCE, AND BLOOD INTO HER

STREETS; AND THE WOUNDED SHALL BE JUDGED IN THE MIDST OF HER BY THE SWORD UPON HER ON EVERY SIDE; AND THEY SHALL KNOW THAT I AM THE LORD.

(24) "AND THERE SHALL BE NO MORE A PRICKING BRIER UNTO THE HOUSE OF ISRAEL, NOR ANY GRIEVING THORN OF ALL WHO ARE ROUND ABOUT THEM, WHO DESPISED THEM; AND THEY SHALL KNOW THAT I AM THE LORD GOD."

The synopsis is:

1. The judgment upon Zidon was suffering but not extinction. Therefore, she exists today; but her history has been one of pestilence and bloodshed.

2. The city was founded by a son of Canaan (Gen. 10:15). It was famous as the shrine of the Virgin Queen of Heaven and her Child. Jezebel was a daughter of the king of Zidon and introduced this degrading form of idolatry into Israel.

3. From all of this, we can surely see how the Lord hates the sin of idolatry. And let all remember, anything that comes between the Believer and Christ is looked at by the Lord as *"idolatry."*

ZIDON

The phrase of Verse 21, addressed to Ezekiel, *"Son of man, set your face against Zidon, and prophesy against it,"* spelled tremendous trouble for this city, even though they would have little believed the Prophet, even had they heard him proclaiming these words. They did not believe in Jehovah.

Sidon is about twenty-five or thirty miles north of Tyre. In fact, they were sister cities, but yet with Tyre serving as the chief city. Even though their sins were the same and required a like punishment, still, the relation of this city to Tyre was one of sufficient independence to justify a separate Oracle from the Holy Spirit. The Prophet was to *"prophesy against it,"* and not *"for it."*

According to tradition, Sidon was the first Phoenician city to be founded and became a principal Canaanite stronghold (Gen. 10:19; I Chron. 1:13). In Isaiah's day, he prophesied that Sennacherib, the Assyrian, would take the city (Isa. 23:2-12).

NOTES

On Sennacherib's death, Sidon revolted and Esarhaddon invaded Sidon, killing its ruler, sacked the port, and reestablished Assyrian authority over the city.

With the decline of the Assyrians, Sidon recovered its independence, only to be besieged again and captured by Nebuchadnezzar. This was in 587 B.C., and was foretold by Jeremiah (Jer. 25:22; 27:3; 47:4). Years later, under the Persians, it provided the majority of the Persian fleet.

About 350 B.C., under Tabnit II, Sidon led the rebellion of Phoenicia and Cyprus against Artaxerxes III. The city was betrayed and 40,000 perished, the survivors burning the city and fleet.

It was a woman from Sidon who came to Christ in order that her daughter may be healed. She was called the Syro-Phoenician (Mk. 7:24-31; Mat. 15:21-29). As well, many Sidonians listened to the teaching of Christ (Mk. 3:8; Lk. 6:17; 10:13-14). Also, Paul visited friends in this city on his way to Rome (Acts 27:3).

OPPOSITION OF THE LORD

The phrase of Verse 22, *"Thus saith the Lord God: behold, I am against you, O Zidon,"* presents a cold and chilling statement! It is one thing to have man against us, but quite something else to have God against us. Sin and rebellion against His Way are the cause of this enmity between God and Zidon, as it is the cause of everything that is negative between God and man.

Zidon was very close to Israel, and could have known Israel's God, but as the hearts of men are set to do evil, she had little interest.

While Israel might be blamed, the truth is, it is doubtful that Zidon would have had any interest, even had Israel been on fire for God. It is the same presently:

How many today, even in the light of the Glorious Gospel of Christ, actually are interested in the Lord? That number is abysmally few! That's the reason that Jesus said:

"Because strait is the gate, and narrow is the way, which leads unto life, and few there be that find it" (Mat. 7:14).

JUDGMENT

Verses 22 and 23 proclaim judgment.

The phrase of Verse 23, *"For I will send into her pestilence and blood into her streets,"* has to do with the terrible invasions she suffered from this time forward, and as previously addressed.

Even though it is seldom mentioned from behind modern pulpits, nevertheless, judgment will be sent by God if a person, city, nation, or group of nations ignore His Word, and rebel against His authority. Sometimes the judgment is long in coming, and because of such delay, many think it will not come at all, but come it shall!

The judgment, and as stated in this Verse, as well as many others, can take the form of disease, war, crime, or any one of many devices and means.

If the calamity is national, the righteous oftentimes suffer along with guilty.

Even though Satan may be greatly instrumental in these Judgments, still, he can do only what God allows him to do; therefore, one must conclude that, as the Lord outlined judgments upon cities and nations of old, he continues to do such presently.

The only thing that can stop personal or national Judgment is Holy Spirit Revival. And to be quickly stated, Revival must always begin at the *"House of God,"* which constitutes the Church (I Pet. 4:17). Then the lost can be saved and a nation brought from the crumbling edge of judgment.

Let it be known that such judgment incorporates the entirety of the world and irrespective of its religious beliefs, but with greater responsibility demanded of those nations which profess to know the Lord (Lk. 12:48).

I AM THE LORD GOD

The phrase of Verse 24, *"And there shall be no more a pricking brier unto the House of Israel,"* refers to Sidon wounding Israel in several different ways. Jezebel was a case in point, as she was the daughter of Ethbaal, priest/king of Tyre and Sidon. She was married to Ahab, the King of the Northern Confederacy of Israel, and introduced Baal worship in Samaria to a degree that it had never been known before.

It should by now be known and understood that the Lord does not look kindly on those who would persecute His Children, and irrespective of their wrongdoing. While fellowship may at times have to be withdrawn, still, Paul said that he should be counted *"not as an enemy, but admonish him as a brother"* (II Thess. 3:15).

The idea is that ancient Judah, as well as the modern Christian, are God's property and His Alone. As such, it is to be respected accordingly and by all!

(25) "THUS SAITH THE LORD GOD; WHEN I SHALL HAVE GATHERED THE HOUSE OF ISRAEL FROM THE PEOPLE AMONG WHOM THEY ARE SCATTERED, AND SHALL BE SANCTIFIED IN THEM IN THE SIGHT OF THE HEATHEN, THEN SHALL THEY DWELL IN THEIR LAND THAT I HAVE GIVEN TO MY SERVANT JACOB.

(26) "AND THEY SHALL DWELL SAFELY THEREIN, AND SHALL BUILD HOUSES, AND PLANT VINEYARDS; YES, THEY SHALL DWELL WITH CONFIDENCE, WHEN I HAVE EXECUTED JUDGMENTS UPON ALL THOSE WHO DESPISE THEM ROUND ABOUT THEM; AND THEY SHALL KNOW THAT I AM THE LORD THEIR GOD."

The exegesis is:

1. The happy future of Israel is contrasted with the extinction of Tyre and the judgment of Zidon.

2. They, the Zidonians, shall get to know, to their sorrow, that I am *"Adonai-Jehovah."*

3. They, the Israelites, shall get to know, to their joy, that I am *"Jehovah, their God."* For the Lord will faithfully fulfill His promise to Jacob and will give them the land.

4. The Great God and Saviour, Jesus Christ (Titus 2:13) can be known as a Judge or as a Saviour. All men must know Him as either. How much wiser to fall as His feet in contrition and faith, and so prove His Grace as a Saviour, than, later, to experience His severity as a Judge.

THE RESTORATION OF ISRAEL

The phrase of Verse 25, *"When I shall have gathered the House of Israel from the people among whom they are scattered,"* refers to a restoration that has already begun. It began in 1948, and has continued ever since, with the greatest influx recently coming from the former Soviet Union.

However, the greatest gathering is yet to take place, which will commence immediately after the Second Coming of the Lord, when Israel, and to a man, will accept the Lord Jesus Christ, not only as their Saviour, but as their Messiah as well!

SANCTIFICATION

The phrase, *"And shall be sanctified in them in the sight of the heathen,"* is, as by now should be obvious, extremely important in the eyes of God. The word, *"sanctified,"* means to *"set apart,"* as for holy use, and for holy use only!

In Sanctification, the Lord is depicted as holy in majesty, mysterious in His Numinous Otherness, loftily removed from man, sin, and Earth.

The people are exhorted to regard the Lord of Hosts as holy (Isa. 8:13), and God says He will sanctify Himself and be sanctified in or by them, as well as recognized in His sovereign claims. His Holiness will be acknowledged through His people's attitude and relationship to Him.

The idea is that God's Holiness will be brought about in His people, either by their lives of Holiness, i.e. obedience or else by Judgment. Among the ungodly, Judgment, but in any case, His Holiness will be vindicated.

THE LAND OF ISRAEL

The phrase of Verse 25, *"Then shall they dwell in their land that I have given to My servant Jacob,"* refers to the longest conflict that has engaged itself on this planet. It is the Land of Israel, and the Lord, in the Passage, plus many others, proclaims His giving such to His people, and exactly where this Land should be.

The Lord told Abraham, *"Unto your seed have I given this Land, from the river of Egypt unto the great river, the river Euphrates"* (Gen. 15:18).

This area includes the Sinai Peninsula all the way to the Suez Canal on the south, to the river Euphrates on the east, which includes modern Syria, as well as part of Iraq and the Arabian Peninsula. It was never fully occupied, even in the prosperous reigns of David and Solomon. It will be fully occupied by Israel in the coming Millennium (Ezek. 47:13-48:29).

When He used the phrase, *"My servant Jacob,"* He, at the same time, is saying that He did not give it to Esau, i.e., the Arabs. Over this Land, the battle has raged and continues even unto the present.

Israel presently signing the Palestinian accord, which proved to be fruitless, and now pressured to sign the *"roadmap"* (2003), all an effort to obtain peace, regrettably, will little solve the problem. Satan continues with his attempt to deny the Land that God originally promised to Abraham and his descendants, namely, the Jews. Consequently, more blood has been spilled in this area than possibly any other area in the world. Regrettably, the bloodshed is not over. The worst days are ahead!

Despite all the promises of the Muslims, their goal is the annihilation of every Jew, and the land in totality coming to them.

It will not happen, but only because of the Second Coming of the Lord (Rev., Chpt. 19).

DWELL SAFELY

The phrase of Verse 26, *"And they shall dwell safely therein,"* refers to that which is yet to come. As is obvious, such is not the case at present.

It is noted that Christ should mention the two cities of this Chapter, Tyre and Zidon (Mat. 11:21; Lk. 10:13) in that their stated position would be spiritually better than the cities of Galilee, which had rejected His Ministry. As well, He Himself passed through the coasts of Tyre and Zidon (Mat. 15:21), and possibly even actually walked the streets of the latter city (Mk. 7:24).

As stated, the Zidonians shall get to know Jehovah, to their sorrow, while the Israelites shall get to know, to their joy, that He is Jehovah their God.

The return of the Jews to the Land of Israel is foretold in many prophecies. (Some of the more striking are: Deut. 30:3-4; Isa. 11:11-13; 27:12-13; Jer. 31:8-10; 32:37; Ezek. 34:13; 37:21; Amos 9:14-15.)

The prediction of this Twenty-sixth Verse will take place at the Second Coming of Christ, which will begin a thousand-year

Reign, with Israel finally realizing her place and position in Christ. At that time, *"They shall know that I am the Lord their God."*

"Stand up, stand up for Jesus, ye soldiers of the Cross;
"Lift high His royal banner, it must not suffer loss:
"From victory unto victory His army shall He lead,
"'Til every foe is vanquished, and Christ is Lord indeed."

"Stand up, stand up for Jesus, the trumpet call obey;
"Forth to the mighty conflict in this His glorious day:
"Ye who are men now serve Him against unnumbered foes;
"Let courage rise with danger, and strength to strength oppose."

"Stand up, stand up for Jesus, stand in His strength alone;
"The arm of flesh will fail you, you dare not trust your own:
"Put on the gospel armor, each piece put on with prayer;
"Where duty calls or danger, be never wanting there."

"Stand up, stand up for Jesus, the strife will not be long;
"This day the noise of battle, the next victor's song:
"To him who overcometh, a crown of life shall be;
"He with the King of Glory shall reign eternally."

CHAPTER 29

(1) "IN THE TENTH YEAR, IN THE TENTH MONTH, IN THE TWELFTH DAY OF THE MONTH, THE WORD OF THE LORD CAME UNTO ME, SAYING,

(2) "SON OF MAN, SET YOUR FACE AGAINST PHARAOH KING OF EGYPT, AND PROPHESY AGAINST HIM, AND AGAINST ALL EGYPT:

(3) "SPEAK, AND SAY, THUS SAITH THE LORD GOD; BEHOLD, I AM AGAINST YOU, PHARAOH KING OF EGYPT, THE GREAT DRAGON THAT LIES IN THE MIDST OF HIS RIVERS, WHICH HAS SAID, MY RIVER IS MY OWN, AND I HAVE MADE IT FOR MYSELF.

(4) "BUT I WILL PUT HOOKS IN YOUR JAWS, AND I WILL CAUSE THE FISH OF YOUR RIVERS TO STICK UNTO YOUR SCALES, AND I WILL BRING YOU UP OUT OF THE MIDST OF YOUR RIVERS, AND ALL THE FISH OF YOUR RIVERS SHALL STICK UNTO YOUR SCALES.

(5) "AND I WILL LEAVE YOU THROWN INTO THE WILDERNESS, YOU AND ALL THE FISH OF YOUR RIVERS: YOU SHALL FALL UPON THE OPEN FIELDS; YOU SHALL NOT BE BROUGHT TOGETHER, NOR GATHERED: I HAVE GIVEN YOU FOR MEAT TO THE BEASTS OF THE FIELD AND TO THE FOWLS OF THE HEAVEN.

(6) "AND ALL THE INHABITANTS OF EGYPT SHALL KNOWN THAT I AM THE LORD, BECAUSE THEY HAVE BEEN A STAFF OF REED TO THE HOUSE OF ISRAEL.

(7) "WHEN THEY TOOK HOLD OF YOU BY YOUR HAND, YOU DID BREAK, AND REND ALL THEIR SHOULDER; AND WHEN THEY LEANED UPON YOU, YOU BROKE, AND MADE ALL THEIR LOINS TO BE AT A STAND.

(8) "THEREFORE THUS SAITH THE LORD GOD; BEHOLD, I WILL BRING A SWORD UPON YOU, AND CUT OFF MAN AND BEAST OUT OF YOU.

(9) "AND THE LAND OF EGYPT SHALL BE DESOLATE AND WASTE; AND THEY SHALL KNOW THAT I AM THE LORD: BECAUSE HE HAS SAID, THE RIVER IS MINE, AND I HAVE MADE IT.

(10) "BEHOLD, THEREFORE I AM AGAINST YOU, AND AGAINST YOUR RIVERS, AND I WILL MAKE THE LAND OF EGYPT UTTERLY WASTE AND DESOLATE, FROM THE TOWER OF SYENE EVEN UNTO THE BORDER OF ETHIOPIA.

(11) "NO FOOT OF MAN SHALL PASS THROUGH IT, NOR FOOT OF BEAST SHALL PASS THROUGH IT, NEITHER SHALL IT BE INHABITED FORTY YEARS.

(12) "AND I WILL MAKE THE LAND OF

EGYPT DESOLATE IN THE MIDST OF THE COUNTRIES THAT ARE DESOLATE, AND HER CITIES AMONG THE CITIES THAT ARE LAID WASTE SHALL BE DESOLATE FORTY YEARS: AND I WILL SCATTER THE EGYPTIANS AMONG THE NATIONS, AND WILL DISPERSE THEM THROUGH THE COUNTRIES.

(13) "YET THUS SAITH THE LORD GOD; AT THE END OF FORTY YEARS WILL I GATHER THE EGYPTIANS FROM THE PEOPLE WHERE THEY WERE SCATTERED:

(14) "AND I WILL BRING AGAIN THE CAPTIVITY OF EGYPT, AND WILL CAUSE THEM TO RETURN INTO THE LAND OF PATHROS, INTO THE LAND OF THEIR HABITATION; AND THEY SHALL BE THERE A BASE KINGDOM.

(15) "IT SHALL BE THE BASEST OF THE KINGDOMS; NEITHER SHALL IT EXALT ITSELF ANY MORE ABOVE THE NATIONS: FOR I WILL DIMINISH THEM, THAT THEY SHALL NO MORE RULE OVER THE NATIONS.

(16) "AND IT SHALL BE NO MORE THE CONFIDENCE OF THE HOUSE OF ISRAEL, WHICH BRINGS THEIR INIQUITY TO REMEMBRANCE, WHEN THEY SHALL LOOK AFTER THEM: BUT THEY SHALL KNOW THAT I AM THE LORD GOD."

The exegesis is:

1. Egypt is the last world kingdom addressed by Ezekiel. The Prophecies concerning this kingdom will cover four Chapters.

2. Herodotus and Josephus state that this Pharaoh — Hopra or Apries — captured Gaza, made himself master of Palestine, recovered what was lost in the battle at Carchemish, and that, because of his successes for twenty-five years, he declared that not even a god could defeat him. But he was overthrown by Nebuchadnezzar and strangled by his own rebellious soldiers.

3. The *"dragon"* of Verse 3 actually refers to the crocodile, which was the national emblem of Egypt, as the eagle is of the United States.

4. Egypt has been a base kingdom exactly as prophesied by Ezekiel, from then until now, and will continue to be until the Second Coming of the Lord.

5. The forty years of desolation and dispersion, as it regards Egypt, closed at the destruction of the Babylonian Empire by the Persians.

EGYPT

This Prophecy was given about six months before Jerusalem fell. In all, several Prophecies will be given, covering some four Chapters, and given over a time period of about two years.

Each of these Prophecies, or else a portion of the Prophecy, was called forth by the political events of the time, and should be studied in connection with them.

The phrase of Verse 2, *"Son of man, set your face against Pharaoh king of Egypt,"* probably pertained to *"Pharaoh Hopra,"* or as he was called by the Greeks, *"Apries."*

At the beginning of this Prophecy, which was about six months, as stated, before the Fall of Jerusalem, Zedekiah, the king of Judah, and his counselors, following in the steps of Hezekiah (Isa., Chpt. 30) and Jehoiakim (Jer., Chpt. 46), had courted Pharaoh's alliance against the Chaldeans. As Ezekiel had previously prophesied, they would find that they were once more leaning on a broken reed.

We now come to 587 B.C., when Jerusalem was actually besieged, but still dreaming of being relieved by an Egyptian army.

The very one who Zedekiah was depending on, Pharaoh Hopra, was being prophesied against by both Ezekiel and Jeremiah. So, there was no excuse for the rebellion. The truth is, despite the Word of the Lord, Judah and Jerusalem determined to lean on the arm of flesh, i.e., Egypt. Tragically, they would see, and in no uncertain terms, just how helpless Egypt actually was.

Tragically, the modern Church follows suit! Any more, it little seeks God, it little believes God! It would rather trust in the arm of flesh.

As there was no help from that source in Ezekiel's day, there is no help from that source presently!

The phrase of Verse 3, *"Speak, and say, Thus saith the Lord God: Behold, I am against you, Pharaoh king of Egypt,"* begins a pronounced judgment against Egypt, which would ensure its denigration, at least until the Second Coming of the Lord. The reasons are manifold and begin in this Verse, continuing until Chapter 32. And yet, beautifully enough, Egypt will be restored in the coming Kingdom Age along with Israel.

Egypt, in Bible symbolism, has always stood for the spirit of the world. It was, as every Bible student knows, the nation that enslaved God's chosen people, the sons of Jacob, who were only delivered as Jehovah made evident His great Power against them.

The phrase, *"The great dragon that lies in the midst of his rivers,"* refers to the Hebrew word, *"tannin,"* which is the crocodile, which was the proper symbol of Egypt, as found on certain coins.

The phrase of Verse 3, *"Which has said, my river is my own, and I have made it for myself,"* refers to the Nile, which, in those times, flooded its banks every year, thereby, making the land, at least in proximity to the river, extremely fertile. But for the Nile and its inundation, Egypt would be as desolate as the deserts on either hand. So sharp is the change from watered land to desert that one, it is said, could stand with one foot in each.

Egypt's agriculture, and, hence, her prosperity depended wholly on this inundation. If the flood was high in a given year, such produced splendid crops that made Egypt's agricultural wealth proverbial. A low Nile would mean drought, while an extremely high Nile would spell great difficulties, as well!

As well, the Nile was Egypt's main arterial highway, with boats sailing both north and south, up and down its wide course.

In the religious beliefs of the Egyptians, the spirit of the Nile-flood was the god, Ha'pi, bringer of fertility and abundance, so-called!

In fact, the river Nile was worshipped by the Egyptians under various names and symbols. It was called *"the father of life"* and *"the father of the gods."*

As well, Pharaoh considered himself a god, and particularly this Pharaoh believed himself so firmly established in his kingdom that there was no God Who could cast him out of it. He thought of himself as the creator of his own power.

The traditional headdress, or crown, of Pharaoh consisted of whatever type of cloth headcovering that was desired, with a coiled serpent made of gold serving as the actual crown. Its cobra-type head would have protruded out over the forehead of Pharaoh, somewhat like a small hood, with two rubies serving as its eyes; therefore, when Moses and Aaron, many years before, stood before Pharaoh of that day demanding the release of the Israelites, and looking into his face, they, as well, looked into the face of the serpent, i.e., symbolic of Satan.

THE WORD OF THE LORD

The phrase of Verse 5, *"I have given you for meat to the beasts of the field and to the fowls of the Heaven,"* proclaims that which most definitely came to pass.

It is said that Pharaoh attacked Tyre and Zidon, and then failed in an enterprise against Cyrene, and was deposed by Amasis in 569 B.C. It is probably this expedition against Cyrene, which led to the revolt of Amasis against Pharaoh Hopra, which resulted in his defeat, to which Verse 5 and others refer!

Pharaoh did not know, and would not have believed had it been related to him, that his destiny was in the Hands of Jehovah, and not his heathenistic gods for which Egypt was famous. In his haughtiness, and especially at this time when Nebuchadnezzar had laid siege to Jerusalem, he would not have believed, or even understood, the thrust of this Prophecy.

In his mind, Judah's God was obviously weaker than the Babylonian gods, much less his, or else, she would not be in this state of defeat! He would not, and could not, have conceived of the idea that Jehovah was purposely allowing Judah to come to this state, and because of her many sins. And, above all, that Jehovah was guiding his destiny, as well, would have been laughable to this heathenistic Monarch.

Nevertheless, his unbelief did not alter the predicted results, as unbelief never alters the predicted results of what the Lord has stated!

As an example, the Book of Revelation is an open account given to the entirety of mankind concerning the coming Judgment upon this world, but little believed by anyone, even the Church; nevertheless, it will happen, and exactly as the Word of God proclaims it.

THE LORD AND HIS PEOPLE

The phrase of Verse 6, *"Because they have been a staff of reed to the house of Israel,"* presents at least one of the causes of God's anger outlined against Egypt, as here recorded. Egypt had promised to deliver Judah from the Babylonians, which caused Judah to depend on them, but they proved to be only a flimsy *"reed."*

It is extremely interesting that the Lord, even though it was His Will that Babylon serve as the chastiser of Judah, still, His anger at Egypt for promising what they could not deliver, and, at least in some fashion, adding to Judah's plight, would now cause judgment to be brought on them.

As we have repeatedly stated in these Volumes, the Lord, even though chastening Judah and Jerusalem, and severely, and because of their many sins, still, would not tolerate any other nation or people maltreating them without bringing Judgment upon themselves. Such should be a lesson to all! When the Lord said: *"Touch not My Anointed, and do My Prophets no harm,"* He meant exactly what He said (Ps. 105:15).

The meaning is clear. Anyone who is truly chosen and called of God belongs to the Lord in a sense that is very special to Him, and should be very special to all others. Certainly, wrongdoing, as in the case of Judah and Jerusalem, cannot be condoned, even though God's called and anointed, still, all punishment and chastisement belong strictly in the domain of the Lord, and are never given to others; consequently, anyone who lifts a hand to such had better be in blessing instead of cursing. Anything else will automatically trigger a negative response from the Lord, which may be a while in coming, but ultimately it will come.

Therefore, whenever man-made Religious Denominations think they can chastise their Preachers, they have just abrogated the Headship of Christ, and incurred the Wrath of God. As stated, it may be a while in coming, but come it will!

As well, those doing the punishing or chastising are oftentimes in far worse spiritual condition than the ones being chastised, hence, the very reason the Lord will not place such in the hands of man.

James addressed this by saying: *"There is One Lawgiver, Who is able to save and to destroy: who are you who judges another?"* (James 4:12).

The Holy Spirit here, through James, plainly tells us that it is the Lord Alone Who is qualified to judge or to chastise. We must not forget that!

In no way does this mean that unrepentant, unconfessed sin can be condoned. If fellowship is withdrawn, as may be necessary in such cases, still, the individual must continue to be treated as a Brother, and not as an enemy (II Thess. 3:15).

EGYPT'S SIN

The phrase of Verse 7, *"When they took hold of you by the hand, and you did break,"* gives us more insight into what actually happened.

One would think that the Lord would little care concerning the perfidiousness of Egypt, especially considering that He had ordained Judah and Jerusalem for severe chastisement; nevertheless, it mattered greatly to Him that Egypt *"broke"* when *"they leaned upon her."*

When Nebuchadnezzar laid siege to Jerusalem, due to the promises of Egypt, Zedekiah thought that Egypt would come to his rescue, and he would, therefore, be saved.

He thought this despite the Prophecies of Jeremiah and Ezekiel to the contrary.

In fact, Egypt did make a thrust against Nebuchadnezzar, causing him to withdraw for a period of time, thereby giving a false hope to Jerusalem; nevertheless, the joy and relief were short-lived, as Egypt was quickly defeated, with Nebuchadnezzar quickly returning to finish the conquest of Jerusalem.

However, as a result of Egypt's promises, Zedekiah held out against Nebuchadnezzar, greatly incensing the Babylonian Monarch, which caused him to wreak a terrible vengeance when the walls of the city of Jerusalem were finally breached, for which Egypt was partly responsible, and of which the Lord here speaks.

A COVENANT GOD

The phrase of Verse 8, *"Therefore thus saith the Lord God,"* refers to the Truth that matters of war and peace, and all else for that matter, are decided exclusively by the Lord.

The title, *"Lord God,"* presents the Lord as a Covenant God Who is always present. He is not simply a God afar off, or a God of past history, or a God Who will appear in that future the Prophets foretell. He is a God Who is present and Who acts at every point of the history and experience of His people, be they Israel or the Church.

Concerning the New Testament, the title, *"Lord,"* attached to *"Jesus,"* or to *"Jesus Christ,"* ascribes Deity to Christ (Lk. 20:42-44). Thomas confessed Him as *"my Lord and my God!"* as well ascribing to Him Deity.

The earliest Chapters of the Book of Acts testify to the truth that after the Resurrection, the Church immediately confessed *"Jesus is Lord;"* and the balance of the New Testament constantly affirms Jesus' Lordship. To recognize Jesus as Lord is to acknowledge His Deity.

THE LORDSHIP OF CHRIST

As Lord, Christ is seated at God's Right Hand, the place of authority. His authority is universal, *"Far above all rule and authority, power and dominion, and every title that can be given, not only in the present age, but also in the one to come"* (Eph. 1:21). All *"Angels, authorities, and powers"* are *"in submission to Him"* (I Pet. 3:22).

As under the old economy of God, the Lordship of Christ is worked out in this present world. Peter explores the situation in which a Believer does what is right but still endures suffering. He reminds us that the *"eyes of the Lord are on the Righteous"* (I Pet. 3:12). Even if we suffer for what is right, we can *"set apart Christ as Lord"* in our hearts; that is, we can remain confident that Christ, as Lord, is superintending events.

In viewing the rendering of the title, *"Lord,"* in both Old and New Testaments, we must come to the conclusion that the ultimate meaning of the title belongs to Jesus Alone (Phil. 2:9-11). It affirms His Deity and His authority over every power — natural and supernatural. As Lord, Jesus governs the sweep of history and guards each individual's step.

One practical implication of the Lordship of Christ as seen in Scriptures' call to us is to abandon judging or attempting to control others. While every Believer is given authority, referred to at times as *"the authority of the Believer,"* that is always over demon spirits, and never over other human beings. The Lord reserves that right exclusively to Himself. Jesus died and rose again that He might actually be Lord in the life of each person who trusts in Him.

In the Old Testament, the title, *"Lord,"* was applied to Christ in His preincarnate state, whereas, it continues to be applied to Him in his incarnate state — human but glorified form.

WASTE

Verses 9 through 13 proclaim the Word of the Lord, as it regards the Judgment brought to pass on Egypt.

The phrase of Verse 9, *"Because He* (Pharaoh) *has said, the river is mine, and I have made it,"* proclaims the Lord drawing attention to the boastful pride of Pharaoh. He claimed the river Nile as his, and even that he had created it. How stupid can a man be! It was God Who created everything, but Pharaoh gave Him no glory for such, and, in fact, didn't even recognize Jehovah.

Is that any different than the teaching of evolution, which denies God as the Creator of man? I think not. In fact, the modern sin is far worse, and, to be sure, it will ultimately be called to account.

The statement of Verse 9, *"And the Land of Egypt shall be desolate and waste,"* refers to the idea that if Pharaoh created the river, surely he can stop the *"desolation and waste"*! But, of course, Pharaoh is helpless to do this, because, despite his bluster, he is just a man and, as such, is helpless in the Face of God.

The phrase of Verse 10, *"From the tower of Syene even unto the border of Ethiopia,"* should read *"from Migdol to Syene, even to the border of Ethiopia."*

Migdol represented the northern extremity of Egypt, as Syene represented the southern. Therefore, the entirety of Egypt is included in the statement.

FORTY YEARS

The phrase of Verse 11, *"Neither shall it be inhabited forty years,"* is mentioned again in both Verses 12 and 13.

The *"utter waste and desolation"* of Verse 10, as well as the *"man"* and *"beast"* of Verse 11, are not to be taken literally. If taken literally, it would mean that for forty years there were no human beings or animals in Egypt, which we know did not happen! It did mean, as referred to, that Egypt would suffer greatly for this period of time, actually being a vassal state of the Babylonian Empire, thereby, experiencing no prosperity whatsoever.

Even though there is no historical records of the fulfillment of these particular Passages, still, knowing that Nebuchadnezzar invaded Egypt after the destruction of Jerusalem, we may assume, with little risk of doubt, that he *"scattered the Egyptians among the nations."* Such was the practice of invaders in order that it would be deprived of its elite, and, therefore, incapable of insurrection.

The *"forty years"* period of time began about twenty-seven years after the first captivity of Judah, which began the seventy year period of Israel's subjugation. It would have taken a period of time for the Babylonians to subjugate Egypt, possibly even some three years, which would total thirty. This would leave the forty years as mentioned.

It is believed that at approximately the time that Israel was allowed by Cyrus of the Medes and the Persians, which had defeated the Babylonians, to go back to the Promised Land, likewise, Egypt was allowed to return to her native land as well!

Cyrus, having Esther as his mother, had been raised as a subject, no doubt, of Mosaic Law and Jewish history. As such, he would have had some, if not excellent, knowledge of the Word of God as it was up to that time. He was quite possibly very well familiar with the Prophecies of both Jeremiah and Ezekiel, and was determined to help fulfill the predictions. He, no doubt, knew that he was named by God in Scripture over 150 years before he was born, or, about 200 years before he made the decree to rebuild Jerusalem and the Temple (Isa. 44:28; 45:1).

A BASE KINGDOM

The phrase of Verse 14, *"And they shall there be a base kingdom,"* means one that is a subordinate kingdom. Such has Egypt been from that day to the present time.

The phrase also of Verse 14, *"And I will bring again the captivity of Egypt,"* states their restoration, which took place at about the same time as Israel's; however, it as well points to the future restoration of Egypt and of Israel at the same time, as predicted in Isaiah, Chapter 19 — for Egypt is to be restored and blessed in the latter day, the coming Kingdom Age.

From the time of her defeat by Nebuchadnezzar to a short time after World War II, Egypt has been under the authority of foreign nations. Not long after World War II, Egypt was granted autonomy by Britain; however, she still remains *"a base kingdom,"* even *"the basest of the kingdoms."*

Egypt is presently the largest of the Arab nations but possesses little power at all. Exactly that which the Lord said would be, has been and is!

CONFIDENCE

The phrase of Verse 16, *"And it shall be no more the confidence of the House of Israel,"* proclaims the last time that Israel leaned on the arm of Egypt. After this, Israel never again placed any trust in Egypt, with a bitter enmity existing between the nations, which continues, at least in part, even unto the present time.

All of this refers to the Biblical Truth that the Lord desires His people, whether Israel of old or the modern Church, to trust solely in Him instead of the world. As this was Israel's great temptation, it is the great temptation of the modern Church, as well!

There are two major spiritual positions to which the Holy Spirit seeks to bring the Believer. They are:

A SCRIPTURAL POSITION

The Word of God is the Rule Book, the Guide Post, the Road Map, the Book of Instructions, and the Pattern for Living. Every single thing in the Believer's life, and irrespective of its nature, is to be brought under the domain of the Word of God. No man, Preacher, family member, Church Denomination, or Religious Organization must abrogate that position. It must be fought for and clung to at all costs!

Sadly and regrettably, most Christians succumb to the conventional wisdom, prevailing winds, or the Denomination line, giving little thought to what the Bible actually says.

Only the Word of the Lord is Truth, and, as such, will lead one to victory. All else is sinking sand!

Nevertheless, to adhere strictly to the Word of God will invite the enmity of not only the world, but, as well, the far greater majority of the Church!

CONFIDENCE EXCLUSIVELY IN THE LORD

The Arm of the Lord is to be leaned on exclusive of man, whether the man is good or bad. While it is certainly better to lean on the arm of a Godly man, rather than one who would lead astray, still, even this is not the perfect Will of God, in that He desires, and actually demands, total dependence on, and trust in, Him (Prov. 3:5-6).

At least one of the reasons the Lord took the Children of Israel through the wilderness is that they would have absolutely no arm to lean on except God. In other words, they had to trust Him for anything and everything.

Oftentimes, the Lord will push the Believer into a spiritual posture, to where he has absolutely no choice but to solely trust God.

It is true that some have taken this to the extreme, even denying life-saving medicine to those who desperately needed it, of which this has no reference, because the Lord will not do for us what we can do for ourselves.

The Believer is to do all that he can in whatever capacity, but placing total trust in the Lord for the ultimate outcome. The Lord will not feed the lazy, nor satisfy the whims of the ignorant. As the Lord will not allow man to abrogate His position as Lord Supreme of the Universe, likewise, He will not allow Himself to abrogate man's position, i.e., do for man what man can do for himself.

(17) "AND IT CAME TO PASS IN THE SEVEN AND TWENTIETH YEAR, IN THE FIRST MONTH, IN THE FIRST DAY OF THE MONTH, THE WORD OF THE LORD CAME UNTO ME, SAYING,

(18) "SON OF MAN, NEBUCHADNEZZAR KING OF BABYLON CAUSED HIS ARMY TO SERVE A GREAT SERVICE AGAINST TYRUS: EVERY HEAD WAS MADE BALD, AND EVERY SHOULDER WAS PEELED: YET HAD HE NO WAGES, NOR HIS ARMY, FOR TYRUS, FOR THE SERVICE THAT HE HAD SERVED AGAINST IT:

(19) "THEREFORE THUS SAITH THE LORD GOD; BEHOLD, I WILL GIVE THE LAND OF EGYPT UNTO NEBUCHADNEZZAR KING OF BABYLON; AND HE SHALL TAKE HER MULTITUDE, AND TAKE HER SPOIL, AND TAKE HER PREY; AND IT SHALL BE THE WAGES FOR HIS ARMY.

(20) "I HAVE GIVEN HIM THE LAND OF EGYPT FOR HIS LABOUR WHEREWITH HE SERVED AGAINST IT, BECAUSE THEY WROUGHT FOR ME, SAITH THE LORD GOD.

(21) "IN THAT DAY WILL I CAUSE THE HORN OF THE HOUSE OF ISRAEL TO BUD FORTH, AND I WILL GIVE YOU THE OPENING OF THE MOUTH IN THE MIDST OF THEM; AND THEY SHALL KNOW THAT I AM THE LORD."

The diagram is:

1. The Prophecy of Verses 17 through 21 was given seventeen years later, but introduced here to secure the unity of the subject.

2. The siege of Tyre by Nebuchadnezzar lasted thirteen years. The Babylonian king undertook it at God's command (Jer. 25:9). He captured the city but secured no treasure, for the Tyrians had removed it, and most of their citizens, to other cities by the sea. Carrying earth and timber for the construction of besieging forts made the soldiers' heads bald, for baskets of Earth and stones were carried on the head, and peeled their shoulders, for timber was carried on the shoulder.

3. Even though Nebuchadnezzar was not aware of such, the Lord paid him for the subjugation of Tyre by giving him the land of Egypt.

NEBUCHADNEZZAR

The phrase of Verse 19, *"Therefore thus saith the Lord God; Behold, I will give the land of Egypt unto Nebuchadnezzar king of Babylon,"* has to do with several things.

(A) Egypt must be punished because of her insolence against God and her deceiving Judah.

(B) Tyre must be punished as well. However, the Babylonian Monarch would receive no compensation for his thirteen years of effort, because of the reasons already given.

(C) The spoil and plunder of the Egyptian cities would serve as *"wages for his army."* This would pay him for Tyre.

(D) In all of this, the participants, though they knew it not, had been working out the Will of the Supreme. They also had been servants of Jehovah, as Jeremiah and Ezekiel, although in a different sense (Jer. 25:9).

All of this proclaims the final disposition of all things, as everything is ultimately being brought to its rightful place and position.

The Lord oversees all, and brings judgment upon that which is due judgment, and He compensates that which is due compensation, even as He here did for Nebuchadnezzar.

To be sure, neither of these Monarchs, the king of Egypt or Babylon, had any idea that they were working out the Will of God. In fact, had such been suggested to them, as stated, it would have been laughable. They considered their particular gods, whatever they were, to be vastly superior to the God of Judah, Jehovah; nevertheless, even though they were unwitting subjects, if they opposed God, which Egypt did, the end result would be dire, even as it was. If they carried out the Will of God, even as did Babylon, even though it, as well, was an unwitting subject, it would be blessed, even as it was.

As then, so now! The Lord rules and controls all.

Coming up to the present time, the United States is the world's only superpower. In fact, the Lord has given the scepter of power to the United States, which pertains to many things, the least not being the protection of Israel. However, this doesn't mean that everything the United States does is sanctioned by the Lord, not at all!

It does mean that God has appointed this nation a powerful place and position in the world of this particular time, and if this nation does His Will, it will be blessed; otherwise, we will face judgment, which the Lord can instigate in any number of ways.

This nation legalizing abortion, resulting in the murder of millions of unborn babies, and now, legalizing homosexual marriages, cries out for judgment. And to be sure, sooner or later, the Lord will call this nation to account as it regards these terrible sins. But once again, I go back to Israel.

In the 1800's and early 1900's, Great Britain held the scepter of power granted to them by the Lord. Among other things, little by little, Great Britain tried to hinder Israel from becoming a nation and tried to hinder her immediately after she became a nation. As a result, Great Britain, which was once the mighty Empire of the world, is presently only a shadow of what it once was. I greatly suspect that the greatest arena of responsibility given by God to the United States presently, with the scepter of world power held in our hands, as stated, is the protection of Israel. We must be very, very careful regarding demands made upon Israel as it regards the Muslims. We must never forget this Land of Israel belongs to God. He gave it to Isaac and not Ishmael. Therefore, it belongs to the sons of *"Isaac,"* i.e., *"Jacob."* If we forget that, forcing Israel into an untenable position, we could bring upon ourselves more trouble than we've ever seen. The minute care that God took then, and I speak of the Israel of Ezekiel's time, He continues to do so presently.

RESTORATION

The phrase of Verse 21, *"In that day will I cause the horn of the House of Israel to bud forth,"* refers to the coming Kingdom Age, when Israel will then accept Christ as their Lord, King, Saviour, and Messiah. Israel must come to terms with Christ, and come to terms they shall, which can only be done by heart repentance.

The phrase, *"And I will give you the opening of the mouth in the midst of them,"* refers to the *"highway"* spoken of by Isaiah, which he said would come *"out of Egypt to Assyria,"* and of necessity will come through the Promised Land.

Isaiah used the same phrase as Ezekiel by saying, *"In that day shall Israel be the third with Egypt and with Assyria, even a*

Blessing in the midst of the land" (Isa. 19:23-24).

As this will be the time that Israel will *"bud forth,"* i.e., the coming restoration, Isaiah further said: *"Whom the LORD of Hosts shall bless saying, Blessed be Egypt My people and Assyria the Work of My Hands, and Israel, My inheritance"* (Isa. 19:25).

As Israel was the cause of their doings of so long ago, likewise, Israel will be the cause of their blessing in that coming glad day!

"God's tomorrow is a day of gladness,
"And its joy shall never fade:"

"No more weeping, no more sense of sadness,
"No more foes to make afraid."

"God's tomorrow is a day of glory:
"We shall wear the crown of life."

"Sing thro' countless years love's old story,
"Free forever from all strife."

CHAPTER 30

(1) "THE WORD OF THE LORD CAME AGAIN UNTO ME, SAYING,

(2) "SON OF MAN, PROPHESY AND SAY, THUS SAITH THE LORD GOD; HOWL YE, WOE WORTH THE DAY!

(3) "FOR THE DAY IS NEAR, EVEN THE DAY OF THE LORD IS NEAR, A CLOUDY DAY; IT SHALL BE THE TIME OF THE HEATHEN.

(4) "AND THE SWORD SHALL COME UPON EGYPT, AND GREAT PAIN SHALL BE IN ETHIOPIA, WHEN THE SLAIN SHALL FALL IN EGYPT, AND THEY SHALL TAKE AWAY HER MULTITUDE, AND HER FOUNDATIONS SHALL BE BROKEN DOWN.

(5) "ETHIOPIA, AND LIBYA, AND LYDIA, AND ALL THE MINGLED PEOPLE, AND CHUB, AND THE MEN OF THE LAND THAT IS IN LEAGUE, SHALL FALL WITH THEM BY THE SWORD.

(6) "THUS SAITH THE LORD; THEY ALSO WHO UPHOLD EGYPT SHALL FALL; AND THE PRIDE OF HER POWER SHALL COME DOWN: FROM THE TOWER OF SYENE SHALL THEY FALL IN IT BY THE SWORD, SAITH THE LORD GOD.

(7) "AND THEY SHALL BE DESOLATE IN THE MIDST OF THE COUNTRIES THAT ARE DESOLATE, AND HER CITIES SHALL BE IN THE MIDST OF THE CITIES THAT ARE WASTED.

(8) "AND THEY SHALL KNOW THAT I AM THE LORD, WHEN I HAVE SET A FIRE IN EGYPT, AND WHEN ALL HER HELPERS SHALL BE DESTROYED.

(9) "IN THAT DAY SHALL MESSENGERS GO FORTH FROM ME IN SHIPS TO MAKE THE CARELESS ETHIOPIANS AFRAID, AND GREAT PAIN SHALL COME UPON THEM, AS IN THE DAY OF EGYPT: FOR, LO, IT COMES.

(10) "THUS SAITH THE LORD GOD; I WILL ALSO MAKE THE MULTITUDE OF EGYPT TO CEASE BY THE HAND OF NEBUCHADNEZZAR KING OF BABYLON.

(11) "HE AND HIS PEOPLE WITH HIM, THE TERRIBLE OF THE NATIONS, SHALL BE BROUGHT TO DESTROY THE LAND: AND THEY SHALL DRAW THEIR SWORDS AGAINST EGYPT, AND FILL THE LAND WITH THE SLAIN.

(12) "AND I WILL MAKE THE RIVERS DRY, AND SELL THE LAND INTO THE HAND OF THE WICKED: AND I WILL MAKE THE LAND WASTE, AND ALL THAT IS THEREIN, BY THE HAND OF STRANGERS: I THE LORD HAVE SPOKEN IT.

(13) "THUS SAITH THE LORD GOD; I WILL ALSO DESTROY THE IDOLS, AND I WILL CAUSE THEIR IMAGES TO CEASE OUT OF NOPH; AND THERE SHALL BE NO MORE A PRINCE OF THE LAND OF EGYPT: AND I WILL PUT A FEAR IN THE LAND OF EGYPT.

(14) "AND I WILL MAKE PATHROS DESOLATE, AND WILL SET FIRE IN ZOAN, AND WILL EXECUTE JUDGMENTS IN NO.

(15) "AND I WILL POUR MY FURY UPON SIN, THE STRENGTH OF EGYPT; AND I WILL CUT OFF THE MULTITUDE OF NO.

(16) "AND I WILL SET FIRE IN EGYPT: SIN SHALL HAVE GREAT PAIN, AND NO SHALL BE RENT ASUNDER, AND NOPH SHALL HAVE DISTRESSES DAILY.

(17) "THE YOUNG MEN OF AVEN AND OF PIBESETH SHALL FALL BY THE SWORD: AND THESE CITIES SHALL GO INTO CAPTIVITY.

(18) "AT TEHAPHNEHES ALSO THE DAY SHALL BE DARKENED, WHEN I SHALL BREAK THERE THE YOKES OF EGYPT: AND THE POMP OF HER STRENGTH SHALL CEASE IN HER: AS FOR HER, A CLOUD SHALL COVER HER, AND HER DAUGHTERS SHALL GO INTO CAPTIVITY.

(19) "THUS WILL I EXECUTE JUDGMENTS IN EGYPT: AND THEY SHALL KNOW THAT I AM THE LORD."

The composition is:

1. The great space given to Egypt in the Bible and the number of Prophecies concerning her is largely due to the attraction which her wealth and idolatry had for Israel. They continually confided in her rather than in Jehovah.

2. Egypt symbolizes the world. The Christian Church leans far too much upon it, rather than upon God. Hence, its religion is copied, and, when money is needed by the Church, the help of *"Egypt"* is sought, and in many and varied ways, and I speak of employing the methods of the world. This leaning on *"Egypt"* destroys the spiritual life of the Church, as the covenant with Egypt destroyed the national independence of Israel.

3. The phrase of Verse 3, *"The Day of the Lord,"* is an idiom expressing Divine intervention in human affairs. It occurs twenty times in the Old Testament, and four times in the New.

THE WORD OF THE LORD

The phrase of Verse 1, *"The Word of the Lord,"* proclaims that which is of extreme importance, irrespective of its direction.

The natural heart quickly wearies of these repeated threatenings of Judgment, hence, the Books of Jeremiah and Ezekiel are, by and large, unpopular in Christendom.

But these repetitions reveal God's heart and man's heart — the One so loving, the other so evil. Love sought continually to save; rebellion refused continually to listen.

Egypt, as previously stated, symbolizes the world. Too oftentimes Egypt's ways are used in the Church, which always brings spiritual death. It's quite satisfactory for the world to copy the ways of the Lord, but not at all satisfactory for the ways of the world to be substituted for the Ways of the Lord. Let it ever be known, if the Church is led by the world, i.e., *"Egypt,"* and not by the Spirit, that which plagued Israel of old will plague the modern Church!

THE WAYS OF EGYPT

Worse than all, the Church has borrowed Egypt's form of deliverance, which is psychology, which, in reality, is no deliverance at all! As a result, and because of almost total dependence upon this humanistic philosophy, the Church has become so psychologized that it has been lulled into a spiritual stupor, and, is, thereby, so deceived that it no longer even knows or realizes its spiritual condition. Anymore, very few messages from behind modern pulpits proclaim the Bible, but, instead, are laced with psychology. Most of the book in Christian bookstores are, likewise, one form of psychology or the other, rather than the Word of God; consequently, Biblical terminology has been changed until it little represents the Bible, and, therefore, the Ways of God, but rather psychology and the ways of the world.

To be frank, most Churches are little more than social centers with religious overtones, while the Pastors are social workers.

THE NEW VOCABULARY

As a result of the psychologizing of the Church, the vocabulary of Christians is steadily changing. It is more and more becoming the vocabulary of Egypt instead of the Bible. The following will explain what I mean:

• In this modern climate, the hapless victim is no longer delivered, but, is rather *"rehabilitated,"* a word, incidentally, which is not even found in the Bible.

• The modern Christian no longer prays through, but, instead, gets *"therapy."*

• No longer do people *"need the Lord,"* but, rather *"professional help."*

• It is no longer sin, but, rather *"psychological maladjustment."*

• It is no longer Christ, but *"counseling!"*

- Churches once considered themselves spiritually strong if they were blessed with prayer warriors, but now, the strong Church is blessed with a Psychologist on its staff.
- The cause once was sin, now it is *"childhood traumas."*
- People were once enabled by the Holy Spirit, but now they are a *"Type A personality."*
- Preachers were once called of God, but now they are furthering their *"career."*
- We once cried to the Lord, but now we make an appointment with the *"counselor."*
- We were once *"saved,"* but now we have a *"religious experience."*
- We were once Sanctified, but now we are in a *"state of denial."*
- We were once Justified, but now we have just gotten rid of our *"religious guilt."*
- The Altar used to be a place of Sacrifice, but it has been replaced with the *"Psychiatrist's couch."*
- Christians once prayed, but now they *"pay the Psychologist."*

I think, by now, it is obvious as to how our vocabulary, and even our thinking, have drastically changed. The leaning on *"Egypt"* destroys the spiritual life of the Church, as the covenant with Egypt destroyed the national independence of Israel of old!

THE COMING GREAT TRIBULATION

This Chapter is basically divided into two sections. Verses 1 through 9 have to do with the coming Great Tribulation Period, while Verses 10 through 26 have to do with the judgment that Egypt was facing from Babylon in Ezekiel's day.

The phrase of Verse 2, *"Woe worth the day,"* actually says, *"Woe be to the day."* It refers, as stated, to the coming Great Tribulation. It actually will be a time when the entirety of the world will *"howl."*

Jesus said it would be a time of such *"great tribulation, such as was not since the beginning of the world to this time, no, nor ever shall be."*

He then said, *"Except those days should be shortened, there should no flesh be saved"* (Mat. 24:21-22). This refers to the destruction of hundreds of millions, or even billions, of people.

The reason for this terrible coming destruction is twofold:

1. *"For the great day of His Wrath is come: and who shall be able to stand?"* (Rev. 6:17). The world has known war, sorrow, and judgment from its inception; however, it has never known the Wrath of God, at least on a worldwide scale. While it is true that His Wrath has been evident at various times and places, still, that will have been nothing in comparison to what is coming. Then it will be on a worldwide basis!

2. During this coming dreaded time, spirit forces from Satan's domain of darkness will be loosed on the world in a fashion it has never known before. It will be so bad that the Scripture says: *"In those days shall men seek death, and shall not find it; and shall desire to die, and death shall flee from them"* (Rev. 9:6). These dreaded happenings will take place under the Judgments of the Seven Seals, the Seven Trumpets, and the Seven Vials.

THE DAY OF THE LORD

The phrase of Verse 3, *"The day of the Lord,"* refers to the Second Advent of Christ and continues through the Millennium, a time frame of one thousand years. The Holy Spirit, through the Prophet, is saying that the Great Tribulation, which is coming upon this Earth, proclaims the fact that the Second Coming *"is near."*

The phrase, *"A cloudy day,"* speaks of the judgments just referred to, which will encompass the whole of humanity. This *"cloudy day"* will last for seven years, called *"Daniel's Seventieth Week"* (Dan. 9:27).

This intervention of the Great Tribulation which is coming upon the world is necessarily punitive; for the Lord's Day terminates and judges man's day. It will be a *"day"* as man has never known before!

Regrettably, the world believes this not at all, continuing to think that man will ultimately solve the problems of the world, finally regaining paradise lost; however, the Bible says otherwise!

Sadder still, the far greater majority of the Church follows the unbelief of the world.

Let all know and understand that the Coming of the Lord is the only hope for this world. The world certainly is not going to heal itself, and neither can it be done by the Church, but only by the Coming of Jesus Christ.

The Second Coming of the Lord is one of the basic cardinal doctrines of the Church. If this doctrine is lost, and it is by and large lost in most Church circles, the Church has then spelled its own doom!

It is sadder still, when one realizes that the major Pentecostal Denominations, which once heralded the great doctrines of *"Salvation by Grace," "the Baptism with the Holy Spirit with the evidence of speaking with other tongues," "Divine Healing," "the preaching of the Cross," "the Rapture,"* and *"the Second Coming of the Lord,"* not only little proclaim these great Doctrines any more, but are Pentecostal in name only. Our Lord said: *"You have a name that you live, and are dead"* (Rev. 3:1).

The modern Pentecostal Denominations (and I am Pentecostal) boast of their size, wealth, and education, while, in spiritual reality, they far more resemble a man who is four hundred pounds overweight. He may be big, but he certainly could not be proclaimed as healthy.

From Holy Ghost Revival we have degenerated to motivational seminars or more symposiums on how to swell our already bloated unsaved rolls with more unsaved.

The phrase of Verse 3, *"It shall be the time of the heathen,"* has two meanings:

1. The Antichrist will make his debut, with his *"religion"* being pandemic. It will embrace much of the world.

2. It will be the time when God's judgment will be poured out on the heathen.

THE OPENING OF THE SECOND SEAL

The phrase of Verse 4, *"The sword shall come upon Egypt,"* refers to the Antichrist attacking Egypt, overcoming her, actually bringing her into his ranks, along with Ethiopia, and Libya, etc. of Verse 5.

This has to do with the opening of the *"second Seal"* in the coming Great Tribulation, when power will be given to the Antichrist to *"take peace from the Earth"* (Rev. 6:4). Even though the Tribulation will be worldwide, its greatest concentration, and according to the Bible, will be in the area around the Mediterranean and Northern Africa.

NOTES

THE THIRD SEAL

The *"desolation"* and the *"waste"* of Verse 7 refer to the opening of the *"third seal."* There it says, *"Come and see. And I beheld, and lo a black horse; and he who sat on him had a pair of balances in his hand"* (Rev. 6:5).

The speaks of terrible famine, which will result in terrible desolation, that will grip Egypt when it is destroyed by the Antichrist.

Even though the Antichrist will attack Egypt, making his bid for world dominion, of which Egypt will be the first, still, the Lord is the One setting the parameters for the Antichrist, and, actually, for all else, as portrayed by the phrase in Verse 8, *"And they shall know that I am the Lord."*

The phrase of Verse 9, *"For, lo, it comes,"* proclaims the certitude of these Prophecies. There is no way that man can avoid them, but with one exception!

I speak of the Rapture of the Church.

The only ones who will escape this coming Judgment will be those who are raptured away to be with the Lord Jesus Christ, which will immediately precede these coming judgments (I Thess. 4:13-18). The Holy Spirit, through the Apostle Paul, spoke concerning the Church: *"For God has not appointed us to wrath, but to obtain Salvation by our Lord Jesus Christ"* (I Thess. 5:9).

This simply means that the Lord has not appointed Christians to go through the Great Tribulation Wrath, the sudden destruction, or the wrath of eternal Hell for that matter, but to be delivered by Rapture so that, whether we live or die, we should live together with Him forever (I Thess. 4:13-18; II Thess. 2:7).

Regrettably, very few in the modern Church have even heard of this cardinal doctrine of the Bible, much less believe in it! But let all know and understand that the *"Rapture"* and the *"Resurrection"* are one and the same. In other words, to believe in the Resurrection, which every true Christian does, is at the same time to believe in the *"Rapture."*

NEBUCHADNEZZAR

The phrase of Verse 10, *"By the hand of Nebuchadnezzar king of Babylon,"* brings us back to the time of Ezekiel, and the destruction of Egypt of so long ago. As is often done with Bible Prophecy, the thrust of direction will automatically change, and without warning. As we have stated, Verses 1 through 9 pertain to the coming Great Tribulation, which, of course, will conclude with the Second Coming, thereby beginning the Kingdom Age. The remainder of this Chapter pertains to Egypt's position, as it was during the time of Ezekiel.

To give another example, Isaiah's Prophecy concerning the coming Messiah, and actually quoted by the Lord at Nazareth, was actually separated in mid-sentence, with the first half pertaining to the First Advent of Christ, and the latter part pertaining to the coming Second Advent (Isa. 61:1-3; Lk. 4:18-19).

Jesus quoted the statement, *"To preach the acceptable year of the Lord,"* and then stopped. The entire sentence given by Isaiah was, *"To proclaim the acceptable year of the Lord, and the day of vengeance of our God."*

Even though it was one sentence in Isaiah's Prophecy, and given by the Holy Spirit, still, the first part, *"to proclaim the acceptable year of the Lord,"* was to be fulfilled by Christ at His First Advent, with the second part, as stated, to be fulfilled at His Second Coming.

Therefore, the fulfillment of that one sentence is divided by at least two thousand years.

The Holy Spirit, no doubt, has many reasons for giving some of these Prophecies in this manner, with not the least of them being the confusion of the mildly curious. He desires the sincere Bible student to probe. Paul wrote, and speaking of Christ: *"In Whom are hid all the treasures of wisdom and knowledge"* (Col. 2:3). The word, *"hid,"* has reference to the Truth that these *"treasures"* are hidden from the merely curious, causing the avid Disciple to probe deep, as a miner would search for gold.

By the mention of *"Nebuchadnezzar,"* we know that the Prophecy changes from the future to the time of Ezekiel.

THE DIVINE JUDGMENTS

The phrase of Verse 11, *"The terrible of the nations,"* refers to the power of the Babylonians as those who were to execute the Divine Judgments.

The tenor of these statements proclaims the fact that the Babylonians were stronger than the Egyptians; however, this was of little consequence, as the Lord was guiding events. In effect, and along with their strength, the Lord was helping the Babylonians. He was not doing so because they were more righteous than the Egyptians, or anyone else. Actually, they were idol worshippers!

His choice of them was made solely on His Plan, which included not only the present, but the future as well!

By this time, the Lord had already begun to give Daniel the outline of these coming world Empires, of which Babylon was the first; therefore, all things done by the Lord have to do not only with the present, but also the eternal.

This means that the Plan is predestined, but they who fit into this Plan is determined to a great extent by *"whosoever will"* (Rev. 22:17).

PREDESTINATION

I realize that the statement we have just made is an oversimplification of an extremely complicated subject; however, it will at least give an idea as to the meaning of *"predestination."*

The word, *"predestine,"* means *"to mark out ahead of time,"* or *"to predetermine."*

The word, *"predestine,"* or *"predestination,"* occurs only six times in the New Testament (Acts 4:28; Rom. 8:29-30; I Cor. 2:7; Eph. 1:5, 11). However, there are other words in Scripture that suggest the same concept — that God has sovereignly determined beforehand that a certain thing shall come to pass. In context, these words affirm God's ultimate control of all things.

In the New Testament, the Greek word, *"prooriv,"* meaning *"to predestine,"* is used with specific focus. That is, just what is predetermined is carefully identified.

For example, Acts 4:28 asserts that the events associated with and culminating in Jesus' Crucifixion were exactly what God's Power and Will had decided beforehand should happen.

Romans 8:29 identifies those who love God as *"predestined to be conformed to the likeness of His Son."* he next Verse adopts the Divine viewpoint of timelessness; however, the predestination concerns only those who love God and does not determine as to who those people will be, but is determined by their own will. The idea is, the Plan, whatever it might be, is predestined, but as to the ones who will be in that Plan, such are determined by *"whosoever will."*

According to I Corinthians 2:7, God's Plan to redeem human beings though Christ was something *"destined for our glory before time began."* In fact, Peter said the same thing (I Pet. 1:18-20). But again, as to who these human beings will be, who will enter into this great Program, is left up to *"whosoever will."* It is only the Redemption Plan that is predestined, not the individuals who will be in it.

THE PLAN

In Ephesians 1:5, Paul affirms that God, out of love for Believers, *"predestined us to be adopted as His sons through Jesus Christ, in accordance with His pleasure and Will."* In the same Chapter, he adds, *"in Him we were also chosen, having been predestined according to the Plan of Him Who works out everything in conformity with the purpose of His Will"* (Eph. 1:11).

However, the *"predestination"* focuses on the Salvation Plan, including the whole wonderful process, specifically Jesus' death, with our adoption into God's family, and our transformation into Jesus' own likeness.

Strikingly, these particular Passages do not relate God's Plan and the human will. Other Passages make it clear that the choice to reject or respond to Christ is the responsibility of those who hear the Gospel.

Paul said: *"For whosoever shall call upon the Name of the Lord shall be saved."*

"How then shall they call on Him in Whom they have not believed? And how shall they believe in Him of Whom they have not heard? And how shall they hear without a Preacher?" (Rom. 10:13-14).

God, being Omnipotent, Omniscient, and Omnipresent is able to sovereignly order history so that the uncoerced choices of human beings harmonize with His Plan.

Another striking Truth is that the Greek verb, *"troorizo"* (predestination), is nowhere used in Scripture to state that some people are predestined by God to be lost. Actually, it is not God's Will that any be lost, but that all come to repentance (II Pet. 3:9). However, we all know that God's Will, at least in these particular matters, is seldom carried out, for most, and sadly, die lost!

What is clear is that each individual's choice invariably coincides with God's foreknowledge and His sovereign Will.

IDOLS

The phrase of Verse 13, *"Thus saith the Lord God; I will also destroy the idols, and I will cause their images to cease out of Noph,"* proclaims God's hatred for this absurd worship.

"Noph" was the Greek Memphis, the capital of lower Egypt, and the chief center of the worship of *"Phthah."* These were destroyed by the invading Babylonians.

The phrase, *"And there shall be no more a prince of the land of Egypt,"* had an immediate fulfillment, for, from the days of the Persians through Roman rule, which lasted for about 1,500 years, the kings of Egypt were not Egyptians by race.

Due to their subjugation, and subsequent decline, and always being under the hand of conquerors, there was a perpetual *"fear in the land of Egypt."*

The phrase of Verse 18, *"And her daughters shall go into captivity,"* has reference, not only to the women being led into captivity, but, as well, to her idols, i. e., *"daughters,"* which were taken by Nebuchadnezzar to Babylon, where he would have ensconced them in the temple of the god Bel. He would have placed them there, and in whatever form they were in, along with the other idols, including the Holy Vessels that had been taken from the Temple in Jerusalem.

I AM THE LORD

The phrase of Verse 19, *"And they shall know that I am the Lord,"* is used repeatedly by the Holy Spirit throughout the Book of Ezekiel. The statement is made in order to counter the boastful, prideful, arrogant attitudes of not only Egypt, but every other nation, as well!

Because these *"judgments"* do not happen immediately, the Word of God is given little credit; however, for any and all, the time will ultimately come, whether here or at the Great White Throne Judgment, that all *"shall know that I am the Lord."*

Most, tragically, at the present time, and for all time for that matter, do not even believe that He exists, and if He does, that He takes little interest in the order of things; nevertheless, there will come a time that all will believe! But for most, as with Egypt, it would be too late!

(20) "AND IT CAME TO PASS IN THE ELEVENTH YEAR, IN THE FIRST MONTH, IN THE SEVENTH DAY OF THE MONTH, THAT THE WORD OF THE LORD CAME UNTO ME, SAYING,

(21) "SON OF MAN, I HAVE BROKEN THE ARM OF PHARAOH KING OF EGYPT; AND, LO, IT SHALL NOT BE BOUND UP TO BE HEALED, TO PUT A ROLLER TO BIND IT, TO MAKE IT STRONG TO HOLD THE SWORD.

(22) "THEREFORE THUS SAITH THE LORD GOD; BEHOLD, I AM AGAINST PHARAOH KING OF EGYPT, AND WILL BREAK HIS ARMS, THE STRONG, AND THAT WHICH WAS BROKEN; AND I WILL CAUSE THE SWORD TO FALL OUT OF HIS HAND.

(23) "AND I WILL SCATTER THE EGYPTIANS AMONG THE NATIONS, AND WILL DISPERSE THEM THROUGH THE COUNTRIES.

(24) "AND I WILL STRENGTHEN THE ARMS OF THE KING OF BABYLON, AND PUT MY SWORD IN HIS HAND: BUT I WILL BREAK PHARAOH'S ARMS, AND HE SHALL GROAN BEFORE HIM WITH THE GROANINGS OF A DEADLY WOUNDED MAN.

(25) "BUT I WILL STRENGTHEN THE ARMS OF THE KING OF BABYLON, AND THE ARMS OF PHARAOH SHALL FALL DOWN; AND THEY SHALL KNOW THAT I AM THE LORD, WHEN I SHALL PUT MY SWORD INTO THE HAND OF THE KING OF BABYLON, AND HE SHALL STRETCH IT OUT UPON THE LAND OF EGYPT.

(26) "AND I WILL SCATTER THE EGYPTIANS AMONG THE NATIONS, AND DISPERSE THEM AMONG THE COUNTRIES; AND THEY SHALL KNOW THAT I AM THE LORD."

The structure is:

1. *"The one arm"* i.e., the army of Pharaoh was broken at Carchemish; the other in Egypt, for, weakened by a revolt, he was easily overthrown by Nebuchadnezzar, and thus, both his arms were broken.

2. Up until this time, Egypt was a mighty nation, and had been so for many centuries; however, from this time forward, even unto this present day (2003), Egypt has been, as is, exactly what God said she would be, *"a base nation."*

3. All of this is a startling example of the manner in which God works. In Old Testament Times, His dealings with nations had to do, as is here obvious, with their relationship with Israel. Presently, nations are judged according to how they affect the great Plan of God in these last days, and, always, as to how the true Church is affected.

THE BROKEN ARMS OF PHARAOH

Verses 20 through 26 seem to have been written at about the time of the abortive attempt of Pharaoh Hopra to come to the relief of Jerusalem. So this is about three months before Jerusalem will fall (II Ki. 25:2-3).

Even though there will be some sixteen years before Nebuchadnezzar will invade Egypt, the Prophecy of what will happen is given to us in these Passages.

The phrase of Verse 21, *"I have broken the arm of the Pharaoh king of Egypt,"* was a commonly used term of that day. It spoke of the strength being destroyed.

The phrase, *"And, lo, it shall not be bound up to be healed,"* refers to the fact that a broken arm could be healed, for the man to fight another day; however, the Lord emphatically states that Pharaoh's wound shall not be healed: and so it has been from then until now!

Ezekiel uses that phrase, *"to put a roller to bind it,"* which refers to the modern process of putting it in *"splints."*

It is interesting that the Hebrew word for *"roller"* is not found elsewhere in Scripture, and Ezekiel's use of it may mean that he had some knowledge of surgery.

The phrase, *"To make it strong to hold the sword,"* refers to the fact of Nebuchadnezzar's destruction of Egypt, and it never rising again as a world power.

The phrase of Verse 22, *"And will break his arms,"* speaks of both arms, which has reference to two distinct engagements. As stated, the first arm was broken at Carchemish by Nebuchadnezzar as prophesied by Jeremiah (Jer. 46:2). The other arm was broken, as well, by Nebuchadnezzar, when he invaded Egypt a few years later, and, thus, both of the arms, proverbially speaking, of Pharaoh were broken.

The phrase of Verse 24, *"And I will strengthen the arms of the king of Babylon,"* refers to exactly what the Lord did, while He would *"weaken the arms of Pharaoh."* As a result, his arms would *"fall down."*

Even though these nations little knew nor understood their destiny, or its source, nevertheless, this in no way hindered the manner in which God ordered events.

It is regrettable that the far greater majority of modern men little read or even believe the Word of God, which leaves them spiritually ignorant concerning the affairs of life; however, as these nations of old, this in no way limits God's rule within their lives, or even entire nations.

Pharaoh had little knowledge that he was being weakened by the Lord, while Nebuchadnezzar had little knowledge that he was being strengthened by the Lord; nevertheless, that's the way it was! As well, the manner in which the Lord did these things, if the truth be known, would have been made up of small events taking place, which at the time was noticed probably very little. But yet, these events, whatever they might have been, turned the tide in the direction desired by the Lord.

Man is extremely limited as to what he can do; however, God is not limited. He uses the elements, the stubbornness or obedience of men, or whatever He so desires to bring about His purpose, design, and Will. It is our business, and by the study of His Word, and our close relationship to Him, to learn the manner in which He works, at least as much as we poor human beings can know. But irrespective of our poverty, the Holy Spirit, through Paul, said: *"But as it is written, Eye has not seen, nor ear heard, neither have entered into the heart of man, the things which God has prepared for them who love Him.*

"But God has revealed them unto us by His Spirit: for the Spirit searches all things, yes, the deep things of God."

The Apostle then said, *"Now we have received, not the spirit of the world, but the Spirit which is of God; that we might know the things that are freely given to us of God"* (I Cor. 2:9-12).

"Immortal Love, forever full,
"Forever flowing free,
"Forever shared, forever whole,
"A never ebbing sea!"

"We may not climb the heavenly steeps
"To bring the Lord Christ down;
"In vain we search the lowest deeps,
"For Him no depths can drown."

"But warm, sweet, tender, even yet
"A present help is He;
"And faith has still its Olivet,
"And love its Galilee."

"The healing of his seamless dress
"Is by our beds of pain;
"We touch Him in life's throng and press,
"And we are whole again."

"O Lord and Master, take our all.
"We own Your Name and sign
"We own Your sway, we hear Your call
"We rest our lives in Thine."

CHAPTER 31

(1) "AND IT CAME TO PASS IN THE ELEVENTH YEAR, IN THE THIRD MONTH, IN THE FIRST DAY OF THE MONTH, THAT THE WORD OF THE LORD CAME UNTO ME, SAYING,

(2) "SON OF MAN, SPEAK UNTO PHARAOH KING OF EGYPT, AND TO HIS MULTITUDE; WHO ARE YOU LIKE IN YOUR GREATNESS?

(3) "BEHOLD, THE ASSYRIAN WAS A CEDAR IN LEBANON WITH FAIR BRANCHES, AND WITH A SHADOWING SHROUD, AND OF AN HIGH STATURE; AND HIS TOP WAS AMONG THE THICK BOUGHS.

(4) "THE WATERS MADE HIM GREAT, THE DEEP SET HIM UP ON HIGH WITH

HER RIVERS RUNNING ROUND ABOUT HIS PLANTS, AND SENT OUT HER LITTLE RIVERS UNTO ALL THE TREES OF THE FIELD.

(5) "THEREFORE HIS HEIGHT WAS EXALTED ABOVE ALL THE TREES OF THE FIELD, AND HIS BOUGHS WERE MULTIPLIED, AND HIS BRANCHES BECAME LONG BECAUSE OF THE MULTITUDE OF WATERS, WHEN HE SHOT FORTH.

(6) "ALL THE FOWLS OF HEAVEN MADE THEIR NESTS IN HIS BOUGHS, AND UNDER HIS BRANCHES DID ALL THE BEASTS OF THE FIELD BRING FORTH THEIR YOUNG, AND UNDER HIS SHADOW DWELT ALL GREAT NATIONS.

(7) "THUS WAS HE FAIR IN HIS GREATNESS, IN THE LENGTH OF HIS BRANCHES: FOR HIS ROOT WAS BY GREAT WATERS.

(8) "THE CEDARS IN THE GARDEN OF GOD COULD NOT HIDE HIM: THE FIR TREES WERE NOT LIKE HIS BOUGHS, AND THE CHESTNUT TREES WERE NOT LIKE HIS BRANCHES; NOR ANY TREE IN THE GARDEN OF GOD WAS LIKE UNTO HIM IN HIS BEAUTY.

(9) "I HAVE MADE HIM FAIR BY THE MULTITUDE OF HIS BRANCHES: SO THAT ALL THE TREES OF EDEN, THAT WERE IN THE GARDEN OF GOD, ENVIED HIM."

The overview is:

1. This Prophecy was uttered about two months before the Fall of Jerusalem.

2. In it, Pharaoh is compared with Sardana-Palus, the last king of Assyria, and conquered by Nebuchadnezzar.

3. The Prophet likens Empires to great trees and their kings to the highest branches.

The Assyrian Empire is here compared to a great cedar — a cedar of Lebanon, a cedar of the Garden of God. These are terms expressing magnitude, strength, and beauty.

EGYPT AND ASSYRIA

This Chapter was written about two or three months before the Fall of Jerusalem. It deals with the ruin of two mighty empires, Egypt and Assyria, and their banishment to eternal Hell. The language is striking, and leaves nothing to the imagination.

NOTES

It should serve as a lesson to the world that *"the wicked shall be turned into Hell, and all the nations that forget God"* (Ps. 9:17). In these Passages, the might and splendor producing pomp and pride, caused these mighty Empires to think of themselves as invincible; however, their invincibility, under the gaze of God, proved to be paper thin, resulting in great destruction. Inasmuch as mighty empires are addressed, and with their Fall cataclysmically outlined, the individual should understand that the message of this Chapter given, is not only national but personal. As such, the Fear of God, of which, and among other things, this Chapter intends to portray, shall be strengthened in every heart.

As these mighty Empires fell, so did those who followed them: Babylon, Medo-Persia, Greece, and mighty Rome. As well, the present might and majesty of the United States, even though founded on Christian principles, and thereby producing the greatest standard of living the world has ever known, along with the greatest freedoms, still, it, too, is imperfect, and, must give way in favor of the coming Perfect Government headed up by the Lord Jesus Christ, Who will replace the imperfect. For that coming glad day, we longingly look. Thankfully, presently it is not nearly as long in coming as it was when Ezekiel wrote these words.

Even though the Message is directed to *"Pharaoh king of Egypt"* of Verse 2, nevertheless, it will give a long historical record of God's dealings with the Assyrians, with a final Prophecy revealing that Pharaoh and all his multitudes shall perish as the Assyrian king and his army.

The question, *"Who are you like in your greatness?"* is speaking of Sardana-Palus, the last king of Assyria, who was conquered by Nebuchadnezzar. Possibly, Pharaoh looked up to this now dead despot; however, his end will be as his, defeated and lost!

RIGHTEOUSNESS

The lessons should not be lost upon the reader that the emulation of men produces no Righteousness. Therefore, the eye of the beholder should be upon Christ. It was this One of Whom Paul spoke, when he said: *"That I may know Him"* (Phil. 3:10).

Regrettably, sports figures, actors, business tycoons, politicians, and educators are held up as examples and role models for the youth of today; consequently, a harvest of shame is repeated, and because the only true model, and that intended to be, is Christ! The same doom met by the last Assyrian king will be met by mighty Pharaoh, as well! The same can be said for all who place men as their champions.

Christ Alone can give Righteousness to man. Nothing that man does will bring about Righteousness, irrespective as to how good it might seem to a fallen world. Righteousness can be obtained only by faith and trust in Christ, and what Christ has done at the Cross. Faith, thus evidenced, will grant to the believing sinner an imputed Righteousness given freely by the Lord, bought and purchased by the Precious Blood of Christ at the Cross of Calvary. It is obtained by Faith, and by Faith only, which refers to Faith in Christ and the Cross. As stated, men cannot reach God except through Christ (Jn. 14:20), likewise, men cannot reach Christ except through the Cross (Jn. 3:16), and, as well, men cannot reach the Cross except by a denial of self (Lk. 9:23).

THE ASSYRIAN

The Prophet likens, by the Holy Spirit, empires to great trees and their kings to the highest branches.

This Prophecy penetrates the world of the dead and reveals the disembodied spirits of deceased kings as no longer royal personages, but members of the general multitude of the dead and the damned.

Thus, this Chapter is one of the few which unveils the mysterious spirit-world.

The phrase of Verse 4, *"The waters made him great,"* pictures the nations that contributed to the wealth of this empire; and the trees of the fields symbolized the subordinate kings. Such are portrayed to proclaim the splendor of this kingdom, and how it was thought to be impossible to be brought to destruction.

At this hour, the United States is the only super-power in the world, with the former Soviet Union now in total disarray. And yet, our nation seems to have little sense of purpose or direction. Actually, it seems to founder at times, as a ship without a rudder. Such portrays that might and majesty, along with wealth and splendor, cannot take the place of God. And yet, America is presently all but bereft of the Leadership and Counsel of the Lord of Glory; hence, it is directionless and purposeless!

The Bible was once the foundation of this land, but presently it is all but banned, and, thereby ignored. America has been blessed because America has once known God. However, this nation is losing its knowledge of God, and thereby its greatness! The lessons of these empires, as outlined in the Bible, should be lessons for us presently, but little are, because they are basically ignored! The truth is, we are living on borrowed time!

EXALTATION

The phrase of Verse 5, *"Therefore his height was exalted above all the trees of the field,"* speaks of the supremacy of the Assyrian empire; however, this supremacy was gained by brute terror and force. Too often, and almost exclusively, the *"height"* of empires enjoyed has been the result of brute terror, and, therefore, at the expense of the subjugated, even their own people; consequently, Joseph Stalin, to bring the former Soviet Union to its *"height"* would slaughter over 50 million fellow Russians, and others in this empire; likewise, over 100 million were ruthlessly slaughtered in order that Communism may subjugate modern China.

America and England, in their status, are two of the few in the world which have gained *"height"* without such terror. Even though its governments are far from perfect, still, their blessings have been brought about by the Bible, but, sadly, the Bible is now being ignored, or even ridiculed. Someone has well said, *"Much Bible, much freedom; little Bible, little freedom; no Bible, no freedom."*

THE GARDEN OF GOD

The short phrase of Verse 8, *"the cedars,"* represents the individual nations of the world of that day.

The phrase, *"In the Garden of God,"* represents the sovereignty of the Lord over these nations, even though they did not know

Him, nor even recognize Him, but, were rather idol worshippers. It was tragic in that it was His *"Garden,"* but the nations within it did not know Him; therefore, they conducted themselves as if He did not exist, and, despite the Light given to Judah, which was supposed to guide them, they went to their doom!

The phrase, *"Nor any tree in the Garden of God was like unto him in his beauty,"* refers to the fact that Assyria, up to this time, was the greatest of all.

The Assyrian empire had its beginning almost immediately after Noah's flood. The Scripture mentions Babylonia and says, *"Out of that land went forth Asshur, and built Nineveh"* (Gen. 10:11). Asshur was the son of Shem, the son of Noah.

Nineveh became the capital of the mighty Assyrian empire. The city was located about three hundred miles north of Babylon. Abraham, in his trek from Ur of the Chaldees on his way to Canaan, and stopping at Haran, and following the Euphrates, would have passed not too far from Nineveh, which was a thriving city during his time; therefore, and even though this empire had its slow beginnings, it would have ruled more or less for nearly 1,500 years; however, its greatest power was about the last three hundred years of its reign, until defeated by Babylon.

For almost all the existence of the Northern Kingdom of Israel, Assyria was a threat, and finally did annihilate these wayward people of God as a nation.

Brazen with their success, they now pushed against the Southern Kingdom of Judah, proposing to take this country as well! They reasoned that both Kingdoms, the North and the South, worshipped the same God, and as the Northern Kingdom of Israel had been ripe for the plucking, with its God little match for them, or so they thought, Judah would, as well, be easy pickings.

However, they were to suffer a humiliating defeat with 185,000 of their soldiers being slain in one night. The God they had ridiculed sent one Angel and disseminated their ranks, and, as well, greatly humiliated their field commander, Sennacherib (II Ki., Chpt. 19).

Therefore, they were to find that Judah's God had such power that they never dreamed!

They would be defeated by the mighty Babylonian Empire, some years later.

(10) "THEREFORE THUS SAITH THE LORD GOD; BECAUSE YOU HAVE LIFTED UP YOURSELF IN HEIGHT, AND HE HAS SHOT UP HIS TOP AMONG THE THICK BOUGHS, AND HIS HEART IS LIFTED UP IN HIS HEIGHT;

(11) "I HAVE THEREFORE DELIVERED HIM INTO THE HAND OF THE MIGHTY ONE OF THE HEATHEN; HE SHALL SURELY DEAL WITH HIM: I HAVE DRIVEN HIM OUT FOR HIS WICKEDNESS.

(12) "AND STRANGERS, THE TERRIBLE OF THE NATIONS, HAVE CUT HIM OFF, AND HAVE LEFT HIM: UPON THE MOUNTAINS AND IN ALL THE VALLEYS HIS BRANCHES ARE FALLEN, AND HIS BOUGHS ARE BROKEN BY ALL THE RIVERS OF THE LAND; AND ALL THE PEOPLE OF THE EARTH ARE GONE DOWN FROM HIS SHADOW, AND HAVE LEFT HIM.

(13) "UPON HIS RUIN SHALL THE FOWLS OF THE HEAVEN REMAIN, AND ALL THE BEASTS OF THE FIELD SHALL BE UPON HIS BRANCHES:

(14) "TO THE END THAT NONE OF ALL THE TREES BY THE WATERS EXALT THEMSELVES FOR THEIR HEIGHT, NEITHER SHOOT UP THEIR TOP AMONG THE THICK BOUGHS, NEITHER THEIR TREES STAND UP IN THEIR HEIGHT, ALL THAT DRINK WATER: FOR THEY ARE ALL DELIVERED UNTO DEATH, TO THE NETHER PARTS OF THE EARTH, IN THE MIDST OF THE CHILDREN OF MEN, WITH THEM WHO GO DOWN TO THE PIT.

(15) "THUS SAITH THE LORD GOD; IN THE DAY WHEN HE WENT DOWN TO THE GRAVE I CAUSED A MOURNING: I COVERED THE DEEP FOR HIM, AND I RESTRAINED THE FLOODS THEREOF, AND THE GREAT WATERS WERE STAYED: AND I CAUSED LEBANON TO MOURN FOR HIM, AND ALL THE TREES OF THE FIELD FAINTED FOR HIM.

(16) "I MADE THE NATIONS TO SHAKE AT THE SOUND OF HIS FALL, WHEN I CAST HIM DOWN TO HELL WITH THEM WHO DESCEND INTO THE PIT: AND ALL THE TREES OF EDEN, THE CHOICE AND

BEST OF LEBANON, ALL WHO DRINK WATER, SHALL BE COMFORTED IN THE NETHER PARTS OF THE EARTH.

(17) "THEY ALSO WENT DOWN INTO HELL WITH HIM UNTO THEM WHO BE SLAIN WITH THE SWORD; AND THEY WHO WERE HIS ARM, WHO DWELT UNDER HIS SHADOW IN THE MIDST OF THE HEATHEN.

(18) "TO WHOM ARE YOU THUS LIKE IN GLORY AND IN GREATNESS AMONG THE TREES OF EDEN? YET SHALL YOU BE BROUGHT DOWN WITH THE TREES OF EDEN UNTO THE NETHER PARTS OF THE EARTH: YOU SHALL LIE IN THE MIDST OF THE UNCIRCUMCISED WITH THEM WHO BE SLAIN BY THE SWORD. THIS IS PHARAOH AND ALL HIS MULTITUDE, SAITH THE LORD GOD."

The synopsis is:

1. As Verse 16 proclaims, it was God Who cast Sardana-Palus down into Hell.

2. Verses 14, 16, and 18 suggest that Hell is situated in the center of the Earth.

3. Verse 14 proclaims the fact that the greatest monarchs rank with the disembodied spirits of the generality of men.

4. Companions in misery derive a sad comfort from mutual suffering.

The death of Pharaoh would be without honor, for he was strangled; and so the Prophet exclaims pointing to him: *"This is Pharaoh."*

PRIDE

The phrase of Verse 10, *"Because you have lifted up yourself in height,"* reveals the reason for the destruction of Assyria, its great pride!

Although building for quite some time, the insulting remarks made against Jehovah, when Sennacherib came against Judah, signaled the beginning of the end for this lordly empire (Isa., Chpt. 37; II Ki., Chpt. 19). Even though it would take about a century before their defeat by the Babylonians, in the mind of God, it was already sealed.

The phrase of Verse 11, *"I have therefore delivered him into the hand of the mighty one of the heathen,"* refers to Nebuchadnezzar. Ironically enough, Nebuchadnezzar would personally suffer for his own pride in later years, but would have the testimony of Daniel to bring him back to sanity (Dan., Chpt. 4).

The phrase, *"I have driven him out for his wickedness,"* refers to his cup of iniquity filling until there was no choice but to remove him. This God did, and this God does!

Mighty nations or individuals may go on in their wickedness for quite some time, but ultimately, the Lord will bring judgment, which holds true for every nation, or person, in the world, and for all time.

For instance, the great Move of God brought about in England by John Wesley, no doubt, gave that powerful country a reprieve. In fact, it was said of those meetings, that had they not taken place, England could very well have gone the way of France, as it regards the terrible bloodletting which took place there. As well, the same could be said for the great Moves of God in America and Canada; nevertheless, and despite the great movings of the Holy Spirit in America, this country, seemingly, and as stated, has made a conscious decision to ignore the Bible, thereby forsaking God, and, therefore, to chart its own course.

Consequently, this nation is probably farther away from God at this moment than it has ever been in its history! Its only hope is a mighty moving of the Holy Spirit, but there seems to be little hunger and thirst for Righteousness in the Churches.

The call that went to Israel of old, *"If My people, which are called by My Name, shall humble themselves, and pray, and seek My face, and turn from their wicked ways; then will I hear from Heaven, and will forgive their sin, and will heal their land"* (II Chron. 7:14), is still apropos today for America, or for any nation, or even any person. Obedience to this passage alone is the only answer and solution.

HELL

The phrase of Verse 14, *"To the end that none of all the trees by the waters exalt themselves,"* proclaims a warning to all the other nations, that the destruction of Assyria should be a lesson to them; however, few, if any, heeded the admonition!

The boasting and arrogant pride of even the mightiest are ultimately *"delivered unto death."* And in their death, they are taken down *"to the nether parts of the Earth."* In this Verse, it is called *"the pit,"* with Verse 17 calling it *"Hell."*

The phrase, *"To the nether parts of the Earth,"* suggests that Hell is situated in the center of the Earth. In that *"pit"* are the greatest Monarchs, joining the disembodied spirits of the lowest rank of men. So, the mightiest and the greatest are *"in the midst of the children of men, with them who go down to the pit."*

What a warning to the whole of humanity, but largely ignored!

The phrase of Verse 16, *"When I cast them down to Hell with them who descend into the pit,"* refers to the Lord casting the last king of the Assyrian Empire, Sardana-Palus, down into Hell.

The phrase, *"Shall be comforted in the nether parts of the Earth,"* refers to the mighty Empires and nations, already fallen and in Hell, which are *"comforted"* with the thought that yet another kingdom mightier than they has fallen as they fell.

Despite the plain Scriptural teaching, it is regrettable that the far greater majority of Preachers in Christendom no longer even believe there is a literal place called Hell, or that the fire there is literal as well! Most, if believing it at all, call it a *"figure of speech,"* giving no credence to Scriptural teaching.

When Jesus told of the experience of the rich man in Hell (Lk., Chpt. 16), he used the phrase concerning what the man said, *"For I am tormented in this flame."* In this Passage, as in all others, there is no hint in Scripture that these are merely *"figures of speech."* The Lord meant what He said and said what He meant. We do not have the prerogative of taking a literal statement from Scripture and making it into a figure of speech. Such will do extreme violence to the Word of God.

If we had this right, we could take the description of the New Jerusalem in Revelation 21:10 as a figure of speech as well! But, of course, such would be preposterous! As well, to describe *"Hell,"* and what is said about it, as a *"figure of speech"* is also preposterous!

The truth, and according to Scripture, is that Hell exists exactly as stated in the Word of God (Mat. 16:18; Lk. 16:19-31).

It is also taught by some that the wicked will be annihilated, and, consequently, that the fire of Hell is not literal; however, Scripture does not teach the annihilation of any part of creation. All Passages in the Word of God teach that the soul is immortal and that the body will be immortal in the Resurrection.

Others erroneously state that men will suffer absolute destruction in Hell; however, the Greek for *"destruction,"* in II Thessalonians 1:9, means ruin, not extinction.

Still others state that the wicked will die and be extinct; however, spiritual death means separation, not annihilation.

Some claim that the experience given by Christ in Luke, Chapter 16 is only a mere parable; however, a parable illustrates certain points and names are not used. To the contrary, in Luke, Chapter 16, no point is illustrated, and at least one person is identified by name.

The truth is, the story, as given by Christ, is a literal one of two beggars — one begged in this life, and the other in the next life.

ETERNAL

As well, the soul of man is immortal. As a consequence, the punishment of Hell must be eternal. Jesus declared in plain terms that the immortality of the soul, and the consciousness of the soul after leaving the body, are a reality.

The Bible teaches that Hell is eternal. It also teaches that the fire of Hell is literal and that the human soul and spirit cannot be burned up. Even when the body is reunited with the soul and spirit in the second resurrection of damnation, the body itself cannot then be destroyed. Pain and punishment are literal, real, and eternal.

Men continue to rebel against the plain teachings of the Word of God, but this opposition does not negate the truthfulness of what God has stated. A terrible price was paid at Calvary's Cross for man's Redemption. Man does not have to go to Hell; he chooses to go there by his unbelief.

HOW MANY, OF AGES PAST, HAVE GONE TO HELL?

The phrase of Verse 17, *"They also went down into Hell with him,"* presents to us a chilling statement. The only way to miss Hell, and, thereby, eternal separation from God, is to accept the Lord Jesus Christ as one's Saviour. He Alone is the Giver of Salvation, and He Alone can rescue men from the powers of darkness; but yet, from the beginning, precious few have accepted Him as their Saviour.

From the time of Adam to Noah's flood, a time of approximately 1,600 years, the Bible only records two individuals who were saved other than Noah and his family. They were Abel and Enoch (Gen. 4:4; 5:22). Possibly others were saved, but there is no record of it. The Scripture says concerning that time: *"And God saw that the wickedness of man was great in the Earth and that every imagination of the thoughts of his heart was only evil continually"* (Gen. 6:5). Therefore, if mankind was to be saved at all, the flood was a necessity.

THE CALL OF ABRAHAM

After the flood, other than Noah and some of his family, the only ones in the entirety of the world living for God, of which we are aware, were Abraham and Sarah, who had been called out of Ur of the Chaldees (Gen. 12:1). Actually, he had been an idol worshipper until the Revelation given to him by the Lord: (we can also include Melchizedek and his family) and then, the only ones in the world living for God were Abraham's offspring.

This offspring, the sons of Jacob, grew into a mighty nation, of which some lived for God; however, only these followers of the true God were saved, with all others dying lost, as recorded here and elsewhere in Scripture.

Even at the present time, with some six billion people on planet Earth, by comparison, only a few are truly saved. Jesus said: *"Because strait is the gate, and narrow is the way, which leads unto life, and few there be who find it"* (Mat. 7:14).

THE LORD JESUS CHRIST

All who have ever been saved, even from the time of Adam, were saved as a result of trusting Jesus Christ as their Saviour. When Adam and Eve were driven from the Garden by the Lord, still, they were given the Plan of Salvation, with the Sacrificial System serving as a symbol, which pointed to the One Who was to come, Who Alone could redeem fallen humanity, the lost sons of Adam's fallen race (Gen. 3:24; 4:4, 7). Even though their knowledge concerning Christ would have been very limited, as would be obvious, still, the Prophecies had been given, and they knew that One was coming, as stated, to Whom the Sacrifices ever pointed.

The animal Sacrifices could not save anyone, but faith and trust evidenced in the One to Whom the Sacrifices pointed, namely Christ, definitely did bring Salvation. This is the reason that the Holy Spirit said of Abel: *"By Faith Abel offered unto God a more excellent Sacrifice than Cain, by which he obtained witness that he was righteous, God testifying of his gifts: and by it* (the One Whom the Sacrifice represented) *he being dead yet speaks"* (Heb. 11:4).

Before the Cross, all men who were truly saved were saved simply by looking forward to that coming event, and thereby placing their faith. Likewise, men are saved presently by looking backward to that event. Before the Cross, men looked forward to a Prophetic Jesus, in other words, the One to Whom the Prophecies pointed (Gen. 3:15; 49:10; Isa., Chpt. 53), and now men look to an Historical Jesus, One Who has come, Who died on the Cross, paying the price demanded by God, which mankind could not pay, thereby redeeming fallen humanity, at least those who will believe (Jn. 3:16; Eph. 2:8-9; Rom. 10:9-10, 13).

Salvation has always come and can only come through Christ. And we may quickly add, it comes through Christ only by and through what He did at the Cross, all on our behalf. This means that the Cross was not an execution, or an assassination, but rather a Sacrifice, meaning that Jesus freely laid down His life, and then took it up again. While the Romans and the Jews may have thought that they were the ones who killed Him, even though their hearts were, in fact, filled with murder, had He desired to stop them, He could have easily done so. In fact, His very reason for coming to this world was to pay the price for lost humanity, which was the Cross (Jn. 10:17-18).

JESUS IS THE SOURCE AND THE CROSS IS THE MEANS

The Revelation of God, as it regards the human race, has always come to us in progressive steps. At the very outset, and I'm speaking of the immediate time after the Fall, the Lord told Satan, through the serpent: *"And I will put enmity* (hatred) *between you and the woman* (Satan has a special hatred for women, in general), *and between your seed* (all of humanity who follow Satan) *and her Seed* (the Lord Jesus Christ); *it* (Christ) *shall bruise your head* (which Christ did at the Cross) *and you shall bruise His heel"* (the suffering of the Cross [Gen. 3:15]).

To symbolize this, the Lord instituted the sacrificial system, and appointed certain animals, such as the lamb, goat, ram, heifer and oxen, to serve as innocent victims, which would be symbolic of the One Who was to come (Gen. 4:4).

The Revelation was fleshed out a little more, as God told Abraham as to exactly how Redemption would be brought about. It would be through death, and the death of the One Who was to come. It was typified by the proposed offering up of Isaac, which was stopped at the last moment (Gen. 22:8-14).

It was not until Moses, some four hundred years after Abraham, that the Lord revealed the *"means"* by which this death would occur, which would be Cross.

It was the time of great failure on the part of Israel, regarding their sojourn in the wilderness. They blamed God and Moses for their plight. The Scripture says: *"And the LORD sent fiery serpents among the people, and they bit the people: and much people of Israel died"* (Num. 21:6).

As the people importuned Moses concerning their plight, Moses went to the Lord: *"And the LORD said unto Moses, Make thee a fiery serpent, and set it upon a pole: and it shall come to pass, that everyone who is bitten, when he looks upon it, shall live"* (Num. 21:8).

The reason the *"serpent"* was placed on the pole is because it was at the Cross where all sin was atoned for, and thereby, defeated. Its power was broken, and its guilt removed (Col. 2:14-15). The *"serpent on the pole"* proclaimed the *"means"* by which the Lord would redeem humanity. It would be by death on the Cross.

Concerning this, Paul said: *"Blotting out the handwriting of ordinances that was against us* (the Ten Commandments), *which was contrary to us* (meaning that due to the Fall, man could not keep the Commandments), *and took it out of the way* (satisfied its just demands), *nailing it to His Cross* (at the Cross, the full price was paid);

"And having spoiled principalities and powers (Satan, his fallen angels, and demon spirits), *He* (Christ) *made a shew of them openly* (defeated them for all of the spirit world to see), *triumphing over them in it* (Satan was completely defeated at the Cross, and done so by all sin being atoned, which took away his legal right to hold man in captivity)" (Col. 2:14-15).

Consequently, if men remain in bondage, it is because they will not trust Christ and what Christ has done at the Cross. As stated, Christ is the *"Source,"* while the Cross is the *"Means."*

BROUGHT DOWN

The phrase in the Eighteenth Verse, *"Yet shall you be brought down with the trees of Eden unto the nether parts of the Earth,"* proclaims the fact that even the mightiest on Earth, whomever they might be, who do not know the Lord, will ultimately conclude their sojourn in Hell itself. It is a chilling thought, but it is true!

The phrase, *"This is Pharaoh and all his multitude, saith the Lord God,"* proclaims the fact that God spotlighted this particular individual, that the world may know, that despite his pomp, claims, and so-called majesty, he did not know Jehovah, did not recognize Jehovah, but despite that, Jehovah controlled his destiny, which was eternal Hell.

So the Holy Spirit dismisses this mighty monarch by saying in sarcasm, and rightly so, *"This is Pharaoh"*! As stated, there is a Hell, and the only way it can be escaped is by the acceptance of Jesus Christ, and what He has done for us at the Cross (Jn. 3:16). All who reject Christ presently as their Saviour will tomorrow face Him as their judge (Rev. 20:11-15).

Ignoring Him, or claiming to serve another god, even as the religions of this present world, in no way absolves such individuals from their destiny regarding Christ. Let us say it again:

It is to Jesus Christ that the world must answer. Your answer to Him can be *"yes,"* and He will be your Saviour, and give you eternal life (Rom. 6:23). Or your answer to Him can be *"no,"* and He will then be your Judge, and the end result, irrespective as to what you might otherwise believe, will be eternal Hell (Rev. 20:15).

"Nearer my God, to Thee, Nearer to Thee!
"E'en tho' it be a Cross that raises me;
"Still all my song shall be,
"Nearer, my God, to Thee."

"Tho' like the wanderer, the sun gone down,
"Darkness be over me, my rest a stone,
"Yet in my dreams I'd be
"Nearer, my God, to Thee."

"There let the way appear steps unto heav'n;
"All that You send me, in mercy given
"Angels to beckon Me
"Nearer, my God, to Thee."

"Then with my waking thoughts, bright with Your praise,
"Out of my stony griefs, Bethel I raise,
"So by my woes to be
"Nearer, my God, to Thee."

"Or if on joyful wing, cleaving the sky,
"Sun, moon, and stars forgot upward I fly,
"Still all my song shall be,
"Nearer, my God, to Thee."

CHAPTER 32

(1) "AND IT CAME TO PASS IN THE TWELFTH YEAR, IN THE TWELFTH MONTH, IN THE FIRST DAY OF THE MONTH, THAT THE WORD OF THE LORD CAME UNTO ME, SAYING,

(2) "SON OF MAN, TAKE UP A LAMENTATION FOR PHARAOH KING OF EGYPT, AND SAY UNTO HIM, YOU ARE LIKE A YOUNG LION OF THE NATIONS, AND YOU ARE AS A WHALE IN THE SEAS: AND YOU CAME FORTH WITH YOUR RIVERS, AND TROUBLED THE WATERS WITH YOUR FEET, AND FOULED THEIR RIVERS.

(3) "THUS SAITH THE LORD GOD; I WILL THEREFORE SPREAD OUT MY NET OVER YOU WITH A COMPANY OF MANY PEOPLE; AND THEY SHALL BRING YOU UP IN MY NET.

(4) "THEN WILL I LEAVE YOU UPON THE LAND, I WILL CAST YOU FORTH UPON THE OPEN FIELD, AND WILL CAUSE ALL THE FOWLS OF THE HEAVEN TO REMAIN UPON YOU, AND I WILL FILL THE BEAST OF THE WHOLE EARTH WITH YOU.

(5) "AND I WILL LAY YOUR FLESH UPON THE MOUNTAINS, AND FILL THE VALLEYS WITH YOUR HEIGHT.

(6) "I WILL ALSO WATER WITH YOUR BLOOD THE LAND WHEREIN YOU SWIM, EVEN TO THE MOUNTAINS; AND THE RIVERS SHALL BE FULL OF YOU.

(7) "AND WHEN I SHALL PUT YOU OUT, I WILL COVER THE HEAVEN, AND MAKE THE STARS THEREOF DARK; I WILL COVER THE SUN WITH A CLOUD, AND THE MOON SHALL NOT GIVE HER LIGHT.

(8) "ALL THE BRIGHT LIGHTS OF HEAVEN WILL I MAKE DARK OVER YOU, AND SET DARKNESS UPON YOUR LAND, SAITH THE LORD GOD.

(9) "I WILL ALSO VEX THE HEARTS OF MANY PEOPLE, WHEN I SHALL BRING YOUR DESTRUCTION AMONG THE NATIONS, INTO THE COUNTRIES WHICH YOU HAVE NOT KNOWN.

(10) "YES, I WILL MAKE MANY PEOPLE AMAZED AT YOU, AND THEIR KINGS SHALL BE HORRIBLY AFRAID FOR YOU, WHEN I SHALL BRANDISH MY SWORD BEFORE THEM; AND THEY SHALL TREMBLE AT EVERY MOMENT, EVERY MAN FOR HIS OWN LIFE, IN THE DAY OF YOUR FALL."

The diagram is:

1. Basically, the same thing is said in this Chapter which was said in the three preceding Chapters.

When the Holy Spirit repeats something, even as He did here, He does so for purpose and reason. The great moral lessons given are meant to be emphasized. By the Holy Spirit doing such, the fact is brought out that the natural heart tends to resist the pleadings of the Love of God.

2. Jerusalem would fall shortly after this Prophecy was uttered.

3. Once again, we should be made aware, from all the evidence here given, as to how the Lord controls the rise and fall of nations.

THE LAMENTATION FOR PHARAOH

The phrase of Verse 2, *"Son of man, take up a Lamentation for Pharaoh king of Egypt,"* proclaims an awful judgment, hence the word *"lamentation"* being used.

This king was *"Pharaoh Hopra."* He was haughty, prideful, and declared himself God, attempting to make Egypt the master of the world. He would reckon without the Babylonian Monarch whom the Lord had appointed.

Pharaoh had no regard for Jehovah, believing himself to be god, he concluded himself to be the master of his own fate. He told the lies, and then believed them!

But in one way or the other, most of the world falls into the same category. While most may not be as boastful as Pharaoh, still, those who aren't born again give little credit to God, if any at all. Most think the world revolves around themselves, and conduct themselves accordingly. Self-importance is the bane of the human race.

MY NET

The phrase of Verse 3, *"And they shall bring you up in My net,"* signifies the Babylonians, who were appointed by the Lord to take Egypt down, which they did.

At this juncture, there was no way that Egypt could survive the onslaught, and no matter the extent of their preparation. The Lord Whom they would not own nor recognize had decreed against them, and their situation was now hopeless.

If one is to notice, the phrase, *"My net,"* signifies that the rise and fall of nations are decided not by the wealth of its citizens or the strength of its military, but by God.

EGYPT, ASSYRIA, AND TYRE

Verses 4 through 6 proclaim in cataclysmic tones, by none other that Jehovah, the coming destruction upon Egypt.

NOTES

If one is to notice, great space is devoted to three major empires: Assyria, Egypt, and Tyre. Actually, Tyre was not an empire, at least in the sense of Egypt and Assyria, but still exerted vast control because of its great wealth, etc. All three, in some respect, had had great opportunity to know and hear the Gospel.

Egypt had known the Power of God as few empires, inasmuch as the Lord had dealt with them severely so long before regarding the deliverance of the Children of Israel. Seeing the Power of God manifested, in a way no nation on Earth had ever seen, was enough to bring them to repentance, but, still, they continued to rebel and to serve their idols.

Likewise, Assyria had been dealt with graciously by the Prophet Jonah, in that this Prophet was sent directly by the Lord to Nineveh, the capital city of Assyria, with a Message of Judgment unless they repented. The Book of Jonah records their great repentance, which, no doubt, staved off their deserved Judgment, but, regrettably, was soon forgotten!

By comparison, Tyre had known a favorable relationship with David, the great King of Israel, as no other Gentile power. As such, they had had great opportunity to know the Lord, and, thereby, to serve Him; however, they continued to cling to their idols, and eventually suffered great destruction.

Therefore, these nations were dealt with according to the Light they had been shown, hence, the space devoted.

LIGHT REJECTED

Verses 7 and 8 proclaim the degree of destruction that will be visited upon Egypt. The phrase of Verse 7, *"And when I shall put you out,"* refers to their light being extinguished. Light rejected is light removed.

This Verse leads back to the plague of darkness that gripped Egypt during the time of Moses (Ex. 10:21). Then it was literal, now, it is poetical, and intending the overthrow of the imperial and executive governments. As such, their light would go out and they would be no more.

The phrase of Verse 8, *"All the bright lights of Heaven will I make dark over you,"* refers to the Light of the Gospel that had once been given to them, but refused, and now would be darkness.

This Verse, although obscure, and little thought of, as its surrounding Passages, has to do greatly with the rise and fall of nations. The degree of their Judgment has to do with the Light once given and rejected.

If one is to notice, only the nations that had at least some contact with Israel or Judah were so judged. Nations afar off, such as China, etc., received no mention, and because no Light was given to them.

Some would argue that it is better to have never known the Light than to know it and turn from it. Such a statement is correct, for Peter said: *"For it had been better for them not to have known the way of Righteousness, than, after they have known it, to turn from the Holy Commandment delivered unto them"* (II Pet. 2:21).

However, those who have the opportunity to be exposed to the Light, and take faithful advantage of that opportunity, are blessed beyond words to compare!

The nations of the world have a choice; they can have the *"Lights of Heaven"* or *"darkness upon the land."* They cannot have both! The *"Lights of Heaven"* will bring unprecedented spiritual, physical, domestical, and economic blessings. The *"darkness"* will bring the very opposite.

HISTORY

In history, only a few nations have, even in small measure, opted for the *"Light."* Of course, the first nation to know God was Israel; and she was raised up by God from the loins of Abraham, and the womb of Sarah, for the express purpose of giving the world the Word of God, and, as well, serving as the womb of the Messiah. They were to evangelize the world also, but failed miserably in the last task, and because of self-righteousness, etc.

Israel was to be the bearer of the *"Lights of Heaven"* and give it to the other nations of the world. Regrettably, in this she woefully failed!

Another empire, and about 1,800 years later, which had a semblance of that *"Light"* was England, which fueled the British Empire, at least in some measure, giving the Gospel to great parts of the world. Due to her influence, Australia, New Zealand, along with parts of Africa, were greatly influenced by the *"Light."* Germany would have also been a recipient of that *"Light"* as the great reformer, Martin Luther, planted a seed for the Gospel, which opposed Roman Catholicism, which, in fact, spread around the entirety of the world.

America and Canada have, as few nations in the world, been recipients of the *"Lights of Heaven."* And consequently, they have been blessed as few nations of the world have been blessed. Every blessing is because of the *"Light,"* as every sorrow is because of the *"darkness."*

Regrettably and sadly, the United States, as presently the greatest bearer of that *"Light,"* is fast opting for *"darkness"*! Only a Move of God can turn that *"darkness."*

As ever, and especially now, others, such as the political process, the great educational institutions, or economic prosperity, are thought to be able to turn the tide; however, such is impossible, even though the intentions may be good.

As well, the *"religious right,"* with its efforts in the political process, will have no more positive effect on the nation than all the other efforts. The only answer is found in II Chronicles 7:14: *"If My people, which are called by My Name, shall humble themselves, and pray, and seek My Face, and turn from their wicked ways; then will I hear from Heaven, and will forgive their sin, and will heal their land."*

REBELLION

The words used in Verse 9, *"I will,"* and, as well, used in other Verses, and concerning the Lord of Glory, signify a control that is so total that it is beyond the scope of imagination to comprehend. And yet, the Lord works within a set of parameters, instituted by Himself, as Creator, which always respects the free will agency of men, and, therefore, never violates those parameters.

To oversimplify a very complicated process, it is quite possible to rebel against God, but it is not possible to succeed in such rebellion. Satan, knowing that the Lord works in these parameters, which include Love, Mercy,

Grace, Compassion, and Longsuffering, makes people believe that because Judgment is not immediately forthcoming that it will not come at all! However, while it is true that it may be long in coming, and thankfully so, still, as here proclaimed, it will come!

The phrase of Verse 10, *"And they shall tremble at every moment,"* proclaims the helplessness of those who had boasted of their invincibility.

Before the actions of the Lord, men can easily boast of their prowess, but, when God begins to make His Power felt, the small efforts of even the strongest men are shown quickly to be insignificant.

The phrase, *"When I shall brandish My sword before them,"* has to do with the Babylonians used as an instrument of God to carry out His Will.

(11) "FOR THUS SAITH THE LORD GOD; THE SWORD OF THE KING OF BABYLON SHALL COME UPON YOU.

(12) "BY THE SWORDS OF THE MIGHTY WILL I CAUSE YOUR MULTITUDE TO FALL, THE TERRIBLE OF THE NATIONS, ALL OF THEM: AND THEY SHALL SPOIL THE POMP OF EGYPT, AND ALL THE MULTITUDE THEREOF SHALL BE DESTROYED.

(13) "I WILL DESTROY ALSO ALL THE BEASTS THEREOF FROM BESIDE THE GREAT WATERS; NEITHER SHALL THE FOOT OF MAN TROUBLE THEM ANY MORE, NOR THE HOOFS OF BEASTS TROUBLE THEM.

(14) "THEN WILL I MAKE THEIR WATERS DEEP, AND CAUSE THEIR RIVERS TO RUN LIKE OIL, SAITH THE LORD GOD.

(15) "WHEN I SHALL MAKE THE LAND OF EGYPT DESOLATE, AND THE COUNTRY SHALL BE DESTITUTE OF THAT WHEREOF IT WAS FULL, WHEN I SHALL SMITE ALL THEM WHO DWELL THEREIN, THEN SHALL THEY KNOW THAT I AM THE LORD.

(16) "THIS IS THE LAMENTATION WHEREWITH THEY SHALL LAMENT HER: THE DAUGHTERS OF THE NATIONS SHALL LAMENT HER: THEY SHALL LAMENT FOR HER, EVEN FOR EGYPT, AND FOR ALL HER MULTITUDE, SAITH THE LORD GOD."

The overview is:

1. Egypt would get to know, and beyond the shadow of a doubt, that God is, and that He judges evil. There is little proof, in any, that they recognized what had happened to them, and why!

2. Most Christians, even the best, little realize the degree of involvement as it regards the Lord and the nations of the world. As stated, the Book of Ezekiel is little studied by most Believers.

3. The prediction was that many nations would lament the fall of Egypt; in fact, Egypt would never rise again, at least to any degree of prominence.

THE LORD GOD

The phrase of Verse 11, *"For thus saith the Lord God,"* proclaims that which follows as that which will definitely take place.

Very plainly the Prophet proclaims the coming destruction of Egypt by the Babylonians and even several years before its actual happening, but with no favorable response from Pharaoh. Pharaoh did not believe Jehovah, so why should he believe His Prophet? However, his unbelief did not make the Word of God of none effect, at it does not make it of none effect for the entirety of mankind.

Anyway, and as previously stated, Pharaoh believed his god to be stronger than the God of Judah, inasmuch as Judah had already fallen to the Babylonians. So why should he listen to Jehovah's Prophets, inasmuch as the Lord could not even save Judah, or so Pharaoh reasoned? Such is the reasoning of the majority of mankind, and because they do not understand God or how He works, and because they do not know His Word.

THE POMP OF EGYPT

The phrase of Verse 12, *"And they shall spoil the pomp of Egypt,"* refers to Egypt's pride, which was boasting itself through Pharaoh-Hopra; however, this *"pomp"* would be destroyed, as he was strangled to death by his own men.

The Egyptians reasoned as all other nations! They figured only in the realm of military and economic might, and, of course, believing in their gods, which were actually no gods at all! In their pantheon of gods, one God Who ruled over all was not understood, or even considered. Each nation had its own god or gods which sometimes overlapped with other nations, but never with the idea of only one God overall.

As well, they thought only of strength, and, if losing in military conflict, that the other god was simply stronger than their god.

Therefore, Jehovah bringing judgment on His own people would have been understood by them only up to a point, and that He controlled their nations, as well, understood not at all!

THE LAMENTATION

Verses 13 through 16 continue with predicted Judgment, which was dire indeed! It is plainly obvious that the anger of the Lord has been aroused.

Verse 16 proclaims the surrounding nations thinking, as well, that Egypt's gods were certainly stronger than the *"Lord God"* of Judah.

And then, when the destruction came, their *"lamentation"* was great, not only for the destruction of Egypt, but the besting of her gods by Jehovah, which put these nations in jeopardy as well!

The idea is not as foreign as one may think!

When Japan entered into its bid for world dominion in the 1930's, she did so on the same premise as these nations of old. She thought her god, i.e., the religion of Shintoism, which consisted chiefly in the cultic devotion to deities of natural forces and veneration of the Emperor as a descendant of the sun-goddess, was greater than the God of the west, i.e., Jesus Christ; consequently, Japan's thinking would have been little different than Egypt and the nations of old, and her *"lamentations"* upon her defeat would have been the same as well!

Immediately following World War II, General Douglas MacArthur, as the supreme overlord of defeated Japan, and seeing their disillusionment with the religion of Shintoism, requested hundreds of Missionaries to be sent from America to Japan. The General knew that Japan, at this present time, and due to her defeat, mentally reasoned that America's God was stronger than her god; therefore,

NOTES

the time of evangelism was ripe. Sadly, the Churches in America responded very little.

At that time, the old-line Denominations had already tragically started down the road of spiritual decay, and were little interested in evangelism, but more so in a social gospel. As such, the few they sent were of little use. Also, the Pentecostal Movements were very small, thereby responding little; consequently, little attention was devoted to Japan, at least at that time.

PROPHECY

Strangely and beautifully enough, in the summer of 1944, which was about a year before the end of World War II, the Lord began to speak through me concerning this very thing, even though I was only nine years old. At that time, He spoke through me with a Prophecy of the invention of the Atomic Bomb, even though it was a year before it would come about.

No, the word *"Atomic"* was not used, only that one bomb would be invented that would be so strong and powerful that it would destroy an entire city with one blast. That was the Atomic Bomb!

I realize that it is somewhat puzzling that the Lord would give such to a nine-year-old child, especially considering the inability, and, also, our small Church, which had little or no influence! Nevertheless, this is what the Lord did, which proved to be amazingly accurate.

With the economic miracle in Japan in the post-war years, the Japanese, once again, resorted to Shintoism and Buddhism, giving credit to these false deities for their prosperity. They closed their eyes to the fact that it was America's largesse, and therefore the influence of Christianity, with its benevolence and kindness, which afforded them such. Nevertheless, their economic prosperity is not spiritual prosperity, and, consequently, Japan today is like a nation without a soul.

As of late, they are finding out that money cannot satisfy the spiritual hunger in their hearts, and, as a result, and for all practical purposes, they are purposeless and directionless.

(17) "IT CAME TO PASS ALSO IN THE

TWELFTH YEAR, IN THE FIFTEENTH DAY OF THE MONTH, THAT THE WORD OF THE LORD CAME UNTO ME, SAYING,

(18) "SON OF MAN, WAIL FOR THE MULTITUDE OF EGYPT, AND CAST THEM DOWN, EVEN HER, AND THE DAUGHTERS OF THE FAMOUS NATIONS, UNTO THE NETHER PARTS OF THE EARTH, WITH THEM WHO GO DOWN INTO THE PIT.

(19) "WHOM DO YOU PASS IN BEAUTY? GO DOWN, AND BE THOU LAID WITH THE UNCIRCUMCISED.

(20) "THEY SHALL FALL IN THE MIDST OF THEM WHO ARE SLAIN BY THE SWORD: SHE IS DELIVERED TO THE SWORD: DRAW HER AND ALL HER MULTITUDES.

(21) "THE STRONG AMONG THE MIGHTY SHALL SPEAK TO HIM OUT OF THE MIDST OF HELL WITH THEM WHO HELP HIM: THEY ARE GONE DOWN, THEY LIE UNCIRCUMCISED, SLAIN BY THE SWORD.

(22) "ASSHUR IS THERE AND ALL HER COMPANY: HIS GRAVES ARE ABOUT HIM: ALL OF THEM SLAIN, FALLEN BY THE SWORD:

(23) "WHOSE GRAVES ARE SET IN THE SIDES OF THE PIT, AND HER COMPANY IS ROUND ABOUT HER GRAVE: ALL OF THEM SLAIN, FALLEN BY THE SWORD, WHICH CAUSED TERROR IN THE LAND OF THE LIVING.

(24) "THERE IS ELAM AND ALL HER MULTITUDE ROUND ABOUT HER GRAVE, ALL OF THEM SLAIN, FALLEN BY THE SWORD, WHICH ARE GONE UNCIRCUMCISED INTO THE NETHER PARTS OF THE EARTH, WHICH CAUSED THEIR TERROR IN THE LAND OF THE LIVING; YET HAVE THEY BORNE THEIR SHAME WITH THEM WHO GO DOWN TO THE PIT.

(25) "THEY HAVE SET HER A BED IN THE MIDST OF THE SLAIN WITH ALL HER MULTITUDE: HER GRAVES ARE ROUND ABOUT HIM: ALL OF THEM UNCIRCUMCISED, SLAIN BY THE SWORD: THOUGH THEIR TERROR WAS CAUSED IN THE LAND OF THE LIVING, YET HAVE THEY BORNE THEIR SHAME WITH THEM WHO GO DOWN TO THE PIT: HE IS PUT IN THE MIDST OF THEM THAT BE SLAIN.

(26) "THERE IS MESHECH, TUBAL, AND ALL HER MULTITUDE: HER GRAVES ARE ROUND ABOUT HIM: ALL OF THEM UNCIRCUMCISED, SLAIN BY THE SWORD, THOUGH THEY CAUSED THEIR TERROR IN THE LAND OF THE LIVING.

(27) "AND THEY SHALL NOT LIE WITH THE MIGHTY WHO ARE FALLEN OF THE UNCIRCUMCISED, WHICH ARE GONE DOWN TO HELL WITH THEIR WEAPONS OF WAR: AND THEY HAVE LAID THEIR SWORDS UNDER THEIR HEADS, BUT THEIR INIQUITIES SHALL BE UPON THEIR BONES, THOUGH THEY WERE THE TERROR OF THE MIGHTY IN THE LAND OF THE LIVING.

(28) "YES, YOU SHALL BE BROKEN IN THE MIDST OF THE UNCIRCUMCISED, AND SHALL LIE WITH THEM WHO ARE SLAIN WITH THE SWORD.

(29) "THERE IS EDOM, HER KINGS, AND ALL HER PRINCES, WHICH WITH THEIR MIGHT ARE LAID BY THEM WHO WERE SLAIN BY THE SWORD: THEY SHALL LIE WITH THE UNCIRCUMCISED, AND WITH THEM WHO GO DOWN TO THE PIT.

(30) "THERE BE THE PRINCES OF THE NORTH, ALL OF THEM, AND ALL THE ZIDONIANS, WHICH ARE GONE DOWN WITH THE SLAIN; WITH THEIR TERROR THEY ARE ASHAMED OF THEIR MIGHT; AND THEY LIE UNCIRCUMCISED WITH THEM WHO BE SLAIN BY THE SWORD, AND BEAR THEIR SHAME WITH THEM WHO GO DOWN TO THE PIT.

(31) "PHARAOH SHALL SEE THEM, AND SHALL BE COMFORTED OVER ALL HIS MULTITUDE, EVEN PHARAOH AND ALL HIS ARMY SLAIN BY THE SWORD, SAITH THE LORD GOD.

(32) "FOR I HAVE CAUSED MY TERROR IN THE LAND OF THE LIVING: AND HE SHALL BE LAID IN THE MIDST OF THE UNCIRCUMCISED WITH THEM WHO ARE SLAIN WITH THE SWORD, EVEN PHARAOH AND ALL HIS MULTITUDE, SAITH THE LORD GOD."

The composition is:

NOTES

1. This is the last Prophecy concerning Egypt. It presents, in chilling detail, the eternal destiny of those in this mighty empire, including Pharaoh, which is eternal Hell. All these, when on Earth, were mighty and caused terror; but in the world of the dead they suffer a common misery and helplessness.

2. These Passages give us a brief glimpse into the mystery of the spirit world of the lost. As stated, it's not a pleasant aspect!

3. The word, *"uncircumcised,"* occurs some ten times in this Prophecy. It expresses the fact that these mentioned were not in the Covenant, and would correspond presently to the modern *"unconverted."*

THE NETHER PARTS OF THE EARTH

Verses 17 through 21 proclaim the eternal destiny of the Egypt of that day. It was eternal Hell. Let the world scoff at the idea of such a place; let most of the Church refuse to believe this which is plainly written in the Word of God; nevertheless, the eternal abode of the unredeemed, the place called *"Hell,"* is a reality. It's not a figment of someone's imagination, and it certainly isn't a joke. But the tragedy is, *"Hell"* is but a joke to most people. In fact, it is a favorite swear word of the unredeemed. But if they knew of its reality, to be sure, they would realize that *"Hell is no joke."* Sadly and regrettably, they will find out soon enough.

THE CROSS

As we've already stated in this Volume, and will no doubt state again, the only thing standing between man and this place called Hell is *"the Cross of Christ."* The Cross, and the Cross alone, is what has made it possible for man to be saved, and, thereby, to not suffer this horror of which we speak, which horror is beyond compare! Even God, that is if He is to be true to His nature, can not save man by the mere fact of His Deity. The price for man's terrible sin had to be paid, and, for sure, it could not be paid by man. So, if it was to be paid, God would have to pay it Himself, which He did by becoming man and going to the Cross. In fact, through foreknowledge God knew, even before the foundation of the world, that He would create man, and that man would fall. So, it was decided by the Godhead, sometime in eternity past, that man would be redeemed by the means of the Cross (I Pet. 1:18-20). So this means that the Cross of Christ is the foundation doctrine of the Christian faith. And to be sure, Satan has ever tried to push the Church away from its true foundation, and, sadly, he has succeeded in many cases. But it has always been from the very beginning, when it looked like Satan would take best, the Lord would lift up a Standard against him. In other words, the Lord would pull the Church back to the Cross. Most definitely, He is doing that presently. And again, as we have already stated several times, the Cross is the dividing line between the True Church and the apostate church. And if that is true, and it most definitely is, then this Message of the Cross had better be heeded (I Cor. 1:17-18).

IS IT WHO JESUS WAS OR WHAT JESUS DID?

Someone asked me that question once! They were insinuating that the Cross was of little significance, but that man was redeemed because of *"Who"* Jesus was.

The answer to that is simple!

Jesus is the Son of God; therefore, Who He is is not only all-important, but it was absolutely necessary as well; and for the simple reason that no one else could have redeemed man. Man himself, and that included every single son and daughter of Adam's fallen race, was tainted, terribly so, by original sin. So the perfection that God demanded would have to be provided by God Himself, and such was not available anywhere else. So, we dare not minimize the significance, the all-importance, of *"Who"* Christ was; however, please note the following:

If man could be redeemed merely because of Who Jesus was, then as Paul said, *"Christ died in vain"* (Gal. 2:21). In other words, if by the mere fact of Christ being Deity within itself would redeem fallen man, then why wasn't the work effected before the Cross?

The truth is, as important as Who He was, it was *"What"* He did, which refers to the Cross, which affected man's Redemption, and that alone (Rom. 5:1-2; 6:3-14; I Cor. 1:17-18, 21, 23; 2:2, 5; Gal. 6:14; Eph. 2:13-18; Col. 2:14-15).

To minimize the Cross in any manner is to minimize Christ, which no sane person desires to do! In fact, Christ must not be separated from the Cross, and by that I refer to the benefits of what He there did.

Of course, Christ is no longer on the Cross, with His perfect Sacrifice done and complete, and so perfect and complete that it will never have to be repeated. Paul said:

"But this Man, after He had offered one Sacrifice for sins forever, sat down on the Right Hand of God;

"From henceforth expecting till His enemies be made His footstool.

"For by one Offering He has perfected forever them who are sanctified" (Heb. 10:12-14).

Understanding all of this, the Apostle then said: *"Having therefore, Brethren, boldness to enter into the Holiest by the Blood of Jesus"* (Heb. 10:19). This Verse plainly tells us that we cannot come into the presence of God except *"by the Blood of Jesus,"* which, as is obvious, refers to the Cross.

While it was definitely necessary for Him to be Who He was, to be sure, it was *"What"* He did, and we speak of the Cross, which affected our Redemption.

EVERYTHING COMES THROUGH THE CROSS

Every single thing that man receives from God, whether it be Salvation, the Baptism with the Holy Spirit, the Fruit of the Spirit, Grace, Mercy, Longsuffering, Power, Glory, answer to prayer, the privilege of His Presence, Love, Gifts of the Spirit, eternal life, in fact, everything, all and without exception, are made possible exclusively by the Cross.

Everything that man received from God before the Cross was received, one might say, *"on credit."* In effect, God gave a promissory note that He would pay the debt, the debt that we could not pay (Gal. 4:28). That *"Promise"* was fulfilled at the Cross of Calvary, and the debt is fully paid, all made possible by the Cross.

That's why we keep saying that the Cross must ever be the object of one's Faith. If it's not the object of one's Faith, which in effect means that something else is the object of our faith, it also means that such a person is committing *"spiritual adultery"* (Rom. 7:1-4). When one looks into the situation, we find that this is the very problem that caused the downfall of Judah, which made the people of God a vassal State. They made something other than the Cross of Christ, typified by the Sacrifices, as the object of their faith. It was the heathenistic idols of the surrounding countries which they adopted. That's the reason that the Lord constantly used strong terminology regarding Israel, saying that they were *"people of whoredoms"* (Ezek. 16:25-26, 34; 23:11, 14, 19).

Is the Church presently doing the same thing?

How many Preachers are *"preaching the Cross"*?

How many Churches are *"proclaiming the Cross"*?

The answer is *"precious few,"* which means that something else is the object of their faith, which also means that God looks at such as *"spiritual adultery,"* i.e., *"whoredoms."* If the Church adopts the ways of the world, the Church will experience the eternal destiny of the world, and that we must remember.

NATIONS WITHOUT GOD

The last Prophecy concerning Egypt, as presented in Verses 17 through 32, presents in vision, in a sense, Pharaoh, and his armies, and the armies of his allies, helpless captives covered with shame, and shut up in the dungeon of Hell, in company with other kings and their armies. All these, when on Earth, were mighty and powerful, and caused terror; but in the world of the dead, they suffer a common misery, ignominy, and helplessness.

The phrase of Verse 17, *"The fifteenth day of the month,"* actually refers to the first month, as in Verse 1. In other words, this part of the Prophecy was given some fifteen days after it began, as recorded in Ezekiel 32:1.

The phrase of Verse 19, *"Whom do you pass in beauty?"* refers to Pharaoh thinking himself greater, richer, and more cultured than any other Monarch. After all, at least in his thinking, Egypt was the oldest of the nations. As such, their knowledge surpassed any and all! However, the Holy Spirit says that all of this, the riches, power, pomp, and glory, will count for nothing in that place called *"Hell."* There the pomp and ceremony, called *"beauty"* by the Holy Spirit, and in an ironical way, is no more! All, the rich and the poor, suffer alike!

HELL

The phrase of Verse 21, *"The strong among the mighty shall speak to him out of the midst of Hell with them who help him,"* refers to the other Pharaohs, along with the other mighty kings, such as the Assyrians, who had already gone to Hell, and would *"speak to him,"* i.e., Pharaoh. That which they will *"speak to him"* will not be words of encouragement or respect or appreciation, but, instead, words of scorn.

These words could well be words of ridicule as to why Pharaoh did not listen to the Prophet Ezekiel; however, their words will too late, and they themselves did not listen when on Earth.

Jesus would relate such terminology in the experience He gave of the rich man who went to Hell and Lazarus who went to Paradise (Lk. 16:19-31).

The rich man in Hell would plead that Lazarus would be sent back to Earth to testify to his five brothers. Abraham answered and said: *"If they hear not Moses and the Prophets, neither will they be persuaded, though one rose from the dead"* (Lk. 16:31).

It is amazing! Those in Hell believe, and believe readily, while those on Earth believe not at all! All the *"strong ones"* in Hell at this time, which constituted the mightiest and the greatest kings who ever lived, were Believers in Jehovah and the Prophets, but precious few on Earth believe.

Why?

Due to the way that man fell in the Garden of Eden, it is much easier to believe a lie than the Truth.

Men laugh and make fun of the Biblical Doctrine of Hell, never dreaming that the Doctrine is true, and if continuing on their present course, will, without fail, find out such Truth to their horror. The old joke used by so many, as to having plenty of company in Hell, will certainly be true, but little appreciated!

ASSHUR, ELAM, MESHECH, TUBAL, EDOM, ZIDON

The word *"graves"* in Verse 22, at least in this instance, refers to the tomb, or sepulcher, the place of the body, and not the place of the soul. It merely means that they died, with the next Verses telling the eternal abode of their souls and spirits.

"Asshur" refers to the Assyrians, which as an empire was defeated some years before by the Babylonians. They have gone the way of all others, all of them slain.

The phrase, *"Fallen by the sword,"* is interesting. As they lived by the sword, they died by the sword.

The truth is, the number of casualties as it regards wars, even from the very beginning of time, is shocking to say the last. The loss of life has been appalling! From the dawn of time, the number of those *"fallen by the sword"* would be shocking indeed!

Regrettably, even at this present time, despite the fact of educational enlightenment, and due to the fact that instruments of war have reached unprecedented proportions, the casualties now are greater than ever. In fact, the world presently has the potential to destroy itself. It will not do so, because it will be interrupted by the Second Coming of the Lord. Otherwise, the Scripture says, *"If those days were not shortened, there should no flesh be saved"* (Mat. 24:22).

The phrase, *"Their shame,"* of Verse 24 refers to the fact that, on Earth, those of Asshur and Elam, plus the other nations named in this Chapter, were robed with honor, but, in Hell, were clothed with shame.

Elam, of Verse 24, is the ancient name for the plain of Khuzistan. The civilization in this area is as old as, and closely connected with, the cultures of lower Mesopotamia; consequently, the Elamites are closely connected with Babylonia. Elam was a son of Shem (Gen. 10:22), and, consequently, a grandson of Noah.

Elamite history is obscure from 1000 B.C. until the campaigns of Sargon of Assyria in 721-705 B.C. Sennacherib and Ashurbanipal subjected the Elamites and deported some of them to Samaria, taking Israelites to Elam (Ezra 4:9; Isa. 11:11).

After the collapse of Assyria, Elam was annexed by the Indo-Europeans, who had gradually gained power in Iran following their invasions, beginning about 1000 B.C. Ultimately, this area was annexed by the Medo-Persian Empire under Cyrus.

Strangely enough, the crowd at Pentecost (Acts 2:9) contained men from as far away as Elam, presumably members of the Jewish communities who were descendants who had remained in exile.

These, as well, were consigned to *"the pit,"* and because of their rejection of God.

"Meshech," of Verse 26, was one of the sons of Japheth (Gen. 10:2). Here and elsewhere he is associated with *"Tubal."*

I Chronicles 1:17 names him as a descendant of Shem by Aram, while the parallel passage (Gen. 10:23) gives the name as *"Mash."* The intermarriage implied by the presence of the same name among the children of Japheth and Shem is not impossible, and probably explains the seeming contradiction.

They occupied a region southeast of the Black Sea, and are mentioned in the annals of the Assyrians.

They are also mentioned by the Holy Spirit as dying without God, and, consequently, going to Hell.

The phrase of Verse 27, *"And they shall not lie with the mighty,"* seems to be a contradiction with Verse 26; however, the difficulty is erased when the statement is interpreted *"shall they not lie . . .?"*

The idea of this Verse is that *"Meshech"* and *"Tubal"* have a lower place in Hell, if such is possible. The phrase, *"Which are gone down to Hell with their weapons of war,"* does not mean that such items are taken down to Hell with the lost soul, but that there was no honor at all in their death, and they were buried without the honors of war. In other words, their swords were not placed beneath their heads at their burial.

For the Scythians, who worshipped the sword, this would be the extreme ignominy.

The phrase of Verse 29, *"There is Edom,"* is used by the Holy Spirit as an exclamation!

It is said thusly because the exultation which the Edomites had shown over the Fall of Jerusalem (Ps. 137:7) had exacerbated their already perilous spiritual condition.

NOTES

The *"Zidonians"* of Verse 30 are suggestive of the direction of Northern Syria, including cities like Damascus, Hamath, Arpad, and others.

These too went to Hell!

PHARAOH

The phrase of Verse 32, *"Even Pharaoh and all his multitude, saith the Lord God,"* closes these Prophecies concerning Egypt. She sought, in self-will and the pride of nature, to take the place which God had given to Babylon. In other words, she thought she was bigger than God!

The mighty empire of Assyria had had to bend to God's gift of supremacy to Nebuchadnezzar; and Pharaoh, though he owned no god but himself, was no better than other Monarchs in power and might. He was uncircumcised like the others; that is, not owned of God, not upheld by Him.

Pride, in effect, characterized Egypt and self-will. She had been the confidence of God's people, but should be no longer; for how could such a principle ever furnish the victories which are only given to Faith?

Egypt shall have her place in the future (Isa., Chpt. 19), but never as a ruler; and her judgment secures Israel's blessing, for the will of man in Pharaoh cannot frustrate the purpose of God in Grace.

The election of Nebuchadnezzar as God's *"sword"* and *"terror"* is one of the great facts of Scripture. That sword humbled Egypt in whom Israel trusted. It humbled also all the neighboring nations, and thus destroyed many snares which entrapped the sons of Israel. All these judgments reached forward to a future day, and will be followed by the establishment in Grace of the redeemed nations in union with the New Israel (Isa., Chpt. 19), so forming the one flock of John 10:16 under the care of the Messiah.

"Some thank the Lord for friends and home,
"For mercies sure and sweet;
"But I would praise Him for His grace
"In prayer I would repeat:"

"Some thank Him for the flowers that grow,
"Some for the stars that shine;

"My heart is filled with joy and praise
"Because I know He's mine."

"I trust in Him from day to day,
"I prove His Saving Grace;
"I'll sing this song of praise to Him
"Until I see His face."

CHAPTER 33

(1) "AGAIN THE WORD OF THE LORD CAME UNTO ME, SAYING,

(2) "SON OF MAN, SPEAK TO THE CHILDREN OF YOUR PEOPLE, AND SAY UNTO THEM, WHEN I BRING THE SWORD UPON A LAND, IF THE PEOPLE OF THE LAND TAKE A MAN OF THEIR COASTS, AND SET HIM FOR THEIR WATCHMAN:

(3) "IF WHEN HE SEES THE SWORD COME UPON THE LAND, HE BLOW THE TRUMPET, AND WARN THE PEOPLE;

(4) "THEN WHOSOEVER HEARS THE SOUND OF THE TRUMPET, AND TAKES NOT WARNING; IF THE SWORD COMES, AND TAKES HIM AWAY, HIS BLOOD SHALL BE UPON HIS OWN HEAD.

(5) "HE HEARD THE SOUND OF THE TRUMPET, AND TOOK NOT WARNING; HIS BLOOD SHALL BE UPON HIM. BUT HE WHO TAKES WARNING SHALL DELIVER HIS SOUL.

(6) "BUT IF THE WATCHMAN SEE THE SWORD COME, AND BLOW NOT THE TRUMPET, AND THE PEOPLE BE NOT WARNED; IF THE SWORD COME, AND TAKE ANY PERSON FROM AMONG THEM, HE IS TAKEN AWAY IN HIS INIQUITY; BUT HIS BLOOD WILL I REQUIRE AT THE WATCHMAN'S HAND."

The composition is:

1. The first Prophecy of this Chapter (Vss. 1-20) was spoken the evening before the arrival of the messenger (Vs. 21) announcing the Fall of Jerusalem.

2. This intelligence liberated him from enjoined silence of Ezekiel 24:15-27; and he was now permitted to resume his Ministry to the Exiles (Williams).

3. Once again, the Holy Spirit emphasizes the fact that all God-called Ministers must, at the same time, be *"watchmen."* This refers not only to preaching the truth, but, as well, pointing out error, and those who propagate the error.

THE WORD OF THE LORD

Verse 1 says, *"Again the Word of the LORD came unto me, saying,"*

It had been between two and three years since Ezekiel had been given a Message from the Lord concerning Israel; however, during this period of time, he did address himself, and according to the Word of the Lord, to foreign nations, even as we have seen. Now His own people are again the object of his Prophetic Office.

No date is given regarding this Prophecy, but some think it was immediately before the Messenger came with the news of the Fall of Jerusalem. In fact, the city would have already fallen some time earlier, but, due to the distance and slow method of transportation, it would have taken some time to have reached Ezekiel and the Exiles in Babylonia.

THE WATCHMAN

The phrase of Verse 2, *"If the people of the land take a man of their coasts, and set him for their watchman,"* presents, once again, the Ministry of the watchman, even as outlined previously in Chapter 3. When the Holy Spirit repeats something of this nature, it is meant to portray the seriousness of that which is being presented. In effect, the Holy Spirit is saying in this Chapter that Judah and Jerusalem fell, and with the slaughter of tens of thousands, simply because of unfaithful watchmen. So, the following message of this Prophecy will address the cause of Judah's terrible judgment, as well as the erroneous thoughts held by the people.

If one is to notice, the problems that plagued Judah of old continue to plague the modern Church.

UNFAITHFUL WATCHMEN

The function of the watchman was to stand upon the tower (II Sam. 18:24-25; II Ki. 9:17; Hab. 2:1), keeping his eye on the distant horizon, and as soon as clouds of dust or the gleam of armor gave notice of the approach of the enemy, to sound the Trumpet of alarm (Amos 3:6; Hos. 8:1; Jer. 4:5).

If he discharged that duty faithfully, then the blood of those who perished through their own negligence would rest upon their own heads; however, Judah lost her way, and even as the modern Church loses its way, because of the unfaithfulness of their *"watchmen."*

In the midst of a myriad of *"unfaithful watchmen,"* Jeremiah and Ezekiel stand out as faithful; however, their Message was not to the liking of the general populace, and especially the civil and religious leadership of Judah, so, the people listened to the false prophets instead! It has not changed at the present, being Satan's chief trump card.

As I write these words in July of 2003, the Church, and for all practical purposes, may be even in a worse state than Judah of old. At least, they had Jeremiah who prophesied truthfully in Jerusalem, while Ezekiel prophesied faithfully in captivity, but the modern Church, seemingly, has no one, at least to whom they will listen; consequently, false doctrine is rampant, with fads, foolishness, and foibles accepted without question.

CHRISTIAN TELEVISION

The program offerings of Christian Television, so-called, can be looked at as a mirror of the modern Church. Of course, there will be some exceptions to this, but, as a whole, I think the following portrays the picture which Television presents, as an idea as to what the modern Church actually is.

PAGAN

I speak of Roman Catholic programming, which advocates prayer to dead Saints and the worship of Mary. Jesus labeled such, when He addressed the woman at Jacob's well, by saying: *"You worship you know not what"* (Jn. 4:22).

There is nothing of the Gospel in Catholicism. One can only conclude it to be paganistic.

A FORM OF GODLINESS

In II Timothy, Chapter 3, Paul gives us a long list of sins which will occur to a greater degree in the last days. Regrettably, this unsavory list speaks of the Church. He closed it by saying:

"Having a form of Godliness, but denying the power thereof: from such turn away" (II Tim. 3:5).

This takes in almost all of the programming of the old-line Churches. They have denied the Holy Spirit, and, consequently, have denied the Power. As stated, Paul said *"from these turn away."* They hold no life, because they have denied the Life.

As well, *"denying the power thereof"* refers to the Cross. Paul also said:

"For the preaching of the Cross is to them who perish foolishness; but to we who are saved it is the Power of God" (I Cor. 1:18).

HOW IS THE CROSS THE POWER OF GOD?

As we've stated previously in this Volume, there is really no power in the wooden beam referred to as the Cross. As well, there was no power in the death of Christ, per se. The truth is, Jesus died *"in weakness"* (II Cor. 13:4). Of course, it was a contrived weakness, as should be obvious. It simply means that He didn't avail Himself of the power at His disposal, but allowed Himself to be offered up.

It is what Calvary accomplished, and I speak of Jesus atoning for all sin, which made this great power possible. In fact, the Power is invested in the Holy Spirit. The Cross made it possible, as stated, by atoning for all sin, for the Holy Spirit to use His great power on behalf of the Saints, at least all who will make the Cross the Object of their Faith (I Cor. 1:17; Rom. 6:3-14; Gal. 6:14).

As it regards the rejection of the Cross, most of the Pentecostal and Charismatic Churches have probably gone more down this road than even the old-line Churches. They have embraced humanistic psychology, I personally believe, to even a greater degree than the old-line Churches. In fact, some strong voices in the old-line Denominations are speaking up forcibly against this humanism; but, there is hardly a sound of this capacity coming from the Pentecostal and Charismatic worlds. So this means, they have rejected the Cross, because one cannot serve

God and mammon. Either one cancels out the other!

ITCHING EARS

Paul said: *"For the time will come when they will not endure sound Doctrine; but after their own lusts shall they heap to themselves teachers, having itching ears;*

"And they shall turn away their ears from the Truth, and shall be turned unto fables" (II Tim. 4:3-4). Regrettably, that time has already come!

This Passage speaks of the people who have *"itching ears,"* who seek Preachers who will tell them what they want to hear. They have little difficulty in finding that particular breed.

In fact, there are scores of these *"watchmen"* who desire only one thing, and that's to find out what the people desire to hear, and then give it to them. In the meantime, they will secure, above all, their financial support.

These unfaithful *"watchmen"* have no desire for *"Thus saith the Lord,"* but, instead, are strictly mercenary in their efforts. They both, the Preachers and the people, have turned their ears from the Truth, and *"are turned unto fables"*; consequently, fads are promoted as Gospel, and the people accept it because they do not desire the *"Truth."*

Tragically, tens of millions, and even hundreds of millions, of dollars are poured into the coffers of these false watchmen. More tragic still, some of that money, even great sums of it, comes from well-meaning Christians, who so little know the Word of God that they are easy prey for these religious hucksters.

FAITHFUL WATCHMEN

As there were so few in the days of Jeremiah and Ezekiel, there are few today; consequently, over Christian television one is hard put to find the True Gospel of Jesus Christ. If, in fact, one is found, he is ridiculed, lampooned, laughed at, jeered, with claims being made that his message is not relative to this hour.

No, his Message is relative, but the people just don't want to hear his Message.

Faithful watchmen preach the Cross, and because all Deliverance is found in the Cross, and the Cross alone!

If the Preacher is not preaching the Cross, while what he's saying might be good, it can only be said that he is preaching about the Gospel, instead of preaching the Gospel.

WHAT DO WE MEAN BY PREACHING THE CROSS?

We are not meaning that every Text has to be about the Cross. That's not the idea! What we are meaning is this:

The belief system of the Preacher must be solely in the Cross of Christ, knowing that this is the Foundation of the Faith. In fact, inasmuch as it was the very first Doctrine formulated by the Godhead, even before the foundation of the Earth, it, of necessity, must be the Foundation for all Doctrine (I Pet. 1:18-20).

It doesn't really matter what the Preacher preaches about, what Text he uses, or what subject he broaches, if the Cross is the Foundation Doctrine of his belief system, it will become quickly obvious.

ARE YOU A DELIVERANCE PREACHER?

Someone wrote, sometime back, asking the question of my heading, *"Are you a deliverance Preacher?"*

The answer to that is simple: every true Preacher of the Gospel is a deliverance Preacher. But what do we mean by that?

When most people think of deliverance Preachers, they're thinking of the Preacher who lays his hands on people, prays for them, with the Power of God supposedly coming upon them, and them being set free from their particular bondage, whatever it might be.

While we definitely believe in praying for people, and we definitely believe in the laying on of hands, still, these things, as helpful as they may be in their own way, will not deliver anybody. There's nothing in the Bible that proclaims deliverance in this fashion, with the exception of casting out demons, and healing the sick (Mk. 16:15-18). As well, hands can be laid on people for them to be baptized with the Holy Spirit (Acts 19:6). Such can refer to *"Blessings"* as well!

But when it comes to delivering people of the bondages of sin, there's nothing in the

Word of God that lends credence to anything of this nature. Jesus said:

"You shall know the Truth, and the Truth shall make you free" (Jn. 8:32).

Jesus also said: *"The Spirit of the Lord is upon Me, because He has anointed Me to . . . preach deliverance to the captives"* (Lk. 4:18).

If it is to be noticed, Jesus didn't say *"to deliver the captives,"* but, rather *"to preach deliverance to the captives."* In other words, Preachers are to preach the Truth, which is the Cross, to men and women, and then Deliverance can be effected. In this Volume, I have done my best to portray to you the Cross, not only as it refers to Salvation, but, as well, as it refers to Sanctification, i.e., *"our everyday walk before God."* In effect, what I have been doing, is *"preaching deliverance"* to you, in effect, telling you how to be delivered through what Jesus has done at the Cross.

In that manner, I am a Deliverance Preacher, but only in that manner. As stated, when most Christians think of a deliverance Preacher, they do not think of that of which I have said, but something else altogether. Preachers cannot deliver people, it is the Truth alone, which is *"Jesus Christ and Him Crucified,"* which can deliver people (I Cor. 1:23; 2:2).

THE BLOWING OF THE TRUMPET

Verse 3 says: *"If when he sees the sword come upon the land, he blows the Trumpet, and warns the people;"*

In these Passages, the responsibility of both the people and the watchman is outlined. The responsibility of the *"watchman"* is to correctly *"see"* and *"warn."* He was to warn by *"blowing the Trumpet."*

Such can be likened presently to *"blowing the Trumpet"* of the True Gospel of Jesus Christ, warning against error that will damn the soul. This is not a pleasant task, and, therefore, most Preachers will have no part of it, claiming that they preach only a *"positive Gospel."*

Admittedly, it's not popular to preach what the people do not want to hear, and will certainly incur the wrath, especially of the false teachers and their adherents. Still, the response of the people is not the responsibility of the true watchman, but rather to properly *"see"* and properly *"warn."*

HEAR WHAT THE SPIRIT IS SAYING TO THE CHURCHES

The phrase of Verse 4 which says, *"Then whosoever hears the sound of the trumpet, and takes not warning,"* presents a demand of the Holy Spirit that the people be allowed to *"hear"* that which is Truth. What they do with it is then upon *"his own head."*

To be sure, it is tragic for men to hear the Truth and turn from it, but more tragic still when they have no opportunity to *"hear the sound of the Trumpet."*

In the last couple of years, the Lord has strongly laid upon our hearts that we must address the error of the *"Word of Faith"* doctrine. It is one thing to address an erroneous doctrine which has only a limited following; however, it's something else again to address a doctrine that is widely accepted, and, in fact, very popular, even as is the Word of Faith doctrine.

Its greatest popularity is that it claims that its teachings will make all Believers financially rich, at least those who adhere to its teaching. Scriptures are pulled out of context, attempting to buttress this doctrine, which makes its followers believe that what is being proposed is Scriptural. Unfortunately, there seems to be a modicum of greed in the hearts of all of us. So when that greed can be justified, or so it seems to be, then it becomes legitimate. Peter addressed this by saying:

"Which they who are unlearned and unstable wrest, as they do also the other Scriptures, unto their own destruction.

"You therefore, beloved, seeing you know these things before, beware lest you also, being led away with the error of the wicked, fall from your own steadfastness" (II Pet. 3:16-17).

As well, this is the group which has attacked the Cross of Christ, as perhaps none other, referring to the Cross as *"past miseries"* and *"the greatest defeat in human history."*

They completely ignore all of Paul's writings, claiming that Jesus took upon Himself the nature of Satan while on the Cross, and then died and went to the burning side of Hell, even as all sinners die and go to Hell.

They teach that He was tortured in Hell by demon spirits for some three days and nights, as stated, suffering the agonies of the damned, when, at the end of that three days and nights, God said, *"It is enough,"* and then Jesus was *"born again,"* just like any sinner is Born-Again. They teach that Jesus was then raised from the dead.

They claim that Salvation was purchased by Jesus suffering this three days and nights in the burning side of Hell, which completely ignores the Cross and the shed Blood of Christ. While they may mention the shedding of His Blood, they say that that alone was not enough to redeem man, but that the suffering in Hell had to be added. The truth is, while they pay lip-service to His Precious Blood being shed for lost humanity, it is lip-service only. The truth is, it is an attack against the Atonement, which is the worst sin of all; for if a person is wrong on the Atonement, in some way, more or less, they are wrong about everything else in the Word of God. Paul addressed this as well by saying:

"Now the Spirit (Holy Spirit) *speaks expressly* (pointedly), *that in the latter times* (the times in which we now live) *some shall depart from the Faith* (Jesus Christ and Him Crucified), *giving heed to seducing spirits, and doctrines of devils"* (I Tim. 4:1).

The Church must hear the sound of the Trumpet, and it must be clear, clean, and completely audible, in other words, with no doubt being as to what is said. By the Grace of God, that's what we intend to do.

THE WARNING

The phrase of Verse 5, *"He heard the sound of the trumpet, and took not warning,"* proclaims the fact that the trumpet must sound, which means that the opportunity to accept or reject is demanded by the Holy Spirit.

It is incumbent upon the Preacher of the Gospel to *"deliver his soul,"* which means to faithfully portray what God has told him to deliver to the people. So, if we as Preachers are to obey God, we must do what the Lord wants done.

But the problem is, far too many Preachers succumb to the *"itching ear crowd,"* which means instead of preaching what the Lord wants them to preach, and which is obvious that they ought to preach, they instead preach what the crowd wants to hear. We must remember, popularity is not the issue, but rather faithfulness!

THE BLOOD OF SOULS

The phrase of Verse 6 which says, *"But if the watchman see the sword come, and blow not the trumpet, and the people be not warned,"* presents a somber warning to the *"watchman."* He is demanded by the Holy Spirit that, upon the threat of danger, to *"blow the trumpet."*

To be sure, those who *"warn the people"* will be ostracized, lampooned, lambasted, and caricatured. To say the least, they will not be applauded!

However, to those *"watchmen"* who cater to the public whim, desiring only to preach a feel-good gospel, the warning of the Holy Spirit is blunt: *"But his blood will I require at the watchman's hand."*

Two types of *"warnings"* are given in this Passage: the *"warning"* that should be given to the people by faithful watchmen, and the *"warning"* given by the Holy Spirit to unfaithful watchmen.

The phrase, *"And the people be not warned,"* presents a startling statement, which characterizes almost all of humanity. Even in Christianized America and Canada, the people are seldom warned. The so-called positive gospel is the rage, with false doctrine seemingly eagerly accepted.

But let every Preacher know and understand, that when he stands before God, he will give account for that which he knew he should do, but didn't do. It is a chilling thought to realize that the blood of these souls will be required at the *"watchman's hand."*

Many Preachers take the position that the Lord hasn't told them to take such a stand, that is, if the Lord is consulted at all, which He isn't in most cases.

The truth is, the Lord has already spoken to us through His Word. As a watchman on the wall, and we see danger coming toward the city, such a watchman doesn't have to wait for the Lord to speak to him and tell him to warn of that danger. In fact, one of the very purposes of his Calling is to warn the people as it regards false doctrine and false apostles. The facts are, the *"warning"* is not given, because most Preachers either are not preaching the Truth themselves, or else, they don't want to take the heat — and to be sure, there will be heat!

(7) "SO THOU, O SON OF MAN, I HAVE SET YOU A WATCHMAN UNTO THE HOUSE OF ISRAEL; THEREFORE YOU SHALL HEAR THE WORD AT MY MOUTH, AND WARN THEM FROM ME.

(8) "WHEN I SAY UNTO THE WICKED, O WICKED MAN, YOU SHALL SURELY DIE; IF YOU DO NOT SPEAK TO WARN THE WICKED FROM HIS WAY, THAT WICKED MAN SHALL DIE IN HIS INIQUITY; BUT HIS BLOOD WILL I REQUIRE AT YOUR HAND.

(9) "NEVERTHELESS, IF YOU WARN THE WICKED OF HIS WAY TO TURN FROM IT; IF HE DOES NOT TURN FROM HIS WAY, HE SHALL DIE IN HIS INIQUITY; BUT YOU HAVE DELIVERED YOUR SOUL.

(10) "THEREFORE, O THOU SON OF MAN, SPEAK UNTO THE HOUSE OF ISRAEL; THUS YOU SPEAK, SAYING, IF OUR TRANSGRESSIONS AND OUR SINS BE UPON US, AND WE PINE AWAY IN THEM, HOW SHOULD WE THEN LIVE?

(11) "SAY UNTO THEM, AS I LIVE, SAITH THE LORD GOD, I HAVE NO PLEASURE IN THE DEATH OF THE WICKED; BUT THAT THE WICKED TURN FROM HIS WAY AND LIVE: TURN YE, TURN YE FROM YOUR EVIL WAYS; FOR WHY WILL YOU DIE, O HOUSE OF ISRAEL?"

The structure is:

1. These Passages proclaim to us vividly that God has no pleasure in the death of the wicked, but the contrary.

2. Very carefully, the Holy Spirit delineates the responsibility of the Preacher. If we as Preachers overlook this, we do so at our peril!

3. The Holy Spirit, through the Prophet, also very carefully delineates as to what is *"right"* and as to what is *"wrong."*

THE COMMISSION

The phrase of Verse 7, *"See thou, O son of man, I have set you a watchman unto the house of Israel,"* proclaims the Commission to Ezekiel once again enjoined. He is called *"O son of man,"* which is the same designation that will be given to *"The Son of Man,"* the Lord Jesus Christ (Mat. 13:37; Lk. 9:44, 56). As this designation, likening Ezekiel to Christ, applied to that Prophet, it applies, as well, to every God-called Preacher at present!

The *"Commission"* was, and is, twofold, but very simple:

YOU SHALL HEAR THE WORD AT MY MOUTH

This, and this alone is the criteria, that we, as Preachers of the Gospel, hear from Heaven, as it regards what the Lord wants said and done.

On the surface it may seem simple, but Satan will fight this more than anything else. The Preacher who hears from God, and will deliver what he has heard, is as scarce as the proverbial hen's teeth.

Far too many Preachers espouse only the denominational line at the expense of the Bible. Others, and as stated, look for those who have itching ears, desiring to preach only what the people desire to hear, and, therefore, guaranteeing their financial support.

As well, to truly hear from the Lord, one has to live a consecrated life dedicated to prayer and the study of the Word.

Sometime ago, a poll was taken among Preachers as to the degree of their prayer life. Anonymity was guaranteed. The results were shocking to say the least! The average was, they prayed less than five minutes a day if that!

To be sure, such Preachers were not hearing from God, because such, at least for the most part, cannot hear from the Lord. Therefore, what is presented from those particular pulpits is not the *"Word"* from the *"Mouth of God,"* but, instead, the word of man. As such, it will save no one, heal no one, unbind no one, or meet any need.

WARN THEM FROM ME

This is the second part of the Commission. The Preacher must faithfully hear what the Lord wants said, and then faithfully deliver what the Lord wants delivered.

In 1982, the Lord spoke to my heart concerning a Message He wanted to deliver to the

Catholics in America and around the world. He told me I was to deliver that Message. To sum it up, it was simple. The Message was *"The just shall live by Faith."* Even though this sounds innocent enough, and is actually the very heart of the Gospel, still, those very words are anathema to the whole of Catholicism, as well as much of the Protestant world. To be sure, it would arouse an unprecedented anger, at least toward my Ministry.

At that time, we had, to my knowledge, the largest television network in the world, virtually covering the entirety of the U.S.A., plus Canada and most of Central and South America. As well, the Telecast covered the Philippines, along with certain countries in Africa, and other parts of the world.

I sought the Lord earnestly regarding what I was to say, and how it was to be said. To be frank, at the first, I attempted to shake off this urgent call within my heart, and for the obvious reasons.

First of all, I had very little knowledge of Catholic dogma and doctrine, and, furthermore, we had, at least to my knowledge, the largest Catholic audience of any Preacher in the world. In turn, they were giving millions of dollars to our Ministry, which we sorely needed for the spreading of the Gospel around the world.

Still, the all-important thing was to hear from the Lord and to deliver what He told me to deliver. This we attempted to do, and with thousands of Catholics all around the world being brought to a saving knowledge of Jesus Christ; nevertheless, the opposition was fierce, to say the least.

It came not only from the Catholic Church itself, which would be obvious, but from my own Denomination and other Pentecostals and Charismatics.

Regrettably, the Pentecostal and Charismatic worlds were attempting then, and are attempting now, to work together with the Catholics in a unified fashion.

Many are claiming that Catholicism is Biblical and that Catholics are saved. In fact, a goodly number of very powerful Preachers in the United States, almost all of them Pentecostal and Charismatic, signed a concordant that they would not attempt to evangelize the Catholics, because, as they said it, *"Catholics are already saved."* Nothing could be farther from the truth. Catholicism is not Biblical, is not in any way Biblical, and, in fact, is pagan.

Others claim that if Catholics have truly come to Christ, they are to remain in the Catholic Church. We were, and are, preaching strongly that if Catholics come to Christ, which many do, that they will have to leave the Catholic Church. The Holy Spirit guides into all Truth, and, to be sure, He will not guide anyone to remain in that which is paganistic error (Jn. 16:13).

It must always be remembered that the Cross of Christ is an offense. That's the way it always has been, and that's the way it is now, and ever shall be (Gal. 5:11).

Many Preachers, regrettably, aren't willing to suffer the *"offense of the Cross,"* which means they preach what the people want to hear instead of what the people need to hear.

THE WICKED

The phrase of Verse 8, *"When I say unto the wicked, O wicked man, you shall surely die,"* presents the Message which is to be straight to the point.

To a great degree, as stated, this Chapter is similar in many ways to Ezekiel, Chapter 3. The repetition, due to the extreme seriousness of the matter, is by design. Several things are said:

1. The wicked, unless they are Born-Again, will surely die in their sins, meaning to be eternally separated from God.

2. Even if they are not warned, and have little or no knowledge of their precarious position, ignorance will not secure them Salvation.

3. It is the responsibility of the God-called Preacher to warn the wicked, and, therefore, the responsibility of the Church to send the Preacher (Rom. 10:14-15).

4. If the wicked aren't warned, their blood will be required at the hand of the *"watchman,"* i.e., Preacher.

This means that it is the responsibility of every single Christian to take the Gospel to a lost world (Mk. 16:15). Admittedly, only a few are truly called to take the Message, but all are called to help support those who are taking the Message. Tragically, only a minute few in the Church really get under the burden to carry out this task, that is the single most important task on the face of the Earth.

Even Christians who many times give substantial sums, for the most part, only give a fraction of what they could truly give, or else, they give it to that which is not really the Gospel.

OPPOSITION

Satan fights the carrying out of the Great Commission more than anything else; and, shockingly enough, uses the Church as his greatest helper. It may come as a shock to most Christians, but the greatest hindrance to the propagation of the Gospel is the Church. Powerful political forces within the Church are at work, who have an agenda of *"money"* and *"control."* They not only have no interest in the Will of God, but, actually, actively oppose the Will of God. Tragically, this is not an isolated case, but involves almost the entirety of what is referred to as *"The Church."* This is almost totally true of Denominations, and, is pandemic in independent religious structures as well!

Also, this is not something that is new, but has prevailed even from the very beginning. Christ's greatest opposition was the religious hierarchy of Israel. As well, Paul's greatest hindrance was opposition from within the Church!

Nevertheless, and to be sure, one day when men stand before God, they will not answer to their Denomination, or to other men, but to Christ Himself. The only criteria then will be the Word of God. Consequently, *"My Denomination does not approve . . ."* will not suffice. Or, *"I thought . . . "* will, as well, be insufficient!

As well, Christians are going to be responsible not only for what they did not support, which was of the Lord, but, what they did support, which was not of God. Tragically, false apostles, with their false doctrine, which cause people to be eternally lost, are kept in operation, and most of the time in grand style, not by the liquor business, or the drug business, or the gambling industry, but, instead, by Christians. It is tragic, but true! (Mat. 7:13-27).

NOTES

TRANSGRESSIONS AND SINS

The phrase of Verse 9, *"But you have delivered your soul,"* proclaims the Preacher of the Gospel who heard from Heaven, and then delivered what the Lord told him to deliver. The response of the people is not his responsibility, although he certainly desires that they respond favorably. His responsibility is that he faithfully deliver the Word. To be sure, Ezekiel *"delivered his soul."*

The phrase of Verse 10, *"If our transgressions and our sins be upon us, and we pine away in them, how should we then live?"* addresses itself to the results of *"transgressions and sins."*

Scorn, incredulity, and derision had been heaped upon the Prophet when he told of the coming Judgment. The people had trusted in the promises of the false prophets (Ezek. 13:6). Now they stand face-to-face with the fulfillment of the Prophet's words.

The question, *"How should we then live?"* proclaims the hopelessness of the people, inasmuch as they now realize the seriousness of their sin.

To be sure, every single person who has not faithfully followed the Lord will one day stand in this same position. The far greater majority have trusted false prophets, and, as always, sooner or later, will reap the bitter results.

Consequently, Satan takes full advantage of such hopelessness, telling them that there is no way out; however, the Holy Spirit, even in the next Verse, shows that it's never too late to turn to God.

REPENTANCE

Verse 11 says several things, and, as always, very important things. We learn from these Passages certain things about the very heart of God: Who He is and What He does! We would do well to carefully read and carefully heed what He says.

NO PLEASURE IN THE DEATH OF THE WICKED

Verse 11 plainly tells us this; therefore, every effort is made by the Holy Spirit to turn the wicked from his sin and transgression and to the Lord, thereby finding life.

Even though the *"wicked"* are opposed to God, have rebelled against God, with many doing so even evidencing great anger toward God, still, the Lord takes no pleasure whatsoever in their spiritual wreckage and the ultimate loss of their eternal souls. The truth is:

"God so loved the world, that He gave His only Begotten Son, that whosoever believes in Him, should not perish, but have Everlasting Life" (Jn. 3:16).

If a person wants to know what God is like, he need only study the four Gospels, as it regards the Life of Christ. As one studies Christ, one is studying God, for Christ is God! We learn from Him, Who He was, what He did, and how He conducted Himself, as to exactly what God is like. To say the least, it is a beautiful picture. It is a picture of God!

BUT THAT THE WICKED TURN FROM HIS WAY AND LIVE

In order for this to be done, God, as stated, has given Heaven's best, and we refer to the Lord Jesus Christ.

As well, the Lord has set in the Church *"Apostles, Prophets, Evangelists, Pastors and Teachers"* (Eph. 4:11). Despite all the false apostles and the false prophets, there are some who are true. The Lord works through these, whomever they might be, to help take the Gospel to the world. In fact, as it regards all who will heed the Voice of the Lord, the Lord, at this very moment, is doing great things to get the Gospel to every person on the face of the Earth. One might say that the Lord is working twenty-four hours a day, seven days a week, for He never sleeps, to bring all of this about. It is for the express purpose that *"the wicked turn from his way and live."*

TURN YE, TURN YE FROM YOUR EVIL WAYS

This is a plea for Repentance. There has never been any other way! What the Lord demanded of Cain, which it seems Cain never heeded, He demands of all, and, that is that they repent. Tragically, the Message of Repentance is not pleasant or even desirable by a self-righteous Church. With the modern Church, Repentance is the ending of Ministry, while with the Lord, it is the beginning of Ministry (Rev. 2:5).

Repentance is ugly, because it confesses sin, which is extremely distasteful to self-righteousness, because it is difficult for it to even admit that such could be possible within its ranks; however, such thinking is the result of conceit, and not of God. The truth is, all need to repent, both the Believer and the unbeliever. To five of the seven Churches of Asia, the Message of Christ was *"Repent"* (Rev., Chpts. 2-3).

FOR WHY WILL YOU DIE. . . ?

This seems to be a sob of the Holy Spirit, considering what the Lord has done to bring men to Himself.

Actually, this question is asked by the Holy Spirit and is directed to every individual who has ever spurned the appeal of the Lord.

(12) "THEREFORE, THOU SON OF MAN, SAY UNTO THE CHILDREN OF YOUR PEOPLE, THE RIGHTEOUSNESS OF THE RIGHTEOUS SHALL NOT DELIVER HIM IN THE DAY OF HIS TRANSGRESSION: AS FOR THE WICKEDNESS OF THE WICKED, HE SHALL NOT FALL THEREBY IN THE DAY THAT HE TURNS FROM HIS WICKEDNESS; NEITHER SHALL THE RIGHTEOUS BE ABLE TO LIVE FOR HIS RIGHTEOUSNESS IN THE DAY THAT HE SINS.

(13) "WHEN I SHALL SAY TO THE RIGHTEOUS, THAT HE SHALL SURELY LIVE; IF HE TRUST TO HIS OWN RIGHTEOUSNESS, AND COMMIT INIQUITY, ALL HIS RIGHTEOUSNESSES SHALL NOT BE REMEMBERED; BUT FOR HIS INIQUITY THAT HE HAS COMMITTED, HE SHALL DIE FOR IT.

(14) "AGAIN, WHEN I SAY UNTO THE WICKED, YOU SHALL SURELY DIE; IF HE TURN FROM HIS SIN, AND DO THAT WHICH IS LAWFUL AND RIGHT;

(15) "IF THE WICKED RESTORE THE PLEDGE, GIVE AGAIN THAT HE HAD ROBBED, WALK IN THE STATUTES OF LIFE, WITHOUT COMMITTING INIQUITY; HE SHALL SURELY LIVE, HE SHALL NOT DIE.

(16) "NONE OF HIS SINS THAT HE HAS COMMITTED SHALL BE MENTIONED UNTO HIM: HE HAS DONE THAT WHICH

IS LAWFUL AND RIGHT; HE SHALL SURELY LIVE.

(17) "YET THE CHILDREN OF YOUR PEOPLE SAY, THE WAY OF THE LORD IS NOT EQUAL: BUT AS FOR THEM, THEIR WAY IS NOT EQUAL.

(18) "WHEN THE RIGHTEOUS TURNS FROM HIS RIGHTEOUSNESS, AND COMMITS INIQUITY, HE SHALL EVEN DIE THEREBY.

(19) "BUT IF THE WICKED TURNS FROM HIS WICKEDNESS, AND DO THAT WHICH IS LAWFUL AND RIGHT, HE SHALL LIVE THEREBY.

(20) "YET YOU SAY, THE WAY OF THE LORD IS NOT EQUAL. O YE HOUSE OF ISRAEL, I WILL JUDGE YOU EVERY ONE AFTER HIS WAYS."

The overview is:

1. The conversion of Zaccheus (Lk. 19:1-10) illustrates the power of the new life in Christ to fulfill the requirements of the Moral Law.

2. Perfect love beams in Verse 11, and perfect justice in Verse 20.

3. We find from these Passages that the Way of Lord is unequivocally *"equal."*

RIGHTEOUSNESS AND WICKEDNESS

Two extremely important Messages are given to us in Verse 12. The first Message concerns the righteous. It is unequivocally clear:

The phrase, *"Therefore, thou son of man, say unto the children of your people, The righteousness of the righteous shall not deliver him in the day of his transgression,"* proclaims the fact, and clearly so, that if a righteous man, which of course is one who has been Born-Again, turn from his righteousness, and commences to live in sin and iniquity, his previous righteousness will not save him. The last phrase of this Verse clearly states *"Neither shall the righteous be able to live for his righteousness in the day that he sins."*

This completely destroys the unscriptural doctrine of *"unconditional eternal security."*

If a Believer ceases to believe, thereby turning his back on God, he is no longer looked at by God as a Believer, and, if he remains in that condition, he will die eternally lost.

Whether it was Israel of old, or modern Believers, the way of Salvation has always been the same. Before the Cross, it was faith in Christ, i.e., *"the coming Redeemer,"* typified by the Sacrifices, which Faith saved the individual. While those in Old Testament times looked forward to Christ and the Cross, those who are saved presently look backward to Christ and the Cross. It was a prophetic Jesus then, while it is an historical Jesus at present.

It's *"faith"* that gets the believing sinner in, and it's *"faith"* which keeps the Believer in. If faith is lost, which will always result in the person going deep into sin, such constitutes a lost condition.

TURNING FROM WICKEDNESS

The second great truth found in Verse 12 is found in the phrase, *"As for the wickedness of the wicked, he shall not fall thereby in the day that he turns from his wickedness."*

As the righteous cannot continue to be saved, if he turns from his righteousness, likewise, the wicked will not be lost, if he turns from his wickedness.

This tells us that past wickedness will not stop anyone from being saved, if they will truly turn to the Lord.

It doesn't matter who a person is, or what a person has done, if that person will turn to Christ, irrespective of the degree of their wickedness, the Lord will always readily receive such an individual, and will receive them with open arms (Mat. 11:28-30; Jn. 7:37; Rev. 22:17).

BLASPHEMING THE HOLY SPIRIT

Some may argue that if one has blasphemed the Holy Spirit, that they then cannot be saved. Of course, that is true; however, if a person has really blasphemed the Holy Spirit, there will be no desire on the part of that person to be saved, no desire to come to Christ, no effort to be saved. The idea that some have tried to be saved, and have pleaded with the Lord to save them, but cannot be saved, and because they had blasphemed the Holy Spirit, is not Scriptural, and, in fact, has never happened.

If anyone would do that, they're simply registering unbelief, meaning that the problem is on their part and not on the part of

God. If they will sincerely turn to the Lord, He will always be faithful to save.

The very idea of a person wanting to be saved comes from the Holy Spirit. And to be sure, the Holy Spirit would never convict a heart of the need of Salvation and then refuse to provide such Salvation.

No! If a person has really blasphemed the Holy Spirit, that person will have no desire to come to Christ, no desire to serve Christ, at least in a Biblical way. In fact, in their apostasy, they will probably think they are saved, even as the Pharisees did when they blasphemed the Holy Spirit by claiming that Christ was casting out demons by using the power of demon spirits (Mat. 12:24-37).

The Scripture emphatically states that anyone who desires to come to the Lord, even as Ezekiel here proclaims, irrespective of their past, will be warmly received by the Lord, and will be gloriously saved. The Lord is ever ready (I Cor. 6:9-11).

PAST RIGHTEOUSNESS

The phrase of Verse 13, *"If he trust to his own righteousness, and commit iniquity, all his righteousnesses shall not be remembered,"* presents a truth that must be heeded.

The idea of this Verse is that the individual who thinks he can trust his past righteousness to save him, when he has committed sin, and continues in that sin, the Holy Spirit plainly says here that his past *"righteousnesses shall not be remembered."* As already stated, this completely refutes the unscriptural doctrine of unconditional eternal security.

As well, this Scripture also refutes the idea, as thought by many, that good and bad are weighed against each other, with the side with most coming out the winner. The Holy Spirit emphatically denies this erroneous thinking.

What has taken place in the past regarding an individual is certainly important; however, whether it be Righteousness or unrighteousness, still, that which he presently *"has"* and presently *"is"* is the determining factor.

THE PROOF OF REDEMPTION

Verses 14 through 16 proclaim the fact that, if a person has truly turned from past wickedness, in which they can expect the blessing and favor of the Lord, such will show up in their daily lives by Godly living. These Passages aren't teaching a *"salvation by works,"* but rather that righteous claims will translate into righteous living. The idea that one can claim salvation, even as millions do, without any change in their lifestyle is completely refuted in these Verses of Scripture. If there is anything that the Gospel of Christ does, it is that it changes men.

In other words, the thief quits stealing, the liar quits lying, and the immoral ceases the immorality.

This doesn't mean that such individuals instantly become perfect. In fact, some new Believers may continue to have problems in some certain areas; however, if they will look to Christ and the Cross, victory will be theirs (Rom. 6:3-14). But irrespective of a problem or two they may continue to have, the change in their lives, still, will be absolutely obvious.

JUSTIFICATION BY FAITH

The phrase of Verse 16, *"None of his sins that he has committed shall be mentioned unto him,"* constitutes *"Justification by Faith."* These sins, whatever they may have been, are not mentioned anymore, because in the mind of God they do not exist, because such a person is now in Christ.

Regrettably, many Christians do not seem to understand, or even believe this statement, in that they feel free to bring up that which the Lord has washed, cleansed, and taken away. Such does despite to the Spirit of Grace, but is a sin committed by many Christians too soon and too often!

Due to the seriousness of this offense, please allow us to say it again:

To bring up sins and trespasses which had once been in the lives of others, which have been properly repented of, washed, cleansed, and forgiven by the Lord, constitutes a grievous sin. To do such casts doubt on the efficacy of the Blood of Christ and, as stated, does despite to the Spirit of Grace (Heb. 10:29).

The phrase of Verse 16, *"He shall surely live,"* constitutes Salvation, which negates any spiritual death. This constitutes the greatest thing that can happen to any human heart and life.

EQUAL WAYS

The phrase of Verse 17, *"Yet the children of your people say, The way of the Lord is not equal,"* constitutes the complaint that man has had against God even from the very beginning.

Israel, as most, were claiming that their righteousness and unrighteousness should be balanced one against the other. They construed the Ways of the Lord as unequal, inasmuch as He did not judge in that manner. In fact, it was not God's Ways which were unequal, but their ways. Actually, as the Lord has given His Word in these Passages, nothing could be more equal than that given by the Lord.

Even in the practical application of life, that which they were contending, the balancing of one against the other, does not hold true.

For instance, if a man lives 1,000 days without taking poison, and then on day 1,001 takes poison, all the previous days free of poison will not assuage the results. Thus, it is true of the righteous who live righteously for a period of time, and then forsake that Righteousness, thereby going into sin. The sin, if not repented of and forsaken, will ultimately destroy them, and irrespective of their previous Righteousness.

As well, if a man has been deathly ill for many years, and then a medicine is given to him which instantly restores his health, no one in their right mind would deny that health to him.

Likewise, when the wicked man turns from his wicked ways, and irrespective of how long he has existed in that condition, and begins to serve the Lord, no one can legitimately deny him that right. To do so is, in fact, to deny themselves!

TURNING FROM RIGHTEOUSNESS

Verse 18 makes it very clear that no matter how long a person may live righteously before God, if that person turns from that righteousness, and begins to live in iniquity, which means they have abandoned their faith, they will lose their soul.

Israel's contention was that inasmuch as they were *"God's chosen,"* and the recipients of the Law, and the people of the Prophets, that such should be balanced against any present sin; therefore, they called the Ways of the Lord *"unequal"*!

Also, some were contending that they had not sinned, but were suffering for the sins of their fathers.

The Holy Spirit is emphatic that the present condition is what counts with God and what should count with man.

Consequently, if the Righteous turn from their Righteousness, and begin to commit iniquity, and refuse to repent, they will be judged according to that present position.

Verse 19 proclaims that the Lord will judge the *"wicked"* exactly as He does the *"Righteous,"* all according to their present status. If the wicked man repents, the Lord will instantly save, wiping out all the past wickedness.

I WILL JUDGE YOU AFTER YOUR WAYS

The phrase of Verse 20, *"I will judge you every one after his ways,"* proclaims to us perfect justice. It is a judgment and justice that are equal, fair, and right, in that *"every one is judged after his ways,"* which shows no partiality. Men, and especially religious men, are exceptionally clever in twisting the Word of God in order for it to say something that it, in fact, does not say. Much of the world has died lost because of that very attitude.

Men are so prone to say regarding spiritual matters, *"Well, I think . . . ,"* as if it matters what they think. It is what the Word of God says, and not what men think.

Most of the human family devise their own Salvation while ignoring God. They, as Israel, think they know more than God, or else they just flatly refuse to believe Him, or else they think that by ignoring Him, or claiming that He does not exist, that such will exempt them from the coming Judgment.

However, such is not to be! All will be judged, and irrespective as to whom they may be or where they live or what they believe, all according to the Word of God.

It is even more tragic when one considers that even the majority of Christians who claim to know God and believe Him, little adhere to His Word. They bow to conventional wisdom or to whatever way the religious political wind is blowing. Very few strictly adhere to the Word of God, and because of self-will, man fear, or the desire to be accepted by others.

To strictly adhere to the Word of God will mean being ostracized by the world, and almost all of the Church. It can, as well, mean, in some cases, the desertion of one's own family. However, Jesus said: *"If any man come to Me, and hate not his father, and mother, and wife, and children, and brothers, and sisters, yes, and his own life also, he cannot be My Disciple"* (Lk. 14:26).

(The word *"hate"* means that one must prefer Christ above all others.)

(21) "AND IT CAME TO PASS IN THE TWELFTH YEAR OF OUR CAPTIVITY, IN THE TENTH MONTH, IN THE FIFTH DAY OF THE MONTH, THAT ONE WHO HAD ESCAPED OUT OF JERUSALEM CAME UNTO ME, SAYING, THE CITY IS SMITTEN.

(22) "NOW THE HAND OF THE LORD WAS UPON ME IN THE EVENING, AFORE HE WHO WAS ESCAPED CAME; AND HAD OPENED MY MOUTH, UNTIL HE CAME TO ME IN THE MORNING; AND MY MOUTH WAS OPENED, AND I WAS NO MORE DUMB.

(23) "THEN THE WORD OF THE LORD CAME UNTO ME, SAYING,

(24) "SON OF MAN, THEY WHO INHABIT THOSE WASTES OF THE LAND OF ISRAEL SPEAK, SAYING, ABRAHAM WAS ONE, AND HE INHERITED THE LAND: BUT WE ARE MANY; THE LAND IS GIVEN US FOR INHERITANCE.

(25) "WHEREFORE SAY UNTO THEM, THUS SAITH THE LORD GOD; YOU EAT WITH THE BLOOD, AND LIFT UP YOUR EYES TOWARD YOUR IDOLS, AND SHED BLOOD: AND SHALL YOU POSSESS THE LAND?

(26) "YOU STAND UPON YOUR SWORD, YOU WORK ABOMINATION, AND YOU DEFILE EVERY ONE HIS NEIGHBOR'S WIFE: AND SHALL YOU POSSESS THE LAND?"

The synopsis is:

1. The contention of the people, as it regards the Fall of Jerusalem, reveals the unbelief, pride, blindness, self-righteousness, rebellion, and self-will of the natural heart.

2. Both companies, those in Jerusalem and those in Exile, claim to be the people of God; they publicly worshipped Him; were proud of their Church position, so to speak; but they lived in idolatry and moral abomination.

3. The faith that said, *"The land is given us for an inheritance,"* was a proud and carnal faith. It was not faith that God would recognize. Judgment upon their iniquities, and not blessing, was their due.

4. Though proudly claiming to be children of Abraham, and, therefore, children of God, they were idolatrous, self-confident, violent, and impure.

THE FALL OF JERUSALEM

The time of this Prophecy was some months after the actual Fall of Jerusalem.

It may seem strange that it would take this long for one to come to Tel-Abib with the news of the Fall of the city; however, Tel-Abib was not on the high road of commerce or travel, and, as well, all previous communications, as it regards Jerusalem, had been cut off by the presence of the Chaldean armies in Judah.

The phrase of Verse 21, *"One who had escaped out of the Jerusalem,"* does not shed any light as to who the individual was. Some have conjectured that it may have been Baruch, who was sent by Jeremiah to bear the tidings of his brother Prophet. Jeremiah 45:5 lends some credence to this possibility.

Tradition ascribes to Baruch a prominent part as a teacher among the Exiles of Babylon, shortly after the destruction of Jerusalem; therefore, even though we cannot know for sure, quite possibly this was Baruch.

The phrase, *"The city is smitten,"* even though said by the Messenger, whoever he was, is given as a sob by the Holy Spirit. How so unnecessary this was, but yet, it was done only after the Lord had exhausted every means to bring the people to Repentance, but to no avail!

PROPHECY TO THE EXILES

The phrase of Verse 22, *"And my mouth was opened and I was no more dumb,"* refers back to Ezekiel 24:26-27. Therefore, if we are to go back to the last date given, which is the *"ninth year, in the tenth month"* (Ezek. 24:1), as it refers to the silence of the Prophet regarding the Exiles, we would be speaking of three years of silence, at least as it regarded Judah and the Exiles. However, there is a possibility that the Prophecy contained in the Twenty-fourth Chapter, and regarding Judah, could have taken several weeks or months; therefore, his silence regarding Judah may have seen somewhat less than three years.

At any rate, during this time, he continued to prophesy regarding foreign powers, to which we have already addressed.

THE INHERITANCE

The phrase of Verse 24, *"Son of man, they who inhabit those wastes of the land of Israel speak, saying,"* present the argument of this ungodly remnant.

They said, *"Abraham was one and he inherited the land: but we are many; and the land is given us for inheritance."*

They argued that if a mighty nation was born of one man, Abraham, and that Abraham's seed possessed and held the Land of Israel, how much more powerful a nation could spring out of the many sons of Abraham, whom the Babylonian king had left in Judah! However, as stated, the faith that said, *"the land is given us for inheritance,"* was not a Spiritual or Scriptural faith, but rather a proud and carnal faith, and, as such, would not be honored by God. Judgment upon their iniquities and not blessings would be the result of this carnal, and thereby ungodly, thinking.

These were boastful claims, and constituted the *"bad figs"* of Jeremiah's Parable, who, in effect, were the least worthy representatives of the seed of Abraham, actually, the assassins of Gedaliah (Jer. 41:1-2).

ABOMINATION

Verses 25 and 26 proclaim, through the phrase, *"You work abomination,"* that this referred not only to past abomination, but to the continued working of such.

The Holy Spirit, through the Prophet Ezekiel, even though many hundreds of miles away from destroyed Judah, still, speaks the same thing as the Prophet Jeremiah had

NOTES

prophesied. Despite the Judgment, this *"remnant"* continued to be idol worshippers, rebels against God, dependent upon their own feeble military preparation, which bordered on idiocy, inasmuch as they were a defeated people.

The question is then asked again, especially considering their present spiritual state, and the ridiculous presumption presented, *"And shall you possess the land?"*

Once again, the answer is obvious!

All of this proves that if one will not accept the pleadings of the Holy Spirit, judgment, miracles, or anything else, will seldom bring the individual to God; therefore, Judgment serves more as a purifying process than the Salvation of souls.

(27) "SAY THOU THUS UNTO THEM, THUS SAITH THE LORD GOD; AS I LIVE, SURELY THEY WHO ARE IN THE WASTES SHALL FALL BY THE SWORD, AND HIM WHO IS IN THE OPEN FIELD WILL I GIVE TO THE BEASTS TO BE DEVOURED, AND THEY WHO BE IN THE FORTS AND IN THE CAVES SHALL DIE OF THE PESTILENCE.

(28) "FOR I WILL LAY THE LAND MOST DESOLATE, AND THE POMP OF HER STRENGTH SHALL CEASE; AND THE MOUNTAINS OF ISRAEL SHALL BE DESOLATE, THAT NONE SHALL PASS THROUGH.

(29) "THEN SHALL THEY KNOW THAT I AM THE LORD, WHEN I HAVE LAID THE LAND MOST DESOLATE BECAUSE OF ALL THEIR ABOMINATIONS WHICH THEY HAVE COMMITTED.

(30) "ALSO, THOU SON OF MAN, THE CHILDREN OF YOUR PEOPLE STILL ARE TALKING AGAINST YOU BY THE WALLS AND IN THE DOORS OF THE HOUSES, AND SPEAK ONE TO ANOTHER, EVERY ONE TO HIS BROTHER, SAYING, COME, I PRAY YOU, AND HEAR WHAT IS THE WORD THAT COMES FORTH FORM THE LORD.

(31) "AND THEY COME UNTO YOU AS THE PEOPLE COME, AND THEY SIT BEFORE YOU AS MY PEOPLE, AND THEY HEAR YOUR WORDS, BUT THEY WILL NOT DO THEM: FOR WITH THEIR MOUTH THEY SHOW MUCH LOVE, BUT

THEIR HEART GOES AFTER THEIR COVETOUSNESS.

(32) "AND, LO, YOU ARE UNTO THEM AS A VERY LOVELY SONG OF ONE WHO HAS A PLEASANT VOICE, AND CAN PLAY WELL ON AN INSTRUMENT: FOR THEY HEAR YOUR WORDS, BUT THEY DO THEM NOT.

(33) "AND WHEN THIS COMES TO PASS, (LO, IT WILL COME,) THEN SHALL THEY KNOW THAT A PROPHET HAS BEEN AMONG THEM."

The exegesis is:

1. *"With their mouth they showed love,"* but it didn't come from their heart, showing that their profession was merely surface.

2. The Exiles were proud of their Prophet Ezekiel. They admired his preaching, and crowded to hear him, but did not for a moment intend any change of conduct. If his straightforward preaching effected no change, and because of their hardened hearts, how can we expect the modern pablum which passes for preaching to effect a change!

3. Curiosity, and not Repentance, prompted their desire to hear the Prophet.

4. The Holy Spirit said that their *"hearts did go after covetousness."*

THE JUDGMENT OF GOD

Verses 27 through 29 proclaim the answer of the Lord, as it regards the demand of the Exiles that they had a greater right to the land than even did Abraham. The answer of the Lord was straight and to the point:

The phrase of Verse 27 says, *"Say thou thus unto them, Thus saith the Lord GOD; As I live, surely they who are in the wastes shall fall by the sword."* The description continues to speak of judgment in every form, even to being attacked by *"beasts."*

The Lord further says in Verse 28, *"For I will lay the land most desolate, and the pomp of her strength shall cease."* Thus was the destruction of the Land of Israel, which was once the Glory of all lands.

The Lord has at His disposal any and all things. He can use a heathen army, exactly as He used Nebuchadnezzar, and He could put down a heathen army, which thought to usurp authority over the Word of God, namely, the Egyptians. He could use the beasts of the field, if He so desired, or the horror of *"pestilence."* In truth, everything is at His disposal, and for His use. So what He wants done, as ought to be obvious, will be done.

To be frank, the people of Judah and Jerusalem believed the things I've just stated. But there were two things they didn't believe:

First of all, they did not believe they were nearly as wicked and sinful as the Prophets Jeremiah and Ezekiel said they were. As already stated, they were trying to balance out their lives, and they always concluded, as all do, that the good outweighed the bad. On that basis, they thought that God would spare them, with Him revealing to them that He does not function on that basis.

And then they reasoned, that inasmuch as this Land was, in fact, God's Land, and that the Temple was His Temple, and that He dwelt between the Mercy Seat and the Cherubim, and above all of that, that they were the people of the Law, who had given the world the Prophets, thereby reasoning that the Lord, and because of these things, would never bring judgment upon them.

The cause of judgment is sin which continues to be repeated, but which refuses Repentance. In other words, the person refuses to see himself or herself as they actually are. The Word of God and the Holy Spirit proclaim to us what we are, and if the Preacher faithfully delivers the Word, there will be no doubt; but unfortunately, most prefer to go to Churches where the Word of God is not really preached, but something else, and then they can feel at ease.

COVETOUSNESS

The word *"against"* in Verse 30 should have been translated *"of"* because these Exiles, it seems, were proud of their Prophet Ezekiel, even admiring his preaching, at least after a fashion. As well, they crowded to hear him, but not for a moment did they intend to change their conduct.

The phrase of Verse 31 says, *"They hear your words, but they will not do them: for with their mouth they show much love, but their heart goes after their covetousness."*

The *"covetousness"* referred to a desire for things which were not of the Lord. In other words, they were not interested in the things of the Lord, or the Will of God, desiring only what pleased them.

Them with *"their mouth showing much love"* characterizes them talking the talk, but not walking the walk. How much does this resemble the modern Church? I personally think that the Church of today is in worse condition, spiritually speaking, than even the Judah and Jerusalem of old, which were destroyed. Israel was a nation and thereby suffered destruction of their national identity. The Church is different, but yet with many similarities to Israel of old.

The Church cannot lose its national identity as it regards a sovereign State, because it is not a sovereign State. It is made up of individuals, wherever they might be, who claim to be *"born again."*

But the Church can lose its national identity in respect to its influence. But the influence is always lost in a way that is the very opposite of what many think.

It's not that the world rejects the Church, but rather that it accepts the Church. And to be sure, it will not accept the Church, unless the Church has become like the world. And that's our present problem!

It is the business of the Church to preach the Gospel, which in its most simple form points out what man's problem actually is, which is sin, and what the solution is, which is Jesus Christ and Him Crucified (I Cor. 1:23; 2:2). But what is the modern Church preaching?

As we've repeatedly stated, the modern Church is little more than a glorified social center with religious overtones. As well, the Pastor is a social worker who doubles as a motivational speaker. While what is preached is very pleasing to the ear, in truth it will set no captive free, because it's not the Gospel of Jesus Christ.

Man doesn't need to be motivated, he needs Salvation from sin, which can only come about by the *"preaching of the Cross"* (I Cor. 1:17-18, 21). But the Cross, regrettably, is little preached.

THE PROPHET

The phrase of Verse 32, *"A very lovely song,"* refers to the people coming to hear Ezekiel as they would to hear a hired singer at a banquet. The Prophet's words passed over them and left no lasting impression.

The phrase, *"For they hear your words, but they do them not,"* proclaims Ezekiel as merely being the instrument, but the Words were from God. The tragedy presently is, very few modern Christians even have the opportunity to hear the true Word of the Lord. Sadder yet, the people love to have it just like it presently is.

In some ways, the Prophet mirrored his Master, the coming Messiah. The people said of Christ, *"Never man spoke like this Man"* (Jn. 7:46), but they would not obey His Words.

"We've a story to tell the nations
"That shall turn their hearts to the right;
"A story of truth and mercy,
"A story of peace and light."

"We've a song to be sung to the nations
"That shall lift their hearts to the Lord;
"A song that shall conquer evil,
"And shatter the spear and sword."

"We've a message to give to the nations
"That the Lord Who reigns above,
"Has sent us His Son to save us,
"And show us that God is love."

"We've a Saviour to show to the nations
"Who the path of sorrow has trod,
"That all of the world's great people
"Might come to the truth of God."

CHAPTER 34

(1) "AND THE WORD OF THE LORD CAME UNTO ME, SAYING,

(2) "SON OF MAN, PROPHESY AGAINST THE SHEPHERDS OF ISRAEL, PROPHESY, AND SAY UNTO THEM, THUS SAITH THE LORD GOD UNTO THE SHEPHERDS; WOE BE TO THE SHEPHERDS OF ISRAEL WHO DO FEED THEMSELVES! SHOULD NOT THE SHEPHERDS FEED THE FLOCKS?

(3) "YOU EAT THE FAT, AND YOU CLOTHE YOURSELVES WITH THE WOOL, YOU KILL THEM WHO ARE FED: BUT YOU FEED NOT THE FLOCK.

(4) "THE DISEASED HAVE YOU NOT STRENGTHENED, NEITHER HAVE YOU HEALED THAT WHICH WAS SICK, NEITHER HAVE YOU BOUND UP THAT WHICH WAS BROKEN, NEITHER HAVE YOU BROUGHT AGAIN THAT WHICH WAS DRIVEN AWAY, NEITHER HAVE YOU SOUGHT THAT WHICH WAS LOST; BUT WITH FORCE AND WITH CRUELTY HAVE YOU RULED THEM.

(5) "AND THEY WERE SCATTERED, BECAUSE THERE IS NO SHEPHERD: AND THEY BECAME MEAT TO ALL THE BEASTS OF THE FIELD, WHEN THEY WERE SCATTERED.

(6) "MY SHEEP WANDERED THROUGH ALL THE MOUNTAINS, AND UPON EVERY HIGH HILL: YES, MY FLOCK WAS SCATTERED UPON ALL THE FACE OF THE EARTH, AND NONE DID SEARCH OR SEEK AFTER THEM.

(7) "THEREFORE, YOU SHEPHERDS, HEAR THE WORD OF THE LORD;

(8) "AS I LIVE, SAITH THE LORD GOD, SURELY BECAUSE MY FLOCK BECAME A PREY, AND MY FLOCK BECAME MEAT TO EVERY BEAST OF THE FIELD, BECAUSE THERE WAS NO SHEPHERD, NEITHER DID MY SHEPHERDS SEARCH FOR MY FLOCK, BUT THE SHEPHERDS FED THEMSELVES, AND FED NOT MY FLOCK;

(9) "THEREFORE, O YE SHEPHERDS, HEAR THE WORD OF THE LORD;"

The diagram is:

1. In this Message, the Holy Spirit contrasts the false shepherds with the True Shepherd, and the false sheep with the true sheep.

2. False shepherds feed themselves; the True Shepherd feeds the sheep.

3. All of this should be a warning to modern Preachers, because the admonitions given then apply now as well!

THE SHEPHERDS

There is no date regarding this particular Prophecy; therefore, it may have immediately followed the Prophecy of the preceding Chapter.

This Chapter has as its New Testament counterpart John, Chapter 10, and graphically outlines the Lord's earthly Ministry, which would transpire at His First Advent.

Not only does this Chapter mark out the True Shepherd, the Lord Jesus Christ, but, as well, marks out the restoration of Israel.

The Prophet had been admonished by the Holy Spirit: *"Therefore you shall hear the Word at My mouth, and warn them from Me"* (Ezek. 33:7), and, faithfully, he will carry out this command.

The greatest need on the face of the Earth, is for Preachers of the Gospel to truly hear from God, and, therefore, faithfully deliver what they hear to the people.

There are presently many voices in the land crying that they have heard from the Lord, with only a precious few who truly have!

The phrase of Verse 2, *"Son of man, prophesy against the shepherds of Israel,"* refers to the rulers of Judah, more specifically the last four kings; however, its general meaning definitely includes spiritual leaders, so-called, of any stripe.

The Kings of Judah, ideally, were to follow in the footsteps of David, as he was ever held up as the example (II Ki. 19:34; 20:6). As David was to serve as the example for the continuing Kings of Judah, likewise, the greater Son of David is to presently serve as the example and the *"Chief Shepherd"* (I Pet. 5:4).

It's one thing to prophesy against whatever, but something else again to prophesy against the leaders, which Ezekiel was commanded to do. It is the same presently!

To prophesy against false doctrine, even as the Lord here commands, and also against those who peddle the false doctrine, is almost unheard of presently. There is, thank the Lord, a lone voice here and there. But virtually all pulpits are silent regarding this necessity.

Just as surely as the Lord commanded Ezekiel to prophesy *"against the shepherds of Israel,"* he has commanded this Ministry (Jimmy Swaggart Ministries) to do the same thing, as it regards the present spiritual declension.

The criteria for Church presently is *"big numbers and big money."* Christlikeness, Righteousness, and Holiness have no place in modern theology, which means that such are not even recognized by God as being *"Church."* It is something else altogether!

There once was a time that people could be saved in Baptist, Methodist, or Nazarene

Churches. While that is still true, for a few, it is only a few.

There was a time that Pentecostal Denominations, such as the Assemblies of God, the Church of God, and the Foursquare, plus others, held up the Standard of Righteousness. While some few still do, the truth is, the far greater majority, as it regards these ranks, are no different than their Baptist and Methodist counterparts.

The Charismatic world, which is extremely large, is almost altogether in the Word of Faith camp. Once again, there are a few exceptions, but not many.

The truth is, it is not even possible for a person to be saved in most Churches. More scarce still are the Churches where Believers are still Baptized with the Holy Spirit, with the evidence of speaking with other tongues (Acts 2:4). In all Churches, irrespective of the name on the door, one is hard put to find a pulpit where the Cross is faithfully preached!

THE APOSTLE PAUL AND THE MODERN CHURCH

What would Paul say were he alive now, as it regards the modern Church? Anyone who is a beginning student of the Word of God knows that Paul *"preached the Cross"* (Rom. 6:3-14; I Cor. 1:17-18, 21, 23; 2:2, 5; Gal. 6:14; Eph. 2:13-18; Col. 2:14-15). As well, it is obvious in the Book of Acts, and the Epistles, that Paul also *"preached the Baptism with the Holy Spirit, with the evidence of speaking with other tongues"* (Acts 19:1-7). It is also obvious, that the Apostle *"preached separation from the world"* (II Cor. 6:14-18).

But what is most of the modern Church preaching?

Instead of preaching the Cross, it's preaching motivation. Instead of preaching the Baptism with the Holy Spirit, it is preaching ways to get rich. Instead of preaching separation from the world, it has joined the world, adopted its ways, and is now accepted by the world.

The phrase of Verse 2, *"They do feed themselves,"* as it regards the false shepherds, proclaims the fact that they had no interest whatsoever in the flock, but only in enriching themselves. How much does this characterize the modern Ministry?

To be frank, there have never been many True Shepherds in comparison to the number of false shepherds. When Paul was imprisoned in Rome, he strongly desired to send a Preacher of the Gospel to Philippi, but stated, *"I have no man like-minded, who will naturally care for your state. For all seek their own, not the things which are Jesus Christ's"* (Phil. 2:20-21).

The modern Word of Faith Ministry claims that if their teaching is followed, then the person will get rich. The truth is, the only ones who get rich are these false shepherds, and at the expense of the flock that is fleeced. As the false shepherds of old, their only motive is to *"feed themselves."*

FORCE AND CRUELTY

The Holy Spirit, in Verses 3 and 4, delineates what these false shepherds were doing. The statement is closed with the phrase in Verse 4, *"But with force and with cruelty have you ruled them."*

The *"diseased"* of Verse 4 refers to weak sheep, while the *"sick"* refers to those who are suffering from more definite maladies.

The *"broken"* are those which have fallen from a rock or some such precipice, and thus maimed themselves. Each case required its appropriate treatment.

As well, the word *"neither,"* used four times, should not be overlooked. The idea is that the Holy Spirit notes each particular need, and the required care for that need by True Shepherds, which these, as described by Ezekiel, were not!

The last four Kings of Judah, following Godly Josiah, did not rule with love, care, and concern, but instead *"with force and with cruelty."*

Even though the *"scheme"* is well laid out, the present methods used by many modern Preachers to get money out of people can be labeled as none other than *"forceful and cruel."*

Whenever a Preacher says *"God told me,"* that's a heady thing! If the Lord has, in fact, related something to a Preacher, or anyone for that matter, they should certainly take to heart that which the Lord has said, and do with it what He intends; however, sadly and regrettably, most of that which claims to be of the Lord is anything but the Lord. In other words, the Lord has not spoken.

Many gimmicks are used; however, the greatest gimmick of all is *"The Lord told me,"* and then, they will relate the great cornucopia of riches which are going to come to them if they will give their money, etc.

Let it ever be known that the Lord cannot bless error, and He certainly cannot bless lies. In fact, there is no worse sin than Preachers lying to people, trying to get their money, and making the Lord a part of their scheme. They would be much better off to go into a bank, and level a .38 caliber revolver at the teller's head, and take that money, rather than include God in their nefarious schemes. Let me give you an example:

I do not personally believe that one single Preacher of the Word of Faith doctrine who has abundantly claimed that the Lord has told them all types of things, and especially about money, has, in fact, ever heard from the Lord, at least in the manner in which it is claimed. As stated, the Lord does not bless error and false doctrine in any capacity.

Do you honestly think that the Lord would have spoken to the Judaizers of Paul's day, who were trying to destroy the Message of the Cross, giving them all type of leading and guidance? I don't think so!

When Preachers stand before a congregation and tell them that the Lord has just spoken to them, that all who give $1,000 will have their homes paid for by the end of the year, or all the bills they presently have, etc., I would have to dogmatically state that they haven't heard from the Lord.

These type of *"schemes"* are carried out constantly, all for the purpose of obtaining money. Now let me make it clear:

The Lord definitely does speak to people, and He definitely does give leading, guidance, and directions. And if the Lord has spoken as it regards the giving of money, or whatever, whatever He has said will definitely come to pass. So we're definitely not excluding the leading of the Holy Spirit, but only that which is obviously false!

SCATTERED SHEEP

The phrase of Verse 5, *"And they became meat to all the beasts of the field,"* refers to those of Israel having no True Shepherd to protect them.

This Passage fits exactly with the experience of Christ where it said: *"But when He saw the multitudes, He was moved with compassion on them, because they fainted and were scattered abroad, as sheep having no shepherd"* (Mat. 9:36).

As these spiritual leaders were in Ezekiel's day, so were they in the day of Christ.

The True Shepherd will be faithful to preach the Word of God to those who are in his care. And that is by far the most important thing. While there may be many other things needful and necessary, the faithful delivery of the Word is, by far, the most important.

Now every Preacher in the world will claim that he is preaching the Word, and doing so without compromise. But we all know that most aren't! In that case, he is not being a True Shepherd to the sheep.

Going back to the doctrine of the Nicolaitanes, which actually means *"control of the laity,"* actually for devious means, this characterizes, sad to say, many Churches.

THE CROSS OF CHRIST

If the Preacher is not preaching the Cross, holding it up as the Standard of Doctrine, in effect, *"Jesus Christ and Him Crucified,"* then whatever is being preached, instead of setting the people free, is actually putting them in bondage. There's only one Message, and that is, as we've just stated, *"Jesus Christ and Him Crucified"* (I Cor. 1:23; 2:2). This Message being neglected, ignored, or even repudiated, the Preacher must resort to something else, which, without fail, in some way, will, as stated, place the people in bondage.

WANDERING SHEEP

The phrase from Verse 6, *"My sheep wandered through all the mountains . . . and none did search or seek after them,"* refers to the statement of Christ. He said: *"If a man have a hundred sheep, and one of them be gone astray, does he not leave the ninety and nine, and go into the mountains, and seek that which is gone astray?"* (Mat. 18:12).

Actually, Denominationalism, which characterizes so much of Christianity, is an antithesis of what the True Shepherd ought to be! It seeks to build the Denomination at the expense of the person. The Denomination becomes the focal point instead of the people; however, let it be known that Christ did not come from Heaven and die on Calvary to save Denominations, but, instead, to save men.

If people aren't put first, as this Verse and so many others demand, self-will, covetousness, luxury, power, and cruelty become the order, and, therefore, the norm.

While it's not wrong to form a Denomination or to belong to a Denomination, it becomes wrong when the Denomination begins to be looked at as something other than what it actually is. Ideally, it is a tool, or is supposed to be, to help get the work of the Lord accomplished. But when men begin to attach spirituality to denominational association, the headship of Christ is then abrogated, and the Holy Spirit vacates the premises.

Unfortunately, whereas most Denominations seem to begin in the right way, after a period of time, it seems they start to lose their way, with the Denomination being run solely by men, and not at all by God. As someone has said, no Denomination, at least in a spiritual sense, can survive the third generation. Whether that's correct or not, I don't really know; however, I suspect that it's pretty close to being factual.

MY FLOCK BECAME A PREY

The phrase of Verse 8, *"As I live, saith the Lord GOD, surely because My flock became a prey,"* presents the fact that Judah and Jerusalem were destroyed because of these false shepherds. They led the people astray, setting an example of ungodliness, a hatred for the Word of God, and a disdain for His Prophets. Consequently, and despite the prophesying of Jeremiah and Ezekiel, the nation was totally destroyed.

As sheep, people will follow their shepherd (at least most), even if he is a false shepherd. Hence, the strong admonition of the Lord concerning the judgment of these false shepherds.

This does not excuse the people, and, in Truth, they by all means should flee these false shepherds, heeding the Word of the Lord; however, tragically, few do! That's the reason they are called *"sheep,"* and, thereby, *"become a prey."*

It is interesting that the Holy Spirit uses the phrase, *"My flock,"* denoting Himself as the Head, but, tragically, ignored!

The leveled accusation by the Holy Spirit is that these *"shepherds"* fed themselves and fed not *"My flock."*

THE CLEAR AND PRESENT DANGER

That which was so prevalent in Ezekiel's day is just as prevalent at present. While there are certainly some True Shepherds presently, still, the number is small by comparison. If the agenda is anything other than the sheep and their spiritual welfare, then the shepherds are false.

That statement should be studied carefully, because it applies to most.

The false shepherd always works under an agenda that is subtle and carefully crafted. As we have previously stated, almost all Denominations fall into this same category, with their Leaders putting the Denomination before the spiritual welfare of the people. Because the compromise is so subtle, the people gradually are led down paths that are not *"paths of Righteousness,"* but instead are *"paths of unrighteousness."*

And yet, it's all done under a cloak of religion, which makes it so seductive, and draws millions into its maw. Before the people realize it, if, in fact, they ever do realize it, they are serving a Denomination instead of Christ. They then *"become a prey,"* and if not financially, they are spiritually fleeced. To be certain, the worst fleecing is not financial, but spiritual!

THE TRUE SHEPHERD AND THE CROSS

As we've already stated, but because it is of such consequence, we must call the attention of the Reader to the fact, if the Preacher doesn't understand the Cross, and I'm referring to the Cross as it regards one's Sanctification, then, without fail, in some way, the people will be led astray. Due to the fact that precious few modern Preachers know anything at all about the Cross of Christ, at least as it refers to Sanctification, this means that the object of faith by the Preacher, and those who sit under such a Preacher, is placed elsewhere other than the Cross. As such, they become easy *"prey."*

As we have repeatedly stated, the dividing line is the *"Cross."* Those who ignore or repudiate the Cross have denied the help of the Holy Spirit, which means that there is absolutely no way that such an individual, be he Preacher or otherwise, can follow the right path. Paul said:

"For the preaching of the Cross is to them who perish foolishness, but to we who are saved, it is the Power of God" (I Cor. 1:18).

To properly live this life for the Lord, the Power of God is that which we must have. The *"power"* comes from the Holy Spirit Who demands at all times that the faith of the Believer ever be anchored in the Cross, which gives Him the legal right to perform His great work within our lives (Rom. 8:2). Without that, we simply cannot live the life we ought to live. And to be sure, the *"Cross"* is the centerpiece of all this of which we have just stated (Rom. 6:3-14; 8:1-2, 11; Gal. 6:14).

(10) "THUS SAITH THE LORD GOD; BEHOLD, I AM AGAINST THE SHEPHERDS; AND I WILL REQUIRE MY FLOCK AT THEIR HAND, AND CAUSE THEM TO CEASE FROM FEEDING THE FLOCK; NEITHER SHALL THE SHEPHERDS FEED THEMSELVES ANY MORE; FOR I WILL DELIVER MY FLOCK FROM THEIR MOUTH, THAT THEY MAY NOT BE MEAT FOR THEM.

(11) "FOR THUS SAITH THE LORD GOD; BEHOLD, I, EVEN I, WILL BOTH SEARCH MY SHEEP, AND SEEK THEM OUT.

(12) "AS A SHEPHERD SEEKS OUT HIS FLOCK IN THE DAY THAT HE IS AMONG HIS SHEEP THAT ARE SCATTERED; SO WILL I SEEK OUT MY SHEEP, AND WILL DELIVER THEM OUT OF ALL PLACES WHERE THEY HAVE BEEN SCATTERED IN THE CLOUDY AND DARK DAY.

(13) "AND I WILL BRING THEM OUT FROM THE PEOPLE, AND GATHER THEM FROM THE COUNTRIES, AND WILL BRING THEM TO THEIR OWN LAND, AND FEED THEM UPON THE MOUNTAINS OF ISRAEL BY THE RIVERS, AND IN ALL THE INHABITED PLACES OF THE COUNTRY.

(14) "I WILL FEED THEM IN A GOOD PASTURE, AND UPON THE HIGH MOUNTAINS OF ISRAEL SHALL THEIR FOLD BE: THERE SHALL THEY LIE IN A GOOD FOLD, AND IN A FAT PASTURE SHALL THEY FEED UPON THE MOUNTAINS OF ISRAEL.

(15) "I WILL FEED MY FLOCK, AND I WILL CAUSE THEM TO LIE DOWN, SAITH THE LORD GOD.

(16) "I WILL SEEK THAT WHICH WAS LOST, AND BRING AGAIN THAT WHICH WAS DRIVEN AWAY, AND WILL BIND UP THAT WHICH WAS BROKEN, AND WILL STRENGTHEN THAT WHICH WAS SICK: BUT I WILL DESTROY THE FAT AND THE STRONG; I WILL FEED THEM WITH JUDGMENT."

The exegesis is:

1. The action, the love, and the unselfishness of the True Shepherd are set out in Verses 11 through 16.

2. The Promise is given, despite the false shepherds, that Israel will ultimately be brought to Christ, and rightly restored to her proper place and position.

3. Even though in a saddened spiritual condition, the Lord still refers to them as *"My flock."*

GOD IS UNALTERABLY OPPOSED TO FALSE SHEPHERDS

The phrase of Verse 10, *"Thus saith the Lord GOD; Behold, I am against the shepherds,"* proclaims the fact that shepherds, i.e., *"Preachers"* are held more responsible than the laity. When the Lord says that He is unalterably opposed to something, as He does here the false shepherds, the prospects, to say the least, are frightful. He was against those of Israel, and to be sure, He is against those presently who follow that same path of unrighteousness.

The reason the responsibility of the shepherd is so great is because they will take many with them, wherever it is they go. In other words, untold millions are in Hell presently, because they followed a false shepherd.

I wish I could say, as one looks at all the Preachers in the world presently, that the false shepherds were strongly in the minority; however, the opposite is true. As an educated guess, maybe one out of a hundred would be classified as a True Shepherd. And I fear that I am being overly extravagant, even at that!

THEY WILL GIVE ACCOUNT FOR MY FLOCK

The phrase from Verse 10, *"And I will require My flock at their hand,"* means that they will personally have to answer to God for their wrongdoing. While the flock will be lost, and will have to answer themselves for following a false shepherd, still, the Truth remains, that most people, where Christianity is proclaimed, either go to Heaven or Hell due to the one they are following. It shouldn't be this way, but, regrettably, it is!

Consequently, you as a Believer who reads these words had better check out what any and every Preacher proclaims, and do so by the Word of God.

THE EXCOMMUNICATING OF THESE SHEPHERDS

The phrase of Verse 10, *"And cause them to cease from feeding the flock,"* refers to far more than these individuals being merely set aside. He stopped them by destroying them, and allowing the Kings of Judah to serve no more in that capacity; consequently, Jehoiachin was the last one, at least recognized by God, as in the lineage of David, and sitting on the Throne, and Zedekiah was the last one to serve as King whatsoever. From that time forth, Judah had no more Kings, at least in the lineage of David, and was always ruled over by foreign powers. Therefore, the Lord did exactly what He said He would do! He *"ceased them from feeding the flock."*

THE REVENUE WAS CUT OFF

The phrase, *"Neither shall the shepherds feed themselves any more,"* refers to the fact, that while the Kings of Judah, at least for the most part, refused to feed the flock, they not at all forgot to feed themselves. They bled the people dry!

While this Passage applied to many, it could probably be said that those who peddle the Word of Faith doctrine *"feed themselves"* more so than any other group. And with these millions of dollars that pour into these coffers, it is used not at all to proclaim the Gospel of Jesus Christ to a hurting world, but rather to embellish their own pyramid scheme, for that's exactly what it is! The ones at the top get it all, while those at the bottom get nothing.

DELIVERANCE OF THE FLOCK

The phrase of Verse 10, *"For I will deliver My flock from their mouth,"* means they were devouring the flock instead of feeding the flock. They were exploited instead of developed.

Even after the Kings were deposed, the Jewish Sanhedrin continued in the same evil role of exploiting the people, and, consequently, crucified Christ, their own Messiah, when He came!

They, too, were totally destroyed in A.D. 70, when Titus' tenth legion destroyed Jerusalem, slaughtering over one million Jews; therefore, the Word of God was fulfilled in totality.

However, a future restoration is coming, which will then see Israel governed by the True Shepherd, the Lord Jesus Christ. They exclaimed that they did not want Him as their Shepherd, but would rather have Caesar instead! They said: *"We have no king but Caesar"* (Jn. 19:15). Caesar has proven to be a hard taskmaster.

THE SEARCHING FOR THE SHEEP

The phrase of Verse 11, *"Behold, I, even I, will both search My sheep, and seek them out,"* concerns first of all, the *"other sheep I have, which are not of this fold"* (Jn. 10:16).

When Christ used the statement *"this fold,"* He was speaking of Israel, with the *"other sheep"* constituting the Church, which had not then even begun; however, beginning with the Day of Pentecost, the *"other sheep"* began to be brought into the fold, although it took some years for the actual occurrence to begin (Acts, Chpt. 10).

However, *"this fold,"* which was Israel, even though constituting the beginnings of the Early Church, soon was eclipsed by the tremendous influx of Gentiles.

The second part of the fulfillment will concern the Restoration of Israel, when they will be brought back to the fold, *"and there shall be one fold and One Shepherd"* (Jn. 10:16).

As the Church has been in the making for nearly 2,000 years, Israel will not come back into the fold until the Second Coming of the Lord. At that time, He will *"seek them out."*

After the Battle of Armageddon and the defeat of the Antichrist by the Coming of the Lord, Israel will finally recognize Him as the Messiah, and will accept Him as a man. As well, the millions of Jews scattered all over the world will also come to Christ, being sought out as the Prophets of old had foretold (Isa. 35:10).

THE CLOUDY AND DARK DAY

The phrase of Verse 12, *"And will deliver them out of all places where they have been scattered in the cloudy and dark day,"* refers to the coming Great Tribulation, which is yet future, when Israel will come close to annihilation. The Prophet Zechariah said that two-thirds of the people will be destroyed at that time (Zech. 13:8).

As a result of the Antichrist breaking his seven-year Covenant with Israel at the midpoint (Dan. 9:27), and declaring war on her, Israel will suffer her first defeat since becoming a nation in 1948. At that time, hundreds of thousands will flee to Petra, where the Lord has a place prepared for them (Rev. 12:6; Isa. 16:1-5; 26:20-21; 63:1-6; Ps. 60:6-12; Dan. 11:40-45). However, many more, possibly even hundreds of thousands, will flee to other parts of the world at that time, where the Lord has promised to *"seek out My sheep."*

The Prophet Isaiah said, and as it regards the Word of the Lord: *"I will bring Your seed from the east, and gather you from the west; I will say to the north, Give up; and to the south, Keep not back; bring My sons from far, and My daughters from the ends of the Earth"* (Isa. 43:5-6).

This will take place immediately after the Second Coming (Rev., Chpt. 19).

THEIR OWN LAND

The phrase of Verse 13, *"To their own land,"* refers to the country promised to Abraham, Isaac, and Jacob; and this is to be theirs forever.

Their occupation of this Land has been contested even from the very beginning, and continues unto the present day. Just ahead, the greatest contention will be with the Antichrist. He will seek, once and for all, to destroy these ancient people, thereby, nullifying the Promises of God, and, but for the Second Coming of Christ, would succeed; however, he will not succeed, but will be totally destroyed and by the Brightness of the Coming of the Lord of Hosts.

The phrase, *"And feed them upon the mountains of Israel,"* refers to Christ, at long last, becoming their Lord, and they, at long last, becoming His people.

This *"Land"* called *"Israel"* is the most contested piece of real estate on the face of the Earth. As stated, it has been contested by Satan, using his various vassal States, as no other piece of real estate, with the argument raging hotter today than ever before. The people presently occupying the land along with Israel, and to be sure, there because of the good graces of Israel, call themselves *"Palestinians,"* when, in reality, there is no such thing. They are Egyptians, Syrians, Jordanians, etc.

As well, the Arab countries have declared war on Israel several times, attempting to destroy her, thereby, as they have declared they would do, to push her into the sea. Had they won any one of these wars, Israel would be no more; but the truth is, Israel, despite the fact of being attacked, has won every war. Each time, they could have dispelled all the Arabs in the land of Israel, and would have been perfectly justified in doing so; however, by their good graces, they allowed hundreds of thousands, now numbering several millions, to remain in the Land, which has ever proved to be a thorn in their side.

The modern world thinks that the great dispute going on in Israel is simply because Israel will not give the Arabs a part of Israel for them to have their own State; however, Israel has, in fact, offered them basically everything for which they have asked, but to no avail. The truth is, the lie that is believed by most of the world, that Israel will not give these people a place, is not the source of contention at all, but rather the excuse. The Arab world wants every Jew dead, and every square foot of Israel belonging to them.

In fact, Israel sits in the middle of a sea of

Arabs, actually over 100 million. The Land in question comprises one sixth of one percent of all the land in the Middle East, with the Arabs controlling the balance.

The problem is not new; it has been raging for thousands of years, and it will continue to rage until the Second Coming of the Lord, which alone will settle the question. And to be sure, when the Lord comes, the question will definitely be settled!

SALVATION FOR ISRAEL

The phrase of Verse 14, *"I will feed them in a good pasture,"* refers to Salvation, which affords a right relationship with Christ, which alone satisfies the hunger of the human heart.

The phrase, *"And upon the high mountains of Israel shall their fold be,"* refers to great and abundant blessings.

All of these Promises guarantee the coming Restoration of Israel. It will happen, and nothing can stop it.

Most of the Promises of God are conditional; however, this Promise is not conditional, but rather guaranteed. Israel will ultimately be that which God originally intended, although, terrible days of horrifying judgment must precede this coming event. It is called *"the time of Jacob's trouble."* But the Prophet Jeremiah further said *"But he shall be saved out of it"* (Jer. 30:7).

I WILL FEED MY FLOCK

The phrase of Verse 15, *"I will feed My flock,"* refers to the tender care of the shepherd watching with an individualizing care over each sheep that has been brought back. Every broken limb will be bound up. Every sickness will be treated with its appropriate means of healing.

The phrase, *"And I will cause them to lie down,"* has a special significance for all, but especially for Israel.

It refers to a total serenity, peace, dependence, trust, and reliance upon the Lord, The Great Shepherd. It speaks of Salvation by Faith, which is given to all who believe.

It seems to be very difficult for man to completely trust God for Salvation. Man desires to contribute something, which he thinks surely he can, but which always frustrates the Grace of God, and, thereby, destroys victory. A total reliance on Him, which can only be done as one properly makes the Cross the Object of his Faith, and ever continues to do so, provides the greatest peace in the world, and which is demanded by God in order to obtain Salvation and Victory.

Concerning this, Paul said of Israel: *"For they being ignorant of God's Righteousness, and going about to establish their own righteousness, have not submitted themselves unto the Righteousness of God"* (Rom. 10:3).

Israel, however, is not alone in this terrible failure. It is very difficult for us, even modern Believers, to come to the place that we will evidence total trust in Christ, depending completely on what He has done at the Cross, and did it all for us, to where we will *"lie down"* in His Presence, where the Holy Spirit is attempting to take us.

THE CROSS

In Romans, Chapter 6, Paul beautifully describes God's Plan for victorious living. And please remember, the Lord only has one plan, and because only one is needed. This means, as ought to be obvious, that all other plans, irrespective as to how good they may look on the surface, are woefully insufficient, and because they are all devised by men.

Paul takes us, in Romans, Chapter 6, first of all to the Cross. He tells us that we are *"baptized into His Death,"* then *"buried with Him by baptism into death,"* and then *"raised with Him in newness of life"* (Rom. 6:3-5).

This presents the Cross, and in no uncertain terms. Jesus Christ is the *"Source,"* and the Cross is the *"Means."* We must never forget that!

Understanding that, we now come to sanctifying faith. Paul also said: *"Likewise reckon (account) ye also yourselves to be dead indeed unto sin* (the sin nature), *but alive unto God through Jesus Christ our Lord"* (through what Christ did at the Cross [Rom. 6:11]).

With our faith abiding constantly in the Cross of Christ, which then gives the Holy Spirit latitude to work within our lives, for He ever works within the parameters of the Finished Work of Christ (Rom. 8:1-2, 11), we now have the assurance that *"sin shall not have dominion over you: for you are not under the Law, but under Grace"* (Rom. 6:14).

This is *"God's Prescribed Order of Victory."* He has no other, as no other is needed. But the sadness is, almost none of the modern Church even remotely understand that of which we have briefly described. And to not know this which the Holy Spirit, through the Apostle, taught us, is to automatically cause one to be placed under the *"Law,"* which is a guarantee for failure.

THE LORD WILL DESTROY THE FAT AND THE STRONG

The phrase in Verse 16, *"But I will destroy the fat and the strong,"* is contrasted with the *"broken and the sick."* The idea is this:

As the Great Shepherd, the Lord Jesus Christ, when He comes, will destroy the *"fat and the strong,"* referring to the nations of the world which threw in their lot with the Antichrist, attempting to destroy Israel, they will be *"fed with judgment,"* and given no more place or position regarding supremacy.

As well, Israel, which has been *"lost, driven away, broken, and sick,"* will be healed and strengthened, and by the Messiah at that, and will take its rightful place as the supreme nation on the face of the Earth.

Such a statement at present seems ludicrous, especially considering the strength of America and other nations of the world; however, the seven-year Tribulation period is going to be so severe that once mighty nations are going to be left destitute and destroyed, with the map of the world rearranged.

As well, and more important, Christ will come back with great Power, with the government of the world upon His Shoulder, and at that time, *"God's Will will be done on Earth, as it is in Heaven."*

His Will shall constitute many things, with not the least of them being the supremacy of Israel, in order to fulfill the Promises made to the Patriarchs and Prophets of old!

(17) "AND AS FOR YOU, O MY FLOCK, THUS SAITH THE LORD GOD; BEHOLD, I JUDGE BETWEEN CATTLE AND CATTLE, BETWEEN THE RAMS AND THE HE GOATS.

(18) "SEEMS IT A SMALL THING UNTO YOU TO HAVE EATEN UP THE GOOD PASTURE, BUT YOU MUST TREAD DOWN WITH YOUR FEET THE RESIDUE OF YOUR PASTURES? AND TO HAVE DRUNK OF THE DEEP WATERS, BUT YOU MUST FOUL THE RESIDUE WITH YOUR FEET?

(19) "AND AS FOR MY FLOCK, THEY EAT THAT WHICH YOU HAVE TRODDEN WITH YOUR FEET; AND THEY DRINK THAT WHICH YOU HAVE FOULED WITH YOUR FEET.

(20) "THEREFORE THUS SAITH THE LORD GOD UNTO THEM; BEHOLD, I, EVEN I, WILL JUDGE BETWEEN THE FAT CATTLE AND BETWEEN THE LEAN CATTLE.

(21) "BECAUSE YOU HAVE THRUST WITH SIDE AND WITH SHOULDER, AND PUSHED ALL THE DISEASED WITH YOUR HORNS, TILL YOU HAVE SCATTERED THEM ABROAD;

(22) "THEREFORE WILL I SAVE MY FLOCK, AND THEY SHALL NO MORE BE A PREY; AND I WILL JUDGE BETWEEN CATTLE AND CATTLE.

(23) "AND I WILL SET UP ONE SHEPHERD OVER THEM, AND HE SHALL FEED THEM, EVEN MY SERVANT DAVID; HE SHALL FEED THEM, AND HE SHALL BE THEIR SHEPHERD."

The structure is:

1. The false sheep are characterized, as the false shepherds, by selfishness and violence.

2. The true sheep, like the True Shepherd, are unselfish and gentle.

3. The word *"David"* means *"The Beloved One,"* i.e., the True David, the Messiah. But yet, David, once the King of Israel, will also, once again, occupy that throne. All of this will be during the coming Kingdom Age.

THE GREAT JUDGE

The phrase of Verse 17, *"Behold, I judge between cattle and cattle, between the rams and the he goats,"* actually has to do with the judgment of the nations, which will take place immediately after the Second Coming of Christ.

Our Lord spoke of this when He said: *"When the Son of Man shall come in His Glory, and all the Holy Angels with Him, then shall He sit upon the Throne of His Glory: and before Him shall be gathered all nations; and He shall separate them one from another, as a shepherd divides his sheep from the goats: and He shall set the sheep on His Right Hand, but the goats on the left"* (Mat. 25:31-33).

Thus will the nations be judged, and according to their treatment of Israel. The purpose of this Judgment is to determine who shall enter the Kingdom, as it regards nations. This means that some nations will literally be no more, while other nations will be allowed into the Kingdom, all by Christ (Dan. 7:9-14, 22; Rev. 11:15). At that time, *"The meek will inherit the Earth"* (Ps. 37:11; Mat. 5:5).

THE NATIONS OF THE WORLD WHICH OPPOSED ISRAEL

The phrase of Verse 18, *"But you must foul the residue with your feet,"* has as its counterpart that given by Christ. He said: *"For I was hungry, and you gave Me no meat: I was thirsty, and you gave Me no drink"* (Mat. 25:42).

This speaks of the nations of the world which have treated Israel with disdain, some of these nations even trying to destroy Israel, as Germany of World War II.

But let it be understood and remembered that every slight toward these ancient people is remembered by the Lord, and ultimately will be called to account.

It should also be understood that anyone who seeks to hinder those truly called of God will ultimately answer to the Lord.

MY FLOCK

The phrase of Verse 19, *"And as for My flock,"* has the idea of those which have been beaten down now being raised to supremacy. In all ages, whether Israel or the Church, God's people have faced ridicule, sarcasm, scorn, persecution, and opposition, even though the *"salt of the Earth and the light of the world."* Actually, the Child of God lives in an alien society, which is opposed to Godliness and our Lord. This has seldom been changed in history.

While is it certainly true that the opposition and persecution have ranged from mild to severe, still, it has never totally left and will increase intensely during the coming Great Tribulation, carried out by the Antichrist, against both Israel and those who will give their hearts to Jesus Christ during this time.

NOTES

Dominion teaching has attempted to assuage this, claiming that Israel is no more, and that the Church will ultimately reign supreme over the entirety of the Earth. At that time, they say, they will then signal Christ to come back!

All of these foibles, and foibles they are, constitute a heady doctrine, and appeal to the prideful heart of man; however, it is blatantly false!

Israel, as should be plainly obvious from these many Scriptures, has not been set aside, but, actually, will be restored, and, as well, the supremacy of the Church is not going to increase, but, rather decrease.

Actually, were it not to be raptured out, the Antichrist would totally destroy it; however, and despite the claims of the Dominion teachers to the contrary, it will be raptured away, at least those who are truly Born-Again (I Thess. 4:13-18).

While it is true that the people of God will possess the Earth, both Glorified Saints and Restored Israel, still, this will not happen until Christ comes back, actually bringing the Saints with Him. Then, the ones referred to as *"My flock,"* which in totality will include the Glorified Saints, but actually refers to Restored Israel, will, under Christ, govern the Earth.

NATIONS WHICH OPPOSE ISRAEL

The phrase of Verse 21, *"Because you have thrust with side and with shoulder,"* characterizes the false shepherds of selfishness and violence.

The world, as well as an apostate church, have always engaged in violence regarding the true people of God, whether Israel of old, or the Church. They have *"thrust with side and with shoulder,"* meaning to show no concern, respect, or kindness, and even to use violence, if necessary!

If one looks at what the Pharisees and Sadducees did to Christ, one is seeing the attitude of the world and especially the apostate church towards God's true children. Jesus said, *"If the world hate you, you know that it hated Me before it hated you"* (Jn. 15:18).

As well, the greatest hatred was evidenced by the apostate Church toward Christ. Actually, the apostate church is a part of the "*world,*" which occasions its hatred of Christ and His followers. What I am about to say is strong, but, nevertheless, true!

THE APOSTATE CHURCH

As almost all of the *"Church"* of Christ's day was apostate, likewise, almost all of that which calls itself *"Church"* at the present is also apostate.

That which constitutes apostasy in the Church is that which is devised by man. In other words, it is something other than the Cross. The Lord's True Church is entirely of Himself, and none of man. Sadly, most Christians, and because they little know the Word of God, blindly follow apostate leaders to destruction.

Some years back, speaking to the religious head of a major Pentecostal Denomination regarding a statement he made, I said to him: *"But, my Brother, what you have just stated is unscriptural!"*

Actually, it was so blatantly unscriptural that even he did not try to defend it, at least Scripturally. His answer was, as he groped a few moments for words, *"It is our tradition."*

Tragically, most of the world has gone to Hell, and most who are alive presently are on their way to eternal darkness because of following man's tradition instead of following the Lord. Jesus said: *"Thus have you made the Commandment of God of none effect by your tradition"* (Mat. 15:6).

He then went on to say: *"You hypocrites, well did Isaiah prophesy of you, saying, "This people draw nigh unto Me with their mouth, and honor Me with their lips; but their heart is far from Me."*

He then said: *"But in vain they do worship Me, teaching for doctrines the commandments of men"* (Mat. 15:7-9).

In those verses just quoted, one will find the cause of apostasy in the Church, and the reason that hundreds of millions die lost without God.

As should be obvious, these *"commandments of men"* do not include the Cross!

BETWEEN SHEEP AND SHEEP

The phrase of Verse 22, *"Between cattle and cattle,"* would have probably been better translated *"between sheep and sheep."*

NOTES

The same Hebrew word is translated elsewhere thusly in the Old Testament, and commonly used of sheep rather than cattle (Gen. 30:34-42; 31:8-12).

The phrase, *"Therefore will I save My flock,"* refers to the coming Kingdom Age, which will immediately follow the Second Coming of Christ.

The phrase of Verse 22, *"And they shall no more be a prey,"* means that the world, of which the apostate church is a part, will no longer be able to persecute the Child of God.

While that is certainly true, the greater thrust of all of this, as is obvious, speaks of Israel. Once again, we are brought face-to-face with the judgment of the nations, *"I will judge between sheep and sheep."*

THE LORD JESUS CHRIST

The phrase of Verse 23, *"And I will set up One Shepherd over them,"* actually reads in the Hebrew text, *"A Shepherd, One."* That is, One pre-eminent and unique Shepherd — the only One of His kind, to Whom none other are comparable.

The phrase, *"Even My servant David,"* actually refers to the True David, the Lord Jesus Christ, the True Messiah of Israel (Isa. 55:3-4; Jer. 30:9; Hos. 3:5).

However, as it refers to the *"Son of David,"* it also refers to *"David,"* the same David who was chosen by God, and anointed by Samuel, and served as the King of Israel. Christ will be the Chief Shepherd (Heb. 13:20; I Pet. 2:25; 5:4), while David will be the under-shepherd.

David, as a Glorified Saint, will come back with Christ, along with all Saints, at the Second Coming. The Prophet Zechariah said: *"And the LORD my God shall come and all the Saints with You"* (Zech. 14:5). As well, the great Patriarchs and Prophets of old, such as Abraham, Isaac, and Jacob, along with Moses, and Samuel, actually every Saint of God who has ever lived, will be in that great number.

(24) "AND I THE LORD WILL BE THEIR GOD, AND MY SERVANT DAVID A PRINCE AMONG THEM: I THE LORD HAVE SPOKEN IT.

(25) "AND I WILL MAKE WITH THEM A COVENANT OF PEACE, AND WILL CAUSE THE EVIL BEASTS TO CEASE

OUT OF THE LAND: AND THEY SHALL DWELL SAFELY IN THE WILDERNESS, AND SLEEP IN THE WOODS.

(26) "AND I WILL MAKE THEM AND THE PLACES ROUND ABOUT MY HILL A BLESSING; AND I WILL CAUSE THE SHOWER TO COME DOWN IN HIS SEASON; THERE SHALL BE SHOWERS OF BLESSING.

(27) "AND THE TREE OF THE FIELD SHALL YIELD HER FRUIT, AND THE EARTH SHALL YIELD HER INCREASE, AND THEY SHALL BE SAFE IN THEIR LAND, AND THEY SHALL KNOW THAT I AM THE LORD, WHEN I HAVE BROKEN THE BANDS OF THEIR YOKE, AND DELIVERED THEM OUT OF THE HAND OF THOSE WHO SERVED THEMSELVES OF THEM.

(28) "AND THEY SHALL NO MORE BE A PREY TO THE HEATHEN, NEITHER SHALL THE BEAST OF THE LAND DEVOUR THEM; BUT THEY SHALL DWELL SAFELY, AND NONE SHALL MAKE THEM AFRAID.

(29) "AND I WILL RAISE UP FOR THEM A PLANT OF RENOWN, AND THEY SHALL BE NO MORE CONSUMED WITH HUNGER IN THE LAND, NEITHER BEAR THE SHAME OF THE HEATHEN ANY MORE.

(30) "THUS SHALL THEY KNOW THAT I THE LORD THEIR GOD AM WITH THEM, AND THAT THEY, EVEN THE HOUSE OF ISRAEL ARE MY PEOPLE, SAITH THE LORD GOD.

(31) "AND YOU MY FLOCK, THE FLOCK OF MY PASTURE, ARE MEN, AND I AM YOUR GOD, SAITH THE LORD GOD."

The synopsis is:

1. Israel will be, in that day, as originally intended by God, a blessing in the midst of the Earth.

2. And because Israel is now in her rightful place, *"There shall be showers of blessings"* over the entirety of the Earth.

3. The Messiah will then be manifested as *"The Plant of Renown."* That *"Plant"* will be so rich with nourishment that they who feed upon it shall be no more pinched with hunger, and their happy condition will secure renown for the *"Plant,"* and not for themselves. All Believers should so live as to win renown for our Lord.

NOTES

A COVENANT OF PEACE

The phrase of Verse 25, *"And I will make with them a Covenant of Peace,"* refers to the fact, that at the Second Coming, *"Peace,"* between the Lord and Israel, will then be established (Isa. 42:6; 49:8; 55:3; 57:8; 59:21; 61:8; Jer. 31:31; Heb. 10:16). Consequently, there will be *"Peace"* in the world, with the cessation of all war.

The phrase of Verse 25, *"And will cause the evil beasts to cease out of the land,"* is a euphemism referring to demon spirits as *"beasts."* Therefore, the cause of sin, shame, war, poverty, ignorance, and rebellion against God is removed, as Satan, along with all his cohorts, are locked in the bottomless pit (Rev. 20:1-3).

Because of Satan, whose defeat began at Calvary, and is now locked away, every place in the world will be safe, and expressed by the statement, *"And they shall dwell safely in the wilderness, and sleep in the woods."*

At the present, entire nations are totally controlled by the powers of darkness, and one could say that every nation in the world, if not totally controlled, is greatly influenced, by demon spirits. That is the cause of all the pain, suffering, and heartache in the world, and, in fact, ever has been!

At the present, in many nations, especially those controlled by Islam, the Gospel is not allowed in any fashion. Where there is absence of the Gospel of Jesus Christ, there is of necessity an absence of Righteousness, and, therefore, an abundance of evil. However, during that Coming Glad Day: *"The Knowledge of the LORD shall cover the Earth as the waters cover the sea"* (Hab. 2:14).

SHOWERS OF BLESSING

The phrase of Verse 26, *"There shall be showers of blessing,"* proclaims Israel at peace with Christ and restored to her place of supremacy, which will guarantee *"showers of blessing"* over the entirety of the Earth.

Let us not lose sight of the fact that this great and glorious cornucopia of Blessings, which will come upon Israel and the entirety of the Earth, and in a fashion that the world has never previously known, are all made possible by what Jesus did at the Cross.

If it is to be noticed, He didn't say *"maybe,"*

or *"hope so,"* but, rather *"There shall be showers of blessing."*

Those *"showers of blessing"* can be had presently by all who make Jesus Christ the Lord of their lives, ever understanding, and as previously stated as it regards all of this, Christ is the Source while the Cross is the Means.

THE EARTH SHALL YIELD HER INCREASE

The phrase of Verse 27 which says, *"And the tree of the field shall yield her fruit, and the Earth shall yield her increase,"* tells us emphatically that the *"increase"* of which the Earth is capable cannot be brought about until Israel is finally in her rightful place as the supreme nation of the world, all under Christ. This is what the Lord originally intended, and which will yet come to pass.

There are two particulars that are noted in this Scripture. The first is *"fruit, increase, and safety."*

The second is *"broken bands and deliverance."*

The former is the result of the latter.

Israel is now delivered from the hands of the Antichrist, and the *"yoke"* they have labored under so long has now been broken.

That *"yoke"* began with the Chaldeans approximately 500 years before the birth of Christ, and became total when they rejected their Messiah, saying, *"We have no king but Caesar"* (Jn. 19:15). They found to their utter dismay that Caesar's yoke was much heavier than the yoke of the Messiah (Mat. 11:30).

But the worst *"yoke"* of all, has not really been the yoke of foreign nations, but rather what brought about the *"yoke"* of the foreign nations, which is *"sin."* Israel rejected Christ and the Cross, which submitted them to a horrifying bondage, both nationally and spiritually.

Sin is the worst bondage of all, and the only answer for sin is *"Jesus Christ and Him Crucified"* (I Cor. 1:23).

SIN AND THE CROSS

This is the reason that Jesus must never be separated from the Cross. It's the reason that Paul said, as stated any number of times, *"We preach Christ Crucified."* That's the reason that he also said, *"For I determined not to know anything among you, save Jesus Christ and Him Crucified"* (I Cor. 2:2). And that is the great sin of the Church, separating Christ from the Cross.

Of course, and as is obvious, Christ is not still on the Cross, because the Cross is a Finished Work, meaning that it is total and complete. That's why Paul referred to it as *"The Everlasting Covenant"* (Heb. 13:20).

At this moment, Christ is seated by the Right Hand of the Father (Heb. 1:3). As well, spiritually speaking, we are seated with Him in the heavenlies (Eph. 2:6).

However, all that we have just quoted is made possible, and in totality, by what Jesus did at the Cross. There all sin was atoned, and Satan and every demon spirit were defeated (Col. 2:14-15).

To separate Jesus from the Cross is to separate Him from the very Work which He came to this Earth to do. The Cross and Redemption are synonymous. If Christ is looked at in any fashion other than by the Cross, we, in fact, are left with *"another Jesus, fostered by another spirit, presenting another gospel"* (II Cor. 11:4).

There's only one answer for sin and that is the Cross. And to be sure, the problem of the human race is sin, and the only answer is Christ and Him Crucified.

SAFE IN THEIR LAND

The phrase of Verse 27, *"And they shall be safe in their land,"* refers to that coming glad day, when Israel will then have accepted Christ as Lord and Messiah.

As is obvious in these Passages, the Holy Spirit portrays a bright destiny for the descendants of Jacob, despite their many problems of the past and present. This destiny involves conversion, followed by restoration, and a reestablishment of a national identity, with the Promised Land fully occupied, and Israel taking her place as the nation of nations.

However, and even though these were God's chosen people, still, many of the physical descendants of Israel had no vital personal relationship with the Lord. Paul argues in Romans, Chapter 9 that *"not all who are descended from Israel are Israel ... it is not the natural children who are God's Children, but it is the children of the Promise* who are regarded as Abraham's offspring" (Rom. 9:6-8).

Paul also presents the stunning fact that, through the Gospel, Gentiles are brought into the Covenant, and, thus, into the sacred community (Eph. 3:6; Heb. 8:1-13). In this limited sense, all Believers are *"Israel"* and Abraham's spiritual descendants.

Nevertheless, this in no way negates the Promises made to Israel as a people and as a nation, which will be fulfilled upon Israel being brought back to God at the Second Coming of the Lord.

Actually, the many different ways in which the name *"Israel"* is used has naturally led to some confusion about the Promises given Israel in the Old Testament. Some have asked, *"Are these Promises merely metaphors? That is, do they present a spiritual meaning that is presently experienced by Christians?"*

"Is Israel of the Old Testament and the Church of the New Testament distinctive aspects of God's Plan, or do they blend together into one?"

"Is the future of the nation of Israel as it is presented in the Old Testament still to be realized in history?"

Of course, these questions are very important, for the answers a person gives shape many aspects of his theology and of his understanding of Scripture.

THE RESTORATION OF ISRAEL

The Bible is clear concerning a Restoration of Israel, with the question asked by the Disciples, *"Are You* (speaking to Christ) *at this time going to restore the Kingdom to Israel?"* (Acts 1:6). Jesus replied that only the Father knows the times and dates (Acts 1:7), portraying the fact, plus all the other Prophecies, that this time will come, when the Kingdom will be actually restored to Israel.

Dealing with this question in depth, Paul devotes Chapters 9 through 11 of Romans to examine the situation of Israel. He portrays the opening of the door of Faith to the Gentiles as the grafting of wild olive branches onto a cultivated tree, and promises that this purposeful setting aside of Israel is not permanent.

Looking back to the Old Testament, Paul praises God, for *"God's Gifts and His Call are irrevocable"* (Rom. 11:29). Thus, the Old Testament's picture of Israel's future still awaits realization at the return of Christ.

ISRAEL

The phrase of Verse 28, *"And they shall no more be a prey to the heathen,"* looks forward to the coming Kingdom Age.

Because of the Lord choosing Abraham to bring this family into the world, who would be called *"Israel,"* and would, thereby, grow into a mighty nation, and, by the design of God, give the world the Bible and the Messiah, Satan has contested these people from their inception.

As a result of them being (at that time) the only followers of the Lord in the world, they were *"a prey to the heathen,"* and a target for the *"beasts of the land,"* which refers to demon spirits. Consequently, the battle raged almost from the very beginning.

When the leaders of Israel, or *"Judah,"* as she later came to be called, trusted Jehovah, the Lord performed mighty miracles on their behalf, keeping them safe from the heathen and the powers of darkness; however, oftentimes, her Faith flagged, and she would resort to rebellion against God, actually throwing in her lot with *"the heathen."* Still, in these compromising positions, which ultimately destroyed her, she never found the safety she desired. In fact, that safety can only be found in Christ, Whom she rejected.

Nevertheless, in the Coming Glad Day, when Israel shall, at long last, accept Christ as her Saviour and Messiah, then she shall no longer be subject to the heathen, nor overpowered by demon spirits, and shall *"dwell safely,"* with none being afraid.

This will all come about through Christ, and, in fact, could have come about some 2,000 years ago if Christ had been accepted as Lord. Instead, they crucified Him and brought upon themselves a sorrow and destruction as no nation in the world has ever known.

But, still, and according to the following Scriptures as well as many others, and due to the Promises, the Lord has watched over them from afar. This is what He says He will do:

A PLANT OF RENOWN

The phrase of Verse 29, *"And I will raise*

up for them a plant of renown," refers to none other than the Lord Jesus Christ, Whom they rejected, but will now accept. That *"Plant"* will be so rich with nourishment that they who feed upon it shall be no more pinched with hunger, and their happy condition will secure *"renown"* for the *"Plant"* and not for themselves; however, in securing it for *"Him,"* they, at the same time, will secure it for themselves. As well, every Christian should so live as to win Renown for our Lord.

The phrase, *"Neither bear the shame of the heathen any more,"* refers to their former lost condition when they resorted to the *"ways of the heathen."* It was a *"shame"* to them, as it a *"shame"* to all! Now, they will no longer follow heathen ways, but the Lord, the *"Plant of Renown,"* which the builders originally rejected, but, which became the *"Head of the corner"* (Lk. 20:17).

All of this will take place at the beginning of the Millennial Reign, or, as it sometimes referred to, *"The Kingdom Age."*

MY PEOPLE

The phrase of Verse 30, *"And that they, even the House of Israel are My people, saith the Lord GOD,"* will come about, but only after Israel accepts Jesus Christ as Lord, Saviour, and Messiah, which will take place at the Second Coming.

Verse 31 says, *"And you are My flock, the flock of My pasture, are men, and I am your God, saith the Lord GOD."*

As they are not now ashamed to call Him *"Lord,"* He is not ashamed, as well, to say to them and the world, *"And I am your God."*

The idea of Verse 31, as well as all of these Verses, is that even though the word *"sheep"* was used as a metaphor, still, the Lord is speaking of *"men,"* and not merely just *"sheep."*

But there is here a deeper meaning. Helpless, sinful *"men"* could never do such marvels, only the God Who is Adonai-Jehovah.

"I will go, I cannot stay,
"From the arms of love away,
"Oh for strength of Faith to say,
"Jesus died for me."

"Though I've tried, tried in vain,
"Tried to break the tempter's chain,

"Yet today I'll try again,
"Jesus died for me."

"Something whispers in my soul,
"Though your sins like mountains roll,
"Jesus' Blood can make you whole,
"Jesus died for me."

"Can it be, Oh can it be,
"There is hope for one like me.
"I will go with Thee my plea,
"Jesus died for me."

CHAPTER 35

(1) "MOREOVER THE WORD OF THE LORD CAME UNTO ME, SAYING,

(2) "SON OF MAN, SET YOUR FACE AGAINST MOUNT SEIR, AND PROPHESY AGAINST IT,

(3) "AND SAY UNTO IT, THUS SAITH THE LORD GOD; BEHOLD, O MOUNT SEIR, I AM AGAINST YOU, AND I WILL STRETCH OUT MY HAND AGAINST YOU, AND I WILL MAKE YOU MOST DESOLATE.

(4) "I WILL LAY YOUR CITIES WASTE, AND YOU SHALL BE DESOLATE, AND YOU SHALL KNOW THAT I AM THE LORD.

(5) "BECAUSE YOU HAVE HAD A PERPETUAL HATRED, AND HAVE SHED THE BLOOD OF THE CHILDREN OF ISRAEL BY THE FORCE OF THE SWORD IN THE TIME OF THEIR CALAMITY, IN THE TIME THAT THEIR INIQUITY HAD AN END:

(6) "THEREFORE, AS I LIVE, SAITH THE LORD GOD, I WILL PREPARE YOU UNTO BLOOD, AND BLOOD SHALL PURSUE YOU: SINCE YOU HAVE NOT HATED BLOOD, EVEN BLOOD SHALL PURSUE YOU.

(7) "THUS WILL I MAKE MOUNT SEIR MOST DESOLATE, AND CUT OFF FROM IT HIM WHO PASSES OUT AND HIM WHO RETURNS.

(8) "AND I WILL FILL HIS MOUNTAINS WITH HIS SLAIN MEN: IN YOUR HILLS, AND IN YOUR VALLEYS, AND IN ALL YOUR RIVERS, SHALL THEY FALL WHO ARE SLAIN WITH THE SWORD.

(9) "I WILL MAKE YOU PERPETUAL DESOLATIONS, AND YOUR CITIES SHALL

NOT RETURN: AND YOU SHALL KNOW THAT I AM THE LORD."

The overview is:

1. The Holy Spirit deals with the subject of Edom, and does so in this manner because it is expressive or symbolic of man's hatred against God, and is this way in every age.

2. This ever-continuing hatred, in other words, opposition to the people of God, was derived from Edom's ancestor, Esau (Gen. 27:41).

3. When Jerusalem fell, Edom rejoiced; the Israelites who fled to Edom, attempting to escape the Babylonians, were either killed by the Edomites or turned over to the Babylonians to be killed. In fact, they proposed to take the entirety of the land of Israel as their own.

EDOM

This Prophecy concerns Edom. Therefore, it leaves the glorious future, even as the Holy Spirit describes Israel in a coming glad day, and returns to the destitute present. The reason for this Prophecy is twofold:

1. Edom's hatred of Israel is, in the Scriptures, not only regarded as personal, but is symbolic of the animosity of the human race against God and His People, in every age.

In a sense, the Edomites, who were descendants of Esau, were half-brothers, so to speak, to Israel, inasmuch as Israel descended from Jacob, Esau's twin brother. So the animosity here is indicative, one might say, of that which divides the True Church from the apostate church. While the world in general has no time for God, as is overly obvious, still, the world does not so much openly oppose the Child of God, except in certain situations. Almost all of the opposition to the true Saint of God comes from those who profess the Lord, but really do not know the Lord.

It must be remembered, it was not Rome which initiated the terrible anger against Christ, which ultimately resulted in His Crucifixion, but rather, the religious clique of that day, the Pharisees, Scribes, Chief Priests, and Sadducees. Thus, it has ever been!

So, Edom's hatred of Israel is long-seated, which hatred continues to fuel the apostate church, even unto this hour.

NOTES

2. As well, the second reason for this Prophecy, even as believed by some, is that the Edomites had been allowed by the Chaldeans to take possession of Israel in payment of services rendered by them against Judah in the siege of Jerusalem.

PROPHESY AGAINST IT

Verse 2 says: *"Son of man, set your face against Mount Seir, and prophesy against it."*

Mount Seir was also called *"Idumea,"* the country of the Edomites.

The Prophet *"setting his face against Mount Seir"* was in reality the Lord setting His Face against that area. To have one nation pitted against another is one thing; however, to have God pitted against a nation, or anyone, or anything for that matter, is something else altogether. From that moment, the destiny of Edom as it regards its destruction was sealed, even though it would be many years in coming. In other words, the Israel that Edom opposed would make it through, even continuing unto this hour, and, in fact, will ever continue, and ultimately will know great Blessings from the Lord, while Edom is no more!

To use a street term, how many would have bought stock in Israel at that particular time? The answer is obvious, none . . . unless they had faith.

That goes for all the mighty empires which came against Israel, such as the Assyrians, the Babylonians, the Medo-Persians, the Greeks, and even mighty Rome. They are all gone, nothing but a faint memory in history books, if that, covered by the sands of time. But Israel continues, which should be a lesson to all. In fact, every single Promise and Prediction that the Lord has made as it concerns these ancient people, or anything for that matter, will most assuredly come to pass.

A LESSON FOR MODERN BELIEVERS

If God has truly called someone, and has given them a mandate, irrespective as to what the present situation may seem to be, that person, whoever they might be, will ultimately come through. So what is the moral of that?

The moral is that Believers should be very, very careful that they follow the man or the woman who has a distinct Calling from the Lord, and I might quickly add, a Calling which is obvious.

If such an individual truly has a Call from God, to be sure, Satan will do everything within his power to hinder and hurt that Call. In fact, if there is little opposition, one can be certain that there is little or no Call from God.

But despite that opposition, ultimately, even as the Patriarch Job said: *"But He knows the way that I take: when He has tried me, I shall come forth as gold"* (Job 23:10).

But unfortunately, it is very difficult for most Believers to *"see by Faith."* Most look at the present circumstances, which are almost always little indicative of what is truly taking place. As someone has said:

"You see what is happening, but you don't know what's going on."

THE LORD GOD

The phrase of Verse 3, *"And say unto it, Thus saith the Lord GOD; Behold, O Mount Seir, I am against you,"* tells us exactly the feelings and the direction of the Lord.

It doesn't matter how something looks presently, how much that individuals may praise its appearance, if the Lord is against that thing, *"doom"* has just been written over its future.

Almost the entirety of the world, that is if they believe in God at all, claim they are on God's side; however, that claim is of little worth. The question is, is God on your side?

The Lord is on our side, only as our heart is after His heart. The great Prophet Isaiah said, as it regards the Lord and His attention toward men: *"But to this man will I look, even to him who is poor and of a contrite spirit, and trembles at My Word"* (Isa. 66:2).

DESOLATION

Verse 4 says: *"I will lay your cities waste, and you shall be desolate, and you shall know that I am the LORD."*

Ezekiel formerly prophesied against Edom (25:12-14), but this was several years before the Fall of Jerusalem. This Prophecy here given is after the Fall of the city, and concerns itself with Edom's disposition at that time, as well as previous sins against God's people.

NOTES

The phrase, *"You shall know that I am the LORD,"* is used frequently by Ezekiel, as is by now obvious, and denotes several things:

1. It speaks of great patience and long-suffering of the Lord before finally bringing Judgment to bear.

2. It speaks of people ignoring the Word of God, and because Judgment is delayed, they mock and say, *"Where is the Promise of His Coming?"* (II Pet. 3:4).

3. Ultimately, all He has said He would do will be brought to pass, and, at that time, *"You shall know. . . ."*

Men today have little regard for God or His Word. Considering the population of the entire world, only a few take Him at His Word, therefore, believing His Word. Almost all the world, and for all time, regards the Word of God as no more than a *"myth,"* if they regard it at all!

Nevertheless, every single Promise given in the Word of God, along with every Prophecy, will be fulfilled in totality, and exactly as the Lord said, with not even a *"jot"* or *"tittle"* being unfulfilled (Mat. 5:18).

(A *"jot"* is the smallest letter of the Hebrew Alphabet, with its use being optional. *"Tittle"* is a variant spelling for *"Title,"* which, in the time it was used, meant a stroke above an abridged word, and then any minor stroke. In other words, it's a little tiny stroke on a letter which distinguishes it from another similar letter.)

HATRED

The phrase of Verse 5, *"Because you have had a perpetual hatred,"* as stated, not only epitomizes the hatred of Edom for Israel, but as well, between *"Satan's seed and her Seed,"* the latter being Jesus Christ (Gen. 3:15). It is the attitude of all men toward Christ, and for all ages, with the exception of those who truly know Christ.

Dealing with Edom, they had been Israel's hereditary foe from the days of Esau and Jacob, with Esau actually being the parent of these people, so to speak (Gen. 25:22; 27:37).

As well, many years before as it regards Israel's wanderings in the wilderness, Edom had refused Israel a passage through their territory, thereby, making the way of Israel harder (Num. 20:14-21; Judg. 11:17).

In the days of Jehoshaphat, they combined with Ammon and Moab to invade Judah (II Chron. 20:10-11).

The phrase of Verse 5, *"And have shed the blood of the Children of Israel by the force of the sword in the time of their calamity,"* according to the Prophet Obadiah, refers to the Fall of Jerusalem, and the rejoicing of Edom that this had taken place. As well, they joined with the foreign invaders in the sacking of the city. At that time, they occupied its gates and guarded the roads leading into the country, so as to prevent the escape of any of the wretched inhabitants, and even cut down with the sword such fugitives as tried to make their escape.

The phrase, *"In the time that their iniquity had an end,"* refers to the final transgression of Judah which brought on their destruction.

One would think that inasmuch as God had marked Judah and Jerusalem for Judgment, that whosoever participated in that Judgment would be blessed; however, the opposite was the case!

Only the Babylonians were marked by God to be used in this capacity, and even they attended this task with too much zeal, and were correspondingly judged by God along with the other nations.

All of this should tell us, that God watches minutely over His Children, whether they are consecrated or unconsecrated. How they are dealt with by others is noted very carefully by Him.

While the Lord may delegate judgment to come upon a wayward Believer, the person or people engaged in this act, although used by God, will be unwitting subjects. In other words, they will have no knowledge that they are being thusly used, even as the Babylonians did not understand they were being used by God as it regarded judgment upon Judah and Jerusalem. But even then, as we have already stated, the Babylonians went too far, and the Lord in turn judged them.

CHRISTIANS PUNISHING OTHER CHRISTIANS

No Believer has the right to punish another Believer. This goes for Denominational heads as well! If a Believer is living in open sin, refusing to repent of that sin, quit what is being done, then fellowship may have to be withdrawn; however, it begins and ends there.

When it comes to taking punitive measures by one Christian against another, the Lord will not tolerate such, and for all the obvious reasons. Concerning this, James plainly said: *"There is one Lawgiver, Who is able to save and to destroy* (which of course speaks of the Lord): *Who are you who judges another?"* (James 4:12). In other words, *"Who do you think you are, thinking you are worthy to judge someone else?"*

At times in the past, we have had Preachers at Family Worship Center, who have tried to cause problems in the Church, and would have to be dismissed. Even though what they were doing was obviously wrong, and even though they may continue in that wrong by unscripturally attempting to start another Church in Baton Rouge, and doing so by attempting to draw people away from our Church, still, even though I cannot have fellowship with that person, and for all the obvious reasons, I am to then turn him over to the Lord. In other words, I am not to lift a hand to try to hurt him in any way. I'm to let the Lord take care of that. In fact, if the occasion arises, and he needs my help, irrespective of the past, I am to provide that help, at least where possible.

FOUR SINS

The phrase of Verse 6, *"Therefore, as I live, saith the Lord GOD, I will prepare you unto blood, and blood shall pursue you,"* proclaims the judgment of God.

Four sins are judged in this Chapter. They are:

1. Hatred (Vs. 5).
2. Anger (Vs. 11).
3. Envy (Vs. 11).
4. Malice (Vs. 15).

Thus, it may be learned how God's anger justly burns against people who rejoice at the sufferings of others, enviously coveting their money, and nourishing feelings of anger and hatred against them. In the Hebrew Text, there is a play upon the words *"Edom"* and *"blood."*

The phrase, *"I will prepare you unto blood,"* means that they will be prepared by the Lord for destruction, a destruction they cannot escape because *"blood shall pursue you."*

In that they did not *"hate"* or detest the shedding of the *"blood"* of the people of Judah and Jerusalem, the Holy Spirit emphasizes the fact, *"that what they have sowed, that shall they reap"* (Gal. 6:7).

(The word *"sith"* in Verse 6 is an Old English word meaning *"since"* or *"afterwards"* or *"seeing that."*)

JUDGMENT

The phrase of Verse 7, *"Thus will I make Mount Seir most desolate,"* proclaims the coming judgment.

In these Passages, the Lord finally decides the controversy between Edom and Israel. To the one, He adjudges perpetual desolation; to the other, ever-enduring prosperity. In fact, this is the last Message to Esau, so to speak. All previous appeals of goodness and severity were rejected, but even then, judgment lingered until about A.D. 300.

The phrase of Verse 8, *"And I will fill his mountains with his slain men,"* seems to argue against the Love of God; however, it is because of Love that the Lord does such a thing! As a cancer has to be excised from the physical body in order that the body be saved, likewise, certain nations, as a cancer, have to be destroyed in order to save the body politic.

As no one, at least in their right mind, would fault a surgeon for removing a malignancy, likewise, no one should fault the Lord for doing the same!

The phrase of Verse 9, *"You shall know that I am the LORD,"* means that Edom would know to her sorrow Jehovah's Power to punish, which she has ignored for so long.

They thought to profit from Judah's problems, but, instead brought upon themselves perpetual desolations. Their cities, that they loved so much, would be destroyed, and *"not return,"* i.e., *"not rebuilt."*

(10) "BECAUSE YOU HAVE SAID, THESE TWO NATIONS AND THESE TWO COUNTRIES SHALL BE MINE, AND WE WILL POSSESS IT; WHEREAS THE LORD WAS THERE:

(11) "THEREFORE, AS I LIVE, SAITH THE LORD GOD, I WILL EVEN DO ACCORDING TO YOUR ANGER, AND ACCORDING TO YOUR ENVY WHICH YOU HAVE USED OUT OF YOUR HATRED AGAINST THEM; AND I WILL MAKE MYSELF KNOWN AMONG THEM, WHEN I HAVE JUDGED YOU.

(12) "AND YOU SHALL KNOW THAT I AM THE LORD, AND THAT I HAVE HEARD ALL YOUR BLASPHEMIES WHICH YOU HAVE SPOKEN AGAINST THE MOUNTAINS OF ISRAEL, SAYING, THEY ARE LAID DESOLATE, THEY ARE GIVEN US TO CONSUME.

(13) "THUS WITH YOUR MOUTH YOU HAVE BOASTED AGAINST ME, AND HAVE MULTIPLIED YOUR WORDS AGAINST ME: I HAVE HEARD THEM.

(14) "THUS SAITH THE LORD GOD; WHEN THE WHOLE EARTH REJOICES, I WILL MAKE YOU DESOLATE.

(15) "AS YOU DID REJOICE AT THE INHERITANCE OF THE HOUSE OF ISRAEL, BECAUSE IT WAS DESOLATE, SO WILL I DO UNTO YOU: YOU SHALL BE DESOLATE, O MOUNT SEIR, AND ALL IDUMEA, EVEN ALL OF IT: AND THEY SHALL KNOW THAT I AM THE LORD."

The overview is:

1. Even though Israel was under the judging Hand of God, still, they were His people, even though the far greater majority of them were spiritually lost. Irrespective of their spiritual condition, they were still His people.

2. When God judges His people, the world rejoices, and even much of the Church, and stretches out to seize their possessions. But the world knows not that the commencement of judgment at the House of God, where in fact it must begin, is the precursor of the eternal doom of the enemy (I Pet. 4:17-18).

3. Edom would come to know the Power of God, but in the realm of judgment, which they would not at all enjoy.

4. If man will not know the Lord as a Saviour, he must know Him as a Destroyer.

5. Williams said: *"God promised Palestine to Abraham* (Gen. 17:8). *Isaac made Jacob by Divine ordination* (Gen. 25:23) *the depository and possessor of the Promise. Esau and his sons disputed the gift with perpetual hatred.*

*"Before birth and after birth, Esau tried

to murder Jacob; and in this Chapter, his sons propose to, at last, seize the land. But God was there. They thought, as Esau did, that they could ignore or defeat Him. These are not parables, or pious poems, or fables, as some Preachers claim presently, but historic facts recorded by the infallible Spirit of God."

6. For approximately 1,000 years after the Prophecy was given concerning the destruction of Edom, men could mock these Prophecies, claiming they had not come to pass, thereby claiming the Word of God was not true. But that no longer can be done, because in the Third Century A.D. every Word was fulfilled, and the fulfillment after so long a period is an overwhelming demonstration of the fact that the Bible is a superhuman Book.

7. Bitter words against God's people are accounted by God as spoken against Himself.

THE BOASTS OF EDOM

The phrase of Verse 10, *"Because you have said, These two nations and these two countries shall be mine,"* refer to the Northern Kingdom of Ephraim, sometimes called Israel, and Judah, the Southern Kingdom. Edom coveted this Land, which, as stated, was promised by God to the sons of Jacob, and not Esau.

The truth is, Edom would have done much better to have coveted any land in the world except this Land; likewise, the Muslims in Israel would do far better to contest any other part of the world except the Land of Israel. To be sure, that which ultimately happened to Edom, will, as well, ultimately happen to the Arabs who are attempting to usurp authority over the Promise of God.

Edom now thought that due to the Fall of Judah and Jerusalem, that the Lord had forsaken His people, and His Land; therefore, as a result, *"We will possess it,"* they said! However, the Lord had not forsaken the people or the Land, and the Holy Spirit emphatically declares, *"The Lord was there."* Admittedly, His Presence was there in a different manner than normally, but He *"was there."*

The idea of the Verse is that the child may become unruly, or even commit a serious offense, thereby needing punishment; however, the parents will administer that punishment themselves, and will never allow anyone else to do so unless express permission is given. Likewise, if God's people need punishment or chastisement, the Lord will administer it, and woe be unto anyone else who thinks otherwise!

As well, when one studies the Books of Jeremiah and Ezekiel, one cannot help but come to the conclusion that if any of these surrounding nations had attempted to help Judah at this tragic time, God would have blessed them for their actions, and despite the Judgment that He was bringing on Judah by the Babylonians. Actually, He would even punish Babylon, and severely, because they took their commission regarding Judah and Jerusalem too far!

POSSESSION

The phrase of Verse 10, *"We will possess it,"* also may have a reference to the Blessing which Esau tried to recover from his brother, Jacob, but in vain, because in Genesis 27:34, 41, so here, Jehovah was present to defeat this impious purpose.

God promised Canaan to Abraham (Gen. 17:8). Isaac made Jacob by Divine Ordination (Gen. 25:23) the depository and possessor of the Promise. Esau and his sons disputed the gift with perpetual hatred.

The last phrase of Verse 10, *"Whereas the LORD was there,"* proclaims the majesty and power of these words, and can literally be felt by the Reader.

ANGER AND ENVY

The phrase of Verse 11, *"Therefore, as I live, saith the Lord GOD, I will even do according to your anger, and according to your envy which you have used out of your hatred against them,"* proclaims the fact that the Lord notes all things. At times, the suffering which people desire for others, sometimes falls upon themselves. Far from Edom securing Israel, she, in fact, would ultimately be deprived of her own land, and perish forever as a nation.

The sense of Verse 11 is that Edom would suffer the indignities they design to heap on Israel.

As well, Edom's misconception as to

Jehovah's relation to the Land and the people of Israel, should be corrected when Jehovah should rise up in Judgment against him. In other words, these Prophecies proclaim, and in glaring terms, that God had not abandoned Israel.

SLANDER

The phrase of Verse 12, *"And that I have heard all your blasphemies which you have spoken against the mountains of Israel,"* proclaims the fact that the Lord had been a silent listener to all of these blasphemies spoken by Edom against Israel, and had reckoned these as blasphemies uttered against Himself.

To persecute those who are God's is to persecute God. Likewise, to slander those who belong to God is to slander God!

As God, He is Omniscient, and thereby knows all!

So, nothing is hidden from Him.

The phrase of Verse 13, *"Thus with your mouth you have boasted against Me,"* proclaims the fact, and as stated, that words spoken against God's people are words spoken against God. The phrase is emphatic, *"I have heard them."*

The meaning is, every single word will be accounted for, and a suitable punishment accordingly designed. Consequently, if we really understand these statements, we will look long and hard before we begin to judge someone's motives, voice our dislike, or even give our opinion.

Please note the following:

1. When we hear something negative about a fellow Christian, we must remember that we are hearing gossip, and should treat it accordingly, which means it is either all lies or else part truth and part lie. At any rate, it should never be acted on, and passed on. To do such is to aid and abet Satan's work, because Satan is the greatest slanderer of all!

2. Even if we think we have inside knowledge as to the actual facts, still, we have precious little knowledge of the spiritual warfare involved, and, therefore, should be very careful before we pass judgment.

3. We should always ask ourselves that if we were placed in the same identical position, engaging in the same type of spiritual warfare, would we have done any better, or even as well?

In effect, Verses 11 through 13 tell us, that when we judge others, we are judging ourselves, because: *"Whatever measure you mete will be measured to you again"* (Mat. 7:1-2).

This in no way is meant to imply that we are to condone sin! However, what is to be done about it can only be carried out by the Lord. Our conduct must always be Scriptural. If Edom had followed that pattern, thereby obeying the Word of God, Edom would not have suffered this terrible Judgment.

THUS SAITH THE LORD GOD

The phrase of Verse 14, *"When the whole Earth rejoices, I will make you desolate,"* carries the idea, that when the sons of the Kingdom enter into joy, their haters shall descend into the gloom.

The phrase of Verse 15, *"You shall be desolate, O Mount Seir,"* sums up this Prophecy.

The time would come that Idumea, once so rich in flocks, so strong in its fortresses and rock-hewn cities, and, as well, so extensive in its commercial relations, and so renowned for the architectural splendor of its palaces, is now a deserted and desolate wilderness. For the most part, its highways are untrodden, its cities are all in ruins.

The area once know as Edom is presently known as Jordan.

The capital of ancient Edom was *"Sela,"* which lay on a small plateau behind Petra. Other important towns were Bozrah and Teman.

Some time ago, I had the opportunity to visit Petra, which nearly 2,000 years ago was one of the great trade cities of that part of the world. As well, it is one of the most unique cities in the world, or at least it was.

The valley in which the city was located stretches for several miles, with very high, mountainous peaks on either side. There is only one way into the area, and it's very narrow, once again, with great cliffs on either side, rising up several hundred feet. For all practical purposes, the city was impregnable.

As stated, during its heyday, it was one of the great trade centers of the world. But today, it is empty! Its temples still stand, and its architecture is a wonder to behold, but no one lives there. It is visited now only by tourists. In the distance, we hear the Prophecies of Ezekiel, and we know from the stark evidence before us that these Prophecies have come to pass, and have done so in totality.

It was done that *"they shall know that I am the LORD."*

"I came to Jesus, weary, worn, and sad,
"He took my sins away, He took my sins away,
"And now His love has made my heart so glad,
"He took my sins away."

"The load of sin was more than I could bear,
"He took them all away, He took them all away,
"And now on Him I roll my every care,
"He took my sins away."

"No condemnation have I in my heart,
"He took my sins away, He took my sins away,
"His perfect peace He did to me impart,
"He took my sins away."

"If you will come to Jesus Christ today,
"He'll take your sins away, He'll take your sins away,
"And keep you happy in His love each day,
"He'll take your sins away."

CHAPTER 36

(1) "ALSO, THOU SON OF MAN, PROPHESY UNTO THE MOUNTAINS OF ISRAEL, AND SAY, YOU MOUNTAINS OF ISRAEL, HEAR THE WORD OF THE LORD:

(2) "THUS SAITH THE LORD GOD; BECAUSE THE ENEMY HAS SAID AGAINST YOU, AHA, EVEN THE ANCIENT HIGH PLACES ARE OURS IN POSSESSION:

(3) "THEREFORE PROPHESY AND SAY, THUS SAITH THE LORD GOD; BECAUSE THEY HAVE MADE YOU DESOLATE, AND SWALLOWED YOU UP ON EVERY SIDE, THAT YOU MIGHT BE A POSSESSION UNTO THE RESIDUE OF THE HEATHEN, AND YOU ARE TAKEN UP IN THE LIPS OF TALKERS, AND ARE AN INFAMY OF THE PEOPLE:

(4) "THEREFORE, YOU MOUNTAINS OF ISRAEL, HEAR THE WORD OF THE LORD GOD; THUS SAITH THE LORD GOD TO THE MOUNTAINS, AND TO THE HILLS, TO THE RIVERS, AND TO THE VALLEYS, TO THE DESOLATE WASTES, AND TO THE CITIES THAT ARE FORSAKEN, WHICH BECAME A PREY AND DERISION TO THE RESIDUE OF THE HEATHEN THAT ARE ROUND ABOUT;

(5) "THEREFORE THUS SAITH THE LORD GOD; SURELY IN THE FIRE OF MY JEALOUSY HAVE I SPOKEN AGAINST THE RESIDUE OF THE HEATHEN, AND AGAINST ALL IDUMEA, WHICH HAVE APPOINTED MY LAND INTO THEIR POSSESSION WITH THE JOY OF ALL THEIR HEART, WITH DESPITEFUL MINDS, TO CAST IT OUT FOR A PREY."

The synopsis is:

1. The double Prophecy of this Chapter predicts the restoration of the Land of Israel and of the People of Israel; and the fundamental moral principle is taught that inward holiness must precede outward prosperity (Williams).

2. There was a limited fulfillment of these Prophecies at the restoration under Zerubbabel; but their total fulfillment, actually that to which these Prophecies point, is yet future.

3. God chastens His people, but He destroys their enemies. His people's shame is temporary; that of their enemies, perpetual.

4. The sense of Verse 3 is that the heathen charged Jehovah with inability to protect His land.

PROPHESY

The phrase of Verse 1, *"Prophesy unto the mountains of Israel,"* has to do with that which pertains to the Land of Israel, and what the Lord will there ultimately do.

Actually, this Prophecy is divided into two parts, with Verses 1 through 15 connected with the previous Chapter, and the second part beginning with Verse 16, and closing at Ezekiel 37:14. The subject of the first part is Israel's Restoration. As it deals with the *"Land"* (Vss. 1-15), the second part deals with the *"People."* The lesson is taught that inward holiness must precede outward prosperity.

The phrase of Verse 2, *"Because the enemy has said against you, Aha,"* portrays this enemy as Edom. They gloated over the fall of Judah and Jerusalem, and did so to all who would hear. What they didn't realize was that their gloat against the people of Israel was a gloat against God. As stated, to slander that which belongs to God is to slander God! As well, as should be here overly obvious, the Lord notes all that takes place, even down to the guttural slurs. He does not take kindly to such being leveled at His people, irrespective of their spiritual condition.

THE TALKERS

The phrase of Verse 3, *"And you are taken up in the lips of talkers, and are an infamy of the people,"* constitutes the only place in the Bible where the word *"talkers"* is found. The Hebrew word is *"lashon,"* which means *"a fork of flame; babbler; evil speaker; accuser; slanderer; calumniate; wag the tongue;"* which all speak of Satan's chief efforts to destroy God's people, as *"the accuser of our Brethren"* (Rev. 12:10).

I would certainly trust that, from all of this, the Reader understands the severity of the situation at hand. When one hears the gossip peddled by many Christians, it becomes quickly obvious that they have never read the Book of Ezekiel.

When a person comes to Christ, they can do so only by virtue of Christ and what He has done for us at the Cross. *"We are bought with a price,"* and, in fact, a price of such magnitude as to defy all description — the death of the Son of God on the Cross of Calvary, which alone could atone for all sin.

Having accepted Christ, and now becoming His child, we are *"an heir of God, a joint-heir with Jesus Christ"* (Rom. 8:17).

Belonging exclusively to the Lord, we are guaranteed of His watchful care. And as you do not appreciate at all someone leveling charges against your children, that is if you have children, likewise, the Lord does not appreciate it when someone levels charges, or even curses, against one for whom He has paid such a price.

Some people think because they are a Christian, likewise bought with a price, that that gives them the right to level charges against another Christian. To say the least, it doesn't! In fact, I personally feel that the Lord looks with even greater disdain on the Christian who would do such a thing, because we should know better!

THE MINISTRY OF RECONCILIATION

The phrase of Verse 4, *"Thus saith the Lord GOD to the mountains, and to the hills, and to the rivers, and to the valleys, and to the desolate wastes, and to the cities that are forsaken,"* proclaims the fact that what the Lord has chastised, He can restore. As someone has said, while God may chasten His people, He, in fact, destroys their enemies. Anything the Lord does with His people, and whatever direction it might take, is that they may be ultimately brought to a place of victory. If Repentance is needed, He works toward that end. Sometimes, He must chastise the individual, and, in fact, He chastises all Believers, and for the obvious reasons (Heb. 12:5-11). If the Christian loses Faith, and begins to drift away, the Holy Spirit continues to make every effort to pull that Believer back to the desired place.

Actually, one of the great Ministries of the Holy Spirit, and one of the most important, is the *"Ministry of Reconciliation,"* which includes *"Restoration."* In fact, before *"Restoration"* can be brought about, *"Reconciliation"* must have already taken place.

Before the Lord can do such with Israel, or any individual for that matter, the enmity, or quarrel, must be bridged over. It implies that the parties being reconciled were formerly hostile to one another. The Bible tells us bluntly that sinners are *"enemies"* of God (Rom. 5:10; Col. 1:21; James 4:4).

We should not minimize the seriousness of these and similar Passages. An enemy is not someone who comes a little short of being a friend. He is in the other camp. He is altogether opposed. The New Testament, as well as the Old, pictures God in vigorous opposition to everything and anything that is evil.

The only way to overcome enmity is to take away the cause of the quarrel. That cause is sin! Christ died to put away our sin. In this way, He dealt with the enmity between man and God. He put it out of the way. He made the way wide open for men to come back to God. He did it all at the Cross! It is this which is described by the term *"Reconciliation,"* which brings about *"Restoration."*

MAN'S SIN

It is interesting to notice that no New Testament Passage speaks of Christ as reconciling God to man. Always, the stress is on man being reconciled. This, in the nature of the case, is very important. It is man's sin which has caused the enmity. It is man's sin that has to be dealt with. Actually, man feels no hostility toward God on account of his sin. The barrier arises because God demands holiness in man. Therefore, what Jesus did at Calvary was far more than defeating Satan and the powers of darkness, but, His Death, as well, assuages the anger of God and satisfied the debt piled up by man and owed to God. Consequently, Calvary was brought about to satisfy the righteous demands of a thrice-Holy God. In atoning for all sin, our Lord, likewise, totally and completely defeated Satan. While the Cross was totally and completely Satan's undoing, that was, in actuality, only a by-product of what the Cross accomplished.

The main purpose of the Cross was to address man's sin, the terrible debt of sin owed by man to God. It was a debt, incidentally, that man could not pay. So, if the debt was to be paid and, thereby, the judgment lifted, God would have to become Man, and pay the debt Himself, which He did, by going to the Cross.

WHY NOT ANOTHER FORM OF SACRIFICE?

No! It had to be a Cross. And there was a reason for that.

Under the Law of Moses, if an Israelite committed a dastardly crime, He was to be stoned to death, and then his body was to be placed on a tree, hanging there as a spectacle for all to see. This showed that he was cursed by God; however, he was not to hang there all night, only for a few hours (Deut. 21:22-23).

The death of Christ was not an execution, nor was it an assassination. The death of Christ was a Sacrifice, with Christ purposefully and willingly laying down His Life. If it was to be a Sacrifice, this is the way it had to be (Jn. 10:17-18).

As well, this Sacrifice must be for all sin, even the worst sin of which one could ever begin to think (I Cor. 6:9-11), and, as well, the very cause of sin (Jn. 1:29).

This was so much planned and recognized by the Lord, that the Holy Spirit, through Peter, said, as he spoke to Israel about Jesus: *"Whom you slew and hanged on a tree"* (Acts 5:30). He also spoke through Paul, saying, *"And when they had fulfilled all that was written of Him, they took Him down from the tree, and laid Him in a sepulchre"* (Acts 13:29). Peter also said: *"Who His Own Self bore our sins in His Own Body on the Tree, that we, being dead to sins, should live unto Righteousness: by Whose stripes you were healed"* (I Pet. 2:24).

As we've already stated in this Volume, the Lord revealed to Abraham the way that Redemption would be afforded, which would be by death (Gen., Chpt. 22). But it was to Moses that He revealed as to what manner this death would be, which would be the Cross (Num., Chpt. 21).

If it is to be remembered, Jesus was placed on the Cross at 9 a.m., which was the time of the morning Sacrifice, and He died at 3 p.m., the time of the evening Sacrifice. As well, His Body was taken down from the Cross before nightfall, totally fulfilling the Scripture regarding Deuteronomy 21:22-23.

While the malefactor was cursed by God, even as Moses said, Jesus, instead, bearing our sin on the Cross, was *"made a curse for us,"* which is totally different (Gal. 3:13). To be *"cursed of God,"* one would have had to have committed the sin, whatever it may have been. Christ committed no sin, so had to be *"made a curse,"* which means that He suffered the penalty we should have suffered, which was death (Jn. 3:16).

Even though Christ most definitely suffered on the Cross, it was not the suffering which redeemed humanity. Even though He was greatly humiliated on the Cross, likewise, it was not humiliation which redeemed us.

It was the giving of Himself as a Sacrifice, and the fact that He was perfect in every respect, which provided a Sacrifice that God could accept as payment. It was payment, the life of Christ poured out, regarding His shed Blood (Eph. 2:13-18), which atoned for all sin, past, present, and future. There are three Greek words, at least the three most often used, which typify Redemption. They are:

1. Garazo: this refers to the price being paid, and, thereby, the slave being purchased out of the market place.

2. Exgarazo: this refers to the fact that the price was so adequately paid, that the person purchased out of the slave market of sin, thereby a captive of Satan, will never again have to be worried about being placed on that particular auction block, so to speak.

3. Lutroo: such a price was paid, that in eternity future, Angels, whether fallen or otherwise, will never be able to say that the price was insufficient.

As well, this *"New Covenant,"* which totally and completely fulfilled the Old Covenant, thereby retiring that great Legislation, is so perfect, so complete, so total, that the Holy Spirit, through Paul, referred to it as *"The Everlasting Covenant,"* meaning that in eternity future, it will never have to be amended (Heb. 13:20).

LOVE

In all of this, we must make it clear that the anger of God against man because of his sin never changes His Love for man. The Bible is very clear that God's Love to man never varies, no matter what man may do; indeed, the whole atoning Work of Christ stems from God's great Love.

It was *"while we were yet sinners"* that *"Christ died for us"* (Rom. 5:8).

This truth must be zealously guarded. But, at the same time, we must not allow ourselves to slip into the position of maintaining that God overlooks sin. That He cannot do! Between God and man there must be Reconciliation. Reconciliation is a purely personal matter concerning man's need. Reconciliation in some sense was effected outside man before anything happened within man. This speaks of the Finished Work of Calvary. A reconciliation that can be *"received"* must be offered, and thus in some sense already accomplished.

NOTES

Israel will experience *"Reconciliation"* and *"Restoration"* immediately after the Second Coming of Christ. Zechariah records this event (Zech. 12:10-14; 13:1-2). Then the enmity will be removed, which will then pave the way for a total Restoration to be carried out.

JEALOUSY

The phrase of Verse 5, *"Surely in the fire of My jealousy have I spoken against the residue of the heathen,"* refers to anger at a white-hot pitch.

Edom not only proposed to take *"My Land,"* but to do so with a *"gleeful joy,"* and with *"despiteful minds,"* i.e., *"with contempt of soul,"* meaning that Edom held Judah in contempt, and, as well, Judah's God, Jehovah.

God is *"jealous"* over His people, and, in fact, all that He is or has. This means that it belongs to Him, and that He doesn't take kindly to someone else attempting to hurt His property, or even take His property. Such, as should be obvious, is a dead-end street. In other words, all who enter that street don't come back!

(6) "PROPHESY THEREFORE CONCERNING THE LAND OF ISRAEL, AND SAY UNTO THE MOUNTAINS, AND TO THE HILLS, TO THE RIVERS, AND TO THE VALLEYS, THUS SAITH THE LORD GOD; BEHOLD, I HAVE SPOKEN IN MY JEALOUSY AND IN MY FURY, BECAUSE YOU HAVE BORNE THE SHAME OF THE HEATHEN:

(7) "THEREFORE THUS SAITH THE LORD GOD; I HAVE LIFTED UP MY HAND, SURELY THE HEATHEN WHO ARE ABOUT YOU, THEY SHALL BEAR THEIR SHAME.

(8) "BUT YOU, O MOUNTAINS OF ISRAEL, YOU SHALL SHOOT FORTH YOUR BRANCHES, AND YIELD YOUR FRUIT TO MY PEOPLE OF ISRAEL; FOR THEY ARE AT HAND TO COME.

(9) "FOR, BEHOLD, I AM FOR YOU, AND I WILL TURN UNTO YOU, AND YOU SHALL BE TILLED AND SOWN:

(10) "AND I WILL MULTIPLY MEN UPON YOU, ALL THE HOUSE OF ISRAEL, EVEN ALL OF IT: AND THE CITIES SHALL BE INHABITED, AND THE WASTES SHALL BE BUILT:

(11) "AND I WILL MULTIPLY UPON

YOU MAN AND BEAST; AND THEY SHALL INCREASE AND BRING FRUIT: AND I WILL SETTLE YOU AFTER YOUR OLD ESTATES, AND WILL DO BETTER UNTO YOU THAN AT YOUR BEGINNINGS: AND YOU SHALL KNOW THAT I AM THE LORD.

(12) "YES, I WILL CAUSE MEN TO WALK UPON YOU, EVEN MY PEOPLE ISRAEL; AND THEY SHALL POSSESS YOU, AND YOU SHALL BE THEIR INHERITANCE, AND YOU SHALL NO MORE HENCEFORTH BEREAVE THEM OF MEN.

(13) "THUS SAITH THE LORD GOD; BECAUSE THEY SAY UNTO YOU, YOUR LAND DEVOURS UP MEN, AND HAS BEREAVED YOUR NATIONS:

(14) "THEREFORE YOU SHALL DEVOUR MEN NO MORE, NEITHER BEREAVE YOUR NATIONS ANY MORE, SAITH THE LORD GOD.

(15) "NEITHER WILL I CAUSE MEN TO HEAR IN YOU THE SHAME OF THE HEATHEN ANY MORE, NEITHER SHALL YOU BEAR THE REPROACH OF THE PEOPLE ANY MORE, NEITHER SHALL YOU CAUSE YOUR NATIONS TO FALL ANY MORE, SAITH THE LORD GOD."

The exegesis is:

1. As fertile as Palestine was in the remote past, it will be much more fruitful in the future.

2. The shame with which the heathen covered Israel, by spreading the evil report that the land devoured its inhabitants, will be obviously reversed, with the Land being greatly blessed, in fact, the garden of the world.

3. The Restoration of the people will synchronize with the restoration of the land.

SHAME

The key to Verse 6 is the phrase *"You have borne the shame of the heathen."* This means, as it regards God's people, shame is temporary, while that of their enemies is perpetual.

The Law of Retribution is demanded by the absolute Righteousness of God. The judicial visitations of God cannot possibly be one-sided. That which has been meted out to Israel for their sin will be meted out to Eden, as well as all other opposing nations.

The phrase of Verse 7, *"I have lifted up My Hand,"* refers to God taking an oath that

NOTES

what He had stated about the heathen and their punishment will most surely come to pass.

As well as ancient Edom, a present example is noted. I speak of the former Soviet Union.

This bastion of Communism caused Christians who were in the Soviet Union to suffer terrible shame, as well as great persecution, and throughout the entirety of its some seventy-two-year reign.

And then, in 1989, and before the entire world, the Soviet Union disintegrated, producing a national shame, especially for Communism, felt all around the world!

Sometimes the shame is slow in coming, sometimes rapidly so, as the example just given, but come it shall! The Lord has made a solemn vow, *"They shall bear their shame,"* and bear their shame they shall!

MORAL ELEVATION

The phrase of Verse 8, *"O mountains of Israel,"* and *"the everlasting hills"* of Genesis 49:26 are terms expressive of the moral elevation of Israel over the physical elevation of Edom. In fact, Edom was mountainous. So this tells us, that when Israel comes back to God, which they will at the Second Coming, and do so by accepting God's Son, the Lord Jesus Christ, that their moral elevation will be the highest of any nation in the world.

The phrase, *"For they are at hand to come,"* has the same connotation as *"lifted up My Hand"* in Verse 7. The Lord takes an oath that, as He swore to punish Edom, and even to make her desolate, conversely, He will bless Israel. This will be during the coming Kingdom Age.

PROSPERITY

The phrase of Verse 9, *"Tilled and sown,"* speaks of prosperity.

As the Lord said that He was *"against"* Edom (35:3), He, conversely, says of Israel, *"I am for you."*

"Prosperity" given by the Lord affects every part and parcel of one's life and living. First of all, there must be *"spiritual prosperity."* This can be gained only by the Believer properly placing his faith in the correct object, which must ever be the Cross of Christ. Let's say it again:

1. The only way to God is through Jesus

Christ (Jn. 14:20).

2. The only way to Christ is through the Cross (Jn. 3:16; Eph. 2:13-18).

3. The only way to the Cross is through a denial of self (Lk. 9:23-24).

When *"spiritual prosperity"* becomes obvious, physical, financial, material, domestical, and social prosperity will then follow. The problem of the Church, and especially the last several decades, it has made financial prosperity its theme, while ignoring the spiritual. Such is not to be, as such cannot be!

The phrase of Verse 10, *"And I will multiply,"* proclaims the degree of Blessing which will be given to Israel in that coming glad day.

As the Lord outlined the destruction of Edom and other nations, He, here, outlines the coming blessing and prosperity of the *"House of Israel."* And then He said *"even all of it,"* meaning that the entirety of the Land would be blessed, which will incorporate both the Northern and Southern Kingdoms, plus all of that which was originally promised to Abraham. It will take in Lebanon, Syria, part of Iraq, and the Arabian Peninsula. This will be during the coming Kingdom Age.

The phrase of Verse 11, *"And will do better unto you than at your beginnings,"* proclaims the fact, that as fertile as Israel was, at least at times, in the remote past, it will be much more fruitful in the future. It will be a condition of prosperity so great that it should surpass any measure or degree of Blessing previously enjoyed, not only by Israel, but any nation in the world.

When one considers the Blessing of the Lord on Israel under Solomon, which made it the premier nation in the world of that day, with silver being as rocks on the ground, then the magnitude of the coming Blessing is on a scale little comprehended.

MY PEOPLE SHALL POSSESS THE LAND

Edom said they would possess the land, and the Lord says, in Verse 12, that *"My People Israel shall possess you,"* speaking of the Land.

The phrase of Verse 12, *"And you shall no more henceforth bereave them of men,"* means that all war will cease, which previously, and greatly so, thinned the ranks. Not only will there be no more war, but due to the trees that will grow beside the River, which will proceed from under the threshold of the Temple, death will be abolished (Ezek. 47:12).

The heathen had said, as Verse 13 proclaims, *"Because they say unto you, Your land devours up men, and has bereaved the nations,"* proclaiming the fact that the heathen spread the evil report that the Land devoured its inhabitants, and, was, therefore, cursed!

The phrase of Verse 14, *"Therefore you shall devour men no more,"* pertains to the blessings which will come upon Israel during the coming Kingdom Age.

The idea of Verse 14 is: the great spiritual conflict between light and darkness had brought about the terrible contest for the Land of Israel which began immediately upon its inception, and continued throughout its history. Even though the contest raged fiercely, with tremendous loss of life and destruction of property, still, it is doubtful if the *"nations"* fully understood, or even understood at all, the cause of the conflict.

In fact, that conflict rages even at this very moment, making Israel possibly the most dangerous place on Earth. It is dangerous not only for what is taking place in the confines of its borders, but what it could bring about as it involves confrontation between other nations. So the conflict remains, and will remain, making the Land of Israel the most dangerous place on Earth, which will remain that way until the Coming of the Lord. In fact, the danger is going to increase tremendously so in the near future, especially with the rise of the Antichrist.

THE WORD OF THE LORD

Verses 15 and 16 proclaim the fact that Israel will be completely restored in the coming Kingdom Age, and beyond the shadow of a doubt. The *"Word of the Lord"* proclaims this fact, and to be sure, that which the Lord has spoken will definitely come true.

That God has ever stooped to use mere mortals to proclaim His Glorious Word will ever be a mystery. It is the *"Treasure in earthen vessels"* (II Cor. 4:7).

In fact, the Word of the Lord is the only Truth in the world, and, in fact, ever has been.

(16) "MOREOVER THE WORD OF THE LORD CAME UNTO ME, SAYING,

(17) "SON OF MAN, WHEN THE HOUSE OF ISRAEL DWELT IN THEIR OWN LAND, THEY DEFILED IT BY THEIR OWN WAY AND BY THEIR DOINGS: THEIR WAY WAS BEFORE ME AS THE UNCLEANNESS OF A REMOVED WOMAN.

(18) "WHEREFORE I POURED MY FURY UPON THEM FOR THE BLOOD THAT THEY HAD SHED UPON THE LAND, AND FOR THEIR IDOLS WHEREWITH THEY HAD POLLUTED IT:

(19) "AND I SCATTERED THEM AMONG THE HEATHEN, AND THEY WERE DISPERSED THROUGH THE COUNTRIES: ACCORDING TO THEIR WAY AND ACCORDING TO THEIR DOINGS I JUDGED THEM.

(20) "AND WHEN THEY ENTERED UNTO THE HEATHEN, WHITHER THEY WENT, THEY PROFANED MY HOLY NAME, WHEN THEY SAID TO THEM, THESE ARE THE PEOPLE OF THE LORD, AND ARE GONE FORTH OUT OF HIS LAND.

(21) "BUT I HAD PITY FOR MY HOLY NAME, WHICH THE HOUSE OF ISRAEL HAD PROFANED AMONG THE HEATHEN, WHITHER THEY WENT."

The exegesis is:

1. Verse 17 admits, *"their own way."* Man's way is defiling and defiles.

2. The uncleanness of Verse 17 pictures the vileness of the sinner in God's sight. The first statement of Verse 29 declares the ability of the Saviour to fully cleanse the sinner.

3. The argument of Verses 19 and 20 is, that not only did Israel profane Jehovah's Name in the land prior to the Exile, but they also profaned it among the heathen during the Exile. Their conduct was so bad as captives that the heathen pointed at them with contempt and revulsion, saying: *"These are the people of Jehovah,"* etc. They profaned God by degrading Him to companionship with the idols of the heathen, and also by their immoral conduct (Williams).

DEFILEMENT

The phrase of Verse 17, *"They defiled it by their own way,"* refers to anything and everything that man does, even Christian man, which is done in his own strength and ability, which means that it's not strictly according to the Word of God, always defiles. As we have stated, man's way is defiling and defiles.

The phrase, *"Their way was before Me as the uncleanness of a removed woman,"* pictures the vileness of the sinner in God's sight. The Lord is here using the symbolism of a woman's monthly period, which women undergo until the change of life, which spiritually is meant to symbolize the uncleanness of the heart, all due to the Fall. It was used as an example of Israel's uncleanness.

Going back to *"man's ways,"* it must be readily understood that if the object of our Faith is anything other than the Cross, the Lord marks it down as *"spiritual uncleanliness,"* which, of course, can never be accepted by the Lord. It is the Cross, and the Cross alone, which makes it possible for the Righteousness of Christ to be freely imputed to the individual, whoever that individual may be. The Righteousness of Christ, which is a pure, spotless, unsullied Righteousness, the only kind that God will accept, cannot be earned, cannot be merited, cannot be purchased. It can only be received as a free gift, and is predicated solely upon Faith, and by that we are speaking of Faith in Christ and what Christ has done for us at the Cross.

That is about as simple as simple can be; however, it is very difficult for man to accept, even religious man, and especially religious man!

There are three kinds of Righteousness, to which the Word of God points, with only one being acceptable to the Lord. This is aptly described by Christ in the Parable of the Pharisee and the Publican. Jesus said:

"Two men went up into the Temple to pray; the one a Pharisee, and the other a Publican.

"The Pharisee stood and prayed thus with himself, God, I thank You, that I am not as other men are, extortioners, unjust, adulterers, or even as this Publican.

"I fast twice in the week, I give tithes of all that I possess.

"And the Publican, standing afar off, would not lift up so much as his eyes unto Heaven, but smote upon his breast, saying,

God be merciful to me a sinner.

"I tell you, this man went down to his house justified rather than the other: for everyone who exalts himself shall be abased; and he who humbles himself shall be exalted" (Lk. 18:10-14).

To be frank, the *"Pharisee"* of Jesus' day was accepted in Israel as being an excellent example of Righteousness. By contrast, the *"Publican,"* who was actually a tax-collector, was looked at as the lowest of the low, with many in Israel thinking that those who functioned in such an occupation could not be saved. In effect, in one way or the other, these particular individuals were in the employ of Rome, which was abhorrent to Israel. So here we have the two men placed in total contrast, and done so by Christ in order to teach a most valuable lesson.

RELATIVE RIGHTEOUSNESS

Jesus drew attention first of all to *"relative righteousness,"* and what is that?

The Pharisee compared himself to others as Verse 11 brings out, claiming that he was better than they were, and, in fact, even better than the Publican who stood some distance behind him, to whom we will address ourselves momentarily.

A great many in the modern Church gauge their Salvation or their walk with God relative to others. In other words, they pick out somebody who has done something very wrong, and because they have not done that thing, they automatically judge themselves as being more righteous than that person, whomever that person might be. Anytime we compare our righteousness to the righteousness of other people, whomever those people might be, we are, in fact, functioning from the position of *"relative righteousness,"* a righteousness, incidentally, which is self-righteousness, and which God can never accept.

The Church has a great problem in understanding how a Christian can do something wrong, and as bad as it might be, earnestly seek the Lord for Mercy, Grace and forgiveness, and, thereby, to be declared perfectly righteous, and to do so in a few moments time. Few can accept that, which means they are rejecting the Righteousness of Christ in favor of a man-devised righteousness.

In no way is this meant to portray sin in a light manner. Sin is awful in any context, and will always have an extremely negative effect upon the Child of God, if committed. That certainly should be understood, and, in fact, well understood!

But the truth is, there is no way the sinner can be saved, or the Christian can be made right, outside of the imputed Righteousness of Christ, which is instantly given upon believing faith. Otherwise, he is placed in the ranks of the *"Pharisee,"* with his *"relative righteousness."*

WORKS RIGHTEOUSNESS

If one is practicing *"relative righteousness,"* it is certain that they will, as well, be plagued with *"works righteousness."* And what is that?

The same Pharisee went on to say, *"I fast twice in the week, I give tithes of all that I possess,"* which means that his faith was resting in his works, which again, God cannot accept. He felt that him doing these things made him righteous in God's sight, which again, is the blight of the modern Church, and, in fact, has always been.

Regrettably, the far greater majority of the modern Church is depending on a *"relative righteousness"* and a *"works righteousness."* Momentarily, I will tell you how I know that.

Our Lord is not here demeaning the paying of tithes or fasting: He is rather condemning faith being placed in those things, thinking that the doing of such earns us something with God. In fact, every good Christian will pay their tithes and give offerings to the Lord. Every good Christian will, at times, *"fast."* The idea is, as stated, that our faith is not to be placed in those things, as helpful as they are in their own right.

IMPUTED RIGHTEOUSNESS

The *"Publican"* could not boast of any of the things to which the *"Pharisee"* alluded. Even if he had done some good things, he never mentioned them, but only exclaimed to the Lord his true self as a sinner. Jesus said of this man that he *"would not lift up so much as his eyes unto Heaven, but smote upon his breast, saying, God be merciful to me a sinner"* (Lk. 18:13).

Now, as the Lord was not condemning the paying of tithes and fasting, neither is He claiming that there is virtue in being a sinner. Quite the contrary!

Our Lord is merely stating that the man admitted what he was, which, of course, God already knew, but which the Pharisee would not admit. The Publican cried for *"Mercy,"* and that's exactly what he received.

In fact, Jesus said that *"This man went down to his house justified rather than the other,"* with the *"other"* speaking of the Pharisee.

This means that the Lord instantly imputed a perfect Righteousness to this man because he admitted what he was, and because he asked for Mercy. So, one moment the man was a *"sinner,"* which means that he had no Righteousness at all, and the next moment he is totally righteous, having been imputed Righteousness freely by the Lord, which is the only way that true Righteousness can be granted and received.

Now the Church, regrettably, has a difficult time accepting this. Let's look at it a little further:

RIGHTEOUSNESS AND THE CROSS

As we've said any number of times in this Volume, for everything that we receive from the Lord, and I mean everything, Christ is always the *"Source,"* and the Cross is the *"Means."*

This means that every single thing that Christ gives us, and whatever it might be, comes to us exclusively through His Sacrifice of Himself on the Cross. In other words, the Cross makes it all possible.

Before the Cross, and I speak of Old Testament times, everything was granted to seeking souls on the basis of a Work that was yet to be developed, i.e., *"the Cross,"* all symbolized in the Sacrifices. Since the Cross, everything is given to us predicated on that Finished Work. Whatever we need, and irrespective as to what it might be, Christ has always had that commodity, be it Righteousness, or whatever; however, it is the Cross which makes it possible for these things to be given to us.

In fact, it is the Holy Spirit Who perfects these things in our lives, and Who Alone can perfect these things. But what He does, is to take that which Christ has made possible by the Cross, and then brings them about in our lives, according to our faith being placed in the correct object, which is the Cross (Rom. 6:3-14; 8:1-2, 11; Gal., Chpt. 5; 6:14; Eph. 2:13-18; Col. 2:14-15).

The Holy Spirit works exclusively within the confines of the parameters of the Sacrifice of Christ, meaning that what Christ did at the Cross gives the Holy Spirit the legal right to do the things which He does. Before the Cross, He could only abide *"with"* the Saints, while since the Cross, He now abides *"in"* the Saints, and does so permanently (Jn. 14:16-17).

THE FURY OF THE LORD

The phrase of Verse 18, *"Wherefore I poured out My fury upon them for the blood that they had shed upon the land,"* proclaims an appalling sin.

This Verse proclaims that the idol worship of Israel produced the shedding of blood in the offering up of little children in human sacrifices. Because of this, the anger of the Lord knew no bounds. As a result, and because they would not repent, He *"poured out His fury upon them."*

The *"fury"* of man is one thing, while the *"fury"* of God is something else altogether.

While all sin is awful in the eyes of God, and should be awful in our eyes as well, still, some sins, as should be obvious, are worse than others. In other words, while God abhors all sin, there are certain sins that anger Him greatly. I think it should be understood, that the offering up of little children as human sacrifices would be one of the most egregious sins of all.

How could Israel do such a thing, especially considering that they gave the world the Word of God, and, in fact, were the only people on the face of the Earth who were privileged to have the Word of God?

All sin, and I speak of Believers, always begins by the Believer's faith being improperly placed. This was so before the Cross, and it is certainly so after the Cross (I Cor. 1:18, 23).

During this time, even while Israel was offering up little children as human sacrifices, they were, at the same time, offering up the lambs as sacrifices at the Temple. But the truth is, they had lost all understanding as to what the sacrificial ritual actually meant. In fact, the ritual of offering up animal sacrifices couldn't save anyone. It was that to which these sacrifices pointed, and which they symbolized, namely Christ, and what He would do at the Cross, which effected Salvation. In fact, this meant that the object of Faith for these Jews was meant to be the Cross, exactly as it is presently.

But when they lost that understanding, treating the animal sacrifices as no more than a ceremony or a ritual, which means they had abandoned the Cross, they were then an open target for Satan to take them ever deeper into sin, which he most definitely did. It is the same presently!

Whenever the object of faith is wrong for the Child of God, whether before the Cross or after the Cross, the results will be the same — abject failure!

If the Believer is not trusting Christ and the Cross, and one cannot trust Christ unless one has his faith anchored squarely in the Cross, failure will result, which is unavoidable, and, in fact, will get worse and worse, and because an improper object of faith stops the Holy Spirit from performing His Work within our lives. And to be sure, without the full work of the Holy Spirit, the Believer simply cannot live a successful Christian life.

SCATTERED

The phrase of Verse 19, *"And I scattered them among the heathen,"* not only concerned Ezekiel's day, but, as well, concerned itself with A.D. 70 when Titus destroyed Jerusalem. This was done because they *"shed the Blood of Christ."* As a result, they were *"scattered"* all over the world, and remained that way until 1948.

Actually, in a sense, the majority of Jews are still scattered, and will only be fully restored at the Second Coming of Christ.

THE PEOPLE OF THE LORD

The phrase of Verse 20, *"These are the people of the LORD,"* was actually said by the heathen and said in derision. In other words, it was said in scorn, bringing great reproach upon the Lord, and, of course, upon His people, all which was purposefully intended.

Actually, the Jews were the only *"people of the LORD"* in the entirety of the world; however, their being defeated caused the heathen to conclude that Jehovah had either behaved capriciously towards His people and cast them off, or had proved unequal to the task of protecting them. In either case, the honor of Jehovah had been lessened in the mind and tarnished by the words of the heathen. This, of course, had been brought about by Israel's sin.

THE HOLY NAME OF THE LORD

The phrase of Verse 21, *"But I had pity for My Holy Name,"* proclaims that the Lord will do certain positive things, but not because of any good in Israel, but because of good in Himself.

Israel had become so corrupt, necessitating the destruction of themselves as a people and a nation, that there was no logical reason that they should be restored. They had not only *"profaned"* the Name of the Lord in their own Land, but had also *"profaned it among the heathen, whither they went."*

However, for His Holy Name's sake, and all it represented, which pertained to His Promises and His Word, which He watches over even above all His Name, for that reason and that reason alone, Israel will be restored, as the following Verses even unto the end of this Chapter will proclaim.

Actually, the tenor of these statements constitutes the foundation of the great Doctrine of Grace. God saves man, not because He sees something good in man, but because there is something good in Himself; consequently, even under the New Covenant, which is predicated on Grace, still, God's dealings with His family, the Church, is predicated basically as it was with Israel of old, that much, if not all, of what He does is because of His own honor which constitutes His Name and His Word. The Psalmist said: *"For You have magnified Your Word above all Your Name"* (Ps. 138:2).

God's Promises are wrapped up in His Name, whereas His performance is wrapped up in His Word. In other words, His performance is always greater than His Promise!

(22) "THEREFORE SAY UNTO THE HOUSE OF ISRAEL, THUS SAITH THE LORD GOD; I DO NOT THIS FOR YOUR SAKES, O HOUSE OF ISRAEL, BUT FOR MY HOLY NAME'S SAKE, WHICH YOU HAVE PROFANED AMONG THE HEATHEN, WHERE YOU WENT.

(23) "AND I WILL SANCTIFY MY GREAT NAME, WHICH WAS PROFANED AMONG THE HEATHEN, WHICH YOU HAVE PROFANED IN THE MIDST OF THEM; AND THE HEATHEN SHALL KNOW THAT I AM THE LORD, SAITH THE LORD GOD, WHEN I SHALL BE SANCTIFIED IN YOU BEFORE THEIR EYES.

(24) "FOR I WILL TAKE YOU FROM AMONG THE HEATHEN, AND GATHER YOU OUT OF ALL COUNTRIES, AND WILL BRING YOU INTO YOUR OWN LAND.

(25) "THEN WILL I SPRINKLE CLEAN WATER UPON YOU, AND YOU SHALL BE CLEAN: FROM ALL YOUR FILTHINESS, AND FROM ALL YOUR IDOLS, WILL I CLEANSE YOU.

(26) "A NEW HEART ALSO WILL I GIVE YOU, AND A NEW SPIRIT WILL I PUT WITHIN YOU: AND I WILL TAKE AWAY THE STONY HEART OUT OF YOUR FLESH, AND I WILL GIVE YOU AN HEART OF FLESH.

(27) "AND I WILL PUT MY SPIRIT WITHIN YOU, AND CAUSE YOU TO WALK IN MY STATUTES, AND YOU SHALL KEEP MY JUDGMENTS, AND DO THEM.

(28) "AND YOU SHALL DWELL IN THE LAND THAT I GAVE TO YOUR FATHERS; AND YOU SHALL BE MY PEOPLE, AND I WILL BE YOUR GOD.

(29) "I WILL ALSO SAVE YOU FROM ALL YOUR UNCLEANNESSES: AND I WILL CALL FOR THE CORN, AND WILL INCREASE IT, AND LAY NO FAMINE UPON YOU.

(30) "AND I WILL MULTIPLY THE FRUIT OF THE TREE, AND THE INCREASE OF THE FIELD, THAT YOU SHALL RECEIVE NO MORE REPROACH OF FAMINE AMONG THE HEATHEN."

The synopsis is:

1. Unless an individual seeks first the Kingdom of God and His Righteousness, material prosperity will not fall out to an increase in Godliness, but rather the very opposite.

2. The sinner's only claim for Life and Righteousness is his sinfulness, i.e., *"to admit his sinfulness."*

3. The *"new heart"* and the *"new spirit"* pertain exclusively to the New Covenant, which Israel rejected, and did so by rejecting Christ, but which they must accept, and, in fact, will accept at the Second Coming.

THE NAME OF THE LORD

Four times in as many Verses, the Holy Spirit, through the Prophet, mentions the Holy Name of the Lord, and how that Israel, as Verse 22 says, *"profaned it among the heathen."*

In fact, if one is to notice, there is much repetition in what the Holy Spirit says through the Prophet, even as it regards all of these Prophecies. This is done by design.

Anything the Lord says is of vital significance; but when He repeats Himself, even as He here does, we are being made to know just how serious all of this is.

Israel had lost her way, and would now have to come under the yoke of Gentile powers, which God never intended. As such, she by and large lost her authority in the world, which, in fact, ultimately caused her total destruction. Even though the situation during the time of Ezekiel was bad, very bad, still, the die was cast when Israel crucified Christ. Jesus said of her at that time, *"Your house is left unto you desolate"* (Mat. 23:38).

THE NEW COVENANT

Profaning the Name of the Lord under the New Covenant is far more subtle than it was under the Old. And yet, in some sense of the word, it is almost identical.

As Israel of old lost sight of what the Sacrifices actually meant, the modern Church has long since forgot what the Cross actually means. So that makes the Old and the New, at least in this capacity, one and the same. As Israel of old went into sin, likewise, the modern Church does the same.

The basic difference is the *"idols"*! While the principle is the same, the type of idols is different now than then. Then it was heathenistic gods, now it basically centers up in *"self."*

When the Believer under the New Covenant attempts to live for the Lord by means other than faith in Christ and what Christ did at the Cross, in the eyes of God, such a Believer has *"profaned the Name of the Lord."* In fact, the first four Verses of Romans, Chapter 7 proclaims such a person as living in *"spiritual adultery."* Christ and the Cross are to be looked to for everything, but when something is substituted in place of the Cross, even though Jesus continues to be praised, the end result is always *"another Jesus"* (II Cor. 11:4).

Paul said if we do such a thing, *"Christ shall profit you nothing"* (Gal. 5:2). In fact, the entirety of the Epistle to the Galatians was written to address this very thing.

Israel was a nation; therefore, she went into bondage to the Gentile Powers and because of *"profaning the Name of the Lord."* The Church is not a nation, but rather individual people, who are supposed to be Born-Again. So the individual Christian doesn't come under the bondage of a nation, but rather of demon spirits (Gal. 5:1).

SANCTIFICATION

The phrase of Verse 23, *"And I will sanctify My great Name, which was profaned among the heathen,"* proclaims that which the Lord did do in sending His Son, the Lord Jesus Christ, to this world.

God's acts of Grace toward guilty men solely because of His Name as Saviour, and not because of any moral excellence in them, are shown in Verses 21, 22, 23, and 32. Therefore, the sinner's only claim for Life and Righteousness is his sinfulness and not his righteousness, of which he has none.

The phrase, *"When I shall be sanctified in you before their eyes,"* refers to the Lord's Name always being *"set apart"* exclusively for sacred use.

The idea regarding *"their eyes"* is that Jehovah, and due to Israel's sinfulness, had been reduced to a feeble and local divinity.

The heathen had no understanding as to Israel's disobedience which resulted in their Judgment. They merely thought that Jehovah was not strong or powerful enough to deliver, which *"in their eyes"* meant that their national gods were stronger than Jehovah.

NOTES

CLEAN WATER

The phrase of Verse 24, *"For I will take you from among the heathen . . . and will bring you unto your own Land,"* proclaims that which is not at all fulfilled, even at this time. Since 1948 Israel has been a State, which, of course, is a fulfillment of Bible Prophecy. As a result, they have come from many countries of the world to make up modern Israel; however, as important and necessary as that is, this is not exactly that which was meant by the Holy Spirit.

It will be fulfilled in totality only at the Second Coming of Christ, when Israel, as the next Verse proclaims, then accepts the Lord.

The phrase of Verse 25, *"Then will I sprinkle clean water upon you, and you shall be clean from all your filthiness,"* by the use of the word *"then,"* marks the time for the fulfillment of all these Prophecies. Israel, as a nation, will not be won to Christ until the Antichrist is defeated by the Second Coming of Christ.

Israel, or any person for that matter, cannot be cleansed until they accept Christ as their Lord and Saviour. The Scripture plainly tells us:

"The Blood of Jesus Christ God's Son cleanses us from all sin" (I Jn. 1:7). That is the only cleansing agent, and, in fact, has always been the only cleansing agent.

HOW DOES THE BLOOD OF JESUS CHRIST CLEANSE FROM ALL SIN?

There is no cleansing agent per se in blood, as should be obvious. What is meant is this:

When Jesus died on the Cross, thereby pouring out His Life's Blood, offering Himself in Sacrifice, His Life, as well as His physical body, was perfect in every respect. In other words, He was not born by natural procreation, but rather by decree of the Holy Spirit. Neither Joseph, nor any other man was His father. In fact, Mary only provided a house for Him, so to speak, for the nine months of Him being formed in His Mother's womb. As a result, He didn't carry the traits of His Mother or foster father, or His brothers and sisters. In fact, His conception and birth were totally unlike any conception and birth which had ever been. He was born without original sin, meaning that He had no sin nature. He was not a product of Adam's Fall.

As well, His Life was perfect, not tainted by sin in any respect, for He never sinned or failed in any respect, not in word, thought, or deed! When He came to the end of His life and was ready to be offered, He said as it regards evil, *"For the prince of this world comes, and has nothing in Me"* (Jn. 14:30).

So when He died on the Cross, He died as a Perfect Sacrifice, which was the pouring out of His Life, which God did accept, and which atoned for all sin (Jn. 1:29). Therefore, when the believing sinner accepts Christ as his Lord and Saviour, and is instantly regenerated by the Holy Spirit, which is the *"born again"* experience, all sin being atoned, spiritually speaking, such a person is *"washed, sanctified, and justified in the Name of the Lord Jesus, and by the Spirit of our God"* (I Cor. 6:11).

When any individual accepts Christ, the atoning work of Christ is accepted as well, which means that the sin debt, as it regards that particular individual, is totally erased and done away. It is no more chargeable to that person, because Christ has paid the price. It is all done because of Him giving Himself on the Cross, shedding His Life's Blood, which alone could effect our Salvation.

THE NEW HEART AND THE NEW SPIRIT

The phrase of Verse 26, *"A new heart also will I give you, and a new spirit will I put within you,"* speaks of the New Birth, and totally refutes the claims of those who say that modern Israel will not be restored, and, that they have no part or parcel in the Gospel program presently, or in the future.

These false teachers claim that this was offered to Israel through Christ, but was rejected and, therefore, forfeited; however, those claims do not match up with these Promises. These Promises proclaim a Restoration, which means there will be no rejection or rebellion against Christ in that Coming Glad Day.

In other words, the Prophecy is not conditional. Through foreknowledge the Lord proclaims what will be done, because of what Israel will do in her acceptance of Christ, which is foretold not only by Ezekiel but Isaiah, Jeremiah, Zechariah, and others!

THE SPIRIT OF THE LORD

The phrase of Verse 27, *"And I will put My Spirit within you,"* refers to the *"born-again"* experience, but, as well, *"the Baptism with the Holy Spirit."* This speaks of the ratification of the New Covenant given on the Day of Pentecost (Acts 2:1-4). This, Israel could have had from the First Advent of Christ, if they had only accepted Him, instead of rejecting Him.

Without the Holy Spirit, it is not possible to *"walk in My Statutes, and keep My Judgments"* (Acts 1:8; Rom. 8:11).

All of this corresponds exactly with that given in the New Testament of the regeneration of the individual soul (Jn. 3:3-8; Rom. 8:2, 5, 9; Gal. 5:22-23; Titus 3:5-6; I Pet. 1:22).

Regarding Salvation, Israel must come in the same manner to Christ as any individual. They must accept Him by Faith as all others do, and that they shall do after the Second Advent.

Some have claimed that there are two kinds of Salvation, one for the Jews and one for the Gentiles! This is error pure and simple, because nowhere in the Bible is it taught that anyone can come to the Father except through Jesus Christ. Jesus said: *"I am the Way, the Truth, and the Life: no man comes unto the Father, but by Me"* (Jn. 14:6).

Before the First Advent of Christ, men were saved by looking forward to the price that would be paid at Calvary, of which the Sacrifices of the Lambs and Bullocks were types. After the Death and Resurrection of Christ, men are saved by looking backward to Calvary and the price paid there.

There aren't two types of Salvation, and, in fact, there never have been. From the time the Lord slew an animal, and *"made coats of skins, and clothed Adam and Eve, which replaced their fig leaves, the Way of Salvation, which was Christ and Him Crucified, was plainly marked"* (Gen. 3:21; Chpt. 4).

THE CROSS

Satan's greatest effort has always been to subtly set Calvary aside as the answer to man's dilemma. He has been amazingly successful. In Paul's day, men attempted to add to the

Finished Work of Christ, by claiming that in order to be saved, one had to accept Christ plus keep the Law (Acts 15:1).

Unfortunately, Satan's efforts did not end with the Early Church. Actually, the Early Church began to apostatize after the death of the Apostle Paul and the Apostles of Christ and those who knew them. By the Third Century, the *"leaven"* of *"works religion"* was insidiously making its way into the Church.

By the Sixth Century A.D., the Church had so apostatized until it was well on its way to becoming the Catholic Church, which is purely a man-made institution. It is no less today! Sadly, much of the Protestant Church follows the same path of *"salvation by works."*

Paul said if works are inserted into that which is to be solely of Faith, that one has *"fallen from Grace"* (Gal. 5:4). In other words, one cannot trust in *"works"* and *"Faith"* at the same time!

Actually, this is what caused Israel to lose her way. Paul said: *"For they being ignorant of God's Righteousness, and going about to establish their own righteousness, have not submitted themselves unto the Righteousness of God"* (Rom. 10:3).

THE GREED MESSAGE

At the present time, Satan's greatest effort against God's True Plan of Salvation is the *"greed message,"* which is the primary message of the Word of Faith doctrine.

This erroneous message, which has made great inroads into Pentecostal and Charismatic Churches, is very subtly presented, and, thereby, very easily deceives its many followers. It is a heady doctrine, because it appeals to greed and pride, which have always been Satan's chief approach (Gen. 3:4-5).

Inasmuch as Scripture is used but subtly twisted in order to sponsor this doctrine, many are deceived. Satan's prime efforts are always cloaked in a heavy panoply of religion; consequently, Israel would kill the Lord in the Name of the Lord!

The greed message subtly sets aside man's real problem, which is sin, and the solution, which is Christ and Him Crucified, and, instead, promotes material blessings and benefits.

In the preaching of this message, which Paul called *"another gospel,"* the Blood of Jesus Christ is subtly, cunningly, and quietly set aside.

Most of the advocates of this spurious doctrine would deny what is being said here; however, if one is to notice, the emphasis, at least for the most part, is not on Christ and Him Crucified, but, instead, on material prosperity.

Inasmuch as there is some Truth in this error, as there is some Truth in most all error, it easily deceives, and, thereby, attracts many followers. As stated, it appeals to greed!

ANOTHER GOSPEL

In fact, most of the preaching presently is little lifting up Christ and Him Crucified as the answer to man's dilemma. It is given lip-service, if at all! The Church is busy trying to *"save society,"* instead of *"saving men out of society,"* which is the true purpose of Christ. The Bible teaches that society is evil, corrupt, and, thereby, doomed! Trying to *"improve society"* is like trying to improve *"self."* It cannot be done! But yet, and to be frank, the *"self-improvement"* gospel is presently the greatest effort of all. It appeals to the flesh, and because it appeals to man's *"pride."* Man likes to think that he can correct his problems of emotional disturbances, wrong direction, lack of confidence, etc., all by *"correcting self."* The pulpits are full of this type of message, which, in fact, doesn't recognize man's true problem, which is *"sin,"* and the true solution, which is *"Jesus Christ and Him Crucified."*

Paul said: *"I determined not to know anything among you, save Jesus Christ and Him Crucified"* (I Cor. 2:2). He said this because man's problem is sin, and, because the only solution to sin is what Christ did at Calvary; consequently, any Church that is not a *"Cross Church"* is not a True Church of Jesus Christ. As well, if the Church goes beyond the Cross, it always goes into heresy.

REGENERATION

Verse 28 says three things:
1. Israel will dwell in the land that God gave to their fathers.

2. Israel will be God's people, as was originally intended.

3. The Lord will be their God, and not idols, etc.

The phrase of Verse 29, *"I will also save you from all your uncleannesses,"* should be the last phrase of Verse 28.

As it regards Salvation, Regeneration and not reformation — a new heart and not a changed heart — is that which must be.

The Holy Spirit never attempts to change the old man, but instead makes a *"new man"* (Rom. 6:6-7; II Cor. 5:17; Gal. 6:15).

(If the word *"change"* is used in the sense of changing from one form to a new form, as in the Resurrection (I Cor. 15:51), then the use is Scriptural, and, thereby, legitimate.)

The phrase of Verse 30, *"That you shall receive no more reproach of famine among the heathen,"* means that in that Coming Glad Day, that Israel will be abundantly blessed, and in every capacity, and so much, in fact, that Israel will be the foremost nation in the world.

(31) "THEN SHALL YOU REMEMBER YOUR OWN EVIL WAYS, AND YOUR DOINGS THAT WERE NOT GOOD, AND SHALL LOATHE YOURSELVES IN YOUR OWN SIGHT FOR YOUR INIQUITIES AND FOR YOUR ABOMINATIONS.

(32) "NOT FOR YOUR SAKES DO I THIS, SAITH THE LORD GOD, BE IT KNOWN UNTO YOU: BE ASHAMED AND CONFOUNDED FOR YOUR OWN WAYS, O HOUSE OF ISRAEL.

(33) "THUS SAITH THE LORD GOD; IN THE DAY THAT I SHALL HAVE CLEANSED YOU FROM ALL YOUR INIQUITIES I WILL ALSO CAUSE YOU TO DWELL IN THE CITIES, AND THE WASTES SHALL BE BUILT.

(34) "AND THE DESOLATE LAND SHALL BE TILLED, WHEREAS IT LAY DESOLATE IN THE SIGHT OF ALL WHO PASSED BY.

(35) "AND THEY SHALL SAY, THIS LAND THAT WAS DESOLATE IS BECOME LIKE THE GARDEN OF EDEN; AND THE WASTE AND DESOLATE AND RUINED CITIES ARE BECOME FENCED, AND ARE INHABITED.

(36) "THEN THE HEATHEN WHO ARE LEFT ROUND ABOUT YOU SHALL KNOW THAT I THE LORD BUILD THE RUINED PLACES, AND PLANT THAT THAT WAS DESOLATE: I THE LORD HAVE SPOKEN IT, AND I WILL DO IT.

(37) "THUS SAITH THE LORD GOD; I WILL YET FOR THIS BE ENQUIRED OF BY THE HOUSE OF ISRAEL, TO DO IT FOR THEM; I WILL INCREASE THEM WITH MEN LIKE A FLOCK.

(38) "AS THE HOLY FLOCK, AS THE FLOCK OF JERUSALEM IN HER SOLEMN FEASTS; SO SHALL THE WASTE CITIES BE FILLED WITH FLOCKS OF MEN: AND THEY SHALL KNOW THAT I AM THE LORD."

The overview is:

1. This new moral nature will be a gift to Israel of the Sovereignty of God; but Israel will ask for it, for this responsibility will attach to them. Sovereign grace and human responsibility are co-existent (Phil. 2:12-13).

2. The effect of Grace is self-judgment.

3. Tyre and Assyria claimed to be like the Garden of Eden. But the similitude belongs only to Israel (28:13; 31:8-9).

4. The theme of these Chapters is the relationship between Jehovah and His people. Hence, there are no details given respecting the First Advent.

THE GRACE OF GOD

The phrase of Verse 31, *"Then shall you remember your own evil ways,"* proclaims the fact that the effect of Grace is always self-judgment.

When men attempt to earn their Salvation by works, as do most, they never really see their *"own evil ways."* Such can only be seen when we properly see the Cross. Then and then only do we see Christ, and seeing Christ puts ourselves in proper perspective, with self then losing its attractiveness.

True Bible Repentance demands that the individual sees himself as God sees him. Paul called it: *"Godly sorrow which works Repentance to Salvation not to be repented of,"* i.e., will not be sorry that he has repented (II Cor. 7:10).

A corrupt Church attempts to build self-esteem, while the Holy Spirit attempts to destroy self-esteem, with self being lost in Christ. The answer is as Paul said: *"For *you are dead and your life is hid with Christ in God"* (Col. 3:3).

The phrase of Verse 32, *"Not for your sakes do I this, saith the Lord GOD,"* goes not only for Israel, but, as well, for all of humanity.

Actually, there was no way that the Lord could do such for their sakes, nor for our sakes for that matter, simply because they, as well as we, lack any merit at all. All that is done for the Child of God is done *"for Christ's sake"* (Eph. 4:32; I Jn. 2:12).

BLESSING

The phrase of Verse 33, *"And the wastes shall be built,"* proclaims the fact that Israel's conversion to Christ will precipitate their Blessing. Only when all iniquities have been *"cleansed"* can the individual then *"dwell"* in the inheritance, with the *"wastes"* then being reclaimed, i.e., *"built."*

As all of this applies to Israel, let it be understood that it applies to us as well! The phrase of Verse 34, *"And the desolate land shall be tilled,"* proclaims the fact that the Land of Israel will be blessed as well as its people. In fact, the people must be blessed first, before the Land can be blessed. Israel getting right with God will bring about *"the desolate land"* being changed.

The phrase of Verse 35, *"Like the Garden of Eden,"* proclaims what this Land will be. If the Holy Spirit refers to Israel, at it regards that Coming Glad Day, as the *"Garden of Eden,"* then it should be obvious that the beauty of such will be beyond imagination.

In the spiritual sense, this is what can happen in the heart and life of every Believer, and, in fact, is what is meant to happen. The Lord desires to make a *"Garden of Eden"* out of our life and living. It can only be done as the Believer firmly looks to Christ and the Cross, understanding that what is needed can only be brought about by the Sacrifice of Christ and our Faith in that Finished Work.

As stated, the world keeps trying to improve self, but can only somewhat decorate the exterior, but even that fades, and fast. It is sadder yet, when the Church has bought into this message of *"self-improvement,"* which it definitely has in the last few years.

As we have repeatedly stated, an improvement of self is not man's need. Outside of Christ, and that goes for the Believer who is not looking solely to Christ and the Cross, *"self"* is ugly, corrupt, ungodly, filthy, and wicked. I realize that's strong, but, in fact, it's not strong enough!

"Self," at least if it is to be what it ought to be, can only be made aright by being placed firmly in Christ, which can only be done by looking to the Cross. Let us say it one more time:

1. The only way to God is through Christ (Jn. 14:6).

2. The only way to Christ is through the Cross (I Cor. 1:17-18, 23).

3. The only way to the Cross is through a denial of self (Lk. 9:23-24).

THE LORD

The phrase of Verse 36, *"Then the heathen who are left round about you shall know that I the LORD build the ruined places,"* proclaims the fact that the Name of the Lord must be glorified in the Earth, which it most definitely will be, at the time of the coming Kingdom Age.

At that time, the entirety of the world will know that Jesus is the Son of God, and that He is the Saviour of mankind, and that He effected Salvation by and through what He did at the Cross.

Then, there will be no more Islam, Hinduism, Catholicism, or Buddhism, etc. As well, all forms of Christianity which have been corrupted will fall by the wayside. There will be nothing left but Christ, and He will rule personally from Jerusalem, and the *"Government shall be upon His shoulder"* (Isa. 9:6).

The phrase of Verse 37, *"I will yet for this be enquired of by the House of Israel,"* refers to the coming Great Tribulation of the future, which will bring Israel to utter desolation, and threatened annihilation, which will precipitate their crying to Him for deliverance. This will bring them to a full Repentance and dependence on the Lord (Isa., Chpt. 64; Zech. 12:10; 13:1; Mat. 23:37-39; Rom. 11:25-29).

The phrase of Verse 38, *"So shall the waste cities be filled with flocks of men,"* proclaims this *"earthly glory and blessing."* This will, as well, trigger the blessing of all the other nations of the world. Even though it is little known, the prosperity of the world hinges on Israel's prosperity. This prosperity is all anchored in Christ and cannot be brought about until Christ is recognized and accepted.

However, it shall happen, because *"the LORD has spoken it, and He will do it."*

"When my life work is ended and I cross
  the swelling tide,
"When the bright and glorious morning I shall see,
"I shall know my Redeemer when I
  reach the other side,
"And His Smile will be the first to welcome me."

"O the soul thrilling rapture when I
  view His blessed Face,
"And the luster of His kindly beaming
  Eye;
"How my full heart will praise Him
  for the Mercy, Love and Grace,
"That prepare for me a mansion in the
  sky."

"O the dear ones in glory, how they
  beckon me to come,
"And our parting at the river I recall;
"To the sweet vales of Eden they will
  sing my welcome home,
"But I long to meet my Saviour first
  of all."

"Thru the gates to the city in a robe of
  spotless white,
"He will lead me where no tears will
  ever fall;
"In the glad song of ages I shall mingle
  with delight,
"But I long to meet my Saviour first
  of all."

CHAPTER 37

(1) "THE HAND OF THE LORD WAS UPON ME, AND CARRIED ME OUT IN THE SPIRIT OF THE LORD, AND SET ME DOWN IN THE MIDST OF THE VALLEY WHICH WAS FULL OF BONES,

(2) "AND CAUSED ME TO PASS BY THEM ROUND ABOUT: AND, BEHOLD, THERE WERE VERY MANY IN THE OPEN VALLEY; AND, LO, THEY WERE VERY DRY.

(3) "AND HE SAID UNTO ME, SON OF MAN, CAN THESE BONES LIVE? AND I ANSWERED, O LORD GOD, YOU KNOW.

(4) "AGAIN HE SAID UNTO ME, PROPHESY UPON THESE BONES, AND SAY UNTO THEM, O YE DRY BONES, HEAR THE WORD OF THE LORD.

(5) "THUS SAITH THE LORD GOD UNTO THESE BONES; BEHOLD, I WILL CAUSE BREATH TO ENTER INTO YOU, AND YOU SHALL LIVE:

(6) "AND I WILL LAY SINEWS UPON YOU, WILL BRING UP FLESH UPON YOU, AND COVER YOU WITH SKIN, AND PUT BREATH IN YOU, AND YOU SHALL LIVE AND YOU SHALL KNOW THAT I AM THE LORD.

(7) "SO I PROPHESIED AS I WAS COMMANDED: AND AS I PROPHESIED, THERE WAS A NOISE, AND BEHOLD A SHAKING, AND THE BONES CAME TOGETHER, BONE TO HIS BONE.

(8) "AND WHEN I BEHELD, LO, THE SINEWS AND THE FLESH CAME UP UPON THEM, AND THE SKIN COVERED THEM ABOVE: BUT THERE WAS NO BREATH IN THEM.

(9) "THEN SAID HE UNTO ME, PROPHESY UNTO THE WIND, PROPHESY, SON OF MAN, AND SAY TO THE WIND, THUS SAITH THE LORD GOD; COME FROM THE FOUR WINDS, O BREATH, AND BREATHE UPON THESE SLAIN, THAT THEY MAY LIVE.

(10) "SO I PROPHESIED AS HE COMMANDED ME, AND THE BREATH CAME INTO THEM, AND THEY LIVED, AND STOOD UP UPON THEIR FEET, AN EXCEEDING GREAT ARMY.

(11) "THEN HE SAID UNTO ME, SON OF MAN, THESE BONES ARE THE WHOLE HOUSE OF ISRAEL: BEHOLD, THEY SAY, OUR BONES ARE DRIED, AND OUR HOPE IS LOST: WE ARE CUT OFF FOR OUR PARTS.

(12) "THEREFORE PROPHESY AND SAY UNTO THEM, THUS SAITH THE LORD GOD; BEHOLD, O MY PEOPLE, I WILL OPEN YOUR GRAVES, AND CAUSE YOU TO COME UP OUT OF YOUR GRAVES, AND BRING YOU INTO THE LAND OF ISRAEL.

(13) "AND YOU SHALL KNOW THAT I AM THE LORD, WHEN I HAVE OPENED YOUR GRAVES, O MY PEOPLE, AND BROUGHT YOU UP OUT OF YOUR GRAVES.

(14) "AND SHALL PUT MY SPIRIT IN YOU, AND YOU SHALL LIVE, AND I SHALL PLACE YOU IN YOUR OWN LAND: THEN SHALL YOU KNOW THAT I THE LORD HAVE SPOKEN IT, AND PERFORMED IT, SAITH THE LORD."

The diagram is:

1. The first Prophecy of this Chapter (Vss. 1-14) foretells the moral, national, and physical resurrection of Israel; the second Prophecy (Vss. 15-28) predicts the unity of the nation, and its happy settlement in the Land of Israel under the Government of the Messiah (Williams).

2. The repetition of *"Behold"* fastens the attention upon the two facts: that the bones were very many and very dry.

3. God demonstrates His existence and power by raising the dead (Jn. 5:21; Rom. 1:4; 4:17; II Cor. 1:9).

4. Professors of Religion may assume all the semblances of Spiritual Life and yet have no life, but be dead before God.

5. The valley was covered over with the bones of men slain by violence, and the graves were filled with the bones of the dead, but God is equal to the resurrection of all.

6. The formula, *"saith Jehovah,"* is to be understood as a confirmation written at the foot of the Prophecy saying: *"This is Jehovah's declaration."*

7. The commanding voice of Cyrus raised the Exiles out of their captivity grave, and restored them to the Land of Israel; however, that voice is not the voice of this Chapter. The Voice of this Chapter will be altogether mightier, and will raise the nation from its present long-continued dispersion and moral death.

THE VALLEY OF DRY BONES

As the last Chapter graphically spoke of Israel's coming Restoration, Ezekiel, Chapter 37 graphically portrays the spiritual manner of that Restoration.

It has been approximately 2,500 years since the Prophet had this Vision, and it is just now coming to pass, but will not be completed until the Second Coming of the Lord. As well, between now and that particular time, Israel is going to face its darkest days yet! However, despite those coming darkened days, which Jesus said would be worse than any had ever been, or ever would be, these Prophecies, and down to the most minute detail, will be fulfilled (Mat. 24:21-22).

Most of Ezekiel's Prophecies begin with the word *"And"* or *"Also"* or *"Moreover."* However, those customary words are missing in this particular Prophesy, indicating something extraordinary, which is obvious.

The phrase in Verse 1, *"In the Spirit of the LORD,"* indicates that this was a Vision, and that Ezekiel was not literally taken to this *"valley,"* etc.

The phrase, *"And set me down in the midst of the valley which was full of bones,"* indicates the spiritual and national identity of Israel as being dead.

Even the most rudimentary Bible student would have to recognize the Truth of the destiny of these people called *"Jews"* or *"Israelites."* If one knows anything at all about their history, one knows that their survival other than God has been an absolute impossibility. Their entire history is one of conflict, persecution, coupled with a sheer determination to remain alive.

Someone has said that the Jew is God's prophetic time clock, and so they are! The only way that these people could have survived through the centuries, and above all now, as a distinct nation in their own Land, is that God has kept them alive for a purpose. That purpose is twofold:

A. To keep the Promises that He made to the Patriarchs and the Prophets (Gen. 12:1-3; II Sam. 7:16).

B. Israel's Restoration will signal the blessings of all the nations of the world under Christ (Ps. 67).

When Judah fell to the Babylonian invader, Jehovah took the scepter of power from the hands of the Kings of Judah and placed it in the hands of the Gentiles. It has remained there ever since, called by Christ *"the times of the Gentiles"* (Lk. 21:24).

THE RESTORATION OF ISRAEL

Upon the Second Coming of the Lord and

Israel's acceptance of Christ as Lord and Messiah, the *"times of the Gentiles"* will come to a close, with Israel once again assuming the role of world leadership under Christ. This is a position that she need not have lost, save for sin, but will then be restored as this Chapter and so many others proclaim.

The world little knows or understands that the prosperity of all the nations of the world hinges on these people. Consequently, even though they are now spiritually dead, and have been for a long, long time, still, God will bless the nation that blesses Israel, and curse the nation that curses Israel (Gen. 12:1-3).

When Israel became a nation in 1948, beginning to fulfill this very Chapter, England opposed her effort strongly. From that day until this, England's power has waned and weakened around the world, until she is only a shell of her former self. Much of this deterioration can be laid at the doorstep of her opposition to these ancient people, and Prophecies being fulfilled. To oppose that which belongs to God, and irrespective of its present spiritual condition, is to oppose God. It is a position in which no man, nation, or kingdom desires to be.

Conversely, the United States strongly aided and abetted Israel in her formation as a nation, and her sustenance since.

Shortly before his death, President Truman was asked as to what he considered to be his most important contribution as the holder of the highest office in the land. His answer shocked the reporter. The President quickly said, *"In helping Israel become a nation."*

In the evening of his life, spiritual matters became very real to President Truman, and evidently the Lord revealed to him the spiritual and political significance of this act.

The only answer to the survival of the Jew, and the national identity of the nation of Israel, is God. There is no other answer, as there can be no other answer!

VERY DRY

The phrase of Verse 2, *"And, lo, they were very dry,"* speaks of a total absence of spirituality. In other words, what is even now happening to Israel is not because of any spirituality on their part, when, in fact, there is none at all, but, rather, signifying that the work is strictly at the behest of the Lord.

Due to them being *"very dry,"* and as a result of having rejected their Messiah, and even crucifying Him, that they have survived the centuries, and especially becoming a nation in 1948, is 100 percent the Hand of God at work.

Even now (2003), there is not an ounce of spirituality in the Land of Israel. In fact, many Jews are atheistic or agnostic.

Even the few who claim to believe the Old Testament are bogged down in legalism and incorrect interpretations of the Bible. Paul said: *"Blindness in part is happened to Israel, until the fulness of the Gentiles be come in"* (Rom. 11:25). That blindness is no less now than it was then, if not deeper!

However, Paul also said, and concerning this very Chapter, and regarding the conclusion of the *"times of the Gentiles,"* that *"all Israel shall be saved"* (Rom. 11:26).

CAN THESE BONES LIVE?

The question of Verse 3, *"And He said unto me, Son of man, can these bones live?"* actually proclaims the impossibility of such a thing, at least as far as human beings are concerned.

An American General, in viewing the horror of the Nazi death camps in 1945, where some 6,000,000 Jews were murdered by Hitler and his henchmen, upon seeing the thousands of dead bodies, and the thousands who were near death, said that this very Passage came to him at that moment, *"Can these bones live?"*

In answer to that question, in 1948, and Israel once again becoming a nation, even after nearly 2,000 years, the Prophecy is beginning to be fulfilled.

Ezekiel's answer to the question of the Lord, *"O Lord GOD, You know,"* signifies that the task within the realm of human endeavor was impossible! And, if they, in fact, were made to *"live,"* it would have to be done by the Hand of God.

Inasmuch as this Prophecy was given shortly after the Fall of Judah and Jerusalem, Ezekiel's mind had to have been filled with these recent events. Whether, at this time, he was able to look beyond that moment to a future day so very, very far away, one can only guess; however, once the Vision of the Restoration of the Land and the graphic design of the Temple were given to him, as is outlined in Chapters 40 through 48, more than likely his understanding of that future day was greatly increased.

PROPHESY

The phrase of Verse 4, *"Again He said unto me, Prophesy upon these bones,"* proclaims the fact that the Lord will give a *"Word"* which will guarantee their Restoration and Revival; however, such could only be done according to the *"Word of the LORD."*

As an aside, many have taken this Passage out of context, thinking they could prophesy things into existence according to their own liking, direction, or will; however, such can be only if it is the Will of God. Therefore, the intimation seems to be, if it is God's Will concerning a particular situation, and irrespective as to how personal or impersonal it may be, one, according to the Word of the Lord, can prophesy upon the situation, which will hasten its success; however, it is only the *"Word of the LORD"* that has the power to bring about the miraculous.

When one considers that these words, uttered some 2,500 years ago, are now beginning to be fulfilled, and before our very eyes, one is made to understand the absolute power of the Word of God.

BREATH

The phrase of Verse 5, *"Behold, I will cause breath to enter into you, and you shall live,"* has the same meaning as Genesis 2:7.

The *"breath"* spoken of is the same breath that God *"breathed into his nostrils the breath of life,"* respecting Adam, and he became *"a living soul."*

The life that is spoken of in this Passage: it speaks of national life and Spiritual Life. The national life has already begun, with Israel having become a nation once again in 1948 and continuing; however, the Spiritual Life will begin in the coming Great Tribulation, when 144,000 Jews will accept Christ as their Saviour, with no doubt others, after the event accepting the Lord as well! (Rev., Chpt. 7). However, the fullness of Spiritual Life will not come until the Second Coming (Zech. 13:1, 9).

As the Spirit of God is the only One Who can breathe life into unregenerate man who is dead in trespasses and sins, likewise, He is the only One Who can bring Israel back. To be sure, the *"Spirit of God,"* Who moved upon the face of a ruined and formless world (Gen. 1:2), will move upon ruined and formless Israel, and, in fact, has already begun to do so!

Ezekiel would later say, in his Vision of the coming Temple, and the River, which is a Type of the Holy Spirit, which will flow out from under the threshold of that house, that *"everything shall live whither the River cometh"* (47:1, 9).

As well, to every weary heart, to every thirsty soul, to everyone who longs for Righteousness, the Lord is saying the same to you that He said of old, concerning Israel, *"I will cause breath to enter into you, and you shall live."*

I AM THE LORD

The phrase of Verse 6, *"And I will lay sinews upon you, and will bring up flesh upon you, and cover you with skin, and put breath in you, and you shall live,"* even though, of course, speaking of Israel, as an aside, proclaims to us the secret of how the Lord originally made man (Gen. 2:7).

As stated, this has already begun regarding Israel's national identity, but will not begin Spiritually until the Great Tribulation, and more specifically at the Second Coming of Christ.

Actually, this Passage specifically speaks of Israel's national and Spiritual identity.

The national identity, which has already begun, speaks of the reconstruction of the external skeleton, by bringing together its different parts and clothing them with *"sinews, flesh, and skin."*

However, the second stage, which is the Spiritual identity, will not be brought about until He breathes Spiritual Life into them.

If, in fact, the first part is already being fulfilled (and it definitely is), this means that we are very close to the second stage being fulfilled. Therefore, how close is the Church to the Rapture?

On July 1, at about 9 a.m., on a Monday

morning, 1985, the Lord gave me a Vision of the world harvest and the coming storm. In the Vision, I saw the heavens that were boiling in blackness as I had never seen before. The Lord told me that He would delay the storm for a short period of time, until the harvest could be gathered.

Even though the Lord did not specifically say such to me, I believe the Vision of the storm, coupled with the *"fields ready to harvest,"* signified the coming great and terrible Tribulation Period.

As we look at these Prophecies, and even the beginning stages of their fulfillment, we know that we're living in the last of the last days.

THE BONES CAME TOGETHER

The phrase of Verse 7, *"And as I prophesied, there was a noise,"* in the Hebrew, actually means *"a voice."*

This *"noise,"* i.e., voice, could actually speak of the *"voice of the Archangel,"* with the *"shaking"* speaking of the Resurrection, signifying the Rapture of the Church.

Actually, Israel will come into full flower at the outset of the Great Tribulation, thinking the Antichrist is the Messiah, which will signify the *"bones coming together,"* even in a greater way; however, as the next Verse suggests, the Antichrist is not the Messiah, and, therefore, he can breathe no breath of life into them, but, in fact, will only bring death.

NO BREATH

The phrase of Verse 8, *"But there was no breath in them,"* concerns their national identity, but definitely not their Spiritual identity.

In fact, Israel will accept the *"man of sin"* as the Messiah, as prophesied by Christ, when He said: *"I am come in My Father's Name, and you received Me not: if another shall come in his own name, him you will receive"* (Jn. 5:43).

The false one whom Israel will receive is the *"another"* spoken of by Christ. As the false Messiah, he can give no *"breath of life."* Only Christ, the True Messiah, can do that!

Actually, as a result of their deception, in the latter half of the Great Tribulation, they will come close to annihilation, with the

NOTES

Antichrist turning on them, and seeking to destroy them as a people and a nation.

At this time, two-thirds, according to the Prophet Zechariah, will die (Zech. 13:8-9).

PROPHESY UNTO THE SPIRIT

The phrase of Verse 9, *"Then said He unto me, Prophesy unto the wind,"* actually says in the Hebrew, *"Prophesy unto the Spirit."*

The phrase, *"Come from the four winds,"* actually says in the Hebrew, *"come from the four breaths."*

The number *"four"* is symbolic of *"fourfold,"* denoting an absolute, total, and complete Restoration.

The phrase, *"And breathe upon these slain, that they may live,"* denotes the Truth, that Israel, in the Mind of God, for all practical and spiritual purposes, is *"dead."*

The word, *"Prophesy,"* denotes the *"Word of the LORD,"* which means that it is *"forever settled in Heaven,"* and cannot be denied, and neither can it fail!

Doubt and unbelief would think it absurd prophesying over *"these bones;"* however, Faith says *"they shall live."*

SPIRITUAL LIFE

The phrase of Verse 10, *"So I prophesied as He commanded me, and the breath came into them, and they lived,"* speaks now of Israel's spiritual identity, signifying their spiritual revival, which will take place at the Second Coming.

The phrase, *"And stood upon their feet,"* pertains to the action part of the Spiritual Life, which enables such to be done.

For a long time, even over 2,000 years, Israel has not *"stood upon their feet"* spiritually. But in the coming Glad Day they shall! Then they shall be an *"exceeding great army,"* but, an *"exceeding great army"* for the Lord.

THE THIRTEEN TRIBES

The phrase in Verse 11, *"The whole House of Israel,"* speaks of the entirety of the thirteen Tribes, and that they will no more be divided, but whole.

The latter part of this Verse, speaking of Israel's exclamation, *"Behold, they say,"* refers to the latter half of the coming Great

Tribulation. At that time, it will look like the entirety of their nation will be totally destroyed, with *"hope lost"* and *"cut off for our parts."* This has reference to Zechariah's Prophecy, when he said, *"Two parts therein shall be cut off and die"* (Zech. 13:8).

At that time, they will be at the conclusion of the second half of the Great Tribulation, and will have, three and one half years before, suffered a terrible defeat at the hands of the Antichrist, with him taking over Jerusalem, and threatening the very existence of these ancient people.

In the Battle of Armageddon, as Ezekiel will describe in Chapters 38 and 39, and as Zechariah prophesied, it will look like *"all hope is lost."* Actually, all hope would be lost, but for the Coming of the Lord; however, He will come, and, as well, He will have *"healing in His Wings"* (Mal. 4:2-3).

GRAVES

The phrase of Verse 12, *"Behold, O My people, I will open your graves, and cause you to come up out of your graves, and bring you into the Land of Israel,"* pertains to a double fulfillment.

As Prophecy sometimes does, the previous Verse spoke of the last few months, or even weeks, before the Coming of the Lord, and, therefore, the relief of Israel, whereas, this Verse goes back even to World War II and forward.

Even though this Verse is symbolic of Israel's destitute spiritual condition, it also is literal.

At the end of the World War II, with 6,000,000 Jews slaughtered by Hitler, the Jews became a cohesive nation some three years later, then literally began the fulfillment of this Passage, and *"cause you to come up out of your graves, and bring you into the Land of Israel."*

Since that time, hundreds of thousands of Jews have come from all over the world, immigrating to the *"Land of Israel,"* with the latest excursion from the former Soviet Union not being the least!

As well, the fulfillment of this Passage concerning the second development will take place after the coming of the Lord, when every Jew on the face of the Earth will be *"brought to the Land of Israel"* (Isa. 11:11-12; 56:8).

The phrase of Verse 13, *"And you shall know that I am the LORD,"* proclaims that which Israel does not yet know; however, this they will *"know"* at the Second Coming.

The phrase, *"And brought you up out of your graves,"* has reference to the fact that Israel, and for all practical purposes, in the Battle of Armageddon, is all but totally destroyed. Actually, there is no earthly way they can be salvaged; however, there is a Heavenly Way! And that Heavenly Way is Christ.

The phrase of Verse 14, *"And shall put My Spirit in you,"* signals the great revival that will take place in Israel at the Coming of the Lord. Zechariah gave in greater detail the happening of this great moving of the Holy Spirit (Zech. 12:10-14; 13:1, 9).

This will actually be the greatest revival or restoration the world has ever known. Almost all Jews, if not all, will accept Christ as their own personal Saviour, thereby recognizing Him at long last as the Messiah.

The formula, *"Saith Jehovah,"* is to be understood as a confirmation written at the foot of the Prophecy, saying, *"This is Jehovah's declaration."*

(15) "THE WORD OF THE LORD CAME AGAIN UNTO ME, SAYING,

(16) "MOREOVER, THOU SON OF MAN, TAKE THEE ONE STICK, AND WRITE UPON IT, FOR JUDAH, AND FOR THE CHILDREN OF ISRAEL HIS COMPANIONS: THEN TAKE ANOTHER STICK, AND WRITE UPON IT, FOR JOSEPH THE STICK OF EPHRAIM AND FOR ALL THE HOUSE OF ISRAEL HIS COMPANIONS:

(17) "AND JOIN THEM ONE TO ANOTHER INTO ONE STICK; AND THEY SHALL BECOME ONE IN YOUR HAND.

(18) "AND WHEN THE CHILDREN OF YOUR PEOPLE SHALL SPEAK UNTO YOU, SAYING, WILL YOU NOT SHOW US WHAT YOU MEAN BY THESE?

(19) "SAY UNTO THEM, THUS SAITH THE LORD GOD; BEHOLD, I WILL TAKE THE STICK OF JOSEPH, WHICH IS IN THE HAND OF EPHRAIM, AND THE TRIBES OF ISRAEL HIS FELLOWS, AND WILL PUT THEM WITH HIM, EVEN WITH THE STICK OF JUDAH, AND MAKE THEM ONE STICK, AND THEY SHALL BE ONE

IN MY HAND.

(20) "AND THE STICKS WHEREON YOU WRITE SHALL BE IN YOUR HAND BEFORE THEIR EYES.

(21) "AND SAY UNTO THEM, THUS SAITH THE LORD GOD; BEHOLD, I WILL TAKE THE CHILDREN OF ISRAEL FROM AMONG THE HEATHEN, WHERE THEY BE GONE, AND WILL GATHER THEM ON EVERY SIDE, AND BRING THEM INTO THEIR OWN LAND:

(22) "AND I WILL MAKE THEM ONE NATION IN THE LAND UPON THE MOUNTAINS OF ISRAEL; AND ONE KING SHALL BE KING TO THEM ALL: AND THEY SHALL BE NO MORE TWO NATIONS, NEITHER SHALL THEY BE DIVIDED INTO TWO KINGDOMS ANY MORE AT ALL.

(23) "NEITHER SHALL THEY DEFILE THEMSELVES ANY MORE WITH THEIR IDOLS, NOR WITH THEIR DETESTABLE THINGS, NOR WITH ANY OF THEIR TRANSGRESSIONS: BUT I WILL SAVE THEM OUT OF ALL THEIR DWELLING PLACES, WHEREIN THEY HAVE SINNED, AND WILL CLEANSE THEM: SO SHALL THEY BE MY PEOPLE, AND I WILL BE THEIR GOD.

(24) "AND DAVID MY SERVANT SHALL BE KING OVER THEM; AND THEY ALL SHALL HAVE ONE SHEPHERD: THEY SHALL ALSO WALK IN MY JUDGMENTS, AND OBSERVE MY STATUTES, AND DO THEM.

(25) "AND THEY SHALL DWELL IN THE LAND THAT I HAVE GIVEN UNTO JACOB MY SERVANT, WHEREIN YOUR FATHERS HAVE DWELT; AND THEY SHALL DWELL THEREIN, EVEN THEY, AND THEIR CHILDREN, AND THEIR CHILDREN'S CHILDREN FOR EVER: AND MY SERVANT DAVID SHALL BE THEIR PRINCE FOR EVER.

(26) "MOREOVER I WILL MAKE A COVENANT OF PEACE WITH THEM; IT SHALL BE AN EVERLASTING COVENANT WITH THEM: AND I WILL PLACE THEM, AND MULTIPLY THEM, AND WILL SET MY SANCTUARY IN THE MIDST OF THEM FOR EVERMORE.

(27) "MY TABERNACLE ALSO SHALL BE WITH THEM: YES, I WILL BE THEIR GOD, AND THEY SHALL BE MY PEOPLE.

(28) "AND THE HEATHEN SHALL KNOW THAT I THE LORD DO SANCTIFY ISRAEL, WHEN MY SANCTUARY SHALL BE IN THE MIDST OF THEM FOR EVERMORE."

The construction is:

1. The second Prophecy of this Chapter, which begins with Verse 15, predicts the future union of the Tribes, their restoration to the Land of Israel, and their settlement there under one Shepherd, teaches that a divinely wrought union is real and enduring, and brings its subjects into fellowship with God, and disposes them around a Divine center, Who and Which is Christ (Williams).

2. Verse 21 was chosen for the legend on the Zionist medal commemoration — the First National Federation (1896) since the days of Titus.

3. *"David My servant"* refers to David, the King of Israel, who will reign under Christ in the Millennial Kingdom, and will do so forever.

4. As the first Restoration from Babylon was opposed by Satan, so will he oppose Israel's future settlement in the Land of Israel, which he is doing presently. The time frame, however, of the great opposition, will be the latter half of the Great Tribulation. The two following Chapters deal with this and foretell the agents Satan will employ.

5. This Chapter destroys the Anglo-Israelite theory, i.e., *"that the United States and Great Britain are part of the lost tribes of Israel."*

THE TWO STICKS

The two *"sticks"* of Verse 16 represent the two Houses of Israel, the Northern Confederation of Israel, sometimes called Ephraim or Samaria, and the Southern Kingdom, known as Judah.

The phrase of Verse 17, *"And join them one to another into one stick,"* predicts that both sticks (both Kingdoms) will now become *"one stick,"* i.e., signifying one people, which will be brought about by the *"Hand of the Lord,"* and will never again be divided.

In fact, the division was never of the Lord, but was brought about because of sin.

Under both David and Solomon, the Land was one, but, with the death of Solomon, the nation divided with some nine Tribes making up the Northern Kingdom, with Judah and Benjamin making up the Southern Kingdom. Levi and Simeon were added to Judah because Simeon's inheritance was within the inheritance of Judah (Josh. 19:1).

The division remained for about 260 years, until the Northern Kingdom of Israel was taken into captivity by the Assyrians, where it remained, leaving only the Southern Kingdom of Judah.

Judah lasted for approximately 133 years after Israel's Fall before falling to the Babylonians.

After the dispersion of some 70 years, parts of the entirety of the thirteen Tribes came back into the Land and formed one nation, as they were upon the Birth of Christ.

The phrase of Verse 19, *"And they shall be one in My Hand,"* proclaims the bringing of these people back together, as the Lord always intended.

The cause was an unlawful breaking off from the House of Judah, and the establishment of an independent Kingdom. The House of Joseph actually said, *"What portion have we in David?" "And we have none inheritance in the son of Jesse"* (II Chron. 10:16).

At that time, the Northern Kingdom forsook all that the Covenant stood for, which promised a coming Redeemer, i.e., *"inheritance."*

Verse 20 says: *"And the sticks whereon you write shall be in your hand before their eyes."*

It is amazing that the Lord would take something that simple, such as *"sticks,"* which Ezekiel, evidently, literally did, to express and portray something of such vital consequence.

THE LAND

The phrase of Verse 22, *"And I will make them one nation in the land upon the mountains of Israel; and one king shall be king to them all,"* refers to the area promised to Abraham (Gen. 12:7).

Its boundary on the West is the Mediterranean; on the South, the Suez Canal, which includes the Arabian Peninsula; on the East, the Euphrates River; on the North, the northern border of Lebanon, plus Syria.

David came closer to occupying the entirety of the Promised Land than anyone else! However, for the greater part of its existence, the territory was much reduced, incorporating basically which was called *"from Dan to Beersheba."* However, in the coming Kingdom Age, all of the original promised territory will be occupied, with possibly even extra space added.

Due to this being promised by the Lord to the sons of Jacob, Satan has contested it mightily! Of course, the entirety of the world is aware of the territorial demands made by the Arabs in Israel, and their being granted the Gaza Strip, plus Jericho, with the entirety of the West Bank possibly to be included.

It is ironical, that in July of 1994, the newly formed state of Palestine advertised the city of Jerusalem as Jerusalem, Palestine. Israel was highly offended by this action, as it should have been! However, it is well known that the nations of the world will not recognize Jerusalem as the capital of Israel, but, instead looking to Tel Aviv.

Irrespective of the present claims, this Land belongs to Israel, and is promised by the Lord, which Promise, and to be sure, will be carried out and fulfilled in totality.

Incidentally, the Arabs in Israel refer to themselves as *"Palestinians,"* but the truth is, there is no such people by that name. The Arabs who occupy part of Israel are Jordanians, Egyptians, Syrians, etc.

DAVID

The phrase of Verse 23, *"Neither shall they defile themselves any more with their idols, nor with their detestable things,"* refers to that which will take place almost immediately after the Second Coming of Christ, and will bring about that which the Lord has always intended, *"His people, and, consequently, their God."*

The phrase of Verse 24, *"And David My servant shall be king over them,"* is meant to be taken literally. David was ever looked at as the example for all the kings of Israel, and will, consequently, serve in this capacity under Christ forever.

A self-righteous Church would have difficulty understanding this, especially due to David's transgression regarding Bathsheba and her husband Uriah; however, only self-righteousness would blanch at such a prospect. Those who truly understand who and what man actually is, and that the Grace of God is our only Hope, this Passage, to such a person, is a source of great comfort.

Even though David suffered terribly so for this transgression, still, this sin, plus all the other sins that David committed, were washed away by the Precious Blood of Jesus Christ. It is called *"Justification by Faith,"* and is the undergirding strength of all who trust in the Name of Christ.

JUSTIFICATION BY FAITH

The great question is: How can God, Who must ever abide by His Righteous Nature, declare a person who is obviously guilty, as *"not guilty"*?

Paul said: *"To declare, I say, at this time His Righteousness: that He might be just, and the Justifier of him which believeth in Jesus"* (Rom. 3:26).

So, the same question may be asked in this way: How can God be just, and at the same time be the justifier of the person who is obviously guilty?

The answer is found in the latter portion of Romans, Chapter 3, Verse 26, *"which believeth in Jesus."*

Justification is a declaration of *"not guilty,"* and to take it even further, it actually means *"totally innocent, having never been guilty of any transgression or iniquity."*

Now we ask the question again: How can God maintain His *"Justice,"* and, at the same time, justify guilty sinners? Once again, the answer is found in Christ, and Christ Alone. More particularly, it is found in what Christ did at the Cross.

SUBSTITUTION AND IDENTIFICATION

For this great work to be carried out, the Work of Justification, God would have to become Man, which we refer to as the *"Incarnation."* He would have to be man's Substitute, doing for man what man could not do for himself. For proper Justification to be carried out, Christ would have to be born of a Virgin, exactly as prophesied by Isaiah (Isa. 7:14). Her name was Mary! His birth had to be in this manner, in order that He not have original sin, which came upon all men after the Fall. It is referred to as the *"fallen sons of Adam's lost race."*

As the perfect Son of God, in fact, the *"Last Adam,"* Jesus had to keep the law perfectly, and in every respect. In other words, He could not sin in word, thought, or deed; had He done so, not only would man be eternally lost, with no possible way for anyone to be saved, but, likewise, God would be defeated, with Satan becoming the lord of the universe. So, everything was riding on the Lord Jesus Christ. In other words, God placed everything in Jesus Christ, and did so because of His great love for fallen humanity (Jn. 3:16).

Not only did Christ have to live a perfect life, thereby keeping the Law in every respect, but, as well, the terrible sin debt, which included every human being who had ever lived, had piled higher and higher through the centuries. This debt had to be addressed, had to be paid, and had to be paid in full. For that to happen, which would atone for all sin, Jesus had to go to the Cross. He had to give His Life, and because His Life was a Perfect Life, which He gave by the shedding of His Blood, which Peter referred to as *"Precious Blood"* (I Pet. 1:19).

God accepted the Sacrifice, meaning that Jesus had taken our place, and now sinful man could be justified.

HOW WAS MAN TO RECEIVE JUSTIFICATION?

Paul said: *"Therefore being Justified by Faith, we have peace with God through our Lord Jesus Christ"* (Rom. 5:1).

So what does it mean to be *"Justified by Faith"*?

In Chapters 4 and 5 of Romans, Paul goes to great length to portray to the human family that Justification is not at all obtained by works or merit, but strictly by Faith.

He goes to this great length, simply because there is something in man that seeks to earn his way with the Lord. It's a result of the Fall, but it is the biggest problem faced by the human family. We keep trying to do for ourselves which we cannot do, and even if we could do, that is, after a measure, God couldn't accept it, because of our fallen condition. God can only accept what His Son, and our Saviour, the Lord Jesus Christ, has done, and that alone!

WHAT DO WE MEAN BY *"FAITH"*?

It means that the believing sinner, and the Christian for that matter, must ever have Christ and the Cross as the Object of his Faith. Christ must not be separated from the Cross, and, of course, the Cross must not be separated from Christ. To evidence Faith in Christ and the Cross proclaims the fact that we firmly believe in what Christ did for us, and accept it at face value (Jn. 3:16; Rom. 6:3-5; Eph. 2:13-18; Col. 2:14-15).

So, the moment the believing sinner evidences Faith in Christ, believing what Jesus did for us at the Cross, at that moment, the Lord imputes to that individual a spotless Righteousness, which, in effect, means that one has been totally and completely justified.

Paul said, and as it concerns Justification by Faith, *"For if by one man's offense* (Adam) *death reigned by one* (as a result of the Fall); *much more they which receive abundance of Grace and the Gift of Righteousness* (which we receive by accepting Christ and what He did for us at the Cross) *shall reign* (rule) *in life by One, Jesus Christ* (Christ is the Source, while the Cross is the Means)" (Rom. 5:17).

The phrase of Verse 25, *"And My servant David shall be their Prince forever,"* goes back to the Messianic Promise of II Samuel 7:12-16.

Some have concluded that the name *"David"*, as used here, refers to the Messiah; however, the Holy Spirit uses the phrase, *"My servant David,"* but never once is Christ called *"My servant David."* So it is obvious that King David is the one predicted here to be *"their prince for ever."*

There is no evidence that Restored Israel will have Glorified Bodies, as all the Saints will have in the coming Resurrection (I Cor. 15:51-57). However, this refers only to the Israel of that particular time. Every Jew before this time who died in Christ will definitely have Glorified Bodies.

In fact, the Glorified Saints will no longer marry and have children, because such is not necessary, due to our living eternally. Jesus said regarding such, *"They are as the Angels"* (Mat. 22:30).

NOTES

However, Restored Israel, not having Glorified Bodies, will continue to marry and have children, even *"forever."* As well, there will be no death, and all will remain youthful and alive by partaking of the fruit and the leaves of the trees beside the river which flows from the Millennial Temple in Jerusalem. The Scripture says: *"And the leaf thereof for medicine"* (Ezek. 47:1, 9, 12).

The Twenty-fifth Verse mentions *"their children, and their children's children, for ever,"* proving that babies will continue to be born by these individuals forever.

Therefore, there will be two types of people on the Earth forever, the Glorified Saints of God, which will be made up of all included in the First Resurrection, both Jews and Gentiles. This will pertain to every person who trusted the Lord for Salvation, from Adam through the Great Tribulation Period.

The second group will be those who live in their natural bodies forever, after having accepted Christ as their eternal Saviour, which will be done after the Second Coming; consequently, the Bible teaches eternal generations of eternal people on Earth. In this second group, there will also be those who will serve God, but will not live for Him. They will ultimately be lost (Rev., Chpt. 20).

THE EVERLASTING COVENANT

The phrase of Verse 26, *"Moreover I will make a Covenant of Peace with them; it shall be an Everlasting Covenant with them,"* pertains to the New Covenant (Heb. 13:20). This is all based on what Jesus did at the Cross, which, in effect, is the very meaning of the New Covenant, i.e., *"Everlasting Covenant."* This Covenant is based on better Promises than all the other Covenants (Heb. 8:6-13), and, in fact, is a perfect Covenant, which means it will never have to be amended.

MY SANCTUARY

Verse 28 says: *"And the heathen shall know that I the LORD do sanctify Israel, when My Sanctuary shall be in the midst of them for evermore."*

God's Presence with Israel is the sign that He is with them, and that the world must, and, in fact, shall recognize this approval.

In fact, the *"Sanctuary"* in the midst of

Israel is the greatest sign of all of God's acceptance and approval!

In fact, the very last phrase in the Book of Ezekiel is *"The LORD is there"* (48:35).

There could be nothing greater!

"Though the angry surges roll on my tempest-driven soul,
"I am peaceful, for I know,
"Wildly though the winds may blow,
"I've an anchor safe and sure, that can evermore endure."

"Mighty tides about me sweep, perils lurk within in the deep,
"Angry clouds o'er-shade the sky,
"And the tempest rises high;
"Still I stand the tempest's shock for my anchor grips the Rock."

"I can feel the anchor fast as I meet each sudden blast,
"And the cable, though unseen,
"Bears the heavy strain between,
"Through the storm I safely ride, till the turning of the tide."

"Troubles almost 'whelm the soul; griefs like billows o'er me roll;
"Tempters seek to lure astray;
"Storms obscure the light of day:
"But in Christ I can be bold, I've an anchor that shall hold."

CHAPTER 38

(1) "AND THE WORD OF THE LORD CAME UNTO ME, SAYING,

(2) "SON OF MAN, SET YOUR FACE AGAINST GOG, THE LAND OF MAGOG, EVEN THE CHIEF PRINCE OF MESHECH AND TUBAL, AND PROPHESY AGAINST HIM,

(3) "AND SAY, THUS SAITH THE LORD GOD; BEHOLD, I AM AGAINST YOU, O GOG, THE CHIEF PRINCE OF MESHECH AND TUBAL:

(4) "AND I WILL TURN YOU BACK, AND PUT HOOKS INTO YOUR JAWS, AND I WILL BRING YOU FORTH, AND ALL YOUR ARMY, HORSES AND HORSEMEN, ALL OF THEM CLOTHED WITH ALL SORTS OF ARMOUR, EVEN A GREAT COMPANY WITH BUCKLERS AND SHIELDS, ALL OF THEM HANDLING SWORDS:

(5) "PERSIA, ETHIOPIA, AND LIBYA WITH THEM; ALL OF THEM WITH SHIELD AND HELMET:

(6) "GOMER, AND ALL HIS BANDS; THE HOUSE OF TOGARMAH OF THE NORTH QUARTERS, AND ALL HIS BANDS: AND MANY PEOPLE WITH YOU.

(7) "BE THOU PREPARED, AND PREPARE FOR YOURSELF, YOU, AND ALL YOUR COMPANY WHO ARE ASSEMBLED UNTO YOU, AND BE THOU A GUARD UNTO THEM.

(8) "AFTER MANY DAYS YOU SHALL BE VISITED: IN THE LATTER YEARS YOU SHALL COME INTO THE LAND THAT IS BROUGHT BACK FROM THE SWORD, AND IS GATHERED OUT OF MANY PEOPLE, AGAINST THE MOUNTAINS OF ISRAEL, WHICH HAVE BEEN ALWAYS WASTE: BUT IT IS BROUGHT FORTH OUT OF THE NATIONS, AND THEY SHALL DWELL SAFELY ALL OF THEM.

(9) "YOU SHALL ASCEND AND COME LIKE A STORM, YOU SHALL BE LIKE A CLOUD TO COVER THE LAND, YOU, AND ALL YOUR BANDS, AND MANY PEOPLE WITH YOU."

The overview is:

1. Chapters 38 and 39 portray the advancement of the Antichrist, and his attack upon Israel, culminating in the Battle of Armageddon.

2. In his bid for world conquest, why is Israel so important to the Antichrist?

More promises and predictions are made in the Bible concerning Israel than anything else; consequently, if the Antichrist can destroy these ancient people, then the Promises of God fall to the ground, making the entirety of the Word of God invalid, which means that if such could happen, Satan will win the day.

3. These two Chapters portray the Second Coming, which will prevent the Antichrist from having his way, and, in fact, will spell the doom of the Man of Sin.

THE WORD OF THE LORD

Verse 1 says: *"And the Word of the LORD came unto me, saying,"*

The Thirty-sixth Chapter of Ezekiel portrays the Restoration of Israel, with the Thirty-seventh and Thirty-eighth Chapters proclaiming how this Restoration will take place. It will be by the Spirit of God.

Immediately upon the coming of the Spirit (Ezek. 37:14), Satan rears his ugly head, because the Thirty-eighth Chapter portrays the highest ascendancy of man, in the form of the Antichrist, empowered by Satan as no man has ever been empowered by the Evil One, attempting to usurp authority over the Holy Spirit and to destroy the ancient people, God's people. It is called *"the Battle of Armageddon."*

THE SPIRIT COMES, AND SATAN OPPOSES

The chronological order of these Chapters, at least in the Spiritual sense, is the pattern always followed by Satan. The Holy Spirit comes, and Satan opposes!

In fact, Satan has no regard at all for the efforts of man, be they ever so religious. His opposition is stirred only upon the advent of the Holy Spirit, as given by Christ; consequently, the far greater majority of the world of religion, even including the Church, experiences no opposition from Satan whatsoever! Actually, he is the author of all religion, and much of that which goes under the guise of *"Christianity."*

Nevertheless, for the few who operate in the realm of the Holy Spirit, and few it is, depending upon His empowerment, leading and anointing, the opposition by the Evil One is fierce indeed! No opposition, no Spirit; much opposition, much Spirit!

These two Chapters (Ezek. 38-39) constitute the greatest detailed account in the Bible of the Battle of Armageddon.

GOG

The phrase of Verse 2, *"Son of man, set your face against Gog, the land of Magog,"* proclaims the very opposite which the Prophet was commanded to do, as it regarded prophesying blessing upon Israel (Ezek. 37:4), which portrayed God's favor. He is commanded to do the very opposite against the confederation of Satan. He will *"prophesy against him."*

NOTES

As the favorable Prophecy concerning the Restoration of Israel is dead certain to be fulfilled, likewise, the unfavorable Prophecy against the Antichrist, Satan's chief henchman, will most assuredly come to pass.

The name or title, *"Gog,"* means *"roof or mountain."* Likewise, this is the name of the giant *"Ishbibenob,"* who tried to kill David at the close of his reign, which means *"dweller on the Mount,"* signifying the efforts of man regarding ascendancy in pomp, pride, and power, with *"Gog"* being the ultimate.

Among the several names that will be used regarding the Antichrist, *"Gog"* is definitely one of those names. By the Holy Spirit ascribing this name to him, in no way means that it is guaranteed that the Antichrist will employ the same. While he may definitely use the name, the main purpose of the Spirit is to portray the fact, that the spirit of the Antichrist is saying that the mountain, i.e., *"the entirety of the Earth,"* is his.

In fact, the Antichrist will go under several names:

1. *"The little horn"* (Dan., Chpts. 7, 8).
2. *"The prince that shall come"* (Dan., Chpt. 9).
3. *"The king of the north"* (Dan., Chpt. 11).
4. *"The man of sin"* (II Thess., Chpt. 2).
5. *"The son of perdition"* (II Thess., Chpt. 2).
6. *"That wicked"* (II Thess., Chpt. 2).
7. *"The king of Babylon"* (Isa., Chpts. 13-14).
8. *"The Assyrian"* (Mic., Chpt. 5).
9. *"The Antichrist"* (I Jn., Chpt. 2).
10. *"The beast"* (Rev., Chpt. 13).

All of these Scriptures speak of a man who will come in the last days, which compares with Ezekiel, Chapters 38 and 39.

The phrase of Verse 2, *"The land of Magog, the chief prince of Meshech and Tubal,"* merely refers to the Gentiles who descended from Japheth. *"Magog, Meshech, and Tubal"* were sons of *"Japheth,"* who was a son of Noah (Gen. 10:1-4).

Some have tried to make the *"land of Magog"* refer to Russia; however, it simply refers to the area populated by the sons of Japheth, who populated Eastern and Western Europe.

To fully understand these phrases, one has

to go back to the time of Noah and make a brief study of his three sons, *"Shem, Ham, and Japheth."* Of these three sons came the entirety of the human family.

As stated, Japheth's descendants settled Europe, which ultimately settled North America, as well as parts of the East. They are known as the Gentiles.

Shem produced those who settled the Middle East, as well as Asia Minor.

Ham's descendants, as well, settled parts of the Middle East, Africa, and ultimately Central and South America (Gen., Chpt. 10).

As is obvious, the descendants of Japheth and Ham make up the greater majority of the greater population of the world, with the sons of Shem basically referring to the Israelites and the Arabs.

Noah actually prophesied what would happen to the descendants of his three sons.

SHEM

The Holy Spirit, through Noah, said, *"Blessed be the Lord God of Shem,"* meaning that the relationship between the Lord and the descendants of Shem would be closer than any other. In fact, through Shem would come the Bible, the Word of God, and, most important of all, Christ would be after this lineage (Gen. 10:21; 11:10; Lk. 3:23-38).

Through the family of Shem would come the Israelites and the Arabs, both in the line of Abraham. The two sons of Abraham, Isaac and Ishmael, would bring forth the entire lineage of Shem. The Israelites, God's Chosen, would come from Isaac, while the Arabs would come from Ishmael; however, the Lord rejected Ishmael as a work of the flesh, even though blessing him (Gen. 17:20). However, the Lord said that He would bless and establish His Covenant with Isaac (Gen. 17:19); consequently, there has been great contention between Isaac and Ishmael ever since!

The True Seed, the Lord Jesus Christ, God manifest in the flesh, came through the lineage of Isaac, while the false seed, Mohammed, came through Ishmael.

Even though the Work of the Spirit, produced through Abraham, the Lord Jesus Christ, has blessed the entirety of the world, the work of the flesh, as produced also by Abraham, resulting in the birth of Ishmael, has brought great contention to the world, as do all *"works of the flesh"* (Gen. 17:19-22).

JAPHETH

The Holy Spirit, through Noah, said of Japheth, *"God shall enlarge Japheth"* (Gen. 9:27).

This Prophecy has come true to the letter, in that the races that sprang from Japheth, the white and the yellow, have been the driving force all over the world, as it pertains to science, government, etc.

The remaining statement concerning Japheth, *"And he shall dwell in the tents of Shem"* (Gen. 9:27), refers to Israel originally destined by God to be the leading people in the world, but forfeited this position because of sin; therefore, that which was promised to Shem, leader of the world, was, instead, given by God to Japheth.

This has reference to Israel losing her way with God, and the scepter of power being transferred from the Kings of Judah to the Gentiles, of which the first was Nebuchadnezzar. The last King of Judah was Zedekiah, and the last King in the Davidic line to grace the Throne of Judah, which was the last King actually recognized by God, was the King who immediately preceded Zedekiah, *"Jehoiachin."* The power has remained with the Gentiles ever since, with Christ calling it *"the times of the Gentiles"* (Lk. 21:24).

This is what is meant by Japheth *"dwelling in the tents of Shem."*

HAM

The Scripture says that the youngest son of Noah *"saw the nakedness of his father"* (Gen. 9:22), which some Bible Scholars think may have included the homosexual act, which included Ham's son, *"Canaan,"* and resulted in the Holy Spirit, through Noah, saying *"Cursed be Canaan."* Consequently, Ham's descendants, through Canaan, have been cursed exactly as prophesied.

The descendants of Canaan settled in the Middle East, making up the Jebusites, Hivites, Philistines, etc., and were ultimately destroyed by Israel, or else made servants upon the taking of the Promised Land. They also populated Africa.

Therefore, as already stated, *"the land of Magog,"* although including Russia, also includes Europe, the Far East, and North America, etc.

THE CHIEF PRINCE OF MESHECH AND TUBAL

The phrase of Verse 3, *"Behold, I am against you, O Gog, the Chief Prince of Meshech and Tubal,"* proclaims the Holy Spirit, some 2,500 years ago, speaking through the Prophet Ezekiel, and portraying the disposition of the Lord as it regards the coming Antichrist.

For many years, Bible teachers have taught that these Passages refer to Russia, but a closer investigation of the statements prove otherwise. As well, the events that have transpired recently, in the area formerly known as the Soviet Union, further emphasize the fact that even though Russia will no doubt play a part in these last-days events, still, it will only be a part of the whole.

Therefore, the phrase, *"Behold, I am against you, O Gog,"* is not really referring to Russia, but, instead, the Antichrist.

For years, Bible Scholars have erroneously attempted to make the name *"Meshech"* mean Moscow, and *"Tubal"* mean Tobolsk, both in Russia; however, these two names, *"Meshech and Tubal,"* have no reference to the cities mentioned, but, instead, refer to the whole of Europe. As well, as Daniel portrays, this fits in perfectly with his Prophecies. Actually, when the Antichrist makes his debut in the Battle of Armageddon, his vast army will include myriads of soldiers from both Europe and the Far East.

THE BATTLE OF ARMAGEDDON

The phrase of Verse 4, *"And I will turn you back, and put hooks into your jaws,"* refers to the Battle of Armageddon, which will be the second invasion by the Antichrist of Israel, in which he will be totally destroyed.

Approximately seven years before, the Antichrist will sign a seven-year peace treaty with Israel and other nations. In fact, all of these accords which we are presently seeing between Israel and the Palestinians so-called, etc., are merely precursors of the seven-year treaty, which will be formulated by the Antichrist. At that time, Israel, thinking the Antichrist is the Messiah, and announcing such to the entirety of the world, will say, *"Peace and safety."* But then Paul said, *"Sudden destruction cometh upon them, as travail upon a woman with child; and they shall not escape"* (I Thess. 5:3).

At the mid-point of this seven-year treaty (Dan. 9:27; 11:40-45; II Thess. 2:3-4; Rev. 11:1-2), the Antichrist will break his treaty with Israel, attacking her, with Israel suffering her first military defeat since her formation as a nation in 1948. Now will truly begin the *"time of Jacob's trouble"* (Jer. 30:6). For that three and one-half years, it will look like the Antichrist will be able to do what Haman, Herod, and Hitler failed to do.

Actually, he would succeed but for the sudden coming of the Lord Jesus Christ, with the armies of Heaven, Who will defeat him in what is called *"the Battle of Armageddon."* The Lord will then set up His Kingdom of Righteousness (Zech. 14:1-15; Rev. 19:11-21).

If one is to notice, words such as *"horses,"* *"bucklers,"* and *"shields,"* as well as *"swords,"* are used because this was the weaponry of that day; however, the weapons that will be used by the Antichrist will be modern weaponry with the latest technology.

The Holy Spirit used these words because they are familiar to all, and properly explain what needs to be explained. In fact, if modern terminology had been used, such as *"jets,"* *"bombers,"* *"machine guns,"* etc., these words would have had no meaning until the recent past; therefore, such would have caused endless controversy among Bible Scholars. The idea is not to name the weaponry, but rather to show that the Antichrist will be fully equipped with all sorts of weapons, determined to destroy Israel.

THE TAUNT

The phrase of Verse 6, *"And many people with you,"* actually names, in both Verses, 5 and 6, some of the nations which will have thrown in their lot with the Antichrist, determined to help him defeat Israel.

The phrase of Verse 7, *"Be thou prepared, and prepare for yourself, you, and all your company who are assembled unto you,"* merely refers to a taunt given by the Holy

Spirit to the Antichrist. In other words, *"prepare yourself, to the very best of your ability, and, still, it will avail you nothing, as you will be totally defeated."*

The phrase, *"And be thou a guard unto them,"* refers to this mighty army under the leadership of the Antichrist, and thinking that, due to their past successes, his leadership will guarantee continued successes.

However, the balance of this Chapter will tell exactly what will happen to all those *"who are assembled unto you."*

THE LATTER YEARS

The two phrases of Verse 8, *"After many days"* and *"in the latter years,"* refer to this present time, and the immediate future; therefore, any claims that this Chapter has already been fulfilled are spurious.

The Holy Spirit, no doubt, gave these phrases through Ezekiel in order to dispel the idea among the Exiles that this particular Prophecy pertained to their times. This which is being said is to be fulfilled in *"the latter years,"* which, as stated, refers to this present time and the near future.

The phrase, *"The land that is brought back from the sword,"* refers to the many conflicts Israel has had since becoming a nation in 1948. Even though the United Nations voted that the Jews be given their ancient homeland, still, it was definitely not a peaceful transition. The Arabs repeatedly tried to stop her, and would have definitely succeeded, and due to their great numbers, had it not been for the help of the Lord. So, Israel was literally *"brought back from the Sword."*

The phrase of Verse 8, *"And is gathered out of many people,"* refers to Jews which were scattered all over the world, but began to come to the newly formed state of Israel, beginning in 1948. In fact, Jews are still coming from many nations of the world to Israel, with the last great influx being from the former Soviet Union.

The phrase, *"Against the mountains of Israel, which have been always waste,"* refers to the Land of Palestine that virtually went to *"waste"* after A.D. 70, when Titus totally destroyed Jerusalem, killing over 1,000,000 Jews and selling other hundreds of thousands as slaves.

NOTES

Coupled with the second onslaught by the Romans in A.D. 150, the Jews were driven all over the world, with their ancient homeland reverting basically to *"waste."*

The phrase, *"But it is brought forth out of the nations,"* refers to the United Nations voting that Israel would become a State, with even Soviet Russia voting her approval.

The last phrase of Verse 8, *"And they shall dwell safely all of them,"* refers to the Jews desiring a homeland, instead of being scattered all over the world. Their feeling was, that if this could be obtained, then they would be *"safe."*

The Holocaust of World War II, which saw some 6,000,000 Jews slaughtered by Hitler, caused the birth of a desire in the hearts of many, many Jews to insist upon this homeland.

One Jew was asked during the tumultuous days of 1948, when Israel was struggling to gain the approval of the United Nations, and especially the United States, thereby, to secure a homeland, exactly why they wanted such? His answer was somewhat enlightening!

With a far-away look in his eyes, and his mind, no doubt, on the horror of the recent Holocaust, he said, *"The next time they'll know where to find us, and we will be ready."*

After nearly 2,000 years, Jacob was finally coming home.

As I dictate these notes, I strongly sense the Presence of God, in that we are so privileged to be living during the time when these great Prophecies of old are beginning to be fulfilled. What a testimony to the veracity of the Word of God! What a testimony to the truthfulness of its eternal composition!

But yet, even though they have in part *"dwelled safely,"* still, the *"safety"* of Israel even from its beginning has been precarious.

In the very near future, Israel, continuing to be pressed from all sides, will eagerly accept the promises of the false Messiah, the Antichrist, thinking he fulfills the Prophecies and will guarantee the *"safety"* for which they have so long sought. But it will prove to be a false hope!

However, upon the Second Coming of Christ, then, and truly, *"They shall dwell safely all of them."*

ARMAGEDDON

The phrase of Verse 9, *"You shall ascend and come like a storm,"* proclaims the Battle of Armageddon. It will be the most horrifying conflict the world has ever known, at least concerning one particular Battle. Hundreds of thousands, and possibly even millions, will die!

The phrase, *"You shall be like a cloud to cover the land,"* refers to tremendous numbers of soldiers of the Antichrist, which will result in many deaths, especially considering that we are speaking of the Lord intervening and Zechariah saying that He will *"fight against those nations, as when He fought in the day of battle"* (Zech. 14:3).

At any rate, the Battle will be so severe, and the deaths of such magnitude, that it is said that the blood (winepress) will flow to *"the horse bridles, by the space of a thousand and six hundred furlongs,"* referring to about one hundred eighty four miles (Rev. 14:20).

So, we are speaking here of something that has never happened in such magnitude as this in the history of the world.

(10) "THUS SAITH THE LORD GOD; IT SHALL ALSO COME TO PASS, THAT AT THE SAME TIME SHALL THINGS COME INTO YOUR MIND, AND YOU SHALL THINK AN EVIL THOUGHT:

(11) "AND YOU SHALL SAY, I WILL GO UP TO THE LAND OF UNWALLED VILLAGES: I WILL GO TO THEM THAT ARE AT REST, WHO DWELL SAFELY, ALL OF THEM DWELLING WITHOUT WALLS, AND HAVING NEITHER BARS NOR GATES,

(12) "TO TAKE A SPOIL, AND TO TAKE A PREY: TO TURN YOUR HAND UPON THE DESOLATE PLACES THAT ARE NOW INHABITED, AND UPON THE PEOPLE WHO ARE GATHERED OUT OF THE NATIONS, WHICH HAVE GOTTEN CATTLE AND GOODS, WHO DWELL IN THE MIDST OF THE LAND.

(13) "SHEBA, AND DEDAN, AND THE MERCHANTS OF TARSHISH, WITH ALL THE YOUNG LIONS THEREOF, SHALL SAY UNTO YOU, ARE YOU COME TO TAKE A SPOIL? HAVE YOU GATHERED YOUR COMPANY TO TAKE A PREY? TO CARRY AWAY SILVER AND GOLD, TO TAKE AWAY CATTLE AND GOODS, TO TAKE A GREAT SPOIL?

(14) "THEREFORE, SON OF MAN, PROPHESY AND SAY UNTO GOG, THUS SAITH THE LORD GOD: IN THAT DAY WHEN MY PEOPLE OF ISRAEL DWELL SAFELY, SHALL YOU NOT KNOW IT?

(15) "AND YOU SHALL COME FROM YOUR PLACE OUT OF THE NORTH PARTS, YOU, AND MANY PEOPLE WITH YOU, ALL OF THEM RIDING UPON HORSES, A GREAT COMPANY, AND A MIGHTY ARMY:

(16) "AND YOU SHALL COME UP AGAINST MY PEOPLE OF ISRAEL, AS A CLOUD TO COVER THE LAND: IT SHALL BE IN THE LATTER DAYS, AND I WILL BRING YOU AGAINST MY LAND, THAT THE HEATHEN MAY KNOW ME, WHEN I SHALL BE SANCTIFIED IN YOU, O GOG, BEFORE THEIR EYES."

The composition is:

1. As in Israel's early history the sons of Ham afflicted her, so will she in the future suffer from the sons of Japheth.

2. The *"evil thought"* of the Antichrist (Vs. 10) constitutes the destruction of Israel. Unfortunately, untold numbers have harbored the same type of thought over the many past centuries, and do so presently.

3. But let it be known that all who harbor evil thoughts against Israel are, at the same time, harboring evil thoughts against God. To say the least, such is a losing operation!

AN EVIL THOUGHT

The phrase of Verse 10, *"And you shall think an evil thought,"* consists of the plans of the Antichrist inspired of Satan to destroy Israel and the Jews. He thinks that he will do what Haman, Herod, and Hitler could not do!

In his hatred of God, and especially the Lord Jesus Christ, and due to the fact that the Church has been raptured away, he will center the focus of his anger and evil on the Jew, who is, by and large, the only people connected to the Lord on the face of the Earth. So, at least in his mind, upon their destruction he will be master and god of the world (II Thess. 2:4).

The worth of the Land of Israel is not actually that important; in fact, it makes up only one sixth of one percent of the land of the Middle East presently held by the Arabs. So why is this so all-important to the Antichrist?

The problem is spiritual, even as it has always been spiritual. God called Abraham out of Ur of the Chaldees, having revealed Himself to the Patriarch, which would be followed by tremendous Promises. In fact, from the loins of Abraham and the womb of Sarah, his wife, would come the people of faith, who were destined by God to give the world the Word of God, and to bring forth the Messiah. Accordingly, they would govern the world; however, they rejected their Messiah, crucifying Him, which means that they refused the Kingdom which was offered to them.

As a result of this, and because of the chastising Hand of God, their nation was destroyed, and they were scattered all over the world. But yet, the Promises remained, and they most definitely will be fulfilled.

Knowing all of this, at least what the Lord has predicted concerning these ancient people, Satan, even from the beginning, has set out to stop the fulfillment of the Promises of God respecting Israel and her Restoration, and even from the beginning. In other words, the opposition has been relentless.

Satan knows, if Israel falls, the Promises of God also fall.

CANNOT SATAN READ THE BIBLE?

The idea is, Satan can certainly read the Bible, and can certainly understand what it says. It predicts his total and complete defeat. So how does he think that he can overcome the Lord?

The truth is, Satan is deceived, even as the billions who follow him. He actually believes that he will win in this conflict. It is the most profound case of *"unbelief"* in the history of man, which has dragged down untold millions, even billions.

But the truth is, he will not succeed; every single Promise and Prediction in the Bible which has not already been fulfilled will be fulfilled to the letter. Of that, one can be certain!

THE ATTACK ON ISRAEL

The phrase of Verse 11, *"And you shall say, I will go up to the land of unwalled villages,"* presents the Antichrist now engaging the final solution, the total destruction of Israel, with every Jew being killed, or so he thinks!

After the Antichrist breaks his seven-year pact with Israel, and actually invades them, making Jerusalem his city, and the Temple his headquarters, Daniel says that he will *"hear tidings out of the East, and out of the North,"* and will have to leave off his subjugation of Israel in order to attend to this pressing business.

Actually, these battles that he will fight at this time will probably take the better part of two years to finish. He will then regroup, with even a larger army, having won these conflicts, and will come down to once and for all annihilate Israel.

Incidentally, there is every evidence that America, at this time, plus all the other nations in the world, with some of them who may have previously thought favorably toward Israel, but, now, remaining neutral (Zech. 12:1-3).

Israel, after having been defeated upon the first invasion of the Antichrist, will have fled to Petra in modern Jordan, and other places. Upon the Antichrist (Gog) going to fight other battles, Israel will then filter back into the Land, reoccupying its cities, and will attempt to make herself strong.

The phrases, *"The land of unwalled villages"* and *"dwelling without walls"* and *"having neither bars nor gates,"* refer to Israel's efforts at mobilization to be rather weak, at least in the mind of the Antichrist. In other words, the Antichrist feels that he will have no problem whatsoever in totally annihilating these people; however, he will reckon without the Coming of the Lord.

TO TAKE A SPOIL

The phrase of Verse 12, *"To take a spoil, and to take a prey,"* presents the plans of the man of sin.

The Antichrist, at least at this time, will be well on his way to taking over the entirety of the world. It seems, by comparing Scripture with Scripture, that by now he will have already conquered many nations of the world, and neutralized most of the others, if not all, by making agreements with them, etc. His ambition is to rule the world, and, due to the power given to him by Satan, as it has never been given to any other man, and his false prophet performing miracles, the nations of the world, at least at the outset, which will no doubt include America, will truly think this man holds the answers to the ills and problems of mankind. This will be man's grandest effort to restore Paradise without the *"Tree of Life,"* Which is Jesus Christ.

However, and according to Revelation, Chapter 6, his conquest of peace will quickly turn into a conquest by war. By now, his strength is so great that it seems nothing can stand in his way. He will set out to take over the entirety of the world, or so he thinks!

This will be the conclusion of man's social system, and man's government. It will be the conclusion of a society that has been corrupt from its very beginning. Now, the corruption will be on a scale heretofore unknown in the history of man. Actually, the world is already being set for the advent of the Antichrist. His rise will be religious as well as political. As such, the Apostate Church is being jockeyed into position to herald his rise in a positive way.

THE QUESTIONS

The questions of Verse 13: *"Are you come to take a spoil? Have you gathered your company to take a prey? To carry away silver and gold, to take away cattle and goods, to take a great spoil?"* addressed to the Antichrist are not meant to proclaim an adversarial position. Here, they merely anticipate and express the true motives of *"Gog"* to fall upon Israel.

Some erroneously teach from this Verse that these nations represent opposition to the Antichrist and will, therefore, throw in their lot with Israel, helping to defend her; however, there is nothing in this Verse that says this, nor any other Verse in the Bible.

Actually, every evidence is, as we have previously stated, that no nation in the world will come to Israel's aid at that time.

No doubt, there will be opposition to the Antichrist in many nations of the world; however, such will be muted, and will offer no viable protest at this incursion.

DWELL SAFELY

The phrase of Verse 14, *"In that day when My people of Israel dwell safely, shall you not know it?"* pertains to the Antichrist getting his attack ready.

The idea of this Verse is, despite the Antichrist invading Israel and defeating her at the mid-point of the Great Tribulation, and breaking his seven-year pact, still, due to pressing business elsewhere (Dan. 11:44), Israel will filter back into the land, reoccupying it, and seemingly, will, once again, dwell there, and with a modicum of safety. The Antichrist will be fighting great battles elsewhere.

But Israel filtering back into the land, and *"dwelling safely,"* will, no doubt, infuriate the *"man of sin,"* and he will set about to handle the situation once and for all!

THE NORTH

The phrase of Verse 15, *"And you shall come from your place out of the north parts,"* does not refer to Russia, as some think, but rather to Syria. This will be where he will gather his army.

However, the Syria of Daniel's Prophecies, of which this speaks, included modern Syria, Iraq, and Iran.

Daniel's Prophecies spoke of the break-up of the Grecian Empire under Alexander the Great. It broke into four parts of which the Syrian division, or northern part, signifies the area from which the Antichrist will come (Dan., Chpt. 11). Therefore, he could come from any one of the three countries mentioned above and still fulfill Bible Prophecy.

At the beginning of the time of the Antichrist, ten kingdoms will be formed inside the old Roman Empire territory. As he begins his quest for the world, he will declare war on three of these kingdoms, quickly overcoming them (Dan. 7:8-9, 21-25); the other six will throw in their lot with him, without conflict, with him now heading up all ten kingdoms (Rev. 17:9-17).

After attacking Israel and defeating her at about the mid-point of the Great Tribulation, in fact breaking his pact with her, this is when the *"tidings of the east and the north"* will come to him (Dan. 11:44).

He will then stop his efforts concerning Israel, going north and east to fight great battles, which will no doubt, at that time, bring Russia, along with possibly China and Japan, under his wing. He will then come down upon Israel, described as the *"Battle of Armageddon"* (Zech. 14:1-5; Rev. 19:11-21).

THE LATTER DAYS

The phrase of Verse 16, *"It shall be in the latter days,"* once again has the Holy Spirit using this phrase.

As stated, it refers to the last of the last days, which pertains to the present and the near future. In other words, these Prophecies have already begun to come to pass, and with each passing day will accelerate their fulfillment.

The phrase, *"When I shall be sanctified in you, O Gog, before their eyes,"* refers to the Lord defending what is His.

The idea is, *"Gog"* will make his boasts all over the world concerning the greatness of his power, and the absence of the Power of God, no doubt using all of the media to accomplish this task. In other words, every Television network in the world will proclaim his intentions.

However, when the Lord does what He has promised to do, all the *"heathen"* will *"know Me."* Then, He will show the world His great Power, which will be made evident at the Second Coming.

(17) "THUS SAITH THE LORD GOD, ARE YOU HE OF WHOM I HAVE SPOKEN IN OLD TIME BY MY SERVANTS THE PROPHETS OF ISRAEL, WHICH PROPHESIED IN THOSE DAYS MANY YEARS THAT I WOULD BRING YOU AGAINST THEM?

(18) "AND IT SHALL COME TO PASS AT THE SAME TIME WHEN GOG SHALL COME AGAINST THE LAND OF ISRAEL, SAITH THE LORD GOD, THAT MY FURY SHALL COME UP IN MY FACE.

(19) "FOR IN MY JEALOUSY AND IN THE FIRE OF MY WRATH HAVE I SPOKEN, SURELY IN THAT DAY THERE SHALL BE A GREAT SHAKING IN THE LAND OF ISRAEL:

(20) "SO THAT THE FISH OF THE SEA, AND THE FOWLS OF THE HEAVEN, AND THE BEASTS OF THE FIELD, AND ALL CREEPING THINGS THAT CREEP UPON THE EARTH, AND ALL THE MEN WHO ARE UPON THE FACE OF THE EARTH, SHALL SHAKE AT MY PRESENCE, AND THE MOUNTAINS SHALL BE THROWN DOWN, AND THE STEEP PLACES SHALL FALL, AND EVERY WALL SHALL FALL TO THE GROUND.

(21) "AND I WILL CALL FOR A SWORD AGAINST HIM THROUGHOUT ALL MY MOUNTAINS, SAITH THE LORD GOD: EVERY MAN'S SWORD SHALL BE AGAINST HIS BROTHER.

(22) "AND I WILL PLEAD AGAINST HIM WITH PESTILENCE AND WITH BLOOD; AND I WILL RAIN UPON HIM, AND UPON HIS BANDS, AND UPON THE MANY PEOPLE WHO ARE WITH HIM, AN OVERFLOWING RAIN, AND GREAT HAILSTONES, FIRE, AND BRIMSTONE.

(23) "THUS WILL I MAGNIFY MYSELF, AND SANCTIFY MYSELF; AND I WILL BE KNOWN IN THE EYES OF MANY NATIONS, AND THEY SHALL KNOW THAT I AM THE LORD."

The structure is:

1. The Antichrist has boasted to the world as to what he is going to do to Israel.

2. The Lord will now proclaim what He is going to do to the Antichrist.

3. Then shall the entirety of the world know and understand, without the shadow of a doubt, *"that I am the Lord."*

THE PROPHETS OF ISRAEL

The phrase of Verse 17, *"Are you he of whom I have spoken in old time by My servants the Prophets of Israel,"* proclaims the fact that the Prophets of Israel were the only ones in the world recognized at that time by God.

The Lord is actually speaking here of the Prophecies given to Ezekiel, of which this is one, as well as Isaiah and Daniel, plus, no doubt, others.

The phrase, *"Old time,"* is in contrast to the *"latter days"* of Verse 16.

As well, the Holy Spirit emphasizes the veracity of these Prophecies of *"old time,"* guaranteeing the certitude of their fulfillment. Actually, the Bible is the only Book in the world that prophetically tells the future of man. This alone is enough to prove its veracity and predictions.

Especially considering that approximately one-third of the Bible is made up of Prophecy, with great portions of it yet unfulfilled, to doubt the inspiration of such is to doubt the Truth that is before one's very eyes. As well, every single Prophecy has come to pass, according to the fullness of its time, which guarantees the fulfillment of those that are to follow.

Of course, the question must be asked as to the Antichrist reading these very Prophecies and then making his plans to circumvent their predictions. That will not be done, and because of the incurable heart of unbelief in man. The Antichrist will be so lifted up in himself, that he will surely think that nothing can stand in his way, and, he will no doubt make himself believe that all these things, despite their accuracy and pinpoint predictions, are mere myths. Actually, almost the entirety of the world does the same thing presently, and, in fact, always has!

FURY

The phrase, *"That My fury shall come up in My face,"* refers to the actual attack by the Antichrist on the Land of Israel. This is the *"Battle of Armageddon."*

In fact, the phrase, *"My fury shall come up in My face,"* corresponds to the statement of Zechariah, *"Then shall the LORD go forth, and fight against those nations, as when He fought in the day of battle"* (Zech. 14:3).

This is anger at a white-hot pitch, and anger from One Who is all-powerful; therefore, the world is going to see a magnitude of judgment that it has never known before. The *"man of sin"* will rue the day that he took on *"God's people and God's Land."*

JEALOUSY

The phrase of Verse 19, *"For in My jealousy, and in the fire of My wrath have I spoken,"* is linked to His *"fury"* and *"wrath."* These are His people and His Land. He is *"jealous"* over them, as He is *"jealous"* over all that belongs to Him, including the Church, and we speak of the True Church.

The phrase, *"Surely in that day there shall be a great shaking in the Land of Israel,"* can refer only to the Battle of Armageddon, for no other prediction can match this description.

THE PRESENCE OF GOD

The phrase of Verse 20, *"And all the men who are upon the face of the Earth shall shake at My Presence,"* presents a display of power such as the world has never know before. As stated, it will take place at the Second Coming.

This tremendous conflict, and we continue to speak of the Second Coming, will affect plant life, animal life, plus all humans, and even the topography of the land. All of this will in no way be caused by the Antichrist, but, instead, by the Power of God. Thusly, one can understand the magnitude of *"My fury that shall come up in My face."*

Actually, the world has never seen, heard, or known of such power being expended in such magnitude. No wonder, the Lord said, *"The heathen may know Me,"* referring to much of the world, which will see this spectacle, more than likely over television even as it transpires, brought into their very homes.

Undoubtedly, there will hundreds, if not thousands, of television cameras there, sponsored by the major networks of the world, and insisted on by the Antichrist in his pomp and pride, as he desires to record, for the entirety of the world, the tremendous victory he is about to win, or so he thinks! However, there will be a victory, but it will not be his!

The tremendous television coverage, meant to impress the entirety of the world, will do just that, but in the opposite direction. The world will see a demonstration of the Power of God as it has never seen before, and, as well, undoubtedly observe Christ with the armies of Heaven, coming back to Earth with a glory that boggles the mind.

This will be quite an event, to say the least, and especially considering that every Born-Again individual who has ever lived, plus those who are reading these very words, who are saved by the Blood of Christ, will be with Christ at His Second Coming (Jude, Vs. 14).

Actually, outside of these Scriptures, there is no way for one to describe the magnitude of this power, because it is a power far beyond the capabilities of man to even comprehend or understand.

It may be argued, that atomic energy falls into the same category; however, as powerful as that is, it is localized, whereas this will cover the entirety of the Land of Israel, plus other areas as well!

Some may argue that all the disturbance in the heavens which will take place at the Second Coming, which Jesus addressed in Matthew, Chapter 24, will knock out all television reception. While that certainly could be, there is every evidence that the Lord will protect the television coverage, for the Scripture says, concerning the Second Coming, in the Words of our Lord: *"And then shall appear the sign of the Son of Man in Heaven: and then shall all the tribes of the Earth mourn, and they shall see the Son of Man coming in the clouds of Heaven with power and great glory"* (Mat. 24:30).

About the only way that all the people of the Earth, which incidentally doesn't mean every single one, but rather the greater bulk of the population, will be able to see Him is by television.

STRANGE HAPPENINGS

The phrase of Verse 21, *"And every man's sword shall be against his brother,"* proclaims one of the methods of destruction employed by the Lord in battles of the past. He has caused the enemy to begin to fight among themselves.

For instance, when Jonathan was fighting the Philistines, the Scripture says, *"The Earth quaked"* and *"They went on beating down one another,"* meaning that the Philistines, for some reason, turned on each other (I Sam. 14:15-16). This will happen, as well, at the Battle of Armageddon.

HAILSTONES, FIRE, AND BRIMSTONE

The phrase of Verse 22, *"And I will plead against him with pestilence and with blood,"* refers to any destructive force, which, in this case, will cause great bloodshed. In fact, the bloodshed will be so great in the Battle of Armageddon, and we speak of blood being shed by the forces of the Antichrist, that the Scripture says that it will flow to the horses' bridles, at least for a certain distance, and will, no doubt, be mixed with water (Rev. 14:20).

The phrase, *"And I will rain upon him, upon his bands, and upon the many people who are with him, an overflowing rain, and great hailstones, fire, and brimstone,"* proclaims that which the Prophet Zechariah meant by the Lord doing battle as in days of old. As He had done so many times in the past, He will do so again at this momentous occasion.

For instance, when Sisera, the Canaanite General, was defeated by Deborah and Barak, the Scripture says, concerning his 900 chariots of iron, *"The Earth trembled, and the Heavens dropped, the clouds also dropped water."* It also said, *"The stars in their courses fought against Sisera"* (Judg. 5:4, 20-21).

Therefore, the Lord will employ the same tactics, but on a magnified scale, in the Battle of Armageddon. He will use the elements over which the Antichrist, nor any other man, will have any control.

THE LORD WILL MAGNIFY AND SANCTIFY HIMSELF

The phrase of Verse 23, *"Thus will I magnify Myself, and sanctify Myself,"* proclaims this being done by the supernatural destruction of the Antichrist, and even all the mighty armies which are with him, which will be destruction and death never before equaled.

The words, *"magnify Myself"* and *"sanctify Myself,"* have terrifying consequences, if used in the negative.

It has reference to anger held in check for a long time, and then exploding with a fury that defies description. It pertains to the honoring of His Name, especially after the Antichrist has blasphemed the Lord for a period of some seven years.

The phrase, *"I will be known in the eyes of many nations,"* refers to this which will be done as described, and, which, no doubt, and as previously stated, will be portrayed all over the world by television as it is happening.

Therefore, not only will the Antichrist be

defeated, but, due to these actions by the Lord, the entirety of the world will instantly know and recognize His Power, Glory, and Majesty. For the Scripture says that He will come back *"King of kings, and Lord of lords"* (Rev. 19:16).

Then, and beyond the shadow of a doubt, *"They shall know that I am the Lord."*

This will begin the glorious Kingdom Age, with Christ reigning personally and Supreme from Jerusalem.

"Be not dismayed whatever betide,
"God will take care of you;
"Beneath His wings of love abide,
"God will take care of you."

"Through days of toil when heart does fail,
"God will take care of you;
"When dangers fierce your path assail,
"God will take care of you."

"All you may need He will provide,
"God will take care of you;
"Nothing you ask will be denied,
"God will take care of you."

"No matter what may be the test,
"God will take care of you;
"Lean weary one upon His breast,
"God will take of you."

CHAPTER 39

(1) "THEREFORE, THOU SON OF MAN, PROPHESY AGAINST GOG, AND SAY, THUS SAITH THE LORD GOD; BEHOLD, I AM AGAINST YOU, O GOG, THE CHIEF PRINCE OF MESHECH AND TUBAL:

(2) "AND I WILL TURN YOU BACK, AND LEAVE BUT THE SIXTH PART OF YOU, AND WILL CAUSE YOU TO COME UP FROM THE NORTH PARTS, AND WILL BRING YOU UPON THE MOUNTAINS OF ISRAEL:

(3) "AND I WILL SMITE YOUR BOW OUT OF YOUR LEFT HAND, AND WILL CAUSE YOUR ARROWS TO FALL OUT OF YOUR RIGHT HAND.

(4) "YOU SHALL FALL UPON THE MOUNTAINS OF ISRAEL, YOU, AND ALL YOUR BANDS, AND THE PEOPLE WHO ARE WITH YOU: I WILL GIVE YOU UNTO THE RAVENOUS BIRDS OF EVERY SORT, AND TO THE BEAST OF THE FIELD TO BE DEVOURED.

(5) "YOU SHALL FALL UPON THE OPEN FIELD: FOR I HAVE SPOKEN IT, SAITH THE LORD GOD.

(6) "AND I WILL SEND A FIRE ON MAGOG, AND AMONG THEM WHO DWELL CARELESSLY IN THE ISLES: AND THEY SHALL KNOW THAT I AM THE LORD."

The structure is:

1. The Lord, as is overly obvious, is *"against the Antichrist;"* therefore, anything the Lord is against cannot ultimately come out to success, irrespective as to how strong it may seem to be at the beginning.

2. The Antichrist will think that his attack on Israel is of his making. But the truth is, it is the Lord Who engineers these events.

3. This Prophecy was given about 2,500 years ago, proclaiming the Omniscience of the Lord, in that He knows all things, past, present and future. What a mighty God we serve!

THE BATTLE OF ARMAGEDDON

The phrase of Verse 1, *"Therefore, thou son of man, prophesy against Gog, and say, Thus saith the Lord GOD; Behold, I am against you, O Gog,"* proclaims in these simple words the doom of the man of sin.

As the Thirty-sixth Chapter told of Israel's coming Restoration, with the Thirty-seventh saying as to how it would be done (by the Spirit of God), and the Thirty-eighth portraying Satan's opposition to the Spirit of God, and this time through the Antichrist, called *"Gog,"* this Chapter proclaims Gog's defeat by the Lord Jesus Christ. It is the Battle of Armageddon as described in Revelation 16:16.

As the last Chapter began, thus this Chapter begins accordingly: *"I am against you, O Gog."*

As previously stated, the phrase, *"The chief prince of Meshech and Tubal,"* has no reference to any particular locality, but, instead, refers to the great confederation of Gentile nations throwing in their lot with the Antichrist, in order to destroy Israel.

One of the reasons the phrase is used

accordingly is because *"Gog,"* the Antichrist, is a Jew, and, at least in these circumstances, it is somewhat strange for Gentile armies to follow a Jew, especially as he attempts to destroy his own people.

(Even though there is no particular Scripture that specifically states that the Antichrist will be Jewish, still, it is virtually impossible that the Jews would proclaim as Messiah anyone who is not Jewish. And at the beginning, they will think this man is the Messiah [Jn. 5: 43].)

THE NORTH PARTS

The phrase of Verse 2, *"And I will turn you back, and leave but the sixth part of you,"* proclaims this, as stated, as the Battle of Armageddon.

Many Bible Teachers claim that Chapters 38 and 39 pertain to another battle other than the Battle of Armageddon; however, a proper interpretation of the Scripture plainly shows that this individual, who is the Antichrist, is going to make a concentrated effort against Israel, which, needless to say, is far more than a police action, but is instead a wholesale invasion of the Land. Also, the manner in which he will be opposed by the Lord, once again, proclaims this as the Battle of Armageddon, and, especially, that Israel is wondrously restored after this, plainly portrays this as the final and concluding conflict.

Immediately after the Thirty-ninth Chapter, the total Restoration of the Land, with the construction of the Temple, even in minute detail, are given to us, which further portrays this conflict as the final one, and, therefore, the Battle of Armageddon.

This portrayal in these two Chapters could not portray the invasion of the Antichrist some three and one half years earlier when he will break his seven-year covenant with Israel (Dan. 9:27), because that particular conflict, which will happen before the Battle of Armageddon, will be somewhat incomplete, simply because the Antichrist will be threatened by other enemies out of the North and East according to Daniel 11:44.

At the end of these three and one-half years of subduing these enemies, and preparing for the total annihilation of Israel, who will have filtered back into the Land

NOTES

during the absence of the Antichrist, he is now prepared for this final conflict, which will be fought on the field of Megiddo, and is called by the Lord *"Armageddon"* (Rev. 16:16).

THE SIXTH PART

Due to the fact that God is Almighty, there is no way that any army, or conglomeration of armies, can defeat the Lord. But still, the incurable heart of man, grossly deceived, even as the heart of the Antichrist will be grossly deceived, still thinks that God can be circumvented, ignored, or even defeated. But it will not happen, as it cannot happen.

This great conflict will signal the Second Coming, which Coming will portray the Lord as a *"man of war."* As previously stated, the Prophet Zechariah said: *"Then* (at this Battle) *shall the LORD go forth and fight against those nations, as when He fought in the day of battle"* (Zech. 14:3).

At this time, and due to the Lord fighting against the man of sin, the entirety of his armies will be destroyed with the exception of a *"sixth part."* How large his army will be we aren't told; however, it no doubt will include many hundreds of thousands of men, possibly even a million or more. At any rate, when it's all over, only one out of six will remain alive.

This we do know, so many men will be killed that blood will flow for a space of about 184 miles to the horses' bridles, which is about five or six feet deep.

Actually, the Scripture does not say that this deluge will all be blood, but, instead, calls it *"the winepress,"* which, no doubt, denotes the *"overflowing rain"* of Ezekiel 38:22 mixed with blood (Rev. 14:20).

THE ROUTE OF THE INVASION

The phrase of Verse 2, *"And will cause you to come up from the north parts, and will bring you upon the mountains of Israel,"* refers to the Lord bringing the Antichrist to this place, despite the fact that the man of sin will think that all of this is his idea.

To which we have previously alluded, many Bible students have concluded that the phrase, *"To come up from the north parts,"* refers to Russia; however, this statement has no reference to Russia, but instead refers to the invasion route being the same as it was for the Assyrians, Babylonians, Grecians, and others in the past.

In fact, many have taught that Ezekiel, Chapters 38 and 39, portrays some type of battle between Russia and Israel, therefore claiming that this is not a description of the Battle of Armageddon. However, the fall and, thereby, destruction of Soviet Communism put that myth to rest. No, these two Chapters describe the Battle of Armageddon, and for the reasons which we have already given.

THE WORD OF THE LORD

The phrase of Verse 3, *"And I will smite your bow out of your left hand,"* proclaims the emphasis on the pronoun *"I."* It is used accordingly in these Passages regarding the destruction of the Antichrist, denoting the fact that the Lord will be his opposer.

While the Antichrist, called *"Gog,"* will think he is fighting Israel only, in Truth, he is fighting the Lord, a battle he cannot hope to win. In fact, all should know and understand this great Truth.

The Lord has never lost a battle, and the Lord will never lose a battle, irrespective as to how small it might be or large it might be. Bringing this into the personal experiences of individual Christians, a tremendous truth should here be well understood.

The Christian should find out what the Lord is doing, which can be done, if self-will is laid aside, and one ardently seeks the Lord, asking for leading and guidance. God uses men, and by that we mean both men and women. So, all Believers should ascertain as to whom the Lord is truly using, and place their support accordingly. But there is a catch to all of this, that most Christians seem not to understand.

THE OPPOSITION OF SATAN

That which the Lord has truly called, and is truly using, will always be opposed greatly by Satan. Unfortunately, it seems that most Christians look for that which is never opposed, thinking somehow that that signals the Blessings of the Lord. It doesn't!

How many modern Christians would have thrown in their lot with Moses, with him spending forty years at the back side of the desert? I can assure you, not many!

How many would have thrown in their lot with David, when he was being hunted by Saul, a period of time which lasted for probably about fifteen years? How many would have thrown in with Job, when he lost everything he had, with even his dearest friends, so-called, blaming him for the tragedy, with even his wife telling him that he should curse God and die? What about Paul, when he languished in prison for several years, even during the prime of his Ministry?

But God ultimately brought these individuals out, as the Lord will always bring His people out.

Opposition by other Christians to the true man of God is not going to hurt the opposed, but it will definitely hurt the opposer.

It seems that all of the nations of the world, at the time of the Battle of Armageddon, will throw in their lot with the Antichrist, or else will remain neutral. In other words, it seems that none will side with Israel; nevertheless, the Lord will side with Israel, and that's all that really matters in any case.

THE COMPLETE DEFEAT

The phrase of Verse 4, *"You shall fall upon the mountains of Israel,"* is a prediction now given about 2,500 years ago, but most assuredly which will come to pass.

The idea of Verse 4 is that the defeat of the Antichrist and his armies will be so severe, vultures and beasts will feed upon the multitudes of dead bodies, littering the *"mountains of Israel."*

The phrase, *"You shall fall,"* signifies not only the defeat of the *"man of sin,"* but, as well, the collapse of corrupt human society, which includes corrupt human government.

Man has ever attempted to rebuild the Garden of Eden, but without the *"Tree of Life,"* symbolic of the Lord Jesus Christ. His efforts have been in vain because it is impossible to do such; however, the grandest effort of all will be in the near future, when the Antichrist will make his debut for world dominion. It will be religious, economical, sociological, military, and governmental; hence, at this time, *"his number is six hundred three-score and six."* It is *"the number of a man,"* denoting man's supreme effort (Rev. 13:18).

THE SECOND COMING

The Second Coming of the Lord will usher in True Government, which will be upon the Shoulder of Christ, referring to Him bearing the responsibility, and, therefore, guaranteeing its success. The *"Tree of Life"* will be back in the Garden, and Paradise will finally be brought back — but only upon the Advent of Christ.

The phrase, *"And the people who are with you,"* proclaims the somber note, that not only will the Antichrist be destroyed, but, as well, all who have thrown in their lot with him, proclaiming that they have made a bad choice. To fight against that which belongs to God is to fight against God! But this is Truth that most seem to never learn.

In fact, untold millions in the world will actually think that the Antichrist is some type of deity, and will worship him accordingly, which worship the Antichrist will ardently seek!

THE FIRE ON MAGOG

Verse 5 says: *"You shall fall upon the open field: for I have spoken it, saith the Lord GOD."*

The phrase, *"Open field,"* refers to the time of the defeat of the Antichrist. It will be in the very midst of the Battle, with the Antichrist bearing down on Jerusalem, and thinking that victory is within his grasp (Zech. 14:1-3).

At the time he is strongest, he will be destroyed, for *"I have spoken it, saith the Lord GOD."*

The phrase of Verse 6, *"And I will send a fire upon Magog,"* simply means that the Lord will personally use the elements of the heavens to destroy the vast Gentile armies following the Antichrist.

The phrase, *"And among them who dwell carelessly in the isles,"* simply refers to other nations of the world, which in their minds are neutral, and are simply turning a blind eye to this wholesale slaughter against Israel by the Antichrist. During the late 1930's, and at the outset of World War II, many nations of the world, including the United States, knew what was taking place regarding the Jews, but, still, did nothing about it; consequently, 6,000,000 Jews were slaughtered by the demon-possessed madmen of Hitlerite Germany. Finally, America did wake up, as well as other countries, but not in time to stop the slaughter.

Whereas there was somewhat of a reprieve extended by the Lord concerning that encounter, there will be no reprieve concerning this final encounter. Every nation will be held accountable! Every nation *"shall know that I am the LORD."*

In the late 1930's, the Lord said little, and did little; however, at this time, the time of the coming Battle of Armageddon, He is going to say much and do much!

In fact, the entirety of the world at that time *"shall know that I am the LORD."*

TELEVISION

To which we have already alluded, it is positive that every major television news network in the world will be represented at the Battle of Armageddon. The Antichrist, the egomaniac which he will be, will want the entirety of the world to see his great victory, as he annihilates Israel. No doubt, he has plans, that which has already been formulated, for the greatest gala event the world has ever known, his enthronement as the King of kings and Lord of lords. And to be sure, it will look like he is going to pull it off.

On a constant basis, news reports will come in from the battlefront, with television coverage of his advance going into billions of homes around the world. Steadily, his gigantic army crowds Jerusalem, with news reports going out constantly that victory is near. In fact, half the city will fall (Zech. 14:2).

But the Prophet Zechariah also predicted something else:

At this time, when it looks like it's all over, when it looks like the Antichrist will do what Haman, Herod, and Hitler could not do, when it looks like Satan is just about ready to administer the final blow, when it looks like these ancient people, Israel, are about to die, and to a man, the following could very well happen:

There will be a strange phenomenon in the heavens. Jesus Himself said: *"For as the* lightning comes out of the east, and shines even unto the west; so shall also the coming of the Son of Man be."

He then said: *"Immediately after the tribulation of those days shall the sun be darkened, and the moon shall not give her light, and the stars shall fall from Heaven, and the powers of the heavens shall be shaken:*

"And then shall appear the sign of the Son of Man in Heaven" (Mat. 24:27-30.)

Thousands of Television cameras will no doubt point toward the heavens, thinking that the Antichrist is about to introduce a new type of weapon. In fact, hundreds, if not thousands, of newscasters may very well be attempting to explain this great phenomenon to all the people of the world, possibly stating that this which the Antichrist is now introducing will surely mean *"finish"* for Israel.

But then, the terminology will change. It is quite possible that the newscasters, in their attempt to explain this phenomenon to the world, will begin to exclaim, *"Is it possible?" "Can it be?"* And then they will say:

"Ladies and gentlemen, see for yourselves, it is millions of white horses, with every one containing a rider, with a startling glory like we've never seen." But then they will say, *"There is One leading them, and with a glory such as has never been witnessed before. And yes, He has a banner stretched around His body with the name written 'King of kings and Lord of lords!'*

"Could it be?" hundreds of announcers will say. *"Is it Jesus Christ?"*

And then the Scripture says: *"Behold, He comes with clouds* (clouds of Saints); *and every eye shall see Him, and they also which pierced Him"* (Rev. 1:7).

The phrase, *"Every eye shall see Him,"* could refer to those in Israel, and especially in the vicinity of Jerusalem; however, due to modern communications, it probably has reference to most of the world, which could only be carried out by Television, to which we have alluded.

HIS COMING

When He came the first time, He came as a lowly human being, raised in the home of peasant parents, in which Isaiah prophesied:

NOTES

"And when we shall see Him, there is no beauty that we should desire Him" (Isa. 53:2).

In fact, at the conclusion of His Life and Ministry, He was spit upon, laughed at, caricatured, beaten, ostracized, ridiculed, lampooned, and put on a Cross; however, when He comes back the second time, it will be totally different than the first time. He will then come back in such a glory as the world has never known before, and as the Scripture has said, *"crowned King of kings and Lord of lords."* In other words, the Second Coming will be the most cataclysmic event, and by far, that the world has ever known. There has been nothing in history that could even remotely compare with this of which the Bible proclaims.

When you consider that every Saint of God who has ever lived will come back with Christ, all with glorified bodies, such will stagger the imagination.

Millions ask the question, *"Will this really happen?"* The answer is simple:

If He came the First Time, and He most definitely did, then, for certain, He will come the Second Time (Rev., Chpt. 19).

(7) "SO WILL I MAKE MY HOLY NAME KNOWN IN THE MIDST OF MY PEOPLE ISRAEL: AND I WILL NOT LET THEM POLLUTE MY HOLY NAME ANY MORE: AND THE HEATHEN SHALL KNOW THAT I AM THE LORD, THE HOLY ONE IN ISRAEL.

(8) "BEHOLD, IT IS COME, AND IT IS DONE, SAITH THE LORD GOD; THIS IS THE DAY WHEREOF I HAVE SPOKEN.

(9) "AND THEY WHO DWELL IN THE CITIES OF ISRAEL SHALL GO FORTH, AND SHALL SET ON FIRE AND BURN THE WEAPONS, BOTH THE SHIELDS AND THE BUCKLERS, THE BOWS AND THE ARROWS, AND THE HANDSTAVES, AND THE SPEARS, AND THEY SHALL BURN THEM WITH FIRE SEVEN YEARS:

(10) "SO THAT THEY SHALL TAKE NO WOOD OUT OF THE FIELD, NEITHER CUT DOWN ANY OUT OF THE FOREST; FOR THEY SHALL BURN THE WEAPONS WITH FIRE: AND THEY SHALL SPOIL THOSE WHO SPOILED THEM, AND ROB THOSE WHO ROBBED THEM, SAITH THE LORD GOD.

(11) "AND IT SHALL COME TO PASS IN THAT DAY, THAT I WILL GIVE UNTO GOG A PLACE THERE OF GRAVES IN ISRAEL, THE VALLEY OF THE PASSENGERS ON THE EAST OF THE SEA: AND IT SHALL STOP THE NOSES OF THE PASSENGERS: AND THERE SHALL THEY BURY GOG AND ALL HIS MULTITUDE: AND THEY SHALL CALL IT THE VALLEY OF HAMON-GOG.

(12) "AND SEVEN MONTHS SHALL THE HOUSE OF ISRAEL BE BURYING OF THEM, THAT THEY MAY CLEANSE THE LAND.

(13) "YES, ALL THE PEOPLE OF THE LAND SHALL BURY THEM; AND IT SHALL BE TO THEM A RENOWN THE DAY THAT I SHALL BE GLORIFIED, SAITH THE LORD GOD.

(14) "AND THEY SHALL SEVER OUT MEN OF CONTINUAL EMPLOYMENT, PASSING THROUGH THE LAND TO BURY WITH THE PASSENGERS THOSE WHO REMAIN UPON THE FACE OF THE EARTH, TO CLEANSE IT: AFTER THE END OF SEVEN MONTHS SHALL THEY SEARCH.

(15) "AND THE PASSENGERS WHO PASS THROUGH THE LAND, WHEN ANY SEES A MAN'S BONE, THEN SHALL HE SET UP A SIGN BY IT, TILL THE BURIERS HAVE BURIED IT IN THE VALLEY OF HAMON-GOG.

(16) "AND ALSO THE NAME OF THE CITY SHALL BE HAMONAH. THUS SHALL THEY CLEANSE THE LAND."

The overview is:

1. The certainty of these events is affirmed in Verse 8.

2. So many of the army of the Antichrist will be killed at the time of the Coming of the Lord that it will take Israel seven months to clean up the battlefield, as it regards burying the dead, and collecting the bones, etc.

3. The word *"renown"* refers to the Lord being highly honored, and all the people of Israel, in fact, the entirety of the world, knowing that the Lord is the One Who has won this battle.

MY HOLY NAME

Verse 7 captures all the Promises made by the Lord to the Patriarchs and Prophets of old! It is as if the Lord has been asleep, but suddenly awakens.

The phrase of Verse 7, *"So will I make My Holy Name known in the midst of My people Israel,"* will be done in several ways:

There has been no moving or operation of the Holy Spirit in Israel, or among Jews, for nearly 2,000 years. This certainly does not mean that individual Jews have not been saved, because some have come to Christ down through the centuries; however, this was all on an individual basis, and had little to do with the great Promises given to the Patriarchs and Prophets of old.

Therefore, the fulfillment of this Promise will be basically in two forms:

A. The Salvation of the 144,000 (Rev., Chpt. 7); the two witnesses (Rev. 11:3-13).

B. The Second Coming of the Lord (Rev., Chpt. 19).

While the other things play a very important part, still, it is the *"Second Coming"* that will open the eyes of Israel, and, in fact, the entirety of the world.

THE POLLUTION OF THE NAME OF THE LORD HAS ENDED

Verse 7 continues to say, *"And I will not let them pollute My Holy Name any more."*

The Antichrist, and for a period of some seven years, will, in fact, greatly *"pollute"* the Name of the Lord. He will actually declare war on the Lord Jesus Christ, and do so in varied ways. He will no doubt confiscate every Bible where he has any power at all, demanding total allegiance to himself, plus hatred for Christ.

The Scripture further says, *"And there was given unto him a mouth speaking great things and blasphemies."* It also says, *"And he opened his mouth in blasphemy against God, to blaspheme His Name, and His Tabernacle, and them who dwell in Heaven"* (Rev. 13:5-6).

At the Second Coming of the Lord, once and for all, the *"pollution"* will end!

THE ENTIRETY OF THE WORLD WILL KNOW THAT JESUS CHRIST IS LORD AND THE MESSIAH OF ISRAEL

The last phrase of Verse 7, *"And the heathen shall know that I am the LORD, the*

Holy One in Israel," will proclaim, once and for all, that Jesus Christ is Lord.

These very Prophecies in Ezekiel, plus the other Prophets, are little believed by the world. Even much of the Church no longer believes that Israel has any part in the great Plan of God; however, this Passage, plus many others, tell us different!

At the Second Coming of the Lord, to which these Passages refer, so dramatic will be the Lord's rescue of Israel that the world will have absolutely no doubt as to Who Israel's Saviour is!

As stated, the Second Coming of Christ will, no doubt, be televised by thousands of television cameras and networks, which are there to record the great victory of the Antichrist, but, instead, will record the great victory of the Lord Jesus Christ.

At the present time (2003), over 5,000,000,000 people in this world have access to a television set, and will, no doubt, at that time, be eagerly watching the events in the Middle East, and will, instead, see far more than they had thought to see. As we have done our best to describe, they will see the Second Coming of Christ, which will, no doubt, be the most dramatic event that has ever happened in human history. Then, and to be sure, *"the heathen shall know."*

THIS IS THE DAY

The phrase of Verse 8, *"Behold, it is come, and it is done, saith the Lord GOD,"* pertains to the coming Great Tribulation Period, and to the events surrounding that Era. Even though these words were spoken approximately 2,500 years ago, they are so certain of fulfillment, that the Holy Spirit says, through the Prophet, *"it is done."* As someone has said, *"Read the last page of the Book, we win!"*

The events leading up to this time, which, in effect, is the very time in which we are now living, are proclaimed by the Scriptures as being a time of spiritual declension.

Economically and numerically, the American Church has never been stronger; however, spiritually speaking, it is at its lowest ebb since the Reformation. Churches are being filled with people clamoring to hear a *"social message."* And, in fact, the most popular of all is the self-improvement message. The tragedy is, none of this is the Gospel of Jesus Christ, but rather a Band-Aid that is being placed over the cancer of sin, with the end result being, as always, acute destruction. The real problem in mankind, as it has always been the real problem, is *"sin."* But the modern Church acts as if sin does not exist, with the subject little being broached, except in a nebulous way. All the while, the bondages of darkness are taking their deadly toll, with this Band-Aid of the social gospel not only not helping the people, but rather harming them, and severely.

THE ONLY ANSWER IS THE CROSS

As stated, man's problem is sin, whether he be redeemed or otherwise, and the only solution for sin, or, in fact, anything that addresses itself to humankind, is the Cross of Christ.

But tragedy of tragedy, the Cross is being preached not at all, with some few remote exceptions. Satan does everything within his power to cover up or to sidetrack the true solution. And tragically, he by and large succeeds with much of the Church.

The theme of our 2003 International Youth Camp, conducted at Family Worship Center in Baton Rouge, Louisiana, was *"breaking the sin cycle."* This was the theme which my grandson, Gabriel Swaggart, who heads up Crossfire, our local youth group, and which sponsors this International Youth Camp, said that the Lord gave to him. His Message on the Friday night of that particular Camp proclaimed the solution to the terrible sin cycle, which alone is the Cross. I was thrilled as I watched the Lord anoint him to proclaim this Message, and to do so in no uncertain terms.

Before it is too late, we must preach the Cross! We must proclaim the Cross! We must hold it up as the only answer to a hurting and dying world (Rom. 5:1; 6:3-14; 8:1-2, 11; I Cor. 1:17-18, 21, 23; 2:2).

Jesus said: *"And I, if I be lifted up from the Earth, will draw all men unto Me.*

"This He said, signifying what death He should die" (Jn. 12:32-33).

As is here obvious, Christ being *"lifted up from the Earth"* has to do with Him being lifted up on the Cross. That and that alone, which paid the price for man's terrible sin problem, can set the captive free.

The phrase of Verse 8, *"This is the day whereof I have spoken,"* pertains to the coming Great Tribulation Period, and, more especially, to these events at the very conclusion of that particular time.

It pertains to the actual day of the Battle of Armageddon, which will, in fact, last only one day (Zech. 14:7); however, this only speaks of the *"day"* of the Coming of the Lord, and does not refer to the many months of preparation for the battle, or other parts of the conflicts which will precede this momentous day.

SEVEN YEARS

Concerning the weapons that will litter the battlefield, Verse 9 says, *"And they shall burn them with fire seven years."*

Most weapons are made of iron, steel, or other types of metals; still, there will be enough material that is combustible that will keep a contingent of people, no doubt appointed for this very task, busy for some seven years.

The phrase of Verse 10 says, *"And they shall spoil those who spoiled them, and rob those who robbed them, saith the Lord GOD,"* refers to the Antichrist coming to an ignominious end, in fact, the very opposite of that which he had planned.

In the so-called *"Peace for Galilee"* campaign, when Israel attempted to destroy the P.L.O., I, along with several of my associates, were invited to Israel where we would be taken into Lebanon at the very height of the conflict. This happened in 1983, if I remember correctly, and was the closest to war that I had ever personally come.

Of all the things seen and experienced, the mile after mile of Israeli tractor-trailers hauling back captured equipment, both damaged and undamaged, was a scene I will not soon forget. Some of the battle tanks looked like they had been opened with a giant can opener, while others seemed to be untouched; as well, there were myriad truckloads of other captured war material, which, no doubt, if usable, were placed in Israel's inventory. At any rate, the amount was staggering, which, at least, gives one an idea as to the fulfillment of this Verse. Whereas the armies just mentioned only numbered tens of thousands, the armies of the Antichrist will number hundreds of thousands, if not many millions!

So, if one could multiply what I witnessed those years ago by a thousand, one would have an idea as to what is meant by these predictions.

Much, if not most, of the weaponry of the world will be gathered at this Battle of Armageddon.

At this moment (2003), and what is little known by the rest of the world, Saudi Arabia has developed several underground bases in their vast land, containing the very latest in technological military equipment, with much, if not most, purchased from America, and costing, at this stage, nearly one-half trillion dollars.

For what does Saudi Arabia need such a vast array of equipment, and, as well, the most technologically advanced? She need have no fear from Israel, but most probably fears her own fellow Arabs!

However, the likelihood of a conflict between Arab States, at least of this magnitude, is unlikely; therefore, that this vast array of weaponry will fall into the hands of the coming Antichrist is a definite possibility. Daniel did say: *"But he shall have power over the treasures of gold and of silver"* (Dan. 11:43). Of course, this which gold and silver can buy will definitely be included!

GOG

The phrase of Verse 11, *"And it shall come to pass in that day, that I will give unto Gog a place there of graves in Israel,"* proclaims the fact that Israel will be the *"grave"* of the Antichrist, and, in fact, all his armies, instead of the place of victory he had so surely thought it would be.

Down through the many past centuries, battle after battle has been fought in the Land of Israel. The conflict has been almost unceasing for the last 3,500 years. But this will be the last conflict, and will, in fact, be the greatest of them all. But it will be a conflict totally different than any that has ever been waged at that particular place, or anywhere else for that matter.

While Israel will definitely be a participant, it will be the Coming of the Lord, when He will fight, and in a manner He has not fought since days of old, which will decide this conflict, and do so in no uncertain terms (Zech. 14:3). Among all the dead, on that great day of battle, will be *"Gog,"* the Antichrist.

His death will herald the demise of Satan's greatest and final effort to usurp authority over Christ. As well, and at this time, Christ will bind Satan with a *"great chain"* and *"cast him into the bottomless pit, and shut him up, and set a seal upon him, that he should deceive the nations no more, till the thousand years should be fulfilled: and after that he must be loosed a little season"* (Rev. 20:1-3).

The phrase, *"And they shall call it the valley of Hamon-gog,"* refers to the valley of Megiddo, which will be called, at least for a time, *"the multitude of Gog."* It actually will refer to the multitude slain by God at this great occasion.

The skeptic and unbeliever would have nothing but criticism for the actions of the Lord regarding the deaths of so many in this momentous conflict; however, such will come about only after repeated efforts by the Lord soliciting Repentance, but to no avail! (Rev. 9:20-21).

As well, the destruction of those who have vowed the destruction of God, and all that belongs to Him, as well as taking peace from the Earth, thereby causing the suffering and deaths of untold hundreds of millions, will be an act of much needed surgery.

Only those who desire unrighteousness, and, thereby, further pain and suffering, would take exception to these happenings. At long last, the question, *"How long?"* will be answered (Rev. 6:10).

HOW DOES SATAN THINK HE CAN DEFEAT THE LORD?

The Lord is Almighty, meaning that He can do anything, and is, in fact, the Creator Who has created all things (Jn. 1:1-3). Satan is but a creature, meaning that in eternity past, Lucifer, the great angel, was created by God, and, of course, created in Righteousness and Holiness. At some point in time, he led a revolution against God, which has raged from then until now. The Battle of Armageddon, for all practical purposes, will be Satan's swan song.

While it is true that he will be loosed a little season from the bottomless pit, where he will be incarcerated, along with all demon spirits and fallen angels, for a thousand years, his efforts at that time will be short-lived (Rev. 20:1-10).

When we speak of Satan attempting to usurp authority over God, and, in fact, defeat Him, there is only one way that Satan can hope to gain his devious ends. Of course, all the Lord has to do is say the Word, and Satan is no more. And, in fact, the reason He hasn't done this before now is actually a *"mystery."* But this we do know, the Lord has His reasons for everything, and, to be sure, He does all things well. So, Him allowing Satan to continue for this period of time has been for good reason, which eternity future will reveal as to its wisdom.

The only way that Satan could ever think of defeating the Lord is by Satan stopping the Word of the Lord from coming to pass. This he has repeatedly tried to do, even from the very beginning. As stated, his greatest effort will be the Antichrist, and especially the Battle of Armageddon.

If he can defeat Israel, then all the many Promises made by the Lord as it regards these ancient people will fall to the ground, and, in effect, Satan will have won the conflict, with God being dethroned, and Satan taking His place. Of course, we know that cannot happen, but Satan is so deceived that he actually believes he can win the day.

In fact, the Word of the Lord, and we speak of the Bible, is of such significance that the Scripture says: *"For You have magnified Your Word above all Your Name"* (Ps. 138:2).

So, everything hinges on the *"Word of the Lord."* That's why Jesus also said: *"For verily I say unto you, Till Heaven and Earth pass, one jot or one tittle shall in no wise pass from the Law, till all be fulfilled"* (Mat. 5:18).

SEVEN MONTHS

Verse 12 says: *"And seven months shall the House of Israel be burying of them, that they may cleanse the land."*

Of course, modern equipment could accomplish this task in a few days; however, the latter phrase, *"that they may cleanse the land,"* refers to every bone being found and gathered, which will take *"seven months."*

The phrase of Verse 13, *"And it shall be to them a renown the day that I shall be glorified, saith the Lord GOD,"* links this spectacle to the sanctifying of the Name of the Lord.

Normally, the Lord sanctifies His Name by love freely offered and freely received; however, if it is not freely received, but, instead, spurned and blasphemously denounced, His Name is *"sanctified"* and *"glorified"* by Judgment.

Therefore, all men will answer to God in one way or the other, whether by Mercy and Grace, or by Judgment, but answer they shall!

The phrase of Verse 14, *"Those who remain,"* indicates that at least some of the *"sixth part"* left of the armies of the Antichrist will be employed in this effort of cleansing the Land.

So, in fact, if that is the case, the prisoners used to bury their comrades will have a double impact of the Power of God, which will include His Coming, and this aftermath of which they will be a part. Many of these hapless individuals may possibly, at that time, turn to Christ.

The phrase of Verse 15, *"Till the buriers have buried it in the valley of Hamon-gog,"* indicates that the battle area will cover large parts of Israel, with the slain covering many miles, perhaps the entire length and breadth of Israel. Quite possibly, it could even spill over into surrounding countries.

It seems that all the bones will be collected and taken to *"the valley of Hamon-gog"* and there buried. If this is the case, it will be done for a reason, the portraying of such as a monument to Satan's defeat, and the victory, even the great victory, of the Lord Jesus Christ.

(17) "AND, THOU SON OF MAN, THUS SAITH THE LORD GOD; SPEAK UNTO EVERY FEATHERED FOWL, AND TO EVERY BEAST OF THE FIELD, ASSEMBLE YOURSELVES, AND COME; GATHER YOURSELVES ON EVERY SIDE TO MY SACRIFICE THAT I DO SACRIFICE FOR YOU, EVEN A GREAT SACRIFICE UPON THE MOUNTAINS OF ISRAEL, THAT YOU MAY EAT FLESH, AND DRINK BLOOD.

(18) "YOU SHALL EAT THE FLESH OF THE MIGHTY, AND DRINK THE BLOOD OF THE PRINCES OF THE EARTH, OF RAMS, OF LAMBS, AND OF GOATS, OF BULLOCKS, ALL OF THEM FATLINGS OF BASHAN.

(19) "AND YOU SHALL EAT FAT TILL YOU BE FULL, AND DRINK BLOOD TILL YOU BE DRUNK, OF MY SACRIFICE WHICH I HAVE SACRIFICED FOR YOU.

(20) "THUS YOU SHALL BE FILLED AT MY TABLE WITH HORSES AND CHARIOTS, WITH MIGHTY MEN, AND WITH ALL MEN OF WAR, SAITH THE LORD GOD.

(21) "AND I WILL SET MY GLORY AMONG THE HEATHEN, AND ALL THE HEATHEN SHALL SEE MY JUDGMENT THAT I HAVE EXECUTED, AND MY HAND THAT I HAVE LAID UPON THEM.

(22) "SO THE HOUSE OF ISRAEL SHALL KNOW THAT I AM THE LORD THEIR GOD FROM THAT DAY AND FORWARD.

(23) "AND THE HEATHEN SHALL KNOW THAT THE HOUSE OF ISRAEL WENT INTO CAPTIVITY FOR THEIR INIQUITY: BECAUSE THEY TRESPASSED AGAINST ME, THEREFORE HID I MY FACE FROM THEM, AND GAVE THEM INTO THE HAND OF THEIR ENEMIES: SO FELL THEY ALL BY THE SWORD.

(24) "ACCORDING TO THEIR UNCLEANNESS AND ACCORDING TO THEIR TRANSGRESSIONS HAVE I DONE UNTO THEM, AND HID MY FACE FROM THEM."

The overview is:

1. The *"great sacrifice"* of Verse 17 proclaims that which will happen to the Antichrist and his armies. It will not be a victory march, but rather *"a sacrifice."*

2. This mighty army will have refused to *"eat the flesh and drink the blood"* of the Son of God, referring to the price that He would pay at the Cross in order that men might be saved, and so, instead, will have their flesh eaten, and their blood drunk by the fowls of the heavens.

3. The animals spoken of in Verse 18 pertain to the great generals serving under the Antichrist, who will die.

4. The entirety of the world will then know Who is Lord. It could not be accomplished

with Mercy and Grace, so it will be accomplished with Judgment.

THE GREAT SACRIFICE

The phrase of Verse 17, *"And, thou son of man, thus saith the Lord GOD; Speak unto every feathered fowl, and to every beast of the field, Assemble yourselves, and come,"* is the same command as Revelation 19:17-18, 20.

It also refers to the statement of Christ when He said, *"Wheresoever the carcase is, there will the eagles be gathered together"* (Mat. 24:27-31), and *"Wheresoever the body is, there will the eagles be gathered together"* (Lk. 17:34-37).

Even though, and no doubt due to the tremendous numbers who will be slaughtered, vultures and beasts will be engaged, as such always is the case, still, the Passage is meant to impress upon the Reader the tremendous numbers that will be killed.

The phrase, *"Gather yourselves on every side to My sacrifice, that I do sacrifice for you, even a great sacrifice upon the mountains of Israel, that you may eat flesh and drink blood,"* points to the Sacrifice of Christ at Calvary, which was rejected, and, conversely, they themselves became *"a great sacrifice."* Therefore, this lesson should not be lost on the Reader, that if the Sacrifice of Christ is rejected, the individual(s) will ultimately become a sacrifice themselves, but a sacrifice which will not save.

The apt description given, *"that you may eat flesh and drink blood,"* is very similar to the statement made by Christ concerning Himself: *"Verily, verily, I say unto you, Except you eat the flesh of the Son of Man and drink His Blood, you have no life in you"* (Jn. 6:53).

The only answer for a hurting, dying, Satanically-bound human race is the Cross of Christ. It was there that Jesus Christ offered up His Body in Sacrifice, and, thereby, poured out His Precious Blood. This alone was and is able to set the captive free.

It simply refers to the Believer evidencing Faith in Christ and what Christ did at the Cross. That is constituted as *"eating His Flesh and drinking His Blood."*

But let the Reader understand, and to which we have already alluded, the Sacrifice of Christ rejected means that the individual, or nation, or even a group of nations, such as here represented, will themselves be a sacrifice. But the latter will be a sacrifice that will not save, but rather will spell *"doom"* for all involved.

THE SACRIFICE OF CLEANSING

The phrase of Verse 18, *"You shall eat the flesh of the mighty, and drink the blood of the princes of the Earth,"* signifies the military and political elite of the army of the Antichrist.

The idea is, the powerful confederation of forces gathered by the Antichrist, and which had made plans for the subjugation of the entire world, with certain areas of the world already parceled out to these *"mighty,"* have all, and without fail, been foiled by the Coming of Christ. As well as the Antichrist being killed, likewise, most, if not all, of his leaders will be killed!

The phrase of Verse 19, *"Till you be drunken of My sacrifice which I have sacrificed for you,"* presents a startling statement.

The idea is, and as stated, that if they would not accept the Sacrifice of Christ at Calvary, then they would be made a sacrifice, of which they were, but which would not save their souls, but would serve as a part of the sacrifice of cleansing.

The Truth presented here concerning the sacrifice is so important that it is repeated again by the Holy Spirit. Christ died as a Sacrifice to save humanity. All who receive that Sacrifice unto themselves and have faith in its atoning Offering will be saved (Jn. 3:16); however, all who refuse to receive it have, in essence, set themselves against God and His Plan for the human family, and will, therefore, be made a sacrifice themselves as stipulated here, in order that the world rid itself of its malignancy; however, the sacrifice recorded here in no way saves the victim, but instead cleanses the world in order that the Righteous may enjoy the Blessings of God.

MY TABLE

The phrase of Verse 20, *"Thus you shall be filled at My Table with horses and chariots, with mighty men,"* contains a wealth of information. The Antichrist has made his plans for world dominion, and after some seven years of carnage, warfare, murder, and mayhem, is well on his way to the realization of his goal. The plans, no doubt, formulated by these demon-possessed sons of darkness, include the death of every single person on the face of the Earth who will not promise total allegiance to the Antichrist, and total denial of the God of Heaven. In other words, *"Gog"* is preparing *"a table"* of sacrifice for anyone on the Earth who does not recognize him as god and offer him worship; however, the Second Coming of the Lord will change the direction of this *"table."* Instead of this son of darkness preparing *"a table,"* he, instead, will become *"a table,"* in effect, *"My table."*

THE HEATHEN

The phrase of Verse 21, *"And I will set My Glory among the heathen,"* pertains to all who do not know the Lord.

The Bible regards all who do not accept the Lord Jesus Christ as their Saviour as *"the heathen."* Therefore, that includes almost all the world.

In effect, every single person in *"Christian America"* who does not know the Lord Jesus Christ as their personal Saviour, as well as any place else in the world, is regarded by the Lord as *"heathen."* Living in a country, such as America, which adheres, at least somewhat, to the principle of Christianity in no way changes the status of the individual person. Only the acceptance of Christ as one's Saviour will change this designation as given by the Holy Spirit.

As well, the idea is put forth that the Antichrist had planned to set his glory over the entire world, but, instead, *"Christ will set His Glory among the heathen."*

The phrase, *"And all the heathen shall see My judgment that I have executed,"* refers to the entirety of the one-thousand-year Millennial Reign, when Christ will rule this world exclusively, and the government shall be upon His Shoulder (Isa. 9:6-7).

However, it, as well, and as previously stated, includes most of the world, actually *"seeing"* the Second Coming portrayed over television, even as it happens.

THE LORD JESUS CHRIST

Verse 22 says: *"So the House of Israel shall know that I am the LORD their God from that day and forward."*

Along with *"the heathen"* seeing this glorious spectacle, likewise, *"the House of Israel"* will now *"know"* exactly Who the Messiah is. They will know that the One they rejected and crucified is actually *"the LORD their God."* They will know it from *"that very day and forward."*

There will be no argument, His identity is obvious, and, more specifically, because of the nail-prints in His Hands.

The Scripture says: *"And one shall say unto Him, What are these wounds in Your hands? Then He shall answer, Those with which I was wounded in the house of My friends"* (Zech. 13:6).

CAPTIVITY

The phrase of Verse 23, *"And the heathen shall know that the House of Israel went into captivity for their iniquity,"* pertains to the entirety of the world being made aware, and understanding exactly, as to what has happened to Israel. It was sin that caused Israel's destruction, and, to be sure, sin will place anyone *"in captivity."*

THE SIN NATURE

The only way the sin cycle can be broken is by the sinner accepting Christ and making Him Lord and Saviour of his life.

Even then, and we refer to the post-conversion experience, if the Believer doesn't maintain his Faith in Christ and the Cross, ever understanding that the Cross is the *"means"* of our victory, the sin nature will once again rule in the Believer's life, bringing untold difficulties and problems. Paul said concerning this very thing:

"Let not sin (the sin nature) *therefore reign* (rule) *in your mortal body, that you should obey it in the lusts thereof"* (Rom. 6:12).

If there were no danger of this, as many teach, then the Holy Spirit, through Paul, wasted all of these instructions. But, of course, we know that the Holy Spirit doesn't mince words.

Some seventeen times in the Sixth

Chapter of Romans alone, Paul mentions *"sin."* Fourteen times the definite article, *"the,"* is placed in front of the word *"sin,"* meaning *"the sin,"* which actually refers to the *"sin nature."* In other words, it's not speaking of particular acts of sin, but rather the principle of sin, in other words, what causes people to sin.

Two of the other times, the word *"sin"* is used as a noun, and not a verb, meaning that Paul is continuing to address himself to the sin nature. So that leaves only one time (Rom. 6:15) that refers to acts of sin.

To counteract this monster, Paul begins his teaching in Chapter 6 with an explanation of the Cross (Rom. 6:3-5), and what it means to the person who has come to Christ. We are *"baptized into His death"* and *"buried with Him by baptism into death"* and then *"raised with Him in newness of life."*

The Sixth Chapter of Romans is the great Sanctification Chapter of the Bible. In other words, it is here that the Holy Spirit, through Paul, tells us how to live a victorious, overcoming Christian life. In other words, that *"the sin nature not have dominion over us"* (Rom. 6:14).

He begins with the Cross, and, in fact, he never leaves the Cross. It is the Cross alone, and our Faith in that Finished Work of Christ, which gives us victory over the world, the flesh, and the Devil (Col. 2:14-15). Otherwise, the Believer will, in some way, be in captivity to Satan. The Believer must understand that, in fact never forgetting that!

THE HIDDEN FACE OF GOD

The phrase of Verse 23, *"Because they trespassed against Me, therefore hid I My face from them, and gave them into the hand of their enemies: so fell they all by the sword,"* proclaims, and in no uncertain terms, the reason why.

Looking at Israel down through the many centuries of their experience, we know that the dispersions under the Assyrians, the Babylonians, and the Romans were all effected by the sword. As well, this pertains to all Jews who have been exiled through the centuries, and, more particularly, the terrible holocaust of World War II. All of this can justly be stated, *"They all fell by the sword."*

NOTES

The equity of God's action with Israel in all periods of their history — past, present, and future — is declared in Verses 22 through 29.

The phrase, *"They trespassed against Me,"* refers to Israel's rebellion from the very beginning, which finally necessitated their destruction and dispersion, which included the Babylonian captivity, as well as the destruction of Jerusalem by Titus in A.D. 70. However, the crowning *"trespass"* of all, was their rejection of Christ and His Crucifixion.

They refused to believe Him, and said, *"Let His Blood be upon us, and on our children"* (Mat. 27:25), and, referring to His Kingship, *"We have no king but Caesar"* (Jn. 19:15). As a result of them not wanting Him, He *"hid His Face from them."*

That lasted for nearly 2,000 years, with them being given over *"into the hand of their enemies."*

In the early 1980's, the Jewish community in the United States grew angry with me, because I brought out these very things over our worldwide Telecast. They were loathe to admit that their terrible problems of the past and present were because of their rejection and Crucifixion of Christ. I answered them as follows:

It is not that the Lord instituted the terrible persecutions that came upon the Jewish people down through the centuries, but, instead, that they did not desire Him, therefore He gave them *"into the hands of their enemies."* It was not the Lord Who did these things to them, but their enemies.

They did not want Him, so the only alternative was Caesar, and Caesar has been a hard taskmaster!

Verse 24 says, *"According to their uncleanness and according to their transgressions have I done unto them, and hid My face from them."*

It is not that the Lord placed the demonic impulses in the madness of Adolf Hitler that he institute the holocaust, but that he was the one that Israel chose instead of Christ. They made their decision, and succeeding generations have continued to make the same decision; therefore, as they did not desire Him, He *"hid His Face from them."* This was all He could do! No one can force themselves on someone else who does not desire him. Israel did not desire Him, and made it very plain as to their wishes. Therefore, they, as all others, have reaped the results.

Regrettably, this scenario has not yet ended. Continuing to reject Him, Israel will, instead, accept *"another"* as their Messiah (Jn. 5:43). This will happen in the very near future, and will bring Israel yet another holocaust! (Mat. 24:21-22).

However, and finally, Israel will come out of the darkness into the light, and will accept Christ as their Saviour and Messiah. The next Passages tell us how!

(25) "THEREFORE THUS SAITH THE LORD GOD; NOW WILL I BRING AGAIN THE CAPTIVITY OF JACOB, AND HAVE MERCY UPON THE WHOLE HOUSE OF ISRAEL, AND WILL BE JEALOUS FOR MY HOLY NAME;

(26) "AFTER THAT THEY HAVE BORNE THEIR SHAME, AND ALL THEIR TRESPASSES WHEREBY THEY HAVE TRESPASSED AGAINST ME, WHEN THEY DWELT SAFELY IN THEIR LAND, AND NONE MADE THEM AFRAID.

(27) "WHEN I HAVE BROUGHT THEM AGAIN FROM THE PEOPLE, AND GATHERED THEM OUT OF THEIR ENEMIES' LANDS, AND AM SANCTIFIED I THEM IN THE SIGHT OF MANY NATIONS;

(28) "THEN SHALL THEY KNOW THAT I AM THE LORD THEIR GOD, WHICH CAUSED THEM TO BE LED INTO CAPTIVITY AMONG THE HEATHEN: BUT I HAVE GATHERED THEM UNTO THEIR OWN LAND, AND HAVE LEFT NONE OF THEM ANY MORE THERE.

(29) "NEITHER WILL I HIDE MY FACE ANY MORE FROM THEM: FOR I HAVE POURED OUT MY SPIRIT UPON THE HOUSE OF ISRAEL, SAITH THE LORD GOD."

The synopsis is:

1. The pardoning love of God fills the repentant heart with self-abhorrence.

2. So certain is the future restoration of Israel that the past tense is here used in predicting it (Vss. 28-29).

3. The Vision opens and closes with a valley of dry bones, for after the vultures and wild beasts shall have finished their feast, nothing but bones will remain. But for these bones, there will be no resurrection to life.

So these two valleys contrast the one with the other — the one a testimony to God's faithfulness and love; the other to His fidelity in judgment (Williams).

MERCY

The phrase of Verse 25, *"And have mercy upon the whole House of Israel,"* becomes possible because of Israel's Repentance. The Lord will always have *"mercy"* on all who will meet His conditions. To be sure, His conditions are not stringent, but *"easy"* and *"light"* (Mat. 11:29-30).

The word *"now"* of Verse 25 gives us the time that this will happen. It will be after the Battle of Armageddon and at the Second Advent of Christ. This will be the occasion of their humbling before Him, and His lifting *"the captivity of Jacob."* That *"captivity"* has lasted for about 2,500 years.

Regrettably, none of it had to be, but was only because of their *"uncleanness"* and *"transgressions."*

As a result, His Mercy will be so extended that it will include *"the whole House of Israel,"* because *"the whole House"* will repent and accept Him as their Lord and Saviour.

The phrase, *"And will be jealous for My Holy Name,"* is a fearsome statement. *"His Holy Name"* stands behind His Word. He is *"jealous"* that His honor be protected, and that every single Prophecy be fulfilled; and, to be sure, that it shall be!

JEALOUSY

The Hebrew root meaning *"jealousy"* portrays a very strong emotion, a passionate desire. The word is used in both a positive and negative sense.

The strong emotion represented by this word can be viewed positively as a high level of commitment when it describes the feeling of a person for something that is rightly his or her own. Here, *"jealousy"* has the sense of intense love. When applied to God, *"jealousy"* communicates the fierce intensity of His commitment to His people, even when they turn from Him.

In giving the Mosaic Law, the Lord announced to the people of Israel that they must remain committed to Him and not turn to idolatry, and He gave this reason for it: *"I, the LORD your God, am a jealous God"* (Ex. 20:5). Therefore, the *"jealousy"* of God is expressed in Old Testament history, both in *"punishing"* and in *"showing love."*

JEALOUSY AS SHOWN IN THE OLD TESTAMENT

In the Old Testament, God is said to be *"jealous"* for His people, for His Land (Joel 2:18), and for Jerusalem and Zion (Zech. 1:14). This is expressed in the New Testament, as well, respecting Israel concerning the Second Coming (Rev., Chpt. 19).

While the anger of God is an expression of God's jealous wrath, the acts of Judgment recorded in the Old Testament continue to be for the ultimate benefit of a people who must be brought back to a right relationship with God if they are to experience blessing.

Neither God nor humans are cold, computer-like beings. Persons have emotions as well as intellect and will, and often these emotions are strong. Jealousy, or zeal, is one of the stronger emotions.

God's jealousy, although it issues in punishment as well as blessing, is viewed as something both righteous and good. In general, human jealousy is viewed with suspicion. Our emotions are too often tainted by the sin that twists human personalities; however, one can experience, as well, strong emotional commitments to what is good as well as strong emotional desires for what is not our own.

As it relates to God, jealousy is of the essence of His moral Character. It is a major cause for worship and confidence on the part of His people and a ground for fear on the part of His enemies, as is given here.

DWELL SAFELY IN THEIR LAND

The phrase of Verse 26, *"After that they have borne their shame, and all their trespasses whereby they have trespassed against Me,"* proclaims the reason for all of the terrible difficulties of Israel through the many centuries.

The implication of this Verse is that all the *"shame"* was unnecessary, and did not need to be. The Jew, sadly and regrettably, has carried this *"shame"* for nearly 2,000 years. They have steadfastly refused to admit that it was because of their *"trespasses."* Consequently, many have been ashamed of their Jewishness, or puzzled by the persecution, thereby blaming Christ and Christians, when, in reality, it's their own *"trespasses"* which have cause the *"shame."*

Even though the *"trespasses"* are the cause, still, the real cause is the refusal to repent of the trespasses. *"Trespasses,"* sadly and regrettably, are incumbent upon all (Rom. 3:23). It is the lack of the admittance of the *"trespasses,"* and the refusal to come to Christ in order that these *"trespasses"* be handled correctly by Faith in His atoning shed Blood, which brings Judgment. Jesus said, *"And you will not come to Me, that you might have life"* (Jn. 5:40).

In David's last song, he said: *"For I have kept the ways of the LORD, and have not wickedly departed from my God"* (II Sam. 22:22).

How could David say this at the end of his life, especially considering that he had committed the terrible sin with Bathsheba, and against her husband Uriah, as well as other grievous sins?

David was not saying that he had not sinned, but that he had not wickedly departed from God's Ways of handling that sin. He admitted it before the Lord, and believed in the Lord, and these sins were washed away by the Precious Blood of Christ (II Sam. 12:13; Ps. 51).

Regarding sin, most men refuse to accept God's Way, instead devising their own ways, which the Lord will not accept.

Men attempt to atone for their sins by joining Churches, becoming religious, giving money, doing good works, ad infinitum; consequently, they depart wickedly from God's Ways, and continue to bear the *"shame."*

The moment one takes his sin to Christ, confessing that he is a sinner, and asking for the Mercy, Grace, and Love of the Lord, the sin is instantly forgiven, cleansed, washed, and put away (I Jn. 1:9).

This Israel would not do, and most all others will not do!

But finally Israel shall. Then they will *"dwell safely in their Land, and none shall make them afraid."*

THE REGATHERING OF ISRAEL

The phrase of Verse 27, *"When I have brought them again from the people, and gathered them out of their enemies' lands,"* proclaims the gathering that will take place after the Second Coming of Christ and will include every Jew from every country in the world who will be brought, and gladly, to Israel.

The word *"again"* proclaims the fact of a second gathering, the first having taken place beginning in 1948.

In every nation of the world, including America, the Jew is looked at, in many cases, with hostility. This is very wrong, but very real!

However, the main reason this phrase *"their enemies' lands"* is used, is because the Lord intends for all Jews to be in the Land of Israel. The phrase, *"And am sanctified in them in the sight of many nations,"* refers to His Plan for them finally being realized; consequently, all the Promises and Predictions given to the Prophets will be brought to pass. Thus will the Lord be *"sanctified in them."*

RESTORATION

The phrase of Verse 28, *"Then shall they know that I am the LORD their God, which caused them to be led into captivity among the heathen,"* has reference to Israel finally recognizing Christ as the Messiah and Lord and Saviour. For some 2,000 years, they have steadfastly denied this fact. But *"then shall they know."* The word *"then"* signifies the time as the Second Coming of the Lord.

The phrase, *"But I have gathered them unto their own Land,"* proclaims the fact that so certain is the future restoration of Israel that the past tense is used here in predicting it.

The phrase, *"And have left none of them anymore there,"* refers to lands other than Israel.

As well, this will not be a forced return, but a joyful return, inasmuch as most, if not all, will accept Christ at this time.

THE POURED OUT SPIRIT

The phrase of Verse 29, *"For I have poured out My Spirit upon the House of Israel, saith the Lord GOD"* proclaims that which will be done, and because Israel has now accepted Christ as Lord and Saviour.

The Spirit of God cannot be poured out on anyone until first the sin question is settled, which can only be done by the individual evidencing Faith in Christ and what Christ has done at the Cross.

The balance of the Chapters in Ezekiel have to do with the coming Millennial Kingdom, and the rebuilding of the Millennial Temple, etc. All of this proves that Chapters 38 and 39 are, in fact, a portrayal of the Battle of Armageddon. The chronology demands this.

Chapter 37 proclaims Israel being brought back as a nation, with Chapters 38 and 39 portraying the advent of the Antichrist in his efforts to destroy Israel, which will culminate in the Battle of Armageddon. That will precipitate the Second Coming of the Lord, with Jesus then reigning in Jerusalem in the restored nation and rebuilt Temple.

"Sowing in the morning, sowing seeds of kindness,
"Sowing in the noontide and the dewy eve;
"Waiting for the harvest and the time of reaping,
"We shall come rejoicing, bringing in the sheaves."

"Sowing in the sunshine, sowing in the shadows;
"Fearing neither clouds nor winter's chilling breeze;
"By and by the harvest and labor ended,
"We shall come rejoicing, bringing in the sheaves."

"Going forth with weeping, sowing for the Master,
"Tho' the loss sustained our spirit often grieves;
"When our weeping's over, He will bid us welcome,
"We shall come rejoicing, bringing in the sheaves."

CHAPTER 40

(1) "IN THE FIVE AND TWENTIETH

YEAR OF OUR CAPTIVITY, IN THE BEGINNING OF THE YEAR, IN THE TENTH DAY OF THE MONTH, IN THE FOURTEENTH YEAR AFTER THAT THE CITY WAS SMITTEN, IN THE SELFSAME DAY THE HAND OF THE LORD WAS UPON ME, AND BROUGHT ME THITHER.

(2) "IN THE VISIONS OF GOD BROUGHT HE ME INTO THE LAND OF ISRAEL, AND SET ME UPON A VERY HIGH MOUNTAIN, BY WHICH WAS AS THE FRAME OF A CITY ON THE SOUTH.

(3) "AND HE BROUGHT ME THITHER, AND, BEHOLD, THERE WAS A MAN, WHOSE APPEARANCE WAS LIKE THE APPEARANCE OF BRASS, WITH A LINE OF FLAX IN HIS HAND, AND A MEASURING REED; AND HE STOOD IN THE GATE.

(4) "AND THE MAN SAID UNTO ME, SON OF MAN, BEHOLD WITH YOUR EYES, AND HEAR WITH YOUR EARS, AND SET YOUR HEART UPON ALL THAT I SHALL SHOW YOU; FOR TO THE INTENT THAT I MIGHT SHOW THEM UNTO YOU ARE YOU BROUGHT HERE: DECLARE ALL THAT YOU SEE TO THE HOUSE OF ISRAEL."

The exegesis is:

1. Jerusalem is the subject of Ezekiel's last Vision, as it is of his first. It is the city of the Great King, the Lord Jesus Christ.

2. In this last Vision, the city appears as the capital of the whole Land; and the great object of both eye and heart is the Palace of the Messiah.

3. The Palace of the Messiah, the City of the Great King, and the Land promised to Abraham appear, therefore, in this Millennial Vision.

4. The Land will extend from the Euphrates on the north to the Nile on the south, and from the Mediterranean on the west to the Indian Ocean on the east. The tongue of the Egyptian Sea will be dried up (Isa. 11:15), thus enlarging Arabia. The Land of Israel will, therefore, in that day, be a magnificent territory embracing a vast portion of the Ancient World.

TIME FRAMES

The phrase of Verse 1, *"In the five and twentieth year of our captivity,"* concerns itself with the first invasion by Babylon of Jerusalem, which occurred in 605 B.C. During this invasion, the city was partly destroyed and many of the people carried away captive. The city was further devastated in 597 B.C., and finally burned and desolated in the 586 B.C.

Therefore, the statement, *"in the fourteenth year after the city was smitten,"* probably has a different time reference than the dates just given. Even though Jerusalem was first invaded by Babylon in 605 B.C., quite possibly Jehoiakin's deportation did not take place until 600 B.C., which would have been fourteen years before the destruction of Jerusalem. Possibly, Ezekiel was calculating his time from that projection.

At any rate, the Jews began their trek back to the Land of Israel in about 535 B.C. With the first invasion taking place in 605 B.C., this would have totaled seventy years, as predicted.

In this twenty-fifth year of the captivity, the Lord will give to the Prophet his next to the last Vision. Actually the last Vision given him was in the twenty-seventh year, and concerned itself with the defeat of Egypt (Ezek. 29:17-21).

Therefore, Israel was redeemed out of Egypt at the beginning, and now saved from Egypt at the last; consequently, this symbolizes the defeat of the Antichrist at the Battle of Armageddon, for Ezekiel 29:21 says: *"In that day will I cause the horn of the House of Israel to bud forth, and I will give you the opening of the mouth in the midst of them; and they shall know that I am the LORD."*

This speaks of the very *"day"* that we've been studying regarding Israel's restoration after the Battle of Armageddon, the defeat of the Antichrist, and the Coming of the Lord.

It is interesting that Ezekiel's statement in 29:17 concerning Egypt's soon defeat, as well as her defeat at the last, symbolizing the Antichrist, is almost identical to the statement in Exodus 12:2. This certainly is not without meaning, and lends more credence to that great future deliverance.

THE VISIONS OF GOD

The phrase of Verse 2, *"In the visions of*

God brought He me into the Land of Israel," pertains to the Restoration of Jerusalem and the Temple.

The events of the Chapters 40 through 48 concern things in the coming Kingdom Age, when Christ will Personally rule from Jerusalem, which will immediately follow the Battle of Armageddon and the Second Coming of the Lord.

The phrase, *"And set me upon a very high mountain,"* gives no indication as to where this is. In fact, such doesn't exist at present.

However, we do know, that upon the Coming of the Lord, a topographical change will take place the moment His Feet stand on the *"Mount of Olives."* The Scripture says, *"And half of the mountain shall remove toward the north, and half of it toward the south."* Therefore, the Holy Spirit is possibly speaking of the part of Olivet that will move toward the north (Zech. 14:4).

THE MAN WITH THE LINE IN HIS HAND

The phrase of Verse 3 says, *"And He brought me thither, and, Behold, there was a Man, Whose appearance was like the appearance of brass."* If we are to compare the descriptions given in Ezekiel 1:26-27; Daniel 10:6 and Revelation 1:15, then this Man is Christ. Personally, He will give the Prophet the information regarding the coming glory and grandeur of restored Jerusalem and the Temple.

The phrase, *"With a line of flax in His Hand, and a measuring reed,"* speaks of Righteousness. The line is, no doubt, linen, because the place to be measured is the Sanctuary, whose Priests are obliged to clothe themselves in linen. It would be a Kingdom of Righteousness; therefore, it would be measured by the All-Righteous One, and by the *"measuring reed"* of Righteousness.

RIGHTEOUSNESS

It signifies that this Kingdom Age will have a Righteousness wholly of God, and, none of man. Regrettably, self-righteousness has characterized mankind from the Fall, and has been the most terrible blight of the Church.

Inasmuch as this information is given at the very outset of the Vision, we are made to realize that the coming Kingdom Age will be characterized by the Righteousness of Christ exclusively; consequently, there will be no more Church Denominations, no more unscriptural man-made Church rules, no more man-made religion.

The word *"Righteousness"* simply means *"uprightness."* It is that which man has none of, at least within himself, and that which only God can provide. The Righteousness which alone comes from the Lord, and, self-righteousness, which characterizes the human family, has ever been the source of spiritual conflict. Man keeps thinking he can provide his own Righteousness, despite the Scripture plainly saying, *"There is none righteous, no, not one"* (Rom. 3:10). However, the Lord will freely impart Righteousness to all who will admit they have none, and, within themselves, cannot obtain such. It is called *"Imputed Righteousness"* (Rom. 4:22-25).

In the Beatitudes, Jesus blesses those who hunger for Righteousness and those who suffer persecution because of Righteousness (Mat. 5:6, 10).

THE LAW AND RIGHTEOUSNESS

Jesus outlined the relationship between the Law and Righteousness. Although His teachings do not abrogate the Law, still, He insists that the Righteousness of His followers must exceed *"that of the Pharisees and Teachers of the Law"* (Mat. 5:20). This was a stunning and shocking teaching in His day, for those Leaders were committed to a life of strict observance of Law.

His emphasis was not on behavior judged by Law, but by the inner heart attitude from which the action springs. Thus, Law prohibits murder, but Jesus says we must be concerned with the anger that leads to murder (Mat. 5:21-23). Again, the Law prohibited adultery, but Jesus says we must be concerned even with a lustful look (Mat. 5:27-30).

Under Grace, Christ took the Command ever further, recalling that the Old Testament called on God's people to love their neighbors, but, that now, He calls on them to love their enemies. This is True Righteousness (Mat. 5:43-48).

RIGHTEOUSNESS FROM THE HEART

Jesus' teaching involved a dramatic shift of focus. Rather than seeing Righteousness in terms of behavior, which self-righteousness always does, Jesus shifted the issue to within the human heart and personality. It is motives, thoughts, and desires that God is concerned with.

The Righteousness given freely by God refers to far more than doing what God says, but, instead, actually being like Him, which is impossible within human ability, but made possible by the impartation of Divine Righteousness acted upon by the Holy Spirit.

Even more stringently, Jesus said that without the inner Righteousness that He called for, one *"will certainly not enter the Kingdom of Heaven"* (Mat. 5:20).

THE THEME OF RIGHTEOUSNESS

In Romans, Chapter 1, Paul introduced, by the guidance of the Holy Spirit, the theme of Righteousness, on which the entirety of Romans focuses. The Book emphasizes the Truth that the Gospel is about a Righteousness that comes from God and is *"by faith from first to last"* (Rom. 1:17).

Consequently, and picking up on the Teachings of Christ, the New Testament shifts emphasis from a righteousness linked with human behavior to a Righteousness that God provides; however, the New Testament reaches back to the Old Testament, emphasizing the theme established in Genesis 15:6; that is, that such Righteousness is imputed to those who have faith. Thus, the Gospel of Christ is Good News, for God through Jesus provides human beings with Righteousness as a free gift. All one can do to receive it is to trust the One Who promises this all-consummate Blessing (Rom. 10:6; Heb. 11:7).

Continuing in Romans, Paul moved on in his study, as given by the Holy Spirit, that Gentile and Jew alike had no Righteousness within themselves.

He emphasized the fact, and, as stated, that *"there is no one Righteous, not even one"* (Rom. 3:10), and that, in fact, the Law silences every human claim to goodness: he said, *"No one will be declared Righteous in* (God's) *sight by observing the Law; instead, through the Law we become conscious of sin"* (Rom. 3:20).

Paul's affirmation, as Christ's, was a bold denial of the view of Judaism in his day. Law and Righteousness, at least in Jewish thinking, were intimately associated in Jewish thought. Paul's linking Law with sin, not Righteousness, must have seemed far worse than merely radical!

RIGHTEOUSNESS AND FAITH

Linking Righteousness with Faith, Paul rebuilds the structure he had torn down. If Righteousness is not linked with Law or human behavior, how can human beings attain it? Paul says that the Old Testament itself testifies to a *"Righteousness from God, apart from Law"* (Rom. 3:21).

Since all have sinned, humanity's only hope is for Redemption. Jesus died as a Sacrifice of Atonement. The Sacrifice of Christ frees God to be just, even while He pronounces the sinner guiltless. It is because Christ took the punishment that we should have taken. It is in Redemption and Atonement, therefore, that we find the key to Righteousness. And it is through Faith that this Righteousness from God is received by the individual.

IMPUTED RIGHTEOUSNESS

Thus, and as we have stated, the *"Righteousness from God"* is, first of all, an Imputed Righteousness. That is, we are given legal standing before God as Righteous persons, upon our Faith in what He did at Calvary and the Resurrection. Upon believing Him, though, in fact, we are sinners, on the basis of Jesus' death for our sins, God acquits all who believe in Him, and pronounces us Righteous.

One can only shout Hallelujah!

As is painfully, painfully obvious, human beings are, in fact, unrighteous, but God, through Christ's death, has found a legal basis on which to declare the Believer Righteous, despite his present condition of unrighteousness.

RIGHTEOUSNESS AND THE CROSS

Inasmuch as the Lord has imputed Righteousness unto us upon believing Him, now,

Christ begins to act in our lives to make us Righteous persons. In other words, to bring our *"state"* up to our *"standing."* We are, upon the reception of the *"Righteousness of God,"* given a *"new self,"* created to be like God in True Righteousness and Holiness (Eph. 4:24). Consequently, after receiving the *"Righteousness of God,"* which the Believer does by trusting in Christ and what Christ has done at the Cross, the Believer then finds that to struggle in his own strength only brings defeat (Rom., Chpt. 7). It's called *"walking after the flesh"* (Rom. 8:1); however, when the Believer accepts his helplessness and applies to his daily life the same principle of faith that brought judicial acquittal, and I speak of finding Salvation, he finds freedom in Christ, in fact, a freedom that is beyond comprehension!

This is done by the Believer understanding that everything he receives from the Lord has come to him, and continues to come to him, exclusively through Christ and what Christ has done at the Cross. As we have repeatedly stated, while Jesus is the *"Source,"* the Cross is the *"Means"* by which all of these things are done for us. The Believer is to ever make the Cross the Object of his Faith. This alone is what it means to fully trust Christ. To try to trust Christ outside of the Cross, or apart from the Cross, concludes by the individual worshipping and serving *"another Jesus"* (II Cor. 11:4).

RIGHTEOUSNESS AND THE HOLY SPIRIT

This is the glorious Righteousness of which Jesus spoke, God acts within Believers to *"give life to our mortal bodies through His Spirit"* (Rom. 8:11) Who lives within. Thus, the Believer is free to actually live a Righteous Life, not because of conformity to an outward standard, but because the inner person is shaped by the Spirit to choose spontaneously what God Himself chooses.

To sum up, True Righteousness means being like God, not simply obeying Him. Therefore, to meet God's approval, the heart, not simply the behavior, must be right.

Thus, the Gospel is Good News, because it announces that God will declare Righteous those who believe in Jesus, Whose life was offered in Atonement for our sins.

"The Lord made Him Who had no sin to be sin for us, so that in Him we might be made the Righteousness of God" (II Cor. 5:21).

Therefore, that which began even at the Fall of man (Gen. 3:15), which was by Grace, and could only be by Grace, and made possible by the Death and Resurrection of Christ, now in the Kingdom Age will flower into the entire Earth. It is all in Christ and what Christ did at the Cross!

As it began in the heart of man, given freely by Christ, it will now, and through Christ, cover the entire Earth, hence, a Kingdom of Righteousness.

The phrase of the Verse 3, *"And He stood in the gate,"* refers to Himself as the *"Door"* to this Kingdom of Righteousness (Jn. 10:9).

DIMENSIONS

The phrase of Verse 4, *"And the Man said unto me, Son of man, behold with your eyes, and hear with your ears,"* portrays the Truth that all given concerning dimensions, portrayals, and specifications have a spiritual reference, with all pertaining to Christ. As the Tabernacle in the wilderness and the Temple in Jerusalem all spoke of Him, likewise, the Millennial Temple speaks exclusively of Him; therefore, everything pertaining to it, down to the most minute detail, portrays Him in some fashion. The measurements, designs, and descriptions given are not merely facts and figures, but, instead, portrayals in some fashion of His Glorious Person and Work.

The phrase, *"And set your heart upon all that I shall show you,"* refers not only to the design of the structures, but, also, that all which will be given in the coming Kingdom Age will exclusively be by Christ, and of Christ. He Alone satisfies the cravings of the human heart. Therefore, every dimension speaks of a Work of Grace provided only by Him.

CHRIST

The phrase, *"For to the intent that I might show them unto you are you brought hither,"* declares His desire that we may know and understand.

However, the carnal heart will see little

blessing in these tedious statements and measurements, and, consequently, will reap little! However, the spiritual heart will dig and probe that these nuggets of spiritual gold may be brought to the surface. Paul said: *"In Whom are hid all the treasures of Wisdom and Knowledge"* (Col. 2:3).

I would pray that as we go through these glorious descriptions, the Lord will help us to find at least some of these treasures.

The phrase, *"Declare all that you see to the House of Israel,"* refers to the nation of Israel being two things in the coming Kingdom Age:

1. A nation of Priests, not only for Israel but for the entire world, and then truly will *"My House be a house of prayer for all nations"* (Mk. 11:17).

2. Israel, under Christ, and, no doubt, aided and abetted by the Glorified Saints of all ages, will evangelize the world (Isa. 66:18-21).

At the outset, to sum up that which Ezekiel will *"see"* and *"hear,"* the following is given. The scene being Millennial, the dimensions of each are on a corresponding scale.

The Land originally promised to Abraham extended from the Euphrates River on the north to the Nile on the south, and from the Mediterranean on the west to the Indian Ocean upon the east. The tongue of the Egyptian Sea will be dried up (Isa. 11:15), thus enlarging Arabia. The Land of Israel will, therefore, in that coming time, be a magnificent territory, embracing a portion of land at least 100 times larger than modern Israel.

The City will have a dimension of 144 square miles, befitting the future metropolis of the world. It will be upon the north side of the very great valley of Zechariah 14:4-5, thus occupying a magnificent position, and will be beautiful for situation, the joy of the whole Earth. Its suburbs will form a square of some 60 miles, that is, 3,600 square miles. The Palace of the Messiah will occupy the center of a reservation called *"The Sanctuary."* This Sanctuary will be a great square of about a mile on each side. The Palace will have a boundary wall enclosing a square of about one fifth of a mile on each face. Within this square will be the Inner Court, a square of about 450 English feet, and within this square will stand the Palace, the Court of the Palace, and the *"Separate Place,"* all forming a square.

Finally, in the middle of the Separate Place will stand the Altar, 18 feet square on a platform about 21 feet square.

Thus, the Altar will be the actual center of the Millennial Sanctuary — the Temple or Palace being immediately to the west of it.

The Messiah, the Lord Jesus Christ, will enter the Great Square of the Sanctuary by the East Gate, and pass through the Courts into the Palace. Then will be fulfilled Ezekiel 43:4 and Matthew 23:39.

The center of the Millennial Earth will, therefore, be an Altar, testifying that all Blessing is founded upon Atonement, the Atonement freely purchased by the shedding of Christ's Own Precious Blood (I Pet. 1:18-20).

(5) "AND BEHOLD A WALL ON THE OUTSIDE OF THE HOUSE ROUND ABOUT, AND IN THE MAN'S HAND A MEASURING REED OF SIX CUBITS LONG BY THE CUBIT AND AN HAND BREADTH: SO HE MEASURED THE BREADTH OF THE BUILDING, ONE REED; AND THE HEIGHT, ONE REED.

(6) "THEN CAME HE UNTO THE GATE WHICH LOOKS TOWARD THE EAST, AND WENT UP THE STAIRS THEREOF, AND MEASURED THE THRESHOLD OF THE GATE, WHICH WAS ONE REED BROAD: AND THE OTHER THRESHOLD OF THE GATE, WHICH WAS ONE REED BROAD.

(7) "AND EVERY LITTLE CHAMBER WAS ONE REED LONG, AND ONE REED BROAD; AND BETWEEN THE LITTLE CHAMBERS WERE FIVE CUBITS: AND THE THRESHOLD OF THE GATE BY THE PORCH OF THE GATE WITHIN WAS ONE REED.

(8) "HE MEASURED ALSO THE PORCH OF THE GATE WITHIN, ONE REED.

(9) "THEN MEASURED HE THE PORCH OF THE GATE, EIGHT CUBITS; AND THE POSTS THEREOF, TWO CUBITS; AND THE PORCH OF THE GATE WAS INWARD.

(10) "AND THE LITTLE CHAMBERS OF THE GATE EASTWARD WERE THREE ON THIS SIDE, AND THREE ON THAT SIDE; THEY THREE WERE OF ONE MEASURE: AND THE POSTS HAD ONE MEASURE ON

THIS SIDE AND ON THAT SIDE.

(11) "AND HE MEASURED THE BREADTH OF THE ENTRY OF THE GATE, TEN CUBITS; AND THE LENGTH OF THE GATE, THIRTEEN CUBITS.

(12) "THE SPACE ALSO BEFORE THE LITTLE CHAMBERS WAS ONE CUBIT ON THIS SIDE, AND THE SPACE WAS ONE CUBIT ON THAT SIDE: AND THE LITTLE CHAMBERS WERE SIX CUBITS ON THIS SIDE, AND SIX CUBITS ON THAT SIDE.

(13) "HE MEASURED THEN THE GATE FROM THE ROOF OF ONE LITTLE CHAMBER TO THE ROOF OF ANOTHER: THE BREADTH WAS FIVE AND TWENTY CUBITS, DOOR AGAINST DOOR.

(14) "HE MADE ALSO POSTS OF THREESCORE CUBITS, EVEN UNTO THE POST OF THE COURT ROUND ABOUT THE GATE.

(15) "AND FROM THE FACE OF THE GATE OF THE ENTRANCE UNTO THE FACE OF THE PORCH OF THE INNER GATE WERE FIFTY CUBITS.

(16) "AND THERE WERE NARROW WINDOWS TO THE LITTLE CHAMBERS, AND TO THEIR POSTS WITHIN THE GATE ROUND ABOUT, AND LIKEWISE TO THE ARCHES: AND WINDOWS WERE ROUND ABOUT INWARD: AND UPON EACH POST WERE PALM TREES.

(17) "THEN BROUGHT HE ME INTO THE OUTWARD COURT, AND, LO, THERE WERE CHAMBERS, AND A PAVEMENT MADE FOR THE COURT ROUND ABOUT: THIRTY CHAMBERS WERE UPON THE PAVEMENT.

(18) "AND THE PAVEMENT BY THE SIDE OF THE GATES OVER AGAINST THE LENGTH OF THE GATES WAS THE LOWER PAVEMENT.

(19) "THEN HE MEASURED THE BREADTH FROM THE FOREFRONT OF THE LOWER GATE UNTO THE FOREFRONT OF THE INNER COURT WITHOUT, AN HUNDRED CUBITS EASTWARD AND NORTHWARD.

(20) "AND THE GATE OF THE OUTWARD COURT THAT LOOKED TOWARD THE NORTH, HE MEASURED THE LENGTH THEREOF, AND THE BREADTH THEREOF.

(21) "AND THE LITTLE CHAMBERS THEREOF WERE THREE ON THIS SIDE AND THREE ON THAT SIDE; AND THE POSTS THEREOF AND THE ARCHES THEREOF WERE AFTER THE MEASURE OF THE FIRST GATE: THE LENGTH THEREOF WAS FIFTY CUBITS, AND THE BREADTH FIVE AND TWENTY CUBITS.

(22) "AND THEIR WINDOWS, AND THEIR ARCHES, AND THEIR PALM TREES, WERE AFTER THE MEASURE OF THE GATE THAT LOOKS TOWARD THE EAST; AND THEY WENT UP UNTO IT BY SEVEN STEPS; AND THE ARCHES THEREOF WERE BEFORE THEM.

(23) "AND THE GATE OF THE INNER COURT WAS OVER AGAINST THE GATE TOWARD THE NORTH, AND TOWARD THE EAST; AND HE MEASURED FROM GATE TO GATE AN HUNDRED CUBITS."

The diagram is:

1. Attention is first directed to the wall enclosing the square in which will stand the Palace. This wall (*"building"*) will be 9 feet high and 9 feet broad.

2. The East Gate is then the subject of Verses 6 through 16. It will be 90 feet high, and will contain 6 posts, three on either side, and the governing figure of its dimensions, as also of those of the Sanctuary and the Oblation, will be five — the number of Grace.

3. Through this magnificent porch, the Messiah will enter; it will then be closed and reserved for the use of the Prince, Who possibly will be David.

4. All the statements about this Gate — its porches, its thresholds, and its measurements teach spiritual lessons concerning the beauties and perfections of Christ as the Way, the Truth, and the Life. But the spiritual vision of Christian people is not often sufficiently keen to recognize them.

5. As Moses was shown in the Mount the Pattern of the Tabernacle, and commanded to make all things according to it (Heb. 8:5), and as David was similarly instructed with reference to the Temple (I Chron. 28:11-19), so was it in the case of Ezekiel as regards the future Millennial Sanctuary. In the construction of these three Places of Worship, nothing was left to man's taste or imagination. Everything, even in the matter of measurements, was commanded by God.

THE WALL

The phrase of Verse 5, *"And behold a wall on the outside of the house round about,"* proclaims that which encloses the square in which will stand the Sacred Palace.

It is interesting that the Tabernacle had no wall, nor did the Temple, or at least a wall that was an essential part of the Sacred Structure. Here, however, the wall constitutes an integral portion of the whole, and is designed *"to make a separation between the Sanctuary and the profane place."* This *"wall"* encloses the square in which will stand the Sacred Palace.

The phrase, *"And in the Man's hand a measuring reed of six cubits long by the cubit and an hand breadth,"* presents the number *"6,"* which incidentally is the number of man. In this, we are led to believe that this specific measurement is used because the entire Plan of God is wrapped up in Christ, of which this building will be His dwelling place, with all of it entirely for man. None of the Great Redemption Plan was for God, but, instead, for man, as emphasized by the most beloved Passage, *"For God so loved the world, that He gave His Only Begotten Son, that whosoever believeth in Him should not perish, but have everlasting life"* (Jn. 3:16).

A *"reed"* represents about 9 feet, while the *"cubit"* represents about 18 inches.

The phrase, *"So He measured the breadth of the building, one reed; and the height, one reed,"* refers to the fact that the wall was about 9 feet wide and about 9 feet high.

THE EASTERN GATE

The phrase of Verse 6, *"Then came He unto the gate which looks toward the east,"* presents the *"East Gate,"* which is the subject of Verses 6 through 16.

The *"East Gate"* was the principal entrance, and stood directly in front of the Porch of the Temple proper. This reason (the entrance) will explain the fullness of description accorded to it rather than to the others. The Eastern Gate represents Christ as the *"Door,"* or the entrance to all things pertaining to God, which was all made possible by the Cross. This is the literal application which portrays the spiritual application as given in John, Chapter 10.

The phrase, *"And went up the stairs thereof,"* pertains to God's Plan of Salvation. Even though the number of steps are not here given, they are mentioned in Verse 22 and 26, concerning the Northern and Southern Gates, as being *"seven."*

"Seven" is God's numbers, implying perfection, completion, and universality. Such is God's Salvation, afforded by Christ Jesus, and offered freely to man.

Man must ascend in heart and mind as they enter the Sanctuary, and the seven steps represent the completeness, at last, of that ascension.

Incidentally, Solomon had *"six steps that led to his throne"* (II Chron. 9:18). The meaning is clear. Even though Solomon's reign represented the glorious reign of Christ, still, it was only a representation, and of man, therefore, the number *"six"* was used, inasmuch as it is man's number, which falls short of fulfillment, totality, and completion; however, the glorious reign of Christ will be a perfect reign, hence, symbolized by *"seven steps."*

The phrase, *"And measured the threshold of the gate, which was one reed broad; and the other threshold of the gate, which was one reed broad,"* represents 9 feet, in either case.

Once again, even though the steps were *"seven,"* representing God's Perfect Plan, the broadness was *"one reed,"* i.e., *"six cubits,"* meaning that this Perfect Salvation was designed exclusively for imperfect man.

THE LITTLE CHAMBERS

The phrase of Verse 7, *"And every little chamber was one reed long, and one reed broad,"* actually means that these small *"chambers"* or rooms are 9 by 9. The phrase, *"And between the little chambers were five cubits,"* represents 7-1/2 feet between each chamber. These are actually guard-chambers intended for the Levite sentinels, who keep guard over the house. It is not that guards are needed, but for decorative purposes only!

Nevertheless, the spiritual application is appropriate. The Child of God is ordered to *"watch"* as well as to *"pray"* (Mk. 13:33).

THE MAN WITH THE LINE IN HIS HAND

The pronoun *"He"* of Verses 8 and 9 refers to the *"Man with the line of flax in His Hand,"* and is, no doubt, Christ. He is the One Who measures, and, as the Lord of Glory, is perfect in His design. As we have stated, even though the Temple and the Altar, along with the entire Sanctuary, are made for man, nevertheless, man has absolutely no part in its design or appearance. All is of Christ as Salvation is totally of Christ.

If one is to notice, the Holy Spirit, with His attention to detail and constant repetition, allows us to observe, but observe only!

If man, in the many centuries past, would have only been content with that which God provided, instead of either attempting to take from it or add to it, many more souls would have been saved, whereas many have been lost!

The *"porch of the gate"* of Verses 8 and 9 sits immediately in front of the Temple facing the east. It is actually between the Temple and the great Altar.

The whole series of Courts and Buildings are located in the middle of the Priests' portion, which is about 60 by 60 square miles, called *"The Holy Oblation."* The Temple is only one of the Buildings located in the Sanctuary, therefore, we cannot speak of the entire series of Buildings as the Temple.

The Temple is surrounded by Chambers (rooms), with the exception of the rear, which is the *"Separate Place,"* and the front, which is the *"Porch."*

Immediately around the Temple area is the *"Inner Court,"* which is 300 cubits x 300 cubits, which means that it is 450 feet long with the same in length. The Temple sits at the immediate back of the *"Inner Court,"* with the Great Altar sitting in the approximate middle of the area.

Around the *"Inner Court"* is the *"Outer Court,"* which is 500 cubits x 500 cubits, i.e., 750 feet wide and the same in length.

Around that area is the *"Most Outer Court"* where is the Profane Place, which is 500 reeds wide and 500 reeds long. This is 3,000 cubits, which would be 4,500 feet wide with the same in length.

NOTES

The *"Porch,"* of course, is the entrance to the Temple. As such, it signifies the area nearest the Holy Place and the Holy of Holies. Actually, the entire Temple area signifies the spiritual place or position occupied by the Child of God.

In our nearness to Christ, are we in the *"Most Outer Court,"* or the *"Outer Court,"* or maybe the *"Inner Court"*?

Spiritually speaking, the ideal place is in the very Temple itself.

FOR MAN

The *"little chambers"* of Verses 10 and 12 are, as stated, 9 by 9. This is done by design, inasmuch as *"six"* denotes man's number, and, therefore, imperfection and incompletion, and that the entirety of this is done for man.

The phrase of Verse 12, *"The space also before the little chambers was one cubit on this side, and the space was one cubit on that side,"* proclaims the *"space"* which was immediately before the *"little chambers."* This, most likely, was to enable the guardsmen, by stepping beyond their cells, to observe the happenings in the Gate without interrupting those coming and going.

Presently, the Temple in which the Holy Spirit resides is the heart and life of the Child of God (I Cor. 3:16).

THE GUARD CHAMBERS

Verse 13 says: *"He measured then the gate from the roof of one little chamber to the roof of another: the breadth was five and twenty cubits, door against door."*

This means that it is about 37-1/2 feet from door to door of the Chambers.

If the Guard Chambers are scrutinized this closely, as to measurement and direction, then the significance should not be lost upon us.

To guard our mind, which is the doorway to our spirit, in order that defilement not enter, is of vast significance, to say the least! This is His House, and it must be reserved for that which is pleasing to Him; consequently, *"There shall in no wise enter into it anything that defileth, neither whatsoever worketh abomination, or makes a lie: but they which are written in the Lamb's Book of Life"* (Rev. 21:27).

THE POSTS

The phrase of Verse 14, *"He made also posts of three-score cubits,"* presents these as 90 feet high, and are different, as is obvious, than the little short posts mentioned in Verse 10.

It is interesting that the Holy Spirit uses the words, *"He made,"* inasmuch as the same thing is said in Revelation 3:12, *"Him who overcomes will I make a pillar in the Temple of my God."* These *"posts"* or *"pillars,"* as is obvious, are quite large.

I think the Holy Spirit does not desire this *"post"* of 90 feet height to be contrasted with the *"little post"* of only 3 feet height, as signified in Verse 9. To serve in any capacity in the Kingdom of God is of utmost significance. As one is needed, the other is needed as well! As one has its own type of duty, the other, as well, has its type.

He said that He would make of us a *"pillar,"* and the type that He makes is at His discretion.

WINDOWS

The phrase of Verse 16, *"And windows were round about inward,"* seems to indicate that there were windows on three sides, amply admitting light, as well as ample observance for the guards.

Likewise, the Christian is to *"guard"* by *"watching,"* as well as *"praying."*

PALM TREES

The phrase of Verse 16, *"And upon each post were palm trees,"* presents the possibility that the *"posts"* or *"pillars"* were shaped like a *"palm tree"* or else, the portrayal of *"palm trees"* was carved into the structure. There is even a possibility that living palm trees were growing out of the posts.

It is notable that the only type of trees mentioned as being a part of the decoration of the Millennial Temple is *"palm trees."*

Why these were selected by the Holy Spirit is not known, unless it is to denote the perfection of harmony.

Inasmuch as the curse will be lifted in the Millennial Earth, it stands to reason that even though the particular seasons of the year will continue as always, still, every indication is that climatic disturbances, such as storms, hurricanes, floods, etc., will be forever ended.

Due to the fall of man, nothing that pertains to man, including the functions of the planet, and even the stars of the heavens, work, function, or perform exactly as they were originally intended. In other words, the harmony of God's creation has been disturbed to where even the Earth *"groans"* for deliverance (Rom. 8:22). Only with Christ can there be harmony; when Christ reigns supreme during that coming Glad Day, *"harmony"* will prevail, hence, the *"palm tree"* as a symbol.

THE OUTER COURT AND THE INNER COURT

The phrase of Verse 17, *"Then brought He me into the outward court,"* and the phrase of Verse 19, *"Then He measured the breadth from the forefront of the lower gate unto the forefront of the inner court without,"* represent the two courts nearest the Great Altar, with, of course, the *"Inner Court"* being the nearest.

The great square of the Outer Court, with its thirty chambers of Verse 17, its pavement, and its superficial measure, is specified in Verses 17 through 19. The Hebrew word for *"pavement"* suggests ornamental pavement.

The Thirty Chambers will be placed all along by the three gates, giving access to the Great Square. It may be assumed that Ten Chambers will be apportioned to each gate, five on the one side and five on the other, and that these Chambers will be attached to the external walls of the gates, and will look out upon the pavement. Thus, each gate will be provided with six internal and ten external Chambers; that is, forty-eight Chambers in all.

As the Prophet, led by the Lord Jesus Christ, steps into the Outer Court, which is the area surrounding the Temple buildings, and the Inner Court, the first thing he observed was the Chambers and the pavement which ran around the Court. The Chambers were cells or rooms (Ezekiel 42:1; I Chron. 9:26). The exact dimensions, sites, and uses are not specified, though, as they were thirty in number, it is probable they were arranged on the East, North, and South Gates of the Court.

Such Chambers existed in the Temple of Solomon, and were large enough to hold up to some thirty people (I Sam. 9:22; Jer. 35:2). They were designed for sacrificial meals and such like purposes, and will probably be used for the same purposes in the Millennial Temple.

As well, in Solomon's Temple, they had been occupied by distinguished persons connected with the Temple Service (II Ki. 23:11; 36:10; Ezra 10:6).

The pavement of the Outer Court was called *"the lower pavement,"* as given in Verse 18, to distinguish it from that laid in the Inner Court, which stood at a higher elevation.

Even though very little information is given regarding the specified use of the *"Thirty Chambers,"* etc., still, we do know that all pertains to the worship of the Lord. To be sure, it will not be ritualistic worship, which characterizes all of religion and much of Christianity, but a heart-felt worship, of which most in the world will participate. To be sure, every Chamber and room, or even the most insignificant part of the Great Temple, will glorify Christ and play an extremely useful role in the worship which will then be unending.

THE GATES

The phrase of Verse 23, *"And He measured from gate to gate an hundred cubits,"* refers to the fact that the distance from each gate from the Great Square to the corresponding Gate of the Inner Court will be 150 feet on each side. This distance is identical from the North, East, and South.

Verses 20 through 23 tell us that each Gate will be constructed as an arcade, and will be about 75 feet long and 30 feet wide. It will have an arched roof and latticed windows. The exit into the Great Square will be ornamented with two square pillars about 90 feet high, and will have palm trees sculptured on them, or shaped like a palm tree, or even with a living palm tree, as stated, growing out of the top.

The North Gate and the South Gate, with their Chambers, pillars, arches, windows, their seven steps, and their measurements, will be exactly as the East Gate. It will be the standard of entrance, utility, strength, and beauty. Through the East Gate, the King of Glory will enter.

There will be no West Gate, for the Messiah, when seated on His Throne within the Temple, will face the East. The worshippers will enter by the North and South Gates, and stand before Him; behind Him will, perhaps, stand the Cherubims of Glory.

The *"seven steps"* of Verse 22, as we have explained, denote perfection, totality, and completion, which is God's number, and applies to Christ Himself.

(24) "AFTER THAT HE BROUGHT ME TOWARD THE SOUTH, AND BEHOLD A GATE TOWARD THE SOUTH: AND HE MEASURED THE POSTS THEREOF AND THE ARCHES THEREOF ACCORDING TO THESE MEASURES.

(25) "AND THERE WERE WINDOWS IN IT AND IN THE ARCHES THEREOF ROUND ABOUT, LIKE THOSE WINDOWS: THE LENGTH WAS FIFTY CUBITS, AND THE BREADTH FIVE AND TWENTY CUBITS.

(26) "AND THERE WERE SEVEN STEPS TO GO UP TO IT, AND THE ARCHES THEREOF WERE BEFORE THEM: AND IT HAD PALM TREES, ONE ON THIS SIDE, AND ANOTHER ON THAT SIDE, UPON THE POSTS THEREOF.

(27) "AND THERE WAS A GATE IN THE INNER COURT TOWARD THE SOUTH: AND HE MEASURED FROM GATE TO GATE TOWARD THE SOUTH AN HUNDRED CUBITS.

(28) "AND HE BROUGHT ME TO THE INNER COURT BY THE SOUTH GATE: AND HE MEASURED THE SOUTH GATE ACCORDING TO THESE MEASURES;

(29) "AND THE LITTLE CHAMBERS THEREOF, AND THE POSTS THEREOF, AND THE ARCHES THEREOF, ACCORDING TO THESE MEASURES: AND THERE WERE WINDOWS IN IT AND IN THE ARCHES THEREOF ROUND ABOUT: IT WAS FIFTY CUBITS LONG, AND FIVE AND TWENTY CUBITS BROAD.

(30) "AND THE ARCHES ROUND ABOUT WERE FIVE AND TWENTY CUBITS LONG, AND FIVE CUBITS BROAD.

(31) "AND THE ARCHES THEREOF WERE TOWARD THE UTTER COURT; AND PALM TREES WERE UPON THE POSTS THEREOF: AND THE GOING UP TO IT HAD EIGHT STEPS.

(32) "AND HE BROUGHT ME INTO THE INNER COURT TOWARD THE EAST: AND HE MEASURED THE GATE ACCORDING TO THESE MEASURES.

(33) "AND THE LITTLE CHAMBERS THEREOF, AND THE POSTS THEREOF, AND THE ARCHES THEREOF, WERE ACCORDING TO THESE MEASURES: AND THERE WERE WINDOWS THEREIN AND IN THE ARCHES THEREOF ROUND ABOUT: IT WAS FIFTY CUBITS LONG, AND FIVE AND TWENTY CUBITS BROAD.

(34) "AND THE ARCHES THEREOF WERE TOWARD THE OUTWARD COURT; AND PALM TREES WERE UPON THE POSTS THEREOF, ON THIS SIDE, AND ON THAT SIDE: AND THE GOING UP TO IT HAD EIGHT STEPS."

The composition is:

1. As the Tabernacle in the wilderness was designed for the worship of God, likewise, the Millennial Temple, as described by Ezekiel, is designed for the same purpose.

2. Everything designed by the Lord has a spiritual significance. As we study the design, avidly seeking the Lord, the Holy Spirit will ultimately reveal to us what that significance is.

3. This which Ezekiel described for us, and on which I am attempting to elaborate, we will one day look upon with our eyes.

SEVEN STEPS

Verse 24 through 26 continue to describe the Temple area, which forms a square with the dimensions identical from all entrances. As well, all three gates, East, North and South, have *"seven steps"* leading up from the outside of the outer wall.

All of this portrays the exactness, the perfection, and harmony of God's Salvation Plan, exemplified in Christ Who is perfect from every side. Any way one looks, he sees nothing but perfection. If he comes through the South Gate, it is identical to that which leads through the North Gate; therefore, whichever way one enters, there is no confusion. What a beautiful picture of True Bible Christianity.

(If one is notice, we have used eighteen inches to the cubit. There are some who use twenty-five inches; however, our investigation seems to portray that eighteen inches is more near the correct dimension.)

THE SOUTH GATE

Verse 27 says, *"And there was a gate in the inner court toward the south."* We find that this Verse is identical to Verse 23 with one exception. Verse 27 speaks of the *"gate"* toward the *"south,"* while Verse 23 speaks of the *"gate"* toward the *"north."* In both cases, the distance is identical, *"one hundred cubits,"* i.e., 150 feet.

EIGHT STEPS

Verses 28 through 31 proclaim the fact that the construction and measurements of the South Inner Gate Court are identical with the Gates in the Outer Court, with only two points of difference. They are:

1. There are *"eight steps"* which led to the South Inner Gate, whereas there were *"seven"* which led to the North Outer Gate. God's number, which is *"seven,"* cannot be improved upon, and is not meant to be improved upon, because it denotes perfection; therefore, the number *"eight,"* respecting the steps that led to the *"Inner Court,"* should be added to the seven, totaling fifteen.

This corresponds to the Pilgrim Psalms, or *"Songs of Degrees,"* or *"Ascents,"* which were fifteen. They are Psalms 120 through 134. They were supposed to have been sung, one upon each step, by the choir of Levites as they ascended first into the Outer and then the Inner Court of Solomon's Temple.

These fifteen Psalms, according to their structure, are divided into five groups of three Psalms each. The first Psalm of each group speaks of distress and trouble (120, 123, 126, 129, 132); the second Psalm of each group speaks of trust and deliverance by God (121, 124, 127, 130, 133); the third Psalm of each group speaks of Blessing and Triumph upon Zion (122, 125, 128, 131, 134).

These *"Songs of Degrees"* symbolize the spiritual journey of every Believer. In our living for God, the great struggle between the Spirit and the flesh commences; consequently, it is a time of distress, as pictured in the first Psalm in each one of these sets. Gradually, the Believer begins to understand the Cross of Christ and what it means, thereby learning to trust, which is symbolized by the second Psalm in each set.

The Believer, as Israel of old, eagerly awaits the day of Triumph, when corruption will put on incorruption and mortality will put on immortality. This is symbolized by the third Psalm in each set of three.

Consequently, this is what the fifteen steps, no doubt, illustrate!

2. The arches are here toward the Outer Court, whereas the arches or wall projections on the Outer Gate were the opposite, toward the Inner Court.

This probably had to do with the nearness of the Temple and Altar area, which would not have been proper to have positioned these *"arches"* otherwise, because the journey to the Temple area was now complete.

Verses 32 through 34 proclaim the fact that the *"East Inner Gate and Court"* are identical to the *"South Inner Gate Court,"* even to the two particulars mentioned concerning the *"eight steps"* and the *"arches toward the Outward Court."* Therefore, the same particulars would apply in that all are identical regarding dimensions.

(35) "AND HE BROUGHT ME TO THE NORTH GATE, AND MEASURED IT ACCORDING TO THESE MEASURES;

(36) "THE LITTLE CHAMBERS THEREOF, THE POSTS THEREOF, AND THE ARCHES THEREOF, AND THE WINDOWS TO IT ROUND ABOUT: THE LENGTH WAS FIFTY CUBITS, AND THE BREADTH FIVE AND TWENTY CUBITS.

(37) "AND THE POSTS THEREOF WERE TOWARD THE UTTER COURT; AND PALM TREES WERE UPON THE POSTS THEREOF, ON THIS SIDE, AND ON THAT SIDE: AND THE GOING UP TO IT HAD EIGHT STEPS.

(38) "AND THE CHAMBERS AND THE ENTRIES THEREOF WERE BY THE POSTS OF THE GATES, WHERE THEY WASHED THE BURNT OFFERING.

(39) "AND IN THE PORCH OF THE GATE WERE TWO TABLES ON THIS SIDE, AND TWO TABLES ON THAT SIDE, TO SLAY THEREON THE BURNT OFFERING AND THE SIN OFFERING AND THE TRESPASS OFFERING.

(40) "AND AT THE SIDE WITHOUT, AS ONE GOES UP TO THE ENTRY OF THE NORTH GATE, WERE TWO TABLES; AND ON THE OTHER SIDE, WHICH WAS AT THE PORCH OF THE GATE, WERE TWO TABLES.

(41) "FOUR TABLES WERE ON THIS SIDE, AND FOUR TABLES ON THAT SIDE, BY THE SIDE OF THE GATE; EIGHT TABLES, WHEREUPON THEY SLEW THEIR SACRIFICES.

(42) "AND THE FOUR TABLES WERE OF HEWN STONE FOR THE BURNT OFFERING, OF A CUBIT AND AN HALF LONG, AND A CUBIT AND AN HALF BROAD, AND ONE CUBIT HIGH: WHEREUPON ALSO THEY LAID THE INSTRUMENTS WHEREWITH THEY SLEW THE BURNT OFFERING AND THE SACRIFICE.

(43) "AND WITHIN WERE HOOKS, AN HAND BROAD, FASTENED ROUND ABOUT: AND UPON THE TABLES WAS THE FLESH OF THE OFFERING.

(44) "AND WITHOUT THE INNER GATE WERE THE CHAMBERS OF THE SINGERS IN THE INNER COURT, WHICH WAS AT THE SIDE OF THE NORTH GATE; AND THEIR PROSPECT WAS TOWARD THE SOUTH: ONE AT THE SIDE OF THE EAST GATE HAVING THE PROSPECT TOWARD THE NORTH.

(45) "AND HE SAID UNTO ME, THIS CHAMBER, WHOSE PROSPECT IS TOWARD THE SOUTH, IS FOR THE PRIESTS, THE KEEPERS OF THE CHARGE OF THE HOUSE.

(46) "AND THE CHAMBER WHOSE PROSPECT IS TOWARD THE NORTH IS FOR THE PRIESTS, THE KEEPERS OF THE CHARGE OF THE ALTAR: THESE ARE THE SONS OF ZADOK AMONG THE SONS OF LEVI, WHICH COME NEAR TO THE LORD TO MINISTER UNTO HIM.

(47) "SO HE MEASURED THE COURT, AN HUNDRED CUBITS LONG, AND AN HUNDRED CUBITS BROAD, FOURSQUARE; AND THE ALTAR THAT WAS BEFORE THE HOUSE.

(48) "AND HE BROUGHT ME TO THE PORCH OF THE HOUSE, AND MEASURED EACH POST OF THE PORCH, FIVE CUBITS ON THIS SIDE, AND FIVE CUBITS ON THAT SIDE: AND THE BREADTH OF THE GATE WAS THREE CUBITS ON THIS SIDE, AND THREE CUBITS ON THAT SIDE.

(49) "THE LENGTH OF THE PORCH WAS TWENTY CUBITS, AND THE BREADTH ELEVEN CUBITS; AND HE BROUGHT ME BY THE STEPS WHEREBY THEY WENT UP TO IT: AND THERE WERE PILLARS BY THE POSTS, ONE ON THIS SIDE, AND ANOTHER ON THAT SIDE."

The overview is:

1. As we can see from the description given in these Passages, animal sacrifices will be re-instituted in the coming Kingdom Age.

2. As the animal sacrifices of the Old Testament couldn't save, likewise, the Sacrifices being re-instituted in the coming Kingdom Age will have no saving grace. They are merely meant to be a reminder that all blessings come through the great price that Jesus paid on Calvary's Cross.

Because of its great significance, let us repeat it: Jesus Christ is the *"Source,"* while the Cross is the *"Means."*

SYMBOLIC OF CHRIST

Verse 35 through 37 proclaim the same minute specifications which are repeated, as if to show that all parts in this divinely-fashioned edifice are of equal moment, and, therefore, symbolize Christ.

THE BURNT OFFERING

The phrase of Verse 38, *"Where they wash the Burnt Offering,"* proclaims the fact that animal sacrifices will be re-instituted in the coming Kingdom Age, which are meant to convey the idea that everything the Lord does for us, every Blessing, are all because of the *"Cross."*

What the *"North Gate"* led to is different than the South or Eastern Gates.

Upon entering the North Gate, there are eight stoned tables, four to the side, which will be for the Offerings. In the Tabernacle of the wilderness, the Sacrifices were also slain on the north side of the Altar (Lev. 1:11; 8:5).

The phrase, *"And the chambers and the entries thereof were by the posts of the gates,"* are different from the guard-rooms in the Gates and the Chambers on the pavement.

These cells were expressly designed for washing *"the inward and the legs"* of the victims brought for Sacrifice (Lev. 1:9).

Actually, three types of Offerings are offered here, the *"Burnt, Sin, and Trespass Offerings."*

SYMBOLIC SACRIFICES

Verses 39 through 43 give the account of the sacrifices.

There were twelve tables in all, eight on which the Sacrifices were placed, and four for placing the instruments employed in killing the animals.

The tables were made of *"hewn stone."* They are small, being only about twenty-seven inches long and twenty-seven inches broad. They are eighteen inches high.

The *"hooks"* are fastened to the walls, and used to hang the animals on while preparing them for Sacrifice. The Sacrifices, although re-instituted, as under the Old Covenant, do not now take away sin any more than they did then (Heb. 10:4).

The Sacrifices are merely symbolic, and are meant to portray the Great Sacrifice made by Christ at Calvary. This is to never be forgotten; the daily offering of the Sacrifices will be a constant ritual, so that the entire world will never forget.

That which saved man, the shed Blood of Jesus Christ at Calvary, did not come cheaply or easily; therefore, it is thought of so highly in the Mind of God, and rightly so, that the never-ending repetition of Sacrifices in the Kingdom Age will constantly be offered as an ongoing reminder.

THE SINGERS

The phrase of Verse 44, *"And without the Inner Gate were the chambers of the singers in the Inner Court,"* doesn't tell us how many singers there will be. We do know from the text that they will be situated in the Inner Court, outside of the Inner Gate, at the side of the North Gate, and look toward the south.

Thus, the *"singers"* whose worship will accompany the Sacrifices, portray the Truth that the great price paid at Calvary brought eternal joy to the human heart, and is ever to be expressed accordingly.

As well, it tells us that all worship must be linked to the Cross, and if it's not linked to the Cross, it is worship that will not be accepted by the Lord.

We find from the Word of God, especially considering that the Book of Psalms is the longest Book in the Bible, that worship according to music and singing is at least one of the highest forms of worship, provided the music and singing are structured correctly.

Jesus said to the woman at Jacob's well: *"God is a Spirit: and they who worship Him must worship Him in spirit and in truth"* (Jn. 4:24).

The *"spirit"* here of which Jesus spoke is the human spirit, meaning that true worship must come from the human spirit, which also means that it must not be *"will worship."*

Paul addressed this by saying: *"Which things have indeed have a show of wisdom in will worship"* (Col. 2:23).

What is will worship?

It is worship that is linked to ceremonies, rituals, laws, which originate with the flesh, and is not from the spirit of man.

However, for the spirit of man to truly worship the Lord, it must, as well, be based on *"Truth,"* which pertains to the Word of God.

Understanding that music and singing, as proclaimed in the Word of God, play such an important part in our worship of the Lord, there is something else we must understand as it regards music.

MUSIC AS DESIGNED BY THE LORD

Music is made up of three parts: rhythm, melody, and harmony. If any one of the three is confused, while the words expressed in the song may be Biblical, and, therefore, right, still, the Believer will not be able to worship. That's the reason that it is impossible to worship the Lord by the means of modern Contemporary Christian Music. The melody and the harmony are, most of the time, confused, and even though the words may be correct, which mostly they aren't, but still one cannot worship, at least that which the Lord will accept.

Before the spirit of man can worship the Lord, at least as it regards music and singing, the words of the song must be according to the Word of God; and, as well, the harmony and the melody must not be confused. Regrettably, many song writers do not know this, and, thereby, oftentimes structure the harmony and the melody in such a way that make it difficult, if not impossible, for the human spirit to worship the Lord, even though the words may be correct.

While what I have said may not be too easy to understand, I would invite the Reader to listen carefully to the special singing in his Church. He will notice that some of the songs institute worship, while some don't. In other words, he will find himself automatically worshipping the Lord from his spirit as some songs are rendered, while with others such is not the case. Almost altogether, as it regards these songs which do not inspire worship, it is because the melody and the harmony have been confused by the writer. In other words, the Lord's structured order as it regards music has been somewhat violated.

In all of this, one must understand that I'm not speaking of style or taste, but rather that which the Lord wants and desires.

As all of this is portrayed in the coming Millennial Temple, as it regards music, singing, and worship, the Truth, as evident here, that if the Church goes further that Calvary, it loses its way with God. As well, if Calvary is ever lifted up as the focal point of man's Redemption, which it most certainly is, then great joy always accompanies this great Truth, which always instigates worship!

THE PRIESTS

Verses 45 and 46 portray the Office of the Priests.

Verse 45 says: *"And He said unto me, This chamber, whose prospect is toward the south, is for the Priests, the keepers of the charge of the house."*

It is really not known if the *"Chamber"* spoken of here is the same as the *"Chambers of the singers"* in the previous Verse; however, the indication is that it pertains to another Chamber, exclusively for the *"Priests."*

The two Chambers mentioned in Verses 45 and 46 both pertain to the Priests, so they must be solely for the Priests. Those in Verse 45 face the South, and they are in charge of the Temple. The one facing North is for those having charge of the Altar.

Under David, there seem to have been two High Priests, *"Abiathar"* and *"Zadok."*

Abiathar proved unfaithful, in that he attempted to usurp authority over the Will of the Lord, and, therefore, the instructions of David regarding Solomon as being his successor. Abiathar attempted to make the usurper, *"Adonijah,"* another son of David, King.

The phrase of Verse 46, *"The keepers of the charge of the Altar: these are the sons of Zadok among the sons of Levi, which come near to the LORD to minister unto Him,"* proclaims, once again, the *"sons of Zadok"* being established as an order in the coming Kingdom Age, regarding the *"charge of the Altar,"* as it regards the Sacrifices. These, of course, are of the Tribe of Levi, the Priestly Tribe.

THE ALTAR

Verse 47 says: *"So He measured the Court, an hundred cubits long, and an hundred cubits broad, foursquare; and the Altar that was before the House."*

The Altar Court was the Most Inner Court and the fourth perfect square of the Sanctuary. It was 100 cubits, or 150 feet, square.

The third square was 300 cubits, or 450 feet, square.

The second was 500 cubits, or 750 feet, square.

The first square is *"500 reeds,"* or about 4,500 feet, square.

The Great Altar was situated in the very center of the four squares, and is eighteen feet square.

Such is the description of the two Courts, the Outer and the Inner. The provision of noble Chambers and abundant food reveals the Love of God for His servants, and makes evident the happy estate of those engaged in so honourable a service.

In this — the Father's earthly House — there will be many mansions; and they are here pictured as lifted up above the Earth, and built in dependence upon the House. This Revelation testifies to the interest of God in His people; He will rebuild His Sanctuary among us; and He has informed us of this fact, and of its details, as a testimony of His faithful Love, and as a Message to our heart and consciences.

Therefore, the Prophet was commanded to show these things to the House of Israel (Vs. 4).

MEASUREMENTS

Verses 48 and 49 portray the fact that the *"Porch"* of the Temple will be 30 feet long and 16-1/2 feet broad. The *"Most Holy Place"* specified in Verse 4 of the following Chapter is larger than the *"Porch of the House"* or entrance, thus signifying that God's Grace is far greater than anything that could be brought to it; consequently, this fact illustrates a great spiritual Truth.

In this building, and its dependences, the measurements of *"foundations"* and the *"posts"* have great importance; for the one word expresses stability, the other permanence.

In the Bible, the *"posts"* of the door mean the whole house is an erect structure, and they figure its strength. This is initiated in the massive stone door-post of the Egyptian Temples. If, therefore, the posts of the doors shake, the whole house shakes.

In this House of Jehovah, all the foundations will be of like measure, signifying its great strength, which is Christ.

"The whole world was lost in the darkness of sin;
"The Light of the world is Jesus;
"Like sunshine at noonday
"His Glory shone in."

"No darkness have we who in Jesus abide,
"The Light of the world is Jesus;
"We walk in the Light
"When we follow our guide."

"You dwellers in darkness with sin-blinded eyes,
"The Light of the world is Jesus;
"Go, wash in His bidding,
"And Light will arise."

"No need of the sunlight in Heaven we're told,
"The Light of the world is Jesus;

"The Lamb is the Light
"In the city of gold."

CHAPTER 41

(1) "AFTERWARD HE BROUGHT ME TO THE TEMPLE, AND MEASURED THE POSTS, SIX CUBITS BROAD ON THE ONE SIDE, AND SIX CUBITS BROAD ON THE OTHER SIDE, WHICH WAS THE BREADTH OF THE TABERNACLE.

(2) "AND THE BREADTH OF THE DOOR WAS TEN CUBITS; AND THE SIDES OF THE DOOR WERE FIVE CUBITS ON THE ONE SIDE, AND FIVE CUBITS ON THE OTHER SIDE: AND HE MEASURED THE LENGTH THEREOF, FORTY CUBITS: AND THE BREADTH, TWENTY CUBITS.

(3) "THEN WENT HE INWARD, AND MEASURED THE POST OF THE DOOR, TWO CUBITS; AND THE DOOR, SIX CUBITS; AND THE BREADTH OF THE DOOR, SEVEN CUBITS.

(4) "SO HE MEASURED THE LENGTH THEREOF, TWENTY CUBITS; AND THE BREADTH, TWENTY CUBITS, BEFORE THE TEMPLE: AND HE SAID UNTO ME, THIS IS THE MOST HOLY PLACE."

The exegesis is:

1. The massiveness and loftiness of the *"posts"* reveal the magnificence of this Building.

2. This House of Jehovah will be a spectacle of surpassing beauty, glory, and magnificence — a fitting Central Temple of Worship for the entire world.

3. But whatever the glory and the grandeur of this Building, Jesus will outshine them all.

SIX

The phrase of Verse 1, *"Afterward He brought me to the temple and measured the posts, six cubits broad on the one side, and six cubits broad on the other side,"* proclaims the massiveness of these *"posts"* or *"pillars."* They were each nine feet broad.

Actually, it would be inaccurate to speak of all the Courts, Porches, and Buildings as the Temple, as the Temple proper only occupied a small part of it.

"Six" are used for a reason, because it denotes the number of man. Jesus said: *"Him who overcomes will I make a Pillar in the Temple of My God"* (Rev. 3:12).

Consequently, these Pillars, as the ones that stood in front of Solomon's Temple, symbolize the Great Gift of God to the human family, which is Salvation, and what the Lord will make of those who follow Him, and, therefore, overcome the world, the flesh, and the Devil.

THE DOOR

The phrase of Verse 2, *"And the breadth of the Door was ten cubits,"* refers to the *"door"* that led into the Holy Place and was fifteen feet wide.

This corresponds again to Jesus as *"the Door"* (Jn. 10:7).

The Holy Place is 60 feet long and 30 feet wide. This is the same dimensions as Solomon's Temple.

The entire frontage of the Holy Place was about 32 cubits in all, or, about 48 feet wide. This would have included the two massive Pillars as well.

The phrase of Verse 3, *"Then went He inward,"* speaks of the Most Holy Place, which was situated immediately behind the Holy Place, just like the Tabernacle of old.

No one but the High Priest could go into the *"Most Holy Place"* and, that, only once a year; therefore, Christ, it seems, went in Alone leaving Ezekiel outside. The phrase, *"And the Door, six cubits,"* probably refers to its height, which is 9 feet.

The *"breadth of the Door, seven cubits"* refers to its width, which is 10-1/2 feet.

The height of the door, as *"six cubits,"* refers to Christ as being the Door to Salvation, and, therefore, man's approach to God, as *"six,"* is man's number, with the width being *"seven cubits,"* which is God's number, speaking of perfection, and, in this case, speaking of God's Perfect Salvation in Christ.

THE MOST HOLY PLACE

The phrase of Verse 4, *"And He said unto me, This is the Most Holy Place,"* presents itself as basically the same as the Tabernacle and Temple of old.

Actually, the dimensions were the same as Solomon's Temple, 30 feet x 30 feet.

At Solomon's Temple, the *"Altar"* was 30 feet x 30 feet, consequently, corresponding to the size of the Most Holy Place. However, in the Millennial Temple, the *"Altar"* will be smaller than the Most Holy Place, only 18 feet square.

Solomon's Altar was larger, because it represented a price yet to be paid, while the *"Altar"* in the Millennial Temple is smaller, thereby representing a price already paid (II Chron. 4:1; Ezek. 43:16).

(5) "AFTER HE MEASURED THE WALL OF THE HOUSE, SIX CUBITS; AND THE BREADTH OF EVERY SIDE CHAMBER, FOUR CUBITS, ROUND ABOUT THE HOUSE ON EVERY SIDE.

(6) "AND THE SIDE CHAMBERS WERE THREE, ONE OVER ANOTHER, AND THIRTY IN ORDER; AND THEY ENTERED INTO THE WALL WHICH WAS OF THE HOUSE FOR THE SIDE CHAMBERS ROUND ABOUT, THAT THEY MIGHT HAVE HOLD, BUT THEY HAD NOT HOLD IN THE WALL OF THE HOUSE.

(7) "AND THERE WAS AN ENLARGING, AND A WINDING ABOUT STILL UPWARD TO THE SIDE CHAMBERS: FOR THE WINDING ABOUT OF THE HOUSE WENT STILL UPWARD ROUND ABOUT THE HOUSE: THEREFORE THE BREADTH OF THE HOUSE WAS STILL UPWARD, AND SO INCREASED FROM THE LOWEST CHAMBER TO THE HIGHEST BY THE MIDST.

(8) "I SAW ALSO THE HEIGHT OF THE HOUSE ROUND ABOUT: THE FOUNDATIONS OF THE SIDE CHAMBERS WERE A FULL REED OF SIX GREAT CUBITS.

(9) "THE THICKNESS OF THE WALL, WHICH WAS FOR THE SIDE CHAMBER WITHOUT, WAS FIVE CUBITS: AND THAT WHICH WAS LEFT WAS THE PLACE OF THE SIDE CHAMBERS THAT WERE WITHIN.

(10) "AND BETWEEN THE CHAMBERS WAS THE WIDENESS OF TWENTY CUBITS ROUND ABOUT THE HOUSE ON EVERY SIDE.

NOTES

(11) "AND THE DOORS OF THE SIDE CHAMBERS WERE TOWARD THE PLACE THAT WAS LEFT, ONE DOOR TOWARD THE NORTH, AND ANOTHER DOOR TOWARD THE SOUTH: AND THE BREADTH OF THE PLACE THAT WAS LEFT WAS FIVE CUBITS ROUND ABOUT.

(12) "NOW THE BUILDING THAT WAS BEFORE THE SEPARATE PLACE AT THE END TOWARD THE WEST WAS SEVENTY CUBITS BROAD; AND THE WALL OF THE BUILDING WAS FIVE CUBITS THICK ROUND ABOUT, AND THE LENGTH THEREOF NINETY CUBITS.

(13) "SO HE MEASURED THE HOUSE, AN HUNDRED CUBITS LONG; AND THE SEPARATE PLACE, AND THE BUILDING, WITH THE WALLS THEREOF, AN HUNDRED CUBITS LONG;

(14) "ALSO THE BREADTH OF THE FACE OF THE HOUSE, AND OF THE SEPARATE PLACE TOWARD THE EAST, AN HUNDRED CUBITS."

The diagram is:

1. The government of the world of that day, and we speak of the Kingdom Age, will be Christ solely. When Isaiah said, *"And the Government shall be upon His Shoulder,"* this is the time frame of which he spoke (Isa. 9:6).

2. The capital city of the world then will not be New York, or Washington, or Tokyo, or London, etc., but rather Jerusalem. And one might well say, *"Jerusalem, D.C."* i.e., *"David's Capital."*

The world will them know peace and prosperity as it has never known before.

THE WALL OF THE HOUSE

The phrase of Verse 5, *"After He measured the wall of the house, six cubits,"* proclaims the wall as being 9 feet thick.

The *"Chambers"* attached to it were 6 feet wide and 6 feet long, which probably served as storehouses for Priests' clothing, Temple utensils, and Temple treasures.

The massive width of the *"wall"* will, no doubt, serve as a symbol of strength and indestructibility concerning Christ as the True Temple. In other words, this House is secure, whereas the house built by man, therefore, fell!

THE CHAMBERS

The phrase of Verse 6, *"And the side chambers were three, one over another, and thirty in order,"* speaks of three stories of Chambers on either side of the Temple, totaling thirty side Chambers in all.

They were not attached to the *"wall of the House,"* i.e., Temple, actually, there was a passage about thirty feet wide between the Chambers and the Temple. These would have agreed, as well, with the Chambers in Solomon's Temple, except Solomon's joined to the Temple, where these seem to not do so.

THE ENLARGING

The phrase of Verse 7, *"And there was an enlarging,"* seems to point to thinner walls, consequently giving more interior space as the house went upward.

The width of the wall at its foundation was 9 feet thick, with the first story being 7-1/2 feet, diminished to 6 feet by the second story, and 4-1/2 feet for the third story. As stated, the enlarging of the rooms seemed to fall out to the walls being thinner.

THE FOUNDATION

The phrase of Verse 8, *"The foundations of the side chambers were a full reed of six great cubits,"* proclaims the *"foundations"* of these Chambers as being 9 feet thick, constituting a *"firm foundation."*

The phrase of Verse 9, *"The thickness of the wall, which was for the side chamber without, was five cubits,"* making it 7-1/2 feet thick, with its foundation being 9 feet thick. The foundation must always be larger.

As Christ gave these measurements, and the Holy Spirit superintended the writing of them through the Prophet Ezekiel, one would certainly have to wonder as to the necessity of the foundation and walls being so large.

The only answer pertains to the spiritual symbols which these dimensions represent. Ancient buildings would have called for walls of similar thickness, etc. However, this New Temple, during the coming Kingdom Age, will be built according to modern engineering standards, and even more so!

NOTES

Therefore, the symbolism is intended here to convey the spiritual message desired, and, in this case, the firm foundation of our spiritual experience in Christ, along with the firm walls denoting the structure of Salvation, and the reign of Christ, as being absolutely secure and eternal in its consequence.

Therefore, one is to understand the entirety of the structure of this coming Sanctuary in that particular light. As the Tabernacle and Temple of old conveyed the same message, therefore, this Temple will no less do so!

THE SEPARATE PLACE

Verse 10 says: *"And between the chambers was the wideness of twenty cubits round about the house on every side."*

As stated, there will be a pavement some thirty feet wide between the Chambers and the *"House,"* i.e., Temple.

The phrase of Verse 12, *"Now the building that was before the separate place at the end toward the west was seventy cubits broad,"* proclaims this building as being separate from the Temple, actually constructed behind the Temple on the west. It was marked off from the rest of the ground on which the Temple with its Courts and Chambers stood, and devoted most likely to less sacred purposes.

Actually, behind Solomon's Temple lay a similar space (II Ki. 23:11; I Chron. 26:18).

This *"separate building"* will be 105 feet wide and 135 feet long. Its walls will be 7-1/2 feet thick; therefore, the building is quite large!

THE LAW OF MOSES?

The phrase of Verse 13, *"So He measured the house,"* along with Verse 14, in fact, the entire description in all of these Chapters, may lead the Reader to think that the Law of Moses is being reinstituted; however, that is not so, inasmuch as Christ *"took it* (the Law) *out of the way, nailing it to His Cross"* (Col. 2:14).

That which is instituted, even though it will contain some of the trappings of the Mosaic Law, still, is carried forth mostly as a symbol or a memorial of what Christ did at Calvary for the human family, in order that men may be saved; therefore, they must never forget the basis of their Salvation, which is Christ as the Source, and the Cross as the Means.

(15) "AND HE MEASURED THE LENGTH OF THE BUILDING OVER AGAINST THE SEPARATE PLACE WHICH WAS BEHIND IT, AND THE GALLERIES THEREOF ON THE ONE SIDE AND ON THE OTHER SIDE, AN HUNDRED CUBITS, WITH THE INNER TEMPLE, AND THE PORCHES OF THE COURT;

(16) "THE DOOR POSTS, AND THE NARROW WINDOWS, AND THE GALLERIES ROUND ABOUT ON THEIR THREE STORIES, OVER AGAINST THE DOOR, CIELED WITH WOOD ROUND ABOUT, AND FROM THE GROUND UP TO THE WINDOWS, AND THE WINDOWS WERE COVERED;

(17) "TO THAT ABOVE THE DOOR, EVEN UNTO THE INNER HOUSE, AND WITHOUT, AND BY ALL THE WALL ROUND ABOUT WITHIN AND WITHOUT, BY MEASURE.

(18) "AND IT WAS MADE WITH CHERUBIMS AND PALM TREES, SO THAT A PALM TREE WAS BETWEEN A CHERUB AND A CHERUB; AND EVERY CHERUB HAD TWO FACES;

(19) "SO THAT THE FACE OF A MAN WAS TOWARD THE PALM TREE ON THE ONE SIDE, AND THE FACE OF A YOUNG LION TOWARD THE PALM TREE ON THE OTHER SIDE: IT WAS MADE THROUGH ALL THE HOUSE ROUND ABOUT.

(20) "FROM THE GROUND UNTO ABOVE THE DOOR WERE CHERUBIMS AND PALM TREES MADE, AND ON THE WALL OF THE TEMPLE.

(21) "THE POSTS OF THE TEMPLE WERE SQUARED, AND THE FACE OF THE SANCTUARY; THE APPEARANCE OF THE ONE AS THE APPEARANCE OF THE OTHER.

(22) "THE ALTAR OF WOOD WAS THREE CUBITS HIGH, AND THE LENGTH THEREOF TWO CUBITS; AND THE CORNERS THEREOF, AND THE LENGTH THEREOF, AND THE WALLS THEREOF, WERE OF WOOD: AND HE SAID UNTO ME, THIS IS THE TABLE THAT IS BEFORE THE LORD.

(23) "AND THE TEMPLE AND THE SANCTUARY HAD TWO DOORS.

(24) "AND THE DOORS HAD TWO LEAVES APIECE, TWO TURNING LEAVES; TWO LEAVES FOR THE ONE DOOR, AND TWO LEAVES FOR THE OTHER DOOR.

(25) "AND THERE WERE MADE ON THEM, ON THE DOORS OF THE TEMPLE, CHERUBIMS AND PALM TREES, LIKE AS WERE MADE UPON THE WALLS; AND THERE WERE THICK PLANKS UPON THE FACE OF THE PORCH WITHOUT.

(26) "AND THERE WERE NARROW WINDOWS AND PALM TREES ON THE ONE SIDE AND ON THE OTHER SIDE, ON THE SIDES OF THE PORCH, AND UPON THE SIDE CHAMBERS OF THE HOUSE, AND THICK PLANKS."

The composition is:

1. In this Temple, there will be no Veil nor Shewbread nor Lampstand. The Messiah, by His very Presence, will abolish these, meaning that there is no need for such.

2. The *"Cherubims"* represent the Holiness of God, while the *"Palm Trees"* represent the perfect serenity of Salvation afforded only by Christ. There will be an *"Altar of Incense"* in the Holy Place, which will be immediately in front of the Holy of Holies, exactly where it sat in the Tabernacle and Solomon's Temple.

THE PORCHES

The phrase of Verse 15, *"And the Porches of the Court,"* proclaims the fact that *"galleries"* or *"porches"* were made on the sides and fronts of the Chambers and the other building in the separate place. These *"galleries"* or *"porches"* seem to be on the second story and even the third. They were held up by pillars, or ledges, in the wall.

WOOD

The phrase of Verse 16, *"Ceiled with wood round about, and from the ground up to the windows, and the windows were covered,"* indicates that all of this is finished off with wooden wainscotting ornamented with Cherubims and Palm Trees.

(Wainscotting does not mean that the entire ceiling is of wood, but that a *"molding"* of wood is placed around the room where the wall joins the ceiling, such as is done in modern buildings.)

The wood, no doubt, typifies the Incarnation of Christ, when God became Man in order to become the Second Adam, and to redeem humanity.

It also seems that the windows have wood-shutters.

THE CHERUBIMS AND PALM TREES

The phrase of Verse 18, *"And it was made with Cherubims and Palm Trees,"* proclaims basically the same as that which was in Solomon's Temple (I Ki. 6:29).

The idea is, the wainscotting will be adorned with artistic carvings of Cherubims and Palm Trees, a Palm Tree and a Cherub standing alternately.

As the *"wood"* denotes the humanity of Christ, likewise, the *"Cherubims"* denote His Holiness.

As previously stated, the *"Palm Trees"* denote the lifting of the curse from Earth and man, with harmony and serenity now prevailing.

THE MAN AND THE LION

The phrase of Verse 19, *"So that the face of a man was toward the Palm Tree on the one side,"* refers to God becoming Man, *"The Man Christ Jesus,"* which He did in order to redeem man and lift and curse.

The phrase, *"And the face of a young lion toward the Palm Tree on the other side,"* refers to Christ coming as a *"Lion from the Tribe of Judah"* (Rev. 5:5). He is not only a Lion, but, in effect, a *"young Lion."* He is the *"Root of David,"* signifying His human lineage.

Upon the Fall of man, Satan felt that it would not be possible for man to be redeemed, therefore, man would be eternally his. He felt this way, because in Adam's loins, in effect, was every human being who would ever be born. Therefore, the Fall of Adam guaranteed the Fall of all! Consequently, every child would be born cursed, fallen, and depraved, and with no hope of saving themselves.

However, Satan reckoned without the *"Last Adam,"* Who would come from the Tribe of Judah, of these people brought forth from the loins of Abraham and the womb of Sarah, who would produce a *"young Lion,"* born of the Virgin Mary, and, consequently without the stain of sin, and, therefore, not a product of the Fall.

All other men were and are weak, and, therefore, unable to save themselves; however, this Man, *"The Man Christ Jesus,"* would not be weak, but would have the strength of a *"young Lion,"* and would, by His Death at Calvary, save lost humanity.

Hence, these emblems will serve throughout the age of Righteousness as a portrayal of what He did.

Verse 20 proclaims the fact, that throughout the Temple, *"even unto the Inner House,"* which is the *"Holy of Holies,"* these symbols will be evident (Vs. 17).

THE SQUARE POSTS

The phrase of Verse 21, *"The posts of the Temple were squared,"* does not pertain to the giant pillars of the porch, but, instead, were of the Temple proper.

They were *"squared,"* which signifies the fourfold Gospel of Jesus Christ: Salvation by the Blood, the Baptism with the Holy Spirit, Divine Healing, and the Second Coming of Christ. All, now, in the Kingdom Age is a reality, hence *"the appearance of the one as the appearance of the other."*

Before, the final results of all this were but a Promise, but now it is a Possession; consequently, it will never change, hence, the *"appearances"* being the same.

THE ALTAR OF INCENSE

The phrase of Verse 22, *"The Altar of wood was three cubits high,"* does not refer to the Altar of Sacrifice, which sits in the center of the hundred-cubit square and in front of the Temple, but, instead, is the *"Altar of Incense."* It is in the Holy Place, immediately in front of the Holy of Holies, exactly where it sat in the Tabernacle and Solomon's Temple.

It is 4-1/2 feet high and 3 feet long. It is made of *"wood."*

The *"Altar of Incense"* in the Tabernacle (Ex. 30:1) and in Solomon's Temple (I Ki. 7:48) was constructed of wood overlaid with gold, signifying both the Humanity and Deity of Christ.

However, in this Temple, it is only of *"wood."*

Does this mean that the Millennial Temple is less significant than the Tabernacle or Solomon's Temple? Not at all! In fact, the Millennial Temple is the greatest of all.

That being the case, why don't we see gold everywhere?

There is no need in the Millennial Temple for the *"wood"* to be overlaid with gold, as it was in the other Temples, simply because Christ is now here in Person.

As well, in the Temple, as stated, there will be no Veil, nor Table of Shewbread, nor Lampstand. The way was opened to the Holy of Holies by the Cross, so there is no more need for a *"Veil."* Jesus is the *"Bread of Life"* and the *"Light;"* therefore, there is no more need for that particular Table or Lampstand. The Messiah, by His Presence, will abolish these. Also, there will be no Ark of the Covenant.

The *"Altar of Incense"* was a type of the Intercession of Christ, all on our behalf, before the Father (Heb. 1:3; 2:17; 7:25; 10:12-14).

The *"Altar of Incense"* continues to be needed, simply because the world, during the time of the Kingdom Age, will continue to need Intercession. In fact, there will be many millions, possibly even hundreds of millions, which will come to Christ during the coming Kingdom Age. The work of Calvary, which guarantees the Intercession, will be greatly needed for these people. It will be needed for Israel, as well, for all those Jews who accept Christ at the Second Coming will not be included in the First Resurrection of Life, and will, therefore, continue to need Intercession. In fact, all the natural people, during that time, including the Jews, will be kept youthful and energetic by partaking of the fruit which will grow on the trees by the side of the river, which comes out from under the threshold of the Temple (Ezek. 47:12). So, as is obvious, Intercession, typified by the *"Altar of Incense,"* will continue to be needed during the Kingdom Age.

TWO DOORS

Verse 23 says: *"And the Temple and the Sanctuary had two doors."*

These *"doors"* led to the *"Holy Place"* and the *"Most Holy Place."* They are described in the following Verses.

The *"Two leaves apiece"* of Verse 24 simply means that each door was composed of two turning (or folding) leaves. It would be the same as a swinging door, separated in the middle, with each side swinging freely either way. As stated, there was no Veil, and because the Death of Christ at Calvary opened up the way for man to come to God, hence, the giant Veil in the Temple was torn from the top to the bottom (Mat. 27:51).

This guaranteed access by any Believer.

Verses 25 and 26 continue to portray the description of the Millennial Temple, all standing for holiness and harmony.

As previously stated, Solomon's Temple was heavily ornamented with gold, whereas such is not present in the Kingdom Temple, and, because Christ, of which the gold represented, is now present, and, therefore, the gold is no longer necessary. The implication is this:

The abundance of gold made Solomon's Temple beautiful; however, Christ will so far eclipse the luster of mere gold, that even if present, it would not be noticed for the Glory of the Lord.

There is no way that the mere mind of man can comprehend the Glory of that coming moment. The Presence of Christ will so permeate this building, providing a luster and beauty, that it will be absolutely indescribable.

No wonder John the Beloved, while on the Isle of Patmos, and closing out the Canon of Scripture, said, *"Even so, come, Lord Jesus"* (Rev. 22:20).

"How firm a foundation, ye Saints of the Lord,
"Is laid for your Faith in His excellent Word!
"What more can He say than to you He has said,
"To you, who for refuge to Jesus have fled?"

"When thro' fiery trials your pathway shall lie,
"My Grace all sufficient shall be thy supply;
"The flames shall not hurt you, I only design,

"Thy dross to consume, and thy gold to refine."

CHAPTER 42

(1) "THEN HE BROUGHT ME FORTH INTO THE UTTER COURT, THE WAY TOWARD THE NORTH: AND HE BROUGHT ME INTO THE CHAMBER THAT WAS OVER AGAINST THE SEPARATE PLACE, AND WHICH WAS BEFORE THE BUILDING TOWARD THE NORTH.

(2) "BEFORE THE LENGTH OF AN HUNDRED CUBITS WAS THE NORTH DOOR, AND THE BREADTH WAS FIFTY CUBITS.

(3) "OVER AGAINST THE TWENTY CUBITS WHICH WERE FOR THE INNER COURT, AND OVER AGAINST THE PAVEMENT WHICH WAS FOR THE UTTER COURT, WAS GALLERY AGAINST GALLERY IN THREE STORIES.

(4) "AND BEFORE THE CHAMBERS WAS A WALK TO TEN CUBITS BREADTH INWARD, A WAY OF ONE CUBIT; AND THEIR DOORS TOWARD THE NORTH.

(5) "NOW THE UPPER CHAMBERS WERE SHORTER: FOR THE GALLERIES WERE HIGHER THAN THESE, THAN THE LOWER, AND THAN THE MIDDLEMOST OF THE BUILDING.

(6) "FOR THEY WERE IN THREE STORIES, BUT HAD NOT PILLARS AS THE PILLARS OF THE COURTS: THEREFORE THE BUILDING WAS STRAITENED MORE THAN THE LOWEST AND THE MIDDLEMOST FROM THE GROUND.

(7) "AND THE WALL THAT WAS WITHOUT OVER AGAINST THE CHAMBERS, TOWARD THE UTTER COURT ON THE FOREPART OF THE CHAMBERS, THE LENGTH THEREOF WAS FIFTY CUBITS.

(8) "FOR THE LENGTH OF THE CHAMBERS THAT WERE IN THE UTTER COURT WAS FIFTY CUBITS: AND, LO, BEFORE THE TEMPLE WERE AN HUNDRED CUBITS.

(9) "AND FROM UNDER THESE CHAMBERS WAS THE ENTRY ON THE EAST SIDE, AS ONE GOES INTO THEM FROM THE UTTER COURT.

(10) "THE CHAMBERS WERE IN THE THICKNESS OF THE WALL OF THE COURT TOWARD THE EAST, OVER AGAINST THE SEPARATE PLACE, AND OVER AGAINST THE BUILDING.

(11) "AND THE WAY BEFORE THEM WAS LIKE THE APPEARANCE OF THE CHAMBERS WHICH WERE TOWARD THE NORTH, AS LONG AS THEY, AND AS BROAD AS THEY: AND ALL THEIR GOINGS OUT WERE BOTH ACCORDING TO THEIR FASHIONS, AND ACCORDING TO THEIR DOORS.

(12) "AND ACCORDING TO THE DOORS OF THE CHAMBERS THAT WERE TOWARD THE SOUTH WAS A DOOR IN THE HEAD OF THE WAY, EVEN THE WAY DIRECTLY BEFORE THE WALL TOWARD THE EAST, AS ONE ENTERS INTO THEM."

The overview is:

1. The Sanctuaries, given by inspiration to Moses and to David, were built, and thus set visibly before the eyes of Israel. The Sanctuary given to Ezekiel in Vision is yet to be built; but its details are revealed in writing as a testimony and instruction to Israel.

2. These details make real God's interest in His ancient people, and give substance to His Promise to establish His home among them. Thus, this Vision is a perpetual call to repentance (Williams).

3. In a Vision, the Lord showed the Prophet all of these things, and it was just as real to him as it will be when it is ultimately built in Jerusalem. Only Jehovah could do such a thing!

THE OUTER COURT

The phrase of Verse 1, *"Then He brought me forth into the Utter Court, the way toward the north,"* actually refers to the *"Outer Court."*

The *"Chamber that was over against the separate place"* is actually on the west of the enclosure, but extends *"before the building toward the north."*

The survey of the Temple has now been completed, and Ezekiel is taken outside by Christ into the *"Outer Court."*

Incidentally, these are not the same Chambers that are mentioned in Ezekiel 40:17, 44.

Ground Plan Of Temple

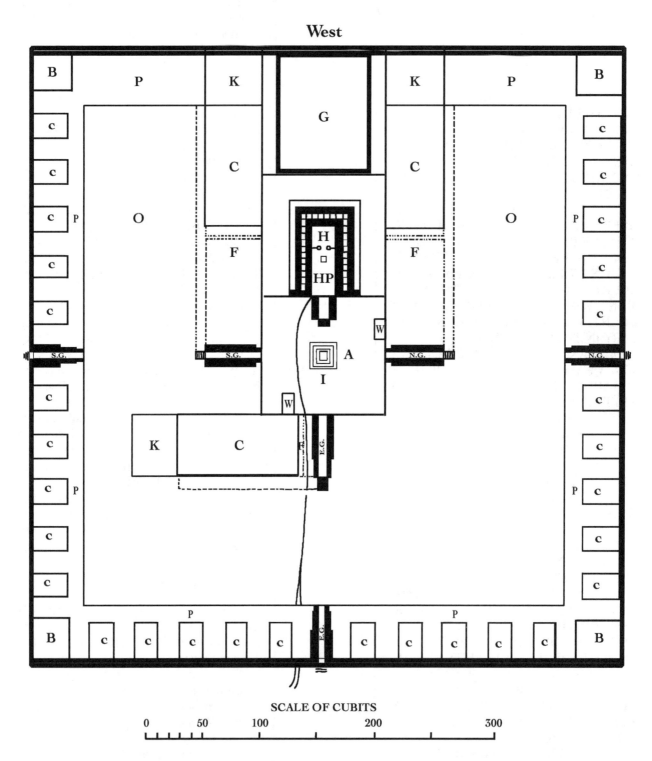

N.G., etc., gateways; **O**, outer court; **P**, pavement; **K**, cooking-chambers for the priests; **B**, boiling-houses for the people; **c**, chambers on the pavement; **G**, the gizrah; **C**, priests' chambers; **F**, fence; **I**, inner court; **E.G.**, **N.G.**, **S.G.**, gates; **A**, Altar of Sacrifice; **W**, watchers' chambers; **HP** and **H**, the house.

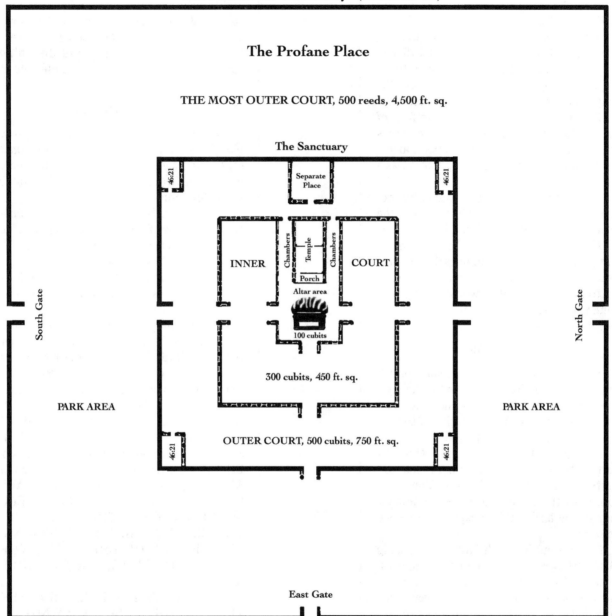

Those were in the Inner Court, while these are in the Outer. These Chambers will describe the area where the Priests are located, and according to their functions in the Temple.

Verses 2 through 5 give more descriptions of the structure.

Verse 2 says that the building containing the Priests' Chambers was 150 feet x 75 feet.

Verse 3 says this building was three stories high, with a *"gallery"* or *"porch"* running the length of the building on all three stories.

The phrase of Verse 4, *"Their doors toward the north,"* makes it clear that the rooms were on the outer wall of the inner court.

Running in front of the Chambers was a walk 15 feet wide.

It seems like the *"way of one cubit"* referred to the space of 18 inches between the walk and the wall of the Chambers.

The phrase of Verse 5, *"Now the upper chambers were shorter,"* implies that the second and third stories were smaller than the bottom floor. In other words, they arose somewhat similar to a pyramid, with the base being wider, etc.

NO PILLARS

The phrase of Verse 6, *"But had not pillars,"* seems to give the reason for the style of structure as a pyramid somewhat! Not having the strong support on the bottom, of necessity, they must diminish in size.

Perhaps, in the spiritual sense, this tells us that the bottom floors being larger suggests enlarged vision enjoyed in Communion, with the upper stories being smaller suggesting an humbling experience gained in service.

In Communion with Him, and sensing His Great Presence, the recipient of this Presence, and for the moment, thinks himself capable of miraculous events; however, the actual service quickly demonstrates the inabilities of the flesh, and humbles the participant. What a beautiful lesson!

The moral is, that our service for Him does not always contain His Presence, and, therefore, quickly humbles us.

THE WALL

Verse 7 says, *"And the Wall that was without over against the chambers toward the Utter Court,"* proclaims the link as being 75 feet.

It seems there was a wall, which height is not given, that was between the Chambers and the Outer Court. This may have been to shield the side windows of the lower Chambers from public gaze, since these were to be occupied as robing and disrobing rooms for the Priests who would officiate in the Temple.

THE CHAMBERS

The phrase of Verse 8, *"For the length of the chambers that were in the Utter Court was fifty cubits,"* refers to the Chambers which had windows and faced the Outer Court for some 75 feet.

The phrase, *"And, lo, before the Temple were an hundred cubits,"* concerns the side of the Chambers which face the Temple, with windows which were 150 feet.

Verses 9 through 12 state that the East and South Gates and their Chambers will be similar to the North Gate and its Chambers.

Quite possibly, the elevation of this building, regarding ground level, will be higher than the Outer Court, but lower than the Temple area; consequently, the *"entry"* is represented as being under the Chambers.

(13) "THEN SAID HE UNTO ME, THE NORTH CHAMBERS AND THE SOUTH CHAMBERS, WHICH ARE BEFORE THE SEPARATE PLACE, THEY BE HOLY CHAMBERS, WHERE THE PRIESTS WHO APPROACH UNTO THE LORD SHALL EAT THE MOST HOLY THINGS: THERE SHALL THEY LAY THE MOST HOLY THINGS, AND THE MEAT OFFERING, AND THE SIN OFFERING, AND THE TRESPASS OFFERING; FOR THE PLACE IS HOLY.

(14) "WHEN THE PRIESTS ENTER THEREIN, THEN SHALL THEY NOT GO OUT OF THE HOLY PLACE INTO THE UTTER COURT, BUT THERE THEY SHALL LAY THEIR GARMENTS WHEREIN THEY MINISTER; FOR THEY ARE HOLY; AND SHALL PUT ON OTHER GARMENTS, AND SHALL APPROACH TO THOSE THINGS WHICH ARE FOR THE PEOPLE.

(15) "NOW WHEN HE HAD MADE AN END OF MEASURING THE INNER

HOUSE, HE BROUGHT ME FORTH TOWARD THE GATE WHOSE PROSPECT IS TOWARD THE EAST, AND MEASURED IT ROUND ABOUT.

(16) "HE MEASURED THE EAST SIDE WITH THE MEASURING REED, FIVE HUNDRED REEDS, WITH THE MEASURING REED ROUND ABOUT.

(17) "HE MEASURED THE NORTH SIDE, FIVE HUNDRED REEDS, WITH THE MEASURING REED ROUND ABOUT.

(18) "HE MEASURED THE SOUTH SIDE, FIVE HUNDRED REEDS, WITH THE MEASURING REED.

(19) "HE TURNED ABOUT TO THE WEST SIDE, AND MEASURED FIVE HUNDRED REEDS WITH THE MEASURING REED.

(20) "HE MEASURED IT BY THE FOUR SIDES: IT HAD A WALL ROUND ABOUT, FIVE HUNDRED REEDS LONG, AND FIVE HUNDRED BROAD, TO MAKE A SEPARATION BETWEEN THE SANCTUARY AND THE PROFANE PLACE."

The structure is:

1. This Temple enclosure will be built to last a thousand years.

2. Every Saint of God who has ever lived, be they Jew or Gentile, will observe these wondrous happenings, but the Temple primarily will be for Israel. She will, at long last, take her place as the Priestly Nation of the world.

3. In fact, Christ, from this Building, will govern the entirety of the world (Isa. 9:7).

SACRIFICES

Verses 13 and 14 state the uses of Chambers just described, and are now called, according to Verse 13, *"Holy Chambers,"* which denote their separation and dedication to sacred purposes.

The phrase of Verse 13, *"Then said He unto me, The north chambers and the south chambers,"* denote two distinct Chambers. They serve as dining-halls and robing rooms for the Priests when they officiate in the Temple.

Parts of the Sacrifices were to be eaten by the Priests, thus signifying the Words of Christ, *"except you eat the flesh of the Son of Man, and drink His Blood, you have no life in you"* (Jn. 6:53).

NOTES

Of course, He was not speaking of literally eating His flesh, for He said, *"It is the Spirit that quickens; the flesh profits nothing: the Words that I speak unto you, they are Spirit, and they are Life"* (Jn. 6:63).

Nevertheless, the eating of parts of the Sacrifices, the Lambs, Bullocks, etc. typified the partaking of Christ and that man does not live by bread alone, but by every Word that proceeds out of the Mouth of God (Mat. 4:4).

This portrayed the Truth in the Old Economy of God, as well as in the New, that Christ is all in all. In other words, if we embrace Christianity as a philosophy, then we have a Christless Christianity, which will bring no Salvation. Christ is Salvation, and must be partaken of in all of His attributes, which can only be done by the Believer evidencing constant faith in the Cross of Christ, in other words, ever making the Cross the Object of his Faith (Rom. 6:3-14; I Cor. 1:17-18, 23; 2:2).

Therefore, and from these Passages, we know that *"Meat Offerings"* (Food Offerings which actually contain no meat, with the word *"meat"* being used for all type of food), and *"Sin Offerings,"* and *"Trespass Offerings"* will be offered. As such, not only are they holy, but where they are prepared is *"holy,"* as well, signified by the statement, *"for the place is holy."*

OTHER GARMENTS

When partaking of the Sacrifices, the Priests would have special garments, called *"other garments"* in Verse 14. When they left this place and went out among the people, they were to put on other clothes.

The reason for the *"other garments"* is because all of the Sacrifices were a memorial of what Christ did at Calvary, therefore, *"most holy."*

Actually, the regulation as to the Priestly garments of the sons of Zadok reveals a feature of the Spiritual Life peculiar to the modern Christian, that there are affections, energies, and ministries which belong exclusively to the life of Communion and Intercession, and must, therefore, be reserved expressly for the Lord.

Refreshed and enabled by this inner communion, the Christian can go out to minister to the world.

A MEMORIAL

From reading these Passages, one would think that the Mosaic Law will be reinstituted in the coming Kingdom Age; however, this is not the case.

While it is true, that certain parts of the Law will be reinstituted, such as the Sacrifices offered by the Priests, etc., still, it is done only as a memorial as to what Christ has already done, and, will serve as a constant reminder that it not be forgotten.

Observing Christ as the King of kings and Lord of lords, and despite the nail-prints in His Hands, resplendent in beauty and glory, one is apt to forget what He did to redeem humanity. These repetitive sacrificial rituals will be a constant reminder, a constant memorial.

THE MEASURING

The phrase of Verse 15, *"Now when He had made an end of measuring the inner house,"* proclaims, as should be by now obvious, that there are spiritual meanings to all of these measurements. To be sure, He measures for Government, Operation, and Service of His Church, all carried out by the Holy Spirit, and all, of course, according to His Word. Jesus said:

"And I say also unto you, that you are Peter, and upon this rock I will build My Church; and the gates of Hell shall not prevail against it" (Mat. 16:18). As His dimensions are exact for the coming Temple, likewise, they are exact for His Church.

Regrettably, man too often treats Christ as a passive Head of the Church, instead of the Active Head He is!

As well, His Word graphically outlines what His Church should be like, and He will tolerate no change of these dimensions, as He will not tolerate a change of dimensions in the coming Millennial Temple.

To be sure, if there is a change, He will occupy no part of it; consequently, the *"Church"* that is actually His, is far smaller than that which calls itself *"Church."* Whatever is His, the Holy Spirit will move and work, and as typified by the river, will flow out from under the threshold of the Temple (Ezekiel 47:1, 9, 12).

Regrettably, man has substituted his own measurements for almost all of that which pertains to the Work of God; consequently, the Holy Spirit will have no part of that which is instituted or instigated by man. Hence, a Spiritless Church, and, therefore, a lifeless Church!

Now He is about to measure the Most Outer Court, which is about 4,500 feet square, therefore, nearly a mile square. In other words, nearly a mile each way, within which the Holy Mountain, so to speak, will stand.

THE SANCTUARY AND THE PROFANE PLACE

Verses 16 through 19 deal with the measurement of the *"Most Outer Court,"* or the *"Profane Place,"* which could be used by the people coming to the Sanctuary itself.

It is called *"Profane,"* meaning for common uses of man instead of Sacred or Divine uses altogether.

Ezekiel 40:5 tells us that a reed is six cubits long. Therefore, 500 reeds would be 3,000 cubits, or 4,500 feet, counting 18 inches to the cubit.

The phrase of Verse 20, *"To make a separation between the Sanctuary and the profane place,"* emphasizes the word *"separation."* To be sure, the word *"separation,"* as it defines the *"Sanctuary"* and the *"profane place,"* exists today just as much as it did in the Temple of old, and shall in the Temple of the future. Any place the Holy Spirit resides is considered *"holy."* Hence, Paul said, *"I beseech you therefore, Brethren, by the Mercies of God, that you present your bodies a Living Sacrifice, holy, acceptable, unto God, which is your reasonable service"* (Rom. 12:1). As well, He said, *"Wherefore come out from among them, and be ye separate, saith the Lord, and touch not the unclean thing: and I will receive you"* (II Cor. 6:17).

While the Bible most definitely teaches *"separation,"* it does not teach *"isolation."* We are in the world, but we are definitely not to be of the world.

When a ship is sailing on the water, it can carry much cargo, thereby helping many people; however, if the water gets in the ship, the cargo can be ruined, and if enough water gets in the ship, the ship can sink.

It's the same way with the world. If a

little of the world gets into the Christian, the *"cargo,"* i.e., *"Work of the Holy Spirit,"* is greatly hindered; however, if too much of the world gets into the Christian, it can come to the place that the Holy Spirit would have to leave, exactly as it happened to Israel long, long ago! In such a case, there is nothing left!

The world holds nothing for the Child of God; Christ provides everything. Jesus said: *"I am the Way, the Truth, and the Life: no man comes unto the Father, but by Me"* (Jn. 14:6).

"Sweet are the Promises, kind is the Word,
"Dearer far than any message man ever heard,
"Pure was the mind of Christ, sinless was He;
"He the great example is, and pattern for me."

"Sweet is the tender love Jesus has shown,
"Sweeter far than any love than mortals have known.
"Kind to the erring one, faithful is He;
"He the great example is and pattern for me."

"List' to His loving words, come unto Me!
"Weary, heavy-laden, there is sweet rest for thee;
"Trust in His Promises, faithful and sure;
"Lean upon the Saviour and your soul is secure."

CHAPTER 43

(1) "AFTERWARD HE BROUGHT ME TO THE GATE, EVEN THE GATE THAT LOOKS TOWARD THE EAST:

(2) "AND, BEHOLD, THE GLORY OF THE GOD OF ISRAEL CAME FROM THE WAY OF THE EAST: AND HIS VOICE WAS LIKE A NOISE OF MANY WATERS: AND THE EARTH SHINED WITH HIS GLORY.

(3) "AND IT WAS ACCORDING TO THE APPEARANCE OF THE VISION WHICH I SAW, EVEN ACCORDING TO THE VISION THAT I SAW WHEN I CAME TO DESTROY THE CITY: AND THE VISIONS WERE LIKE THE VISION THAT I SAW BY THE RIVER CHEBAR; AND I FELL UPON MY FACE.

(4) "AND THE GLORY OF THE LORD CAME INTO THE HOUSE BY THE WAY OF THE GATE WHOSE PROSPECT IS TOWARD THE EAST.

(5) "SO THE SPIRIT TOOK ME UP, AND BROUGHT ME INTO THE INNER COURT; AND, BEHOLD, THE GLORY OF THE LORD FILLED THE HOUSE.

(6) "AND I HEARD HIM SPEAKING UNTO ME OUT OF THE HOUSE; AND THE MAN STOOD BY ME.

(7) "AND HE SAID UNTO ME, SON OF MAN, THE PLACE OF MY THRONE, AND THE PLACE OF THE SOLES OF MY FEET, WHERE I WILL DWELL IN THE MIDST OF THE CHILDREN OF ISRAEL FOR EVER, AND MY HOLY NAME, SHALL THE HOUSE OF ISRAEL NO MORE DEFILE, NEITHER THEY, NOR THEIR KINGS, BY THEIR WHOREDOM, NOR BY THE CARCASSES OF THEIR KINGS IN THEIR HIGH PLACES.

(8) "IN THEIR SETTING OF THEIR THRESHOLD BY MY THRESHOLDS, AND THEIR POST BY MY POSTS, AND THE WALL BETWEEN ME AND THEM, THEY HAVE EVEN DEFILED MY HOLY NAME BY THEIR ABOMINATIONS THAT THEY HAVE COMMITTED: WHEREFORE I HAVE CONSUMED THEM IN MINE ANGER.

(9) "NOW LET THEM PUT AWAY THEIR WHOREDOM, AND THE CARCASSES OF THEIR KINGS, FAR FROM ME, AND I WILL DWELL IN THE MIDST OF THEM FOR EVER.

(10) "THOU SON OF MAN, SHOW THE HOUSE TO THE HOUSE OF ISRAEL, THAT THEY MAY BE ASHAMED OF THEIR INIQUITIES: AND LET THEM MEASURE THE PATTERN.

(11) "AND IF THEY BE ASHAMED OF ALL THAT THEY HAVE DONE, SHOW THEM THE FORM OF THE HOUSE, AND THE FASHION THEREOF, AND THE GOINGS OUT THEREOF, AND THE COMINGS

IN THEREOF, AND ALL THE FORMS THEREOF, AND ALL THE ORDINANCES THEREOF, AND ALL THE FORMS THEREOF, AND ALL THE LAWS THEREOF: AND WRITE IT IN THEIR SIGHT, THAT THEY MAY KEEP THE WHOLE FORM THEREOF, AND ALL THE ORDINANCES THEREOF, AND DO THEM.

(12) "THIS IS THE LAW OF THE HOUSE; UPON THE TOP OF THE MOUNTAIN THE WHOLE LIMIT THEREOF ROUND ABOUT SHALL BE MOST HOLY. BEHOLD, THIS IS THE LAW OF THE HOUSE.

(13) "AND THESE ARE THE MEASURES OF THE ALTAR AFTER THE CUBITS: THE CUBIT IS A CUBIT AND AN HAND BREADTH, EVEN THE BOTTOM SHALL BE A CUBIT, AND THE BREADTH A CUBIT, AND THE BORDER THEREOF BY THE EDGE THEREOF ROUND ABOUT SHALL BE A SPAN: AND THIS SHALL BE THE HIGHER PLACE OF THE ALTAR.

(14) "AND FROM THE BOTTOM UPON THE GROUND EVEN TO THE LOWER SETTLE SHALL BE TWO CUBITS, AND THE BREADTH ONE CUBIT; AND FROM THE LESSER SETTLE EVEN TO THE GREATER SETTLE SHALL BE FOUR CUBITS, AND THE BREADTH ONE CUBIT.

(15) "SO THE ALTAR SHALL BE FOUR CUBITS; AND FROM THE ALTAR AND UPWARD SHALL BE FOUR HORNS.

(16) "AND THE ALTAR SHALL BE TWELVE CUBITS LONG, TWELVE BROAD, SQUARE IN THE FOUR SQUARES THEREOF.

(17) "AND THE SETTLE SHALL BE FOURTEEN CUBITS LONG AND FOURTEEN BROAD IN THE FOUR SQUARES THEREOF; AND THE BORDER ABOUT IT SHALL BE HALF A CUBIT; AND THE BOTTOM THEREOF SHALL BE A CUBIT ABOUT; AND HIS STAIRS SHALL LOOK TOWARD THE EAST."

The overview is:

1. Atonement, as the eternal foundation of God's relationship with man, is the keynote of this Chapter.

2. The Temple being now ready, the Glory of Jehovah (Messiah) enters.

3. His reluctant departure of Ezekiel 11:23 contrasts here with His swift return.

LOOK TOWARD THE EAST

Verse 1 says: *"Afterward He brought me to the gate, even the gate that looks toward the east:"*

This Chapter is glorious indeed, inasmuch as it heralds the return of the Holy Spirit to the Temple, and, therefore, to Israel. Ezekiel saw Him leave (Ezek. 11:23), now he sees Him return. As of now, the time period has been some 2,500 years, and from the events now happening, fulfilling Bible Prophecy, it cannot be too long before this glorious event transpires.

However, before this takes place, the Rapture of the Church must be brought about (I Thess. 4:16-17), which will occasion the rise of the Antichrist (II Thess. 2:6-8), which will bring about the Great Tribulation (Mat. 24:21), and at its conclusion, the Battle of Armageddon (Ezek., Chpts. 38, 39), which will occasion the Second Coming of the Lord. Immediately after the Second Coming will begin the Kingdom Age, and the building of this Temple, which will occasion *"the Glory of the God of Israel."*

Atonement, as the eternal foundation of God's relationship with man, is the keynote of this Chapter, which will occasion the coming of the Holy Spirit.

The attention now is drawn toward *"the Gate that looks toward the East,"* in other words, *"The Eastern Gate."*

This is not only the principal entrance to the Sanctuary, but, as well, it is the Gate through which Christ will pass, hence its great significance.

The Sanctuary is now ready, so the Lord will return. His departure, as outlined in Ezekiel 11:23, was reluctant. Such contrasts here with His glorious and swift return.

ATONEMENT IS THE ETERNAL FOUNDATION OF GOD'S RELATIONSHIP WITH MAN

Everything centers around the Cross! Salvation is made possible by the Cross, and the Baptism with the Holy Spirit is all made possible by the Cross. In fact, every single attribute of God, everything which He gives to His people, all, and without exception, are made possible by the Cross.

And yet, the modern Church preaches a

gospel presently which totally and completely, at least in most cases, ignores the Cross. In fact, since the Reformation, the Cross has never been more repudiated than it is presently. The Word of Faith doctrine has been the villain in this terrible scenario.

As well, the Church has all but eliminated *"sin"* from its vocabulary, claiming other things as the problem. In other words, it has adopted the ways and the proposed solutions of the world, which, in fact, are no solutions at all. But the real problem of mankind, which includes the Church, is the problem of sin. And to be sure, the only answer for sin, the only solution for sin, is the Cross of Christ.

Without an acceptance of Christ and the Cross, the sinner cannot be saved; and unless the Believer places his faith totally and completely in Christ and the Cross, he cannot live a consecrated, dedicated, Christian life.

As we've previously stated, the key to this understanding is found in Romans, Chapter 6. But the tragedy is, most Preachers have almost no understanding of this Chapter, which means that those who sit under them have no understanding as well. As a result, the *"sin nature"* rules and reigns in the lives of most Christians, and despite the outward bravado, makes the life miserable (Rom. 7:24).

THE GLORY OF THE GOD OF ISRAEL

The phrase of Verse 2, *"And, behold, the Glory of the God of Israel came from the way of the east,"* presents at least one of the greatest moments in history, whether history past or history future. For the first time in over 2,500 years, except for the First Advent of Christ, the Glory of the Lord has returned to Israel.

Such will not only be of utmost blessing and prosperity for Israel proper, but, in fact, for the entirety of the world. Israel being in the place that she ought to be spiritually will signal blessing and prosperity for all of mankind, as it has never previously known.

Some 2,500 years ago, Israel rejected the Lord, and so He left! Now Israel has been washed and cleansed by the Blood of the Lamb, and, therefore, He returns.

So one might say, other than the First Advent of Christ, there is no greater moment for Israel than this moment. Now, and at long last, *"the Glory of the God of Israel"* comes back, and to stay! He will never leave again!

Actually, He will come back the same way he left, *"The East Gate of the LORD's House"* (Ezek. 10:19).

HIS VOICE

The phrase, *"And His voice was like the noise of many waters,"* in many ways, resembles that which took place at Sinai, when the Law was given, and more specifically, the Ten Commandments. The Voice of God at that time was so awesome, and accompanied by *"thunderings,"* and *"lightnings,"* and *"the noise of the trumpet,"* that the people fled (Ex. 20:18-21); however, due to the latter being under Grace and not under Law, with the people cleansed by the Blood of Christ, quite possibly the reaction will then be different. It will not be of fear, but of joy!

HIS GLORY

The phrase of Verse 2, *"And the Earth shined with His Glory,"* proclaims the fact that the entirety of the *"Earth"* at that time will be affected in a positive sense.

The possibility definitely exists that the entirety of the world, or at least those who have television sets, which includes most of the world, will, with all wonder, observe this event in some fashion by television, exactly as it happens.

This I do know, when the Holy Spirit anoints a message or a song, etc., and when it is aired at that time or later over television, the same Anointing carries through to the people who are watching in their homes, etc.

If the Lord would allow such to take place, and He possibly shall, then the entirety of the Earth will shine with *"His Glory."*

As a result of this glorious event, the Earth will enter into a period of peace and prosperity such as it has never known before. For the first time, the Earth will be viewed as God originally created it, as well as man. No one has ever seen the Earth or man as God originally created them, except when Christ was observed during His First Advent.

All that is presently seen is the result of the Fall, which has brought a horrible curse, resulting in pain, suffering, sickness, and sorrow. Now that time of pain and suffering will end, with Blessing, Peace, Prosperity, Glory, and Grace covering the entirety of the world.

As well, all the religions of the world will be thrown into Hell with their maker, namely Satan. His false ways of Salvation will be exposed for what they are, Satanic. Jesus Christ will reign Gloriously Supreme and *"the Earth will shine with His Glory."*

THE VISION

The phrase of Verse 3, *"And it was according to the appearance of the Vision which I saw, even according to the Vision that I saw when I came to destroy the city,"* refers to the Prophecy given to Ezekiel by the Lord, which announced the destruction of that place. It did not mean that Ezekiel personally destroyed it, but that he was the announcer of this tragic event!

The idea of Ezekiel's terminology is that, in the past, God had shown Himself as One of Justice and Judgment by overturning and destroying the old; likewise, He will now exhibit Himself as a God of Grace and Mercy by condescending to establish His abode in the New. Consequently, Ezekiel saw the destruction and the restoration, and unlike any other Prophet before or since!

THE POWER OF GOD

The phrase, *"And the Visions were like the Vision that I saw by the river Chebar; and I fell upon my face,"* proclaims the proper position in the Presence of the Lord of Glory. To see that which He has made, and we refer to *"the Temple,"* is one thing; to see Him is quite another!

In the Presence of such Holiness and Purity, one is stricken, and extensively so, by one's own unworthiness. And to think that One such as this would come down here to this mortal coil, and, as a Peasant at that, and then die for lost humanity!

He came the first time as a *"Lamb,"* in other words to be offered, which He was on the Cross of Calvary. Now He comes as a *"Lion,"* the *"Lion of the Tribe of Judah"* (Rev. 5:5). He came the first time as a Peasant, now He comes as *"King of kings, and Lord of lords"* (Rev. 19:16). The first time He came by man unheralded, now He comes *"with Glory."*

Ezekiel says that the Glory and Grandeur of this Coming is *"according to the appearance of the Vision"* which he saw, as is recorded in Chapter 10; however, there is a vast difference:

Then, He came to *"destroy the city,"* now He will come to *"build the city."*

When the Prophet likens the appearance, he is only speaking of the *"Glory of the LORD,"* and not the purpose of the Lord.

THE HOUSE OF THE LORD

Verse 4 reads: *"And the Glory of the LORD came into the House by the way of the gate whose prospect is toward the east."*

Let us emphasize again, the *"Great Altar,"* which will sit in the exact center of the Earth, and will be the centerpiece, so to speak, of this great Temple, and where the Sacrifices will be offered, had to be expressed in detail, before the Glory of the Lord could come. This tells us, when the Cross of Christ is preached, thereby held up as the means by which God gives all things to His people, to be sure, the Spirit of God is not long behind.

Before the Spirit of God could come on the Day of Pentecost, Calvary had to be a fact, which it was. This paved the way, and, in fact, made the way, for the Holy Spirit to come in full flower, and because all sin had been atoned. The Holy Spirit can function only on that which has been cleansed of all sin, which can only be done by the shed Blood of Christ, and Faith in that Finished Work.

In the great Latter Rain outpouring, which began at approximately the beginning of the Twentieth Century, in the great Revivals which swept the world in the late 1800's, the Cross, at that particular time, was gloriously and wondrously preached and proclaimed. The Church had to be brought back to the Cross, before this great outpouring of the Spirit could take place.

THE CROSS AND THIS PRESENT TIME

In the last few decades, at least as I dictate these notes (2003), the Cross of Christ has been vilified and repudiated, as possibly never before in history. As repeatedly stated, the Word of Faith doctrine, more than anything else, has been the principal means of this repudiation. It is so subtle, and because it claims to be Spirit-led. Its major theme is *"money,"* which promises to make its devotees rich, and coupled with great claims of the Spirit, provides a heady doctrine, which seems to find a ready lodging place.

The truth is, there is no *"Faith"* in this doctrine, at least that which God will recognize. As well, the only ones who get rich are the Preachers. Pure and simple, it is *"another Jesus, presented by another spirit, with the end result being another gospel"* (II Cor. 11:4). It is presented by an *"angel of light"* (II Cor. 11:14), and, therefore, seems to be right; however, Paul said that those who preach this type of message are *"Satan's ministers"* (II Cor. 11:15). They are *"transformed as the ministers of Righteousness,"* but are the very opposite!

Nevertheless, despite this powerful attack by Satan, once again, the Cross of Christ is beginning to be preached.

In 1997, the Lord began to give me a Revelation of the Cross that answered all of my questions regarding victorious living, and which has revolutionized my life and ministry. I use the phrase, *"Began to give me,"* and because this Revelation has not stopped unto this moment, with the Lord continuing to open up that which He gave to Paul nearly 2,000 years ago. Admittedly, what we have is not new; it is, as stated, what the Lord gave to the great Apostle, which, in effect, is the meaning of the New Covenant.

I personally believe that the Lord is going to send a mighty moving of the Spirit once again over this world. In other words, I don't think this great Latter Rain outpouring is over. I believe that which is to come, and will come shortly, will be greater than anything this world has ever known, possibly even eclipsing, if possible, the great outpouring in the Early Church. To be sure, the Lord never *"takes from,"* but always *"adds to."* In other words, His Revelation is always a Progressive Revelation.

The Cross is being preached (I Cor. 1:23; 2:2), which will increase and intensify, and which must be done in order for the Spirit of God to move, which I believe will be the last great move before the Rapture, that is, if the Lord does, in fact, delay the Rapture at all!

THE HOLY SPIRIT

The phrase of Verse 5, *"So the Spirit took me up, and brought me into the Inner Court,"* pertains to the area immediately surrounding the Temple and the Great Altar. It will be about 450 feet square.

The Lord is now entering into and taking possession of the *"House,"* as formerly He had entered into and taken possession of the Tabernacle and the Temple of old (Ex. 40:34-35; I Ki. 8:10-11).

The phrase, *"So the Spirit took me up,"* refers to him being taken by the Holy Spirit by Vision into the *"Inner Court."* There he saw the *"Glory of the LORD fill the house."*

As we have said previously, and so say we again, Chapters 40 through 42 proclaim the building of the Temple, as well as the great Altar, on which the Sacrifices were to be re-established. The preparation for the Sacrifices being established, which means that the Cross of Christ was placed as the centerpiece of all things, then the Holy Spirit could make His entrance. The Holy Spirit works so closely with Christ, as it refers to His sacrificial, atoning work, that, in fact, the Holy Spirit will not move, and, in fact, cannot move, until faith in the Cross is properly established (Jn. 14:16-17; Rev. 5:6).

PERSONAL EXPERIENCE

I personally believe that the Revelation of the Cross which the Lord has given this Evangelist, beginning in 1997 and continuing unto this hour, is a prelude to the greatest outpouring of the Holy Spirit that the world has ever known. I have had small amounts of information come my way that the Lord is giving this same Word to others in other parts of the world, which I definitely believe. It is not something new, having been given to the Apostle Paul nearly 2,000 years ago. In fact, it is the meaning of the New Covenant, the meaning of all that the Lord has ever done for the human race. It is all wrapped up in the phrase, *"Jesus Christ and Him Crucified"* (I Cor. 1:17-18, 21, 23; 2:2; Eph. 2:13-18; Col. 2:14-15).

THE LORD JESUS CHRIST

Verse 6 reads: *"And I heard Him speaking unto me out of the House; and the Man stood by me."*

Two questions arise out of this Verse:

A. Who was speaking to Ezekiel? The answer is obvious! It was the Holy Spirit, as is stated in Verse 5. The Holy Spirit is the One Who occupied the Holy of Holies, and dwelt between the Mercy Seat and the Cherubims, in the Tabernacle and the Temple of old. He will likewise occupy this House.

At the present, and due to what Christ did at Calvary, the Believer becomes the House in which the Holy Spirit now resides (I Cor. 3:16).

As God, He can occupy Heaven, the Believer, and the Temple which will be built in the coming Kingdom Age. In other words, He is Omnipresent.

Let the Reader understand, that the Moving and Operation of the Holy Spirit in His present Work as it regards Believers, and especially the fact that He can abide within us permanently, were all made possible by what Jesus did at the Cross. As I have emphasized this any number of times, I must continue to emphasize it, in that the Reader will understand the great significance of Calvary.

Before the Cross, the Holy Spirit was very limited as to what He could do in this Earth, because the sin debt remained, even over the Godliest, and because the blood of bulls and goats could not take away sins (Heb. 10:4). But the Cross completely removed the sin debt, in fact, taking away our sin (Jn. 1:29), that Satan can no longer level the charge of sin against true Believers. It was all handled at the Cross of Calvary.

We gain the benefits of the Cross, solely by evidencing Faith in Christ and what Christ did at the Cross. Please allow me once again to repeat myself, and because of the tremendous significance of what is said.

CHRIST MUST NEVER BE SEPARATED FROM THE CROSS

The moment the Preacher attempts to preach Christ without preaching the Cross, he is left with *"another Jesus, fostered by another spirit, which presents another gospel"* (II Cor. 11:4). And that's exactly what the modern Church is presently doing.

Revelation 5:6 portrays the *"slain lamb,"* which typifies Christ and what He did at the Cross. John sees all of this at the Throne of God, which means that access can never be granted until the Believer's Faith rests solely in Christ and His Finished Work (Eph. 2:13-18).

John said this slain lamb had *"seven horns and seven eyes, which are the seven Spirits of God sent forth into all the Earth."* In fact, the slain Lamb and the Holy Spirit are so closely intertwined that they cannot be separated. In fact, this one Passage tells us that the full Work of the Holy Spirit, which is a sevenfold work, cannot be brought about in the heart and life of the Believer until the Believer understands, and does so totally, that everything comes to him from God by virtue of the Cross of Christ.

While the Holy Spirit will do all that He can for the Believer, and in whatever circumstance, the truth is, until the Believer fully understands the Cross, in other words, gets his Faith right, which means it's properly placed, which means it's placed exclusively in the Sacrificial, Atoning Work of Christ, the sevenfold work of the Spirit in one's life cannot be brought about. And what is that sevenfold work?

THE SEVENFOLD WORK OF THE SPIRIT

The sevenfold work of the Spirit is found in the writings of the Prophet Isaiah. The Prophet said:

"And the Spirit of the LORD shall rest upon Him, the Spirit of Wisdom and Understanding, the Spirit of Counsel and Might, the Spirit of Knowledge and of the Fear of the LORD" (Isa. 11:2).

This is broken down as follows:
1. The Spirit of the LORD.
2. The Spirit of Wisdom.
3. The Spirit of Understanding.
4. The Spirit of Counsel.
5. The Spirit of Might.
6. The Spirit of Knowledge.
7. The Spirit of the Fear of the LORD.

This is the sevenfold Work of the Spirit,

mentioned by John as it regards his Vision.

(The pronoun *"Him"* in Isaiah 11:2 refers to Christ. It is on Him that all of this rests, even as John the Beloved said.)

As well, John the Baptist also said, and speaking of Christ: *"He shall baptize you with the Holy Spirit and with fire."* (Mat. 3:11). All of this means that the Holy Spirit functions exclusively in the realm of what Christ desires, with the attributes of the Spirit made possible solely by the Sacrifice of Christ, which demands the Faith of the Believer.

THE MEANING OF THE SEVEN HORNS AND THE SEVEN EYES

Continuing to refer to the Vision of John in Revelation 5:6, the number *"seven"* is God's number of perfection, totality, and universality. In the Bible, *"horns"* speak of dominion. Inasmuch as the Holy Spirit is here portrayed as having *"seven horns,"* this means that total and complete dominion will be given to the Believer upon proper faith, which is always in Christ and the Cross. This means that no Believer need have the sin nature rule him in any capacity. In fact, if we properly look to Christ and the Cross, Paul said, *"The sin nature will not have dominion over us"* (Rom. 6:14).

So, if the Believer is being dominated by the sin nature in any respect, this means that his Faith is not properly placed in the Cross. Proper Faith will always guarantee a complete deliverance and victory (Rom. 6:3-14).

The *"seven eyes"* speak of total and complete illumination, and speak of a proper understanding of the Word. All the false doctrine presently seen, and the Church sadly is full of false doctrine, is caused by improper illumination. In other words, it is not possible for the Believer to properly understand the Bible unless the Believer properly understands the Cross. The story of the Bible is the story of the Cross, as the story of the Cross is the story of the Bible. In fact, it's virtually impossible for the Christian to properly spot false doctrine without a proper understanding of the Cross. And because the modern Church little understands the Cross, the modern Church is sadly filled with false doctrine.

WHO IS THE MAN WHO STANDS BY EZEKIEL?

B. This is the second question of Verse 6. This *"Man"* is Christ Jesus, Who has conducted Ezekiel through the entirety of this manifestation (Ezek. 40:3-4).

What an honor to be accompanied by Christ, and led by the Spirit! And yet, this is the privilege of every Believer in this Glorious Day of Grace (Rev. 3:20).

THE PLACE OF MY THRONE

The words of Verse 7, *"This is"* are to be supplied before *"the place of My Throne."*

The phrase, *"The place of My Throne,"* is peculiar to Ezekiel; however, similar statements were made in earlier writings, although pertaining to His Presence as dwelling between the Mercy Seat and the Cherubim (Ex. 25:22; I Sam. 4:4; II Ki. 19:15; Isa. 37:16).

These statements concerned His Presence; this statement in Ezekiel concerns more than His Presence, even His Person.

The phrase, *"And the place of the soles of My feet,"* was used, in one form or the other, denoting the Ark of the Covenant (I Chron. 28:2; Ps. 99:5; 132:7).

However, whereas there was an *"Ark of the Covenant"* in the Tabernacle and Solomon's Temple, such will not be in the Millennial Temple, because Christ will be present in Person.

THE COMING RESTORATION

The phrase of Verse 7, *"Where I will dwell in the midst of the Children of Israel forever,"* goes beyond anything that had been spoken concerning either the Tabernacle of Moses or the Temple of Solomon. Once again, we state the fact, that while His Presence occupied these former structures, both His Presence and His Person will occupy the coming Millennial Temple.

The phrase, *"And My Holy Name shall the House of Israel no more defile,"* speaks of the times they did defile it by building the altars for dead idols in the very Temple Court. This had been done by more Kings than one in Judah (II Ki. 16:11; 21:4-7).

The coming Millennial Temple will never

see such a thing, and because Israel's rebellion is ever past.

THE DEFILEMENT OF GOD'S HOLY NAME

The phrase of Verse 8, *"They have even defiled My Holy Name by their abominations that they have committed,"* must be looked at in the present light as well.

As modern Believers read these words about Israel of old, which caused the Lord to *"consume them in His anger,"* the modern Believer must as well understand that such is happening presently.

Any vice allowed by the Believer in his heart is constituted by the Lord as being an idol, the same as Israel of old! Looking at the religious side, any Believer who places his or her faith in anything other than the Sacrifice of Christ has, once again, made such an idol. It is a sobering thought, but it is true.

And, in fact, if this actually is true, and it most definitely is, then virtually the entirety of the modern Church is presently engaging in idol worship. That's the reason that John the Beloved said: *"Little children, keep yourselves from idols"* (I Jn. 5:21).

PUT AWAY YOUR WHOREDOMS

The phrase of Verse 9, *"Now let them put away their whoredom,"* presents a theology that harmonizes with that of the Old and New Testament writers, who invariably proclaimed the necessity of purity of heart and life as a necessary condition of God's abiding in the heart, while asserting that such Divine indwelling in the heart is the only certain Creator of such purity, for one cannot create such himself (Isa. 1:16, 25; 26:12; Jn. 14:23; II Cor. 6:17; James 4:8).

Let us say it again:

If one places one's faith in anything other than the Cross of Christ, such is looked at by the Lord as *"spiritual whoredoms,"* which are labeled in the New Testament as *"spiritual adultery"* (Rom. 7:1-4).

Second, there is no way that the Believer can rid himself of such by his own strength, ability, and personal power.

I realize that virtually every Christian claims that such is not being done by his own personal strength, but rather by the Lord; however, irrespective of such claims being made, if the Believer doesn't understand the Cross, and how his faith there must be properly placed, whatever he claims, he, in fact, is attempting to clean up his life by his own strength and power. In other words, the Holy Spirit must do these things, and He doesn't do them automatically.

The Holy Spirit works in our lives exclusively on the premise of what Christ did at the Cross, and our Faith in that Finished Work. As we've repeatedly stated, the Holy Spirit doesn't demand much of us, but He does demand Faith. But for it to be Faith that God will recognize, which gives the Holy Spirit the latitude to work, it must be Faith in Christ and the Cross.

Let us say it again:

Christ is the *"Source,"* while the Cross is the *"Means."*

The phrase of Verse 9, *"And I will dwell in the midst of them forever,"* concerns the fact that lust and the Lord cannot at the same time dwell in this Temple.

MEASURE THE PATTERN

The phrase of Verse 10, *"That they may be ashamed of their iniquities,"* refers to iniquities of the past and not of the present. The idea is that all the glory Israel beholds could have been theirs for the asking, even from the beginning, had they only obeyed the Lord. Observing what is here now, and realizing what they have missed all of these centuries, makes them *"ashamed of their iniquities."*

As well, as such words will be spoken to Israel in that Coming Glad Day, they are spoken presently to any and all.

Even though the Millennium, constituting the reign of Christ, is not yet here, still, in Spirit the same Truth applies. It is *"our iniquities"* that separate us from God (Isa. 59:2).

The phrase, *"Let them measure the pattern,"* concerns itself with the Great Sanctuary, which will be the dwelling place of the Lord, and, comparing this Glorious Palace with the Pagan and Papal temples of idolatrous worship, the people will then be ashamed of shrines, both ancient and modern, of which they are now so proud.

Similarly, a comparison between the Way of Salvation and Holiness patterned in the Scriptures and those invented by man fills the contrite heart with self-condemnation.

THE VATICAN IN ROME

On a recent trip to Rome, we visited the Vatican, the Papal shrine of Catholicism.

At a certain place in this enclosure, there is a set of stairs, numbering, I suppose, 100 or so, that is supposed to be built over an ancient Church in Rome. People are led to believe if they crawl up those steps on their hands and knees, that such will bless them, etc.

I stood there that day, observing the scene as scores of people crawled over those filthy steps on their hands and knees, with some of them even kissing each step as they climbed upward. They thought that by doing so, that this was gaining them something with the Lord.

My heart grieved as I observed this situation, but yet at the same time, I believe the Holy Spirit spoke to my heart, that many in the Protestant world are, in some way, doing the same thing. While it may not be crawling up these stairs in Rome, it is faith and trust placed in something other than the Cross, which, in the eyes of God, puts all of this, the stairs and other faith objects, in the same category.

In fact, I was greatly convicted of my own actions of the past, knowing that, in spirit, I had done the same thing.

It is so easy for faith to be placed in religious things other than the Cross, and because they are religious things, we tend to think that what is being done is holy, and, thereby, recognized by God. It isn't!

The Lord recognizes alone our Faith in Christ and the Vicarious, Atoning Work of Christ.

THE HOUSE

The phrase of Verse 11, *"And if they be ashamed of all that they have done, show them the form of the house, and the fashion thereof,"* proclaims God's Way.

The *"House,"* and Who it represented, namely Christ, is to be of such splendor and glory that it defies description!

The idea is, that the miserable efforts of man to form his own Salvation will seem as nothing in comparison to God's Salvation.

The idea of this statement pertains to the place where God dwells. He will not dwell in anything except that which He Himself has made. All else, and especially of religion, is polluted, diseased, corrupt, unclean, leprous, and defiling. Such would include all religions such as Buddhism, Islam, Shintoism, Hinduism, Mormonism, Catholicism, as well as parts of Christianity which have apostatized. Only that which is of God, all of God, and only of God, can be accepted. Therefore, almost all are excluded, and for all the obvious reasons.

THE LAW OF THE HOUSE

The phrase of Verse 12, *"This is the Law of House,"* proclaims the Word of the Lord. The House is Holy because there the Lord resides. Anything made by man is unholy, irrespective of its religious intent. Therefore, all of Catholicism is unholy; all of that among Protestant Churches which is unscriptural is unholy. *"This is the Law of the House."*

THE MEASURES OF THE ALTAR

The phrase of Verse 13, *"And these are the measures of the Altar after the cubits,"* proclaims the Atonement as the eternal foundation of God's relationship with man, of which *"the Altar"* is symbolic. In fact, this characterizes the entirety of the Chapter.

The *"Altar"* of Verses 13 through 17 is to be distinguished from the *"Table of Jehovah"* (Ezek. 41:22). That Table will be of wood, and will stand within the Temple; the Altar will occupy the center of the Court of the Priests, and, therefore, the center of all the other square Courts, and of the Land, and of the world.

Such symbolizes Calvary and will forever serve as a reminder, and a memorial of what Christ did in order that humanity be redeemed.

The *"Altar"* is a place of death, but from this death comes life.

When Jesus died on Calvary, He died to save us from sin and self. Some understand the problem of sin, but few understand the problem of *"self."*

Sin is immediately eradicated, cleansed, and washed upon acceptance of Christ as Saviour; however, the dependence on self is not as easily eradicated. It can be explained perhaps this way:

The Children of Israel being delivered from Egypt was a type of Salvation, which saves from sin; however, the taking of the Promised Land is a type of victory over self.

All the people had to do upon deliverance from Egypt was simply believe Moses and follow him; however, the taking of the Land was a different matter altogether. The battles were many! The demand upon Faith was constant! As there were victories, there were also defeats.

The same is true of *"self."* Victory does not come easily, with many defeats along the way. But, ultimately, if we believe God and follow Him, thereby placing our faith exclusively in Christ and the Cross, even though the battles will be severe, the victory is certain (Rom. 6:3-14). Self will ultimately be hidden in Christ, for that is where self must abide, if we are to have the victory that Christ Alone affords (Lk. 9:23-24; Gal. 2:20-21).

So, as Christ died on the Altar for the Salvation of mankind, likewise, the Christian has to die on the *"Altar"* through Christ and the crucifixion of self (Col. 2:20; 3:1-3). Spiritually speaking, this is what is meant by *"the measures of the Altar."*

Verses 14 through 17 proclaim the fact, that is if our measurement of the cubit is correct, this Altar is 18 feet long and 18 feet wide.

As previously stated, it is somewhat smaller than the Altar which was built in front of Solomon's Temple, inasmuch as that Altar was 30 feet wide and 30 feet long.

It is smaller, simply because the sacrifices offered thereon will be symbolic only, and will not be nearly as many as the Altar of old. The Cross forever handled the problem of sin.

(18) "AND HE SAID UNTO ME, SON OF MAN, THUS SAITH THE LORD GOD; THESE ARE THE ORDINANCES OF THE ALTAR IN THE DAY WHEN THEY SHALL MAKE IT, TO OFFER BURNT OFFERINGS THEREON, AND TO SPRINKLE BLOOD THEREON.

(19) "AND YOU SHALL GIVE TO THE PRIESTS THE LEVITES THAT BE OF THE SEED OF ZADOK, WHICH APPROACH UNTO ME, TO MINISTER UNTO ME, SAITH THE LORD GOD, A YOUNG BULLOCK FOR A SIN OFFERING.

(20) "AND YOU SHALL TAKE OF THE BLOOD THEREOF, AND PUT IT ON THE FOUR HORNS OF IT, AND ON THE FOUR CORNERS OF THE SETTLE, AND UPON THE BORDER ROUND ABOUT: THUS SHALL YOU CLEANSE AND PURGE IT.

(21) "YOU SHALL TAKE THE BULLOCK ALSO OF THE SIN OFFERING, AND HE SHALL BURN IT IN THE APPOINTED PLACE OF THE HOUSE, WITHOUT THE SANCTUARY.

(22) "AND ON THE SECOND DAY YOU SHALL OFFER A KID OF THE GOATS WITHOUT BLEMISH FOR A SIN OFFERING; AND THEY SHALL CLEANSE THE ALTAR, AS THEY DID CLEANSE IT WITH THE BULLOCK.

(23) "WHEN YOU HAVE MADE AN END OF CLEANSING IT, YOU SHALL OFFER A YOUNG BULLOCK WITHOUT BLEMISH AND A RAM OUT OF THE FLOCK WITHOUT BLEMISH.

(24) "AND YOU SHALL OFFER THEM BEFORE THE LORD, AND THE PRIESTS SHALL CAST SALT UPON THEM, AND THEY SHALL OFFER THEM UP FOR A BURNT OFFERING UNTO THE LORD.

(25) "SEVEN DAYS SHALL YOU PREPARE EVERY DAY A GOAT FOR A SIN OFFERING: THEY SHALL ALSO PREPARE A YOUNG BULLOCK, AND A RAM OUT OF THE FLOCK, WITHOUT BLEMISH.

(26) "SEVEN DAYS SHALL THEY PURGE THE ALTAR AND PURIFY IT; AND THEY SHALL CONSECRATE THEMSELVES.

(27) "AND WHEN THESE DAYS ARE EXPIRED, IT SHALL BE, THAT UPON THE EIGHTH DAY, AND SO FORWARD, THE PRIESTS SHALL MAKE YOUR BURNT OFFERINGS UPON THE ALTAR, AND YOUR PEACE OFFERINGS; AND I WILL ACCEPT YOU, SAITH THE LORD GOD."

The overview is:

1. The instructions for the Sacrifices, which will continue throughout the Kingdom Age, once again, present the Cross as the means by which God has blessed humanity.

2. The story of the Bible is the story of Jesus Christ and Him Crucified. That alone is the answer for the fallen sons of Adam's lost race.

3. As we've said repeatedly, Christ is the Source, while the Cross is the Means.

THE ORDINANCES OF THE ALTAR

The phrase of Verse 18, *"And He said unto me, Son of man, thus saith the Lord GOD; these are the ordinances of the Altar,"* presents the consecration of the Altar.

The *"Ordinances"* here given do not pertain to the regulations for the sacrificial worship to be afterwards performed upon this Altar, for the rites to be observed at this time are for its consecration only. Such were done regarding the Altar in the Tabernacle (Ex. 29:1-46; Lev. 8:11-33), and in Solomon's Temple (I Ki. 8:63-66; II Chron. 7:4-10). It was to be dedicated by a special ceremony before being brought into ordinary use.

All things, as well as man being sin-defiled, Atonement will be made for the Altar. The perfection of the Atonement appears in the seven days of its action, hence it will need no repetition. The Altar was to be used for two purposes only:

TO OFFER BURNT OFFERINGS THEREON

Burnt Offerings consisted of the whole of the animal, minus its skin, being offered on the Altar. Such signified that God gave His all for humanity, and that we are to give our all to the Lord. This speaks of the tremendous price that Jesus paid at the Cross, and the victory there won.

Such were done, not only to defeat the powers of darkness, which it definitely did, but, even more so, to satisfy the justice of God concerning man's sin and guilt (Col. 2:14-15).

TO SPRINKLE BLOOD THEREON

The shedding of the Precious Blood of Christ was that which satisfied the demands of a thrice-Holy God. In the Garden, the punishment for sin was death, which was spiritual death, separation from God; therefore, the price for life is also death.

However, the death must be that of a Perfect Sacrifice, Which Blood could not be tainted by sin. The Scripture says: *"The life of the flesh is in the blood"* (Lev. 17:11); however, the blood of man would not suffice, because it was tainted by sin as a result of the Fall. Therefore, there had to be a Substitute. That Substitute was Christ. He became Man, while never ceasing to be God. He was born of the Virgin Mary, and, therefore, not of the seed of man, and, therefore, not defiled. His Blood was pure and untainted!

Therefore, when He died, shedding His Life's Blood, it was perfect and pure Blood, untainted by sin, and, therefore, His Life was acceptable unto God as a Perfect Sacrifice, which would atone for the sins of all who would believe (Jn. 3:16; Rom. 10:9-10, 13; Rev. 22:17).

A CROSS CHURCH

Consequently, if the Church in any manner compromises the Doctrine of the precious shed Blood of Christ, thereby denigrating what He did at Calvary, the Church then loses its way. Every Church must be a *"Cross Church."* If it majors in anything else other than *"Christ and Him Crucified,"* then it is not proclaiming the Gospel of Jesus Christ (I Cor. 1:17-18, 21, 23; 2:2). This is the only thing that will set the captive free, and, hence, if we go beyond Calvary, we lose our way.

Tragically, only a precious few Preachers of the Gospel, in this day and age, believe that which has just been stated. Most of the Preachers in the old-line Denominations have long since compromised this all-important Doctrine. As well, many in the Pentecostal and Charismatic ranks are doing the same thing by placing the emphasis on things other than *"Christ and Him Crucified."*

The significance placed here on the Sacrificial, Atoning Work of Christ, in the coming Kingdom Age, which will be carried out, not only in the Millennium, but, as well, throughout eternity, portrays to us the thoughts of the Holy Spirit regarding the Altar and what it represents; consequently, our attention, dedication, priority, and devotion to this all-important event must never be abrogated!

As the Levitical Offerings predicted the preciousness and sufficiency of the offering up of Christ Himself, so will the Millennial Sacrifices recall and testify to that Great Offering as an accomplished fact.

These Sacrifices will be necessary; for when Israel, and the world, look upon the resplendent form of Immanuel as He will appear on this Mount of Glory, they will be disposed, despite the nail-prints in His Hands, to forget that He hung in Blood and Death for their sins upon the Cross of Calvary.

This Great Blood-sprinkled Altar, with its burning fire, will vividly instruct them; and it will help them to feel that they were sinners, or that they are sinners, as some will be, and that the precious Blood of the Lamb of God, shed for them, is the One and only necessary Atonement, and the foundation of all their Millennial happiness.

THE PRIESTS

The phrase of Verse 19, *"And you shall give to the Priests the Levites that be of the seed of Zadok,"* harks back to David's faithful High Priest. This means that only those who derive their descent from Zadok are to participate.

Hence, by the choosing of these *"sons of Zadok,"* the Holy Spirit proclaims to us the value of faithfully adhering to the Will of God, instead of the will of man. The implication is this:

Just before David died, his son *"Adonijah exalted himself, saying, I will be King"* (I Ki. 1:5). (He had the same mother as Absalom, and, as well, had the Absalom spirit.)

Abiathar, who shared the High Priestly duties with Zadok, joined in with Adonijah, even though they knew it was God's Will that Solomon be King. They were religious opportunists, which characterizes so much of modern Christendom, which is even more political than secular politics. Such has no desire for the Will of God, only the desire to further its own interests. Regrettably, the Church is full of *"Adonijahs"* and *"Abiathars."*

The Scripture plainly says that *"Zadok the Priest was not with Adonijah"* (I Ki. 1:8).

NOTES

He threw in his lot with David, and, hence, eternally the Greater Son of David, the Lord Jesus Christ. As a result, and by the Will of God, and for his faithfulness to that Will, *"Zadok"* was made the sole High Priest, and, consequently, anointed Solomon to be King (I Ki. 1:39).

MINISTER UNTO ME

The phrase, *"To minister unto Me, saith the Lord GOD,"* has more meaning than meets the eye. Zadok, in his decision of Righteousness, ministered unto the Lord instead of himself. As a result, his *"seed"* will continue to minister in this high and exalted position.

(At this time, Zadok of old, and with a Glorified Body, will, no doubt, be there to worship, instruct, and help.)

The phrase, *"A young bullock for a Sin Offering,"* refers to Christ, Who died in the very flower of His Manhood, as will be symbolized by this animal.

THE BLOOD

The phrase of Verse 20, *"And you shall take of the blood thereof,"* forms an integral part of every expiatory Offering.

However, there was a difference in the *"Sin Offering"* and the other Offerings. In the other Offerings, the blood was poured out at the base of the Altar, whereas the *"Sin Offering"* blood was to be smeared on the four horns of the Altar, with a horn at each corner, specifying all points of the compass, hence, Calvary is for all.

As well, it was to be smeared on the *"four corners of the settle,"* which formed a part of the base or foundation of the Altar.

"Blood" was also to be smeared on the *"border,"* which was immediately below the *"settle."* The implication is that the Blood was smeared around the entire border. Thus was the *"Altar cleansed and purged."*

This was not for the cleansing of the people, but for the *"Altar"* itself. Without an atoned-for Altar, there could be no atoned-for people! It stood in need of cleansing, because the sins of the people were transferred to it. Consequently, when Christ died on Calvary, His Blood, which stained the Cross and the Earth beneath it, purged and cleansed this most vile form of death.

One must understand that, due to the Fall, every single thing on the planet, including man, the Earth, and all forms of creation, were polluted and defiled; hence, the very Cross on which Christ hung, and the Earth in which it was fastened, were polluted and defiled, but were cleansed by the precious Blood of Christ.

THE JESUS DIED SPIRITUALLY DOCTRINE

This doctrine, as propagated by the Word of Faith people, claims that Jesus, while on the Cross, took upon Himself the Satanic nature, actually became demon-possessed, and thereby died as a sinner and went to the burning side of Hell, where He suffered there for three days and three nights. This means that He suffered with all the other myriad of sinners who had preceded Him in Hell.

At the end of the three days and nights, God said, *"It is enough,"* and Jesus, according to this teaching, was *"born again,"* and then raised from the dead.

The trouble with this, there is not a shred of this teaching found anywhere in the Bible. This teaching completely eliminates the veracity of the Cross, which makes the shedding of the Blood of Christ of no effect.

But what does the Bible say?

"But now in Christ Jesus you who in times past were far off are made near by the Blood of Christ."

The Scripture then says, *"And that He might reconcile both* (Jews and Gentiles) *unto God in one Body* (the Church) *by the Cross* (where the victory was there won), *having slain the enmity* (between God and man) *thereby"* (Eph. 2:13, 16).

There is nothing said in these Passages, or any other Passages in the Bible for that matter, which supports the fallacy of the erroneous doctrine that Jesus Died Spiritually on the Cross. The Word of God rather extols the virtue of the shed Blood and the place where that Blood was shed, which was the Cross. Any deviation from that destroys the Atonement and is a grievous sin, perhaps the worst sin that can be committed, other than blaspheming the Holy Spirit.

No, the Cross is where the great price was paid, the great victory was won, and Salvation was thereby effected. There is no record in the Word of God that Jesus ever went to the burning side of Hell. He did go down into Paradise, and, as well, did preach to the spirits in prison, which were fallen angels (I Pet. 3:18-20). But that is the extent of His sojourn in the nether world. In fact, He delivered all the souls that were in Paradise, taking them back with Him to the portals of glory, with that place now being empty (Eph. 4:8-9). No, the work was begun and finished at Calvary. This is proven by the *"rent Veil,"* which took place on the Cross the moment that Jesus said, *"It is finished"* (Mat. 27:51).

THE SIN OFFERING

Verse 21 reads: *"You shall take the bullock also of the Sin Offering, and you shall burn it in the appointed place of the house, without the Sanctuary."*

The idea is that the skin and dung of the bullock should be burned without the camp (Ex. 29:14; Lev. 4:12, 21; 9:11, 15). As well, Hebrews 13:13 mentions such!

The place where these items were to be burned was *"without the Sanctuary."* This is the *"Separate Place,"* which is mentioned in Ezekiel 41:12, which was a part of the house in the widest sense, and yet belonged not to the *"Sanctuary"* in the strictest sense.

(The Separate Place is located at the extreme western part of the Outer Court, and is not attached directly to the Sanctuary or the Temple in any manner.)

The phrase of Verse 22, *"And on the second day you shall offer a kid of the goats without blemish for a Sin Offering,"* represents a different animal, but otherwise a repetition of the first day of cleansing.

The Reader must wonder as to need the for different animals or another animal at all?

Actually, there were five Levitical Offerings given in the Law of Moses, with all typifying what Christ would do at Calvary. In other words, it took five Offerings to wholly portray His One Sacrificial Offering on the Cross (Lev., Chpts. 1-5).

Incidentally, five is the number of Grace, in that Christ was given one Name with five meanings (Isa. 9:6). As well, Christ suffered five wounds at Calvary.

The different types of animals, among other things, expressed His different types of Ministry. They also correspond to the four Gospels.

1. Ram: This animal speaks of Christ as King, and corresponds with Matthew, and, as well, of His Sacrificial Offering, hence, the dying of a King.

2. Bullock: This spoke of Christ as the Servant, and corresponds with the Gospel according to Mark. As a bullock was made, at times, to pull a plow and served in the servant capacity, so did Christ. He was a King, but yet a Servant.

3. Goat: This spoke of Christ as the Prophet and, hence, a Man, which corresponds with the Gospel according to Luke.

4. Lamb: This corresponds with the Gospel according to John, and, hence, speaks of Christ as God, and, in this case, *"the Lamb of God."*

BURNT OFFERING

Verses 23 and 24 should be compared with the Book of Leviticus. There, the Burnt Offering preceded the Sin Offering; here it follows.

Then Faith praised and looked forward to the Sin Offering of Calvary; in the future day, Faith will praise looking back to Calvary. Thus the Great Sin Offering of the Lamb of God stands in the midst of the ages and is preceded and followed by praise, the latter typified by the *"Burnt Offering."* Actually, there will be no Day of Atonement in Millennial Worship; for the Sacrifices then will recall the One all-suffering Atonement perfected at Golgotha.

It seems that the Offering of these animals will be immediately after the cleansing of the Altar on the second day, and presumably also on the succeeding days.

The phrase of Verse 24, *"And the Priests shall cast salt upon them,"* referring to the Offerings, has reference to the Word of God. In other words, all of this is according to the Word of God, typified by *"salt."*

SEVEN DAYS

Verse 25 reads: *"Seven days shall you prepare every day a goat for a Sin Offering: they shall also prepare a young bullock, and a ram out of the flock, without blemish."*

As we have stated, the perfection of the Atonement appears in the seven days of its action. As such, it will need no repetition. *"Seven,"* as God's number, denotes perfection, completion, fulfillment, totality, and universality.

Every day for seven days three animals will be offered, *"a goat," "a young bullock,"* and *"a ram."*

As they were *"without blemish,"* they symbolized His perfect Life as the incomparable One.

As well as the Altar being purified, likewise, *"they consecrated themselves,"* speaking of the Priests, the *"seed"* of Zadok.

Likewise, as this consecrated the Priests, it consecrates all who believe in the Vicarious Atoning Offering of Christ at Calvary.

THE EIGHTH DAY

Verse 27 reads: *"And when these days are expired, it shall be, that upon the eighth day, and so forward, the Priests shall make your Burnt Offerings upon the Altar, and your Peace Offerings; and I will accept you, saith the Lord GOD."* Both the *"Altar"* and the *"Priests"* are now cleansed, which speak of the *"seven days"* of Offerings being finished. Thereby, on the *"eighth day,"* regular Sacrifices will commence, and will continue throughout the Kingdom Age, and do so every single day.

The *"eighth day"* speaks of Resurrection. Jesus was resurrected on the eighth day, the first day of the week. It speaks of a new beginning.

So, the entirety of the Earth at that particular time will have a new beginning, enjoying peace and prosperity as it has never known before. It will have all been made possible by what Christ did at the Cross. This we must never forget!

"What can take away my sins, nothing but the Blood of Jesus.

"What can make me whole again, nothing but the Blood of Jesus.

"O precious is the flow, that washes white as snow.

"No other fount I know, nothing but the Blood of Jesus."

CHAPTER 44

(1) "THEN HE BROUGHT ME BACK THE WAY OF THE GATE OF THE OUTWARD SANCTUARY WHICH LOOKS TOWARD THE EAST; AND IT WAS SHUT.

(2) "THEN SAID THE LORD UNTO ME; THIS GATE SHALL BE SHUT, IT SHALL NOT BE OPENED, AND NO MAN SHALL ENTER IN BY IT; BECAUSE THE LORD, THE GOD OF ISRAEL, HAS ENTERED IN BY IT, THEREFORE IT SHALL BE SHUT.

(3) "IT IS FOR THE PRINCE; THE PRINCE, HE SHALL SIT IN IT TO EAT BREAD BEFORE THE LORD; HE SHALL ENTER BY THE WAY OF THE PORCH OF THAT GATE, AND SHALL GO OUT BY THE WAY OF THE SAME.

(4) "THEN BROUGHT HE ME THE WAY OF THE NORTH GATE BEFORE THE HOUSE: AND I LOOKED, AND, BEHOLD, THE GLORY OF THE LORD FILLED THE HOUSE OF THE LORD: AND I FELL UPON MY FACE.

(5) "AND THE LORD SAID UNTO ME, SON OF MAN, MARK WELL, AND BEHOLD WITH YOUR EYES, AND HEAR WITH YOUR EARS ALL THAT I SAY UNTO YOU CONCERNING ALL THE ORDINANCES OF THE HOUSE OF THE LORD, AND ALL THE LAWS THEREOF; AND MARK WELL THE ENTERING IN OF THE HOUSE, WITH EVERY GOING FORTH OF THE SANCTUARY.

(6) "AND YOU SHALL SAY TO THE REBELLIOUS, EVEN TO THE HOUSE OF ISRAEL, THUS SAITH THE LORD GOD; O YE HOUSE OF ISRAEL, LET IT SUFFICE YOU OF ALL YOUR ABOMINATIONS.

(7) "IN THAT YOU HAVE BROUGHT INTO MY SANCTUARY STRANGERS, UNCIRCUMCISED IN HEART, AND UNCIRCUMCISED IN FLESH, TO BE IN MY SANCTUARY, TO POLLUTE IT, EVEN MY HOUSE, WHEN YE OFFER MY BREAD, THE FAT AND THE BLOOD, AND THEY HAVE BROKEN MY COVENANT BECAUSE OF ALL YOUR ABOMINATIONS.

(8) "AND YOU HAVE NOT KEPT THE CHARGE OF MY HOLY THINGS: BUT YOU HAVE SET KEEPERS OF MY CHARGE IN MY SANCTUARY FOR YOURSELVES."

The diagram is:

1. The Messiah, having entered His Temple, the Inner Gate of the Eastern entry shall be shut, thus giving a memorial of the fact, and an assurance that He will never again forsake His Temple.

2. The Prince, who could be the High Priest, shall enter the Outer Porch of the Eastern Gate and advance to the Inner exit, but no farther. He shall sit there and eat the sacrificial meal. The congregation of worshippers will take its place in front of, and outside of, the gate. The Prince, having worshipped, will then retire as he entered.

3. In the Temple and its functions the world of the Kingdom Age will see the Ways of the Lord.

THE EASTERN GATE

Verse 1 reads: *"Then He brought me back the way of the gate of the outward Sanctuary which looks toward the east; and it was shut."*

The Eastern Gate being shut to the general public, except on Sabbaths and New Moons (Ezek. 46:1-3), proclaims the fact that the Lord will never again forsake His Temple, as He did, and, in fact, was forced to do, and because of the idol worship of Judah, which resulted in her being taken over by the Babylonians. This happened some 500 years before Christ. But those days are now over, and will never again be repeated, symbolized by the Messiah having entered His Temple, and the gate being shut.

The phrase of Verse 2, *"Then said the LORD unto me; this gate shall be shut, it shall not be opened, and no man shall enter in by it,"* proclaims the fact that the North and South Gates will be the principal entry points for worshippers, day and night, who, no doubt, will come from all over the world, and do so continually.

Jerusalem will be so resplendent with the Glory of God, literally emanating His Presence, with so many hundreds of millions desiring its association, that, quite possibly, different parts of the Earth, and regarding their coming to worship, may, possibly, need to be regulated. Now it is difficult to get anyone to worship the Lord, even in Church! However, on this coming Glad and Glorious Day, the entirety of the Earth will worship Him, Who made all things, and redeemed man, thereby bringing him from darkness to Light (Ps. 150).

THE PRINCE

The phrase of Verse 3, *"It is for the Prince; the Prince, he shall sit in it to eat bread before the LORD,"* proclaims this man, who will probably be the High Priest, entering the Outer Porch of the Eastern Gate and advancing to the Inner exit, but no farther. He shall sit there and eat the Sacrificial Meal.

"To eat bread before the LORD" is, in the Scriptures, an act of worship (Gen. 31:54; Ex. 18:12; 24:11; I Cor. 10:18).

THE GLORY OF THE LORD

The phrase, *"And I looked, and behold the Glory of the LORD filled the House of the LORD: and I fell upon my face,"* is what makes the Church different than all earthly organizations. In Truth, the Church should be a heavenly organization on Earth! The only thing that can make it thus so is the *"Glory."* And yet, the number of Churches that would fall into this category are minuscule, to say the least! The idea is this:

The Man measuring the dimensions of the Sanctuary is Christ. The Holy Spirit, Who is correspondent with the Glory of God, will occupy only that which is *"measured"* by the *"Man," "The Man Christ Jesus."* Consequently, He does not occupy much, simply because most all of that which calls itself *"Church"* is a work (measurement) of man, and not God.

The rule of measurement is the Bible, but, sadly, in most Church circles, it is used only as window dressing!

This probably can be said to be Satan's greatest area of conflict. He attempts to substitute his measurements of the Church in the place of the Lord's. He does it through religious man, and does it well!

The result of the *"Glory of the LORD"* filling the House was Ezekiel falling on his face; thus is man humbled.

The Church designed by man institutes ungodly pride, while the Church designed by the Lord institutes humility.

THE ORDINANCES OF THE HOUSE OF THE LORD

The phrase of Verse 5, *"And the LORD said unto me, Son of man, mark well, and behold with your eyes, and hear with your ears all that I say unto you concerning all the ordinances of the House of the LORD,"* means *"set the heart upon."* The heart, the eyes, the ears are all to be engaged with Jehovah's House and its Ordinances, Laws, and Statutes. On entering God's Presence, it is of the utmost importance that the heart should be deeply affected; and, as well, it should be as deeply exercised when going forth from the Divine Presence.

Previously (Ezek. 40:4), the Lord had told the Prophet, concerning the Temple, *"Set your heart upon all that I shall show you."* Now He tells him to do so concerning the Bible, for this is the kernel of this Passage. He is told, and concerning this admonition, to *"mark well."* It means to set the heart upon learning all these things. He says no less to the Modern Church!

The Word of God is to be the criteria in all things. And yet, most Christians, even Preachers, little know the Word of God!

There was a time that theology was the queen of the sciences in all universities, secular or otherwise; consequently, the foundation of all learning, at least in those days, was based on the Bible; consequently, America became great. However, those days are long since past. Today, psychology is the queen of the sciences instead of theology, and not only in secular universities, but Bible Colleges and Seminaries, as well!

THE CROSS HAS BEEN ABANDONED BY THE CHURCH

The Holy Spirit through Peter said that the Word of God *"gives unto us all things that pertain unto life and Godliness, through the knowledge of Him Who has called us to Glory and Virtue"* (II Pet. 1:3).

Sadly, the *"all things"* given to us by the Lord, and we speak of that which pertains to life and living, have been abandoned in favor of humanistic psychology. One cannot have it both ways! If one embraces the Cross, humanistic psychology must be abandoned. If one embraces humanistic psychology, the Cross must be abandoned. And regrettably, the Church, totally and completely, has opted for humanistic psychology. Some parts of it may still claim to cling to the Cross, but, as stated, it is impossible for such to be. Either the Lord gave us *"all things which pertain to life and Godliness,"* or He didn't tell the truth, and we should look elsewhere.

I happen to believe that the Lord told the truth, and that He did give us *"all things."*

The answer to man's dilemma, which is sin, is found in the Cross, and is found only in the Cross. There the Lord Jesus Christ satisfied the demands of the broken law, and thereby atoned for all sin. With all sin atoned, past, present, and future, at least for those who will believe, Satan lost his legal right to hold man in bondage. Sin was that right, but with all sin atoned, there is no more sin, and again, at least for all who will believe (Jn. 3:16; Col. 2:14-15).

In fact, it is impossible for anyone to live a life of victory over the world, the flesh, and the Devil without looking exclusively to the Cross, which gives the Holy Spirit latitude to work in one's life (Rom. 8:11). The idea that man can make himself what he ought to be is so foolish as to defy description. That's what makes it so difficult to understand!

How can Preachers, who claim to be Spirit-filled, look to the world for their help, which, in fact, contains no help? Is it because of ignorance of the Cross or unbelief?

THE CROSS IS ALWAYS REJECTED ON MORAL GROUNDS

Let's look at that statement closely!

The Cross is never rejected on theological grounds, meaning that it's too difficult to understand, but rather on moral grounds. What does that mean?

It is certainly true that many are ignorant of the Cross as it regards our Sanctification. In other words, most really do not understand Romans, Chapter 6. Not understanding Romans, Chapter 6 means that they do not understand God's Prescribed Order of Victory.

However, I have found that when the Scriptural explanation of this great Chapter is given, that the far greater majority of *"Christians"* either ignore what is being said or else outright reject what is being said. The rejection is not brought about because of a lack of understanding, but simply because of unbelief. This means that it becomes a moral problem. It is because of pride, self-will, or whatever! Irrespective, it is a rejection of God's Prescribed Order of Victory, and, to be sure, the Lord has only one Prescribed Order. To reject that, is to reject the Lord!

REBELLION

The phrase of Verse 6, *"And you shall say to the rebellious, even to the House of Israel,"* takes the Prophet back to the original happenings at the North Gate, for this was the scene of the *"abominations,"* which, at least in part, caused the original destruction of Judah and Jerusalem (Ezek. 8:5). Consequently, a stern reminder and warning is given that the nation should now be preserved from lapsing into similar transgressions. Thankfully, there will be no repeating of these *"abominations."*

Verse 7 proclaims the fact that Israel will serve as the High Priestly Nation for the entirety of the world in the coming Kingdom Age. The position originally outlined by the Lord for His people will now finally be realized! They were intended to serve as an example of Righteousness, and, thereby, to lead the Gentile World to Christ. In this they miserably failed, regarding the past, but now will gloriously succeed.

THREE TYPES OF PEOPLE

During the thousand year Kingdom Age, there will actually be three types of people in the world: A. Jews; B. Gentiles; and, C. Glorified Saints.

The Jews and Gentiles will be those who are alive at the Second Coming, and, as well, those who will be born during the Kingdom Age. At the outset, the number of Jews will be small, considering that the majority will be killed in the last three and one-half years of the Great Tribulation, and especially the Battle of Armageddon; however, their numbers will increase speedily, due to the Blessings of the Lord during the Kingdom Age.

The Gentiles will number into the hundreds of millions, if not two or three billion. As well, vast numbers of these will be killed during the Great Tribulation. Jesus said, *"And except those days should be shortened, there should no flesh be saved"* (Mat. 24:22).

After the Second Coming, many Gentiles will accept Christ as Lord and Saviour. They, as the Jews, upon accepting Christ, will live forever in their natural state, by virtue of the *"Tree of Life"* (Ezek. 47:12; Rev. 22:1-2).

The third group will be the Glorified Saints, made up of both Jews and Gentiles of all ages, who accepted the Lord as their Saviour, and had part in the First Resurrection (Rev. 20:6). These, which at least will number in the tens of millions, will help Christ administer the affairs of the Earth, and of all His Creation, forever! Their Glorified Bodies will be the same as Christ's Body, when He was raised from the dead (Rom. 8:17, 30). John the Beloved said: *"Now are we the sons of God, and it does not yet appear what we shall be: but we know that, when He shall appear, we shall be like Him; for we shall see Him as He is"* (I Jn. 3:2).

KEEPING THE CHARGE

Verse 8 reads: *"And you have not kept the charge of My holy things: but you have set keepers of My charge in My Sanctuary for yourselves."*

The implication is that in the Old Economy of God, the Levites, who were supposed to attend to the duties of the Temple, grew weary of this service and engaged others, even Gentiles and, therefore, uncircumcised in the flesh or heart, to discharge the services.

This happened even after the dispersion and the return of Israel from captivity. Upon the rebuilding of the Temple, Eliashib, the High Priest, allowed Tobiah, a Gentile, to actually have a Chamber in the Temple. It says that the High Priest was allied unto him (Neh. 13:3-5).

As a result, Nehemiah *"cast forth all the household stuff of Tobiah out of the Chamber"* (Neh. 13:7-9).

All of this means that Israel of old departed from the Word of God, making up their own rules, ignoring what the Lord had commanded.

NOTES

In modern Christendom, I wonder what the Lord thinks of religious offices, which, in fact, have no Scriptural foundation?

I speak of positions such as Pope, Cardinals, Priests, Bishops, Superintendents, Overseers, etc. (The titles or designations of *"Bishop, Presbyter, Overseer, and Elder"* are all different names for the one position of a Pastor of a local Church. Scripturally, they refer to no office other than that position. Beginning in about the Third Century, or even before that, the Church began to apostatize, consequently, devising man-made positions, which had no Scriptural validity.)

CHURCH GOVERNMENT

In fact, some of these positions, such as Superintendent, or Overseer, etc., are not unscriptural as long as the individuals occupying these offices understand that they carry no Scriptural authority, but are administrative only. But regrettably, the incurable evil of the hearts of men quickly adopts that for which the Bible gives no authority, and claims these positions as one of Spiritual authority. As such, they sin!

The Man with a line in His Hand, as described in these Chapters, did not measure such. There is nothing in the New Testament that gives any higher Spiritual authority than the Apostle; however, such authority is always over demon spirits, and never over other people.

The local Pastor is, as well, given a very high position Scripturally, as it regards Church government.

When Jesus addressed His statement to the seven Churches of Asia, He did not address His Letter to any Denominational or Church headquarters, but, instead, to each individual Church, and, more particularly, to each individual Pastor (Rev., Chpts. 2-3). He did this because there was no such thing as a *"headquarters"* which served as a Spiritual authority over these Churches. Even Jerusalem had no Spiritual authority over the local Churches, which constituted what is referred to as the *"Early Church."*

Consequently, there was no such thing as a Denomination at that time, and there certainly was nothing such as a religious hierarchy. Remembering that Jesus is the

Builder of His Church, and that the Holy Spirit carried out this design, one should be very fearful of changing it (Mat. 16:18).

(9) "THUS SAITH THE LORD GOD; NO STRANGER, UNCIRCUMCISED IN HEART, NOR UNCIRCUMCISED IN FLESH, SHALL ENTER INTO MY SANCTUARY, OF ANY STRANGER WHO IS AMONG THE CHILDREN OF ISRAEL.

(10) "AND THE LEVITES WHO ARE GONE AWAY FAR FROM ME, WHEN ISRAEL WENT ASTRAY, WHICH WENT ASTRAY AWAY FROM ME AFTER THEIR IDOLS; THEY SHALL EVEN BEAR THEIR INIQUITY.

(11) "YET THEY SHALL BE MINISTERS IN MY SANCTUARY, HAVING CHARGE AT THE GATES OF THE HOUSE, AND MINISTERING TO THE HOUSE: THEY SHALL SLAY THE BURNT OFFERING AND THE SACRIFICE FOR THE PEOPLE, AND THEY SHALL STAND BEFORE THEM TO MINISTER UNTO THEM.

(12) "BECAUSE THEY MINISTERED UNTO THEM BEFORE THEIR IDOLS, AND CAUSED THE HOUSE OF ISRAEL TO FALL INTO INIQUITY; THEREFORE HAVE I LIFTED UP MY HAND AGAINST THEM, SAITH THE LORD GOD, AND THEY SHALL BEAR THEIR INIQUITY.

(13) "AND THEY SHALL NOT COME NEAR UNTO ME, TO DO THE OFFICE OF A PRIEST UNTO ME, NOR TO COME NEAR TO ANY OF MY HOLY THINGS, IN THE MOST HOLY PLACE: BUT THEY SHALL BEAR THEIR SHAME, AND THEIR ABOMINATIONS WHICH THEY HAVE COMMITTED.

(14) "BUT I WILL MAKE THEM KEEPERS OF THE CHARGE OF THE HOUSE, FOR ALL THE SERVICE THEREOF, AND FOR ALL THAT SHALL BE DONE THEREIN."

The exegesis is:

1. The Levites appointed to teach the Law turned from that Holy Book and taught man's way of salvation. In this they have many modern imitators.

2. As a consequence, they will be confined to the Court of the Priests and not permitted to enter the Temple itself. Such will be their punishment all through the Millennial Age.

3. God's Way is the Cross. To substitute something else presents itself as a gross sin, actually, one of the worst sins that one could commit.

THE STRANGER

The phrase of Verse 9, *"Thus saith the Lord GOD; No stranger, uncircumcised in heart, nor uncircumcised in flesh, shall enter into My Sanctuary,"* seems to refer to all Gentiles, and even certain Jews.

It seems in the coming Kingdom Age, that the Lord intends for Israel only to serve in the Temple, and even certain ones in Israel, *"the sons of Zadok,"* with the *"Levites"* in lesser positions. They are to be what He intended for them to be at the very beginning, *"a Kingdom of Priests"* (Ex. 19:6).

THE LEVITES

The phrase of Verse 10, *"And the Levites who are gone away far from me, when Israel went astray,"* delegates, in the following Verses, what they are to do as it regards service in the Sanctuary.

Verse 11 reads: *"Yet they shall be ministers in My Sanctuary, having charge at the gates of the House, and ministering to the House: they shall slay the Burnt Offering and the sacrifice for the people, and they shall stand before them to minister unto them."*

As is here given, the duties are laid out for the Levites, in which they are to render service throughout the Kingdom Age.

Some may think it cruel that this sentence be imposed upon these Levites who had nothing to do with the sins committed by their fathers nearly 3,000 years in the past; however, the Lord is not holding them responsible personally, but only the Order of Levites itself! Actually, it is Grace fueled by Love that affords them even this privilege, and a privilege it is to function in any capacity in the Sanctuary.

The phrase of Verse 12, *"Because they ministered unto them before their idols, and caused the House of Israel to fall into iniquity,"* refers to the Levites, who had a very honored and privileged position in the Sanctuary, and who were appointed to teach the

Law, but turned from the Word of God and inserted man's way, which has been the bane of humanity since the very beginning of time, at least in one way or the other.

This shows that corrupt leadership, and I speak of that which strays from the Word of God, will not only bring ruin to themselves, but to all those who have the misfortune of sitting under their preaching and teaching. To be sure, this will not absolve the hearers from responsibility, but it does mean that the bearer of false doctrine will be held doubly responsible!

The phrase of Verse 13, *"And they shall not come near unto Me, to do the Office of a Priest unto Me,"* portrays the Levites confined to the Court of the Priests and not permitted to enter the Temple itself. Such will be their punishment all through the Millennial Age.

The phrase of Verse 14, *"But I will make them keepers of the charge of the House,"* presents them privileged still!

As stated, to have any part in the Sanctuary, no matter how seemingly menial it might be, is still a privilege of unparalleled proportions. Every indication is that these Levites will discharge their duties with happiness and joy, thankful for the opportunity to do so, and realizing that Grace has given them this which they will have.

(15) "BUT THE PRIESTS THE LEVITES, THE SONS OF ZADOK, WHO KEPT THE CHARGE OF MY SANCTUARY WHEN THE CHILDREN OF ISRAEL WENT ASTRAY FROM ME, THEY SHALL COME NEAR TO ME, TO MINISTER UNTO ME, AND THEY SHALL STAND BEFORE ME TO OFFER UNTO ME THE FAT AND THE BLOOD, SAITH THE LORD GOD:

(16) "THEY SHALL ENTER INTO MY SANCTUARY, AND THEY SHALL COME NEAR TO MY TABLE, TO MINISTER UNTO ME, AND THEY SHALL KEEP MY CHARGE.

(17) "AND IT SHALL COME TO PASS, THAT WHEN THEY ENTER IN AT THE GATES OF THE INNER COURT, THEY SHALL BE CLOTHED WITH LINEN GARMENTS; AND NO WOOL SHALL COME UPON THEM, WHILE THEY MINISTER IN THE GATES OF THE INNER COURT, AND WITHIN.

NOTES

(18) "THEY SHALL HAVE LINEN BONNETS UPON THEIR HEADS, AND SHALL HAVE LINEN BREECHES UPON THEIR LOINS; THEY SHALL NOT GIRD THEMSELVES WITH ANY THING THAT CAUSES SWEAT.

(19) "AND WHEN THEY GO FORTH INTO THE UTTER COURT, EVEN INTO THE UTTER COURT TO THE PEOPLE, THEY SHALL PUT OFF THEIR GARMENTS WHEREIN THEY MINISTERED, AND LAY THEM IN THE HOLY CHAMBERS, AND THEY SHALL PUT ON OTHER GARMENTS; AND THEY SHALL NOT SANCTIFY THE PEOPLE WITH THEIR GARMENTS.

(20) "NEITHER SHALL THEY SHAVE THEIR HEADS, NOR SUFFER THEIR LOCKS TO GROW LONG; THEY SHALL ONLY POLL THEIR HEADS.

(21) "NEITHER SHALL ANY PRIEST DRINK WINE, WHEN THEY ENTER INTO THE INNER COURT.

(22) "NEITHER SHALL THEY TAKE FOR THEIR WIVES A WIDOW, NOR HER WHO IS PUT AWAY: BUT THEY SHALL TAKE MAIDENS OF THE SEED OF THE HOUSE OF ISRAEL, OR A WIDOW WHO HAD A PRIEST BEFORE.

(23) "AND THEY SHALL TEACH MY PEOPLE THE DIFFERENCE BETWEEN THE HOLY AND PROFANE, AND CAUSE THEM TO DISCERN BETWEEN THE UNCLEAN AND THE CLEAN.

(24) "AND IN CONTROVERSY THEY SHALL STAND IN JUDGMENT; AND THEY SHALL JUDGE IT ACCORDING TO MY JUDGMENTS: AND THEY SHALL KEEP MY LAWS AND MY STATUTES IN ALL MY ASSEMBLIES; AND THEY SHALL HALLOW MY SABBATHS.

(25) "AND THEY SHALL COME AT NO DEAD PERSON TO DEFILE THEMSELVES: BUT FOR FATHER, OR FOR MOTHER, OR FOR SON, OR FOR DAUGHTER, FOR BROTHER, OR FOR SISTER WHO HAS HAD NO HUSBAND, THEY MAY DEFILE THEMSELVES.

(26) "AND AFTER HE IS CLEANSED, THEY SHALL RECKON UNTO HIM SEVEN DAYS."

The synopsis is:

1. The *"fat and the blood"* of Verse 15 stand for prosperity and cleansing.

2. The *"linen garments,"* which the Priests were to wear, symbolize Righteousness — the Righteousness of Christ.

3. *"Sweat"* is not to be caused, symbolizing the fact that Salvation, and everything that goes with Salvation, is all by Grace and never by works.

THE SONS OF ZADOK

The phrase of Verse 15, *"But the Priests the Levites, the sons of Zadok, who kept the charge of My Sanctuary when the Children of Israel went astray from Me, they shall come near to Me, to minister unto Me,"* proclaims those of the Levites who are permitted to serve as Priests. All who functioned in Temple duties of any kind were to be of the Tribe of Levi, the Priestly Tribe; however, those of the family of Zadok alone will be permitted to serve as Priests, and due to the problems mentioned in previous Verses.

The phrase of Verse 16, *"They shall enter into My Sanctuary,"* proclaims their privilege.

I am certain that the other Levites who were assigned less responsible tasks, and because of the sins of their forefathers, had no complaint whatsoever. They will be delighted to have any part of the service at all! One can be assured that there will be no jealousy or envy on the part of these Levites regarding the *"sons of Zadok,"* who will do service in all the confines of the Temple.

LINEN GARMENTS

The phrase of Verse 17, *"They shall be clothed with linen garments,"* suggests the Righteousness of Christ, of which these garments were symbols.

The phrase, *"And no wool shall come upon them, while they minister,"* pertains to that which would cause sweat, and would, therefore, symbolize one's own efforts. *"Salvation is not of works, lest any should boast, it is the Gift of God"* (Eph. 2:8-9).

NO SWEAT

The phrase of Verse 18, *"They shall have linen bonnets upon their heads,"* implies that they are to understand, and understand fully, that their Righteousness is of Christ, and not at all of themselves.

The phrase, *"And shall have linen breeches upon their loins,"* symbolizes the truth that all that is done for Christ is due to His Righteousness freely imputed to us who believe, and not to our own abilities.

The phrase, *"They shall not gird themselves with any thing that causes sweat,"* is to signify that man's own efforts regarding Salvation can never be recognized by God. Therefore, all that man does to earn his Salvation, in Truth, earns nothing at all! Salvation is free, and, therefore, freely given, and must be freely received.

SALVATION AND THE CROSS

Salvation has to do with Faith and Faith alone, and refers to Faith exclusively in the Cross of Christ. If we attempt to make anything else the object of the our Faith, it is Faith, thereby, which God will not recognize.

And yet, this is the biggest problem faced by the Christian. God recognizes no one except His Son, and our Saviour, the Lord Jesus Christ. As a result, He recognizes nothing but that which Christ has done as it regards our Redemption, and I continue to speak of the Cross. Anything else is out! In fact, as previously stated, the entire story of the Bible is the story of Jesus Christ and Him Crucified. Any deviation from that can never be accepted by the Lord, can never be blessed by the Lord.

THE OUTER COURT

The phrase of Verse 19, *"And when they go forth into the Utter Court,"* pertains to the fact that they had been attending to their duties in the Inner Court. While attending to the Sacrifices, which were holy, the Priests were to wear certain types of garments, which signified such holiness, i.e., the Righteousness of Christ. These were the linen garments.

However, when they finished these duties and went to the *"Outer Court,"* they were to change from these holy garments, and *"put on other garments."*

The phrase, *"And they shall not sanctify the people with their garments,"* speaking of the linen garments, is meant to make a statement.

The statement is simple: Man is unholy, while Christ is holy! As well, there is nothing that man can do within himself to obtain holiness, except freely admit that he is unholy, and throw himself on the Mercy and Grace of Jesus Christ, Who will then freely impute to the Believer Holiness and Righteousness. In other words, to qualify, one has to be unqualified, and know it.

The idea of all of this is, the Priests could not transfer their Righteousness to the people, which Righteousness their linen garments signify. In other words, Righteousness can never be of ritual or ceremony; therefore, to make this crystal clear to the people, their linen garments were not to be worn in the Outer Court.

HAIR

Verse 20 reads: *"Neither shall they shave their heads, nor suffer their locks to grow long; they shall only poll their heads."*

The *"shaved head"* was a symbol of dependence on self, and not on the Lord. In a sense, the hair signified man's need for God.

Conversely, long hair on a man symbolizes weakness. Inasmuch as the Priests were types of Christ, they could not show weakness, hence they were not to have long hair.

They were merely, at certain times, to cut their hair, leaving it so as it would not be shaved or long.

STRONG DRINK

Verse 21 reads: *"Neither shall any Priest drink wine when they enter into the Inner Court."*

The Hebrew word for *"wine"* used here is *"yayan,"* and, in this case, means *"an intoxicating beverage,"* in other words, the kind of drink that will make one drunk.

If it is to be remembered, Nadab and Abihu, sons of Aaron, offered up strange fire before the Lord, which means they selected coals of fire from some other ignition other than the Brazen Altar, which typified the Cross. They placed this *"strange fire"* on the Altar of Incense, which stood immediately before the Veil, which led to the Holy of Holies. They were stricken dead immediately (Lev. 10:1-2).

The idea is, the Brazen Altar stood for the Cross of Christ, and the price that He paid for the Redemption of humanity. The Altar of Incense stood for the Intercession of Christ before the Father, even at the Throne of God, all on our behalf (Heb. 1:3; 7:25). Intercession is made on our behalf, solely by and through what Jesus did at the Cross, hence the command being that all coals of fire placed on the Altar of Incense must come from the Brazen Altar, as stated, which was a type of the Cross (Heb. 10:12-14).

The evidence is, Nadab and Abihu were drunk when they offered up this *"strange fire."* The Scripture plainly said: *"Do not drink wine nor strong drink, you, nor your sons with you, when you go into the Tabernacle of the congregation, lest you die: it shall be a Statute forever throughout your generations"* (Lev. 10:9).

The idea is not offered here, as it would seem to be on the surface, that it was satisfactory to drink elsewhere. The idea is, no intoxicating beverage must be consumed at all, not even a small amount. The Priests, under the Old Economy of God, had to offer up Incense twice a day, seven days a week. While all of this was done by courses, meaning that the Priests only served a few weeks out of the year, whichever period of time was their course, still, the ruling held permanently.

THE REAL CAUSE OF DEATH

While strong drink played a part in the deaths of Nadab and Abihu, of that scene so long ago, the alcohol was a result of their real sin, which was that they ignored the Cross. In other words, they tried to effect Intercession without the benefit of the Cross. This means that anything that diverts our total allegiance to *"Jesus Christ and Him Crucified"* must be avoided at all cost. That's why Paul said:

"And be not drunk with wine wherein is excess; but be filled with the Spirit" (Eph. 5:18).

The *"wine"* symbolizes the ways of the world, while, of course, the Holy Sprit portrays that which is of the Lord.

If one follows the Holy Spirit, which is referred to as *"walking after the Spirit,"* then one will know total and complete victory.

HOW DO WE WALK AFTER THE SPIRIT?

Paul said: *"There is therefore now no condemnation to them which are in Christ Jesus, who walk not after the flesh, but after the Spirit"* (Rom. 8:1).

Someone sent me, through the mail, a study course taught by a particular Preacher, and, incidentally, a man who had been a dear friend of mine, but who is now with the Lord. In fact, he was one of the greatest men of God I ever personally knew. The title of the course was *"Walking in the Spirit."* While the information given was excellent, in actuality it told no one how to *"walk after the Spirit,"* but rather what would happen after one was walking after the Spirit. The truth is, one doesn't have to be too much concerned as to what will happen after one *"walks after the Spirit,"* and because, for all practical purposes, that will, by and large, take care of itself. The great question is *"How does one walk after the Spirit?"* That is the question.

In truth it's very simple! It seems complicated, simply because all the methods proposed, which are varied and many, are devised by man, which means they aren't devised by God, which means, in simple terminology, that following these methods will not fall out to *"walking after the Spirit,"* but rather *"walking after the flesh."*

First of all, the word *"walk,"* as it's used by Paul, refers to the manner in which we order our behavior; in other words, how one lives for the Lord. It is our *"daily walk before the Lord,"* and done so on a perpetual basis.

We are told in the phrase, *"Walking after the Spirit,"* that the only way this can successfully be done is by the Holy Spirit accomplishing the task. The truth is, it is impossible for any Believer, even the Godliest, even the most dedicated, to *"walk"* as one should walk, if he tries to do so by his own willpower, strength, and ability.

So, knowing that the Holy Spirit is the only One Who can carry out in our lives what needs to be carried out, we need to know how He does these things.

The first thing we must realize is, the help of the Holy Spirit is not an automatic process. Were it an automatic process for Believers, there would never be a single failure of any nature or kind, which should be overly obvious. But considering that there are many failures in the hearts and lives of Christians, it becomes overly obvious that the work and help of the Spirit are not automatic.

We are given the key to walking after the Spirit in Romans 8:2. Paul there said:

"For the Law (a Law devised by the Godhead in eternity past) *of the Spirit* (Holy Spirit) *of life* (all life flows from Christ by the means of the Cross, but is delegated by the Holy Spirit) *in Christ Jesus* (this short phrase refers to what Christ did on the Cross, by and through which the Holy Spirit works) *has made me free from the Law of sin and death."*

IN CHRIST JESUS

Anytime Paul uses the short phrase, *"in Christ Jesus,"* or one of its derivatives, such as *"in Him,"* etc., which he does well over 100 times in his fourteen Epistles, without exception he is referring to what Christ did at the Cross. Consequently, and according to the teaching of the great Apostle, which incidentally the Holy Spirit gave to him, the subject matter of our faith must always be the Cross. While we certainly must have faith that the Holy Spirit will carry out this great work within our lives, the emphasis must always be on what makes all of this possible, which is Christ Jesus and what He did at the Cross.

That's the reason that Jesus said, and concerning the Holy Spirit: *"Howbeit when He, the Spirit of Truth is come, He will guide you into all Truth: for He shall not speak of Himself; but whatsoever He shall hear, that shall He speak: and He will show you things to come.*

"He shall glorify Me: for He shall receive of Mine, and shall show it unto you" (Jn. 16:13-14).

When Jesus spoke about *"receiving of Mine,"* He was speaking of what He did at the Cross, and that the Holy Spirit would show this, the things He there did for us, to us.

So, *"walking after the Spirit"* refers to understanding that it is the Spirit of God

Who Alone can carry out in our lives what needs to be carried out. And the way He does this is by and through what Jesus did at the Cross, hence, the phrase constantly being used, *"in Christ Jesus."* According to Romans, Chapter 6, we as Believers, and on an unending basis, are to place our Faith exclusively in Christ and what He did for us at the Cross, ever understanding, and even as we have constantly stated, that the Source is Jesus and the Means is the Cross. When we place our faith exclusively in the Cross, and leave our faith exclusively in the Cross, understanding that all things the Lord does for us comes 100 percent through the Sacrifice of Christ, that is *"walking after the Spirit."*

PERSONAL RELATIONSHIPS

The phrase of Verse 22, *"Neither shall they take for their wives a widow, nor her who is put away,"* proclaims a higher standard than is normal. In fact, as to whom the Priest could marry is given in Verse 22.

All of this tells us that celibacy is not advised or sanctioned, except in certain cases; hence, the celibacy of the Roman Catholic Priests has occasioned untold problems for the Catholic Church, in that it is unnatural and unscriptural.

Celibacy is certainly not wrong, providing that is what the Lord wants one to do, which in fact He did want Paul to do; however, that was the exception and not the norm.

THE UNCLEAN AND THE CLEAN

Verse 23 reads: *"And they* (the Priests) *shall teach My people the difference between the holy and profane, and cause them to discern between the unclean and the clean."*

The *"difference"* between the *"holy and profane"* and the *"unclean and the clean"* has always been the duty of the God-called Preacher of the Gospel, whether as Priests under the Old Economy, or the new one to come, or Preachers under the New Covenant. That's the reason Paul told Timothy: *"I charge you therefore before God, and the Lord Jesus Christ, Who shall judge the quick* (living) *and the dead at His appearing and His Kingdom;*

"Preach the Word; be instant in season,

NOTES

out of season; reprove, rebuke, exhort with all longsuffering and Doctrine" (II Tim. 4:1-2).

This means that the Preacher of the Gospel is to plainly and clearly state, *"This is wrong, and that is right."* This means that such a Preacher is not looking for people who have itching ears, that he might tell them what they want to hear. The true Preacher will hear from God and tell the people what they need to hear, irrespective as to their response. And if the Preacher doesn't do this, who will?

Some Preachers brag that they never preach anything but a positive Gospel. They should stop and think that for something to be positive, at the same time, something must be negative. Perhaps the following should be looked at a little more closely:

There was a day that Preachers preached a lot of negative Gospel, which fell out to a lot of positive living. Nowadays, it seems that most preach a positive Gospel exclusively, which falls out to negative living.

While the Preacher definitely must not be opposed to all things, he definitely must be opposed to some things, and should say so. The Scripture plainly tells us here that some things are *"holy"* and some things are *"unholy,"* i.e. *"profane."* Some things are *"unclean"* and some things are *"clean."* We should carefully delineate between the two, as to where the people will have absolutely no doubt as to what we are saying.

Far too many Preachers are, in reality, politicians, who try to say things that will offend no one, and satisfy everybody. As a result, they actually say nothing!

JUDGMENT

The phrase of Verse 24, *"And in controversy they shall stand in Judgment,"* refers to the fact, that if the Preacher preaches what he ought to preach, it will definitely be controversial. Many Preachers oppose things that almost everyone else opposes; in other words, it causes no controversy; however, how many Preachers oppose things which are definitely wrong, and we refer to being unscriptural, when, in fact, the error is accepted by most all?

As an example, the Word of Faith doctrine, which is presently prevalent, and to which we have addressed ourselves many times in this Volume, is accepted by most of the Church, and especially the Pentecostal and Charismatic varieties. In fact, almost all the Charismatics accept this erroneous doctrine.

So to cry out against this error guarantees that there is going to be a controversy, and, thereby, guarantees much opposition. Most Preachers, to be factual, simply don't want the controversy or the opposition. So they say nothing, which is exactly what Satan wants and desires.

In fact, the Lord has instructed this Ministry (Jimmy Swaggart Ministries) to *"prophesy against these false prophets"* (Ezek. 13:2). While virtually every Minister in our organization is being used of the Lord in this capacity, it is Donnie who has taken the brunt of the opposition, and because the voice with which he speaks, I personally believe, is a Prophetic Voice. Nevertheless, irrespective of the opposition, or even persecution, as a true Minister of the Gospel, we must not be *"disobedient to the heavenly vision."*

The phrase of Verse 24, *"And they shall judge it according to My Judgments,"* refers to the fact that everything must be judged according to the Word of God. It is *"His Judgments"* and not ours, or anyone else, for that matter. The question must always be, *"Is it Scriptural?"* If it's not, we must cry out against it, for the Word of God is the criteria.

DEATH

The phrase of Verse 25, *"And they shall come at no dead person to defile themselves,"* has some exceptions, as the balance of the Verse brings out; however, the Priests will not be allowed to touch any dead person, with the exception of very close relatives. The reason being, death is symbolic of the fruit of sin, and, therefore, the prohibition (Rom. 6:23).

As well, this Passage tells us that certain people will die during the coming Kingdom Age. In other words, death will not be totally eradicated; however, it will only be in rare cases, where individuals have rebelled against God, and, therefore, commit death penalty sins, and, as such, have

NOTES

to be executed (Isa. 65:20).

Or quite possibly, some will refuse to eat of the *"leaves"* and *"fruit"* that will grow on the trees which will be situated on either side of the Millennial River (Ezek. 47:7, 12), which will be for *"medicine,"* and will keep people alive and youthful indefinitely!

There will be a healing and preservation of life qualities about these *"leaves"* and *"fruit,"* which will cause human bodies to live on and on, without sickness and disease. It is inconceivable that some people may refuse to eat of this provision; however, considering the incurable evil of the human heart, it should be no surprise.

However, in comparison to the present, deaths will be few and far between in this coming glad time.

SEVEN DAYS

Verse 26 reads: *"And after he* (the Priest) *is cleansed, they shall reckon unto him seven days."*

The number *"seven"* is God's number, and speaks, at least in this case, of the perfect Salvation afforded by Christ from the terrible wages of sin, which is death.

If Priests have to touch a dead body, they will be required to go through a ceremonial cleansing for some seven days.

(27) "AND IN THE DAY THAT HE GOES INTO THE SANCTUARY, UNTO THE INNER COURT, TO MINISTER IN THE SANCTUARY, HE SHALL OFFER HIS SIN OFFERING, SAITH THE LORD GOD.

(28) "AND IT SHALL BE UNTO THEM FOR AN INHERITANCE: I AM THEIR INHERITANCE: AND YOU SHALL GIVE THEM NO POSSESSION IN ISRAEL: I AM THEIR POSSESSION.

(29) "THEY SHALL EAT THE MEAT OFFERING, AND THE SIN OFFERING, AND THE TRESPASS OFFERING: AND EVERY DEDICATED THING IN ISRAEL SHALL BE THEIRS.

(30) "AND THE FIRST OF ALL THE FIRSTFRUITS OF ALL THINGS, AND EVERY OBLATION OF ALL, OF EVERY SORT OF YOUR OBLATIONS, SHALL BE THE PRIEST'S: YOU SHALL ALSO GIVE UNTO THE PRIEST THE FIRST OF YOUR DOUGH, THAT HE MAY CAUSE THE

BLESSING TO REST IN YOUR HOUSE.

(31) "THE PRIESTS SHALL NOT EAT OF ANY THING THAT IS DEAD OF ITSELF, OR TORN, WHETHER IT BE FOWL OR BEAST."

The composition is:

1. In the offering up of sacrifices, which will be carried out throughout the Millennial Reign, it will be shown that Calvary is the Divine center of God's purposes of Grace and wrath.

2. It is conceivable that only by such object lessons will it be possible to properly interpret the Book of Leviticus to the various nations of the Millennium Earth, and, in this way, to vindicate God's action in the past and in the future.

3. Israel, having in the past failed to observe the legislation of Leviticus, and so to testify of the one great Sacrifice that was to come, must, by the perfect observance of the future sacrifices, witness of an Atoning Saviour Who has come.

THE SIN OFFERING

The phrase of Verse 27, *"He shall offer his Sin Offering, saith the Lord GOD,"* proclaims the fact, that upon the touching of a dead body, even the closest of relatives, the Priest is required to offer his Sin Offering. The *"Sin Offering"* secured relationships, for such had been broken because of pollution and contamination. It was not so much that the Priest willfully sinned, but that his required duties, which pertained to the touching of a dead body, even a close relative, spoke of the awful effects of sin; consequently, this had to be cleansed, and could only be done so by the *"Sin Offering,"* which demanded *"a young bullock."* In this, one should realize the horror of sin.

All of this tells us, and in no uncertain terms, that the Cross of Christ is the only solution for sin.

Even though the stipulation will be incumbent upon the Priests, it will not apply to all others, as they will continue to function under Grace, and the New Covenant.

In reality, these Offerings by the Priests are symbolic only, as they effect no cleansing from sin, but merely reflect what Christ did at Calvary, and will serve as a constant reminder of that terrible price that was paid.

THE INHERITANCE

The phrase of Verse 28, *"And it shall be unto them for an inheritance,"* proclaims that all Priests should have as their possession Jehovah, and not any territorial possession or tribal tract, such as should be assigned to the other Tribes (Ezek., Chpt. 48). However, this is not a negative, but rather a positive, in that the life wholly surrendered in heart to the Lord, which will typify these *"sons of Zadok,"* ensures the Lord giving the best of everything, for He is the greatest Inheritance of all, and by far!

The phrase, *"I am their possession,"* speaks of fellowship, communion, and relationship. This is the highest form of Blessing.

EATING THE OFFERINGS

Verse 29 reads: *"They shall eat the Meat Offering, and the Sin Offering, and the Trespass Offering: and every dedicated thing in Israel shall be theirs."*

The eating of these *"Offerings"* means the animal is killed, and then the skin is pulled from the carcass. As well, the fat is removed from certain body organs and burned on the Altar. The blood is poured out at the base of the Altar.

The Priests then could take the balance of the carcass for themselves, with the eating of these portions symbolizing what Christ said about Himself:

"I am the Living Bread which came down from Heaven: if any man eat of this Bread, he shall live forever: and the Bread that I will give is My flesh, which I will give for the life of the world" (Jn. 6:51).

The way that one now *"eats the flesh of the Son of God, and drinks His Blood"* is to place his faith in Christ and what Christ did at the Cross, in the giving of Himself. It does not have a literal meaning, as it was not supposed to have a literal meaning.

The *"eating of His flesh"* constitutes the Believer accepting, without reservation, what Christ did at the Cross in the giving of Himself in Sacrifice.

In the coming Kingdom Age, the Priests, in the eating of these Sacrifices, will symbolically portray to the world Who Christ is and what Christ has done.

THE BLESSING ON THE HOUSE

Verse 30 says, *"And the first of all the firstfruits of all things, and every oblation of all, of every sort of your oblations* (the sacrifices), *shall be the Priest's,"* presents itself as symbolic of Christ, and the Offerings which we as Believers bring to Him.

As this will be true of Israel in that coming glad day, and I speak of the *"blessings to rest upon their houses,"* it is likewise true at present under the New Covenant.

When the Believer gives to the Work of God, and we speak of the *"firstfruits,"* which speaks of a *"tithe,"* thereby giving such to Christ and His Work, we are assured that the *"Blessing will rest upon our house."* What a beautiful Promise!

As well, all of this infers that if we do not obey the Lord as it regards the firstfruits of our increase, the Blessing will cease. As stated, as it will be true in the coming Kingdom Age, as it regards Israel, it is true presently as well.

THE SACRIFICE

Verse 31 reads: *"The Priests shall not eat of anything that is dead of itself, or torn, whether it be fowl or beast."*

The idea is that the animals brought for Sacrifice must not be animals that have died of natural causes, or killed by other beasts, but, instead, the healthiest of the healthy. The Lord gives His best, and He demands, as He should, our best.

However, the real meaning here has to do with Cross of Calvary. The death of Christ was not an incident, accident, assassination, or execution. It was a Sacrifice, meaning that He freely laid down His Life, and, as well, took it up again. In fact, He said:

"Therefore does My Father love Me, because I lay down My Life, that I may take it again.

"No man takes it from Me, but I lay it down of Myself. I have power to lay it down, and I have power to take it again" (Jn. 10:17-18).

While it definitely is true that both the Jews and the Romans killed Christ, still, they were able to do so only because He allowed such. But the idea is, His death was a *"Sacrifice,"* which was necessary in order that the sin debt be paid, thereby satisfying the Righteousness of God, which, in turn, would redeem fallen man, that is, upon proper faith (Jn. 3:16; Rom. 10:9-10, 13; Rev. 22:17).

Thus Calvary, in all of this, is shown to be the Divine Center of God's purposes of Grace and Wrath.

> *"Gracious Spirit, dwell with me: I myself would gracious be;*
> *"And with words that help and heal,*
> *"Would Thy life in mine reveal;*
> *"And with actions bold and meek, would for Christ My Saviour speak."*
>
> *"Truthful Spirit, dwell with me: I myself would truthful be;*
> *"And, with wisdom kind and clear,*
> *"Let Your life in mine appear;*
> *"And with actions brotherly, speak my Lord's sincerity."*
>
> *"Mighty Spirit, dwell with me: I myself would mighty be;*
> *"Mighty so as to prevail*
> *"Where unaided man must fail;*
> *"Ever by a mighty hope pressing on and bearing up."*
>
> *"Holy Spirit, dwell with me: I myself would holy be;*
> *"Separate from sin, I would choose and cherish all things good;*
> *"And whatever I can be*
> *"Give to Him Who gave Me Thee."*

CHAPTER 45

(1) "MOREOVER, WHEN YOU SHALL DIVIDE BY LOT THE LAND FOR INHERITANCE, YOU SHALL OFFER AN OBLATION UNTO THE LORD, AN HOLY PORTION OF THE LAND: THE LENGTH SHALL BE THE LENGTH OF FIVE AND TWENTY THOUSAND REEDS, AND THE BREADTH SHALL BE TEN THOUSAND. THIS SHALL BE HOLY IN ALL THE BORDERS THEREOF ROUND ABOUT.

(2) "OF THIS THERE SHALL BE FOR THE SANCTUARY FIVE HUNDRED IN

LENGTH, WITH FIVE HUNDRED IN BREADTH, SQUARE ROUND ABOUT; AND FIFTY CUBITS ROUND ABOUT FOR THE SUBURBS THEREOF.

(3) "AND OF THIS MEASURE SHALL YOU MEASURE THE LENGTH OF FIVE AND TWENTY THOUSAND, AND THE BREADTH OF TEN THOUSAND: AND IN IT SHALL BE THE SANCTUARY AND THE MOST HOLY PLACE.

(4) "THE HOLY PORTION OF THE LAND SHALL BE FOR THE PRIESTS THE MINISTERS OF THE SANCTUARY, WHICH SHALL COME NEAR TO MINISTER UNTO THE LORD: AND IT SHALL BE A PLACE FOR THEIR HOUSES, AND AN HOLY PLACE FOR THE SANCTUARY.

(5) "AND THE FIVE AND TWENTY THOUSAND OF LENGTH, AND THE TEN THOUSAND OF BREADTH SHALL ALSO THE LEVITES, THE MINISTERS OF THE HOUSE, HAVE FOR THEMSELVES, FOR A POSSESSION FOR TWENTY CHAMBERS."

The exegesis is:

1. The *"Oblation"* addressed here speaks of the entirety of the city which will be built, but more particularly, of the Temple area, and most specific of all, the Great Altar, where Sacrifices are offered. All of this is a Gift to the Lord, so to speak, which means that it will be totally set apart for His Service

2. This city, so to speak, will be 45 miles x 45 miles, in other words, 45 miles wide and 45 miles long. These numbers are correct, if, in fact, the cubit is actually 18 inches long. As previously stated, it has been judged at various different lengths.

3. The possessions of the Levites and of the Priests will be equal, i.e., 45 miles x 18 miles each. The Sanctuary will stand at the center of the Priests' possession.

4. The Sanctuary will occupy an area of about 1 square mile.

THE OBLATION

The phrase of Verse 1, *"Moreover, when you shall divide by lot the land for inheritance, you shall offer an oblation unto the LORD, an holy portion of the Land,"* has to do with the entirety of the city, and, in fact, it will be the capital city of the world. It is *"holy"* because it represents Christ and what He did at Calvary in order to redeem humanity. The Temple will form the center of the *"Oblation,"* which refers to a Gift to the Lord, and because it is to be used strictly for His Holy Purposes.

The Temple forming the center of the *"Oblation,"* with the Great Altar sitting in the exact geographical center of the world, will, in effect, so to speak, be the nerve center of the world.

As stated, the length of this city will be approximately 45 miles, with the width being approximately the same thing; however, it is divided up into several sections, with at least a couple of those sections being 10,000 reeds wide, totaling approximately 18 miles.

THE SANCTUARY

The phrase of Verse 2, *"Of this there shall be for the Sanctuary five hundred in length, with five hundred in breadth, a square round about,"* probably refers to cubits. This would mean it would be 750 feet square. This area includes not only the Outer Court, but the Inner Court, as well as the Temple and Altar area. All of it is looked at primarily as the *"Sanctuary."*

THE MEASURE

The phrase of Verse 3, *"And of this measure shall you measure the length of five and twenty thousand, and the breadth of ten thousand,"* refers to the particular area in which the Sanctuary will be located. This means it is not a repetition of Verse 1, but is explanatory and additional.

The phrase of Verse 4, *"The holy portion of the land shall be for the Priests the ministers of the Sanctuary,"* refers not only to the area occupied by the Sanctuary, but, as well, the *"houses"* of the Priests. So, in that area of approximately 45 miles long and 18 miles wide will be the most strategic part of this city, housing the Temple area, as well as the domiciles of the Priests, so they will have ready access to the Temple services, where will be the area of their ministry.

THE LEVITES

Verse 5 proclaims the fact that the Levites will have an area the same size as those of the Priests, approximately 45 miles x 18 miles. In other words, their portion will be, as it regards size, the same as the portion of the Priests.

All Priests are Levites, but all Levites are not Priests; nevertheless, to serve in any type of function concerning the Sanctuary, one must be a Levite; therefore, these, although having less sacred duties than the Priests, *"the sons of Zadok,"* still, attend to many functions pertaining to the Sanctuary, although not the Sacrifices.

The statement in Verse 5, *"a possession for twenty Chambers,"* pertains to dwelling houses, and, no doubt, refers to sections of houses, in other words, twenty to a section, etc.

(6) "AND YOU SHALL APPOINT THE POSSESSION OF THE CITY FIVE THOUSAND BROAD, AND FIVE AND TWENTY THOUSAND LONG, OVER AGAINST HE OBLATION OF THE HOLY PORTION: IT SHALL BE FOR THE WHOLE HOUSE OF ISRAEL.

(7) "AND A PORTION SHALL BE FOR THE PRINCE ON THE ONE SIDE AND ON THE OTHER SIDE OF THE OBLATION OF THE HOLY PORTION, AND OF THE POSSESSION OF THE CITY, BEFORE THE OBLATION OF THE HOLY PORTION, AND BEFORE THE POSSESSION OF THE CITY, FROM THE WEST SIDE WESTWARD, AND FROM THE EAST SIDE EASTWARD: AND THE LENGTH SHALL BE OVER AGAINST ONE OF THE PORTIONS, FROM THE WEST BORDER UNTO THE EAST BORDER.

(8) "IN THE LAND SHALL BE HIS POSSESSION IN ISRAEL: AND MY PRINCES SHALL NO MORE OPPRESS MY PEOPLE; AND THE REST OF THE LAND SHALL THEY GIVE TO THE HOUSE OF ISRAEL ACCORDING TO THEIR TRIBES."

The diagram is:

1. This Great Square of 45 miles to the side, concerning the city, will be sub-divided into three portions: the possession of the Levites on the north, the possession of the Priests in the center, and the possession of the City in the south. Actually, I have labeled the entirety of the area as the *"City,"* although it is sectioned off, as is here obvious.

NOTES

2. God's love for man, and His hatred of injustice, appear in His making His Dwelling-Place among them.

3. This will be the governmental center of the world, all centered up in Christ, and based upon His Substitutionary Atonement.

THE CITY

The phrase of Verse 6, *"And you shall appoint the possession of the city five thousand broad, and five and twenty thousand long,"* refers to an area approximately 45 miles long and about 9 miles wide.

This will be the area where business is conducted, as in any major city; however, this city will have no slums, no gangs of criminals, and, in fact, no crime of any kind. Neither will there be alcohol, nicotine, drugs, or immorality.

To the majority of the world, at least presently speaking, this will be a dull city; however, they would reckon accordingly simply because they have no knowledge of the Lord or His Presence. Actually, it will be the most exciting, glorious, and wonderful city the world, up to that time, has ever known. The Presence of the Lord will give it a fervor, and a sense of well-being, such as man has never experienced, and all because of Christ.

Actually, the entirety of the Land will bask in prosperity, well-being, and growth. What with the huge amounts of money now being spent for weapons and armaments being spent, at that time, for development, government will function as it should!

As well, there will be equal distribution, without the majority of the wealth given over to a tiny percentage, while the majority suffer! Distribution will be fair and equal with plenty for all. And, as stated, it is all because of Christ, and what He has done for us at the Cross.

The phrase, *"It shall be for the whole house of Israel,"* refers to the fact that this will actually not be a Gentile city, but rather a Jewish city. Israel will now be in her rightful place, as the leading nation in the world, which God always intended, but under Christ. To be sure, they tried it without Christ, but it miserably failed, as fail it must; but with Christ, there can be no failure.

THE PRINCE

The phrase of Verse 7, *"And a portion shall be for the Prince on the one side and on the other side of the Oblation of the Holy Portion,"* doesn't tell us exactly how large these *"portions"* will be; as well, the indication is that, whatever size the portions will be, they will lie on both sides of the Holy Portions, i.e., the portions of the Priests and the Levites.

The *"Prince"* will probably be the High Priest, and he will be in charge of all Millennial worship (Vss. 16-17).

GOVERNMENT

The phrase of Verse 8, *"In the land shall be His possession in Israel: and My Princes shall no more oppress My people,"* proclaims the fact that all rulers, at that time, who will serve under Christ, will deal honestly, forthrightly, and circumspectly. As such, honest government is guaranteed. As well, it will serve as a model for the rest of the world, as portrayed in the next Verse.

(9) "THUS SAITH THE LORD GOD; LET IT SUFFICE YOU, O PRINCES OF ISRAEL: REMOVE VIOLENCE AND SPOIL, AND EXECUTE JUDGMENT AND JUSTICE, TAKE AWAY YOUR EXACTIONS FROM MY PEOPLE, SAITH THE LORD GOD.

(10) "YOU SHALL HAVE JUST BALANCES, AND A JUST EPHAH, AND A JUST BATH.

(11) "THE EPHAH AND THE BATH SHALL BE OF ONE MEASURE THAT THE BATH MAY CONTAIN THE TENTH PART OF AN HOMER, AND THE EPHAH THE TENTH PART OF AN HOMER: THE MEASURE THEREOF SHALL BE AFTER THE HOMER.

(12) "AND THE SHEKEL SHALL BE TWENTY GERAHS: TWENTY SHEKELS, FIVE AND TWENTY SHEKELS, FIFTEEN SHEKELS, SHALL BE YOUR MANEH.

(13) "THIS IS THE OBLATION THAT YOU SHALL OFFER; THE SIXTH PART OF AN EPHAH OF AN HOMER OF WHEAT, AND YOU SHALL GIVE THE SIXTH PART OF AN EPHAH OF AN HOMER OF BARLEY:

(14) "CONCERNING THE ORDINANCE OF OIL, THE BATH OF OIL, YOU SHALL OFFER THE TENTH PART OF A BATH OUT OF THE COR, WHICH IS AN HOMER OF TEN BATHS; FOR TEN BATHS ARE AN HOMER.

(15) "AND ONE LAMB OUT OF THE FLOCK, OUT OF TWO HUNDRED, OUT OF THE FAT PASTURES OF ISRAEL; FOR A MEAT OFFERING, AND FOR A BURNT OFFERING, AND FOR PEACE OFFERINGS, TO MAKE RECONCILIATION FOR THEM, SAITH THE LORD GOD.

(16) "ALL THE PEOPLE OF THE LAND SHALL GIVE THIS OBLATION FOR THE PRINCE IN ISRAEL.

(17) "AND IT SHALL BE THE PRINCE'S PART TO GIVE BURNT OFFERINGS, AND MEAT OFFERINGS, AND DRINK OFFERINGS, IN THE FEASTS, AND IN THE NEW MOONS, AND IN THE SABBATHS, IN ALL SOLEMNITIES OF THE HOUSE OF ISRAEL: HE SHALL PREPARE THE SIN OFFERING, AND THE MEAT OFFERING, AND THE BURNT OFFERING, AND THE PEACE OFFERINGS, TO MAKE RECONCILIATION FOR THE HOUSE OF ISRAEL."

The construction is:

1. The *"homer"* equals about 8 bushels. An *"omer"* equals a little bit short of a bushel.

2. For the first time, the world will know honesty, as it must know honesty.

3. The *"Offerings,"* i.e., *"Sacrifices,"* will be offered continually, once again, as a constant reminder of what Jesus has done at the Cross, which makes this glorious prosperity possible.

HONESTY

Verses 9 through 12 proclaim the honesty that must prevail if any nation, and in this case the world, is to be what it ought to be.

Regrettably, up until that coming day, the world, except perhaps in some isolated cases, and for short periods of time, if that, has never known fairness, equality, and justice, and due to the corrupt and wicked hearts of men. However, in the coming Kingdom Age, when Christ rules supreme, the *"crooked shall be made straight"* (Isa. 40:4).

Incidentally, the *"shekel,"* as it is portrayed in Verse 12, should be worth about $15 in 2003 currency. This alone tells us how strong the currency will be in that day, and, as well, it will not suffer inflation or deflation, but will retain its integrity.

SUPPORT

The word *"oblation"* sets the stage for Verses 13 through 15.

The word *"oblation"* means that which is offered as a Sacrifice or Gift to the Lord.

The amounts represented here are the equivalency in money and are to be given to the Sanctuary by all Israelites, in order to support the rulers of Israel.

It is not certain whether each person is to give the amount stipulated, or a representative head of each family; however, several things are noted as a result of these commands:

1. All in Israel will be so wealthy that this will present no burden whatsoever, and, actually, will be considered a joy and privilege.

2. As the wealth of the people is abundant, likewise, an abundance will be given for the rulers of Israel, which will guarantee their comfortable upkeep.

3. There will never be a shortage of ingredients for the Sacrifices, as there were many times under the old Law of Moses.

4. If one is to notice, the honesty and integrity of *"just weights,"* and the stability of the economy, are tied to the Offerings given to the Lord. This, at least in part, guarantees the prosperity of not only Israel, but the entirety of the world.

However, this is not something new, as God has always generously blessed those who give to His Work; therefore, what is done then, the giving to the Lord, which will include everyone, now only includes a precious few, hence, the poverty that grips most of the world.

THE OFFERINGS

Verse 17 proclaims the fact that *"Burnt Offerings,"* and *"Meat Offerings,"* and *"Drink Offerings,"* and *"Peace Offerings"* will be offered constantly in Israel during the Kingdom Age. Although not mentioned here, *"Trespass Offerings"* and *"Sin Offerings"* will be included as well; in other words, the entirety of the fivefold Offerings of the Levitical Law, which were practiced by Israel by the command of the Lord during the centuries before the Cross, will be reinstituted in the Kingdom Age.

These *"Offerings"* all symbolized Christ, in His Substitutionary, Mediatorial, Intercessory, Atoning Work, regarding the Redemption of humanity.

RECONCILIATION

The phrase, *"To make reconciliation for the House of Israel,"* refers to Atonement; however, this is to be ever understood, that it is only symbolic, as Christ has already made Atonement, thereby reconciling Israel, as well as all of the world, to God, by His death at Calvary.

The offering up of these Sacrifices, and on a continuous basis, at least throughout the Kingdom Age, will be a constant reminder to Israel, as well as the entirety of the world, that the great peace and prosperity that will reign on the Earth at that time, and, above all, the Redemption of humanity, were all brought about as a result of the price paid by Christ at the Cross of Calvary. Over and over again, and in every conceivable way possible, the Holy Spirit constantly emphasizes and re-emphasizes this obvious Truth. It is through the Cross that every Blessing comes from God. It is through the Cross that every Blessing is made possible. It is through the Cross that man can be reconciled to God, and only through the Cross. It is through the Cross that the Christian presently can live a victorious, overcoming, Christian life, and, once again, only through the Cross!

As surely we here see the obvious, it is impossible to overstate the Cross, to overemphasize the Cross. In fact, the crowning sin of the Church is the making too little of the Cross, or ignoring it altogether! The Scripture ever says, *"For God so loved the world, that He gave . . ."* (Jn. 3:16). That which He gave was His Only Son, and He gave Him as a Sacrifice, Which Alone would redeem the fallen sons of Adam's lost race. Let us never forget that!

(18) "THUS SAITH THE LORD GOD; IN THE FIRST MONTH, IN THE FIRST DAY OF THE MONTH, YOU SHALL TAKE A YOUNG BULLOCK WITHOUT BLEMISH, AND CLEANSE THE SANCTUARY.

(19) "AND THE PRIEST SHALL TAKE OF THE BLOOD OF THE SIN OFFERING, AND PUT IT UPON THE POSTS OF THE HOUSE, AND UPON THE FOUR CORNERS OF THE SETTLE OF THE ALTAR, AND UPON THE POSTS OF THE GATE OF THE INNER COURT.

(20) "AND SO YOU SHALL DO THE SEVENTH DAY OF THE MONTH FOR EVERY ONE WHO ERRS, AND FOR HIM WHO IS SIMPLE: SO SHALL YOU RECONCILE THE HOUSE.

(21) "IN THE FIRST MONTH, IN THE FOURTEENTH DAY OF THE MONTH, YOU SHALL HAVE THE PASSOVER, A FEAST OF SEVEN DAYS; UNLEAVENED BREAD SHALL BE EATEN.

(22) "AND UPON THAT DAY SHALL THE PRINCE PREPARE FOR HIMSELF AND FOR ALL THE PEOPLE OF THE LAND A BULLOCK FOR A SIN OFFERING.

(23) "AND SEVEN DAYS OF THE FEAST HE SHALL PREPARE A BURNT OFFERING TO THE LORD, SEVEN BULLOCKS AND SEVEN RAMS WITHOUT BLEMISH DAILY THE SEVEN DAYS; AND A KID OF THE GOATS DAILY FOR A SIN OFFERING.

(24) "AND HE SHALL PREPARE A MEAT OFFERING OF AN EPHAH FOR A BULLOCK, AND AN EPHAH FOR A RAM, AND AN HIN OF OIL FOR AN EPHAH.

(25) "IN THE SEVENTH MONTH, IN THE FIFTEENTH DAY OF THE MONTH, SHALL HE DO THE LIKE IN THE FEAST OF THE SEVEN DAYS, ACCORDING TO THE SIN OFFERING, ACCORDING TO THE BURNT OFFERING, AND ACCORDING TO THE MEAT OFFERING, AND ACCORDING TO THE OIL."

The structure is:

1. There is a Ministry to God only (Vs. 20), and there is a ministry to man (Vs. 24). In Christian service, this distinction must be observed; and the richer will be the ministry to man if that to God be given the first place.

2. Everything done here, and without exception, all, and in its entirety, portray Christ in His great Work of Redemption.

3. Some may ask the reason for the sacrificial system of the Old Testament being reinstituted in the Kingdom Age, considering that Jesus has already fulfilled the Law in every respect? There is no implication here that anything of the old Law was left unfulfilled by Christ, but rather, that it never be forgotten, that He did fulfill all the Law, and in every respect, by His Atoning Death. The reinstitution of the sacrificial system is meant to proclaim that fact, and that it never be forgotten. To be sure, these object lessons will ever hold up the Cross before the world of that coming day.

THE SANCTUARY

Verse 18 reads: *"Thus saith the Lord GOD; in the first month, in the first day of the month, you shall take a young bullock without blemish, and cleanse the Sanctuary:"*

The contrast between the legislation of Verses 18 through 25 and that of Leviticus emphasizes the difference between Mosaic and Millennial worship. Here the year begins with the demonstration of accomplished Redemption, and the provision of a pure ground of worship. Thus shall Atonement be made for the house on the first day, and for the worshippers on the seventh day. The year will, therefore, begin with the Memorial of a perfected Atonement for sin; in Leviticus, the year closed with an Atonement pointing forward to a cleansing and purging yet to be accomplished.

As the *"Sanctuary"* will be occupied by men not glorified, though redeemed, it, of necessity, will need cleansing.

Those who are glorified, which will include all who have part in the First Resurrection, which will include everyone, both Jews and Gentiles, from the time of Adam through the Great Tribulation, will have no sin nature, and, therefore, all possibility of future sin (I Cor. 15:51-57).

Conversely, all of Israel, at least the Israel of that day, though redeemed, will not be in a Glorified State, and will still have the sin nature. As such, they will continue to come short of the Glory of God, although being continually cleansed by the intercession of Christ, as it regards what He did at the Cross in the shedding of His Precious Blood (Rom. 3:23; Heb. 7:25; I Jn. 1:7). Nevertheless, with Satan and his demon spirits locked away in the bottomless pit, the sin nature will, by and large, be dormant, thereby providing a perfect environment, and a sin-free lifestyle, at least as far as outward actions are concerned (Rev. 20:1-3).

THE FIRST RESURRECTION

There is some indication that the Jews and Gentiles who will be alive at the beginning of the Kingdom Age, and accepting Christ as their Saviour, will remain in this redeemed state forever. In other words, they will not be glorified as those who have part in the First Resurrection (I Cor., Chpt. 15). It seems from the Scripture that these natural earthly nations who have lived from the Tribulation through the Millennium (people who are Born-Again) will multiply and replenish the Earth, and carry out the original program of God on Earth, as Adam and others would have done if man had not sinned. These are the sheep nations of Matthew 25:31-46.

The Scripture says, *"And the nations of them which are saved shall walk in the light of it: and the kings of the Earth do bring their glory and honor into it"* (Rev. 21:24). This is speaking of the New Jerusalem, which will come down from God out of Heaven to exist on Earth forever, thereby changing the headquarters of the Lord from Heaven to Earth.

THE BLOOD

The phrase of Verse 19, *"And the Priest shall take of the blood of the Sin Offering,"* pertains to the *"young bullock"* of Verse 18, which typified Christ Who died in the prime of His Manhood. Verse 19 typifies the Precious shed Blood of Christ on which the foundation of Salvation is based.

Inasmuch as these Sacrifices will be carried on forever, and strictly as a memorial of what Christ did at Calvary, this should, by all means, portray to us the value here placed by the Lord on this action. Considering the tremendous activity involved, coupled with its duration, which is forever, we get at least some idea of its importance!

Therefore, every Church should be a *"Cross Church,"* and every Preacher a *"Cross Preacher"* (I Cor. 1:17-18, 21, 23; 2:2).

The death of Christ at Calvary satisfied the demands of God regarding the terrible sin debt owed by the human family, which broke the back of Satan, so to speak, thereby destroying his strangle-hold over mankind (Col. 2:14-15).

Man's problem is sin, not money, education, environment, government, etc., and his solution is the Saviour, Who paid the price at Calvary's Cross; however, for man to avail himself of the tremendous benefits of the Finished Work of Christ, man must accept Christ and what He did at the Cross. In other words, the Cross, as I would certainly trust is overly obvious in these Passages, must never be separated from Christ.

It is not that Christ is still on the Cross, for He certainly isn't. In fact, He is at the Right Hand of the Father (Heb. 1:3). As well, as Believers, and spiritually speaking, we are presently seated with Him in Heavenly Places (Eph. 2:6).

This of which we speak pertains to the benefits of the Cross, and benefits, I might quickly add, which will never end.

THE CROSS

The Sixth Chapter of Romans outlines God's Prescribed Order of Victory. It tells the Believer how to live a Godly life, how to walk in perpetual victory, how that Righteousness and Holiness are developed in the heart and life of the Believer.

First of all, the Apostle takes us to the Cross (Rom. 6:3-5). But in this particular passage, he doesn't so much tell us what Jesus did there, although that definitely is included, as he does, or rather the Spirit through him, how the Believer fits into the Cross.

We are told in those Passages that we are *"baptized into His death, buried with Him by Baptism into death, and then raised with Him in newness of life."* And, of course, it must be understood that Paul is not speaking here of Water Baptism. In fact, Water Baptism has absolutely nothing to do with the Sixth Chapter of Romans. He's talking about the death of Christ and our part in that death, which in the Mind of God puts us into Christ upon the Believer evidencing Faith in what Jesus did at the Cross.

So, as it regards victorious living, the Holy Spirit, through Paul, takes us straight to the

Cross, where the *"old man"* dies, and we are raised a *"new creation"* (II Cor. 5:17).

He then tells us, in Romans 6:11, that due to the Cross, we must *"account ourselves as being dead unto the sin nature, but alive unto God through Jesus Christ."* This means that we are to continue to evidence faith, even on a daily basis (Lk. 9:23), in what Jesus did for us at the Cross, fully understanding that the Cross is the total and complete means of our victory. Paul said:

"But God forbid that I should glory, save in the Cross of our Lord Jesus Christ, by Whom the world is crucified unto me, and I unto the world" (Gal. 6:14).

Understanding this, and continuing to evidence faith in Christ and what He did at the Cross, we are then assured that *"sin shall not have dominion over us"* (Rom. 6:14).

First it is the Cross, and then it is our faith evidenced in the Cross, and then the Holy Spirit, Who works entirely within the parameters of the Finished Work of Christ, performs in our lives that which only He can do (Rom. 8:1-2, 11). In fact, anything that's done of the Lord in our lives must be carried out in totality by the Holy Spirit. He doesn't require much of us, but He does require that we evidence Faith constantly in the Sacrifice of Christ, which gives Him the legal right to carry out His Work in our lives (Rom. 8:2).

SIN

Verse 20 reads: *"And so you shall do the seventh day of the month for everyone who errs, and for him who is simple: so shall you reconcile the house."*

The phrase, *"Everyone who errs,"* refers to those who have drifted from the straight path through ignorance or foolishness.

The *"simple"* pertains to the one who, for whatever reason, does not fully understand the ramifications of his actions.

These passages portray to us the absolute abhorrence of sin by the Lord and, therefore, the absolute perfection demanded. Inasmuch as such is not possible even for redeemed man, provision is here made.

SEVEN

Verse 21 reads: *"In the first month, in the fourteenth day of the month, you shall have the Passover, a Feast of seven days; unleavened bread shall be eaten."*

The two Feasts of Passover and Tabernacles will be marked by sevenfold Offerings in contrast to the twofold ones of Leviticus; and this because these Offerings will testify to the perfection of the cleansing for sin fulfilled at Calvary.

The character of worship in that future day, and the sense of the sufficiency of Christ's Sacrifice of Himself as the Sin Offering and the Burnt Offering, will be perfect.

Thus, these two Feasts will celebrate the perfection and sufficiency of the Atoning Work of Christ, and, together with Feasts of Sabbath and the New Moon, testify to the fulfillment of God's Promises to Israel in bringing them into rest, and making them to be a light to the Gentiles (Isa., Chpts. 60, 66).

Under the First Covenant, the Passover was a domestic and family Feast; under the New Covenant, it will be a princely and national one.

THE HIGH PRIEST

Verses 22 through 25 proclaim the leadership of the High Priest as it regards these various Offerings. He will be totally in charge of these Sacrifices. If one is to notice, even though the type of animals remains the same, the number differs from the Law of Moses.

There, two bullocks, one ram, and seven lambs were offered daily, while here *"seven bullocks and seven rams,"* along with one *"lamb"* (kid of the goats) are offered daily for the seven days.

The number *"seven"* being God's Perfect number, and denoting perfection and completion, signifies the work finished, while the Levitical Offerings signified the work yet to be done.

The Passover will be celebrated *"in the first month"* (Vs. 21), with the other of the Feasts celebrated in the seventh month, with the latter representing the Feasts of Tabernacles.

"Joys are flowing like a river
"Since the Comforter has come;
"He abides with us forever,
"Makes the trusting heart His home."

"Bringing life and health and gladness

"All around, this Heav'nly Guest
"Banished unbelief and sadness,
"Changed our weariness to rest."

"Like the rain that falls from Heaven,
"Like the sunlight from the sky,
"So the Holy Spirit is given,
"Coming on us from on high."

"See, a fruitful field is growing,
"Blessed fruit of Righteousness;
"And the streams of life are flowing
"In the lonely wilderness."

"What a wonderful Salvation,
"Where we always see His Face!
"What a perfect habitation,
"What a quiet resting place!"

CHAPTER 46

(1) "THUS SAITH THE LORD GOD; THE GATE OF THE INNER COURT THAT LOOKS TOWARD THE EAST SHALL BE SHUT THE SIX WORKING DAYS; BUT ON THE SABBATH IT SHALL BE OPENED, AND IN THE DAY OF THE NEW MOON IT SHALL BE OPENED.

(2) "AND THE PRINCE SHALL ENTER BY THE WAY OF THE PORCH OF THAT GATE WITHOUT, AND SHALL STAND BY THE POST OF THE GATE, AND THE PRIESTS SHALL PREPARE HIS BURNT OFFERING AND HIS PEACE OFFERINGS, AND HE SHALL WORSHIP AT THE THRESHOLD OF THE GATE: THEN HE SHALL GO FORTH; BUT THE GATE SHALL NOT BE SHUT UNTIL THE EVENING.

(3) "LIKEWISE THE PEOPLE OF THE LAND SHALL WORSHIP AT THE DOOR OF THIS GATE BEFORE THE LORD IN THE SABBATHS AND IN THE NEW MOONS.

(4) "AND THE BURNT OFFERING THAT THE PRINCE SHALL OFFER UNTO THE LORD IN THE SABBATH DAY SHALL BE SIX LAMBS WITHOUT BLEMISH, AND A RAM WITHOUT BLEMISH.

(5) "AND THE MEAT OFFERING SHALL BE AN EPHAH FOR A RAM, AND THE MEAT OFFERING FOR THE LAMBS AS HE SHALL BE ABLE TO GIVE, AND AN HIN OF OIL TO AN EPHAH.

(6) "AND IN THE DAY OF THE NEW MOON IT SHALL BE A YOUNG BULLOCK WITHOUT BLEMISH, AND SIX LAMBS, AND A RAM: THEY SHALL BE WITHOUT BLEMISH.

(7) "AND HE SHALL PREPARE A MEAT OFFERING, AN EPHAH FOR A BULLOCK, AND AN EPHAH FOR A RAM, AND FOR THE LAMBS ACCORDING AS HIS HAND SHALL ATTAIN UNTO, AND AN HIN OF OIL TO AN EPHAH.

(8) "AND WHEN THE PRINCE SHALL ENTER, HE SHALL GO IN BY THE WAY OF THE PORCH OF THAT GATE, AND HE SHALL GO FORTH BY THE WAY THEREOF."

The overview is:

1. On the Feasts of the Sabbath and the New Moon, the Prince shall enter by the East Gate and worship at its extremity in front of the Temple; but he shall not go beyond the inner door. And the people shall worship standing in front of the Eastern entry of this gate. (Williams).

2. The Divine foundation being laid — the blood and the oil — the heart is given freedom to express its joy and its communion in the Meal Offering, i.e., fellowship with God in the enjoyment of Christ, as the Bread that came down, and comes down, from Heaven, whereof if a man eat, he shall never die.

3. The slain animals for the Sacrifices will shed *"Blood,"* typifying the price that Jesus paid at Calvary, and the *"Oil"* typifies the Holy Spirit. The moral is, the Holy Spirit works entirely within the framework of the Finished Work of Christ. This is a great Truth, that must not be lost upon the Child of God.

THUS SAITH THE LORD GOD

This Chapter opens with *"Thus saith the Lord GOD,"* emphasizing the seriousness of these commands, inasmuch as their being obeyed guarantees the prosperity, both spiritually and economically, of the entirety of the world. Isaiah said, *"And the Gentiles shall come to Your light, and kings to the brightness of Your rising"* (Isa. 60:3).

Even though these directions, as given by the Lord for this future day, may seem tedious even to Christians, nevertheless, in that coming Glad Day, every Gentile will know and understand this of which Israel does, and, will rejoice in their carrying out of it. Isaiah further said: *"And their seed shall be known among the Gentiles, and their offspring among the people: all who see them shall acknowledge them, that they are the seed which the LORD has blessed"* (Isa. 61:9).

As well, as stated, the faithfulness of Israel in the carrying out of all of these duties will determine the prosperity of the world; therefore, every Gentile nation, and, in fact, every singular individual, will get to know these rules laid down by the Lord, and will come to the understanding of all of these Sacrifices, and, above all, how that everything points to Christ. Their continued prosperity depends on such. We say these things, not that there will be any slackness on the part of Israel, but to explain what is being done, and why it is being done.

THE EASTERN GATE

The phrase of Verse 1, *"The gate of the Inner Court that looks toward the east shall be shut the six working days; but on the Sabbath day it shall be opened, and in the day of the new moon it shall be opened,"* proclaims this gate as being done this way for two reasons:

1. This will be the Gate through which the Messiah will enter in order to take up abode in the Sanctuary, and is, therefore, reserved for His use exclusively, as well as the High Priest, who is a Type of Christ.

2. It was through the Eastern Gate of Old Jerusalem that Jesus entered immediately before His Crucifixion, and referred to as the *"triumphant entry,"* but rejected by Israel (Mat. 21:1-11).

THE PRINCE

The phrase of Verse 2, *"And the Prince shall enter by the way of the porch of that gate without, and shall stand by the post of the gate,"* probably represents the High Priest. On the Feasts of the Sabbath and the New Moon, at this time, the Prince (High Priest) shall enter by the East Gate, and worship a short distance from it in front of the Sanctuary; but he shall not go beyond that inner door.

The Prince (High Priest) will provide the Offerings and the other Priests will present them. The Offerings of the Sabbath shall number seven, denoting the perfection of Christ.

WORSHIP

Verse 3 reads: *"Likewise the people of the land shall worship at the door of this Gate before the LORD in the Sabbaths and in the New Moons."*

The people of Israel will be allowed to worship *"at the door of this Gate before the LORD,"* but not on the porch, as the Prince. This will be done only, and, as stated, on the *"Sabbaths,"* and *"the New Moons."*

The reason the Prince has greater access, even unto the porch, is because he is Type of Christ; however, even he cannot go beyond the inner door.

The people are allowed to worship (at the Gate) because such typifies Christ as *"the Door"* (Jn. 10:9).

The *"Sabbath"* signifies the *"rest"* afforded only in Christ, which Israel will truly have in the coming Kingdom Age.

The *"New Moon"* signifies the perpetuity of this *"rest,"* guaranteeing its existence forever.

THE BLOOD AND THE OIL

Verse 4 reads: *"And the Burnt Offering that the Prince shall offer unto the LORD in the Sabbath Day shall be six lambs without blemish, and a ram without blemish."*

The offering up of these animals signifies the shedding of much blood, which is meant to typify the great price paid for humanity, as it regards the Cross of Christ.

Verse 5 reads, *"And the Meat Offering shall be an ephah for a ram, and the Meat Offering for the lambs as he shall be able to give, and an hin of oil to the ephah."*

The *"oil"* typifies the Holy Spirit, which always must be preceded by the *"Shed Blood."* When the Cross is properly held up, the Holy Spirit will soon follow.

The Divine foundation being laid — the Blood and the Oil — the heart can now express its joy and its communion in the Meal Offering, which signifies fellowship with

God in the enjoyment of Christ.

THE SACRIFICES

Verses 6 through 8 continue to proclaim the fact of the Sacrifices, which pertain to *"worship."* The truth is, it is impossible to properly worship the Lord, unless it's done on the basis of the Sacrifice of Christ, which, in fact, is demanded by the Holy Spirit.

Jesus said: *"God is a Spirit: and they who worship Him must worship Him in spirit and in truth"* (Jn. 4:24).

"Truth," of course, pertains to Christ and what Christ did at the Cross. Our Faith expressed in that Finished Work, the Holy Spirit works on our renewed spirit, leading the Believer into worship. It is the only type of worship that God will accept — that which is based on the Sacrifice of Christ.

(9) "BUT WHEN THE PEOPLE OF THE LAND SHALL COME BEFORE THE LORD IN THE SOLEMN FEASTS, HE WHO ENTERS IN BY THE WAY OF THE NORTH GATE TO WORSHIP SHALL GO OUT BY THE WAY OF THE SOUTH GATE; AND HE WHO ENTERS BY THE WAY OF THE SOUTH GATE SHALL GO FORTH BY THE WAY OF THE NORTH GATE: HE SHALL NOT RETURN BY THE WAY OF THE GATE WHEREBY HE CAME IN, BUT SHALL GO FORTH OVER AGAINST IT.

(10) "AND THE PRINCE IN THE MIDST OF THEM, WHEN THEY GO IN, SHALL GO IN; AND WHEN THEY GO FORTH, SHALL GO FORTH.

(11) "AND IN THE FEASTS AND IN THE SOLEMNITIES THE MEAT OFFERING SHALL BE AN EPHAH TO A BULLOCK, AND AN EPHAH TO A RAM, AND TO THE LAMBS AS HE IS ABLE TO GIVE, AND AN HIN OF OIL TO AN EPHAH.

(12) "NOW WHEN THE PRINCE SHALL PREPARE A VOLUNTARY BURNT OFFERING OR PEACE OFFERINGS VOLUNTARILY UNTO THE LORD, ONE SHALL THEN OPEN HIM THE GATE THAT LOOKS TOWARD THE EAST, AND HE SHALL PREPARE HIS BURNT OFFERING AND HIS PEACE OFFERINGS, AS HE DID ON THE SABBATH DAY: THEN HE SHALL GO FORTH; AND AFTER HIS GOING FORTH ONE SHALL SHUT THE GATE.

(13) "YOU SHALL DAILY PREPARE A BURNT OFFERING UNTO THE LORD OF A LAMB OF THE FIRST YEAR WITHOUT BLEMISH: YOU SHALL PREPARE IT EVERY MORNING.

(14) "AND YOU SHALL PREPARE A MEAT OFFERING FOR IT EVERY MORNING, THE SIXTH PART OF AN EPHAH, AND THE THIRD PART OF AN HIN OF OIL, TO TEMPER WITH THE FINE FLOUR; A MEAT OFFERING CONTINUALLY BY A PERPETUAL ORDINANCE UNTO THE LORD.

(15) "THUS SHALL THEY PREPARE THE LAMB, AND THE MEAT OFFERING, AND THE OIL, EVERY MORNING FOR A CONTINUAL BURNT OFFERING."

The synopsis is:

1. In the National Feasts, the Prince (High Priest) will worship with, and among, the people on the common ground of brotherhood and fellowship. For these Feasts, he will provide the Meal Offering. There is no such command in Leviticus.

2. Under the Law, there was the Morning and Evening sacrifice, but under Grace, there will be only the Morning Lamb; for to that Day there shall be no evening.

3. Even though all of this is similar to Leviticus, still, Leviticus looked forward to a coming Work, while Millennium Worship looks back to a Finished Work. There is a vast difference!

THE NORTH GATE AND THE SOUTH GATE

The phrase of Verse 9, *"But when the people of the Land shall come before the LORD in the solemn Feasts, he who enters in by way of the North Gate to worship shall go out by way of the South Gate,"* also presents the opposite for those who come in by the South Gate.

If the people enter the place of worship by the way of the *"North Gate,"* they are not allowed to exit that way, but must exit by way of the *"South Gate."* Conversely, if they enter by the way of the *"South Gate,"* they must exit by the way of the *"North Gate."*

There is a spiritual reason for this of far greater import than just the matter of entrance and exit.

The idea is that one is to partake of all of Christ and not just part of Christ. To go all the way through, and irrespective of what side one came in, signified the partaking of all. Many today accept Christ only partially. They accept Salvation, but not the Baptism with the Holy Spirit, with the evidence of speaking with other tongues. Others accept both Salvation and the infilling of the Spirit, but look at the Holy Spirit as rather a goal than the gateway which it really is! Consequently, they only go part way. Regrettably, at this present time, there seems to be few who go all the way.

In the coming Kingdom Age, and which will last forever, every Israelite who comes in at either one of the side Gates, will, upon the completion of his solemn worship, exit at the opposite Gate, thereby signifying the intentions of Christ that they did not stop short, but, instead, did *"eat the flesh of the Son of Man, and drink His Blood"* (Jn. 6:53).

THE PRINCE

The phrase of Verse 10, *"And the Prince in the midst of them, when they go in, shall go in,"* implies that, in such times of worship, the Prince shall stand on a level with the people, and both enter and retire by the same door as they.

This signifies Christ, Who became One with the people in the Incarnation; however, He did not become one with them in their sin. The *"Prince"* conducted himself accordingly, only associating with the worship of the people on a certain level and at certain times, because he is type of Christ.

THE MORNING SACRIFICE

Verses 11 through 15 continue to proclaim the various Offerings.

As repeatedly stated, all the Offerings typified Christ, and will be done as Memorial of what He did at Calvary. Thus, this momentous occasion, which happened so long ago, will never lose its significance and meaning among the people, and will continue to portray the reason for their deliverance and blessing.

If it is to be noticed, in Millennial Worship, there will only be a morning sacrifice, which will be offered at 9 a.m. Under the old Law of Moses, there were the morning and evening sacrifices, 9 a.m. and 3 p.m. Why the difference?

The reason is, spiritually speaking, regarding that coming Glad Day, there will only be a morning, and no evening.

(16) "THUS SAITH THE LORD GOD; IF THE PRINCE GIVE A GIFT UNTO ANY OF HIS SONS, THE INHERITANCE THEREOF SHALL BE HIS SONS'; IT SHALL BE THEIR POSSESSION BY INHERITANCE.

(17) "BUT IF HE GIVE A GIFT OF HIS INHERITANCE TO ONE OF HIS SERVANTS, THEN IT SHALL BE HIS TO THE YEAR OF LIBERTY; AFTER IT SHALL RETURN TO THE PRINCE: BUT HIS INHERITANCE SHALL BE HIS SONS' FOR THEM.

(18) "MOREOVER THE PRINCE SHALL NOT TAKE OF THE PEOPLE'S INHERITANCE BY OPPRESSION, TO THRUST THEM OUT OF THEIR POSSESSION; BUT HE SHALL GIVE HIS SONS INHERITANCE OUT OF HIS OWN POSSESSION: THAT MY PEOPLE BE NOT SCATTERED EVERY MAN FROM HIS POSSESSION.

(19) "AFTER HE BROUGHT ME THROUGH THE ENTRY, WHICH WAS AT THE SIDE OF THE GATE, INTO THE HOLY CHAMBERS OF THE PRIESTS, WHICH LOOKED TOWARD THE NORTH: AND, BEHOLD, THERE WAS A PLACE ON THE TWO SIDES WESTWARD.

(20) "THEN SAID HE UNTO ME, THIS IS THE PLACE WHERE THE PRIESTS SHALL BOIL THE TRESPASS OFFERING AND THE SIN OFFERING, WHERE THEY SHALL BAKE THE MEAT OFFERING; THAT THEY BEAR THEM NOT OUT INTO THE UTTER COURT, TO SANCTIFY THE PEOPLE.

(21) "THEN HE BROUGHT ME FORTH INTO THE UTTER COURT, AND CAUSED ME TO PASS BY THE FOUR CORNERS OF THE COURT; AND, BEHOLD, IN EVERY CORNER OF THE COURT THERE WAS A COURT.

(22) "IN THE FOUR CORNERS OF THE COURT THERE WERE COURTS JOINED OF FORTY CUBITS LONG AND THIRTY BROAD: THESE FOUR CORNERS WERE OF ONE MEASURE.

(23) "AND THERE WAS A ROW OF BUILDING ROUND ABOUT IN THEM, ROUND ABOUT THEM FOUR, AND IT WAS MADE WITH BOILING PLACES UNDER THE ROWS ROUND ABOUT.

(24) "THEN SAID HE UNTO ME, THESE ARE THE PLACES OF THEM WHO BOIL, WHERE THE MINISTERS OF THE HOUSE SHALL BOIL THE SACRIFICE OF THE PEOPLE."

The exegesis is:

1. God's hatred of robbery, oppression, and injustice appears in the legislation of Verses 16 through 18.

2. His loving care for the physical needs of His servants is shown in Verses 19 through 24.

3. In the detail of these duties, Israel will finally begin to function as God originally intended; however, these things will be done, and with joy, and carried out correctly, and throughout the entirety of the Kingdom Age, ensuring the prosperity of the world, but only because Christ has finally been enthroned in the hearts of His ancient people.

THE INHERITANCE

The phrase of Verse 16, *"Thus saith the Lord GOD; If the Prince give a gift unto any of his sons,"* proves that this *"Prince"* will be an ordinary man, and not resurrected David, etc. — he will have sons, which, of course, Glorified Saints will not have.

The idea of this Verse is that if the Prince desires to give an *"inheritance"* unto *"his sons,"* he is allowed to do this. This is important, simply because the Prince will never die, staying alive forever, by virtue of the life qualities of the leaves and fruit which grow on the trees by the side of the river that flows from the Temple, which we will study in the next Chapter.

However, if he gives them an inheritance, it is theirs forever, unless they desire to give it to their sons, etc.

THE YEAR OF LIBERTY

Verse 17 proclaims the fact that gifts given by the High Priest to one of his servants, which he is free to do, but with the understanding, that this gift will be only until *"the year of liberty,"* i.e., *"year of Jubilee,"* which comes every 50 years. At this time, the *"gift"* will be returned to the Prince.

This tells us that the year of Jubilee will be celebrated in the Kingdom Age, but possibly only among the Jews in the confines of the Land of Israel. As well, the *"Year of Jubilee"* signifies the freedom that is found only in Christ, which was purchased for us by the Cross of Calvary.

THE ENTRY

The phrase of Verse 19, *"After He brought me through the entry, which was at the side of the gate,"* refers to the Man with the line in His Hand, Who continues to serve as a Guide for the Prophet. A long time ago, Jesus said to His Disciples, *"Follow Me"* (Mat. 4:19). He is still saying the same today.

The Gate in question is the Northern Gate, where the *"Holy Chambers of the Priests"* are located.

To follow Christ, and to follow Him in all things, is the most wonderful, glorious life that one could ever know or have. However, let it be understood, that Christ cannot be successfully followed, unless we do so by the virtue of His Finished Work. In other words, we must ever understand that it is the Cross which has made it possible for us to follow Christ. This is the case now, and, in fact, has always been the case, even from the dawn of time. The Fourth Chapter of Genesis proclaims this!

THE MINISTRY TO GOD

The phrase of Verse 20, *"Then said He unto me, This is the place where the Priests shall boil the Trespass Offering and the Sin Offering,"* presents this Ministry by the Priests as being dedicated to God only. While there is a ministry to man, typified in Verse 24, still, the ministry to man will never be what it ought to be, unless there is a proper Ministry to God.

The idea of Verse 20 is that such Offerings were for the Priests only, and, thereby, typified their personal worship of the Lord.

Most of the duties of the Priests concerned him acting as a mediator between the Lord and the people; therefore, much of what was done was for the people; however, inasmuch as the Priests are only men, they, too, must offer up Sacrifices for themselves. This consisted of the *"Trespass Offering"* and the *"Sin Offering."* Along with it, they offered the *"Meat Offering"* (Meal Offering).

This typified that, even though they were God's chosen, and even Priests, still, they needed the redemptive process of Christ as much as anyone.

THE SACRIFICES

Verses 21 through 24 proclaim that, in all four corners of the Outer Court, there were places located that the Priests may prepare Sacrifices for the people.

The Sacrifices were to be prepared in a certain way, and these places were designated for that preparation.

It seems that these buildings, or at least a portion of them, were used respecting these Sacrifices.

After the Sacrifice was offered by the individual, whoever he may have been, certain parts of certain Sacrifices were to be eaten by the Priests. Such were prepared and carried out in these designated areas. The people, upon the bringing of their Sacrifices to be offered, would have only witnessed a part of the Offering. According to the type of Sacrifice, the animal would have been skinned appropriately, with a part of it being offered on the Great Altar. The other part would have been eaten by the Priests, which the people could not see, but which was required for the Sacrifice to be acceptable.

Likewise, the Believer, upon accepting Christ as his Saviour, only understands a small part of what was done, because that which was carried out by Christ, as our Great High Priest, with the shedding of His Precious Blood, all had to be done in order that His once-for-all Sacrifice be viable (Heb. 10:12-14).

It is here shown to us that we may know and understand the magnitude of the price paid at Calvary.

"Shall I empty-handed be, when beside the crystal sea
"I shall stand before the everlasting throne?
"Must I have a heart of shame as I answer to my name,
"With no works that my Redeemer there can own?"

"When the harvest days are past, shall I hear Him say at last,
"Welcome pilgrim, I've prepared for you a place?
"Shall I bring Him golden sheaves, ripened fruit, and faded leaves,
"When I see the blessed Saviour face-to-face?"

"When the books are opened wide, and the deeds of all are tried,
"May I have a record whiter than the snow;
"When my race on Earth is run, may I hear Him say, Well done,
"Take the crown that Love immortal does bestow."

CHAPTER 47

(1) "AFTERWARD HE BROUGHT ME AGAIN UNTO THE DOOR OF THE HOUSE; AND, BEHOLD, WATERS ISSUED OUT FROM UNDER THE THRESHOLD OF THE HOUSE EASTWARD: FOR THE FOREFRONT OF THE HOUSE STOOD TOWARD THE EAST, AND THE WATERS CAME DOWN FROM UNDER FROM THE RIGHT SIDE OF THE HOUSE, AT THE SOUTH SIDE OF THE ALTAR.

(2) "THEN BROUGHT HE ME OUT OF THE WAY OF THE GATE NORTHWARD, AND LED ME ABOUT THE WAY WITHOUT UNTO THE UTTER GATE BY THE WAY THAT LOOKS EASTWARD; AND, BEHOLD, THERE RAN OUT WATERS ON THE RIGHT SIDE.

(3) "AND WHEN THE MAN WHO HAD THE LINE IN HIS HAND WENT FORTH EASTWARD, HE MEASURED A THOUSAND CUBITS, AND HE BROUGHT ME THROUGH THE WATERS; THE WATERS WERE TO THE ANKLES.

(4) "AGAIN HE MEASURED A THOUSAND, AND BROUGHT ME THROUGH THE WATERS; THE WATERS WERE TO THE KNEES. AGAIN HE MEASURED A THOUSAND, AND BROUGHT ME

THROUGH; THE WATERS WERE TO THE LOINS.

(5) "AFTERWARD HE MEASURED A THOUSAND; AND IT WAS A RIVER THAT I COULD NOT PASS OVER: FOR THE WATERS WERE RISEN, WATERS TO SWIM IN, A RIVER THAT COULD NOT BE PASSED OVER."

The diagram is:

1. The Scripture doesn't say *"water,"* but rather *"waters,"* which issued from the House — their source, the Throne of Jehovah; their channel, the Altar of Jehovah, i.e., Calvary (Joel 3:18; Zech. 14:8; Rev. 22:1).

2. These *"waters"* shall grow of themselves, and not, as in nature, by accession from side streams.

3. The Messiah will go in by the East Gate, and the waters will flow out by the same Gate. Christ ascended into Heaven, and, as a result, the Holy Spirit descended from Heaven.

WATERS

The phrase of Verse 1, *"Afterward He brought me again unto the door of the house,"* speaks of the Sanctuary from which these waters will flow. As well, the *"Door"* is Christ, and *"No man comes unto the Father, but by Me"* (Jn. 14:6).

This means that one cannot get to God through Mohammed, the Catholic Church, Joseph Smith, or any other fake luminary. If the world believes in God at all, it erroneously thinks He can be reached through many and varied sources; however, there is only one Door, and that Door is Christ.

Consequently, Satan has fought Christ, and understandably so, as no other! As a result, Christianity is fast becoming a Christless philosophy or, more particularly, it embraces Christ, and especially much of the Church, without the Cross. As a result, most of the Church serves *"another Jesus, fostered by another spirit, presenting another gospel"* (II Cor. 11:4).

Let it ever be known that Christianity without Christ and the Cross is left with no more meaning than the mindless mumblings of witchcraft and voodoo. To accept Christianity without Christ and the Cross, or even to accept Christ and ignore the Cross, is to degenerate into mere religion, which offers

NOTES

no life, and, instead, guarantees death. For without Christ and what He did at the Cross, there is no life (Jn. 14:6; I Cor. 1:17-18, 23; 2:2).

THE THRESHOLD

The phrase *"And, behold, waters issued out from under the threshold of the house eastward,"* proclaims a symbolism of the Holy Spirit, Who issues forth from Christ.

This is a symbolic fulfillment of the Promise of Christ when He said: *"If any man thirst, let him come unto Me, and drink.*

"He who believes on Me, as the Scripture has said, out of his innermost being shall flow Rivers of living water.

"But this spoke He of the Spirit" (Jn. 7:37-39).

This River began to flow on the Day of Pentecost (Acts, Chpt. 2), and has been flowing ever since, and will flow ever so abundantly during the coming Kingdom Age, which will bring life to the entirety of the world. To be sure, the Holy Spirit has been here from the very beginning, actually moving on the chaotic Earth, bringing order out of disorder (Gen. 1:2); however, until the Day of Pentecost, His activities were more hidden than visible, due to the fact that the sin debt remained unpaid, in that the blood of bulls and goats could not take away sins (Heb. 10:4).

On the Day of Pentecost, this river of the Spirit, so to speak, began to flow, because Jesus had paid that price at Calvary's Cross, in effect, satisfying the totality of the sin debt, and for all time, past, present, and future, at least for all who will believe (Heb. 10:12-14).

The *"threshold"* speaks of place and position. It speaks of the floor and denotes humility; hence, Naomi would tell Ruth, *"Get thee down to the floor,"* referring to a place of humility concerning Boaz (Ruth 3:3).

John the Baptist spoke of Christ baptizing with the Holy Spirit, and with fire, *"Whose shoes I am not worthy to bear"* (Mat. 3:11).

The phrase concerning the shoes spoke of a slave, who would remove the shoes of visitors upon entering the House, and wash their feet. It was the job, incidentally, of the lowliest slave.

HUMILITY

John was portraying that humility was a requirement for receiving the Holy Spirit, which is the opposite of pride.

Likewise, the *"threshold"* typifies the individual, who must get down on their knees, spiritually speaking, putting their head down in order to drink the water; regrettably, millions have desired this life-giving stream, but have not been willing to humble themselves; consequently, and in this fashion, it is impossible to partake of this gift without, as Naomi told Ruth, *"getting down to the floor."*

THE ALTAR

The phrase, *"For the forefront of the House stood toward the east, and the waters came down from under the right side of the House, at the south side of the Altar,"* denotes the channel, or course, of the River. It is the Altar of Jehovah, i.e., Calvary.

This portrays to us the Truth that the Holy Spirit could not take up abode, at least not permanently, in believing man, until Jesus paid the price for man's Redemption at Calvary's Cross, thereby satisfying the claims of Heavenly Justice (Jn. 14:16-17).

Due to this *"Altar,"* God can now look at man exactly as He looks at His Own Son, the Lord Jesus Christ. For upon acceptance of Him, He becomes our Substitute, and, therefore, in God's Eyes, we are perfect as His Son is perfect; however, it is all by Faith in Him, and not any of our works.

The cleansing afforded by the Precious Blood of Jesus Christ made it possible for our bodies to literally become the House, or Temple, of the Holy Spirit, where He comes to abide (I Cor. 3:16).

Therefore, the Church must ever remember that the course of this Great River, symbolic of the Holy Spirit, is the Cross of Christ. Even though the Cross is now history, still, its benefits continue on unto this hour, and, in fact, will never be discontinued. That is why Paul referred to the Cross, which made possible the New Covenant, as *"The Everlasting Covenant,"* meaning that it will never have to be amended, abridged, or changed in any way, because it is perfect (Heb. 13:20).

Consequently, it is blasphemous for some Charismatic Preachers to claim they have gone beyond the Cross, and, thereby, the songs of the Blood are no longer needed!

Let it ever be understood, if one attempts to go beyond the Cross, one loses one's way! To try to go beyond the Cross, is to claim an unfinished work, an unfinished Atonement. As stated, such an attitude can be constituted as none other than *"blasphemy."*

THE LEADING

The phrase of Verse 2, *"Then brought He me out of the way of the gate northward,"* simply means that the East Inner Gate was shut, and, as well, the East Outer Gate was shut, therefore, the Lord led him outside of the Inner and Outer Courts by the North Gates.

There is, of course, spiritual meaning in this seemingly obscure passage.

For instance, many hungry hearts desire the Baptism with the Holy Spirit, but, because of not being totally led by Christ, they become discouraged, not quite knowing the way or the route in order to receive.

Admittedly, the course, although direct, is seldom reached in a direct way. Some receive easily, some do not! However, all will receive who persist, because all are invited to come (Rev. 22:17).

The River flows through the Eastern Gate, but yet one cannot go through that Gate, but has to go through the Northern Gate in order to arrive at the appointed place. Therefore, if one is not led *"by the Man with the line in His Hand,"* one will be confused, and, therefore, discouraged, and fail to receive.

Consequently, Spirit-filled Believers should themselves be led by Christ in their dealing with those who are hungry for the Holy Spirit. If earthly wisdom is used rather than Heavenly wisdom, the individual will be led astray; however, if the Spirit-filled Believer is led by Christ in taking the person to the River, so to speak, all will arrive safely and will receive of its life-changing properties.

Someone has said that as revolutionary as Salvation is to the unbeliever, likewise, as revolutionary is the infilling of the Holy Spirit to the Believer.

While Salvation separates the sinner from the world, the Baptism with the Holy Spirit separates the Christian from dead, cold, lifeless formalism, in other words, for what passes for Christianity.

THE FLOWING OF THE WATERS

The phrase, *"And, behold, there ran out waters on the right side,"* pertains to the River flowing out from the Sanctuary into the desert.

This River is not meant to be kept within the confines of the Sanctuary, but is meant to flow out into the world, thereby bringing life; consequently, if the Holy Spirit is not allowed to function in the life of the Believer as He desires, which is to flow out to others, He will soon cease operations. He does not do things our way, but we do things His Way. As a result, many Christians, who have once been truly Spirit-filled, now show no evidence of the Operation of the Holy Spirit within their lives, simply because He has been misused, or else we would not allow Him to use us as He desires.

THE HOLY SPIRIT AND THE CROSS

The Holy Spirit works strictly within the confines of the Sacrifice of Christ. In other words, what Christ did at the Cross gives the Holy Spirit the legal right to carry forth His Work in the heart and life of the Believer (Jn. 14:16-17; Rom. 8:2, 11).

The Denominational world, believing not at all in the Baptism with the Holy Spirit, with the evidence of speaking with other tongues, have little understanding as it regards the Spirit; consequently, He is given almost no place whatsoever in those circles.

The Pentecostal world, which is supposed to specialize in the Holy Spirit, has, in fact, for all practical purposes, drifted so far away from His Leading and Guidance that if He is thought about at all, it is thought and believed that speaking in other tongues is the beginning and the end of whatever happens; therefore, He is taken for granted, thinking that whatever He does is automatic.

A little thinking would help us to come to the conclusion that the Holy Spirit doesn't just work automatically. If He did, there would be no failing Christians whatsoever. As well, all would be spiritually mature, etc. But again, we know that's not the case.

Regarding the Charismatic world, which is very large, the Holy Spirit, for all practical purposes, is divorced completely from the Cross of Christ. While that is done, as well, in the Pentecostal ranks, it is not nearly as blatant in those ranks as it is in the Charismatic world. In fact, in much of the Charismatic world, the Cross is ridiculed, lampooned, even blasphemed, as being the *"greatest defeat in human history,"* as they say, or as someone said, *"past miseries."*

At approximately the turn of the Twentieth Century, with the outpouring of the Holy Spirit beginning, as it regards the Latter Rain (Joel 2:23), the Denominational world attempted to preach the Cross without the Holy Spirit, with the upshot being that they now preach much of nothing. The Pentecostal world attempted to preach the Holy Spirit without the Cross, and now they are accepting *"spirits,"* thinking it's the Holy Spirit.

HOW THE HOLY SPIRIT WORKS

As stated, the Holy Spirit, the Third Person of the Triune Godhead, so to speak, works entirely within the parameters of the Finished Work of Christ. This is so set in concrete, proverbially speaking, that it is referred to as a *"Law,"* called *"the Law of the Spirit of life in Christ Jesus"* (Rom. 8:2).

This means that the Holy Spirit will not divert from this *"Law,"* as should be overly obvious. It was formulated by the Godhead sometime in eternity past.

This *"Law"* is *"in Christ Jesus,"* which refers to what Christ did at the Cross, all on our behalf.

The only thing the Holy Spirit requires of us, as it regards Him working within our hearts and lives, is that we ever make the Cross of Christ the Object of our Faith (Rom. 6:3-14; I Cor. 1:17-18, 23; 2:2; Gal. 6:14; Col. 2:14-15).

If we anchor our Faith in the Cross of Christ, in other words, ever making the Cross the Object of our Faith, Jesus said that the Holy Spirit *"shall receive of Mine* (what Christ did for us at the Cross), *and shall show it unto you"* (Jn. 16:14). The reason the Holy Spirit little works in the hearts and lives of most Believers, even though they are baptized with the Spirit, is simply because their faith is placed in something other than the Cross of Christ.

SPIRITUAL ADULTERY

Whether the Believer realizes it or not, when we place our Faith elsewhere, we are, in effect, saying that the Atonement is incomplete, in other words, what Christ did at the Cross did not quite finish the task, and we have to add our efforts to His Work. To be sure, and as should be overly obvious, that is an insult to Christ, thereby causing the Holy Spirit to do little within our lives.

In fact, even as Paul wrote in the first four Verses of Romans, Chapter 7, when Believers, who are married to Christ, are, in fact, unfaithful to Christ, which is done by the Believer looking elsewhere other than Christ and the Cross, the Holy Spirit labels such as *"spiritual adultery"* (Rom. 7:2-4). As once again it should be obvious, the Holy Spirit is definitely not going to aid and abet a Christian in such an endeavor. But regrettably, most modern Christians are living in a state of *"spiritual adultery,"* simply because they little understand, or understand not at all, what Paul told us in the Sixth Chapter of Romans, which tells us *"how to live for the Lord."* In other words, Romans, Chapter 6 is the great *"how to Chapter"* in the Word of God. Without a proper understanding of that Chapter, it is impossible for the Believer to live a victorious, overcoming Christian life.

THE MAN WITH THE LINE IN HIS HAND

The phrase of Verse 3, *"And when the Man Who had the line in His Hand went forth eastward, He measured a thousand cubits,"* which pertains to about 1,500 feet. This means that the River, which issues out from under the threshold of the Sanctuary, is about 1,500 feet wide at this particular juncture. As it flows eastward, the channel begins to widen. And as we shall see, this River will ultimately become quite large. At the outset, it will flow Eastward, and then turn Southward, dividing at some point and becoming two great Rivers. One half or one River will flow into the Dead Sea, causing that body of water to come alive, and the other will flow into the Mediterranean.

Even though the measurement is literal, still, the progression, as evidenced in this and the next two Verses, represents great spiritual Truths. If one is to notice, it is a fourfold progression, corresponding with the fourfold Gospel.

THE ANKLES

The phrase of Verse 3, *"And He brought me through the waters; the waters were to the ankles,"* represents the entrance into the River, which portrays Salvation. Ankles give direction to the motion, and, upon entering the River of Salvation, and the life-giving qualities of the Holy Spirit, one's direction changes. By the Grace of God, he can now walk straight instead of crooked, as he once did.

But let us go back again to what we've just given you regarding the Holy Spirit.

The Reader must remember, this River is symbolic of the Holy Spirit. The Man with the line in His Hand is Christ. At Salvation, the Holy Spirit leads the believing sinner to Christ. After Salvation, Christ leads the new Believer to the Holy Spirit.

THE HOLY SPIRIT

Anything that's done in the heart and life of the Believer must, of necessity, be done through the Person, Work, Ministry, and Power of the Holy Spirit. And as we've already stated, He works exclusively within the parameters of the Sacrifice of Christ. So, if the Believer is to *"walk straight,"* which the *"ankles"* represent, then the Believer must follow God's Prescribed Order.

Again, as previously stated, that *"Order"* is found exclusively, at least in its totality, in Romans, Chapter 6.

Although we have given the following elsewhere in this Volume, due to its vast significance, please allow me the latitude of giving it again.

The following will be brief, but I think helpful.

FOCUS

The Believer must always focus on Christ. Christ is always the Source.

OBJECT OF FAITH

While Christ is the Source, the Cross is the Means, and, in fact, the only means. By that, we mean that every single thing we receive from the Lord comes to us exclusively through Christ and what Christ has done for us at the Cross. We must never forget that.

POWER SOURCE

Understanding that Christ is the Source, and that the Cross is the Means, by which we receive all things from the Lord and, thereby, ever placing our Faith in the Cross of Christ, the Holy Spirit will then be our Power Source, which will always guarantee that for which Christ died.

RESULTS

The results, in such a case, will always be victory (Rom. 6:3-14; 8:1-2, 11; Eph. 2:13-18; Col. 2:14-15).

THE KNEES

The phrase of Verse 4, *"Again He measured a thousand, and brought me through the waters; the waters were to the knees."* This proclaims another 1,500 feet being measured. The *"Man"* bids the Prophet to follow, as He bids all to follow, and *"the waters were to the knees."*

As the *"ankles"* portrayed Salvation, the *"knees"* portray prayer, and a total dependence on the Lord. One might even say it portrays the Holy Spirit, because nothing will be done for the Lord outside of the Power of the Holy Spirit.

Sadly, many only wade out to the ankles, and never progress to the *"knee"* experience; consequently, most of that which is attempted in the Work of the Lord is an attempt of the flesh, and not the Spirit, and, therefore, of no value.

The implication in these Passages is that the *"Man with the line in His Hand,"* be followed, as this is what He intends!

Sadly, many will not follow Him, because they follow other voices. They follow Denominations, erroneous doctrines, fads, etc., but will not follow Christ. Paul said: *"Be ye followers of Me, even as I also am of Christ"* (I Cor. 11:1).

It is certainly true that we should follow those whom the Lord has called, such as *"Apostles; and some, Prophets; and some, Evangelists; and some, Pastors and Teachers"* (Eph. 4:11). However, they are to be followed only as they follow Christ, which means they must adhere to His Word. If they are not following the Word, they should not be followed at all! But sadly, many Christians do not know the Word well enough to know what is false and what is true.

THE LOINS

The phrase, *"Again He measured a thousand, and brought me through; the waters were to the loins,"* speaks of another 1,500 feet.

Once again, the Lord is beckoning to the Prophet to follow, as He beckons all to follow Him. Now, *"the waters are to the loins,"* signifying another progression of depth, and, as well, a portrayal of the miracle-working Power of God, representing the manner in which the Holy Spirit works on this Earth.

The *"loins"* of a man are his procreative area. As it is physically, the Holy Spirit here means for it to be spiritually as well.

Men and women, even boys and girls, who truly have a touch with God are those who bring about great things in this world. But that which is procreative cannot be brought about unless the individual first of all has come to the depth relative to the *"knees."* Each succession is dependent on the other. Without a proper prayer life, signified by the knees, the Holy Spirit cannot bring about the great things which He Alone will do. And, as we have previously stated, all of this must be anchored in the Cross, inasmuch as this River flows as a result of the *"Altar."* In other words, it is made possible to the human family by what Jesus did at the Cross.

A RIVER

The phrase of Verse 5, *"Afterward He measured a thousand; and it was a River that I could not pass over,"* proclaims the fact that the Baptism with the Holy Spirit is not a goal at which one arrives and remains, but, instead, a gateway to the things of God, which are unending. This is emphasized by the statement, *"that I could not pass over."*

It's amazing that much of the Church world claims that one receives all at Salvation, thereby denying the Baptism with the Holy Spirit as a viable Work of Grace.

It is certainly true that upon conversion one is truly and completely saved, and, in fact, cannot be more saved than at that moment; however, Salvation, one might say, is only the entrance into the things of the Lord, which are actually unending! In fact, one doesn't receive it all when one is Baptized with the Holy Spirit. It is impossible to receive all that God has, for He is Infinite.

The *"River"* represents the last progression, with itself open-ended, which symbolizes the whole Gospel for the whole man.

As well, and even as we shall see, this *"River"* contains life-giving properties, which cannot be found anywhere else, thus a proper representative of the Gospel.

(6) "AND HE SAID UNTO ME, SON OF MAN, HAVE YOU SEEN THIS? THEN HE BROUGHT ME, AND CAUSED ME TO RETURN TO THE BRINK OF THE RIVER.

(7) "NOW WHEN I HAD RETURNED, BEHOLD, AT THE BANK OF THE RIVER WERE VERY MANY TREES ON THE ONE SIDE AND ON THE OTHER.

(8) "THEN SAID HE UNTO ME, THESE WATERS ISSUE OUT TOWARD THE EAST COUNTRY, AND GO DOWN INTO THE DESERT, AND GO INTO THE SEA: WHICH BEING BROUGHT FORTH INTO THE SEA, THE WATERS SHALL BE HEALED.

(9) "AND IT SHALL COME TO PASS, THAT EVERY THING THAT LIVES, WHICH MOVES, WHITHERSOEVER THE RIVERS SHALL COME, SHALL LIVE: AND THERE SHALL BE A VERY GREAT MULTITUDE OF FISH, BECAUSE THESE WATERS SHALL COME THITHER: FOR THEY SHALL BE HEALED; AND EVERY THING SHALL LIVE WHERE THE RIVER COMES.

(10) "AND IT SHALL COME TO PASS, THAT THE FISHERS SHALL STAND UPON IT FROM ENGEDI EVEN UNTO ENEGLAIM; THEY SHALL BE A PLACE TO SPREAD FORTH NETS; THEIR FISH SHALL BE ACCORDING TO THEIR KINDS, AS THE FISH OF THE GREAT SEA, EXCEEDING MANY.

(11) "BUT THE MIRY PLACES THEREOF AND THE MARISHES THEREOF SHALL NOT BE HEALED; THEY SHALL BE GIVEN TO SALT.

(12) "AND BY THE RIVER UPON THE BANK THEREOF, ON THIS SIDE AND ON THAT SIDE, SHALL GROW ALL TREES FOR MEAT, WHOSE LEAF SHALL NOT FADE, NEITHER SHALL THE FRUIT THEREOF BE CONSUMED: IT SHALL BRING FORTH NEW FRUIT ACCORDING TO HIS MONTHS, BECAUSE THEIR WATERS THEY ISSUED OUT OF THE SANCTUARY: AND THE FRUIT THEREOF SHALL BE FOR MEAT, AND THE LEAF THEREOF FOR MEDICINE."

The overview is:

1. The waters shall be living and life-giving; but there shall be no healing for the miry places, proclaiming the fact that imperfection will exist during the Millennium, for man will still be under trial. He will have freedom of choice. If he accepts the rule of the Messiah, he will enjoy the blessings; but if he rejects that government, he, like Lot's wife, proverbially speaking, will be turned into salt, for Grace despised involves bitterness and death.

2. Millennium Blessing will be powerful and abiding, it will greatly surmount and almost efface evil, but not entirely; for only in the New Heaven and New Earth will there be perfection.

3. The trees shall perpetually bring forth new fruit because nourished by waters issuing from the Sanctuary. The fruit will heal as well as nourish. Such is the character of a life and ministry based upon Calvary, and energized by the Holy Spirit.

THE FORCE OF THE RIVER

The question of Verse 6, *"And He said unto me, Son of man, have you seen this?"* portrays Christ turning the attention of Ezekiel from the *"Course"* of the River to the *"Force"* of the River. Therefore, in all of this, we have the following scenario:

1. The *"Source"* of this River is the Sanctuary, which, in all of its many appointments, portrays Christ, and only Christ.

2. The *"Course"* is by the Altar, which portrays Calvary, making the Cross the means by which these things are done.

3. The *"Force"* portrays that which the River does, which, in effect, symbolizes the Holy Spirit.

So, we have the *"Source,"* which is Christ, the *"Course,"* which is the Cross, and the *"Force,"* which symbolizes the Holy Spirit.

THE BRINK OF THE RIVER

The phrase, *"Then He brought Me, and caused me to return to the brink of the River,"* portrays what the River does, which is astounding, to say the least! The Holy Spirit, of which the River is a symbol, does not come into our hearts and lives as a matter of mere ornamentation. He is there to accomplish a work, which, in fact, only He can do. And if allowed His Way, we will discover *"Life,"* and we will discover *"fruit."*

TREES

Verse 7 reads: *"Now when I had returned, behold, at the bank of the River were very many trees on the one side and on the other."*

Up to now, nothing has been mentioned about the trees which line both banks. Quite possibly, the Prophet had seen them, but did not, at least not at that time, know or understand that these Trees are different than any the world has ever known.

The phraseology suggests the fact that there is an abundant growth, and on both sides of the River.

"Trees" in Bible symbolism signify, at least if the right kind, as these certainly are, the production of fruit (Mat. 7:17). Such is the productive Spirit-filled life! The *"very many trees"* signify *"much fruit"* (Jn. 15:5).

THE DESERT AND THE SEA

The phrase of Verse 8, *"Then said He unto me, these waters issue out toward the east country, and go down into the Desert, and go into the Sea,"* now proclaims what this River can and will do.

The idea of the River is to bring life to the *"desert,"* as the Holy Spirit Alone, through Christ, can bring life to unregenerate man, who is dead in trespasses and sins. Literally, this speaks of the Dead Sea, which contains no life whatsoever. The River will flow into this lifeless Sea, and will change it dramatically!

NOTES

The Dead Sea, also called the Salt Sea, is about 340 square miles in area, and its surface is nearly 1,300 feet below the Mediterranean Sea level.

There is absolutely no life in the Dead Sea, which spiritually portrays the spiritual lifelessness of man. Man, being dead in trespasses and sins, has nothing of God within him, unless he is regenerated by the Power of the Holy Spirit. Spiritually speaking, man is a *"desert,"* and a *"lifeless sea."*

He keeps trying to rejuvenate himself with various means and methods, always with no success. The reason is simple:

Man's problem is not economical, physical, or educational. Man's problem is spiritual. While his spiritual problem definitely affects every other aspect of life and living, the truth is, until the spiritual problem is resolved, man cannot be whole, irrespective as to what he might do or be otherwise. As a result of Adam's Fall, man is born in sin, meaning that death shrouds him in everything that he does, and because *"the wages of sin is death"* (Rom. 6:23).

THE HEALING OF THE WATERS

The phrase, *"Which being brought forth into the sea, the waters shall be healed,"* presents the healing of the Dead Sea. The idea is that if the waters of the Dead Sea can be healed, then anything can be healed! It is the Spirit of God Who will revive the dead bones at Ezekiel 37:14, and the Spirit of God Which will heal the waters of the Dead Sea, symbolizing what the Lord can do for Israel, and, in fact, will do, and, as well, for any individual who will put themselves in His Hands. What Jesus did at the Cross, which the Holy Spirit will make real to the individual, can change any life. And, in fact, there is no other way that man can truly be changed.

While the unredeemed look to witchcraft, or New Year's resolutions, or a hundred and one other things, to try to change themselves, there is no help whatsoever from those sources. In fact, within himself, man has no answer to his dilemma. The answer has to come from the outside, and I refer to Christ, and Christ Alone.

This is the only answer for the Church. Without this River of God, the Holy Spirit, there is no life in the Church. And, as well, if there is no life, it can be obtained if one will get in the River and get the River in them, so to speak.

This is the only true *"healing"* for the Body of Christ. Seminars will not do it! Symposiums will not do it! The elevating of self-esteem will not do it! Psychological counseling will not do it! Neither will new buildings insert life! Only the Holy Spirit can do this. But yet, and tragically, the Church seems determined to try anything and everything except the one thing that will truly bring healing, the Holy Spirit.

THE BAPTISM WITH THE HOLY SPIRIT

The Baptism with the Spirit, which follows conversion, and for which one must ask, is not really optional, but rather a command of our Lord. It is not for the purpose of Salvation, that being afforded by Faith in Christ and what Christ did at the Cross. It is for worship, service, and direction.

Jesus said to His followers immediately before His Ascension: *"Being assembled together with them, commanded them that they should not depart from Jerusalem, but wait for the Promise of the Father, which, said He, You have heard of Me.*

"For John truly baptized with water, but you shall be baptized with the Holy Spirit not many days hence" (Acts 1:4-5).

As is obvious here, this is a *"command."*

In effect, He was telling them that they should not go preach, try to win souls, or attempt anything as it regards the Work of the Lord, until they were first baptized with the Holy Spirit. When that happens, He further said:

"But you shall receive power, after that the Holy Spirit is come upon you: and you shall be witnesses unto Me both in Jerusalem, and in all Judaea, and in Samaria, and unto the uttermost part of the earth" (Acts 1:8).

THE HOLY SPIRIT AT CONVERSION

While it is certainly true that the Holy Spirit definitely comes into the heart and life of the Believer at conversion, that is different than being Baptized with the Holy Spirit, of which Jesus is addressing here. In other words, there is a vast difference in being *"born of the Spirit"* than being *"baptized with the Spirit."*

While the Holy Spirit, as stated, comes into the heart and life at conversion, until one is Baptized with the Spirit, His Work within us is greatly curtailed. A Baptism with the Spirit effects a surrender, which opens up the heart, the mind, the soul, and the spirit to the Spirit, in effect, giving Him control. In fact, without the Baptism with the Holy Spirit, there can be very little true worship, or proper leading, as it regards service for the Lord. While there definitely can be some worship and some leading, without the Baptism with the Spirit, such are very limited.

As someone has well said, *"Salvation liberates one from the world, while the Baptism with the Spirit liberates one from cold, dead religious formalism."* Without the Baptism with the Spirit, while there may be much religious activity, there is actually going to be very little truly done for the Lord.

THE BAPTISM WITH THE HOLY SPIRIT FOLLOWS CONVERSION

I think it should be overly obvious that the followers of Christ were saved before the Day of Pentecost. In fact, Jesus said of them, *"But rather rejoice, because your names are written in Heaven"* (Lk. 10:20).

As well, the converts of Philip, when he preached the meeting in the particular city of Samaria, first gave their hearts to Christ. The Bible said of them, *"But when they believed Philip preaching the things concerning the Kingdom of God, and the Name of Jesus Christ, they were baptized, both men and women"* (Acts 8:12). In other words, these people were saved. They had given their hearts and lives to Christ.

However, they were not, at that time, Baptized with the Holy Spirit. The Scripture further said:

"Now when the Apostles which were at Jerusalem heard that Samaria had received the Word of God, they sent unto them Peter and John:

"Who, when they were come down, prayed for them, that they might receive the Holy Spirit:

*"For as yet He was fallen upon none of them: only they were baptized in the Name of Lord Jesus.

"Then laid they their hands on them, and they received the Holy Spirit"* (Acts 8:14-17).

In Acts, Chapter 9, the account is given of Paul being saved on the road to Damascus. But some three days after he was saved, the Scripture says that Ananias said to Paul, *"The Lord, even Jesus, Who appeared unto you in the way as you came, has sent me, that you might receive your sight, and be filled with the Holy Spirit"* (Acts 9:17).

In Acts, Chapter 10, the account is given of the Salvation of Cornelius and his household, at which time they also were baptized with the Holy Spirit (Acts 10:44-48).

In Acts, Chapter 19, we are given another account of the followers of Christ who lived in Ephesus. Paul said unto them: *"Have you received the Holy Spirit since you believed?"*

The Scripture says that Paul then *"laid his hands upon them, and the Holy Spirit came on them; and they spoke with tongues and prophesied"* (Acts 19:1-7).

So, the Scripture is replete with the Truth that the Baptism with the Spirit always follows conversion. In fact, Jesus told His Disciples that it was impossible for the unredeemed to be baptized with the Spirit. He said: *"And I will pray the Father, and He shall give you another Comforter, that He may abide with you forever;*

"Even the Spirit of Truth; Whom the world cannot receive, because it sees Him not, neither knows Him" (Jn. 14:16-17).

Therefore, to be baptized with the Holy Spirit, one must first be saved, which is an absolute requirement, as is overly obvious from the Scriptures.

THE INITIAL, PHYSICAL EVIDENCE OF THE BAPTISM WITH THE SPIRIT

According to the Scriptures, we believe that everyone who is Baptized with the Holy Spirit speaks with other tongues, as the Spirit of God gives the utterance. We also believe that if that particular initial evidence is not obvious, then one, despite what else might happen, has not been Baptized with the Spirit. We believe the Scriptures are replete with this.

Concerning the Day of Pentecost, which was the Day the Holy Spirit came to this world in a new dimension, and because of what Jesus had done at the Cross, the Scripture says, as it regards those who had gathered in the Temple, *"And they were all filled with the Holy Spirit, and began to speak with other tongues, as the Spirit gave them utterance"* (Acts 2:4).

Furthermore, the following Passages proclaim the fact that *"speaking with other tongues"* is not gibberish, incoherent babble, or anything of that nature, but rather a language, spoken by some people somewhere in the world, but not known by the speaker.

All that Day, on whom the Spirit was outpoured, seemed to be *"Galileans"* (Acts 2:7).

And then, quite a number of other indigenous people, most who were Jews or proselyte Gentiles, who were in Jerusalem at that time in order to keep the Feast, and who spoke both Hebrew and their indigenous language where they lived, which was somewhere in the Roman Empire, heard all these languages being spoken (Acts 2:7-12).

So, this establishes the fact that *"tongues,"* as it regards the Baptism with the Holy Spirit, are indeed languages spoken somewhere in the world.

In Acts, Chapter 8, as hands were laid on the Samaritans by Peter and John, nothing is said about what happened as it regards tongues, etc.; however, we do know that Simon the Sorcerer tried to buy this gift from Peter and John, when he saw them lay hands on the Samaritans, and they received the Holy Spirit. I cannot imagine that this man would have desired to have parted with his money if there was nothing more than the laying on of hands. No, he saw and heard something that took place, and, according to other Scriptures, it was *"tongues."*

In fact, when he tried to buy this gift from Peter, the Apostle said unto him: *"Your money perish with you, because you have thought that the Gift of God may be purchased with money.*

"You have neither part not lot in this matter: for your heart is not right in the

Sight of God" (Acts 8:20-21).

In fact, the word *"matter"* should have been translated *"utterance,"* for that is what it actually means from the original Greek word used here by Peter.

In Acts, Chapter 9, as it regards the account of Paul being saved and baptized with the Spirit, it doesn't say anything about what happened, only that Ananias prayed for him, and the Scripture says that he was *"filled with the Holy Spirit"* (Acts 9:17).

However, he said in his first Letter to the Church at Corinth: *"I thank my God, I speak with Tongues more than you all"* (I Cor. 14:18).

No, Paul wasn't speaking of the fact that he was fluent in several languages. Actually, the entirety of I Corinthians, Chapter 14, is given over to an explanation of *"tongues,"* and how they are to be used.

In fact, the Scriptural evidence is replete; the Believers in the Early Church were taught Salvation by Grace through Faith (Eph. 2:8-9), and the Baptism with the Holy Spirit with the evidence of speaking with other Tongues, as we are addressing here. In other words, they didn't teach that one is baptized with the Holy Spirit at conversion, but rather that the Baptism with the Spirit is an experience subsequent to Salvation, and is always accompanied by speaking with other tongues.

In Acts, Chapter 10, and as it regarded Cornelius and those who heard Peter preach that day, the Scripture says, *"For they heard them speak with tongues, and magnify God"* (Acts 10:46).

Concerning the Ephesian Believers, the Scripture says, *"And they spoke with tongues, and prophesied"* (Acts 19:6).

WHAT GOOD ARE TONGUES?

Many have asked that particular question. First of all, allow me to say that anything that God gives, whether we fully understand it or not, is of vast significance. And to question what God does is to question Him, thereby, casting doubt and aspersions on His Word, which is not exactly the sensible thing to do.

Let's look at what the Scriptures say, as it regards this all-important aspect of our experience with the Lord.

NOTES

1. It is the Word of the Lord: *"In the Law it is written, With men of other tongues and other lips will I speak unto this people"* (I Cor. 14:21).

2. When one prays in tongues, one's spirit prays: *"For if I pray in an unknown Tongue, my spirit prays"* (I Cor. 14:14).

3. It is a sign to unbelievers: *"Wherefore Tongues are for a sign, not to them who believe, but to them who believe not"* (I Cor. 14:22).

4. When one speaks with other tongues, one *"speaks unto God"*: *"For he who speaks in an unknown Tongue speaks not unto men, but unto God"* (I Cor. 14:2).

5. When one speaks in tongues, one speaks the wonderful works of God: *"We do hear them speak in our tongues the wonderful Works of God"* (Acts 2:11).

6. Speaking in tongues affords a *"rest"* and *"refreshing"* for the soul and the spirit of the individual: *"For with stammering lips and another tongue will He speak to this people. To whom He said, This is the rest wherewith you may cause the weary to rest; and this is the refreshing"* (Isa. 28:11-12).

7. Speaking with other tongues spiritually builds one up: *"But you, Beloved, building up yourselves on your most Holy Faith, praying in the Holy Spirit"* (Jude, Vs. 20).

LIFE

The phrase of Verse 9, *"And it shall come to pass, that everything that lives, which moves, whithersoever the Rivers shall come, shall live,"* presents the answer for every soul.

In fact, this is the only answer for the hurting heart, for the wasted life, for every bondage, every lifeless marriage, every lifeless Church.

The word *"rivers"* signifies two great rivers.

This River will flow out from the Sanctuary eastward, and then will turn south toward the Dead Sea. At some point on the southern journey, it will split, with one side continuing to the Dead Sea, with the other going to the Mediterranean (Zech. 14:8).

As someone has very well said, *"The moving of the Spirit is the beginning of Life"* (Gen. 1:1-2). In fact, and as we have repeatedly stated, the Holy Spirit takes that which

Christ has done at the Cross of Calvary, and makes it real to the heart and life (Jn. 16:13-15). In fact, the Holy Spirit works exclusively within the parameters of the Sacrifice of Christ. He does nothing outside those parameters, and everything within those parameters. That's why it is demanded that we ever evidence faith in Christ and the Cross (Rom. 6:3-14; I Cor. 1:17-18, 21, 23; 2:2; Gal. 6:14; Eph. 2:13-18; Col. 2:14-15).

A VERY GREAT MULTITUDE

The phrase, *"And there shall be a very great multitude of fish, because these waters shall come thither,"* concerns the Dead Sea being made alive by these waters, resulting in a Sea full of fish. That is the literal meaning; however, the spiritual meaning has to do with the following:

It refers to great numbers of souls being saved. It goes back to the words of the Master to His Disciples: *"Follow Me, and I will make you fishers of men"* (Mat. 4:19).

Where the Spirit of God is truly working, souls will be saved. In fact, souls cannot be saved unless the Spirit of God moves upon the heart, convicting the person of sin, and, as well, making Christ real to that lost soul (Jn. 3:5-8). In fact, the only thing that makes the Church different than anything else in the world is the Holy Spirit. Without the Spirit, it is just another religious effort, not so much unlike the other religions of the world, all of which were instituted by Satan. For the Church to be what the Church ought to be, the Holy Spirit must be prominent in all things. For the individual to be what the individual ought to be, the Holy Spirit must have the preeminence, in which He will always glorify Christ.

THE RIVER OF LIFE

The phrase, *"And everything shall live whither the River cometh,"* presents the answer to any and every problem. If the individual will only allow the Spirit of God to have His place within our hearts and lives, there is not a problem that cannot be solved. The idea is, and as we have previously stated, if this River, which is symbolic of the Holy Spirit, can make the Dead Sea come alive, a Sea, incidentally, which presently contains no life whatsoever, then there is nothing the Holy Spirit cannot do. He can take your *"desert"* and turn it into a verdant garden. He can take your emptiness and fill it up, your lack and make it plenty, your sickness and turn it to health, your death and turn it to life, your sin and turn it to Salvation, etc.

EXCEEDING MANY

The phrase of Verse 10, *"Their fish shall be according to their kinds, as the fish of the great Sea, exceeding many,"* speaks of the Dead Sea coming to life, and coming to life with many different kinds of fish, *"exceeding many."*

Once again, I go back to that which is beyond the literal meaning of this text, and I refer to the spiritual meaning. I speak of souls, great numbers of souls being brought to Christ!

Anytime the Spirit of God moves exceedingly, many souls are saved. There is much presently which is claimed to be the Spirit, but which is marked by the terrible fact that virtually no one is being saved in these meetings, etc.

As a case in point, the Word of Faith doctrine sees almost no one saved. In fact, there is absolutely no one that is saved as it regards that particular doctrine, and because it is grossly unscriptural. While there may be a few people saved in those meetings, it is because of other things, and not that error which is preached.

In fact, its principal Teachers claim that their ministry is not to get people saved, but rather to tell them how to get a lot of money, etc.

The Truth is, they don't get people saved because the Holy Spirit is not truly working in their midst, despite all of their claims otherwise.

All of these things in the Forty-seventh Chapter of Ezekiel will take place in the coming Millennial Reign. Then, many, many souls will be saved, as will be obvious, here typified by the words *"exceeding many."*

But I also believe that an even greater harvest is coming upon this world, and I speak of many souls being saved, which I personally think will take place immediately before the Rapture. Now let me hasten to say the following:

There is absolutely nothing in the Word of God which stipulates that the Rapture will be delayed. In fact, we are to expect His imminent return at any time (Rev. 22:20). So the following thoughts are my own.

THE DREAMS OF PHARAOH

Going back to the time of Joseph, the Scripture records a dream given to the Egyptian Monarch, but which he or his magicians could not interpret, and which troubled him greatly.

Joseph was called in before Pharaoh because the Monarch had been told that Joseph, who was then in prison, could interpret dreams.

As he related the dream to Joseph, he spoke of seven fat cattle, and then seven poor cattle, which came up after them. He also spoke of seven fat and healthy stalks of grain, and with seven blasted stalks coming up after them.

Joseph interpreted the dream according to that present time, to which it most definitely pointed; however, the dream of Pharaoh and Joseph's interpretation definitely have a greater prophetic meaning, pertaining to the last days.

The seven lean cattle and the seven withered stalks of grain present a double application, which are obvious. The first application pertains to the famine which came upon Egypt about seven years later, as well as the entirety of the Middle East. But the second part to that dream, in that it was doubled, pertains to the last days.

The seven years of great trouble pertain to the coming Great Tribulation, which is to come upon Israel, and the world. As the history of the first application brought Jacob to Joseph, the second application is going to bring Israel to Jesus, which is its intended purpose.

However, before the seven lean cattle and the seven blasted stalks of grain, there were seven fat cattle and seven healthy stalks of grain. Once again, that has a double application.

The first application pertains to the historical narrative of seven years of plenty, as it regards Egypt, with granaries filled to overflowing.

The second application, I believe, refers to a harvest in these last of the last days, which will be the concluding days of the Church. As the second application of trouble refers to the coming Great Tribulation, and if that is correct, and it definitely is, then I believe a great harvest of souls is going to come about immediately preceding the Rapture.

As I dictate these notes (August 10, 2003), there are probably fewer people being saved presently than at any time since the Reformation. That is tragic, but true! As well, there are fewer people being baptized with the Holy Spirit than at any time since the great Latter Rain outpouring began at the turn of the Twentieth Century (Joel 2:23). Personally, I do not believe the Lord is going to come back for a Church that is so woefully unprepared. I personally believe there is going to be a great Move of God, which will begin very shortly, that will usher millions into the Kingdom, and, as well, see untold thousands baptized with the Holy Spirit. In fact, the Scriptures further proclaim such. Peter said, and quoting the Prophet Joel:

"And on My servants and on My handmaidens I will pour out in those days of My Spirit; and they shall prophesy:

"And I will show wonders in Heaven above, and signs in the Earth beneath; blood, and fire, and vapor of smoke:

"The sun shall be turned into darkness, and the moon into blood, before that great and notable Day of the Lord come:

"And it shall come to pass, that whosoever shall call on the Name of Lord shall be saved" (Acts 2:18-21).

These Passages pertain to the entirety of time from the Day of Pentecost unto the present, now totaling approximately 2,000 years; however, the Scriptural indication is that there will be even a greater outpouring immediately before the coming Great Tribulation, which, incidentally, will follow the Rapture of the Church.

All of this doesn't mean that the Church is going to embrace the Gospel. In fact, most in the modern Church will do the very opposite. And as we have repeatedly stated, the Cross of Christ is the dividing line between the True Church and the apostate church. But for those who believe the Lord, I believe great and wonderful things are going to happen!

MIRY PLACES

Verse 11 reads: *"But the miry places thereof and the marishes thereof shall not be healed; they shall be given to salt."*

Even though these Waters shall be living and life-giving in the coming Kingdom Age, still, there will be no healing for the miry places. The reason is, imperfection will continue to exist during the Millennium, for man will still be under trial. He will have freedom of choice. If he accepts the rule of the Messiah, he will enjoy the Blessings pictured in Verses 1 through 10 and in Verse 12. But if he rejects that government, he, like Lot's wife, spiritually speaking, will be turned into salt; Grace despised involves bitterness and death.

Millennium Blessing will be powerful and abiding, it will greatly surmount and almost efface evil, but not entirely; for only in the New Heaven and New Earth will there be perfection.

TREES FOR MEAT

The phrase of Verse 12, *"And by the River upon the bank thereof, on this side and on that side, shall grow all trees for meat,"* which will have properties totally different than that which has been previously produced. The properties contained in this fruit, no doubt nourished by the waters, will cause human bodies to be free from sickness, and thereby to live on without death. One could even refer to them as *"trees of life."*

Of course, all the Saints who have ever lived from the time of Abel and on through the Great Tribulation will have glorified bodies and will not need such; however, there will be hundreds of millions of people in the world at that time who will not have glorified bodies. In fact, Israel as a nation will fall into that category, as well as millions of Gentiles. Not having Glorified Bodies, these will need something to sustain the physical body, and this particular *"fruit"* is designed by the Lord to do that.

NOTES

NEW FRUIT

The phrase, *"Whose leaf shall not fade, neither shall the fruit thereof be consumed: it shall bring forth new fruit according to his months,"* refers to an abundance of everything.

In the first place, it seems there will be multiple thousands of these trees, which will line both Rivers, with one River going to the former Dead Sea, and the second River going to the Mediterranean. As well, whereas most trees produce annually, these will produce a new crop monthly, and will suffice for the entirety of the world.

THE SANCTUARY

The phrase, *"Because their waters they issued out of the Sanctuary,"* proclaims the Source of this River which has the life-giving properties, which will nourish these *"trees."*

The *"Sanctuary,"* in all of its many appointments, and whatever they might be, totally and completely represent Christ, whether in His Mediatorial, Intercessory, or Atoning Work. Christ is always the Source.

However, as the Scripture abundantly points out, these waters which will *"issue out from under the threshold of the house eastward . . . and shall come down from under the right side of the house, at the south side of the Altar,"* pertain to the fact that the *"Altar,"* i.e., *"the Cross,"* is the *"Means,"* by which Christ does all of these things. Everything from God to man, and irrespective as to what it might be, comes from Christ through the Cross.

MEDICINE

The phrase, *"And the fruit thereof shall be for meat, and the leaf thereof for medicine,"* pertains to life-giving properties, and, as well, physical healing properties.

This tells us that the physical bodies of those who are living at that time, will at times, have problems; however, the *"fruit"* from these *"trees"* will instantly heal whatever that problem might be.

As an aside, this tells us that it is not wrong for a Christian to take medicine, nor does it show a lack of faith. The practice of medicine, as it refers to Doctors, is, as would be obvious, an uncertain science, because man's knowledge is not perfect; still, many medicines have been effective, which greatly help the physical body, and, if needed by the Christian, there is no Scriptural reason why such medicine should not be taken.

But whereas medicine presently only helps, then, the *"medicine"* of this fruit that is to come will totally and completely heal, and without failure. As well, whereas there are many different types of medicines presently, then, this *"fruit"* will be sufficient for all illnesses, whatever they might be. In fact, all sickness and illness at that time, by the eating of this fruit, which will be abundant for all, will be stopped, even before it begins.

I realize that all of this seems too good to be true; however, to be sure, it is true, and will definitely come to pass, exactly as the Word of the Lord proclaims.

(13) "THUS SAITH THE LORD GOD; THIS SHALL BE THE BORDER, WHEREBY YOU SHALL INHERIT THE LAND ACCORDING TO THE TWELVE TRIBES OF ISRAEL: JOSEPH SHALL HAVE TWO PORTIONS.

(14) "AND YOU SHALL INHERIT IT, ONE AS WELL AS ANOTHER CONCERNING THE WHICH I LIFTED UP MY HAND TO GIVE IT UNTO YOUR FATHERS: AND THIS LAND SHALL FALL UNTO YOU FOR INHERITANCE.

(15) "AND THIS SHALL BE THE BORDER OF THE LAND TOWARD THE NORTH SIDE, FROM THE GREAT SEA, THE WAY OF HETHLON, AS MEN GO TO ZEDAD;

(16) "HAMATH, BEROTHAH, SIBRAIM, WHICH IS BETWEEN THE BORDER OF DAMASCUS AND THE BORDER OF HAMATH; HAZARHATTICON, WHICH IS BY THE COAST OF HAURAN.

(17) "AND THE BORDER FROM THE SEA SHALL BE HAZARENAN, THE BORDER OF DAMASCUS, AND THE NORTH NORTHWARD, AND THE BORDER OF HAMATH, AND THIS IS THE NORTH SIDE.

(18) "AND THE EAST SIDE YOU SHALL MEASURE FROM HAURAN AND FROM DAMASCUS, AND FROM GILEAD, AND FROM THE LAND OF ISRAEL BY JORDAN, FROM THE BORDER UNTO THE EAST SEA. AND THIS IS THE EAST SIDE.

(19) "AND THE SOUTH SIDE SOUTHWARD, FROM TAMAR EVEN TO THE WATERS OF STRIFE IN KADESH, THE RIVER TO THE GREAT SEA. AND THIS IS THE SOUTH SIDE SOUTHWARD.

(20) "THE WEST SIDE ALSO SHALL BE THE GREAT SEA FROM THE BORDER, TILL A MAN COME OVER AGAINST HAMATH. THIS IS THE WEST SIDE.

(21) "SO SHALL YOU DIVIDE THIS LAND UNTO YOU ACCORDING TO THE TRIBES OF ISRAEL.

(22) "AND IT SHALL COME TO PASS, THAT YOU SHALL DIVIDE IT BY LOT FOR AN INHERITANCE UNTO YOU, AND TO THE STRANGERS WHO SOJOURN AMONG YOU, WHICH SHALL BEGET CHILDREN AMONG YOU: AND THEY SHALL BE UNTO YOU AS BORN IN THE COUNTRY AMONG THE CHILDREN OF ISRAEL; THEY SHALL HAVE INHERITANCE WITH YOU AMONG THE TRIBES OF ISRAEL.

(23) "AND IT SHALL COME TO PASS, THAT IN WHAT TRIBE THE STRANGER SOJOURNS, THERE SHALL YOU GIVE HIM HIS INHERITANCE, SAITH THE LORD GOD."

The diagram is:

1. In Joshua, the land was divided from south to north. In the coming Day of Restoration, it will be apportioned from north to south.

2. Inheritance was forbidden under Law to the Gentile; but, in the Millennium, it will be fully granted.

3. Then will God's original purpose be effected; Israel will first be possessed, and then the greater territory promised to Abraham secured.

JOSEPH

The phrase of Verse 13, *"Joseph shall have two portions,"* is because he personally received none, but, instead, it went to his two sons, Manasseh and Ephraim.

Counting the *"two portions"* given to Joseph, which will be in the name of his two sons, there will be thirteen portions in all, divided among the Twelve Tribes of Israel.

At the present time, other than possibly

the Tribe of Levi, most, if any Jews, know not as to exactly what Tribe they belong; however, this information will be easily ascertained whenever Jesus comes back, and Israel is given her rightful place. To be sure, Heaven keeps the record.

THE INHERITANCE

The phrase of Verse 14, *"And you shall inherit it, one as well as another,"* refers to each Tribe, irrespective of their size, receiving equal portions.

Upon the first distribution under Joshua, it was not handled this way, with some Tribes receiving a larger portion than others; nevertheless, in the Kingdom Age, the allotments will be equal.

The phrase, *"Concerning the which I lifted up My Hand to give it unto your fathers,"* proclaims the certitude of this action.

From the very beginning of this Promise, Satan has contested its fulfillment. In fact, the battle rages even unto today.

The Arabs presently occupying Israel refer to themselves as *"Palestinians"*; however, that name is a misnomer, meaning that it is made up out of whole cloth. In fact, the Arabs now in Israel, and claiming, in fact, all of the Land of Israel, are Jordanians, Syrians, Egyptians, etc. The truth is, they have no rightful claim to any of this land, even as these Passages in Ezekiel proclaim.

Of all the areas of the Middle East and North Africa which belong to the Arabs, the Land of Israel only comprises one-sixth of 1 percent of this entire area. There is plenty of room in all of the other Arab lands for these *"Palestinians,"* so-called. That being the case, why is it that they want the Land of Israel?

The truth is, they don't even really know themselves. Satan is the instigator in all of this, which means that these people are being used as tools of Satan to try to circumvent the great Promises of God; irrespective, and to be sure, God's Word, which promised this Land to the Jews, will be given to the Jews. The Truth further is, the problems in the Middle East will not be solved until the Second Coming of our Lord. In fact, the hardest days for Israel are just ahead. The Prophet Jeremiah referred to it as *"the time of Jacob's trouble."* But then the Prophet said, *"But he shall be saved out of it"* (Jer. 30:7).

The Promise of the Lord is emphatic as it regards the Land of Israel, and *"this land shall fall unto you for inheritance."*

THE NORTHERN BORDER

Verses 15 through 17 proclaim the fact that the *"North Border"* of the Promised Land, at least in that coming Millennial Day, will begin on the Mediterranean and take in Damascus, actually going as far north as Hazarenan, which is approximately 75 miles north of Damascus. In fact, all of modern Syria will then be in the domain of Israel.

THE EAST BORDER

The eastern border of Israel, in the coming Millennial Reign, will go all the way to the Persian Gulf, for that is the Eastern Sea. It will extend to the Euphrates, which will take in most of modern Iraq.

THE SOUTH BORDER

Verse 19 proclaims the fact that the southern border of Israel will extend all the way to the Suez Canal, and some even think to the River Nile. But more than likely it only includes the Sinai Peninsula, which will stop at the Suez Canal. In fact, counting the entirety of the Southern and Eastern borders, the entirety of the Arabian Peninsula will be included, which, of course, takes in a great part of modern Saudi Arabia.

THE WESTERN BORDER

This is easily defined, as it is the Mediterranean Sea.

Thus, we have these borders, which will enlarge modern Israel to approximately 100 times its present size, if not much larger. All that promised to Abraham will totally and completely be realized. In fact, it could have been realized a long, long time ago, had Israel only accepted Christ. But her rejection of Him greatly extended the process.

THE TRIBES

Verses 21 through 23 deal with the different Tribes of Israel.

The word *"strangers"* in Verse 22 refers to

Gentiles. Inheritance, as stated, was forbidden under the Law of Moses to the Gentiles; but, in the Millennium, it will be fully granted, with, of course, some limitations.

Quite possibly, the Gentiles will become proselyte Jews. As well, there is a possibility that many Gentiles, at least in that day, shall desire this association, and rightly so.

Because of the Jews being God's chosen people, they have suffered terrible opposition from Satan, as well as the animosity of much of the world; also, that suffering has been greatly exacerbated because of their Crucifixion of Christ, thereby, denying God's only Son, their Messiah and Saviour.

However, in that coming Glad Day, such animosity will be removed, and Jewish people will be looked at by all the world with great respect and honor (Isa. 62:4).

"Father Almighty, grant us now Your blessing,
"Answer in love Your children's supplication:
"Hear Thou our prayer, the spoken and unspoken;
"Hear us, our Father."

"Shepherd of souls, Who brings all who seek You
"To pastures green, beside the peaceful waters;
"Tenderest Guide, in ways of cheerful duty,
"Lead us, good Shepherd."

"Father of mercy, from Your watch and keeping
"No place can part nor hour of time remove us:
"Give us Your good, and save us from our evil,
"Infinite Spirit!"

CHAPTER 48

(1) "NOW THESE ARE THE NAMES OF THE TRIBES. FROM THE NORTH END TO THE COAST OF THE WAY OF HETHLON, AS ONE GOES TO HAMATH, HAZARENAN, THE BORDER OF DAMASCUS NORTHWARD, TO THE COAST OF HAMATH; FOR THESE ARE HIS SIDES EAST AND WEST; A PORTION FOR DAN.

(2) "AND BY THE BORDER OF DAN, FROM THE EAST SIDE UNTO THE WEST SIDE, A PORTION FOR ASHER.

(3) "AND BY THE BORDER OF ASHER, FROM THE EAST SIDE EVEN UNTO THE WEST SIDE, A PORTION FOR NAPHTALI.

(4) "AND BY THE BORDER OF NAPHTALI, FROM THE EAST SIDE UNTO THE WEST SIDE, A PORTION FOR MANASSEH.

(5) "AND BY THE BORDER OF MANASSEH, FROM THE EAST SIDE UNTO THE WEST SIDE, A PORTION FOR EPHRAIM.

(6) "AND BY THE BORDER OF EPHRAIM, FROM THE EAST SIDE EVEN UNTO THE WEST SIDE, A PORTION FOR REUBEN.

(7) "AND BY THE BORDER OF REUBEN, FROM THE EAST SIDE UNTO THE WEST SIDE, A PORTION FOR JUDAH.

(8) "AND BY THE BORDER OF JUDAH, FROM THE EAST SIDE UNTO THE WEST SIDE, SHALL BE THE OFFERING WHICH YOU SHALL OFFER OF FIVE AND TWENTY THOUSAND REEDS IN BREADTH, AND IN LENGTH AS ONE OF THE OTHER PARTS, FROM THE EAST SIDE UNTO THE WEST SIDE: AND THE SANCTUARY SHALL BE IN THE MIDST OF IT."

The construction is:

1. Seven Tribes will have their possession north of the Temple, and five Tribes south of the Temple.

2. The children of Leah and Rachel will be placed near the Temple; those of Bilhah and Zilpah (Gen. 30:5, 10), the servant ladies, more distant from the Temple.

3. The city will be foursquare, with twelve gates, three on each side. In a sense, it will be a copy of the city of Revelation, Chapters 21 and 22.

THE TRIBES

The phrase of Verse 1, *"Now these are the names of the Tribes . . . a portion for Dan,"* portrays this Tribe mentioned first.

Concerning the 144,000 Jews who will be

saved in the Great Tribulation, with 12,000 from each Tribe, Dan is not mentioned there.

The question is, *"Why?"*

Some think that the Antichrist, being Jewish, will be of the Tribe of Dan.

In Jacob's Prophesy concerning the various Tribes, he said of Dan, *"Dan shall be a serpent by the way, and an adder in the path, that bites the horses' heels, so that his rider shall fall backward"* (Gen. 49:17).

Irrespective of the difficulties in Revelation, the entirety of the Tribe of Dan will now have accepted the Lord as their Saviour and Messiah. As such, Grace gives them the first portion.

(Actually, Ephraim is not mentioned in the Revelation account either, as the names of Levi and Joseph, Ephraim's father take their places.)

JUDAH

Of the seven Tribes mentioned in Verses 1 through 7, the Seventh Verse closes with the phrase, *"A portion for Judah."*

These sons of Jacob, with the exception of Joseph, and probably Benjamin, could hardly have been called examples of Righteousness. (Joseph is represented by his sons, Manasseh and Ephraim.) Some of them were even murderous in heart, even desiring to kill their brother, Joseph. They then lied to their Father, Jacob, saying that Joseph had undoubtedly been killed by wild beasts, and nothing but his coat of colors was left, causing the Patriarch untold sorrow and heartache (Gen., Chpt. 37).

As well, Judah, as the head of the Tribe from which Christ would come, committed terrible sin, as recorded in Genesis, Chapter 38; likewise, Reuben, Jacob's firstborn, committed grievous sin with *"Bilhah, his Father's concubine"* (Gen. 35:22).

And then there was the perfidiousness of Levi and Simeon in murdering all the males of Shechem, because one of them had defiled their sister Dinah (Gen., Chpt. 34).

Considering the checkered past of these men, and now the Blessings given to them in the coming Kingdom Age, along with their names being eternally inscribed on the Gates of the New Jerusalem, which will come down from God out of Heaven, thereby making planet Earth the headquarters of the Lord, the self-righteous would be hard put to agree to such!

However, these things were *"past"* and covered by the Blood of Christ, and there is every evidence that the latter years of their lives were spent in serving God. Such is Grace!

To be sure, when one looks at these men, one is looking at oneself. As the Lord showed Grace unto them, He will likewise show Grace to anyone who will trust Him.

The only qualification to receive Grace is to be disqualified, and know it! The problem is not the qualification, which is unqualification, which pertains to all, but in getting men to admit it!

THE SANCTUARY

The phrase of Verse 8, *"And the Sanctuary shall be in the midst of it,"* concerns the Temple being in the very middle of this city.

As everything about the Sanctuary speaks of Christ, and, in fact, is symbolic of Him, and from where in actuality He shall rule, all of this tells us that everything is in Christ, even as everything has always been in Christ.

(9) "THE OBLATION THAT YOU SHALL OFFER UNTO THE LORD SHALL BE OF FIVE AND TWENTY THOUSAND IN LENGTH, AND OF TEN THOUSAND IN BREADTH.

(10) "AND FOR THEM, EVEN FOR THE PRIESTS, SHALL BE THIS HOLY OBLATION; TOWARD THE NORTH FIVE AND TWENTY THOUSAND IN LENGTH, AND TOWARD THE WEST TEN THOUSAND IN BREADTH, AND TOWARD THE EAST TEN THOUSAND IN BREADTH, AND TOWARD THE SOUTH FIVE AND TWENTY THOUSAND IN LENGTH: AND THE SANCTUARY OF THE LORD SHALL BE IN THE MIDST THEREOF.

(11) "IT SHALL BE FOR THE PRIESTS WHO ARE SANCTIFIED OF THE SONS OF ZADOK; WHICH HAVE KEPT MY CHARGE, WHICH WENT NOT ASTRAY WHEN THE CHILDREN OF ISRAEL WENT ASTRAY, AS THE LEVITES WENT ASTRAY.

(12) "AND THIS OBLATION OF THE LAND THAT IS OFFERED SHALL BE UNTO THEM A THING MOST HOLY BY THE BORDER OF THE LEVITES.

(13) "AND OVER AGAINST THE BORDER OF THE PRIESTS THE LEVITES SHALL HAVE FIVE AND TWENTY THOUSAND IN LENGTH, AND TEN THOUSAND IN BREADTH: ALL THE LENGTH SHALL BE FIVE AND TWENTY THOUSAND, AND THE BREADTH TEN THOUSAND.

(14) "AND THEY SHALL NOT SELL OF IT, NEITHER EXCHANGE, NOR ALIENATE THE FIRSTFRUITS OF THE LAND: FOR IT IS HOLY UNTO THE LORD."

The exegesis is:

1. The "Oblation" addressed here pertains to the entirety of this city, and whatever its function, as belonging solely to the Lord, in other words, a gift to Him.

2. The Book of Ezekiel teaches that God's purposes may be deferred but cannot be defeated; for Israel will be restored, the Temple of Jehovah certainly built in Jerusalem, and memorial sacrifices once again offered. Christ will be enthroned, and national worship established.

3. In the Inner Court of that Temple, there will be neither Ark, Shewbread, Lampstand, nor Veil, for the actual presence of the Messiah will abolish these. A Risen Lord in the midst abolishes memorials of His absence (Williams).

THE OBLATION

The phrase of Verse 9, *"The Oblation that you shall offer unto the LORD,"* concerns, as stated, the entirety of this city being given as a Gift to the Lord.

In fact, and as should be overly obvious, it is His to begin with, even as everything is His, and we refer to that which is good, wholesome, righteous, and true. He gives it to us, and we, in turn, are to give it back to Him.

All of this, at least as it refers to the Child of God, is a test of our faithfulness regarding stewardship.

THE SANCTUARY OF THE LORD

The phrase of Verse 10, *"And the Sanctuary of the LORD shall be in the midst thereof,"* pertains to the very center of this Holy Oblation, i.e., *"the city."*

As all the Tribes were proportioned around the Tabernacle in the wilderness (Num., Chpts. 1-3), they are likewise proportioned here, although not in the same order.

And yet, as everything was in proportion to the Tabernacle then, everything is in proportion to the Sanctuary now. The reason is simple; it is where the Lord dwells! This is the crowning Truth portrayed by the Holy Spirit in these directions and instructions.

Then, the entirety of the world will look toward Jerusalem, not because of its geographical location or riches, but because *"the LORD is there"* (Ezek. 48:35). Then, prosperity will reign, as prosperity could have reigned all the time, had the Lord been the Center of all activity.

However, man, engineered by Satan, has usurped authority over the Lord and His Ways, instituting his own, which lead only to death. Now, Christ, as the Center of all, will bring everlasting joy and prosperity.

As well, if the Lord is the Center of our Churches, marriages, businesses, homes, education, activities, etc., untold Blessing will be the portion of that person, Church, or nation.

THE SONS OF ZADOK

The phrase of Verse 11, *"It shall be for the Priests who are sanctified of the sons of Zadok,"* speaks of the faithfulness of *"Zadok"* (I Ki. 1:8). Their faithfulness is ever called to account, as faithfulness will ever be called to account.

Concerning *"faithfulness,"* Jesus did not say, *"Well done, thou good and successful servant,"* but rather, *"Well done, thou good and faithful servant: you have been faithful over a few things, I will make you ruler over many things: enter thou into the joy of your Lord"* (Mat. 25:21).

The area in the Twelfth Verse called *"Most Holy"* is the area of the *"Sanctuary."*

Therefore, the reason for the prosperity throughout the world of that day, both spiritual and economical, will be because that from which it emanates is *"Most Holy,"* which speaks of Christ.

There is nothing about this Land that makes it holy, as well as the sons of Zadok, only because Christ there resides.

As well, there is nothing about any mortal, irrespective of whom they may be, that could remotely be called holy, except our relationship with Christ.

THE LEVITES

Verses 13 and 14 proclaim the area apportioned to the Levites. They will have part in the Sanctuary duties, but not the Sacrifices. That will be attended to by the *"sons of Zadok."*

Their portion will be about 17 miles wide and 42 miles long, that is, if our calculations are correct concerning measurements. They will not be able to *"sell, exchange, nor alienate it."*

As well, the *"firstfruits of the Land,"* or the first crop the land produces each year, are not to be sold, but, instead, given to the Lord as an Offering.

This typifies our inheritance in Christ. As Naboth's vineyard, it is not for sale, nor can it be exchanged.

As well, in both the Old and New Testaments, the *"firstfruits,"* or *"tithe"* belong to the Lord.

Therefore, the principle in this Chapter given, concerning the portion of the Levites, is the same regarding the Christian experience in the spiritual sense.

(15) "AND THE FIVE THOUSAND, THAT ARE LEFT IN THE BREADTH OVER AGAINST THE FIVE AND TWENTY THOUSAND, SHALL BE A PROFANE PLACE FOR THE CITY, FOR DWELLING, AND FOR SUBURBS: AND THE CITY SHALL BE IN THE MIDST THEREOF.

(16) "AND THESE SHALL BE THE MEASURES THEREOF; THE NORTH SIDE FOUR THOUSAND AND FIVE HUNDRED, AND THE SOUTH SIDE FOUR THOUSAND AND FIVE HUNDRED, AND ON THE EAST SIDE FOUR THOUSAND AND FIVE HUNDRED, AND THE WEST SIDE FOUR THOUSAND AND FIVE HUNDRED.

(17) "AND THE SUBURBS OF THE CITY SHALL BE TOWARD THE NORTH TWO HUNDRED AND FIFTY, AND TOWARD THE SOUTH TWO HUNDRED AND FIFTY, AND TOWARD THE EAST TWO HUNDRED AND FIFTY, AND TOWARD THE WEST TWO HUNDRED AND FIFTY.

(18) "AND THE RESIDUE IN LENGTH OVER AGAINST THE OBLATION OF THE HOLY PORTION SHALL BE TEN THOUSAND EASTWARD, AND TEN THOUSAND WESTWARD: AND IT SHALL BE OVER AGAINST THE OBLATION OF THE HOLY PORTION; AND THE INCREASE THEREOF SHALL BE FOR FOOD UNTO THEM WHO SERVE THE CITY.

(19) "AND THEY WHO SERVE THE CITY SHALL SERVE IT OUT OF ALL THE TRIBES OF ISRAEL.

(20) "ALL THE OBLATION SHALL BE FIVE AND TWENTY THOUSAND BY FIVE AND TWENTY THOUSAND: YOU SHALL OFFER THE HOLY OBLATION FOURSQUARE, WITH THE POSSESSION OF THE CITY.

(21) "AND THE RESIDUE SHALL BE FOR THE PRINCE, ON THE ONE SIDE AND ON THE OTHER OF THE HOLY OBLATION, AND OF THE POSSESSION OF THE CITY, OVER AGAINST THE FIVE AND TWENTY THOUSAND OF THE OBLATION TOWARD THE EAST BORDER, AND WESTWARD OVER AGAINST THE FIVE AND TWENTY THOUSAND TOWARD THE WEST BORDER, OVER AGAINST THE PORTIONS FOR THE PRINCE: AND IT SHALL BE THE HOLY OBLATION; AND THE SANCTUARY OF THE HOUSE SHALL BE IN THE MIDST THEREOF.

(22) "MOREOVER FROM THE POSSESSION OF THE LEVITES, AND FROM THE POSSESSION OF THE CITY, BEING IN THE MIDST OF THAT WHICH IS THE PRINCE'S, BETWEEN THE BORDER OF JUDAH AND THE BORDER OF BENJAMIN, SHALL BE FOR THE PRINCE."

The structure is:

1. All of these measurements and directions may seem tedious and of little consequence; however, to be sure, the entirety of the Gentile world of that day will look toward, and understand, all of this, even in minute detail. The reason is, Israel's place and position, and her faithfulness to these responsibilities as the Priestly nation, will guarantee the prosperity of the world.

2. The Feasts of the Outer Court will be the Sabbath, the New Moon, Passover, and Tabernacles; but no Pentecost or Day of Atonement, for these cannot be repeated.

3. Atonement and spiritual birth will be the base of Millennial Blessing.

4. Israel's possession of the Land under Joshua was founded upon the Passover (Josh. 5:10). Millennial possession of the Land will be based upon that which the Passover foreshadowed.

THE CITY

The phrase of Verse 15, *"And the city shall be in the midst thereof,"* is where business will be conducted. It is called a *"profane place,"* not meaning that it is evil, but that it is not dedicated to sacred use in the sense that the Sanctuary area is.

This area will be about 8 miles wide and 42 miles long.

The phrase, *"For dwelling, and for suburbs,"* pertains to the area where houses will be built, as well as business activity. No doubt, many more people than there is room for will desire to live in Jerusalem.

Inasmuch as the Glory of God will constantly cover the city, it will be the most desirable place on Earth. No doubt, both Jews and Gentiles will live in this area.

As it regards this city, it will be unlike any city the world has ever seen or known. It will be a city free from crime, poverty, hunger, hate, war, greed, etc. Even though every other city in the world, at that time, will fall, in a sense, into the same category, still, none will have the Glory of God as this *"city."*

Isaiah said, concerning the Jerusalem of that day, *"And the Gentiles shall see Your Righteousness, and all kings Your Glory: and You shall be called by a new name, which the Mouth of the LORD shall name.*

"You shall also be a Crown of Glory in the Hand of the LORD, and a royal diadem in the Hand of your God" (Isa. 62:2-3).

MEASUREMENTS

Verse 16 pertains to the dimensions of the city proper, as it pertains to business, etc. It will be about 5 miles square.

The measurement is given for each side of the city in repetition, in order that it may be known that this city is just as grand on one side as the other. In other words, there will be no slums in this city, as there are presently in every city in the world.

Verse 17 speaks of the *"suburbs,"* which will probably be reserved as a garden or park.

NOTES

Verses 18 and 19 proclaim the fact that two sections of Land will be set aside, reserved for farming, on either side of the city. Each side will measure about 8 x 17 miles.

This will be ample Land to support the city with food, plus the Sanctuary area. Inasmuch as the curse will be lifted, the abundance then produced will be more than enough.

The Nineteenth Verse seems to imply that *"they who serve the city,"* i.e., conduct business there, etc., will be drawn from representatives from all the Tribes of Israel. Therefore, there will be no partiality shown, nor favoritism.

THE OBLATION

The phrase of Verse 20, *"All the oblation,"* concerns the entirety of the area, including city, suburbs, farming land, and the place of the Sanctuary. All will measure approximately 42 miles x 42 miles, that is, if we are correct in our measurements.

The phrase of Verse 20, *"You shall offer the holy oblation foursquare,"* signifies the totality of the Gospel of Jesus Christ, as the whole Gospel, for the whole man. Of all the world, this area will be the most important on Earth, and because Christ is there. No longer will Washington, Tokyo, or London occupy this position. It will be Jerusalem, but, more importantly, the Sanctuary, and, more important still, Christ. It will be a Government such as the world has never known, for it will be upon His Shoulder (Isa. 9:4-6).

Answers to every question will flow from this area, be it spiritual, economical, domestic, or physical; consequently, the entirety of the complexion of the world will change, because the wisdom then given will not be earthly wisdom, which is sensual and devilish, but Heavenly Wisdom (James 3:14-18).

THE PRINCE

The phrase of Verse 21, *"And the residue shall be for the prince,"* probably speaks of the Great High Priest.

The Land east and west of the Holy Oblation will be for the Prince of Israel. This area on both sides is called *"the residue."*

It seems these portions given to him will be about 8-1/2 miles x 8-1/2 miles. They will be on East and West corners, respectively; therefore, he will have access to whatever he needs from either side.

Once again, the Holy Spirit repeats the phrase, *"And the Sanctuary of the House shall be in the midst thereof,"* and by design. It is meant to impress upon the Believer that all Blessing flows from the Sanctuary, and, therefore, from Christ. Even though these dimensions are given and explained, and will, no doubt, be grand and glorious, still, all of it is because of *"Him,"* the Messiah, the Saviour of man, the Lord of Glory.

Verse 22 proclaims the fact that one portion of the Prince will border *"Judah,"* while the other portion borders *"Benjamin."* These were the two Tribes that remained true to the Temple and the worship of God, when the nation of Israel was divided upon the death of Solomon; therefore, their faithfulness is not forgotten, but will ever portray their allegiance to the Lord of Glory, and His Word.

(23) "AS FOR THE REST OF THE TRIBES, FROM THE EAST SIDE UNTO THE WEST SIDE, BENJAMIN SHALL HAVE A PORTION.

(24) "AND BY THE BORDER OF BENJAMIN, FROM THE EAST SIDE UNTO THE WEST SIDE, SIMEON SHALL HAVE A PORTION.

(25) "AND BY THE BORDER OF SIMEON, FROM THE EAST SIDE UNTO THE WEST SIDE, ISSACHAR A PORTION.

(26) "AND BY THE BORDER OF ISSACHAR, FROM THE EAST SIDE UNTO THE WEST SIDE, ZEBULON A PORTION.

(27) "AND BY THE BORDER OF ZEBULON, FROM THE EAST SIDE UNTO THE WEST SIDE, GAD A PORTION.

(28) "AND BY THE BORDER OF GAD, AT THE SOUTH SIDE SOUTHWARD, THE BORDER SHALL BE EVEN FROM TAMAR UNTO THE WATERS OF STRIFE IN KADESH, AND TO THE RIVER TOWARD THE GREAT SEA.

(29) "THIS IS THE LAND WHICH YOU SHALL DIVIDE BY LOT UNTO THE TRIBES OF ISRAEL FOR INHERITANCE, AND THESE ARE THEIR PORTIONS, SAITH THE LORD GOD.

NOTES

(30) "AND THESE ARE THE GOINGS OUT OF THE CITY ON THE NORTH SIDE, FOUR THOUSAND AND FIVE HUNDRED MEASURES.

(31) "AND THE GATES OF THE CITY SHALL BE AFTER THE NAMES OF THE TRIBES OF ISRAEL: THREE GATES NORTHWARD; ONE GATE OF REUBEN, ONE GATE OF JUDAH, ONE GATE OF LEVI.

(32) "AND AT THE EAST SIDE FOUR THOUSAND AND FIVE HUNDRED: AND THREE GATES; AND ONE GATE OF JOSEPH, ONE GATE OF BENJAMIN, ONE GATE OF DAN.

(33) "AND AT THE SOUTH SIDE FOUR THOUSAND AND FIVE HUNDRED MEASURES: AND THREE GATES; ONE GATE OF SIMEON, ONE GATE OF ISSACHAR, ONE GATE OF ZEBULUN.

(34) "AT THE WEST SIDE FOUR THOUSAND AND FIVE HUNDRED, WITH THEIR THREE GATES; ONE GATE OF GAD, ONE GATE OF ASHER, ONE GATE OF NAPHTALI.

(35) "IT WAS ROUND ABOUT EIGHTEEN THOUSAND MEASURES: AND THE NAME OF THE CITY FROM THAT DAY SHALL BE, THE LORD IS THERE."

The overview is:

1. The Bible student, as well as the Hebrew Prophet, is commanded, and invited, to behold with his eyes, to hear with his ears, and to set his heart upon all that God reveals in this Book of Ezekiel.

2. Everything in Ezekiel's Temple was measured by the Man Who had the reed and the line. Christ, the Head of Church, the Divine Man, measures and tests everything in a professed temple. His instrument of measurement is the Bible.

3. The Christian is a temple (I Cor. 3:16), having walls, gates, chambers, narrow windows, etc., i.e., limitations, openings, emotions, and prejudices. These must be tested by the *"reed"* and the *"line."*

4. In the South Chambers, there were sunshine and service; in the North Chambers, Sacrifice and Intercession.

5. This last Vision, which spans Chapters 40 through 48, predicts that Israel will be the Divine center of government in the Earth; that in its center will be placed the Temple

of God's Glory; and that in its center will be the Throne of God, so to speak, and the Altar of Burnt Offering, typifying the Cross. Thus, Christ and the Cross will be the center of the future Kingdom of God on Earth. Overall will be the bridal canopy of the Glory of God (Isa. 4:5).

DIVIDE BY LOT

Verses 23 through 29 present the borders of the various Tribes.

The phrase of Verse 29, *"Divide by Lot,"* originally referred to the Urim and Thummin, which were held by the High Priest, and used to discern the Mind of God (Josh. 13:7; 15:1; 16:1; 17:1). Therefore, the statement, as recorded here, simply means that each possession and its boundary have been decided by the Holy Spirit.

The first time the Land was portioned out, after Joshua had gained victory over the inhabitants, because of Israel's continued sin, the Land was mightily contested by the enemy; however, it will not be contested again. *"These are their portions, saith the Lord GOD,"* and they are portions that will never be changed or taken by an enemy.

THE GATES

Verses 30 through 34 proclaim the fact that the final portion is dedicated to the gates, dimensions, and name of the city. The phrase of Verse 30, *"And these are the goings out of the city,"* refers to the walls around the city, and its measurement.

The phrase, *"The North side,"* also refers to every side, *"four thousand and five hundred measures (reeds);"* therefore, the city will be about 7-1/2 miles on each side.

The city will be foursquare, with three gates to the side, totaling twelve gates. The phrase of Verse 31, *"And the gates of the city shall be after the names of the Tribes of Israel,"* presents itself as very similar to the New Jerusalem, which will come down from God out of Heaven, and is recorded in Chapters 21 and 22 of the Book of Revelation. Even though this city is a miniature, at least in some ways, of the New Jerusalem, which will come down from God out of Heaven upon the New Earth (Rev. 21:12-16), still, the differences will be great. The earthly city will be about 7-1/2 miles square, while the Heavenly one will be 1,500 miles square, and the same measurement high, which defies all comprehension and imagination.

THE LORD IS THERE

The phrase of Verse 35, *"The name of the city from that day shall be, The LORD is there,"* presents only one of the number of new names for the eternal earthly Jerusalem.

The phrase, *"The LORD is there,"* means, in Hebrew, *"Adonai-Shammah,"* or *"Jehovah-Shammah,"* meaning literally what it says. For the Messiah will be there reigning visibly and eternally in Israel (Isa. 9:6-7; Lk. 1:32-33; Rev. 11:15; 20:4-10).

As well, the Holy Spirit said through the Prophet Isaiah, that the city would be called *"Hephzibah,"* meaning *"delight,"* or *"in whom is My delight"* (Isa. 62:4).

It will be called that by the Lord, and *"The LORD is there"* by the population of the world.

The whole vast structure, from its platform base to its glorious summit, will be a place of Glory, with the *"Tree of Life"* in its very center, i.e., *"Christ."*

"THE LORD IS THERE"

Hallelujah!

THE CONCLUSION

It is August 11, 2003, as I conclude the rewrite on the Book of Ezekiel. I have learned so very much in the writing of this, thereby hoping that the Reader will benefit accordingly.

I have tried my best to portray these great Visions, as given to the Prophet Ezekiel, exactly as they were given, learning that all that Israel was, and shall be, is centered up in the Atonement. But, of course, *"the Atonement"* is the centerpiece of the entirety of the Bible.

THE BOOK OF EZEKIEL

In this great Book, we have the cause of the Fall of Israel, which was sin. As well, it is tragically amazing at the similarity of the Israel of that day of so long ago with the modern Church. The earmarks are too plentiful to be ignored.

Also, in these great Visions given to the

Prophet, we are given a *"look,"* so to speak, into the regions of Hell itself. In fact, the great Prophet describes it, at least from the viewpoint given him by the Holy Spirit, as no place otherwise found in the Word of God.

And then in Chapter 37, we are given a preview of the Restoration of Israel, which, in fact, has already begun. That should be a sobering thought to all concerned, helping us to realize how close we are to the very end — the end of the Church Age.

Chapters 38 and 39 portray the Battle of Armageddon as no other account given in the Word of God.

Immediately following this avid description, Chapter 40 proclaims the Restoration of Israel, with her finally fulfilling that which God had intended from the very beginning. This description continues through the end of the Book.

Understanding that the supremacy of Israel begins with Chapter 40, we understand from this that Chapters 38 and 39 must, of necessity, portray the Battle of Armageddon.

So, Chapter 37 is in the process of fulfillment now, with the balance of the Book yet to be fulfilled.

A TREMENDOUS LESSON

It is a shame that the Book of Ezekiel is studied so little by the modern Church. As stated, the similarities between the Israel that lost her way and the modern Church are striking. It is meant by the Holy Spirit that the modern Church take a lesson from this.

But despite all the problems of Israel of old, Chapters 40 through 48 proclaim the fact that these beleaguered people will be brought back, with the Promises made to Abraham and the Patriarchs of old made good, and in every respect. Despite every attack by Satan, despite his unrelenting efforts to destroy these ancient people, the Book closes with the beautiful proclamation, *"The LORD is there."*

Nothing could be greater!

"Thy Word is a Lamp to my feet,
"A light to my path always,
"To guide and to save me from sin,
"And show me the Heav'nly Way."

"Forever, O Lord, is Thy Word
"Established and fixed on high;
"Thy faithfulness unto all men
"Abideth forever nigh."

"At morning, at noon, and at night
"I ever will give You praise;
"For You are my portion, O Lord,
"And shall be through all my days!"

"Thro' Him Whom Thy Word has foretold,
"The Saviour and Morning Star,
"Salvation and Peace have been bro't
"To those who have strayed afar."

BIBLIOGRAPHY

The Student's Commentary on the Holy Scriptures — Williams.

The Pulpit Commentary.

The New Bible Dictionary.

Ellicott's Commentary on the Whole Bible.

Theological Wordbook of the Old Testament.

Strong's Exhaustive Concordance of the Bible.

INDEX

The index is listed according to subjects. The treatment may include a complete dissertation or no more than a paragraph. But hopefully it will provide some help.

As well, even though extended treatment of a subject may not be carried in this Commentary, one of the other Commentaries may well include the desired material.

A FORM OF GODLINESS, 321
A LESSON FOR MODERN BELIEVERS, 351
ABOMINATION, 48, 118, 120, 153, 333
ABORTION, 184
ACCEPTANCE, 169
ACCEPTANCE OF THE CROSS, 99
ALIENATION, 202
ALL TRUTH IS GOD'S TRUTH?, 267
ALMIGHTY GOD, 63
ALTAR, 223, 424, 478
ALTAR OF INCENSE, 429
AMMONITES, 225, 227
ANGEL OF THE HIGHEST RANK, 273
ANGELS OF LIGHT, 247
ANGER, 216
ANGER AND ENVY, 355
ANKLES, 480
ANOINTED CHERUB, 277
ANOINTING, 11
ANOTHER GOSPEL, 269, 370
ANOTHER JESUS, ANOTHER SPIRIT, AND ANOTHER GOSPEL, 35
APOCRYPHA, 241, 243
APOSTASY, 222
APOSTATE CHURCH, 346
APOSTLE PAUL AND THE MODERN CHURCH, 337
APOSTLES AND PROPHETS, 97
ARE YOU A DELIVERANCE PREACHER?, 322
ARMAGEDDON, 388
ASSHUR, ELAM, MESHECH, TUBAL, EDOM, ZIDON, 318
ASSYRIAN, 304

ATONEMENT IS THE ETERNAL FOUNDATION OF GOD'S RELATIONSHIP WITH MAN, 438
ATTACK ON ISRAEL, 389
BABYLON AND EGYPT, 145
BABYLONIANS, 201
BAPTISM WITH THE HOLY SPIRIT FOLLOWS CONVERSION, 484
BAROMETER OF THE CHURCH, 277
BASE KINGDOM, 292
BATTLE OF ARMAGEDDON, 386, 394
BEAUTY, 272
BECAUSE OF SIN, 146
BENEFITS OF THE CROSS, 54
BETWEEN SHEEP AND SHEEP, 346
BIBLE, 76
BITTER WATERS, 203
BLASPHEMING THE HOLY SPIRIT, 329
BLESSING, 372
BLESSING OF THE LORD, 187
BLESSING ON THE HOUSE, 463
BLOOD, 216, 448, 469
BLOOD AND THE OIL, 472
BLOOD OF JESUS CHRIST, 242
BLOOD OF SOULS, 324
BLOOD ON THE HANDS, 210
BLOWING OF THE TRUMPET, 323
BOASTS OF EDOM, 355
BONDAGE OF DARKNESS, 274
BOOK OF REVELATION, 258
BOTTOMLESS PIT, 240
BRAZEN ALTAR, 56
BREATH, 376
BRINK OF THE RIVER, 483

BROKEN ARMS OF PHARAOH, 301
BROKEN COVENANT, 128
BURDEN, 173
BURNT OFFERING, 422, 450
BUSINESS, 249
BY FAITH, 203
CAIN AND ABEL, 223
CALL OF ABRAHAM, 308
CALVARY, 118
CAN A HOMOSEXUAL BE SAVED?, 120
CANAAN, 111
CANNOT SATAN READ THE BIBLE?, 389
CAPTIVITY, 1, 83, 405
CAUSE, 172
CHAINS, 144
CHAMBERS, 434
CHANGING OF THE WORD OF GOD, 22
CHERUBIM, 3, 62, 71
CHERUBIMS AND PALM TREES, 429
CHIEF PRINCE OF MESHECH AND TUBAL, 386
CHOICE, 246
CHRIST MUST NEVER BE SEPARATED FROM THE CROSS, 442
CHRISTIAN AND GRACE, 124
CHRISTIAN CONTEMPORARY MUSIC, 275
CHRISTIAN TELEVISION, 321
CHRISTIAN WHO TRIES TO LIVE UNDER LAW, 123
CHRISTIANS PUNISHING OTHER CHRISTIANS, 353
CHURCH, 221
CHURCH GOVERNMENT, 454
CIRCUMCISION, 270
CITY, 465
CLEAR AND PLAIN PREACHING, 211
CLEAR AND PRESENT DANGER, 339
CLOUDY AND DARK DAY, 342
COMING GREAT TRIBULATION, 297
COMING RESTORATION, 443
COMMISSION, 325
CONDEMNATION, 141
CONFIDENCE, 292
CONFIDENCE EXCLUSIVELY IN THE LORD, 293
CONSECRATION OF THE PROPHET, 220
CONSENT OF THE GOVERNED, 281
CONSPIRACY, 192
CONTINUED VICTORY?, 61
CONTROL OF THE HOLY SPIRIT, 17
CONVERSION OF ZEDEKIAH?, 131

COUNSELING, 182
COVENANT, 130, 188
COVENANT GOD, 290
COVENANT OF PEACE, 347
COVERING, 200
COVETOUSNESS, 334
CROSS, 2, 4, 35, 49, 54, 64, 151, 189, 209, 217, 240, 316, 343, 369, 469
CROSS AND THIS PRESENT TIME, 440
CROSS CHURCH, 447
CROSS HAS BEEN ABANDONED BY THE CHURCH, 452
CROSS IS ALWAYS REJECTED ON MORAL GROUNDS, 453
CROSS IS THE MEANS, 65
CROSS OF CHRIST, 23, 31, 338
CROSS OF CHRIST MUST EVER BE THE OBJECT OF FAITH, 69, 257
CROSS, A PLACE OF DEFEAT OR VICTORY?, 26
CROSS, THE MEANS OF THIS DEATH, 70
CROSS, THE ONLY SOLUTION FOR PRIDE, 265
CROSS, THE RATIFICATION OF THE COVENANT, 189
CULTURE, 248
CURSE OF THE LAW, 162
DAILY, 37
DAVID, 231, 380
DAY OF THE LORD, 297
DEAD TO THE SIN NATURE, 280
DEATH, 75, 77, 461
DECEPTION, 63, 106
DECEPTION AND THE CROSS, 106
DEEPENING ERROR, 242
DEFILEMENT, 363
DEFILEMENT OF GOD'S HOLY NAME, 444
DELIVERANCE OF THE FLOCK, 341
DENIAL, 103
DEPARTING FROM THE FAITH, 24
DEPARTURE, 79
DEPENDENCE!, 200
DESERT AND THE SEA, 483
DESIRE OF THE EYES, 219
DESOLATION, 84, 145, 352
DESTRUCTION, 57, 226, 235, 254, 264
DESTRUCTION OF SATAN, 281
DIADEM, 177
DIMENSIONS, 413
DISCRIMINATION, 248
DISHONEST GAIN, 186

DISPENSATION OF GRACE, 206
DIVIDE BY LOT, 498
DIVINE JUDGMENTS, 299
DOCTRINE OF SELF-ESTEEM IS A DOCTRINE OF DEVILS, 266
DOES A PROPER UNDERSTANDING OF THE CROSS GUARANTEE VICTORY?, 197
DOES GOD JUDGE BELIEVERS?, 32
DOESN'T THE MODERN CHURCH BELIEVE THIS GREAT TRUTH OF TOTAL VICTORY IN THE CROSS?, 24
DOOM OF THE FALSE PROPHETS, 90
DOOR, 425
DREAMS OF PHARAOH, 488
DROSS, 190
DWELL SAFELY IN THEIR LAND, 408
DYING TO SELF!, 205
EARTH SHALL YIELD HER INCREASE, 348
EAST BORDER, 491
EASTERN GATE, 416, 451, 472
EATING THE OFFERINGS, 462
EDOM, 229, 351
EGYPT, 129, 153, 206, 288
EGYPT AND ASSYRIA, 303
EGYPT, ASSYRIA, AND TYRE, 311
EGYPT'S SIN, 290
EGYPTIAN IDOLATRY, 52
EIGHTH DAY, 450
ELDERS, 169
EQUAL, 140
EQUAL WAYS, 331
ERRONEOUS INTERPRETATION, 138
ETERNAL, 307
ETERNAL SECURITY, 14
ETHICS, 122
EVANGELISM, 251
EVERLASTING COVENANT, 123, 382
EVERYTHING COMES THROUGH THE CROSS, 317
EVIL THOUGHT, 388
EXALTATION, 304
EXAMPLE OF METHODS OTHER THAN THE CROSS, 169
EXCOMMUNICATING OF THESE SHEPHERDS, 341
EXILES, 166
EZEKIEL, 221
FAIR JEWELS, 117
FAITH, 4, 60, 257

FAITH AND ITS CORRECT OBJECT, 258
FAITH IN THE CROSS, 135
FAITHFUL WATCHMEN, 322
FALL OF JERUSALEM, 332
FALLING FROM GRACE, 232
FALSE DOCTRINE, 52, 133, 192, 246
FALSE HELP, 211
FALSE MESSAGE, 74, 86
FALSE PEACE, 93
FALSE PROPHETS, 87, 95
FIRE ON MAGOG, 397
FIRST RESURRECTION, 469
FIRSTBORN?, 28
FLESH, 212
FLESH AND THE SPIRIT, 231
FLOWING OF THE WATERS, 479
FOCUS, 480
FOOLISH PROPHETS, 88
FORCE AND CRUELTY, 337
FORCE OF THE RIVER, 482
FOREVER, 283
FORSAKING GOD, 208
FOUNDATION, 427
FOUNDING OF TYRE, 235
FOUR SINS, 353
FOUR SINS OF SODOM, 120
FRUITFUL, 146
FURY, 392
FURY OF THE LORD, 365
GAMBLING SPIRIT, 187
GAPS AND THE HEDGE, 88
GARDEN OF GOD, 273, 304
GATES, 419, 498
GLOAT OF SATAN OVER THE FALL OF JUDAH AND JERUSALEM, 234
GLORY OF GOD, 4, 6, 78
GLORY OF THE GOD OF ISRAEL, 439
GLORY OF THE LORD, 17, 63, 452
GOD IS UNALTERABLY OPPOSED TO FALSE SHEPHERDS, 340
GOD'S ANSWER TO PRIDE, 264
GOD'S JUDGMENT AGAINST SIN, 62
GOD'S PRESCRIBED ORDER OF VICTORY, 32, 59, 90, 279
GOD'S WAY, 176
GOD'S WISDOM, 272
GOG, 384, 401
GOSPEL, 244
GOSPEL OF GREED, 262

GOSPEL OF SELF-ESTEEM, 265
GOVERNMENT, 466
GRACE, 104, 112
GRACE OF GOD, 232, 371
GRACE OR LAW, 105
GRAVES, 378
GREAT JUDGE, 344
GREAT SACRIFICE, 404
GREED, 185
GREED MESSAGE, 370
GUARD CHAMBERS, 417
HAILSTONES, FIRE, AND BRIMSTONE, 393
HAM, 385
HATRED, 352
HEALING OF THE WATERS, 483
HEAR WHAT THE SPIRIT IS SAYING TO THE CHURCHES, 323
HEATHEN, 166, 212, 227, 405
HELL, 27, 239, 306, 318
HIDDEN FACE OF GOD, 406
HIGH PRIEST, 470
HIS GLORY, 439
HIS VOICE, 439
HISTORY, 312
HISTORY OF ISRAEL, 149
HOLY NAME OF THE LORD, 366
HOLY PLACES, 46
HOLY SPIRIT, 2, 4, 7, 12, 43, 53, 60, 68, 73, 100, 151, 196, 249
HOLY SPIRIT AND THE CROSS, 479
HOLY SPIRIT AT CONVERSION, 484
HOLY SPIRIT AT THE PRESENT TIME, 79
HOLY THINGS, 181
HONESTY, 466
HOUSE OF GOD, 56
HOUSE OF THE LORD, 440
HOW DO WE STAY DEAD?, 91
HOW DO WE WALK AFTER THE SPIRIT?, 459
HOW DOES GOD REACT TO REBELLION?, 215
HOW DOES SATAN THINK HE CAN DEFEAT THE LORD?, 402
HOW DOES THE BLOOD OF JESUS CHRIST CLEANSE FROM ALL SIN?, 368
HOW DOES THE LAW AFFECT THE MODERN CHRISTIAN?, 159
HOW IS REBELLION AS THE SIN OF WITCHCRAFT?, 81
HOW IS THE CROSS THE POWER OF GOD?, 210, 321
HOW MANY, OF AGES PAST, HAVE GONE TO HELL?, 307
HOW SHOULD THIS HISTORY AFFECT MODERN CHRISTIANS?, 145
HOW THE HOLY SPIRIT WORKS, 66, 69, 479
HOW TO LIVE YOUR LIFE!, 124
HOW WAS MAN TO RECEIVE JUSTIFICATION?, 381
HUMAN SACRIFICE, 210
HUMANISTIC PSYCHOLOGY, 193
HUMBLED, 121
HUMILITY, 270, 478
I WILL JUDGE YOU AFTER YOUR WAYS, 331
IDOLATRY, 34, 145, 213
IDOLATRY AND THE MODERN CHURCH, 35
IDOLS, 100, 155, 300
IGNORANCE, 103
ILLEGITIMATE?, 185
IMAGE OF JEALOUSY, 49, 52
IMPUTED RIGHTEOUSNESS, 364, 412
IN CHRIST JESUS, 459
INCREASE OF WICKEDNESS, 114
INDICTMENT, 115
INDIVIDUAL RESPONSIBILITY, 136
INFALLIBILITY OF THE NEW COVENANT, 189
INHERITANCE, 187, 462, 475, 491
INIQUITY, 20, 278
INIQUITY OF JERUSALEM, 180
INITIAL, PHYSICAL EVIDENCE OF THE BAPTISM WITH THE SPIRIT, 485
INTERCESSION, 151
INTERCESSION AND THE HOLY SPIRIT, 212
IS IT THE CROSS OR THE THRONE?, 29
IS IT WHO JESUS WAS OR WHAT JESUS DID?, 316
IS PREACHING THE CROSS PREACHING DEATH?, 29
IS THE RESURRECTION THE PRINCIPAL PLACE OF VICTORY?, 26
ISLAM, 228
ISRAEL, 225, 349
ISRAEL AND THE CHURCH, 256
ITCHING EARS, 322
JAPHETH, 385
JEALOUS GOD, 225
JEALOUSY, 360, 392, 407
JEALOUSY AS SHOWN IN THE OLD TESTAMENT, 408

JEHOAHAZ, 144
JEHOIAKIM, 144
JEREMIAH, 48, 185
JERUSALEM, 21, 111, 176
JESUS, 151
JESUS CHRIST IS THE SOURCE AND THE CROSS IS THE MEANS, 4, 64, 308
JESUS DIED PHYSICALLY, NOT SPIRITUALLY, 27
JESUS DIED SPIRITUALLY DOCTRINE, 25, 26, 449
JOHN THE BAPTIST, 185
JOSEPH, 490
JOSIAH, 144
JUDAH, 199, 218, 250, 493
JUDGMENT, 32, 34, 87, 117, 140, 161, 178, 207, 228, 284, 354, 460
JUDGMENT MULTIPLIED, 75
JUDGMENT OF GOD, 43
JUSTIFICATION BY FAITH, 330, 381
KEEPING THE CHARGE, 454
KEY TO VICTORY, 138
KING OF BABYLON, 175
KINGDOM NOW PHILOSOPHY, 41
KNEES, 481
LAKE OF FIRE, 240
LAMENTATION, 143, 314
LAMENTATION FOR PHARAOH, 311
LAND OF ISRAEL, 226, 286
LATTER DAYS, 391
LATTER YEARS, 387
LAW, 67, 105, 135, 158
LAW AND RIGHTEOUSNESS, 411
LAW OF MOSES?, 427
LAW OF THE HOUSE, 445
LAW OF THE SPIRIT OF LIFE IN CHRIST JESUS, 68
LAWFUL AND RIGHT, 133
LEADING AND GUIDANCE, 175
LET MY PEOPLE GO, 154
LEVITES, 455, 464, 495
LICENSE, 103
LIES, 217
LIFE, 486
LIGHT REJECTED, 311
LINEN GARMENTS, 457
LITTLE CHAMBERS, 416
LITTLE SANCTUARY, 77
LOINS, 481

LORD AND HIS PEOPLE, 290
LORD IS THERE, 498
LORD JESUS CHRIST, 346
LORD WILL MAGNIFY AND SANCTIFY HIMSELF, 393
LORD'S SUPPER, 50
LORDSHIP OF CHRIST, 291
LOVE, 112, 360
LUCIFER, 271
MAIN EMPHASIS OF THE BELIEVER'S INHERITANCE, 188
MAKING OF THE CROSS OF CHRIST OF NONE EFFECT, 31
MAN, 56
MAN AND GOD, 261
MAN AND THE LION, 429
MAN WITH THE LINE IN HIS HAND, 411, 417, 480
MAN'S ATTEMPT TO PLAY GOD, 267
MAN'S SIN, 359
MASADA, 253
MEANING OF PRAYER, 150
MEANING OF THE SEVEN HORNS AND THE SEVEN EYES, 443
MEASURE, 464
MEASURE THE PATTERN, 444
MEASUREMENTS, 424, 496
MEASURES OF THE ALTAR, 445
MEASURING, 436
MEDICINE, 489
MEMORIAL, 436
MERCHANDISE, 251, 278
MERCY, 118, 163, 407
MESSAGE OF THE CROSS, 94, 98
MESSAGE OF THE CROSS IS NOT OPTIONAL, 223
MESSIAH, 251
MIND OF MAN, 75
MINISTRY OF RECONCILIATION, 358
MINISTRY OF THE WATCHMAN, 15
MINISTRY TO GOD, 475
MIRY PLACES, 489
MOAB AND SEIR, 227
MODERN ABOMINATIONS, 49
MODERN BELIEVER AND THE LAW, 123
MODERN CHURCH, 164
MODERN CHURCH AND THE HOLY SPIRIT, 12
MODERN PREACHERS, 181

MODERN TEACHING THAT EQUATES TO
    IDOLS, 155
MONEY, 275
MONEY GOSPEL, 74
MORAL ELEVATION, 361
MORE ABUNDANT LIFE, 153
MORNING SACRIFICE, 474
MOSAIC LAW, 162
MOST HOLY PLACE, 425
MOVING OF THE SPIRIT, 42
MUSIC, 274
MUSIC AS DESIGNED BY THE LORD, 423
MUSIC WAS ORIGINALLY CREATED BY GOD, 276
MY FLOCK, 345
MY FLOCK BECAME A PREY, 339
MY GOD, MY GOD, WHY HAVE YOU FORSAKEN
    ME?, 28
MY HOLY NAME, 399
MY PEOPLE, 350
MY SANCTUARY, 382
MY TABLE, 404
NAHAH, 176
NAME OF THE LORD, 157, 367
NATIONS OF THE WORLD, 229
NATIONS OF THE WORLD WHICH OPPOSED
    ISRAEL, 345
NATIONS WHICH OPPOSE ISRAEL, 345
NATIONS WITHOUT GOD, 317
NEBUCHADNEZZAR, 236, 293, 298
NEGATIVE MESSAGE, 9
NETHER PARTS OF THE EARTH, 316
NEW BIRTH, 142
NEW COVENANT, 189, 270, 367
NEW FRUIT, 489
NEW HEART AND THE NEW SPIRIT, 369
NEW REFORMATION, 266
NEW SPIRIT, 78
NEW TESTAMENT AND IDOLS, 101
NEW VOCABULARY, 296
NO MORE PITY, 59
NO PLEASURE IN THE DEATH OF THE
    WICKED, 327
NO SWEAT, 457
NOAH, DANIEL, AND JOB, 108
NORTH GATE AND THE SOUTH GATE, 473
NORTH PARTS, 395
NORTHERN BORDER, 491
OBEDIENCE, 163
OBJECT OF OUR FAITH, 159, 182, 481

OBLATION, 464, 494, 496
OFFERINGS, 467
OFFICE OF THE PROPHET, 95, 96
OLD TYRE, 237
ONLY ANSWER IS THE CROSS, 400
ONLY WAY TO LIVE FOR GOD, 37
OPENING OF THE SECOND SEAL, 298
OPPOSITE OF THE ECONOMY OF GOD, 263
OPPOSITION, 327
OPPOSITION OF GOD, 235
OPPOSITION OF SATAN, 396
OPPOSITION OF THE LORD, 284
ORDINANCES OF THE ALTAR, 447
ORDINANCES OF THE HOUSE OF THE
    LORD, 452
OTHER GARMENTS, 435
OUTER COURT, 431, 457
OUTER COURT AND THE INNER COURT, 418
PAGAN, 321
PALM TREES, 418
PARABLE, 126
PARADISE, 239
PAST RIGHTEOUSNESS, 330
PAUL AND THE CROSS, 36
PERFECTION, 278
PERSECUTION, 97
PERSONAL RELATIONSHIPS, 460
PERSONAL RESPONSIBILITY, 137
PERVERSION OF SACRED MUSIC, 277
PHARAOH, 319
PHILISTINES, 230
PILLOW PROPHETS, 98
PLACE CALLED HELL, 238
PLACE OF MY THRONE, 443
PLANT OF RENOWN, 349
PLAYED THE WHORE, 115
POLLUTION OF THE NAME OF THE LORD HAS
    ENDED, 399
POMP OF EGYPT, 313
POSITION AND CONDITION, 160
POSSESSION, 355
POURED OUT SPIRIT, 409
POWER, 164
POWER OF GOD, 83, 440
POWER OF THE SPIRIT, 135
POWER SOURCE, 183, 481
POWERS OF DARKNESS, 197
PRAYER, 150
PREACHER OF RIGHTEOUSNESS, 8

PREACHING AND TEACHING, 96
PREACHING OF THE CROSS, 90
PREDESTINATION, 139, 299
PRESENCE OF GOD, 392
PRESENT CHURCH, 148
PRESIDENT TRUMAN, 253
PRIDE, 121, 259, 281, 306
PRIDE AND HUMANITY, 260
PRIDE AND ITS EFFECT, 261
PRIDE AND JUDGMENT, 259
PRIDE AND SATAN, 260
PRIDE HAS BUDDED, 44
PRIESTS, 423, 448
PRINCE, 452, 466, 472, 474, 496
PRINCE OF TYRUS, 256
PROOF OF REDEMPTION, 330
PROPHECY, 314
PROPHECY FULFILLED, 214
PROPHECY TO THE EXILES, 332
PROPHESY, 74, 171, 357, 376
PROPHESY UNTO THE SPIRIT, 377
PROPHET, 8, 335
PROPHETS OF ISRAEL, 391
PROSPERITY, 107, 361
PSYCHOLOGY, 202
PURGATORY, 240
PURGE, 217
PUT AWAY YOUR WHOREDOMS, 444
QUESTIONS, 390
REAL CAUSE OF DEATH, 458
REAL REASON IS AN IMPROPER UNDERSTANDING OF THE CROSS, 154
REBELLION, 109, 156, 214, 312, 453
REBELLION AGAINST GOD'S WAY, 60
REBELLION AGAINST THE CROSS, 215
REBELLIOUS HOUSE, 80
RECONCILIATION, 467
REGENERATION, 141, 370
RELATIONSHIP, 152
RELATIVE RIGHTEOUSNESS, 364
REMNANT, 39
REPENTANCE, 101, 141, 218, 327
REPENTANCE AND THE CROSS, 102
REPETITION, 198
REPROACH, 181
RESPONSE OF THE CHURCH TO THE CROSS, 216
RESTORATION, 131, 169, 294, 409
RESTORATION OF ISRAEL, 285, 349, 374

RESULTS, 481
RESURRECTION, 29
REVEALED TRUTH, 223
REVELATION, 125
RIGHT KIND OF PRIDE, 259
RIGHTEOUS AND THE WICKED, 172
RIGHTEOUSNESS, 137, 142, 303, 411
RIGHTEOUSNESS AND FAITH, 412
RIGHTEOUSNESS AND THE CROSS, 365, 412
RIGHTEOUSNESS AND THE HOLY SPIRIT, 413
RIGHTEOUSNESS AND WICKEDNESS, 329
RIVER, 481
RIVER OF LIFE, 487
ROMAN CATHOLIC EXPLANATION, 241
ROMANS, 90
ROMANS, CHAPTER 7, 91
ROUTE OF THE INVASION, 395
RUIN, 252
RULE, 167
SABBATH, 159
SACRIFICE OF CLEANSING, 404
SACRIFICES, 435, 463, 473, 476
SALVATION AND THE CROSS, 457
SALVATION FOR ISRAEL, 343
SAMARIA, 196
SANCTIFICATION, 160, 286, 368
SANCTUARY, 211, 221, 464, 468, 489, 493
SANCTUARY AND THE PROFANE PLACE, 436
SANCTUARY OF THE LORD, 494
SATAN'S LAST FLING AT THE CHURCH, 31
SAVING THE LIFE OF THE MOTHER?, 185
SCATTERED SHEEP, 338
SEARCHING FOR THE SHEEP, 341
SECOND COMING, 397
SELF, 205, 268
SEPTEMBER 11, 2001, 57
SERIOUSNESS OF SPIRITUAL ADULTERY, 204
SEVEN, 470
SEVEN DAYS, 461
SEVEN MONTHS, 402
SEVEN YEARS, 401
SEVENFOLD WORK OF THE SPIRIT, 442
SHAME, 361
SHARPENED SWORD, 173
SHEM, 385
SHEPHERDS, 336
SHOWERS OF BLESSING, 347
SIGNS, 18, 81, 224
SIGNS OF THE TIMES, 18

SIN, 53, 142, 188, 279, 470
SIN AND THE CROSS, 348
SIN NATURE, 102, 405
SIN OFFERING, 449, 462
SINGERS, 422
SIXTH PART, 395
SLANDER, 356
SLAYER, 174
SODOM, SAMARIA, AND JERUSALEM, 119
SONS OF ZADOK, 457, 494
SOULS, 133
SOUTH BORDER, 491
SOVEREIGN, 236
SPIRIT OF THE LORD, 222, 369
SPIRIT OF THE WORLD, 144
SPIRIT WORLD, 5, 55
SPIRITS OF THE PROPHETS, 96
SPIRITUAL ADULTERY, 113, 196, 210, 480
SPIRITUAL ADULTERY AND THE MODERN CHURCH, 113
SPIRITUAL CONDITION, 156
SPIRITUAL HARM, 89
SPIRITUAL LIFE, 377
SPIRITUAL PERVERSION, 204
SPIRITUAL SYMBOL, 188
STRANGE HAPPENINGS, 393
STRANGERS, 75, 455
STRONG DRINK, 458
STRUCTURE OF MUSIC, 277
STRUGGLE, 104
STUMBLINGBLOCK OF THEIR INIQUITY, 45
SUBSTITUTION AND IDENTIFICATION, 381
SUBTLE WAYS OF SATAN, 209
SUCCESS, 247
SUN WORSHIPERS, 54
SWORD, 83, 172
SYMBOLIC SACRIFICES, 422
TAKE UP THE CROSS DAILY, 37
TAKING OF THE GOSPEL TO THE WORLD, 250
TAKING UP THE CROSS, 268
TALKERS, 358
TAMMUZ, 54
TARTARUS, 238
TAUNT, 386
TELEVISION, 397
THE INHERITANCE, 333
THE JUDGMENT OF GOD, 334
THE LORD WILL DESTROY THE FAT AND THE STRONG, 344
THE REGATHERING OF ISRAEL, 409
THEME OF RIGHTEOUSNESS, 412
THIRD SEAL, 298
THIRTEEN TRIBES, 377
THREE TYPES OF PEOPLE, 453
THRESHOLD, 477
THUS SAITH THE LORD, 77
TIME FRAMES, 410
TO MAKE UP THE HEDGE AND STAND IN THE GAP, 193
TO OFFER BURNT OFFERINGS THEREON, 447
TO TAKE A SPOIL, 389
TRAFFIC OF SIN, 282
TRANSGRESSIONS AND SINS, 327
TREES, 483
TREES FOR MEAT, 489
TRIBES, 491, 492
TRIBULATION, 168
TRUE BLESSINGS OF GOD, 263
TRUE PROPHET, 95
TRUE SHEPHERD AND THE CROSS, 339
TURN, AND LIVE, 142
TURNING FROM RIGHTEOUSNESS, 331
TURNING FROM WICKEDNESS, 329
TWO DOORS, 430
TWO STICKS, 379
TYRE, 234
UNBELIEF, 24, 92, 172
UNCLEAN AND THE CLEAN, 460
UNCONDITIONAL ETERNAL SECURITY, 139
UNFAITHFUL WATCHMEN, 320
UNITED STATES, 249
UNWORTHILY, 50
VAIN REASONING, 166
VAIN VISION, 89
VALLEY OF DRY BONES, 374
VANITY AND LYING DIVINATION, 88
VATICAN IN ROME, 445
VEIL IN THE TEMPLE, 28
VENGEANCE, 230
VICTORY!, 91
VICTORY OVER SIN, 134
VICTORY SINCE THE CROSS, 134
VILE SINS, 183
VINE, 109
VISION, 1, 49, 79, 440
VISION OF GOD, 48, 410
WALL, 416, 434

WANDERING SHEEP, 338
WARN THEM FROM ME, 325
WARNING, 324
WAS JESUS CURSED BY GOD ON THE CROSS?, 71
WASTE, 291
WATCHMAN, 14, 320
WATERS, 477
WAYS OF EGYPT, 296
WEALTH, 261
WESTERN BORDER, 491
WHAT DID THE CROSS ACCOMPLISH?, 66
WHAT DO WE MEAN BY *"FAITH"*?, 382
WHAT DO WE MEAN BY PREACHING THE CROSS?, 322
WHAT DO WE MEAN, UNDERSTAND THE CROSS AS IT REFERS TO SANCTIFICATION?, 105
WHAT GOOD ARE TONGUES?, 486
WHAT IS MAN?, 268
WHAT IS MEANT BY THE TERM *"APOCRYPHA"*?, 242
WHAT IS THE CONDITION OF THE MODERN CHURCH?, 92
WHAT IS THE SIN NATURE?, 102
WHAT IS THE STATUS OF THEM WHO HAVE NEVER HAD THE PRIVILEGE TO HEAR THE GOSPEL?, 15
WHAT IS TRUE REPENTANCE?, 102
WHAT SHOULD THE POLICY OF AMERICA BE TOWARD MUSLIM COUNTRIES?, 228
WHEELS, 64
WHO IS THE MAN WHO STANDS BY EZEKIEL?, 443
WHOREDOMS, 195
WHY A CROSS?, 70
WHY A SERPENT?, 70
WHY JESUS WENT TO THE CROSS, 69
WHY NOT ANOTHER FORM OF SACRIFICE?, 359
WHY WILL PEOPLE FOLLOW FALSE PROPHETS?, 39
WHY WILL THE BELIEVER NOT LOOK TO GOD?, 205
WICKED, 326
WICKED COUNSEL, 73
WILDERNESS, 161
WISDOM, 261, 272
WISDOM CORRUPTED, 282
WITHOUT GOD, 145
WORD FROM THE LORD, 166

WORD OF FAITH DOCTRINE, 25, 186
WORD OF GOD, 11, 217, 250
WORD OF THE LORD, 19, 148, 170, 245, 256, 289, 296, 362
WORKS OF THE FLESH, 59
WORKS RIGHTEOUSNESS, 364
WORLDLINESS, 201
WORSHIP, 472
WORTHLESS, 109
WRATH OF GOD, 95, 117
YEAR OF LIBERTY, 475
YOU SHALL HEAR THE WORD AT MY MOUTH, 325
ZEDEKIAH, 81, 147
ZIDON, 284

For all information concerning the *Jimmy Swaggart Bible Commentary*, please request a Gift Catalog.

You may inquire by using Books of the Bible.

- Genesis (639 pages) (11-201)
- Exodus (639 pages) (11-202)
- Leviticus (435 pages) (11-203)
- Numbers
  Deuteronomy (493 pages) (11-204)
- Joshua
  Judges
  Ruth (329 pages) (11-205)
- I Samuel
  II Samuel (528 pages) (11-206)
- I Kings
  II Kings (560 pages) (11-207)
- I Chronicles
  II Chronicles (528 pages) (11-226)
- Ezra
  Nehemiah
  Esther (288 pages) (11-208)
- Job (320 pages) (11-225)
- Psalms (688 pages) (11-216)
- Proverbs (320 pages) (11-227)
- Ecclesiastes
  Song Of Solomon (245 pages) (11-228)
- Isaiah (688 pages) (11-220)
- Jeremiah
  Lamentations (688 pages) (11-070)
- Ezekiel (508 pages) (11-223)
- Daniel (403 pages) (11-224)
- Hosea
  Joel
  Amos (496 pages) (11-229)
- Obadiah
  Jonah
  Micah
  Nahum
  Habakkuk
  Zephaniah *(will be ready Spring 2013)* (11-230)

- Matthew (625 pages) (11-073)
- Mark (606 pages) (11-074)
- Luke (626 pages) (11-075)
- John (532 pages) (11-076)
- Acts (697 pages) (11-077)
- Romans (536 pages) (11-078)
- I Corinthians (632 pages) (11-079)
- II Corinthians (589 pages) (11-080)
- Galatians (478 pages) (11-081)
- Ephesians (550 pages) (11-082)
- Philippians (476 pages) (11-083)
- Colossians (374 pages) (11-084)
- I Thessalonians
  II Thessalonians (498 pages) (11-085)
- I Timothy
  II Timothy
  Titus
  Philemon (687 pages) (11-086)
- Hebrews (831 pages) (11-087)
- James
  I Peter
  II Peter (730 pages) (11-088)
- I John
  II John
  III John
  Jude (377 pages) (11-089)
- Revelation (602 pages) (11-090)

For telephone orders you may call 1-800-288-8350 with bankcard information. All Baton Rouge residents please use (225) 768-7000. For mail orders send to:

Jimmy Swaggart Ministries
P.O. Box 262550 • Baton Rouge, LA 70826-2550
Visit our website: www.jsm.org

NOTES

NOTES

NOTES

NOTES

NOTES

NOTES

NOTES

NOTES

NOTES

NOTES

NOTES

NOTES

NOTES